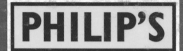

PHILIP'S

C000259955

STREET

Dorset

Bournemouth and Poole

www.philips-maps.co.uk

First published in 2002 by

Philip's, a division of
Octopus Publishing Group Ltd
www.octopusbooks.co.uk
2-4 Heron Quays, London E14 4JP
An Hachette Livre UK Company
www.hachettelivre.co.uk

Second edition 2006
Second impression with revisions 2008
DORBB

ISBN 978-0-540-08774-7 (spiral)

© Philip's 2008

o|s Ordnance Survey®

This product includes mapping data licensed
from Ordnance Survey® with the permission of
the Controller of Her Majesty's Stationery Office.
© Crown copyright 2008. All rights reserved.
Licence number 100011710.

Printed by Toppan, China

Contents

III   **Key to map symbols**

IV   **Key to map pages**

VI   **Route planning**

X   **Administrative and Postcode boundaries**

1   **Street maps** at 3½ inches to 1 mile

188   **Street maps** at 1¾ inches to 1 mile

212   **Street map** at 3½ inches to 1 mile

213   **Index** of towns and villages

216   **Index** of streets, hospitals, industrial estates, railway stations, schools, shopping centres, universities and places of interest

Digital Data

The exceptionally high-quality mapping found in this atlas is available as digital data in TIFF format, which is easily convertible to other bitmapped (raster) image formats.

The index is also available in digital form as a standard database table. It contains all the details found in the printed index together with the National Grid reference for the map square in which each entry is named.

For further information and to discuss your requirements, please contact james.mann@philips-maps.co.uk

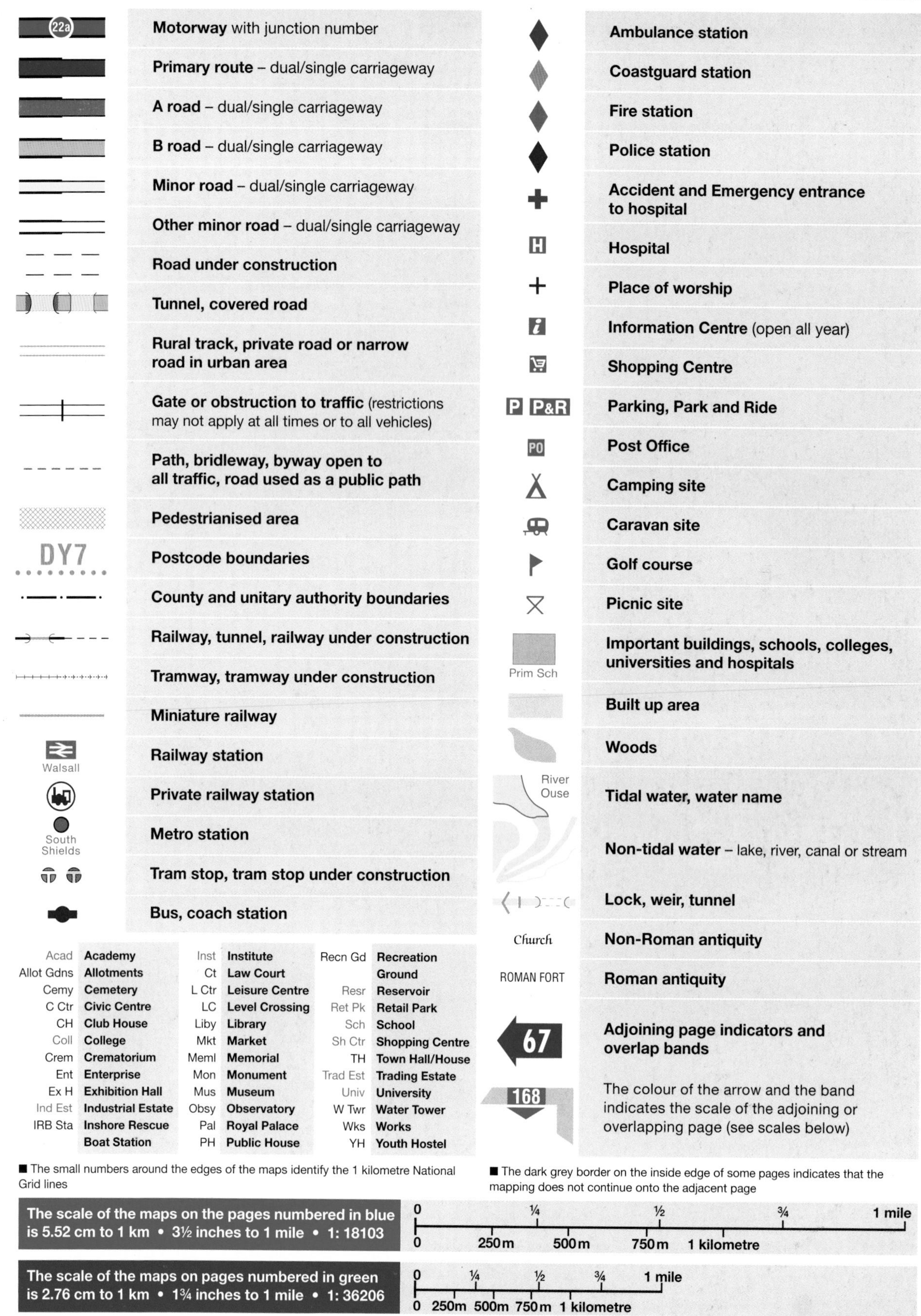

Motorway with junction number		◆	**Ambulance station**
Primary route – dual/single carriageway		◆	**Coastguard station**
A road – dual/single carriageway		◆	**Fire station**
B road – dual/single carriageway		◆	**Police station**
Minor road – dual/single carriageway		✚	**Accident and Emergency entrance to hospital**
Other minor road – dual/single carriageway		**H**	**Hospital**
Road under construction		+	**Place of worship**
Tunnel, covered road		**i**	**Information Centre** (open all year)
Rural track, private road or narrow road in urban area		🛒	**Shopping Centre**
Gate or obstruction to traffic (restrictions may not apply at all times or to all vehicles)		**P** **P&R**	**Parking, Park and Ride**
Path, bridleway, byway open to all traffic, road used as a public path		**PO**	**Post Office**
Pedestrianised area		Ⓧ	**Camping site**
DY7 **Postcode boundaries**		🚐	**Caravan site**
County and unitary authority boundaries		▶	**Golf course**
Railway, tunnel, railway under construction		⊠	**Picnic site**
Tramway, tramway under construction		Prim Sch	**Important buildings, schools, colleges, universities and hospitals**
Miniature railway			**Built up area**
Railway station Walsall			**Woods**
Private railway station		River Ouse	**Tidal water, water name**
Metro station South Shields			**Non-tidal water** – lake, river, canal or stream
Tram stop, tram stop under construction			**Lock, weir, tunnel**
Bus, coach station		*Church*	**Non-Roman antiquity**
		ROMAN FORT	**Roman antiquity**

Acad	**Academy**	Inst	**Institute**	Recn Gd	**Recreation Ground**
Allot Gdns	**Allotments**	Ct	**Law Court**		
Cemy	**Cemetery**	L Ctr	**Leisure Centre**	Resr	**Reservoir**
C Ctr	**Civic Centre**	LC	**Level Crossing**	Ret Pk	**Retail Park**
CH	**Club House**	Liby	**Library**	Sch	**School**
Coll	**College**	Mkt	**Market**	Sh Ctr	**Shopping Centre**
Crem	**Crematorium**	Meml	**Memorial**	TH	**Town Hall/House**
Ent	**Enterprise**	Mon	**Monument**	Trad Est	**Trading Estate**
Ex H	**Exhibition Hall**	Mus	**Museum**	Univ	**University**
Ind Est	**Industrial Estate**	Obsy	**Observatory**	W Twr	**Water Tower**
IRB Sta	**Inshore Rescue Boat Station**	Pal	**Royal Palace**	Wks	**Works**
		PH	**Public House**	YH	**Youth Hostel**

◀ **67** **Adjoining page indicators and overlap bands**

▼ **168** The colour of the arrow and the band indicates the scale of the adjoining or overlapping page (see scales below)

■ The small numbers around the edges of the maps identify the 1 kilometre National Grid lines

■ The dark grey border on the inside edge of some pages indicates that the mapping does not continue onto the adjacent page

The scale of the maps on the pages numbered in blue is 5.52 cm to 1 km • 3½ inches to 1 mile • 1: 18103

0	¼	½	¾	1 mile
0	250m	500m	750m	1 kilometre

The scale of the maps on pages numbered in green is 2.76 cm to 1 km • 1¾ inches to 1 mile • 1: 36206

0	¼	½	¾	1 mile
0	250m	500m	750m	1 kilometre

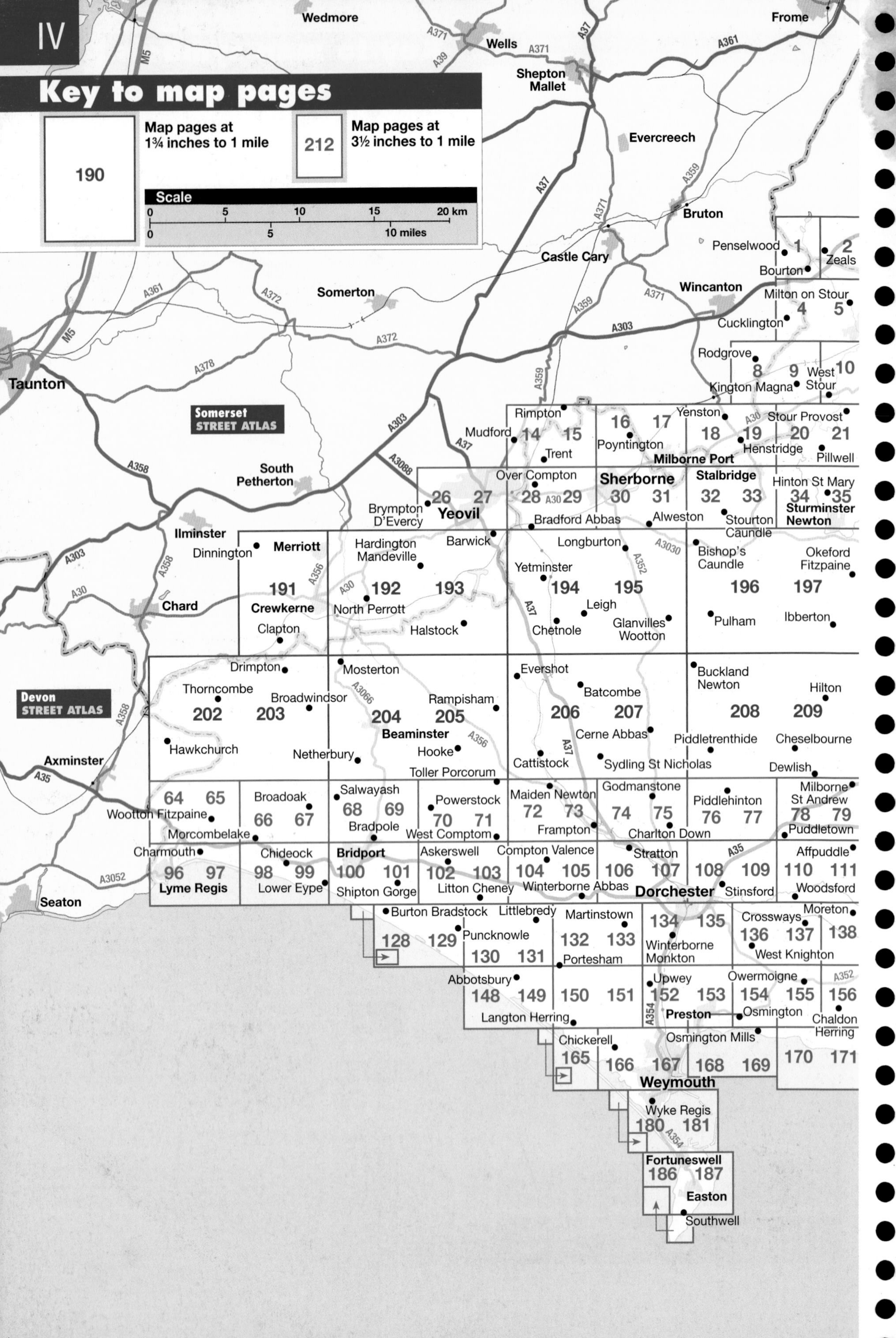

Key to map pages

Map pages at 1¾ inches to 1 mile   190

Map pages at 3½ inches to 1 mile   212

Scale

0   5   10   15   20 km

0   5   10 miles

Wedmore
Wells
Frome
Shepton Mallet
Evercreech
Bruton
Penselwood 1   2 Zeals
Somerton
Castle Cary
Wincanton
Bourton
Milton on Stour
Cucklington 4   5
Rodgrove
8   9 West 10 Stour
Kington Magna
Taunton
Somerset STREET ATLAS
Rimpton
Yenston Stour Provost
Mudford 14   15   16   17   18   19   20   21
Trent Poyntington Henstridge Pillwell
Milborne Port
South Petherton
Over Compton 28 A30 29 Sherborne Stalbridge Hinton St Mary
26   27 28   29   30   31   32   33   34   35
Yeovil Bradford Abbas Alweston Stourton Sturminster Newton
Brympton D'Evercy Caundle
Ilminster
Hardington Mandeville Barwick Longburton Bishop's Caundle Okeford Fitzpaine
Dinnington Merriott
Yetminster A3030
191   192   193   194   195   196   197
Crewkerne North Perrott Leigh Pulham Ibberton
Chard Clapton Halstock Chetnole Glanvilles Wootton
Drimpton Mosterton Evershot Buckland Newton Hilton
Thorncombe Broadwindsor Rampisham Batcombe
Devon STREET ATLAS
202   203   204   205   206   207   208   209
Beaminster Cerne Abbas Piddletrenthide Cheselbourne
Hawkchurch Netherbury Hooke Cattistock Sydling St Nicholas Dewlish
Axminster Toller Porcorum
Maiden Newton Godmanstone Milborne St Andrew
64   65 Broadoak Salwayash Powerstock 72   73   74   75   76   77   78   79
Wootton Fitzpaine 66   67 68   69 70   71 Frampton Charlton Down Puddletown
Morcombelake Bradpole West Compton Affpuddle
Charmouth Chideock Bridport Askerswell Compton Valence Stratton 110   111
96   97 98   99 100   101 102   103 104   105 106   107 108   109 Woodsford
Lyme Regis Lower Eype Shipton Gorge Litton Cheney Winterborne Abbas Dorchester Stinsford
Seaton
Burton Bradstock Littlebredy Martinstown 134   135 Crossways Moreton
128   129 Puncknowle 132   133 136   137   138
130   131 Winterborne Monkton West Knighton
Abbotsbury Portesham Upwey Owermoigne A352
148   149 150   151 152   153 154   155   156
Langton Herring Preston Osmington Chaldon Herring
Chickerell Osmington Mills
165   166   167   168   169 170   171
Weymouth
Wyke Regis
180   181
Fortuneswell
186   187
Easton
Southwell

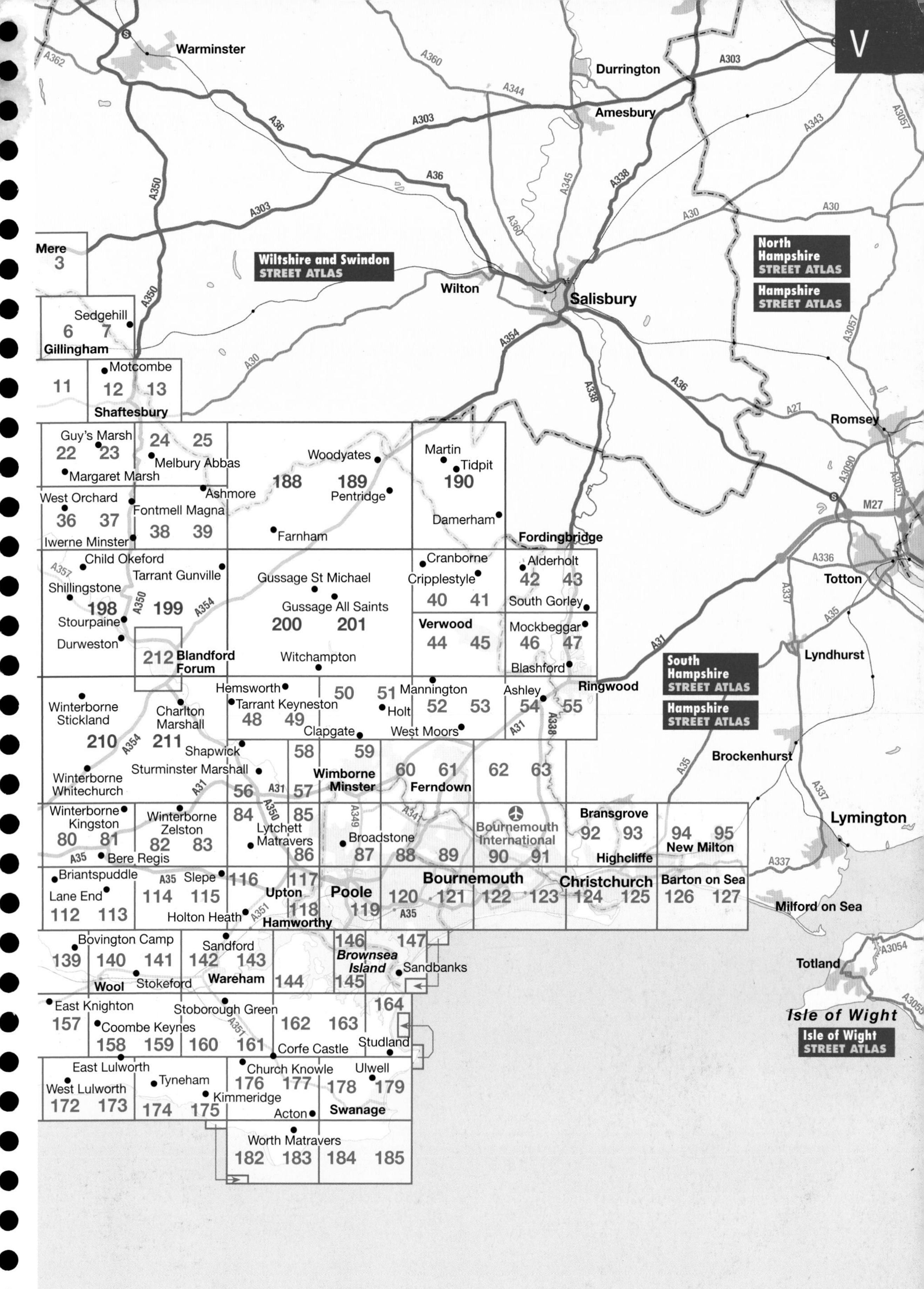
Warminster
A362
A360
Durrington
A303
A344
Amesbury
A36
A303
A3057
A343
A350
A36
A345
A338
A303
A360
A30
A30
Mere
3
Wiltshire and Swindon
STREET ATLAS
Wilton
Salisbury
North
Hampshire
STREET ATLAS
Hampshire
STREET ATLAS
Sedgehill
6
7
Gillingham
A350
A30
A354
A3057
Motcombe
11
12
13
Shaftesbury
A338
A36
A27
Romsey
Guy's Marsh
22
23
24
25
Melbury Abbas
Margaret Marsh
Woodyates
188
189
Pentridge
Martin
Tidpit
190
A3090
M27
West Orchard
36
37
Ashmore
Fontmell Magna
38
39
Iwerne Minster
Farnham
Damerham
Fordingbridge
A336
Child Okeford
A357
Tarrant Gunville
Shillingstone
198
A350
199
A354
Stourpaine
Durweston
Gussage St Michael
Gussage All Saints
200
201
Cranborne
Cripplestyle
40
41
Alderholt
42
43
South Gorley
Totton
A337
A35
Verwood
44
45
Mockbeggar
46
47
Blashford
A31
Lyndhurst
212
Blandford
Forum
Witchampton
Ringwood
Hemsworth
50
51
Mannington
Ashley
Winterborne
Stickland
Charlton
Marshall
Tarrant Keynston
48
49
Holt
52
53
54
55
A338
A31
South
Hampshire
STREET ATLAS
Hampshire
STREET ATLAS
Clapgate
West Moors
210
A354
211
Shapwick
58
59
Brockenhurst
A35
Winterborne
Whitechurch
Sturminster Marshall
A31
56
A31
57
Wimborne
Minster
60
61
Ferndown
62
63
A337
Winterborne
Kingston
80
81
Winterborne
Zelston
82
83
84
A350
85
Lytchett
Matravers
A349
A341
Broadstone
86
87
88
89
Bournemouth
International
90
91
Bransgrove
92
93
Highcliffe
94
95
New Milton
Lymington
A35
Bere Regis
A337
Briantspuddle
Lane End
112
113
A35
Slepe
114
115
Holton Heath
116
117
Upton
118
A351
Hamworthy
Poole
119
120
A35
121
Bournemouth
122
123
Christchurch
124
125
Barton on Sea
126
127
Milford on Sea
Bovington Camp
139
140
141
Sandford
142
143
Wareham
144
146
Brownsea
Island
145
147
Sandbanks
Wool
Stokeford
Totland
A3054
East Knighton
157
Coombe Keynes
158
159
160
Stoborough Green
A351
161
162
163
164
Corfe Castle
Studland
Isle of Wight
A3055
Isle of Wight
STREET ATLAS
East Lulworth
West Lulworth
172
173
Tyneham
174
175
Kimmeridge
Church Knowle
176
177
Ulwell
178
179
Acton
Swanage
Worth Matravers
182
183
184
185

Route planning

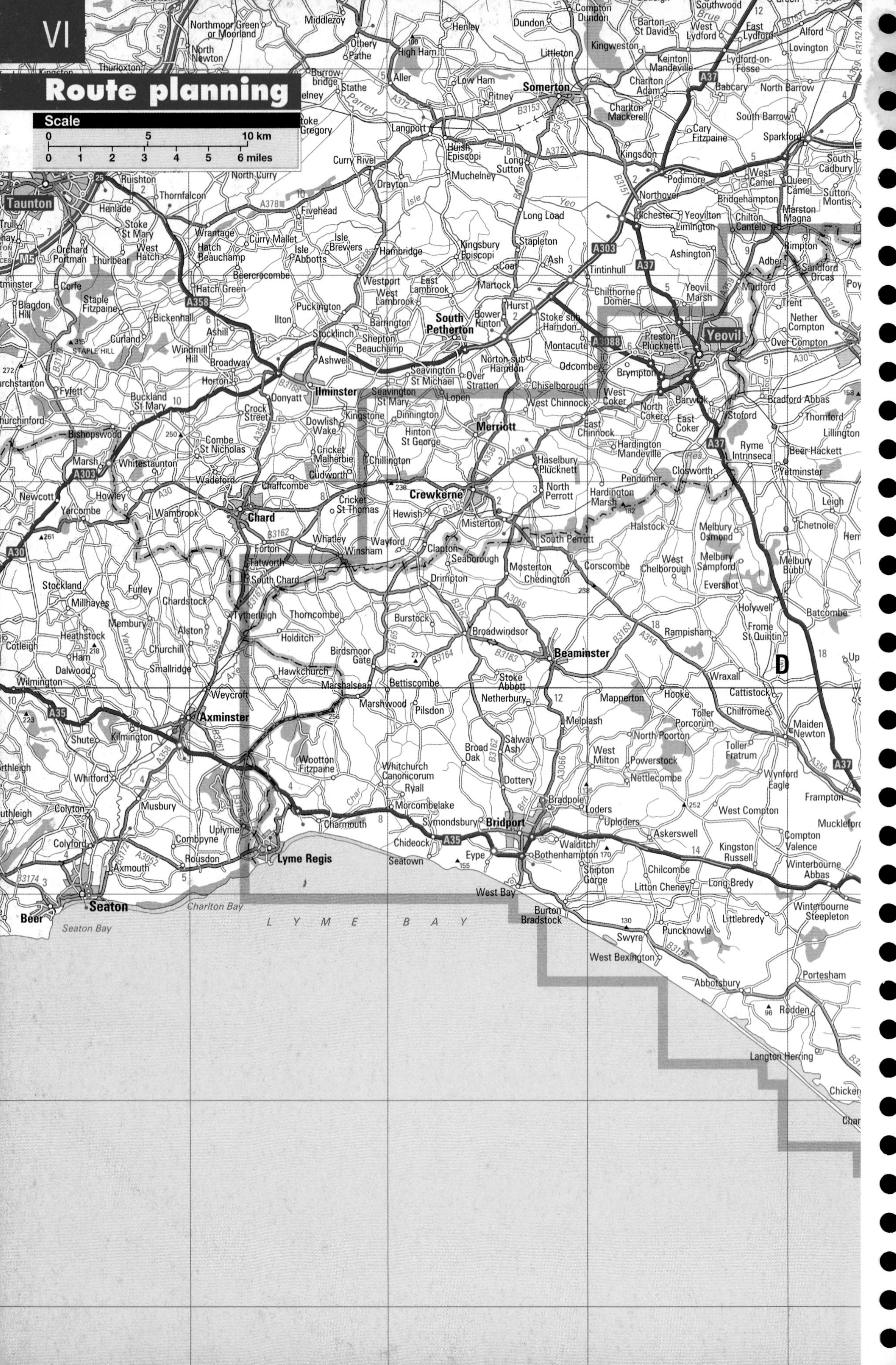
Scale
0
5
10 km
0
1
2
3
4
5
6 miles
Taunton
Somerton
Langport
Yeovil
South Petherton
Ilminster
Chard
Crewkerne
Merriott
Beaminster
Axminster
Lyme Regis
Seaton
Beer
Bridport
Charmouth
Seatown
West Bay
Burton Bradstock
Swyre
West Bexington
Abbotsbury
Portesham
Rodden
Langton Herring
L Y M E B A Y
Charlton Bay
Seaton Bay
Northmoor Green or Moorland
North Newton
Middlezoy
Othery
Pathe
High Ham
Henley
Low Ham
Aller
Pitney
Burrowbridge
Stathe
Stoke Gregory
Curry Rivel
Huish Episcopi
Muchelney
Long Sutton
Drayton
Long Load
Dundon
Compton Dundon
Littleton
Butleigh
Barton St David
Kingweston
Southwood
West Lydford
East Lydford
Lydford-on-Fosse
Alford
Lovington
Keinton Mandeville
Charlton Adam
Charlton Mackerell
Babcary
North Barrow
South Barrow
Cary Fitzpaine
Sparkford
Kingsdon
Podimore
Northover
Ilchester
Yeovilton
Limington
West Camel
Queen Camel
Bridgehampton
Chilton Cantelo
Marston Magna
Sutton Montis
South Cadbury
Ashington
Rimpton
Adber
Sandford Orcas
Mudford
Trent
Nether Compton
Over Compton
Bradford Abbas
Thornford
Lillington
Yeovil Marsh
Preston Plucknett
Brympton
Barwick
Stoford
Ryme Intrinseca
Beer Hackett
Yetminster
Leigh
Chetnole
Tintinhull
Chilthorne Domer
Stoke sub Hamdon
Montacute
Odcombe
Norton sub Hamdon
Over Stratton
Chiselborough
West Chinnock
West Coker
North Coker
East Coker
East Chinnock
Hardington Mandeville
Pendomer
Closworth
Hardington Marsh
Halstock
Melbury Osmond
Melbury Sampford
Melbury Bubb
Evershot
West Chelborough
Corscombe
Haselbury Plucknett
North Perrott
South Perrott
Misterton
Mosterton
Chedington
Rampisham
Holywell
Frome St Quintin
Batcombe
Cattistock
Chilfrome
Maiden Newton
Wraxall
Hooke
Toller Porcorum
Toller Fratrum
Wynford Eagle
Frampton
Kingsbury Episcopi
Stapleton
Ash
Coat
Martock
Hurst
Bower Hinton
East Lambrook
West Lambrook
Hambridge
Isle Brewers
Isle Abbotts
Fivehead
Curry Mallet
Westport
Puckington
Barrington
Ilton
Stocklinch
Shepton Beauchamp
Ashwell
Seavington St Mary
Seavington St Michael
Lopen
Kingstone
Dinnington
Hinton St George
Dowlish Wake
Cricket Malherbie
Chillington
Cudworth
Cricket St Thomas
Hewish
Whatley
Winsham
Wayford
Clapton
Seaborough
Drimpton
Chaffcombe
Donyatt
Crock Street
Combe St Nicholas
Wadeford
Whitestaunton
Buckland St Mary
Broadway
Horton
Ashill
Windmill Hill
Bickenhall
Curland
Staple Fitzpaine
Hatch Green
Hatch Beauchamp
Beercrocombe
Wrantage
Thornfalcon
Ruishton
Henlade
Stoke St Mary
West Hatch
Orchard Portman
Thurlbear
Corfe
Blagdon Hill
Staple Hill
Fyfett
Bishopswood
Marsh
Howley
Yarcombe
Newcott
Wambrook
Forton
Tatworth
South Chard
Stockland
Furley
Millhayes
Chardstock
Membury
Alston
Tytherleigh
Thorncombe
Holditch
Heathstock
Cotleigh
Ham
Dalwood
Churchill
Smallridge
Wilmington
Weycroft
Hawkchurch
Birdsmoor Gate
Marshalsea
Marshwood
Bettiscombe
Pilsdon
Burstock
Broadwindsor
Stoke Abbott
Netherbury
Mapperton
Melplash
Salway Ash
Broad Oak
Dottery
Whitchurch Canonicorum
Ryall
Morcombelake
Wootton Fitzpaine
Symondsbury
Chideock
Eype
Bradpole
Loders
Uploders
Walditch
Bothenhampton
Shipton Gorge
Askerswell
West Milton
North Poorton
Powerstock
Nettlecombe
West Compton
Compton Valence
Kingston Russell
Chilcombe
Litton Cheney
Long Bredy
Winterbourne Abbas
Winterbourne Steepleton
Littlebredy
Puncknowle
Shute
Kilmington
Whitford
Musbury
Colyton
Colyford
Combpyne
Uplyme
Rousdon
Axmouth
Yarty
Axe
Char
Brit
Parrett
Isle
Yeo
Brue
Res
M5
A30
A35
A37
A38
A303
A358
A372
A378
A356
A3066
A3088
A3052
A359
B3151
B3153
B3165
B3168
B3162
B3163
B3164
B3167
B3170
B3172
B3174
B3261
B3148
B3157
D

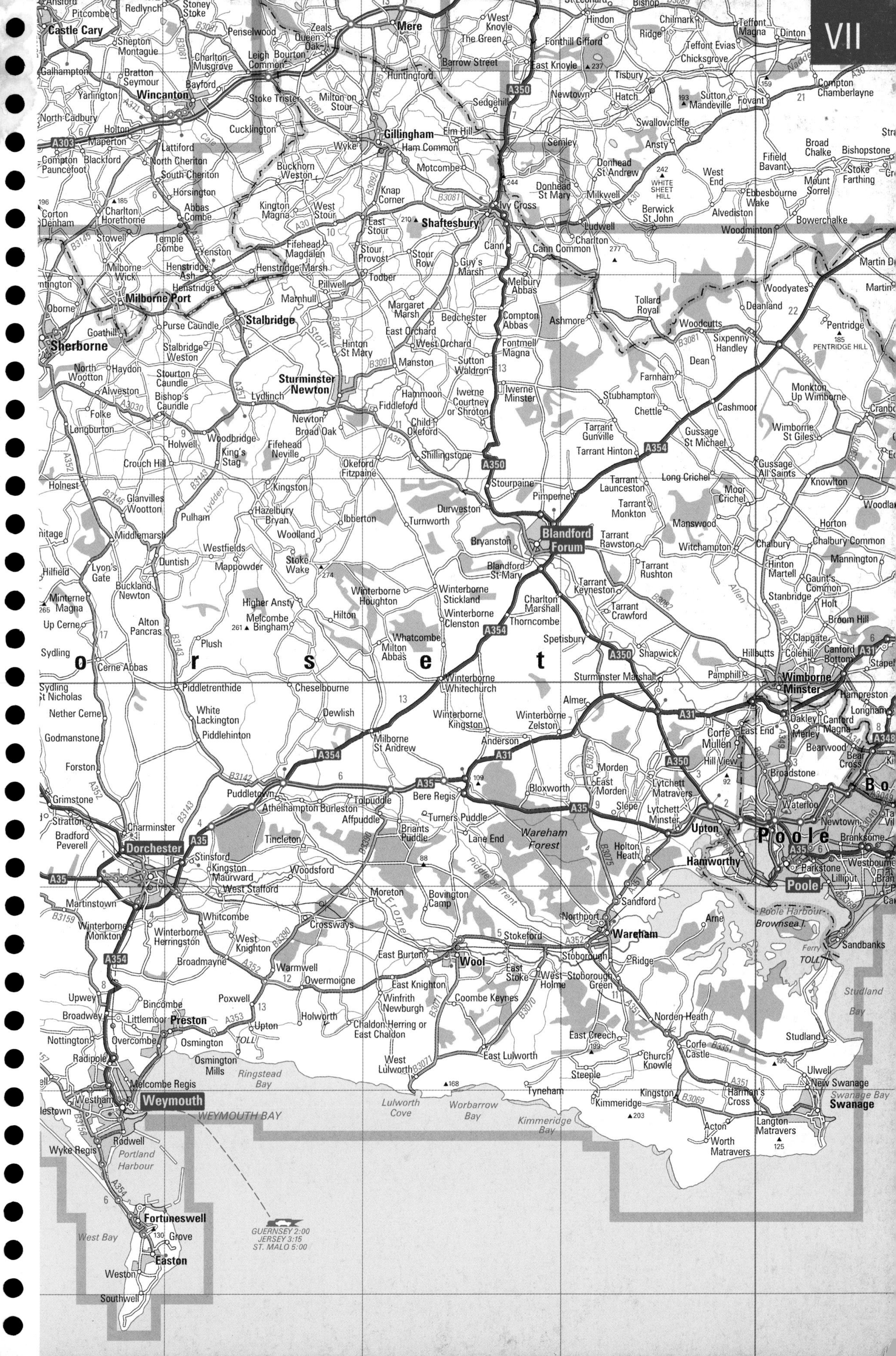
Ansford
Pitcombe
Castle Cary
Redlynch
Stoney Stoke
Shepton Montague
Galhampton
Bratton Seymour
Yarlington
Wincanton
North Cadbury
Holton
Maperton
A303
Compton Pauncefoot
Blackford
Lattiford
North Cheriton
South Cheriton
Horsington
Charlton Horethorne
Corton Denham
Abbas Combe
Temple Combe
Stowell
Yenston
Milborne Wick
Henstridge Ash
Henstridge
Milborne Port
Oborne
Goathill
Sherborne
Purse Caundle
Stalbridge
Stalbridge Weston
North Wootton
Haydon
Stourton Caundle
Alweston
Bishop's Caundle
Folke
Longburton
Holwell
Woodbridge
King's Stag
Crouch Hill
Holnest
Glanvilles Wootton
Pulham
Middlemarsh
Hilfield
Lyon's Gate
Buckland Newton
Duntish
Minterne Magna
Up Cerne
Alton Pancras
Sydling
Cerne Abbas
Sydling St Nicholas
Nether Cerne
Godmanstone
Forston
Grimstone
Stratton
Bradford Peverell
Charminster
Dorchester
A35
Martinstown
Winterborne Monkton
A354
Upwey
Broadwey
Nottington
Radipole
Melcombe Regis
Westham
Weymouth
WEYMOUTH BAY
Wyke Regis
Rodwell
Portland Harbour
Fortuneswell
West Bay
Grove
Easton
Weston
Southwell
GUERNSEY 2:00
JERSEY 3:15
ST. MALO 5:00
Penselwood
Zeals
Queen Oak
Mere
Charlton Musgrove
Leigh Common
Bourton
Bayford
Stoke Trister
Milton on Stour
Cucklington
Gillingham
Wyke
Ham Common
Motcombe
Buckhorn Weston
Kington Magna
West Stour
East Stour
Knap Corner
Shaftesbury
Fifehead Magdalen
Stour Provost
Stour Row
Henstridge Marsh
Pillwell
Todber
Marnhull
Margaret Marsh
East Orchard
West Orchard
Hinton St Mary
Manston
Sturminster Newton
Lydlinch
Hammoon
Fiddleford
Newton
Broad Oak
Child Okeford
Fifehead Neville
Okeford Fitzpaine
Kingston
Hazelbury Bryan
Ibberton
Woolland
Turnworth
Westfields
Mappowder
Stoke Wake
Winterborne Houghton
Higher Ansty
Melcombe Bingham
Hilton
Plush
Whatcombe
Milton Abbas
Winterborne Stickland
Winterborne Clenston
Piddletrenthide
Cheselbourne
White Lackington
Piddlehinton
Dewlish
Milborne St Andrew
Puddletown
Athelhampton
Burleston
Tolpuddle
Affpuddle
Tincleton
Stinsford
Kingston Maurward
West Stafford
Woodsford
Whitcombe
Winterborne Herringston
West Knighton
Broadmayne
Crossways
Warmwell
Owermoigne
Poxwell
Bincombe
Littlemoor
Preston
Overcombe
Osmington
Osmington Mills
Upton
Ringstead Bay
Holworth
Chaldon Herring or East Chaldon
West Lulworth
Lulworth Cove
Worbarrow Bay
Kimmeridge Bay
Moreton
Bovington Camp
East Burton
Wool
East Knighton
Winfrith Newburgh
Coombe Keynes
East Stoke
East Lulworth
Tyneham
Barrow Street
West Knoyle
The Green
Huntingford
Sedgehill
Elm Hill
Semley
A350
Ivy Cross
Cann
Cann Common
Guy's Marsh
Melbury Abbas
Bedchester
Compton Abbas
Fontmell Magna
Sutton Waldron
Iwerne Minster
Iwerne Courtney or Shroton
Shillingstone
Stourpaine
Durweston
Bryanston
Blandford Forum
Blandford St Mary
Pimperne
Charlton Marshall
Thorncombe
Spetisbury
Winterborne Whitechurch
Winterborne Kingston
Anderson
Winterborne Zelston
Almer
Sturminster Marshall
Bere Regis
Turners Puddle
Briants Puddle
Lane End
Wareham Forest
Bloxworth
Morden
East Morden
Slepe
Lytchett Matravers
Lytchett Minster
Holton Heath
Sandford
Northport
Wareham
Stokeford
Stoborough
Ridge
West Holme
Stoborough Green
East Creech
Norden Heath
Corfe Castle
Church Knowle
Steeple
Kingston
Kimmeridge
Harman's Cross
Acton
Worth Matravers
Langton Matravers
Swanage
New Swanage
Swanage Bay
Ulwell
Studland
Studland Bay
Sandbanks
Ferry
TOLL
Poole Harbour
Brownsea I.
Arne
St Leonard
Hindon
Bishop
Chilmark
Teffont Magna
Dinton
Fonthill Gifford
Ridge
Teffont Evias
Chicksgrove
East Knoyle
Tisbury
Newtown
Hatch
Sutton Mandeville
Fovant
Compton Chamberlayne
Swallowcliffe
Ansty
Donhead St Andrew
Donhead St Mary
WHITE SHEET HILL
Milkwell
Berwick St John
West End
Ludwell
Charlton
Alvediston
Ebbesbourne Wake
Fifield Bavant
Broad Chalke
Bishopstone
Stoke Farthing
Mount Sorrel
Bowerchalke
Woodminton
Ashmore
Tollard Royal
Deanland
Woodyates
Martin Down
Martin
Woodcutts
Sixpenny Handley
Pentridge
PENTRIDGE HILL
Dean
Farnham
Stubhampton
Chettle
Cashmoor
Tarrant Gunville
Tarrant Hinton
A354
Gussage St Michael
Monkton Up Wimborne
Wimborne St Giles
Gussage All Saints
Long Crichel
Moor Crichel
Knowlton
Tarrant Launceston
Tarrant Monkton
Manswood
Witchampton
Tarrant Rawston
Tarrant Rushton
Tarrant Keyneston
Tarrant Crawford
Shapwick
Chalbury
Chalbury Common
Horton
Hinton Martell
Gaunt's Common
Mannington
Stanbridge
Holt
Broom Hill
Clapgate
Colehill
Canford Bottom
Hillbutts
Pamphill
Wimborne Minster
A31
Hampreston
Longham
Oakley
Canford Magna
Merley
Bearwood
Corfe Mullen
East End
Hill View
Broadstone
Upton
Hamworthy
Waterloo
Poole
Newtown
Branksome
Parkstone
Lilliput
Westbourne
Dorset

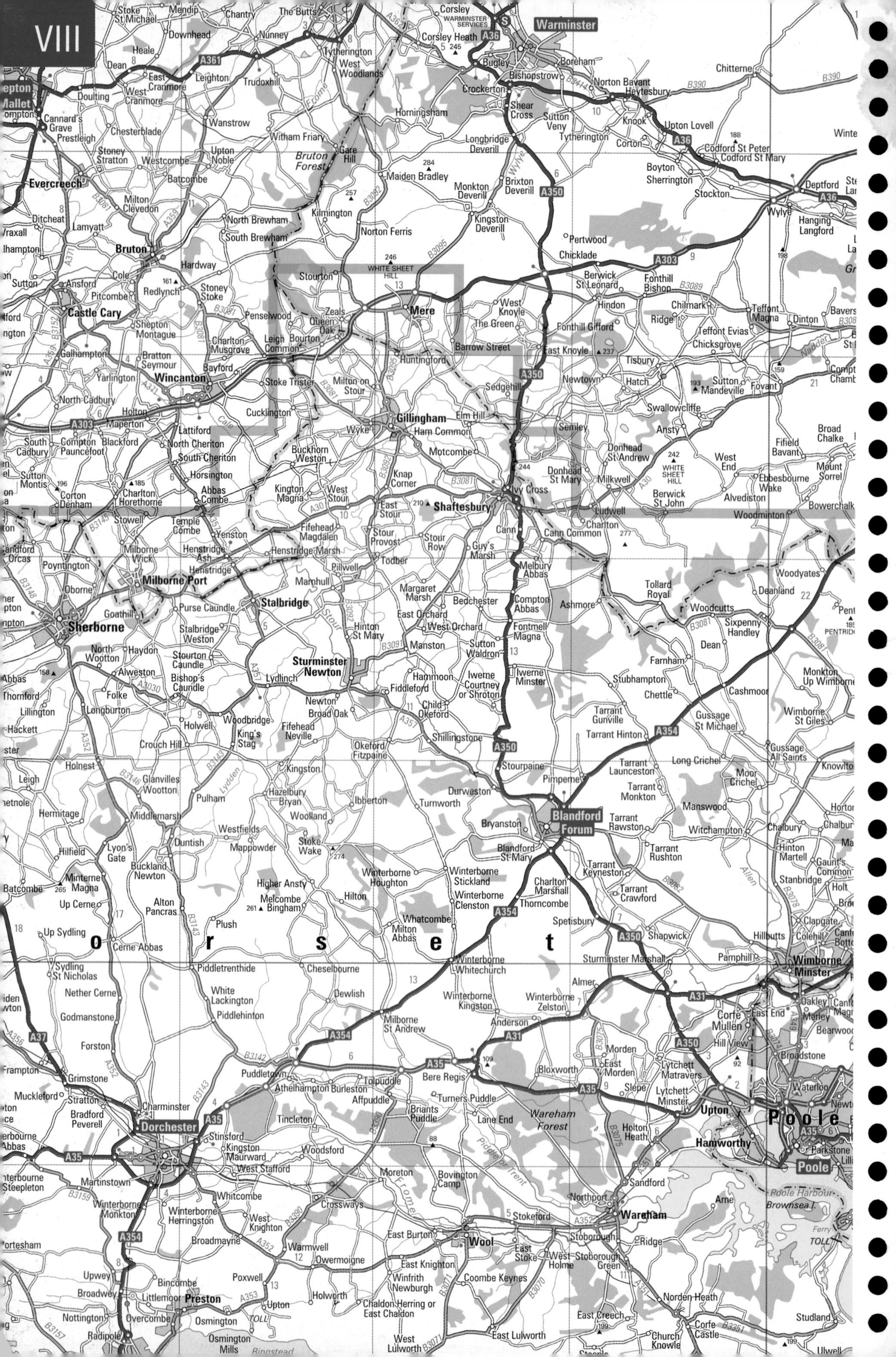

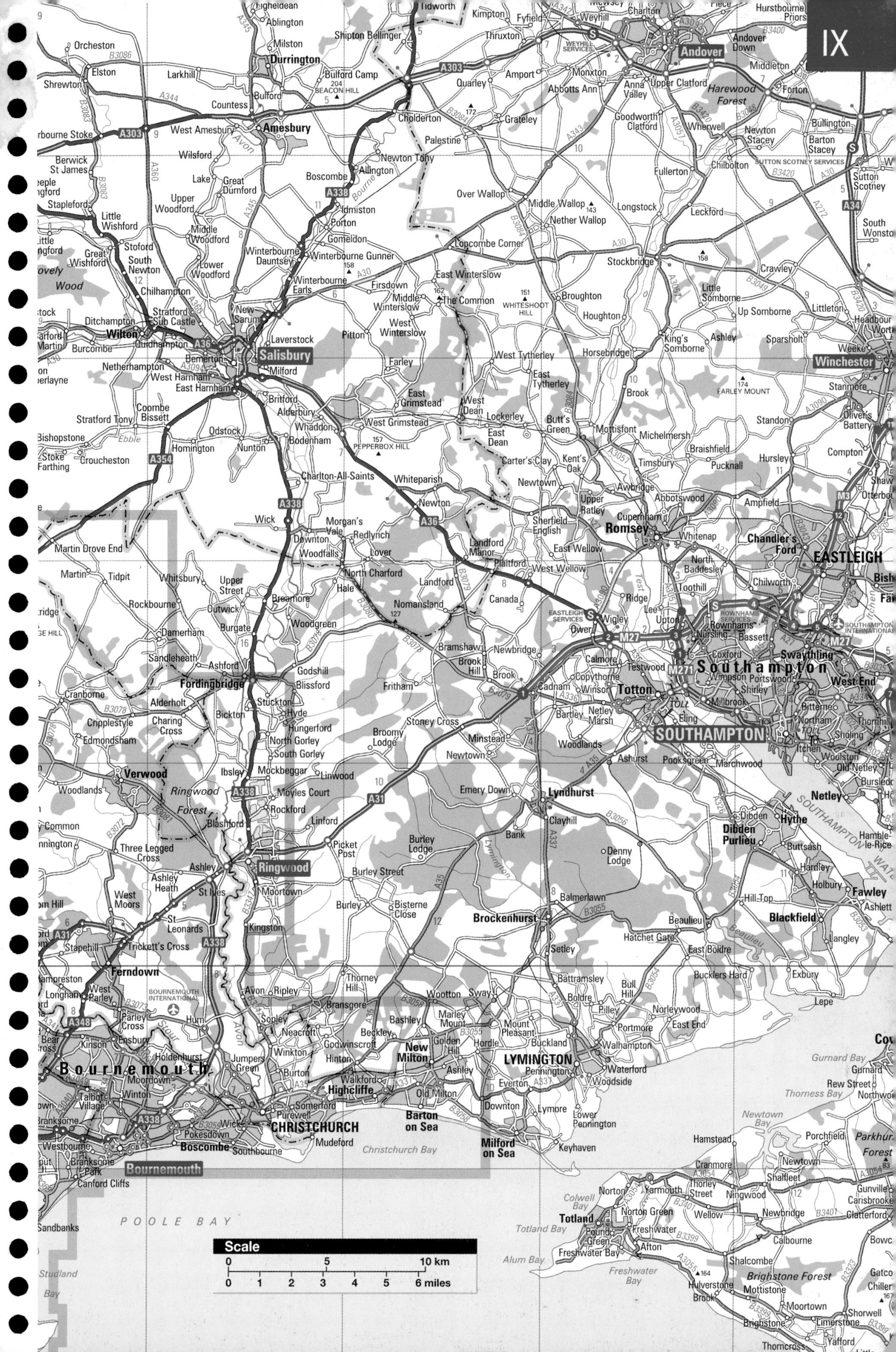
Andover
Salisbury
Winchester
Romsey
EASTLEIGH
Southampton
SOUTHAMPTON
Ringwood
Bournemouth
CHRISTCHURCH
LYMINGTON
Lyndhurst
Brockenhurst
Fordingbridge
Amesbury
Durrington
Wilton
Totton
Hythe
Fawley
Blackfield
Dibden Purlieu
New Milton
Highcliffe
Barton on Sea
Milford on Sea
Verwood
Ferndown
Boscombe
Totland
Yarmouth
Freshwater
Tidworth
Weyhill
Harewood Forest
Stockbridge
Middle Wallop
Over Wallop
Nether Wallop
King's Somborne
Mottisfont
Whiteparish
West Tytherley
Downton
Woodfalls
Redlynch
Breamore
Cranborne
Alderholt
Ashley Heath
St Leonards
St Ives
West Moors
Burley
Minstead
Ashurst
Beaulieu
Sway
Bransgore
Burton
Mudeford
Keyhaven
Lymore
Pennington
Everton
Downton
Ashley
Hordle
Bashley
Netley
Marchwood
Woolston
Bitterne
Shirley
Swaythling
Bassett
Chilworth
Chandler's Ford
Rownhams
Nursling
Upton
Ower
Wigley
Cadnam
Brook
Bramshaw
Fritham
Godshill
Linwood
Picket Post
Emery Down
Bank
Denny Lodge
Balmerlawn
Setley
Battramsley
Boldre
East End
Bucklers Hard
Exbury
Lepe
A303
A338
A36
A354
A31
A35
A337
A34
A30
M27
M271
M3
A348
Christchurch Bay
POOLE BAY
Studland Bay
Gurnard Bay
Thorness Bay
Newtown Bay
Colwell Bay
Totland Bay
Alum Bay
Freshwater Bay
Brighstone Forest
Parkhurst Forest
Ringwood Forest
Scale
0
5
10 km
0
1
2
3
4
5
6 miles

Administrative and Postcode boundaries

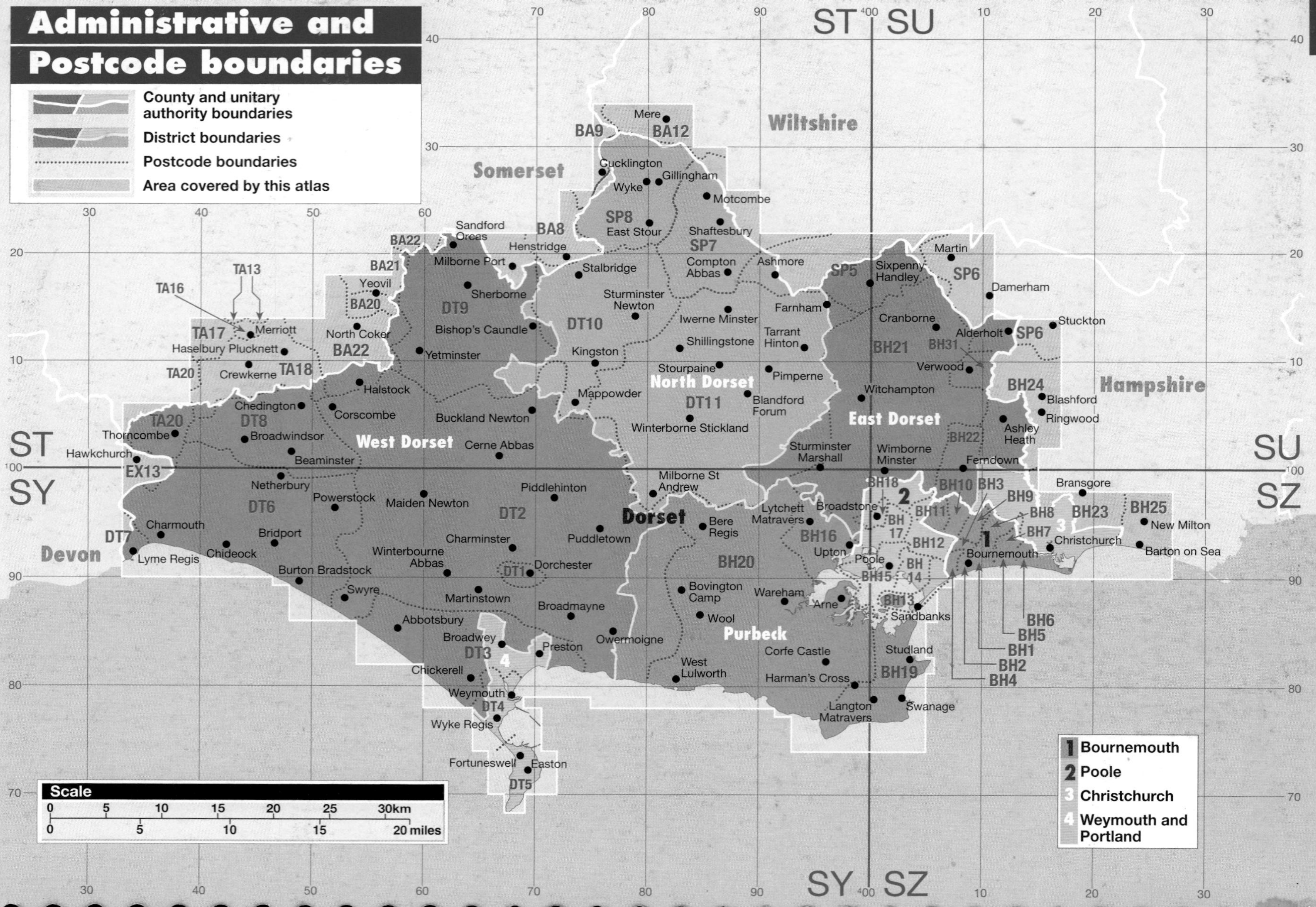

County and unitary authority boundaries
District boundaries
Postcode boundaries
Area covered by this atlas

Legend
1 Bournemouth
2 Poole
3 Christchurch
4 Weymouth and Portland

Scale
0 5 10 15 20 25 30km
0 5 10 15 20 miles

Devon
Somerset
Wiltshire
Hampshire
Dorset
West Dorset
North Dorset
East Dorset
Purbeck

Hawkchurch
Thorncombe
Charmouth
Lyme Regis
Chideock
Netherbury
Chedington
Broadwindsor
Beaminster
Bridport
Burton Bradstock
Swyre
Powerstock
Maiden Newton
Winterbourne Abbas
Abbotsbury
Chickerell
Wyke Regis
Weymouth
Fortuneswell
Easton
Broadwey
Preston
Osmington
Owermoigne
Broadmayne
Martinstown
Charminster
Dorchester
Puddletown
Piddlehinton
Piddletrenthide
Cerne Abbas
Buckland Newton
Corscombe
Halstock
North Coker
Yeovil
Merriott
Haselbury Plucknett
Crewkerne
Sandford Orcas
Milborne Port
Henstridge
Sherborne
Bishop's Caundle
Yetminster
Stalbridge
Kingston
Mappowder
Winterborne Stickland
Milborne St Andrew
Bere Regis
Wool
West Lulworth
Bovington Camp
Wareham
Arne
Corfe Castle
Harman's Cross
Langton Matravers
Swanage
Studland
Sandbanks
Poole
Upton
Lytchett Matravers
Broadstone
Wimborne Minster
Blandford Forum
Pimperne
Tarrant Hinton
Iwerne Minster
Shillingstone
Stourpaine
Sturminster Newton
East Stour
Gillingham
Wyke
Cucklington
Mere
Motcombe
Shaftesbury
Compton Abbas
Ashmore
Farnham
Sixpenny Handley
Martin
Damerham
Cranborne
Witchampton
Sturminster Marshall
Verwood
Alderholt
Stuckton
Blashford
Ringwood
Ashley Heath
Ferndown
Bransgore
New Milton
Barton on Sea
Christchurch
Bournemouth

Postcode areas: EX13, DT7, DT6, DT8, DT2, DT11, DT10, DT9, BA22, BA21, BA20, TA18, TA20, TA17, TA16, TA13, SP8, SP7, SP5, SP6, BA8, BA9, BA12, DT1, DT3, DT4, DT5, BH20, BH16, BH18, BH17, BH15, BH12, BH11, BH10, BH22, BH21, BH24, BH31, BH9, BH8, BH7, BH3, BH10, BH19, BH14, BH13, BH1, BH2, BH4, BH5, BH6, BH23, BH25

ST SU
ST 400 SU
ST SY
SY SZ
SU SZ
SY

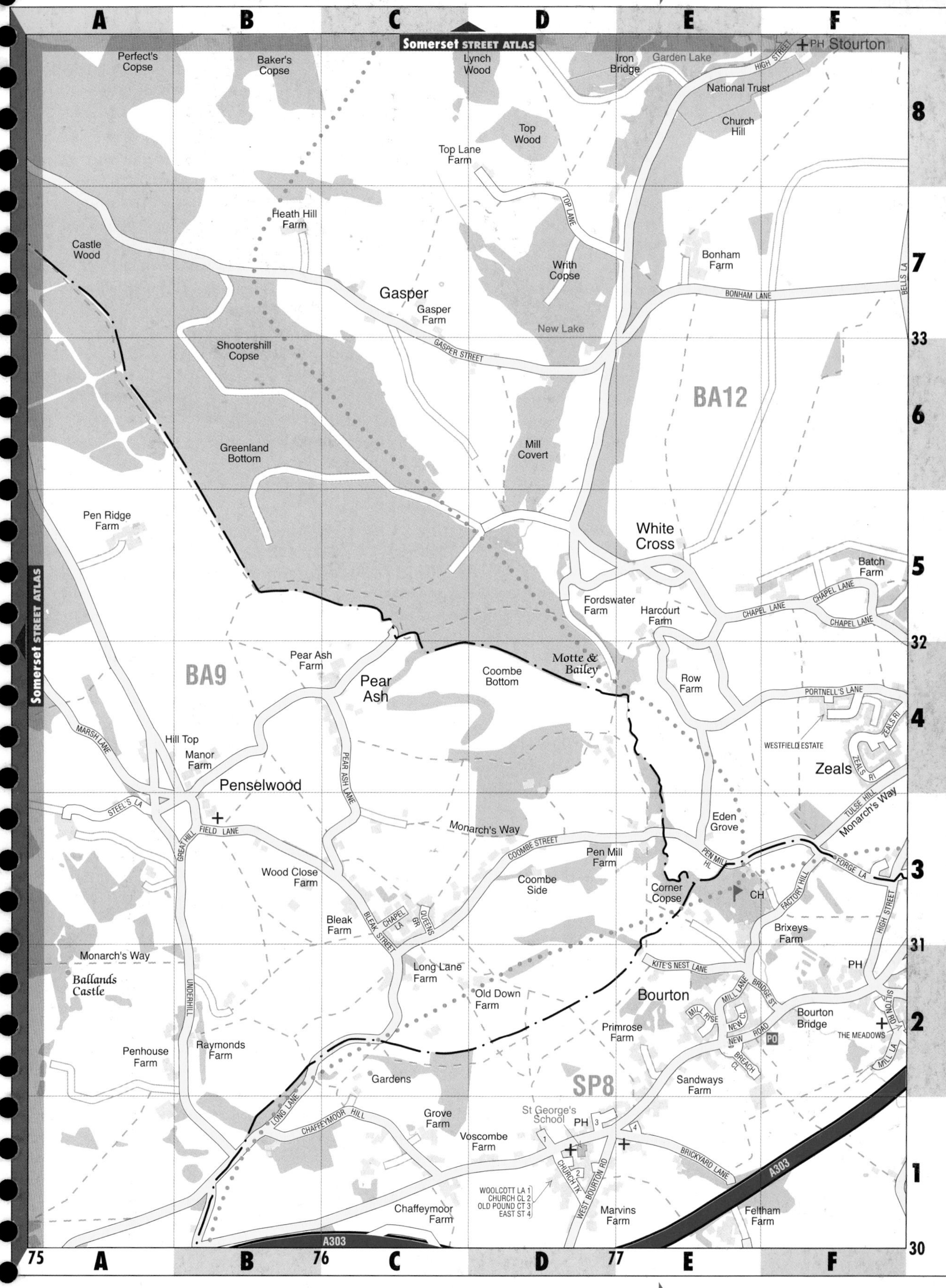

Somerset STREET ATLAS

A   B   C   D   E   F

8

7

33

6

5

32

4

31

2

1

30

Stourton
PH

Garden Lake
Iron
Bridge
National Trust
Church
Hill

BA12

Perfect's
Copse

Baker's
Copse

Lynch
Wood

Top
Wood

Top Lane
Farm

Heath Hill
Farm

Writh
Copse

Bonham
Farm

Castle
Wood

Gasper

Gasper
Farm

Gasper Street

New Lake

BONHAM LANE

BELL'S LA

Shootershill
Copse

Batch
Farm

Greenland
Bottom

Mill
Covert

White
Cross

CHAPEL LANE

CHAPEL LANE

Pen Ridge
Farm

Fordswater
Farm

Harcourt
Farm

Row
Farm

PORTNELL'S LANE

ZEALS RD

BA9

Pear Ash
Farm

Coombe
Bottom

Motte &
Bailey

WESTFIELD ESTATE

Zeals

ZEALS RD

Pear
Ash

MARSH LANE

Hill Top
Manor
Farm

PEAR ASH LANE

Monarch's Way

Eden
Grove

TULSE HILL

Monarch's Way

STEEL'S LA

Penselwood

Wood Close
Farm

Coombe Street

Pen Mill
Farm

PEN MILL HL

FORGE LA

HIGH STREET

GREAT HILL

FIELD LANE

Coombe
Side

Corner
Copse

CH

FACTORY HILL

Bleak
Farm

BLEAK STREET

CHAPEL LA

QUEENS GR

Brixeys
Farm

PH

Monarch's Way

UNDERHILL

Long Lane
Farm

KITE'S NEST LANE

Bourton

MILL LANE

BRIDGE ST

Bourton
Bridge

MILL LA

Ballands
Castle

Old Down
Farm

Primrose
Farm

MILL RISE

NEW CL

THE MEADOWS

Penhouse
Farm

Raymonds
Farm

NEW ROAD

PO

BREACH CL

Gardens

SP8

Sandways
Farm

LONG LANE

CHAFFEYMOOR HILL

Grove
Farm

St George's
School
PH

BRICKYARD LANE

A303

Voscombe
Farm

WEST BOURTON RD

CHURCH TK

Chaffeymoor
Farm

WOOLCOTT LA 1
CHURCH CL 2
OLD POUND CT 3
EAST ST 4

Marvins
Farm

Feltham
Farm

A303

75   A   B   76   C   D   77   E   F   30

Somerset STREET ATLAS

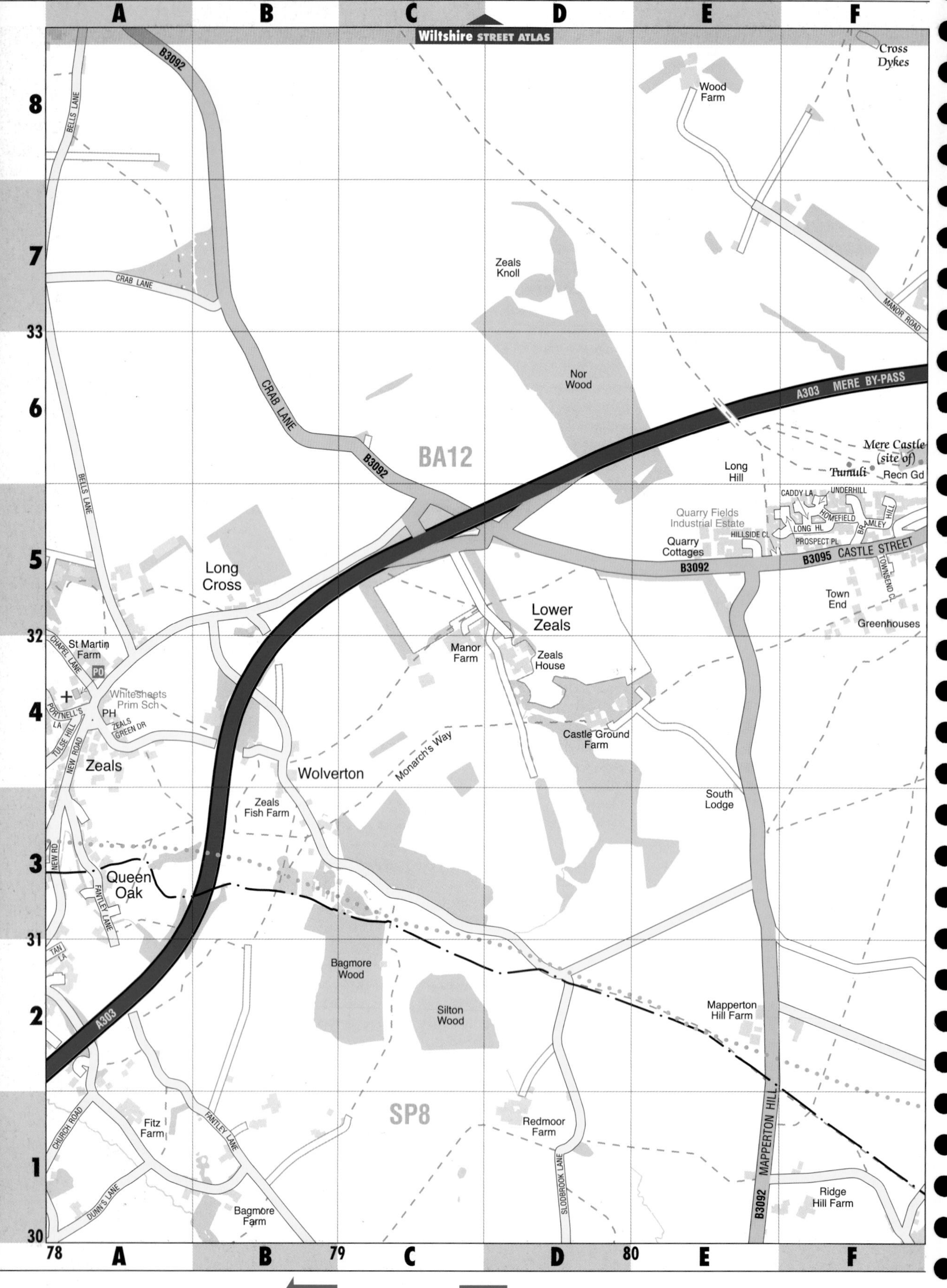
A
B
C
D
E
F
Wiltshire STREET ATLAS
8
7
33
6
5
32
4
3
31
2
1
30
78
79
80
B3092
BELLS LANE
Cross Dykes
Wood Farm
CRAB LANE
Zeals Knoll
MANOR ROAD
Nor Wood
A303 MERE BY-PASS
CRAB LANE
B3092
BA12
Mere Castle (site of)
Long Hill
Tumuli
Recn Gd
CADDY LA
UNDERHILL
HOMEFIELD
Quarry Fields Industrial Estate
HILLSIDE CL
LONG HL
PROSPECT PL
Quarry Cottages
B3095 CASTLE STREET
B3092
TOWNSEND CL
Long Cross
Lower Zeals
Town End
Greenhouses
St Martin Farm
CHAPEL LANE
PO
Manor Farm
Zeals House
Whitesheets Prim Sch
PORTNELL'S LA
PH
ZEALS GREEN DR
TULSE HILL
NEW ROAD
Castle Ground Farm
Monarch's Way
Zeals
Wolverton
South Lodge
Zeals Fish Farm
NEW RD
Queen Oak
FANTLEY LANE
TAN LA
Bagmore Wood
Silton Wood
Mapperton Hill Farm
A303
CHURCH ROAD
Fitz Farm
FANTLEY LANE
SP8
Redmoor Farm
SLODBROOK LANE
MAPPERTON HILL
B3092
DUNN'S LANE
Bagmore Farm
Ridge Hill Farm

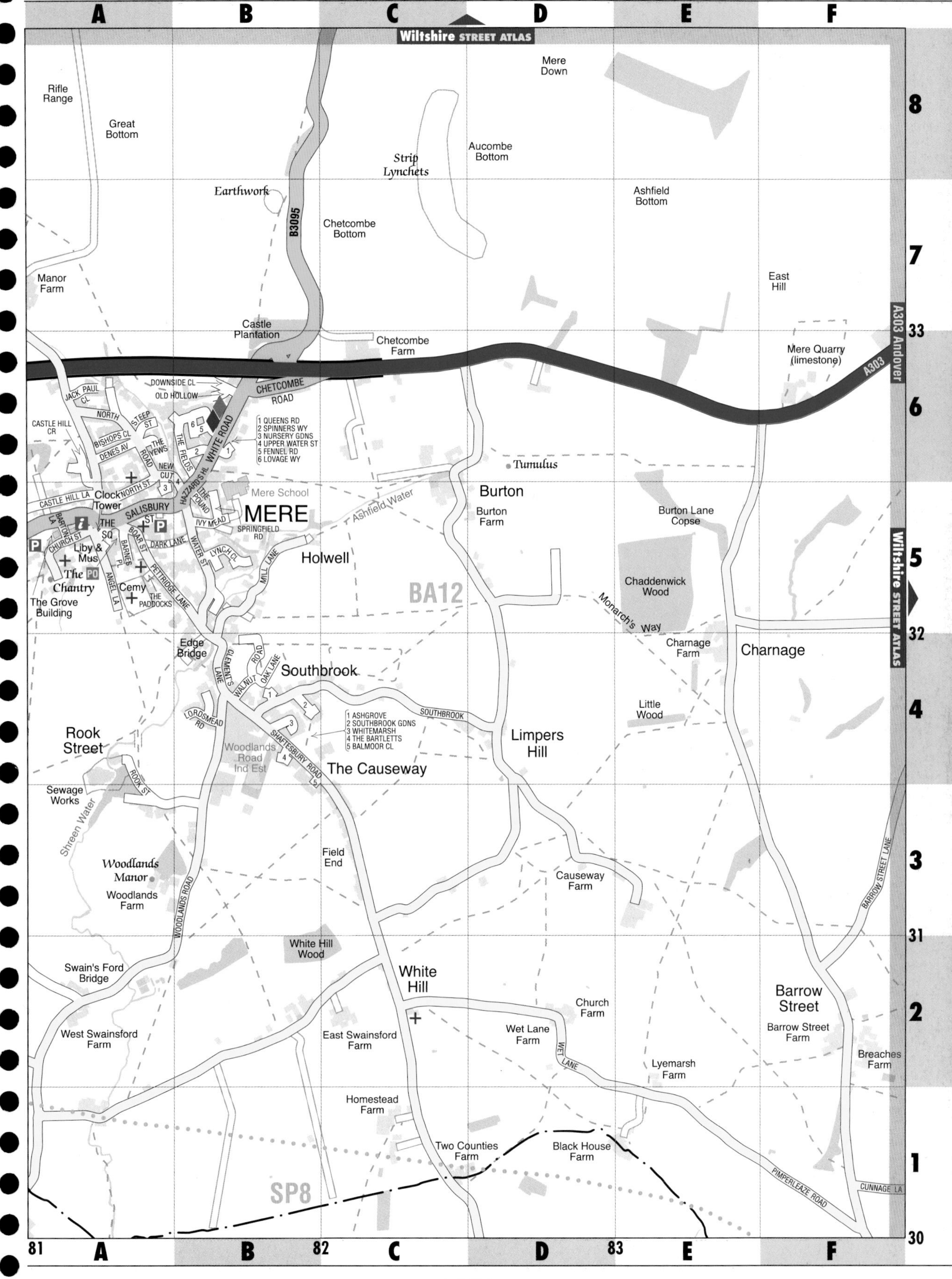

A B C D E F

8

7

33

6

5

32

4

3

31

2

1

30

A B C D E F

81 82 83

Wiltshire STREET ATLAS

A303 Andover

Rifle Range
Great Bottom
Mere Down
Earthwork
Strip Lynchets
Aucombe Bottom
Ashfield Bottom
Chetcombe Bottom
B3095
Manor Farm
East Hill
Castle Plantation
Chetcombe Farm
Mere Quarry (limestone)
DOWNSIDE CL
OLD HOLLOW
CHETCOMBE ROAD
JACK PAUL CL
NORTH
CASTLE HILL CR
STEEP ST
BISHOPS CL
THE VIEWS
DENES AV
WHITE ROAD
1 QUEENS RD
2 SPINNERS WY
3 NURSERY GDNS
4 UPPER WATER ST
5 FENNEL RD
6 LOVAGE WY
Tumulus
NEW CUT
Burton
Burton Farm
Burton Lane Copse
CASTLE HILL LA
Clock Tower
NORTH ST
SALISBURY ST
Mere School
MERE
Chaddenwick Wood
BARTON LA
CHURCH ST
THE SQ
BARNES PL
DARK LANE
IVY MEAD
SPRINGFIELD RD
Liby & Mus
The Chantry
ANGEL LA
WATER ST
LYNCH CL
Holwell
BA12
Monarch's Way
Charnage Farm
Charnage
The Grove Building
Cemy
THE PADDOCKS
MILL LANE
Little Wood
Edge Bridge
CLEMENT'S LANE
WALNUT RD
OAK LANE
Southbrook
1 ASHGROVE
2 SOUTHBROOK GDNS
3 WHITEMARSH
4 THE BARTLETTS
5 BALMOOR CL
SOUTHBROOK
Limpers Hill
Rook Street
LORDSMEAD RD
Woodlands Road Ind Est
SHAFTESBURY ROAD
The Causeway
Sewage Works
ROOK ST
Sheeen Water
Woodlands Manor
Woodlands Farm
Field End
Causeway Farm
WOODLANDS ROAD
BARROW STREET LANE
Swain's Ford Bridge
White Hill Wood
White Hill
Church Farm
Barrow Street
Barrow Street Farm
West Swainsford Farm
East Swainsford Farm
Wet Lane Farm
WET LANE
Lyemarsh Farm
Breaches Farm
Homestead Farm
Two Counties Farm
Black House Farm
PIMPERLEAZE ROAD
CUNNAGE LA
SP8

1

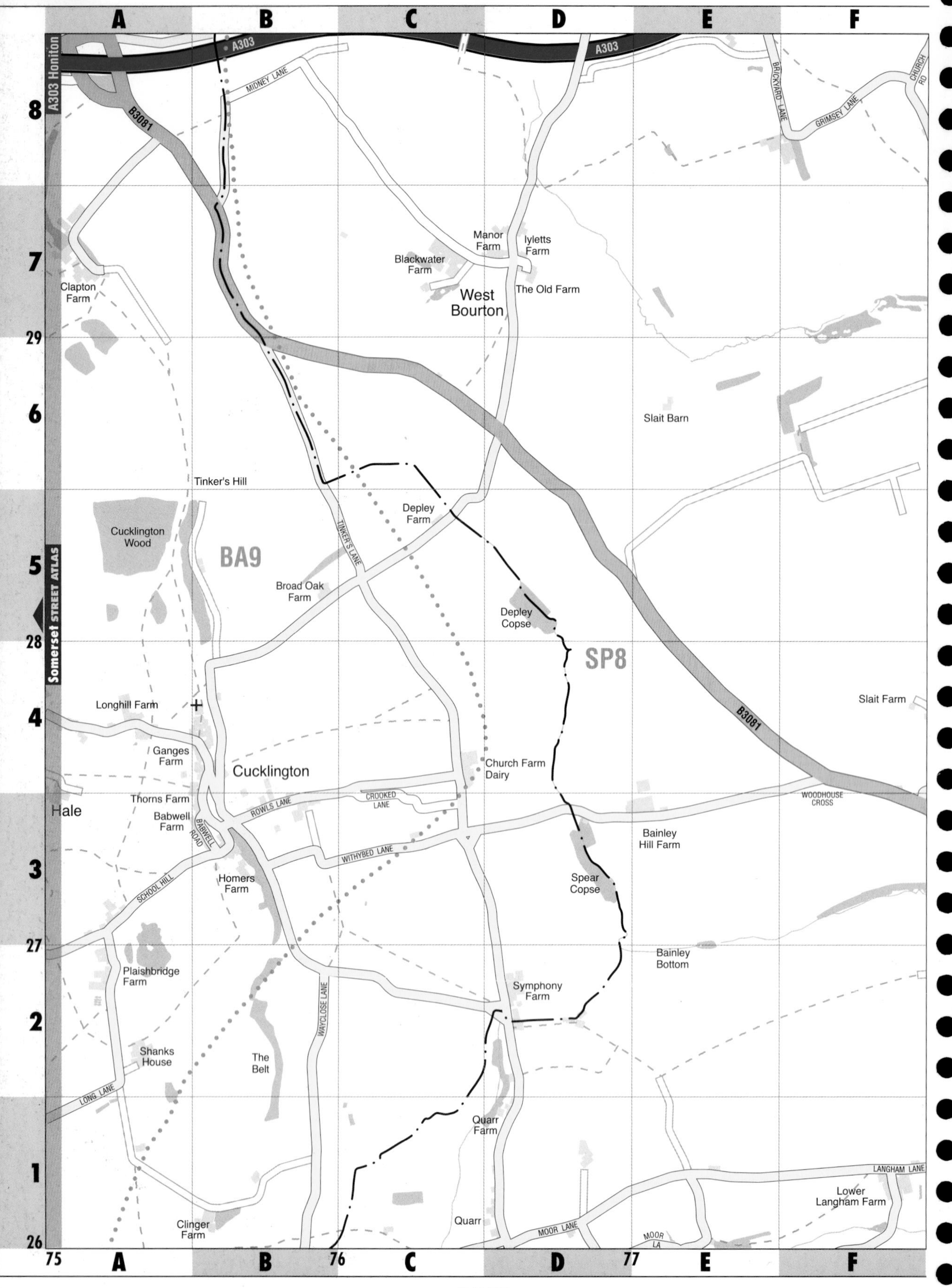
A
B
C
D
E
F
A303 Honiton
A303
A303
MIDNEY LANE
B3081
BRICKYARD LANE
GRIMSEY LANE
CHURCH RD
8
7
29
6
5
28
4
3
27
2
1
26
Manor Farm
Iyletts Farm
Blackwater Farm
The Old Farm
West Bourton
Clapton Farm
Slait Barn
Tinker's Hill
Cucklington Wood
BA9
TINKER'S LANE
Depley Farm
Broad Oak Farm
Depley Copse
SP8
Somerset STREET ATLAS
Longhill Farm
Slait Farm
B3081
Ganges Farm
Cucklington
Church Farm Dairy
Thorns Farm
Hale
CROOKED LANE
ROWLS LANE
WOODHOUSE CROSS
Babwell Farm
BABWELL ROAD
WITHYBED LANE
Bainley Hill Farm
SCHOOL HILL
Homers Farm
Spear Copse
Plaishbridge Farm
Bainley Bottom
WAYCLOSE LANE
Symphony Farm
Shanks House
The Belt
LONG LANE
Quarr Farm
LANGHAM LANE
Lower Langham Farm
Clinger Farm
Quarr
MOOR LANE
MOOR LA
75
76
77

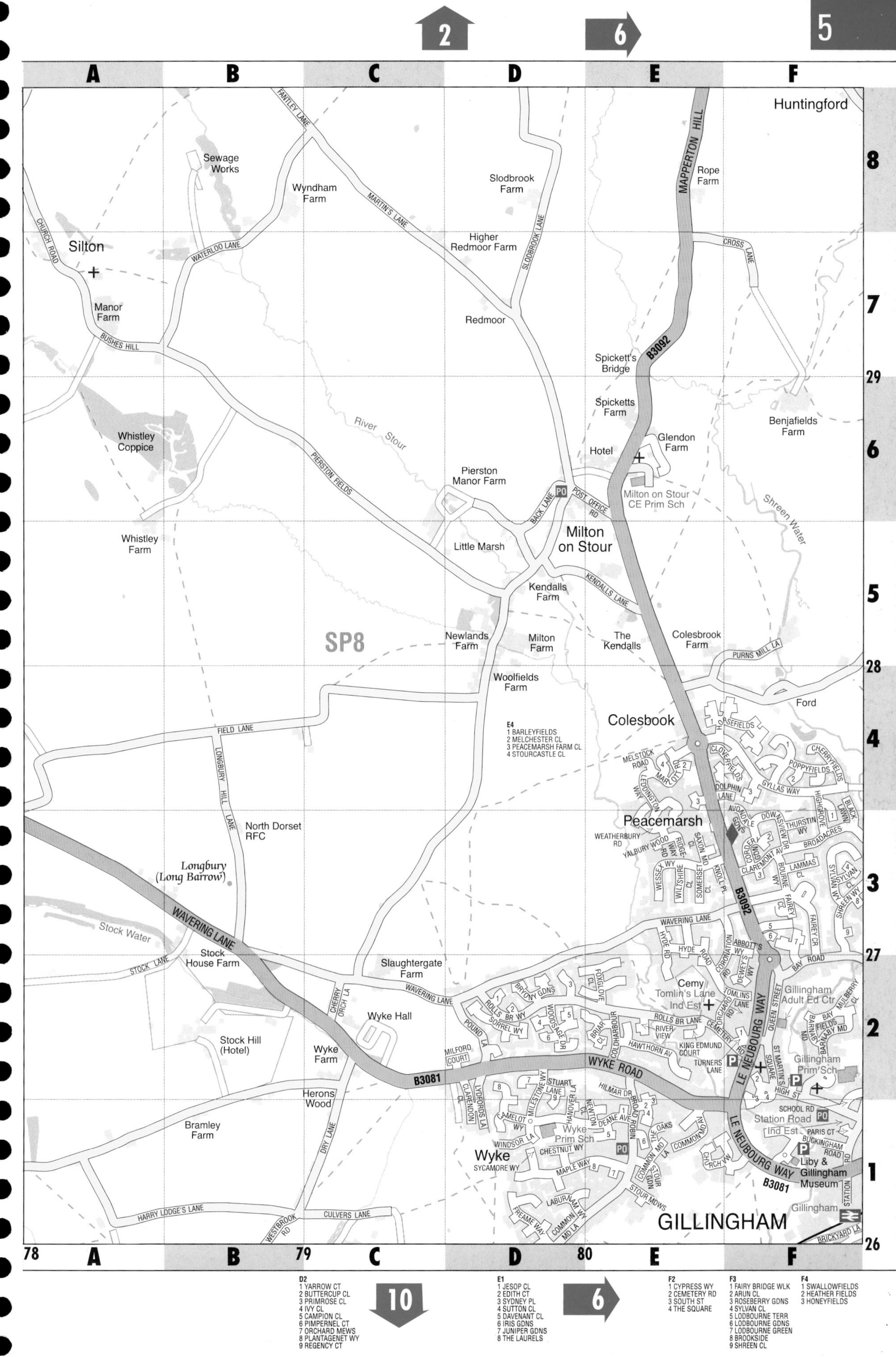

5
2
6
A
B
C
D
E
F
Huntingford
Sewage Works
Wyndham Farm
Slodbrook Farm
Rope Farm
MAPPERTON HILL
FANTLEY LANE
MARTIN'S LANE
CHURCH ROAD
Silton
WATERLOO LANE
Higher Redmoor Farm
SLODBROOK LANE
CROSS LANE
Manor Farm
Redmoor
BUSHES HILL
B3092
Spickett's Bridge
Spicketts Farm
Benjafields Farm
Whistley Coppice
River Stour
Hotel
Glendon Farm
Pierston Manor Farm
PIERSTON FIELDS
PO
POST OFFICE RD
BACK LANE
Milton on Stour CE Prim Sch
Shreen Water
Whistley Farm
Little Marsh
Milton on Stour
KENDALLS LANE
Kendalls Farm
SP8
Newlands Farm
Milton Farm
The Kendalls
Colesbrook Farm
PURNS MILL LA
Woolfields Farm
Ford
Colesbook
FIELD LANE
E4
1 BARLEYFIELDS
2 MELCHESTER CL
3 PEACEMARSH FARM CL
4 STOURCASTLE CL
HORSEFIELDS
MELSTOCK ROAD
CLOVERFIELDS
POPPYFIELDS
CHERRYFIELDS
LONGBURY HILL LANE
LEDDINGTON WAY
DOLPHIN LANE
GYLLAS WAY
North Dorset RFC
Peacemarsh
WEATHERBURY RD
YALBURY WOOD
THURSTIN WY
BROADACRES
Longbury (Long Barrow)
WESSEX WY
WILTSHIRE CL
SOMERSET CL
SAXON MD
KNOLL PL
CLAREMONT AV
LAMMAS CL
BOURNE WAY
SYLVAN WY
SHREEN WAY
Stock Water
WAVERING LANE
HYDE RD
HYDE ROAD
CORONATION RD
ABBOTT'S WY
DEWEY'S WY
FAIREY CR
BAY ROAD
STOCK LANE
Stock House Farm
Slaughtergate Farm
FOXGLOVE CL
Cemy
Tomlin's Lane Ind Est
TOMLINS LANE
Gillingham Adult Ed Ctr
MULBERRY CL
BRYONY GDNS
CHERRY ORCH LA
ROLLS BR WY
SORREL WY
WOODSAGE DR
POUND LA
BRIAR CL
COLDHARBOUR
ROLLS BR LANE
RIVER VIEW
ORCHARD RD
CEMETERY RD
LE NEUBOURG WAY
QUEEN STREET
BAY FIELDS
BARNABY MD
Wyke Hall
Stock Hill (Hotel)
Wyke Farm
MILFORD COURT
HAWTHORN AV
KING EDMUND COURT
TURNERS LANE
P
ST MARTIN'S SQUARE
Gillingham Prim Sch
B3081
WYKE ROAD
STUART LANE
HILMAR DR
HIGH ST
Herons Wood
CLARENDON CL
LYDFORDS LA
MILESTONE WAY
HANOVER LA
NEWTON RD
BROAD ROBIN
SCHOOL RD
Station Road Ind Est
PARIS CT
BUCKINGHAM ROAD
Bramley Farm
DRY LANE
CAMELOT WY
DEANE AVE
THE OAKS
COMMON MD AV
Wyke Prim Sch
WINDSOR LA
CHESTNUT WY
Wyke
SYCAMORE WY
MAPLE WAY
CHURCH WK
Liby & Gillingham Museum
LABURNUM WY
STOUR GDN
STOUR MDWS
STATION RD
FREAME WAY
COMMON MD LA
HARRY LODGE'S LANE
WESTBROOK RD
CULVERS LANE
GILLINGHAM
Gillingham
BRICKYARD LA
78
79
80
8
7
29
6
5
28
4
3
27
2
1
26
D2
1 YARROW CT
2 BUTTERCUP CL
3 PRIMROSE CL
4 IVY CL
5 CAMPION CL
6 PIMPERNEL CT
7 ORCHARD MEWS
8 PLANTAGENET WY
9 REGENCY CT
10
E1
1 JESOP CL
2 EDITH CT
3 SYDNEY PL
4 SUTTON CL
5 DAVENANT CL
6 IRIS GDNS
7 JUNIPER GDNS
8 THE LAURELS
6
F2
1 CYPRESS WY
2 CEMETERY RD
3 SOUTH ST
4 THE SQUARE
F3
1 FAIRY BRIDGE WLK
2 ARUN CL
3 ROSEBERRY GDNS
4 SYLVAN CL
5 LODBOURNE TERR
6 LODBOURNE GDNS
7 LODBOURNE GREEN
8 BROOKSIDE
9 SHREEN CL
F4
1 SWALLOWFIELDS
2 HEATHER FIELDS
3 HONEYFIELDS

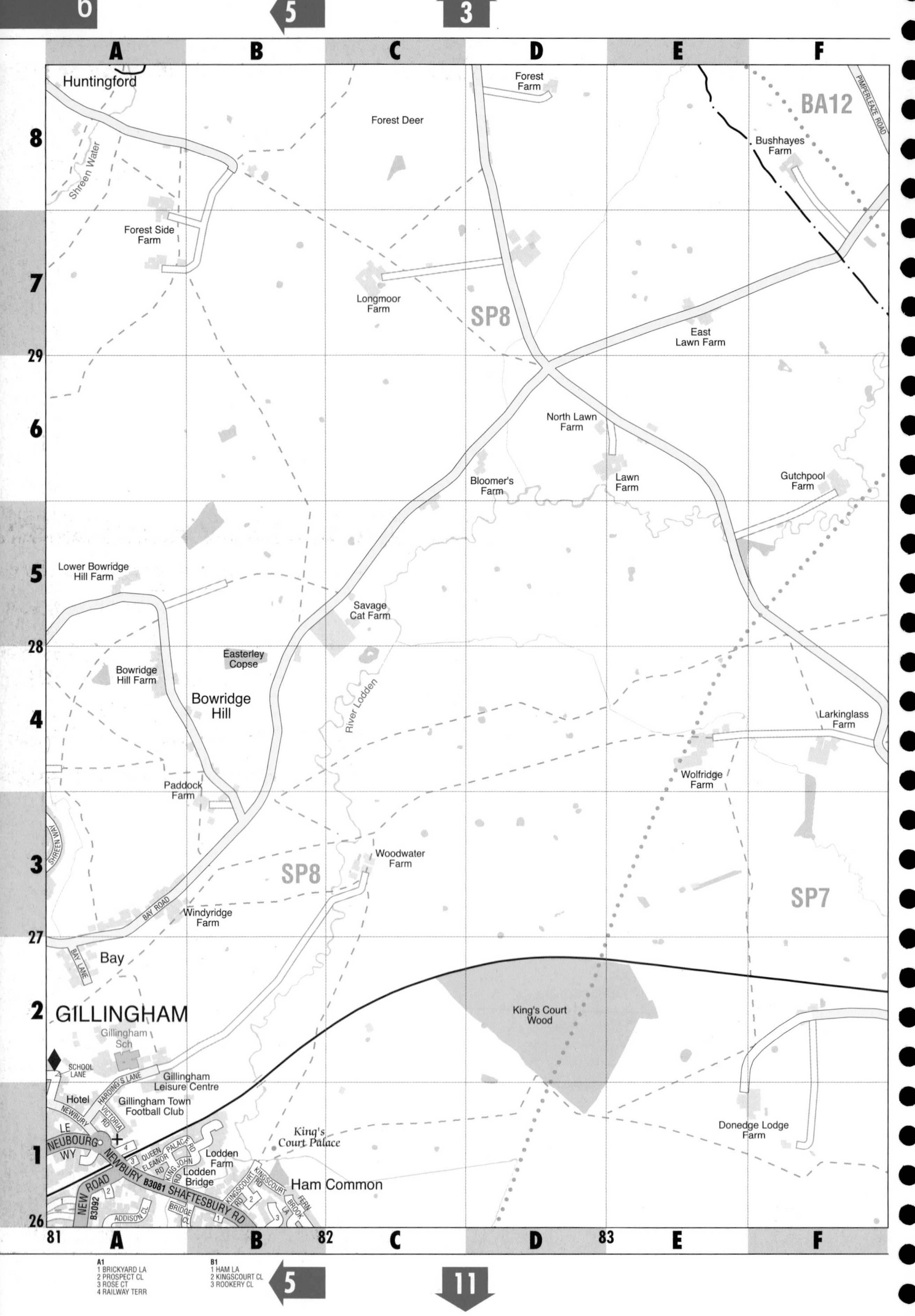

BA12

PIMPERLEAZE ROAD

A   B   C   D   E   F

Huntingford

Forest Farm

Forest Deer

8

Bushhayes Farm

Shreen Water

Forest Side Farm

7

Longmoor Farm

SP8

East Lawn Farm

29

6

North Lawn Farm

Bloomer's Farm

Lawn Farm

Gutchpool Farm

Lower Bowridge Hill Farm

5

Savage Cat Farm

28

Easterley Copse

Bowridge Hill Farm

Bowridge Hill

River Lodden

4

Larkinglass Farm

Wolfridge Farm

Paddock Farm

3

SP8

Woodwater Farm

SP7

BAY ROAD

Windyridge Farm

27

King's Court Wood

Bay

2

GILLINGHAM

Gillingham Sch

SCHOOL LANE

Gillingham Leisure Centre

HARDING'S LANE

Hotel

NEWBURY

VICTORIA RD

Gillingham Town Football Club

Donedge Lodge Farm

LE NEUBOURG WY

NEWBURY

B3092

QUEEN ELEANOR RD

KING JOHN RD

King's Court Palace

Lodden Farm

Lodden Bridge

KINGSCOURT RD

Ham Common

1

B3081 SHAFTESBURY RD

FERN BROOK LA

ADDISON CL

26

NEW ROAD

BRIDGE

81   A   B   82   C   D   83   E   F

A1
1 BRICKYARD LA
2 PROSPECT CL
3 ROSE CT
4 RAILWAY TERR

B1
1 HAM LA
2 KINGSCOURT CL
3 ROOKERY CL

5

11

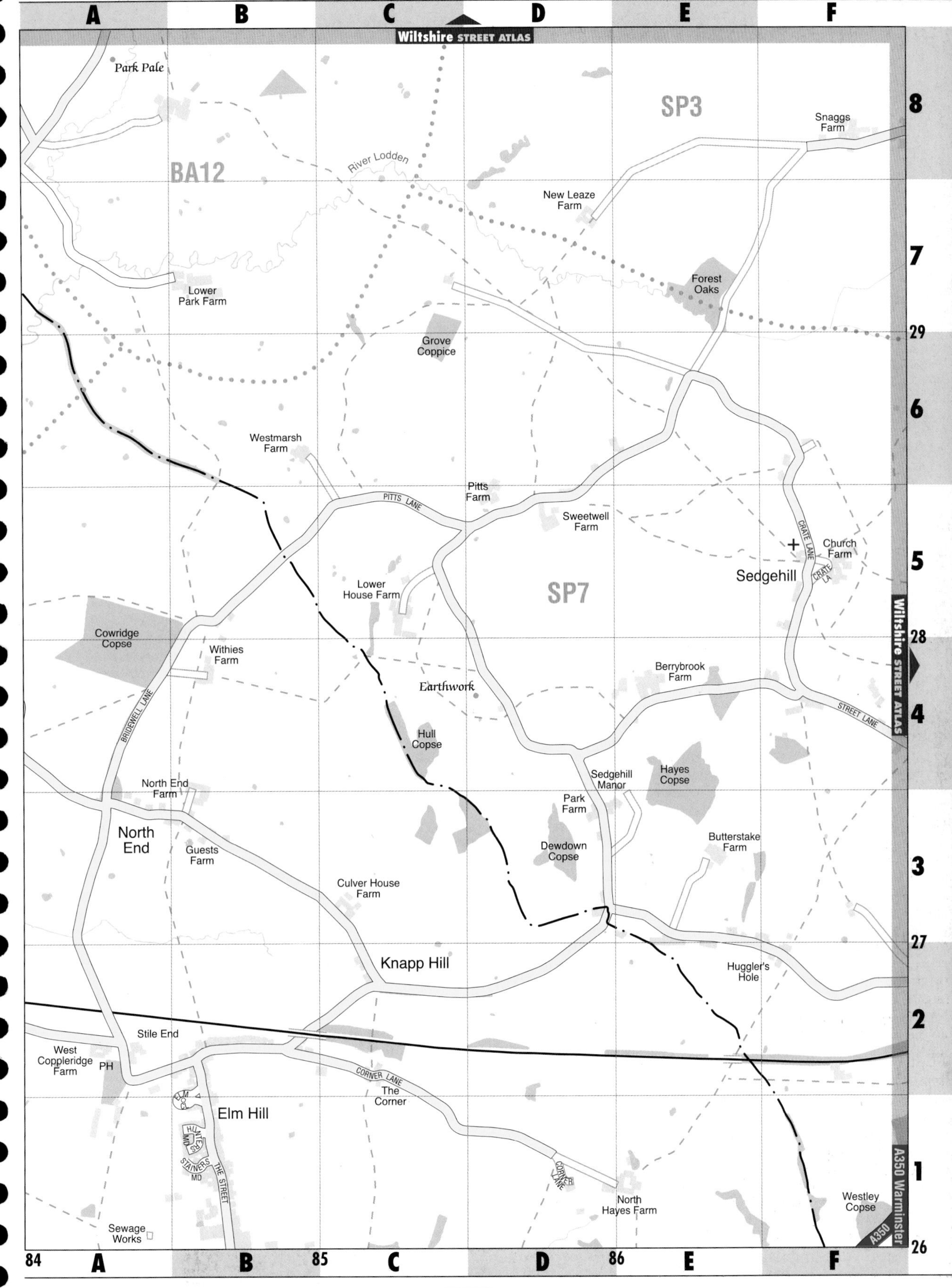

Park Pale

BA12

River Lodden

SP3

Snaggs
Farm

New Leaze
Farm

8

Lower
Park Farm

Forest
Oaks

7

Grove
Coppice

29

Westmarsh
Farm

PITTS LANE

Pitts
Farm

Sweetwell
Farm

6

GRATE LANE

Church
Farm

Sedgehill

GRATE LA.

5

Lower
House Farm

SP7

Cowridge
Copse

Withies
Farm

28

Earthwork

Berrybrook
Farm

BRIDEWELL LANE

STREET LANE

4

Hull
Copse

North End
Farm

Sedgehill
Manor

Hayes
Copse

North
End

Guests
Farm

Park
Farm

Butterstake
Farm

3

Culver House
Farm

Dewdown
Copse

27

Knapp Hill

Huggler's
Hole

Stile End

2

West
Coppleridge
Farm

PH

CORNER LANE

The
Corner

ELM CL

HUNTERS MD

STAINERS MD

THE STREET

Elm Hill

CORNER LANE

North
Hayes Farm

Westley
Copse

1

Sewage
Works

Wiltshire STREET ATLAS

A350 Warminster

A350

26

84   A   B   85   C   D   86   E   F

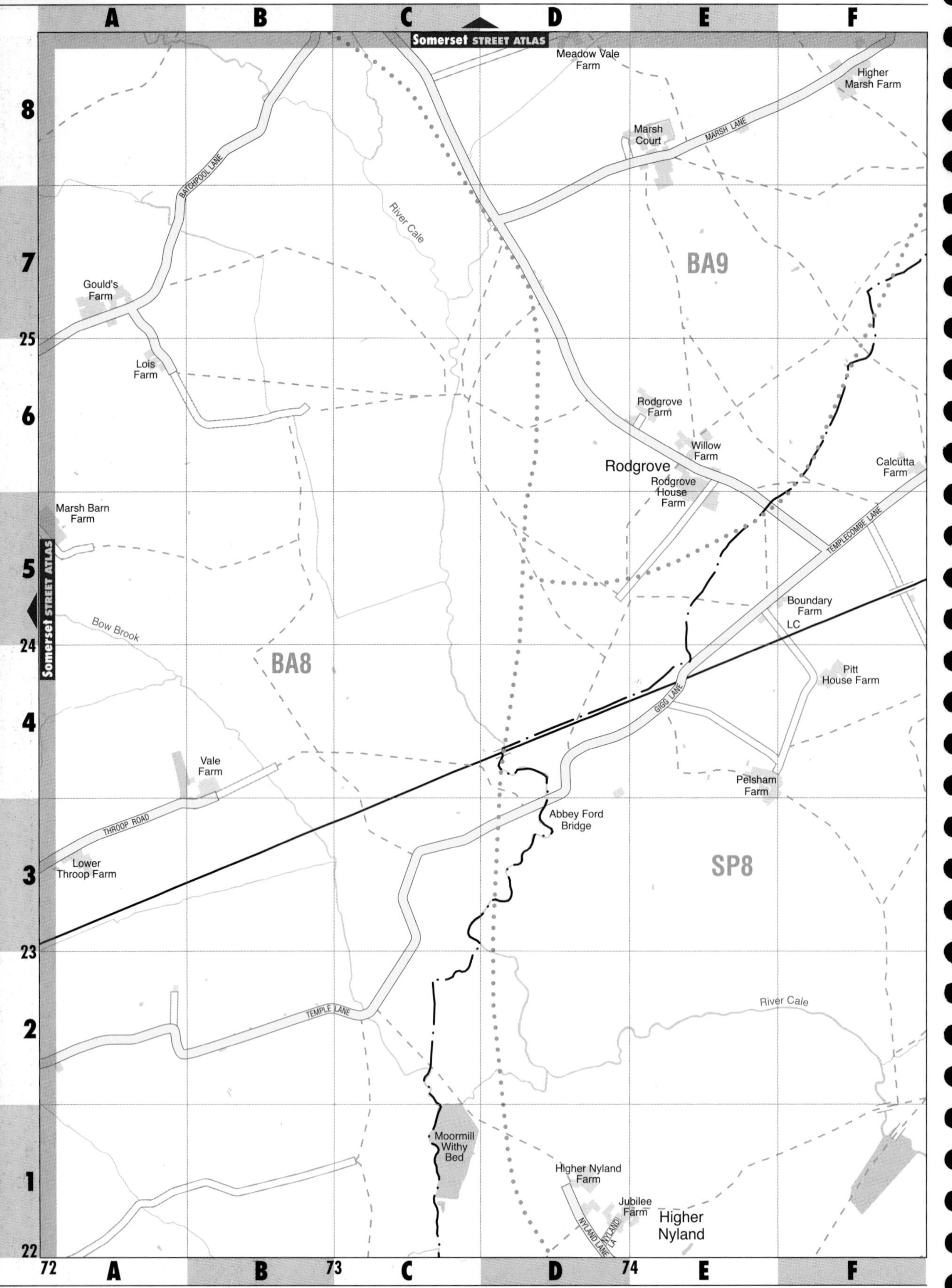

Meadow Vale Farm

Higher Marsh Farm

Marsh Court

MARSH LANE

BA9

River Cale

BATCHPOOL LANE

Gould's Farm

Lois Farm

Rodgrove Farm

Willow Farm

Rodgrove

Calcutta Farm

Rodgrove House Farm

Marsh Barn Farm

TEMPLECOMBE LANE

Boundary Farm LC

BA8

Bow Brook

Pitt House Farm

GIGG LANE

Vale Farm

Pelsham Farm

THROOP ROAD

Abbey Ford Bridge

SP8

Lower Throop Farm

River Cale

TEMPLE LANE

Moormill Withy Bed

Higher Nyland Farm

Jubilee Farm

NYLAND LANE

Higher Nyland

4
10

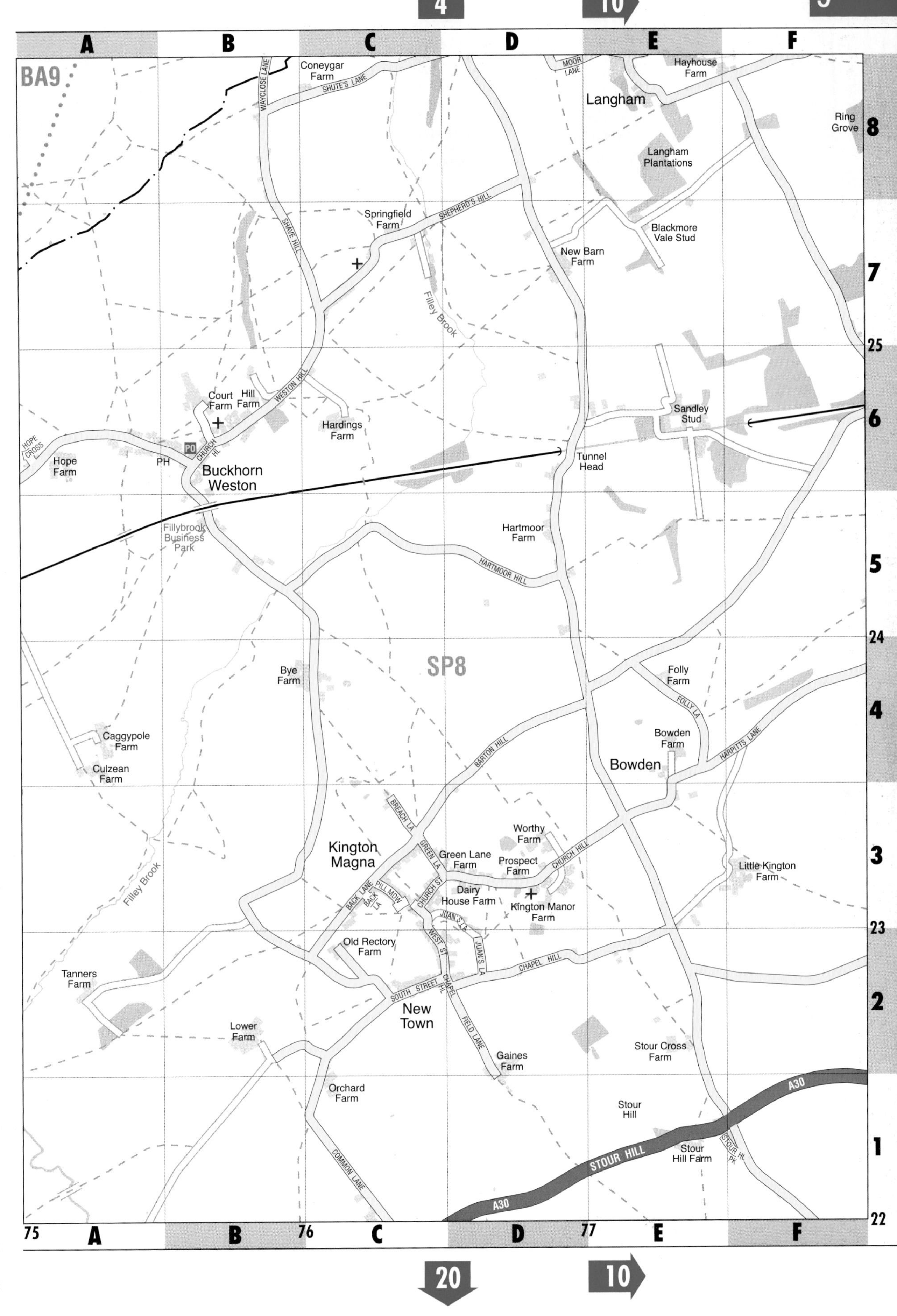

A B C D E F
BA9
Coneygar Farm
SHUTE'S LANE
WAYCLOSE LANE
MOOR LANE
Hayhouse Farm
Langham
Ring Grove
Langham Plantations
Springfield Farm
SHEPHERD'S HILL
SHAVE HILL
Blackmore Vale Stud
New Barn Farm
Filley Brook
Court Farm
Hill Farm
WESTON HILL
Hardings Farm
Sandley Stud
HOPE CROSS
Hope Farm
PH
PO
CHURCH HL
Buckhorn Weston
Tunnel Head
Fillybrook Business Park
Hartmoor Farm
HARTMOOR HILL
SP8
Bye Farm
Folly Farm
FOLLY LA
Caggypole Farm
Culzean Farm
BARTON HILL
Bowden Farm
Bowden
HARPITTS LANE
BREACH LA
Worthy Farm
Kington Magna
GREEN LA
Green Lane Farm
Prospect Farm
CHURCH HILL
Little Kington Farm
Filley Brook
BACK LANE
PILL MDW
BACK LA
CHURCH ST
Dairy House Farm
Kington Manor Farm
JUAN'S LA
WEST ST
Old Rectory Farm
CHAPEL HILL
Tanners Farm
SOUTH STREET
CHAPEL HL
New Town
Lower Farm
FIELD LANE
Gaines Farm
Stour Cross Farm
Orchard Farm
A30
Stour Hill
STOUR HILL
Stour Hill Farm
STOUR HL
STOUR PK
COMMON LANE
A30
8
7
25
6
5
24
4
3
23
2
1
22
75
76
77

20
10

A B C D E F

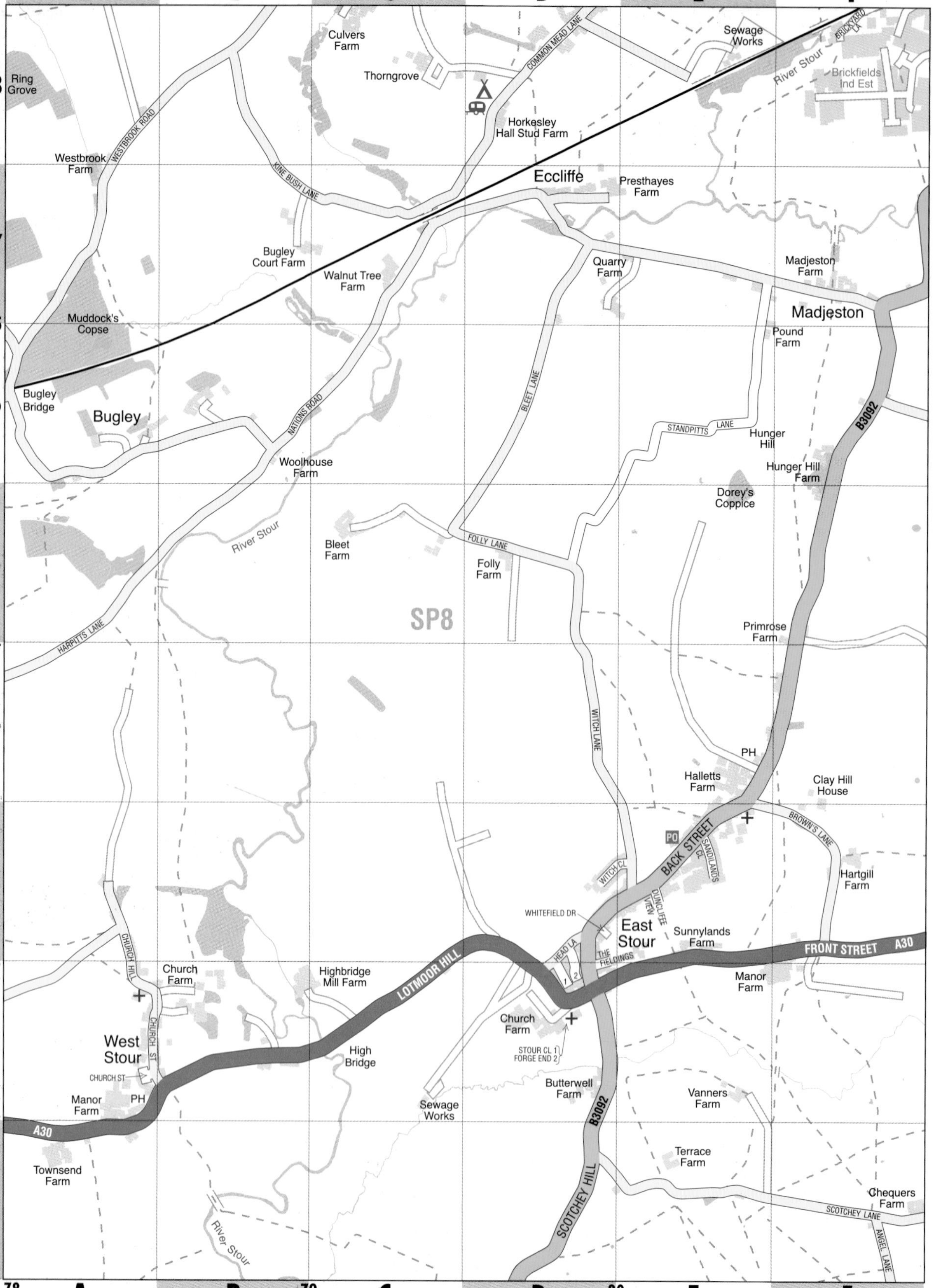

8
Ring Grove
Culvers Farm
Thorngrove
Sewage Works
River Stour
Brickfields Ind Est
Westbrook Farm
WESTBROOK ROAD
Horkesley Hall Stud Farm
Eccliffe
Presthayes Farm
KINE BUSH LANE

7
Bugley Court Farm
Walnut Tree Farm
Quarry Farm
Madjeston Farm
Madjeston

25
Muddock's Copse
Pound Farm
B3092

6
Bugley Bridge
Bugley
NATIONS ROAD
BLEET LANE
STANDPITTS LANE
Hunger Hill
Hunger Hill Farm
Woolhouse Farm
Dorey's Coppice

5
River Stour
Bleet Farm
FOLLY LANE
Folly Farm
SP8
Primrose Farm

24
HARPITTS LANE

4
WITCH LANE
PH
Halletts Farm
Clay Hill House

3
Witch Cl
BACK STREET
SANDYLANDS
Hartgill Farm
WHITEFIELD DR
East Stour
Sunnylands Farm
PO
DUNCLIFFE VIEW
BROWN'S LANE

23
Church Farm
Highbridge Mill Farm
LOTMOOR HILL
HEAD LA
THE HELDINGS
FRONT STREET A30
Manor Farm
CHURCH HILL

2
West Stour
CHURCH ST
High Bridge
Church Farm
STOUR CL 1
FORGE END 2
Vanners Farm
Manor Farm
PH
CHURCH ST
Sewage Works
Butterwell Farm
B3092
Terrace Farm

1
A30
Townsend Farm
SCOTCHEY HILL
Chequers Farm
SCOTCHEY LANE
ANGEL LANE

22
River Stour

78 A B 79 C D 80 E F

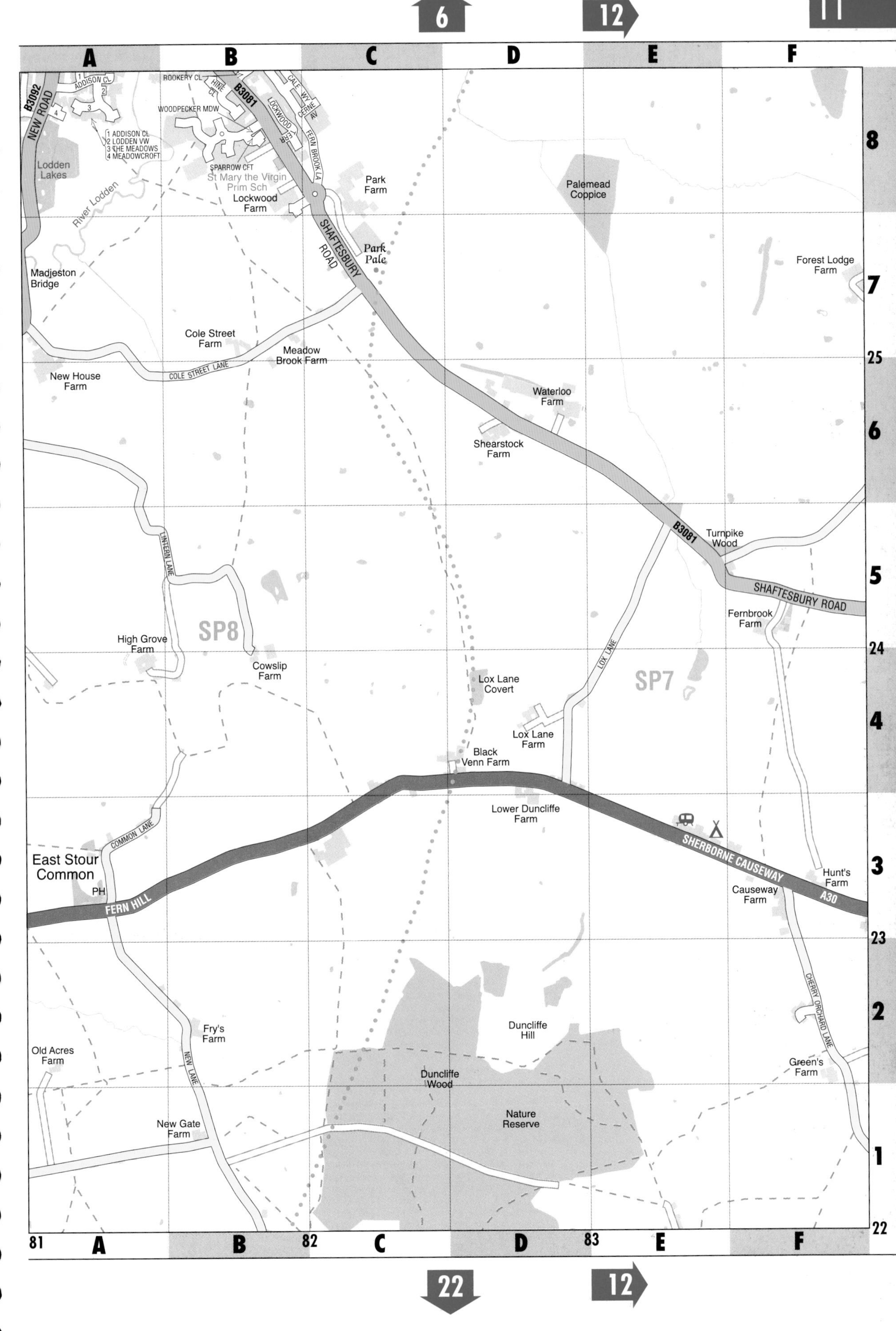
6
12
A
B
C
D
E
F
8
7
25
6
5
24
4
3
23
2
1
22
81
82
83
22
12
B3092
NEW ROAD
ADDISON CL
ROOKERY CL
HINE CL
B3081
LOCKWOOD
CALE WY
CERNE AV
FERN BROOK LA
WOODPECKER MDW
1 ADDISON CL
2 LODDEN VW
3 THE MEADOWS
4 MEADOWCROFT
SPARROW CFT
St Mary the Virgin
Prim Sch
Lodden Lakes
River Lodden
Lockwood Farm
Park Farm
Palemead Coppice
SHAFTESBURY ROAD
Park Pale
Madjeston Bridge
Forest Lodge Farm
Cole Street Farm
Meadow Brook Farm
COLE STREET LANE
New House Farm
Waterloo Farm
Shearstock Farm
B3081
Turnpike Wood
SHAFTESBURY ROAD
LINTERN LANE
SP8
High Grove Farm
Cowslip Farm
Fernbrook Farm
LOX LANE
SP7
Lox Lane Covert
Lox Lane Farm
Black Venn Farm
Lower Duncliffe Farm
COMMON LANE
East Stour Common
PH
FERN HILL
SHERBORNE CAUSEWAY
A30
Hunt's Farm
Causeway Farm
CHERRY ORCHARD LANE
Fry's Farm
Old Acres Farm
Duncliffe Hill
Duncliffe Wood
Nature Reserve
NEW LANE
New Gate Farm
Green's Farm

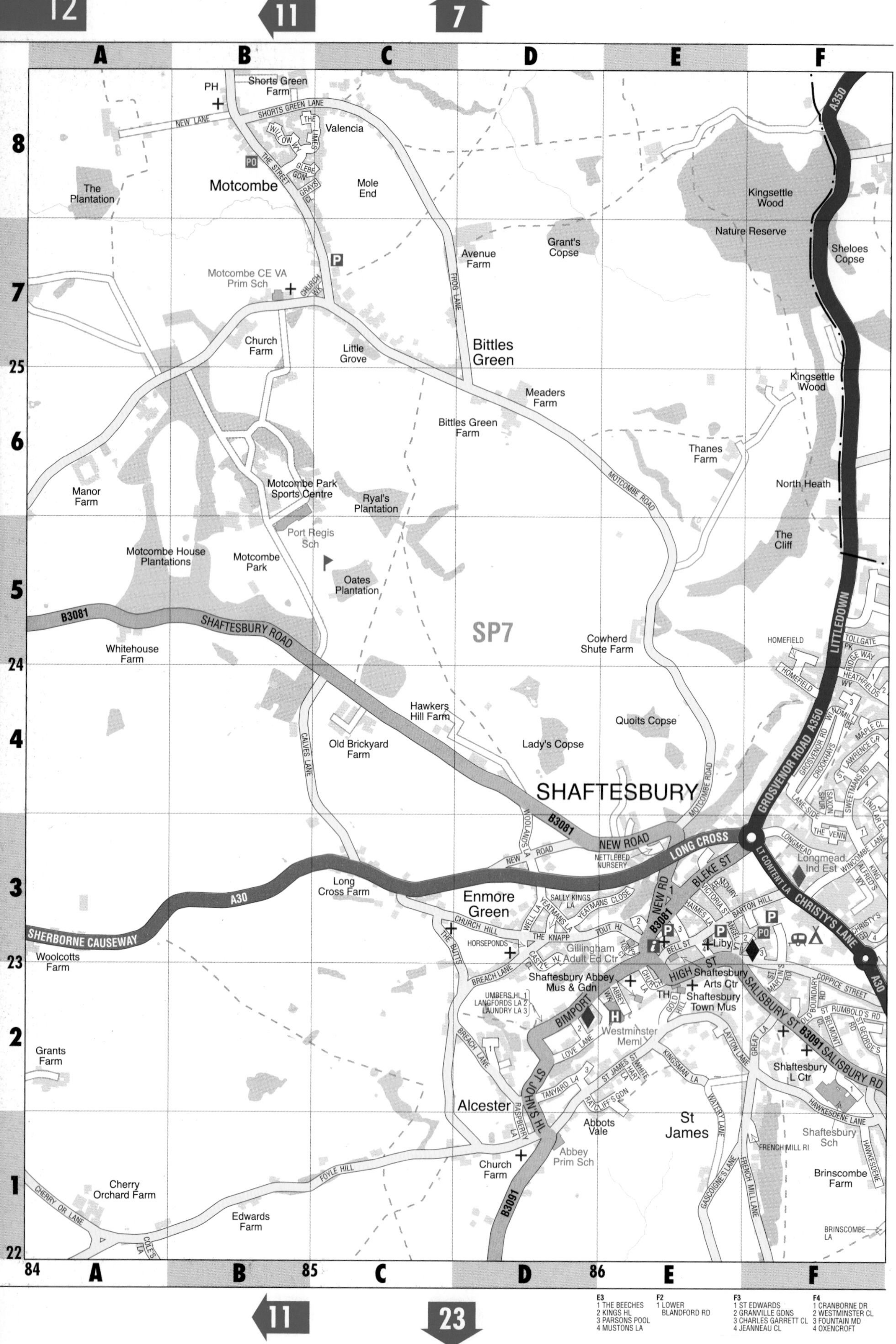

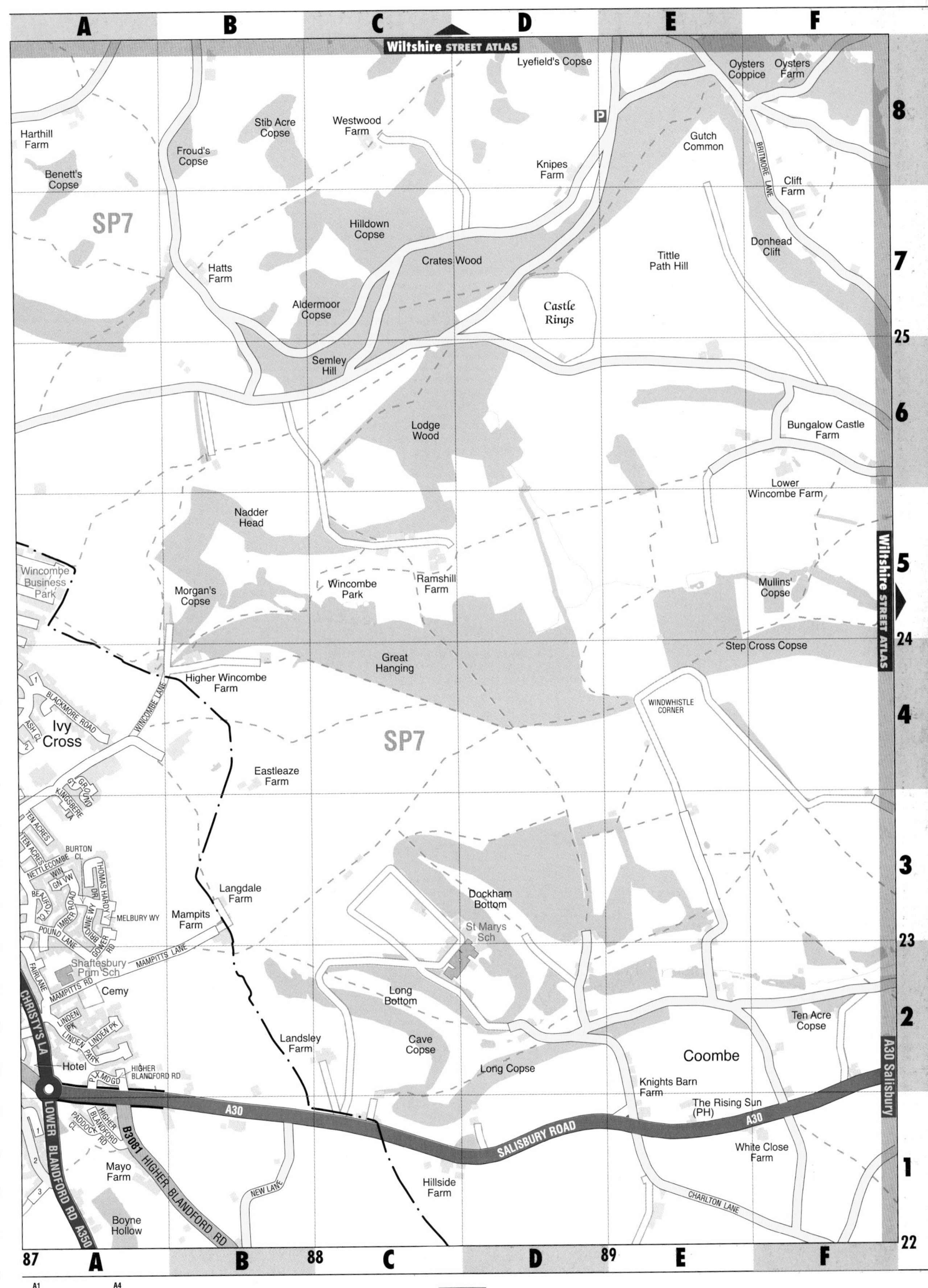

Lyefield's Copse

Oysters Coppice

Oysters Farm

8

Harthill Farm

Stib Acre Copse

Westwood Farm

Gutch Common

BRITMORE LANE

Clift Farm

Benett's Copse

Froud's Copse

Knipes Farm

Donhead Clift

SP7

Hatts Farm

Hilldown Copse

Crates Wood

Tittle Path Hill

7

Aldermoor Copse

Castle Rings

25

Semley Hill

6

Lodge Wood

Bungalow Castle Farm

Nadder Head

Lower Wincombe Farm

Wincombe Business Park

Morgan's Copse

Wincombe Park

Ramshill Farm

Mullins' Copse

5

Step Cross Copse

24

Higher Wincombe Farm

Great Hanging

WINDWHISTLE CORNER

4

Ivy Cross

SP7

BLACKMORE ROAD

ASH CL

Eastleaze Farm

3

G. GROUND

KINGSBERE LA

Langdale Farm

Dockham Bottom

TEN ACRES

BURTON CL

NETTLECOMBE CL

THOMAS HARDY DR

Mampits Farm

St Marys Sch

23

AMBER RD

SNNE WY

MELBURY WY

Shaftesbury Prim Sch

MAMPITTS LANE

Long Bottom

Cemy

LINDEN RD

FAIR LANE

MAMPITTS RD

LINDEN PK

Landsley Farm

Cave Copse

Ten Acre Copse

2

CHRISTY'S LA

Hotel

HIGHER BLANDFORD RD

Coombe

A30 Salisbury

LOWER BLANDFORD RD A350

B3081 HIGHER BLANDFORD RD

A30

Long Copse

Knights Barn Farm

The Rising Sun (PH)

A30

Mayo Farm

NEW LANE

Hillside Farm

SALISBURY ROAD

White Close Farm

1

Boyne Hollow

CHARLTON LANE

22

A1
1 BUTTS MD
2 LWR BLANDFORD RD
3 BRINSCOMBE LA

A4
1 HAWTHORN CL
2 SPRINGFIELD CL

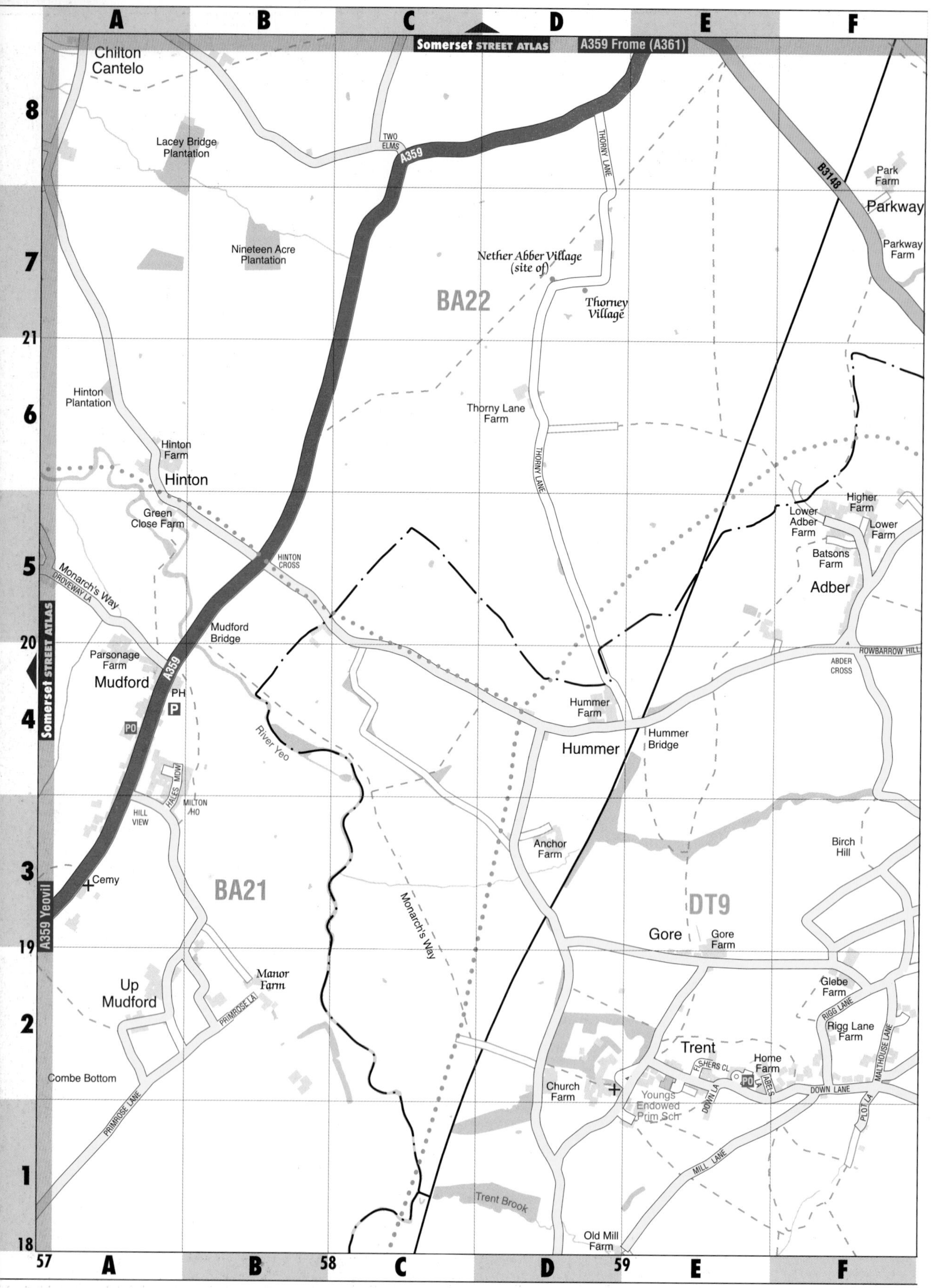

A359 Frome (A361)

Chilton
Cantelo

Lacey Bridge
Plantation

Nineteen Acre
Plantation

B3148

Park
Farm

Parkway

Parkway
Farm

Nether Abber Village
(site of)

BA22

Thorney
Village

Hinton
Plantation

Thorny Lane
Farm

THORNY LANE

Hinton
Farm

Hinton

Green
Close Farm

HINTON
CROSS

Lower
Adber
Farm

Higher
Farm

Lower
Farm

Batsons
Farm

Adber

Monarch's Way
DROVEWAY LA

Mudford
Bridge

ROWBARROW HILL

ABDER
CROSS

Parsonage
Farm

A359

Somerset STREET ATLAS

Mudford

PH

P

PO

River Yeo

HALES MDW

HILL
VIEW

MILTON
HO

Hummer
Farm

Hummer
Bridge

Hummer

Birch
Hill

Cemy

BA21

Monarch's Way

Anchor
Farm

DT9

Gore

Gore
Farm

A359 Yeovil

Up
Mudford

Manor
Farm

PRIMROSE LA

PRIMROSE LANE

Glebe
Farm

RIGG LANE

Rigg Lane
Farm

MALTHOUSE LANE

Trent

Combe Bottom

FISHERS CL

Home
Farm

PO

DOWN LA

ABERS

DOWN LANE

PLOT LA

Church
Farm

Youngs
Endowed
Prim Sch

MILL LANE

Trent Brook

Old Mill
Farm

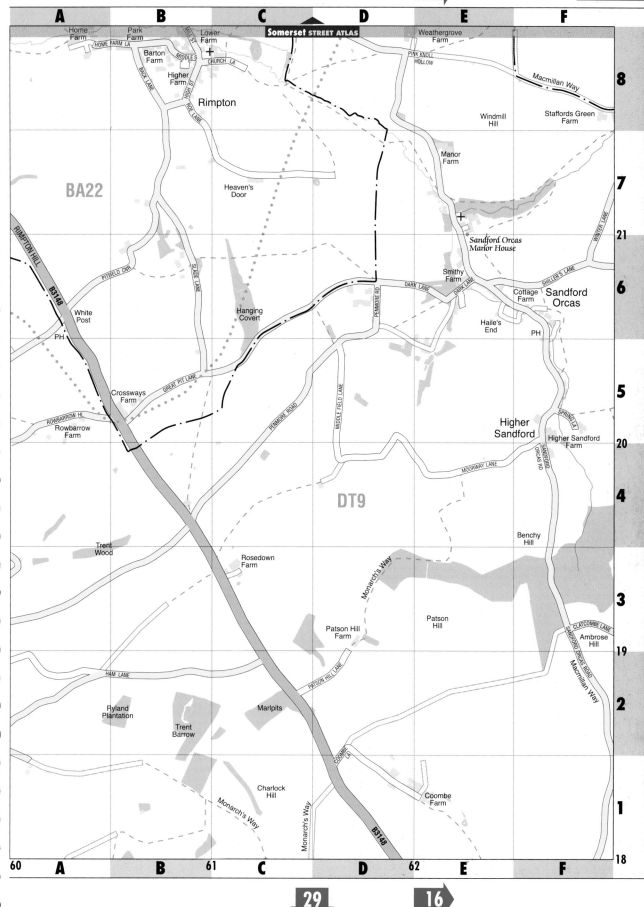

Somerset STREET ATLAS

Home Farm
Park Farm
Barton Farm
Higher Farm
Lower Farm
Weathergrove Farm
HOME FARM LA
MILL ST
MIDDLE ST
BACK LANE
CHURCH LA
PINK KNOLL HOLLOW
Macmillan Way
8
Rimpton
HIGH ST
ROE LANE
Heaven's Door
Windmill Hill
Staffords Green Farm
BA22
Manor Farm
7
Sandford Orcas Manor House
WINTER LANE
21
PITFIELD CNR
SLADE LANE
Smithy Farm
Dark Lane
DARK LANE
SHILLER'S LANE
Cottage Farm
Sandford Orcas
6
RIMPTON HILL
B3148
White Post
Hanging Covert
PENMORE RD
Haile's End
PH
PH
5
PH
Crossways Farm
GREAT PIT LANE
PENMORE ROAD
MIDDLE FIELD LANE
Higher Sandford
SPRING LA
Higher Sandford Farm
20
ROWBARROW HL
Rowbarrow Farm
MOORWAY LANE
SANDFORD ORCAS RD
DT9
4
Trent Wood
Benchy Hill
Rosedown Farm
Monarch's Way
3
Patson Hill
CLATCOMBE LANE
Ambrose Hill
Patson Hill Farm
19
HAM LANE
PATSON HILL LANE
SANDFORD ORCAS ROAD
Macmillan Way
2
Ryland Plantation
Marlpits
Trent Barrow
COOMBE LA
Charlock Hill
Coombe Farm
1
Monarch's Way
Monarch's Way
B3148
18

60   A   B   61   C   D   62   E   F

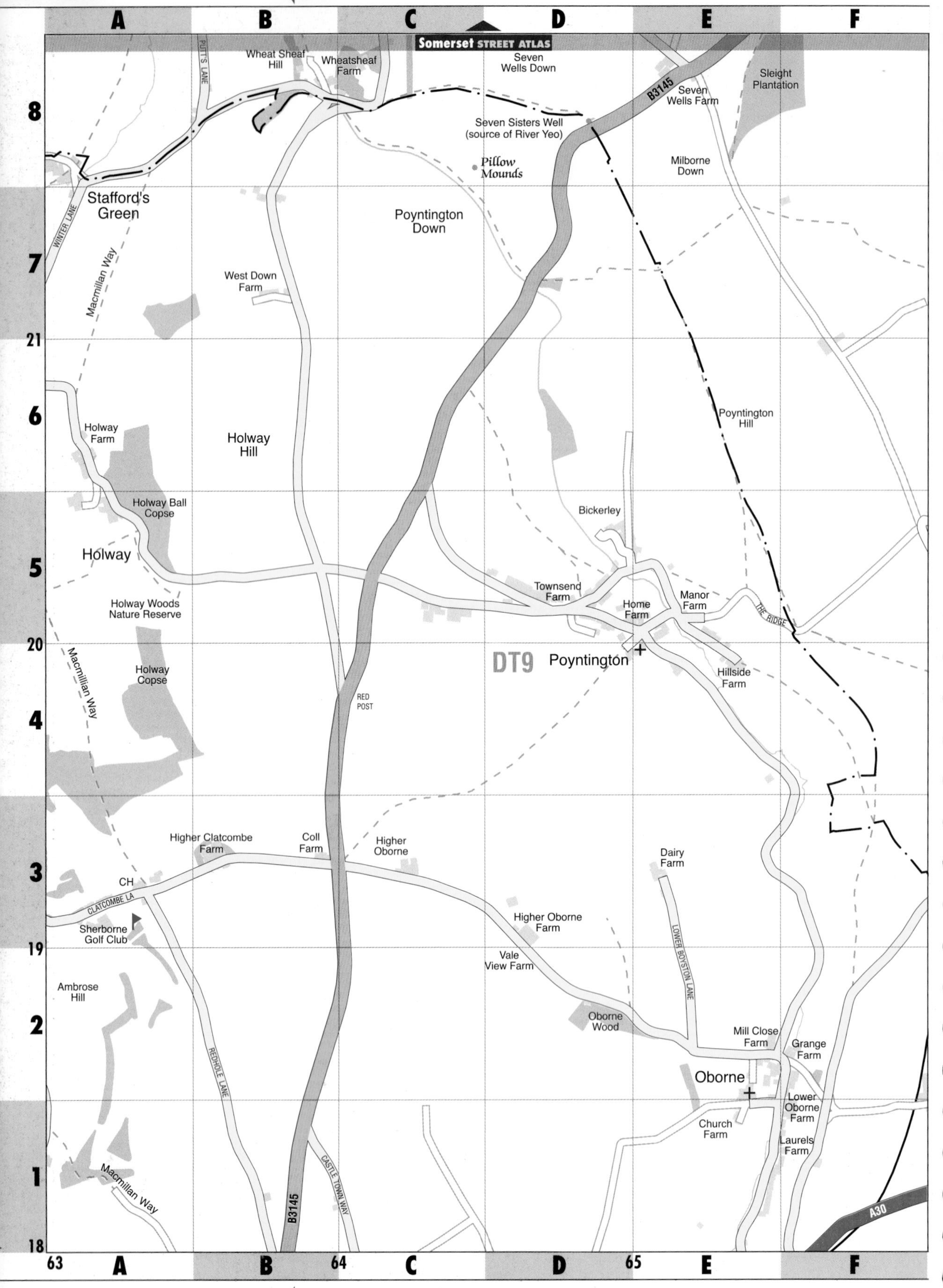

Somerset STREET ATLAS

A B C D E F

8

Wheat Sheaf Hill
Wheatsheaf Farm
Seven Wells Down
Seven Wells Farm
Sleight Plantation
B3145

Seven Sisters Well (source of River Yeo)
Milborne Down

Stafford's Green

Poyntington Down
Pillow Mounds

7

West Down Farm

Macmillan Way

21

Poyntington Hill

6

Holway Farm
Holway Hill

Holway Ball Copse

Bickerley

5

Holway
Townsend Farm
Home Farm
Manor Farm
THE RIDGE

Holway Woods Nature Reserve

20

Holway Copse

Macmillan Way

DT9 Poyntington

RED POST

Hillside Farm

4

Higher Clatcombe Farm
Coll Farm
Higher Oborne

Dairy Farm

3

CH
CLATCOMBE LA

Higher Oborne Farm

LOWER BOYSTON LANE

Sherborne Golf Club

19

Vale View Farm

Ambrose Hill

Oborne Wood

Mill Close Farm
Grange Farm

2

REDHOLE LANE

Oborne
Lower Oborne Farm
Church Farm
Laurels Farm

1

Macmillan Way
B3145
CASTLE TOWN WAY

A30

18

63   A   B   64   C   D   65   E   F

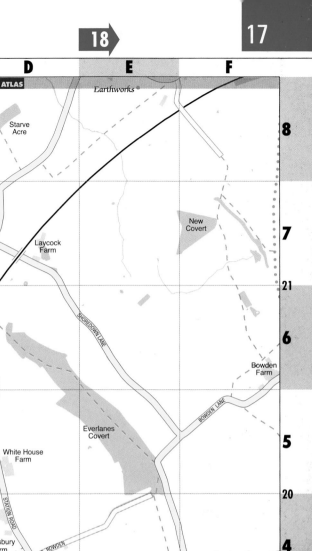

Somerset STREET ATLAS

C2
1 BAUNTONS CL
2 PLOVER CL
3 PRANKERDS RD
4 LAMBERT CL

◀ 31

D1
1 CANNON CT MS
2 PUD BROOK

18 ▶

D2
1 WHEATHILL CL
2 GLOVERS CL
3 LIMERICK CL
4 LOWER GUNVILLE
5 HIGHER GUNVILLE
6 SANSOME'S HL
7 CHAPEL LA

17

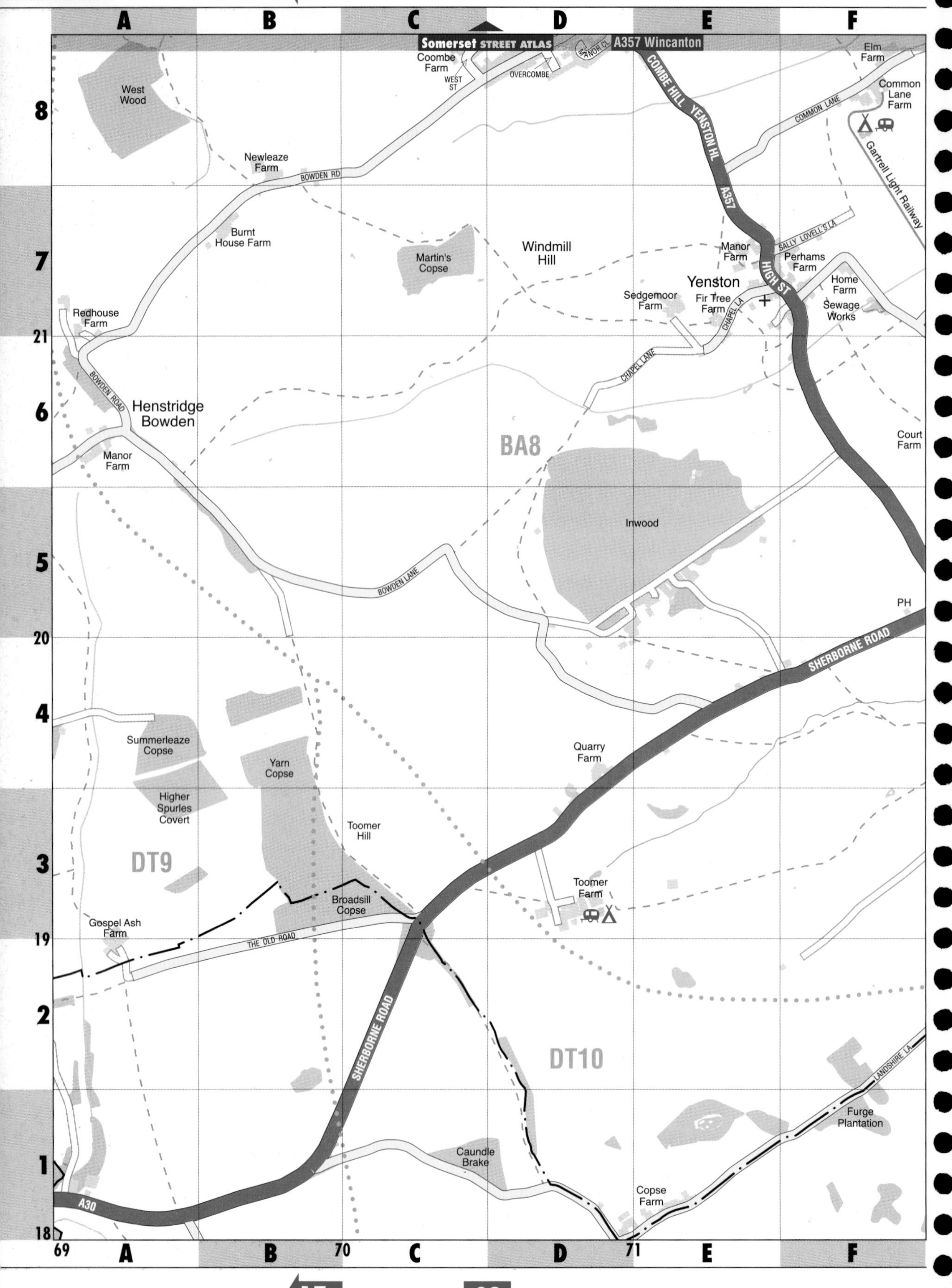

A
B
C
D
E
F
Somerset STREET ATLAS
A357 Wincanton
8
7
21
6
5
20
4
3
19
2
1
18
69
70
71
West Wood
Coombe Farm
WEST ST
OVERCOMBE
MANOR CL
COMBE HILL
YENSTON HL
A357
Elm Farm
Common Lane Farm
COMMON LANE
Gartrell Light Railway
Newleaze Farm
BOWDEN RD
Burnt House Farm
Martin's Copse
Windmill Hill
Manor Farm
SALLY LOVELL'S LA
HIGH ST
Perhams Farm
Yenston
Home Farm
Sedgemoor Farm
Fir Tree Farm
CHAPEL LA
Sewage Works
Redhouse Farm
BOWDEN ROAD
CHAPEL LANE
Henstridge Bowden
BA8
Court Farm
Manor Farm
Inwood
BOWDEN LANE
PH
SHERBORNE ROAD
Summerleaze Copse
Yarn Copse
Quarry Farm
Higher Spurles Covert
Toomer Hill
DT9
Toomer Farm
Broadsill Copse
Gospel Ash Farm
THE OLD ROAD
SHERBORNE ROAD
DT10
LANDSHIRE LA
Furge Plantation
Caundle Brake
Copse Farm
A30

17

32

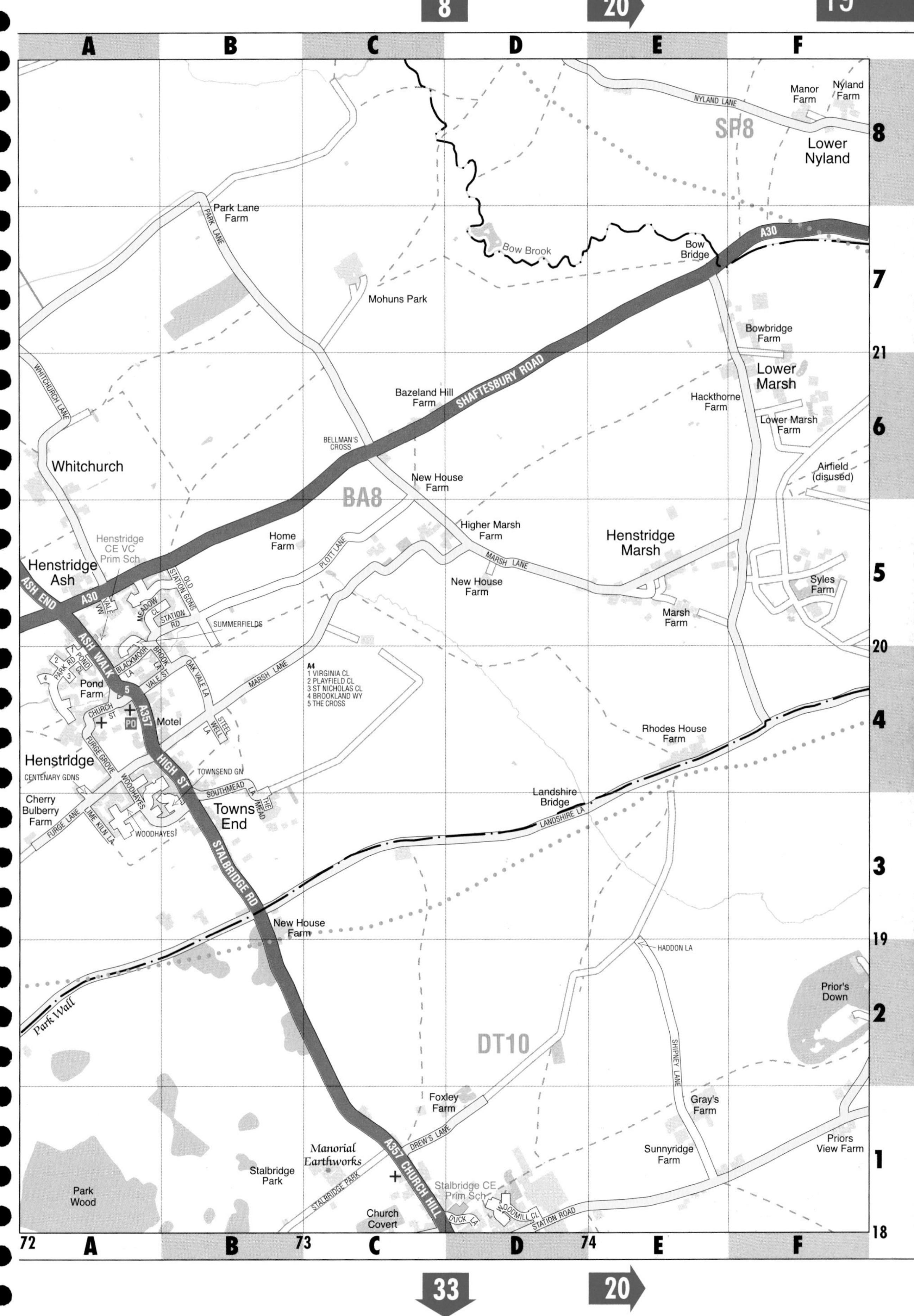
A
B
C
D
E
F
SP8
Manor Farm
Nyland Farm
NYLAND LANE
Lower Nyland
Park Lane Farm
PARK LANE
Bow Brook
Bow Bridge
A30
Mohuns Park
Bowbridge Farm
Lower Marsh
Hackthorne Farm
Lower Marsh Farm
WHITCHURCH LANE
Bazeland Hill Farm
SHAFTESBURY ROAD
BELLMAN'S CROSS
Whitchurch
New House Farm
BA8
Airfield (disused)
Henstridge CE VC Prim Sch
Home Farm
Higher Marsh Farm
Henstridge Marsh
Henstridge Ash
PLOTT LANE
MARSH LANE
ASH END
OLD STATION GDNS
New House Farm
Syles Farm
MEADOW CL
STATION RD
SUMMERFIELDS
Marsh Farm
ASH WALK
BLACKMOOR LA
BROOK LA
VALE ST
OAK VALE LA
MARSH LANE
A4
1 VIRGINIA CL
2 PLAYFIELD CL
3 ST NICHOLAS CL
4 BROOKLAND WY
5 THE CROSS
PARK RD
POND CL
Pond Farm
CHURCH ST
A357
PO
Motel
STEEL WELL LA
Rhodes House Farm
Henstridge
FURGE GROVE
HIGH ST
TOWNSEND GN
CENTENARY GDNS
WOODHAYES
SOUTHMEAD LA
THE MEAD
Landshire Bridge
Cherry Bulberry Farm
Towns End
LANDSHIRE LA
FURGE LANE
LIME KILN LA
WOODHAYES
STALBRIDGE RD
New House Farm
HADDON LA
Park Wall
Prior's Down
DT10
SHIPNEY LANE
Foxley Farm
Gray's Farm
DREW'S LANE
Manorial Earthworks
A357 CHURCH HILL
Sunnyridge Farm
Priors View Farm
Stalbridge Park
Park Wood
STALBRIDGE PARK
Stalbridge CE Prim Sch
Church Covert
DUCK LA
WOODMILL CL
STATION ROAD
8
7
21
6
5
20
4
3
19
2
1
18
72
73
74

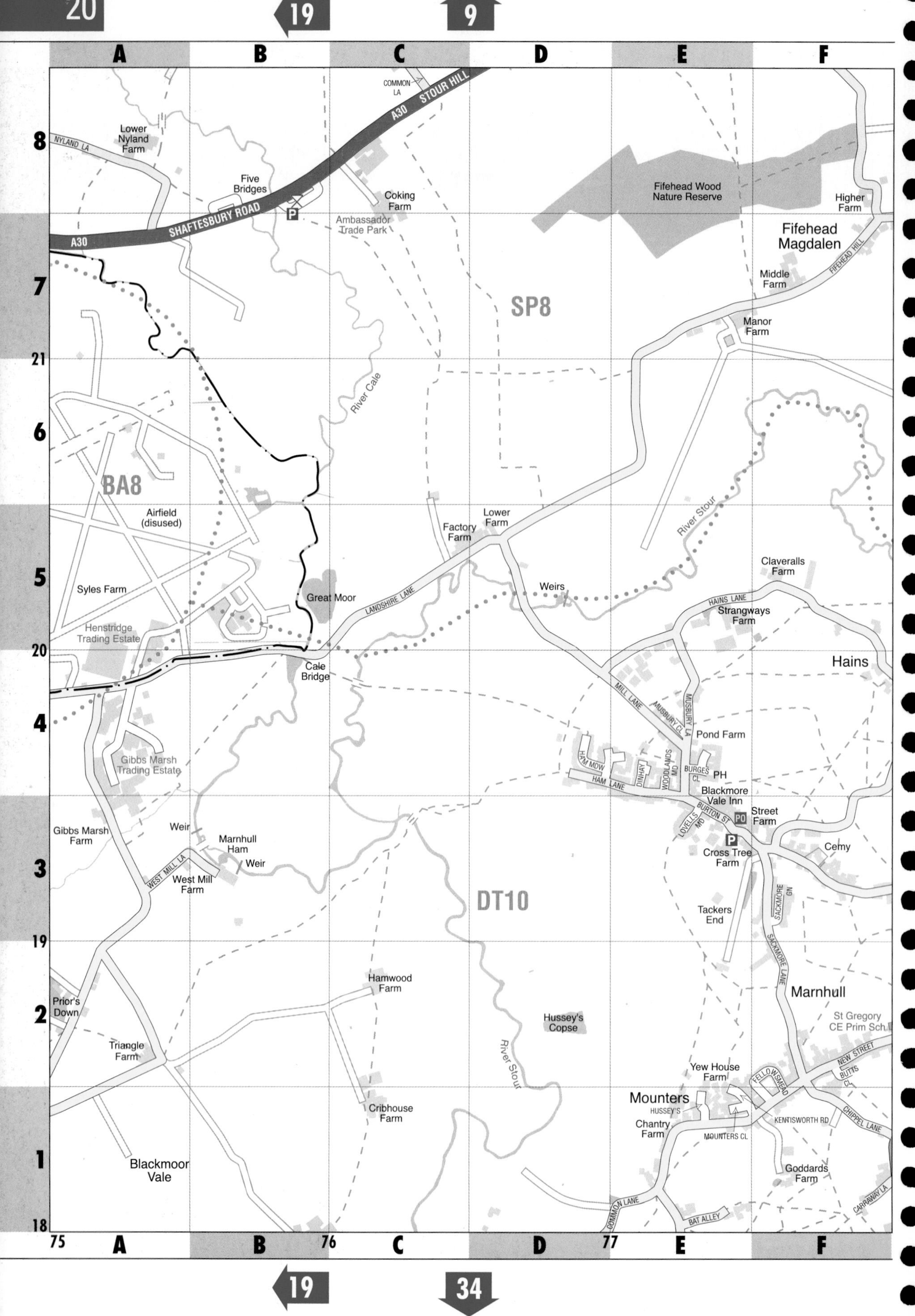

A B C D E F

8

NYLAND LA

Lower Nyland Farm

COMMON LA

A30 STOUR HILL

SHAFTESBURY ROAD

A30

Five Bridges

P

Coking Farm

Ambassador Trade Park

Fifehead Wood Nature Reserve

Higher Farm

Fifehead Magdalen

7

SP8

FIFEHEAD HILL

Middle Farm

Manor Farm

21

River Cale

6

BA8

Airfield (disused)

River Stour

5

Syles Farm

Factory Farm

Lower Farm

Weirs

LANDSHIRE LANE

Great Moor

HAINS LANE

Claveralls Farm

Strangways Farm

20

Henstridge Trading Estate

Cale Bridge

Hains

4

Gibbs Marsh Trading Estate

MILL LANE

AMISBURY LA

Pond Farm

PH

HAM MDW

DINHAY

WOODLANDS

BURGES CL

Blackmore Vale Inn

Street Farm

Cemy

HAM LANE

BURTON ST

PO

3

Gibbs Marsh Farm

Weir

Marnhull Ham

Weir

WEST MILL LA

West Mill Farm

DT10

LOVELLS MD

Cross Tree Farm

P

SACKMORE GN

SACKMORE LANE

Tackers End

Marnhull

19

St Gregory CE Prim Sch.

2

Prior's Down

Hamwood Farm

Hussey's Copse

NEW STREET

BUTTS CL

CHIPPEL LANE

Triangle Farm

River Stour

Yew House Farm

FELLOWSMEAD

Mounters

HUSSEY'S

Cribhouse Farm

Chantry Farm

KENTISWORTH RD

MOUNTERS CL

Goddards Farm

CARRAWAY LA

1

Blackmoor Vale

18

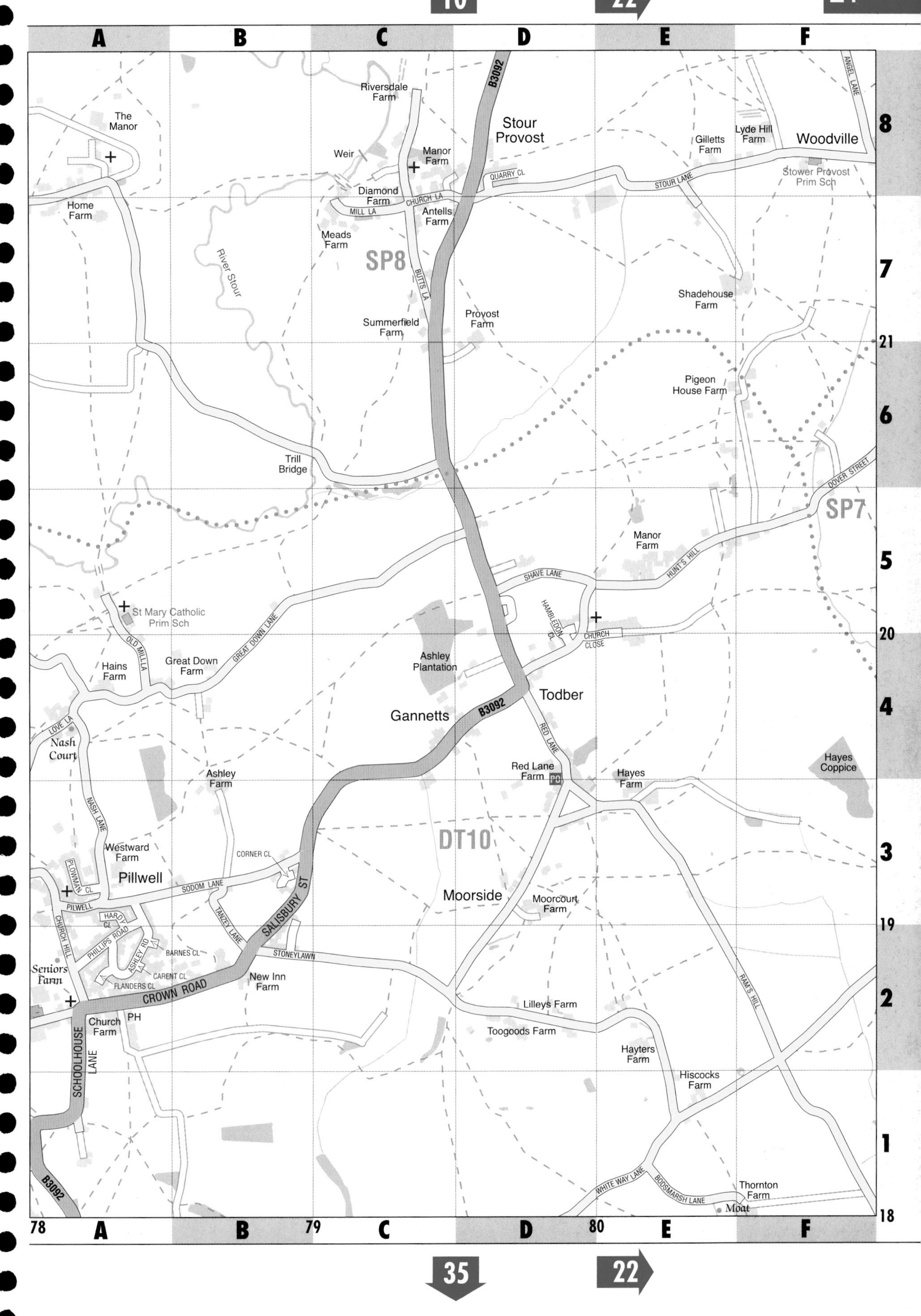
10
22
A
B
C
D
E
F
B3092
Riversdale Farm
Stour Provost
The Manor
Weir
Manor Farm
Diamond Farm
MILL LA
CHURCH LA
QUARRY CL
Antells Farm
Home Farm
Meads Farm
SP8
BUTTS LA
River Stour
Gilletts Farm
Lyde Hill Farm
Woodville
ANGEL LANE
STOUR LANE
Stower Provost Prim Sch
Shadehouse Farm
Summerfield Farm
Provost Farm
Pigeon House Farm
Trill Bridge
DOVER STREET
SP7
Manor Farm
HUNT'S HILL
SHAVE LANE
HAMBLEDON CL
CHURCH CLOSE
St Mary Catholic Prim Sch
OLD MILLLA
GREAT DOWN LANE
Hains Farm
Great Down Farm
Ashley Plantation
Todber
Gannetts
LOVE LA
Nash Court
RED LANE
Red Lane Farm
PO
Hayes Farm
Hayes Coppice
Ashley Farm
NASH LANE
DT10
Westward Farm
CORNER CL
PLOWMAN CL
Pillwell
SODOM LANE
SALISBURY ST
Moorside
Moorcourt Farm
PILLWELL
HARDY CL
CHURCH HILL
PHILLIPS ROAD
ASHLEY RD
BARNES CL
TANZEY LANE
STONEYLAWN
Seniors Farm
CARENT CL
FLANDERS CL
New Inn Farm
CROWN ROAD
Lilleys Farm
Church Farm
PH
Toogoods Farm
RAM'S HILL
SCHOOLHOUSE LANE
Hayters Farm
Hiscocks Farm
WHITE WAY LANE
BOODSMARSH LANE
Thornton Farm
Moat
8
7
21
6
5
20
4
3
19
2
1
18
78
79
80
35
22

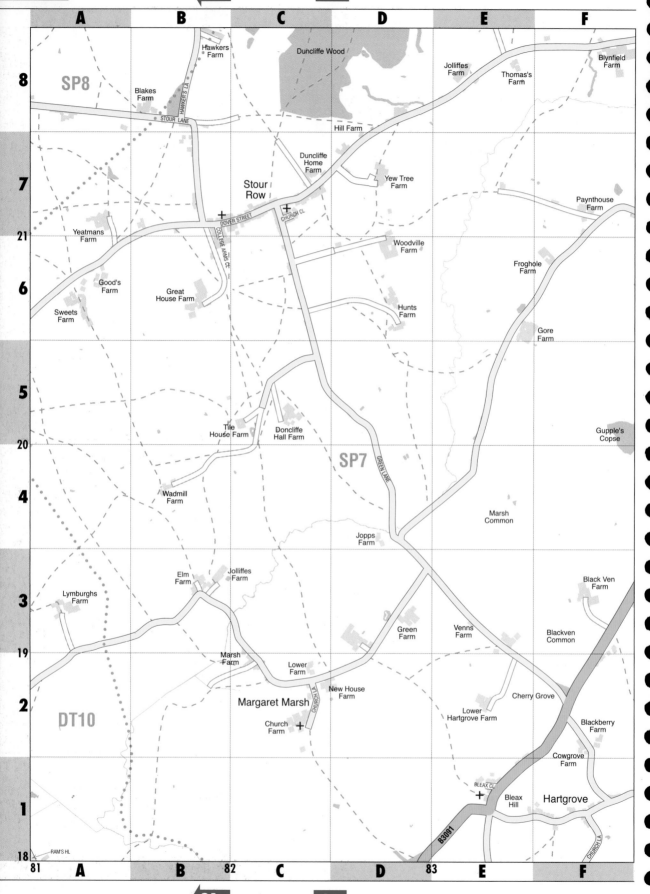

A B C D E F

8 SP8

Hawkers Farm

Duncliffe Wood

Jolliffes Farm
Thomas's Farm
Blynfield Farm

Blakes Farm

STOUR LANE
HAWKER'S LA

Hill Farm

7 Duncliffe Home Farm

Stour Row
Yew Tree Farm

Paynthouse Farm

DOVER STREET
CHURCH CL

21 Yeatmans Farm

COLLEGE ARMS CL

Woodville Farm

Froghole Farm

6 Good's Farm

Great House Farm

Hunts Farm

Gore Farm

Sweets Farm

5

Gupple's Copse

Tile House Farm
Doncliffe Hall Farm

20 SP7

GREEN LANE

4 Wadmill Farm

Marsh Common

Jopps Farm

3 Lymburghs Farm

Elm Farm
Jolliffes Farm

Black Ven Farm

Green Farm
Venns Farm

Blackven Common

19 Marsh Farm

Lower Farm

2 DT10

Margaret Marsh

CHURCH LA

New House Farm

Lower Hartgrove Farm

Cherry Grove

Blackberry Farm

Church Farm

Cowgrove Farm

BLEAX CL

1 Bleax Hill

Hartgrove

18 RAM'S HL

B3091

CHURCH LA

81 A B 82 C D 83 E F

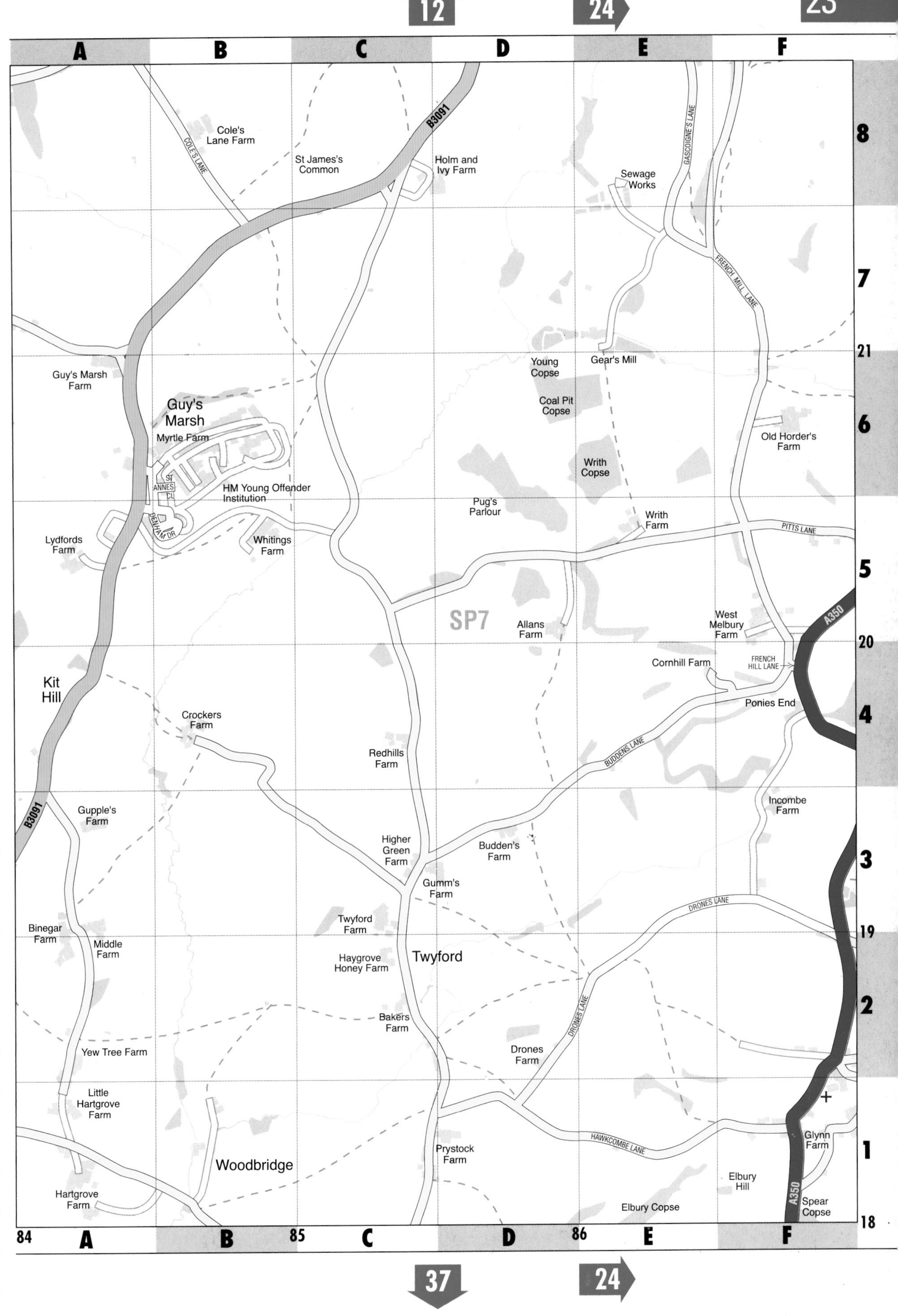
12
24
A
B
C
D
E
F
8
7
21
6
5
20
4
3
19
2
1
18
84
85
86
Cole's
Lane Farm
COLE'S LANE
St James's
Common
B3091
Holm and
Ivy Farm
Sewage
Works
GASCOIGNE'S LANE
FRENCH MILL LANE
Guy's Marsh
Farm
Guy's
Marsh
Myrtle Farm
ST
ANNES
CL
HM Young Offender
Institution
DENHAM DR
Young
Copse
Gear's Mill
Coal Pit
Copse
Old Horder's
Farm
Writh
Copse
Pug's
Parlour
Writh
Farm
PITTS LANE
Lydfords
Farm
Whitings
Farm
SP7
Allans
Farm
West
Melbury
Farm
A350
Cornhill Farm
FRENCH
HILL LANE
Kit
Hill
Ponies End
Crockers
Farm
BUDDENS LANE
Redhills
Farm
Incombe
Farm
Gupple's
Farm
B3091
Higher
Green
Farm
Budden's
Farm
Gumm's
Farm
DRONES LANE
Binegar
Farm
Twyford
Farm
Middle
Farm
Haygrove
Honey Farm
Twyford
Bakers
Farm
DRONES LANE
Yew Tree Farm
Drones
Farm
Little
Hartgrove
Farm
HAWKCOMBE LANE
Glynn
Farm
Prystock
Farm
Woodbridge
Elbury
Hill
A350
Spear
Copse
Hartgrove
Farm
Elbury Copse
37
24

23
13

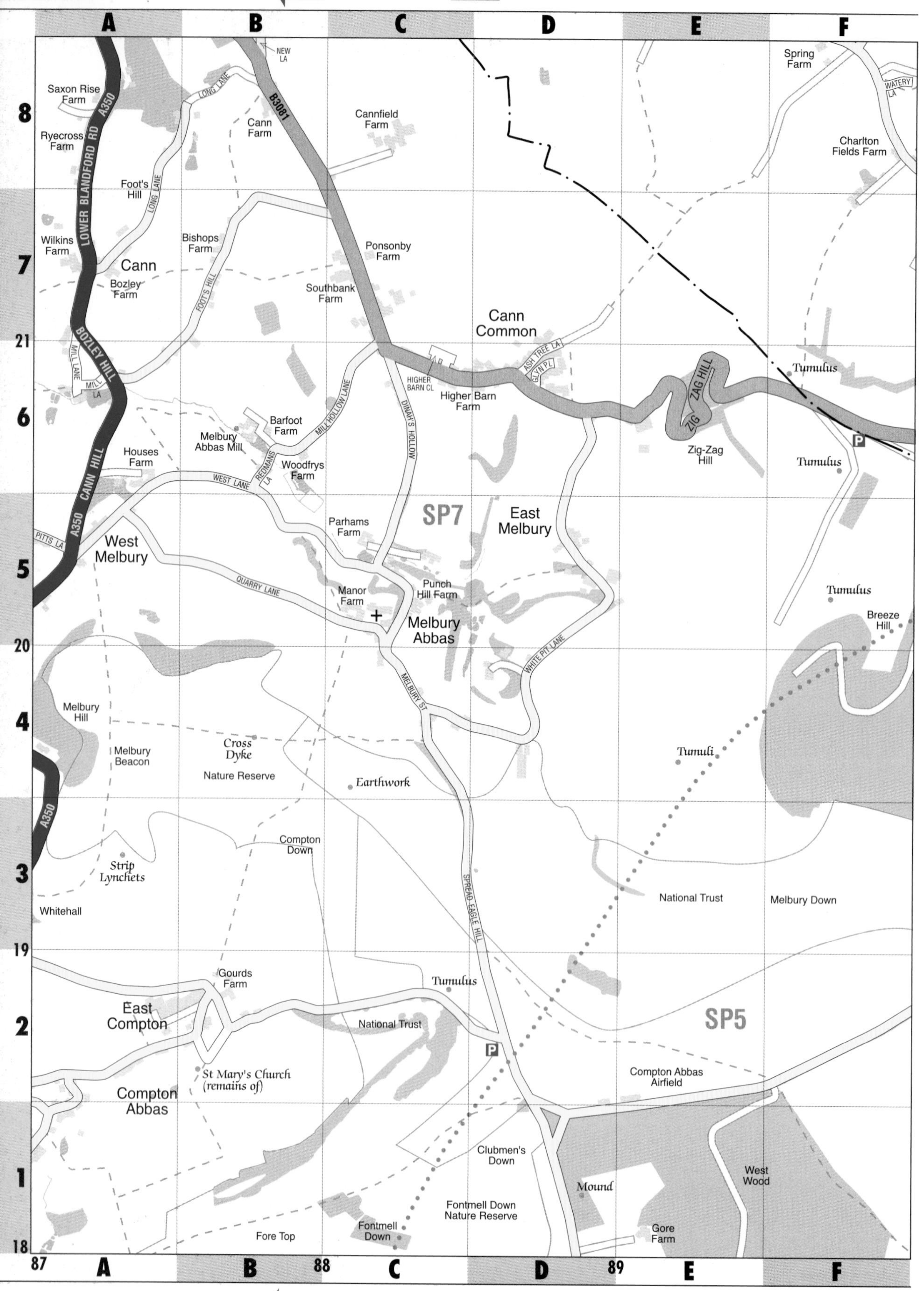
A
B
C
D
E
F
8
7
21
6
5
20
4
3
19
2
1
18
87
88
89
Saxon Rise Farm
Ryecross Farm
Foot's Hill
Wilkins Farm
Cann
Bozley Farm
Cann Farm
Cannfield Farm
Bishops Farm
Ponsonby Farm
Southbank Farm
Cann Common
Spring Farm
Charlton Fields Farm
Tumulus
Higher Barn Farm
Zig-Zag Hill
Barfoot Farm
Melbury Abbas Mill
Woodfrys Farm
Houses Farm
Parhams Farm
SP7
East Melbury
West Melbury
Manor Farm
Punch Hill Farm
Melbury Abbas
Breeze Hill
Melbury Hill
Melbury Beacon
Cross Dyke
Nature Reserve
Earthwork
Tumuli
Compton Down
Strip Lynchets
Whitehall
National Trust
Melbury Down
Gourds Farm
East Compton
SP5
Compton Abbas
St Mary's Church (remains of)
Compton Abbas Airfield
Clubmen's Down
West Wood
Mound
Fontmell Down Nature Reserve
Fontmell Down
Fore Top
Gore Farm
A350
B3081
LOWER BLANDFORD RD
BOZLEY HILL
CANN HILL
MILL LANE
MILL LA
LONG LANE
NEW LA
FOOT'S HILL
MILL HOLLOW LANE
DINAH'S HOLLOW
HIGHER BARN CL
ASH TREE LA
GLYN PL
ZIG ZAG HILL
WATERY LA
REDMANS LA
WEST LANE
PITTS LA
QUARRY LANE
WHITE PIT LANE
MELBURY ST
SPREAD EAGLE HILL

23
38

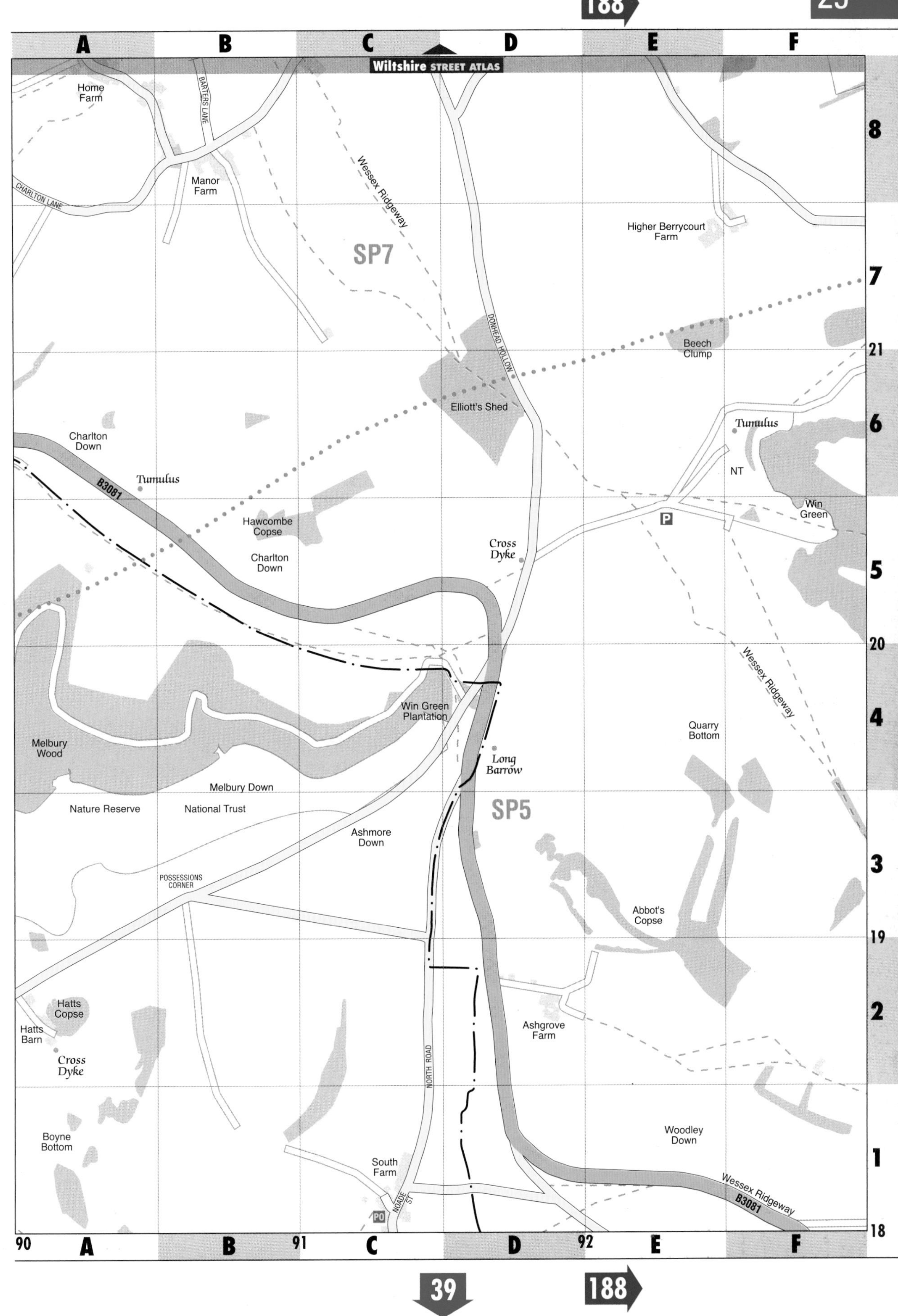
A
B
C
D
E
F
Wiltshire STREET ATLAS
Home Farm
BARTERS LANE
CHARLTON LANE
Manor Farm
Wessex Ridgeway
SP7
Higher Berrycourt Farm
DONHEAD HOLLOW
Beech Clump
Elliott's Shed
Charlton Down
Tumulus
B3081
Hawcombe Copse
Charlton Down
Cross Dyke
Tumulus
NT
Win Green
P
Wessex Ridgeway
Win Green Plantation
Melbury Wood
Long Barrow
Quarry Bottom
Melbury Down
Nature Reserve
National Trust
SP5
Ashmore Down
POSSESSIONS CORNER
Abbot's Copse
Hatts Copse
Hatts Barn
Cross Dyke
Ashgrove Farm
NORTH ROAD
Boyne Bottom
Woodley Down
South Farm
NOADE ST
PO
Wessex Ridgeway
B3081
8
7
21
6
5
20
4
3
19
2
1
18
90
91
92

Somerset STREET ATLAS

A B C D E F

8 7 17 6 5 16 4 15 3 2 14 1 14

Somerset STREET ATLAS

A3088 Ilminster (A303)

Manor Farm

Thorne Coffin

Mast

Shrewsbury Rd

Oak Farm

Lufton Manor Coll

Lufton Trading Estate

Yeovil Coll

Yeovil Town Football Club

Memorial Rd

Yeovil Coll

Guard Avenue

Houndstone

Manor Farm

Lufton

A3088

George Smith Way

Artillery Road

Murray-Smith Av

Buckle

Black Mere

Samways Close

Hawks Rise

Superstore

Poppy Cl

Crem

BA21

The Forum

Cannington Coll

Preston City Comp Sch

Bartletts Place

Houndstone Close

Tithe Barn

Preston Plucknett

High Leaze Farm

BA22

Alvington

Alvington Farm

New Road

Clarks Close

Lower Odcombe

Bank Farm

Brympton Avenue

Home Farm

Brympton House

Brympton D'Evercy

Bunford Lane

Playing Field

Lynx West Trading Estate

Watercombe Pk

Lynx Trading Estate

BA20

Lysander Road

Woodcote

Pye Corner

Leaze Cottages

Camp Hill

Broadleaze Farm

Dry Copse

Sampson's Wood

Ash Copse

Nathan Cl

A3088

A30

Watercombe La A3088

Camp Road

Goldsacre Lane

Feebarrow

West Coker Rd

A30

Nash Farm

51 A 52 B C 52 C D 53 D E F

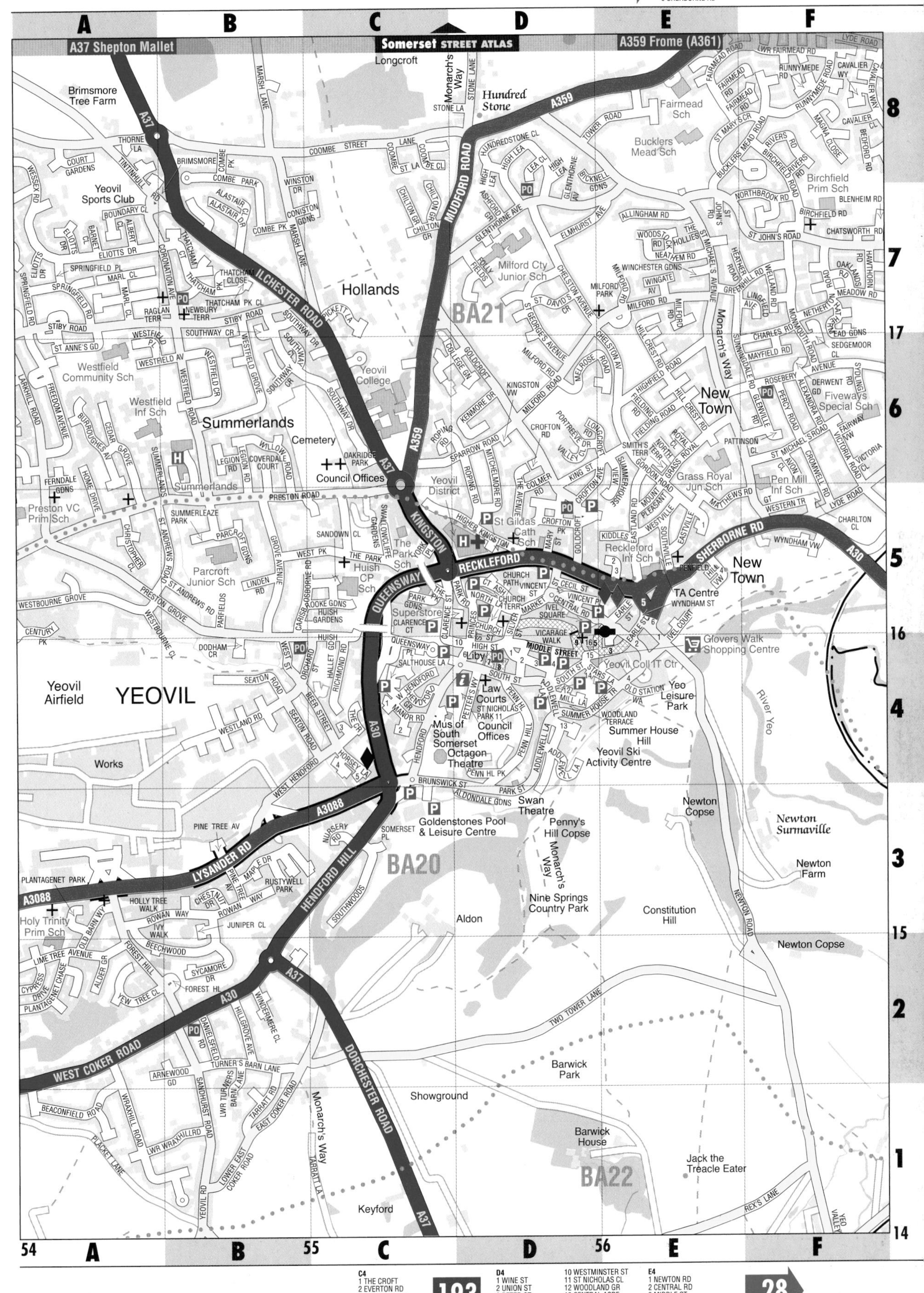

A   B   C   D   E   F

8

1 CORTON CL
2 ADBER CL
3 COMPTON CL
4 SANDLEWOOD CL
5 ASHWOOD DR

YEOVIL

Trent Brook

BRIAR
CONSTABLE CL
REDWOOD RD
TRENT CL
GAINSBOROUGH WAY
CAVALIER WY
BEDFORD
HERTFORD RD
WILTON DR
ROMSEY RD
LYDE ROAD

7

BLENHEIM RD

St JOHN'S RD
LYDE RD
WELBECK RD
MONTROSE RD
LOWTHER
OXFORD RD
OXFORD ROAD
BABYLON VIEW

17

MEADOW RD
WOBURN RD
WENTWORTH RD
MARLBOROUGH RD
MEADOW RD
ARUNDEL RD
PEMBROKE CL
BELVEDERE RD
LYDE LA

Glebe Farm
Lower Dairy Farm
Nether Compton
Bucklers Farm
FOLLY LA
CROSSFIELDS

Over Compton
St MICHAELS CL
WESTERN ST
WESTERN ST
FLAX LA
PLUM ORCHARD
Plum Orchard Farm
Lower Farm

6

ROSEBERY AVE
SANDRINGHAM
BALMORAL
HOWARD RD
LYDE RD
CLAYTON
CL
Pen Mill
Yeovil Coll
BUCKLAND ROAD
Pen Mill Trading Estate
Sewage Works

HERBLAY CL
CAMBORNE
CAMBORNE PL

Lower Farm
Higher Farm

COMPTON ROAD
River Yeo

Compton Manor Farm
Butterfly House

5

FLUSHING MDW
Yeovil Pen Mill
Sewage Works

BA21

Babylon Hill

BABYLON HILL

Noor Farm

16

SHERBORNE ROAD
A30
BABYLON HILL

DT9

4

CH
Yeovil Golf Club

Tilly's Hill

LEAZE LANE

East Farm

Park House

3

UNDERDOWN HOLLOW
Coombe

15

BA20

QUARRY LANE
WESTBURY

2

River Yeo

Manor Farm
FARM ROAD
PETTITTS CL
CROSS WY
CROSS ROAD
NORTH ST

QUEENS RD
AMBROSE CL
BISHOP'S LANE
MANOR CLOSE
SOUTH VW

LC

1

Yeovil Junction

BA22

HIGHER WESTBURY
Bradford Abbas
CHURCHWELL ST
WESSEX DR
BACK LA
PO
Church Rd
St Mary CE Prim Sch

14

D1
1 BAKEHOUSE LA
2 THE CROSS
3 CHURCHWELL CL

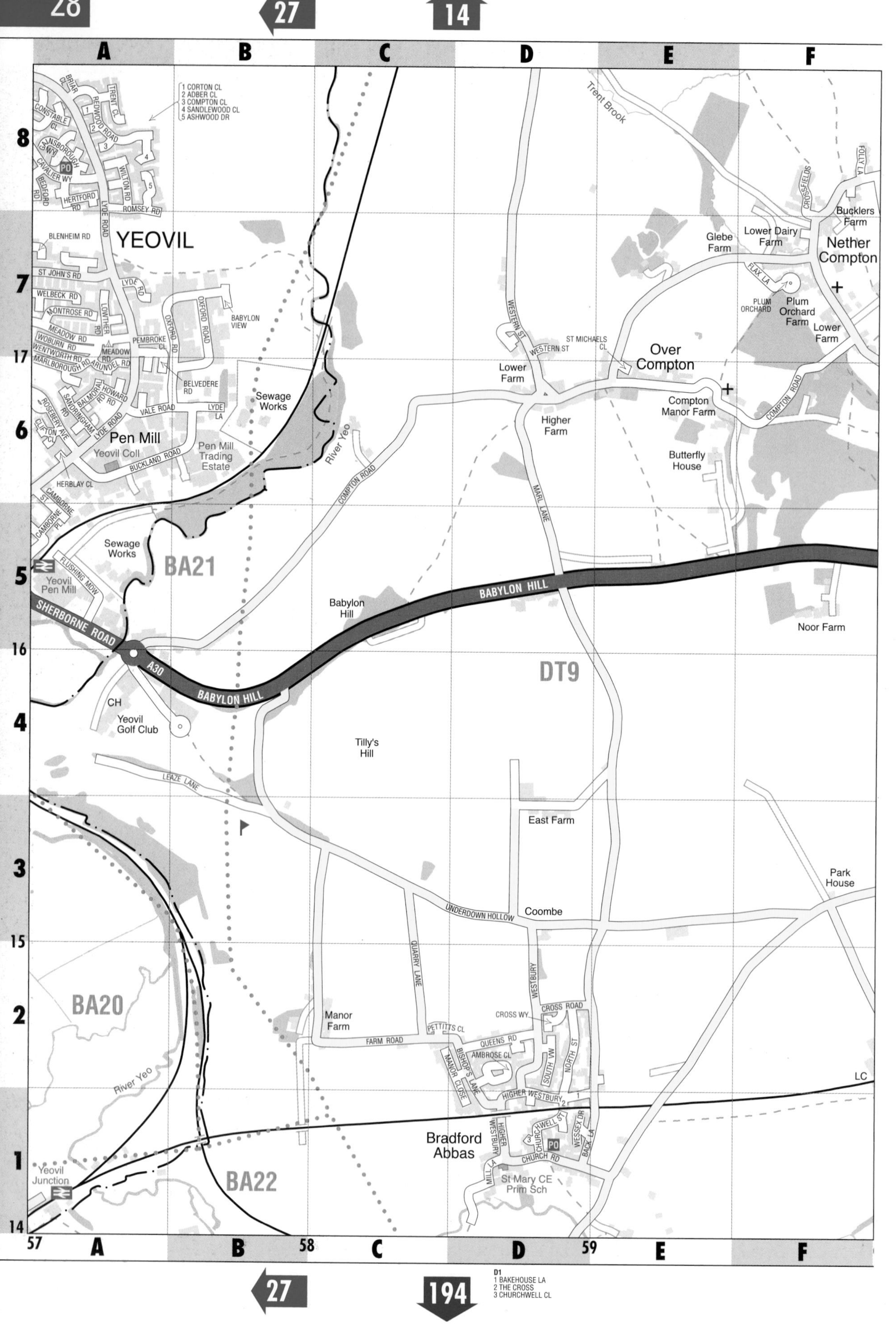

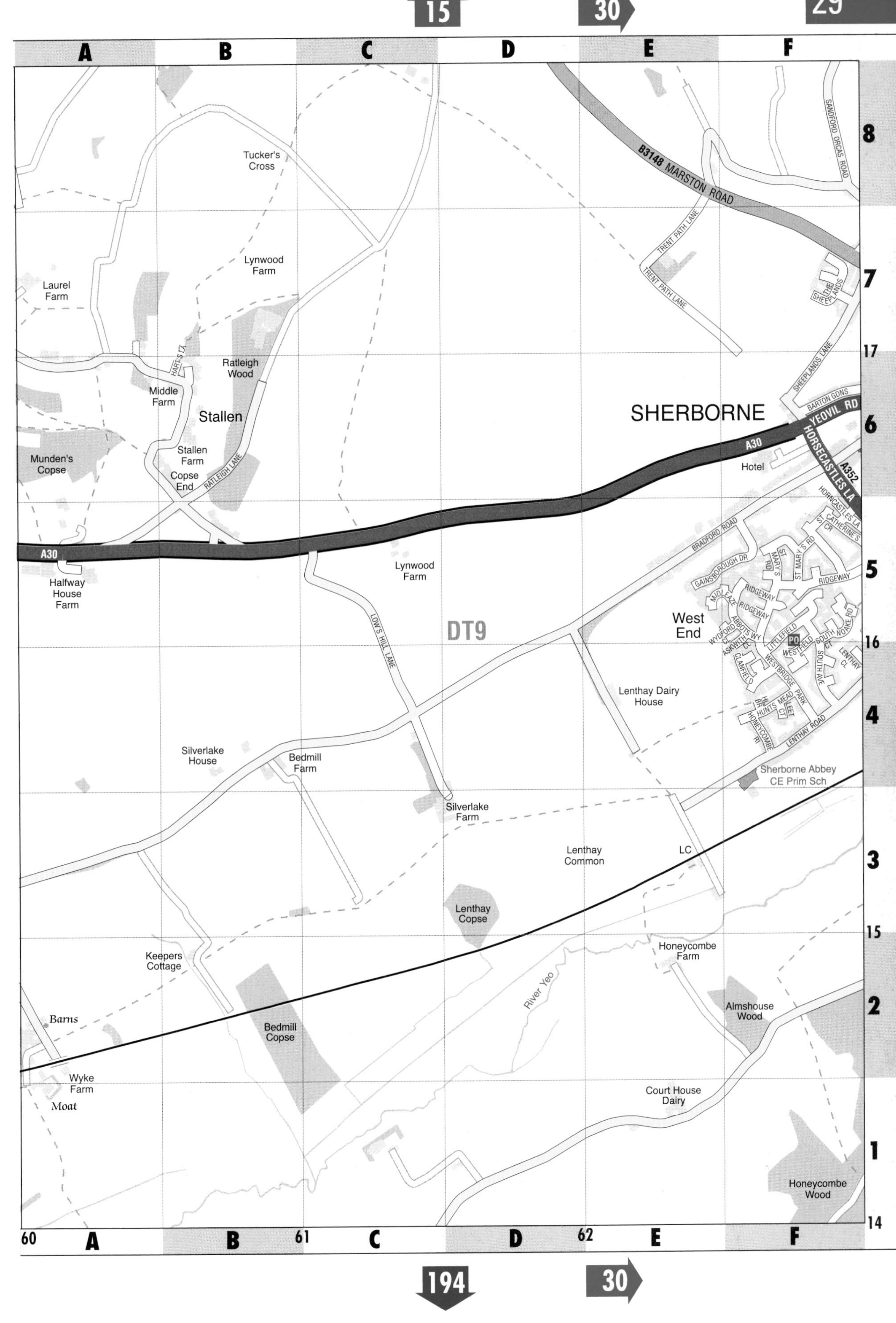

A   B   C   D   E   F

8

B3148 MARSTON ROAD

SANDFORD ORCAS ROAD

Tucker's
Cross

TRENT PATH LANE

7

Lynwood
Farm

SHEEPLANDS LANE

SHEEPLANDS LA

17

Laurel
Farm

Middle
Farm

Ratleigh
Wood

SHERBORNE

BARTON GDNS

YEOVIL RD

HORSECASTLES LA

6

HART'S CR

Stallen

A30

Hotel

A352

Munden's
Copse

Stallen
Farm

Copse
End

RATLEIGH LANE

BRADFORD ROAD

ST CATHERINE'S

ST CR

GAINSBOROUGH DR

MEAD LANE

RIDGEWAY

ST MARY'S RD

RIDGEWAY

A30

A30

Halfway
House
Farm

LOW'S HILL LANE

Lynwood
Farm

DT9

West
End

WYCFORD

ASKWITH'S WY

ABBOTS WY

LITTLEFIELD

WESTFIELD

PO

SOUTH AVE

SOUTH NOKE RD

RIDGEWAY

5

16

Lenthay Dairy
House

HUNTS MEAD

WESTBRIDGE PARK

LENTHAY ROAD

LENTHAY
CT

4

Silverlake
House

Bedmill
Farm

Silverlake
Farm

Sherborne Abbey
CE Prim Sch

Lenthay
Common

LC

3

Lenthay
Copse

15

Keepers
Cottage

Honeycombe
Farm

River Yeo

Almshouse
Wood

2

Barns

Bedmill
Copse

Wyke
Farm

Court House
Dairy

Moat

1

Honeycombe
Wood

14

60   A   B   61   C   D   62   E   F

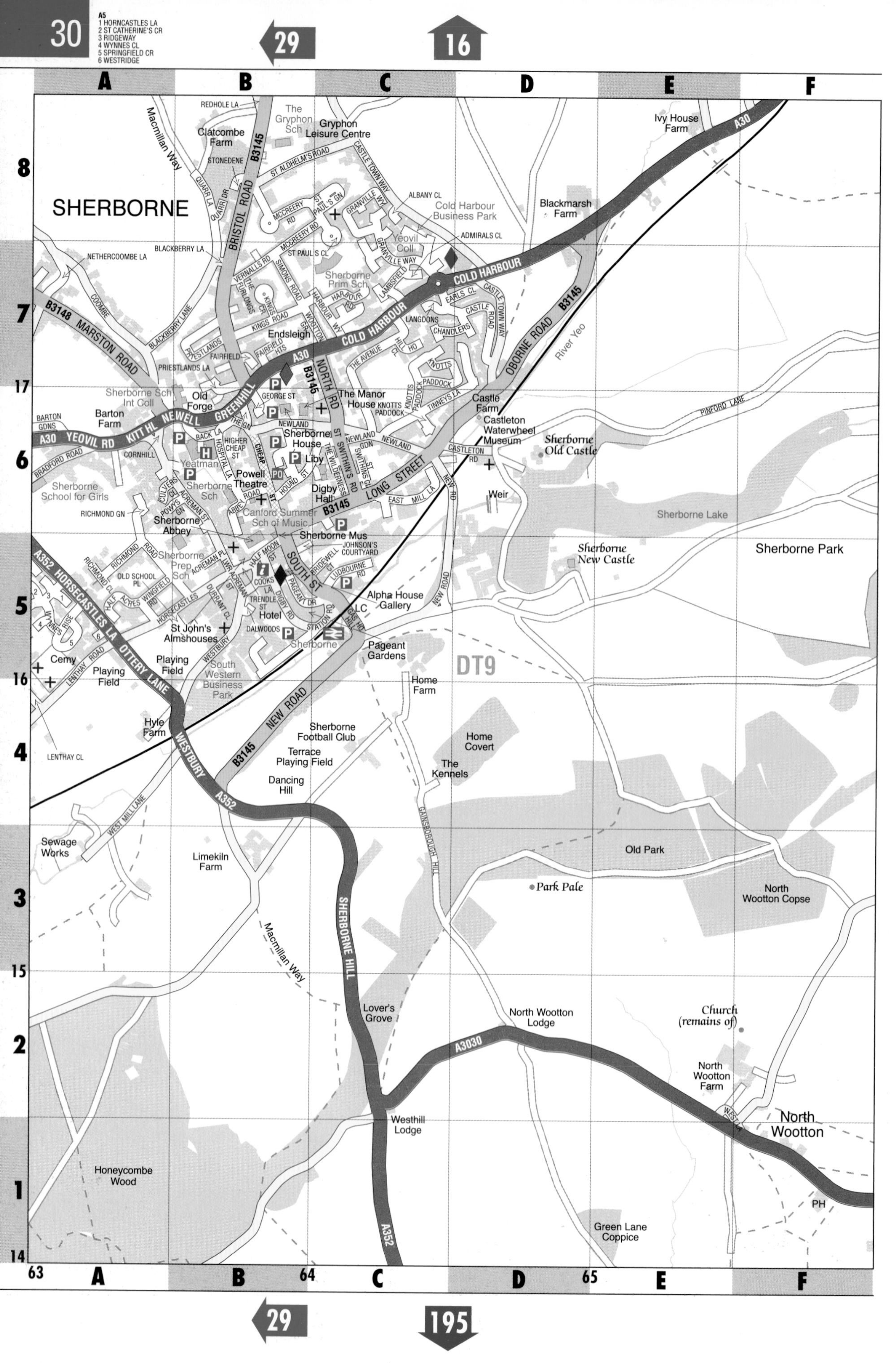
SHERBORNE
Clatcombe Farm
The Gryphon Sch
Gryphon Leisure Centre
Ivy House Farm
Blackmarsh Farm
Cold Harbour Business Park
Yeovil Coll
Sherborne Prim Sch
Endsleigh
Sherborne Sch Int Coll
Old Forge
Barton Farm
The Manor House
Castle Farm
Castleton Waterwheel Museum
Sherborne Old Castle
Sherborne House
Liby
Yeatman
Powell Theatre
Sherborne Sch
Digby Hall
Sherborne School for Girls
Canford Summer Sch of Music
Sherborne Abbey
Sherborne Mus
Weir
Sherborne Lake
Sherborne Park
Sherborne New Castle
Sherborne Prep Sch
Alpha House Gallery
Hotel
St John's Almshouses
Sherborne
Pageant Gardens
DT9
Cemy
Playing Field
South Western Business Park
Home Farm
Hyle Farm
Sherborne Football Club
Home Covert
Terrace Playing Field
The Kennels
Dancing Hill
Sewage Works
Limekiln Farm
Old Park
Park Pale
North Wootton Copse
Macmillan Way
Lover's Grove
North Wootton Lodge
Church (remains of)
North Wootton Farm
North Wootton
Westhill Lodge
Honeycombe Wood
Green Lane Coppice
PH
A30
A352
A3030
B3145
B3148
COLD HARBOUR
OBORNE ROAD
LONG STREET
NEW ROAD
SHERBORNE HILL
WESTBURY
HORSECASTLES LA
OTTERY LANE
MARSTON ROAD
YEOVIL RD
BRISTOL ROAD
NORTH RD
SOUTH ST
River Yeo

17
32

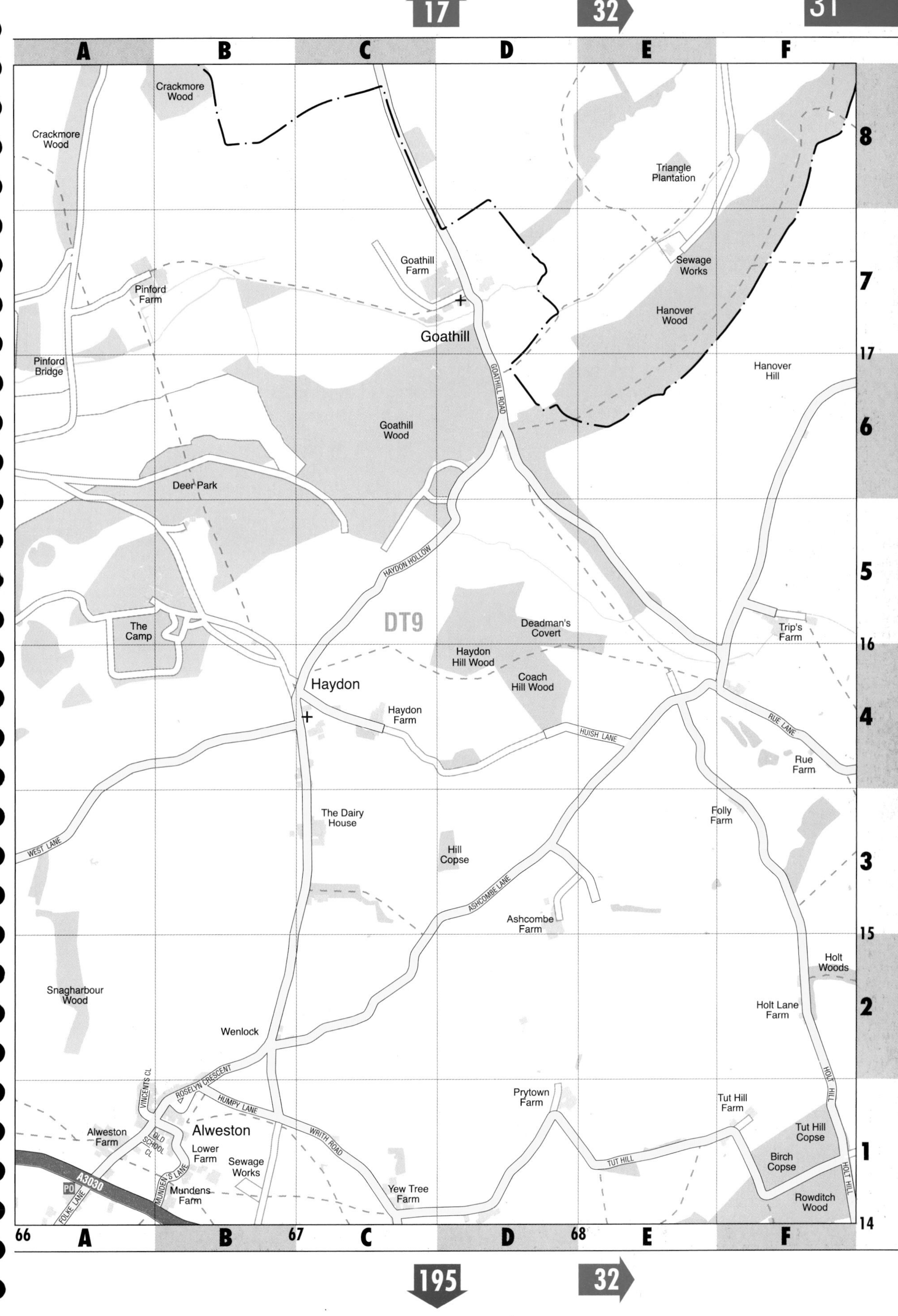
A
B
C
D
E
F
Crackmore Wood
Crackmore Wood
Triangle Plantation
Sewage Works
Goathill Farm
Pinford Farm
Hanover Wood
Goathill
Pinford Bridge
Hanover Hill
GOATHILL ROAD
Goathill Wood
Deer Park
HAYDON HOLLOW
The Camp
DT9
Deadman's Covert
Trip's Farm
Haydon Hill Wood
Coach Hill Wood
Haydon
Haydon Farm
HUISH LANE
RUE LANE
Rue Farm
The Dairy House
Folly Farm
WEST LANE
Hill Copse
ASHCOMBE LANE
Ashcombe Farm
Holt Woods
Snagharbour Wood
Holt Lane Farm
Wenlock
VINCENTS CL
ROSELYN CRESCENT
HUMPY LANE
Prytown Farm
Tut Hill Farm
HOLT HILL
Alweston Farm
Alweston
OLD SCHOOL CL
Lower Farm
WRITH ROAD
Sewage Works
TUT HILL
Tut Hill Copse
Birch Copse
A3030
PO
FOLKE LANE
MUNDEN'S LANE
Mundens Farm
Yew Tree Farm
Rowditch Wood
8
7
17
6
5
16
4
3
15
2
1
14
66
67
68

195
32

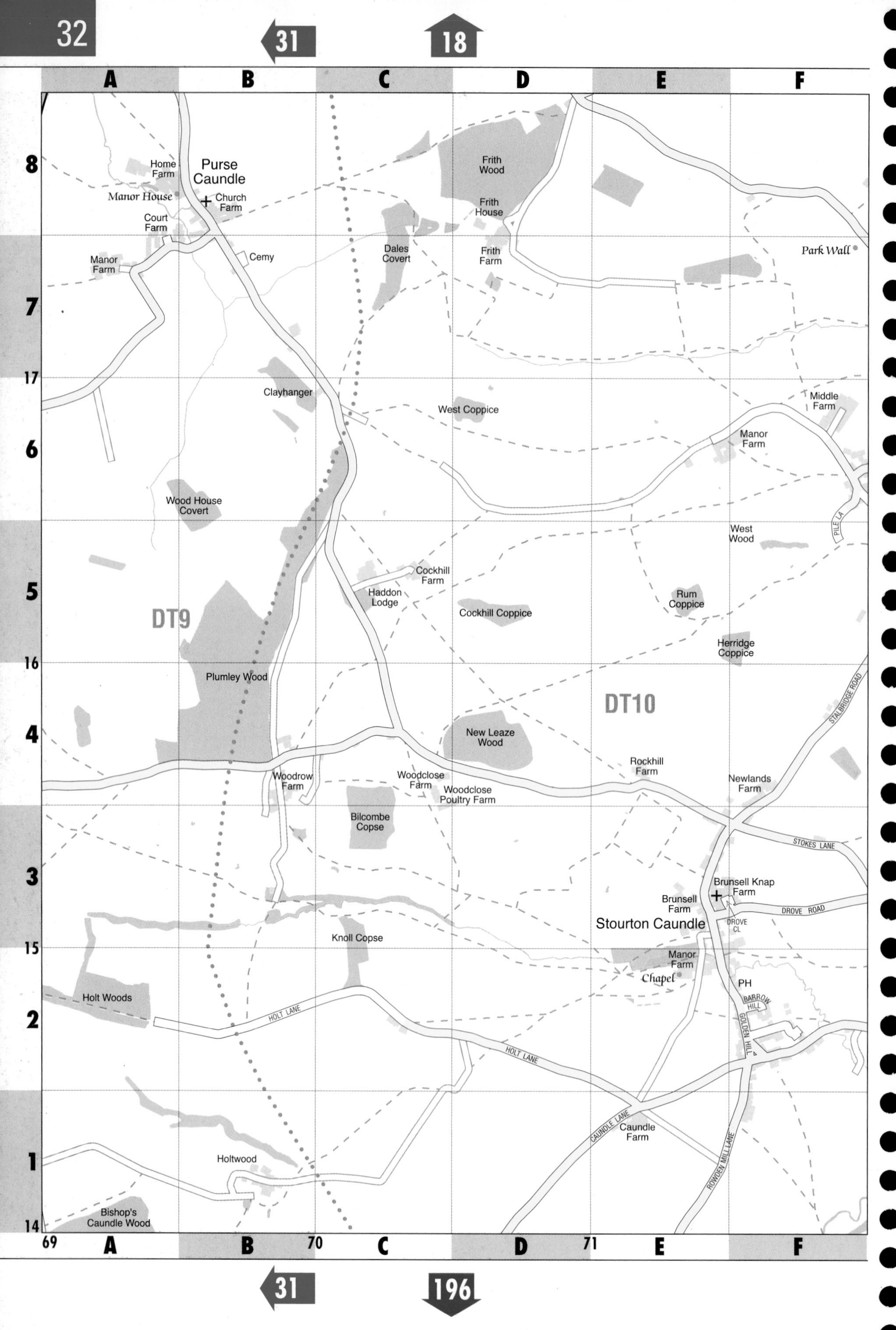
31
18
A
B
C
D
E
F
8
7
17
6
5
16
4
3
15
2
1
14
69
70
71
Home Farm
Purse Caundle
Manor House
Church Farm
Court Farm
Manor Farm
Cemy
Frith Wood
Frith House
Frith Farm
Dales Covert
Park Wall
Clayhanger
West Coppice
Middle Farm
Manor Farm
Wood House Covert
West Wood
PILE LA
Cockhill Farm
Haddon Lodge
Cockhill Coppice
Rum Coppice
Herridge Coppice
DT9
DT10
Plumley Wood
STALBRIDGE ROAD
New Leaze Wood
Rockhill Farm
Newlands Farm
Woodrow Farm
Woodclose Farm
Woodclose Poultry Farm
Bilcombe Copse
STOKES LANE
Brunsell Knap Farm
Brunsell Farm
DROVE ROAD
DROVE CL
Stourton Caundle
Knoll Copse
Manor Farm
Chapel
PH
BARROW HILL
GOLDEN HILL
Holt Woods
HOLT LANE
HOLT LANE
CAUNDLE LANE
Caundle Farm
ROWDEN MILL LANE
Holtwood
Bishop's Caundle Wood
31
196

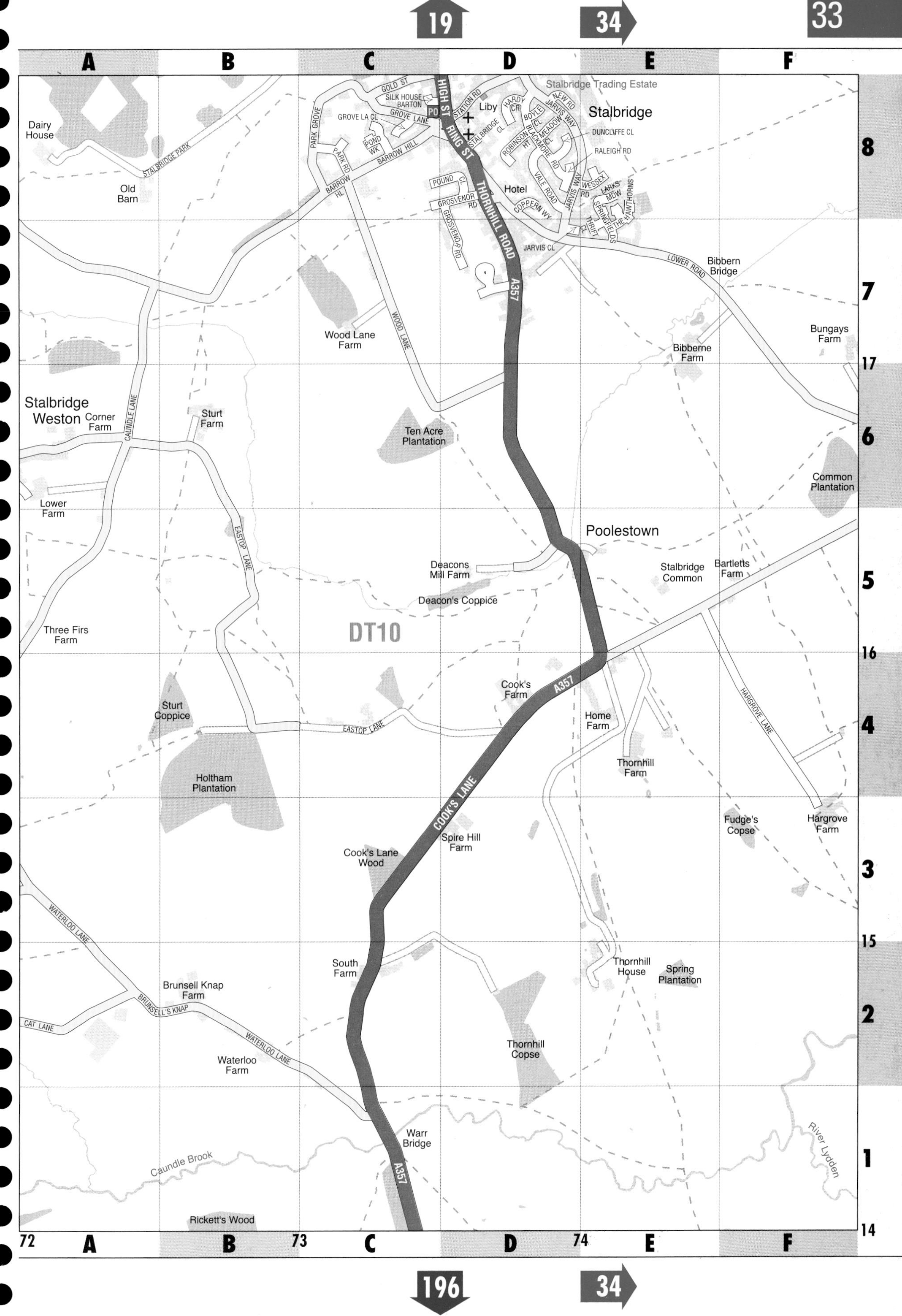

A   B   C   D   E   F

Dairy House

Old Barn

Stalbridge Park

Stalbridge Weston   Corner Farm

Lower Farm

Three Firs Farm

CAUNDLE LANE

Sturt Farm

EASTOP LANE

Sturt Coppice

Holtham Plantation

WATERLOO LANE

Brunsell Knap Farm

BRUNSELL'S KNAP

CAT LANE

WATERLOO LANE

Waterloo Farm

Caundle Brook

Rickett's Wood

PARK GROVE

BARROW HL

PARK RD

WOOD LANE

Wood Lane Farm

Ten Acre Plantation

Deacons Mill Farm

Deacon's Coppice

DT10

EASTOP LANE

Cook's Farm

COOK'S LANE

Cook's Lane Wood

Spire Hill Farm

South Farm

Warr Bridge

A357

PARK GROVE   GOLD ST   SILK HOUSE BARTON   GROVE LA CL   GROVE LANE   POND WK

HIGH ST   RING ST   PO   STATION RD

GROSVENOR RD   GROSVENOR P RD   POUND

THORNHILL ROAD   A357

Liby   Stalbridge Trading Estate

NEW RD   JARVIS WAY   Stalbridge

HARDY CR   BOTL   BLACKMORE RD   ROBINSON CL   STALBRIDGE CL

DUNCLIFFE CL   RALEIGH RD

Hotel   VALE ROAD   CLIPPERM WY

JARVIS CL

WESSEX RD   JARVIS WAY   LARKS MDW   SPRINGFIELDS   THE CAWTHORNS   THRIFT

LOWER ROAD

Bibbern Bridge

Bibberne Farm

Bungays Farm

Common Plantation

Poolestown

Stalbridge Common   Bartletts Farm

A357

HARGROVE LANE

Home Farm

Thornhill Farm

Fudge's Copse

Hargrove Farm

Thornhill House

Spring Plantation

Thornhill Copse

River Lydden

8   7   17   6   5   16   4   15   3   2   1   14

72   A   B   73   C   D   74   E   F

A B C D E F

8

Gomershay Farm

Bibbern Brook

River Stour

COMMON LANE

Crosses Farm

Pleck

Walton Elm

Shepherds Close Farm

MOWES LA

COMMON LANE

Antells Farm

7

Hewletts Farm

COX HILL

King's Mill Farm

Yardgrove Farm

COX HILL

17

Bungays Farm

Grove Farm

King's Mill Bridge

KING'S MILL ROAD

6

LOWER ROAD

River Lydden

Weirs

CUTT MILL LANE

Cutt Mill

Halletts Farm

Lower Bagber Farm

Joyce's Coppice

5

Marsh Farm

Lower Ryalls Farm

DT10

PENTRIDGE LANE

Pentridge Farm

16

Ryalls Farm

PENTRIDGE LANE

Bagber Wood

Lovell's Coppice

4

Bagber Bridge

Bagber House Farm

Manor Farm

STALBRIDGE LANE

3

River Lydden

Rushay Farm

Blackwater Bridge

15

Ash Tree Farm

Pleak House Farm

Queen's Coppice

STALBRIDGE LA

2

Longacres Farm

Oaks Farm

Mullins' Farm

Meadow Farm

Horsehill Farm

Medieval Village of Colber (site of)

1

Perry Farm

Higher Farm

Oaklea Farm

Bagber Common

14

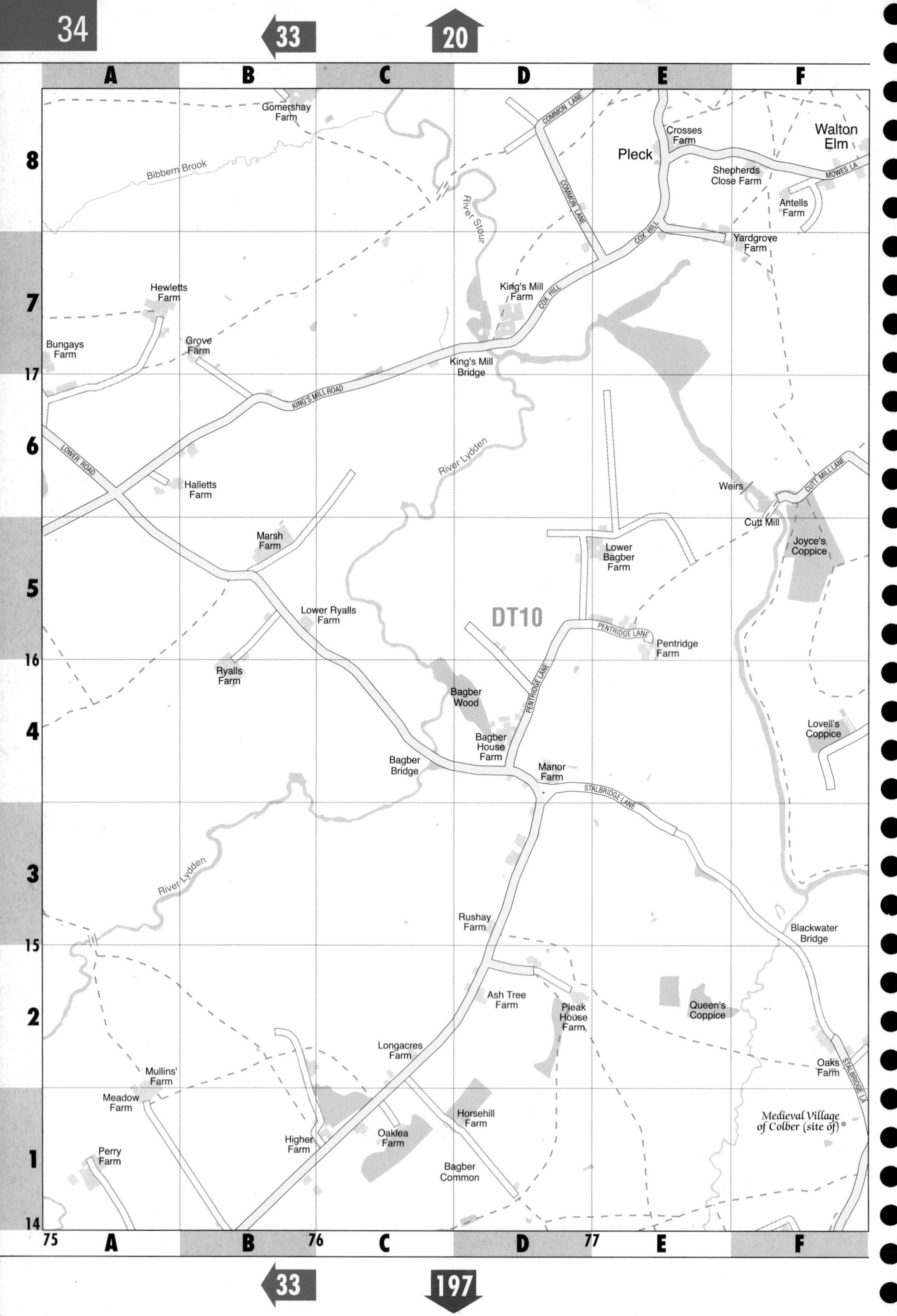

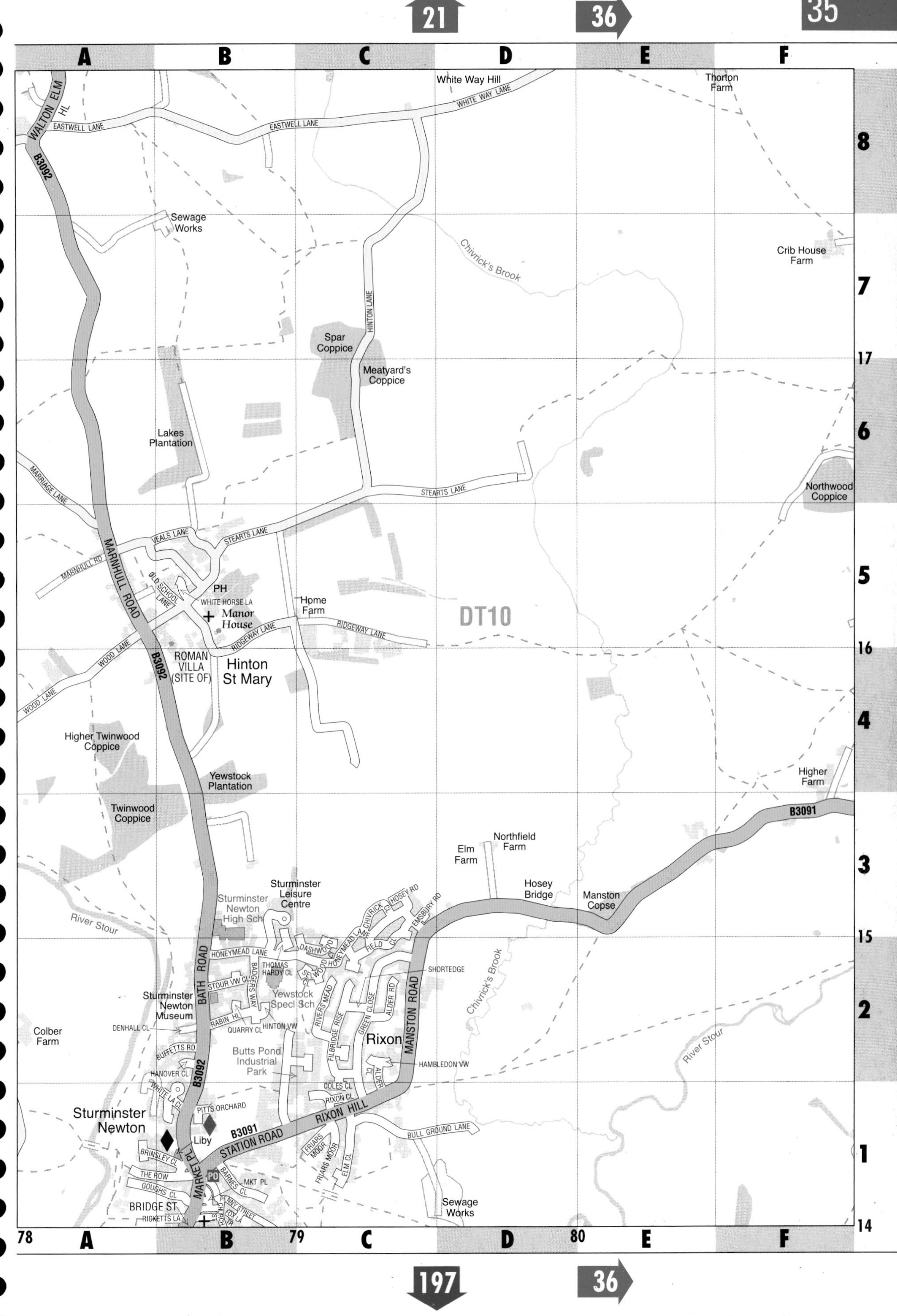
21
36
A
B
C
D
E
F
White Way Hill
WHITE WAY LANE
Thorton Farm
WALTON ELM
HL
EASTWELL LANE
EASTWELL LANE
8
B3092
Sewage Works
Chivrick's Brook
Crib House Farm
HINTON LANE
7
Spar Coppice
Meatyard's Coppice
17
Lakes Plantation
6
MARRIAGE LANE
STEARTS LANE
Northwood Coppice
VEALS LANE
STEARTS LANE
MARNHULL RD
MARNHULL ROAD
OLD SCHOOL LANE
PH
WHITE HORSE LA
Manor House
Home Farm
RIDGEWAY LANE
RIDGEWAY LANE
DT10
5
16
WOOD LANE
WOOD LANE
B3092
ROMAN VILLA (SITE OF)
Hinton St Mary
4
Higher Twinwood Coppice
Yewstock Plantation
Higher Farm
Twinwood Coppice
B3091
Northfield Farm
Elm Farm
3
Sturminster Leisure Centre
Hosey Bridge
Manston Copse
Sturminster Newton High Sch
River Stour
HOSEY RD
EMSBURY RD
CHIVRICK
DASHWOOD
HONEYMEAD LANE
FIELD CL
15
HONEYMEAD LANE
THOMAS HARDY CL
BADGERS WAY
SHORTEDGE
STOUR VW CL
BATH ROAD
Sturminster Newton Museum
Yewstock Specl Sch
RIVERS MEAD
GREEN CLOSE
ALDER RD
MANSTON ROAD
Chivrick's Brook
2
RABIN HL
HINTON VW
DENHALL CL
QUARRY CL
Colber Farm
Rixon
FILBRIDGE RISE
River Stour
BUFFETTS RD
Butts Pond Industrial Park
HAMBLEDON VW
HANOVER CL
B3092
ALDER CL
WHITE LA CL
COLES CL
RIXON CL
PITTS ORCHARD
RIXON HILL
Sturminster Newton
B3091
Liby
STATION ROAD
BULL GROUND LANE
FRIARS MOOR
FRIARS MOOR
ELM CL
1
BRINSLEY CL
MARKET PL
THE ROW
PO
BARNES CL
MKT PL
GOUGHS CL
Sewage Works
BRIDGE ST
PENNY STREET
FOX LA
CHURCH ST
RICKETTS LA
14
78
A
B
79
C
D
80
E
F
197
36

A B C D E F

8

Lushes Farm

B3091

East Orchard

Swainscombe Farm

Trapdoor Farm

CHURCH LANE

Breach Farm

Keybrook Farm

Henbury Farm

7

RAM'S HILL

Key Brook

Higher Keybrook Farm

CHURCH LANE

17

Ramshill Farm

Lower Breach Farm

SP7

Manor Farm

Bowling Green Farm

6

Northwood Farm

School House Farm

Gullivers Farm

DROVE LANE

Meads Farm

Folly Farm

West Orchard

FISHEY LANE

5

Conegar Farm

Winchells Farm

Manor Farm

PH

Naish's Farm

DT10

16

4

Sewage Works

Manston Brook

Middle Farm

B3091

Manston

3

Lower Farm

Manston Farm

DT11

15

Manston House

River Stour

2

Weir

Fontmell Farm

Manor Farm

Cross

Fontmell Parva

Hammoon

Porter's Hill

GALLOWS CORNER

LOWER COMMON ROAD

Hazel Copse

1

Newbury Copse

Ridgeway Farm

14

81 A B 82 C D 83 E F

23
38

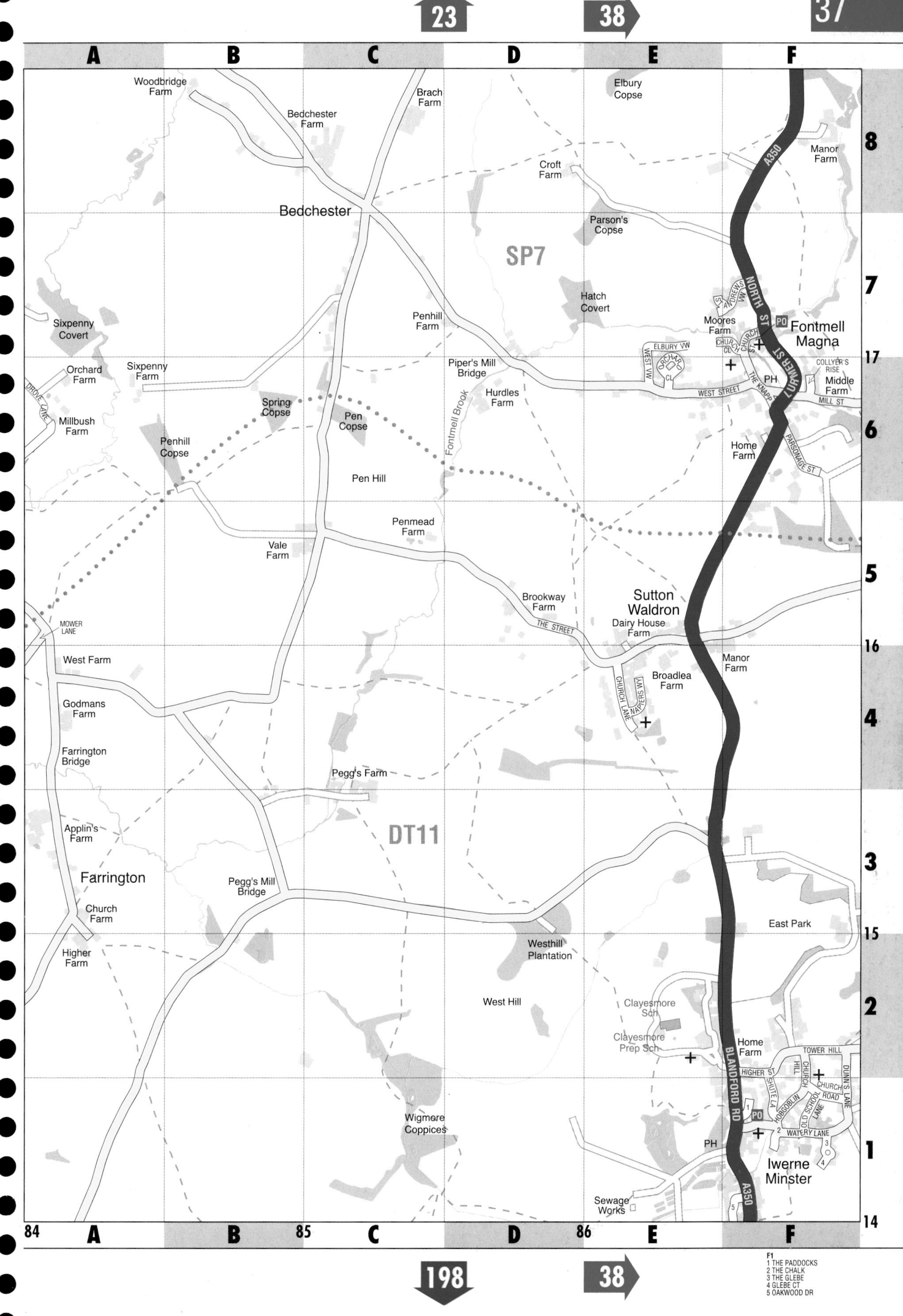
A
B
C
D
E
F
Woodbridge Farm
Bedchester Farm
Brach Farm
Elbury Copse
Manor Farm
Croft Farm
Bedchester
Parson's Copse
SP7
A350
Hatch Covert
Sixpenny Covert
Penhill Farm
Moores Farm
NORTH ST
PO
Fontmell Magna
ST ANDREWS WAY
CHURCH ST
CHURCH CL
ELBURY VW
WEST VW
ORCHARD CL
COLLYER'S RISE
Orchard Farm
Sixpenny Farm
Piper's Mill Bridge
Hurdles Farm
PH
LURMER ST
Middle Farm
DROVE LANE
WEST STREET
THE KNAPP
MILL ST
Spring Copse
Millbush Farm
Pen Copse
Fontmell Brook
Penhill Copse
Home Farm
PARSONAGE ST
Pen Hill
Penmead Farm
Vale Farm
Brookway Farm
Sutton Waldron
MOWER LANE
Dairy House Farm
THE STREET
West Farm
Manor Farm
Broadlea Farm
Godmans Farm
CHURCH LANE
NAPIERS WAY
Farrington Bridge
Pegg's Farm
DT11
Applin's Farm
Farrington
Pegg's Mill Bridge
Church Farm
East Park
Higher Farm
Westhill Plantation
West Hill
Clayesmore Sch
Clayesmore Prep Sch
Home Farm
BLANDFORD RD
TOWER HILL
HIGHER ST
SHUTE LA
CHURCH HILL
CHURCH ROAD
DUNN'S LANE
HOBGOBLIN
OLD SCHOOL LANE
WATERY LANE
Wigmore Coppices
PH
Iwerne Minster
Sewage Works
84
85
86
8
7
17
6
5
16
4
3
15
2
1
14
F1
1 THE PADDOCKS
2 THE CHALK
3 THE GLEBE
4 GLEBE CT
5 OAKWOOD DR

198
38

A B C D E F

8

Fontmell Down

Fore Top

National Trust

Longcombe Bottom

West Wood

SP5

Cross Dyke

Shepherd's Bottom

7

SP7

Fontmell Wood

Littlecombe Bottom

Fontmell Hill House

17

Springhead Farm

MILL STREET

6

Washers Pit

Strip Lynchets

Balfour's Wood

STUBHAMPTON BOTTOM

Washers Pit Coppice

5

Enclosure

Stubhamton Bottom

Combe Bottom

STUBHAMPTON BOTTOM

16

Sutton Hill Farm

Sutton Hill

4

West Lodge

DT11

Higher Barn Plantation

Folly Barrow

Spinney Pits Coppice

Higher Barn Plantation

Freak's Coppice

Lower Freaks Coppice

3

Bareden Down

Tumuli

15

Tumuli

Bareden Wood

Payne Coppice

Wales Wood

Common Bushes

2

Iwerne Hill

TOWER HILL

Great Peakey Coppice

TOWER HILL

Hill Farm

1

Brookman's Valley

BOYNE'S LANE

Heron Grove Coppice

14

Rolf's Wood

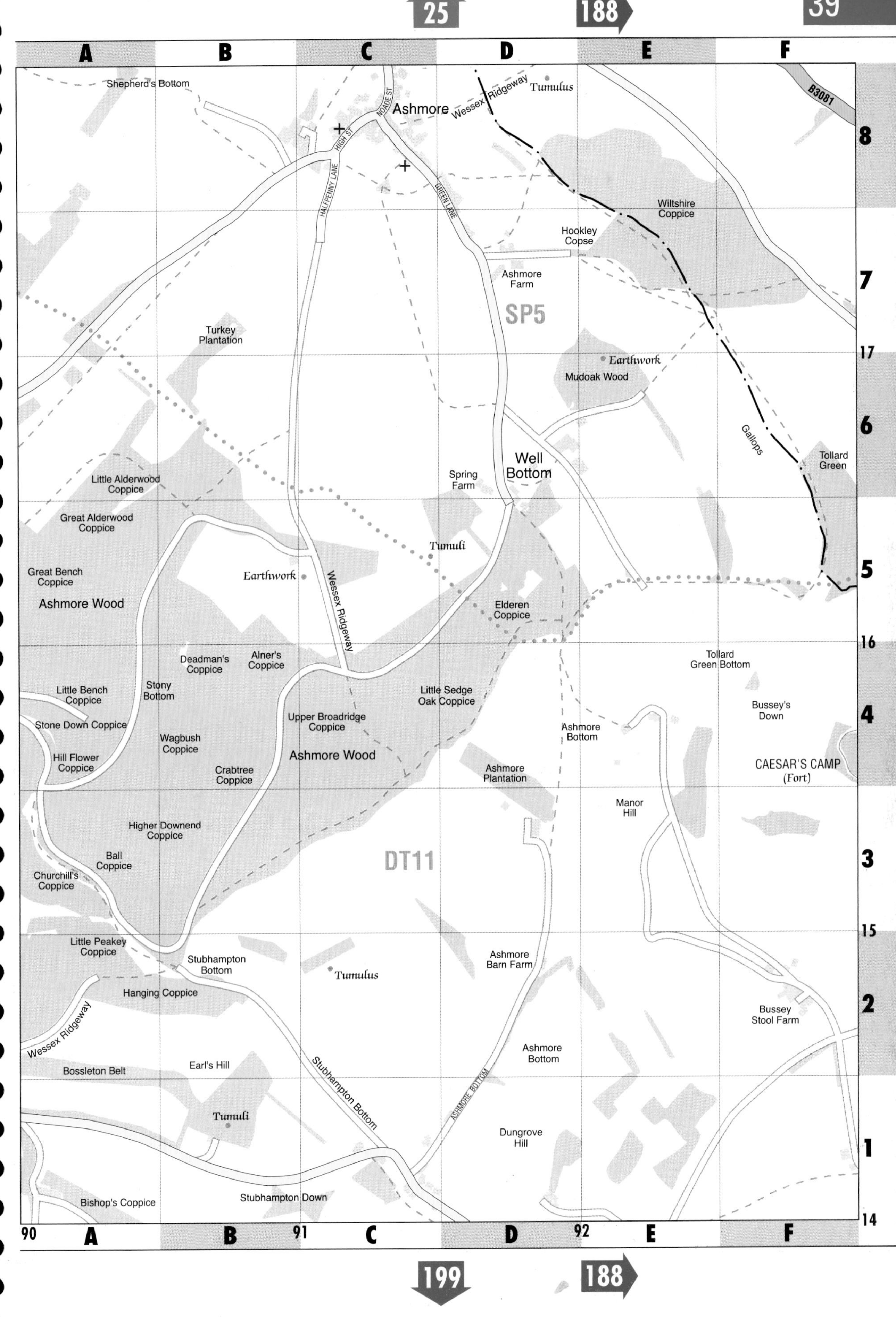

A   B   C   D   E   F

8
7
17
6
5
16
4
3
15
2
1
14

Shepherd's Bottom

Ashmore

Wessex Ridgeway

Tumulus

B3081

Wiltshire
Coppice

Hookley
Copse

Ashmore
Farm

SP5

Turkey
Plantation

Earthwork

Mudoak Wood

HALFPENNY LANE

HIGH ST

NORDE ST

GREEN LANE

Gallops

Tollard
Green

Well
Bottom

Spring
Farm

Little Alderwood
Coppice

Great Alderwood
Coppice

Great Bench
Coppice

Ashmore Wood

Earthwork

Wessex Ridgeway

Tumuli

Elderen
Coppice

Tollard
Green Bottom

Bussey's
Down

Deadman's
Coppice

Alner's
Coppice

Stony
Bottom

Little Bench
Coppice

Little Sedge
Oak Coppice

Ashmore
Bottom

Stone Down Coppice

Wagbush
Coppice

Upper Broadridge
Coppice

Ashmore Wood

Ashmore
Plantation

Manor
Hill

CAESAR'S CAMP
(Fort)

Hill Flower
Coppice

Crabtree
Coppice

DT11

Higher Downend
Coppice

Ball
Coppice

Churchill's
Coppice

Little Peakey
Coppice

Stubhampton
Bottom

Tumulus

Ashmore
Barn Farm

Bussey
Stool Farm

Hanging Coppice

Wessex Ridgeway

Earl's Hill

Stubhampton Bottom

ASHMORE BOTTOM

Ashmore
Bottom

Bossleton Belt

Tumuli

Dungrove
Hill

Bishop's Coppice

Stubhampton Down

90   A   B   91   C   D   92   E   F

201
190

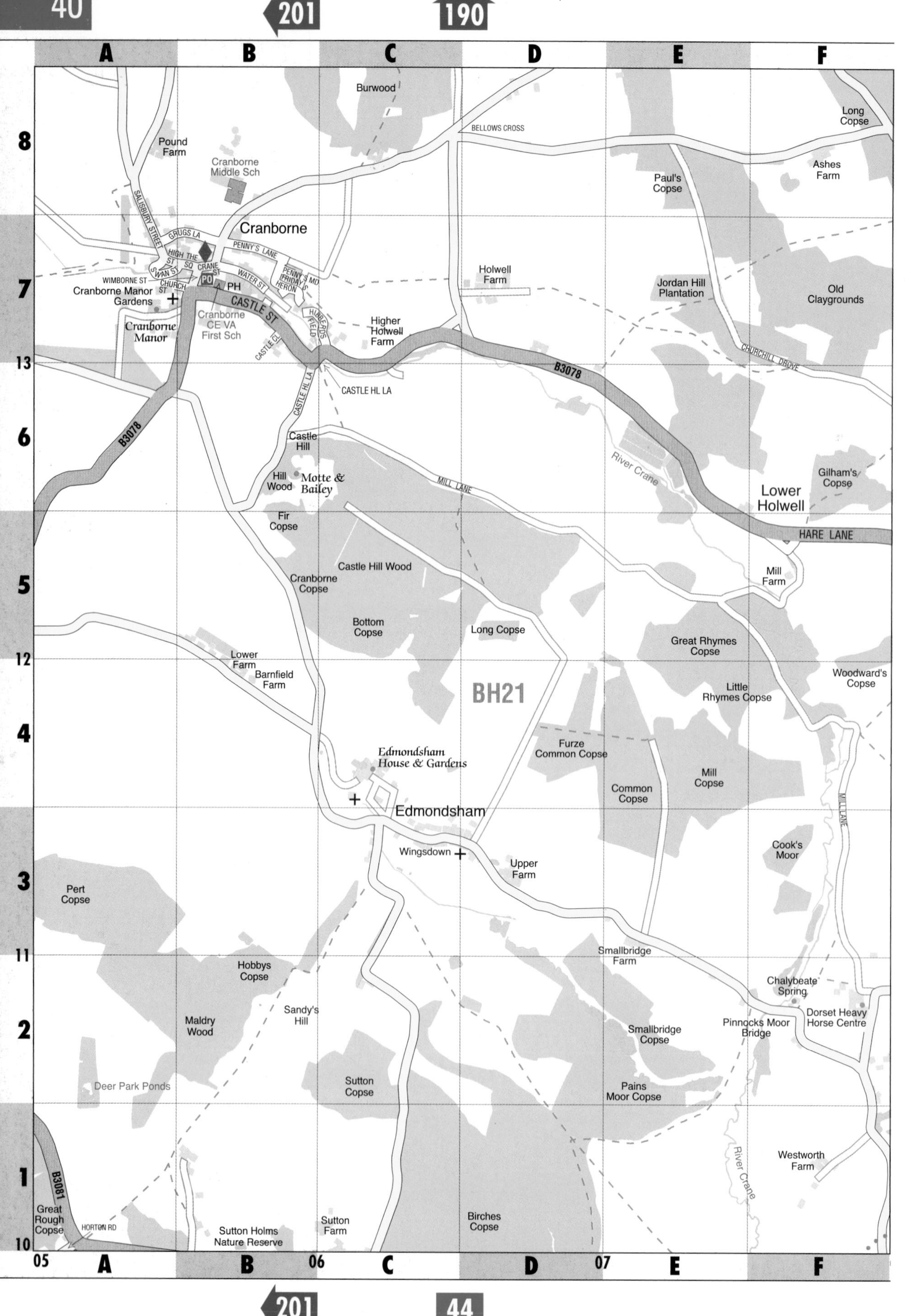
A
B
C
D
E
F
8
7
13
6
5
12
4
3
11
2
1
10
05
06
07
Burwood
Long Copse
Pound Farm
Cranborne Middle Sch
BELLOWS CROSS
Paul's Copse
Ashes Farm
Cranborne
SALISBURY STREET
GRUGS LA
PENNY'S LANE
HIGH THE ST
SWAN ST
SQ
CRANE ST
WATER ST
PENNY'S MD
FRIDAYS
HERON
WIMBORNE ST
CHURCH ST
PO
PH
Cranborne Manor Gardens
CASTLE ST
Cranborne CE VA First Sch
Cranborne Manor
HIBBERDS FIELD
CASTLE CL
Holwell Farm
Jordan Hill Plantation
Old Claygrounds
Higher Holwell Farm
CHURCHILL DROVE
B3078
CASTLE HL LA
Castle Hill
Hill Wood
Motte & Bailey
MILL LANE
River Crane
Gilham's Copse
Lower Holwell
HARE LANE
Fir Copse
Castle Hill Wood
Cranborne Copse
Mill Farm
Bottom Copse
Long Copse
Great Rhymes Copse
Lower Farm
Barnfield Farm
Woodward's Copse
Little Rhymes Copse
BH21
Furze Common Copse
Edmondsham House & Gardens
Mill Copse
Common Copse
Edmondsham
Wingsdown
Upper Farm
Cook's Moor
Pert Copse
Smallbridge Farm
Hobbys Copse
Chalybeate Spring
Sandy's Hill
Maldry Wood
Smallbridge Copse
Pinnocks Moor Bridge
Dorset Heavy Horse Centre
Deer Park Ponds
Sutton Copse
Pains Moor Copse
Westworth Farm
B3081
Great Rough Copse
HORTON RD
Sutton Holms Nature Reserve
Sutton Farm
Birches Copse

201
44

190
42

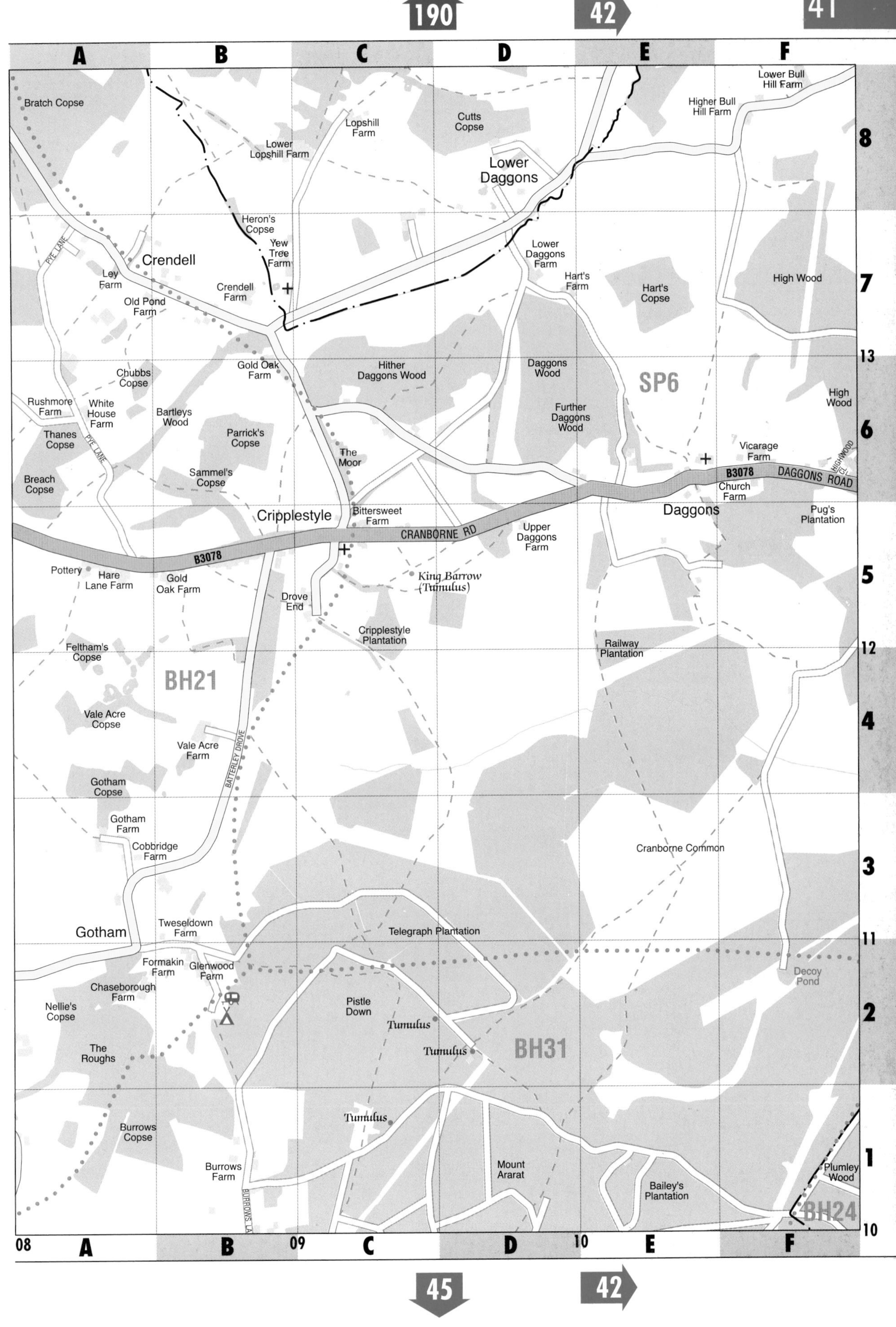
A
B
C
D
E
F
Bratch Copse
Lopshill Farm
Lower Lopshill Farm
Cutts Copse
Lower Bull Hill Farm
Higher Bull Hill Farm
Lower Daggons
Heron's Copse
Yew Tree Farm
Crendell
Ley Farm
Pye Lane
Crendell Farm
Old Pond Farm
Lower Daggons Farm
Hart's Farm
Hart's Copse
High Wood
Chubbs Copse
Gold Oak Farm
Hither Daggons Wood
Daggons Wood
SP6
High Wood
Rushmore Farm
White House Farm
Bartleys Wood
Parrick's Copse
Further Daggons Wood
Thanes Copse
The Moor
Vicarage Farm
Highwood Cl
Breach Copse
Sammel's Copse
B3078
Daggons Road
Church Farm
Cripplestyle
Bittersweet Farm
Daggons
Pug's Plantation
Cranborne Rd
Upper Daggons Farm
B3078
Pottery
Hare Lane Farm
Gold Oak Farm
King Barrow (Tumulus)
Drove End
Cripplestyle Plantation
Railway Plantation
Feltham's Copse
BH21
Vale Acre Copse
Vale Acre Farm
Batterley Drove
Gotham Copse
Gotham Farm
Cobbridge Farm
Cranborne Common
Gotham
Tweseldown Farm
Telegraph Plantation
Formakin Farm
Glenwood Farm
Decoy Pond
Chaseborough Farm
Nellie's Copse
Pistle Down
Tumulus
Tumulus
BH31
The Roughs
Tumulus
Burrows Copse
Burrows Farm
Burrows La
Mount Ararat
Bailey's Plantation
Plumley Wood
BH24
8
7
13
6
5
12
4
3
11
2
1
10
08
09
10

45
42

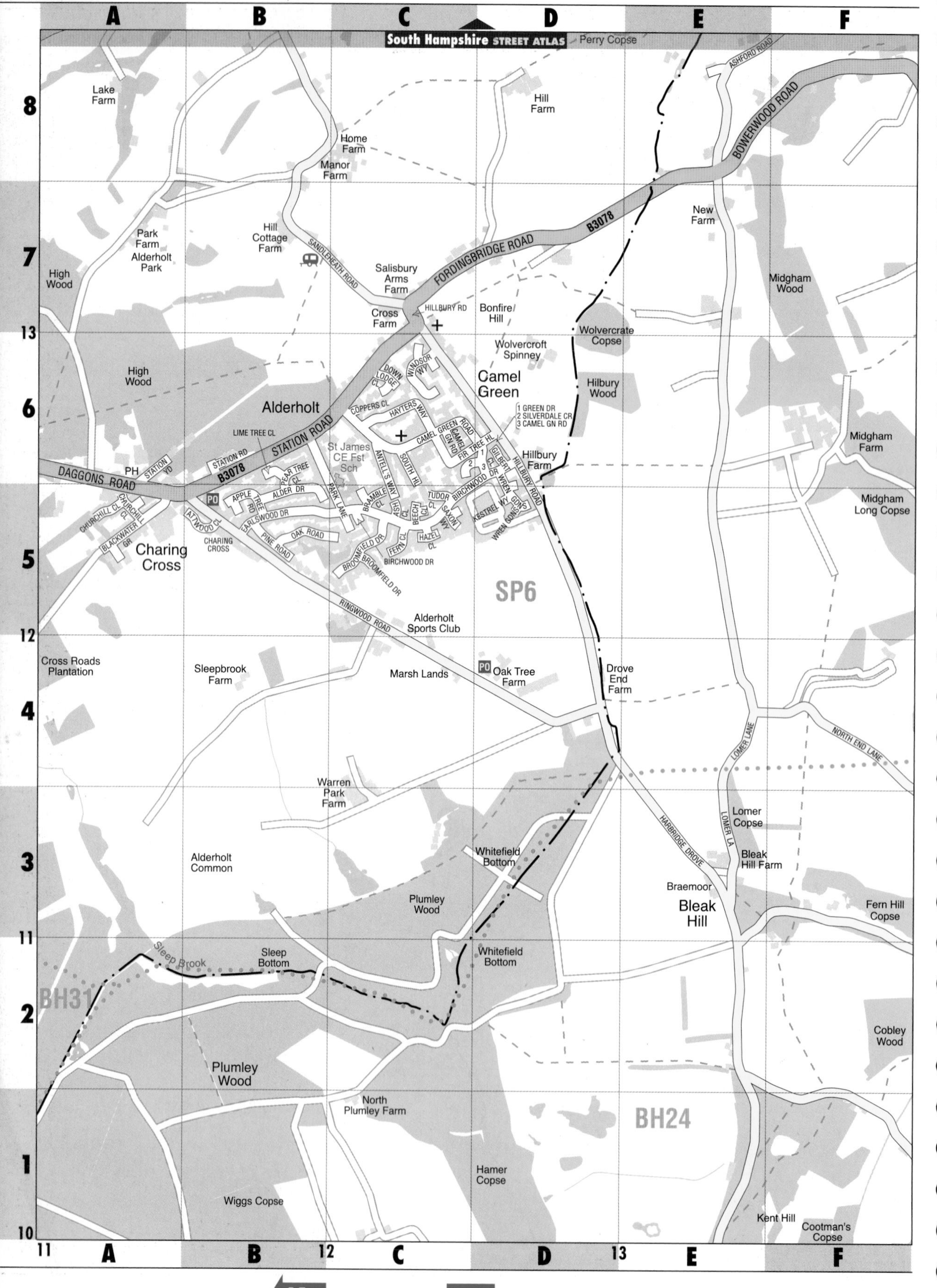

Perry Copse
Ashford Road
BOWERWOOD ROAD
Lake Farm
Hill Farm
8
Home Farm
Manor Farm
New Farm
B3078
Midgham Wood
High Wood
Park Farm
Alderholt Park
Hill Cottage Farm
SANDLEHEATH ROAD
Salisbury Arms Farm
FORDINGBRIDGE ROAD
7
High Wood
13
Cross Farm
HILLBURY RD
Bonfire Hill
Wolvercrate Copse
Wolvercroft Spinney
High Wood
Camel Green
Hilbury Wood
Midgham Farm
6
Alderholt
DOWN LODGE CL
WINDSOR WY
COPPERS CL
HAYTERS WY
1 GREEN DR
2 SILVERDALE CR
3 CAMEL GN RD
HILLBURY ROAD
Midgham Long Copse
LIME TREE CL
St James CE Fst Sch
CAMEL GREEN ROAD
SOUTH HL
ANTELL'S WAY
FIR TREE HL
GILBERT CL
Hillbury Farm
STATION RD
STATION ROAD
B3078
PH
STATION
PEAR TREE CL
APPLE TREE RD
ALDER DR
PARK LANE
BRAMBLE CL
HAZEL CL
TUDOR CL
SAXON
BIRCHWOOD
WREN GDNS
KESTREL
Daggons Road
PO
CHURCHILL CL
CHURCHILL
BLACKWATER
ATWOOD
CHARING CROSS
EARLSWOOD DR
PINE ROAD
OAK ROAD
BROOMFIELD DR
FERN CL
BEECH
5
Charing Cross
BROOMFIELD DR
BIRCHWOOD DR
SP6
12
Cross Roads Plantation
RINGWOOD ROAD
Alderholt Sports Club
Drove End Farm
Sleepbrook Farm
Marsh Lands
PO Oak Tree Farm
4
LOWER LANE
NORTH END LANE
Warren Park Farm
Lomer Copse
LOMER LA
HARBRIDGE DROVE
3
Alderholt Common
Whitefield Bottom
Bleak Hill Farm
Braemoor
Fern Hill Copse
Plumley Wood
Bleak Hill
11
Sleep Brook
Sleep Bottom
Whitefield Bottom
BH31
2
Cobley Wood
Plumley Wood
North Plumley Farm
BH24
1
Hamer Copse
Kent Hill
Cootman's Copse
Wiggs Copse
10

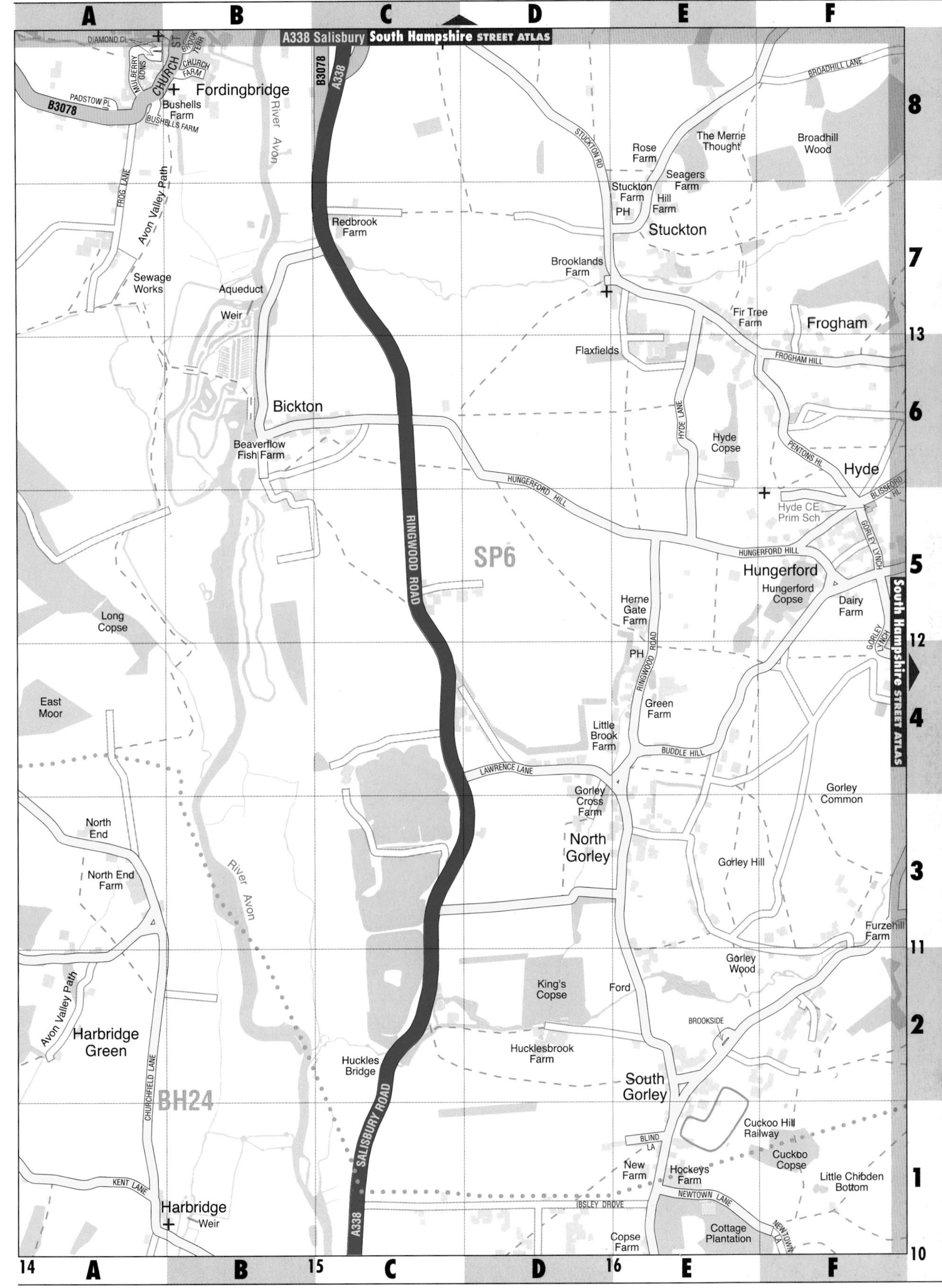
A338 Salisbury
South Hampshire STREET ATLAS
Fordingbridge
Bushells Farm
River Avon
Avon Valley Path
Sewage Works
Aqueduct
Weir
Redbrook Farm
Bickton
Beaverflow Fish Farm
Long Copse
East Moor
North End
North End Farm
Harbridge Green
Harbridge
Huckles Bridge
BH24
SP6
RINGWOOD ROAD
SALISBURY ROAD
LAWRENCE LANE
Stuckton
Rose Farm
The Merrie Thought
Broadhill Wood
Seagers Farm
Stuckton Farm
Hill Farm
PH
Brooklands Farm
Fir Tree Farm
Frogham
Flaxfields
FROGHAM HILL
HYDE LANE
Hyde Copse
Hyde
Hyde CE Prim Sch
HUNGERFORD HILL
Hungerford
Hungerford Copse
Dairy Farm
Herne Gate Farm
Green Farm
Little Brook Farm
BUDDLE HILL
Gorley Cross Farm
North Gorley
Gorley Common
Gorley Hill
Furzehill Farm
Gorley Wood
King's Copse
Ford
BROOKSIDE
Hucklesbrook Farm
South Gorley
Cuckoo Hill Railway
Cuckoo Copse
Little Chibden Bottom
New Farm
Hockeys Farm
NEWTOWN LANE
IBSLEY DROVE
Copse Farm
Cottage Plantation
CHURCHFIELD LANE
KENT LANE
FROG LANE
PADSTOW PL
B3078
DIAMOND CL
CHURCH ST
STUCKTON RD
BROADHILL LANE
PENTONS HL
GORLEY LYNCH
BLISSFORD HL
BLIND LA
14
15
16
10
11
12
13

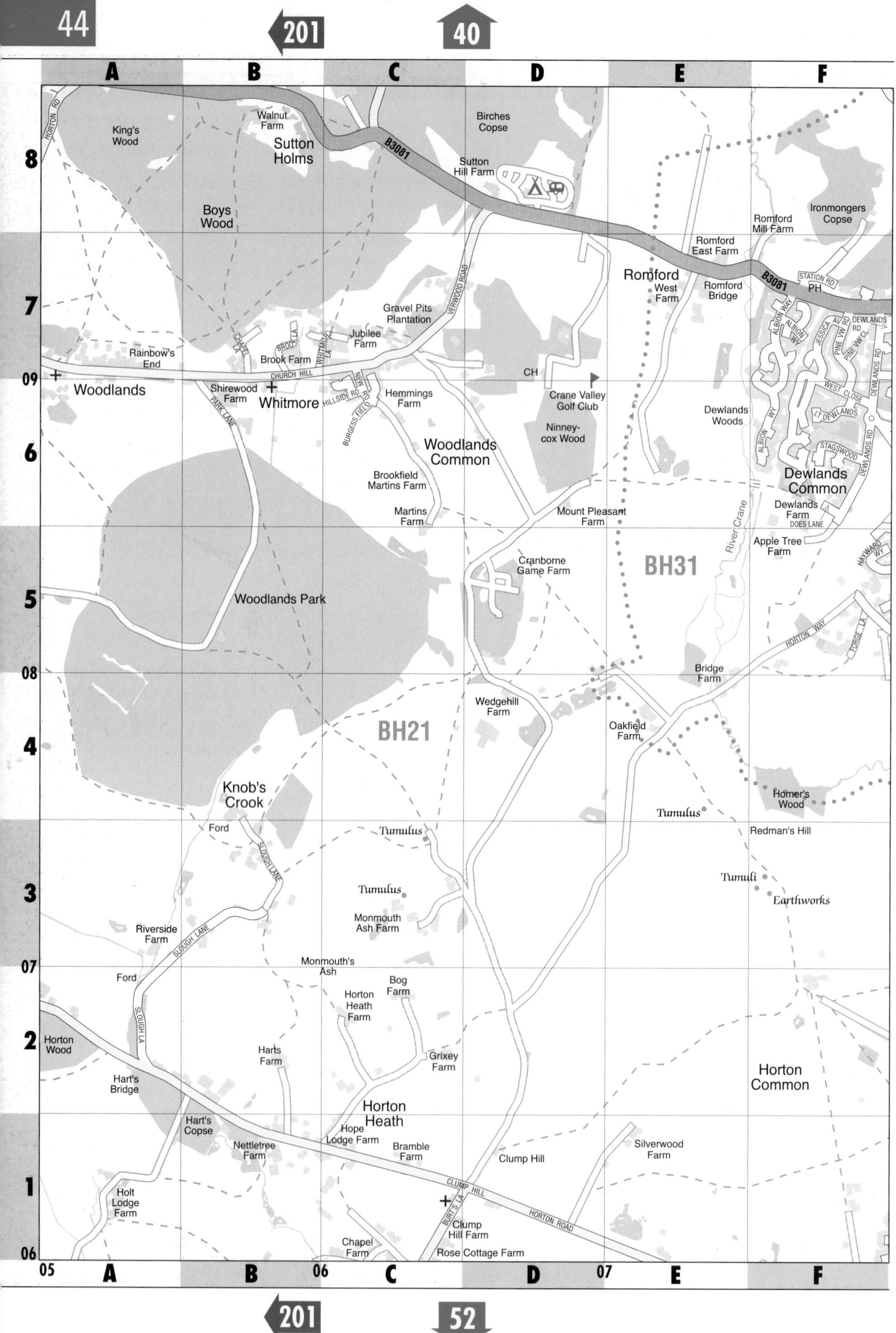

201
40

A | **B** | **C** | **D** | **E** | **F**

HORTON RD

King's
Wood

Walnut
Farm

Sutton
Holms

Birches
Copse

B3081

Boys
Wood

Sutton
Hill Farm

Romford
Mill Farm

Ironmongers
Copse

Romford
East Farm

Romford
West Farm

Romford
Bridge

B3081

STATION RD

PH

Rainbow's
End

Gravel Pits
Plantation

VERWOOD ROAD

Jubilee
Farm

WHITMORE LA

BROCK LA

Brook
Farm

CHURCH HILL

ALBION WAY

ALBION WAY

JESSICA AV RD

PINE VW RD

PINE VW CL

DEWLANDS RD

WEST CLOSE

DEWLANDS RD

Woodlands

Shirewood
Farm

Whitmore

HILLSIDE RD

BURGESS FIELD LA

Hemmings
Farm

CH

Crane Valley
Golf Club

Dewlands
Woods

LT DEWLANDS

STAGSWOOD

Dewlands
Common

PARK LANE

Ninney-
cox Wood

Woodlands
Common

Brookfield
Martins Farm

Dewlands
Farm

DOES LANE

HAYWARD WY

Martins
Farm

Mount Pleasant
Farm

River Crane

Apple Tree
Farm

Woodlands Park

Cranborne
Game Farm

BH31

HORTON WAY

FORGE LA

Bridge
Farm

Homer's
Wood

Wedgehill
Farm

Oakfield
Farm

BH21

Knob's
Crook

Tumulus

Redman's Hill

Ford

SLOUGH LANE

Tumulus

Tumuli

Earthworks

Riverside
Farm

SLOUGH LANE

Tumulus

Monmouth
Ash Farm

Ford

Monmouth's
Ash

SLOUGH LA

Bog
Farm

Horton
Heath
Farm

Horton
Wood

Harts
Farm

Grixey
Farm

Horton
Common

Hart's
Bridge

Horton
Heath

Hart's
Copse

Hope
Lodge Farm

Bramble
Farm

Clump Hill

Silverwood
Farm

Nettletree
Farm

CLUMP HILL

Holt
Lodge
Farm

BURT'S LA

Clump
Hill Farm

HORTON ROAD

Chapel
Farm

Rose Cottage Farm

05 | **A** | **B** | 06 | **C** | **D** | 07 | **E** | **F**

201
52

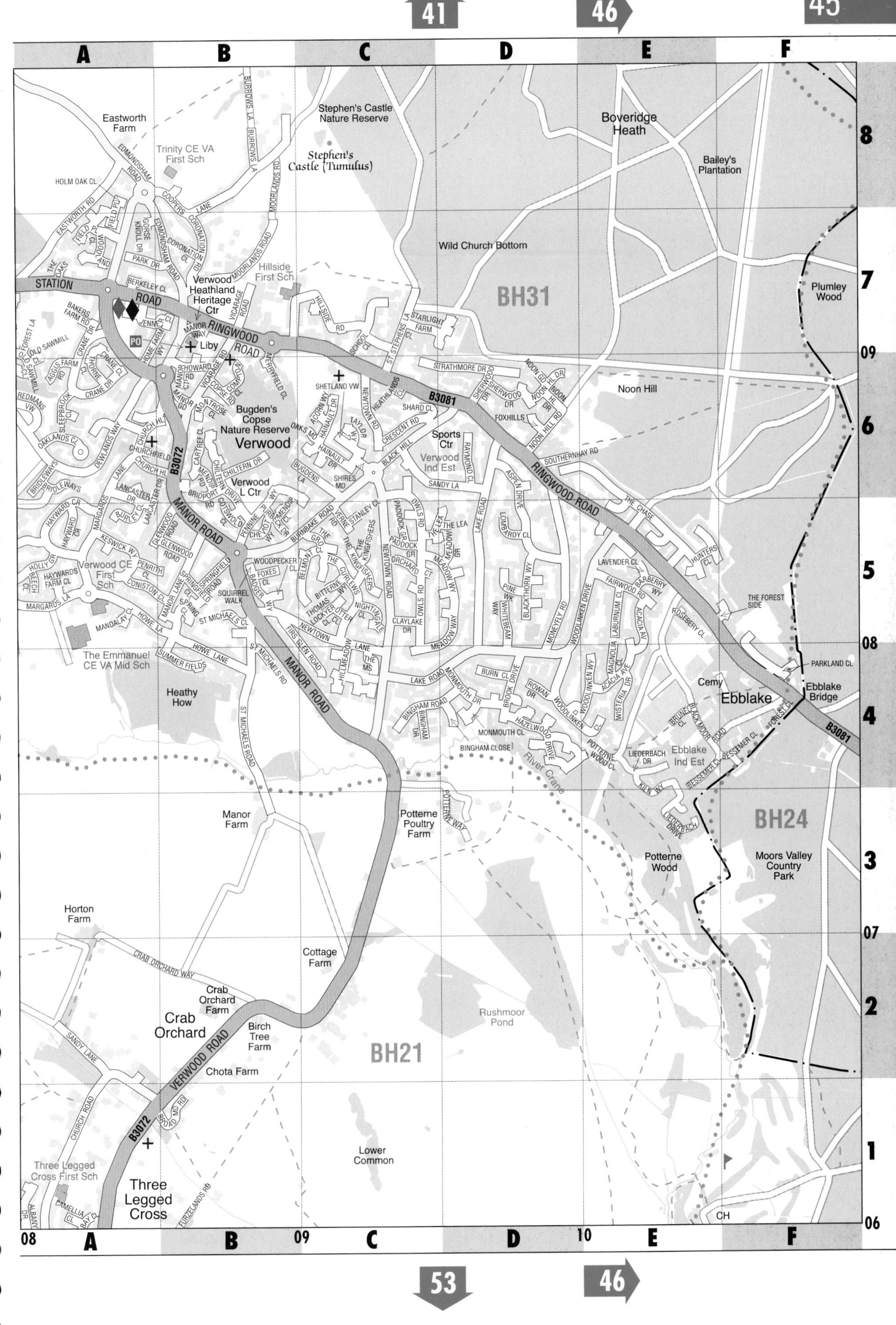

41
46
A
B
C
D
E
F
8
7
09
6
5
08
4
3
07
2
1
06
08
09
10
53
46
Eastworth Farm
Trinity CE VA First Sch
Stephen's Castle Nature Reserve
Stephen's Castle (Tumulus)
Boveridge Heath
Bailey's Plantation
Wild Church Bottom
Hillside First Sch
Verwood Heathland Heritage Ctr
BH31
Plumley Wood
STATION ROAD
RINGWOOD ROAD
Liby
Noon Hill
B3081
Bugden's Copse Nature Reserve
Verwood
Sports Ctr
Verwood Ind Est
Verwood L Ctr
B3072
MANOR ROAD
Verwood CE First Sch
The Emmanuel CE VA Mid Sch
Heathy How
THE FOREST SIDE
PARKLAND CL
Cemy
Ebblake
Ebblake Bridge
Ebblake Ind Est
River Crane
Manor Farm
Potterne Poultry Farm
BH24
Potterne Wood
Moors Valley Country Park
Horton Farm
Cottage Farm
Crab Orchard Farm
Crab Orchard
Birch Tree Farm
Rushmoor Pond
BH21
Chota Farm
VERWOOD ROAD
Lower Common
Three Legged Cross First Sch
Three Legged Cross
CH

45
42

A B C D E F

8

Plumley Wood

Wiggs Copse

Hamer Copse

Kent Hill Plantation

Cootman's Copse

Harbridge Farm

Harbridge Sch

Turmer

Ford

Plumley Farm

7

Harefield Plantation

Lower Turmer

09

6

Reservoir Cottage

Home Farm

SHEPHERDS LA

SHEPHERDS HILL

CHESTNUT AVENUE

Home Wood

Dog Kennel Wood

ELLINGHAM DRIVE

New Bridge

5

Ringwood Forest

VERWOOD ROAD

NEA DRIVE

Nursery Cottages

Somerley Park

Somerley

08

BH24

ELLINGHAM DR

NEA DR

4

Bluehaze

Park Cottage

3

Sunderton Wood

07

DUNCOMBE DRIVE

ASHLEY DRIVE

Withybed Copse

2

Tumulus

Tumuli

Sunderton Wood

Ashley Heath

Duncombe Lodge

B3081

1

Moors Valley Country Park

VERWOOD ROAD

Ashley Farm

06

11 A B 12 C D 13 E F

B3081

Baker's Hanging

45
54

43

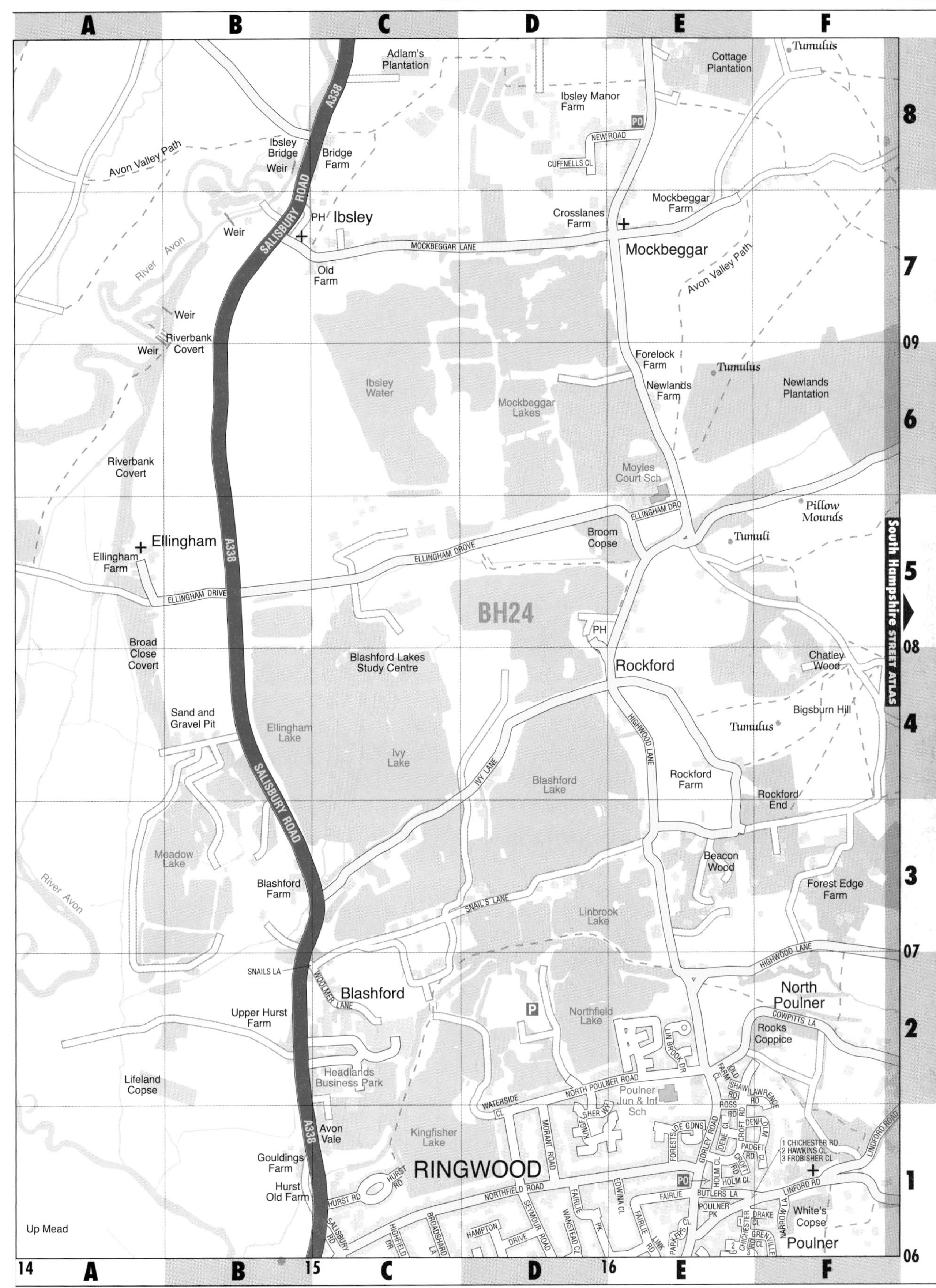

A
B
C
D
E
F
Adlam's Plantation
Cottage Plantation
Tumulus
Ibsley Manor Farm
NEW ROAD
CUFFNELLS CL
Avon Valley Path
Ibsley Bridge
Bridge Farm
Weir
SALISBURY ROAD
A338
PH
Ibsley
Weir
River Avon
Old Farm
MOCKBEGGAR LANE
Crosslanes Farm
Mockbeggar Farm
Mockbeggar
Avon Valley Path
Weir
Riverbank Covert
Weir
Forelock Farm
Tumulus
Newlands Farm
Newlands Plantation
Ibsley Water
Mockbeggar Lakes
Riverbank Covert
Moyles Court Sch
ELLINGHAM DRO
Pillow Mounds
Ellingham
Ellingham Farm
ELLINGHAM DRIVE
ELLINGHAM DRIVE
Broom Copse
Tumuli
BH24
PH
Broad Close Covert
Blashford Lakes Study Centre
Rockford
Chatley Wood
Sand and Gravel Pit
Ellingham Lake
HIGHWOOD LANE
Bigsburn Hill
Tumulus
Ivy Lake
IVY LANE
Blashford Lake
Rockford Farm
Rockford End
Meadow Lake
Beacon Wood
River Avon
Blashford Farm
SNAIL'S LANE
Linbrook Lake
Forest Edge Farm
HIGHWOOD LANE
SNAILS LA
WOOLMER LANE
Blashford
North Poulner
COWPITTS LA
Upper Hurst Farm
Northfield Lake
Rooks Coppice
LIN BROOK DR
Headlands Business Park
Lifeland Copse
WATERSIDE CL
NORTH POULNER ROAD
Poulner Jun & Inf Sch
Avon Vale
Kingfisher Lake
MORANT ROAD
FORESTSIDE GDNS
GORLEY ROAD
1 CHICHESTER RD
2 HAWKINS CL
3 FROBISHER CL
LINFORD ROAD
Gouldings Farm
HURST RD
RINGWOOD
BUTLERS LA
LINFORD RD
Hurst Old Farm
HURST RD
NORTHFIELD ROAD
FAIRLIE
POULNER PK
White's Copse
Poulner
Up Mead
SALISBURY RD
HIGHFIELD DR
BROADSHARD LA
HAMPTON DRIVE
SEYMOUR ROAD
WANSTEAD CL
EDWINA CL
FAIRLIE PK
LINK RD
PARKERS CL
NARROW LA
GRENVILLE CL
South Hampshire STREET ATLAS
8
7
09
6
5
08
4
3
07
2
1
06
14
15
16

55

211
200

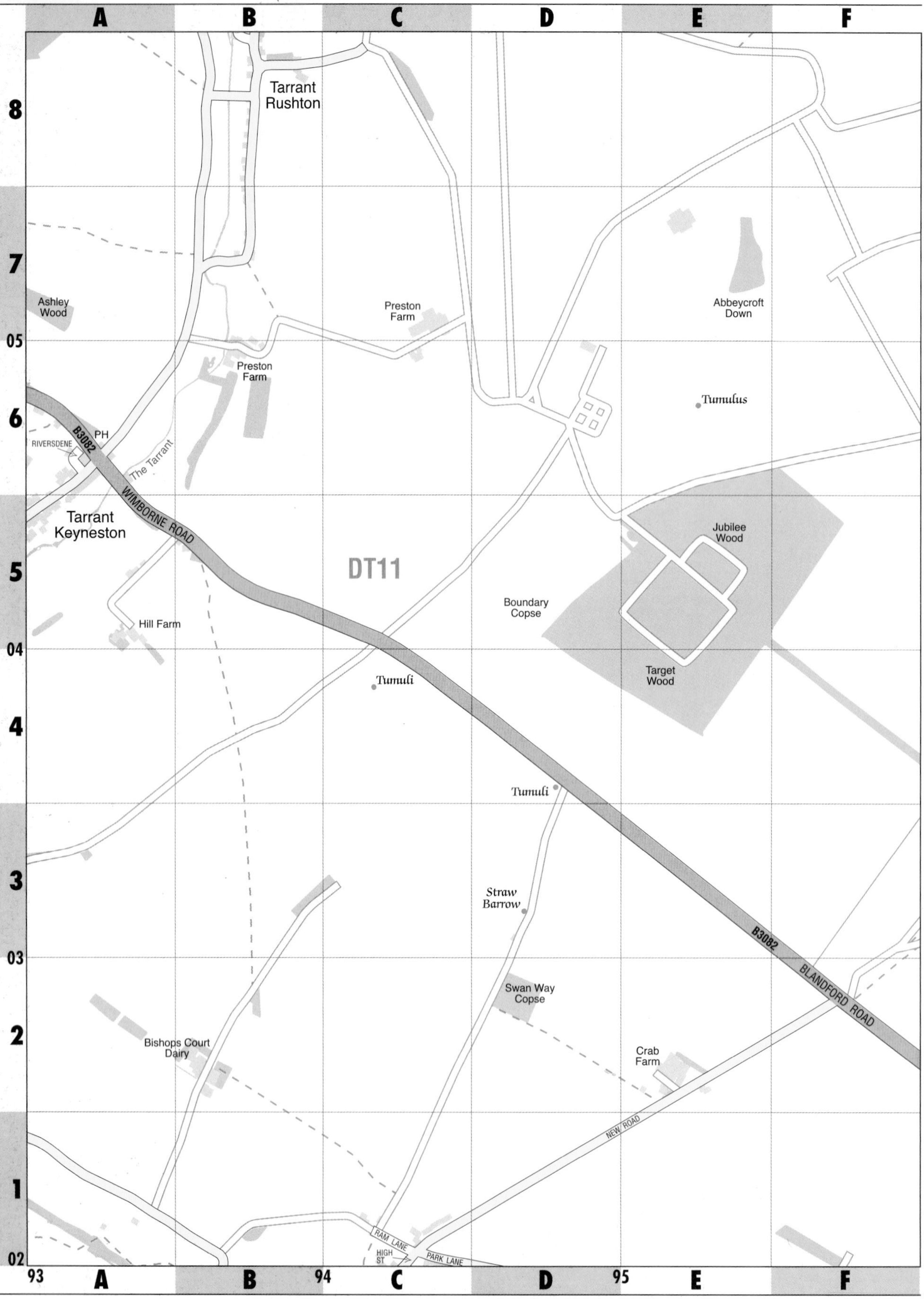

| | A | B | C | D | E | F |

8

Tarrant
Rushton

7

Ashley
Wood

Preston
Farm

Abbeycroft
Down

05

Preston
Farm

Tumulus

6

PH

RIVERSDENE

B3082

The Tarrant

Jubilee
Wood

Tarrant
Keyneston

WIMBORNE ROAD

DT11

Boundary
Copse

5

Hill Farm

Target
Wood

04

Tumuli

4

Tumuli

3

Straw
Barrow

B3082

BLANDFORD ROAD

03

Swan Way
Copse

2

Bishops Court
Dairy

Crab
Farm

NEW ROAD

1

RAM LANE

HIGH
ST

PARK LANE

02

| 93 | A | | B | 94 | C | | D | 95 | E | | F |

211

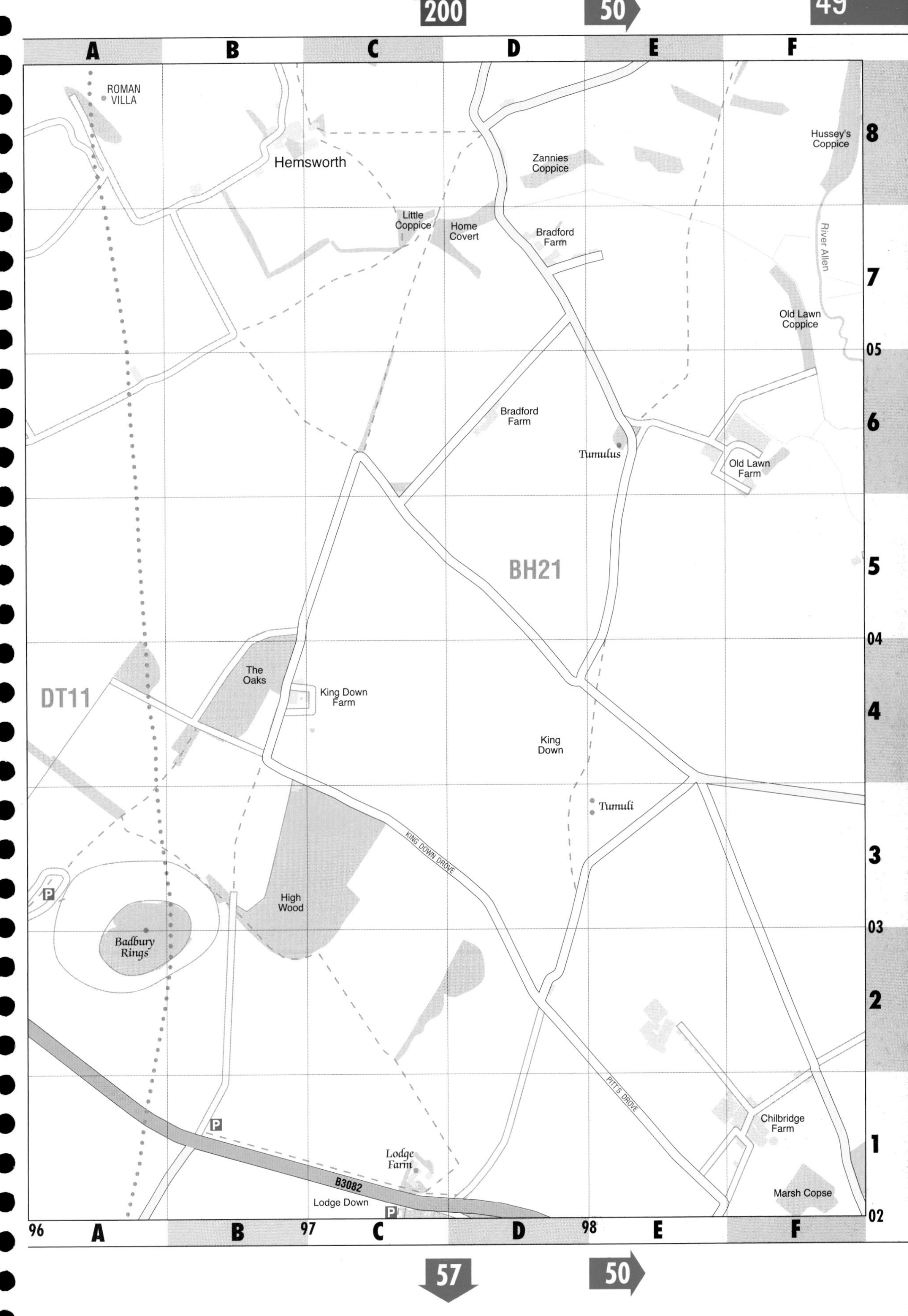
200
50
A
B
C
D
E
F
ROMAN VILLA
Hemsworth
Zannies Coppice
Hussey's Coppice
Little Coppice
Home Covert
Bradford Farm
River Allen
Old Lawn Coppice
Bradford Farm
Tumulus
Old Lawn Farm
BH21
The Oaks
King Down Farm
DT11
King Down
Tumuli
KING DOWN DROVE
High Wood
Badbury Rings
PITT'S DROVE
Chilbridge Farm
Lodge Farm
B3082
Lodge Down
Marsh Copse
8
7
05
6
5
04
4
3
03
2
1
02
96
97
98
57
50

49 201

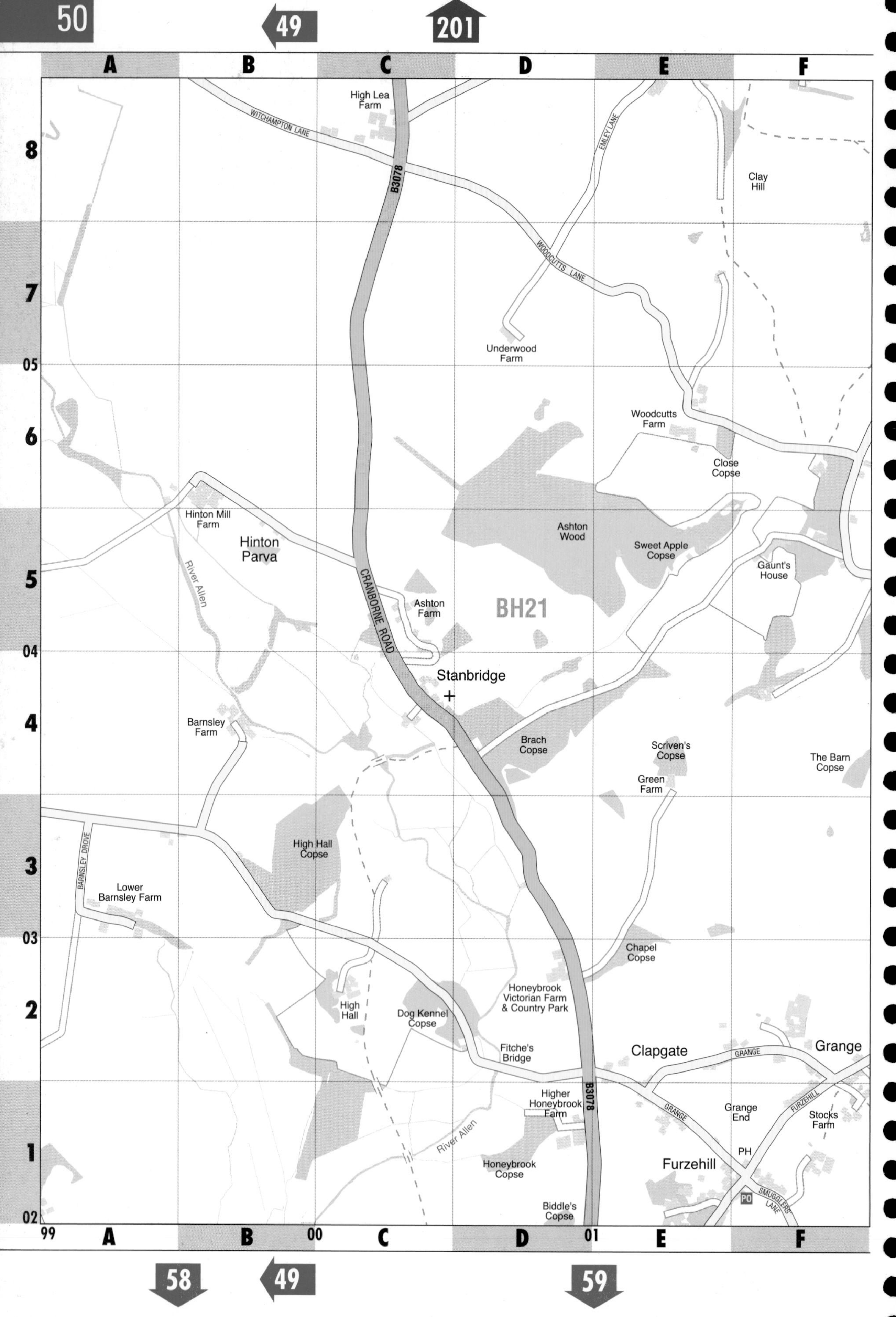

A B C D E F
8 7 05 6 5 04 4 3 03 2 1 02
99 00 01
High Lea Farm
WITCHAMPTON LANE
B3078
EMLEY LANE
Clay Hill
WOODCUTTS LANE
Underwood Farm
Woodcutts Farm
Close Copse
Ashton Wood
Sweet Apple Copse
Gaunt's House
Hinton Mill Farm
Hinton Parva
River Allen
CRANBORNE ROAD
Ashton Farm
BH21
Stanbridge
Barnsley Farm
Brach Copse
Scriven's Copse
The Barn Copse
Green Farm
High Hall Copse
BARNSLEY DROVE
Lower Barnsley Farm
Chapel Copse
Honeybrook Victorian Farm & Country Park
High Hall
Dog Kennel Copse
Fitche's Bridge
Clapgate
GRANGE
Grange
Higher Honeybrook Farm
Grange End
FURZEHILL
Stocks Farm
River Allen
PH
Honeybrook Copse
Furzehill
PO
SMUGGLERS LANE
Biddle's Copse

58 49 59

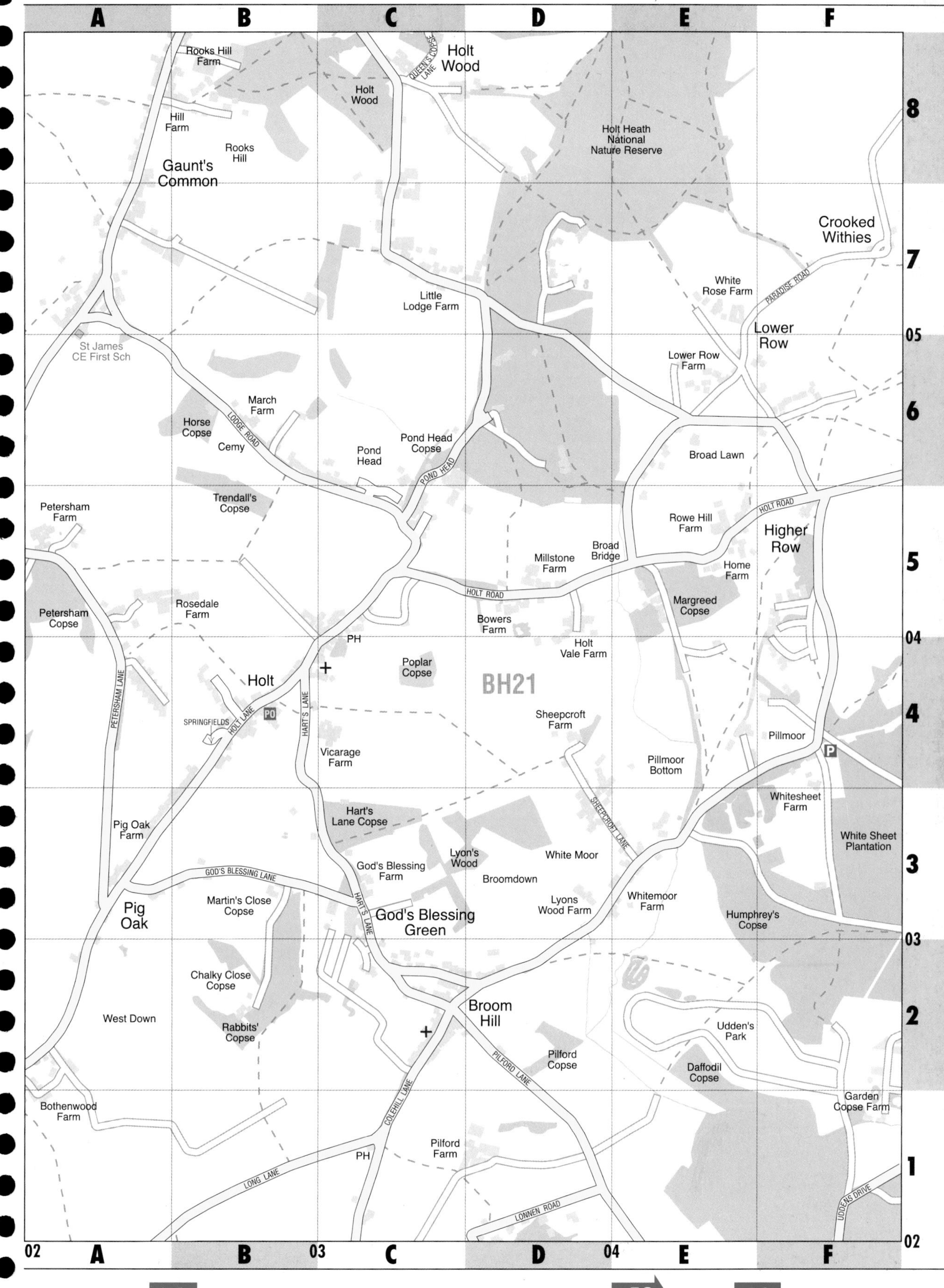
201
52
A B C D E F
Rooks Hill Farm
Holt Wood
Queen's Copse Lane
Holt Wood
Hill Farm
Rooks Hill
Gaunt's Common
Holt Heath National Nature Reserve
Crooked Withies
White Rose Farm
Paradise Road
Little Lodge Farm
Lower Row
St James CE First Sch
Lower Row Farm
March Farm
Horse Copse
Lodge Road
Cemy
Pond Head Copse
Pond Head
Pond Head
Broad Lawn
Trendall's Copse
Petersham Farm
Holt Road
Rowe Hill Farm
Higher Row
Broad Bridge
Millstone Farm
Home Farm
Holt Road
Margreed Copse
Petersham Copse
Rosedale Farm
Bowers Farm
PH
Holt Vale Farm
Poplar Copse
BH21
Holt
Petersham Lane
Springfields
Holt Lane
PO
Hart's Lane
Sheepcroft Farm
Pillmoor
P
Vicarage Farm
Pillmoor Bottom
Hart's Lane Copse
Whitesheet Farm
Pig Oak Farm
Sheepcroft Lane
White Sheet Plantation
Lyon's Wood
White Moor
God's Blessing Lane
God's Blessing Farm
Broomdown
Martin's Close Copse
Hart's Lane
Whitemoor Farm
Pig Oak
God's Blessing Green
Lyons Wood Farm
Humphrey's Copse
Chalky Close Copse
Broom Hill
West Down
Rabbits' Copse
Udden's Park
Pilford Lane
Pilford Copse
Daffodil Copse
Bothenwood Farm
Garden Copse Farm
Colehill Lane
Pilford Farm
PH
Long Lane
Lonnen Road
Uddens Drive
8 7 05 6 5 04 4 3 03 2 1 02
02 03 04
59
52
60

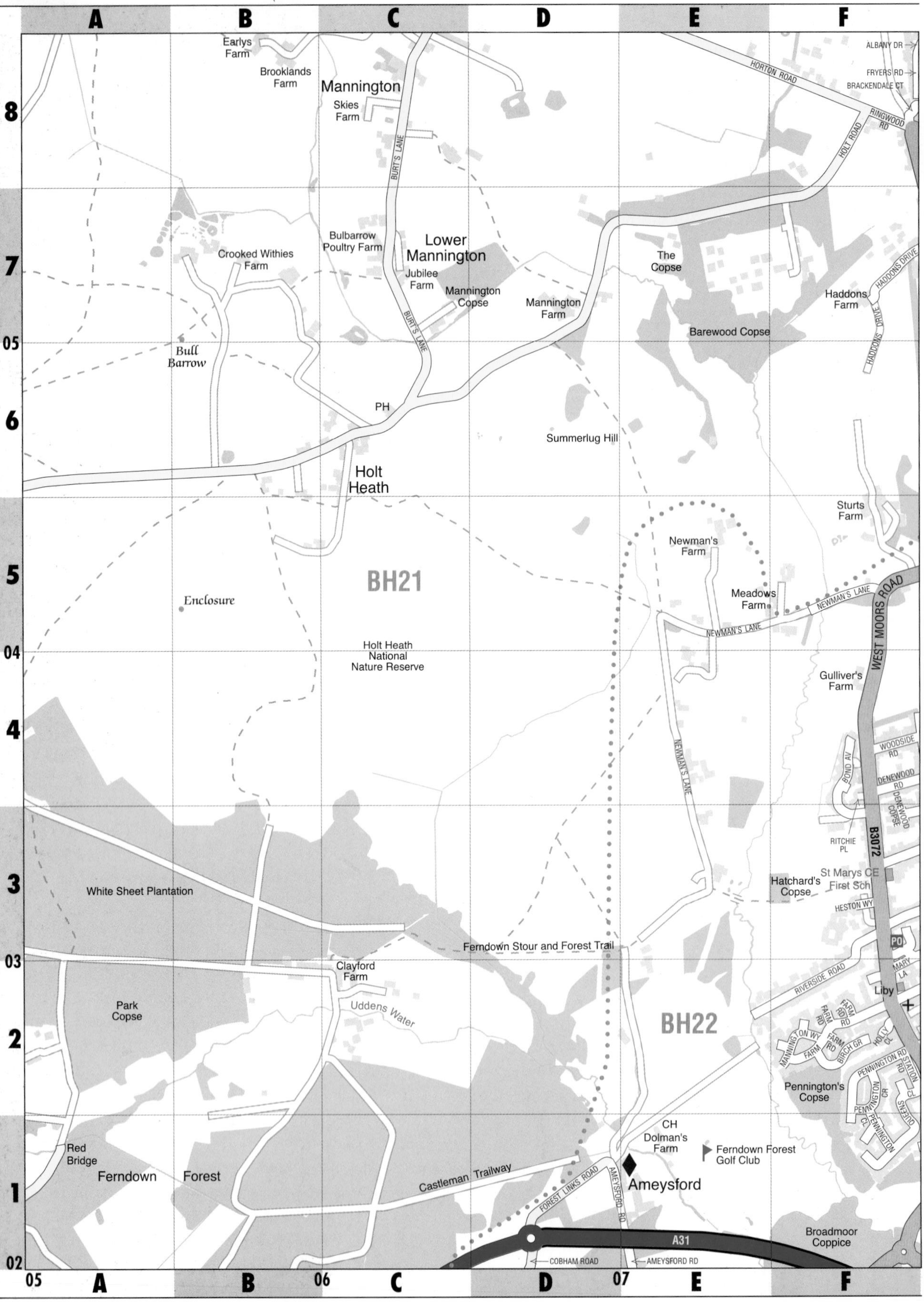

A B C D E F

8

7

05

6

5

04

4

3

03

2

1

02

ALBANY DR
FRYERS RD
BRACKENDALE CT
RINGWOOD RD

Earlys Farm

Brooklands Farm

Mannington

Skies Farm

BURT'S LANE

HORTON ROAD

HOLT ROAD

Crooked Withies Farm

Bulbarrow Poultry Farm

Lower Mannington

Jubilee Farm

Mannington Copse

Mannington Farm

The Copse

Barewood Copse

Haddons Farm

HADDONS DRIVE

Bull Barrow

PH

Summerlug Hill

Sturts Farm

Holt Heath

Newman's Farm

Meadows Farm

NEWMAN'S LANE

WEST MOORS ROAD

BH21

Enclosure

Holt Heath National Nature Reserve

Gulliver's Farm

WOODSIDE RD

BOND AV

DENEWOOD RD

DENEWOOD COPSE

B3072

RITCHIE PL

White Sheet Plantation

Hatchard's Copse

St Marys CE First Sch

HESTON WY

NEWMAN'S LANE

Ferndown Stour and Forest Trail

PO

Clayford Farm

Uddens Water

RIVERSIDE ROAD

Liby

ST MARY LA

Park Copse

BH22

MANNINGTON WY
FARM RD
FARM RD
BIRCH GR
HOLLY CL

Pennington's Copse

PENNINGTON RD
STATION RD
STATION CL
SPEEDS

PENNINGTON CR

Red Bridge

Ferndown Forest

Castleman Trailway

CH
Dolman's Farm

Ferndown Forest Golf Club

FOREST LINKS ROAD

AMEYSFORD RD

Ameysford

Broadmoor Coppice

A31

COBHAM ROAD

AMEYSFORD RD

05 A 06 B C 07 D E F

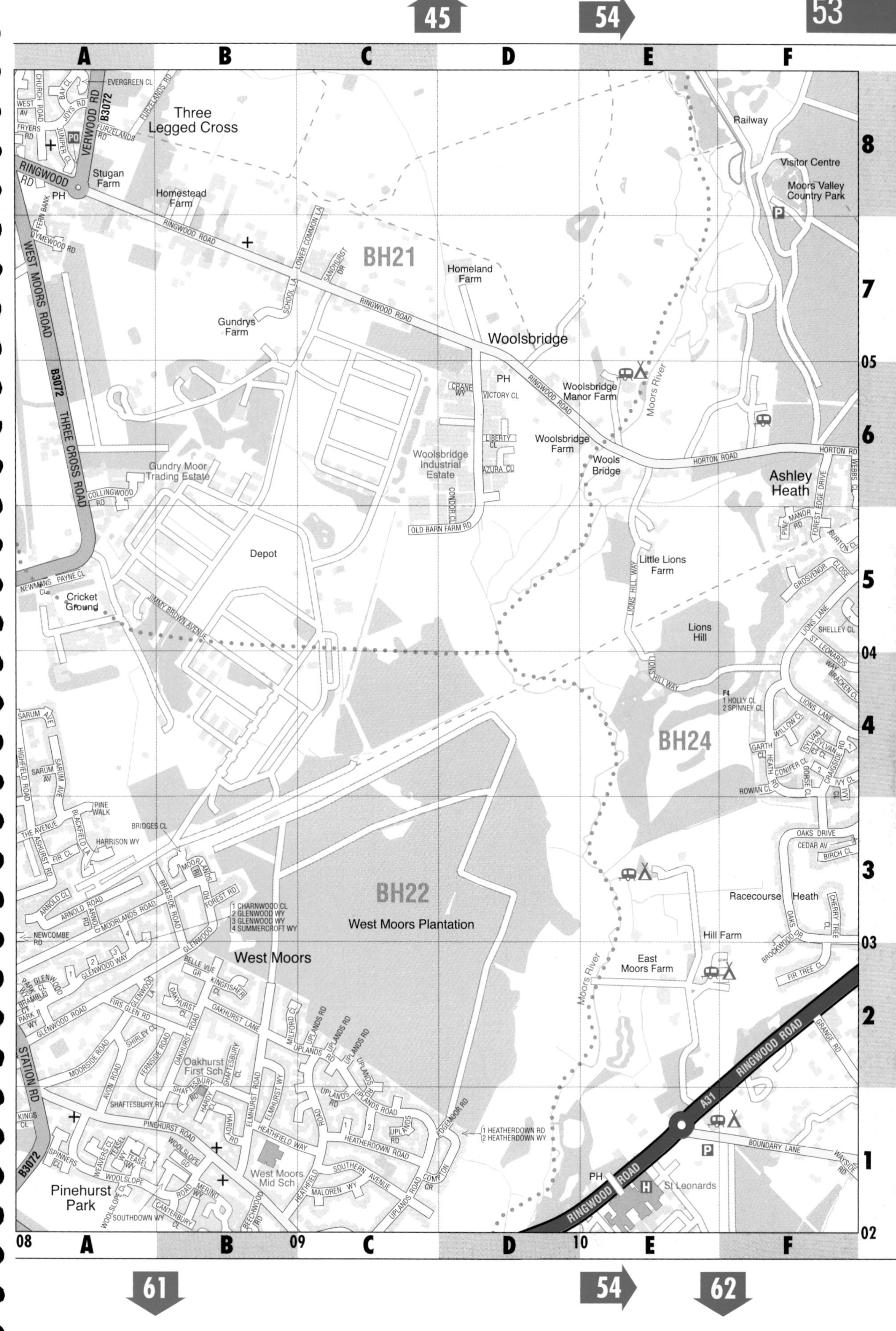
45
54
Three Legged Cross
Stugan Farm
Homestead Farm
Gundrys Farm
Homeland Farm
Woolsbridge
Woolsbridge Manor Farm
Woolsbridge Farm
Wools Bridge
Woolsbridge Industrial Estate
Gundry Moor Trading Estate
Depot
Cricket Ground
Railway
Visitor Centre
Moors Valley Country Park
Ashley Heath
Little Lions Farm
Lions Hill
BH21
BH22
BH24
West Moors Plantation
West Moors
Racecourse Heath
Hill Farm
East Moors Farm
Oakhurst First Sch
West Moors Mid Sch
Pinehurst Park
St Leonards
Moors River
RINGWOOD ROAD
HORTON ROAD
WEST MOORS ROAD
THREE CROSS ROAD
VERWOOD RD
STATION RD
B3072
A31
61
54
62

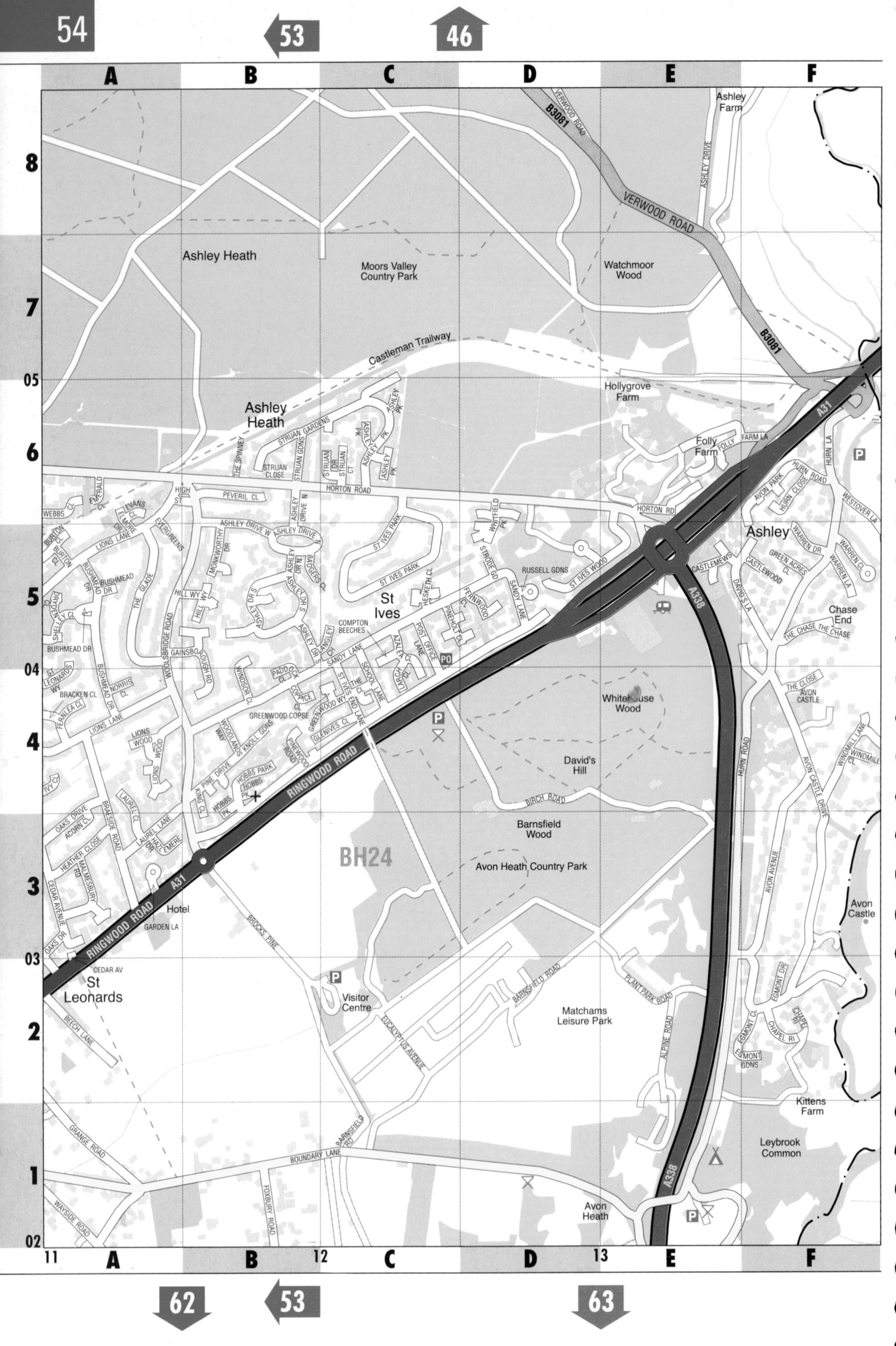
53
46
A
B
C
D
E
F
8
7
05
6
5
04
4
3
03
2
1
02
11
12
13
Ashley Farm
B3081
VERWOOD ROAD
ASHLEY DRIVE
Ashley Heath
Moors Valley Country Park
Watchmoor Wood
Castleman Trailway
Hollygrove Farm
Ashley Heath
STRUAN GARDENS
STRUAN GDNS
STRUAN CLOSE
THE SPINNEY
ASHLEY PK
Folly Farm
FOLLY
FARM LA
A31
HURN LA
HURN ROAD
AVON PARK
HURN CLOSE
WESTOVER LA
HORTON ROAD
HORTON RD
PEVERIL CL
HIGH ST
EVERALD CL
WEBBS CL
EVANS CL
ELMORE DR
EVERGREENS
BURTON CL
LIONS LANE
ASHLEY DRIVE W
ASHLEY DRIVE N
ST IVES PARK
WHITFIELD PK
STRIDE GD
RUSSELL GDNS
ST IVES WOOD
Ashley
WARREN DR
WARREN CL
WARREN LA
GREEN ACRES CL
CASTLEMEWS
CASTLEWOOD
DAVIS LA
Chase End
THE CHASE
BUSHMEAD DR
BUSHMEAD
THE GLADE
MONKWORTHY DR
HILL WY
BADGERS CL
HESKETH CL
St Ives
FERNWOOD CL
SANDY LANE
PINEHOLT CL
COMPTON BEECHES
POST OFFICE LANE
AZALEA CL
LARCH CL
SCHOOL LANE
PO
WOOLSBRIDGE ROAD
GAINSBOROUGH RD
WINDSOR CL
PADDOCK CL
COPSE CL
GREENWOOD WY
ST IVES END LANE
THE CL
GREENWOOD COPSE
GLENIVES CL
ST LEONARDS WY
BRACKEN CL
NORRIS CL
FERNLEA CL
LIONS WOOD
WOODLANDS WAY
KNOLL GDNS
PINEWOOD ROAD
RINGWOOD ROAD
HOBBS PARK
HOBBS PK
PINE DRIVE
KING CL
Whitehouse Wood
THE CLOSE
AVON CASTLE
David's Hill
BIRCH ROAD
HURN ROAD
A338
WINDMILL LANE
WINDMILL CL
AVON CASTLE DRIVE
IVY CL
OAKS DRIVE
ACORN CL
BRAESIDE ROAD
LAUREL CL
LAUREL LANE
HAZLEMERE DR
HEATHER CLOSE
MALMESBURY RD
CEDAR AVENUE
Barnsfield Wood
BH24
Avon Heath Country Park
AVON AVENUE
Avon Castle
Hotel
GARDEN LA
OAKS DR
BROCKS PINE
CEDAR AV
St Leonards
Visitor Centre
BARNSFIELD ROAD
PLANT PARK ROAD
Matchams Leisure Park
EUCALYPTUS AVENUE
ALPINE ROAD
EGMONT DR
EGMONT CL
CHAPEL RI
EGMONT GDNS
BEECH LANE
Kittens Farm
Leybrook Common
GRANGE ROAD
BARNSFIELD RD
BOUNDARY LANE
FOXBURY ROAD
WAYSIDE ROAD
Avon Heath
P

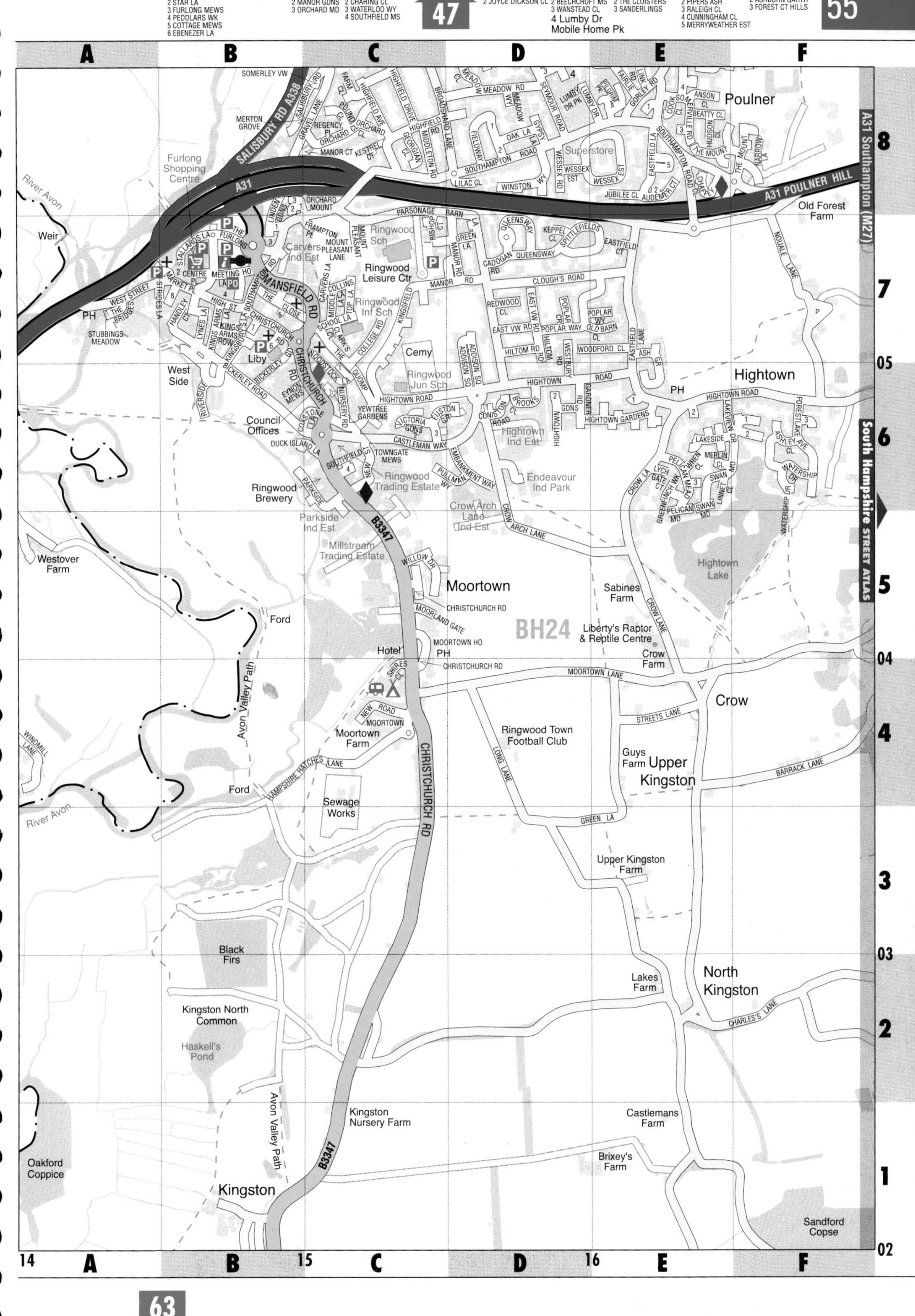

B7
1 THE SWEEP
2 STAR LA
3 FURLONG MEWS
4 PEDDLARS WK
5 COTTAGE MEWS
6 EBENEZER LA

7 GOOSEBERRY LA
8 DEWEYS LA

B8
1 LINDEN GDNS
2 MANOR GDNS
3 ORCHARD MD

C6
1 HARRY BARROW CL
2 CHARING CL
3 WATERLOO WY
4 SOUTHFIELD MS

D6
1 CROW ARCH LA
2 JOYCE DICKSON CL

D8
1 BEECHCROFT LA
2 BEECHCROFT MS
3 WANSTEAD CL
4 Lumby Dr
Mobile Home Pk

E6
1 OLD STACKS GDNS
2 THE CLOISTERS
3 SANDERLINGS

E8
1 WHITEHART FIELDS
2 PIPERS ASH
3 RALEIGH CL
4 CUNNINGHAM CL
5 MERRYWEATHER EST

F6
1 HOLMWOOD GARTH
2 ASHBURN GARTH
3 FOREST CT HILLS

47

55

A B C D E F

8

Tumulus

Bishops Court Farm
Hyde Farm
WEST STREET
PH
HIGH STREET
CHURCH ST
Kings Farm
STEWARD'S LANE
Shapwick
PICCADILLY LANE

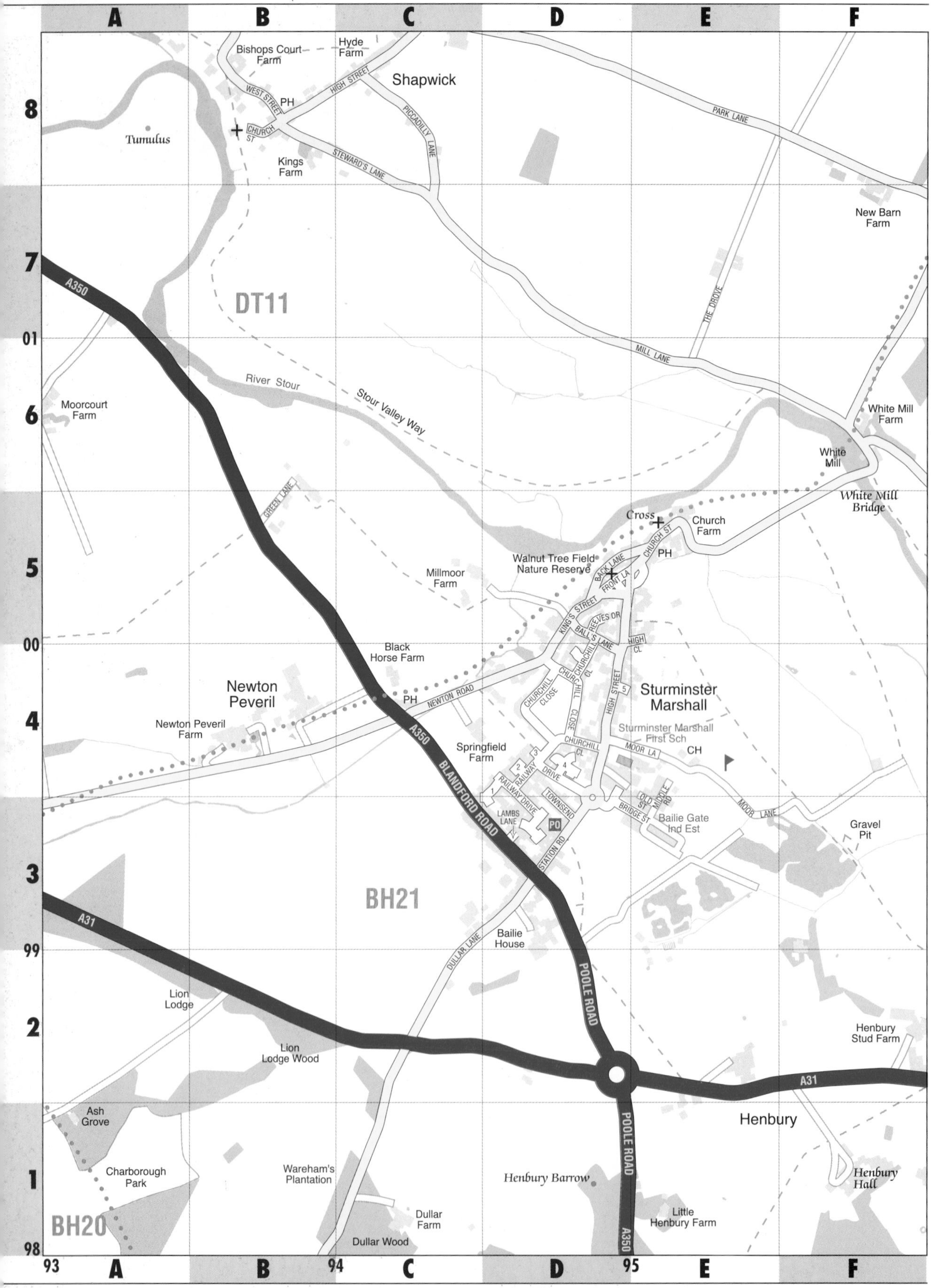

PARK LANE

New Barn Farm

7

A350

DT11

01

River Stour

GREEN LANE

Stour Valley Way

MILL LANE

THE DROVE

White Mill Farm

6

Moorcourt Farm

White Mill

White Mill Bridge

Cross
Church St
Church Farm
PH

5

Millmoor Farm

Walnut Tree Field Nature Reserve
BACK LANE
FRONT LA
CHURCH ST

00

Black Horse Farm

PH
NEWTON ROAD
KING'S STREET
BALL'S LANE
REEVES DR
CHURCH CL
HIGH CL

Newton Peveril

Newton Peveril Farm

A350

Springfield Farm

CHURCHILL CLOSE
CHURCHILL CL
HIGH STREET

Sturminster Marshall
Sturminster Marshall First Sch
MOOR LA
CH
MOOR LANE

4

RAILWAY DRIVE
DRIVE
TOWNSEND
OLD MIDDLE RD
BRIDGE ST
Bailie Gate Ind Est

BLANDFORD ROAD

LAMBS LANE
PO
STATION RD

Gravel Pit

3

BH21

A31

99

DULLAR LANE

Bailie House

POOLE ROAD

Lion Lodge

2

Lion Lodge Wood

Henbury Stud Farm

A31

POOLE ROAD

Henbury

Ash Grove

1

Charborough Park

Wareham's Plantation

Henbury Barrow

Henbury Hall

Dullar Farm

A350

Little Henbury Farm

BH20

Dullar Wood

98

D4
1 CHARBOROUGH WY
2 HAYCOCK WY
3 PARKELEA
4 TATTERSHALL GDNS
5 SHERIDEN WY

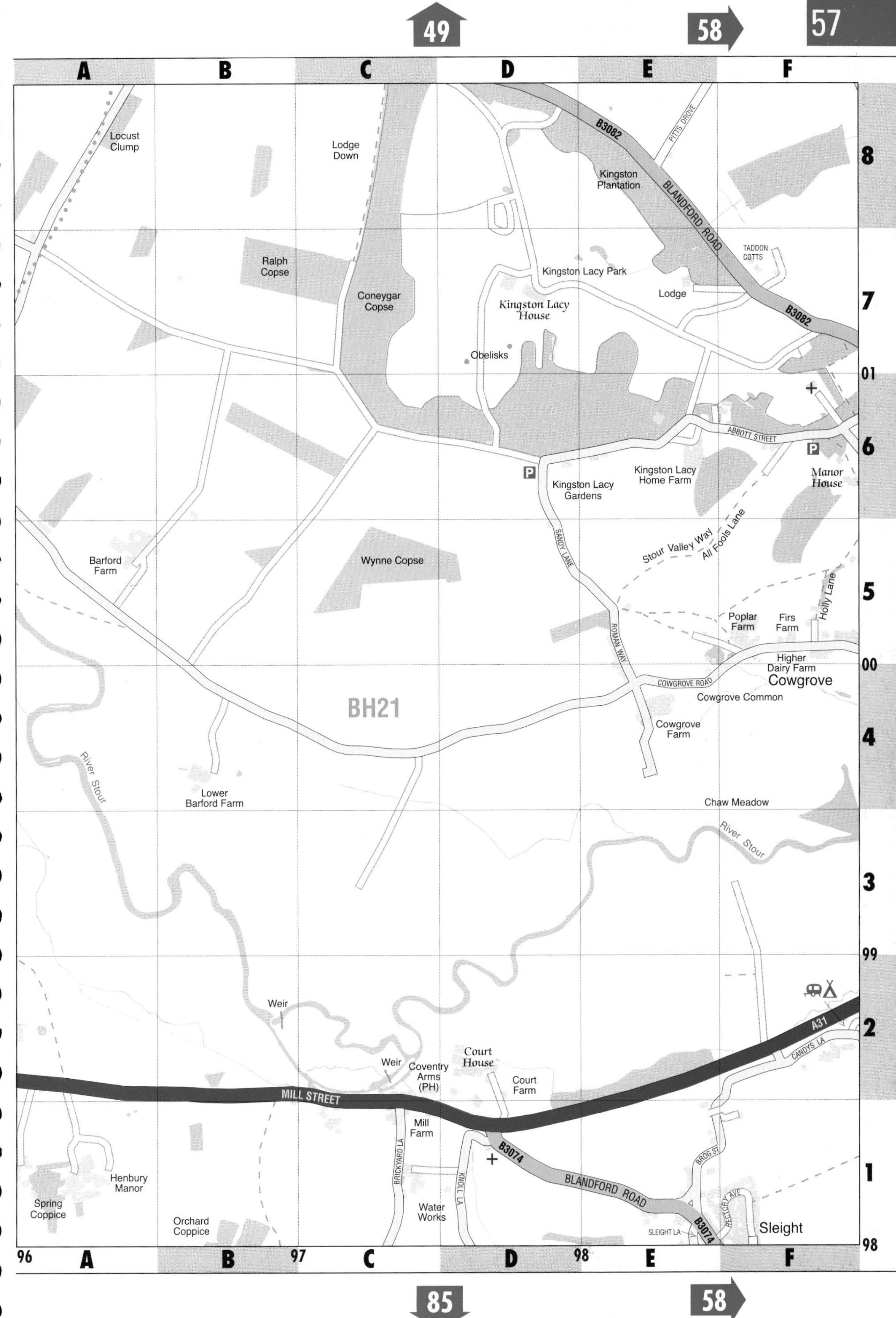
49
58
A
B
C
D
E
F
8
7
01
6
5
00
4
3
99
2
1
98
96
97
98
Locust Clump
Lodge Down
Ralph Copse
Coneygar Copse
Kingston Plantation
B3082
BLANDFORD ROAD
PITTS DROVE
TADDON COTTS
Kingston Lacy Park
Lodge
Kingston Lacy House
Obelisks
ABBOTT STREET
Kingston Lacy Gardens
Kingston Lacy Home Farm
Manor House
SANDY LANE
Stour Valley Way
All Fools Lane
Barford Farm
Wynne Copse
Holly Lane
Poplar Farm
Firs Farm
ROMAN WAY
Higher Dairy Farm
Cowgrove
COWGROVE ROAD
Cowgrove Common
BH21
Cowgrove Farm
River Stour
Lower Barford Farm
Chaw Meadow
Weir
A31
CANDYS LA
Court House
Coventry Arms (PH)
Court Farm
MILL STREET
Mill Farm
BRICKYARD LA
KNOLL LA
B3074
BLANDFORD ROAD
BROG ST
RECTORY AVE
Henbury Manor
Spring Coppice
Orchard Coppice
Water Works
SLEIGHT LA
Sleight
85
58

49 57 50
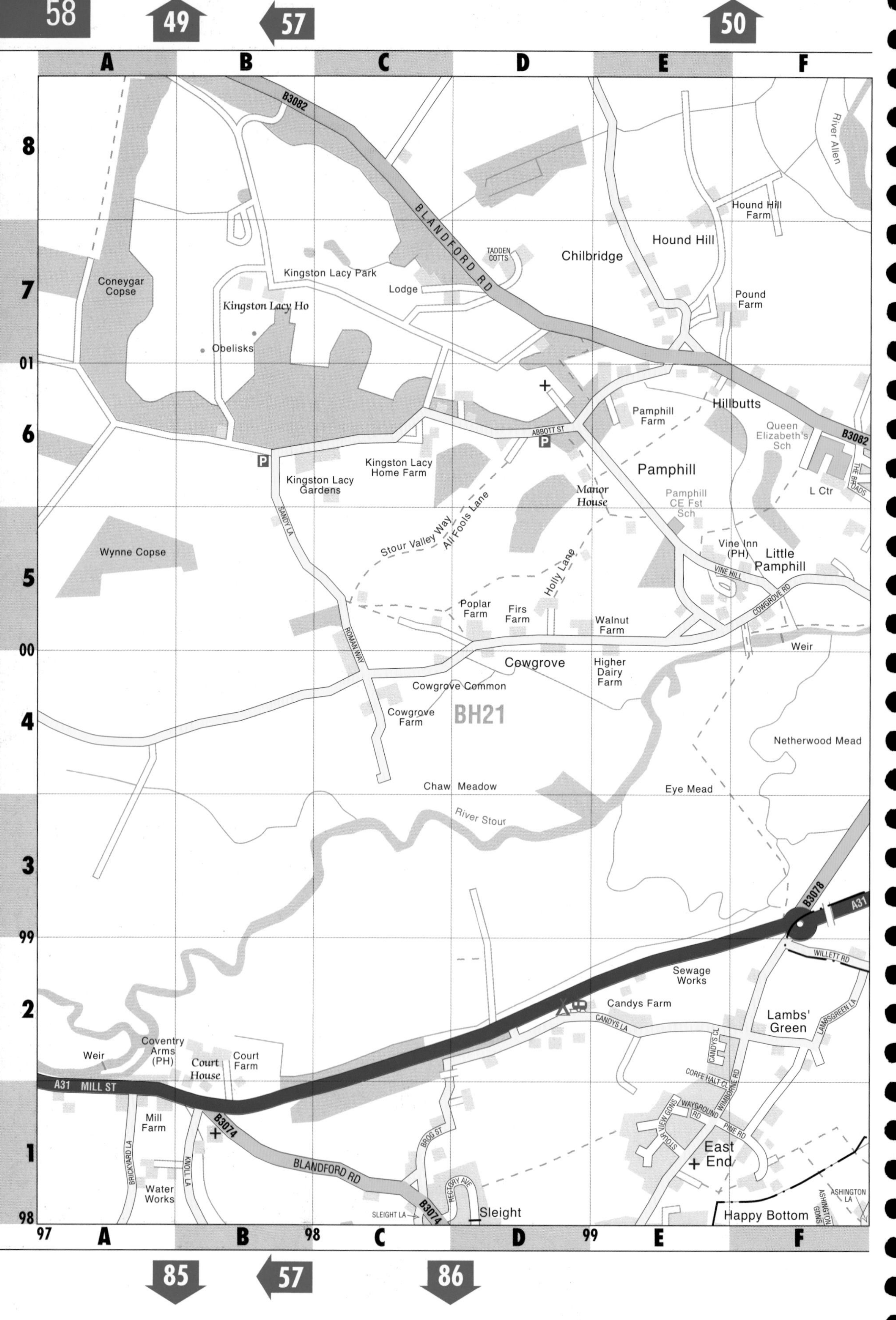

A B C D E F
8 7 01 6 5 00 4 3 99 2 1 98
97 98 99
B3082
BLANDFORD RD
Coneygar Copse
Kingston Lacy Park
Kingston Lacy Ho
Obelisks
Lodge
TADDEN COTTS
Chilbridge
Hound Hill
Hound Hill Farm
Pound Farm
River Allen
Hillbutts
Pamphill Farm
Queen Elizabeth's Sch
ABBOTT ST
Kingston Lacy Home Farm
Kingston Lacy Gardens
Pamphill
Manor House
Pamphill CE Fst Sch
L Ctr
THE BRADS
SANDY LA
Wynne Copse
Stour Valley Way
All Fools Lane
Holly Lane
Vine Inn (PH)
Little Pamphill
VINE HILL
COWGROVE RD
Poplar Farm
Firs Farm
Walnut Farm
ROMAN WAY
Weir
Cowgrove
Higher Dairy Farm
Cowgrove Common
Cowgrove Farm
BH21
Netherwood Mead
Chaw Meadow
Eye Mead
River Stour
B3078
A31
WILLETT RD
Sewage Works
Candys Farm
CANDYS LA
Lambs' Green
LAMBSGREEN LA
CANDYS CL
CORFE HALT CL
WIMBORNE RD
Coventry Arms (PH)
Weir
Court House
Court Farm
A31 MILL ST
Mill Farm
B3074
BLANDFORD RD
BRICKYARD LA
KNOLL LA
Water Works
BROG ST
RECTORY AVE
SLEIGHT LA
Sleight
STOUR VIEW GDNS
WAYGROUND RD
PINE RD
East End
Happy Bottom
ASHINGTON LA
ASHINGTON GDNS

85 57 86

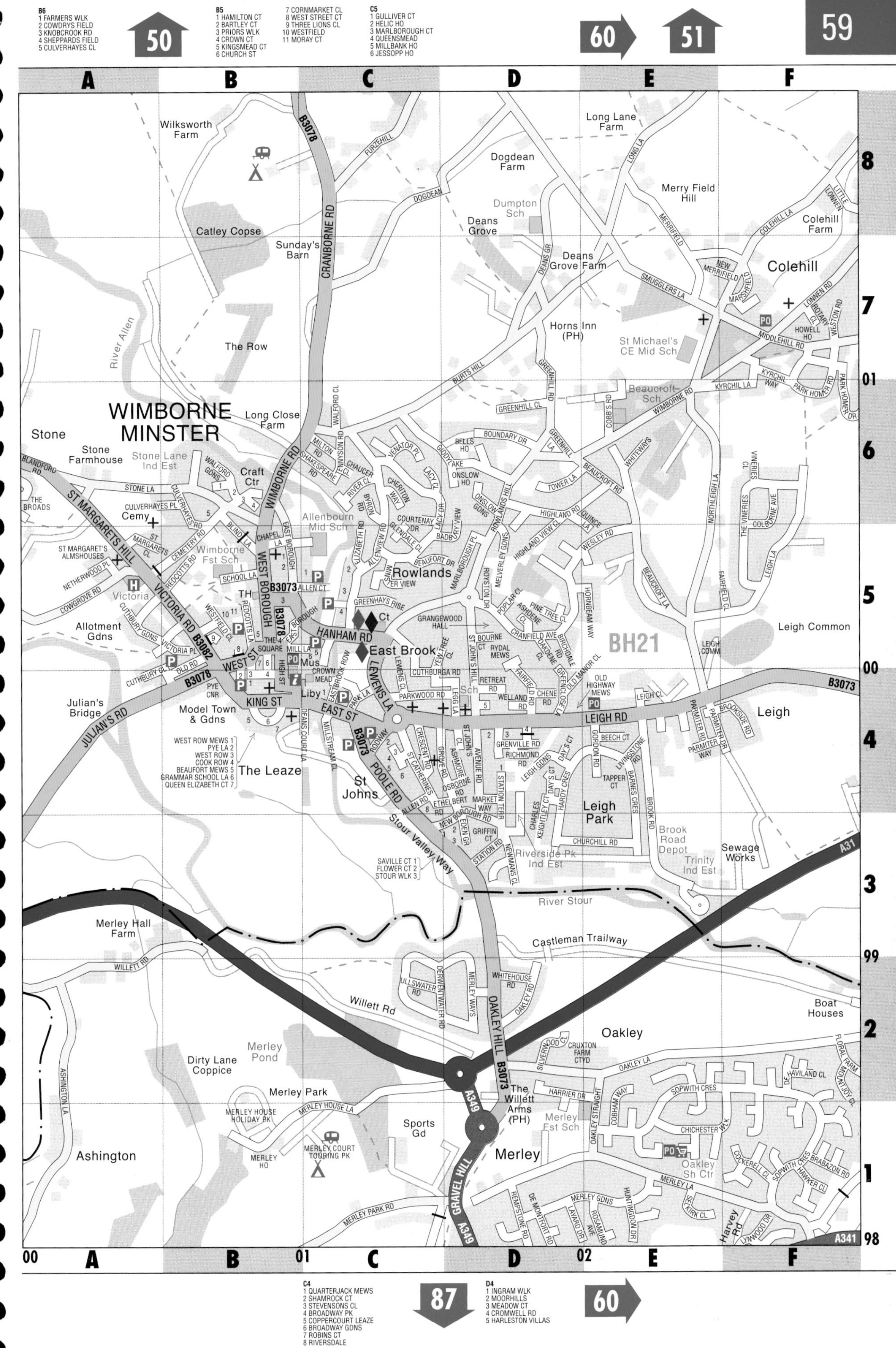

B6
1 FARMERS WLK
2 COWDRYS FIELD
3 KNOBCROOK RD
4 SHEPPARDS FIELD
5 CULVERHAYES CL

B5
1 HAMILTON CT
2 BARTLEY CT
3 PRIORS WLK
4 CROWN CT
5 KINGSMEAD CT
6 CHURCH ST

7 CORNMARKET CL
8 WEST STREET CT
9 THREE LIONS CL
10 WESTFIELD
11 MORAY CT

C5
1 GULLIVER CT
2 HELIC HO
3 MARLBOROUGH CT
4 QUEENSMEAD
5 MILLBANK HO
6 JESSOPP HO

Wilksworth Farm

Catley Copse

Sunday's Barn

B3078

CRANBORNE RD

FURZEHILL

DOGDEAN

Long Lane Farm

Dogdean Farm

Deans Grove

Dumpton Sch

Merry Field Hill

LONG LA

MERRIFIELD

NEW MERRIFIELD

Colehill

COLEHILL LA

Colehill Farm

The Row

River Allen

Stone

WIMBORNE MINSTER

Long Close Farm

WALFORD CL

BURTS HILL

Horns Inn (PH)

GREENHILL RD

St Michael's CE Mid Sch

Beaucroft Sch

WIMBORNE RD

SMUGGLERS LA

COBB'S RD

MARSHFIELD

MIDDLEHILL RD

HOWELL HO

LONNEN RD

NEWBOROUGH WAY

KYRCHIL WAY

PARK HOMER RD

PARK HOMER DR

KYRCHIL LA

8

7

01

6

Stone Farmhouse

Stone Lane Ind Est

Craft Ctr

WALFORD CL

MILTON RD

SHAKESPEARE RD

CHAUCER RD

TENNYSON RD

RIVER CL

ELIZABETH RD

VENATOR PL

CHERITON

BYRON RD

GOODY LAKE

BELLS HO

BOUNDARY DR

GREENHILL CL

GREENHILL

BEAUCROFT RD

WHITEWAYS

NORTHLEIGH LA

THE VINERIES

COLBORNE AVE

BH21

Leigh Common

BLANDFORD RD

THE BROADS

ST MARGARET'S HILL

Cemy

STONE LA

CULVERHAYES PL

CULVERHAYES RD

MARGARETS CL

CEMETERY RD

St Margaret's Almshouses

NETHERWOOD RD

COWGROVE RD

Victoria

VICTORIA RD

REDCOTTS RD

REDCOTTS LA

CUTHBURY GDNS

CUTHBURY CL

VICTORIA PL

B3082

WESTFIELD CL

Allotment Gdns

B3078

OLD RD

WEST ST

KING ST

Julian's Bridge

JULIAN'S RD

Model Town & Gdns

DEANS COURT LA

MILLSTREAM CL

POOLE RD

B3073

St Johns

The Leaze

CUTHBURY

CHAPEL LA

WEST BOROUGH

SCHOOL LA

Wimborne Fst Sch

Allenbourn Mid Sch

B3073

ALLEN CT

TH

THE SQUARE

HANHAM RD

Mus

Liby

CROWN MEAD

EASTBROOK ROW

LEWENS LA

EAST ST

EASTBROOK ROW

Rowlands

Ct

Greenhays Rise

East Brook

CUTHBURGA RD

PARKWOOD RD

GLENDALE CL

COURTENAY DR

BEAUFORT DR

Grangewood Hall

Cranfield Ave

YEW TREE

BOURNE

RYDAL MEWS

JOHN'S HILL

RETREAT

WELLAND RD

CHENE RD

ONSLOW GDNS

HIGHLAND VIEW CL

WESLEY RD

TOWER RD

HIGHLAND RD

QUINCE LA

LEIGH LA

FAIRFIELD RD

BEAUCROFT LA

LEIGH RD

Leigh

B3073

LEIGH COMM

5

00

4

WEST ROW MEWS 1
PYE LA 2
WEST ROW 3
COOK ROW 4
BEAUFORT MEWS 5
GRAMMAR SCHOOL LA 6
QUEEN ELIZABETH CT 7

PYE CNR

SAVILLE CT 1
FLOWER CT 2
STOUR WLK 3

Stour Valley Way

Riverside Pk Ind Est

GRENVILLE RD

RICHMOND RD

AVENUE RD

STATION RD

MARKET WAY

NEW BOROUGH RD

GRIFFIN RD

ST CATHERINES

ST JOHN'S RD

OSBORNE RD

ETHELBERT RD

CHARLES ST

KEIGHTLEY CRES

HARDY CRES

DAL'S CT

BARNES CRES

LEIGH GDNS

BEECH CT

GORDON RD

TAPPER CT

Leigh Park

CHURCHILL RD

Brook Road Depot

Trinity Ind Est

Sewage Works

LIVINGSTONE RD

PARMITER DR

PARMITER WAY

BROOK RD

BROOKSIDE RD

A31

3

99

2

Merley Hall Farm

ASHINGTON LA

WILLETT RD

Willett Rd

Dirty Lane Coppice

Merley Pond

Merley Park

MERLEY HOUSE LA

Merley House Holiday Pk

Merley Ho

MERLEY COURT TOURING PK

Ashington

Merley Park Rd

Sports Gd

GRAVEL HILL

A349

B3073

OAKLEY HILL

ULLSWATER RD

DERWENTWATER RD

MERLEY WAYS

WHITEHOUSE RD

OAKLEY RD

Castleman Trailway

River Stour

Boat Houses

Oakley

Cruxton Farm Ctyd

SILVERWOOD

The Willett Arms (PH)

Merley Fst Sch

HARRIER DR

Merley

MERLEY GDNS

DE MONTFORT RD

HEMPSTONE RD

HUNTINGDON DR

ROSAMUND AVE

MERLEY PARK RD

OAKLEY STRAIGHT

COBHAM WAY

SOPWITH CRES

CHICHESTER WAY

Oakley Sh Ctr

OAKLEY SH LA

COCKERELL CL

SOPWITH CL

HAWKER CL

BRABAZON RD

AVILAND CL

FLORAL FARM

MOUNTJOY DR

HARVEY RD

A341

1

98

C4
1 QUARTERJACK MEWS
2 SHAMROCK CT
3 STEVENSONS CL
4 BROADWAY PK
5 COPPERCOURT LEAZE
6 BROADWAY GDNS
7 ROBINS CT
8 RIVERSDALE

D4
1 INGRAM WLK
2 MOORHILLS
3 MEADOW CT
4 CROMWELL RD
5 HARLESTON VILLAS

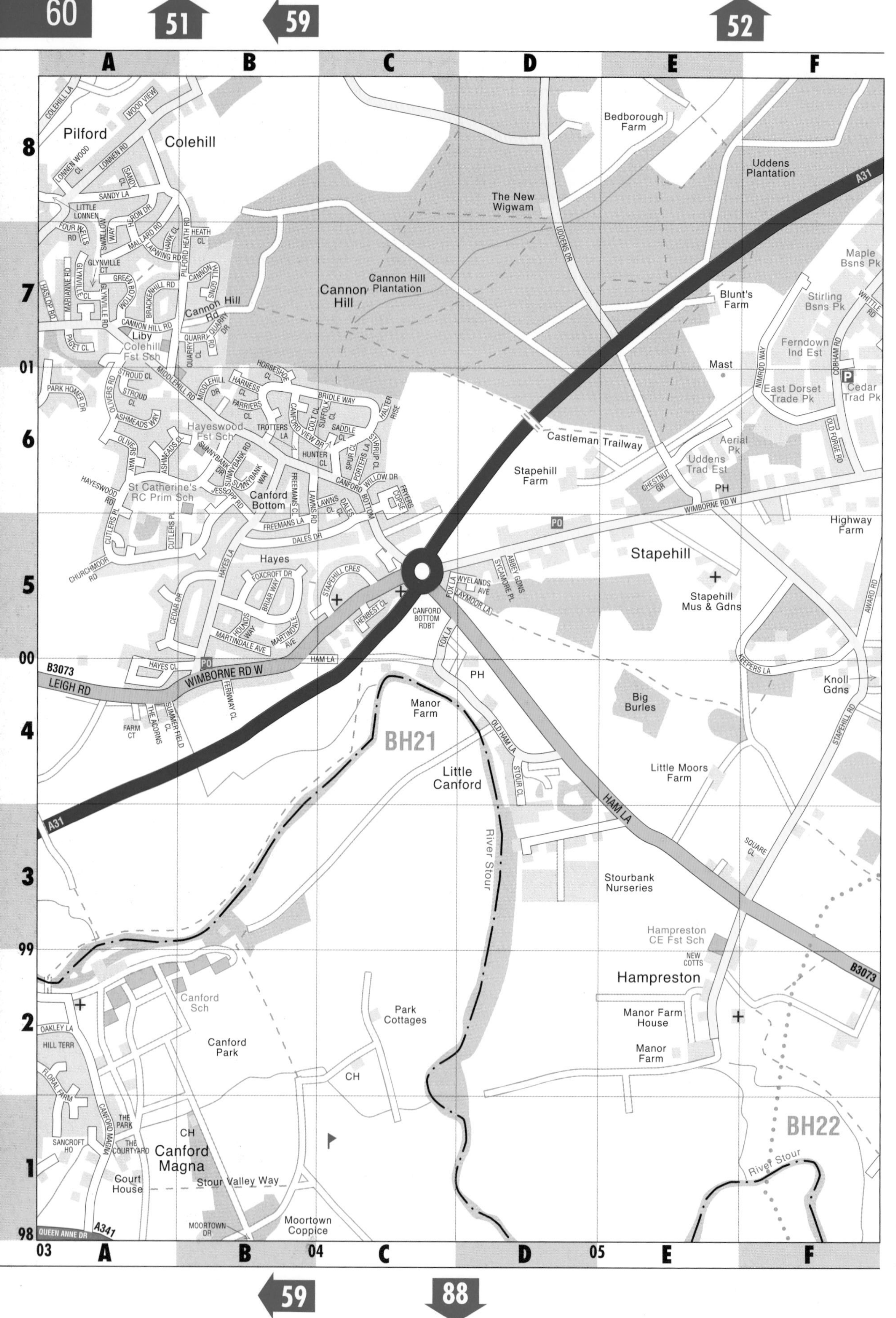
51
59
52
Pilford
Colehill
Bedborough Farm
Uddens Plantation
The New Wigwam
Cannon Hill
Cannon Hill Plantation
Blunt's Farm
Maple Bsns Pk
Stirling Bsns Pk
Ferndown Ind Est
Mast
East Dorset Trade Pk
Cedar Trad Pk
Liby
Colehill Fst Sch
Hayeswood Fst Sch
St Catherine's RC Prim Sch
Canford Bottom
Castleman Trailway
Stapehill Farm
Aerial Pk
Uddens Trad Est
PH
Highway Farm
Hayes
Stapehill
Stapehill Mus & Gdns
Canford Bottom Rdbt
Manor Farm
BH21
Little Canford
Big Burles
Knoll Gdns
Little Moors Farm
River Stour
Stourbank Nurseries
Hampreston CE Fst Sch
Hampreston
Manor Farm House
Manor Farm
Canford Sch
Canford Park
Park Cottages
CH
Canford Magna
Court House
Stour Valley Way
Moortown Coppice
BH22
A31
B3073
A341
Leigh Rd
Wimborne Rd W
Ham La
59
88

52
62
53

Uddens Plantation
Fernside Bsns Pk
Ferndown Ind Est
Ferndown Upper Sch
Sports Ctr
Playing Field
Ferndown
Ferndown Mid Sch
Ferndown Fst Sch
BH22
BH21
Great Barrow
The Roughs
Big Copse
Beacon Farm
Longham Bsns Ctr
Holmwood House
Holmwood Park
Dudsbury Hill
Longham
Dudsbury
West Parley
Parley Fst Sch
Trickett's Cross
Parley Common
Ralph's Barrow
Parley Wood
Uddens Water
Cemy
Superstore
WIMBORNE RD E
VICTORIA RD
WEST MOORS RD
RINGWOOD RD
NEW RD
CHRISTCHURCH RD
HAM LA
A31
A347
A348
B3072
B3073

89
62

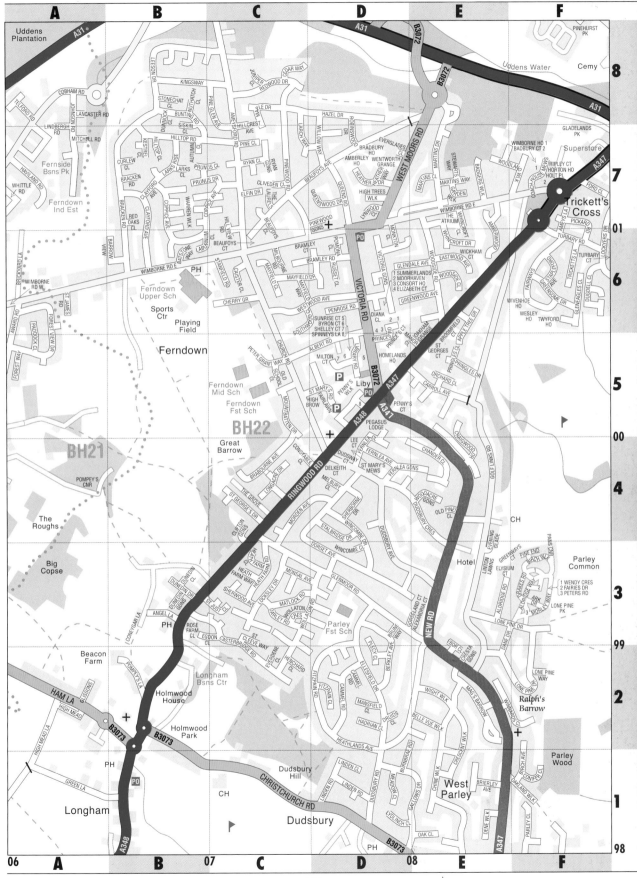

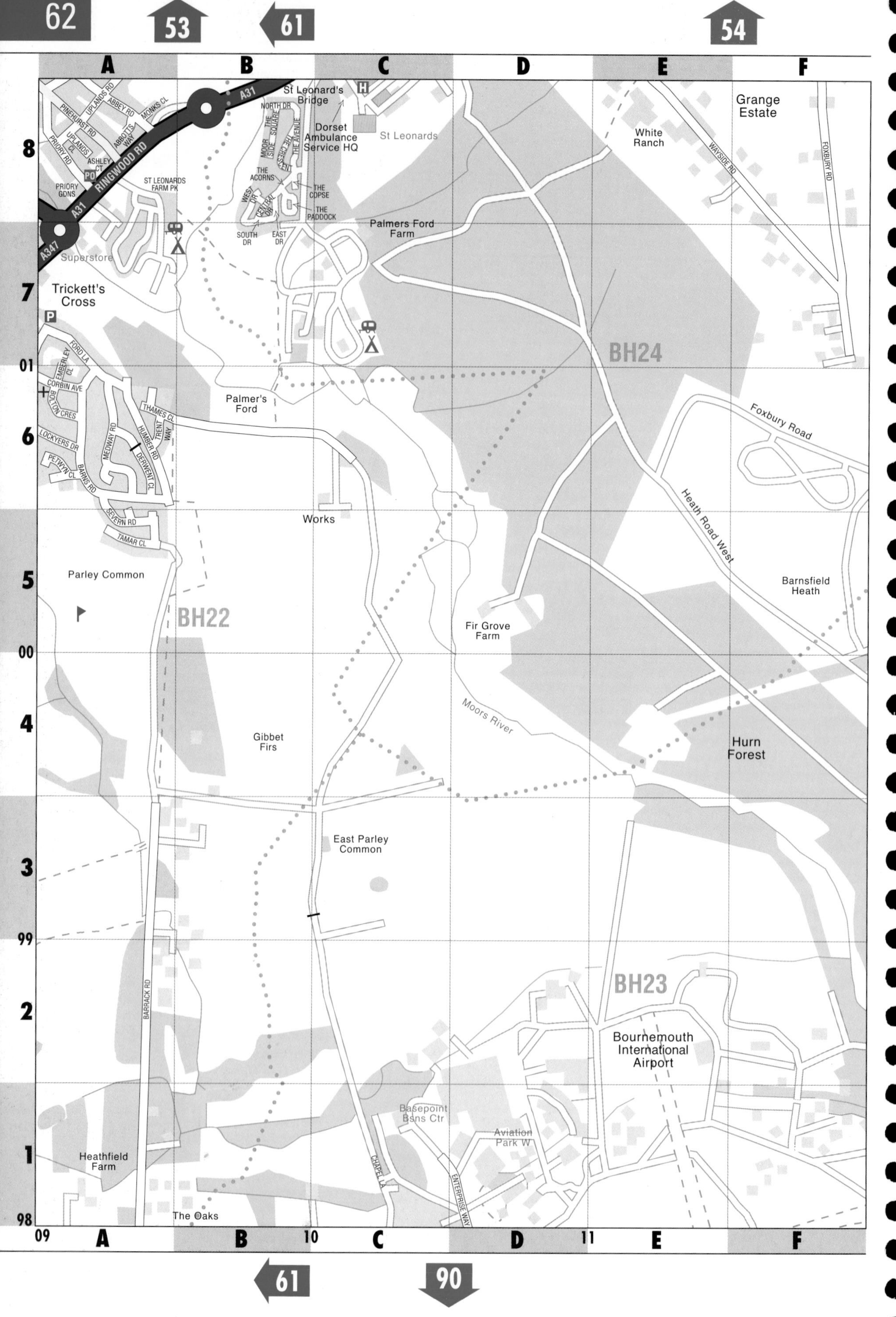

A31
Ringwood Rd
A31
A347
Superstore
Trickett's Cross
P

St Leonard's Bridge
H
St Leonards
Dorset Ambulance Service HQ
Palmers Ford Farm

BH24

White Ranch
Grange Estate
Watside Rd
Foxbury Rd

Uplands Rd
Abbey Rd
Monks Cl
Pinehurst Rd
Abbotts Way
Uplands Cl
Priory Rd
Ashley Ct
PO
Priory Gdns
St Leonards Farm Pk
North Dr
The Avenue
Moorside Cres
The Square
The Acorns
West Dr
Central Dr
The Copse
The Paddock
South Dr
East Dr

Palmer's Ford
Emberley Cl
Ford La
Corbin Ave
Colton Cres
Lockyers Dr
Medway Rd
Thames Cl
Humber Rd
Penny's Way
Derwent Cl
Pelwyn Cl
Barns Rd
Severn Rd
Tamar Cl

Works

Parley Common
BH22

Fir Grove Farm
Foxbury Road

Heath Road West
Barnsfield Heath

Gibbet Firs
Moors River
Hurn Forest

East Parley Common

Barrack Rd

BH23

Bournemouth International Airport

Basepoint Bsns Ctr
Aviation Park W
Chapel La
Enterprise Way

Heathfield Farm
The Oaks

8
01
7
6
5
00
4
3
99
2
1
98

A B C D E F

Avon Heath
Ctry Pk
(South Park)

HURN RD

A338

Kingston

B3347

DRAGON LA

8

Matchams
Farm

MATCHAMS DL

Wattons Ford
Common

Wattons Ford

Dean's
Farm

Matcham's
House

Alder Bed
Copse

Avon Valley Path

7

BH24

Parsonage
Wood

01

Matcham's
Park

Stadium

River Avon

The
Warren

6

Ppg
Sta

Lower Side
Copse

Bisterne

B3347

Hill Road

Week
Wood

South Hampshire STREET ATLAS

5

Foxbury Hill

North End
Copse

Watermain Road

Week
Farm

North End
Farm

00

Plantation Road

Bostwick
Farm

Week
Common

Watermeadows

B3347

4

MATCHAMS LA

Heath Road East

Ski Ctr

BH23

Tyrrell's
Ford
(Hotel)

Watermeadows

Sabines
Farm

3

Fillybrook
Bottom

AVON FARM
COTTS

Avon Tyrrell
Farm

P

London
Farm

99

LONDON LA

Furzy
Copse

New Queen
Inn
(PH)

COUNCIL
HOS

Avon

2

Fillybrook

Coronation
Cottages

Avon
Common

Pithouse
Farm

Watermeadows

A338

Valley
Farm

B3347

1

98

A B C D E F

12 13 14

202

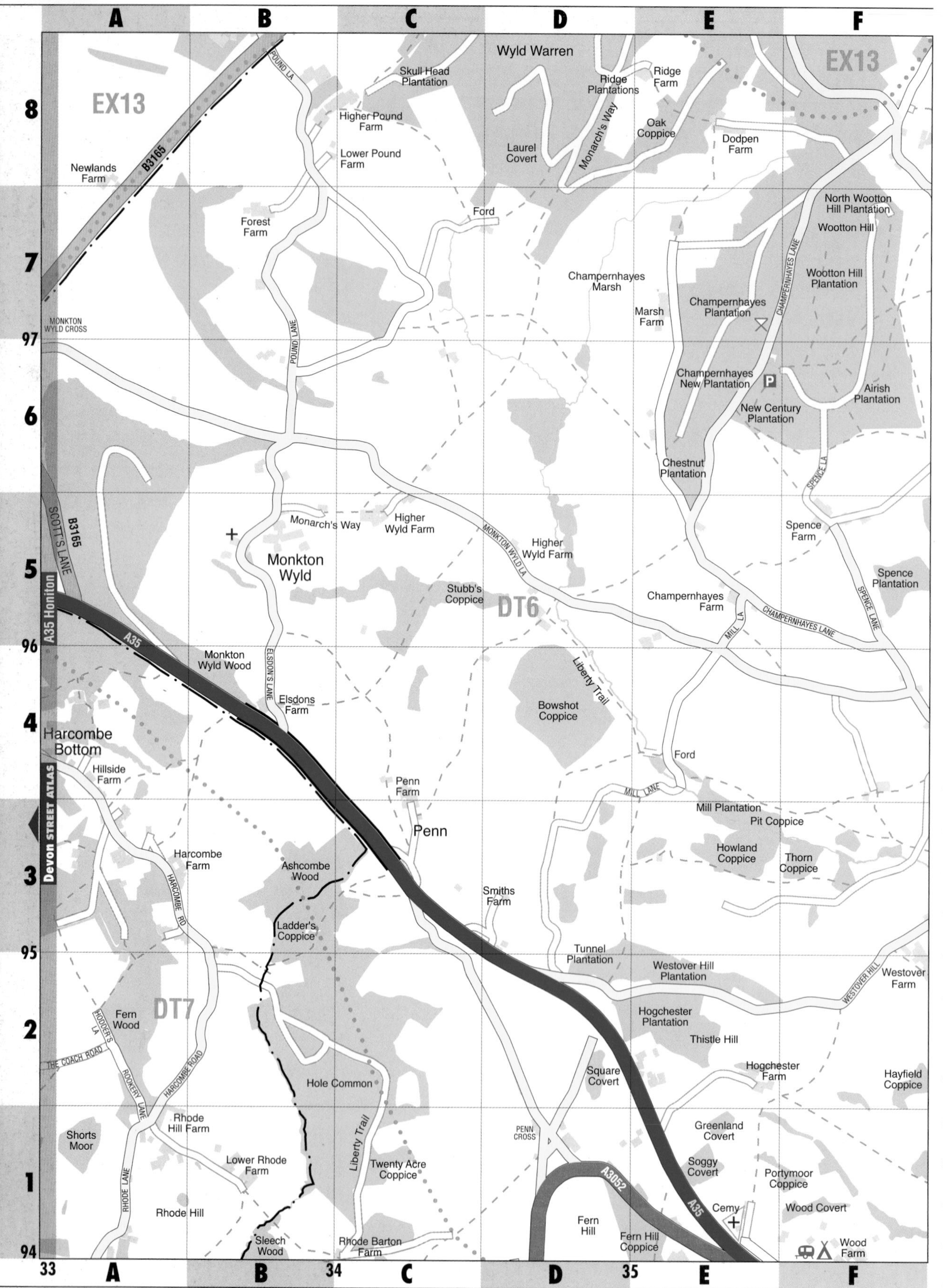

A B C D E F
8 7 6 5 4 3 2 1
97 96 95 94
33 34 35
EX13
Wyld Warren
Skull Head Plantation
Ridge Plantations
Ridge Farm
Higher Pound Farm
Lower Pound Farm
Newlands Farm
Laurel Covert
Monarch's Way
Oak Coppice
Dodpen Farm
Forest Farm
Ford
North Wootton Hill Plantation
Wootton Hill
Wootton Hill Plantation
Champernhayes Marsh
Marsh Farm
Champernhayes Plantation
MONKTON WYLD CROSS
Champernhayes New Plantation
New Century Plantation
Airish Plantation
Chestnut Plantation
Monarch's Way
Higher Wyld Farm
Spence Farm
Monkton Wyld
Higher Wyld Farm
Stubb's Coppice
DT6
Champernhayes Farm
Spence Plantation
Monkton Wyld Wood
Liberty Trail
Elsdons Farm
Bowshot Coppice
Harcombe Bottom
Ford
Hillside Farm
Penn Farm
Mill Plantation
Pit Coppice
Penn
Harcombe Farm
Ashcombe Wood
Howland Coppice
Thorn Coppice
Smiths Farm
Ladder's Coppice
Tunnel Plantation
Westover Hill Plantation
Westover Farm
Fern Wood
DT7
Hogchester Plantation
Thistle Hill
Square Covert
Hogchester Farm
Hayfield Coppice
Hole Common
Rhode Hill Farm
Shorts Moor
Greenland Covert
Liberty Trail
PENN CROSS
Lower Rhode Farm
Twenty Acre Coppice
Soggy Covert
Portymoor Coppice
Rhode Hill
Cemy
Wood Covert
Fern Hill
Fern Hill Coppice
Sleech Wood
Rhode Barton Farm
Wood Farm
B3165
SCOTT'S LANE
POUND LA
POUND LANE
ELSDON'S LANE
MONKTON WYLD LA
CHAMPERNHAYES LANE
MILL LA
MILL LANE
SPENCE LA
SPENCE LANE
HARCOMBE RD
HARCOMBE ROAD
HODDER'S LA
THE COACH ROAD
ROOKERY LANE
RHODE LANE
WESTOVER HILL
A35
A3052
A35 Honiton
Devon STREET ATLAS

96

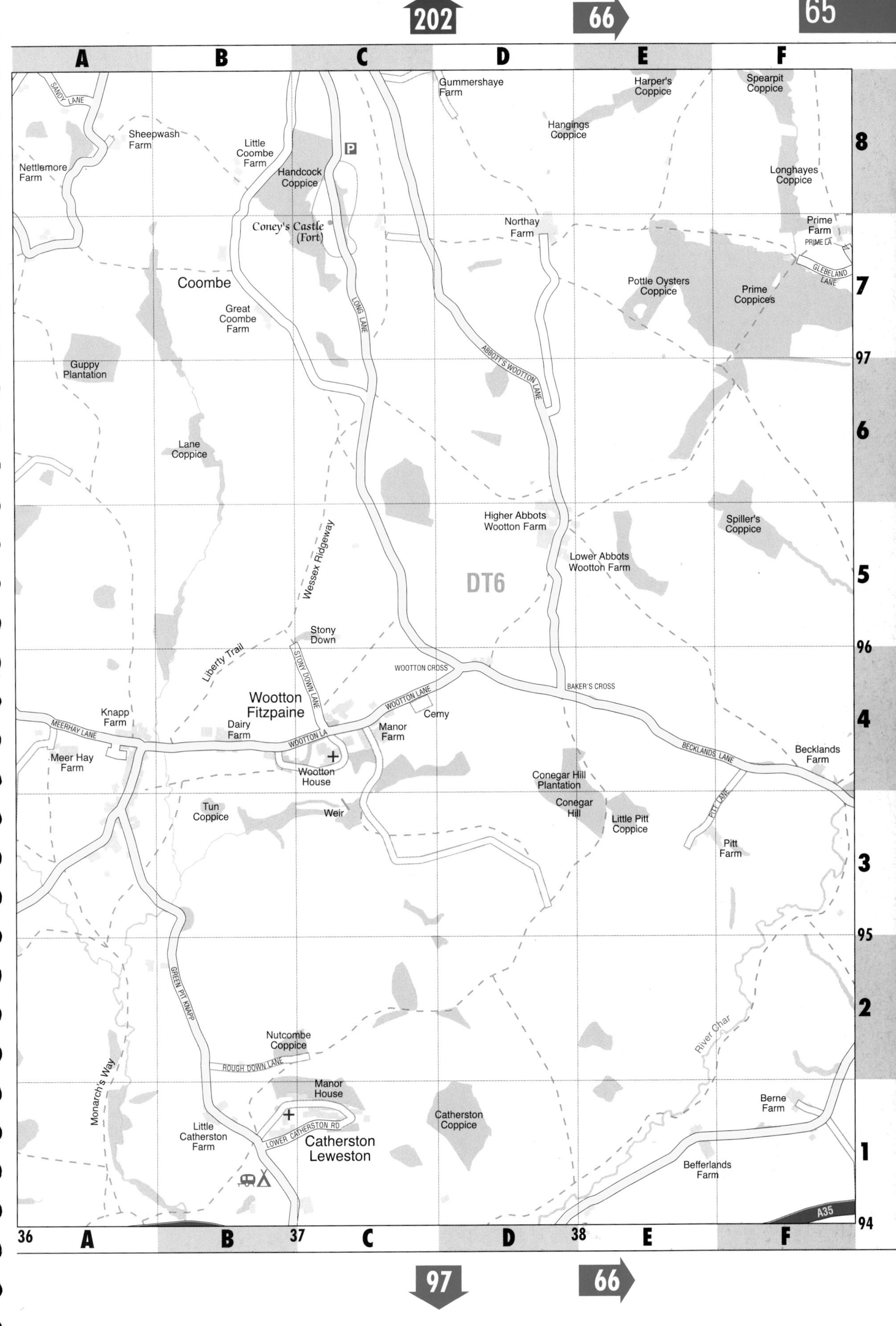
A
B
C
D
E
F
Sandy Lane
Gummershaye Farm
Harper's Coppice
Spearpit Coppice
Sheepwash Farm
Little Coombe Farm
Hangings Coppice
8
Nettlemore Farm
Handcock Coppice
Longhayes Coppice
Coney's Castle (Fort)
Northay Farm
Prime Farm
Prime La
Glebeland Lane
Coombe
Pottle Oysters Coppice
Prime Coppices
7
Great Coombe Farm
Long Lane
Abbott's Wootton Lane
Guppy Plantation
97
Lane Coppice
6
Higher Abbots Wootton Farm
Spiller's Coppice
Wessex Ridgeway
Lower Abbots Wootton Farm
DT6
5
Stony Down
Liberty Trail
Stony Down Lane
96
Wootton Cross
Baker's Cross
Wootton Lane
Knapp Farm
Wootton Fitzpaine
Cemy
4
Meerhay Lane
Dairy Farm
Wootton La
Manor Farm
Becklands Lane
Becklands Farm
Meer Hay Farm
Wootton House
Conegar Hill Plantation
Tun Coppice
Weir
Conegar Hill
Little Pitt Coppice
Pitt Lane
Pitt Farm
3
95
Green Pit Knapp
2
Nutcombe Coppice
River Char
Rough Down Lane
Monarch's Way
Manor House
Berne Farm
Catherston Coppice
Lower Catherston Rd
Little Catherston Farm
Catherston Leweston
1
Befferlands Farm
A35
94
36
A
B
37
C
D
38
E
F

65
203

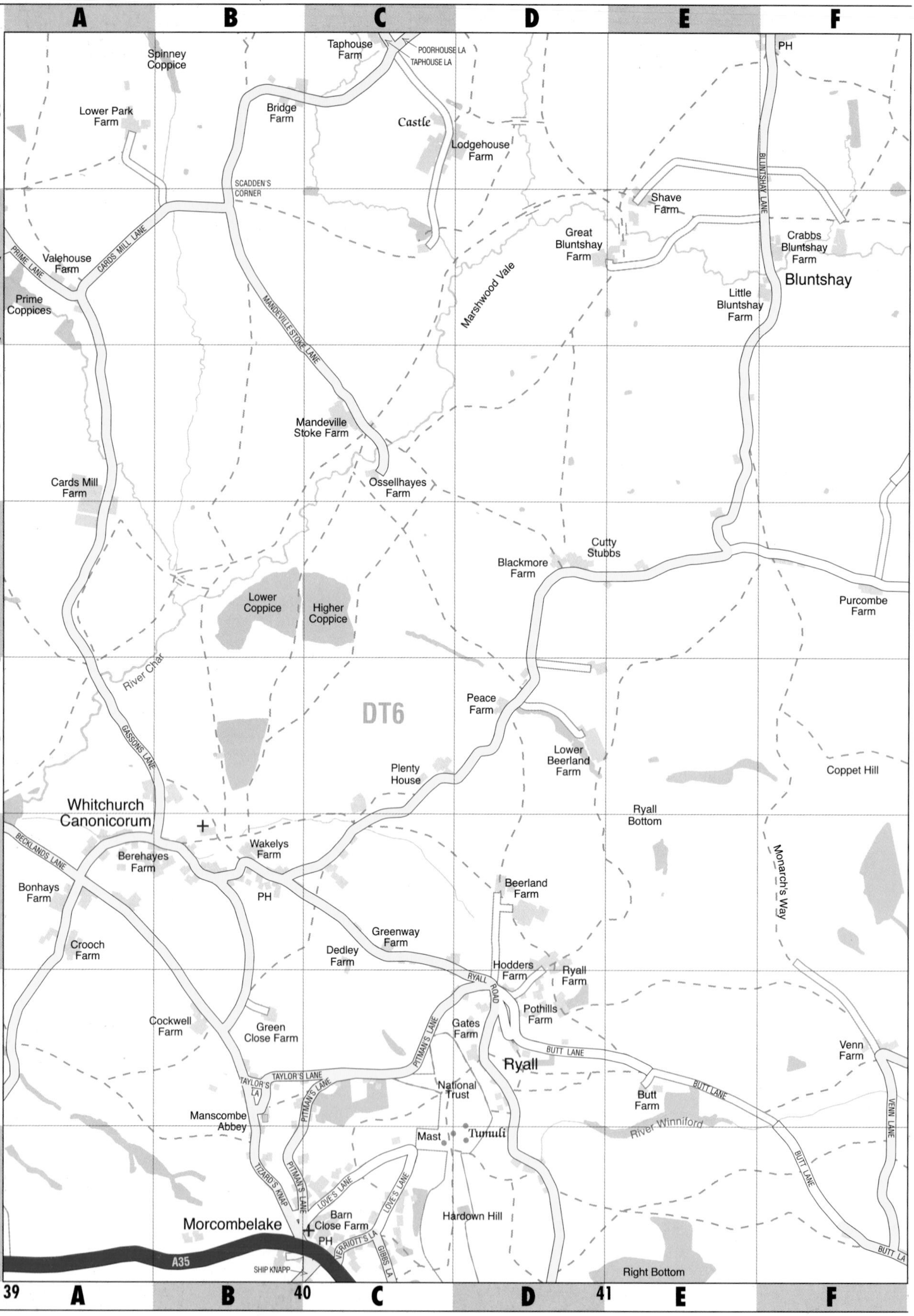

A B C D E F

8

7

97

6

5

96

4

3

95

2

1

94

Spinney
Coppice

Taphouse
Farm

POORHOUSE LA
TAPHOUSE LA

PH

Lower Park
Farm

Bridge
Farm

Castle

Lodgehouse
Farm

Shave
Farm

BLUNTSHAY LANE

Great
Bluntshay
Farm

Crabbs
Bluntshay
Farm

SCADDEN'S
CORNER

Valehouse
Farm

CARDS MILL LANE

PRIME LANE

Prime
Coppices

MANDEVILLE STOKE LANE

Marshwood Vale

Little
Bluntshay
Farm

Bluntshay

Cards Mill
Farm

Mandeville
Stoke Farm

Ossellhayes
Farm

Cutty
Stubbs

Blackmore
Farm

Purcombe
Farm

Lower
Coppice

Higher
Coppice

River Char

DT6

Peace
Farm

Plenty
House

Lower
Beerland
Farm

Coppet Hill

Ryall
Bottom

GASSONS LANE

Whitchurch
Canonicorum

Wakelys
Farm

Monarch's Way

Berehayes
Farm

PH

Beerland
Farm

BECKLANDS LANE

Bonhays
Farm

Greenway
Farm

Crooch
Farm

Dedley
Farm

RYALL ROAD

Hodders
Farm

Ryall
Farm

Venn
Farm

Cockwell
Farm

Green
Close Farm

PITMAN'S LANE

Gates
Farm

Pothills
Farm

BUTT LANE

Ryall

VENN LANE

TAYLOR'S LANE

TAYLOR'S
LA

National
Trust

Butt
Farm

BUTT LANE

Manscombe
Abbey

TIZARD'S KNAP

PITMAN'S LANE

LOVE'S LANE

Mast

Tumuli

River Winniford

BUTT LANE

Morcombelake

Barn
Close Farm

LOVE'S LANE

BIBBS LA

Hardown Hill

A35

SHIP KNAPP

PH

HERRIOTT'S LA

Right Bottom

39 A B 40 C D 41 E F

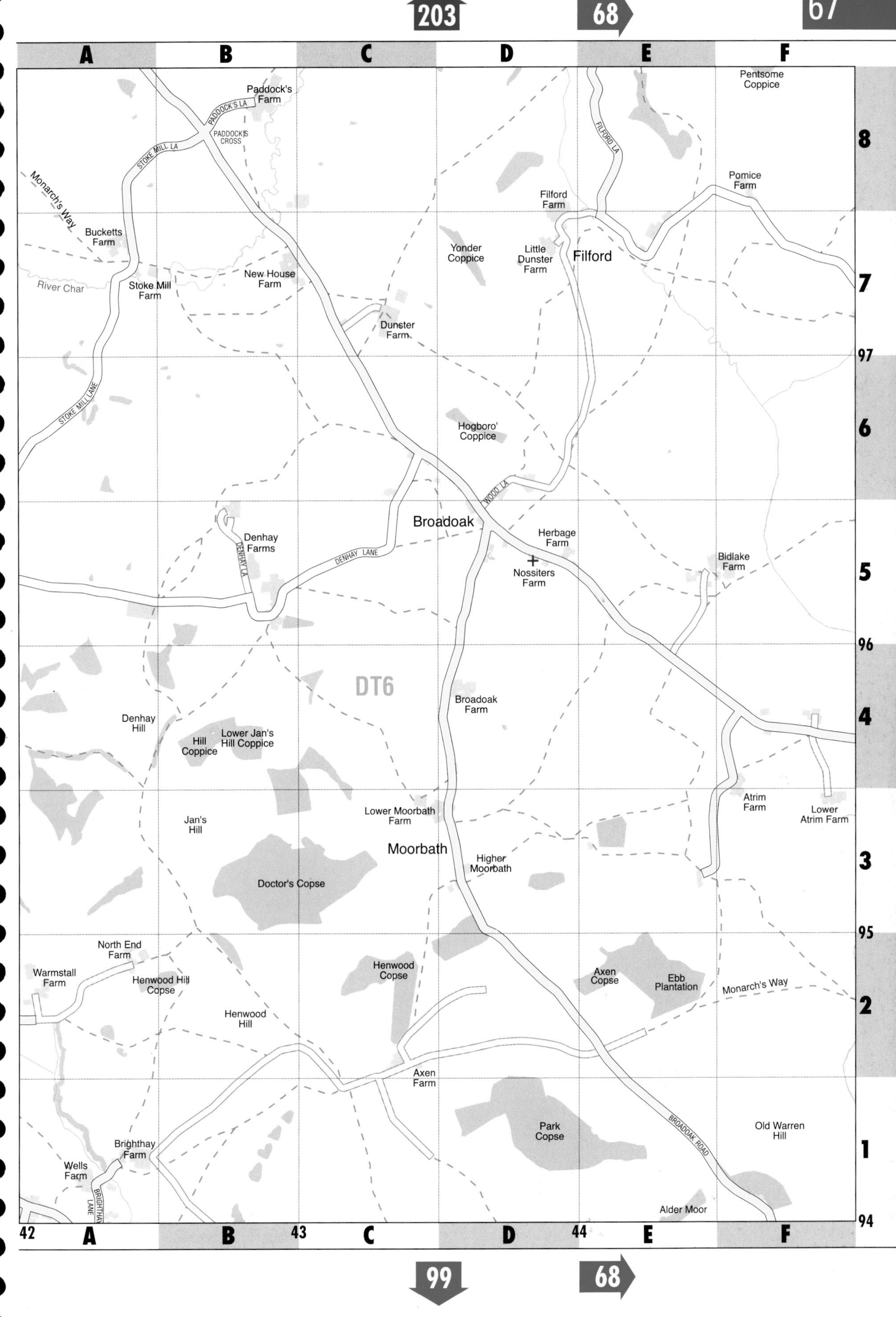

A   B   C   D   E   F

8

Pentsome Coppice

FILFORD LA

Monarch's Way

Bucketts Farm

River Char

Paddock's Farm

PADDOCK'S LA

STOKE MILL LA

PADDOCK'S CROSS

New House Farm

Stoke Mill Farm

STOKE MILL LANE

Dunster Farm

Yonder Coppice

Filford Farm

Little Dunster Farm

Filford

Pomice Farm

7

97

Hogboro' Coppice

WOOD LA

6

Broadoak

Herbage Farm

Denhay Farms

DENHAY LA

DENHAY LANE

+ Nossiters Farm

Bidlake Farm

5

96

DT6

Denhay Hill

Hill Coppice

Lower Jan's Hill Coppice

Broadoak Farm

4

Jan's Hill

Lower Moorbath Farm

Atrim Farm

Lower Atrim Farm

Doctor's Copse

Moorbath

Higher Moorbath

3

95

North End Farm

Warmstall Farm

Henwood Hill Copse

Henwood Copse

Axen Copse

Ebb Plantation

Monarch's Way

2

Henwood Hill

Axen Farm

Park Copse

BROADOAK ROAD

Old Warren Hill

1

Brighthay Farm

Wells Farm

BRIGHTHAY LANE

Alder Moor

94

A B C D E F

8

Higher
Kingsland Farm
Kershay
Farms
Nurserymead
Coppice
Shatcombe
Coppice
Kingsland
B3162
Long Bottom
Coppice
Salway Ash CE
Prim Sch
WHITHAY LA
Higher Kershay
Farm
Lower
Kershay Farm
Perhay
Farm
SLAPE HILL
Myrtle
Farm
Waytown
White House
Farm
Way Farm
Oxbridge
Oxbridge
Farm

7

STRONGATE
LA
STRONGATE LA
Strongate
Farm
Church
Grounds
WHITHAY LANE
Brinsham
Farm
Ash
Farm
FIR TREE
CL
Marlis
Farm
PINEAPPLE LANE
Elwell
Lodge
Camesworth

97

Hill
Farm
PH
SALWAY DR
FITCHERS
Salwayash
Pineapple
Farm
Higher Ford
Farm
Pineapple
Business Park
Elwell
Farms
Higher
Elwell
Farm
Snailscroft
Farm
River Brit
Foxmoor
Coppice

6

B3162
Broadenham
Farm
Ash Lane
Farm
Ash
ASH LANE
Seaview
Farm
Lambrook
Lambrook
Farm
Bingham's
Farm

5

96

Limbury
Ashleigh
Farm
Sewage
Works
Higher
Ash Farm
DT6
Higher
Wooth Farm

4

Atrim
Colly Farm
Dottery
Lower Ash
Farm
PYMORE LANE
Wooth
Farm
Wooth Old
Farm
Wooth

3

95

Bilshay
Farm
BILSHAY LANE
Higher
Pymore Farm
WATFORD LANE
Watford
Farm

2

Monarch's Way
New Close
Farm
DOTTERY ROAD
Middle
Pymore
Farm
Washingpool
Farm
Lower
Pymore
Farm
THREAD MILL
LA
Factory
PYMORE ROAD
PH
Pymore
Gore Cross
Business Park
GORE
CROSS
A3066
BEAMINSTER RD
GORE LANE
BLIND LANE CL
TOWNSEND WY
HEALEYS CL
CORBIN WAY
RIDGEWAY
BEAMINSTER ROAD
HILLVIEW
The Sir John
Colfox Sch
QUEENWELL
DODHAMS
FARM CL
BANTON
SHARD
COURT CL
PAGEANTS CL
DREW
VILLAGE RD
GORE CROSS WY

1

River Simene
B3162
Seymour
Farm
River Brit
GIPSY LANE
ST ANDREW'S
ROAD
KNIGHTSTONE RI
FISHWEIR
TRINITY WY
TRINITY
LA

94

45 A 46 B C 47 D E F

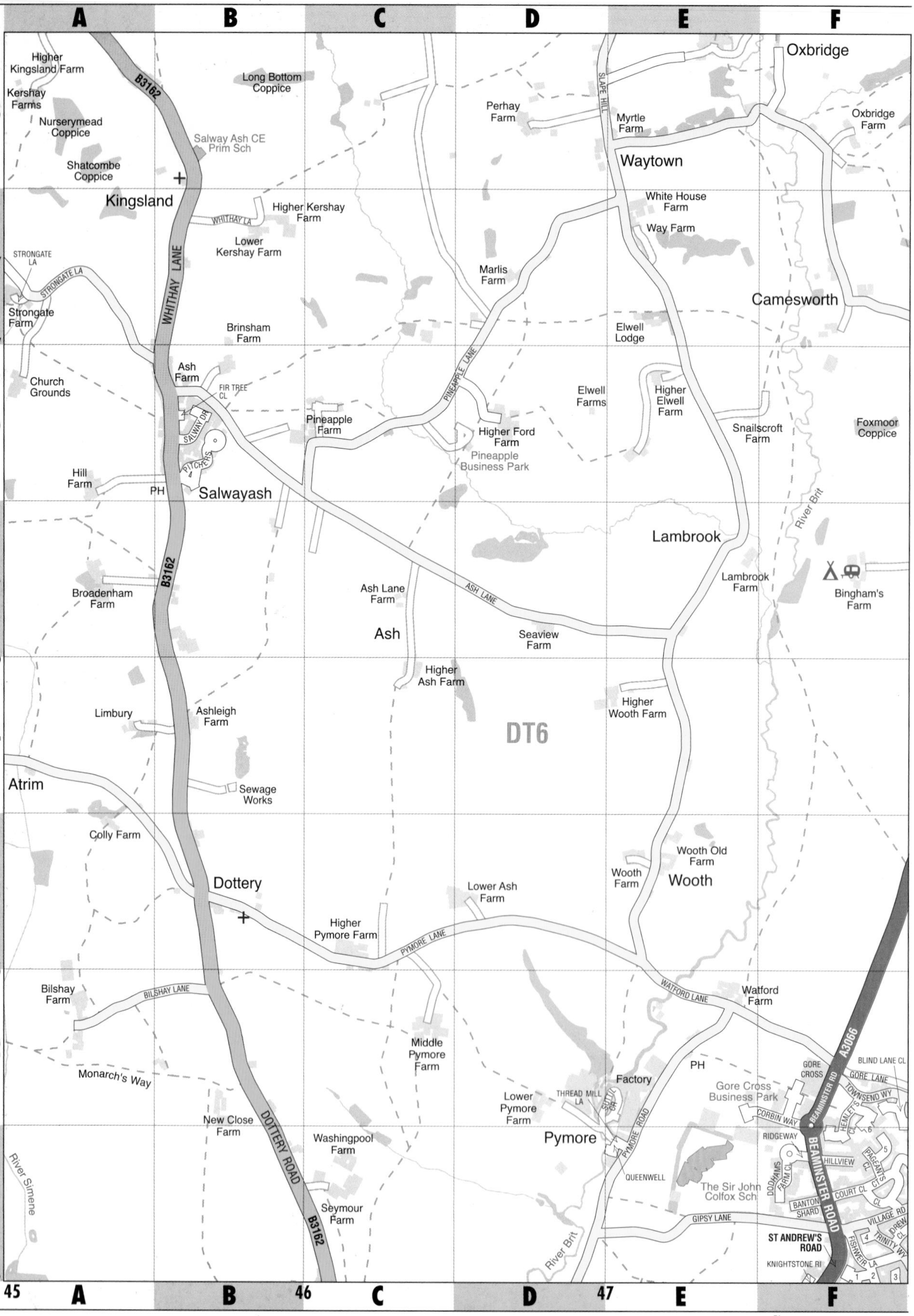

F1
1 FISHWEIR FIELDS
2 ACER AV
3 WHITE CL
4 SPRING CL
5 GORE CROSS WY
6 BATH ORCHARD

204

70

A
B
C
D
E
F
Little Fern Coppice
BUCKHORN CL
TWINWAYS LANE
A3066
MAPPERTON LANE
Charity Farm
Merryhill Farm
Loscombe
Sunnyside Farm
Bull's Hill Coppice
Great Fern Coppice
PH
Hincknowle Fruit Farm
Bull's Hill
Long Mead Coppice
RIDGEBACK LANE
Hincknowle
Hincknowle Coppice
Walnut Farm
Hincknowle Hill
Beningfield Wood Nature Reserve
CAMESWORTH LANE
The Mount
Lower Mount Farm
Mount Meadow Farm
Tumulus
Marlpitts Farm
Mount Coppice
Elcombe Farm
New Barn Farm
Knight's Hill
Mangerton Hill
RUSCOMBE LANE
West Milton
Court House Farm
Lawrence Farm
Church Farm
Gravel Hill
Church
LARCOMBE LANE
Lynch Farm
Pitcher's Hill
Highgrove Farm
Earnscombe Copse
DT6
Round Knoll
Mangerton
Mangerton Water Mill
Lower Mangerton Farm
Corfe Farm
Way's Hill
Welcome Hill
Broad Road Farm
Mangerton River
Presswood Copse
MANGERTON LANE
New House Farm
Old House Farm
Cloverleaf Farm
YELLOW LANE
WADDON WAY
Bell Farm
Symes's Hill Copse
Waddon Hill
Waddon Copse
Tumulus
CHURCH CL
ST JAMES PK
SMISHOPS LA
WHETLAND'S LA
Peascombe Nature Reserve
Hole House Farm
HIGHER ST
Old Post Farm
Loders
MIDDLE ST
FORSTERS LA
PO
River Asker
PH
Loders CE Prim Sch
NEW ST LANE
HIGHACRES
Hillway Copse
Bradpole
FOX CL
CALEY WAY
NEW STREET LA
Stepps Farm
8
7
97
6
5
96
4
3
95
2
1
94
48
49
50

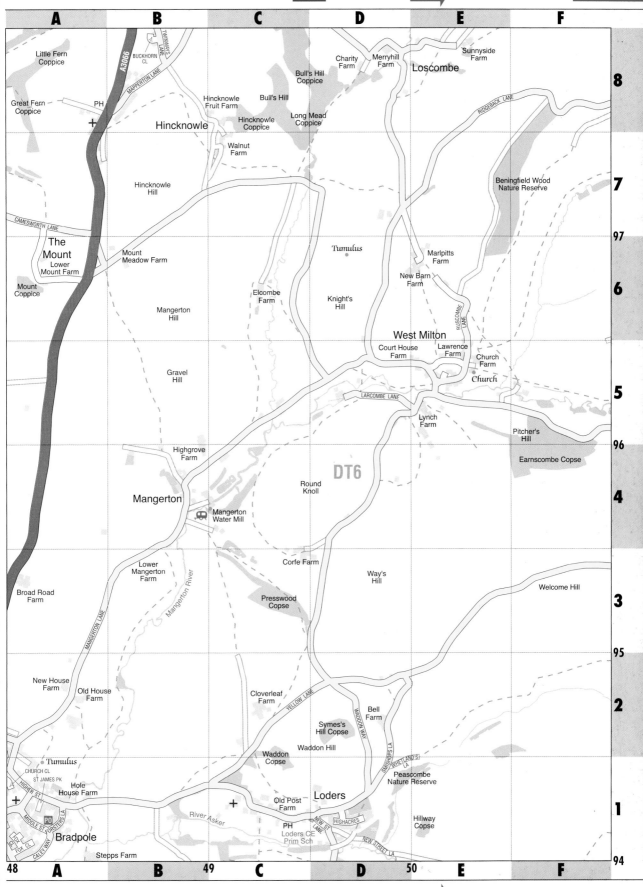

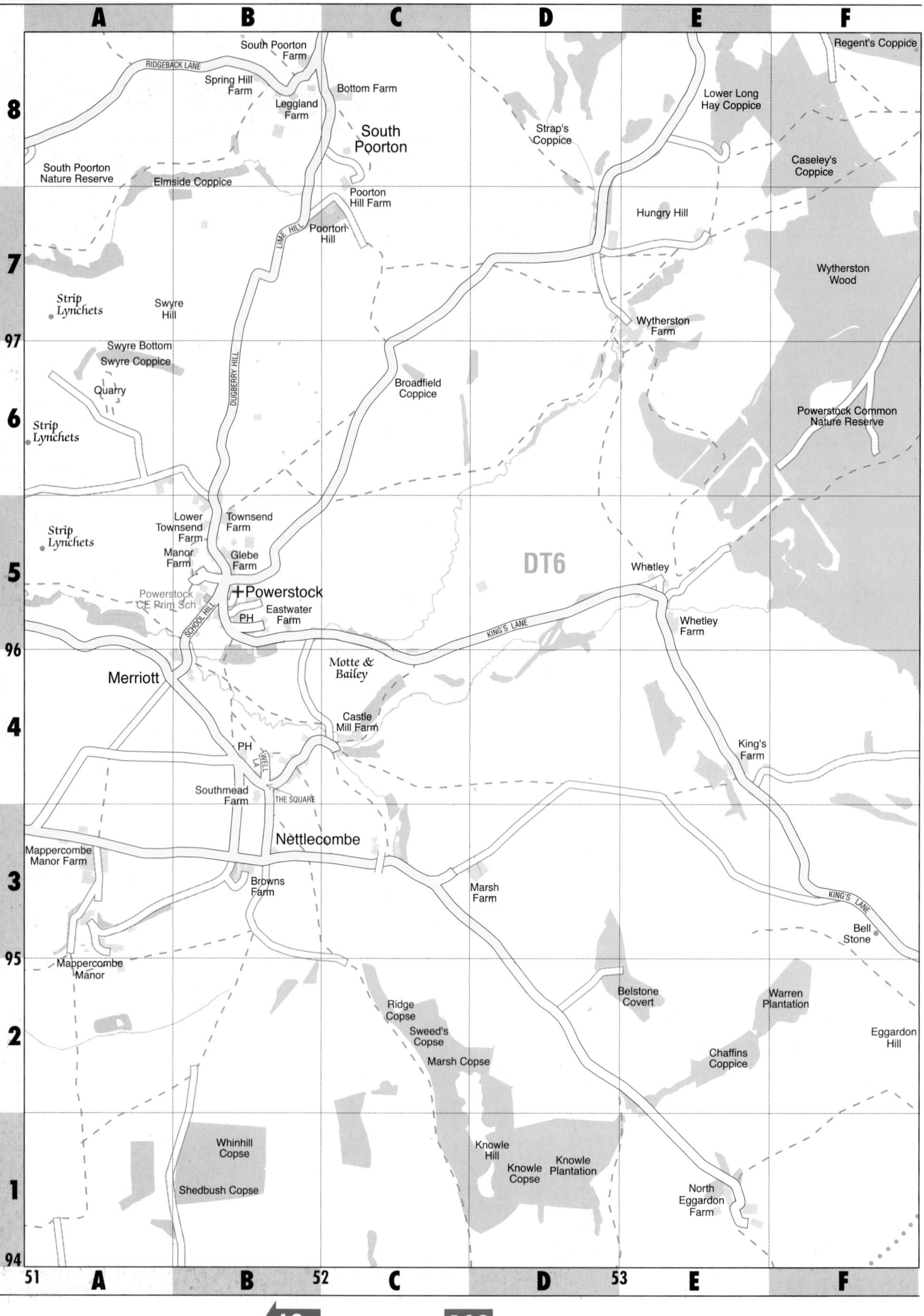

A B C D E F

Regent's Coppice

South Poorton
Farm

RIDGEBACK LANE

Spring Hill
Farm

Bottom Farm

Leggland
Farm

South
Poorton

Strap's
Coppice

Lower Long
Hay Coppice

Caseley's
Coppice

South Poorton
Nature Reserve

Elmside Coppice

Poorton
Hill Farm

Hungry Hill

LIME HILL

Poorton
Farm

Poorton
Hill

7

Wytherston
Wood

Strip
Lynchets

Swyre
Hill

97

Wytherston
Farm

Swyre Bottom
Swyre Coppice

DUGBERRY HILL

Broadfield
Coppice

6

Quarry

Powerstock Common
Nature Reserve

Strip
Lynchets

Lower
Townsend
Farm

Townsend
Farm

Strip
Lynchets

Manor
Farm

Glebe
Farm

DT6

Whetley

5

+ Powerstock

Powerstock
CE Prim Sch

SCHOOL HILL

PH

Eastwater
Farm

Whetley
Farm

KING'S LANE

96

Motte &
Bailey

Merriott

Castle
Mill Farm

4

PH

YWELL LA

King's
Farm

Southmead
Farm

THE SQUARE

Nettlecombe

Mappercombe
Manor Farm

Browns
Farm

Marsh
Farm

KING'S LANE

3

Bell
Stone

95

Mappercombe
Manor

Belstone
Covert

Warren
Plantation

Ridge
Copse

2

Sweed's
Copse

Chaffins
Coppice

Eggardon
Hill

Marsh Copse

Whinhill
Copse

Knowle
Hill

Knowle
Plantation

1

Shedbush Copse

Knowle
Copse

North
Eggardon
Farm

51 A B 52 C D 53 E F

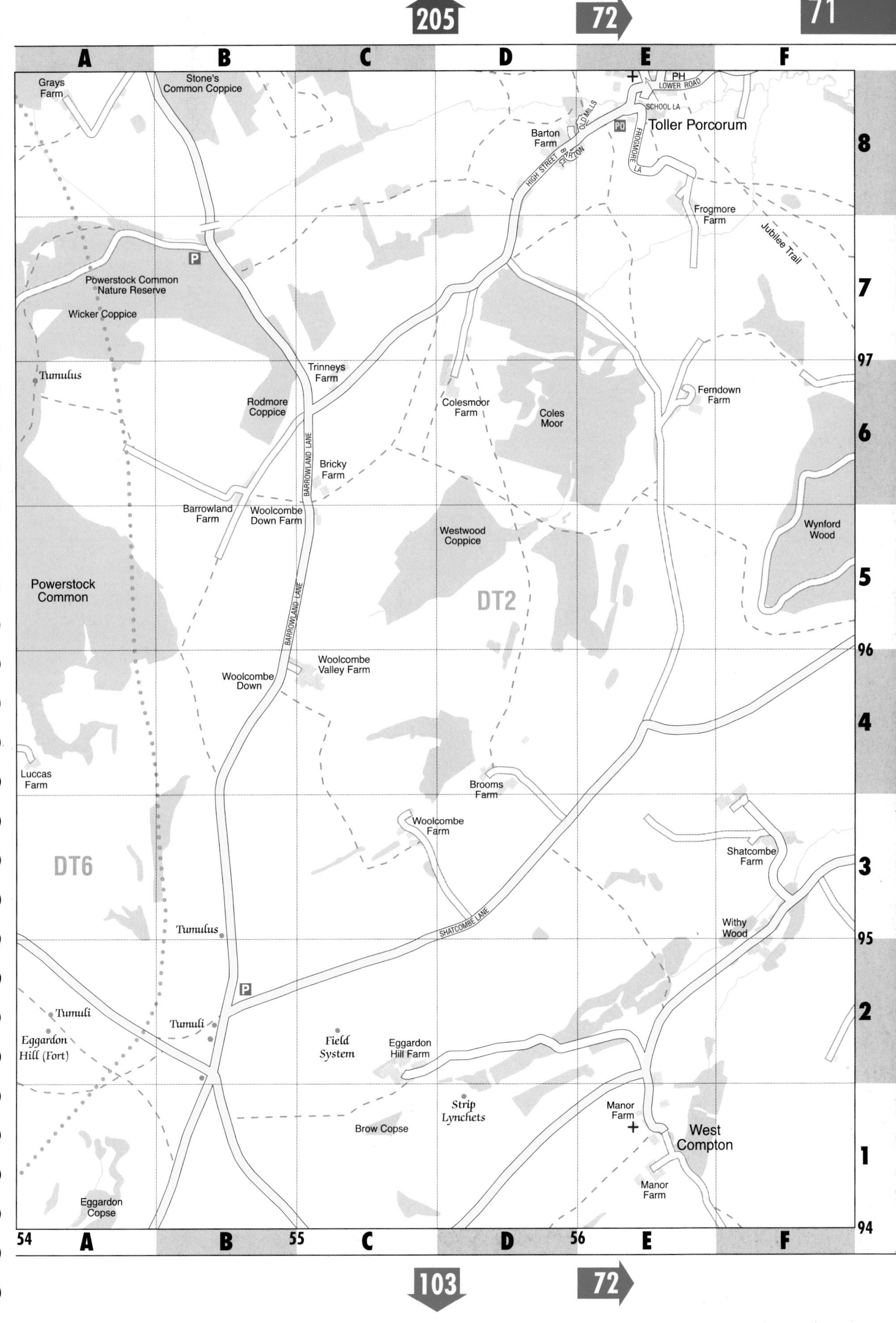
A B C D E F

Grays
Farm

Stone's
Common Coppice

Toller Porcorum

+ PH
LOWER ROAD

SCHOOL LA

Barton
Farm

HIGH STREET
TO CLIFTON

OLD MILLS

P

FROGMORE LA

Frogmore
Farm

Jubilee Trail

8

P

Powerstock Common
Nature Reserve

Wicker Coppice

7

97

Tumulus

Trinneys
Farm

Rodmore
Coppice

BARROWLAND LANE

Colesmoor
Farm

Coles
Moor

Ferndown
Farm

6

Bricky
Farm

Westwood
Coppice

Wynford
Wood

Barrowland
Farm

Woolcombe
Down Farm

BARROWLAND LANE

DT2

5

96

Powerstock
Common

Woolcombe
Valley Farm

Woolcombe
Down

4

Luccas
Farm

Brooms
Farm

Shatcombe
Farm

3

DT6

Woolcombe
Farm

SHATCOMBE LANE

Withy
Wood

95

Tumulus

Tumuli

P

2

Tumuli

*Field
System*

Eggardon
Hill Farm

*Eggardon
Hill (Fort)*

*Strip
Lynchets*

Manor
Farm
+

West
Compton

1

Brow Copse

Manor
Farm

*Eggardon
Copse*

94

54 A 55 B C 55 D 56 E F

71
206

A356

Station Road Ind Est

Greenford CE Prim Sch

Tollerford

PH

WHITEHORSE MWS

KINGSLEY PADDOCK

Cemy

Beacon Farm

GREENFORD LA

BACK LANE

FROME LANE

FROME

Frome Vauchurch

Toller Fratrum Farm

Toller Fratrum

River Hooke

Blanchard's Plantation

Frome Vauchurch Farm

Jubilee Trail

Chammen's Hill

Fore Hill Plantation

Wynford Wood

Thistle Farm

DT2

Manor Farm

Wynford Eagle

GREENFORD LANE

Tumulus

Brookside Farm

Wynford House

Round Hill Plantations

Greenford Farm

Winholes Coppice

Winholes Plantation

Jubilee Trail

Notton Hill Barn

Soapers Hill Plantation

Macmillan Way

206
74

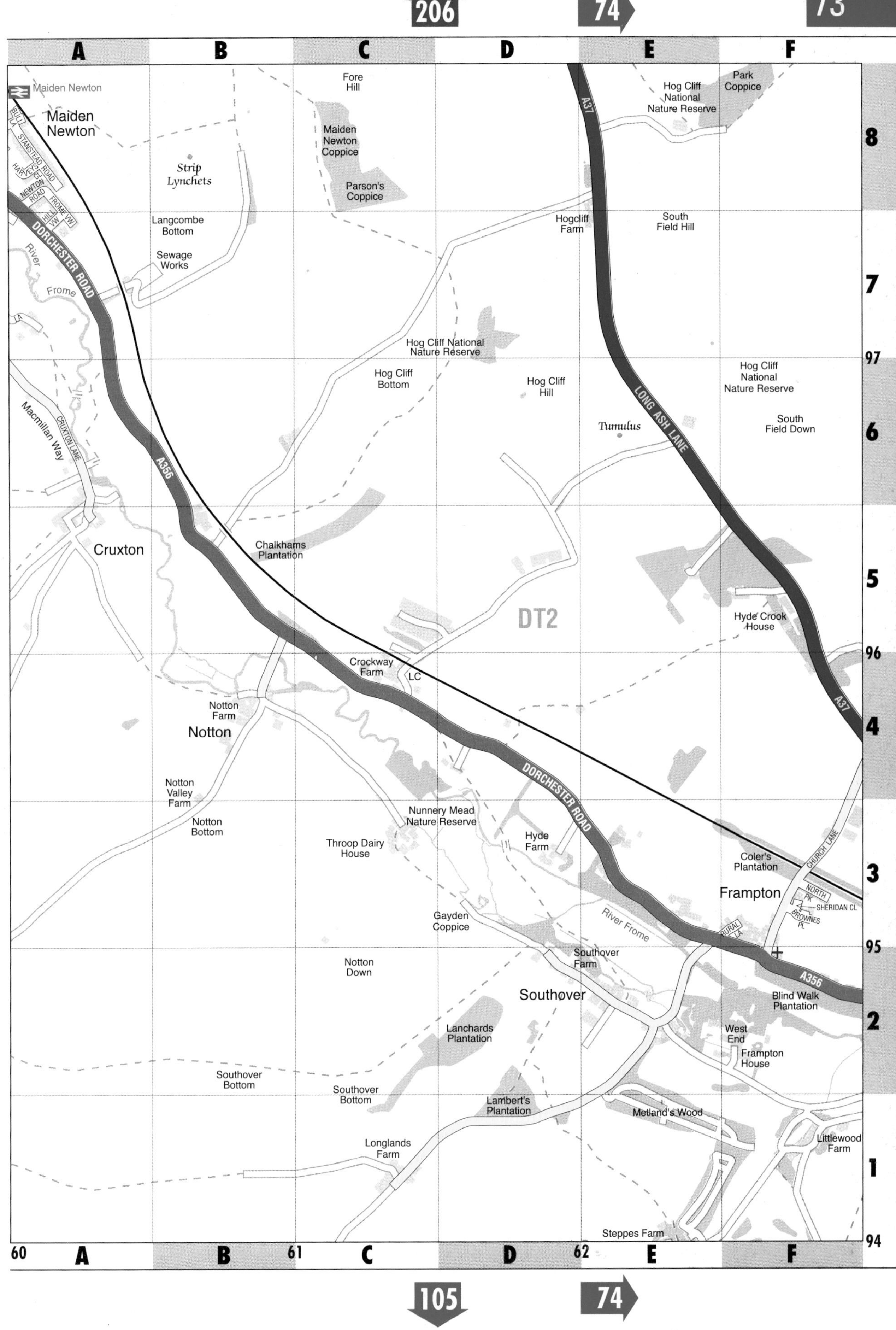
A
B
C
D
E
F
Maiden Newton
Maiden Newton
Fore Hill
Maiden Newton Coppice
Parson's Coppice
Hog Cliff National Nature Reserve
Park Coppice
8
Strip Lynchets
Langcombe Bottom
Sewage Works
River Frome
DORCHESTER ROAD
Hogcliff Farm
South Field Hill
7
Hog Cliff National Nature Reserve
97
Hog Cliff Bottom
Hog Cliff Hill
Hog Cliff National Nature Reserve
Macmillan Way
CRUXTON LANE
Tumulus
LONG ASH LANE
South Field Down
6
A356
A37
Cruxton
Chalkhams Plantation
5
DT2
Hyde Crook House
96
Crockway Farm
LC
Notton Farm
Notton
4
Notton Valley Farm
Notton Bottom
Nunnery Mead Nature Reserve
Throop Dairy House
Hyde Farm
Coler's Plantation
CHURCH LANE
3
Frampton
NORTH PK
SHERIDAN CL
BROWNES PL
RURAL LA
River Frome
Gayden Coppice
95
Notton Down
Southover Farm
Southover
Blind Walk Plantation
2
Lanchards Plantation
West End
Frampton House
Southover Bottom
Southover Bottom
Lambert's Plantation
Metland's Wood
Littlewood Farm
Longlands Farm
1
Steppes Farm
94
60
61
62

105
74

A **B** **C** **D** **E** **F**

8

Huish
Plantation

Tumulus

7

Bushes
Barn

Crete
Bottom

Crete
Hill

Magiston
Hill

97

Tumulus

South
Field Down

6

Crete
Bottom

Syalling Water

Magiston
Farm

5

Coronation
Plantation

Lower
Magiston

Cross Dyke

Stratton
Down

Watcombe
Bottom

96

Jackman's
Plantation

Kidney
Plantation

Langford
Farm

Jackman's
Coppice

DT2

Howdes Barrow
Plantation

4

PICKETTS CROSS

Settlement

Lawyer's
Plantation

Tumulus

A37

Galhampton
Farm

CHURCH LA

Grimstone
Down

Tumuli

LONG ASH LANE

3

Stratton
Down

Half Moon
Plantation

Long
Plantation

Stratton
Down
Plantation

Great War
Plantation

95

Prisoner's of War
Plantation

Hog
Hill

Tumulus

Stratton
Down

Stratton
Bottom

2

A356

Syalling Water

Blind Walk
Plantation

DORCHESTER RD

Peacock
Plantation

DORCHESTER ROAD

Strip
Lynchets

1

River Frome

Manor
Farm

A37

Grimstone

94

63 **A** 64 **B** **C** **D** 65 **E** **F**

207
76

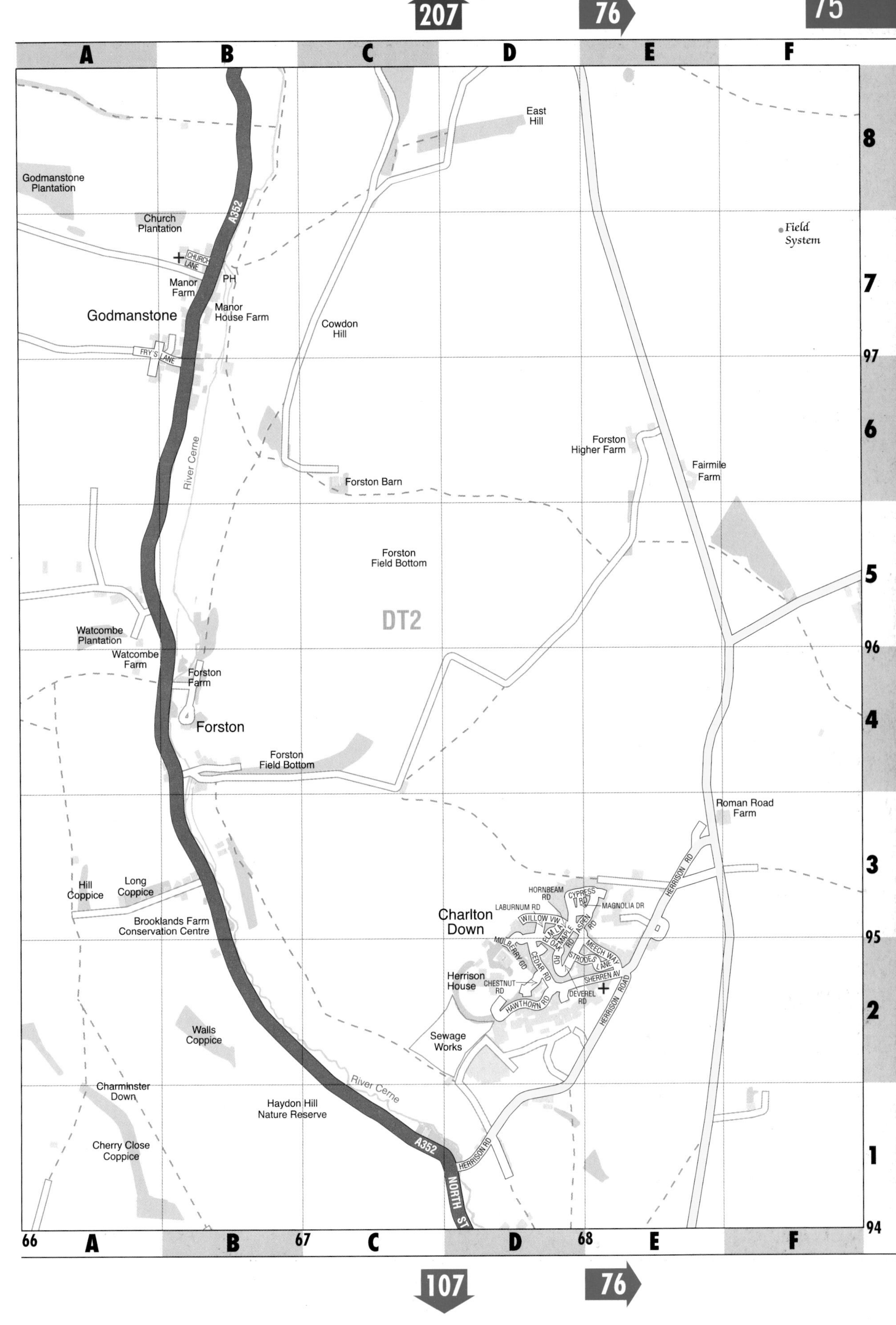
A
B
C
D
E
F
East Hill
Godmanstone Plantation
Church Plantation
Church Lane
Manor Farm
PH
Manor House Farm
Godmanstone
Fry's Lane
A352
Cowdon Hill
Field System
River Cerne
Forston Barn
Forston Higher Farm
Fairmile Farm
Forston Field Bottom
DT2
Watcombe Plantation
Watcombe Farm
Forston Farm
Forston
Forston Field Bottom
Roman Road Farm
Hill Coppice
Long Coppice
Brooklands Farm Conservation Centre
Charlton Down
Hornbeam Rd
Laburnum Rd
Cypress Rd
Magnolia Dr
Willow Vw
Elm La
Oak
Maple Rd
Aspen Rd
Mulberry Gd
Cedar Rd
Meech Way
Strodes Lane
Sherren Av
Herrison House
Chestnut Rd
Deverel Rd
Hawthorn Rd
Herrison Road
Herrison Rd
Sewage Works
Walls Coppice
Charminster Down
Haydon Hill Nature Reserve
Cherry Close Coppice
North St
8
7
97
6
5
96
4
3
95
2
1
94
66
67
68

107
76

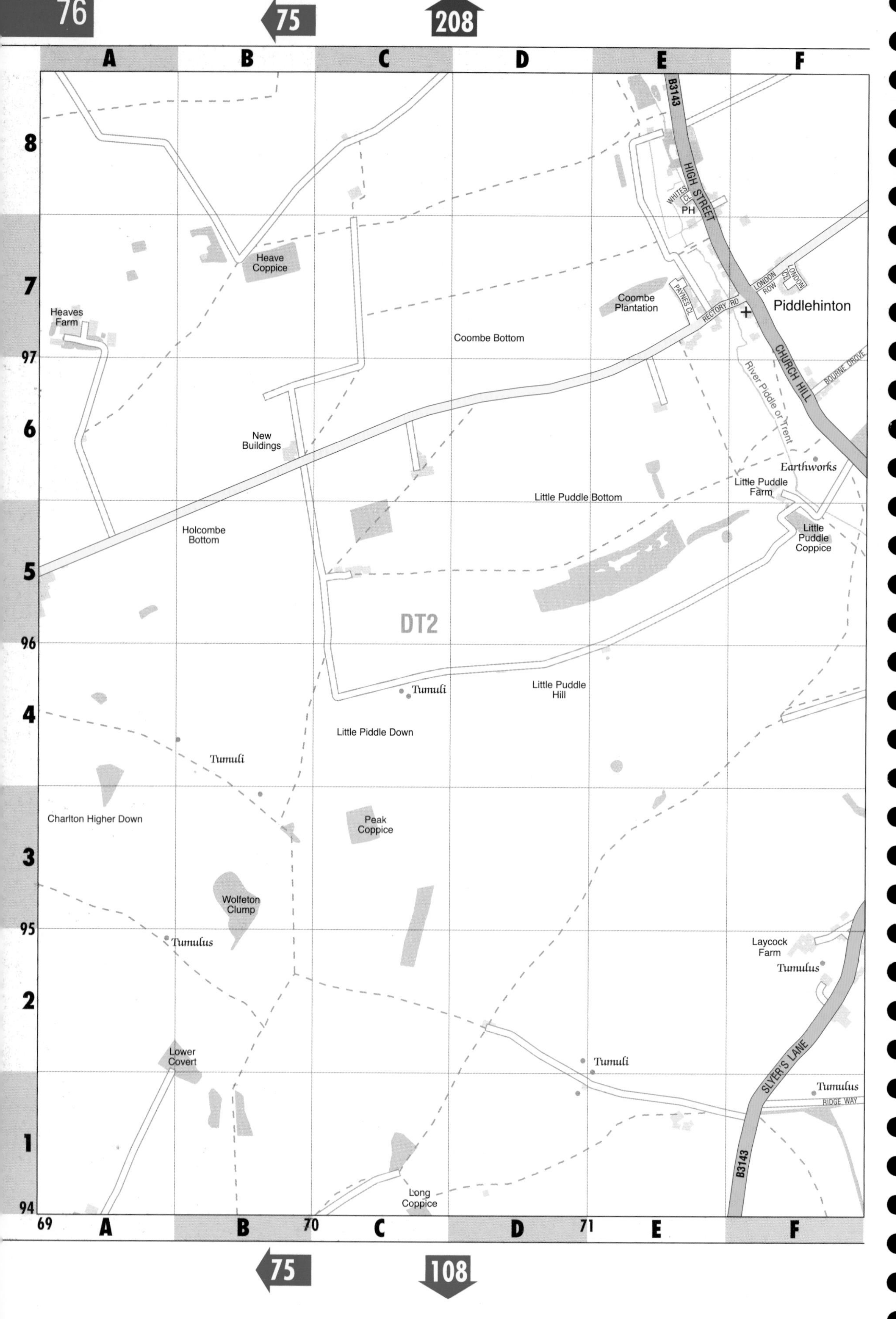

8

7

97

6

5

96

4

3

95

2

1

94

Heaves
Farm

Heave
Coppice

New
Buildings

Holcombe
Bottom

Coombe Bottom

Coombe
Plantation

B3143

HIGH STREET

WHITES CL
PH

PAYNES CL

RECTORY RD

LONDON ROW
LONDON CL

Piddlehinton

CHURCH HILL

BOURNE DROVE

River Piddle or Trent

Earthworks

Little Puddle
Farm

Little
Puddle
Coppice

Little Puddle Bottom

DT2

Tumuli

Little Puddle
Hill

Little Piddle Down

Tumuli

Charlton Higher Down

Peak
Coppice

Wolfeton
Clump

Tumulus

Laycock
Farm

Tumulus

Lower
Covert

Tumuli

SLYER'S LANE

Tumulus

RIDGE WAY

B3143

Long
Coppice

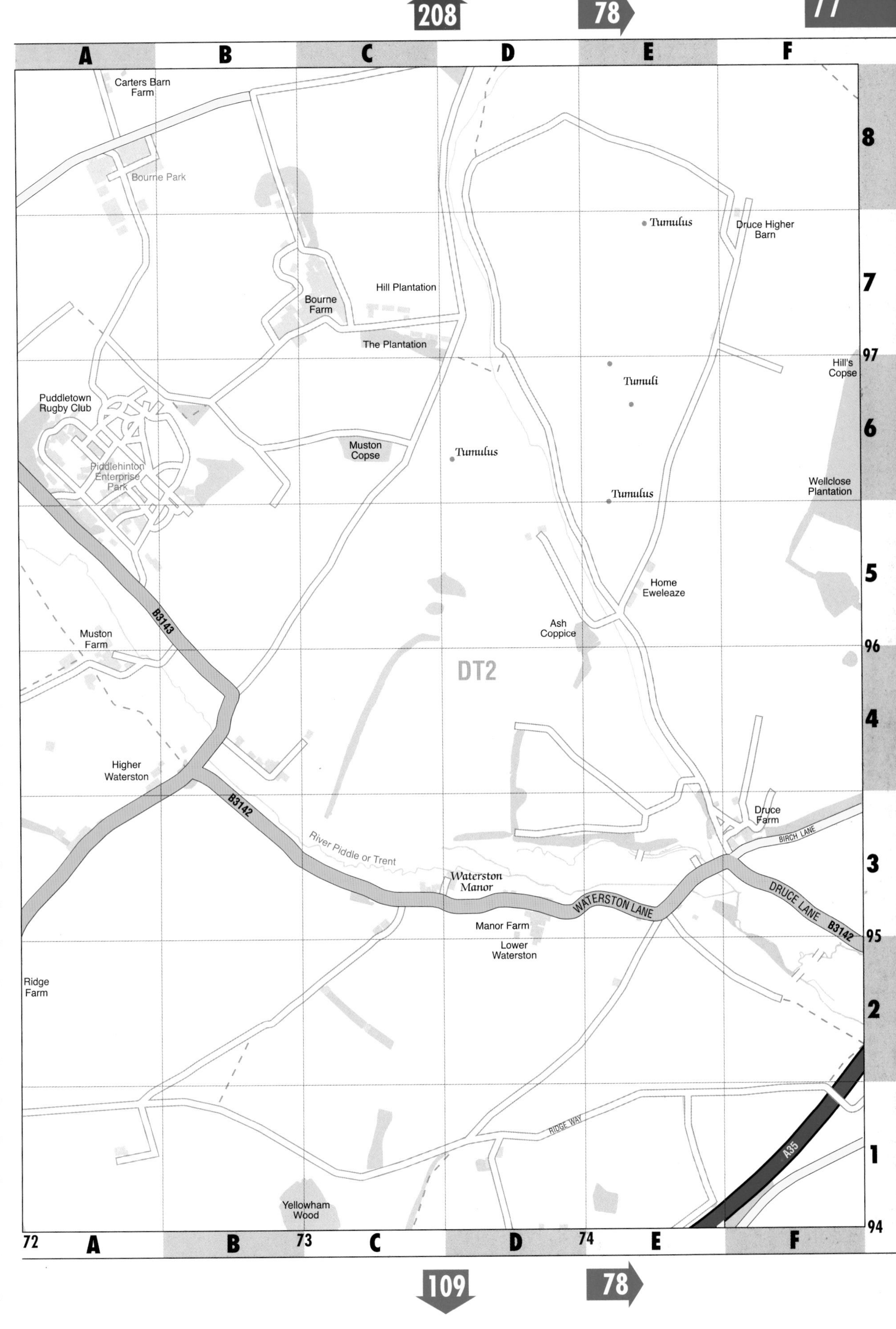

A   B   C   D   E   F

Carters Barn Farm

Bourne Park

Tumulus

Druce Higher Barn

8

Hill Plantation

Bourne Farm

7

The Plantation

Hill's Copse

97

Tumuli

Puddletown Rugby Club

Piddlehinton Enterprise Park

Muston Copse

Tumulus

6

Wellclose Plantation

B3143

Muston Farm

Tumulus

Home Eweleaze

5

Ash Coppice

96

DT2

4

Higher Waterston

B3142

Druce Farm

BIRCH LANE

River Piddle or Trent

Druce Lane B3142

3

Waterston Manor

WATERSTON LANE

Manor Farm

95

Lower Waterston

Ridge Farm

2

RIDGE WAY

A35

1

Yellowham Wood

94

A   B   C   D   E   F

8

7

97

6

5

96

4

3

95

2

1

94

Tumuli

Puddletown
Down

Hill's
Copse

Hazel
Copse

Shailes
Copse

Dewlish House

Park Hill

Warren
Plantation

Lower Farm

JOCK'S HILL

Crawthorne
Farm

Devil's Brook

Warren Hill
Farm

Wreden
Plantation

DT2

Basan
Plantation

Basan Hill

BASAN HILL

Fryer's
Bridge

Tumuli

Burleston
Down

WARREN HILL

WARREN ROAD

WARREN ROAD

BIRCH LANE

LONG LANE

A354

Bardolf
Manor

Burleston
Plantation

B3142

Hill Top

A35

DRUCE LANE

Northbrook

Stafford
Park Farm

PH

DRUCE LANE

THE MOOR

LONG LA

BACKWATER

THOMPSON CL

THREE
LANES
WY

GREENACRES CL

KINGS RD

River Piddle or Trent

Bardolfeston
Village

Home
Farm

BURLESTON DROVE

A35

Puddletown

Puddletown CE
First Sch

St Marys CE
Middle Sch

PH

PO

Liby

STYLES
LA

ORFORD
LA

MILL STREET

THE SQUARE

Ilsington House

HIGH ST

NEW STREET

COOMBE ROAD

HIGH STREET

ROD HILL

THE LA

BUTT HILL

BEECH RD

MILOM LANE

Little Knoll
Copse

Henroost
Wood

Athelhampton

ATHELHAMPTON ROAD

Athelhampton
House & Gardens

West
End

Burleston

75   A   B   76   C   D   77   E   F

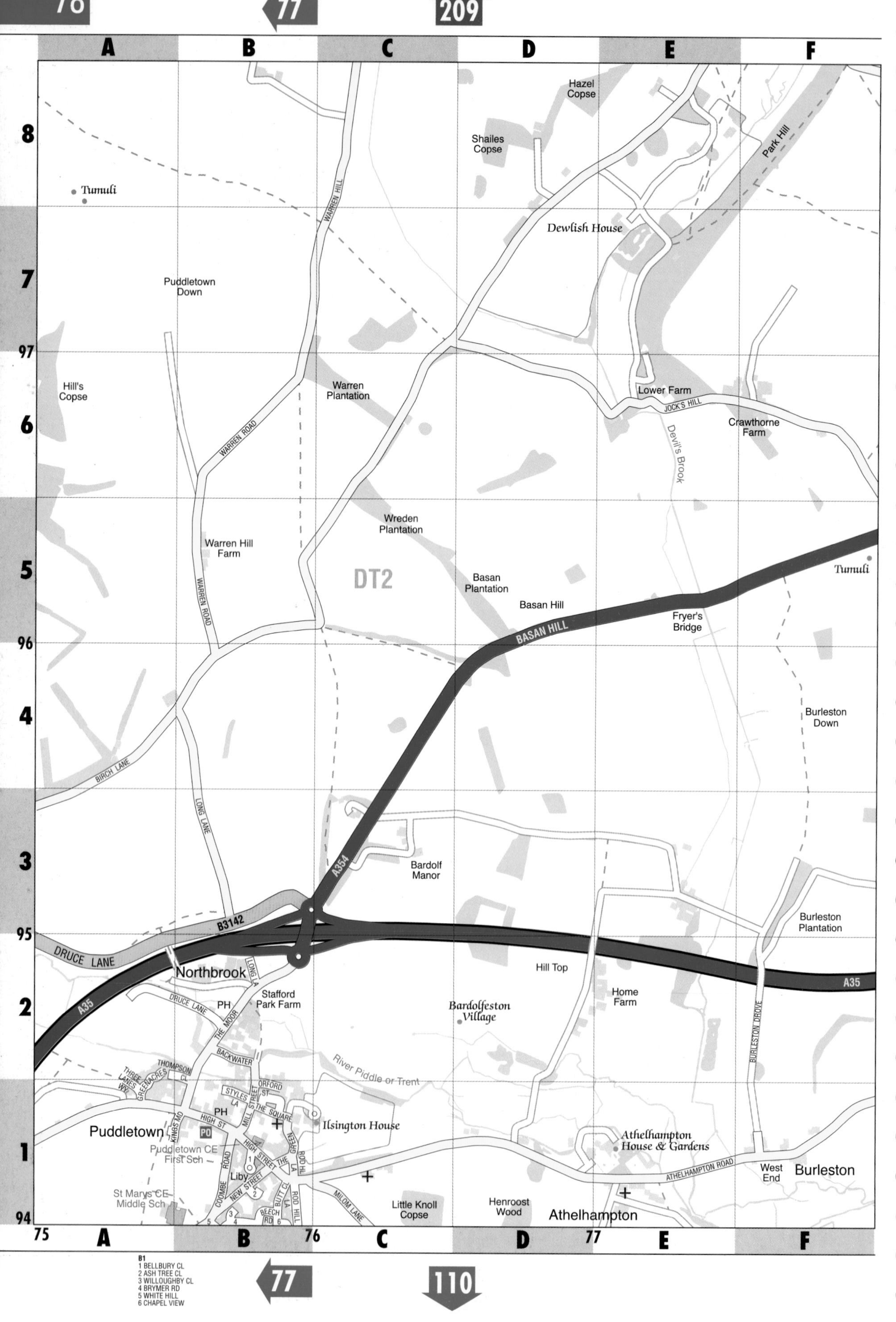

B1
1 BELLBURY CL
2 ASH TREE CL
3 WILLOUGHBY CL
4 BRYMER RD
5 WHITE HILL
6 CHAPEL VIEW

209
80

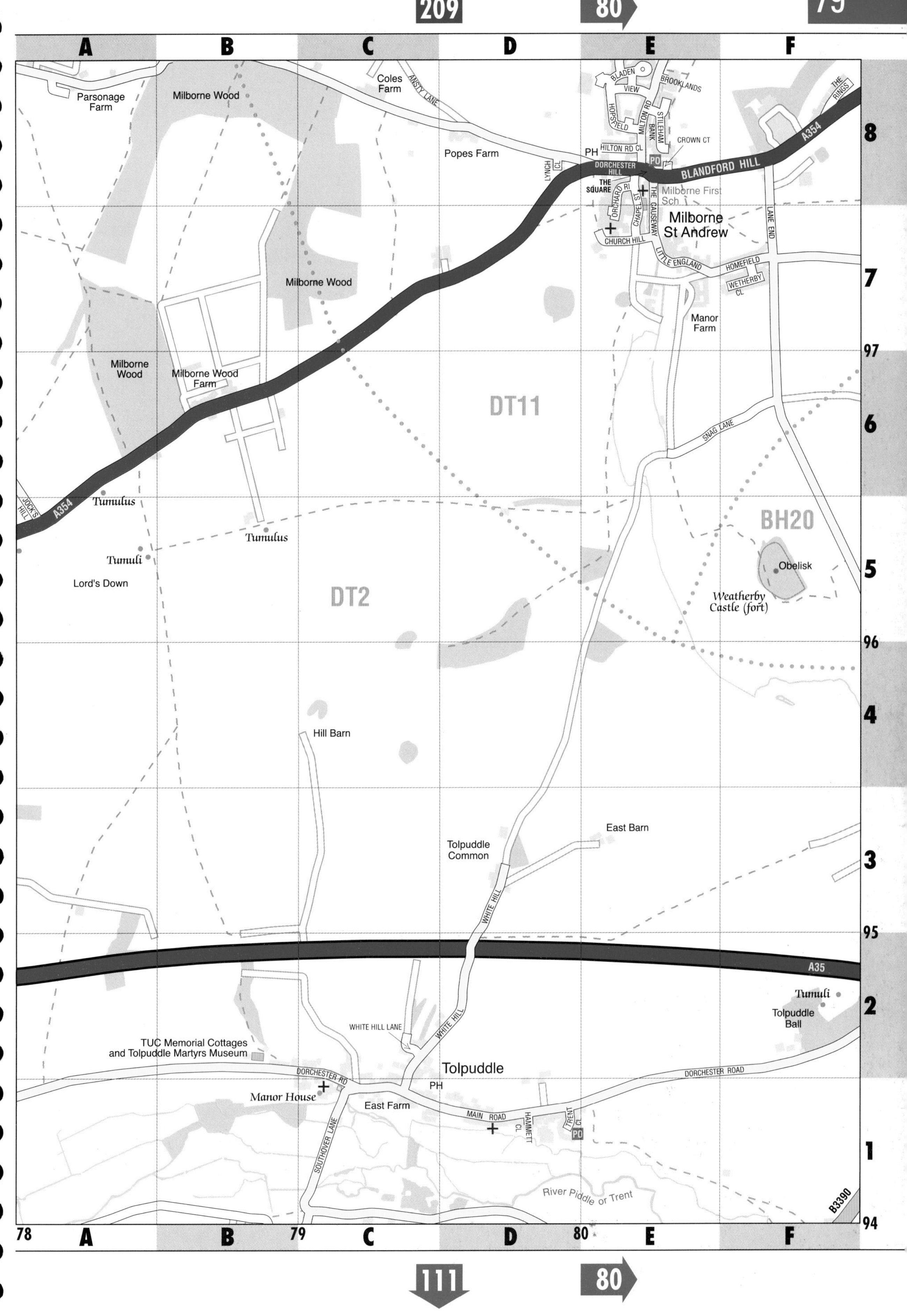
A
B
C
D
E
F
Parsonage Farm
Milborne Wood
Coles Farm
ANSTY LANE
BLADEN VIEW
BROOKLANDS
HOPSFIELD
MILTON RD
STILEHAM BANK
THE RINGS
A354
8
HILTON RD CL
CROWN CT
Popes Farm
PH
LYNCH CL
DORCHESTER HILL
PO
BLANDFORD HILL
THE SQUARE
ORCHARD RI
Milborne First Sch
CHAPEL ST
THE CAUSEWAY
Milborne St Andrew
LANE END
CHURCH HILL
LITTLE ENGLAND
HOMEFIELD
WETHERBY CL
Milborne Wood
7
Manor Farm
97
Milborne Wood
Milborne Wood Farm
DT11
6
SNAG LANE
JOCK'S HILL
A354
Tumulus
Tumulus
BH20
Tumuli
Obelisk
5
Lord's Down
DT2
Weatherby Castle (fort)
96
4
Hill Barn
East Barn
Tolpuddle Common
3
WHITE HILL
95
A35
Tumuli
2
Tolpuddle Ball
WHITE HILL LANE
WHITE HILL
TUC Memorial Cottages and Tolpuddle Martyrs Museum
Tolpuddle
DORCHESTER RD
DORCHESTER ROAD
PH
Manor House
East Farm
MAIN ROAD
HAMMETT CL
TRENT CL
PO
1
SOUTHOVER LANE
River Piddle or Trent
B3390
78
79
80
94

111
80

79 210

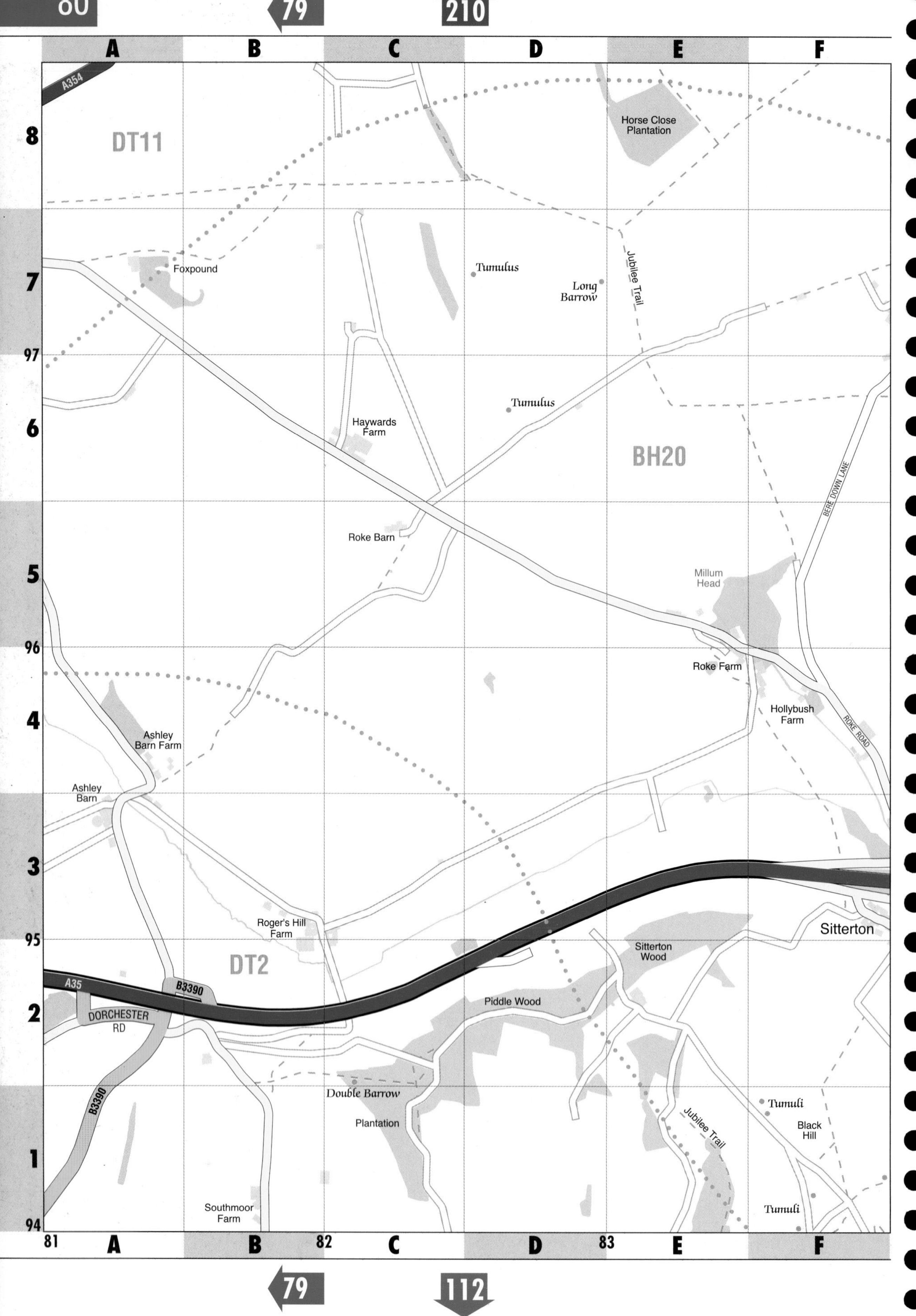
A
B
C
D
E
F
A354
DT11
8
Horse Close
Plantation
Foxpound
7
Tumulus
Long
Barrow
Jubilee Trail
97
Tumulus
Haywards
Farm
6
BH20
BERE DOWN LANE
Roke Barn
5
Millum
Head
96
Roke Farm
Hollybush
Farm
ROKE ROAD
4
Ashley
Barn Farm
Ashley
Barn
3
Roger's Hill
Farm
Sitterton
95
Sitterton
Wood
DT2
A35
B3390
Piddle Wood
2
DORCHESTER
RD
Double Barrow
Plantation
B3390
Tumuli
Jubilee Trail
Black
Hill
1
Southmoor
Farm
Tumuli
94
81
82
83

79 112

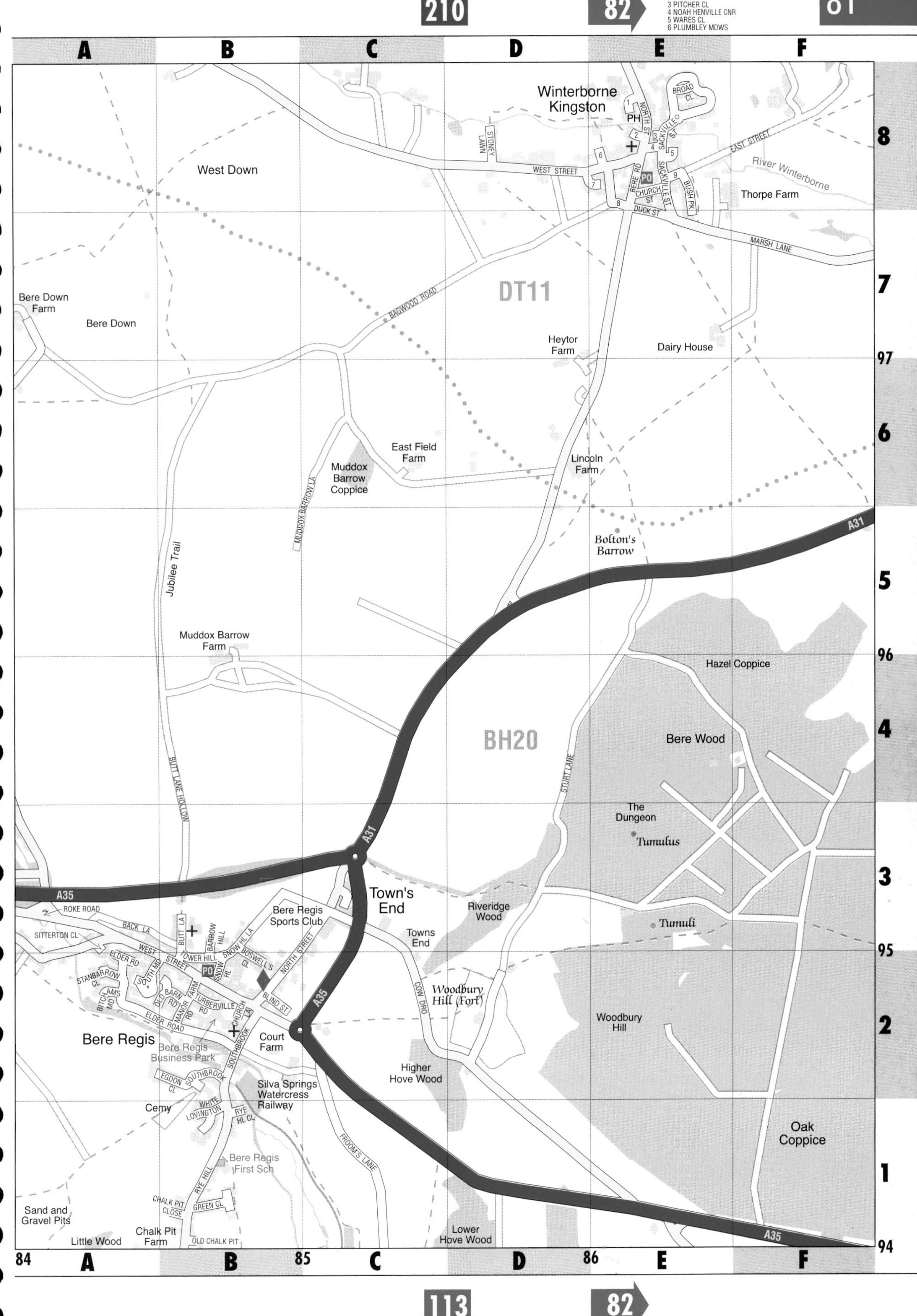

E8
1 WIND WHISTLE FM
2 CLYPETTS
3 PITCHER CL
4 NOAH HENVILLE CNR
5 WARES CL
6 PLUMBLEY MDWS

7 ORCHARD LA
8 BAGWOOD RD
9 EAST ST

A B C D E F

Winterborne Kingston

BROAD CL

PH

NORTH ST

SACKVILLE ST

BERE RD

PO

BUSH PK

WEST STREET

CHURCH ST

DUCK ST

EAST STREET

River Winterborne

Thorpe Farm

MARSH LANE

West Down

DT11

8

7

97

6

Bere Down Farm

Bere Down

Bere Down

Heytor Farm

Dairy House

Muddox Barrow Coppice

East Field Farm

MUDDOX BARROW LA

Lincoln Farm

Bolton's Barrow

A31

Jubilee Trail

Muddox Barrow Farm

5

Hazel Coppice

96

BH20

Bere Wood

4

BUTT LANE HOLLOW

STURT LANE

The Dungeon

Tumulus

A31

A35

Town's End

ROKE ROAD

Bere Regis Sports Club

Riveridge Wood

Tumuli

3

SITTERTON CL

BACK LA

BUTT LA

BARROW HILL

SNOW HILL

NORTH STREET

Towns End

95

WEST STREET

TOWER HILL

PO

BOSWELL'S

A35

Woodbury Hill (Fort)

STANBARROW CL

BIRCH CL

ELDER RD

AMS RD

SO. JTR. MD

BARN

MANOR FARM RD

TURBERVILLE RD

BLIND ST

COW DRO

Woodbury Hill

2

Bere Regis

ELDER ROAD

SOUTHBROOK

Court Farm

Higher Hove Wood

Bere Regis Business Park

EGDON CL

SOUTHBROOK

WHITE LOVINGTON

RYE HL CL

Silva Springs Watercress Railway

Cemy

Oak Coppice

RYE HILL

Bere Regis First Sch

GREEN CL

FROOM'S LANE

1

Sand and Gravel Pits

CHALK PIT CLOSE

Little Wood

Chalk Pit Farm

OLD CHALK PIT

Lower Hove Wood

A35

94

84 A B 85 C D 86 E F

81
211

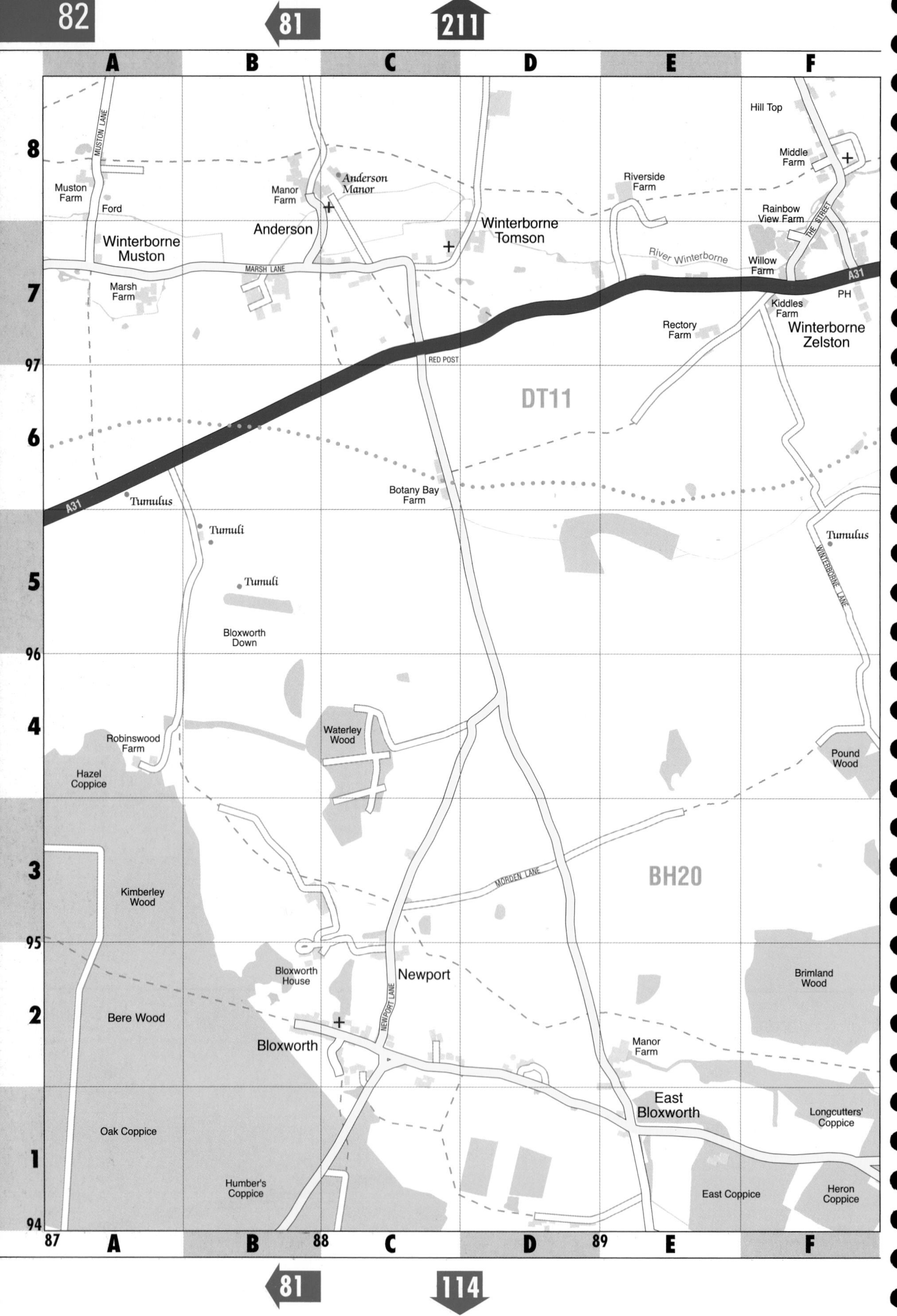
A
B
C
D
E
F
8
7
97
6
5
96
4
3
95
2
1
94
87
88
89
Hill Top
Middle Farm
Muston Farm
Ford
Manor Farm
Anderson Manor
Riverside Farm
Winterborne Muston
Anderson
Winterborne Tomson
Rainbow View Farm
THE STREET
River Winterborne
Willow Farm
MUSTON LANE
MARSH LANE
Marsh Farm
A31
PH
Kiddles Farm
Rectory Farm
Winterborne Zelston
RED POST
DT11
Botany Bay Farm
Tumulus
Tumuli
Tumuli
Tumulus
WINTERBORNE LANE
Bloxworth Down
Waterley Wood
Robinswood Farm
Hazel Coppice
Pound Wood
Kimberley Wood
MORDEN LANE
BH20
Bloxworth House
Newport
NEWPORT LANE
Brimland Wood
Bere Wood
Bloxworth
Manor Farm
East Bloxworth
Longcutters' Coppice
Oak Coppice
Humber's Coppice
East Coppice
Heron Coppice

81
114

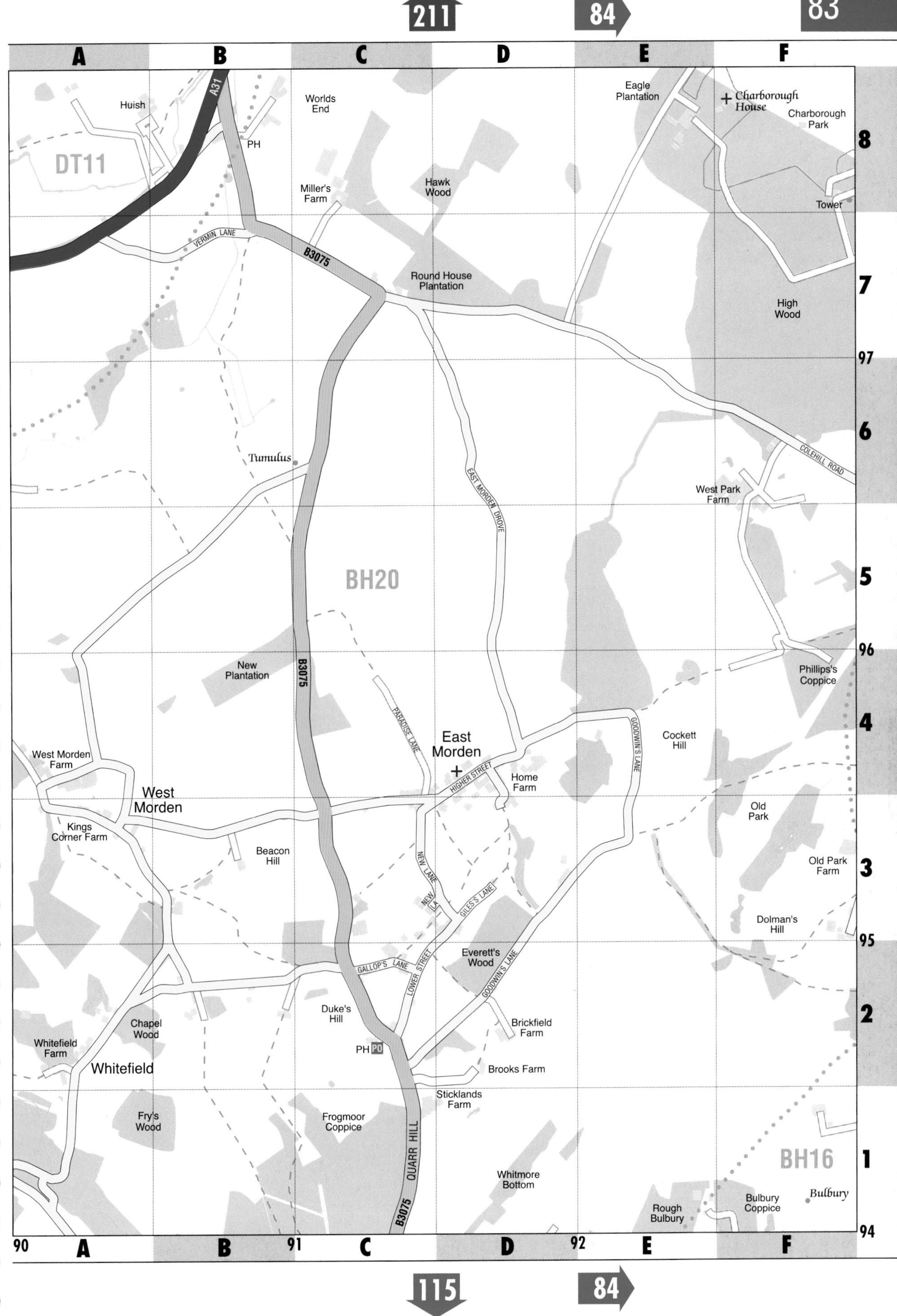
211
84
A
B
C
D
E
F
Huish
A31
PH
Worlds End
Eagle Plantation
Charborough House
Charborough Park
DT11
Miller's Farm
Hawk Wood
Tower
VERMIN LANE
B3075
Round House Plantation
High Wood
Tumulus
EAST MORDEN DROVE
COLEHILL ROAD
West Park Farm
BH20
New Plantation
Phillips's Coppice
PARADISE LANE
GOODWIN'S LANE
East Morden
Cockett Hill
West Morden Farm
HIGHER STREET
Home Farm
West Morden
Old Park
Kings Corner Farm
Beacon Hill
NEW LANE
Old Park Farm
GILES'S LANE
Dolman's Hill
Everett's Wood
GALLOP'S LANE
LOWER STREET
Chapel Wood
Duke's Hill
Brickfield Farm
Whitefield Farm
Whitefield
PH
PO
Brooks Farm
Sticklands Farm
Fry's Wood
Frogmoor Coppice
QUARR HILL
BH16
Whitmore Bottom
Bulbury
Bulbury Coppice
Rough Bulbury
8
7
97
6
5
96
4
3
95
2
1
94
90
91
92
115
84

83 56

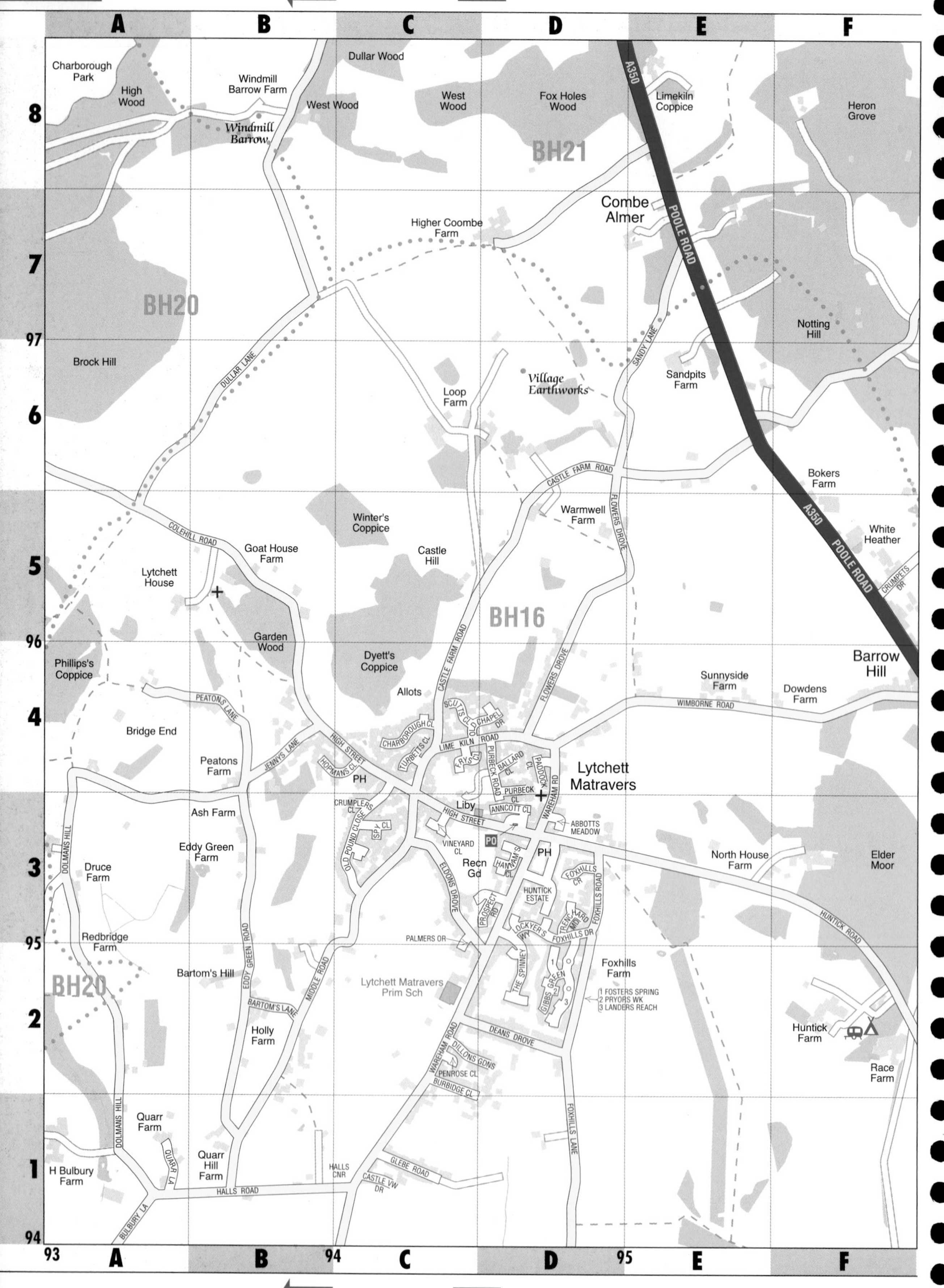
A
B
C
D
E
F
8
7
97
6
5
96
4
3
95
2
1
94
93
94
95
Charborough Park
High Wood
Windmill Barrow Farm
Windmill Barrow
Dullar Wood
West Wood
West Wood
Fox Holes Wood
BH21
A350
Limekiln Coppice
Heron Grove
Combe Almer
POOLE ROAD
Higher Coombe Farm
BH20
Notting Hill
Brock Hill
DULLAR LANE
Loop Farm
Village Earthworks
SANDY LANE
Sandpits Farm
CASTLE FARM ROAD
Bokers Farm
Warmwell Farm
FLOWERS DROVE
Winter's Coppice
COLEHILL ROAD
Goat House Farm
Castle Hill
White Heather
Lytchett House
BH16
CRUMPETS DR
Garden Wood
Phillips's Coppice
Dyett's Coppice
CASTLE FARM ROAD
FLOWERS DROVE
Barrow Hill
Sunnyside Farm
Dowdens Farm
WIMBORNE ROAD
Allots
PEATONS LANE
Bridge End
SCUTTS CL
CHAPEL DR
CHARBOROUGH CL
TURBETTS CL
LIME KILN ROAD
Peatons Farm
JENNYS LANE
HIGH STREET
HOPMANS CL
PH
FRYS CL
PURBECK ROAD
BALLARD CL
PADDOCK CL
WAREHAM RD
Lytchett Matravers
PURBECK CL
ANNCOTT CL
CRUMPLERS CL
Liby
HIGH STREET
ABBOTTS MEADOW
Ash Farm
DOLMANS HILL
Eddy Green Farm
OLD POUND CLOSE
SPY CL
VINEYARD CL
PO
HANHAM'S CL
PH
North House Farm
Elder Moor
Druce Farm
Recn Gd
ELDONS DROVE
FOXHILLS CR
FOXHILLS ROAD
HUNTICK ESTATE
PROSPECT RD
HUNTICK ROAD
Redbridge Farm
EDDY GREEN ROAD
PALMERS OR
LOCKYER'S WY
TRENCHARD MD
FOXHILLS DR
Foxhills Farm
BH20
Bartom's Hill
MIDDLE ROAD
Lytchett Matravers Prim Sch
THE SPINNEY
GIBBS GREEN
1 FOSTERS SPRING
2 PRYORS WK
3 LANDERS REACH
BARTOM'S LANE
Huntick Farm
Holly Farm
WAREHAM ROAD
DEANS DROVE
DILLONS GDNS
Race Farm
PENROSE CL
BURBIDGE CL
FOXHILLS LANE
DOLMANS HILL
Quarr Farm
QUARR LA
Quarr Hill Farm
HALLS CNR
GLEBE ROAD
H Bulbury Farm
CASTLE VW DR
HALLS ROAD
BULBURY LA

83 116

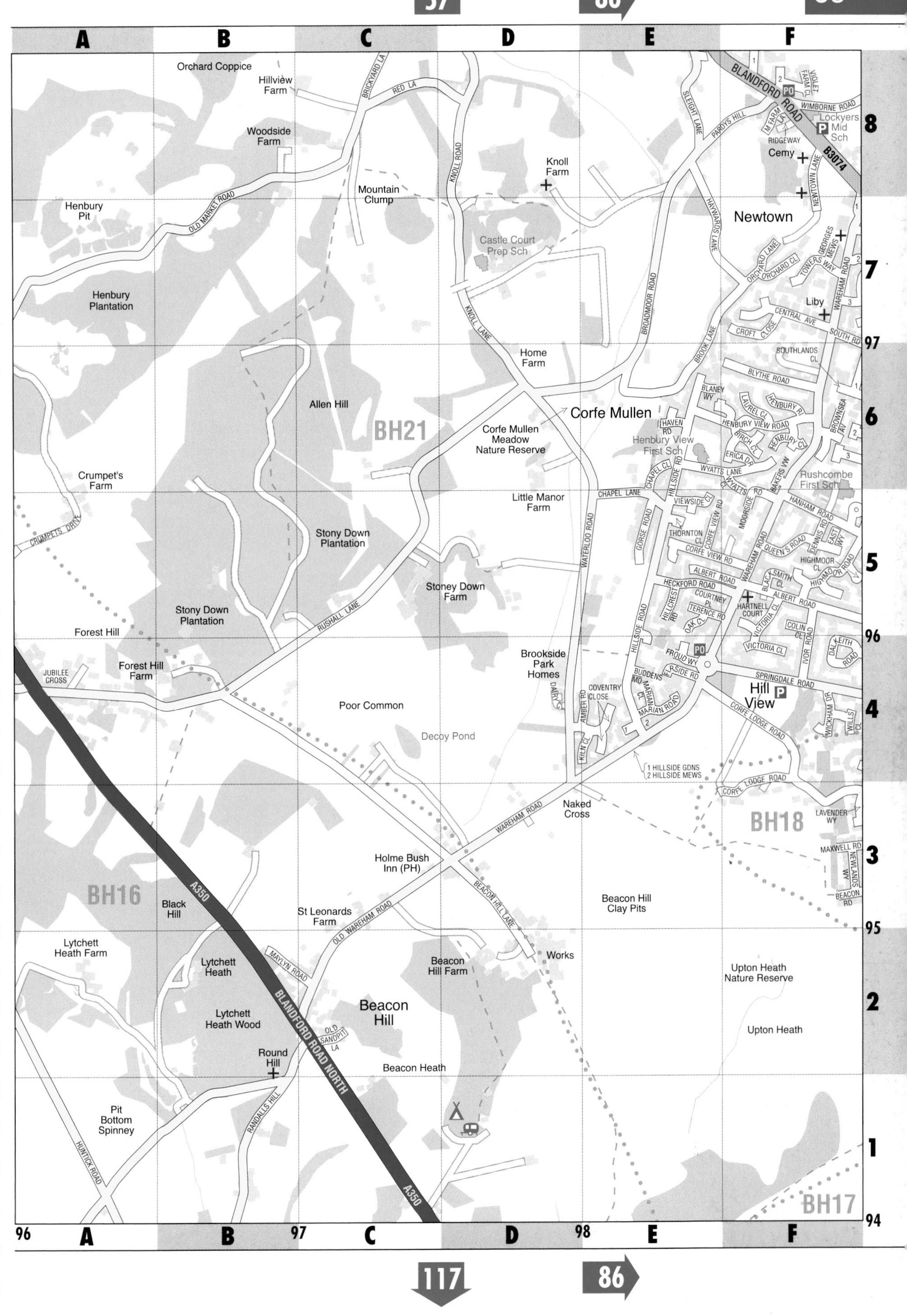
Orchard Coppice
Hillview Farm
Woodside Farm
Henbury Pit
Henbury Plantation
Mountain Clump
Knoll Farm
Castle Court Prep Sch
Newtown
Lockyers Mid Sch
Cemy
Liby
Allen Hill
BH21
Home Farm
Corfe Mullen
Corfe Mullen Meadow Nature Reserve
Henbury View First Sch
Rushcombe First Sch
Crumpet's Farm
Little Manor Farm
Stony Down Plantation
Stoney Down Farm
Forest Hill
Forest Hill Farm
Jubilee Cross
Brookside Park Homes
Hill View
Poor Common
Decoy Pond
Naked Cross
BH18
Holme Bush Inn (PH)
BH16
Black Hill
St Leonards Farm
Beacon Hill Clay Pits
Lytchett Heath Farm
Lytchett Heath
Lytchett Heath Wood
Beacon Hill Farm
Works
Upton Heath Nature Reserve
Beacon Hill
Upton Heath
Round Hill
Beacon Heath
Pit Bottom Spinney
BH17
A350
BLANDFORD ROAD NORTH
B3074
BLANDFORD ROAD
OLD MARKET ROAD
RUSHALL LANE
WAREHAM ROAD
OLD WAREHAM ROAD
BEACON HILL LANE
CORFE LODGE ROAD
1 HILLSIDE GDNS
2 HILLSIDE MEWS
A B C D E F
96 97 98
94 95 96 97
8 7 6 5 4 3 2 1

57 85 58

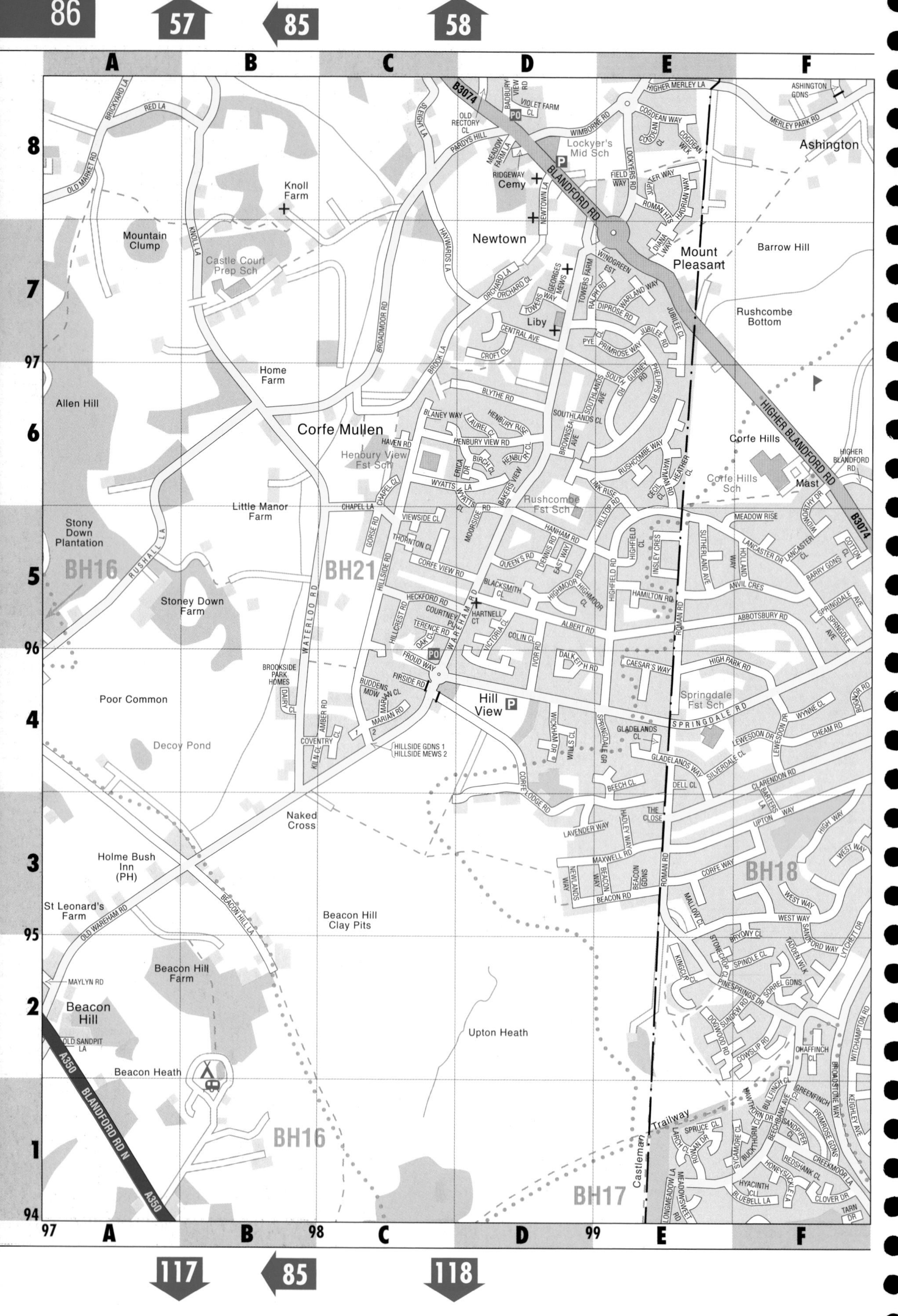
A B C D E F
8 7 97 6 5 96 4 3 95 2 1 94
97 98 99
Knoll Farm
Mountain Clump
Castle Court Prep Sch
Home Farm
Allen Hill
Corfe Mullen
Henbury View Fst Sch
Little Manor Farm
Stony Down Plantation
BH16
BH21
Stoney Down Farm
Poor Common
Decoy Pond
Naked Cross
Holme Bush Inn (PH)
St Leonard's Farm
Beacon Hill Clay Pits
Beacon Hill Farm
Beacon Hill
Beacon Heath
BH16
Upton Heath
BH17
Castleman Trailway
Newtown
Lockyer's Mid Sch
Cemy
Liby
Mount Pleasant
Ashington
Barrow Hill
Rushcombe Bottom
Corfe Hills
Corfe Hills Sch
Mast
Rushcombe Fst Sch
Hill View
Springdale Fst Sch
BH18
B3074
BLANDFORD RD
HIGHER BLANDFORD RD
WIMBORNE RD
HIGHER MERLEY LA
MERLEY PARK RD
RED LA
BRICKYARD LA
OLD MARKET RD
KNOLL LA
SLEIGHT LA
PARDYS HILL
HAYWARDS LA
BROADMOOR RD
BROOK LA
RUSHALL LA
WATERLOO RD
WAREHAM RD
CHAPEL LA
BLYTHE RD
HENBURY VIEW RD
CENTRAL AVE
SOUTHLANDS CL
RUSHCOMBE WAY
JUBILEE CL
HEATHER CL
HANHAM RD
CORFE VIEW RD
HECKFORD RD
ALBERT RD
HIGHFIELD RD
ROMAN RD
ABBOTSBURY RD
HIGH PARK RD
SPRINGDALE RD
ANVIL CRES
LANCASTER DR
CLARENDON RD
UPTON WAY
CORFE WAY
CORFE LODGE RD
LAVENDER WAY
MAXWELL RD
BEACON RD
WEST WAY
SANDFORD WAY
PINESPRINGS DR
BROADSTONE WAY
OLD WAREHAM RD
BEACON HILL LA
MAYLYN RD
OLD SANDPIT LA
A350
BLANDFORD RD N
HILLSIDE GDNS 1
HILLSIDE MEWS 2
LONGMEADOW LA
MEADOWSWEET RD

117 85 118

59
88

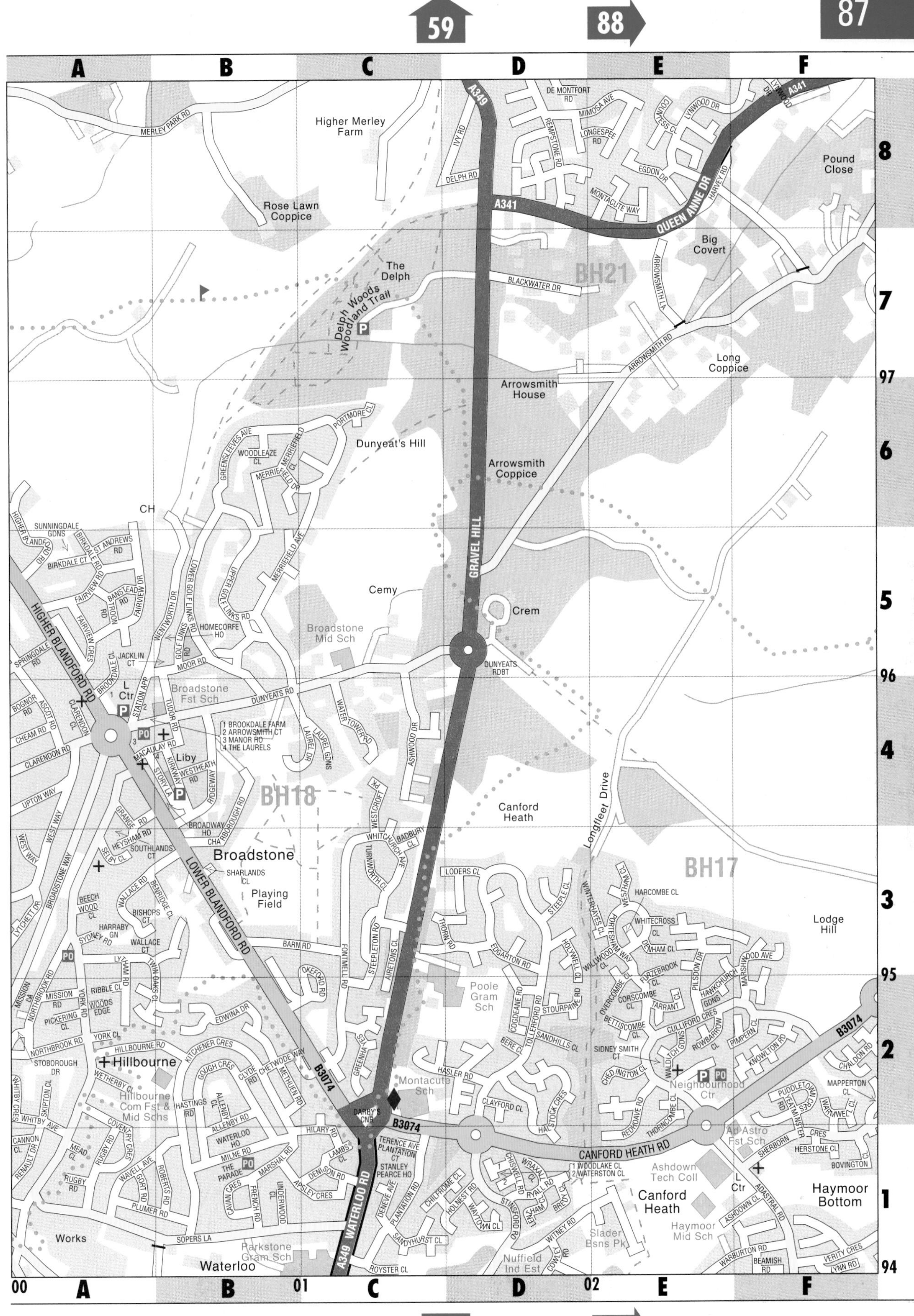
A
B
C
D
E
F
Higher Merley Farm
MERLEY PARK RD
Rose Lawn Coppice
The Delph
Delph Woods Woodland Trail
DE MONTFORT RD
MIMOSA AVE
LONGESPEE RD
REMPSTONE RD
DELPH RD
IVY RD
A349
A341
QUEEN ANNE DR
LYNWOOD DR
COUNTESS CL
EGDON DR
MONTACUTE WAY
HARVEY RD
Pound Close
Big Covert
BH21
BLACKWATER DR
ARROWSMITH LA
ARROWSMITH RD
Long Coppice
Arrowsmith House
Dunyeat's Hill
Arrowsmith Coppice
PORTMORE CL
GREENSLEEVES AVE
WOODLEAZE CL
MERRIEFIELD DR
MERRIEFIELD AVE
CH
SUNNINGDALE GDNS
BIRKDALE RD
BIRKDALE CT
ST ANDREWS RD
FAIRVIEW RD
FAIRVIEW DR
FAIRVIEW CRES
BANSTEAD RD
TROON RD
HIGHER BLANDFORD RD
GRAVEL HILL
Cemy
Crem
Broadstone Mid Sch
HOMECORFE HO
WENTWORTH DR
LOWER GOLF LINKS RD
UPPER GOLF LINKS RD
GOLF LINKS RD
MOOR RD
JACKLIN CT
SPRINGDALE RD
BROOKDALE CL
L Ctr
STATION APP
Broadstone Fst Sch
DUNYEATS RD
DUNYEATS RDBT
WATER TOWER RD
ASHWOOD DR
LAUREL DR
LAUREL GDNS
TUDOR RD
1 BROOKDALE FARM
2 ARROWSMITH CT
3 MANOR HO
4 THE LAURELS
BOGNOR RD
ASCOT RD
CLARENDON RD
CHEAM RD
MACAULAY RD
Liby
KIRKWAY
WESTHEATH RD
RIDGEWAY
STORY LA
UPTON WAY
WEST WAY
BH18
BROADWAY HO
ROXBOROUGH RD
GRANGE RD
HEYSHAM RD
SELBY CL
SOUTHLANDS CT
Broadstone
SHARLANDS CL
Playing Field
LOWER BLANDFORD RD
WESTCROFT PK
WHITCHURCH AVE
BADBURY CL
TURNWORTH CL
Canford Heath
Longfleet Drive
BH17
BROADSTONE WAY
LYTCHETT DR
BEECH WOOD CL
WALLACE RD
BENBRIDGE CL
BISHOPS CT
HARRABY GN
SYDNEY RD
WALLACE CT
LYTHAM RD
TWIN OAKS CL
BARN RD
FONTMELL RD
STEEPLETON RD
AIRETONS CL
LODERS CL
THORN RD
EDGARTON RD
STEEPLE CL
HOLYWELL CL
WINTERHAYES CL
WILLWOOD CL
PORTESHAM WAY
WESTHAM CL
HARCOMBE CL
WHITECROSS CL
DEVHAM CL
FURZEBROOK CL
PILSDON DR
HAWKCHURCH GDNS
MARSHWOOD AVE
Lodge Hill
MISSION RD
NORTHBROOK RD
RIBBLE CL
YORK RD
WOODS EDGE
PICKERING CL
OKEFORD RD
Poole Gram Sch
COGDEANE RD
TOLLERFORD RD
STOURPAINE RD
OVERCOMBE CL
CORSCOMBE CL
TARRANT CL
BETTISCOMBE CL
CULLIFORD CRES
ROWBARROW CL
PIMPERN CL
YORK CL
NORTHBROOK RD
HILLBOURNE RD
EDWINA DR
KITCHENER CRES
STOBOROUGH DR
Hillbourne
WETHERBY CL
GOUGH CRES
CLYDE RD
CHETWODE WAY
METHUEN RD
B3074
GREENHAYES
BERE CL
SANDHILLS CL
SIDNEY SMITH CT
WALDITCH GDNS
KNOWLTON RD
CHALDON RD
Montacute Sch
HASLER RD
CHEDINGTON CL
Neighbourhood Ctr
MAPPERTON CL
WARMWELL CL
PUDDLETOWN CRES
WHITBY CRES
SKIPTON CL
WHITBY AVE
Hillbourne Com Fst & Mid Schs
HASTINGS RD
ALLENBY CL
ALLENBY RD
COVENTRY CRES
WATERLOO HO
HILARY RD
DARBY'S CNR
CLAYFORD CL
HALSTOCK CRES
REDHAVE RD
THORNCOMBE CL
Ashdown Astro
Fst Sch
YEATMINSTER RD
HERSTONE CL
CRES
CANFORD HEATH RD
SHERBORN CRES
BOVINGTON CL
CANNON CL
RENAULT DR
MEAD CL
RUGBY RD
WAVELL AVE
GORT RD
ROBERTS RD
MILNE RD
THE PARADE
MARSHAL RD
LAMBS CL
TERENCE AVE
PLANTATION CT
STANLEY PEARCE HO
CHILTROME CL
HOLNEST RD
CHISWELL RD
WRAXALL CL
RYALL RD
1 WOODLAKE CL
2 WATERSTON CL
Ashdown Tech Coll
L Ctr
ADASTRAL RD
Haymoor Bottom
RUGBY RD
PLUMER RD
CAVAN CRES
FRENCH RD
UNDERWOOD
DENISON RD
APSLEY CRES
WATERLOO RD
DENEVE AVE
PLANTATION RD
WAYTOWN CL
STINSFORD RD
LEIGHAM CL
BRIDY CL
WITNEY RD
Canford Heath
Haymoor Mid Sch
ASHDOWN CL
Works
SOPERS LA
Parkstone Gram Sch
SANDYHURST CL
Slader Bsns Pk
Waterloo
A349
ROYSTER CL
Nuffield Ind Est
COWLEY RD
WARBURTON RD
BEAMISH RD
VERITY CRES
LYNN RD
00
01
02
94
95
96
97
1
2
3
4
5
6
7
8

119
88

87
60

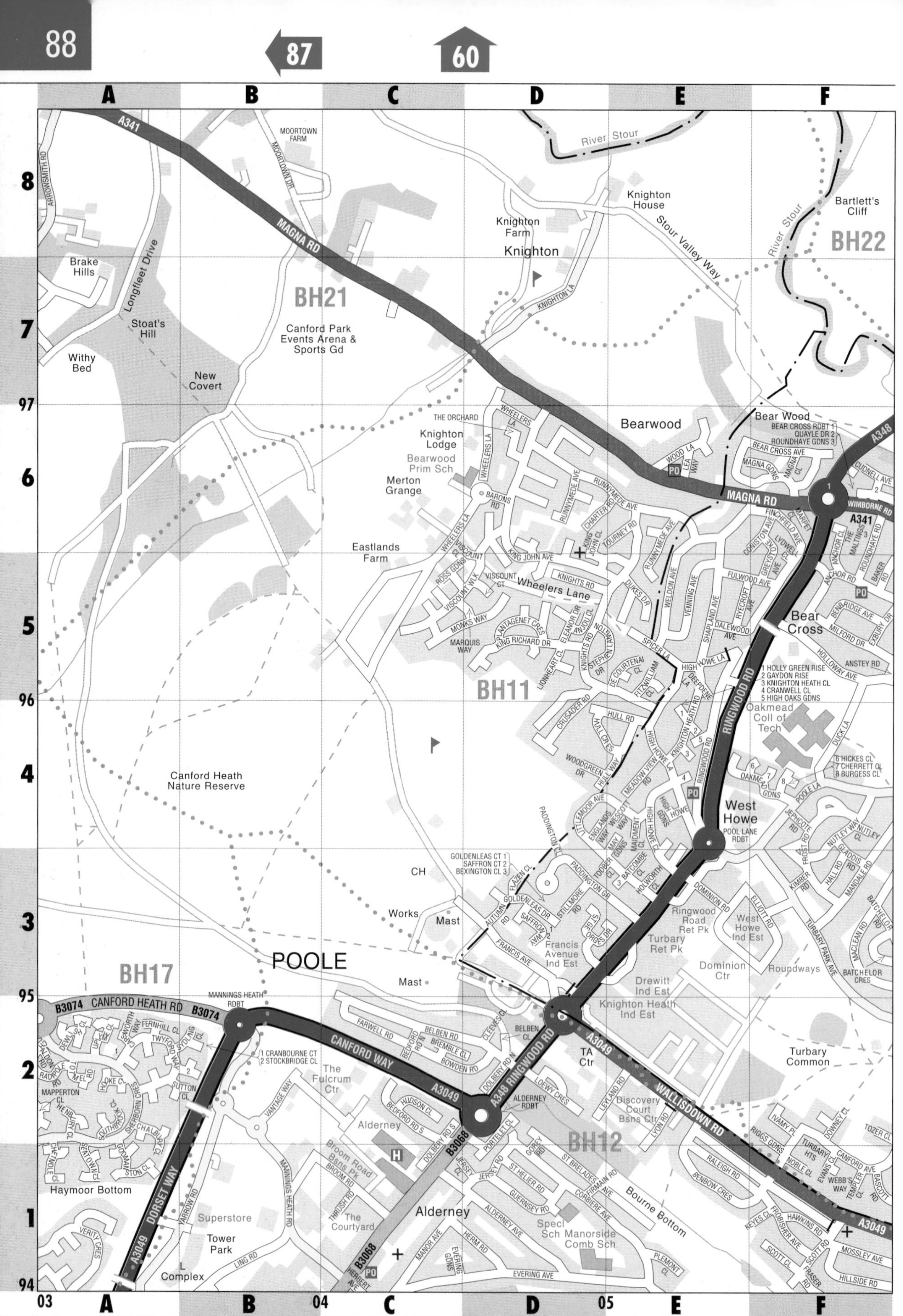
A
B
C
D
E
F
8
7
97
6
5
96
4
3
95
2
1
94
03
04
05
A341
MAGNA RD
River Stour
Knighton House
Knighton Farm
Knighton
Stour Valley Way
Bartlett's Cliff
BH22
Brake Hills
Longfleet Drive
Stoat's Hill
Withy Bed
New Covert
BH21
Canford Park Events Arena & Sports Gd
KNIGHTON LA
MOORTOWN FARM
MOORTOWN DR
ARROWSMITH RD
Bearwood
Bear Wood
Knighton Lodge
Bearwood Prim Sch
Merton Grange
Eastlands Farm
Wheelers Lane
BH11
Bear Cross
RINGWOOD RD
Oakmead Coll of Tech
West Howe
POOL LANE RDBT
Canford Heath Nature Reserve
CH
Works
Mast
POOLE
BH17
Francis Avenue Ind Est
Ringwood Road Ret Pk
Turbary Ret Pk
West Howe Ind Est
Dominion Ctr
Roundways
Drewitt Ind Est
Knighton Heath Ind Est
B3074 CANFORD HEATH RD
MANNINGS HEATH RDBT
CANFORD WAY
A3049
The Fulcrum Ctr
TA Ctr
WALLISDOWN RD
Turbary Common
Discovery Court Bsns Ctr
A348 RINGWOOD RD
ALDERNEY RDBT
Alderney
BH12
Broom Road Bsns Pk
The Courtyard
Haymoor Bottom
DORSET WAY
Superstore
Tower Park
L Complex
Alderney
B3068
Specl Sch
Manorside Comb Sch
Bourne Bottom
WIMBORNE RD
A348

87
120

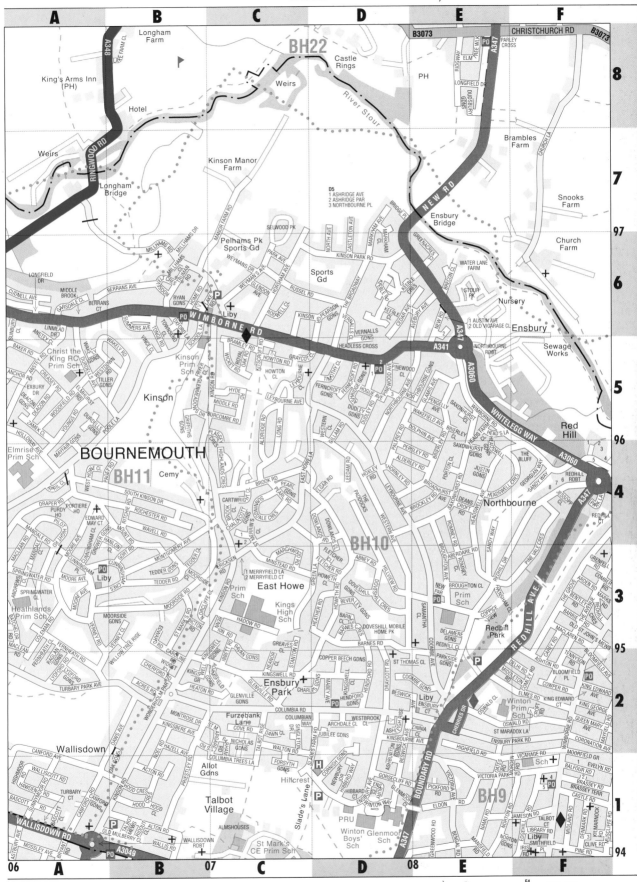

F1
1 EVELYN MEWS
2 ST JOHN'S GDNS
3 NORWAY CL
4 VICTORIA PARK PL
5 LAMPTON GDNS

F4
1 REDHILL PARK HOMES
2 WHEATPLOT PARK HOMES
3 KINGFISHER PARK HOMES
4 RIVERSIDE
5 WIMBORNE HO
6 MAGNOLIA HO
7 WISTERIA HO
8 LABURNUM HO

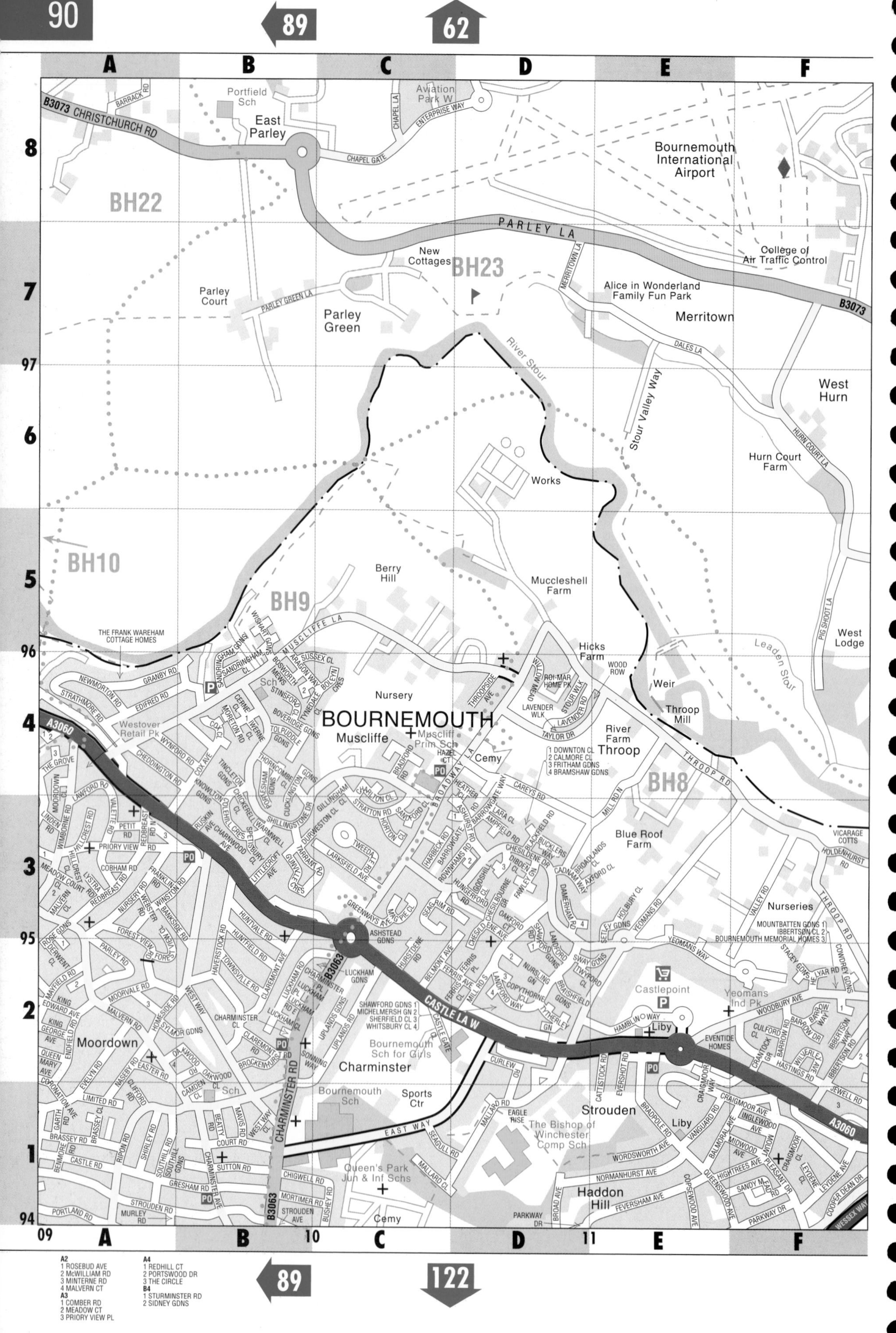

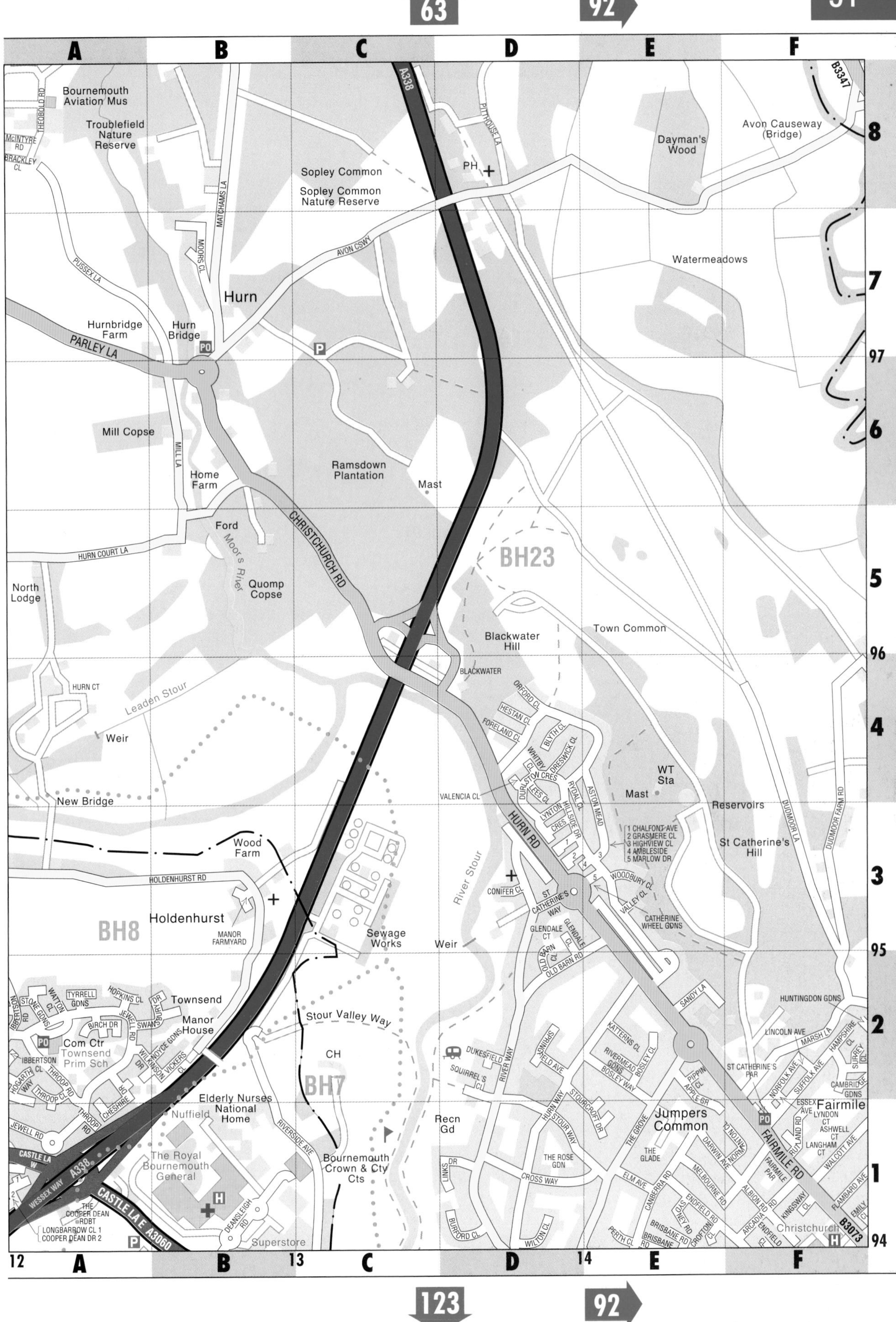
63
92
123
Bournemouth Aviation Mus
Troublefield Nature Reserve
Sopley Common
Sopley Common Nature Reserve
Dayman's Wood
Avon Causeway (Bridge)
Watermeadows
Hurn
Hurnbridge Farm
Hurn Bridge
PARLEY LA
Mill Copse
Home Farm
Ramsdown Plantation
Mast
Ford
Moors River
Quomp Copse
North Lodge
BH23
Blackwater Hill
Town Common
Leaden Stour
Weir
New Bridge
Wood Farm
HOLDENHURST RD
Holdenhurst
BH8
MANOR FARMYARD
Sewage Works
River Stour
WT Sta
Reservoirs
St Catherine's Hill
1 CHALFONT AVE
2 GRASMERE CL
3 HIGHVIEW CL
4 AMBLESIDE
5 MARLOW DR
HURN RD
CHRISTCHURCH RD
HURN COURT LA
AVON CSWY
Townsend
Manor House
Com Ctr
Townsend Prim Sch
Stour Valley Way
CH
BH7
Elderly Nurses National Home
Nuffield
The Royal Bournemouth General
Recn Gd
Bournemouth Crown & Cty Cts
Superstore
Jumpers Common
Fairmile
FAIRMILE RD
Christchurch
CASTLE LA E A3060
WESSEX WAY
THE COOPER DEAN RDBT
LONGBARROW CL 1
COOPER DEAN DR 2
A338
B3347
B3073
A B C D E F
8 7 97 6 5 96 4 3 95 2 1 94
12 13 14

91

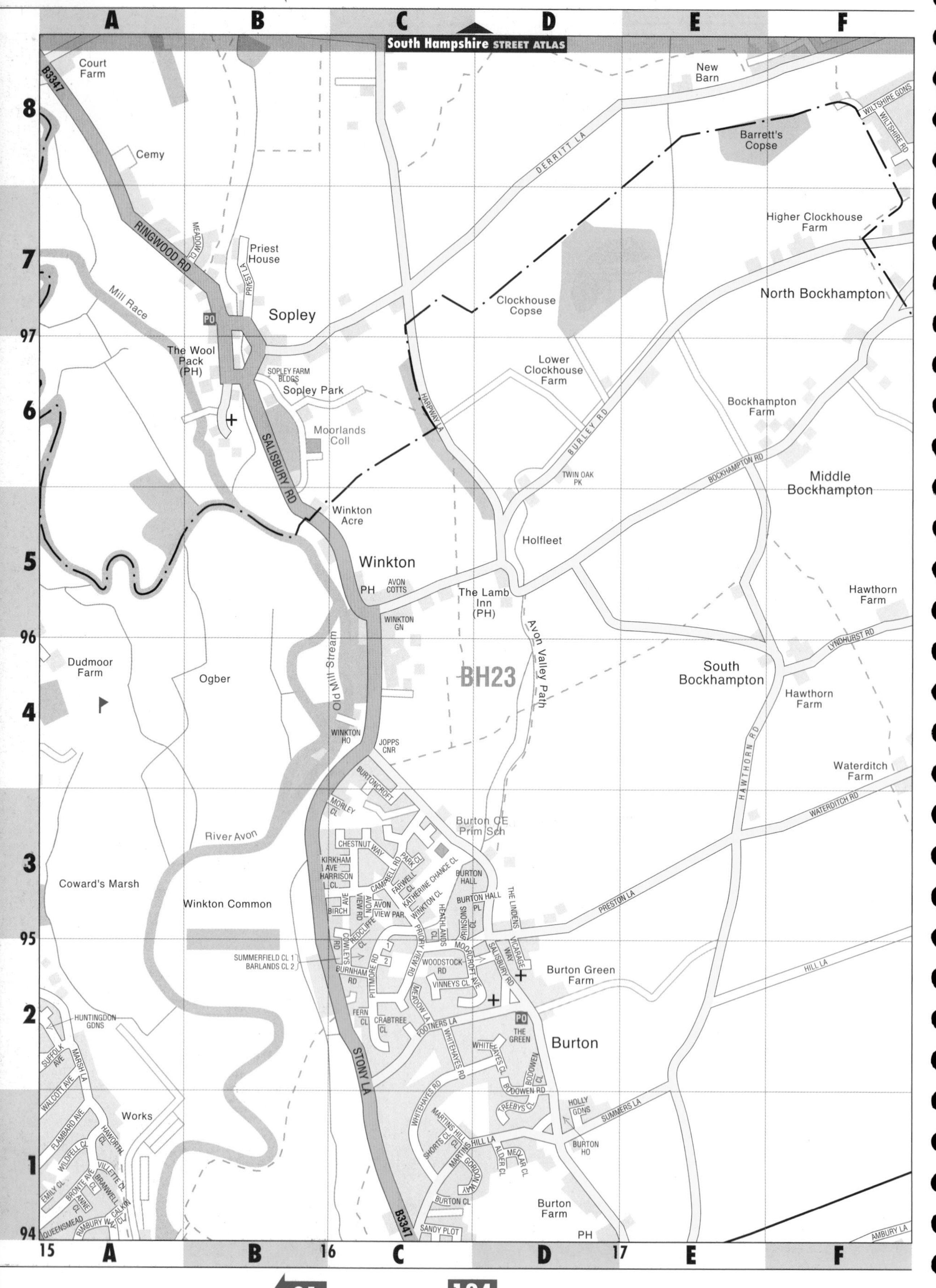

South Hampshire STREET ATLAS
A
B
C
D
E
F
8
7
97
6
5
96
4
3
95
2
1
94
15
16
17
Court Farm
Cemy
New Barn
Barrett's Copse
WILTSHIRE GDNS
WILTSHIRE RD
DERRITT LA
RINGWOOD RD
B3347
MEADOW CL
PRIEST LA
Priest House
Sopley
Mill Race
Higher Clockhouse Farm
North Bockhampton
Clockhouse Copse
The Wool Pack (PH)
SOPLEY FARM BLDGS
Sopley Park
Lower Clockhouse Farm
Moorlands Coll
HARPWAY LA
BURLEY RD
Bockhampton Farm
SALISBURY RD
TWIN OAK PK
BOCKHAMPTON RD
Middle Bockhampton
Winkton Acre
Holfleet
Winkton
PH
AVON COTTS
The Lamb Inn (PH)
Hawthorn Farm
WINKTON GN
Avon Valley Path
Dudmoor Farm
Old Mill Stream
BH23
Ogber
South Bockhampton
LYNDHURST RD
Hawthorn Farm
WINKTON HO
JOPPS CNR
HAWTHORN RD
Waterditch Farm
BURTONCROFT
MORLEY CL
WATERDITCH RD
River Avon
Burton CE Prim Sch
CHESTNUT WAY
KIRKHAM AVE
HARRISON CL
CAMPBELL RD
PARK CL
FARWELL CL
KATHERINE CHANCE CL
BURTON HALL
Coward's Marsh
Winkton Common
BIRCH AVE
AVON VIEW RD
AVON VIEW PAR
REDCLIFFE CL
WINKTON CL
HEATHLANDS CL
SIMMONS CL
BURTON HALL PL
THE LINDENS
PRESTON LA
COWLEYS RD
PRIORY VIEW RD
MOORCROFT AVE
SALISBURY RD
VICARAGE WAY
SUMMERFIELD CL 1
BARLANDS CL 2
BURNHAM RD
PITTMORE RD
WOODSTOCK RD
VINNEYS CL
Burton Green Farm
HILL LA
HUNTINGDON GDNS
FERN CL
CRABTREE CL
MEADOW LA
FOOTNERS LA
PO
THE GREEN
Burton
WHITEHAYES CL
WHITEHAYES RD
BODOWEN CL
BODOWEN RD
SUFFOLK AVE
MARSH LA
WALCOTT AVE
STONY LA
Works
FLAMBARD AVE
HAWORTH CL
HOLLY GDNS
SUMMERS LA
FREEBYS CL
MARTINS HILL CL
SHORTS CL
MARTINS HILL LA
ALDER CL
MEDLAR CL
BURTON HO
WILDFELL CL
VILLETTE CL
BRONTE AVE
EMILY CL
ANNE CL
BRANWELL CL
CALKIN CL
GORDON WAY
BURTON CL
Burton Farm
QUEENSMEAD
RIMBURY WAY
SANDY PLOT
PH
AMBURY LA

91
124

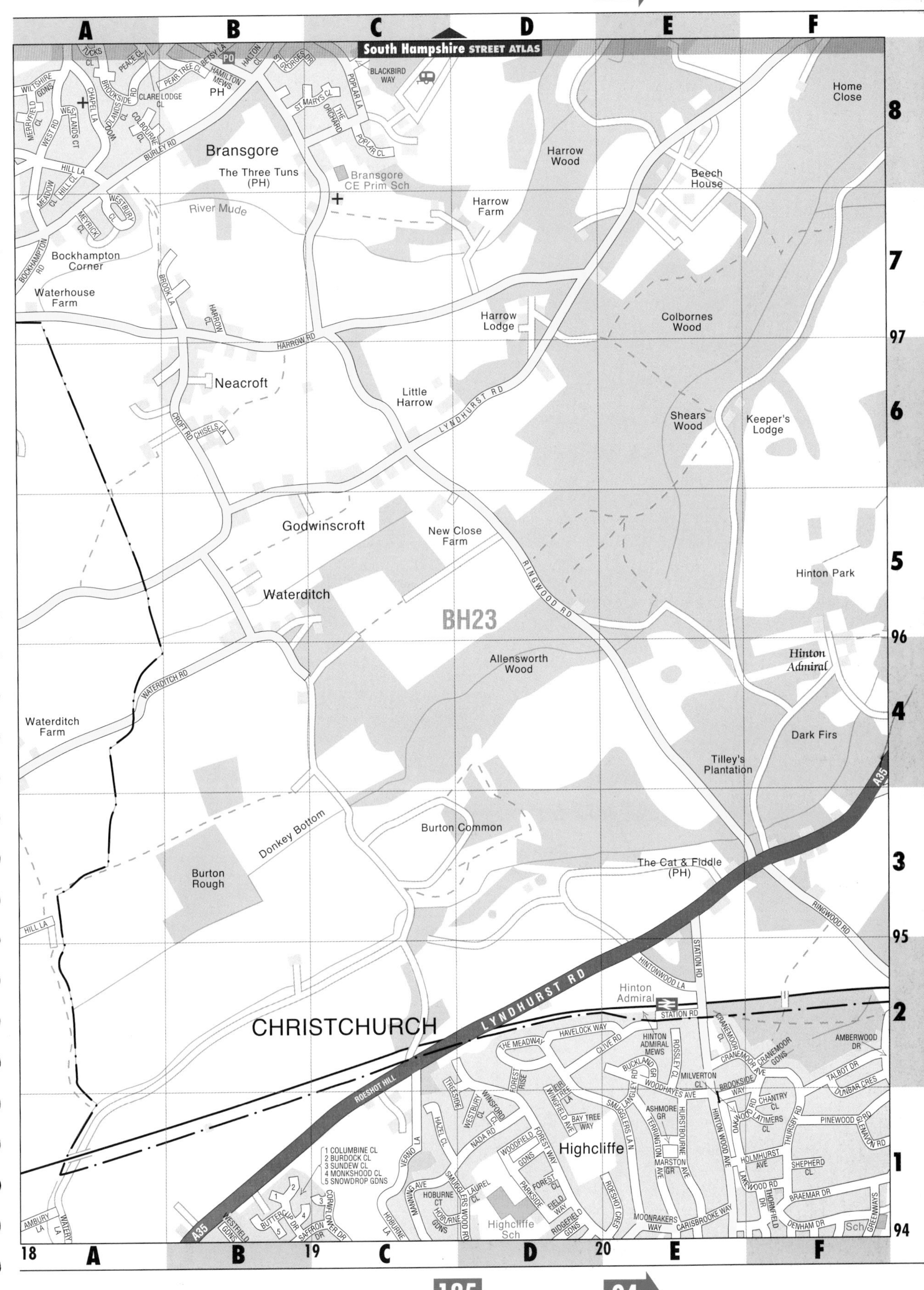

South Hampshire STREET ATLAS

94
B
C
D
F
8
7
97
6
5
96
4
3
95
2
1
94
18
19
20
Home Close
Bransgore
The Three Tuns (PH)
Bransgore CE Prim Sch
River Mude
Harrow Wood
Harrow Farm
Beech House
Bockhampton Corner
Waterhouse Farm
Harrow Lodge
Colbornes Wood
HARROW RD
Neacroft
Little Harrow
LYNDHURST RD
Shears Wood
Keeper's Lodge
Godwinscroft
New Close Farm
Waterditch
BH23
RINGWOOD RD
Hinton Park
Allensworth Wood
Hinton Admiral
WATERDITCH RD
Waterditch Farm
Dark Firs
Tilley's Plantation
A35
Burton Common
Donkey Bottom
Burton Rough
The Cat & Fiddle (PH)
HILL LA
STATION RD
HINTONWOOD LA
Hinton Admiral
CHRISTCHURCH
LYNDHURST RD
ROESHOT HILL
Highcliffe
Highcliffe Sch
1 COLUMBINE CL
2 BURDOCK CL
3 SUNDEW CL
4 MONKSHOOD CL
5 SNOWDROP GDNS
WESTFIELD GDNS
AMBURY LA
WATERY LA
Sch
125
94

93

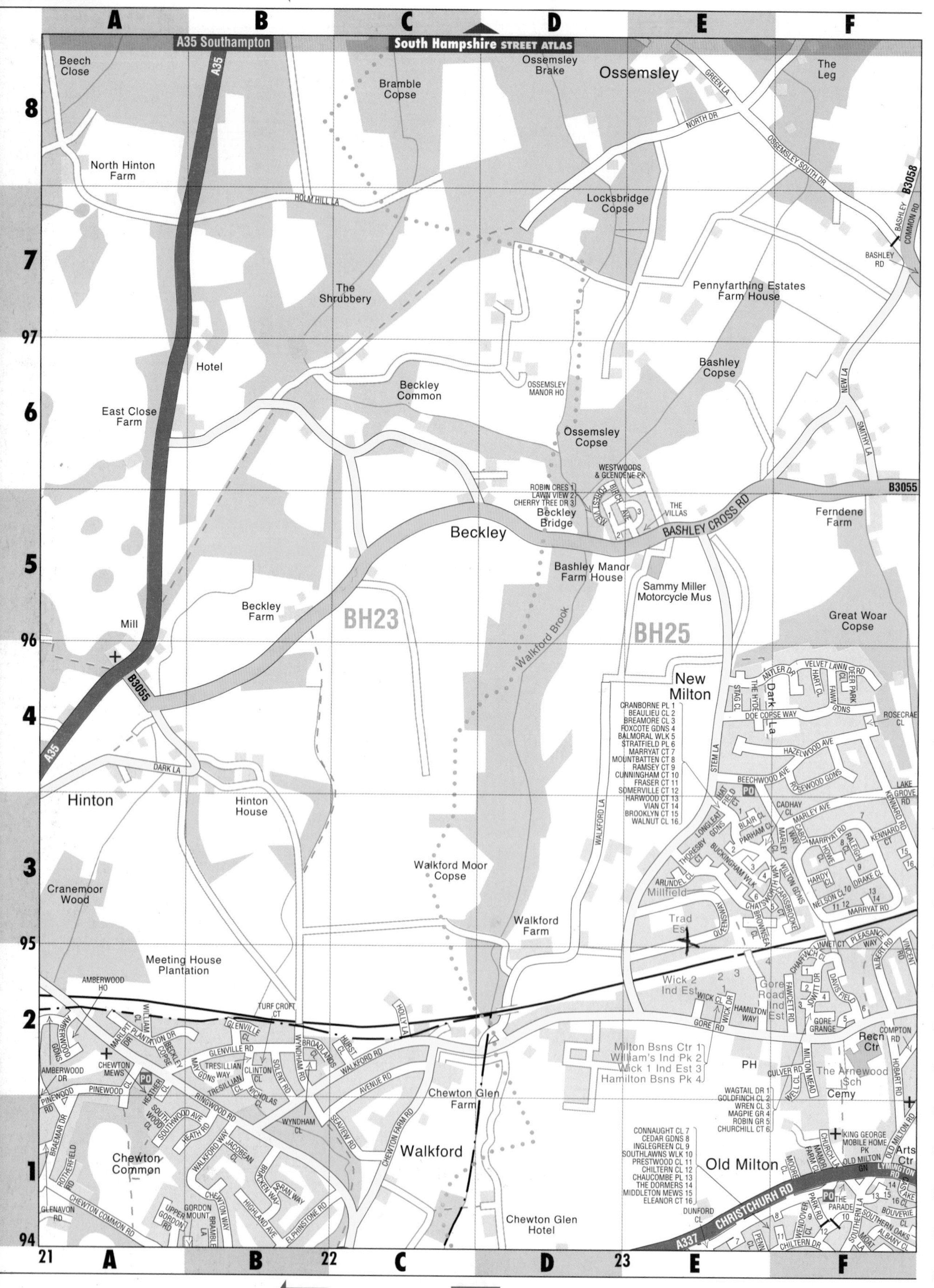
A35 Southampton
South Hampshire STREET ATLAS
Beech Close
Bramble Copse
Ossemsley Brake
Ossemsley
The Leg
North Hinton Farm
HOLM HILL LA
Locksbridge Copse
The Shrubbery
Pennyfarthing Estates Farm House
Hotel
Beckley Common
OSSEMSLEY MANOR HO
Bashley Copse
East Close Farm
Ossemsley Copse
Beckley Bridge
Beckley
BASHLEY CROSS RD
B3055
Ferndene Farm
Bashley Manor Farm House
Sammy Miller Motorcycle Mus
Beckley Farm
BH23
BH25
Great Woar Copse
Mill
Walkford Brook
New Milton
Hinton
DARK LA
Hinton House
Cranemoor Wood
Walkford Moor Copse
Walkford Farm
Meeting House Plantation
Millfield
Trad Est
Wick 2 Ind Est
Gore Road Ind Est
Milton Bsns Ctr 1
William's Ind Pk 2
Wick 1 Ind Est 3
Hamilton Bsns Pk 4
Chewton Glen Farm
Walkford
Chewton Common
Old Milton
Chewton Glen Hotel
The Arnewood Sch
Cemy
Recn Ctr
CHRISTCHURCH RD
A337
CRANBORNE PL 1
BEAULIEU CL 2
BREAMORE CL 3
FOXCOTE GDNS 4
BALMORAL WLK 5
STRATFIELD PL 6
MARRYAT CT 7
MOUNTBATTEN CT 8
RAMSEY CT 9
CUNNINGHAM CT 10
FRASER CT 11
SOMERVILLE CT 12
HARWOOD CT 13
VIAN CT 14
BROOKLYN CT 15
WALNUT CL 16
WAGTAIL DR 1
GOLDFINCH CL 2
WREN CL 3
MAGPIE GR 4
ROBIN GR 5
CHURCHILL CT 6
CONNAUGHT CL 7
CEDAR GDNS 8
INGLEGREEN CL 9
SOUTHLAWNS WLK 10
PRESTWOOD CL 11
CHILTERN CL 12
CHAUCOMBE PL 13
THE DORMERS 14
MIDDLETON MEWS 15
ELEANOR CT 16
ROBIN CRES 1
LAWN VIEW 2
CHERRY TREE DR 3
WESTWOODS & GLENDENE PK
THE VILLAS
KING GEORGE MOBILE HOME PK
A B C D E F
21 22 23
94 1 2 95 3 4 96 5 6 97 7 8

93
126

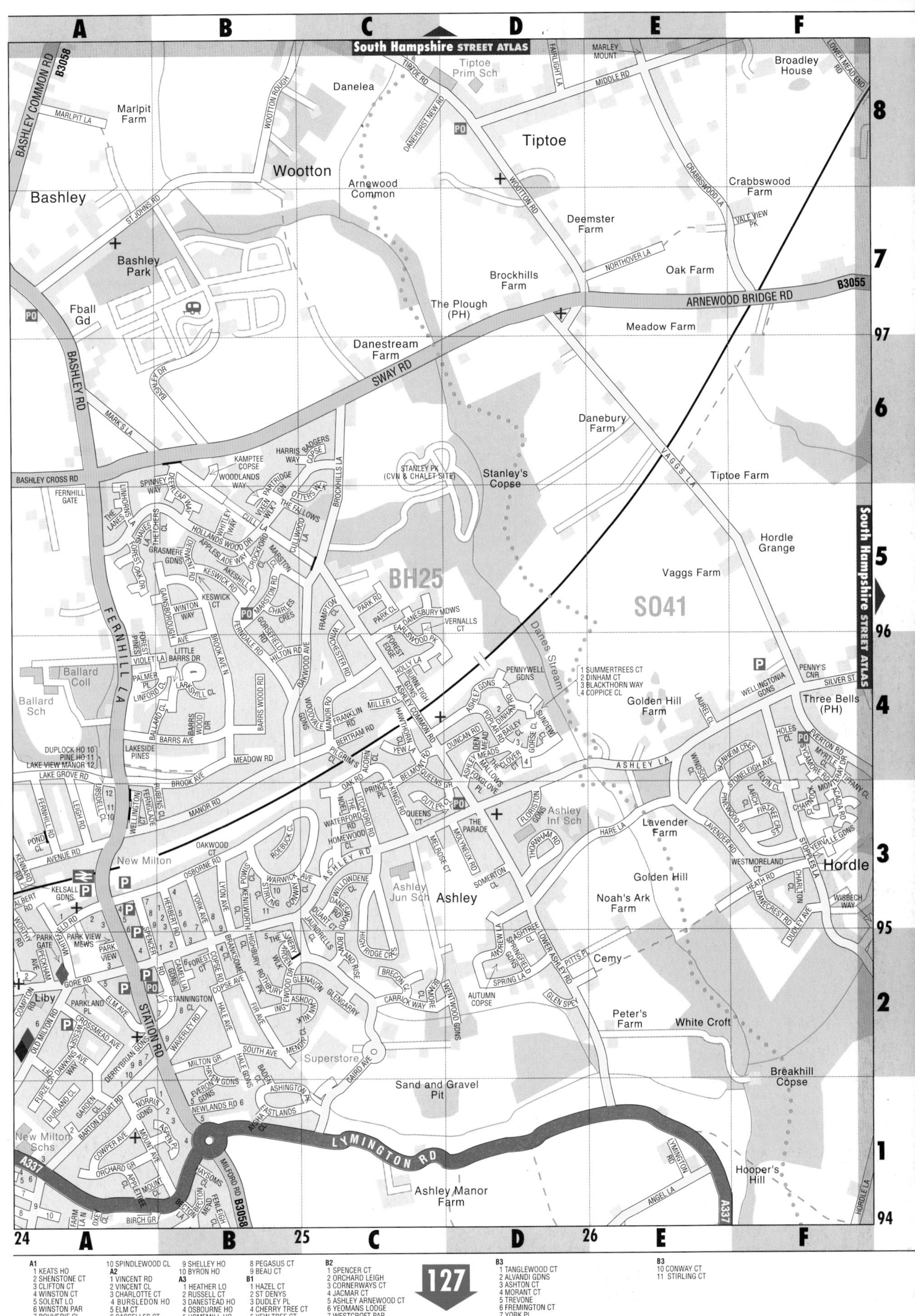

64

C5
1 BRIDGE ST
2 DOLPHIN CL
3 SHERBOURNE LA
4 POOLE'S CT
5 MONMOUTH ST

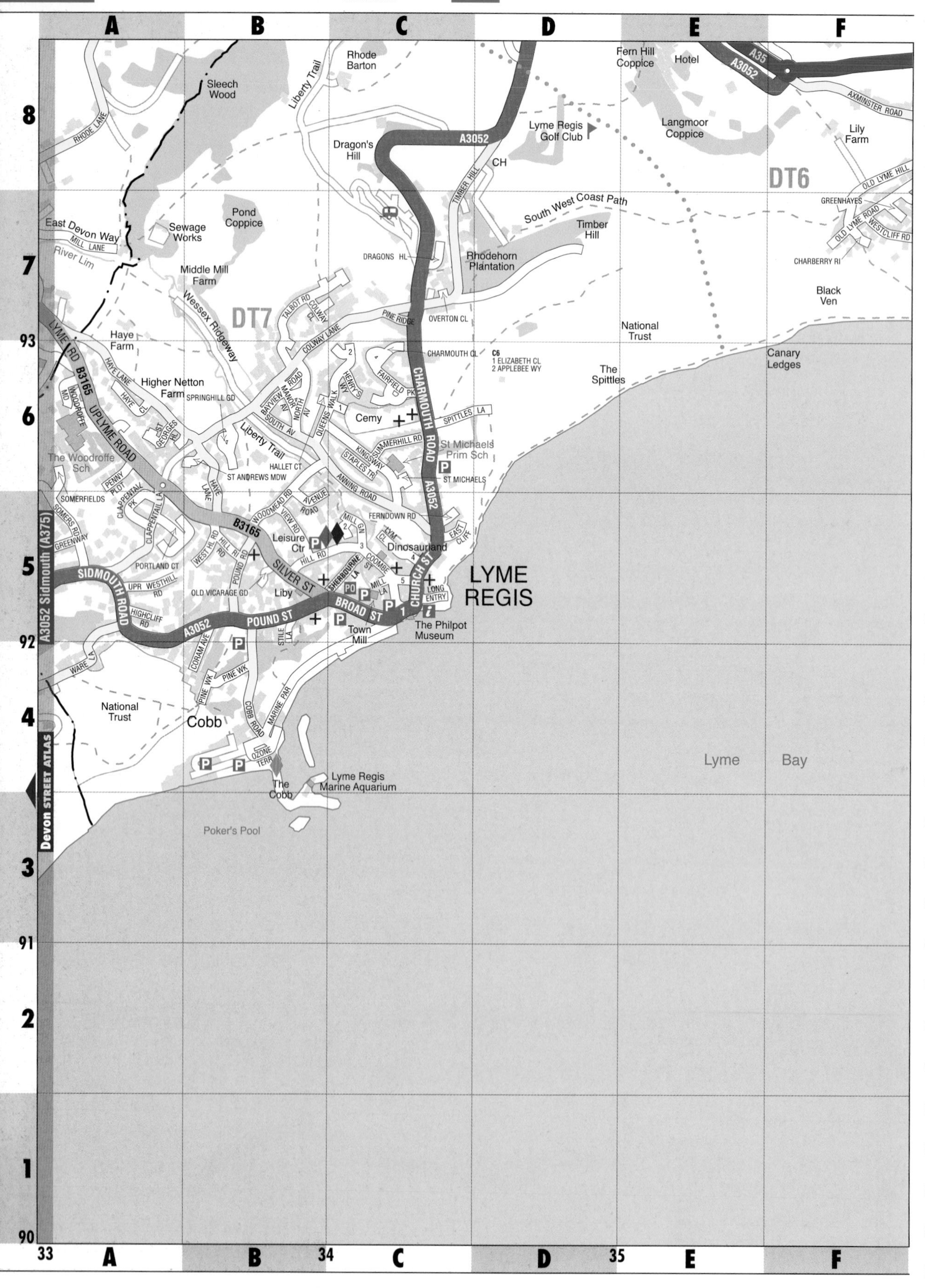

LYME REGIS

Lyme Bay

Devon STREET ATLAS

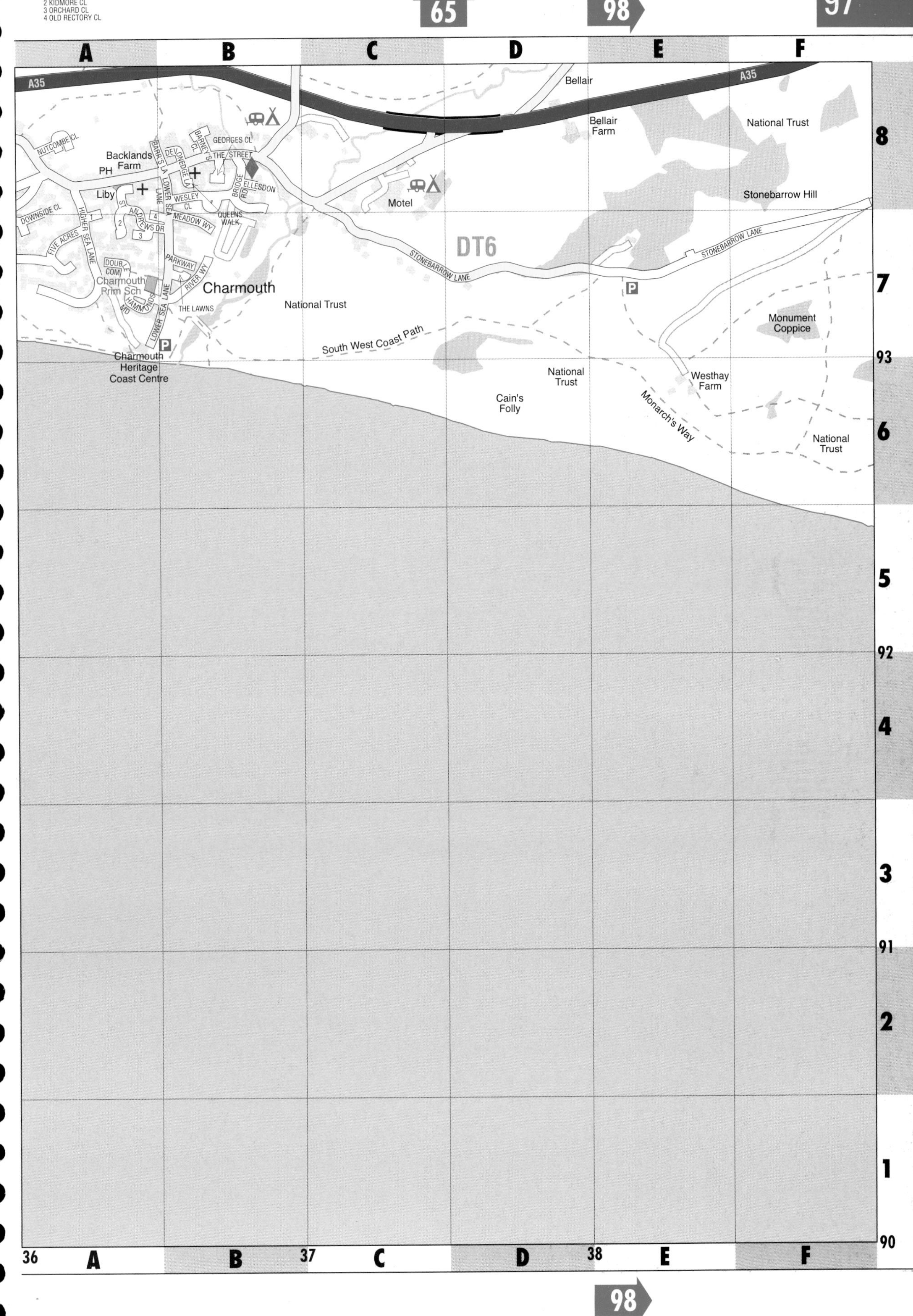

97
66

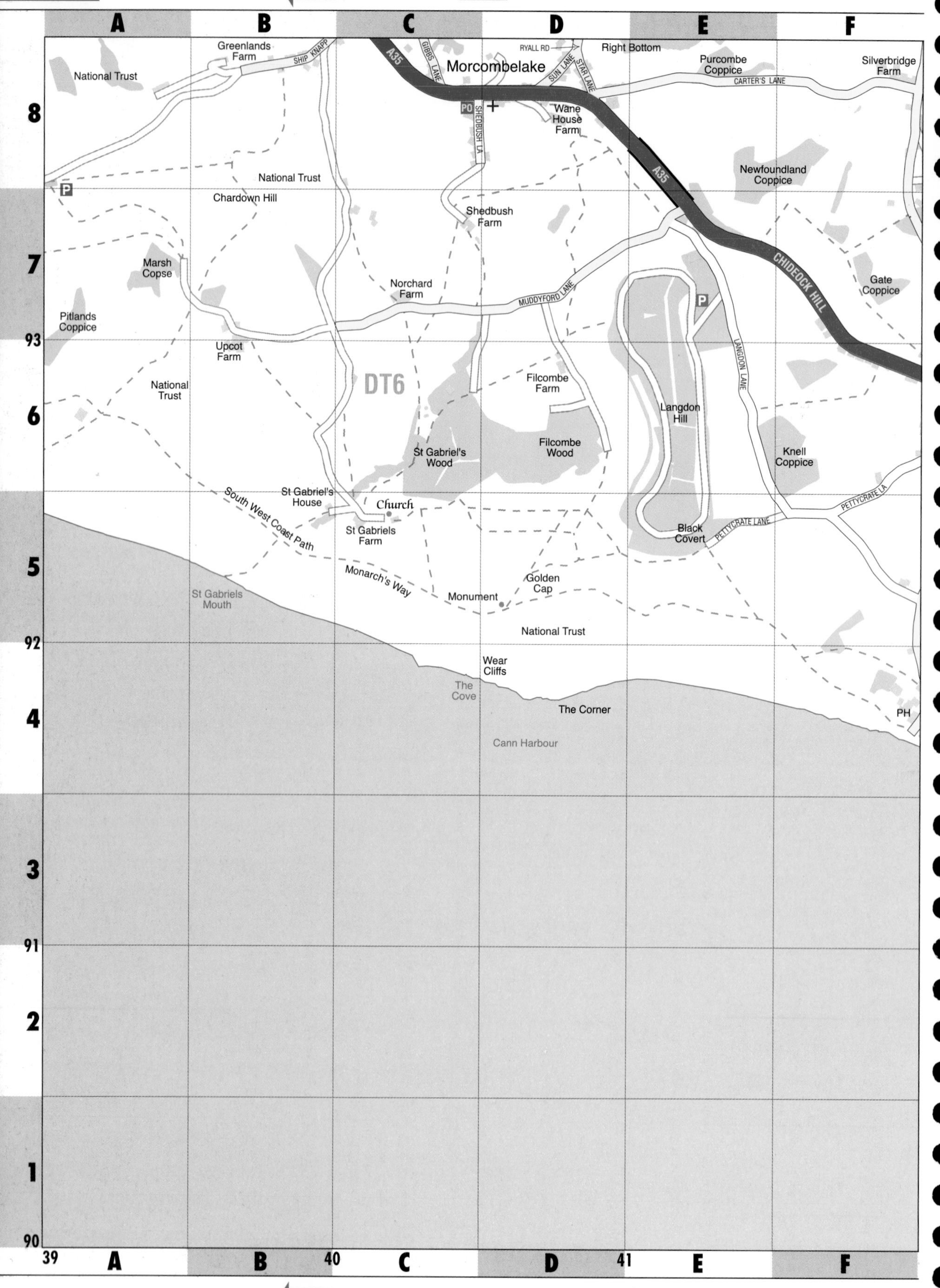
A
B
C
D
E
F
National Trust
Greenlands Farm
SHIP KNAPP
A35
GIBBS LANE
Morcombelake
RYALL RD
SUN LANE
STAR LANE
Right Bottom
Purcombe Coppice
CARTER'S LANE
Silverbridge Farm
PO
SHEDBUSH LA
Wane House Farm
8
National Trust
Chardown Hill
P
Newfoundland Coppice
Shedbush Farm
7
Marsh Copse
Norchard Farm
MUDDYFORD LANE
CHIDEOCK HILL
Gate Coppice
Pitlands Coppice
93
Upcot Farm
DT6
LANGDON LANE
National Trust
Filcombe Farm
Langdon Hill
6
St Gabriel's Wood
Filcombe Wood
Knell Coppice
St Gabriel's House
Church
South West Coast Path
St Gabriels Farm
Black Covert
PETTYCRATE LANE
PETTYCRATE LA
5
Monarch's Way
Golden Cap
St Gabriels Mouth
Monument
National Trust
92
Wear Cliffs
The Cove
4
The Corner
PH
Cann Harbour
3
91
2
1
90
39
40
41

97

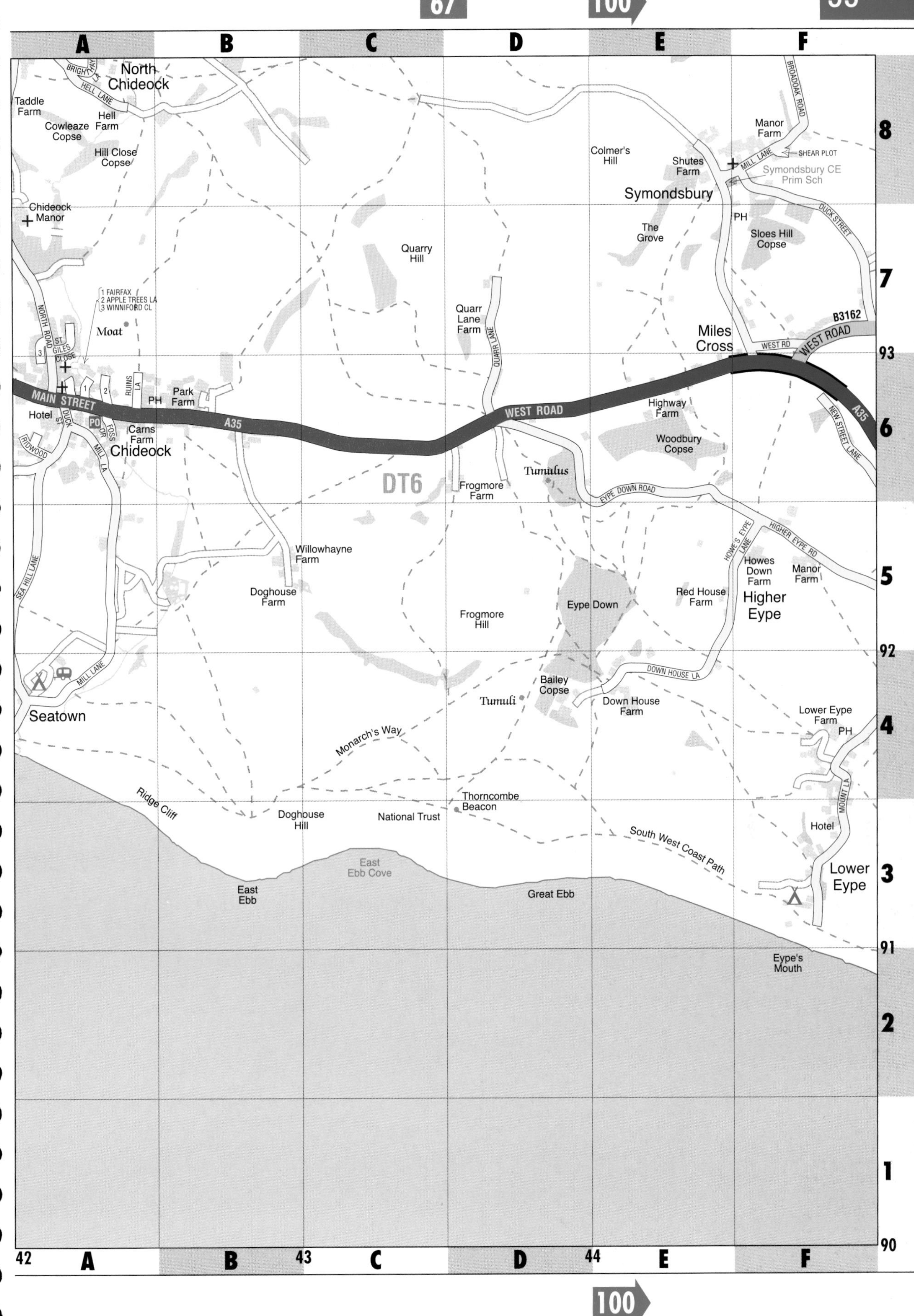

A B C D E F

North Chideock
Taddle Farm
Cowleaze Copse
Hell Farm
Hill Close Copse
Chideock Manor
1 FAIRFAX
2 APPLE TREES LA
3 WINNIFORD CL
Moat
HELL LANE
BRIGHT'S LANE
NORTH ROAD
ST GILES CLOSE
RUINS LA
Park Farm
PH
Quarry Hill
Colmer's Hill
Manor Farm
Shutes Farm
SHEAR PLOT
MILL LANE
BROADOAK ROAD
Symondsbury
Symondsbury CE Prim Sch
DUCK STREET
The Grove
PH
Sloes Hill Copse
Quarr Lane Farm
B3162
Miles Cross
WEST RD
WEST ROAD
93
MAIN STREET
Hotel
PO
Carns Farm
Chideock
A35
WEST ROAD
Highway Farm
A35
NEW STREET LANE
6
DUCK ST
FOSS
MILL LA
RIDWOOD
DT6
Frogmore Farm
Tumulus
Woodbury Copse
EYPE DOWN ROAD
QUARR LANE
Willowhayne Farm
HOWES EYPE LANE
HIGHER EYPE RD
Howes Down Farm
Manor Farm
Red House Farm
Higher Eype
5
Doghouse Farm
Frogmore Hill
Eype Down
92
SEA HILL LANE
MILL LANE
Tumuli
Bailey Copse
DOWN HOUSE LA
Down House Farm
Lower Eype Farm
PH
4
Seatown
Monarch's Way
Thorncombe Beacon
National Trust
South West Coast Path
Hotel
MOUNT LA
Lower Eype
3
Ridge Cliff
Doghouse Hill
East Ebb Cove
East Ebb
Great Ebb
Eype's Mouth
91

2

1

90

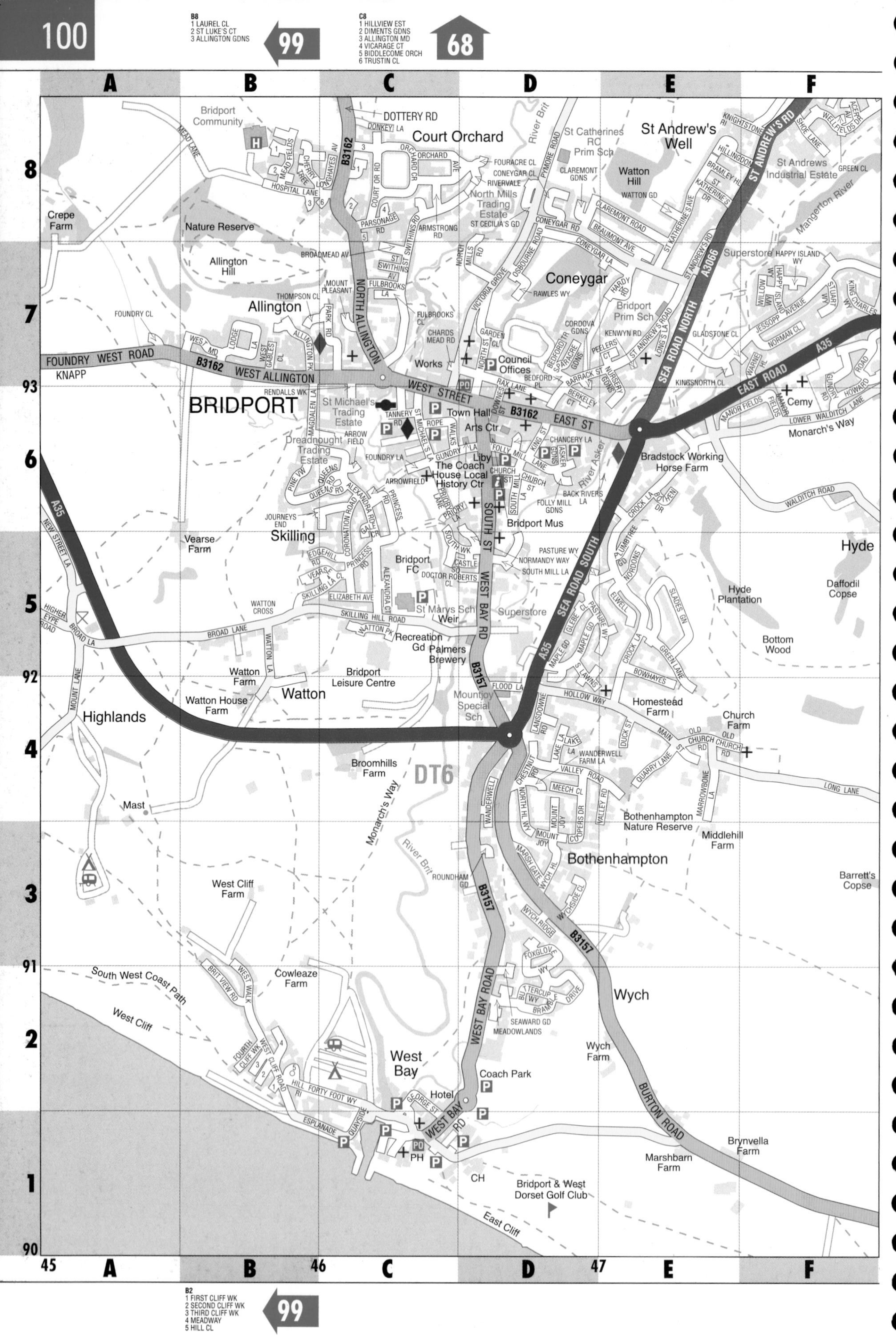

69
102

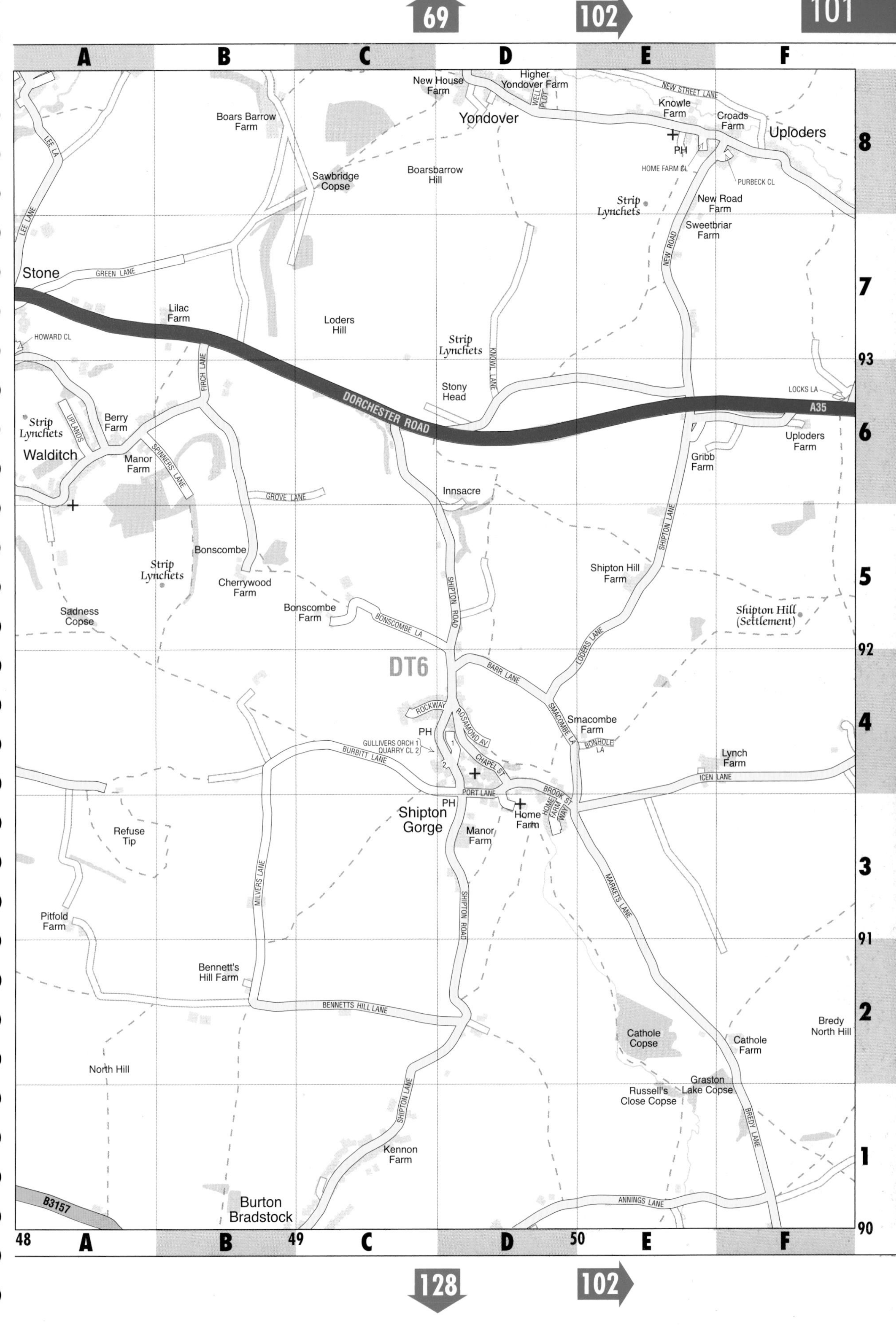
A
B
C
D
E
F
New House Farm
Higher Yondover Farm
WELL PLOT
NEW STREET LANE
Yondover
Boars Barrow Farm
Knowle Farm
Croads Farm
Uploders
PH
HOME FARM CL
PURBECK CL
LEE LA
Sawbridge Copse
Boarsbarrow Hill
Strip Lynchets
New Road Farm
Sweetbriar Farm
LEE LANE
NEW ROAD
Stone
GREEN LANE
Lilac Farm
Loders Hill
HOWARD CL
Strip Lynchets
KNOWL LANE
FIRCH LANE
Stony Head
LOCKS LA
A35
DORCHESTER ROAD
Strip Lynchets
UPLANDS
Berry Farm
Uploders Farm
Walditch
Manor Farm
SPINNERS LANE
Gribb Farm
Innsacre
GROVE LANE
SHIPTON LANE
Bonscombe
Strip Lynchets
Cherrywood Farm
Shipton Hill Farm
Sadness Copse
Bonscombe Farm
BONSCOMBE LA
SHIPTON ROAD
Shipton Hill (Settlement)
LODERS LANE
DT6
BARR LANE
ROCKWAY
ROSAMOND AV
SMACOMBE LA
Smacombe Farm
PH
GULLIVERS ORCH 1
QUARRY CL 2
BURBITT LANE
BONHOLE LA
Lynch Farm
CHAPEL ST
ICEN LANE
PORT LANE
BROOK ST
PH
HOME FARM WAY
Shipton Gorge
Home Farm
Manor Farm
Refuse Tip
MILVERS LANE
SHIPTON ROAD
MARKETS LANE
Pitfold Farm
Bennett's Hill Farm
BENNETTS HILL LANE
Cathole Copse
Cathole Farm
Bredy North Hill
North Hill
Graston Lake Copse
Russell's Close Copse
SHIPTON LANE
BREDY LANE
Kennon Farm
B3157
ANNINGS LANE
Burton Bradstock
8
7
93
6
5
92
4
3
91
2
1
90
48
49
50

128
102

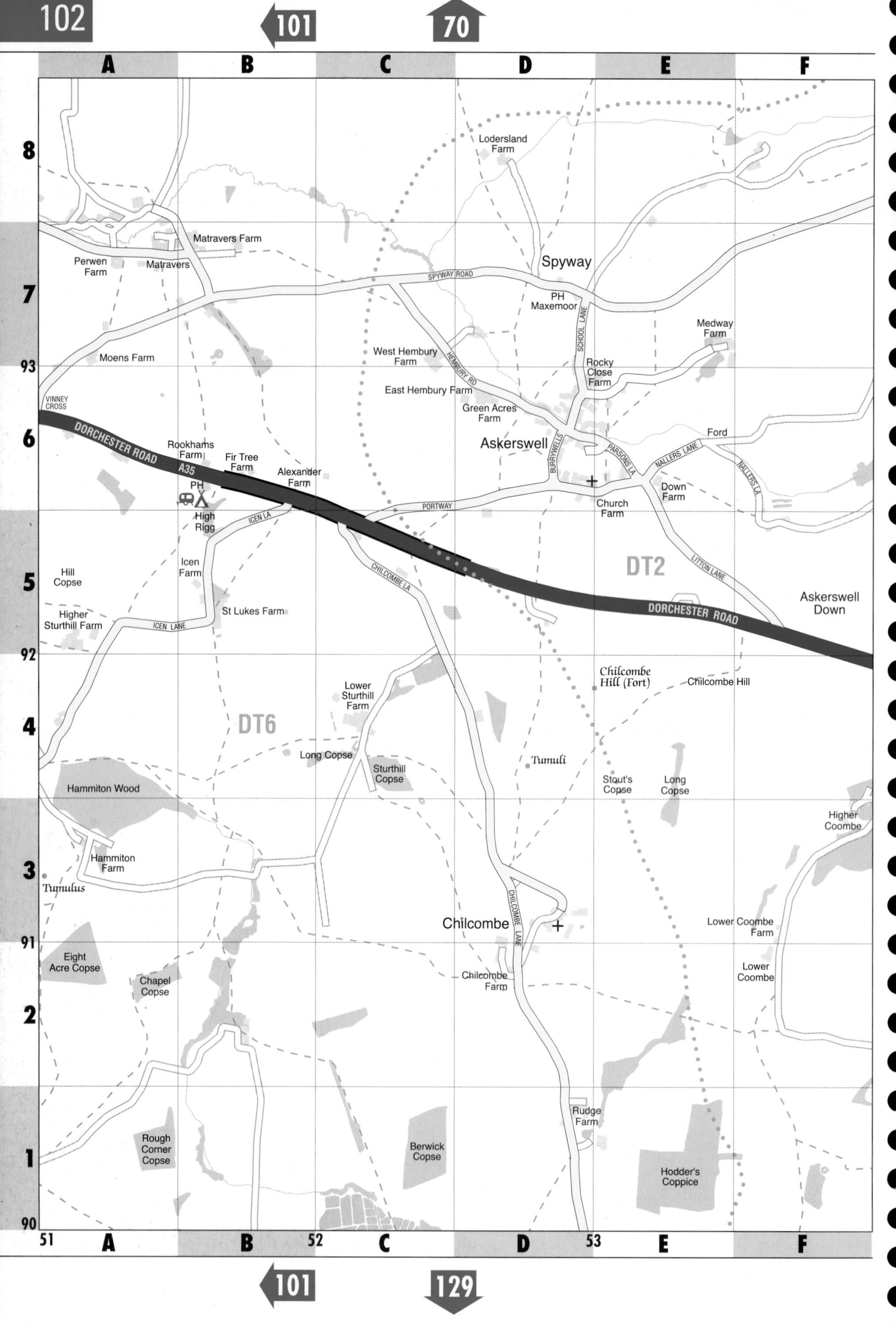

101
70

A B C D E F

8

Lodersland
Farm

Spyway

Matravers Farm

7 Perwen
Farm   Matravers

SPYWAY ROAD

PH
Maxemoor

School Lane

93 Moens Farm

West Hembury
Farm

Medway
Farm

VINNEY
CROSS

East Hembury Farm

Rocky
Close
Farm

DORCHESTER ROAD

Green Acres
Farm

6 A35 Rookhams
Farm   Fir Tree
Farm   Alexander
Farm

Askerswell

Barrwells

Ford

Down
Farm

Nallers Lane

Nallers La

PH

ICEN LA

PORTWAY

Church
Farm

Parsons La

DT2

High
Rigg

Litton Lane

5 Hill
Copse

Icen
Farm

CHILCOMBE LA

DORCHESTER ROAD

Askerswell
Down

Higher
Sturthill Farm

ICEN LANE

St Lukes Farm

92

Lower
Sturthill
Farm

Chilcombe
Hill (Fort)

Chilcombe Hill

4 DT6

Long Copse

Sturthill
Copse

Tumuli

Stout's
Copse

Long
Copse

Hammiton Wood

Higher
Coombe

3 Hammiton
Farm

Chilcombe
Chilcombe
Lane

Lower Coombe
Farm

Tumulus

91 Eight
Acre Copse

Chapel
Copse

Chilcombe
Farm

Lower
Coombe

2

Rudge
Farm

1 Rough
Corner
Copse

Berwick
Copse

Hodder's
Coppice

90

51 A 52 B C 52 D 53 E F

101
129

71
104

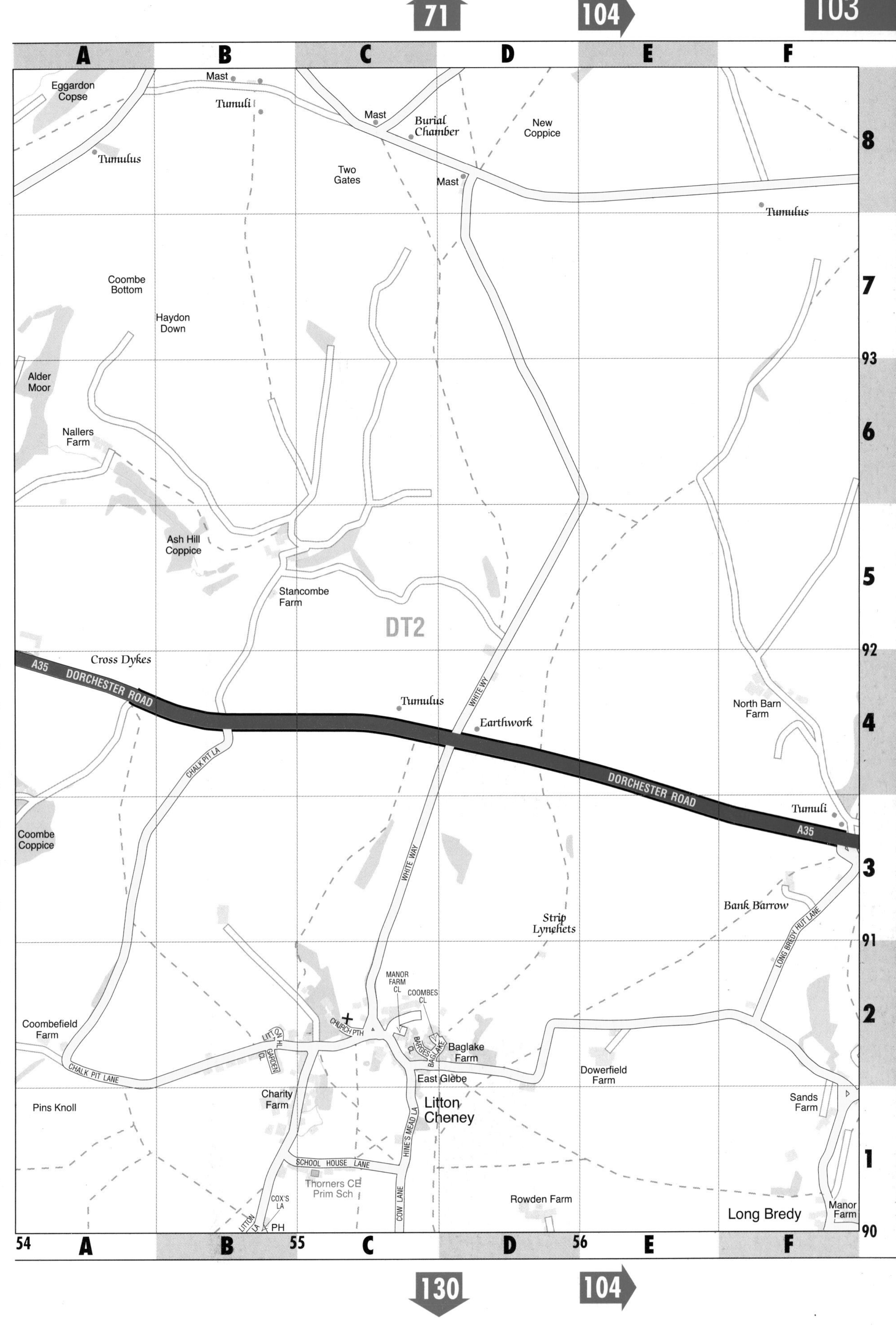
A
B
C
D
E
F
Eggardon Coppice
Mast
Tumuli
Mast
Burial Chamber
New Coppice
Tumulus
Two Gates
Mast
Tumulus
Coombe Bottom
Haydon Down
Alder Moor
Nallers Farm
Ash Hill Coppice
Stancombe Farm
DT2
Cross Dykes
A35
DORCHESTER ROAD
Tumulus
WHITE WY
Earthwork
North Barn Farm
CHALK PIT LA
DORCHESTER ROAD
Tumuli
A35
Coombe Coppice
WHITE WAY
Bank Barrow
Strip Lynchets
LONG BREDY HUT LANE
MANOR FARM CL
COOMBES CL
Coombefield Farm
CHURCH PTH
LITTON HL
GARDEN CL
BARGES CL
BAGLAKE
Baglake Farm
East Glebe
Dowerfield Farm
CHALK PIT LANE
Charity Farm
Pins Knoll
Litton Cheney
HINE'S MEAD LA
Sands Farm
SCHOOL HOUSE LANE
Thorners CE Prim Sch
COW LANE
COX'S LA
Rowden Farm
Long Bredy
Manor Farm
LITTON LA
PH
8
7
93
6
5
92
4
3
91
2
1
90
54
55
56

130
104

103
72

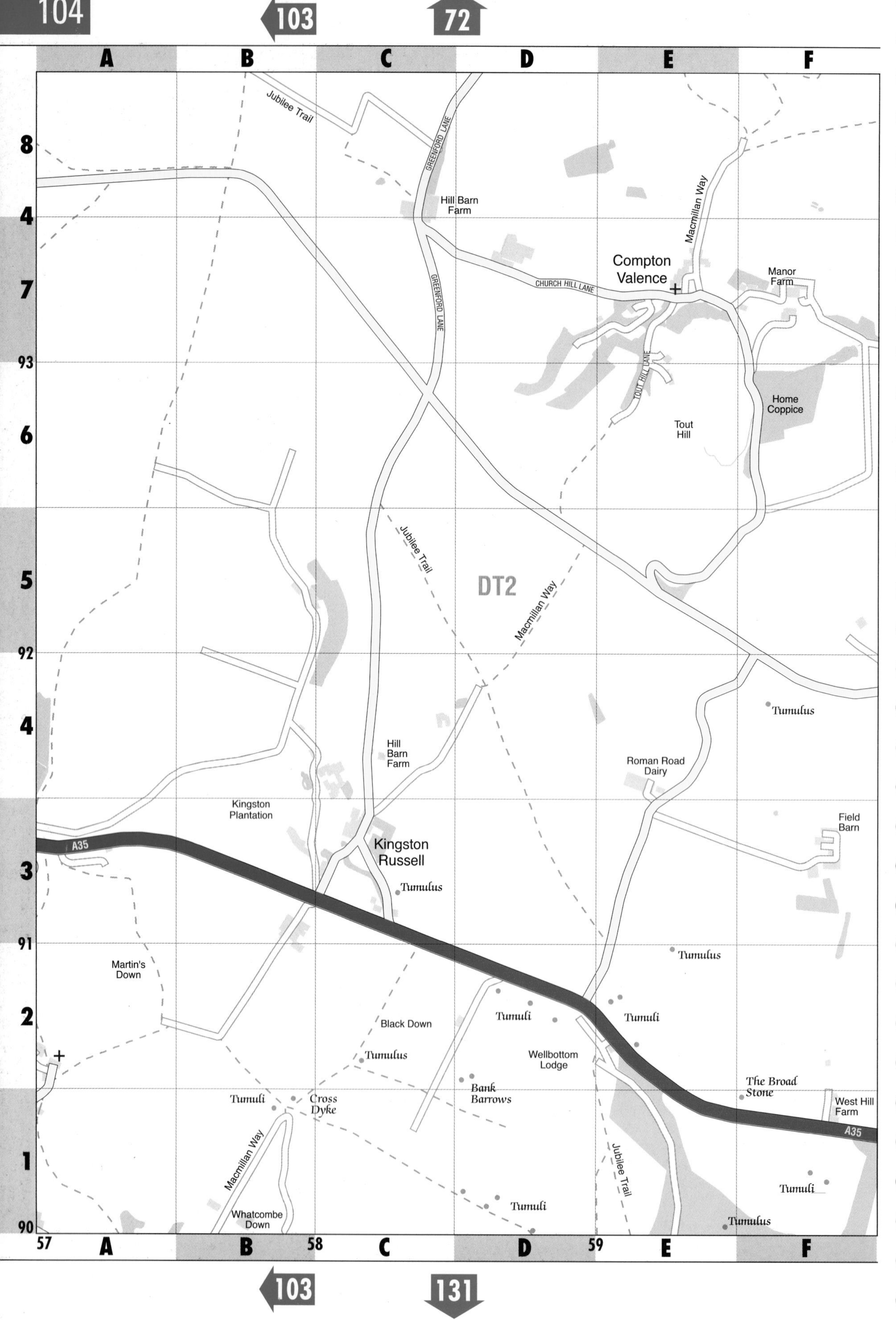
A
B
C
D
E
F
8
4
7
93
6
5
92
4
3
91
2
1
90
57
58
59
Jubilee Trail
GREENFORD LANE
Hill Barn
Farm
Macmillan Way
Compton
Valence
CHURCH HILL LANE
Manor
Farm
TOUT HILL LANE
Home
Coppice
Tout
Hill
DT2
Tumulus
Roman Road
Dairy
Hill
Barn
Farm
Kingston
Plantation
Field
Barn
A35
Kingston
Russell
Martin's
Down
Tumuli
Black Down
Wellbottom
Lodge
The Broad
Stone
West Hill
Farm
Cross
Dyke
Bank
Barrows
Whatcombe
Down

103
131

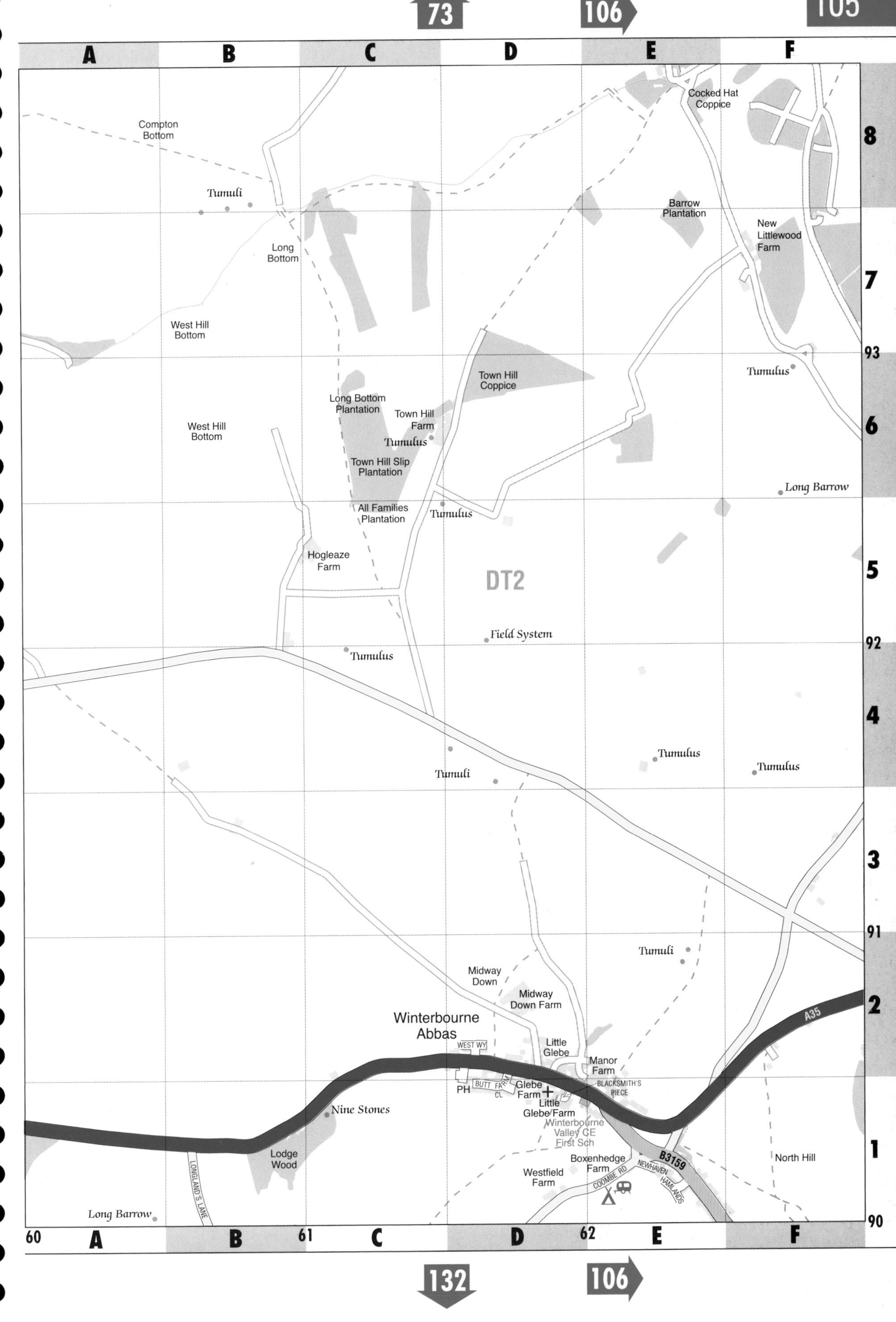

A B C D E F

Compton Bottom

Cocked Hat Coppice

8

Tumuli

Long Bottom

Barrow Plantation

New Littlewood Farm

7

West Hill Bottom

93

Town Hill Coppice

Long Bottom Plantation

Town Hill Farm

6

West Hill Bottom

Tumulus

Town Hill Slip Plantation

Long Barrow

All Families Plantation

Tumulus

5

Hogleaze Farm

DT2

Field System

92

Tumulus

4

Tumulus

Tumulus

Tumuli

Tumuli

3

91

Tumuli

Midway Down

2

Midway Down Farm

A35

Winterbourne Abbas

Little Glebe

Manor Farm

WEST WY

BLACKSMITH'S PIECE

BUTT FM CL

Glebe Farm

PH

Little Glebe Farm

Nine Stones

Winterbourne Valley CE First Sch

North Hill

1

Lodge Wood

LONGLANDS LANE

Boxenhedge Farm

Westfield Farm

COOMBE RD

B3159

NEWHAVEN HAMLANDS

Long Barrow

90

60 A B 61 C D 62 E F

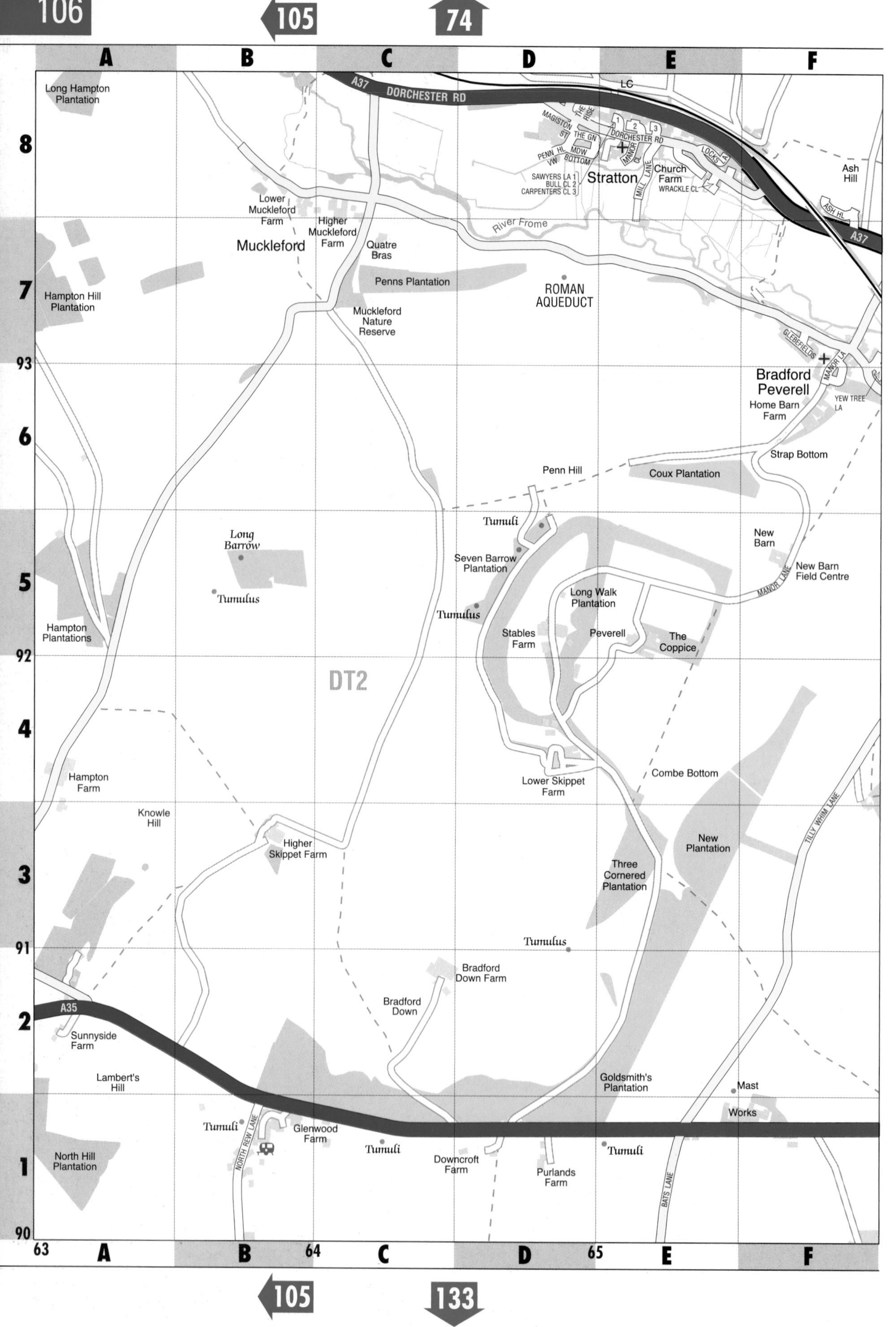

A B C D E F

8

Long Hampton
Plantation

A37 DORCHESTER RD LC

MAGISTON
ST THE GN DORCHESTER RD 1 2 3

PENN HL MDW 3
VW BOTTOM

SAWYERS LA 1
BULL CL 2
CARPENTERS CL 3

Stratton

Church
Farm

WRACKLE CL

Ash
Hill

ASH HL

A37

Lower
Muckleford
Farm

Higher
Muckleford
Farm

Muckleford

Quatre
Bras

River Frome

7

Hampton Hill
Plantation

Penns Plantation

Muckleford
Nature
Reserve

ROMAN
AQUEDUCT

GLEBEFIELDS

93

Bradford
Peverell

Home Barn
Farm

YEW TREE
LA

MANOR LA

6

Strap Bottom

Penn Hill

Coux Plantation

New
Barn

New Barn
Field Centre

Long
Barrow

Tumuli

Seven Barrow
Plantation

Long Walk
Plantation

MANOR LANE

5

Tumulus

Tumulus

Stables
Farm

Peverell

The
Coppice

Hampton
Plantations

92

DT2

4

Hampton
Farm

Lower Skippet
Farm

Combe Bottom

TILLY WHIM LANE

Knowle
Hill

Higher
Skippet Farm

Three
Cornered
Plantation

New
Plantation

3

91

Tumulus

Bradford
Down Farm

2

A35

Sunnyside
Farm

Bradford
Down

Goldsmith's
Plantation

Mast

Works

Lambert's
Hill

NORTH PEW LANE

Tumuli

Glenwood
Farm

Tumuli

Downcroft
Farm

Purlands
Farm

Tumuli

BATS LANE

1

North Hill
Plantation

90

63 A B 64 C D 65 E F

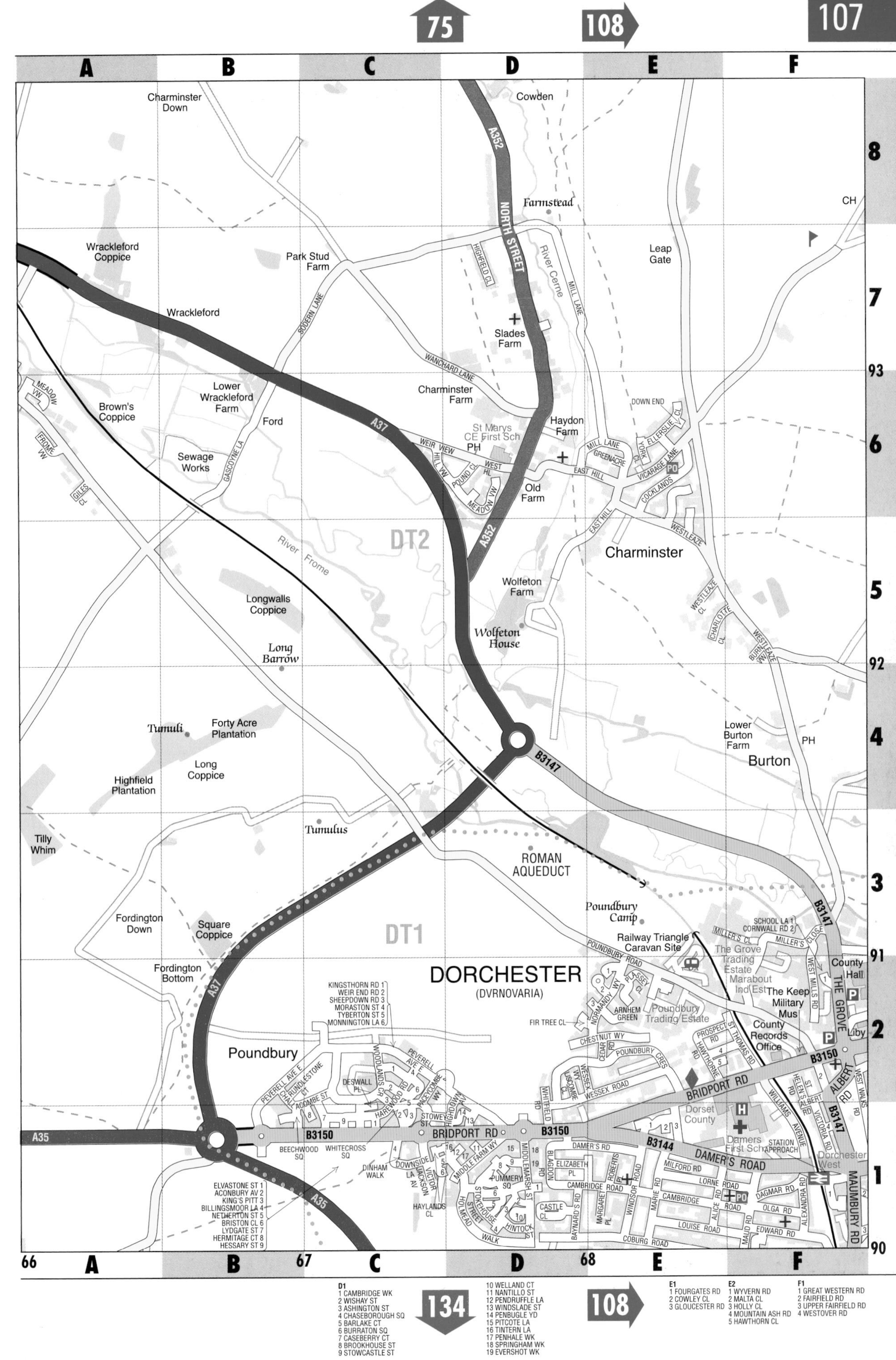
75
108
A
B
C
D
E
F
8
7
93
6
5
92
4
3
91
2
1
90
66
67
68
Charminster Down
Cowden
A352
Farmstead
NORTH STREET
CH
Wrackleford Coppice
Park Stud Farm
HIGHFIELD CL
River Cerne
MILL LANE
Leap Gate
Wrackleford
SODERN LANE
Slades Farm
WANCHARD LANE
Lower Wrackleford Farm
Charminster Farm
MEADOW VW
Brown's Coppice
Ford
A37
DOWN END
Haydon Farm
St Marys CE First Sch
ELLERSLIE CL
FROME VW
Sewage Works
GASCOYNE LA
WEIR VIEW
PH
MILL LANE
GREENACRE
YORK CL
VICARAGE LANE
PO
HILL VW
POUND CL
WEST HL
EAST HILL
GILES CL
MEADOW VW
Old Farm
COCKLANDS
EAST HILL
WESTLEAZE
DT2
River Frome
Charminster
A352
Wolfeton Farm
Longwalls Coppice
WESTLEAZE CL
CHARLOTTE CL
Wolfeton House
Long Barrow
WESTLEAZE
BURN VW
Tumuli
Forty Acre Plantation
Lower Burton Farm
PH
B3147
Burton
Long Coppice
Highfield Plantation
Tilly Whim
Tumulus
ROMAN AQUEDUCT
Poundbury Camp
B3147
SCHOOL LA 1
CORNWALL RD 2
Fordington Down
Square Coppice
DT1
Railway Triangle Caravan Site
MILLER'S CL
MILLER'S CLOSE
POUNDBURY ROAD
The Grove Trading Estate
WEST MILLS RD
County Hall
Fordington Bottom
DORCHESTER
(DVRNOVARIA)
Marabout Ind Est
The Keep Military Mus
THE GROVE
PLASSEY CL
NORMANDY WY
ARNHEM GREEN
Poundbury Trading Estate
County Records Office
KINGSTHORN RD 1
WEIR END RD 2
SHEEPDOWN RD 3
MORASTON ST 4
TYBERTON ST 5
MONNINGTON LA 6
FIR TREE CL
CHESTNUT WY
CEDAR RD
PROSPECT RD
ST THOMAS RD
Liby
Poundbury
POUNDBURY CRES
HAWTHORNE RD
B3150
ALBERT RD
PEVERELL AVE E
CHALL
TRUNDLESTONE CT
DESWALL PL
WOODLANDS CR
PEVERELL AVE E
WESSEX WY
LISCOMBE ST
WESSEX ROAD
WHITFIELD RD
BRIDPORT RD
WEST WALKS RD
PEVERELL AVE E
ACOMBE ST
HAREWOOD PL
PACEYCOMBE WY
HIGHDOWN AV
STOWEY ST
Dorset County
H
HELEN'S ST
ST ALBERT RD
VICTORIA RD
WILLIAMS AVENUE
B3147
A35
B3150
BRIDPORT RD
B3150
B3144
DAMER'S RD
Damers First Sch
STATION APPROACH
BEECHWOOD SQ
WHITECROSS SQ
MIDDLE FARM WY
MIDDLEMARSH ST
BLAGDON RD
ELIZABETH PL
ROBERTS PL
DAMER'S ROAD
Dorchester West
DINHAM WALK
DOWNSIDE LA
JACKSON AV
VICTOR ST
PUMMERY SQ
CAMBRIDGE ROAD
WINDSOR ROAD
MARIE RD
MILFORD RD
LORNE ROAD
DAGMAR RD
MAUMBURY RD
ELVASTONE ST 1
ACONBURY AV 2
KING'S PITT 3
BILLINGSMOOR LA 4
NETHERTON ST 5
BRISTON CL 6
LYDGATE ST 7
HERMITAGE CT 8
HESSARY ST 9
A35
HAYLANDS CL
HOLMEAD WALK
STOKEHOUSE STREET
HINTOCK ST
CASTLE CL
BAYNARD'S RD
MARGARET PL
CAMBRIDGE
ALICE ROAD
OLGA RD
ALEXANDRA RD
LOUISE ROAD
MAUD RD
EDWARD RD
COBURG ROAD
PO
D1
1 CAMBRIDGE WK
2 WISHAY ST
3 ASHINGTON ST
4 CHASEBOROUGH SQ
5 BARLAKE CT
6 BURRATON SQ
7 CASEBERRY CT
8 BROOKHOUSE ST
9 STOWCASTLE ST
10 WELLAND CT
11 NANTILLO ST
12 PENDRUFFLE LA
13 WINDSLADE ST
14 PENBUGLE YD
15 PITCOTE LA
16 TINTERN LA
17 PENHALE WK
18 SPRINGHAM WK
19 EVERSHOT WK
134
108
E1
1 FOURGATES RD
2 COWLEY CL
3 GLOUCESTER RD
E2
1 WYVERN RD
2 MALTA CL
3 HOLLY CL
4 MOUNTAIN ASH RD
5 HAWTHORN CL
F1
1 GREAT WESTERN RD
2 FAIRFIELD RD
3 UPPER FAIRFIELD RD
4 WESTOVER RD

Hill Barn

Square Coppice

Home Farm

B3143

DT2

Limekiln Copse

Higher Kingston Farm

Higher Burton Farm

Badgers Copse

SLYER'S LANE

A35

Frome Whitfield Farm

Birkin House

Frome Whitfield

HOLLOW HILL

Coker's Frome

B3143

B3150

STINSFORD HILL

Stinsford

Kingston Maurward College

Dorset Fire & Rescue Service HQ
County Hall
Dorchester HM Prison

GREY SCHOOL PASSAGE

DT1

CHURCH LA

NEWCOMBE LA

Visitor Centre

Kingston Maurward Gardens & Animal Park

Manor House

CATERS PL

Tutankhamun Exhibition

Terracotta Warriors Mus

Aboretom

Kingston Maurward

Old Crown Ct & Cells

Dinosaur Mus

Casterbridge Ind Est

FRIARY RD

FROME TERR

PORCH. ST

COLLITON ST

CORNHILL

LONDON RD

GLYDE PTH RD

HIGH W ST

HIGH E ST

Greys Bridge

Cty Mus

B3150

HARVEYS TERR

HARDY AVE

DURNOVER CT

Recreation Ground

Mus

DURNGATE

HIGH STREET FORDINGTON

HOLLOWAY ROAD

B3143

PRINCE'S ST

SOUTH ST

CHARLES ST

TRINITY ST

SALISBURY ST

ALL SAINTS RD

VICTORIA TERR

Victoria Buildings

DORCHESTER
(DVRNOVARIA)

SOMER'S RD

WOLLASTON RD

LINDEN AVE

SOUTH WALKS RD

KINGS ROAD

ROBIN'S GTH

ST LUKE'S RD

ALFRED PL

HEATHCOTE RD

LITTLE BRITAIN

LUBBECKE WY

Weir

River Frome

B3144

GT WESTERN RD

SOUTH WALKS RD

Sunninghill Prep Sch

ARBOURS

YORK RD

CULLIFORD RD

Dorchester Prep Sch

KEEN WAY CL

ALFRED RD

ACKERMAN RD

WILSON RD

EDDISON AVENUE

ST GEORGES ROAD

Stinsford View

ST GEORGES RD

ST GEORGES RD

FENWAY CL

Louds Mill Sewage Treatment Works

PRINCE OF WALES ROAD

Tudor Arcade Shopping Centre

Dorchester Market

Dorchester South

STATION APP

WEYMOUTH AVE

LANCASTER RD

MAEN GDNS

B3144

ALINGTON ROAD

FRIARS CL

SMOKEY HOLE LANE

ST GEORGES RD

SYWARD RD

SYWARD CL

A35

Adult Ed Ctr

Sandringham Sports Ctr

ALFRED RD

MONMOUTH RD

A1	A2	B1	B2	C1
1 WEST WALKS RD	1 NORTHERNHAY	1 EARL CL	1 LONDON CL	1 ALINGTON AVE
2 NEW ST	2 NORTH SQ	2 ATHELSTAN RD	2 POUND LANE	2 SANDRINGHAM CT
3 WEYMOUTH AVE	3 THE BOW	3 FORDINGTON GDNS	3 CHURCH ACRE	
4 FAIRFIELD RD	4 ALINGTON ST	4 SYDENHAM WAY	4 CHANNONS CT	
5 UPPER FAIRFIELD RD	5 CHURCH ST	5 BARNES WAY	5 FORDINGTON GN	
6 CROMWELL RD	6 CHURCH CL	6 CULLIFORD RD NTH	6 ALINGTON TERR	
	7 ACLAND RD		7 GREENINGS CT	
	8 ANTELOPE WK			
	9 ALEXANDRA TERR			

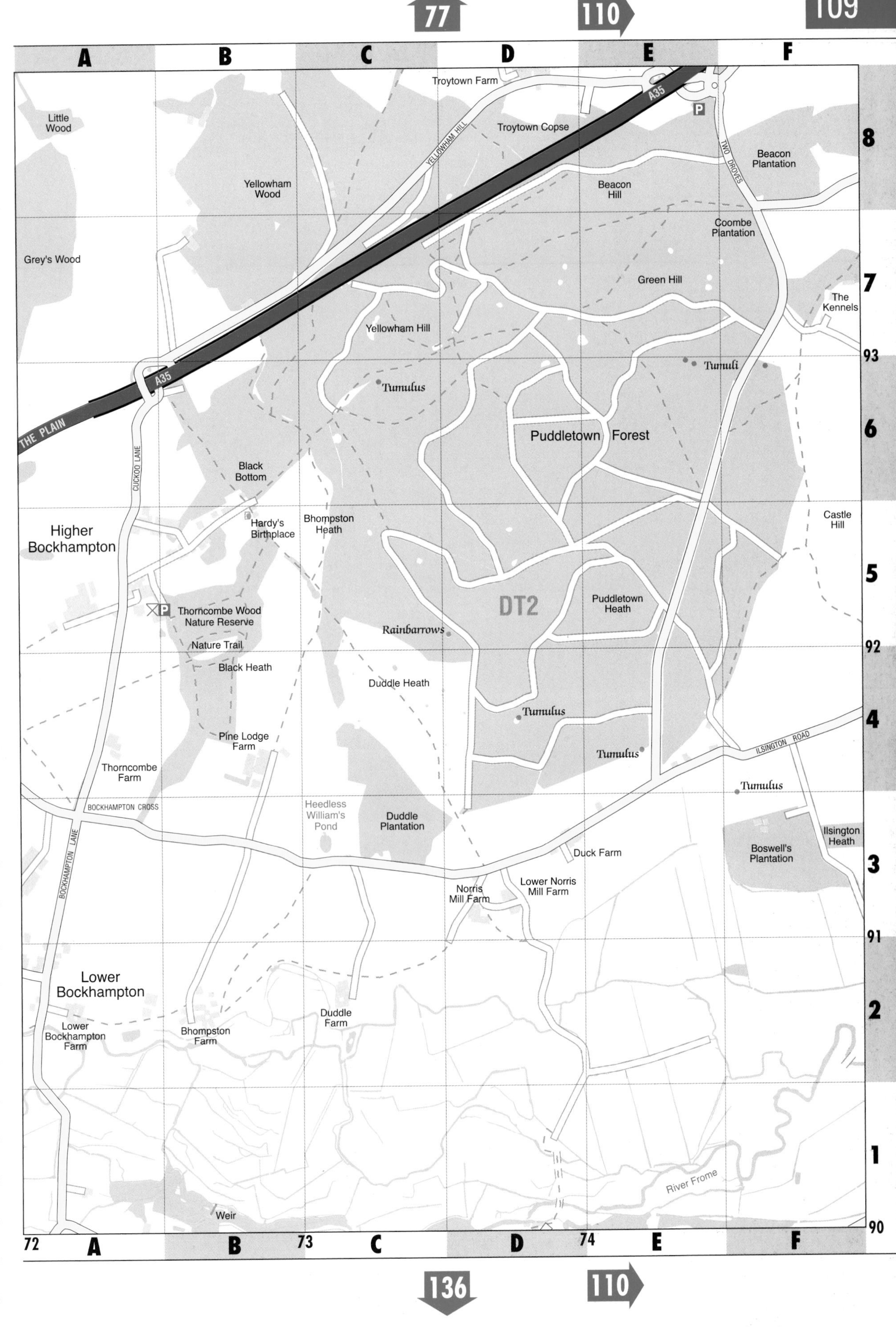
77
110
A
B
C
D
E
F
Troytown Farm
A35
P
Little Wood
Yellowham Hill
Troytown Copse
8
Two Droves
Beacon Plantation
Yellowham Wood
Beacon Hill
Coombe Plantation
Grey's Wood
Green Hill
7
The Kennels
Yellowham Hill
93
Tumuli
A35
Tumulus
The Plain
Puddletown Forest
6
Cuckoo Lane
Black Bottom
Castle Hill
Higher Bockhampton
Hardy's Birthplace
Bhompston Heath
5
DT2
Puddletown Heath
P
Thorncombe Wood Nature Reserve
Rainbarrows
Nature Trail
92
Black Heath
Duddle Heath
Tumulus
4
Pine Lodge Farm
Tumulus
Ilsington Road
Thorncombe Farm
Tumulus
Bockhampton Cross
Heedless William's Pond
Duddle Plantation
Ilsington Heath
Bockhampton Lane
Duck Farm
Boswell's Plantation
3
Norris Mill Farm
Lower Norris Mill Farm
91
Lower Bockhampton
2
Duddle Farm
Lower Bockhampton Farm
Bhompston Farm
1
River Frome
Weir
90
72
A
B
73
C
D
74
E
F
136
110

109
78

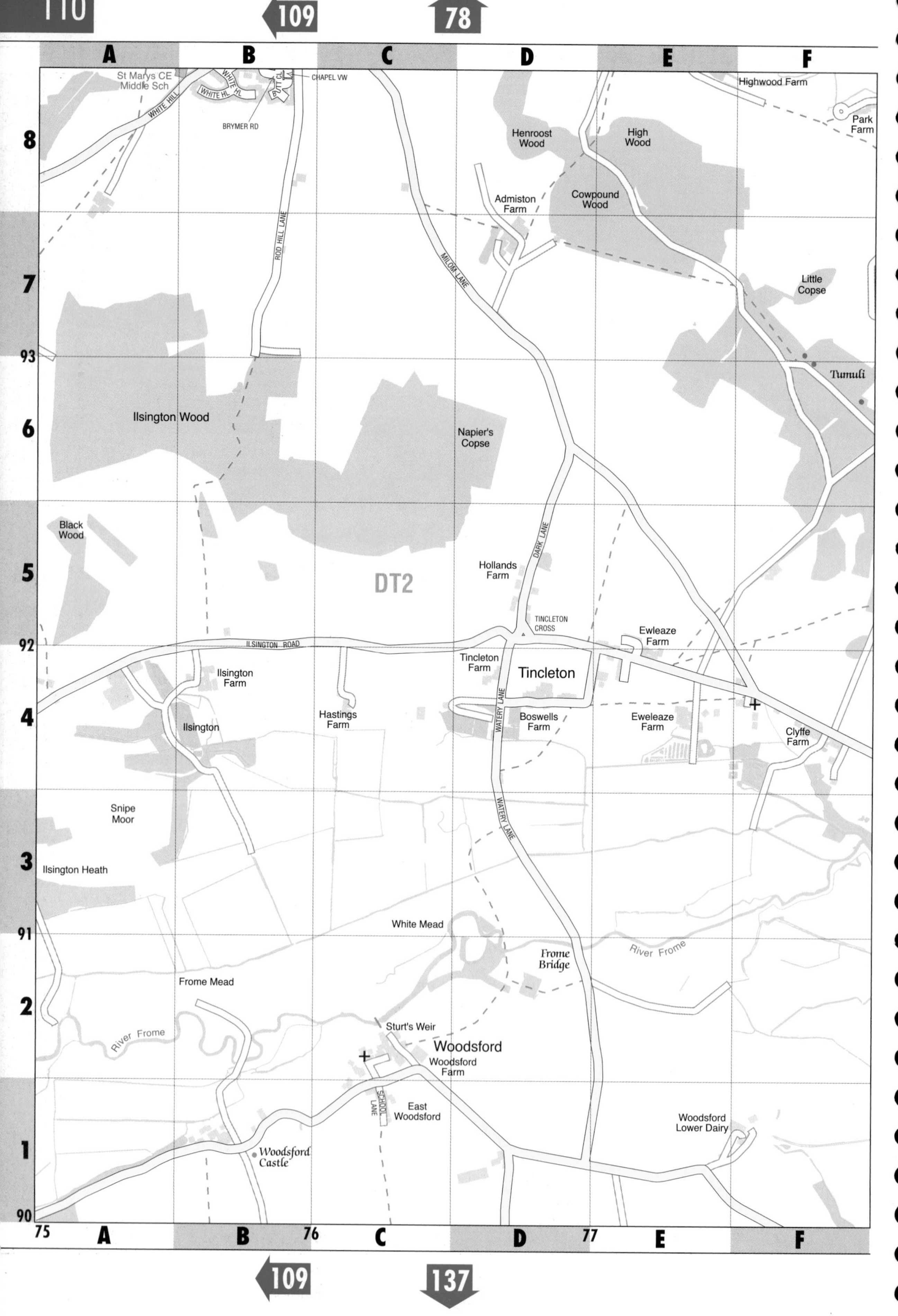
A
B
C
D
E
F
St Marys CE Middle Sch
WHITE HILL
WHITE HL
BUTT CL
CHAPEL VW
BRYMER RD
Highwood Farm
Park Farm
Henroost Wood
High Wood
Admiston Farm
Cowpound Wood
ROD HILL LANE
MILOM LANE
Little Copse
Tumuli
Ilsington Wood
Napier's Copse
Black Wood
DARK LANE
Hollands Farm
DT2
TINCLETON CROSS
Ewleaze Farm
ILSINGTON ROAD
Ilsington Farm
Tincleton Farm
Tincleton
Hastings Farm
Ilsington
WATERY LANE
Boswells Farm
Eweleaze Farm
Clyffe Farm
Snipe Moor
Ilsington Heath
White Mead
Frome Bridge
River Frome
Frome Mead
Sturt's Weir
Woodsford
Woodsford Farm
SCHOOL LANE
East Woodsford
Woodsford Lower Dairy
Woodsford Castle
8
7
93
6
5
92
4
3
91
2
1
90
75
76
77

109
137

79
112

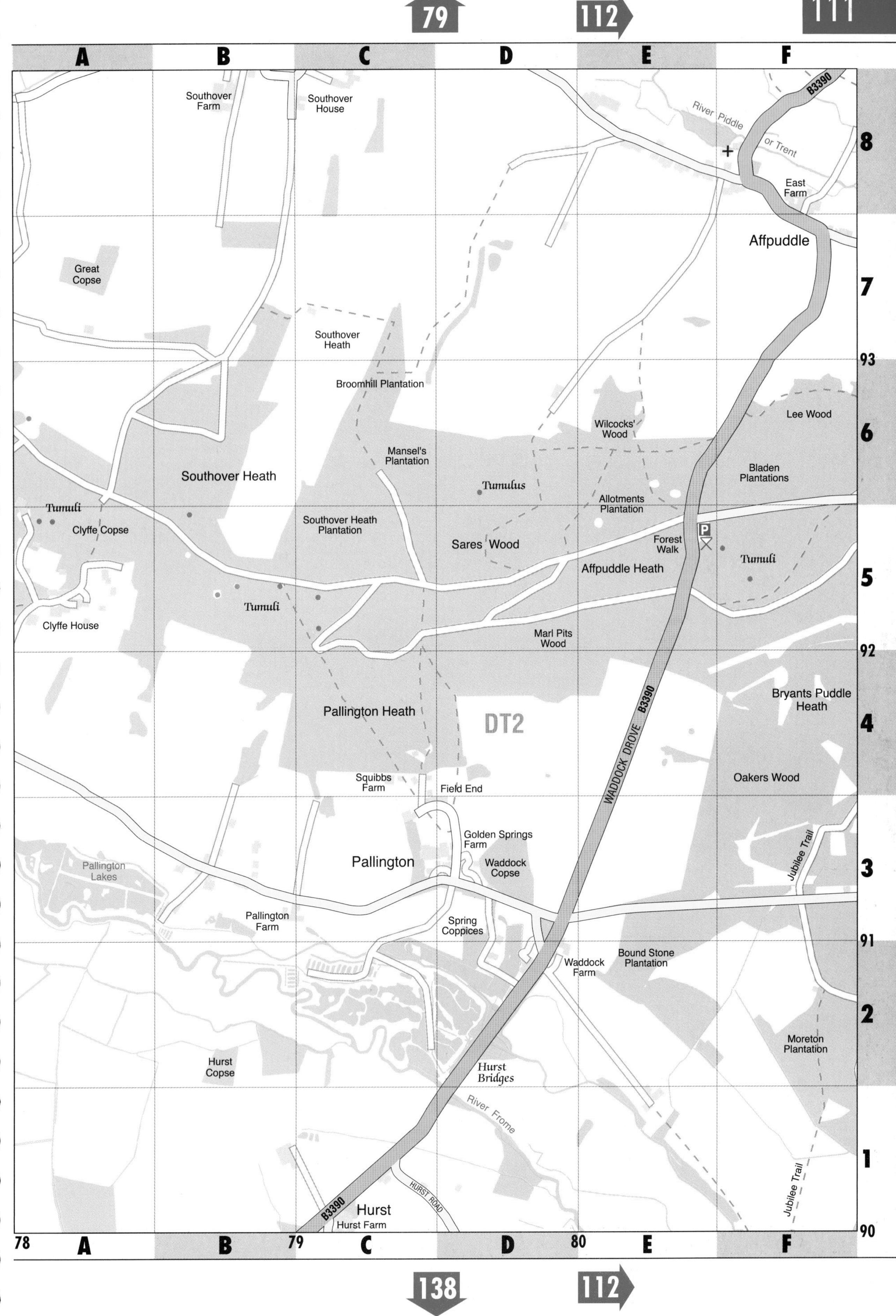
A
B
C
D
E
F
Southover Farm
Southover House
River Piddle or Trent
B3390
East Farm
Affpuddle
Great Copse
Southover Heath
Broomhill Plantation
Lee Wood
Wilcocks' Wood
Mansel's Plantation
Bladen Plantations
Southover Heath
Tumulus
Allotments Plantation
Tumuli
Clyffe Copse
Southover Heath Plantation
Sares Wood
Forest Walk
Tumuli
Affpuddle Heath
Clyffe House
Tumuli
Marl Pits Wood
Pallington Heath
DT2
Bryants Puddle Heath
WADDOCK DROVE
B3390
Squibbs Farm
Field End
Oakers Wood
Golden Springs Farm
Pallington Lakes
Pallington
Waddock Copse
Jubilee Trail
Pallington Farm
Spring Coppices
Waddock Farm
Bound Stone Plantation
Moreton Plantation
Hurst Copse
Hurst Bridges
River Frome
Jubilee Trail
B3390
Hurst
HURST ROAD
Hurst Farm
8
7
93
6
5
92
4
3
91
2
1
90
78
79
80

138
112

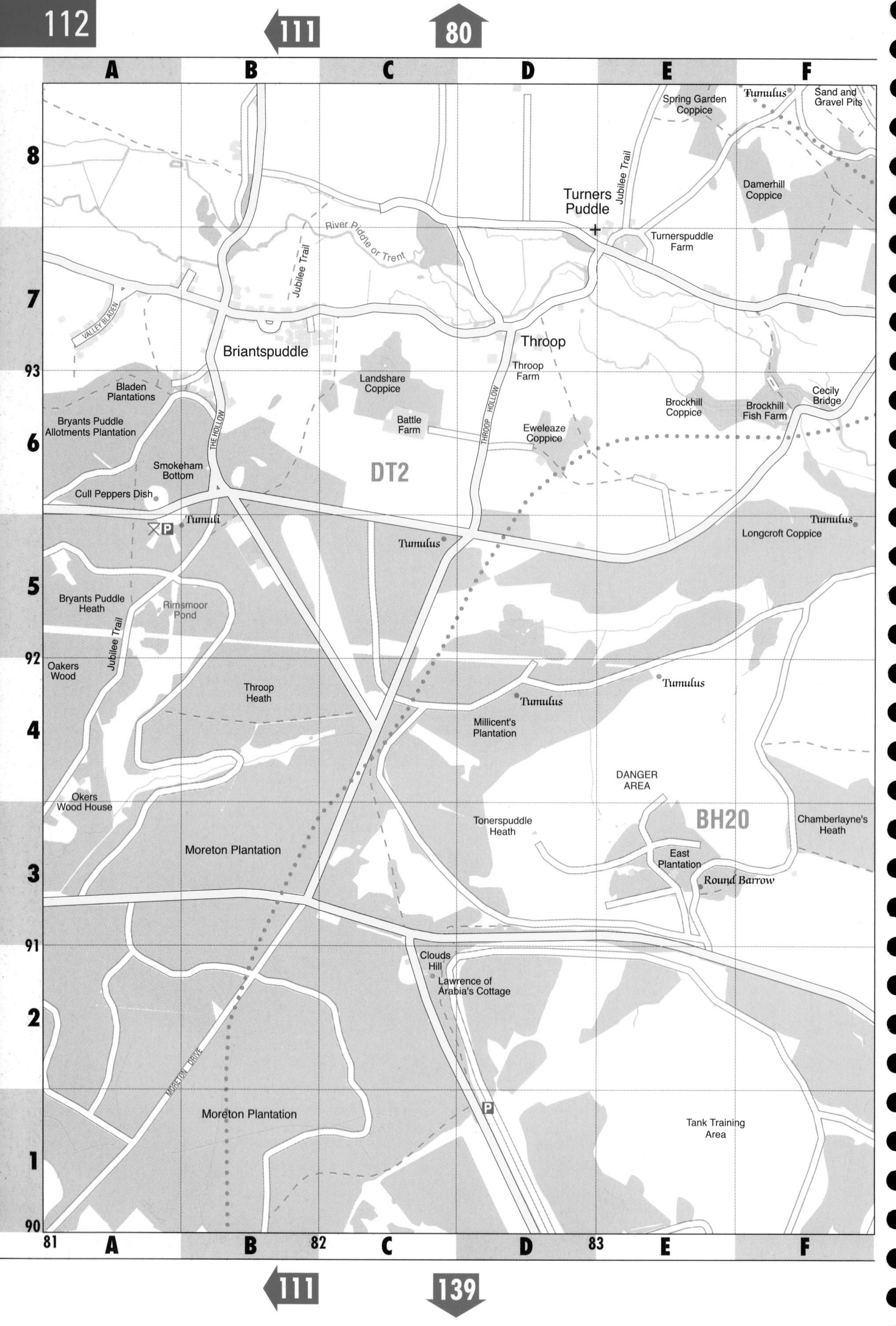

Turners Puddle

Spring Garden Coppice

Tumulus

Sand and Gravel Pits

Damerhill Coppice

Turnerspuddle Farm

Throop

Throop Farm

Briantspuddle

Landshare Coppice

Brockhill Coppice

Brockhill Fish Farm

Cecily Bridge

Bladen Plantations

Bryants Puddle Allotments Plantation

Battle Farm

Eweleaze Coppice

DT2

Smokeham Bottom

Cull Peppers Dish

Tumuli

Tumulus

Tumulus

Longcroft Coppice

Bryants Puddle Heath

Rimsmoor Pond

Oakers Wood

Throop Heath

Tumulus

Tumulus

Millicent's Plantation

DANGER AREA

BH20

Okers Wood House

Tonerspuddle Heath

East Plantation

Chamberlayne's Heath

Moreton Plantation

Round Barrow

Clouds Hill

Lawrence of Arabia's Cottage

Moreton Plantation

Tank Training Area

Jubilee Trail

River Piddle or Trent

THE HOLLOW

THROOP HOLLOW

VALLEY BLADEN

MORETON DRIVE

8 7 93 6 5 92 4 3 91 2 1 90

A B C D E F

81 82 83

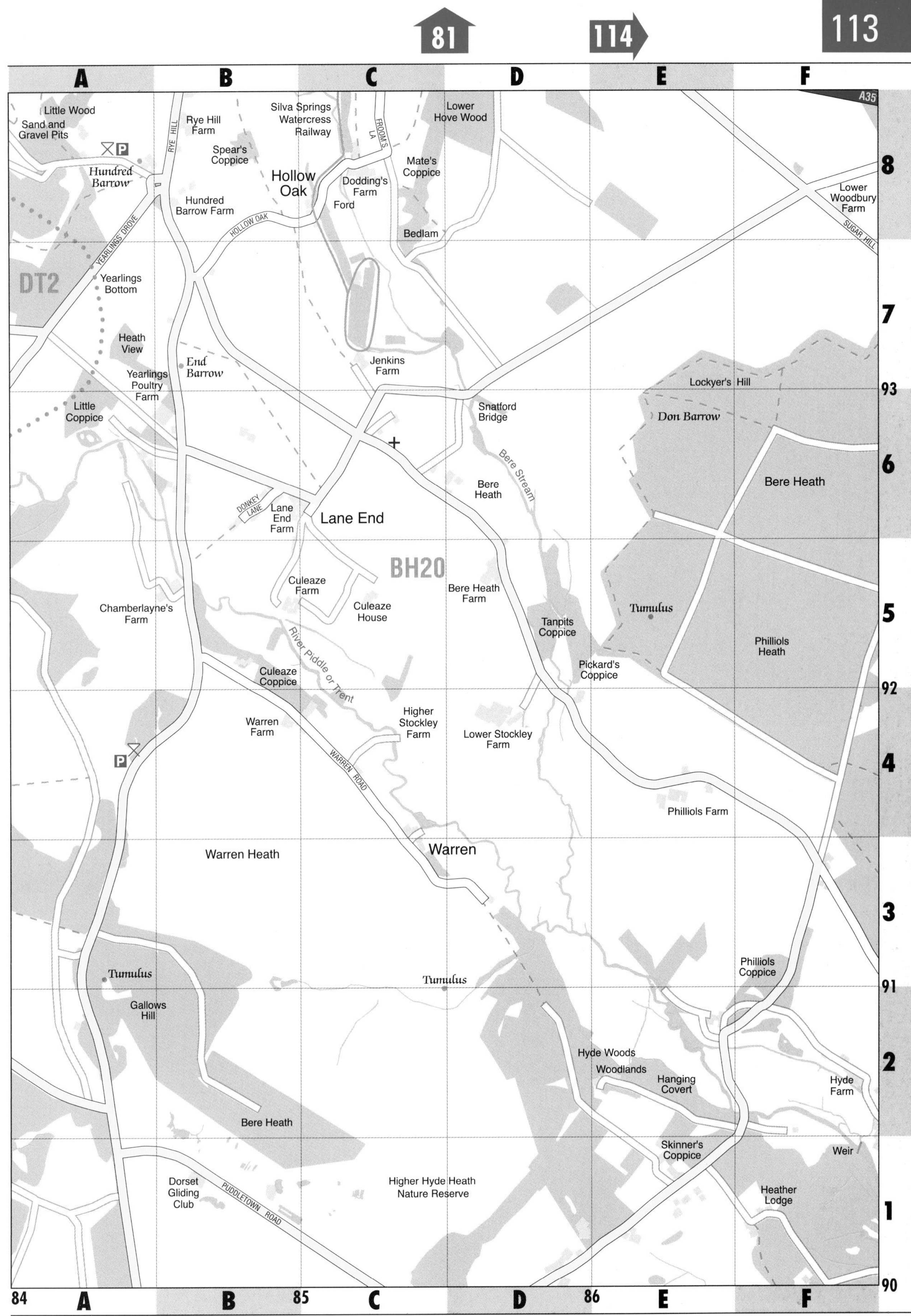

81
114
A
B
C
D
E
F
A35
Little Wood
Sand and Gravel Pits
Hundred Barrow
Rye Hill
Rye Hill Farm
Spear's Coppice
Silva Springs Watercress Railway
Frome's La
Lower Hove Wood
Mate's Coppice
Hollow Oak
Dodding's Farm
Ford
Hundred Barrow Farm
Hollow Oak
Bedlam
Lower Woodbury Farm
Sugar Hill
Yearlings' Drove
DT2
Yearlings Bottom
Heath View
End Barrow
Yearlings Poultry Farm
Jenkins Farm
Little Coppice
Snatford Bridge
Lockyer's Hill
Don Barrow
Bere Stream
Bere Heath
Bere Heath
Donkey Lane
Lane End Farm
Lane End
BH20
Culeaze Farm
Culeaze House
Bere Heath Farm
Chamberlayne's Farm
Tumulus
Tanpits Coppice
Philliols Heath
River Piddle or Trent
Culeaze Coppice
Pickard's Coppice
Warren Farm
Higher Stockley Farm
Lower Stockley Farm
Warren Road
Philliols Farm
Warren Heath
Warren
Philliols Coppice
Tumulus
Tumulus
Gallows Hill
Hyde Woods
Woodlands
Hanging Covert
Hyde Farm
Bere Heath
Skinner's Coppice
Weir
Dorset Gliding Club
Puddletown Road
Higher Hyde Heath Nature Reserve
Heather Lodge
8
7
93
6
5
92
4
3
91
2
1
90
84
85
86
140
114

113
82

A   B   C   D   E   F

A35

Humber's
Coppice

Larch
Plantation

Scotch
Plantation

Snailsbreach
Farm

8

Mast

Ford

Black
Heath

Snail's
Bridge

Oak
Hill

7

93

Bere
Heath

SUGAR HILL

Woolsbarrow
(Fort)

6

Sugar
Hill

Bloxworth
Heath

Morden Heath

5

92

BH20

Wareham Forest

4

P

Stroud
Bridge

Old Ram
Plantation

3

Lower Hyde
Heath

91

North Trigon
Farm

2

Trent
Vale Farm

Hyde House
Country Club

1

Weir

Pond
Plantation

Trigon Hill
Plantation

90

87   A   B   88   C   D   89   E   F

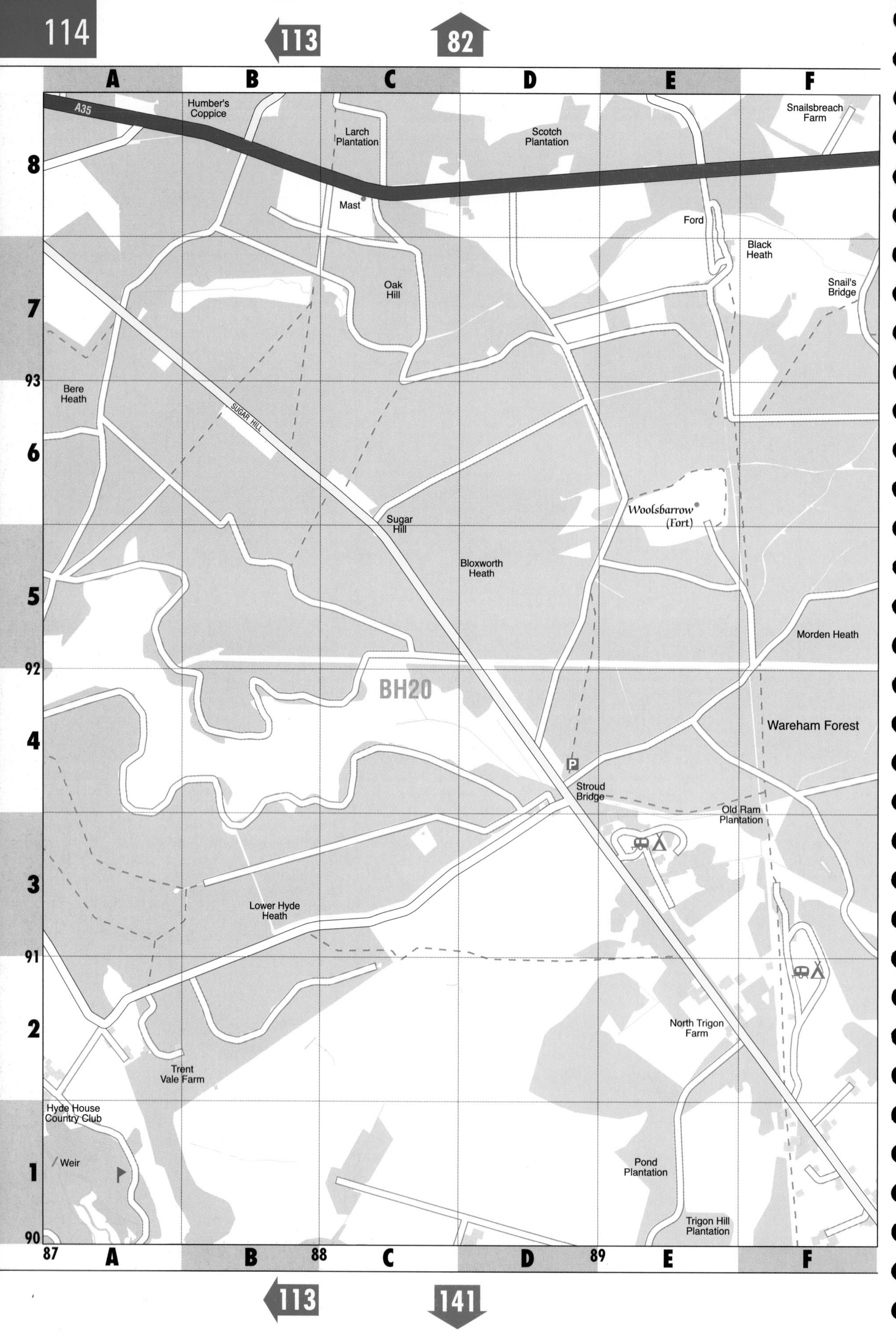

113
141

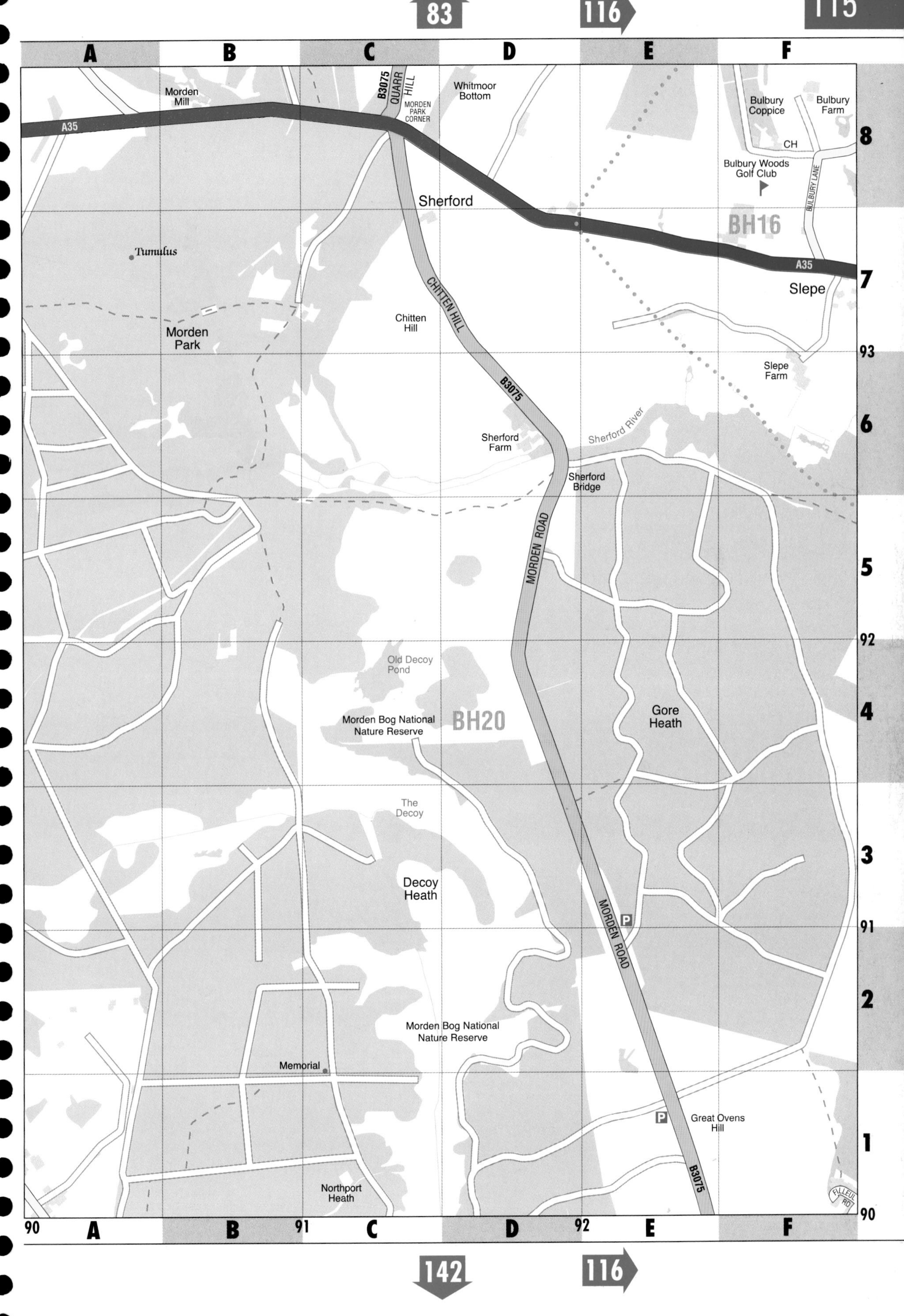

83
116
142
116

Morden Mill

B3075 QUARR HILL

MORDEN PARK CORNER

Whitmoor Bottom

Bulbury Coppice

Bulbury Farm

CH

BULBURY LANE

Bulbury Woods Golf Club

Sherford

BH16

A35

A35

Slepe

Tumulus

CHITTEN HILL

Slepe Farm

Morden Park

Chitten Hill

B3075

Sherford River

Sherford Farm

Sherford Bridge

MORDEN ROAD

Old Decoy Pond

BH20

Gore Heath

Morden Bog National Nature Reserve

The Decoy

Decoy Heath

MORDEN ROAD

P

Morden Bog National Nature Reserve

Memorial

P

Great Ovens Hill

B3075

Northport Heath

FILLEUL RD

115   84

A   B   C   D   E   F

8

Bulbury Lane

Hill Wood

Post Green Farm

Lytchett Minster Sch

Shot Lake Wood

Bere Farm

Post Green

7   A35

Newton Farm

Hill Farm

New Road

Lytchett Minster

93

Pike's Farm

Post Green Road

OLD FORGE CL

ORCHARD CL

B3067

French's Coppice

Cuzenage Coppice

Charity Farm

6

Wareham Road

BH16

PH

Organford

King's Bridge

A35

Higher Wood

Farmer Palmer's Farm Park

King's Bridge Coppice

Holton Heath

5

Lower Wood

A351

Organford Bridge

Sherford River

92

Youngs Farm

Heatherdene

Gore Heath

Wareham Road

4

Organford Road

Pear Tree Farm

FANCY'S ROW

Heath View

CHESTNUT AV

Holton Heath

BH20

ASH AVE   OAK AVE   PINE   FIR   PH   ELM AVE   SYCAMORE AV   PARK DRIVE   CRESCENT

St Martin's Hill

Blackhill Road

Holton Heath National Nature Reserve

3

BIRCH AV   BEECH AVE   LAUREL AVENUE   CHESTNUT   WILLOW

Wareham Road

STATION RD

Black Hill

BLACKHILL ROW   KING'S ROW

HOLTON RD

91

Rustlings Farm

Sandford Drive

Holton Heath Industrial Estate

Blackhill Row   King's Row

Holton Road

2

Sandford House

Sandford Road

Admiralty Research Establishment

Holton Heath

1

Sandford Middle Sch

STATION ROAD

LC Holton Heath

90   A351   FILLEUL RD   WOODLANDS   CEDAR DR   DR 1,2

93   A   B   94   C   D   95   E   F

A1
1 LABURNUM CL
2 HOLLY CL
3 ALDER CL

115   143

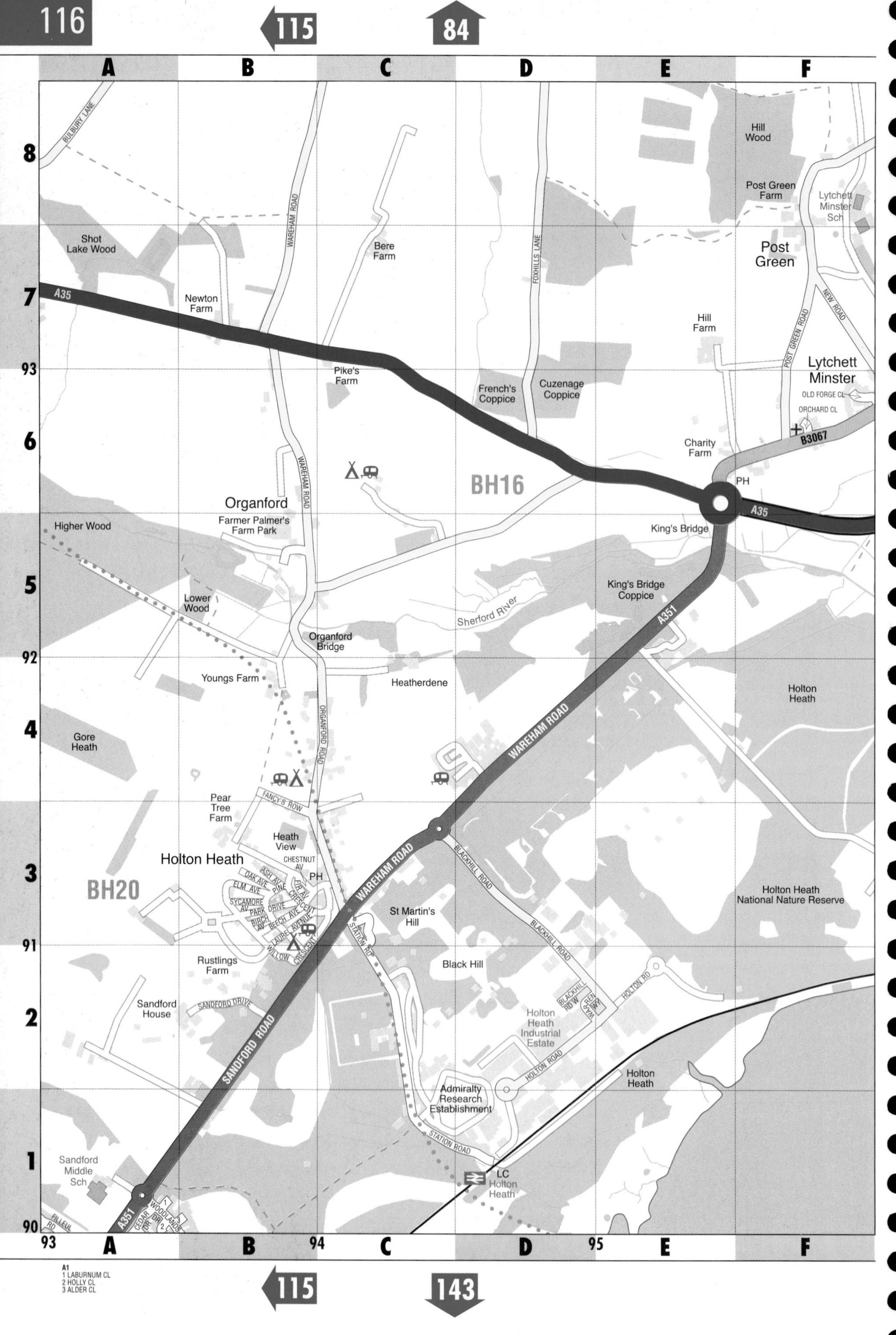

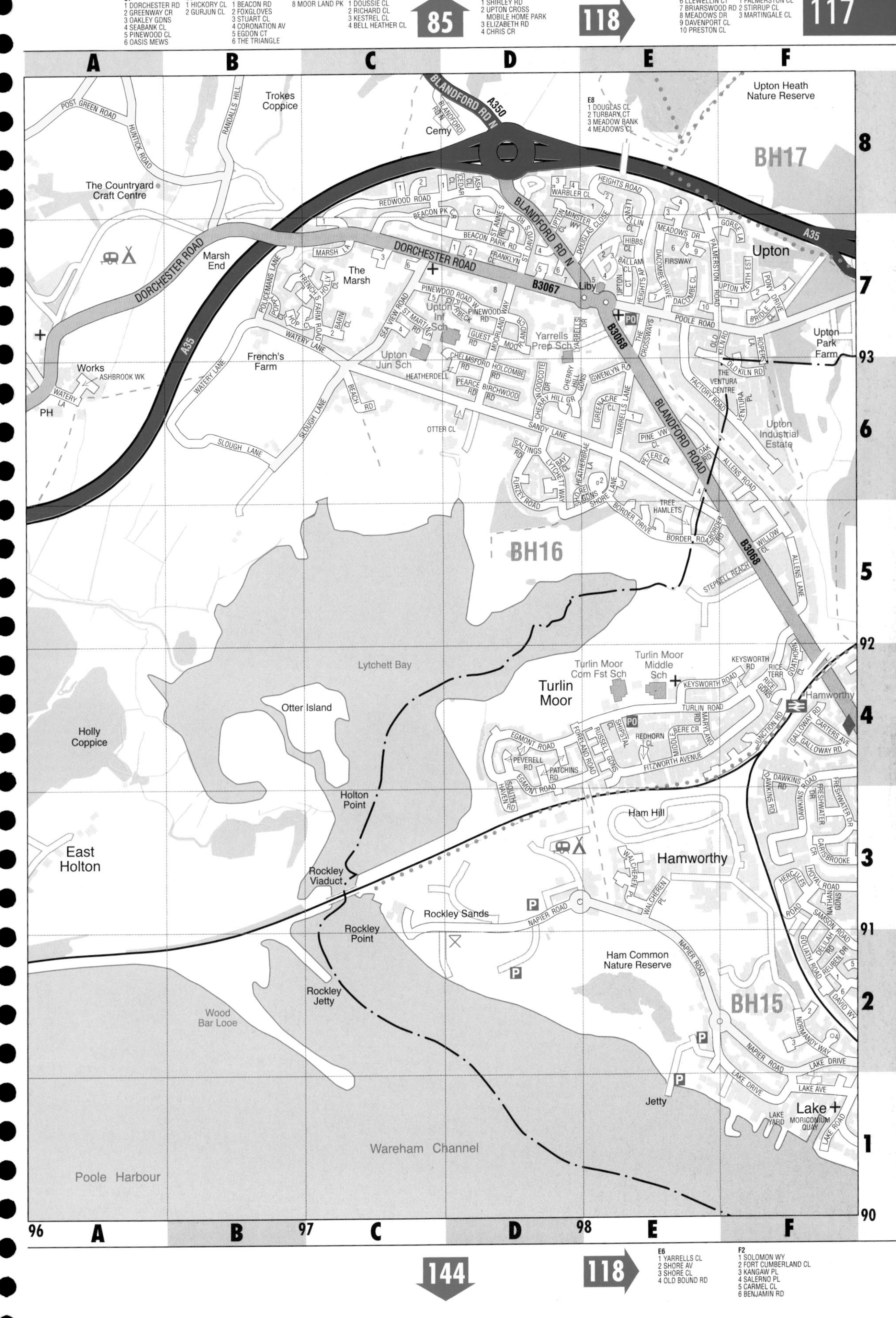
117
C7
1 DORCHESTER RD
2 GREENWAY CR
3 OAKLEY GDNS
4 SEABANK CL
5 PINEWOOD CL
6 OASIS MEWS
C8
1 HICKORY CL
2 GURJUN CL
D7
1 BEACON RD
2 FOXGLOVES
3 STUART CL
4 CORONATION AV
5 EGDON CT
6 THE TRIANGLE
7 DARIAN CT
8 MOOR LAND PK
D8
1 DOUSSIE CL
2 RICHARD CL
3 KESTREL CL
4 BELL HEATHER CL
85
E7
1 SHIRLEY RD
2 UPTON CROSS MOBILE HOME PARK
3 ELIZABETH RD
4 CHRIS CR
118
5 MAPLE LO
6 LLEWELLIN CT
7 BRIARSWOOD RD
8 MEADOWS DR
9 DAVENPORT CL
10 PRESTON CL
F7
1 PALMERSTON CL
2 STIRRUP CL
3 MARTINGALE CL
A B C D E F
E8
1 DOUGLAS CL
2 TURBARY CT
3 MEADOW BANK
4 MEADOWS CL
Upton Heath Nature Reserve
BH17
Trokes Coppice
Cemy
BLANDFORD RD N
A350
A35
The Countryard Craft Centre
Marsh End
DORCHESTER ROAD
The Marsh
B3067
Upton
Liby
PO
B3068
Upton Inf Sch
Upton Jun Sch
Yarrells Prep Sch
French's Farm
Works
PH
Upton Park Farm
Upton Industrial Estate
BLANDFORD ROAD
BH16
Lytchett Bay
Otter Island
Holly Coppice
Holton Point
Turlin Moor
Turlin Moor Com Fst Sch
Turlin Moor Middle Sch
Hamworthy
Ham Hill
East Holton
Rockley Viaduct
Rockley Sands
Rockley Point
Rockley Jetty
Ham Common Nature Reserve
BH15
Wood Bar Looe
Jetty
Lake
Wareham Channel
Poole Harbour
8
7
93
6
5
92
4
3
91
2
1
90
96
97
98
144
118
E6
1 YARRELLS CL
2 SHORE AV
3 SHORE CL
4 OLD BOUND RD
F2
1 SOLOMON WY
2 FORT CUMBERLAND CL
3 KANGAW PL
4 SALERNO PL
5 CARMEL CL
6 BENJAMIN RD

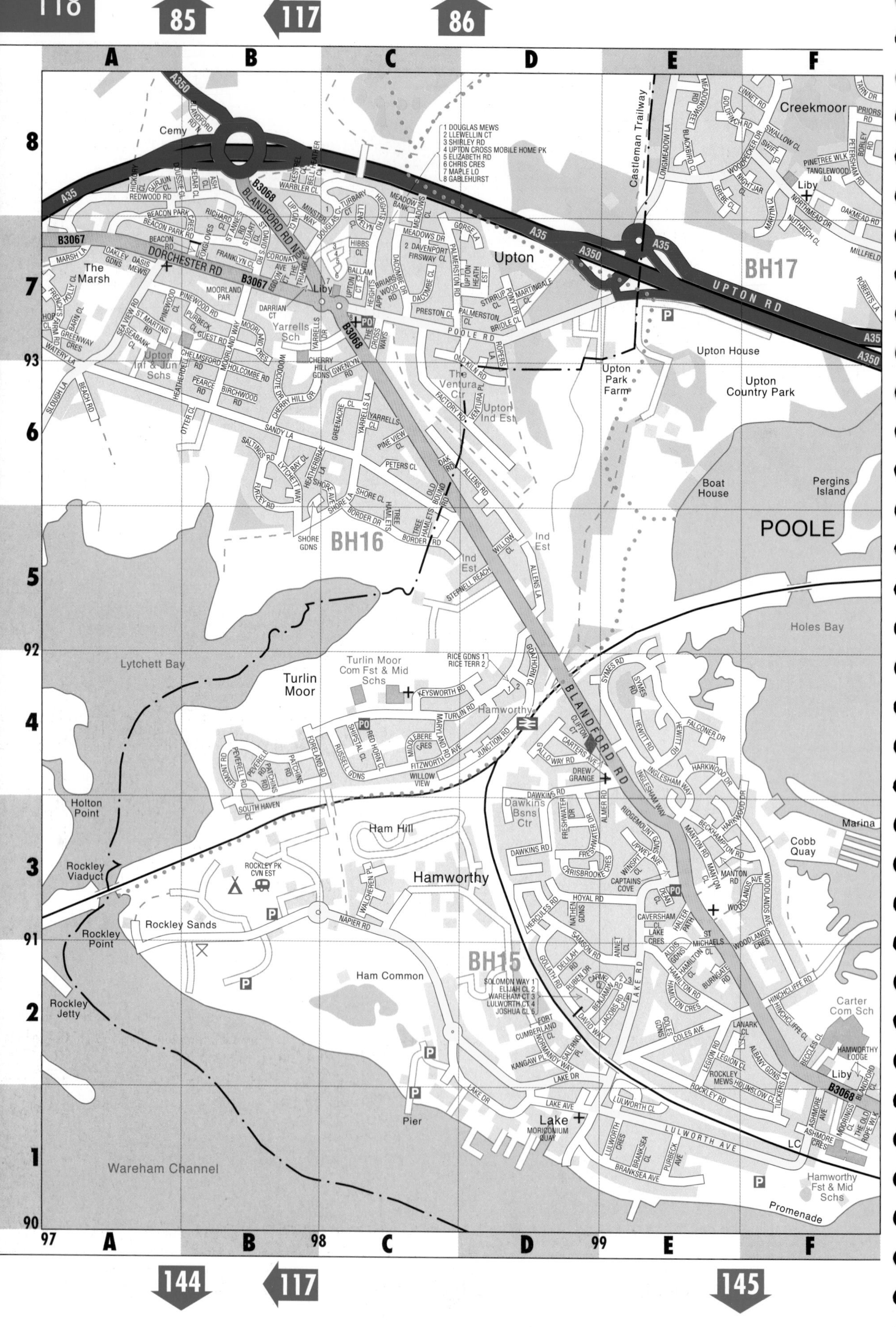

85 | 117 | 86

1 DOUGLAS MEWS
2 LLEWELLIN CT
3 SHIRLEY RD
4 UPTON CROSS MOBILE HOME PK
5 ELIZABETH RD
6 CHRIS CRES
7 MAPLE LO
8 GABLEHURST

Creekmoor

BH17

Upton

UPTON RD

Upton House

Upton Park Farm

Upton Country Park

Boat House

Pergins Island

POOLE

Holes Bay

The Marsh

Dorchester Rd

B3067

B3068

Liby

Yarrells Sch

The Ventura Ctr

Upton Ind Est

BH16

Lytchett Bay

Turlin Moor Com Fst & Mid Schs

Turlin Moor

Rice Gdns 1
Rice Terr 2

Hamworthy

Ind Est

Ind Est

Holton Point

Ham Hill

Hamworthy

Dawkins Bsns Ctr

Marina

Cobb Quay

Rockley Viaduct

Rockley Pk CVN Est

Rockley Sands

Carter Com Sch

Rockley Point

Ham Common

BH15

Solomon Way 1
Elijah Cl 2
Wareham Ct 3
Lulworth Ct 4
Joshua Cl 6

Hamworthy Lodge

Liby

B3068

Rockley Jetty

Pier

Lake

Moriconium Quay

Hamworthy Fst & Mid Schs

Wareham Channel

Promenade

144 | 117 | 145

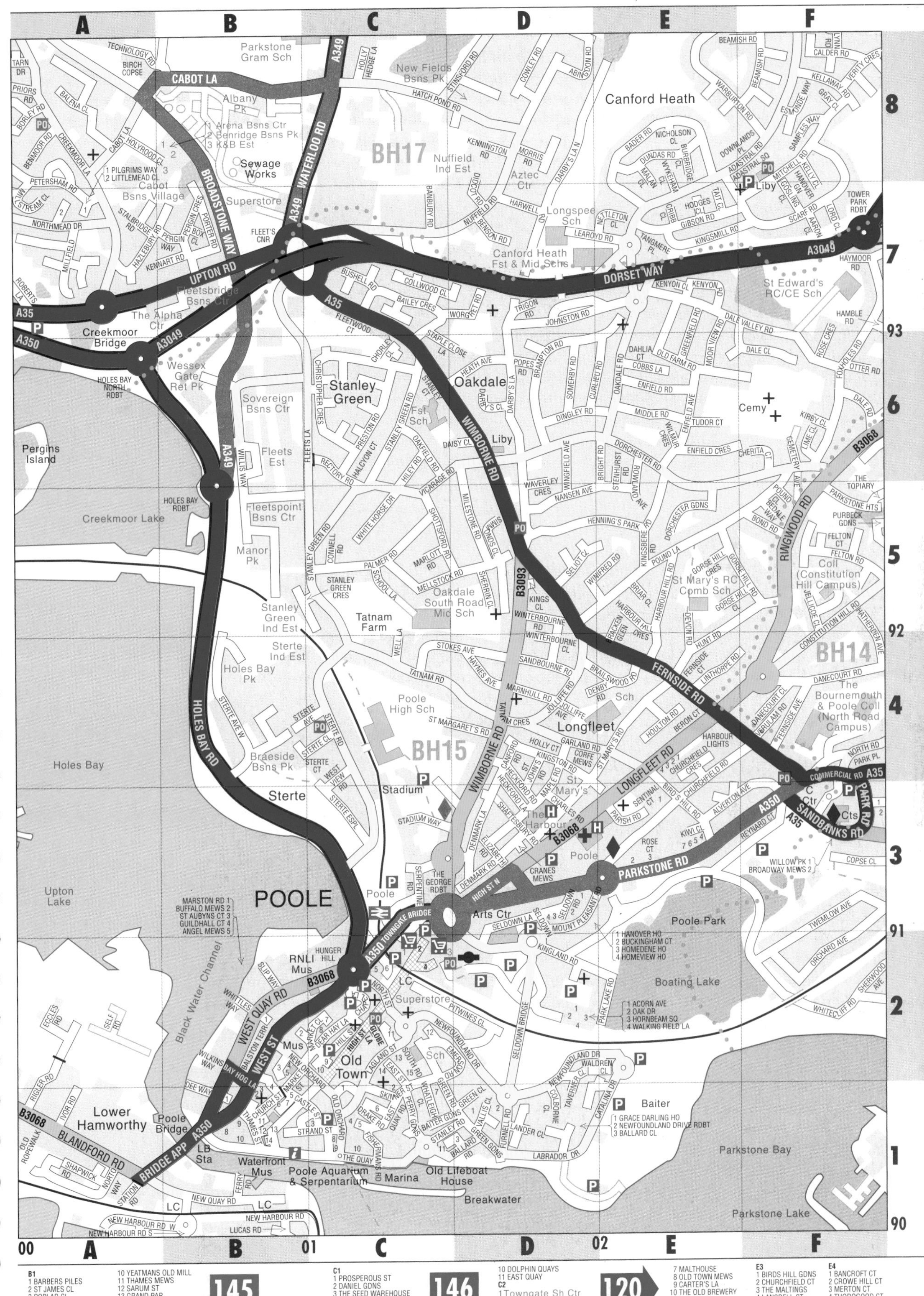

B1
1 BARBERS PILES
2 ST JAMES CL
3 POPLAR CL
4 LEVET'S LA
5 NEW ST
6 ST GEORGE'S ALMSHOS
7 CINNAMON LA
8 BARBERS WHARF
9 BARBERS GATE
10 YEATMANS OLD MILL
11 THAMES MEWS
12 SARUM ST
13 GRAND PAR
14 PARADISE ST

145

C1
1 PROSPEROUS ST
2 DANIEL GDNS
3 THE SEED WAREHOUSE
4 DRAKE CT
5 GRAY'S YD
6 TAYLOR'S BLDGS
7 RODNEY CT
8 QUAY POINT
9 THE KIOSKS

146

C2
1 Towngate Sh Ctr
2 FALKLAND SQ
3 Dolphin Ctr
4 KINGLAND CRES
5 WINCHESTER PL
6 VANGUARD RD

10 DOLPHIN QUAYS
11 EAST QUAY

120

7 MALTHOUSE
8 OLD TOWN MEWS
9 CARTER'S LA
10 THE OLD BREWERY
11 THE BROMBYS
12 EMERSON CL
13 NELSON CT
14 LAGLAND CT
15 GRENVILLE CT

E3
1 BIRDS HILL GDNS
2 CHURCHFIELD CT
3 THE MALTINGS
4 LANSDELL CT
5 GARDENS CT
6 SUNNINGDALE
7 PARK VIEW

E4
1 BANCROFT CT
2 CROWE HILL CT
3 MERTON CT
4 THOROGOOD CT

119
88

F7
1 GREENFIELDS
2 HANDLEY LODGE
3 SHILLINGSTONE GDNS
4 CASHMOOR CL
5 BROADMAYNE RD
6 ROWE GDNS
7 ALDER HEIGHTS

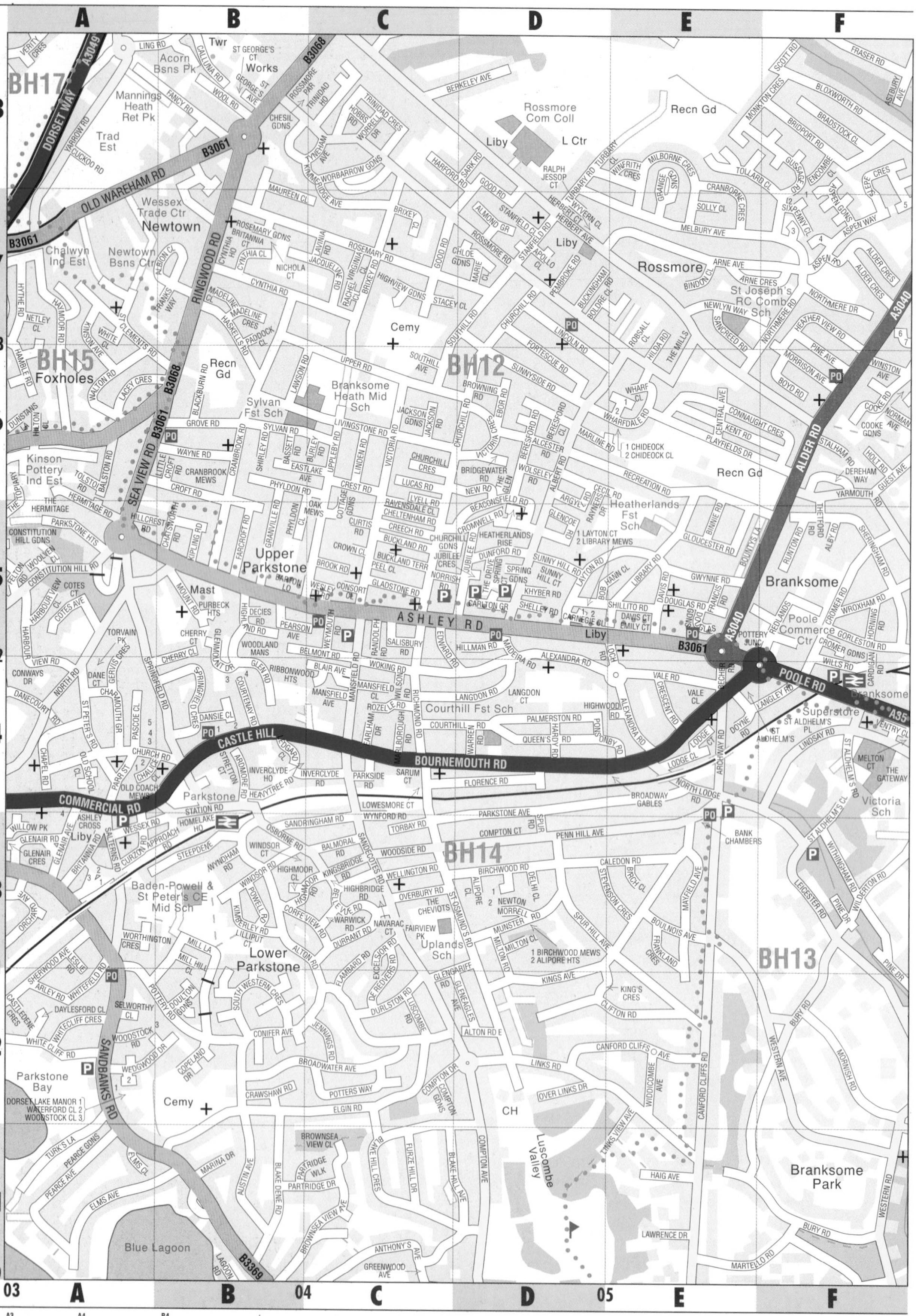

BH17

BH15
Foxholes

BH12

Rossmore

Branksome

BH14

BH13

Upper Parkstone

Lower Parkstone

Parkstone

Parkstone Bay

Blue Lagoon

Branksome Park

Luscombe Valley

Newtown

119
147

A4
1 BURLING TERR
2 CORAL CT
3 LINDUM CT
4 DARWIN CT
5 EAGLHURST
6 STOUR CT
7 AVON CT
8 PRINCES CT
9 HOLLENDEN
10 RUTLAND MANOR
11 LINDSAY MANOR
12 THE OASIS
13 HOLLY LO
14 MELTON CT
15 LINDSAY PK
16 PINE PARK MANS
17 ALBANY HO
18 CEDAR GRANGE
19 LINDSAY CT
20 WOODLANDS
21 PELHAM

C4
1 BENELLEN TWRS
2 GUILDFORD CT
3 MILBURN CL
4 BENNETT HO

C4
5 BICKNELL CT
6 BLENHEIM MEWS
7 GORDON CT

D4
1 KENSINGTON DR
2 BARONSMEDE
3 LEIGHTON LO
4 WHEATON GRANGE
5 HAMPTON CT
6 THE WOODRISINGS
7 RIVERSIDE CT
8 SURREY LO
9 BOURNE RIVER CT

89

10 BRACKEN CT
11 GRENVILLE CT
12 THE TARRANTS
13 LAWN CT
14 OTTERBOURNE
15 ENGLISH CT
16 QUEENS CT

122

F4
1 WYCHWOOD GRANGE
2 COPPER BEECHES
3 FAIRTHORN CT
4 BOURNE PINES
5 HORSESHOE CT
6 ALBANY CT
7 MEYRICK PARK MANS
8 EAST CLIFF
9 WEST CLIFF

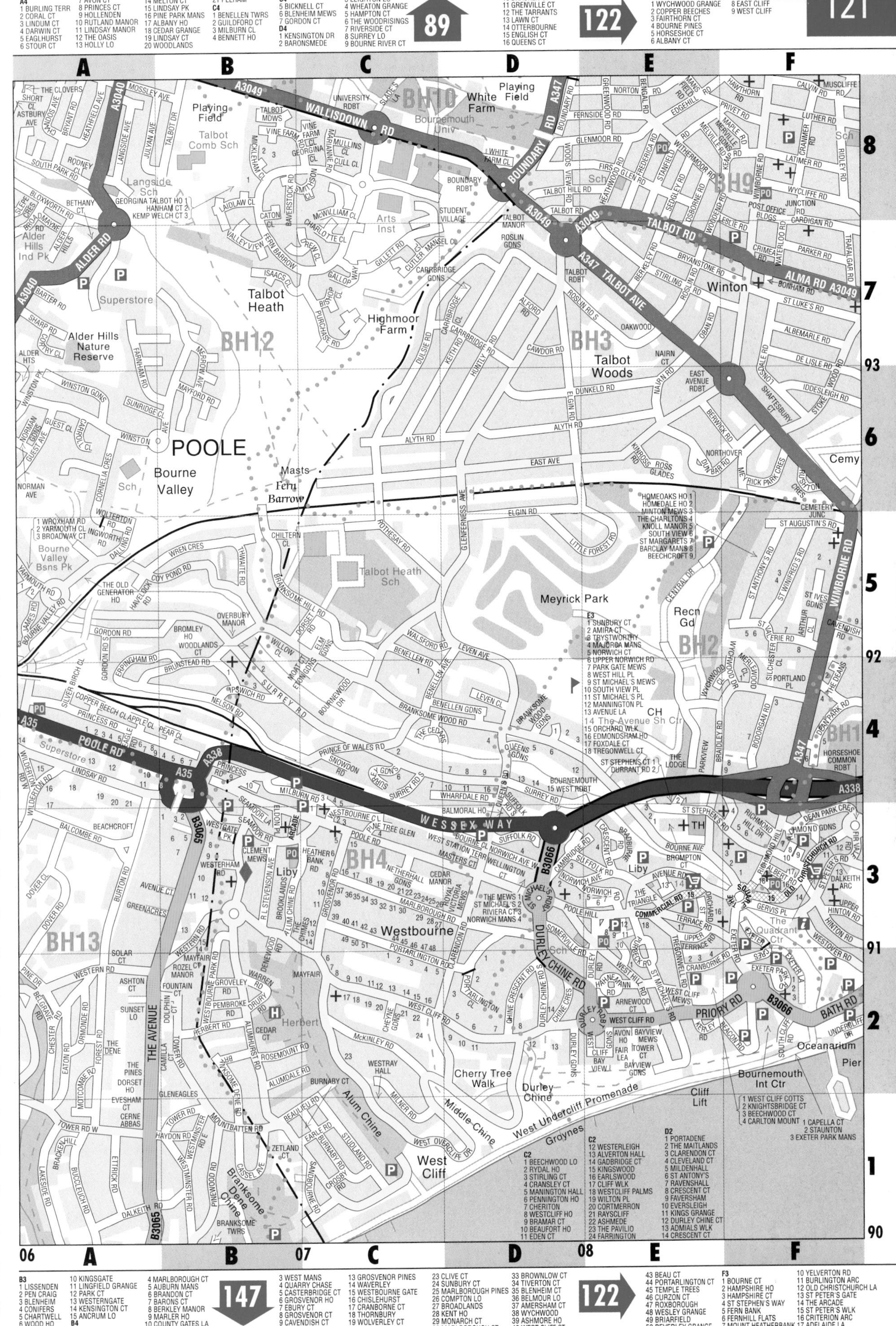

B3
1 LISSENDEN
2 PEN CRAIG
3 BLENHEIM
4 CONIFERS
5 CHARTWELL
6 WOOD HO
7 WESTERHAM
8 BELVOIR PK
9 HEADINGLEA
10 KINGSGATE
11 LINGFIELD GRANGE
12 PARK CT
13 WESTERNGATE
14 KENSINGTON CT
15 ANCRUM LO

B4
1 BRUNSTEAD PL
2 KERNELLS CT
3 CRUSADER CT
4 MARLBOROUGH CT
5 AUBURN MANS
6 BRANDON CT
7 BARONS CT
8 BERKLEY MANOR
9 MARLER HO
10 COUNTY GATES LA

C3
1 LANDSEER RD
2 ANGLEWOOD MANS

147

3 WEST MANS
4 QUARRY CHASE
5 CASTERBRIDGE CT
6 GROSVENOR HO
7 EBURY CT
8 GROSVENOR CT
9 CAVENDISH CT
10 SHELLEY CT
11 PARKLANDS
12 EDENHURST
13 GROSVENOR PINES
14 WAVERLEY
15 WESTBOURNE GATE
16 CHISLEHURST
17 CRANBORNE CT
18 THORNBURY
19 WOLVERLEY CT
20 STUDLAND CT
21 STOURTON CT
22 ALINGTON
23 CLIVE CT
24 SUNBURY CT
25 MARLBOROUGH PINES
26 COMPTON LO
27 BROADLANDS
28 KENT HO
29 MONARCH CT
30 MARLBOROUGH CT
31 BOSTON LO
32 GREENACRES
33 BROWNLOW CT
34 TIVERTON CT
35 BLENHEIM CT
36 BELMOUR LO
37 AMERSHAM CT
38 WYCHWOOD
39 ASHMORE HO
40 WEST CLIFF CT
41 SUNNINGDALE
42 BEECHFIELD

122

43 BEAU CT
44 PORTARLINGTON CT
45 TEMPLE TREES
46 CURZON CT
47 ROXBOROUGH
48 WESLEY GRANGE
49 BRIARFIELD
50 BEVERLEY GRANGE
51 ROMNEY CT

F3
1 BOURNE CT
2 HAMPSHIRE HO
3 HAMPSHIRE CT
4 ST STEPHEN'S WAY
5 FERN BANK
6 FERNHILL FLATS
7 MOUNT HEATHERBANK
8 VERULAM PL
9 GRANVILLE PL
10 YELVERTON RD
11 BURLINGTON ARC
12 OLD CHRISTCHURCH LA
13 ST PETER'S GATE
14 THE ARCADE
15 ST PETER'S WLK
16 CRITERION ARC
17 ADELAIDE LA
18 POST OFFICE RD

A5
1 CULFORD CT
2 APSLEY CT
3 TRELOEN CT
4 RAVANA CT
5 HOMELEIGH HO
6 BEECHEY CT
7 WELLINGTON CT
8 MORINGTON CT
9 PARSONAGE CT

B5
1 HAMILTON CT
2 MOORLEA
3 PORCHESTER CT

121

C5
1 OPHIR GDNS
2 METHUEN CL
3 LOWTHER GDNS
4 THE LANE LOTHER GDNS
5 STEWART CL
6 HENVILLE RD
7 MALMESBURY PARK PL
8 WESLEY CL

90

E5
1 ST ANN'S CT
2 ST GEORGE'S CT
3 ST DAVID'S CT
4 ST JOHN'S CT

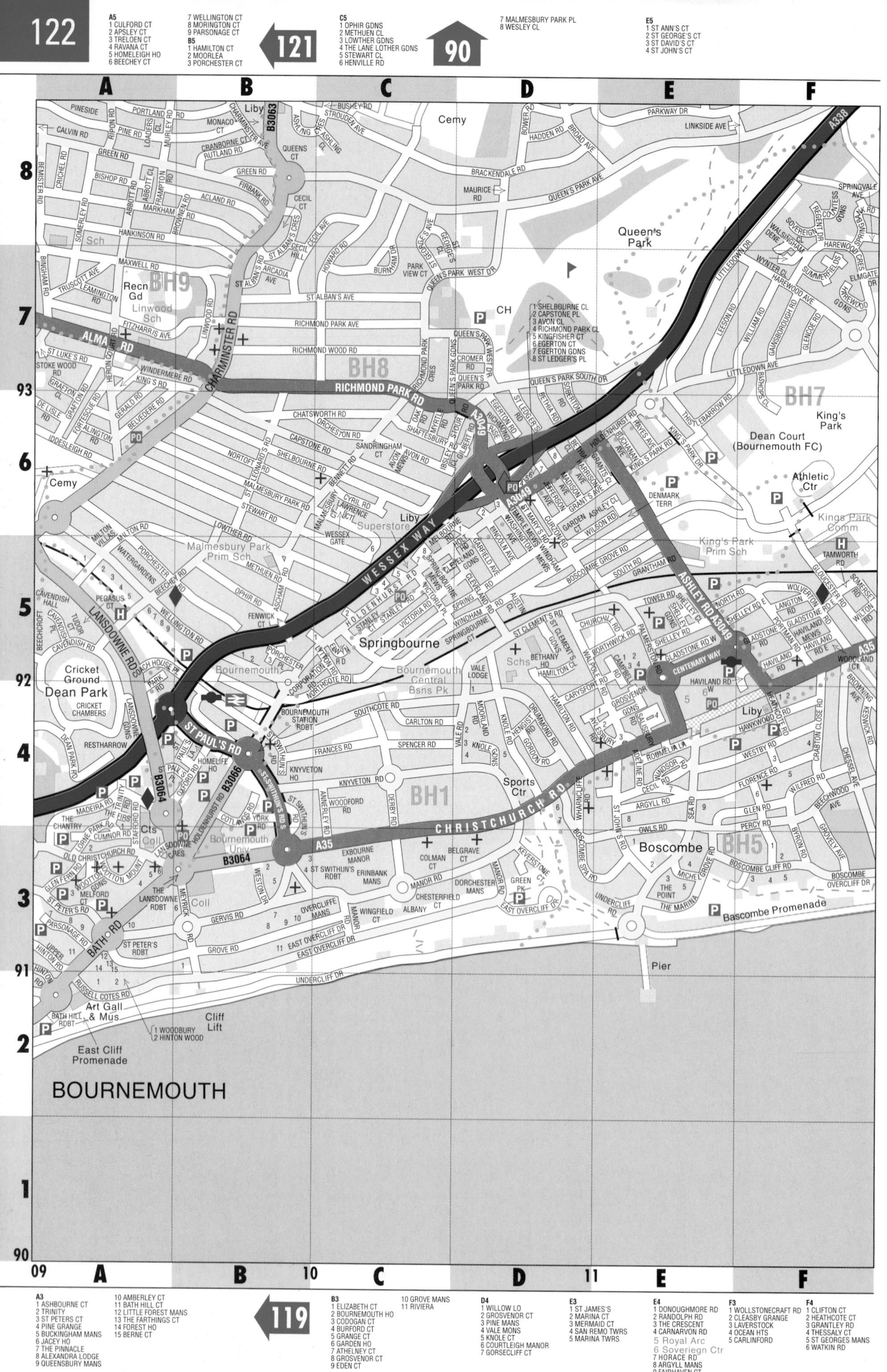

A3
1 ASHBOURNE CT
2 TRINITY
3 ST PETERS CT
4 PINE GRANGE
5 BUCKINGHAM MANS
6 JACEY HO
7 THE PINNACLE
8 ALEXANDRA LODGE
9 QUEENSBURY MANS
10 AMBERLEY CT
11 BATH HILL CT
12 LITTLE FOREST MANS
13 THE FARTHINGS CT
14 FOREST HO
15 BERNE CT

119

B3
1 ELIZABETH CT
2 BOURNEMOUTH HO
3 CODOGAN CT
4 BURFORD CT
5 GRANGE CT
6 GARDEN HO
7 ATHELNEY CT
8 GROSVENOR CT
9 EDEN CT
10 GROVE MANS
11 RIVIERA

D4
1 WILLOW LO
2 GROSVENOR CT
3 PINE MANS
4 VALE MONS
5 KNOLE CT
6 COURTLEIGH MANOR
7 GORSECLIFF CT

E3
1 ST JAMES'S
2 MARINA CT
3 MERMAID CT
4 SAN REMO TWRS
5 MARINA TWRS

E4
1 DONOUGHMORE RD
2 RANDOLPH RD
3 THE CRESCENT
4 CARNARVON RD
5 Royal Arc
6 Soveriegn Ctr
7 HORACE RD
8 ARGYLL MANS
9 FAIRHAVEN CT

F3
1 WOLLSTONECRAFT RD
2 CLEASBY GRANGE
3 LAVERSTOCK
4 OCEAN HTS
5 CARLINFORD

F4
1 CLIFTON CT
2 HEATHCOTE CT
3 GRANTLEY RD
4 THESSALY CT
5 ST GEORGES MANS
6 WATKIN RD

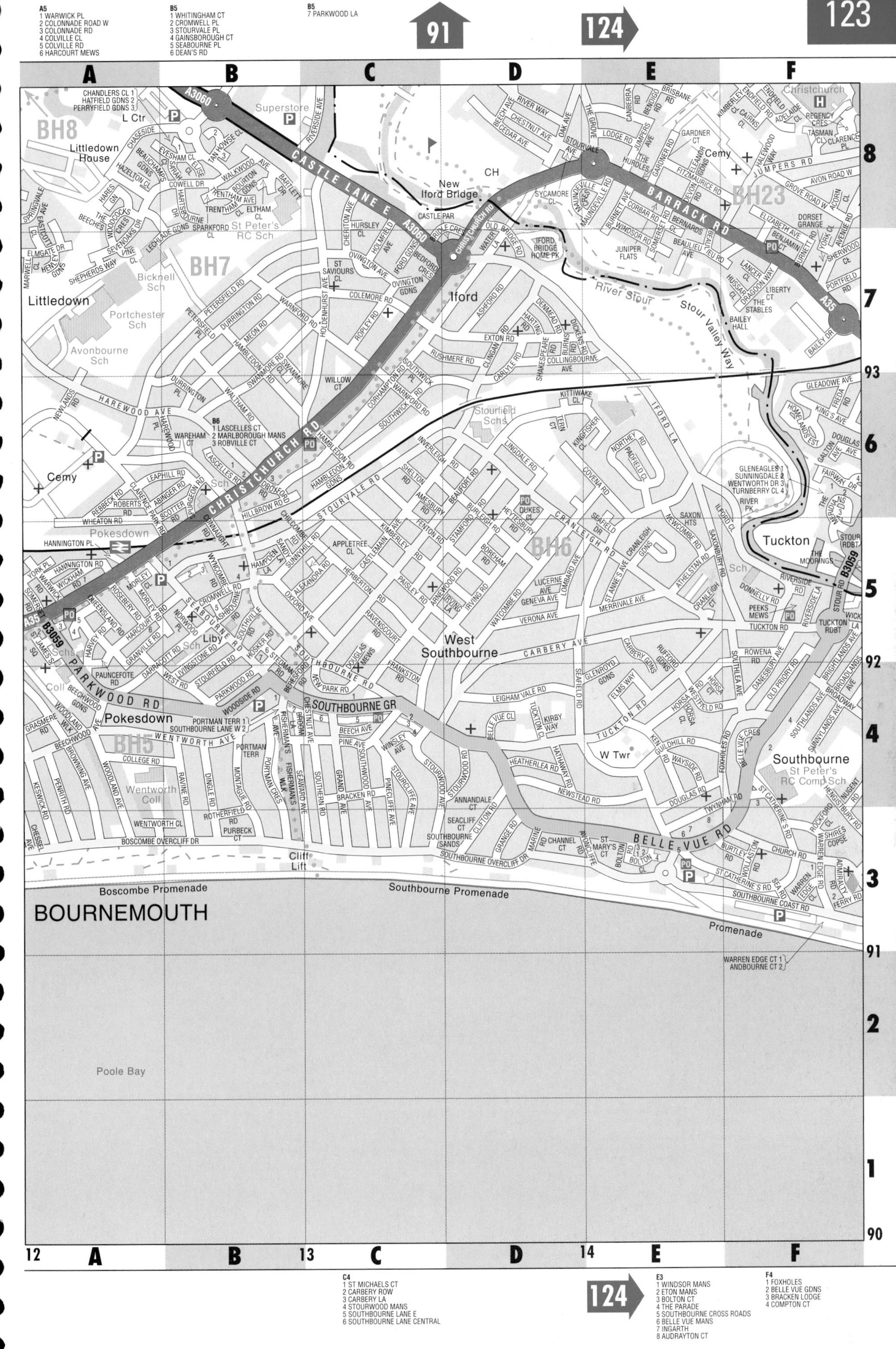
A5
1 WARWICK PL
2 COLONNADE ROAD W
3 COLONNADE RD
4 COLVILLE CL
5 COLVILLE RD
6 HARCOURT MEWS
B5
1 WHITINGHAM CT
2 CROMWELL PL
3 STOURVALE PL
4 GAINSBOROUGH CT
5 SEABOURNE PL
6 DEAN'S RD
B5
7 PARKWOOD LA
91
124
B6
1 LASCELLES CT
2 MARLBOROUGH MANS
3 ROBVILLE CT
CHANDLERS CL 1
HATFIELD GDNS 2
PERRYFIELD GDNS 3
GLENEAGLES 1
SUNNINGDALE 2
WENTWORTH DR 3
TURNBERRY CL 4
WARREN EDGE CT 1
ANDBOURNE CT 2
BH8
BH7
BH6
BH5
BH23
Littledown House
Littledown
Cemy
Pokesdown
Iford
New Iford Bridge
West Southbourne
Tuckton
Southbourne
Christchurch
River Stour
Stour Valley Way
CASTLE LANE E
CHRISTCHURCH RD
BARRACK RD
PARKWOOD RD
SOUTHBOURNE GR
BELLE VUE RD
Boscombe Promenade
Southbourne Promenade
Promenade
BOURNEMOUTH
Poole Bay
124
C4
1 ST MICHAELS CT
2 CARBERY ROW
3 CARBERY LA
4 STOURWOOD MANS
5 SOUTHBOURNE LANE E
6 SOUTHBOURNE LANE CENTRAL
E3
1 WINDSOR MANS
2 ETON MANS
3 BOLTON CT
4 THE PARADE
5 SOUTHBOURNE CROSS ROADS
6 BELLE VUE MANS
7 INGARTH
8 AUDRAYTON CT
F4
1 FOXHOLES
2 BELLE VUE GDNS
3 BRACKEN LODGE
4 COMPTON CT

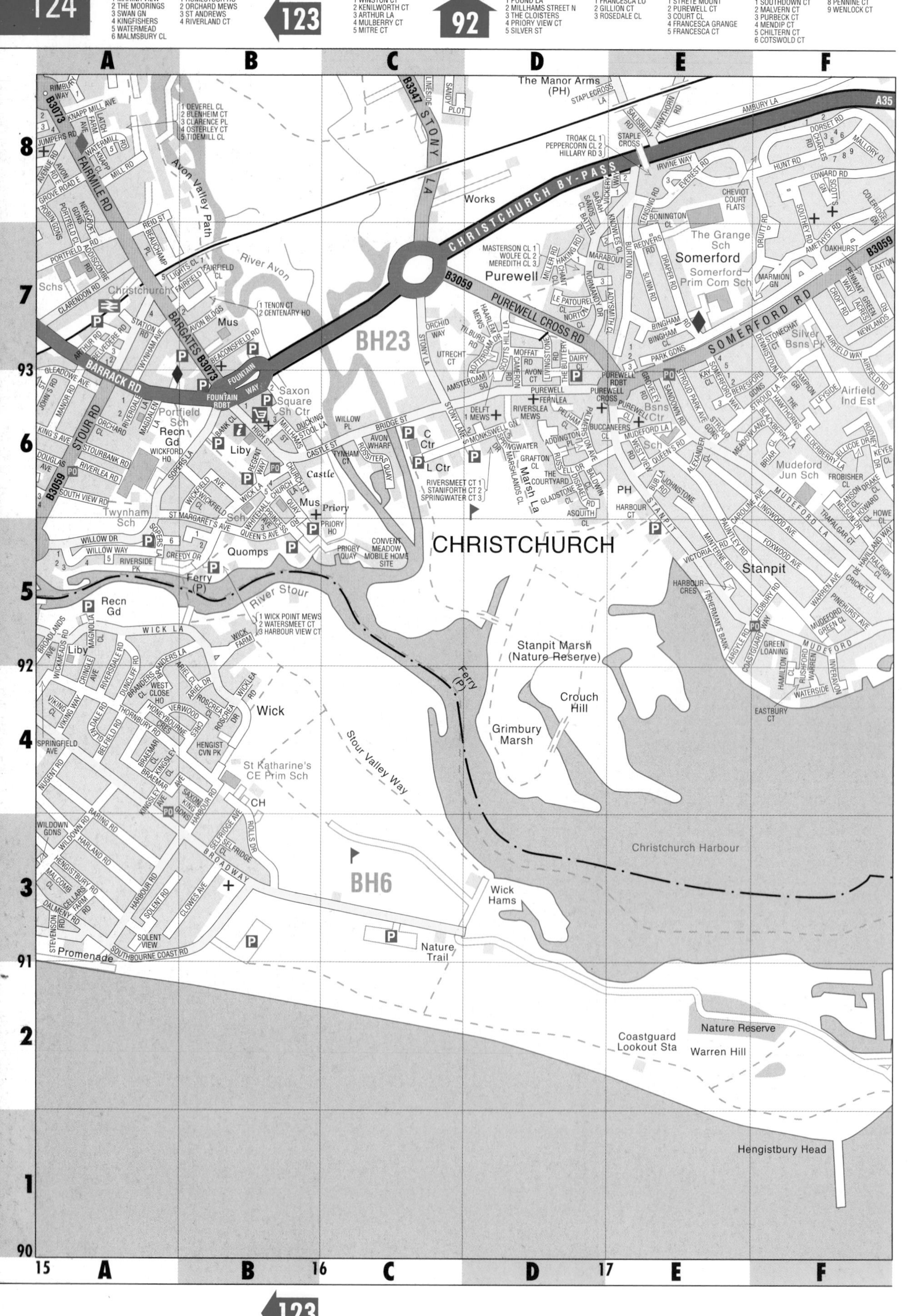
A5
1 MARINA VIEW
2 THE MOORINGS
3 SWAN GN
4 KINGFISHERS
5 WATERMEAD
6 MALMSBURY CL
A6
1 HOMESTOUR HO
2 ORCHARD MEWS
3 ST ANDREWS
4 RIVERLAND CT
123
A7
1 WINSTON CT
2 KENILWORTH CT
3 ARTHUR LA
4 MULBERRY CT
5 MITRE CT
92
B6
1 POUND LA
2 MILLHAMS STREET N
3 THE CLOISTERS
4 PRIORY VIEW CT
5 SILVER ST
E6
1 FRANCESCA LO
2 GILLION CT
3 ROSEDALE CL
E7
1 STRETE MOUNT
2 PUREWELL CT
3 COURT CL
4 FRANCESCA GRANGE
5 FRANCESCA CT
F8
1 SOUTHDOWN CT
2 MALVERN CT
3 PURBECK CT
4 MENDIP CT
5 CHILTERN CT
6 COTSWOLD CT
7 QUANTOCK CT
8 PENNINE CT
9 WENLOCK CT
A
B
C
D
E
F
The Manor Arms (PH)
A35
CHRISTCHURCH BY-PASS
B3073
B3347
B3059
BH23
Avon Valley Path
River Avon
Works
Purewell
Somerford
The Grange Sch
Somerford Prim Com Sch
Silver Bsns Pk
Airfield Ind Est
Christchurch
Schs
Mus
Saxon Square Sh Ctr
Portfield Sch
Recn Gd
Liby
Castle
Priory
C Ctr
L Ctr
Twynham Sch
Quomps
Ferry (P)
River Stour
CHRISTCHURCH
Mudeford Jun Sch
Stanpit
Stanpit Marsh (Nature Reserve)
Crouch Hill
Grimbury Marsh
Wick
St Katharine's CE Prim Sch
Stour Valley Way
BH6
Christchurch Harbour
Wick Hams
Nature Trail
Promenade
Coastguard Lookout Sta
Nature Reserve
Warren Hill
Hengistbury Head
8
7
93
6
5
92
4
3
91
2
1
90
15
16
17
123

93
126

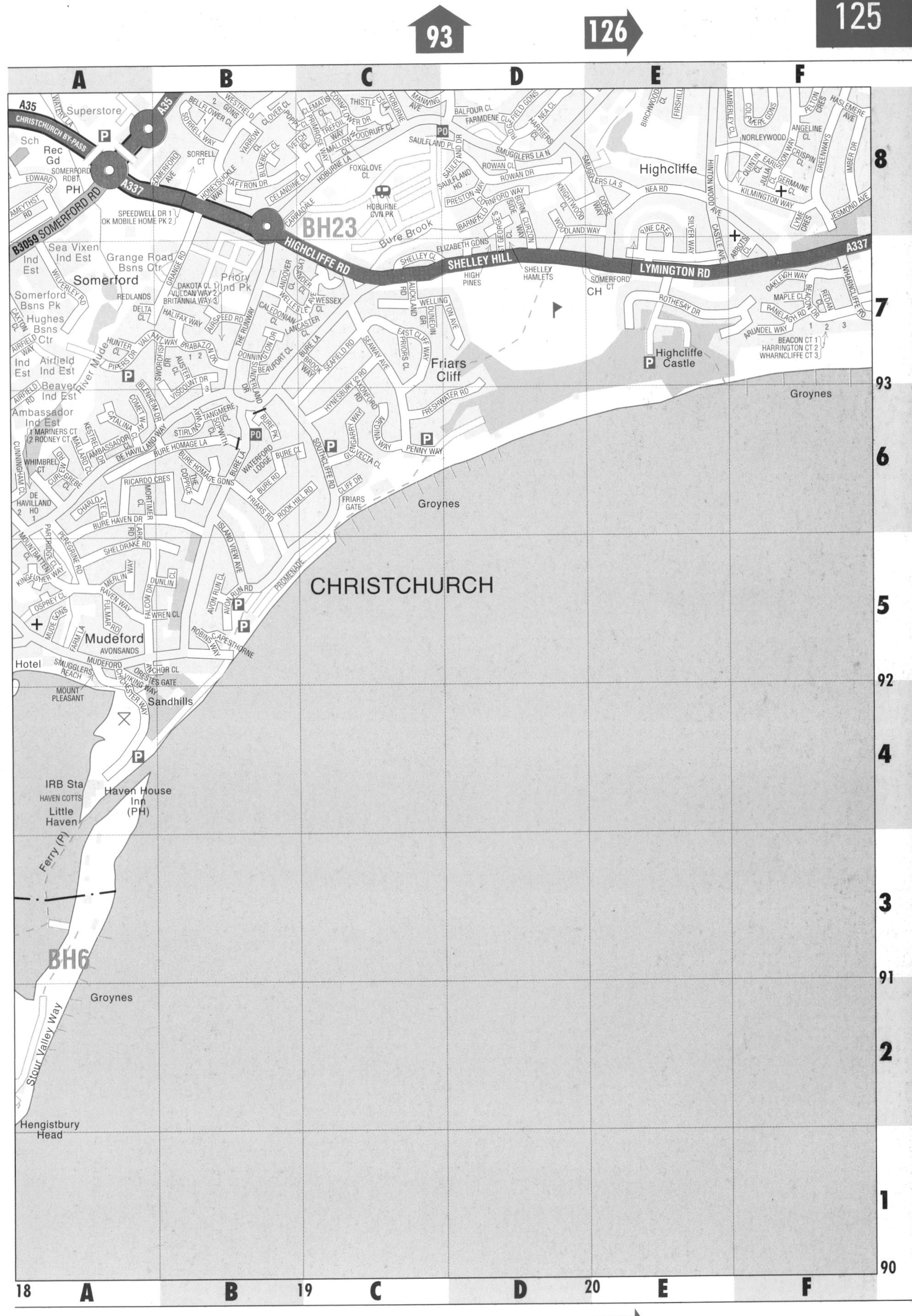

A
B
C
D
E
F
8
7
93
6
5
92
4
3
91
2
1
90
18
19
20
A35
CHRISTCHURCH BY-PASS
Superstore
Sch
Rec Gd
SOMERFORD RDBT
PH
A337
B3059 SOMERFORD RD
SPEEDWELL DR 1
OK MOBILE HOME PK 2
Sea Vixen Ind Est
Grange Road Bsns Ctr
Ind Est
Somerford
Somerford Bsns Pk
Hughes Bsns Ctr
Airfield Ind Est
Ind Est
Beaver Ind Est
Ambassador Ind Est
1 MARINERS CT
2 RODNEY CT
River Mude
DAKOTA CL 1
VULCAN WAY 2
BRITANNIA WAY 3
Priory Ind Pk
BH23
HIGHCLIFFE RD
Bure Brook
HOBURNE CVN PK
FOXGLOVE CL
SAULFLAND PL
PO
SHELLEY HILL
HIGH PINES
SHELLEY HAMLETS
LYMINGTON RD
SOMERFORD CT
CH
Highcliffe
NEA RD
Highcliffe Castle
BEACON CT 1
HARRINGTON CT 2
WHARNCLIFFE CT 3
Groynes
Friars Cliff
PENNY WAY
FRIARS GATE
Groynes
PROMENADE
CHRISTCHURCH
Mudeford
AVONSANDS
Hotel
SMUGGLERS REACH
MOUNT PLEASANT
Sandhills
IRB Sta
HAVEN COTTS
Little Haven
Haven House Inn (PH)
Ferry (P)
BH6
Groynes
Stour Valley Way
Hengistbury Head

126

125
94

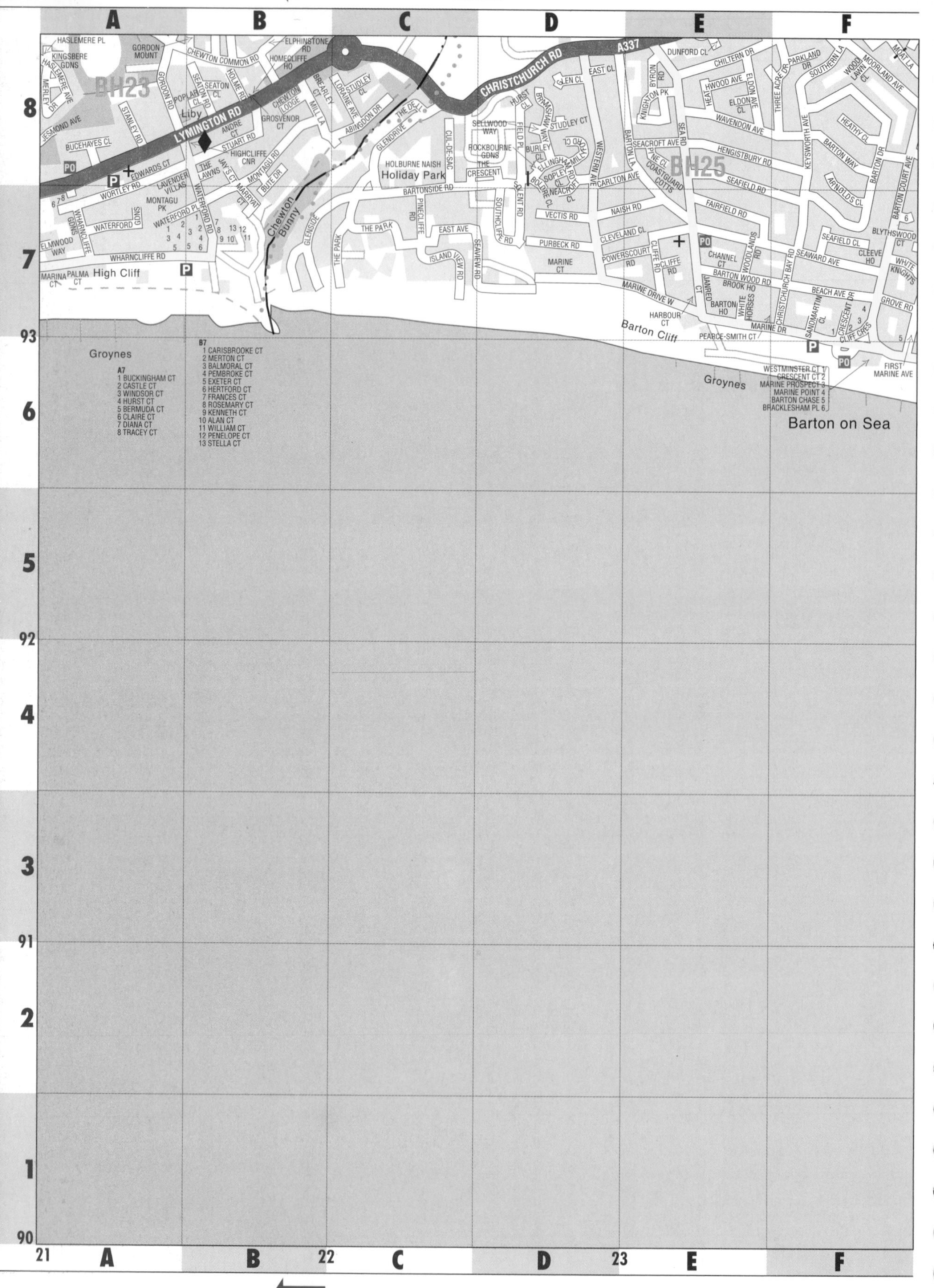
A
B
C
D
E
F
8
7
93
6
5
92
4
3
91
2
1
90
21
22
23
LYMINGTON RD
CHRISTCHURCH RD
A337
BH23
BH25
HASLEMERE PL
KINGSBERE GDNS
GORDON MOUNT
GORDON RD
CHEWTON COMMON RD
ELPHINSTONE RD
HOMECLIFFE HO
SEATON CL
HOLME RD
POPLAR CL
Liby
JESMOND AVE
STANLEY RD
BUCEHAYES CL
EDWARDS CT
WORTLEY RD
LAVENDER VILLAS
MONTAGU PK
WATERFORD GDNS
WATERFORD PL
WATERFORD RD
WHARNCLIFFE GDNS
WHARNCLIFFE RD
ELMWOOD WAY
MARINA CT
PALMA CT
High Cliff
ANDRE CT
STUART RD
HIGHCLIFFE CNR
THE LAWNS
JAY'S CT
MONTAGU RD
BUTE DR
MARRYAT CT
GROSVENOR CT
CHEWTON LODGE
MILL LA
BEARLEY CT
LORAINE AVE
STUDLEY CL
ABINGDON DR
GLENDRIVE
THE DENE
Chewton Bunny
GLENSIDE
THE PARK
PINECLIFFE RD
CUL-DE-SAC
HOLBURNE NAISH
Holiday Park
BARTONSIDE RD
EAST AVE
ISLAND VIEW RD
SEAVIEW RD
SELLWOOD WAY
ROCKBOURNE GDNS
THE CRESCENT
FIELD PL
HURST CL
SOUTHCLIFFE RD
SOLENT RD
BURLEY CL
BRAMSHAW WAY
GLEN CL
STUDLEY CT
ELLINGHAM RD
SOPLEY CL
NEACROFT CL
BOLDRE CL
VECTIS RD
PURBECK RD
MARINE CT
EAST CL
WESTERN AVE
BARTON LA
CARLTON AVE
NAISH RD
CLEVELAND CL
POWERSCOURT RD
CLIFFE RD
MARINE DRIVE W
HARBOUR CT
Barton Cliff
DUNFORD CL
KNIGHTON PK
BYRON RD
SEA RD
SEACROFT AVE
PINE CL
COASTGUARD COTTS
CHILTERN DR
HEATHWOOD AVE
ELDON AVE
ELDON CL
WAVENDON AVE
HENGISTBURY RD
SEAFIELD RD
FAIRFIELD RD
CHANNEL CT
JANRED CT
BARTON WOOD RD
BROOK HO
BARTON HO
WHITE HORSES
WOODLANDS RD
CHRISTCHURCH BAY RD
MARINE DR
PEARCE-SMITH CT
THREE ACRE DR
PARKLAND DR
SOUTHERN LA
WOOD LAWN CL
MOORLAND AVE
MOAT LA
KEYSWORTH AVE
HEATHY CL
BARTON WAY
ARNOLDS CL
BARTON DR
BARTON COURT AVE
BLYTHSWOOD CT
SEAFIELD CL
SEAWARD AVE
CLEEVE HO
WHITE KNIGHTS
BEACH AVE
GROVE RD
SANDMARTIN CL
CRESCENT DR
CLIFF CRES
FIRST MARINE AVE
WESTMINSTER CT 1
CRESCENT CT 2
MARINE PROSPECT 3
MARINE POINT 4
BARTON CHASE 5
BRACKLESHAM PL 6
Groynes
Barton on Sea
A7
1 BUCKINGHAM CT
2 CASTLE CT
3 WINDSOR CT
4 HURST CT
5 BERMUDA CT
6 CLAIRE CT
7 DIANA CT
8 TRACEY CT
B7
1 CARISBROOKE CT
2 MERTON CT
3 BALMORAL CT
4 PEMBROKE CT
5 EXETER CT
6 HERTFORD CT
7 FRANCES CT
8 ROSEMARY CT
9 KENNETH CT
10 ALAN CT
11 WILLIAM CT
12 PENELOPE CT
13 STELLA CT

125

95

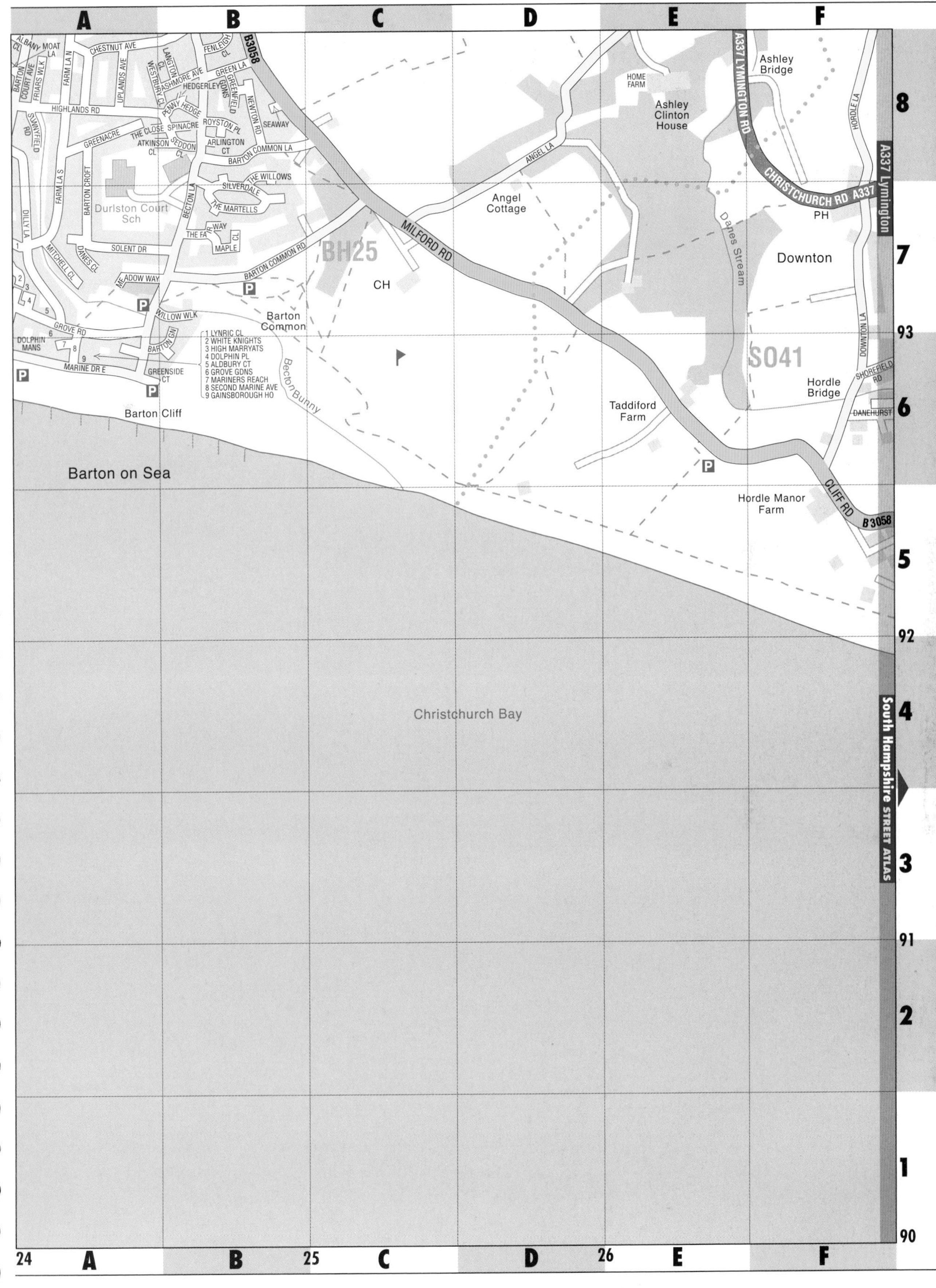

A
B
C
D
E
F
8
7
93
6
5
92
4
3
91
2
1
90
24
25
26
B3058
MILFORD RD
BH25
CH
Barton Common
Becton Bunny
Barton Cliff
Barton on Sea
Durlston Court Sch
Angel Cottage
ANGEL LA
HOME FARM
Ashley Clinton House
Ashley Bridge
A337 LYMINGTON RD
CHRISTCHURCH RD A337
A337 Lymington
PH
Downton
Danes Stream
SO41
Hordle Bridge
DOWNTON LA
HORDLE LA
SHOREFIELD RD
DANEHURST
Taddiford Farm
Hordle Manor Farm
CLIFF RD
B3058
Christchurch Bay
South Hampshire STREET ATLAS
CHESTNUT AVE
HIGHLANDS RD
GREENACRE
SOLENT DR
MARINE DR E
GROVE RD
DOLPHIN MANS
BARTON COMMON RD
BARTON COMMON LA
WILLOW WLK
GREENSIDE CT
BARTON GN
1 LYNRIC CL
2 WHITE KNIGHTS
3 HIGH MARRYATS
4 DOLPHIN PL
5 ALDBURY CT
6 GROVE GDNS
7 MARINERS REACH
8 SECOND MARINE AVE
9 GAINSBOROUGH HO

B8
1 HOWARTH CL
2 SOUTH ANNINGS
3 GROVE ORCHARD
4 ST LAWRENCE
5 DONKEY LA
6 DARBY LA

A B C D E F

Burton Bradstock

Peacehaven Farm

Bredy Farm

BURTON ROAD

Graston Copse

Graston Farm

BREDY LANE

SHIPTON LANE

NORTH HL CL

Shadrach

8

Works

B3157

BARROWFIELD CL

CHARLES RD

SHADRACH

MIDDLE ST

LOWER TOWNSEND

NORTHOVER

ANNINGS LANE

NORTHOVER CLOSE

GROVE ROAD

Liby

Magnolia Farm

BARR LANE

CHURCH ST

Burton Bradstock CE Prim Sch

BREDY ROAD

River Bride

MILL

Manor Farm

HIGH ST

PH

7

National Trust

Burton Cliff

SOUTHOVER

Southover

CLIFF ROAD

COMMON LANE

DT6

Tumulus

Cliff Farm

HIVE CL

Cogden Farm

89

BEACH ROAD

BINDBARROW ROAD

6

Burton Beach

South West Coast Path

Bind Barrow

P

National Trust

Old Coastguard House

B3157

5

Cliff End

P

100

47   48

East Cliff

DT6

89   89

Cogden Beach

Burton Mere

88

4

89   89

3

47   48

87

2

1

86

48   A   B   49   C   D   50   E   F

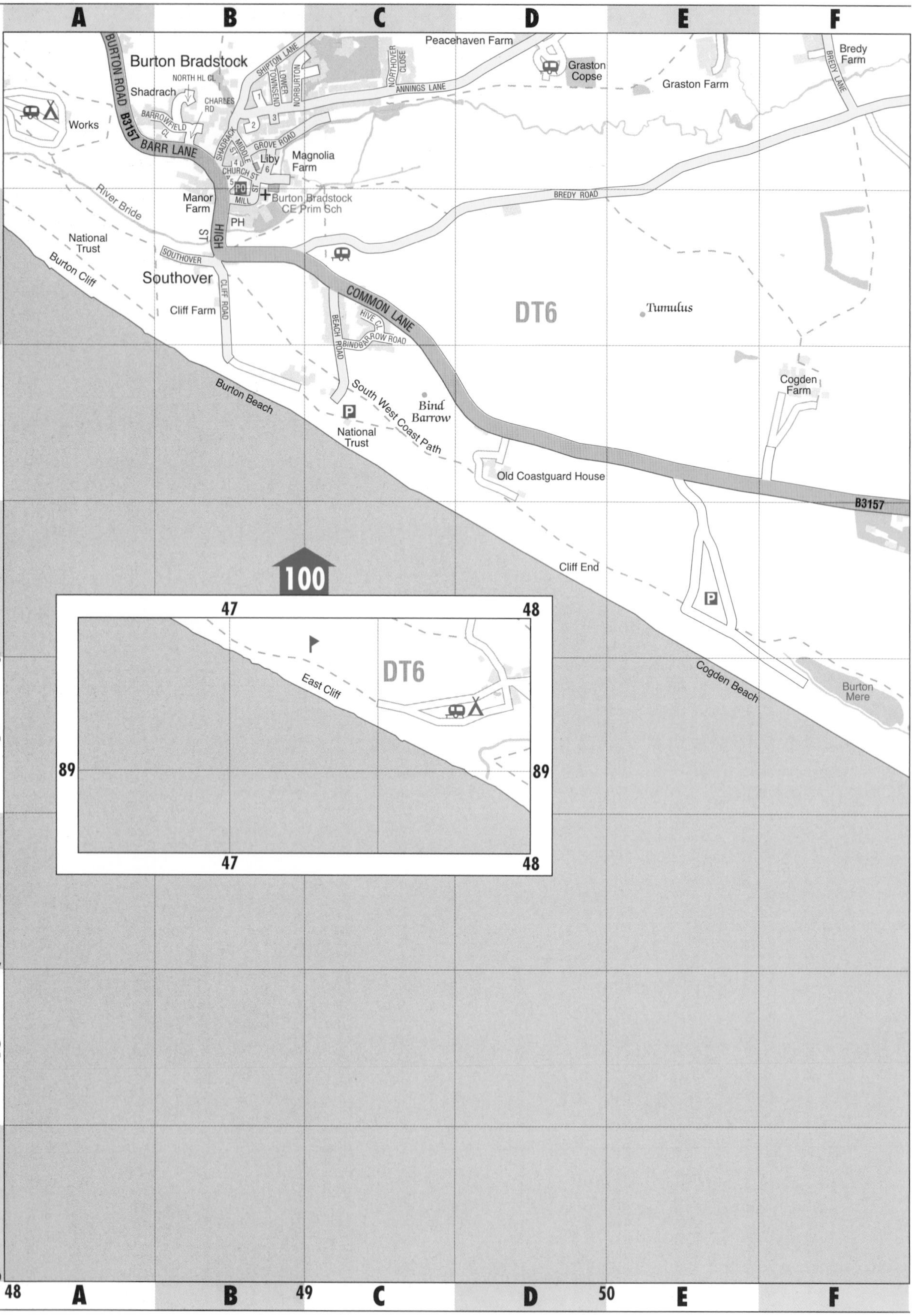

102
130

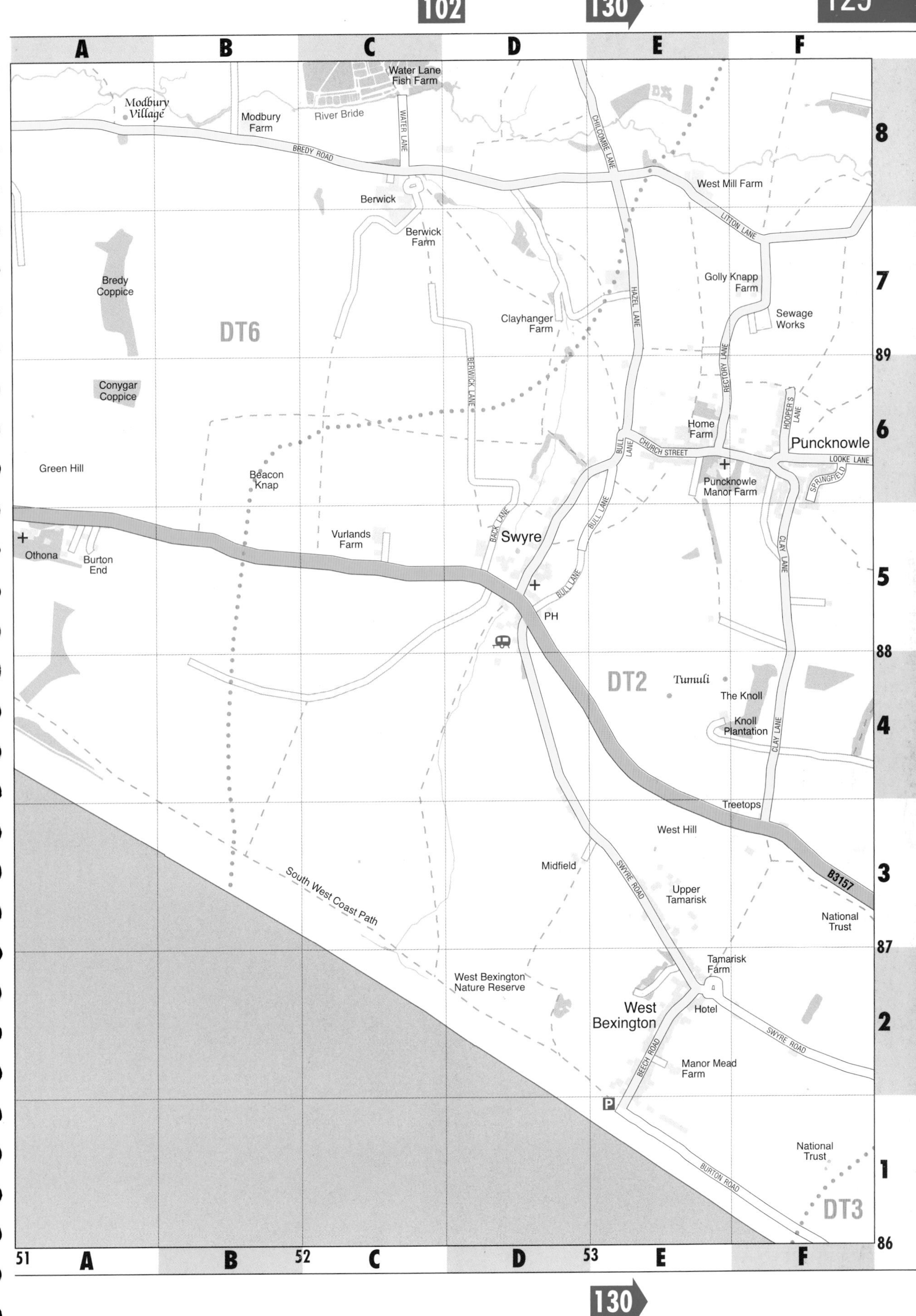
A
B
C
D
E
F
Water Lane Fish Farm
Modbury Village
Modbury Farm
River Bride
WATER LANE
BREDY ROAD
CHILCOMBE LANE
8
West Mill Farm
Berwick
Berwick Farm
LITTON LANE
Bredy Coppice
Golly Knapp Farm
7
HAZEL LANE
Clayhanger Farm
Sewage Works
DT6
RECTORY LANE
89
Conygar Coppice
BERWICK LANE
HOOPER'S LANE
Home Farm
6
Punckknowle
CHURCH STREET
BULL LANE
LOOKE LANE
Green Hill
Beacon Knap
Punckknowle Manor Farm
SPRINGFIELD
BACK LANE
BULL LANE
Vurlands Farm
Swyre
Othona
Burton End
CLAY LANE
5
BULL LANE
PH
88
DT2
Tumuli
The Knoll
Knoll Plantation
4
CLAY LANE
Treetops
West Hill
Midfield
3
SWYRE ROAD
B3157
South West Coast Path
Upper Tamarisk
National Trust
87
Tamarisk Farm
West Bexington Nature Reserve
West Bexington
Hotel
2
SWYRE ROAD
BEECH ROAD
Manor Mead Farm
P
National Trust
1
BURTON ROAD
DT3
86
51
A
B
52
C
D
53
E
F

130

129
103

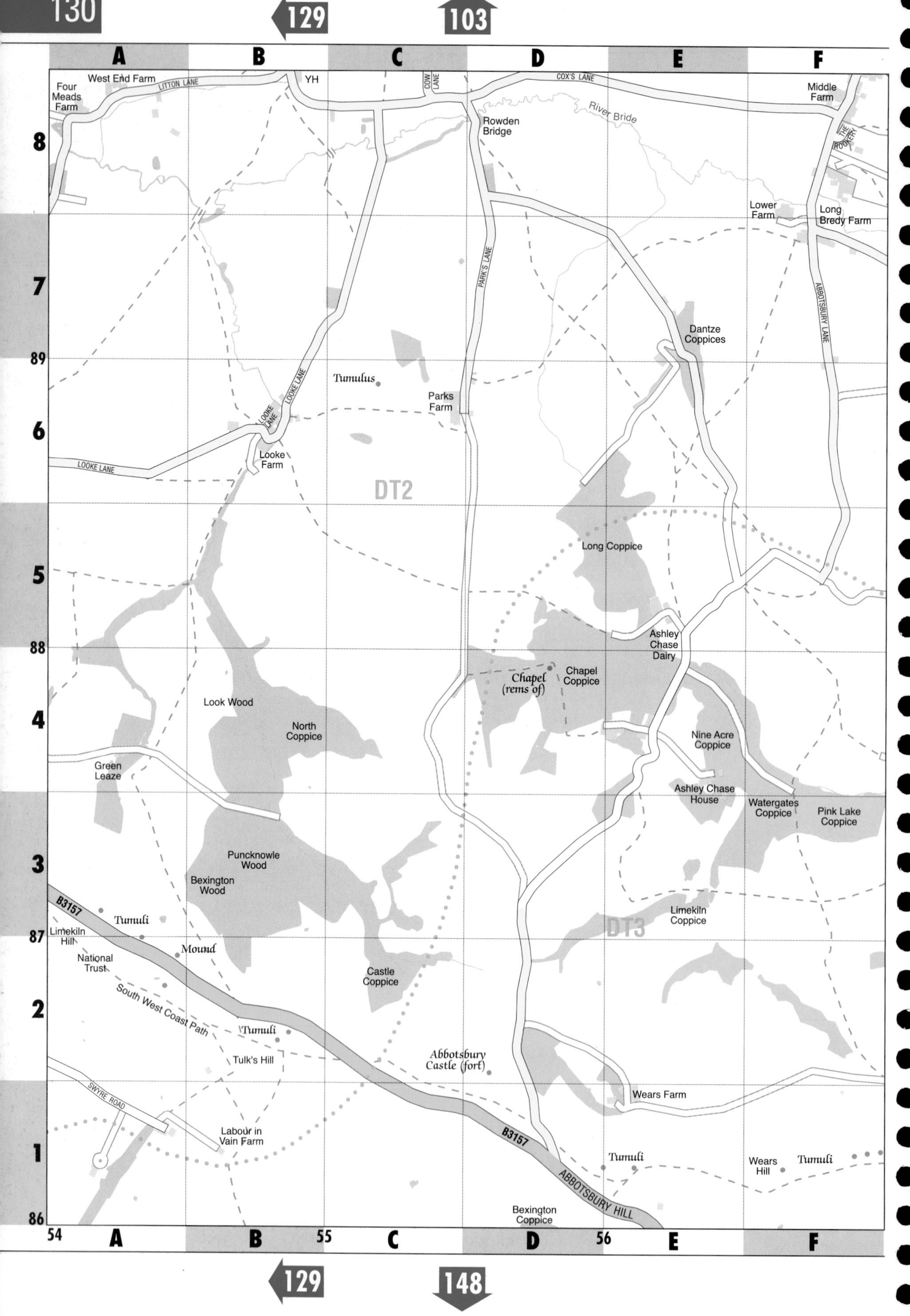
A
B
C
D
E
F
8
7
89
6
5
88
4
3
87
2
1
86
54
55
56
West End Farm
Four Meads Farm
LITTON LANE
YH
COW LANE
COX'S LANE
River Bride
Rowden Bridge
Middle Farm
THE ROOKERY
Lower Farm
Long Bredy Farm
PARK'S LANE
ABBOTSBURY LANE
Dantze Coppices
Tumulus
Parks Farm
LOOKE LANE
Looke Farm
DT2
Long Coppice
Ashley Chase Dairy
Chapel (rems of)
Chapel Coppice
Look Wood
North Coppice
Nine Acre Coppice
Green Leaze
Ashley Chase House
Watergates Coppice
Pink Lake Coppice
Puncknowle Wood
Bexington Wood
B3157
Tumuli
Limekiln Hill
Mound
National Trust
Limekiln Coppice
DT3
Castle Coppice
South West Coast Path
Tumuli
Tulk's Hill
Abbotsbury Castle (fort)
Wears Farm
SWYRE ROAD
Labour in Vain Farm
B3157
Tumuli
Wears Hill
Tumuli
ABBOTSBURY HILL
Bexington Coppice

129
148

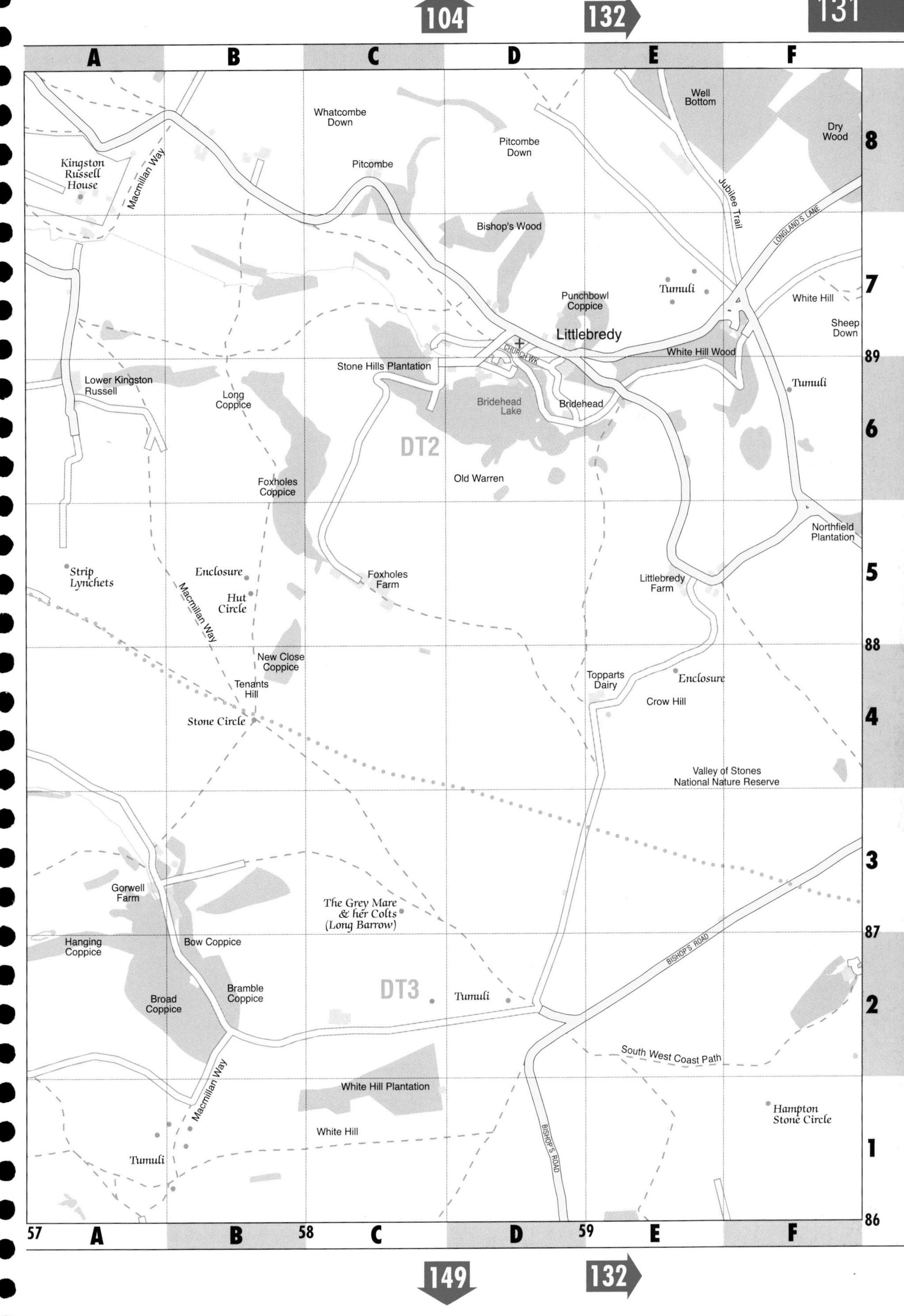

A   B   C   D   E   F

8

Well
Bottom

Dry
Wood

Whatcombe
Down

Pitcombe
Down

Pitcombe

Kingston
Russell
House

Macmillan Way

Bishop's Wood

Jubilee Trail

LONGLANDS LANE

7

Tumuli

White Hill

Punchbowl
Coppice

Sheep
Down

Littlebredy

89

Stone Hills Plantation

CHURCH WK

White Hill Wood

Lower Kingston
Russell

Long
Coppice

Tumuli

6

Bridehead
Lake

Bridehead

DT2

Old Warren

Foxholes
Coppice

Northfield
Plantation

5

Strip
Lynchets

Enclosure

Foxholes
Farm

Littlebredy
Farm

Macmillan Way

Hut
Circle

88

New Close
Coppice

Topparts
Dairy

Enclosure

Tenants
Hill

Crow Hill

4

Stone Circle

Valley of Stones
National Nature Reserve

3

Gorwell
Farm

The Grey Mare
& her Colts
(Long Barrow)

BISHOP'S ROAD

87

Hanging
Coppice

Bow Coppice

Broad
Coppice

Bramble
Coppice

DT3

Tumuli

2

Macmillan Way

South West Coast Path

Hampton
Stone Circle

White Hill Plantation

BISHOP'S ROAD

White Hill

1

Tumuli

86

57   A   B   58   C   D   59   E   F

A B C D E F

8

Longlands

Tumuli

Dry
Wood

LONGLAND'S LANE

Big
Wood

Tumulus

Coombe
Farm

COOMBE ROAD

Strip
Lynchets

Steepleton
Farm

B3159

Greater
Whitway Farm

Manor
Farm

Winterbourne
Steepleton

7

Jubilee Trail

Loscombe
Plantation

Loscombe
Farm

Loscombe
Down

Tumulus

Dairy

Mast

89

Sheep
Down

Tumuli

COOMBE ROAD

Loscombe
Wood

Tumulus

DT2

Tumulus

Ballarat
Farm

6

Long
Barrow

Conygar
Meadow
Coppice

Jubilee Trail

Tumulus

East Rew
Farm

5

Enclosure

88

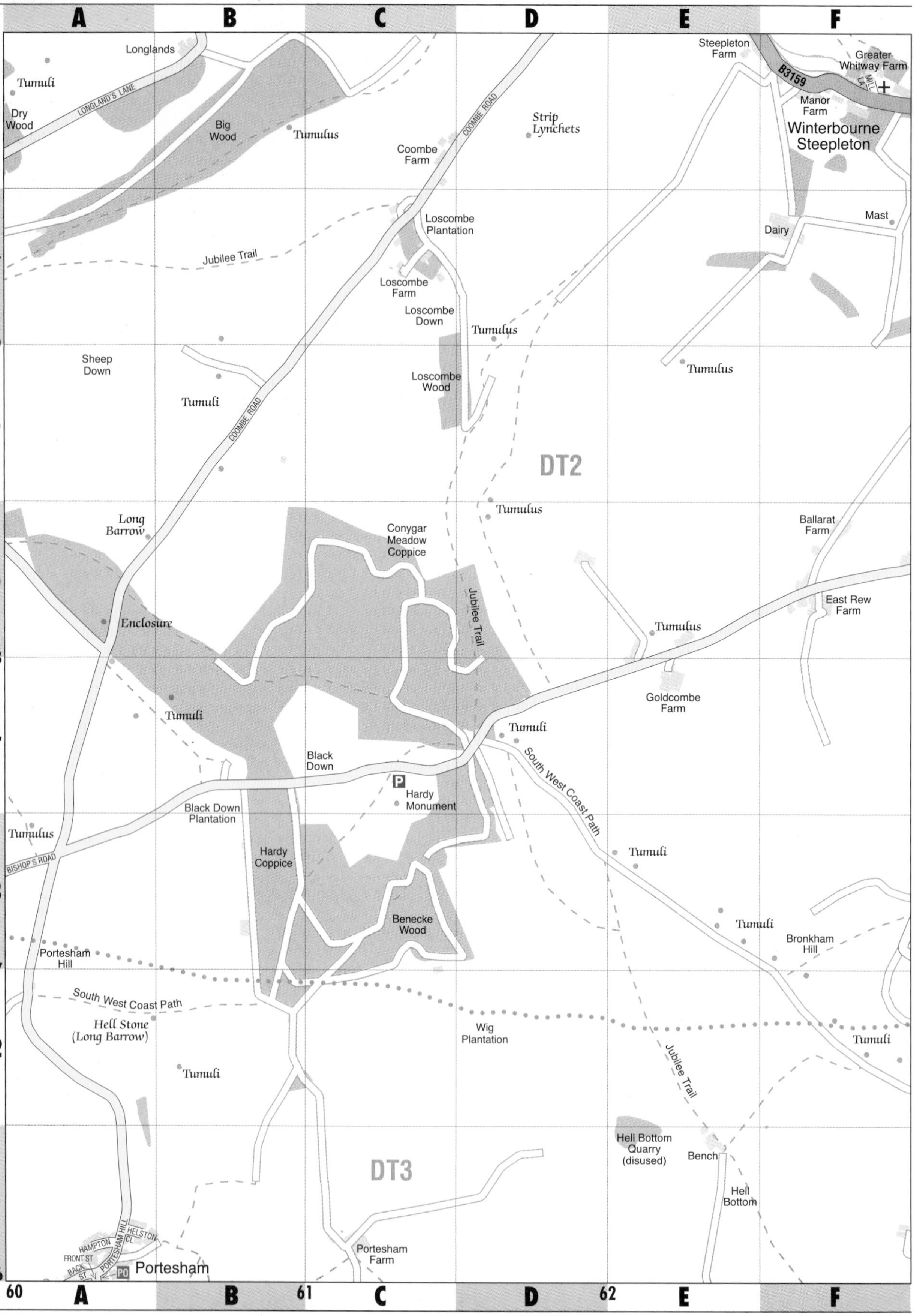

Goldcombe
Farm

4

Tumuli

Black
Down

P

Hardy
Monument

Tumuli

South West Coast Path

Tumuli

Tumulus

Black Down
Plantation

Hardy
Coppice

Tumuli

Bronkham
Hill

3

BISHOP'S ROAD

Benecke
Wood

87

Portesham
Hill

South West Coast Path

Wig
Plantation

Jubilee Trail

Tumuli

2

Hell Stone
(Long Barrow)

Tumuli

Hell Bottom
Quarry
(disused)

Bench

Hell
Bottom

1

DT3

HAMPTON HILL

HELSTON CL

FRONT ST

BACK ST

PORTESHAM HILL

PO

Portesham

Portesham
Farm

86

60 A B 61 C D 62 E F

106
134

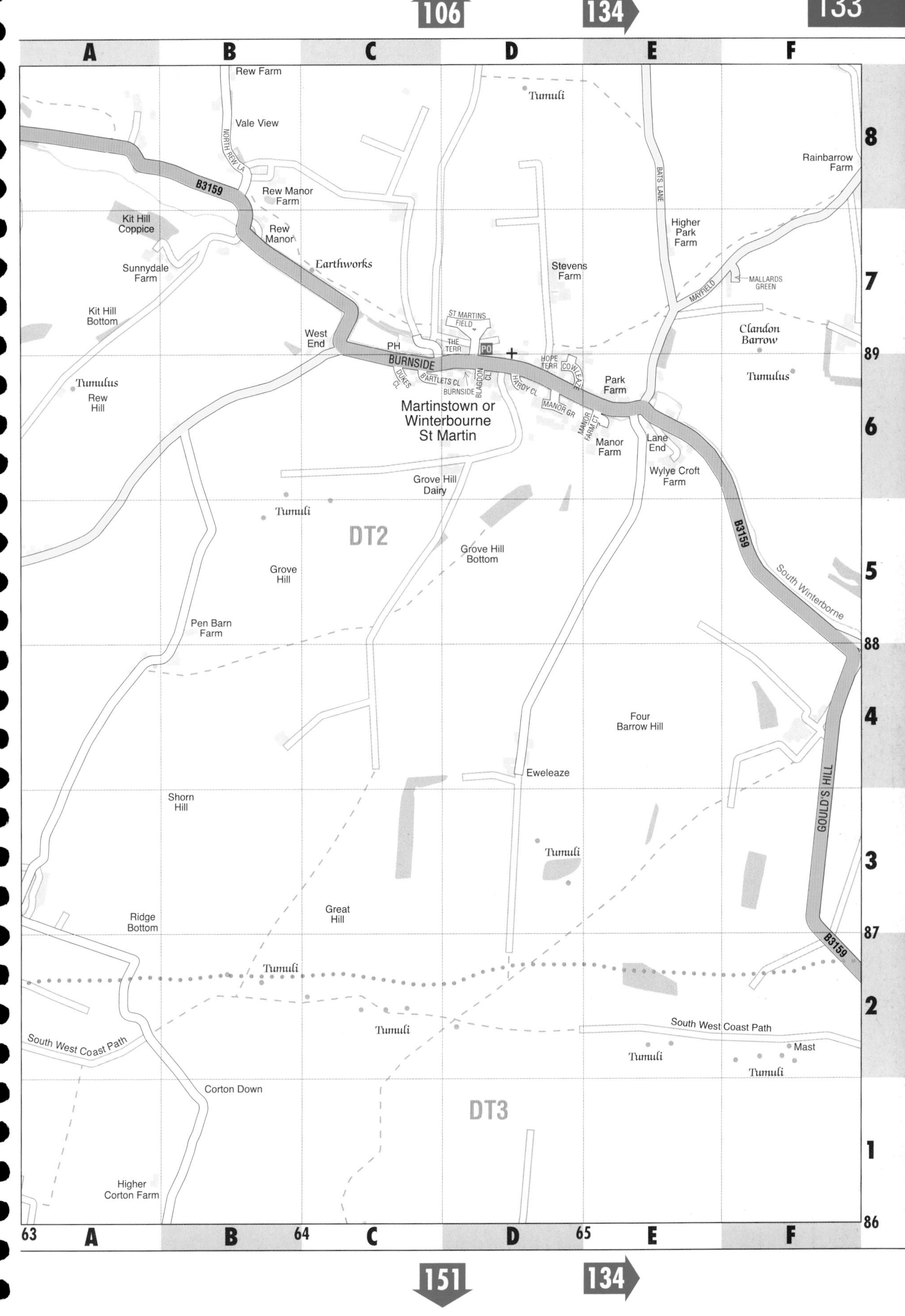
A
B
C
D
E
F
Rew Farm
Tumuli
Vale View
NORTH REW LA
B3159
Rew Manor
Farm
Rainbarrow
Farm
BATS LANE
Kit Hill
Coppice
Rew
Manor
Higher
Park
Farm
Earthworks
Stevens
Farm
Sunnydale
Farm
MAYFIELD
MALLARDS
GREEN
Kit Hill
Bottom
ST MARTINS
FIELD
West
End
Clandon
Barrow
PH
THE
TERR
PO
BURNSIDE
HOPE
TERR
COWLEAZE
DUKES
CL
BARTLETS CL
BURNSIDE
BLAGDON
CL
HARDY CL
Park
Farm
Tumulus
Tumulus
Rew
Hill
Martinstown or
Winterbourne
St Martin
MANOR GR
MANOR
FARM CT
Manor
Farm
Lane
End
Wylye Croft
Farm
Grove Hill
Dairy
Tumuli
DT2
B3159
Grove Hill
Bottom
Grove
Hill
South Winterborne
Pen Barn
Farm
Four
Barrow Hill
GOULD'S HILL
Eweleaze
Shorn
Hill
Tumuli
Ridge
Bottom
Great
Hill
B3159
Tumuli
Tumuli
South West Coast Path
Mast
South West Coast Path
Tumuli
Tumuli
Corton Down
DT3
Higher
Corton Farm
8
7
89
6
5
88
4
3
87
2
1
86
63
64
65

151
134

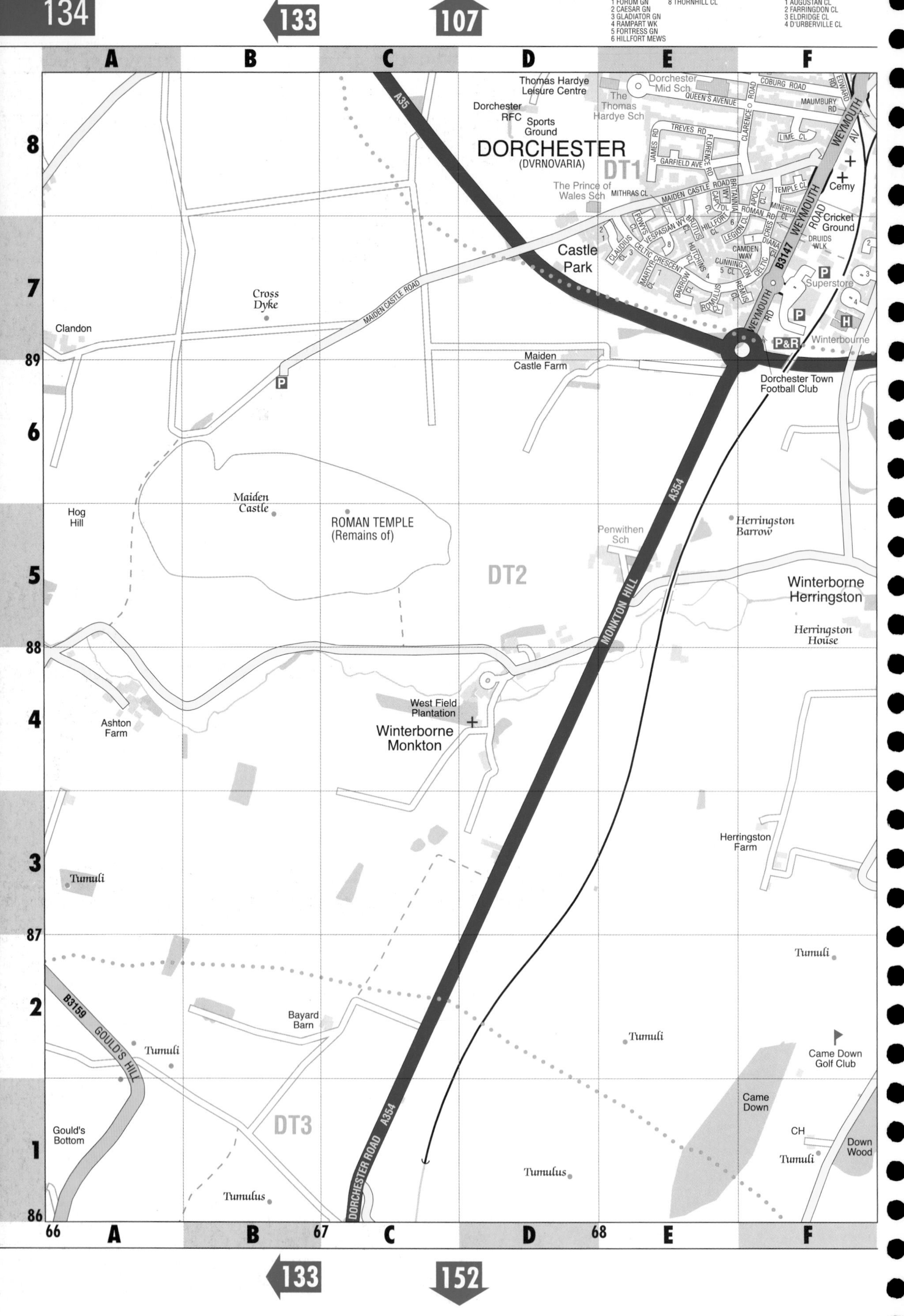
133
107
E7
1 FORUM GN
2 CAESAR GN
3 GLADIATOR GN
4 RAMPART WK
5 FORTRESS GN
6 HILLFORT MEWS
7 FOSSE GN
8 THORNHILL CL
F7
1 AUGUSTAN CL
2 FARRINGDON CL
3 ELDRIDGE CL
4 D'URBERVILLE CL
A
B
C
D
E
F
8
7
89
6
5
88
4
3
87
2
1
86
66
67
68
Thomas Hardye Leisure Centre
Dorchester Mid Sch
The Thomas Hardye Sch
Dorchester RFC
Sports Ground
DORCHESTER
(DVRNOVARIA)
DT1
The Prince of Wales Sch
MITHRAS CL
MAIDEN CASTLE ROAD
QUEEN'S AVENUE
COBURG ROAD
MAUMBURY RD
EDWARD RD
CLARENCE ROAD
TREVES RD
JAMES RD
GARFIELD AVE
FLORENCE RD
LIME CL
TEMPLE CL
WEYMOUTH AV
WEYMOUTH ROAD
B3147
Cemy
Cricket Ground
DRUIDS WLK
Castle Park
Superstore
P&R
Winterbourne
A35
Cross Dyke
Clandon
MAIDEN CASTLE ROAD
Maiden Castle Farm
Dorchester Town Football Club
Maiden Castle
ROMAN TEMPLE
(Remains of)
Hog Hill
Penwithen Sch
Herringston Barrow
DT2
A354
MONKTON HILL
Winterborne Herringston
Herringston House
Ashton Farm
West Field Plantation
Winterborne Monkton
Herringston Farm
Tumuli
Tumuli
Bayard Barn
B3159
GOULD'S HILL
Tumuli
Tumuli
Came Down Golf Club
Came Down
CH
Tumuli
Down Wood
Gould's Bottom
DT3
DORCHESTER ROAD
A354
Tumulus
Tumulus
A
B
C
D
E
F
133
152

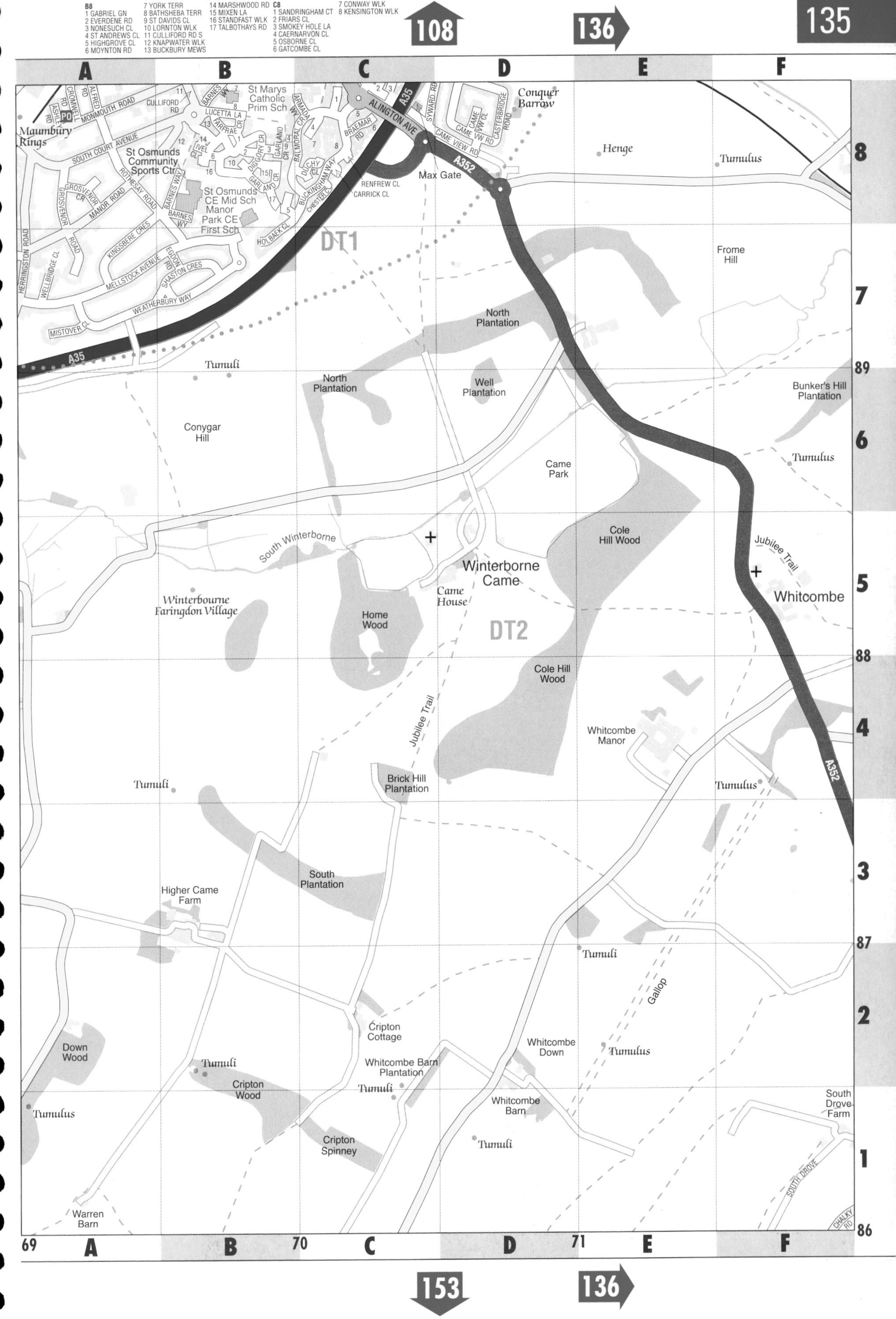
B8
1 GABRIEL GN
2 EVERDENE RD
3 NONESUCH CL
4 ST ANDREWS CL
5 HIGHGROVE CL
6 MOYNTON RD
7 YORK TERR
8 BATHSHEBA TERR
9 ST DAVIDS CL
10 LORNTON WLK
11 CULLIFORD RD S
12 KNAPWATER WLK
13 BUCKBURY MEWS
14 MARSHWOOD RD
15 MIXEN LA
16 STANDFAST WLK
17 TALBOTHAYS RD
C8
1 SANDRINGHAM CT
2 FRIARS CL
3 SMOKEY HOLE LA
4 CAERNARVON CL
5 OSBORNE CL
6 GATCOMBE CL
7 CONWAY WLK
8 KENSINGTON WLK
108
136
A
B
C
D
E
F
Maumbury Rings
St Marys Catholic Prim Sch
Conquer Barrow
St Osmunds Community Sports Ctr
St Osmunds CE Mid Sch
Manor Park CE First Sch
Max Gate
Henge
Tumulus
DT1
Frome Hill
North Plantation
Well Plantation
Tumuli
Conygar Hill
Bunker's Hill Plantation
Came Park
South Winterborne
Cole Hill Wood
Jubilee Trail
Winterborne Came
Came House
Whitcombe
Winterbourne Faringdon Village
Home Wood
DT2
Cole Hill Wood
Whitcombe Manor
Brick Hill Plantation
South Plantation
Higher Came Farm
Gallop
Cripton Cottage
Whitcombe Down
Down Wood
Cripton Wood
Whitcombe Barn Plantation
Whitcombe Barn
Cripton Spinney
South Drove Farm
Warren Barn
A35
A352
ALINGTON AVE
MONMOUTH ROAD
SOUTH COURT AVENUE
MANOR ROAD
ROTHESAY ROAD
KINGSBERE CRES
MELLSTOCK AVENUE
SHASTON CRES
WEATHERBURY WAY
MISTOVER CL
HERRINGSTON ROAD
WELLBRIDGE CL
GROSVENOR CR
GROSVENOR ROAD
BARNES WAY
CULLIFORD RD
LUCETTA LA
FARFRAE CR
IVEL CL
DIGGORY CR
GARLAND CR
BALMORAL CR
ARMADA WY
BRAEMAR RD
DUCHY CL
BUCKINGHAM WAY
CHESTER CL
HOLBAEK CL
RENFREW CL
CARRICK CL
SYWARD RD
CAME VIEW RD
CAME VW CL
CASTERBRIDGE ROAD
EDDON RD
SOUTH DROVE
CHALKY RD
8
7
89
6
5
88
4
3
87
2
1
86
69
70
71
153
136

135
109

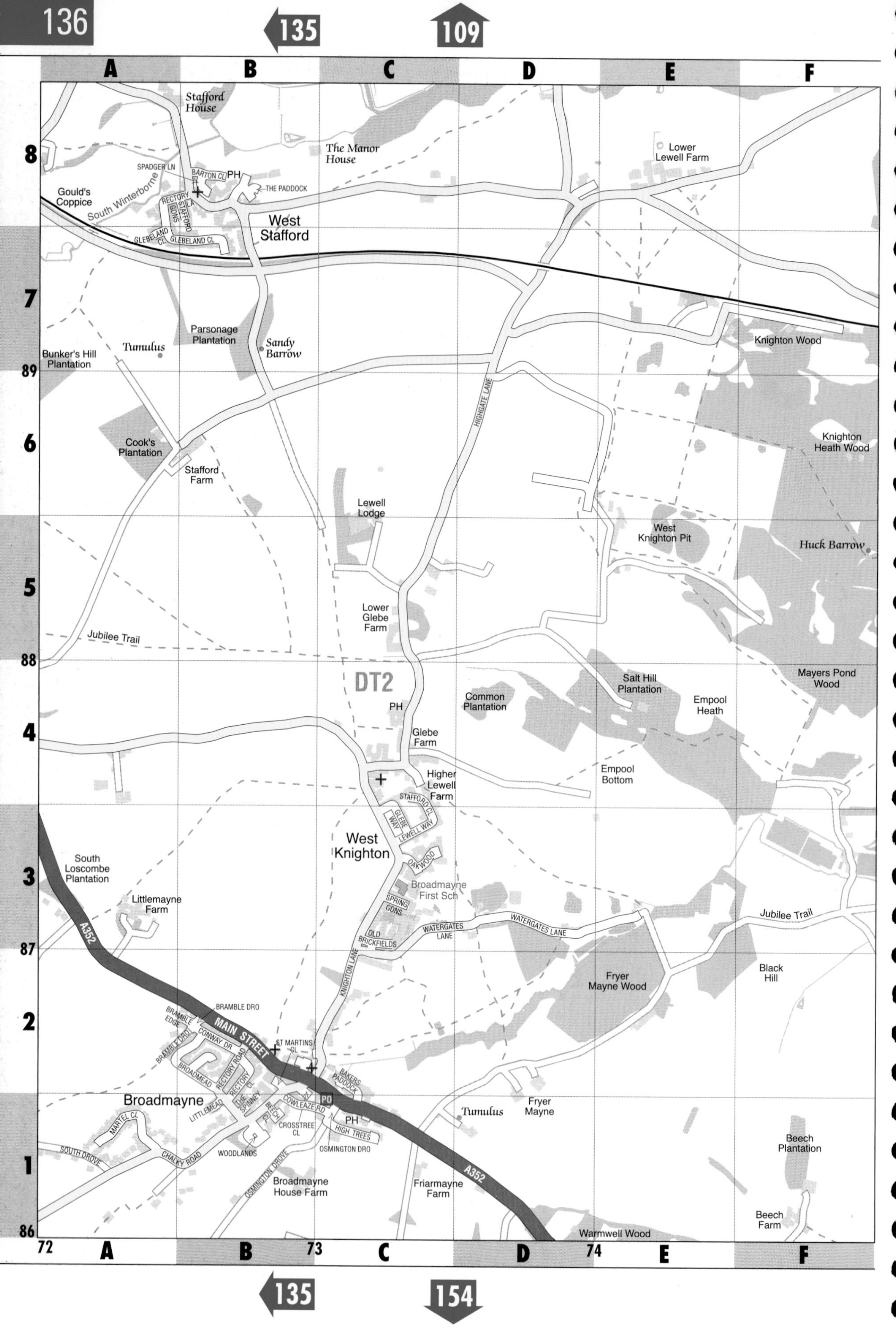
A
B
C
D
E
F
8
7
89
6
5
88
4
3
87
2
1
86
72
73
74
Stafford House
The Manor House
Lower Lewell Farm
SPADGER LN
BARTON CL
PH
THE PADDOCK
Gould's Coppice
South Winterborne
RECTORY GDNS
STAFFORD LA
West Stafford
GLEBELAND CL
GLEBELAND CL
Parsonage Plantation
Sandy Barrow
Tumulus
Bunker's Hill Plantation
Knighton Wood
HIGHGATE LANE
Cook's Plantation
Stafford Farm
Knighton Heath Wood
Lewell Lodge
West Knighton Pit
Huck Barrow
Lower Glebe Farm
Jubilee Trail
DT2
PH
Salt Hill Plantation
Common Plantation
Empool Heath
Mayers Pond Wood
Glebe Farm
Higher Lewell Farm
Empool Bottom
STAFFORD CL
GLEBE WAY
LEWELL WAY
West Knighton
OAKWOOD
South Loscombe Plantation
Broadmayne First Sch
Littlemayne Farm
SPRING GDNS
WATERGATES LANE
WATERGATES LANE
Jubilee Trail
OLD BRICKFIELDS
A352
KNIGHTON LANE
Fryer Mayne Wood
Black Hill
BRAMBLE DRO
BRAMBLE EDGE
MAIN STREET
BRAMBLE DRO
CONWAY DR
ST MARTINS CL
RECTORY ROAD
BROADMEAD
RECTORY CL
BAKERS PADDOCK
Broadmayne
LITTLEMEAD
THE SPINNEY
BEECH CL
COWLEAZE RD
PO
Tumulus
Fryer Mayne
MARTEL CL
CROSSTREE CL
PH
HIGH TREES
Beech Plantation
SOUTH DROVE
CHALKY ROAD
WOODLANDS
OSMINGTON DRO
OSMINGTON DROVE
A352
Broadmayne House Farm
Friarmayne Farm
Beech Farm
Warmwell Wood

135
154

110
138

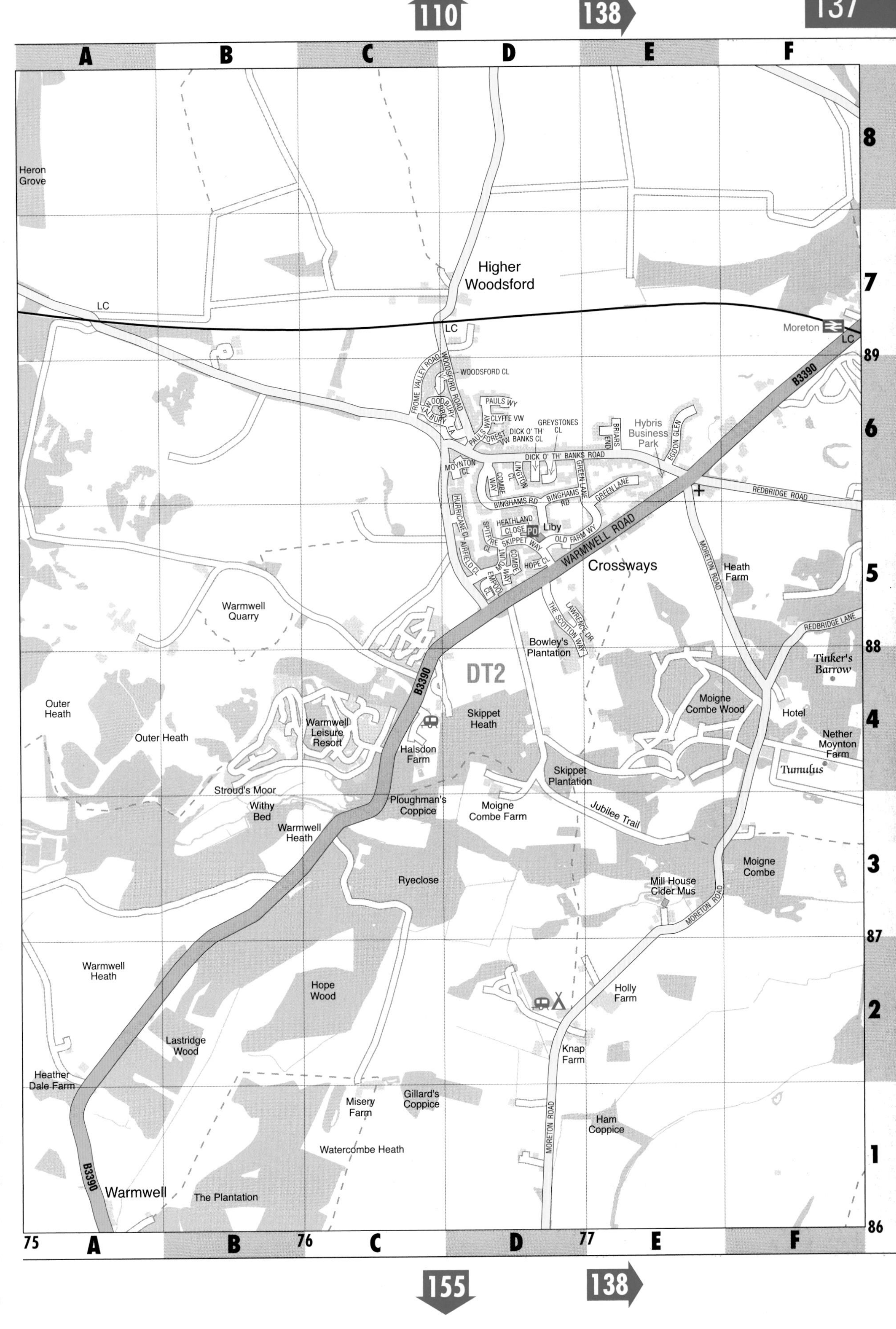
A
B
C
D
E
F
8
7
6
5
4
3
2
1
89
88
87
86
75
76
77
Heron Grove
Higher Woodsford
LC
Moreton
WOODSFORD CL
FROME VALLEY ROAD
WOODSFORD ROAD
PAULS WY
CLYFFE VW
GREYSTONES CL
DICK O' TH' BANKS CL
DICK O' TH' BANKS ROAD
Hybris Business Park
BRIARS END
EGDON GLEN
MOYNTON CL
GREEN LANE
BINGHAMS RD
REDBRIDGE ROAD
HURRICANE CL
HEATHLAND CLOSE
Liby
SKIPPET WAY
OLD FARM WY
WARMWELL ROAD
B3390
HOPE CL
Crossways
MORETON ROAD
Heath Farm
AIRFIELD CL
Warmwell Quarry
THE SCOTTON WAY
LAWRENCE DR
Bowley's Plantation
REDBRIDGE LANE
Tinker's Barrow
DT2
Outer Heath
Warmwell Leisure Resort
Skippet Heath
Moigne Combe Wood
Hotel
Nether Moynton Farm
Halsdon Farm
Tumulus
Skippet Plantation
Stroud's Moor
Withy Bed
Ploughman's Coppice
Moigne Combe Farm
Jubilee Trail
Warmwell Heath
Moigne Combe
Ryeclose
Mill House Cider Mus
Warmwell Heath
Hope Wood
Holly Farm
Lastridge Wood
Knap Farm
Heather Dale Farm
Gillard's Coppice
Misery Farm
Ham Coppice
Watercombe Heath
Warmwell
The Plantation

155
138

137
111

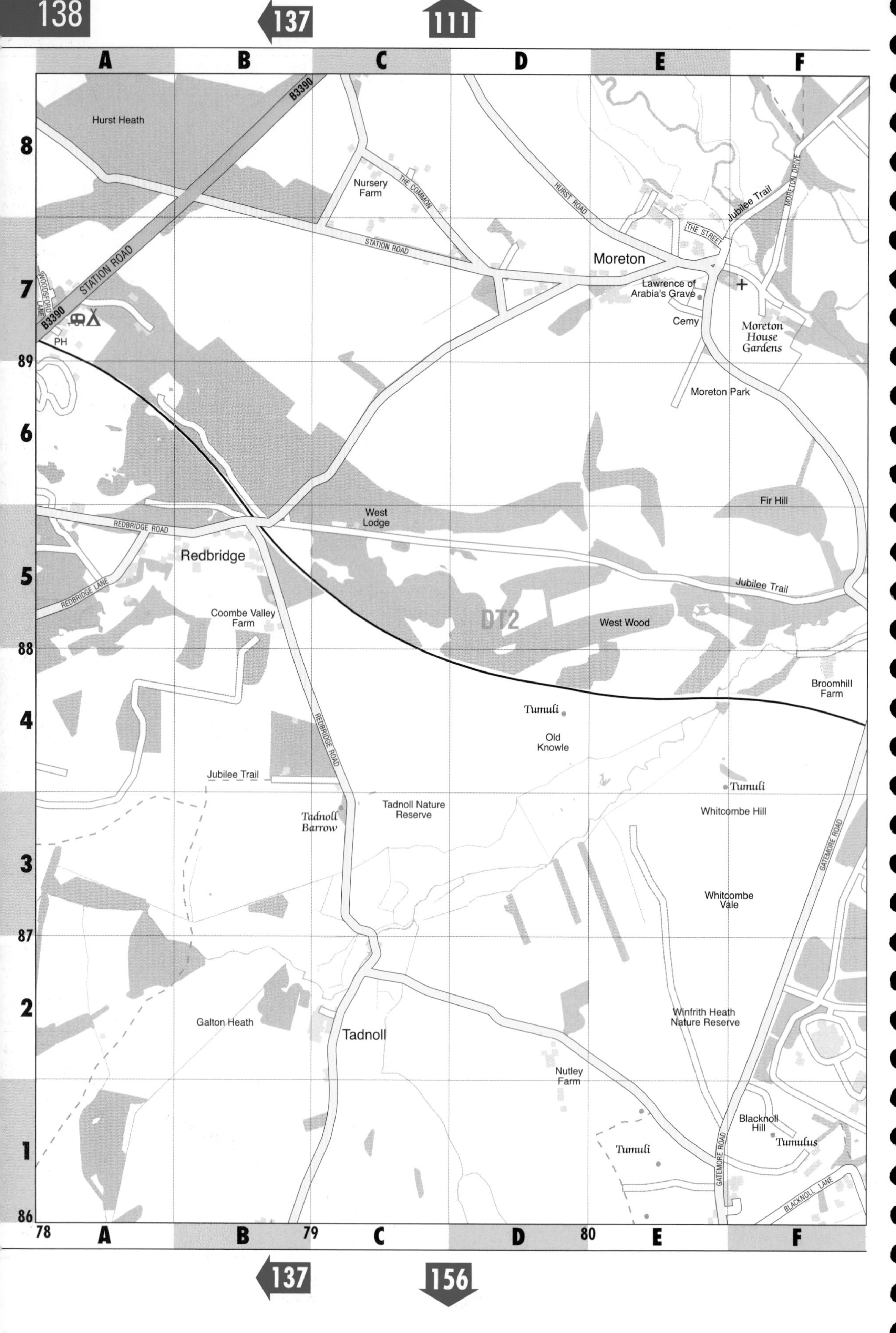
A
B
C
D
E
F
Hurst Heath
B3390
Nursery Farm
THE COMMON
HURST ROAD
Jubilee Trail
MORETON DRIVE
THE STREET
STATION ROAD
Moreton
Lawrence of Arabia's Grave
Cemy
Moreton House Gardens
WOODSFORD LANE
PH
Moreton Park
Fir Hill
West Lodge
REDBRIDGE ROAD
Redbridge
REDBRIDGE LANE
Coombe Valley Farm
DT2
West Wood
Broomhill Farm
Tumuli
Old Knowle
Jubilee Trail
Tadnoll Nature Reserve
Tadnoll Barrow
Whitcombe Hill
Whitcombe Vale
GATEMORE ROAD
Galton Heath
Tadnoll
Winfrith Heath Nature Reserve
Nutley Farm
Blacknoll Hill
Tumulus
BLACKNOLL LANE
8
7
89
6
5
88
4
3
87
2
1
86
78
79
80

137
156

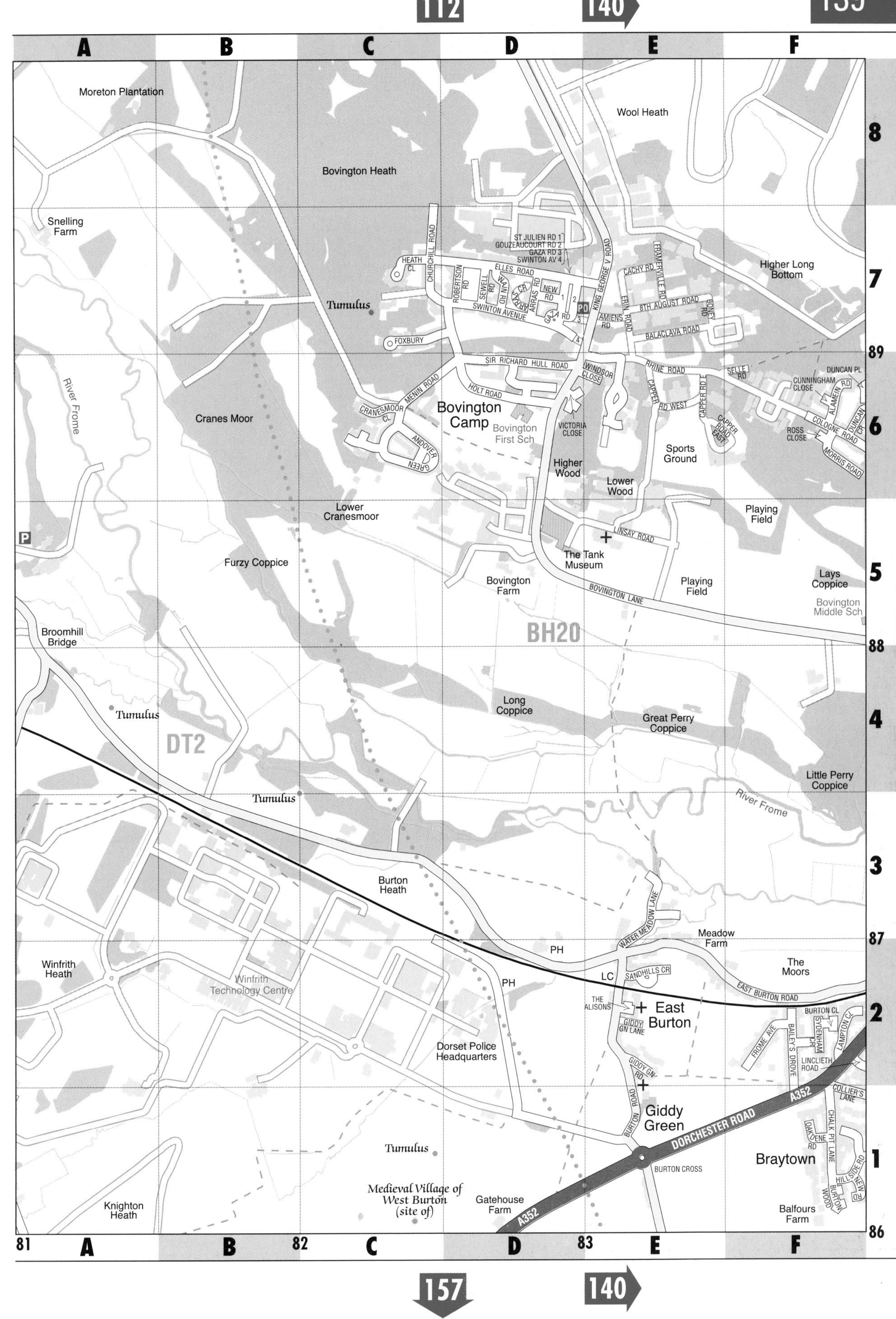

112
140
157
140

A B C D E F

Moreton Plantation

Wool Heath

8

Snelling Farm

Bovington Heath

Higher Long Bottom

7

ST JULIEN RD 1
GOUZEAUCOURT RD 2
GAZA RD 3
SWINTON AV 4

HEATH CL

Tumulus

FOXBURY

ELLES ROAD

CHURCHILL ROAD

ROBERTSON RD

SEWELL RD

MENIN RD

ARRAS RD

NEW RD

KING GEORGE V ROAD

CACHY RD

FRANKVILLE RD

AMIENS RD

ETIN RD

8TH AUGUST ROAD

BONEY RD

BALACLAVA ROAD

89

SWINTON AVENUE

SIR RICHARD HULL ROAD

WINDSOR CLOSE

RHINE ROAD

CAPPER RD

CAPPER RD WEST

CAPPER ROAD EAST

SELLE RD

CUNNINGHAM CLOSE

AMIENS

DUNCAN PL

DUNCAN CL

6

Cranes Moor

CRANESMOOR CL

MENIN ROAD

HOLT ROAD

Bovington Camp

Bovington First Sch

VICTORIA CLOSE

ROSS CLOSE

COLOGNE ROAD

MORRIS ROAD

ANDOVER GREEN

Higher Wood

Lower Wood

Sports Ground

Playing Field

Lower Cranesmoor

LINSAY ROAD

The Tank Museum

Playing Field

Lays Coppice

5

Furzy Coppice

Bovington Farm

BOVINGTON LANE

Bovington Middle Sch

88

Broomhill Bridge

River Frome

P

BH20

Long Coppice

Great Perry Coppice

4

Tumulus

DT2

Little Perry Coppice

River Frome

Tumulus

3

Burton Heath

Meadow Farm

87

Winfrith Heath

Winfrith Technology Centre

PH

PH

WATER MEADOW LANE

LC

SANDHILLS CR

EAST BURTON ROAD

The Moors

THE ALISONS

East Burton

GIDDY GN LANE

BURTON CL

SYDENHAM CL

FROME AVE

BAILEY'S DRIVE

LAMPTON CL

2

Dorset Police Headquarters

GIDDY GN RD

LINCLIETH ROAD

COLLIER'S LANE

A352

Tumulus

BURTON ROAD

Giddy Green

DORCHESTER ROAD

A352

Braytown

CHALK PIT LANE

DARCENE RD

NEW RD

HILLSIDE RD

BURTON WOOD

1

Knighton Heath

Medieval Village of West Burton (site of)

Gatehouse Farm

BURTON CROSS

A352

Balfours Farm

86

81 A 82 B C 82 D 83 E F

A   B   C   D   E   F

8

Stoke
Heath

CH

Grants
Farm

7

Longthorns
Farm

Tumuli

PUDDLETOWN ROAD

89

Woolbridge
Heath

Birch Wood

Great
Plantation

Sand and
Gravel Pit

Lower Long
Bottom

6

DUNCAN CRES

COLOGNE ROAD

Monkey
World Ape
Rescue
Centre

Battery
Bank

5

Bovington
Middle Sch

Hethfelton

Sand and
Gravel Pits

88

BOVINGTON LA

COLOGNE RD

LYTCHETT LANE

LYTCHETT LANE

TOUT HILL

Tout
Hill

BH20

4

Stokeford Common

3

Wool
Bridge

A352

River Frome

Holly Wood

Stony
Weir

Hethfelton
Farm

PH

Stokeford

87

LC

Wool

East Burton Rd

STATION RD

DORCHESTER ROAD

HYDE
RD

PH

St Marys RC
First Sch

BREACH FIELD

HIGH ST

HIGH ST CL

1 JEREMY CL
2 BINDON WY
3 THE CROSS

Manor
Farm

Wool

Bindon Abbey
(rems)

Church

Manor
Farm

2

FOLLY LA

MEADOW
LANE

Liby

COLLIER'S LANE

PO

KINGS CL

East Stoke Fen
Nature Reserve

East
Stoke

KNOWLE HL

DUCK ST

LULWORTH ROAD

B3071

CHURCH LANE

COLUMBELL

MACKVILLE AV

Wool CE
First Sch

Bindon Lane

1

LWR HILLSIDE RD

Braytown

Quarr
Hill

Cole
Wood

Inglewood
Farm

86

84   A   B   85   C   D   86   E   F

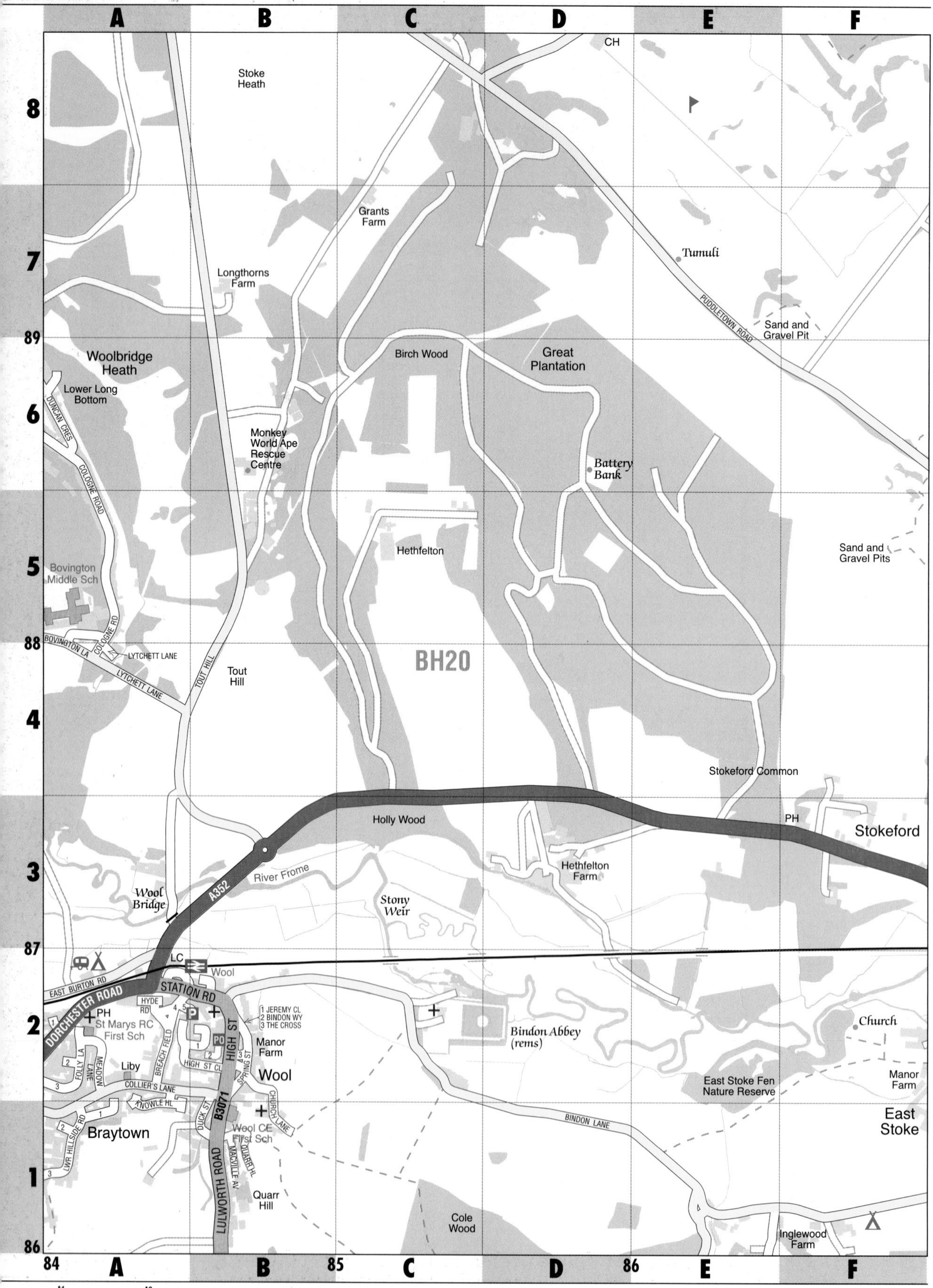

A1
1 KNOWLE WOOD KNAP
2 VICARAGE CL
3 HILLSIDE RD

A2
1 CEDAR CL
2 COTTAGE CL
3 LINCLIETH RD
4 BREACH FIELD
5 LOCKS PIECE

114
142

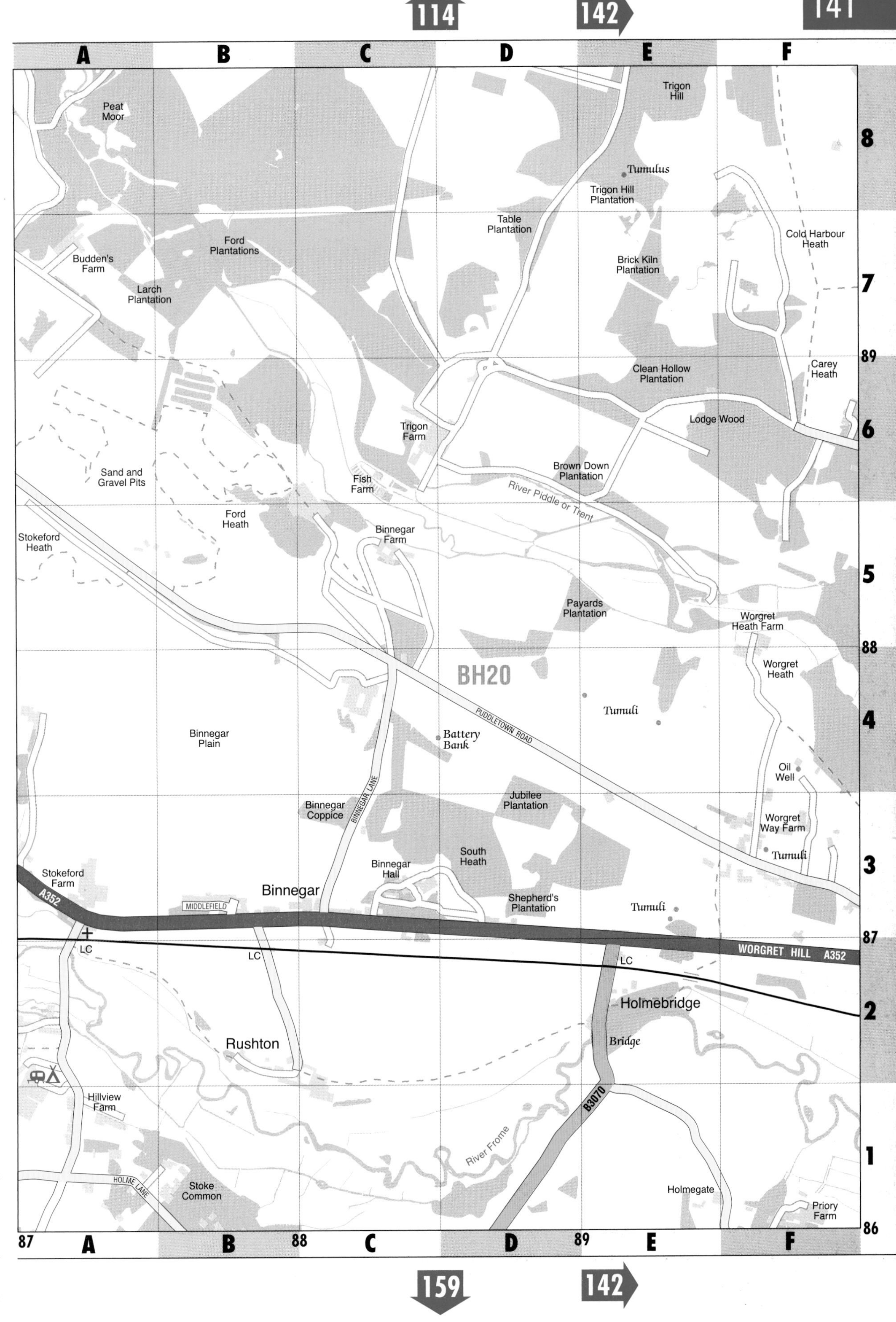
A
B
C
D
E
F
Peat Moor
Trigon Hill
Tumulus
Trigon Hill Plantation
Table Plantation
Cold Harbour Heath
Budden's Farm
Ford Plantations
Brick Kiln Plantation
Larch Plantation
Carey Heath
Clean Hollow Plantation
Lodge Wood
Trigon Farm
Sand and Gravel Pits
Fish Farm
Brown Down Plantation
River Piddle or Trent
Ford Heath
Binnegar Farm
Stokeford Heath
Payards Plantation
Worgret Heath Farm
Worgret Heath
BH20
Tumuli
Puddletown Road
Battery Bank
Binnegar Plain
Oil Well
Binnegar Lane
Jubilee Plantation
Binnegar Coppice
Worgret Way Farm
Tumuli
South Heath
Binnegar Hall
Stokeford Farm
A352
Binnegar
Shepherd's Plantation
Tumuli
Middlefield
LC
LC
LC
Worgret Hill A352
Holmebridge
Bridge
Rushton
B3070
Hillview Farm
River Frome
Holme Lane
Stoke Common
Holmegate
Priory Farm
8
7
89
6
5
88
4
3
87
2
1
86
87
88
89

159
142

A B C D E F

8

7

89

6

5

88

4

3

87

2

1

86

Coldharbour Farm
Cold Harbour
Silent Woman Farm
PH
Cold Harbour Heath
Alpha Farm
P ✕
Northport Heath
Sandford
Sandford Woods
MILES AVE
GORE HILL
ROGETT CR
ELWOOD PL
SHAW DRIVE
FOREST EDGE ROAD
GORE HILL
MORDEN ROAD
Camp Farm
SANDFORD ROAD
POTTERY PH
Carey Heath
Middle Copse
Seven Barrows
Northmoor
GREAT OWLES DR
CH
NORTHMOOR WY
COURTENAY CL

Seven Barrows Farm
Mast
SEVEN BARROWS
STOCKLEY RD
NORTHMOOR DR
BURNS
TARRANT RD
STOUR DR
SHERFORD DRIVE
Northmoor Park
SHERFORD DRIVE
A351
SANDFORD RD
ADMIRAL'S
Justin Business Park
PO
Anglebury Business Park
Sandford Lane Ind Est
North Bestwall Wood

Drive Plantation
FAIRWAY DR
MORDEN DR
MIDDLEBERE DR
BOURNE
TREAT DR
WILLOW WY
DANIEL DR
BERE ROAD
TANTINBOY LA
DRAKE
PRESTON LANE
RYAN CL
DRAX
SANDFORD ROAD
Leanne Business Centre
SANDFORD LA
Northport

Garden Wood
Carey House
BH20
Wareham Forest Way
Westminster Rd Ind Est
MISTOVER ROAD
WESTMINSTER ROAD
CAREY ROAD
HUMBER CH
MELLSTOCK CRES
CAREY
WEST MILL WALLS
CRES
CAREY
ST MARY'S CL
WESSEX OVAL
WESSEX OVAL
CAREY RD
CAREY
JOHN'S
RD
CAREY PPP
PO
ST WALLS
CAUSEWAY CL
TH CH
HIBBS CL
CALCRAFT RD
CAUSEWAY
WAREHAM
North Bestwall Wood

New Meadow Coppice
Ferncroft Farm
Wareham
WAREHAM

Worgret Heath
River Piddle or Trent
West Mills
A351
North Bridge
SHATTER'S HILL
WALLS
NORTH STREET
ST MARTIN'S LA
BRIXE
MOUNT PLEASANT
FOLLY LANE
EDWARD CR
NORTH BESTWALL RD
Swanage & Wareham RFC
1 DALER CT
2 KNIGHTSTONE CT

Tumuli
Oil Well
Little Farm
PUDDLETOWN ROAD
A352
WORGRET HILL
Manor Farm
Worgret
The Lady St Mary CE First School
Wareham Middle School
Rec Gnd
H
MONMOUTH ROAD
NORTH STREET
TINKER
ST MARY'S LANE
COW LANE
ROPERS LANE
MILL LANE
ROPERS
TRINITY
B3075
Wareham Town Mus
HOWARD'S
EAST STREET
BELL'S ORCH
CHURCH LA
WYATT'S LA
CONIGER LA
MEADOW VIEW CL
The Priory
BESTWALL ROAD
BESTWALL BR

Oil Well
The Purbeck School
Purbeck Adult Ed Centre
Purbeck Sports Centre & Swimming Pool
BARNES RD
SHIRLEY RD
FROME RD
STOWELL CR
HARDY RD
B3070
WORGRET ROAD
Magistrates Courts
WEST STREET
Castle (Site of)
POUND LA
Liby
SOUTH ST
PH
Council Offices
South Br
SOUTH CAUSEWAY
Purbeck Way

River Frome
A351
PO
PH
Stoborough
Stoborough CE First Sch
CORFE ROAD
HOLLOW OAK RD
OAKTREE CL
WEST LA
NUTCRACK LANE
Goodens Farm
MELANCHOLY LA
B3075
STOBOROUGH MDW

90 A B 91 C D 92 E F

E3
1 HEMSBACH CT
2 CHURCH GN
3 THE QUAY
4 ABBOTS QUAY
5 TANNER'S LA
6 ST MICHAEL'S RD
7 HILLARD CT
8 REMPSTONE SHOPPING ARCADE
9 MORETON'S LA

E4
1 ST MARTIN'S CL
2 COOPER'S CL
3 DOLLIN'S LA
4 CARRION LA
5 KENNINGTON SQ

116
144

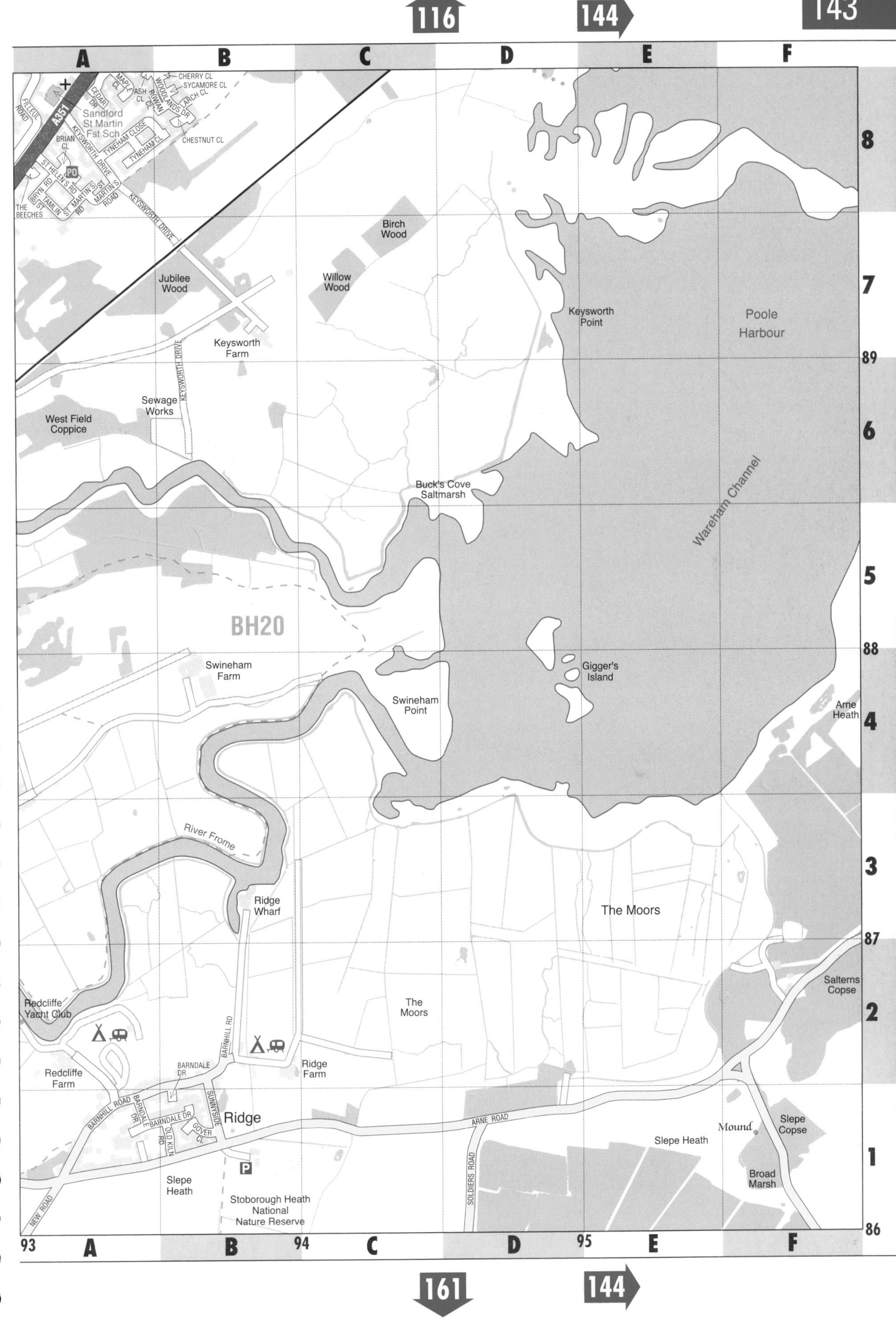
A
B
C
D
E
F
8
7
89
6
5
88
4
3
87
2
1
86
93
94
95
CHERRY CL
SYCAMORE CL
LARCH CL
WOODLANDS DR
ROWAN CL
ASH CL
MAPLE CL
CEDAR DR
FILLEUL ROAD
A351
Sandford
St Martin
Fst Sch
BRIAN CL
KEYSWORTH DRIVE
TYNEHAM CLOSE
TYNEHAM CL
CHESTNUT CL
PO
ST HELEN'S RD
BRYN RD
TAMLIN ST
ST MARTIN'S RD
ST MARTIN'S ROAD
THE BEECHES
KEYSWORTH DRIVE
Birch
Wood
Willow
Wood
Jubilee
Wood
Keysworth
Point
Poole
Harbour
Keysworth
Farm
Sewage
Works
West Field
Coppice
Buck's Cove
Saltmarsh
Wareham Channel
BH20
Swineham
Farm
Gigger's
Island
Swineham
Point
Arne
Heath
River Frome
Ridge
Wharf
The Moors
The
Moors
Salterns
Copse
Redcliffe
Yacht Club
BARNHILL RD
BARNDALE DR
Ridge
Farm
Redcliffe
Farm
BARNHILL ROAD
BARNDALE DR
SUNNYSIDE
Ridge
ARNE ROAD
OLD KILN RD
GOVER CL
Slepe Heath
Mound
Slepe
Copse
P
Slepe
Heath
SOLDIERS ROAD
Broad
Marsh
Stoborough Heath
National
Nature Reserve
NEW ROAD

161
144

143
117
118

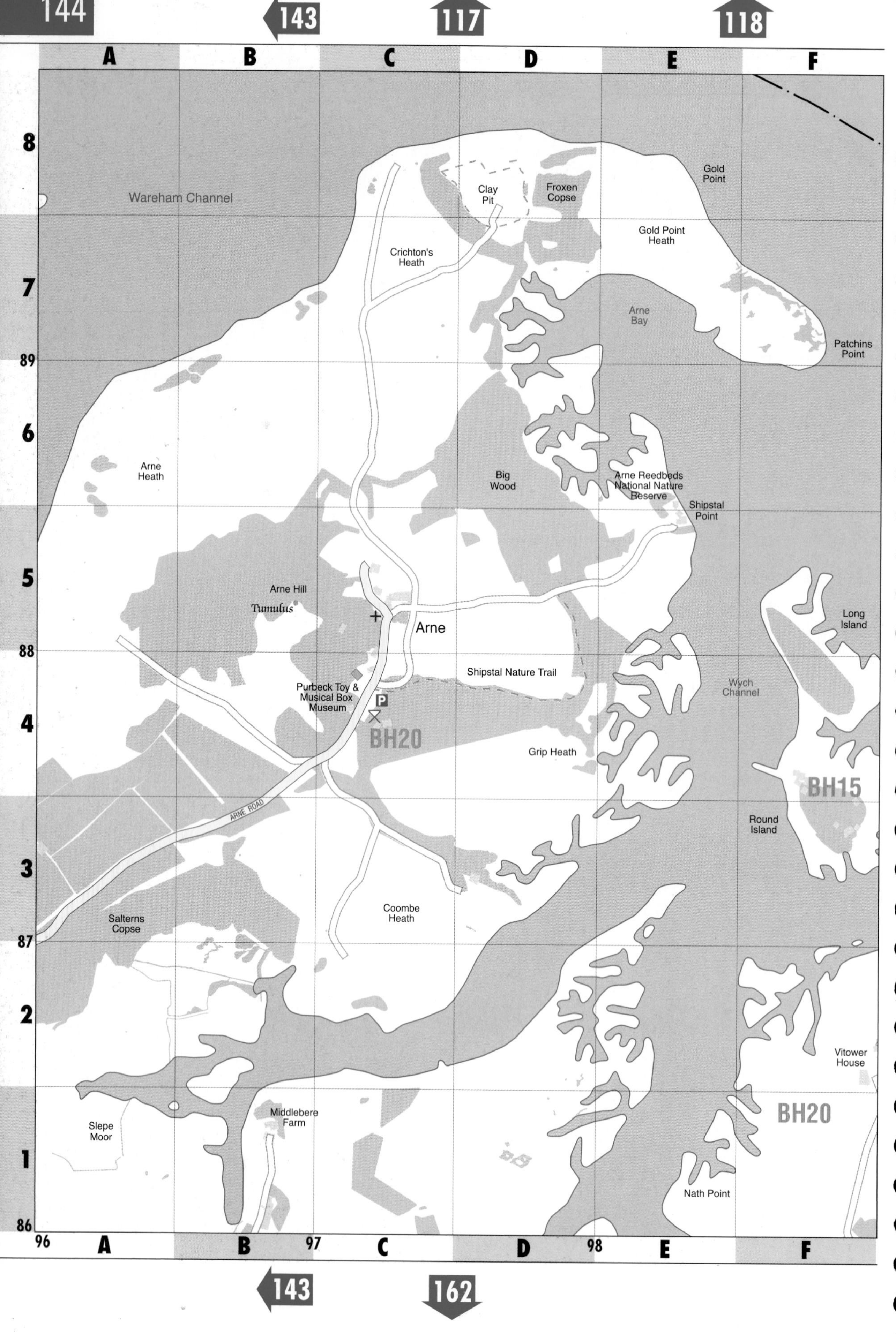

A   B   C   D   E   F

8

Wareham Channel

Clay Pit

Froxen Copse

Gold Point

7

Crichton's Heath

Gold Point Heath

Arne Bay

89

Patchins Point

6

Arne Heath

Big Wood

Arne Reedbeds National Nature Reserve

Shipstal Point

5

Arne Hill

Tumulus

Arne

Long Island

88

Shipstal Nature Trail

Wych Channel

Purbeck Toy & Musical Box Museum

P

BH20

Grip Heath

BH15

4

ARNE ROAD

3

Round Island

Salterns Copse

Coombe Heath

87

2

Vitower House

BH20

1

Slepe Moor

Middlebere Farm

Nath Point

86

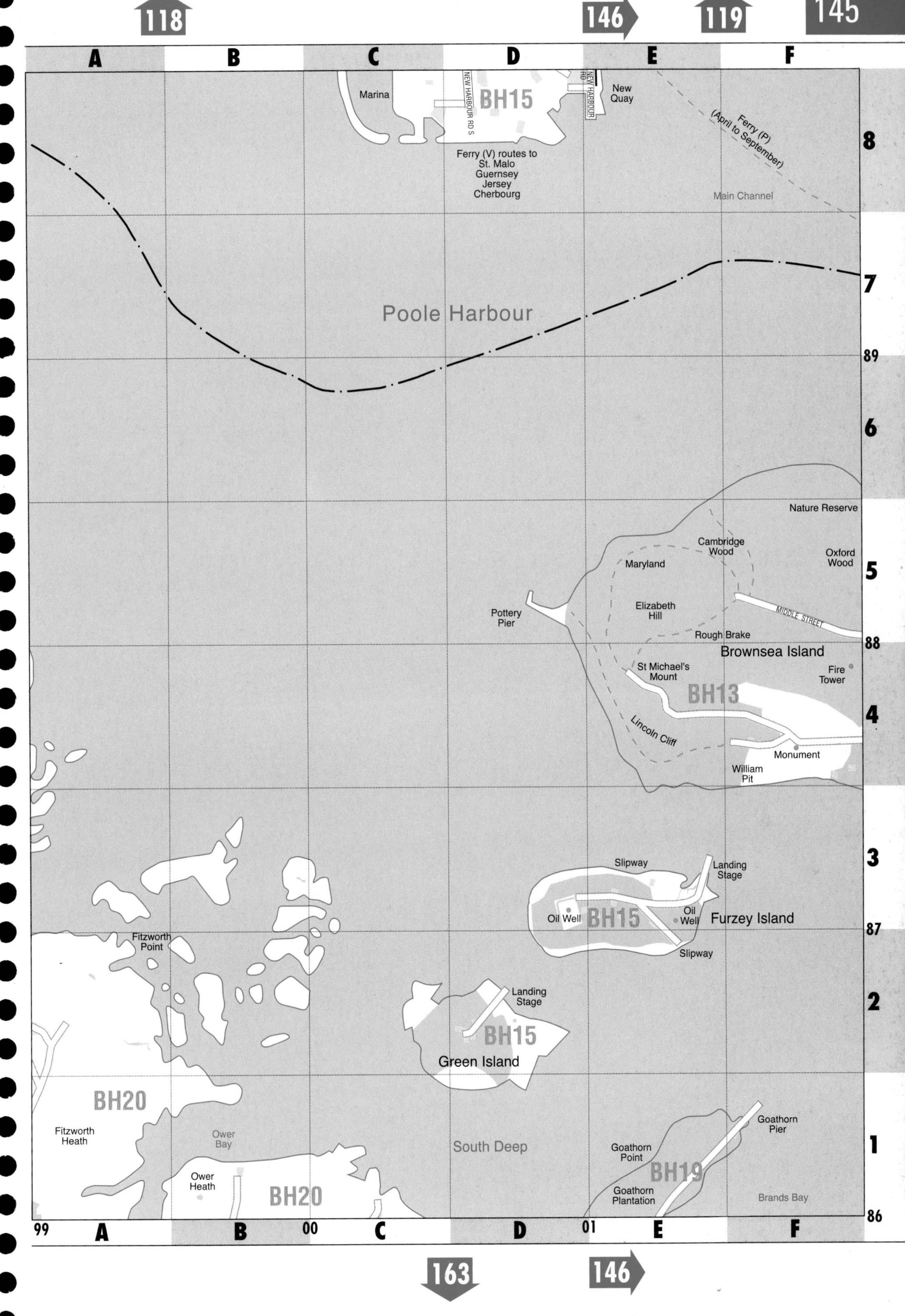

118
146
119

A   B   C   D   E   F

Marina

NEW HARBOUR RD S

BH15

NEW HARBOUR RD

New Quay

Ferry (P) (April to September)

8

Ferry (V) routes to St. Malo Guernsey Jersey Cherbourg

Main Channel

Poole Harbour

7

89

6

Nature Reserve

Cambridge Wood

Oxford Wood

Maryland

5

Pottery Pier

Elizabeth Hill

MIDDLE STREET

88

Rough Brake

Brownsea Island

St Michael's Mount

Fire Tower

BH13

4

Lincoln Cliff

Monument

William Pit

Slipway

Landing Stage

3

Oil Well

BH15

Oil Well

Furzey Island

87

Fitzworth Point

Slipway

Landing Stage

2

BH15

Green Island

BH20

South Deep

Goathorn Pier

1

Fitzworth Heath

Ower Bay

Goathorn Point

BH19

Ower Heath

BH20

Goathorn Plantation

Brands Bay

86

99   A   B   00   C   D   01   E   F

163
146

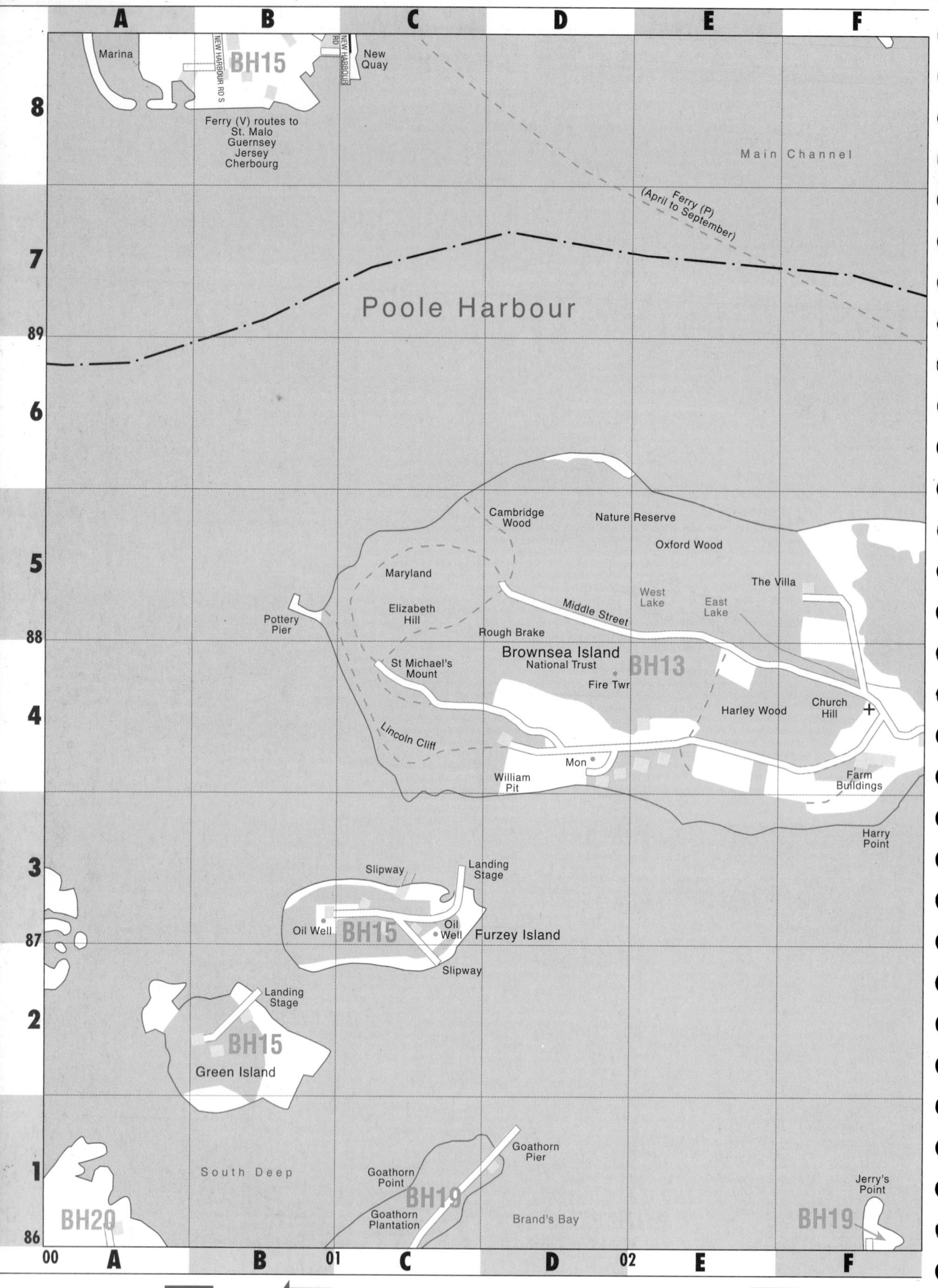

Marina

New Harbour Rd S

New Harbour Rd

BH15

New Quay

8

Ferry (V) routes to
St. Malo
Guernsey
Jersey
Cherbourg

Main Channel

7

Ferry (P)
(April to September)

Poole Harbour

89

6

Cambridge Wood

Nature Reserve

Oxford Wood

5

Maryland

West Lake

East Lake

The Villa

Elizabeth Hill

Middle Street

Pottery Pier

88

Rough Brake

St Michael's Mount

Brownsea Island
National Trust

BH13

Fire Twr

Harley Wood

Church Hill

4

Lincoln Cliff

Mon

William Pit

Farm Buildings

Harry Point

3

Slipway

Landing Stage

Oil Well

BH15

Oil Well

Furzey Island

87

Slipway

Landing Stage

2

BH15

Green Island

Goathorn Pier

1

South Deep

Goathorn Point

BH19

Jerry's Point

BH20

Goathorn Plantation

Brand's Bay

BH19

86

00   A   B   01   C   D   02   E   F

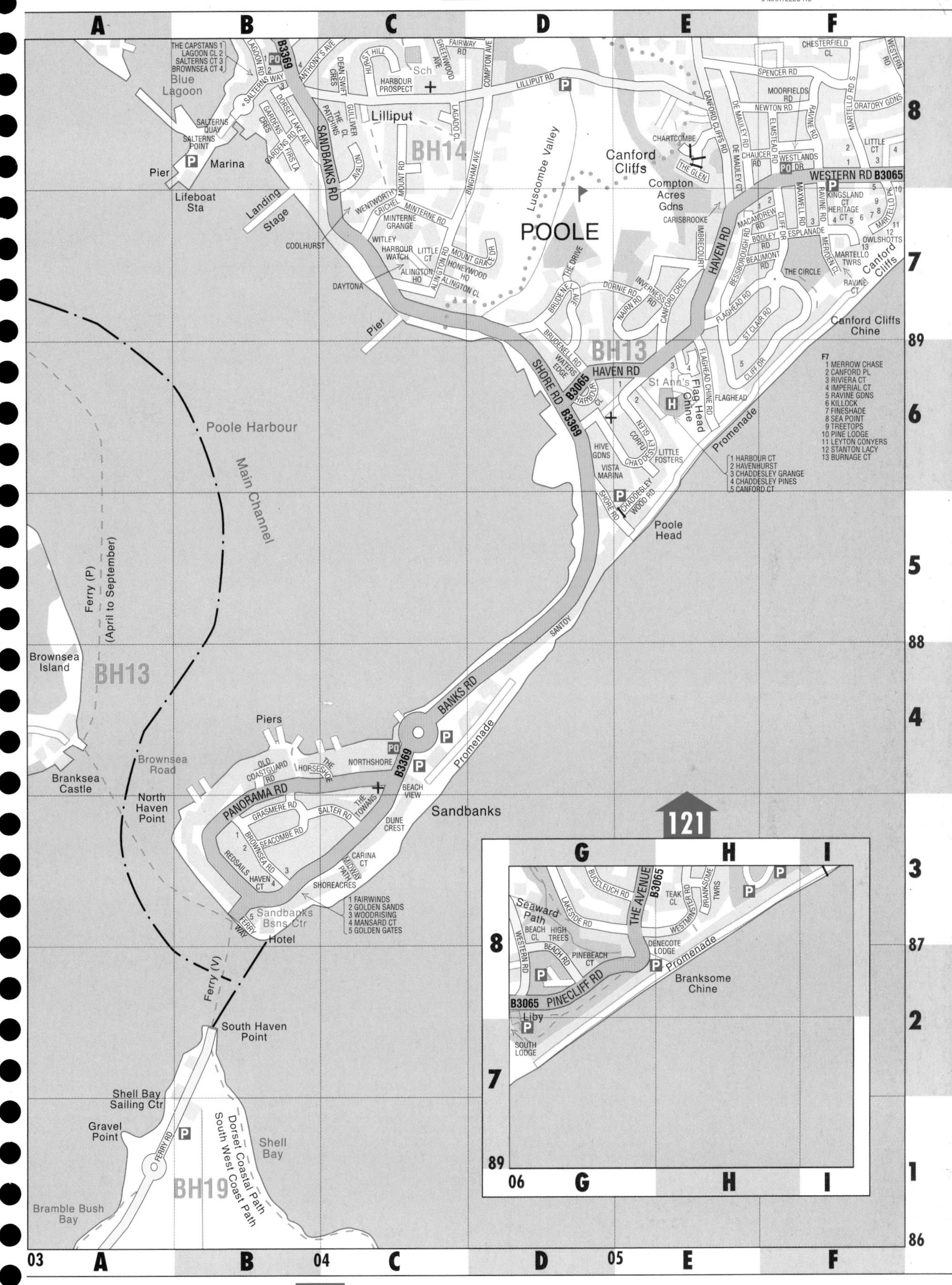

F8
1 KENILWORTH CT
2 BRACKENS WAY
3 STONELEIGH
4 BRANKSOME CT
5 MARTELLO HO

THE CAPSTANS 1
LAGOON CL 2
SALTERNS CT 3
BROWNSEA CT 4

Blue
Lagoon

SALTERNS
QUAY
SALTERNS
POINT

Pier

Marina

Lifeboat
Sta

Landing
Stage

COOLHURST

DAYTONA

Pier

Lilliput

BH14

Luscombe Valley

POOLE

Canford
Cliffs

Compton
Acres
Gdns

CARISBROOKE

CHARTCOMBE

THE GLEN

WESTERN RD B3065

CHESTERFIELD
CL

OWLSHOTTS

Canford
Cliffs

BH13

HAVEN RD

St Ann's

Canford Cliffs
Chine

89

8

7

F7
1 MERROW CHASE
2 CANFORD PL
3 RIVIERA CT
4 IMPERIAL CT
5 RAVINE GDNS
6 KILLOCK
7 FINESHADE
8 SEA POINT
9 TREETOPS
10 PINE LODGE
11 LEYTON CONYERS
12 STANTON LACY
13 BURNAGE CT

Poole Harbour

Main Channel

Ferry (P)
(April to September)

Brownsea
Island

BH13

Brownsea
Road

Branksea
Castle

North
Haven
Point

Piers

PANORAMA RD

OLD
COASTGUARD

NORTHSHORE

Sandbanks

BANKS RD

Promenade

1 HARBOUR CT
2 HAVENHURST
3 CHADDESLEY GRANGE
4 CHADDESLEY PINES
5 CANFORD CT

Poole
Head

6

5

88

4

1 FAIRWINDS
2 GOLDEN SANDS
3 WOODRISING
4 MANSARD CT
5 GOLDEN GATES

Sandbanks
Bsns Ctr

Hotel

Ferry (V)

South Haven
Point

Shell Bay
Sailing Ctr

Gravel
Point

BH19

Bramble Bush
Bay

Shell
Bay

Dorset Coastal Path
South West Coast Path

G   H   I

Seaward
Path

THE AVENUE

B3065

Branksome
Chine

Promenade

PINECLIFF RD

B3065

Liby

SOUTH
LODGE

8

7

87

2

89   1

06   G   H   I

03   A   B   04   C   D   05   E   F

3

86

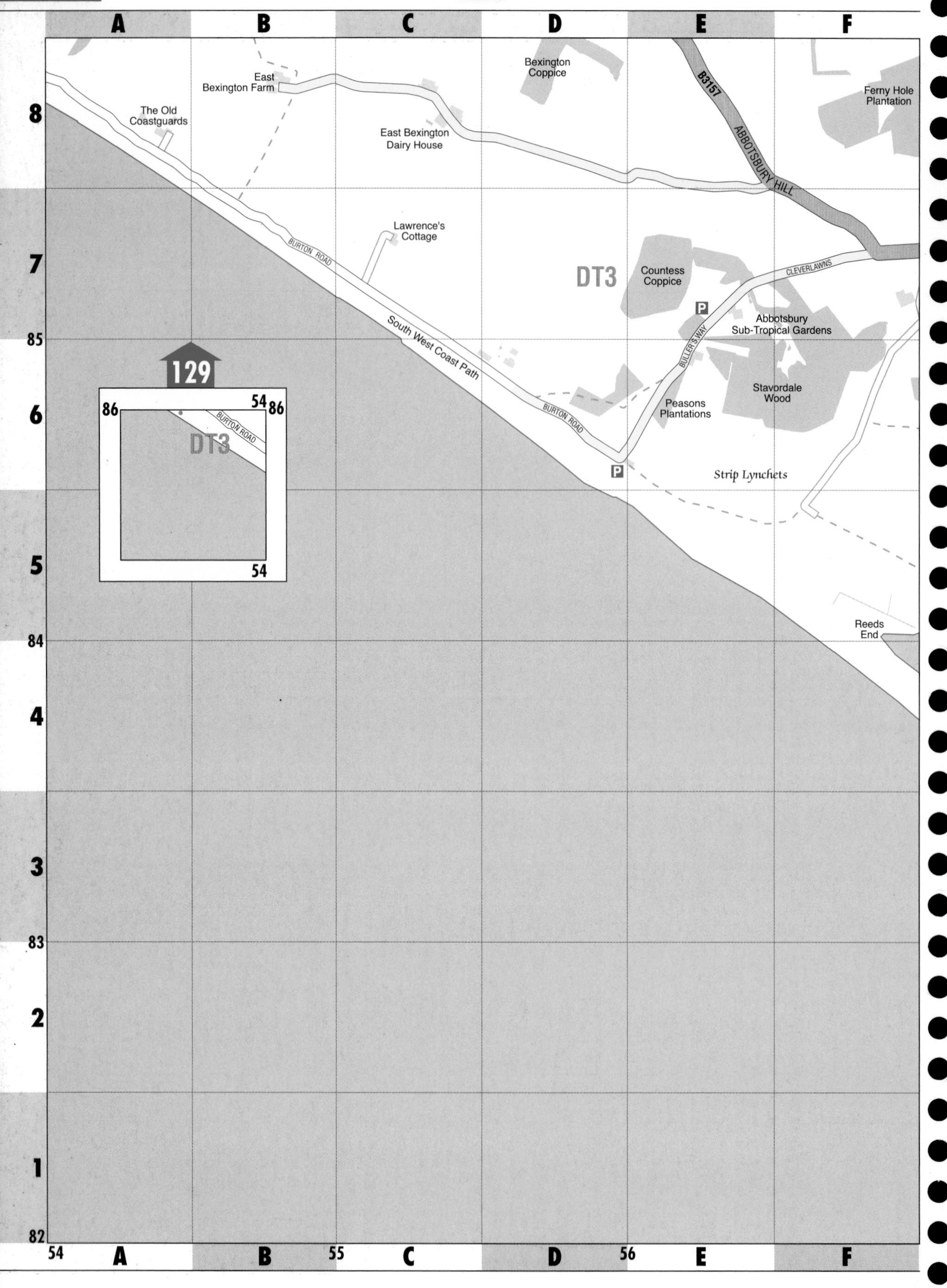

130

A B C D E F

The Old
Coastguards

East
Bexington Farm

East Bexington
Dairy House

Bexington
Coppice

Ferny Hole
Plantation

B3157

ABBOTSBURY HILL

Burton Road

Lawrence's
Cottage

South West Coast Path

DT3

Countess
Coppice

CLEVERLAWNS

P

Abbotsbury
Sub-Tropical Gardens

BULLER'S WAY

129

86   54
      86

DT3

BURTON ROAD

Burton Road

Peasons
Plantations

Stavordale
Wood

54

P

Strip Lynchets

Reeds
End

8

7

85

6

84

5

4

83

3

82

2

1

54   A   B   55   C   D   56   E   F

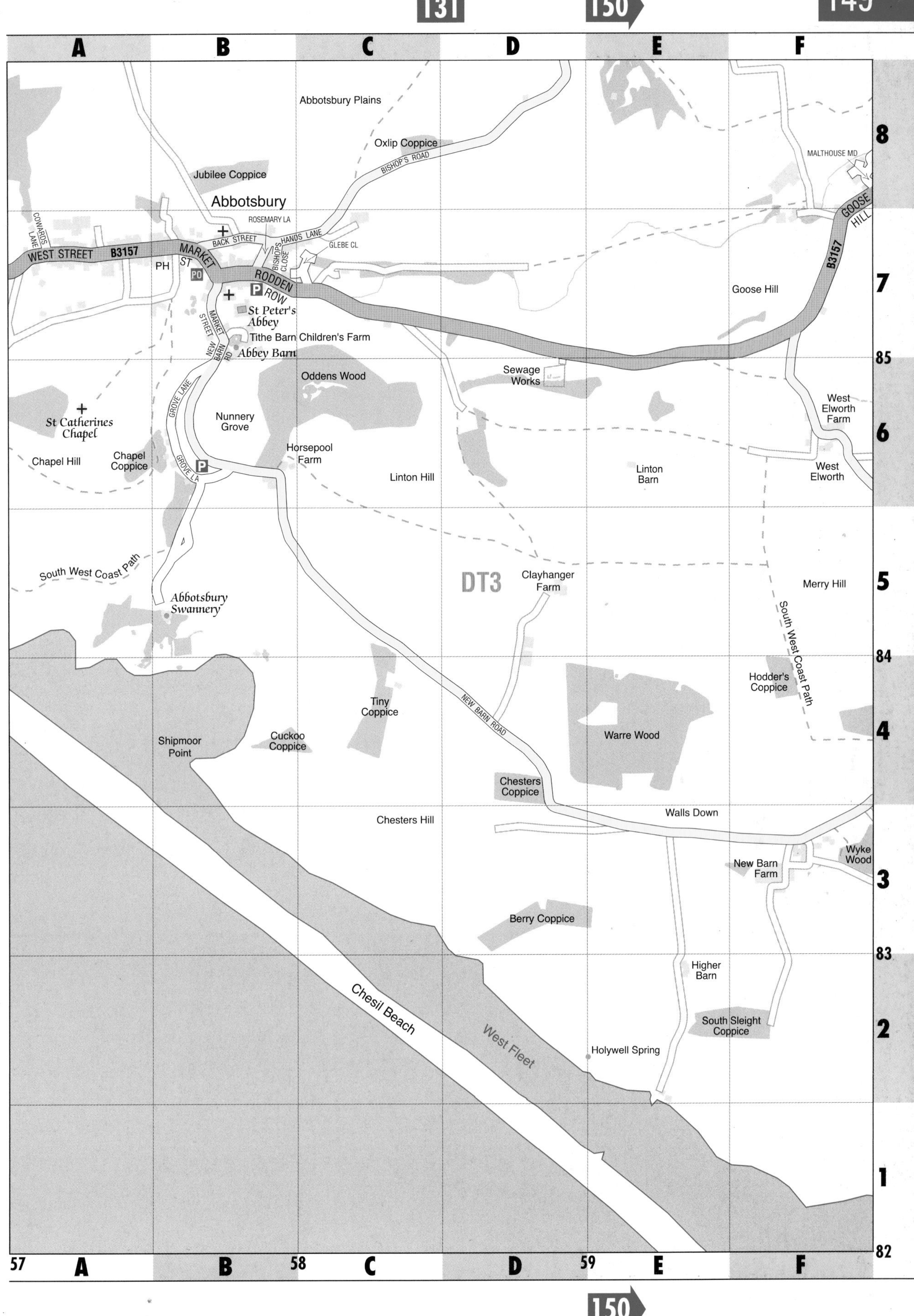

A B C D E F

8
7
85
6
5
84
4
83
2
1
82

Abbotsbury Plains

Oxlip Coppice

BISHOP'S ROAD

Jubilee Coppice

MALTHOUSE MD

Abbotsbury

ROSEMARY LA

GOOSE HILL

BACK STREET

BISHOPS
HANDS LANE

GLEBE CL

COWARDS LANE

WEST STREET B3157

MARKET ST

PH

ST

PO

RODDEN ROW

P

B3157

Goose Hill

St Peter's Abbey

P

Tithe Barn Children's Farm

MARKET STREET NEW RD

Abbey Barn

Oddens Wood

Sewage Works

West Elworth Farm

St Catherines Chapel

GROVE LANE

Nunnery Grove

Horsepool Farm

Linton Barn

West Elworth

Chapel Hill

Chapel Coppice

GROVE LA

P

Linton Hill

South West Coast Path

DT3

Clayhanger Farm

Merry Hill

Abbotsbury Swannery

South West Coast Path

Hodder's Coppice

Tiny Coppice

NEW BARN ROAD

Warre Wood

Shipmoor Point

Cuckoo Coppice

Chesters Coppice

Walls Down

Chesters Hill

Wyke Wood

New Barn Farm

Berry Coppice

Chesil Beach

West Fleet

Higher Barn

South Sleight Coppice

Holywell Spring

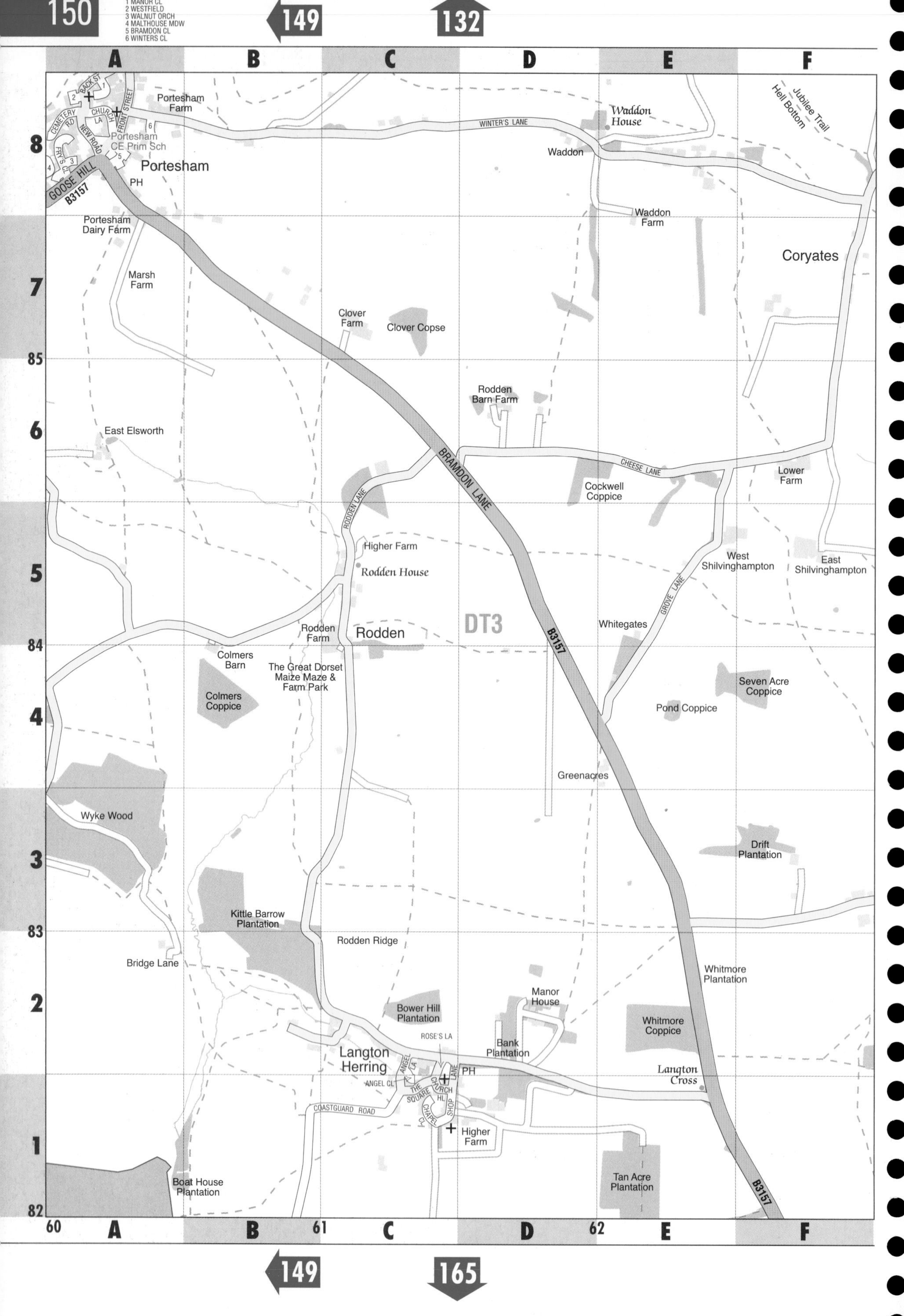

150

A8
1 MANOR CL
2 WESTFIELD
3 WALNUT ORCH
4 MALTHOUSE MDW
5 BRAMDON CL
6 WINTERS CL

149   132

A   B   C   D   E   F

Portesham Farm

WINTER'S LANE

Waddon House

Jubilee Trail

Hell Bottom

Portesham CE Prim Sch

Waddon

CEMETERY RD   CHURCH LA   FRONT STREET

8

FRY'S   NEW ROAD

Portesham

PH

GOOSE HILL   B3157

Waddon Farm

Coryates

Portesham Dairy Farm

Marsh Farm

7

Clover Farm

Clover Copse

85

Rodden Barn Farm

6

East Elsworth

CHEESE LANE

Lower Farm

BRAMDON LANE

Cockwell Coppice

RODDEN LANE

Higher Farm

West Shilvinghampton

East Shilvinghampton

5

Rodden House

GROVE LANE

84

Rodden Farm

Rodden

Whitegates

DT3

Colmers Barn

The Great Dorset Maize Maze & Farm Park

Seven Acre Coppice

B3157

Colmers Coppice

Pond Coppice

4

Greenacres

Drift Plantation

Wyke Wood

3

Kittle Barrow Plantation

83

Rodden Ridge

Whitmore Plantation

Bridge Lane

Bower Hill Plantation

Manor House

2

ROSE'S LA

Whitmore Coppice

Langton Herring

ANGEL CL   THE SQUARE   ANGEL CL   CHURCH HL   CHAPEL CL   SHOP LANE   PH

Bank Plantation

Langton Cross

COASTGUARD ROAD

Higher Farm

1

Boat House Plantation

Tan Acre Plantation

B3157

82

60   A   B   61   C   D   62   E   F

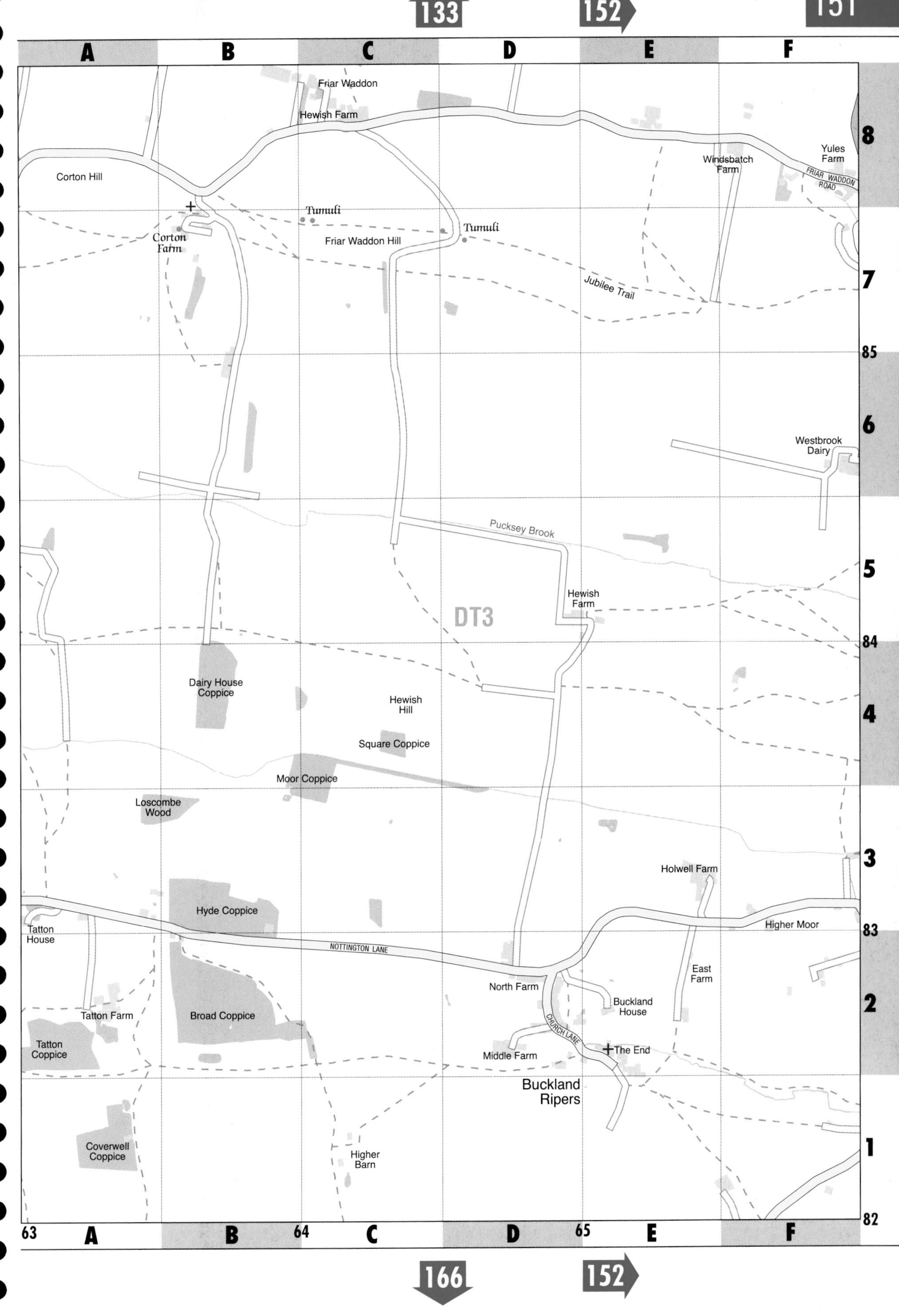

A B C D E F

8

Friar Waddon
Hewish Farm

Corton Hill

Yules
Farm

Windsbatch
Farm

FRIAR WADDON
ROAD

Tumuli

Corton
Farm

7

Friar Waddon Hill

Tumuli

Jubilee Trail

85

6

Westbrook
Dairy

Pucksey Brook

DT3

Hewish
Farm

5

84

Dairy House
Coppice

Hewish
Hill

4

Square Coppice

Moor Coppice

Loscombe
Wood

Holwell Farm

3

Hyde Coppice

Higher Moor

83

Tatton
House

NOTTINGTON LANE

East
Farm

North Farm

Buckland
House

2

Tatton Farm

Broad Coppice

CHURCH LANE

Tatton
Coppice

Middle Farm

+ The End

Buckland
Ripers

1

Coverwell
Coppice

Higher
Barn

82

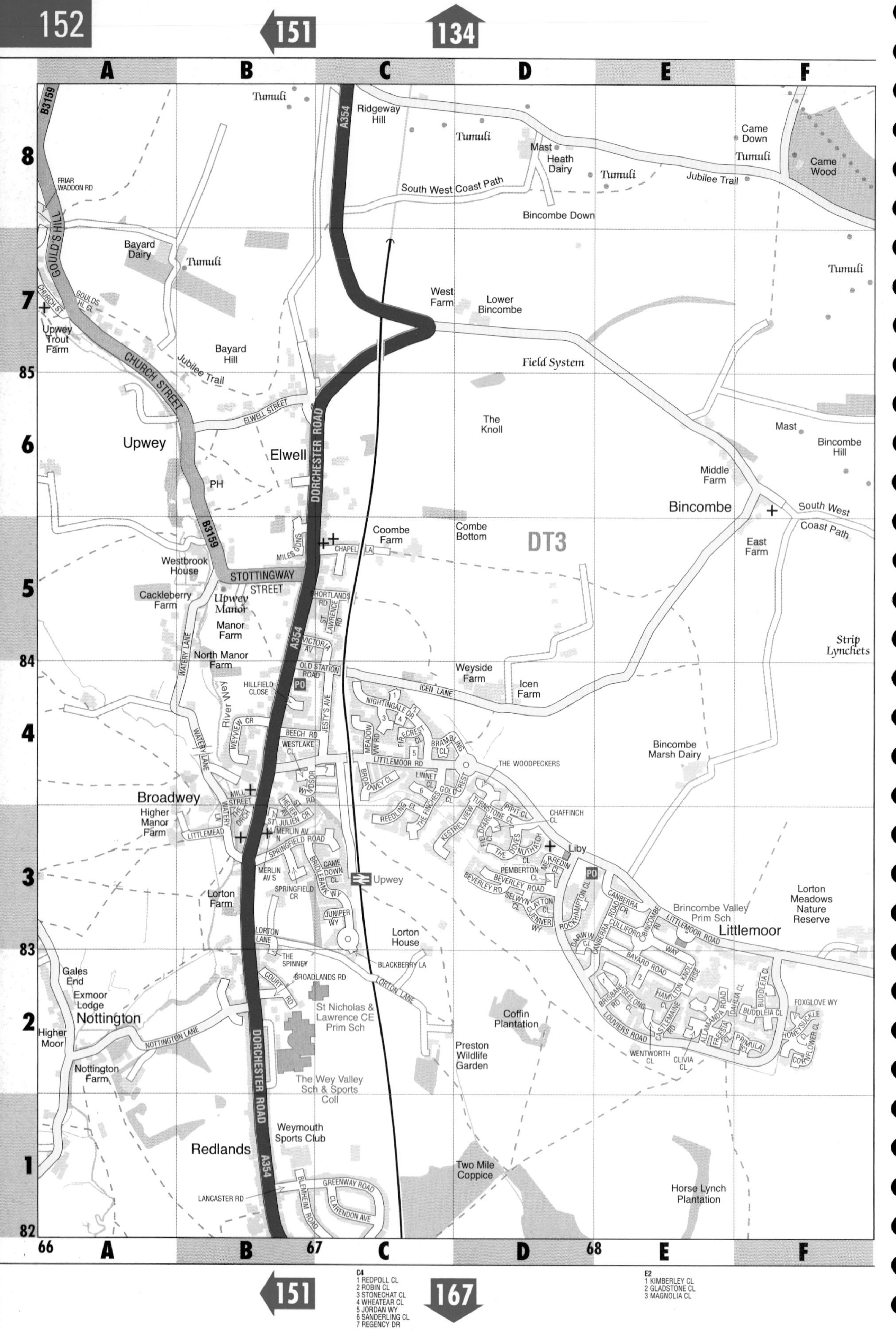

A B C D E F

8

Came Wood

Tumuli

DT2

Holcombe
Bottom

Tumuli

Tumuli

Bank
Barrow

Tumulus

CHALKY ROAD

Half Moon
Coppice

7

SOUTH DV

85

Tumuli

Tumuli

South West Coast Path

6

White
Horse Hill

Spring
Bottom

East
Hill

*White
Horse*

Tumuli

5

Green
Hill

PLAISTERS LANE

84

Chalbury

COOMBE VALLEY ROAD

Rimbrow
Coppice

Water Supply
Museum

SUTTON
CT LAWNS

MISSION CR

HALL LANE

WHITE
HORSE
LA
PH

SILVER ST

SUTTON RD

Sutton
Poyntz

4

SUTTON
CL

PLAISTERS LA

SILVER STREET

OLD
BINCOMBE LA

CORNHILL
WY

BROOKMEAD CL

3

SUNNYFIELDS

REYNARDS
CL

MILLERS
CL

RIMBROW CL

WINSLOW RD

WHITE HORSE DR

White Horse
Farm

DT3

STROUDLEY
CR

WAINWRIGHT CL

RYMBURY
CL

OLD GRANARY

PUDDLEDOCK LANE

SEVEN
ACRES
RD

SEVEN ACRES ROAD

SUTTON ROAD

THE WEIR

VALLEY
CLOSE

STATION RD

VERLANDS RD

Westfield
Tech Coll

BRUNEL
DR

BRUNEL DRIVE

CHURCHWARD AV

COLLETT

MAUNSELL AVENUE

HAWKESWORTH

FIR DR

PO

PRESTON ROAD

A353

83

RHOSEWOOD
DR

STANIER ROAD

BARTON
DR

TELFORD CL

BAYDON CL

ALLBERRY
GDNS

St Andrews
CE Prim Sch

COOMBE VALLEY ROAD

MOORCOMBE DR

LITTLEMOOR ROAD

PRESTON ROAD

Preston

1 HALSTOCK CL
2 BROOKSIDE CL
3 HORYFORD CL

FISHERBRIDGE
Road

TALLIDGE
CL

BIRCH RD

HOLCOMBE CL

Osmington Hill

2

Wyke Oliver
Farm

CHALBURY
CLOSE

MEDWAY
DR

CEDAR DRIVE

WILLOW
CRES

FOREHILL
CLOSE

River Jordan

EMWORTH ROAD

WYKE OLIVER ROAD

OAKBURY DRIVE

ELDON CL

SANDBOURNE RD

ORCHARD DR

FURZY CL

SUNNINGDALE RI

OVERCOMBE DRIVE

1

BUDMOUTH
AV

KINGSBERE
RD

MELSTOCK
AV

RINGSTEAD CRESCENT

A353

Overcombe

ROMAN
TEMPLE

New
Barn

BOWLEAZE COVEWAY

82

B2
1 CHALBURY LODGE
2 HAZEL DR
3 WINGREEN CL
4 MAPLE CL
5 DEANSLEIGH CL

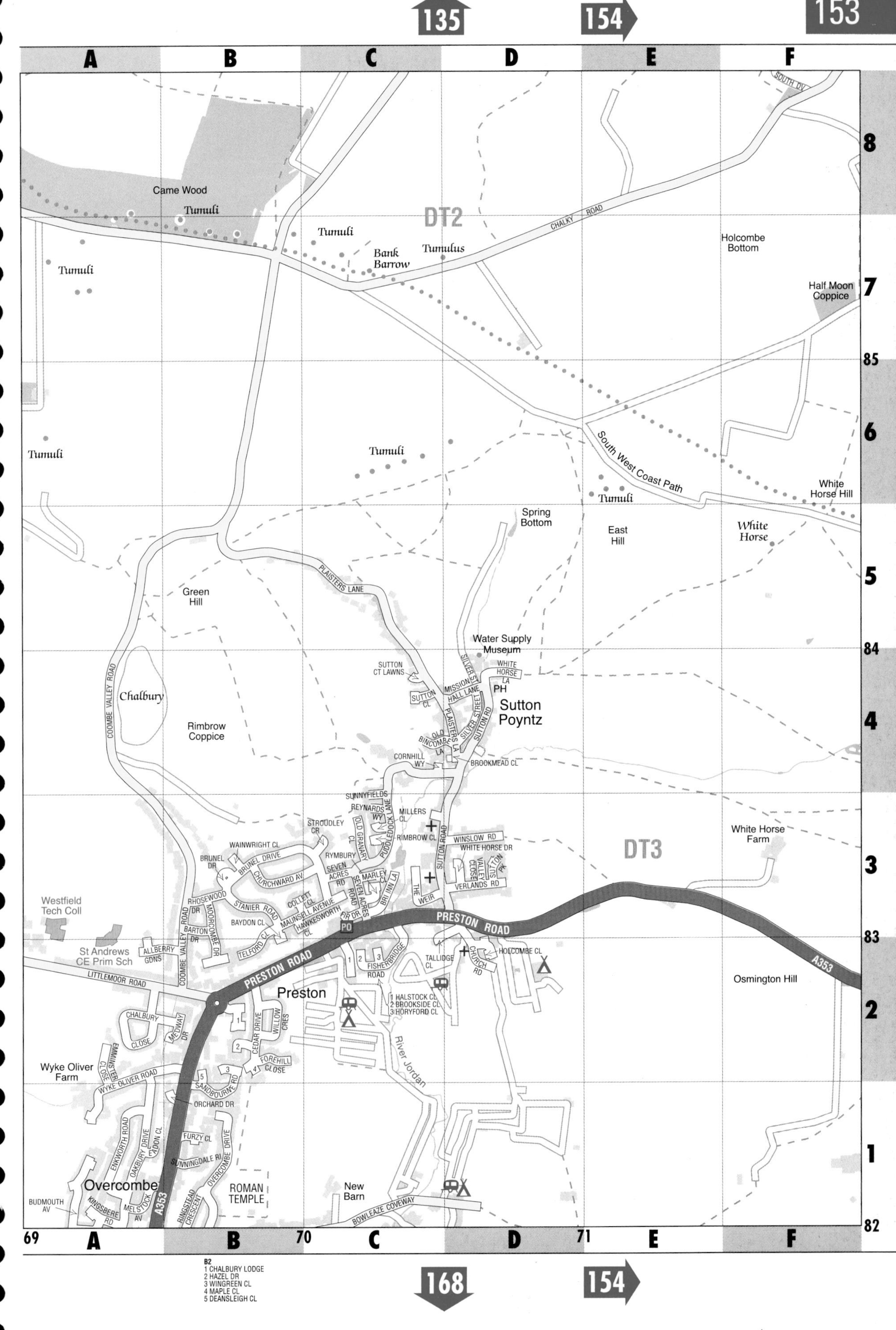

A   B   C   D   E   F

8 Glebe Farm

Conygar
Roman Hill Farm
Roman Hill Trading Estate
Nordale Farm
A352
WARMWELL DRO
Friarmayne Farm
Brick Hill

7 Warmwell Down Barn
Warmwell Cross Farm
A353

85

6 Poxwell Grove

POXWELL DROVE

5 DT2
Manor Farm
Tumuli
Poxwell
Tumulus

84 Pixon Barn
Coombe Bottom
Strip Lynchets
Poxwell Manor

4 South West Coast Path
Strip Lynchets
Poxwell Cairn Circle

Halls Farm
Strip Lynchets

3 Netherton Farm
Grove Farmhouse
Strip Lynchets
Abbeyfeale Farm
Lower Dairy Farm
Poxwell Big Wood

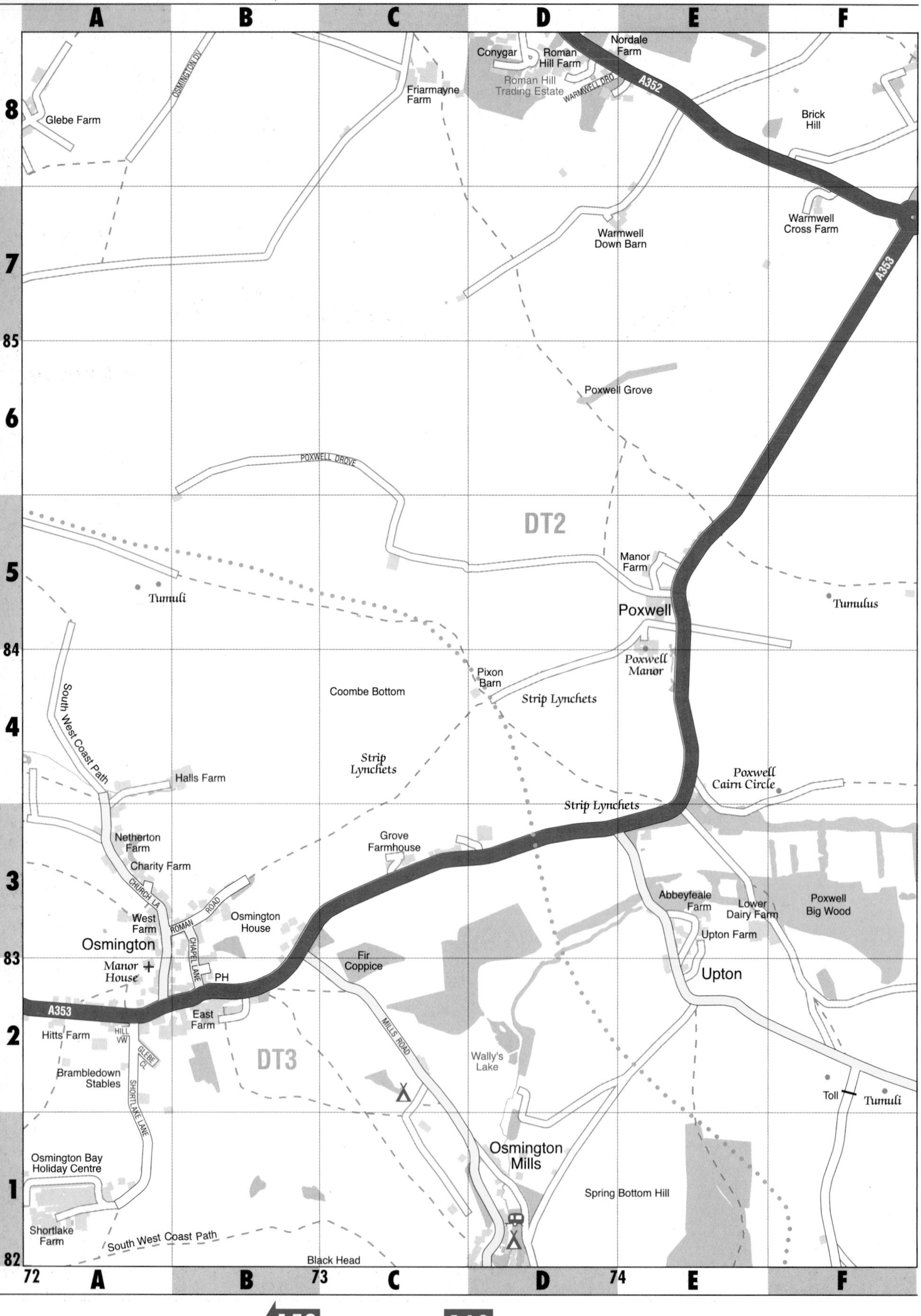

Charity Farm
CHURCH LA
West Farm
ROMAN ROAD
Osmington House
Upton Farm

Osmington
CHAPEL LANE
83 Manor House
PH
Fir Coppice
Upton

2 A353
East Farm
Hitts Farm
HILL VW
GLEBE CL
DT3
MILLS ROAD
Wally's Lake
Toll
Tumuli

Brambledown Stables
SHORTLAKE LANE

1 Osmington Bay Holiday Centre
Osmington Mills
Spring Bottom Hill

Shortlake Farm
South West Coast Path

82 Black Head

72   A   B   73   C   D   74   E   F

137
156

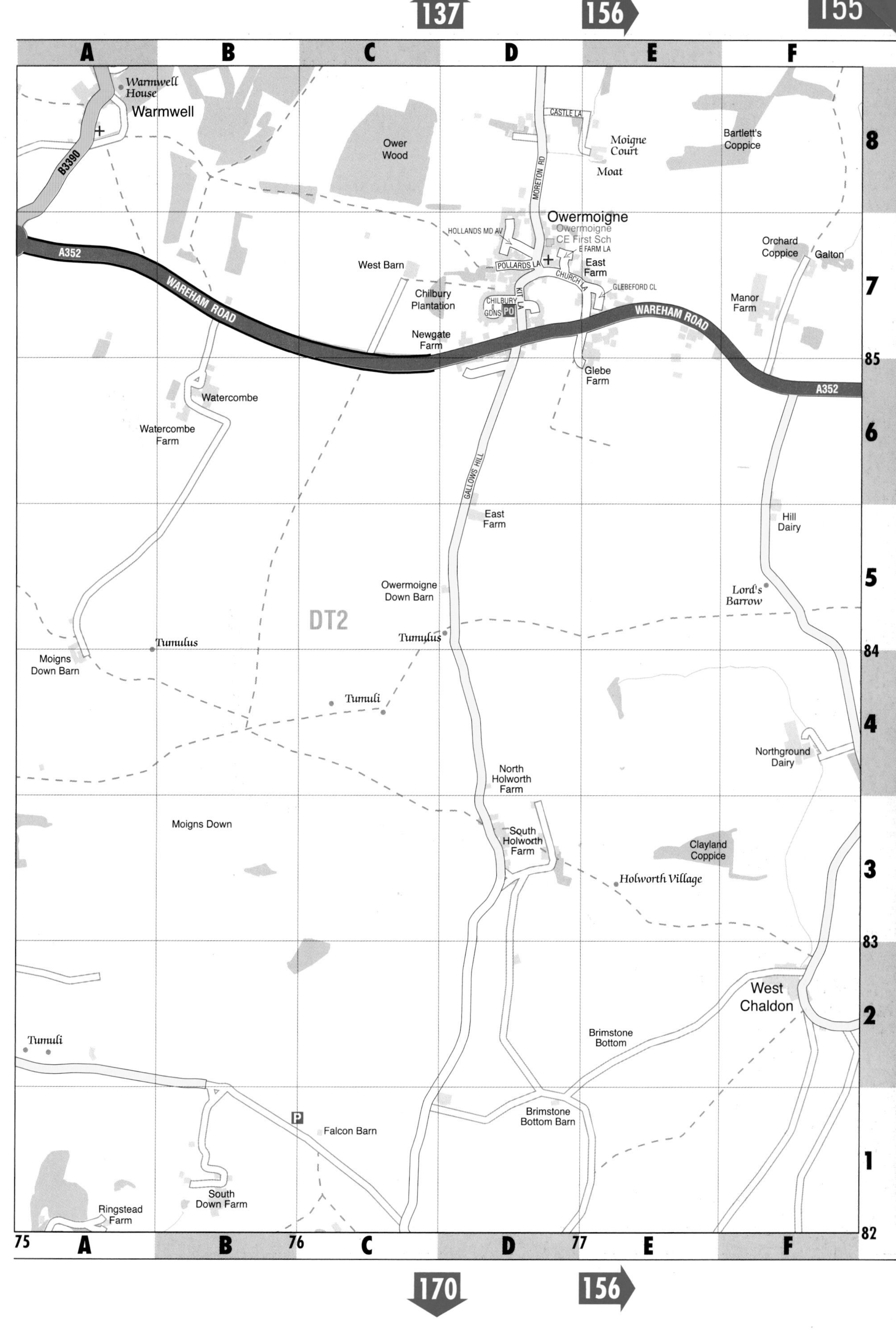
A
B
C
D
E
F
Warmwell House
Warmwell
B3390
Ower Wood
CASTLE LA
MORETON RD
Moigne Court
Moat
Bartlett's Coppice
8
Owermoigne
Owermoigne CE First Sch
HOLLANDS MD AV
E FARM LA
POLLARDS LA
East Farm
CHURCH LA
GLEBEFORD CL
A352
West Barn
Chilbury Plantation
CHILBURY GDNS
KIT LA
PO
WAREHAM ROAD
Newgate Farm
Orchard Coppice
Galton
Manor Farm
7
85
Glebe Farm
Watercombe
Watercombe Farm
6
GALLOWS HILL
East Farm
Hill Dairy
Owermoigne Down Barn
DT2
Lord's Barrow
5
Tumulus
Moigns Down Barn
84
Tumuli
Northground Dairy
4
North Holworth Farm
Moigns Down
South Holworth Farm
Clayland Coppice
Holworth Village
3
83
West Chaldon
Brimstone Bottom
2
Brimstone Bottom Barn
Falcon Barn
P
South Down Farm
Ringstead Farm
1
75
76
77
82

170
156

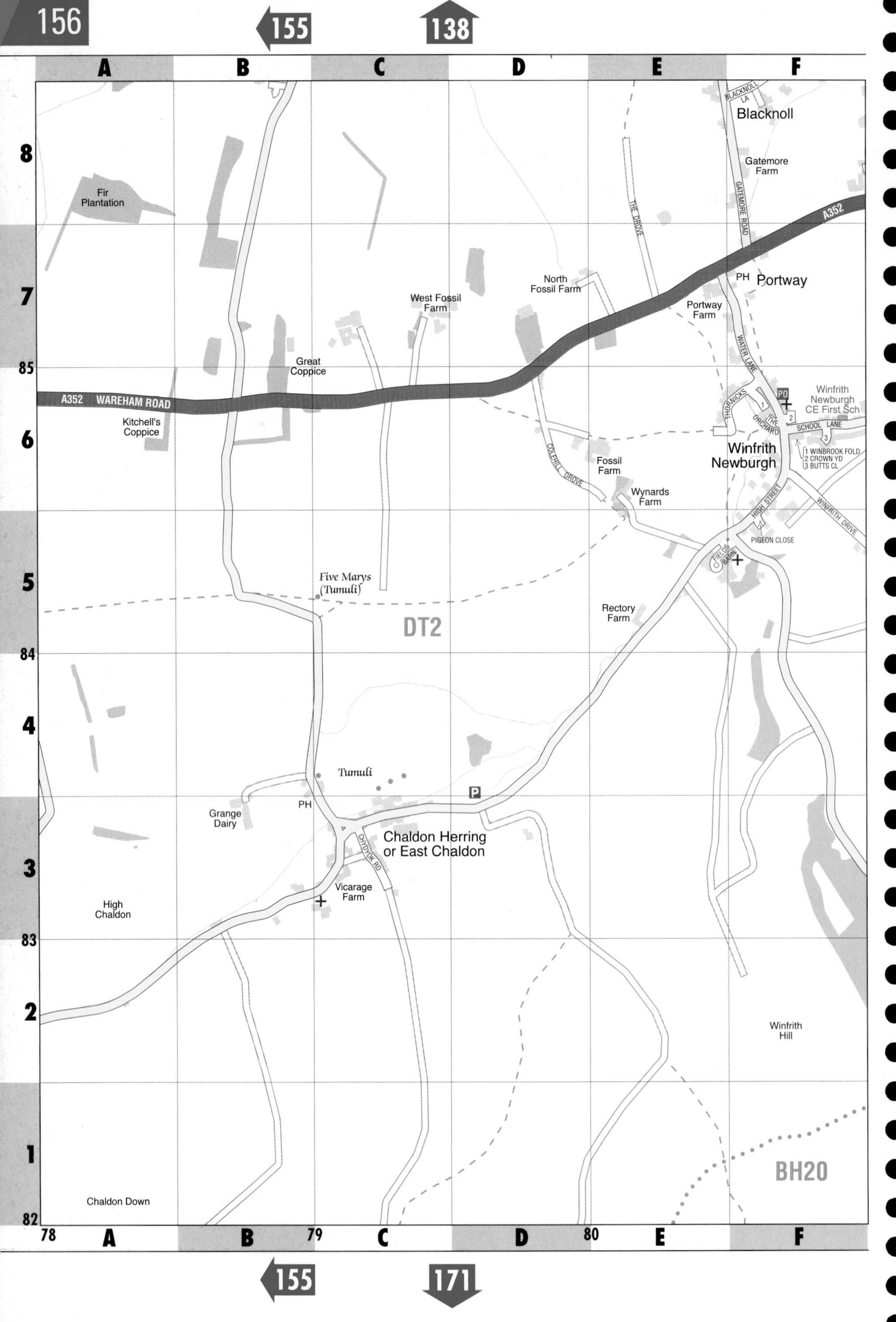

155
138

Blacknoll

Gatemore
Farm

A352

PH Portway

North
Fossil Farm

West Fossil
Farm

Portway
Farm

Fir
Plantation

THE DROVE

GATEMORE ROAD

BLACKNOLL LA

Great
Coppice

WATER LANE

THORNICKS

PO

Winfrith
Newburgh
CE First Sch

A352 WAREHAM ROAD

Kitchell's
Coppice

COLEHILL DROVE

Fossil
Farm

THE ORCHARD

SCHOOL LANE

Winfrith
Newburgh

1 WINBROOK FOLD
2 CROWN YD
3 BUTTS CL

Wynards
Farm

High Street

WINFRITH DRIVE

Five Marys
(Tumuli)

DT2

PIGEON CLOSE

FIELDS BARN

Rectory
Farm

Tumuli

P

Grange
Dairy

PH

CHYDYOK RD

Chaldon Herring
or East Chaldon

High
Chaldon

Vicarage
Farm

Winfrith
Hill

BH20

Chaldon Down

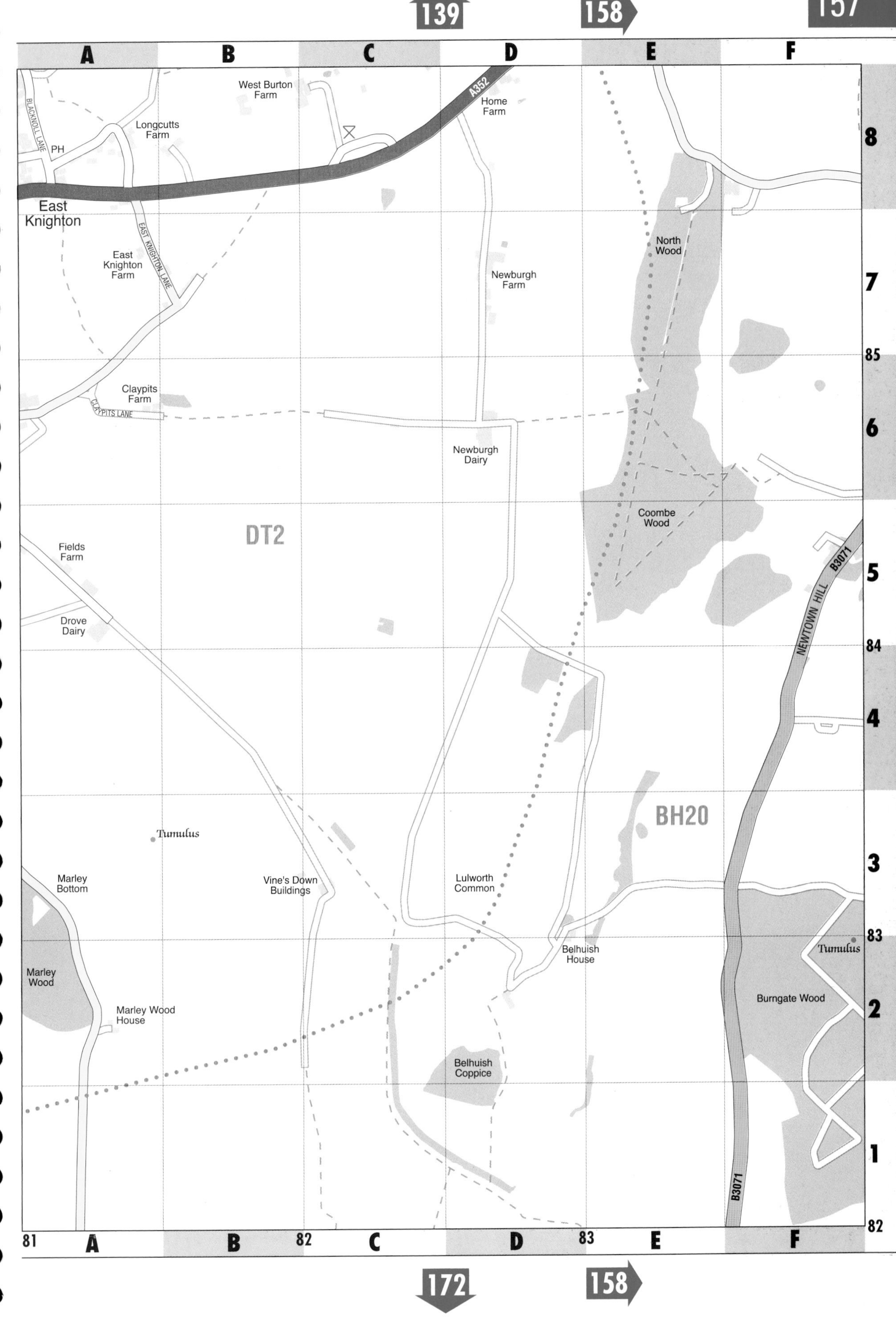

A B C D E F

8
7
85
6
5
84
4
3
83
2
1
82

81 82 83

West Burton Farm

Home Farm

A352

Longcutts Farm

PH

East Knighton

East Knighton Farm

EAST KNIGHTON LANE

BLACKNOLL LANE

Newburgh Farm

North Wood

Claypits Farm

CLAYPITS LANE

Newburgh Dairy

Coombe Wood

DT2

Fields Farm

Drove Dairy

NEWTOWN HILL

B3071

Tumulus

Marley Bottom

Vine's Down Buildings

Lulworth Common

BH20

Belhuish House

Tumulus

Marley Wood

Marley Wood House

Belhuish Coppice

Burngate Wood

B3071

157 140

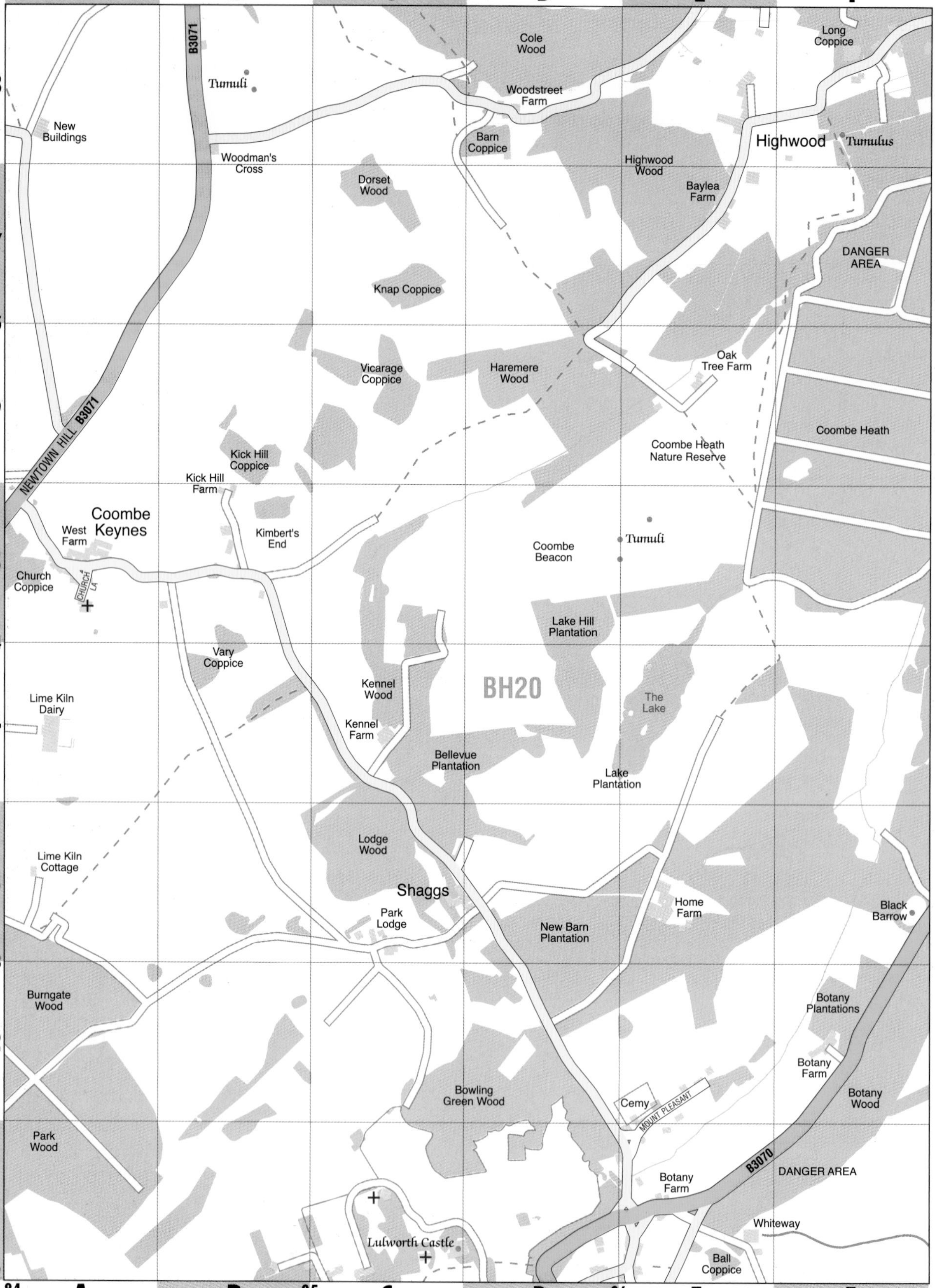

A B C D E F

8

7

85

6

5

84

4

3

83

2

1

82

New Buildings

B3071

Tumuli

Woodman's Cross

NEWTOWN HILL B3071

Cole Wood

Woodstreet Farm

Barn Coppice

Dorset Wood

Knap Coppice

Vicarage Coppice

Haremere Wood

Long Coppice

Highwood   Tumulus

Highwood Wood

Baylea Farm

DANGER AREA

Oak Tree Farm

Coombe Heath Nature Reserve

Coombe Heath

Kick Hill Coppice

Kick Hill Farm

Coombe Keynes

West Farm

Church Coppice

CHURCH LA

Kimbert's End

Coombe Beacon

Tumuli

Lake Hill Plantation

Vary Coppice

Lime Kiln Dairy

Kennel Wood

Kennel Farm

BH20

The Lake

Bellevue Plantation

Lake Plantation

Lodge Wood

Lime Kiln Cottage

Shaggs

Park Lodge

New Barn Plantation

Home Farm

Black Barrow

Burngate Wood

Botany Plantations

Botany Farm

Park Wood

Bowling Green Wood

Cemy

MOUNT PLEASANT

Botany Farm

Botany Wood

B3070

DANGER AREA

Whiteway

Lulworth Castle

Ball Coppice

84 A B 85 C D 86 E F

157 173

141
160

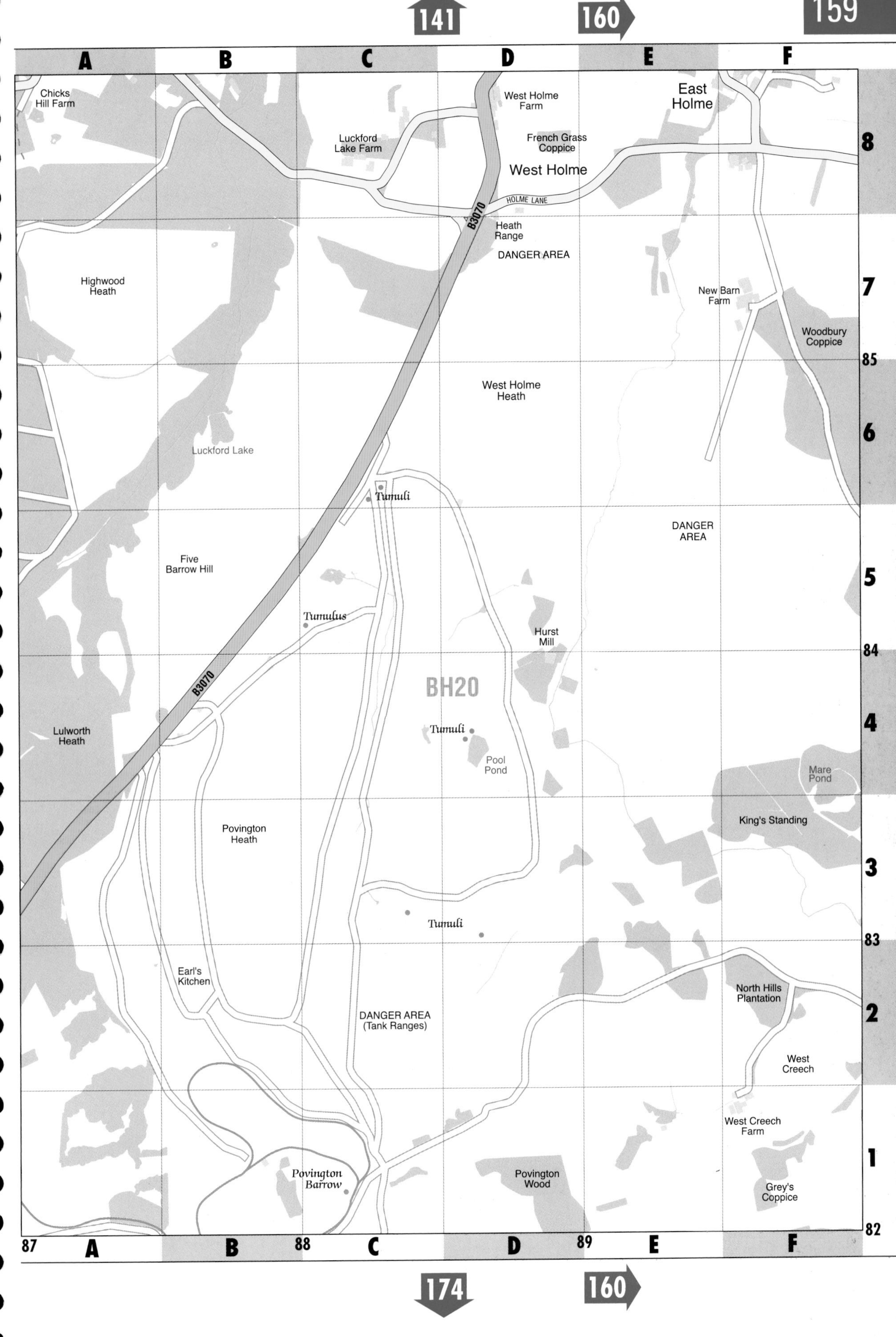
A
B
C
D
E
F
Chicks Hill Farm
West Holme Farm
East Holme
Luckford Lake Farm
French Grass Coppice
West Holme
HOLME LANE
B3070
Heath Range
DANGER AREA
Highwood Heath
New Barn Farm
Woodbury Coppice
West Holme Heath
Luckford Lake
Tumuli
DANGER AREA
Five Barrow Hill
Tumulus
Hurst Mill
BH20
B3070
Lulworth Heath
Tumuli
Pool Pond
Mare Pond
King's Standing
Povington Heath
Tumuli
Earl's Kitchen
North Hills Plantation
DANGER AREA (Tank Ranges)
West Creech
West Creech Farm
Povington Barrow
Povington Wood
Grey's Coppice
8
7
85
6
5
84
4
3
83
2
1
82
87
88
89

174
160

159
142

A B C D E F

8
7
85
6
5
84
4
3
83
2
83
2
1
82

Holme Lane Plantation
HOLME LANE
Tumulus
King's Barrow
WEST LANE
Hotel
Stocks Wood
Stoborough Heath
Doreys Farm
Battle Plain
Rifle Range
Three Lords' Barrow
Tumulus
LC
Holme Heath
Tumuli
New Hall Farm
Creech Bottom
Grange Barn
Creech Heath
DANGER AREA
BH20
Snug Farm
Icen Barrow
GRANGE ROAD
Tumulus
Grange Heath
Haskells Farm
Clay Pits
Drinking Barrow
Tumulus
Creech
Smithys Farm
Tumuli
DANGER AREA
Breach Plantation
John's Plantation
Cotness
Great Plantation
Mine
Whitehall
Mine (dis)
East Creech
Alder Moor
Little Wood
Grange Farm
Creech Barrow Hill
Mine
Creech Grange
Tumulus
Stonehill Down Nature Reserve
Tumulus
GRANGE HILL
Great Wood
Tumulus
Stonehill Down

A351
CORFE ROAD
B3075
NEW ROAD
OLD FURZEBROOK RD
TUCKERS MILL CL
OVAL GDN
THE DROVE
STOBOROUGH MDW
SCOTT CL

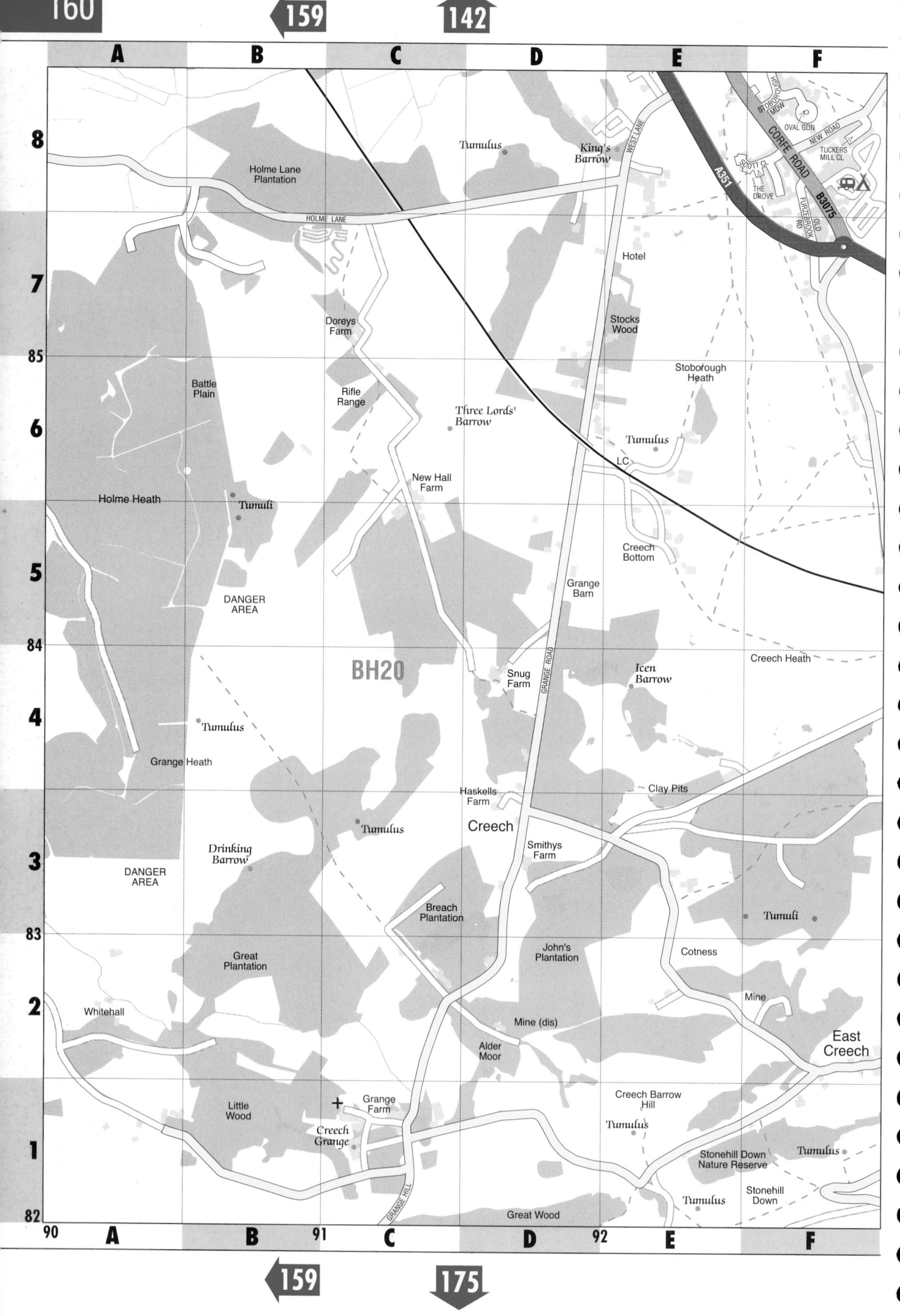

159
175

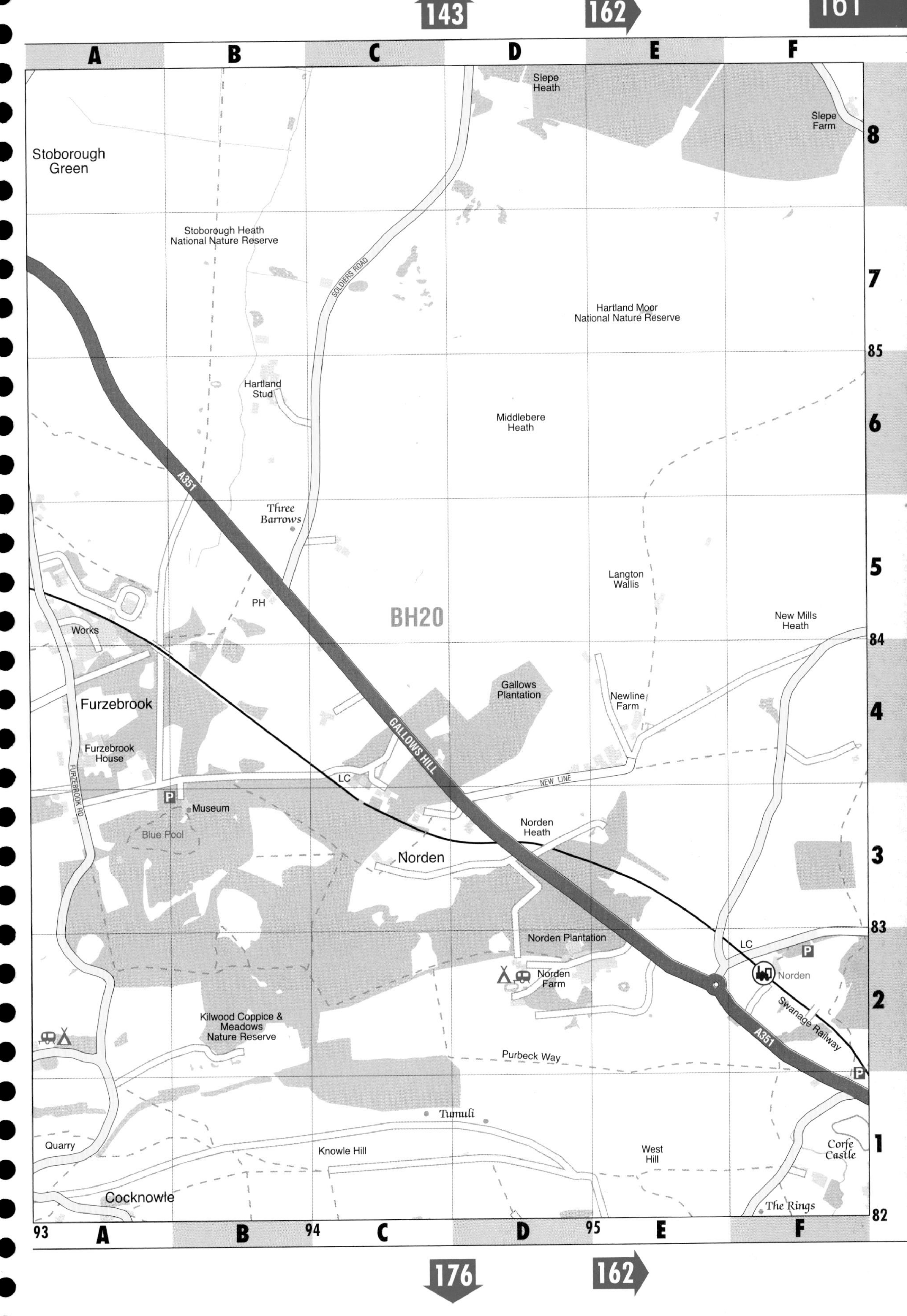
143
162
A
B
C
D
E
F
Slepe Heath
Slepe Farm
Stoborough Green
Stoborough Heath National Nature Reserve
SOLDIERS ROAD
Hartland Moor National Nature Reserve
Hartland Stud
Middlebere Heath
A351
Three Barrows
Langton Wallis
PH
BH20
New Mills Heath
Works
Gallows Plantation
Newline Farm
Furzebrook
GALLOWS HILL
Furzebrook House
FURZEBROOK RD
LC
NEW LINE
Museum
Blue Pool
Norden Heath
Norden
Norden Plantation
LC
Norden Farm
Norden
Swanage Railway
Kilwood Coppice & Meadows Nature Reserve
A351
Purbeck Way
Tumuli
Quarry
Knowle Hill
West Hill
Corfe Castle
Cocknowle
The Rings
8
7
85
6
5
84
4
3
83
2
1
82
93
94
95
176
162

161
144

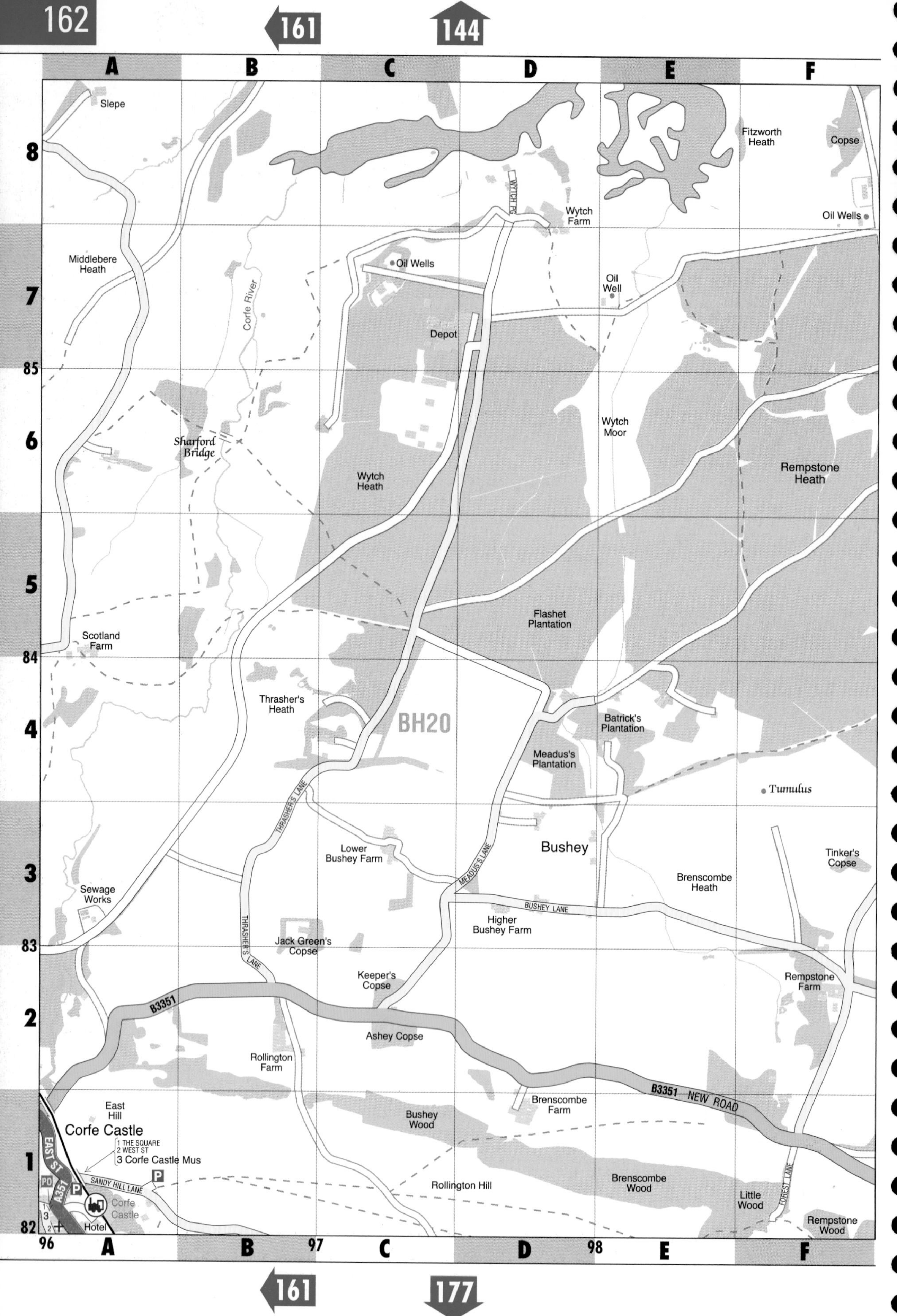
A
B
C
D
E
F
8
7
85
6
5
84
4
3
83
2
1
82
96
97
98
Slepe
Fitzworth Heath
Copse
Oil Wells
Wytch Farm
WYTCH PG
Middlebere Heath
Oil Wells
Oil Well
Corfe River
Depot
Sharford Bridge
Wytch Moor
Wytch Heath
Rempstone Heath
Flashet Plantation
Scotland Farm
Thrasher's Heath
BH20
Batrick's Plantation
Meadus's Plantation
Tumulus
THRASHER'S LANE
Bushey
Lower Bushey Farm
MEADUS'S LANE
Tinker's Copse
Brenscombe Heath
Sewage Works
BUSHEY LANE
Higher Bushey Farm
Jack Green's Copse
Keeper's Copse
Rempstone Farm
B3351
Ashey Copse
Rollington Farm
B3351 NEW ROAD
East Hill
Brenscombe Farm
Corfe Castle
Bushey Wood
EAST ST
1 THE SQUARE
2 WEST ST
3 Corfe Castle Mus
PO
P
A351
SANDY HILL LANE
Corfe Castle
Hotel
Rollington Hill
Brenscombe Wood
Little Wood
FOREST LANE
Rempstone Wood

161
177

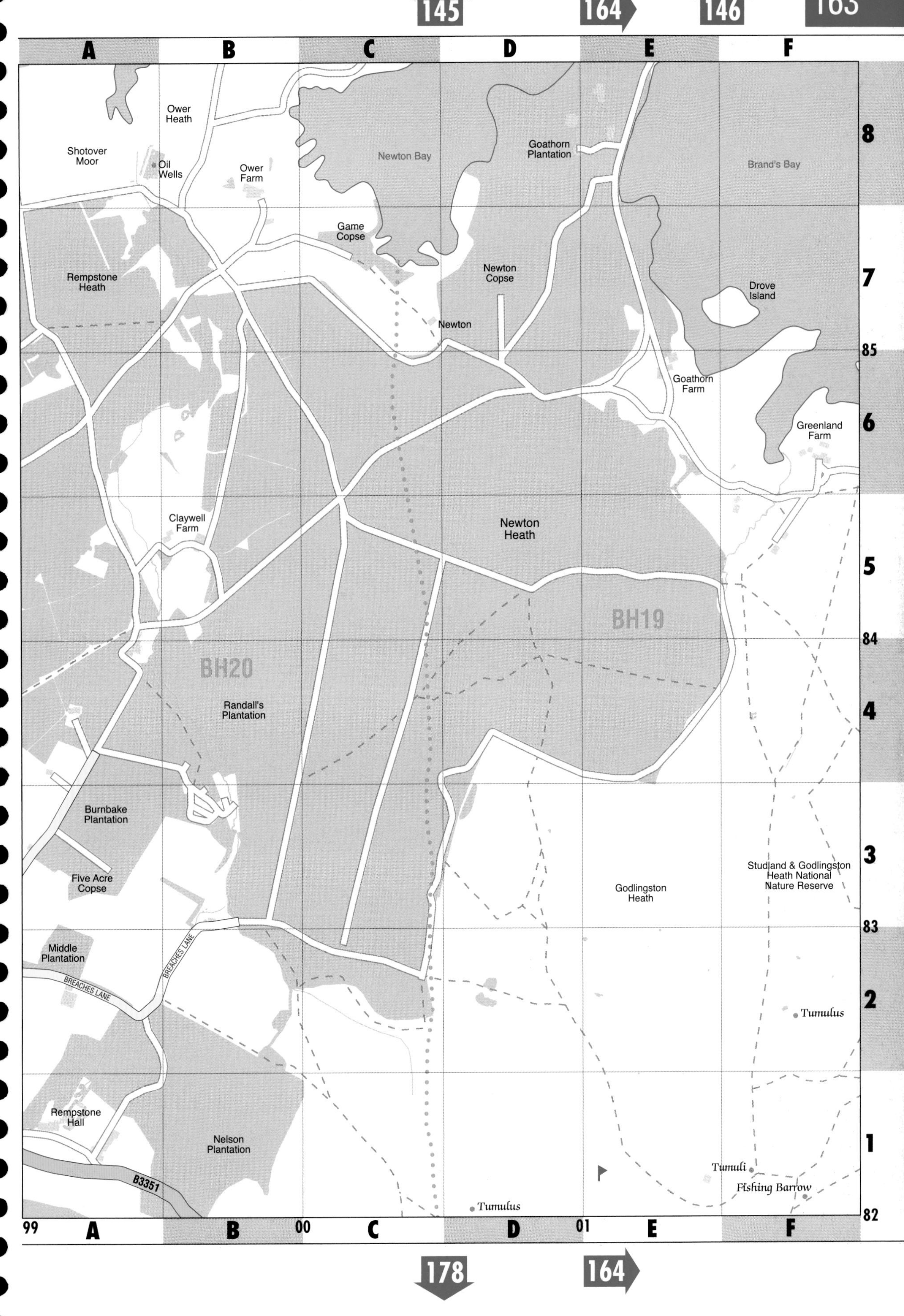

A   B   C   D   E   F

8

Ower Heath

Shotover Moor

Oil Wells

Ower Farm

Newton Bay

Goathorn Plantation

Brand's Bay

Game Copse

Rempstone Heath

Newton Copse

Drove Island

7

Newton

85

Goathorn Farm

6

Greenland Farm

Claywell Farm

Newton Heath

BH19

5

84

BH20

Randall's Plantation

4

Burnbake Plantation

3

Studland & Godlingston Heath National Nature Reserve

Five Acre Copse

Godlingston Heath

83

Middle Plantation

BREACHES LANE

BREACHES LANE

2

Tumulus

Rempstone Hall

Nelson Plantation

1

Tumuli

Fishing Barrow

B3351

Tumulus

82

99   A   B   00   C   D   01   E   F

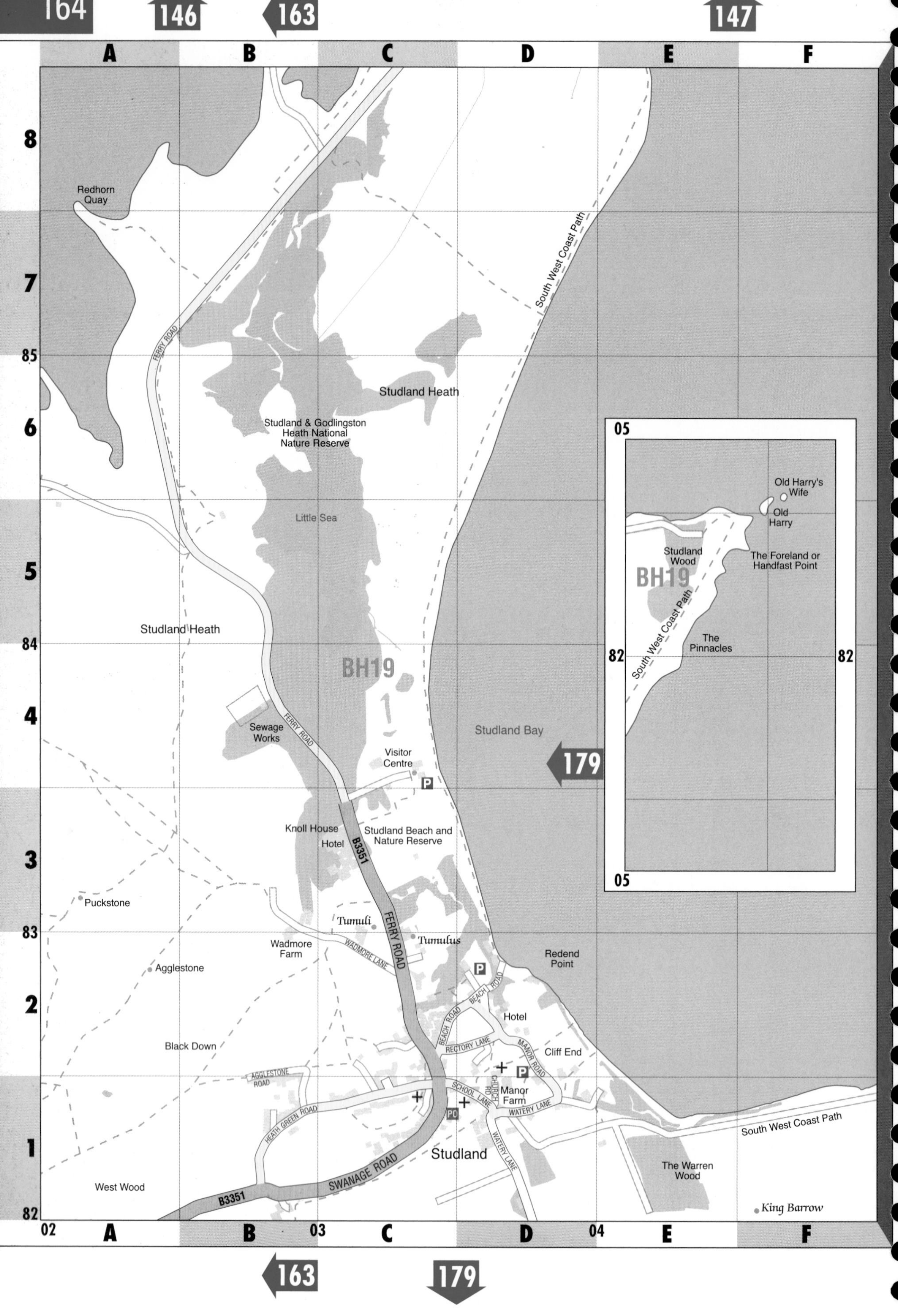

8

Redhorn
Quay

7

85

Studland Heath

6

Studland & Godlingston
Heath National
Nature Reserve

Little Sea

5

84

Studland Heath

BH19

4

Sewage
Works

Visitor
Centre

P

3

Knoll House
Hotel

B3351

Studland Beach and
Nature Reserve

Puckstone

83

Tumuli

Wadmore
Farm

WADMORE LANE

Tumulus

FERRY ROAD

Redend
Point

Agglestone

2

P

BEACH ROAD

BEACH ROAD

Hotel

Black Down

RECTORY LANE

MANOR ROAD

Cliff End

AGGLESTONE
ROAD

P

HEATH GREEN ROAD

SCHOOL LANE

CHURCH
ROAD

Manor
Farm

WATERY LANE

PO

1

West Wood

B3351

SWANAGE ROAD

Studland

WATERY LANE

The Warren
Wood

South West Coast Path

82

King Barrow

S
o
u
t
h

W
e
s
t

C
o
a
s
t

P
a
t
h

Studland Bay

179

FERRY ROAD

05

Old Harry's
Wife

Old
Harry

Studland
Wood

The Foreland or
Handfast Point

BH19

82

South West Coast Path

The
Pinnacles

82

05

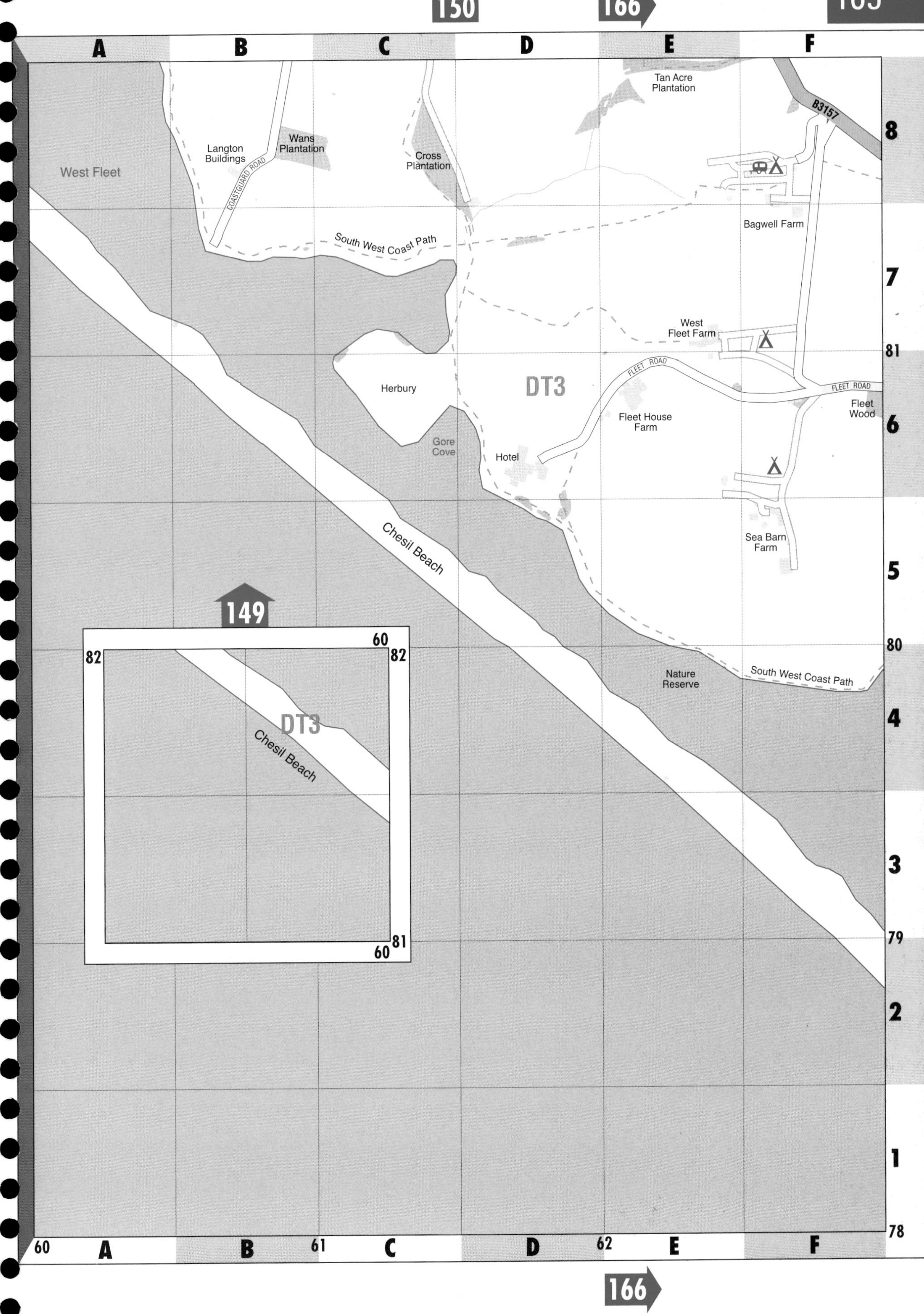

West Fleet

Langton Buildings

Wans Plantation

COASTGUARD ROAD

Cross Plantation

South West Coast Path

Tan Acre Plantation

B3157

Bagwell Farm

West Fleet Farm

DT3

Herbury

FLEET ROAD

Gore Cove

Fleet House Farm

Hotel

FLEET ROAD

Fleet Wood

Chesil Beach

Sea Barn Farm

149

60 82

82

DT3

Chesil Beach

Nature Reserve

South West Coast Path

60 81

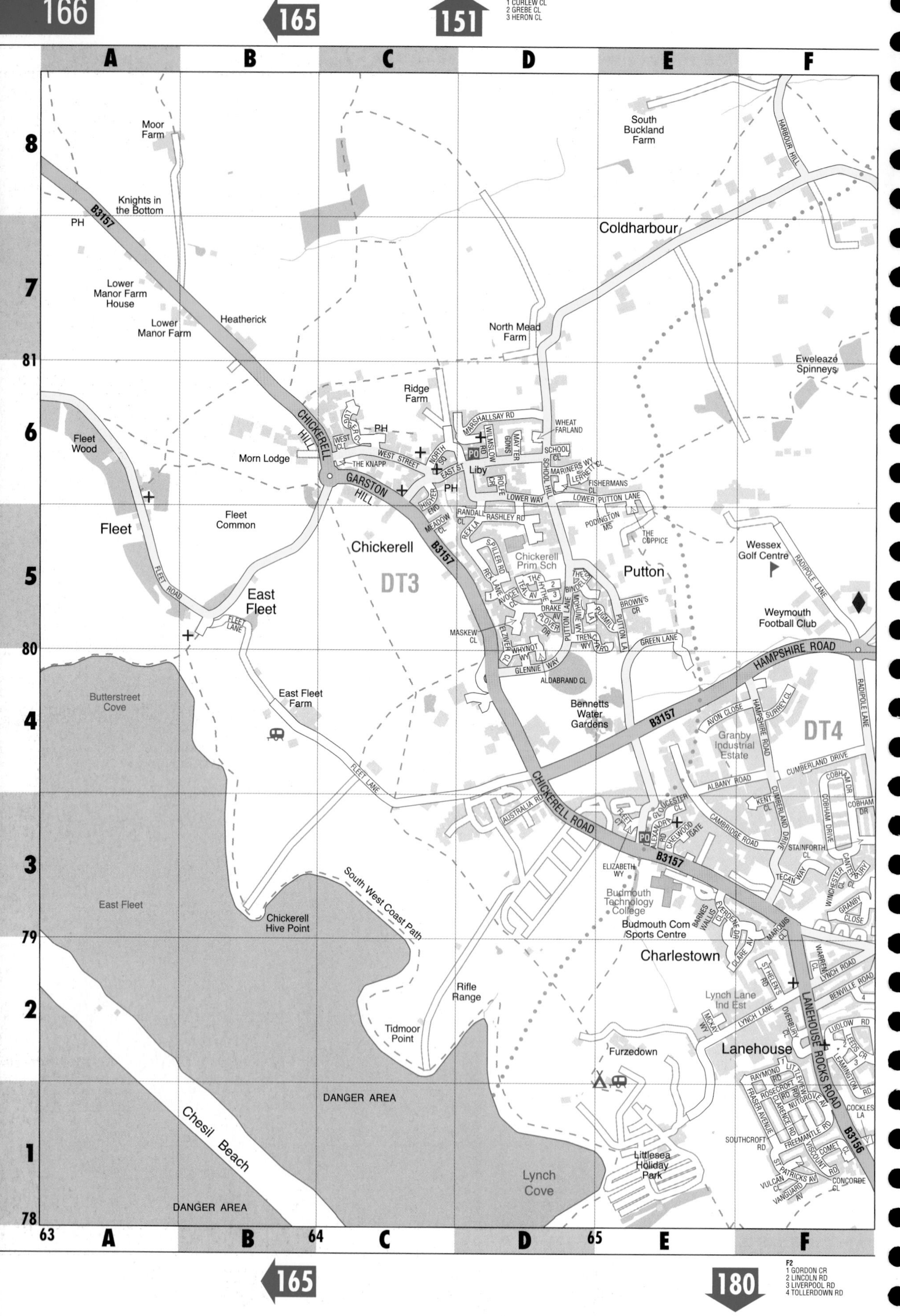

A B C D E F

8

Moor
Farm

Knights in
the Bottom

PH
B3157

7

Lower
Manor Farm
House

Heatherick

Lower
Manor Farm

81

South
Buckland
Farm

Coldharbour

North Mead
Farm

Eweleaze
Spinneys

6

Fleet
Wood

Chickerell Hill

Morn Lodge

THE KNAPP

Ridge
Farm

PH

WEST
CL

USER CL

WEST STREET

NORTH
RD

EAST ST

MARSHALLSAY RD

WILMSLOW
RD

MAY FER
GDNS

Liby

ROLFE
CR

SCHOOL
CL

SCHOOL HILL

WHEAT
FARLAND

MARINERS WY

LERRET
CL

FISHERMANS

PH

GARSTON HILL

THICKBA

MEADOW
CL

END

LOWER WAY

Lower Putton Lane

PODINGTON
MS

THE
COPPICE

Wessex
Golf Centre

Fleet

+

FLEET ROAD

Fleet
Common

Chickerell

DT3

SULLER
CR LA

RANDALL
CL

REX LA

RASHLEY RD

Chickerell
Prim Sch

Putton

RADIPOLE LANE

Weymouth
Football Club

5

East
Fleet

FLEET
LANE

+

AVOCET
DR

THE
TEAL

THE
AV

DRAKE
AV

BROWN'S
CR

PLOVER CL

ELZVER
WY

MASKEW
CL

PUTTON LANE

MOORHEN WY

PILGRIM

PUTTON LA

BINDBS

TRENCHARD
WY

GREEN LANE

80

Butterstreet
Cove

East Fleet
Farm

WHYNOT
WY

GLENNIE WAY

ALDABRAND CL

Bennetts
Water
Gardens

HAMPSHIRE ROAD

B3157

AVON CLOSE

Granby
Industrial
Estate

HAMPSHIRE ROAD

SURREY CL

DT4

CUMBERLAND DRIVE

COBHAM
CL

COBHAM DR

RADIPOLE LANE

4

FLEET LANE

ALBANY ROAD

KENT
CL

CAMBRIDGE ROAD

CUMBERLAND DRIVE

STAINFORTH
CL

COBHAM
DR

3

South West Coast Path

Chickerell
Hive Point

Chickerell Road

AUSTRALIA

GLOUCESTER
RD

ALEXANDRA
RD

PO

CHELWOOD
GATE

ELIZABETH
WY

Budmouth
Technology
College

Budmouth Com
Sports Centre

B3157

BARNES
WALLIS

EVERDENE

CLARE AV

WINCHESTER CL

TEGAN
CL

CANTLE CROFT

GRANBY
CLOSE

St HELEN'S

79

East Fleet

Rifle
Range

Charlestown

Lynch Lane
Ind Est

LYNCH
RD

MACKAY

BENVILLE RD

LANEHOUSE ROCKS ROAD

+

LUDLOW
RD

LEES CR

LEMINGTON

2

Tidmoor
Point

Lynch
Cove

Furzedown

Lanehouse

LYNCH LANE

WARREN
RD

LONGCROFT

COCKLES
LA

B3156

1

Chesil Beach

DANGER AREA

Littlesea
Holiday
Park

SOUTHCROFT
RD

RAYMOND
RD

ROSECROFT
RD

FRASER AVENUE

FREEMANTLE RD

ARNOLD RD

NETHERCOOMBE

VULCAN
CL

St PATRICKS
CL

VANGUARD AV

COMET
CL

VISCOUNT RD

VANGUARD
AV

CONCORDE
CL

78

DANGER AREA

63 A B 64 C D 65 E F

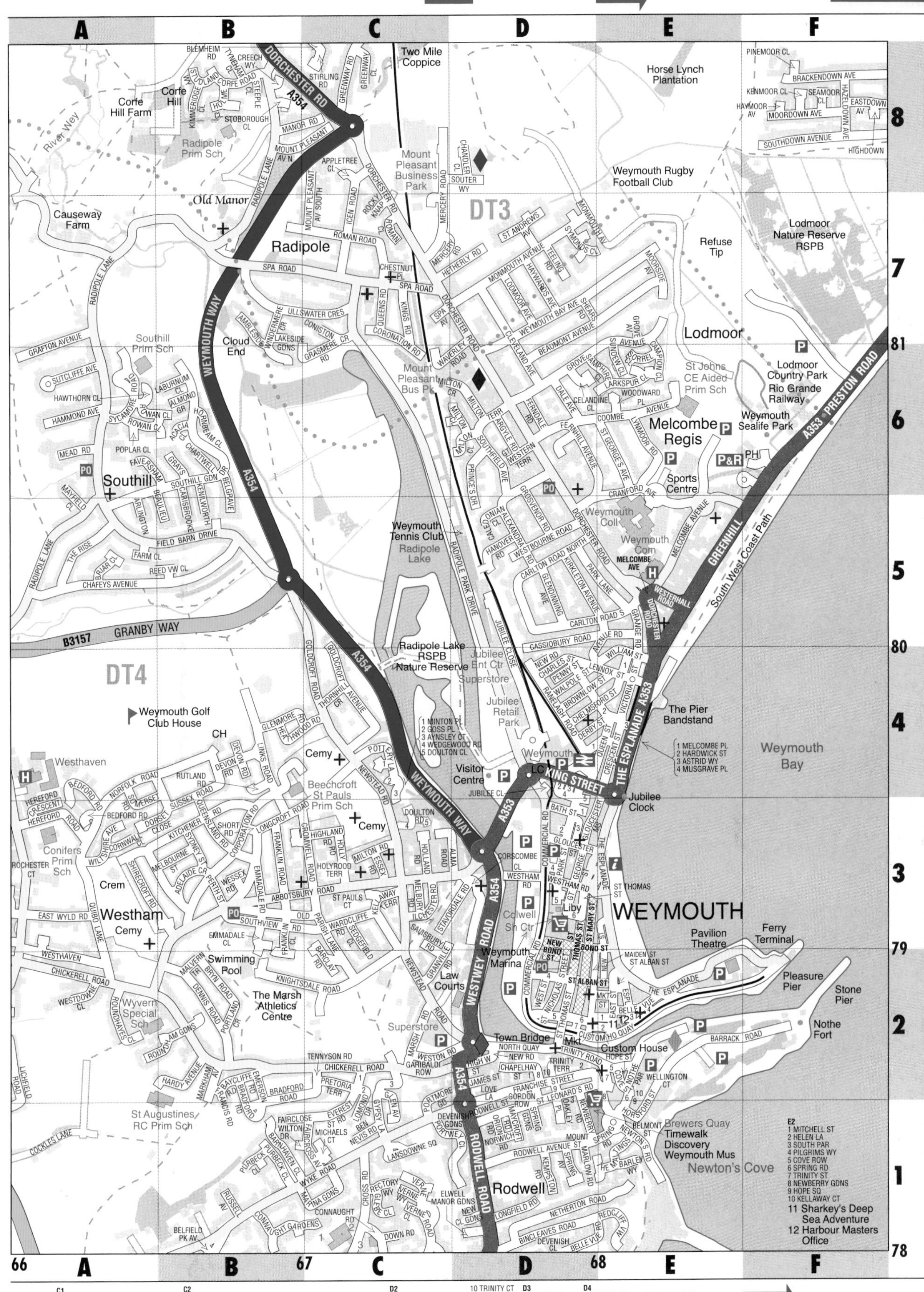

C1
1 Holy Trinity CE Inf Sch
2 Holy Trinity CE Jun Sch
3 Thornlow Prep Sch

C2
1 ASHTON RD
2 GYPSY LA
3 PRINCE OF WALES RD

180

D2
1 CHAPELHAY HEIGHTS
2 HARTLEBURY TERR
3 SPRING LA
4 LOWER ST ALBAN ST
5 ST EDMUND ST
6 ST EDMUND ST
7 ST MARY ST
8 DORSET TERR
9 PROSPECT PL

10 TRINITY CT

D3
1 CLIFTON PL
2 QUEBEC PL
3 TURTON ST
4 WOOPERTON ST
5 CAROLINE PL
6 SCHOOL ST

D4
1 STANLEY ST
2 UPWAY ST
3 TERMINUS ST
4 EDWARD ST
5 ALBERT ST

181 168

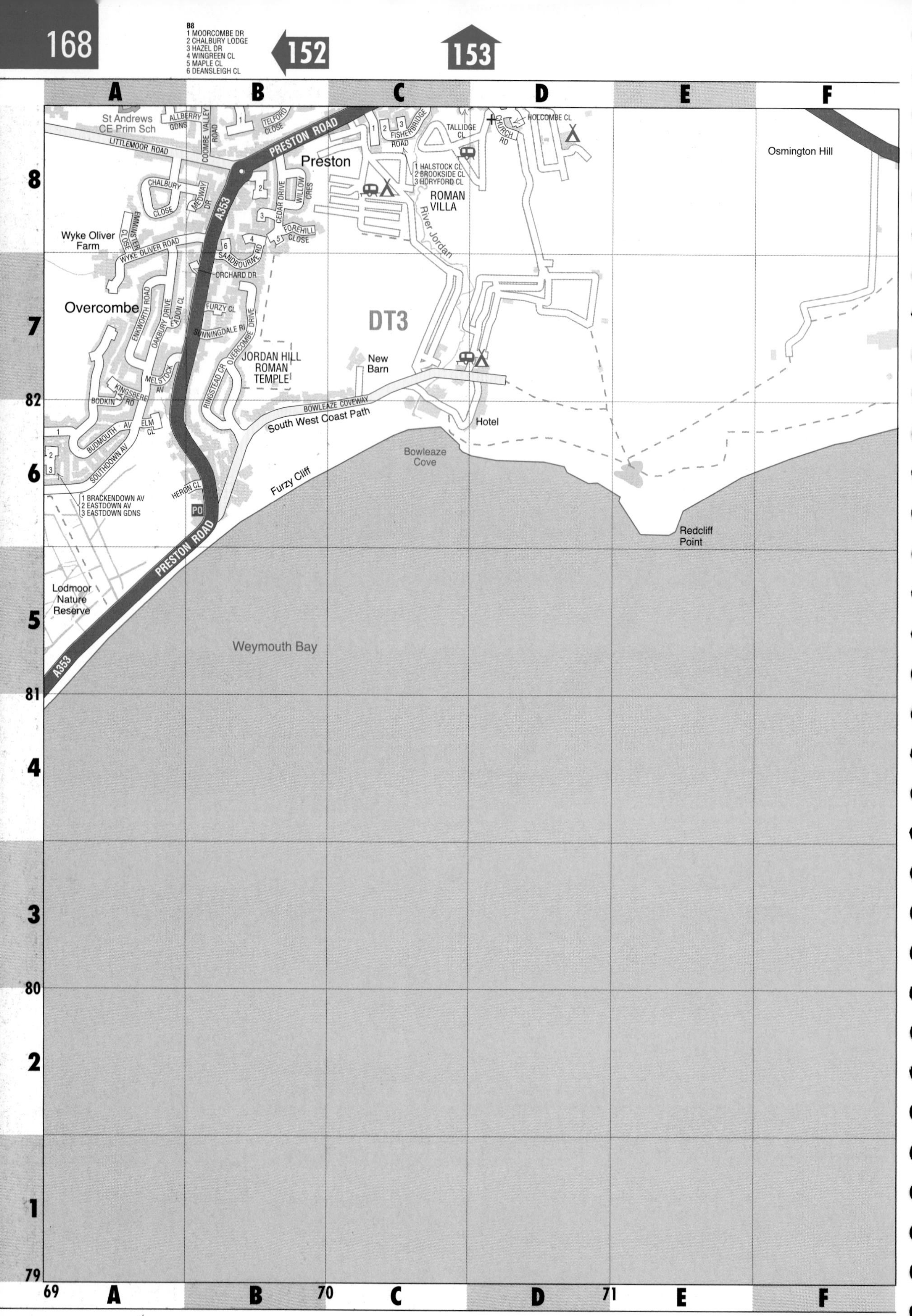

B8
1 MOORCOMBE DR
2 CHALBURY LODGE
3 HAZEL DR
4 WINGREEN CL
5 MAPLE CL
6 DEANSLEIGH CL

152

153

Osmington Hill

St Andrews
CE Prim Sch

ALLBERRY
GDNS

TELFORD
CLOSE

PRESTON ROAD

Preston

LITTLEMOOR ROAD

COOMBE VALLEY ROAD

FISHERBRIDGE
ROAD

TALLIDGE
CL

HOLCOMBE CL

CHURCH RD

CHALBURY
DR

MCWAY

A353

CEDAR DRIVE

WILLOW CRES

FOREHILL CLOSE

1 HALSTOCK CL
2 BROOKSIDE CL
3 HORYFORD CL

ROMAN
VILLA

EMMINSTER CLOSE

Wyke Oliver
Farm

WYKE OLIVER ROAD

ORCHARD DR

River Jordan

DT3

Overcombe

OAKBURY DRIVE

SUNNINGDALE RI

OVERCOMBE DRIVE

JORDAN HILL
ROMAN
TEMPLE

New
Barn

82

RINGSTEAD CR

MELSTOCK AV

KINGSBERE RD

BODKIN

ELM CL

BOWLEAZE COVEWAY

South West Coast Path

Hotel

6

BUDMOUTH AV

SOUTHDOWN AV

1
2
3

1 BRACKENDOWN AV
2 EASTDOWN AV
3 EASTDOWN GDNS

HERON CL

PO

Furzy Cliff

Bowleaze
Cove

Redcliff
Point

5

Lodmoor
Nature
Reserve

A353

PRESTON ROAD

Weymouth Bay

81

4

3

80

2

1

79

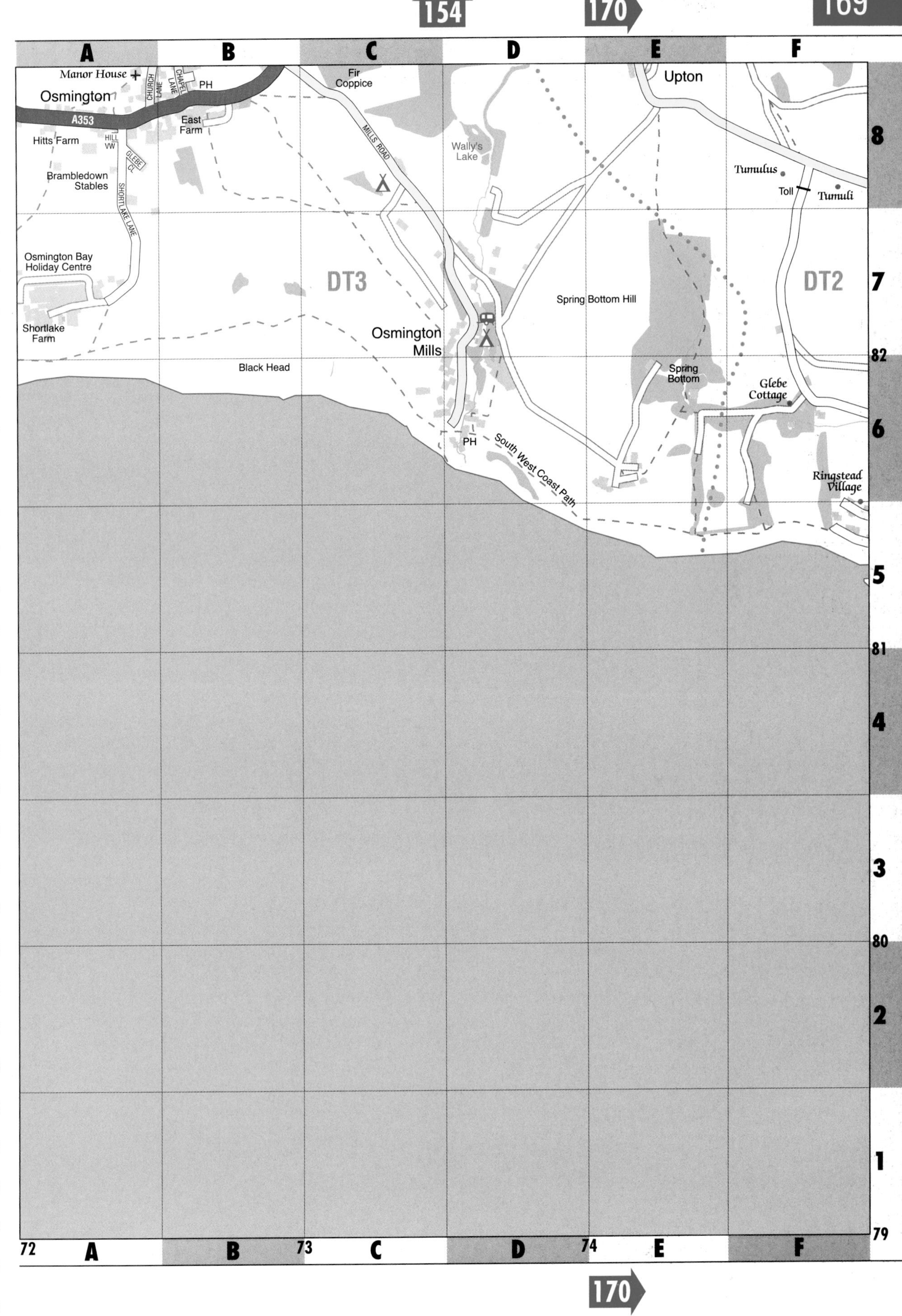
154
170
A
B
C
D
E
F
Manor House
Osmington
PH
CHURCH LANE
CHAPEL LANE
A353
East Farm
Hitts Farm
HILL VW
GLEBE CL
Brambledown Stables
SHORTLAKE LANE
Fir Coppice
MILLS ROAD
Wally's Lake
Upton
Tumulus
Toll
Tumuli
Osmington Bay Holiday Centre
DT3
Spring Bottom Hill
DT2
Shortlake Farm
Osmington Mills
Black Head
Spring Bottom
Glebe Cottage
PH
South West Coast Path
Ringstead Village
8
7
82
6
5
81
4
3
80
2
1
79
72
73
74
170

A B C D E F

8

National
Trust

Sea Barn
Farm

Down
Barn

Holworth
House

Burning
Cliff

DT2

7

Ringstead
Bay

National Trust
Nature Reserve

South West Coast Path

Tumuli

81

Whitenothe
Cottages

Tumuli

6

White
Nothe

5

80

4

3

79

2

1

78

FISHERS PL

P

75 A B 76 C D 77 E F

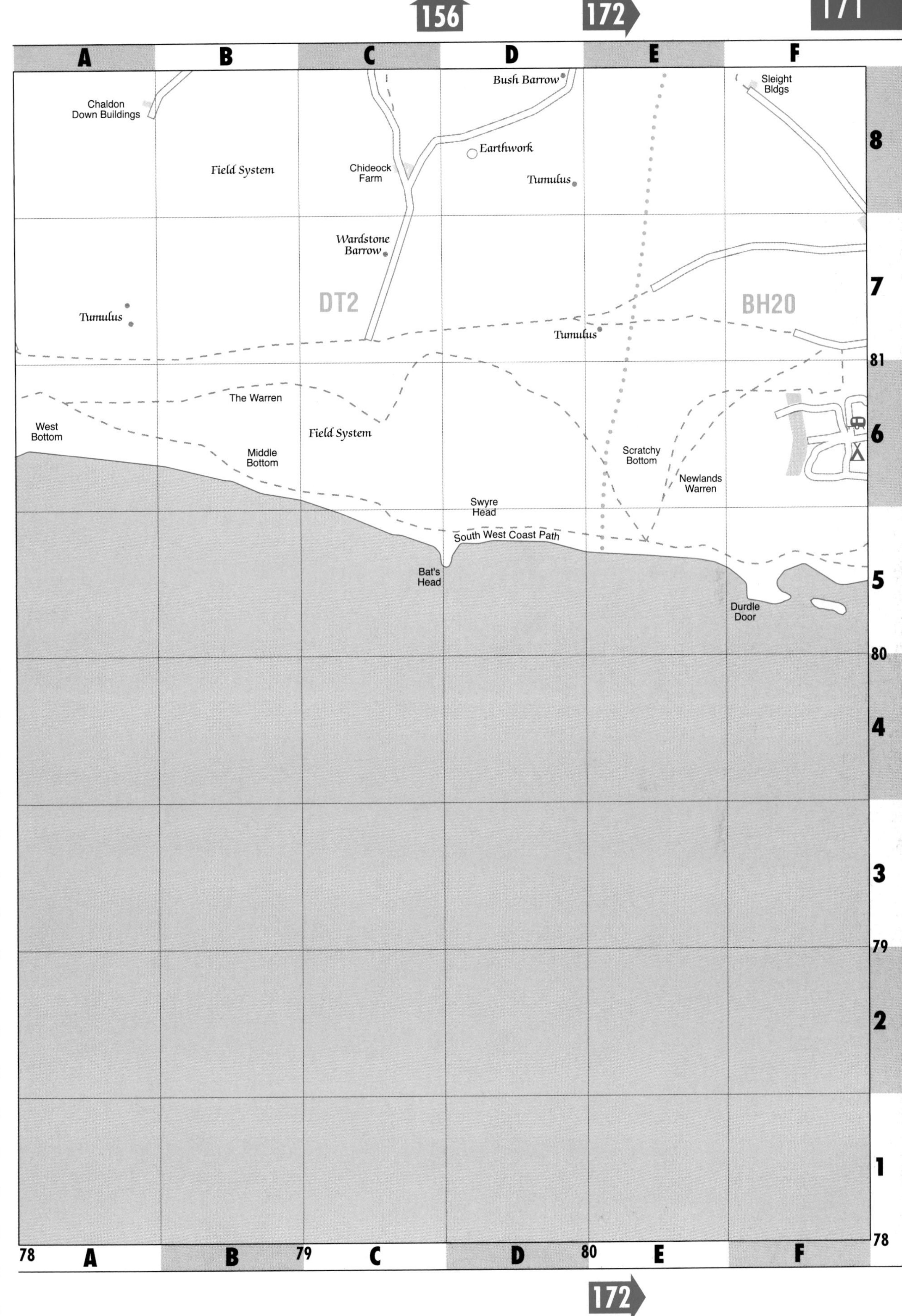

Chaldon
Down Buildings

Field System

Bush Barrow

Sleight
Bldgs

Earthwork

Chideock
Farm

Tumulus

Wardstone
Barrow

DT2

Tumulus

BH20

Tumulus

The Warren

West
Bottom

Field System

Scratchy
Bottom

Middle
Bottom

Newlands
Warren

Swyre
Head

South West Coast Path

Bat's
Head

Durdle
Door

A B C D E F

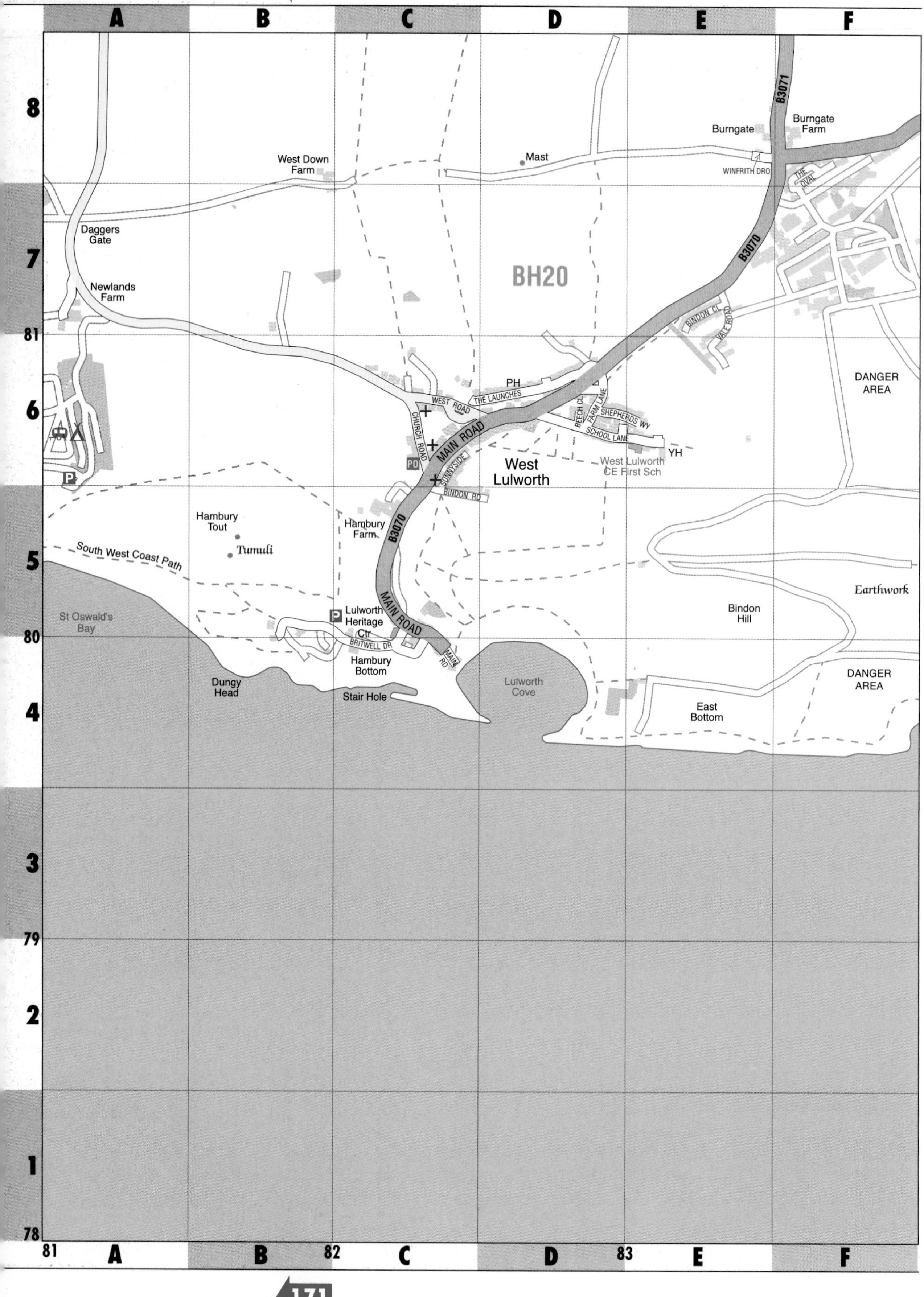

8

West Down Farm

Mast

Burngate

Burngate Farm

B3071

WINFRITH DRO

THE OVAL

Daggers Gate

7

Newlands Farm

BH20

B3070

BINDON CL

VALE ROAD

81

DANGER AREA

6

PH

THE LAUNCHES

WEST ROAD

CHURCH ROAD

MAIN ROAD

BEECH CL

FARM LANE

SHEPHERDS WY

SCHOOL LANE

YH

PO

SUNNYSIDE

West Lulworth

West Lulworth CE First Sch

BINDON RD

Hambury Tout

Tumuli

Hambury Farm

B3070

South West Coast Path

5

St Oswald's Bay

Lulworth Heritage Ctr

MAIN ROAD

Bindon Hill

Earthwork

80

BRITWELL DR

Hambury Bottom

MAIN RD

Dungy Head

Stair Hole

Lulworth Cove

DANGER AREA

4

East Bottom

3

79

2

1

78

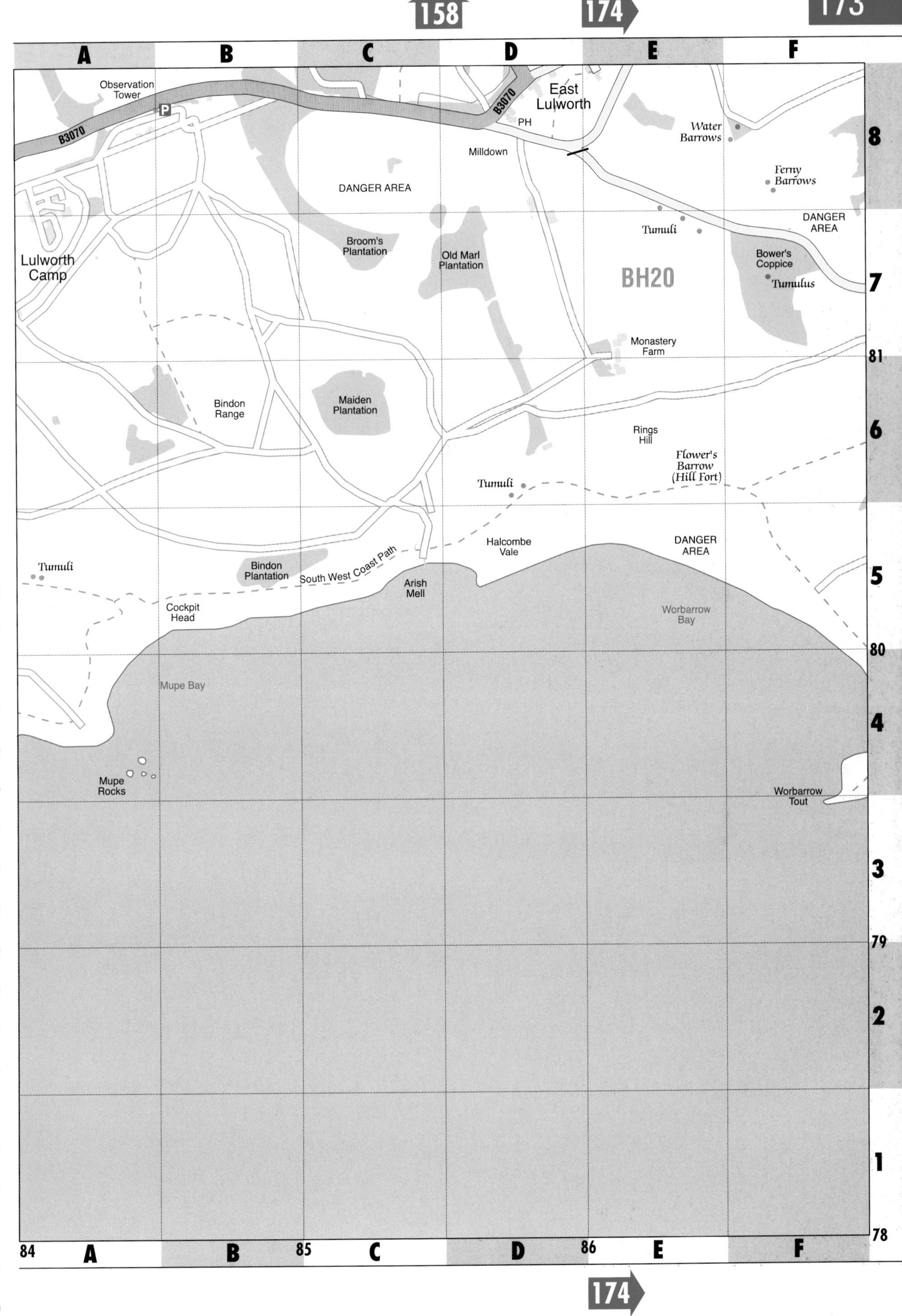

Observation Tower
P
B3070
Lulworth Camp
DANGER AREA
Broom's Plantation
Old Marl Plantation
Bindon Range
Maiden Plantation
Tumuli
Bindon Plantation
South West Coast Path
Cockpit Head
Mupe Bay
Mupe Rocks
Arish Mell
Halcombe Vale
Tumuli
Rings Hill
Flower's Barrow (Hill Fort)
Monastery Farm
East Lulworth
PH
Milldown
B3070
Water Barrows
Ferny Barrows
Tumuli
DANGER AREA
BH20
Bower's Coppice
Tumulus
DANGER AREA
Worbarrow Bay
Worbarrow Tout

A   B   C   D   E   F

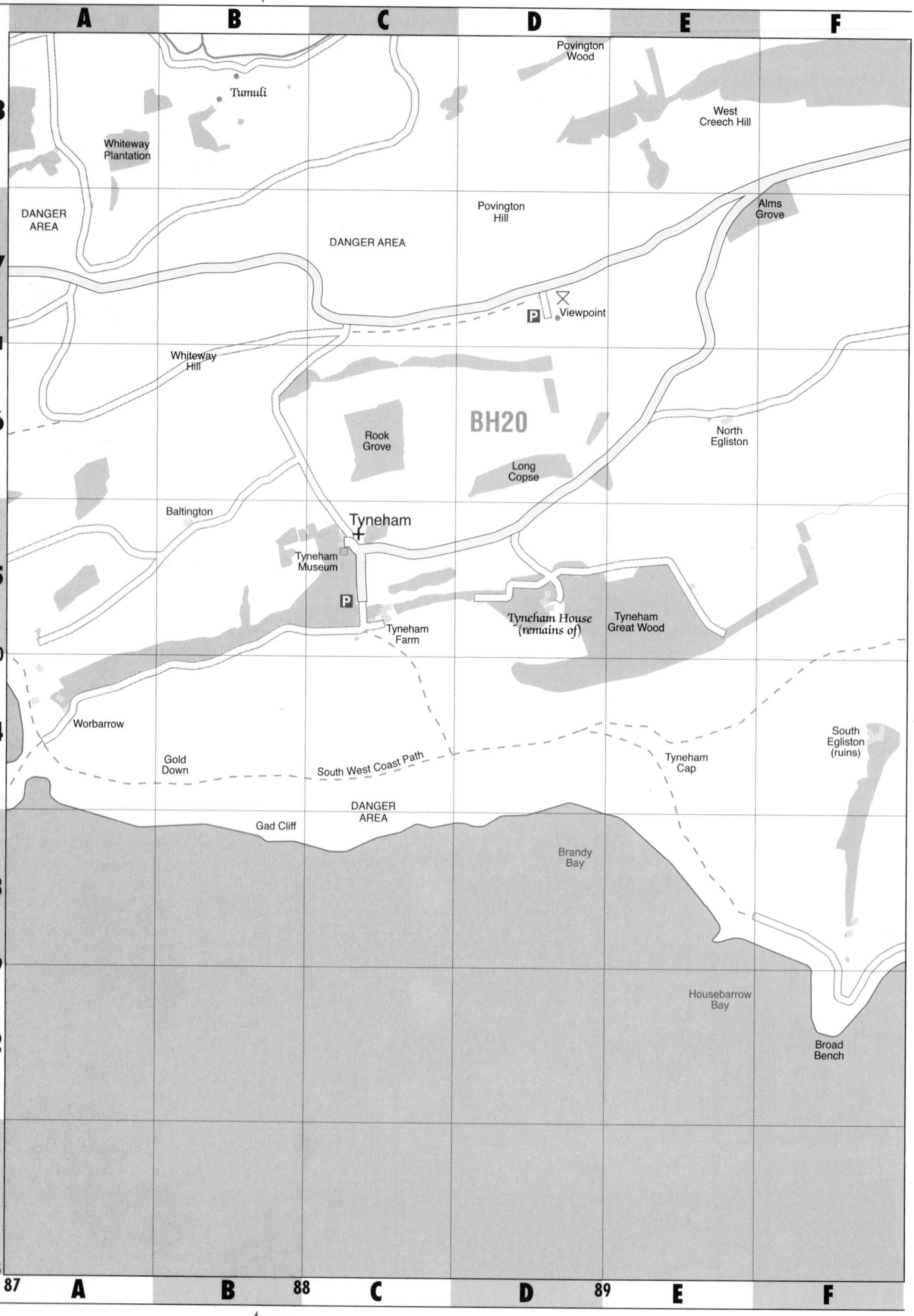

Povington Wood

West Creech Hill

8

Whiteway Plantation

Tumuli

DANGER AREA

Povington Hill

Alms Grove

DANGER AREA

7

P Viewpoint

81

Whiteway Hill

BH20

6

Rook Grove

Long Copse

North Egliston

Baltington

Tyneham

5

Tyneham Museum

P

Tyneham House (remains of)

Tyneham Great Wood

80

Tyneham Farm

4

Worbarrow

Gold Down

South West Coast Path

Tyneham Cap

South Egliston (ruins)

DANGER AREA

Gad Cliff

Brandy Bay

3

79

Housebarrow Bay

2

Broad Bench

1

78

160
176

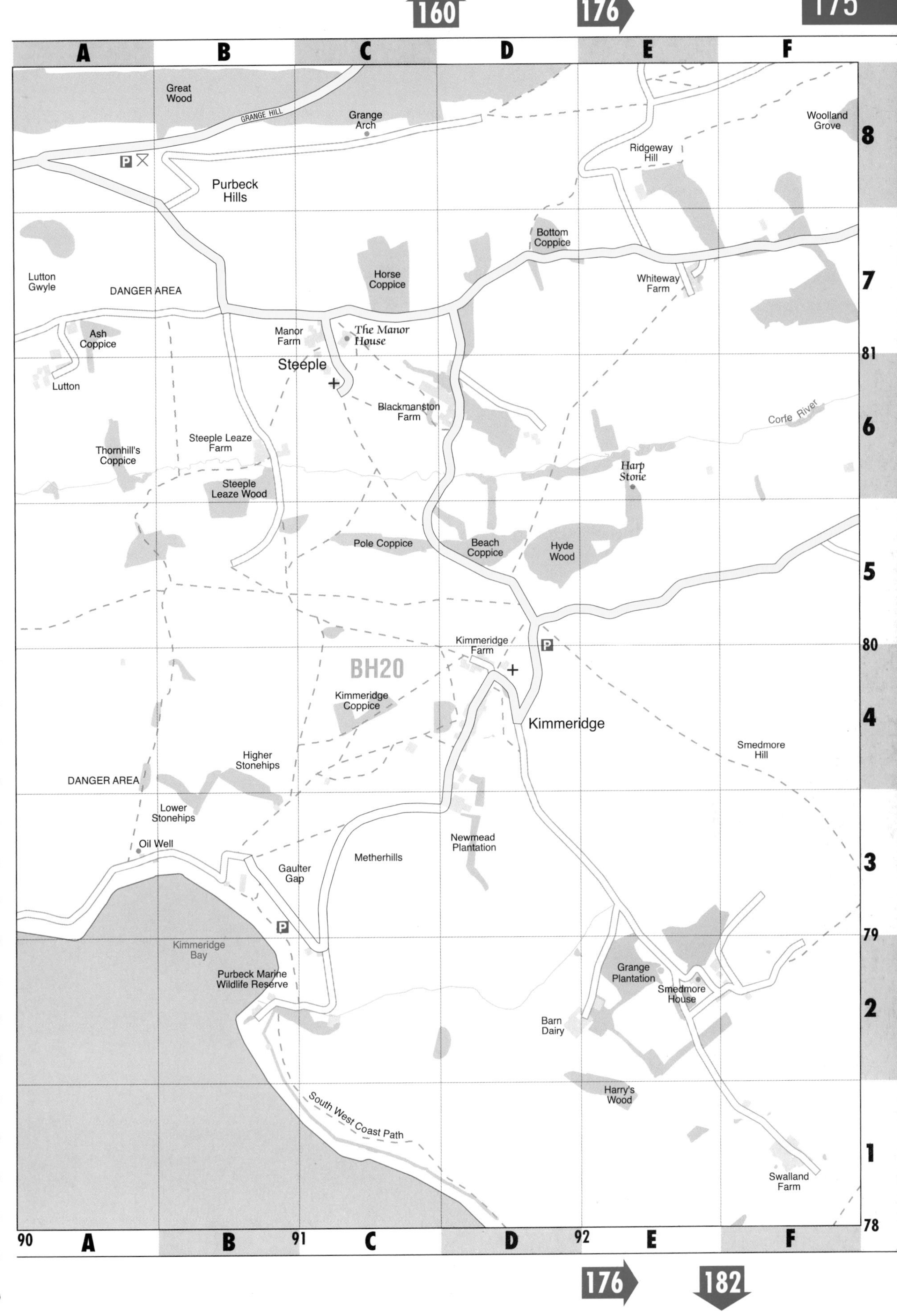
A
B
C
D
E
F
Great Wood
GRANGE HILL
Grange Arch
Woolland Grove
8
Ridgeway Hill
Purbeck Hills
Bottom Coppice
Lutton Gwyle
DANGER AREA
Horse Coppice
Whiteway Farm
7
Ash Coppice
Manor Farm
The Manor House
81
Lutton
Steeple
Blackmanston Farm
Corfe River
6
Thornhill's Coppice
Steeple Leaze Farm
Steeple Leaze Wood
Harp Stone
Pole Coppice
Beach Coppice
Hyde Wood
5
Kimmeridge Farm
80
BH20
Kimmeridge Coppice
Kimmeridge
4
Smedmore Hill
Higher Stonehips
DANGER AREA
Lower Stonehips
Newmead Plantation
Oil Well
Metherhills
Gaulter Gap
3
79
Kimmeridge Bay
Purbeck Marine Wildlife Reserve
Grange Plantation
Smedmore House
2
Barn Dairy
Harry's Wood
South West Coast Path
1
Swalland Farm
78
90
A
B
91
C
D
92
E
F

176
182

175
161

A   B   C   D   E   F

8

Heath View

Church Farm

Church Knowle

PH

Barneston Manor

Church Knowle Animal Sanctuary

Glebe Farm

Cemy

HOLLANDS CLOSE

WEST STREET

WEBBERS CL.

Bucknowle House

Isle of Purbeck

7

West Bucknowle House

81

Puddlemill Farm

Tumuli

6

West Orchard Farm

East Orchard

Corfe Common

Bridle Farm

Chettle Wood

Blashenwell Farm

5

BH20

Willwood Plantation

West Lynch

Lynch Farm

80

Bradle Barn

Orchard Hill Farm

KINGSTON HILL

WEST ST

THE LANE

4

Newfoundland

WEST STREET

PH

Kingston

B3069

P

3

Quarry Wood

The Plantation

P

SOUTH STREET

79

Polar Wood

John Strange Wood

2

Long Wood

Encombe House

Broadley Wood

Westhill Farm

Swyre Wood

Tumulus

Swyre Head

1

Big Wood

Westhill Wood

Field Systems

78

93   A   B   94   C   D   95   E   F

175
182

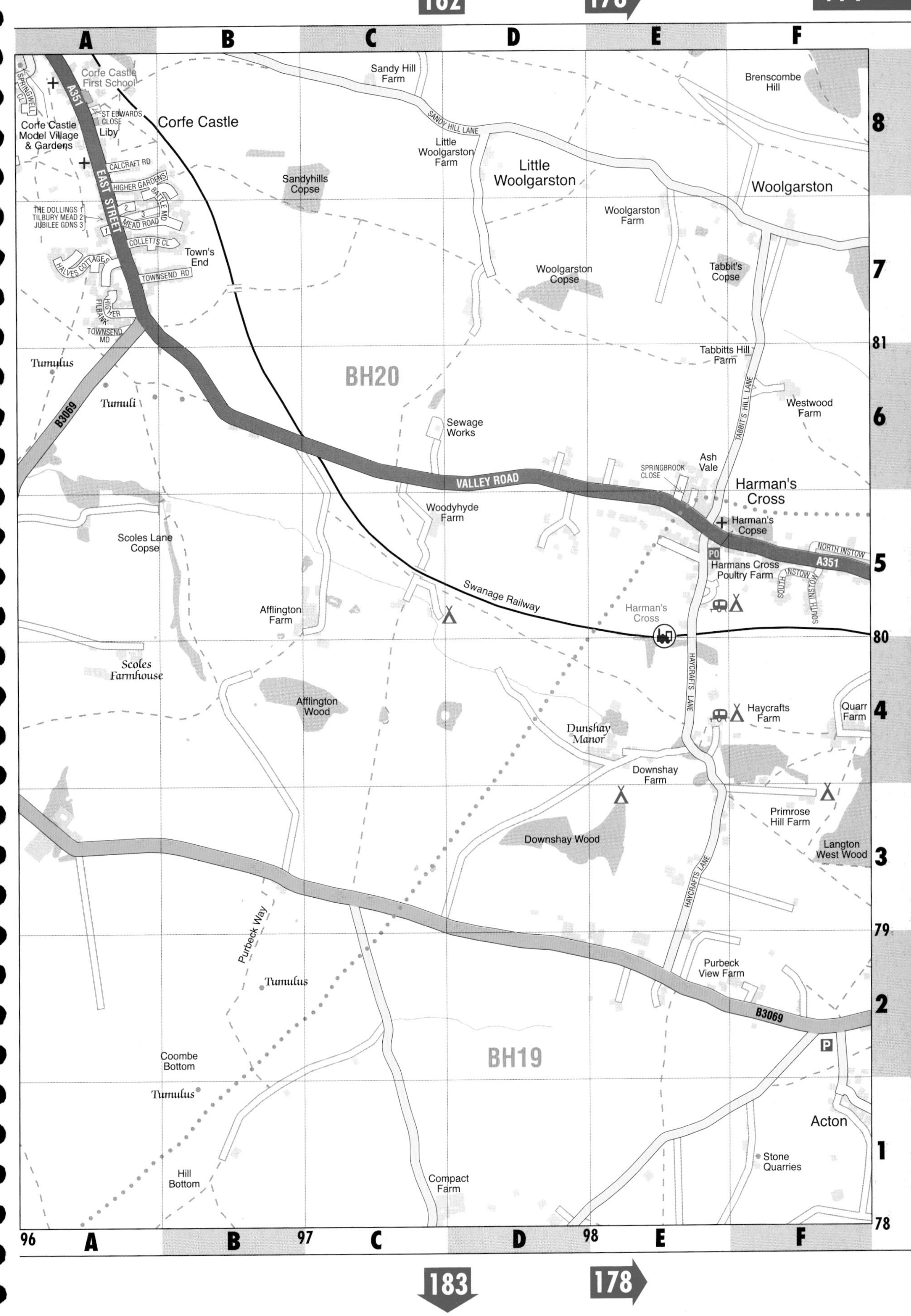

8

Brenscombe Hill

Corfe Castle First School

Corfe Castle

St Edwards Close

Liby

Corfe Castle Model Village & Gardens

Sandy Hill Farm

SANDY HILL LANE

Little Woolgarston Farm

Little Woolgarston

Woolgarston

CALCRAFT RD

HIGHER GARDENS

Sandyhills Copse

Woolgarston Farm

BATTLE MD

THE DOLLINGS 1
TILBURY MEAD 2
JUBILEE GDNS 3

MEAD ROAD

COLLETT'S CL

Town's End

Woolgarston Copse

Tabbit's Copse

7

HALVES COTTAGES

TOWNSEND RD

HIGHER FILBANK

TOWNSEND MD

Tabbitts Hill Farm

81

Tumulus

BH20

TABBIT'S HILL LANE

Westwood Farm

6

B3069

Tumuli

Sewage Works

Ash Vale

SPRINGBROOK CLOSE

Harman's Cross

VALLEY ROAD

Harman's Copse

Scoles Lane Copse

Woodyhyde Farm

PO

NORTH INSTOW

Harmans Cross Poultry Farm

A351

5

Swanage Railway

INSTOW

SOUTH INSTOW

Afflington Farm

Harman's Cross

80

Scoles Farmhouse

Afflington Wood

Dunshay Manor

HAYCRAFTS LANE

Haycrafts Farm

Quarr Farm

4

Downshay Farm

Primrose Hill Farm

Langton West Wood

3

Purbeck Way

Downshay Wood

79

Tumulus

HAYCRAFTS LANE

Purbeck View Farm

B3069

2

Coombe Bottom

BH19

P

Tumulus

Acton

1

Hill Bottom

Compact Farm

Stone Quarries

78

A B C D E F

8 Rempstone Wood B3351 Kingswood Farm Tumuli Isle of Purbeck Golf Club CH
King's Wood
Dean Hill
Purbeck Way
Currendon Farm

7 Ailwood Farm BH20 Godlingston Hill
Giant's Grave Bottom Tumuli

81 Oakwood Farm Knaveswell Farm Nine Barrow Down Round Down
Lower Grove Knitson Farm Strip Lynchets

6 Cow Leaze Copse Godlingston Wood

5 Rickett's Copse North Lease Farm Godlingston Manor
A351 Seekings Farm Marsh Copse Cerny
New Buildings

80 LC Greyseed Farm VALLEY ROAD Herston Yards Farm Alderbury Copse

4 Wilkswood Farm New Barn Square Copse BH19 Great Linnings Copse
Langton West Wood Talbot's Wood Quince Hill Wood Serrell's Copse Swanage Railway

3 CRACK LANE Farm Wood Litchfield Copse Swanage Middle Sch Herston Halt Victoria Avenue Industrial Estate
Langton Matravers Langton Matravers Mus AIGBURTH RD ANCASTER RD

79 St Georges CE First Sch LOWER STEPPES SERRELLS MD THREE ACRE LANE Herston A351 Superstore
The Old Malthouse Sch St George's CL COOMBE HILL B3069 HIGH STREET St Marks CE VA First Sch
Castle View NORTH ST EAST DROVE STEPPES HILL Coombe Farm

2 B3069 HIGH STREET PO GYPSHAYES Putlake Adventure Farm HOLMES RD MARS
CAPSTAN FIELD DURNFORD DROVE TOMS FIELD RD Leeson House Field Studies Centre SYDENHAM RD DAYS RD PRIEST'S WAY

1 Lighthouse Langton House Belle Vue Farm

78 Blacklands Verney Farm

E2
1 ANVIL CL
2 KINGSWOOD CL
3 BAY VIEW
4 CASTERBRIDGE CL

F2
1 VICTORIA AV
2 LEESON CL
3 GLOBE CL
4 SHASTON CL
5 ALDERBURY CL
6 SANDBOURNE CL
7 SHOTTSFORD CL
8 QUARRY CL
9 PURBECK VW

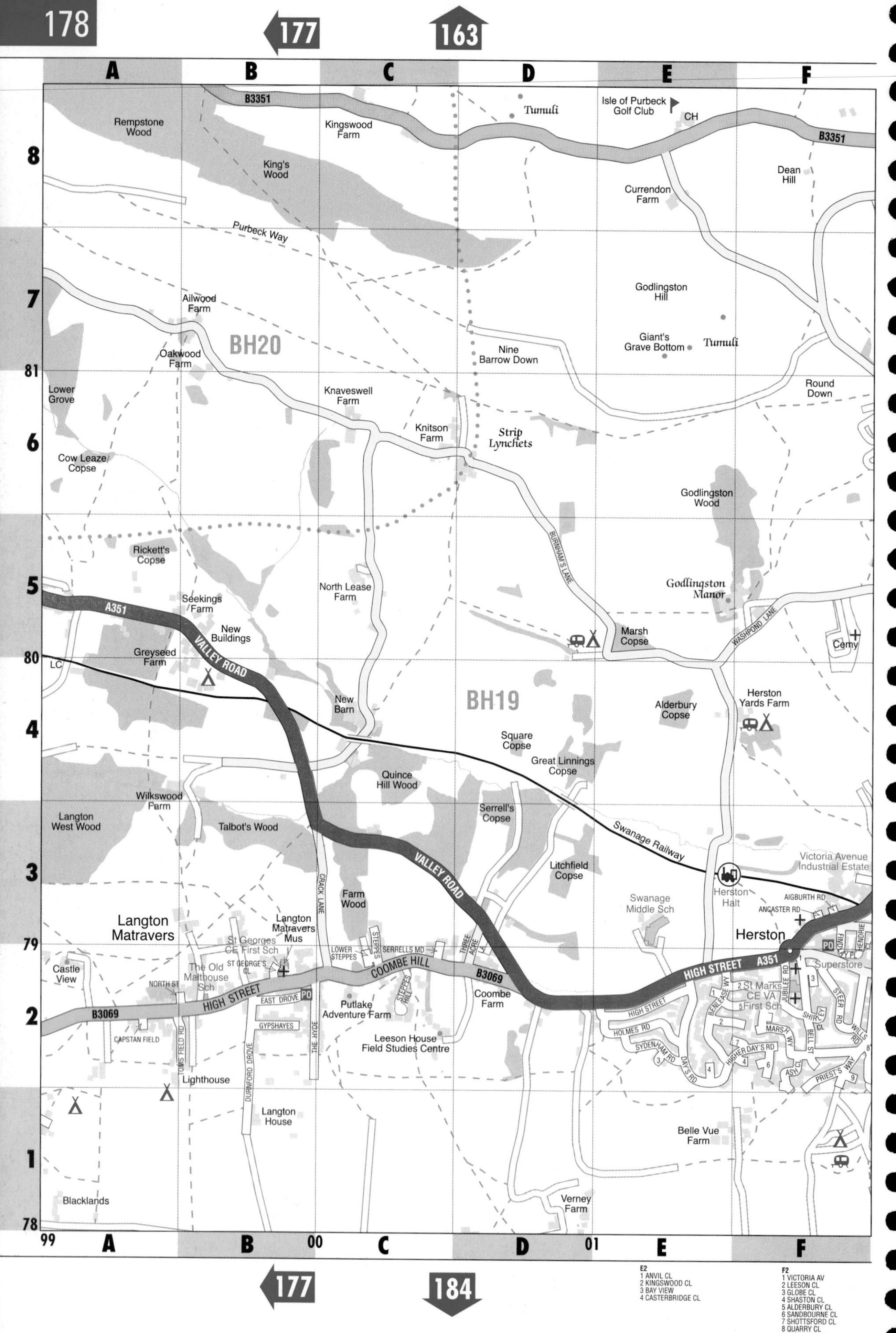

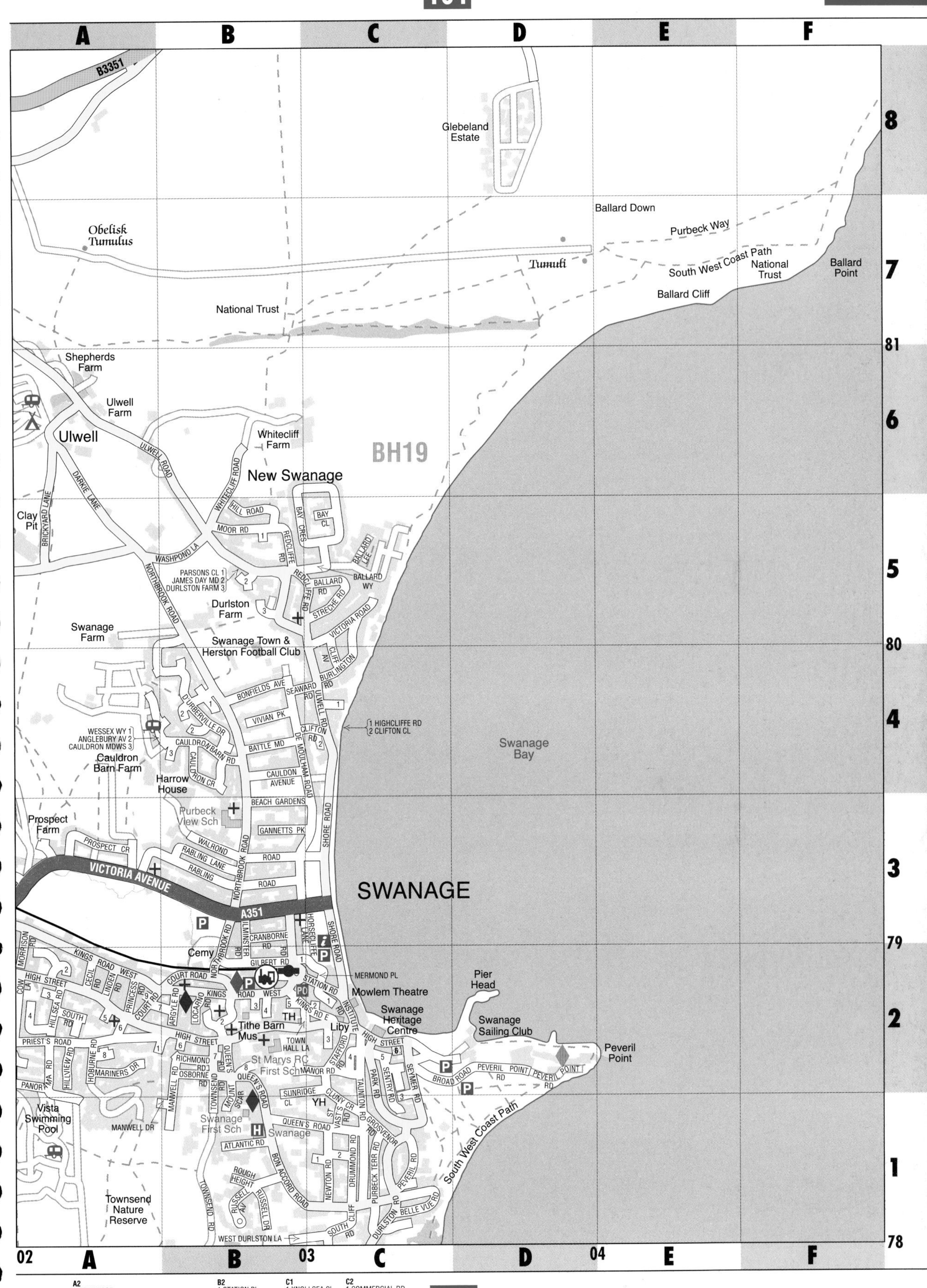

Map grid columns: A B C D E F
Map grid rows: 8 81 7 6 5 80 4 3 79 2 1 78
Bottom references: 02 A 03 B C 04 D E F

A2
1 COWLEASE
2 NEWTON MANOR CL
3 WEST DR
4 NEWTON RISE
5 HOWARD RD
6 GORDON RD
7 HANBURY RD
8 FOXHILL CL
9 BISHOPS ROW

B2
1 STATION PL
2 CHURCH HL
3 CHURCH CL
4 SPRINGFIELD RD
5 ELDON TERR
6 MANWELL'S LA
7 DUNFORD PL
8 QUEENS MD

C1
1 KNOLLSEA CL
2 SALISBURY RD
3 BELVEDERE RD

C2
1 COMMERCIAL RD
2 CORNWALL RD
3 MOUNT PLEASANT LA
4 EXETER RD
5 MARSHALL ROW
6 BURT'S PL

B3351
Glebeland Estate
Obelisk Tumulus
Ballard Down
Purbeck Way
Tumuli
South West Coast Path National Trust
Ballard Point
National Trust
Ballard Cliff
Shepherds Farm
Ulwell Farm
Whitecliff Farm
Clay Pit
Ulwell
New Swanage
BH19
Hill Road
Bay Cres
Bay Cl
Moor Rd
Washpond La
Parsons Cl 1
James Day Md 2
Durlston Farm 3
Durlston Farm
Ballard Rd
Streche Rd
Ballard Wy
Swanage Farm
Swanage Town & Herston Football Club
Victoria Road
Bonfields Ave
Seaward
Ulwell Rd
Burlington
1 Highcliffe Rd
2 Clifton Cl
Swanage Bay
Wessex Wy 1
Anglebury Av 2
Cauldron Mdws 3
Cauldron Barn Rd
Vivian Pk
Battle Md
De Moulham Road
Cauldon Avenue
Cauldron Barn Farm
Harrow House
Clifton Rd
Prospect Farm
Beach Gardens
Purbeck View Sch
Gannetts Pk
Shore Road
Prospect Cr
Walrond Road
Rabling Lane
Rabling Road
SWANAGE
VICTORIA AVENUE
A351
Northbrook Road
Cranborne Rd
Lymington Rd
Horsecliff
P
Cemy
Gilbert Rd
Mermond Pl
Pier Head
Station Rd
Kings Rd E
Mowlem Theatre
Swanage Heritage Centre
Swanage Sailing Club
Morrison Rd
Kings Road West
High Street
Cecil Rd
Linden Rd
Princess Rd
Court Road
Locarno
Argyle Rd
Kings Road West
TH
Liby
Institute Rd
Peveril Point
Hillsea Rd
South Rd
Priest's Road
Hoburne Rd
Hillview Rd
Park Rd
Stafford Rd
Broad Road
Peveril Point Rd
Peveril Point
Cow La
High Street
Richmond Rd
Osborne Rd
St Marys RC First Sch
Town Hall La
Taunton Rd
Cluny Cr
Sentry Rd
Seymer Rd
Panor
Mariners Dr
Manwell Rd
Townsend Rd
Queen's Road
Sunridge Cl
Vast's Rd
Grosvenor Rd
Vista Swimming Pool
Manwell Dr
Swanage First Sch
H Swanage
Atlantic Rd
Queen's Road
YH
Drummond Rd
Purbeck Terr Rd
Belle Vue Rd
South West Coast Path
Townsend Nature Reserve
Rough Heights
Bon Accord Road
Rissell Cl
Russell Dr
Newton Rd
South Cliff Rd
Durlston Rd
West Durlston La

166

167

B8
1 BEACHVIEW CL
2 JASMINE WY
3 CUNNINGHAM CL
4 FOSSETT WY
5 WESTHILL CL

C8
1 LANEHOUSE ROCKS RD
2 WYKE RD
3 LYMES CL
4 CHURCHILL CL
5 SWAFFIELD GDNS
6 MARTLEAVES CL

7 WYKE SQ

D7
1 HILLBOURNE RD
2 DOWNCLOSE

D8
1 BELFIELD PK DR
2 BUXTON CL
3 BELFIELD CL
4 CARRINGTON CL

E8
1 CROSS RD
2 CONNAUGHT RD

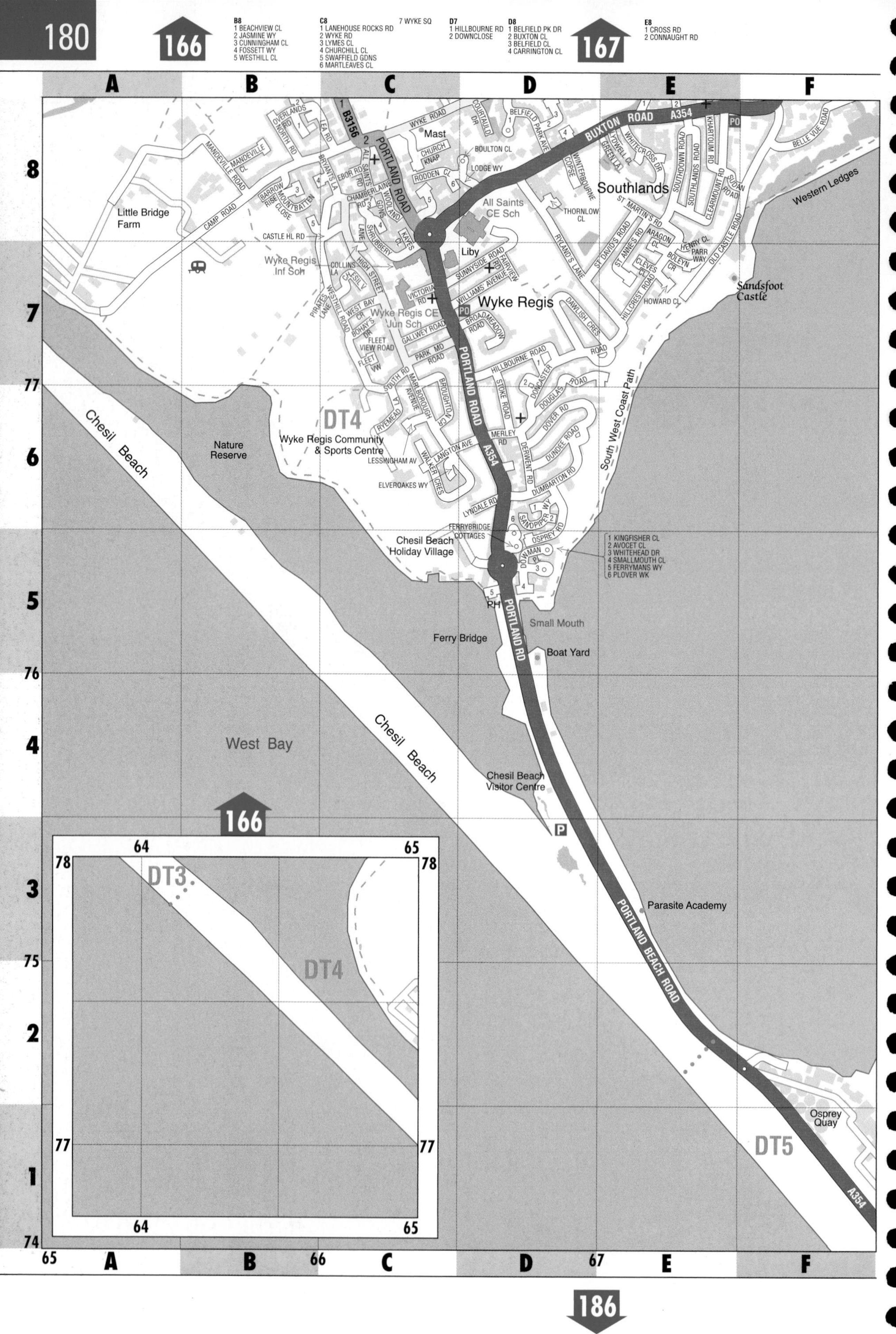

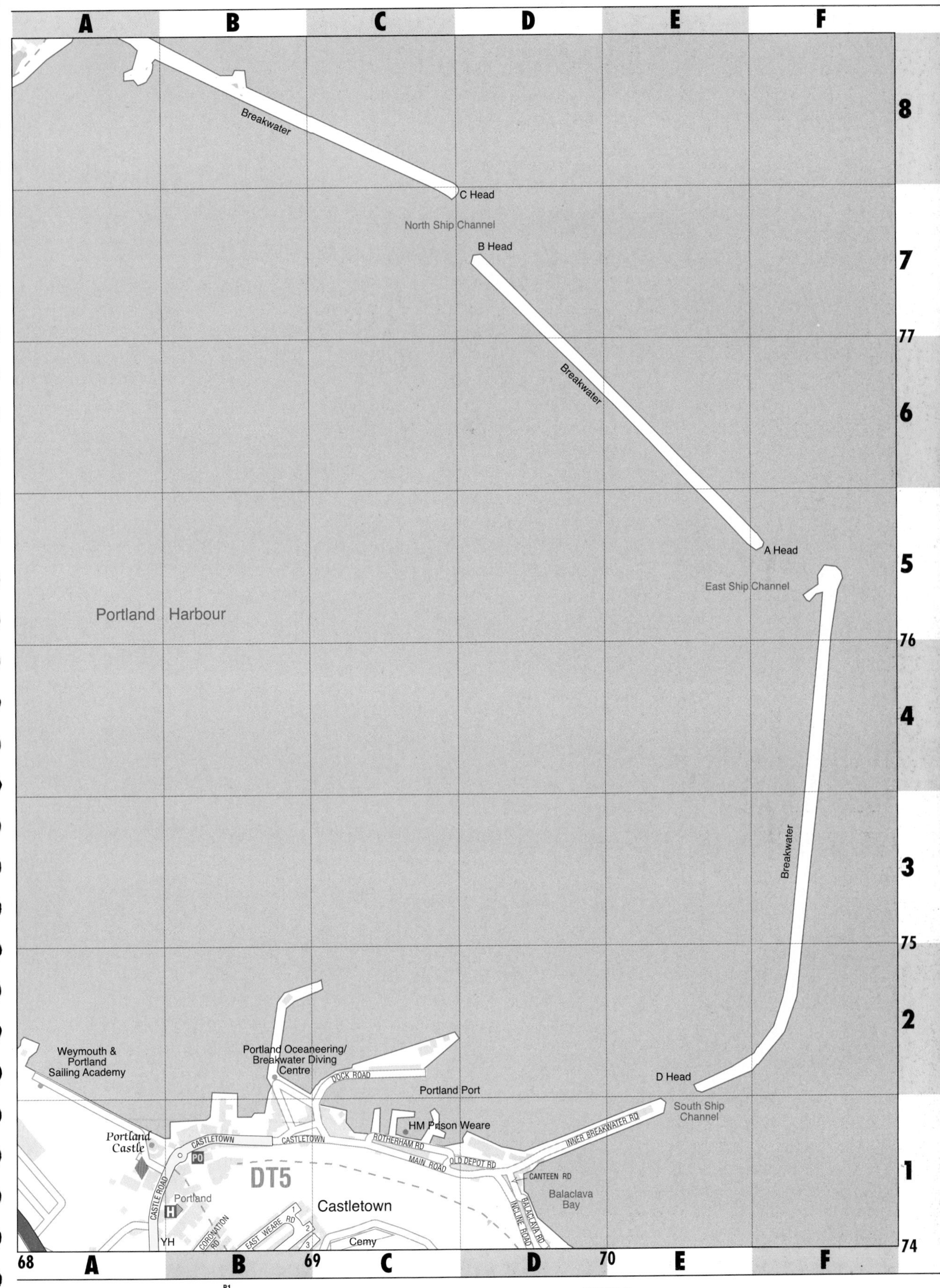

8

7

77

6

5

76

4

3

75

2

1

74

A   B   C   D   E   F

Breakwater

C Head

North Ship Channel

B Head

Breakwater

A Head

East Ship Channel

Portland Harbour

Breakwater

Weymouth &
Portland
Sailing Academy

Portland Oceaneering/
Breakwater Diving
Centre

DOCK ROAD

Portland Port

HM Prison Weare

ROTHERHAM RD

D Head

South Ship
Channel

INNER BREAKWATER RD

Portland
Castle

CASTLETOWN

CASTLETOWN

MAIN ROAD

OLD DEPOT RD

CANTEEN RD

Balaclava
Bay

PO

DT5

Castletown

Cemy

Portland

H

YH

CASTLE ROAD

CORONATION RD

EAST WEARE RD

BALACLAVA RD

INCLINE ROAD

68   A   69   B   C   69   D   70   E   F

B1
1 LEET CL
2 BEEL CL
3 AMELIA CL

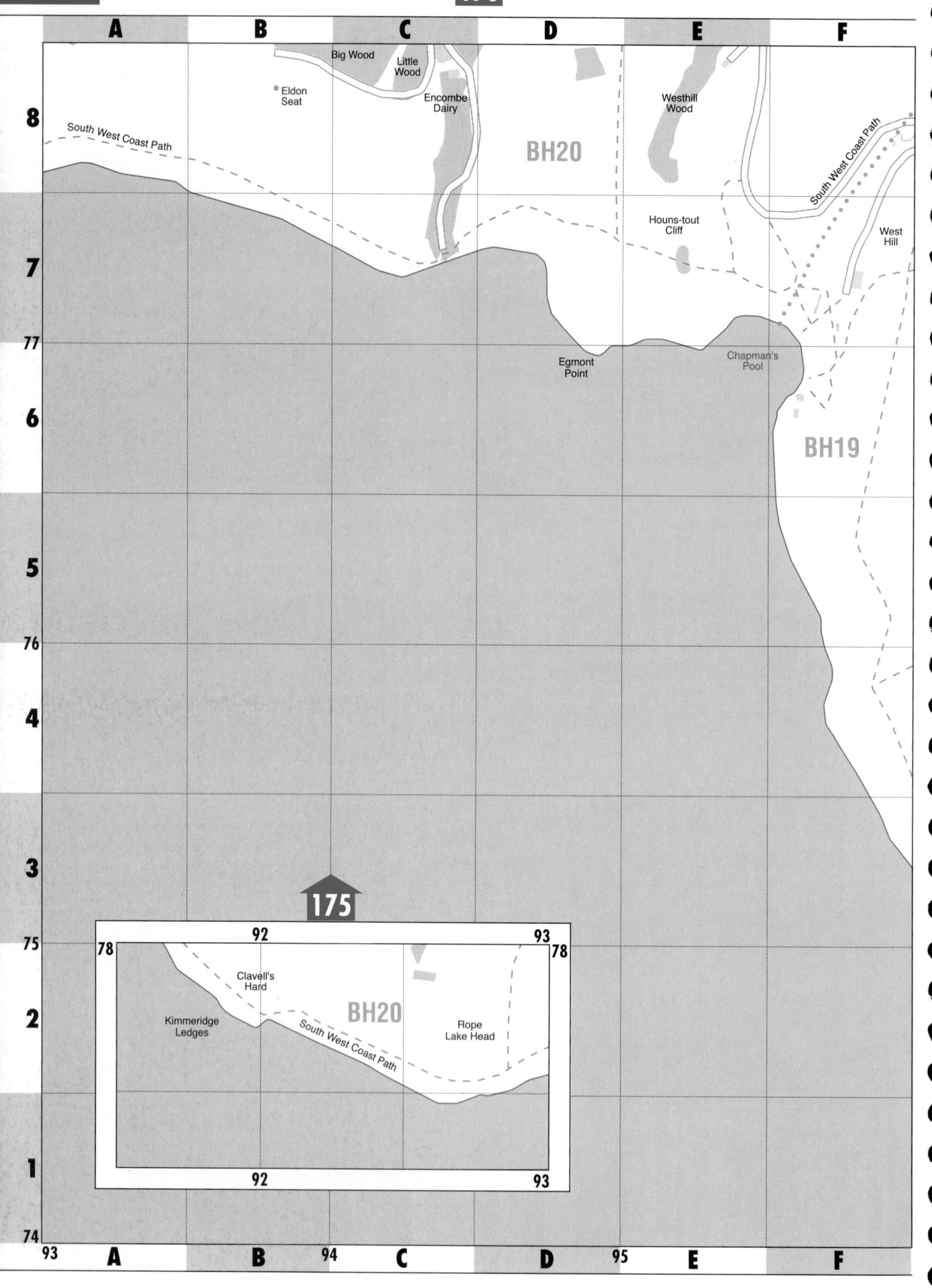

South West Coast Path

Big Wood

Little Wood

Eldon Seat

Encombe Dairy

Westhill Wood

BH20

Houns-tout Cliff

South West Coast Path

West Hill

Egmont Point

Chapman's Pool

BH19

175

Clavell's Hard

BH20

Kimmeridge Ledges

South West Coast Path

Rope Lake Head

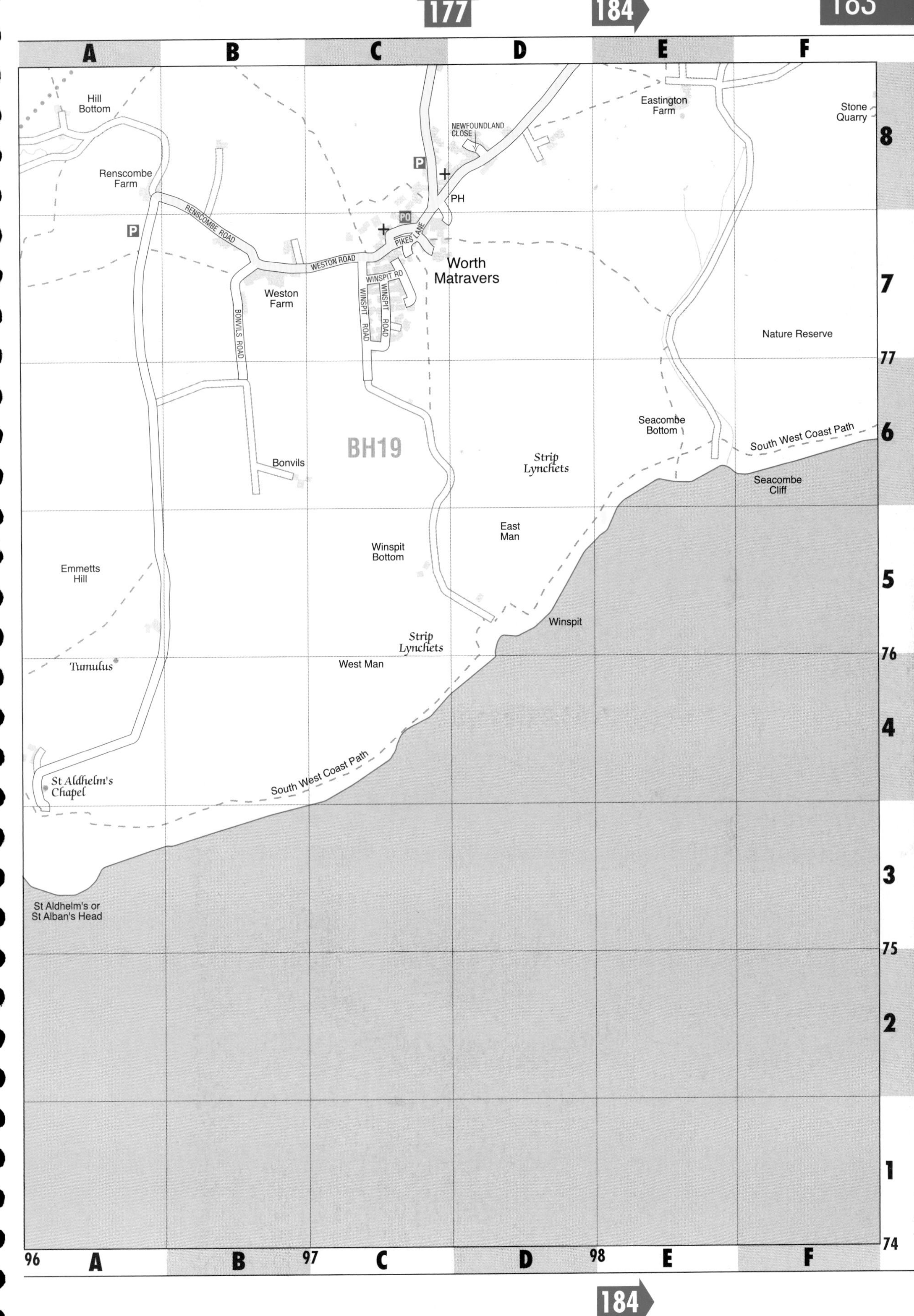
A
B
C
D
E
F
Hill Bottom
Renscombe Farm
P
RENSCOMBE ROAD
NEWFOUNDLAND CLOSE
P
PH
PO
PIKES LANE
WESTON ROAD
Worth Matravers
WINSPIT RD
WINSPIT ROAD
WINSPIT ROAD
Weston Farm
BONVILS ROAD
Eastington Farm
Stone Quarry
Nature Reserve
Seacombe Bottom
South West Coast Path
Seacombe Cliff
BH19
Bonvils
Strip Lynchets
East Man
Winspit Bottom
Emmetts Hill
Winspit
Strip Lynchets
West Man
Tumulus
South West Coast Path
St Aldhelm's Chapel
St Aldhelm's or St Alban's Head
8
7
77
6
5
76
4
3
75
2
1
74
96
97
98

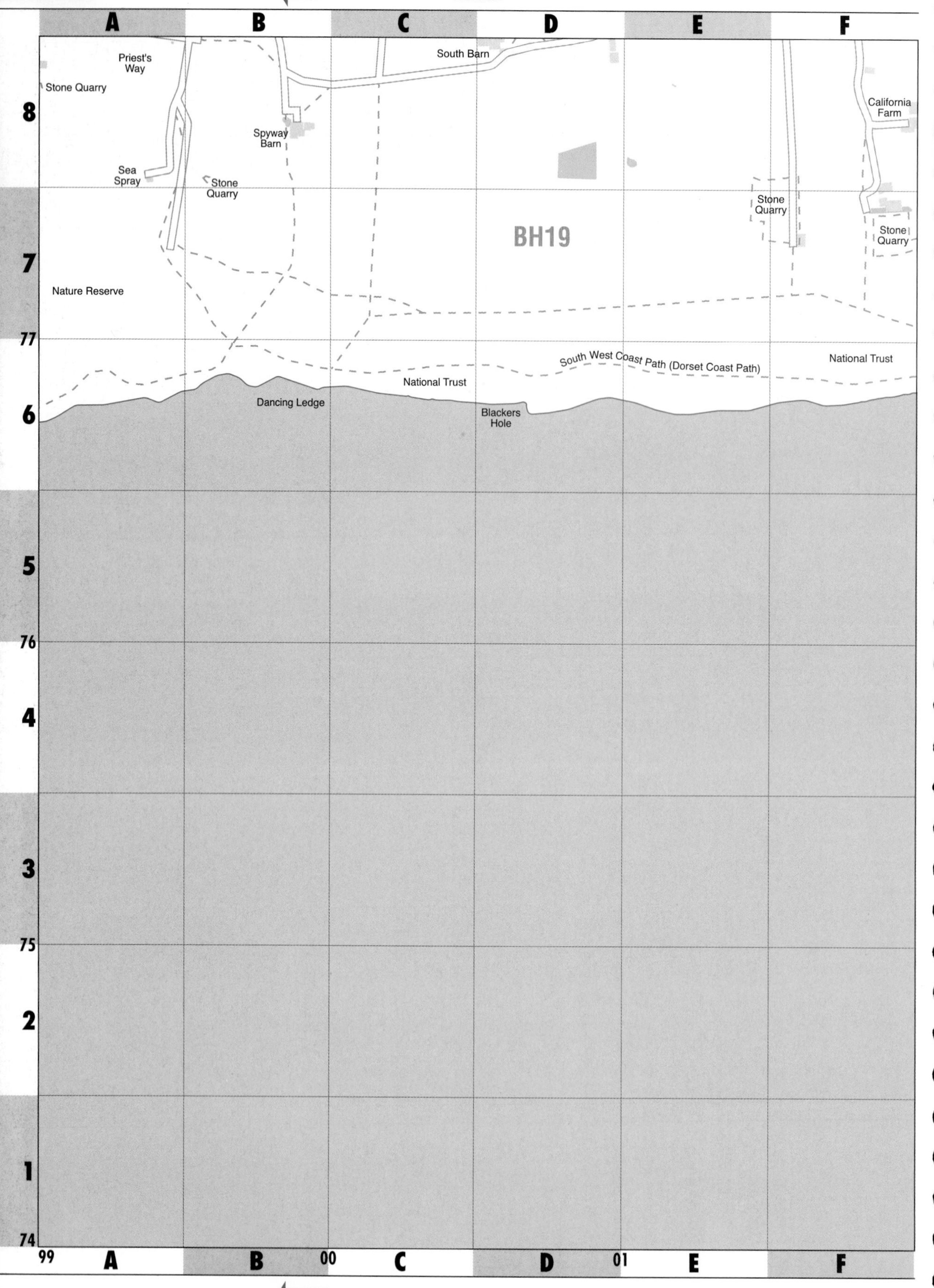

A B C D E F

8

7

77

6

5

76

4

3

75

2

1

74

99 A B 00 C D 01 E F

BH19

Priest's Way

Stone Quarry

South Barn

California Farm

Spyway Barn

Sea Spray

Stone Quarry

Stone Quarry

Stone Quarry

Nature Reserve

South West Coast Path (Dorset Coast Path)

National Trust

National Trust

Dancing Ledge

Blackers Hole

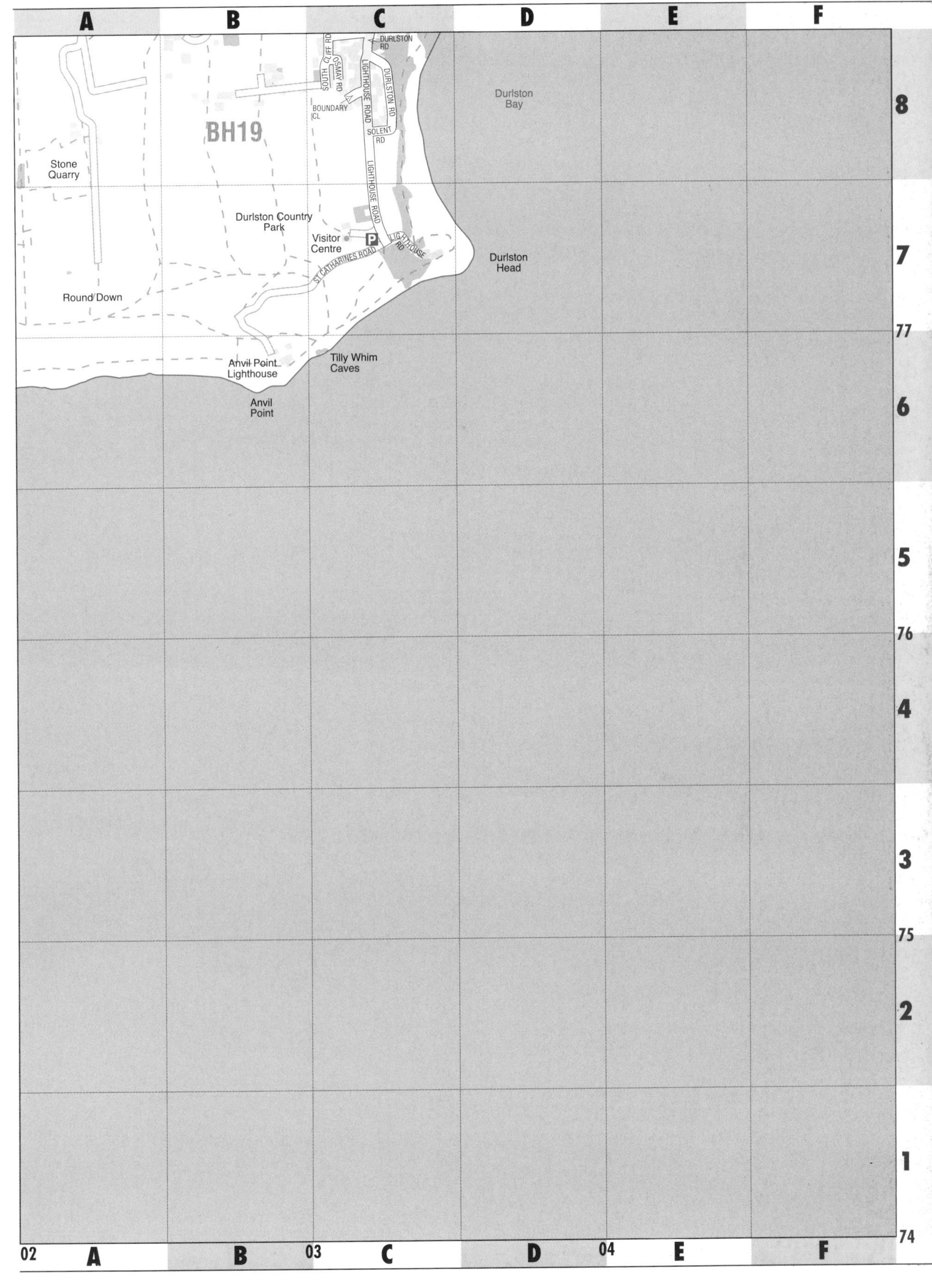

BH19

Stone Quarry

Round Down

Durlston Country Park

Visitor Centre

P

ST CATHARINES ROAD

SOUTH CLIFF RD

GSWAY RD

BOUNDARY CL

DURLSTON RD

LIGHTHOUSE ROAD

SOLENT RD

DURLSTON RD

LIGHTHOUSE ROAD

LIGHTHOUSE RD

Durlston Bay

Durlston Head

Anvil Point Lighthouse

Tilly Whim Caves

Anvil Point

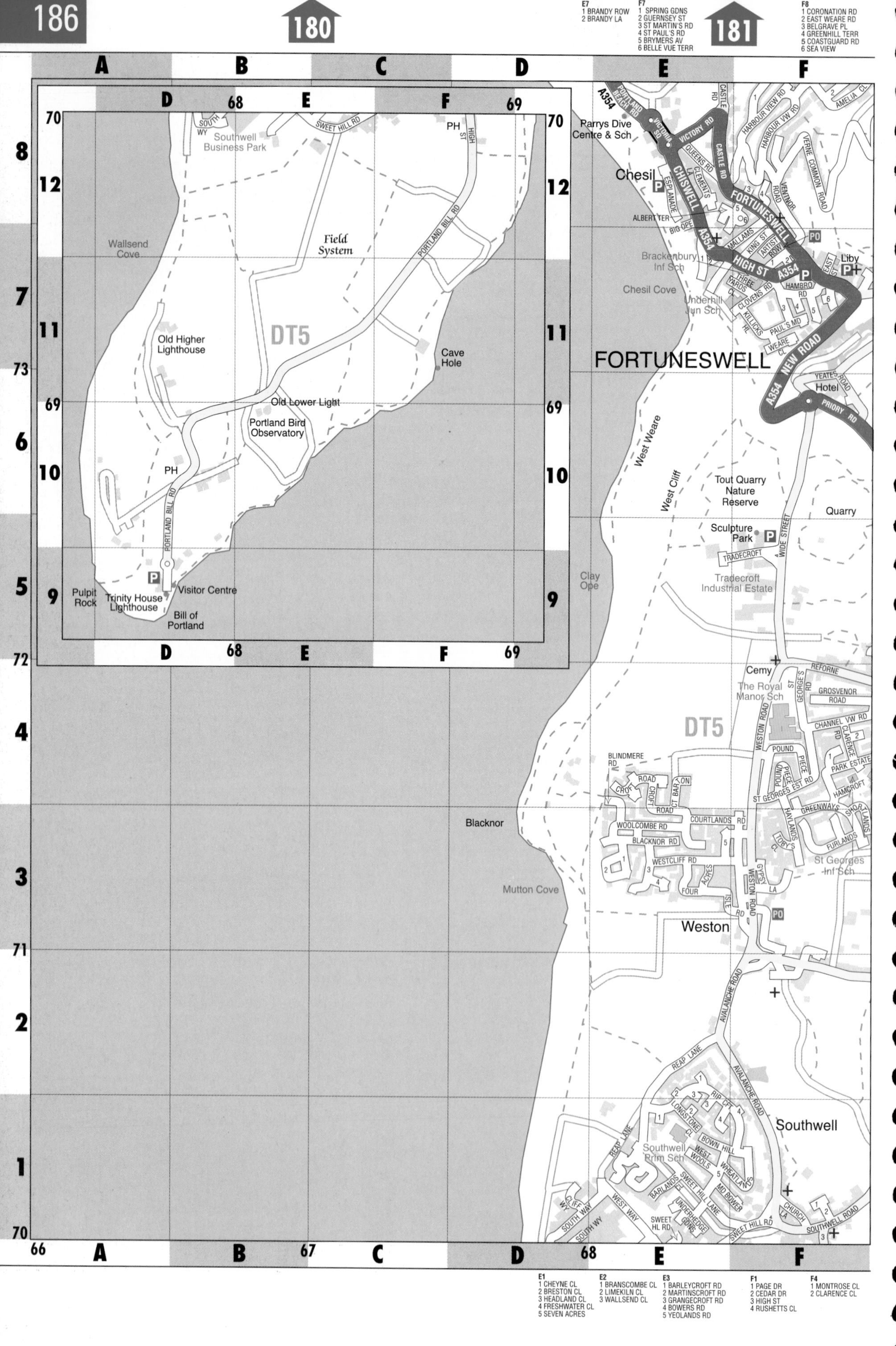
180
181
E7
1 BRANDY ROW
2 BRANDY LA
F7
1 SPRING GDNS
2 GUERNSEY ST
3 ST MARTIN'S RD
4 ST PAUL'S RD
5 BRYMERS AV
6 BELLE VUE TERR
F8
1 CORONATION RD
2 EAST WEARE RD
3 BELGRAVE PL
4 GREENHILL TERR
5 COASTGUARD RD
6 SEA VIEW
Southwell Business Park
Wallsend Cove
Field System
DT5
Old Higher Lighthouse
Cave Hole
Old Lower Light
Portland Bird Observatory
PH
PORTLAND BILL RD
Visitor Centre
Pulpit Rock
Trinity House Lighthouse
Bill of Portland
Parrys Dive Centre & Sch
Chesil
CHISWELL
FORTUNESWELL
HIGH ST
A354
Brackenbury Inf Sch
Chesil Cove
Underhill Jun Sch
FORTUNESWELL
NEW ROAD
Hotel
PRIORY RD
Liby
West Weare
West Cliff
Tout Quarry Nature Reserve
Quarry
Sculpture Park
WIDE STREET
TRADECROFT
Tradecroft Industrial Estate
Clay Ope
Cemy
The Royal Manor Sch
DT5
REFORNE
GROSVENOR ROAD
CHANNEL VW RD
WESTON ROAD
Blacknor
WOOLCOMBE RD
BLACKNOR RD
WESTCLIFF RD
COURTLANDS RD
St Georges Inf Sch
Mutton Cove
Weston
AVALANCHE ROAD
REAP LANE
Southwell
Southwell Prim Sch
SWEET HILL RD
SOUTHWELL ROAD
E1
1 CHEYNE CL
2 BRESTON CL
3 HEADLAND CL
4 FRESHWATER CL
5 SEVEN ACRES
E2
1 BRANSCOMBE CL
2 LIMEKILN CL
3 WALLSEND CL
E3
1 BARLEYCROFT RD
2 MARTINSCROFT RD
3 GRANGECROFT RD
4 BOWERS RD
5 YEOLANDS RD
F1
1 PAGE DR
2 CEDAR DR
3 HIGH ST
4 RUSHETTS CL
F4
1 MONTROSE CL
2 CLARENCE CL

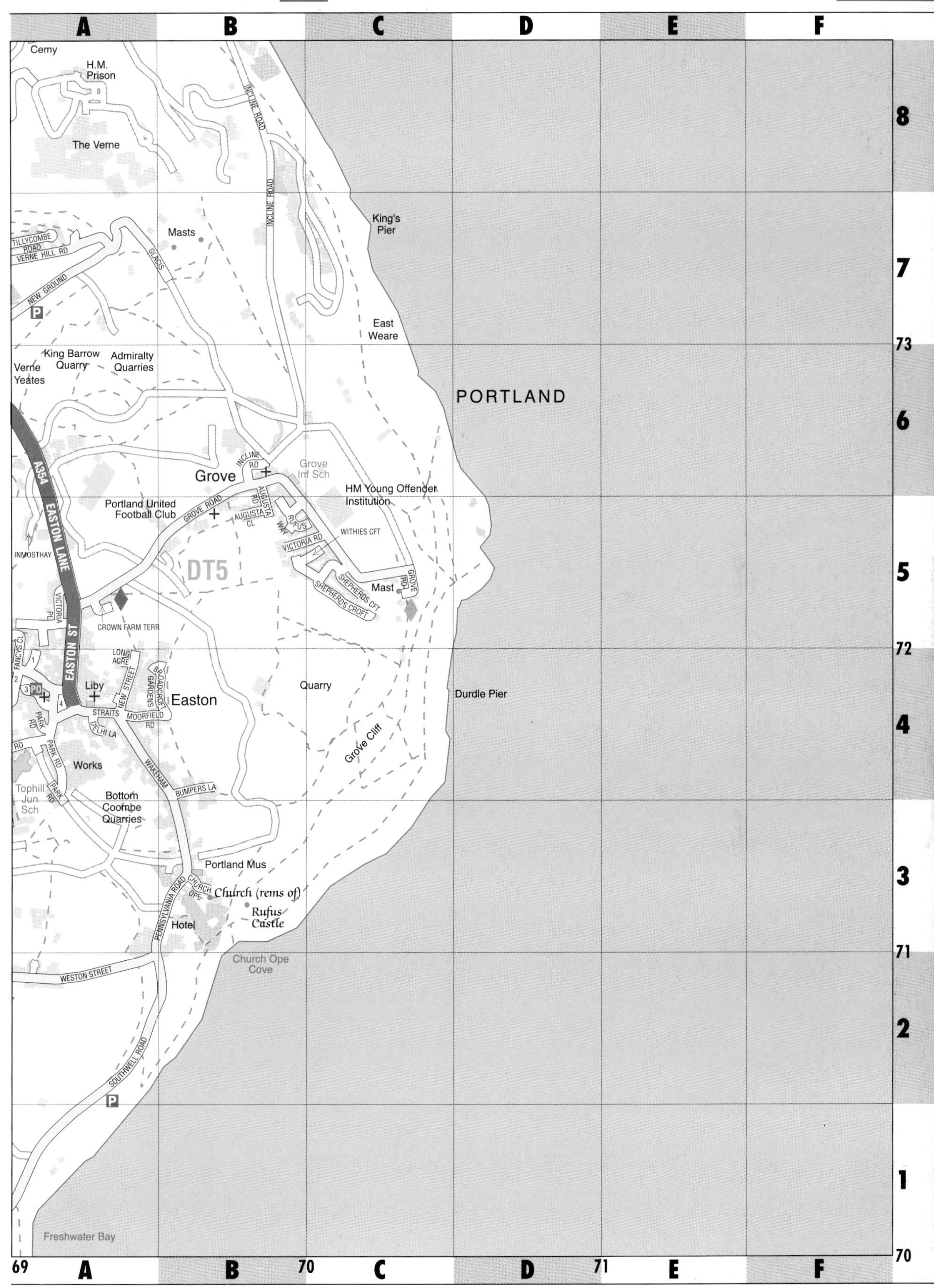

PORTLAND

Grove

Portland United
Football Club

DT5

Easton

Liby

Works

Bottom
Coombe
Quarries

Portland Mus

Church (rems of)

Rufus
Castle

Hotel

Church Ope
Cove

Freshwater Bay

Cemy

H.M.
Prison

The Verne

Masts

King's
Pier

East
Weare

King Barrow
Quarry

Admiralty
Quarries

Verne
Yeates

Grove
Inf Sch

HM Young Offender
Institution

WITHIES CFT

Mast

Quarry

Grove Cliff

Durdle Pier

Crown Farm Terr

Tophill
Jun
Sch

TILLYCOMBE
ROAD

VERNE HILL RD

NEW GROUND

GLACIS

INCLINE ROAD

A354

EASTON LANE

INMOSTHAY

VICTORIA PL

EASTON ST

FANCYS CL

PARK RD

PARK RD

PARK LANE

NEW STREET

STRAITS

DELHI LA

LONG ACRE

MOORFIELD RD

BROADCROFT GARDENS

WAKEHAM

BUMPERS LA

PENNSYLVANIA ROAD

CHURCH OPE

WESTON STREET

SOUTHWELL ROAD

INCLINE RD

GROVE ROAD

AUGUSTA CL

AUGUSTA RD

RUFUS WY

VICTORIA RD

SHEPHERDS CROFT

SHEPHERDS CFT

GROVE RD

A4
1 REFORNE CL
2 STATION RD
3 LADYMD CL
4 EASTON SQ

Scale: 1¾ inches to 1 mile

0 ¼ ½ mile
0 250m 500m 750m 1 km

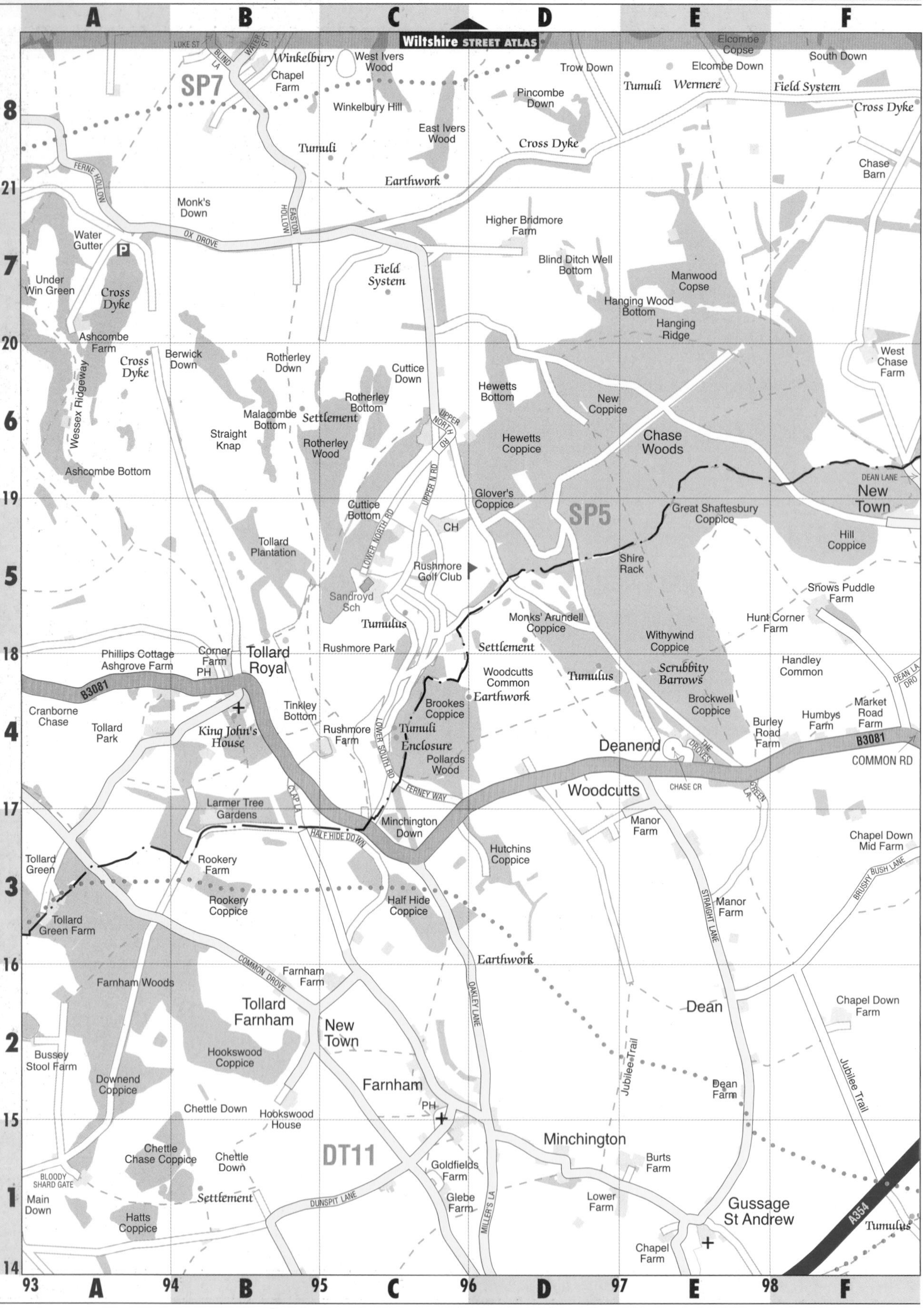

Wiltshire STREET ATLAS

SP7

Luke St
Winkelbury
West Ivers Wood
Trow Down
Elcombe Copse
Elcombe Down
South Down
Chapel Farm
Blind La
Water St
Easton Hollow
Winkelbury Hill
Tumuli
Wermere
Field System
Cross Dyke

Ferne Hollow
Monk's Down
Ox Drove
East Ivers Wood
Pincombe Down
Cross Dyke
Tumuli
Chase Barn

Earthwork
Higher Bridmore Farm
Blind Ditch Well Bottom
Manwood Copse

Water Gutter
Field System
Hanging Wood Bottom
Hanging Ridge

Under Win Green
Cross Dyke
West Chase Farm

Ashcombe Farm
Berwick Down
Rotherley Down
Cuttice Down
Hewetts Bottom
New Coppice
Chase Woods
Dean Lane

Cross Dyke
Wessex Ridgeway
Malacombe Bottom
Rotherley Bottom
Settlement
Hewetts Coppice
SP5
New Town

Straight Knap
Rotherley Wood
Upper North Rd
Glover's Coppice
Great Shaftesbury Coppice
Hill Coppice

Ashcombe Bottom
Cuttice Bottom
Shire Rack
Snows Puddle Farm

Tollard Plantation
Lower North Rd
CH
Rushmore Golf Club
Monks' Arundell Coppice
Withywind Coppice
Hunt Corner Farm

Sandroyd Sch
Tumulus
Settlement
Handley Common
Dean Lane Drd

Phillips Cottage
Ashgrove Farm
Corner Farm PH
Tollard Royal
Rushmore Park
Woodcutts Common
Earthwork
Tumulus
Scrubbity Barrows
Brockwell Coppice
Burley Road Farm
Humbys Farm
Market Road Farm

B3081
Tinkley Bottom
Brookes Coppice
Deanend
B3081
COMMON RD

Cranborne Chase
Tollard Park
King John's House
Rushmore Farm
Lower South Rd
Tumuli
Enclosure
Pollards Wood
Woodcutts
Chase Cr
The Droves
Green

Larmer Tree Gardens
Capel Rd
Ferney Way
Minchington Down
Manor Farm
Straight Lane
Chapel Down Mid Farm

Tollard Green
Half Hide Down
Hutchins Coppice
Brushy Bush Lane

Rookery Farm
Manor Farm

Tollard Green Farm
Rookery Coppice
Half Hide Coppice
Earthwork
Dean
Chapel Down Farm

Farnham Woods
Common Drove
Farnham Farm
New Town
Oakley Lane
Jubilee Trail
Jubilee Trail

Tollard Farnham
Hookswood Coppice
Farnham
Dean Farm

Bussey Stool Farm
Downend Coppice
Chettle Down
Hookswood House
PH
Minchington
Burts Farm

Chettle Chase Coppice
Chettle Down
DT11
Goldfields Farm
Lower Farm
Gussage St Andrew
A354
Tumulus

Bloody Shard Gate
Main Down
Settlement
Hatts Coppice
Dunspit Lane
Glebe Farm
Chapel Farm

93 94 95 96 97 98

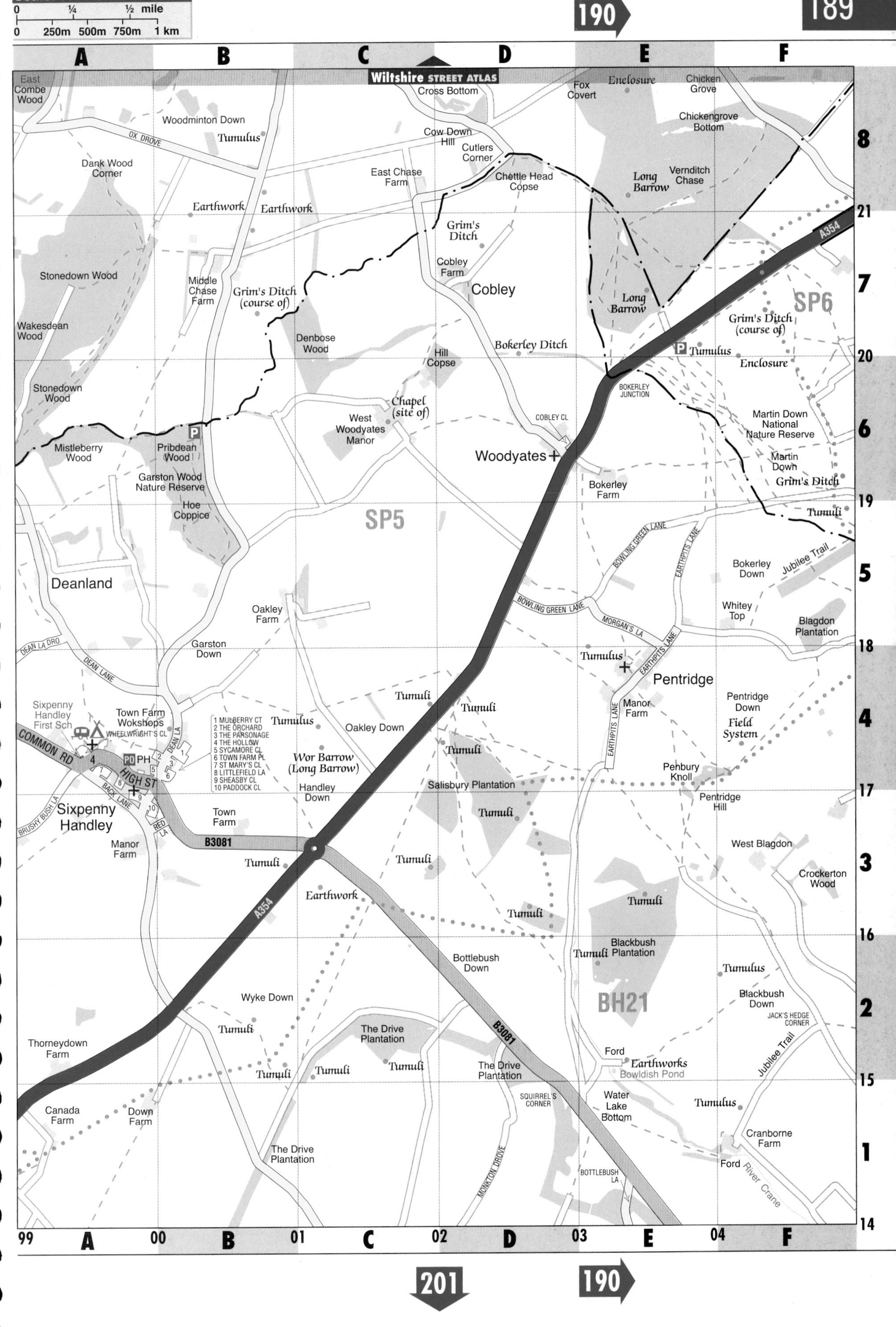
Scale: 1¾ inches to 1 mile
0 ¼ ½ mile
0 250m 500m 750m 1 km
190
Wiltshire STREET ATLAS
East Combe Wood
Cross Bottom
Fox Covert
Enclosure
Chicken Grove
Woodminton Down
Tumulus
OX DROVE
Cow Down Hill
Cutlers Corner
Chickengrove Bottom
Dank Wood Corner
East Chase Farm
Chettle Head Copse
Long Barrow
Vernditch Chase
Earthwork
Earthwork
Grim's Ditch
Cobley Farm
Cobley
Stonedown Wood
Middle Chase Farm
Grim's Ditch (course of)
Long Barrow
SP6
Grim's Ditch (course of)
Wakesdean Wood
Denbose Wood
Hill Copse
Bokerley Ditch
Tumulus
Enclosure
A354
Stonedown Wood
BOKERLEY JUNCTION
Chapel (site of)
West Woodyates Manor
COBLEY CL
Martin Down National Nature Reserve
Mistleberry Wood
Pribdean Wood
Woodyates
Martin Down
Grim's Ditch
Garston Wood Nature Reserve
Bokerley Farm
Hoe Coppice
SP5
Tumuli
BOWLING GREEN LANE
EARTHPITS LANE
Bokerley Down
Jubilee Trail
Deanland
BOWLING GREEN LANE
Oakley Farm
Whitey Top
Blagdon Plantation
MORGAN'S LA
DEAN LA DRO
DEAN LANE
Garston Down
Tumulus
EARTHPITS LANE
Pentridge
Sixpenny Handley First Sch
Town Farm Workshops
WHEELWRIGHT'S CL
Tumuli
Tumuli
Manor Farm
Pentridge Down
Field System
1 MULBERRY CT
2 THE ORCHARD
3 THE PARSONAGE
4 THE HOLLOW
5 SYCAMORE CL
6 TOWN FARM PL
7 ST MARY'S CL
8 LITTLEFIELD LA
9 SHEASBY CL
10 PADDOCK CL
Tumulus
Oakley Down
COMMON RD
DEAN LA
PH
HIGH ST
Wor Barrow (Long Barrow)
Tumuli
EARTHPITS LANE
Penbury Knoll
BACK LANE
Handley Down
Salisbury Plantation
Pentridge Hill
BRUSHY BUSH LA
Sixpenny Handley
Town Farm
RED LA
Tumuli
Manor Farm
B3081
West Blagdon
Tumuli
Tumuli
Crockerton Wood
Earthwork
Tumuli
Tumuli
Bottlebush Down
Tumuli
Blackbush Plantation
Tumulus
Wyke Down
BH21
Blackbush Down
JACK'S HEDGE CORNER
Tumuli
The Drive Plantation
B3081
Thorneydown Farm
Tumuli
Tumuli
Tumuli
The Drive Plantation
Ford
Earthworks
Bowldish Pond
Jubilee Trail
SQUIRREL'S CORNER
Water Lake Bottom
Tumulus
Canada Farm
Down Farm
Cranborne Farm
The Drive Plantation
MONKTON DROVE
BOTTLEBUSH LA
Ford
River Crane
A B C D E F
8 21 7 20 6 19 5 18 4 17 3 16 2 15 1 14
99 00 01 02 03 04
201
190

Scale: 1¾ inches to 1 mile

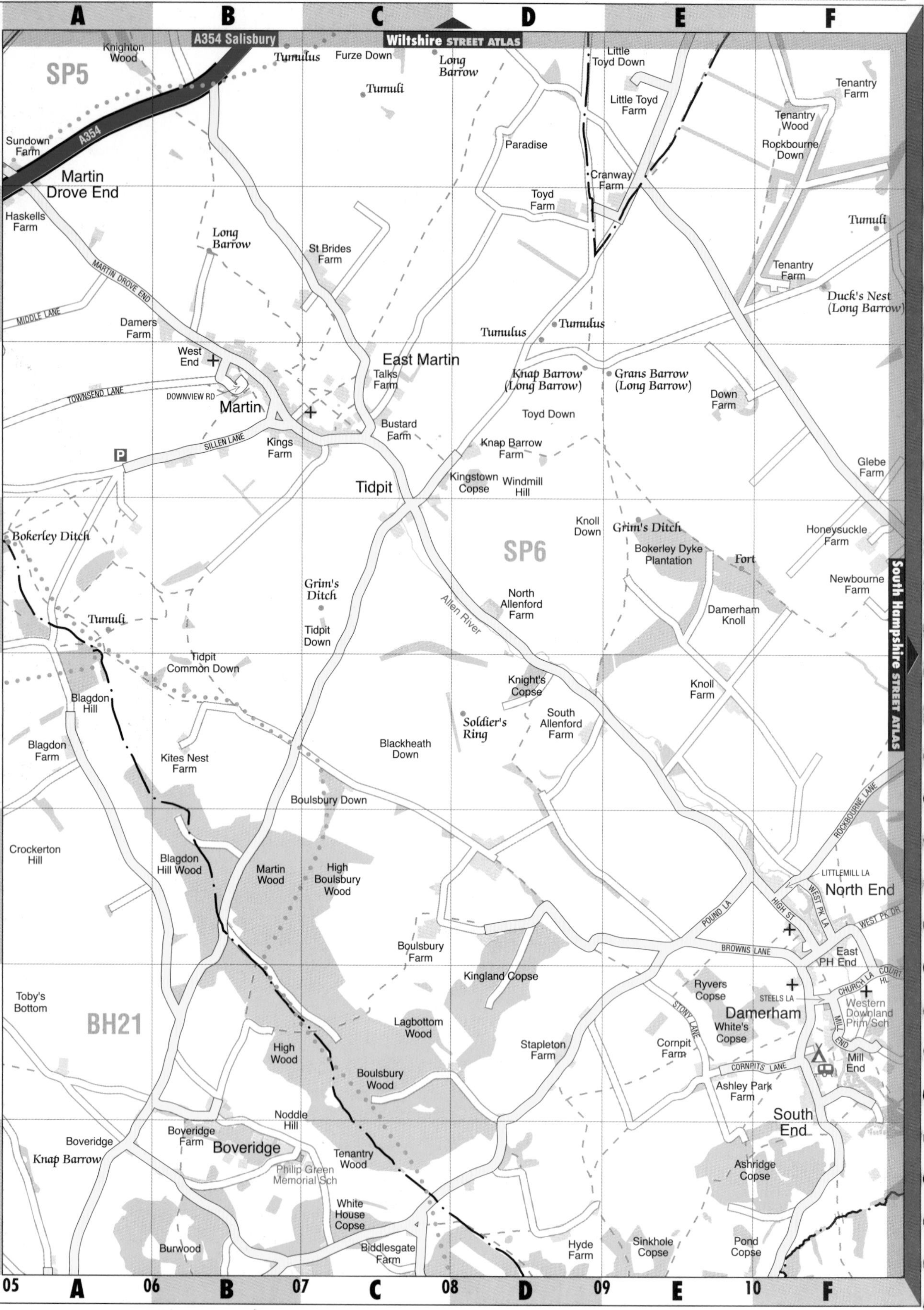

0   ¼   ½ mile
0   250m   500m   750m   1 km

South Hampshire STREET ATLAS

SP5

Knighton Wood

A354 Salisbury

Tumulus

Furze Down

Long Barrow

Little Toyd Down

Little Toyd Farm

Tenantry Farm

Tumuli

Tenantry Wood

Sundown Farm

A354

Paradise

Rockbourne Down

Martin Drove End

Cranway Farm

Toyd Farm

Tenantry Farm

Tumuli

Haskells Farm

Long Barrow

St Brides Farm

Tenantry Farm

Duck's Nest (Long Barrow)

MARTIN DROVE END

MIDDLE LANE

Damers Farm

West End

East Martin

Tumulus

Tumulus

Knap Barrow (Long Barrow)

Grans Barrow (Long Barrow)

Down Farm

TOWNSEND LANE

Talks Farm

DOWNVIEW RD

Martin

Toyd Down

Glebe Farm

SILLEN LANE

Kings Farm

Bustard Farm

Knap Barrow Farm

Tidpit

Kingstown Copse

Windmill Hill

SP6

Bokerley Ditch

Knoll Down

Grim's Ditch

Bokerley Dyke Plantation

Honeysuckle Farm

Grim's Ditch

North Allenford Farm

Fort

Damerham Knoll

Newbourne Farm

Tumuli

Tidpit Down

Allen River

Tidpit Common Down

Knight's Copse

Knoll Farm

Blagdon Hill

Soldier's Ring

South Allenford Farm

Blagdon Farm

Kites Nest Farm

Blackheath Down

Crockerton Hill

Boulsbury Down

ROCKBOURNE LANE

Blagdon Hill Wood

Martin Wood

High Boulsbury Wood

LITTLEMILL LA

North End

HIGH ST

WEST PK LA

WEST PK CR

Boulsbury Farm

POUND LA

Toby's Bottom

BH21

Kingland Copse

BROWNS LANE

East PH End

CHURCH LA COURT HL

Western Downland Prim Sch

High Wood

Lagbottom Wood

Ryvers Copse

STEELS LA

Damerham

MILL END

Mill End

Stapleton Farm

STONY LANE

White's Copse

Cornpit Farm

Boulsbury Wood

CORNPITS LANE

Noddle Hill

Ashley Park Farm

South End

Boveridge Farm

Boveridge

Knap Barrow

Philip Green Memorial Sch

Tenantry Wood

Ashridge Copse

White House Copse

Hyde Farm

Sinkhole Copse

Pond Copse

Burwood

Biddlesgate Farm

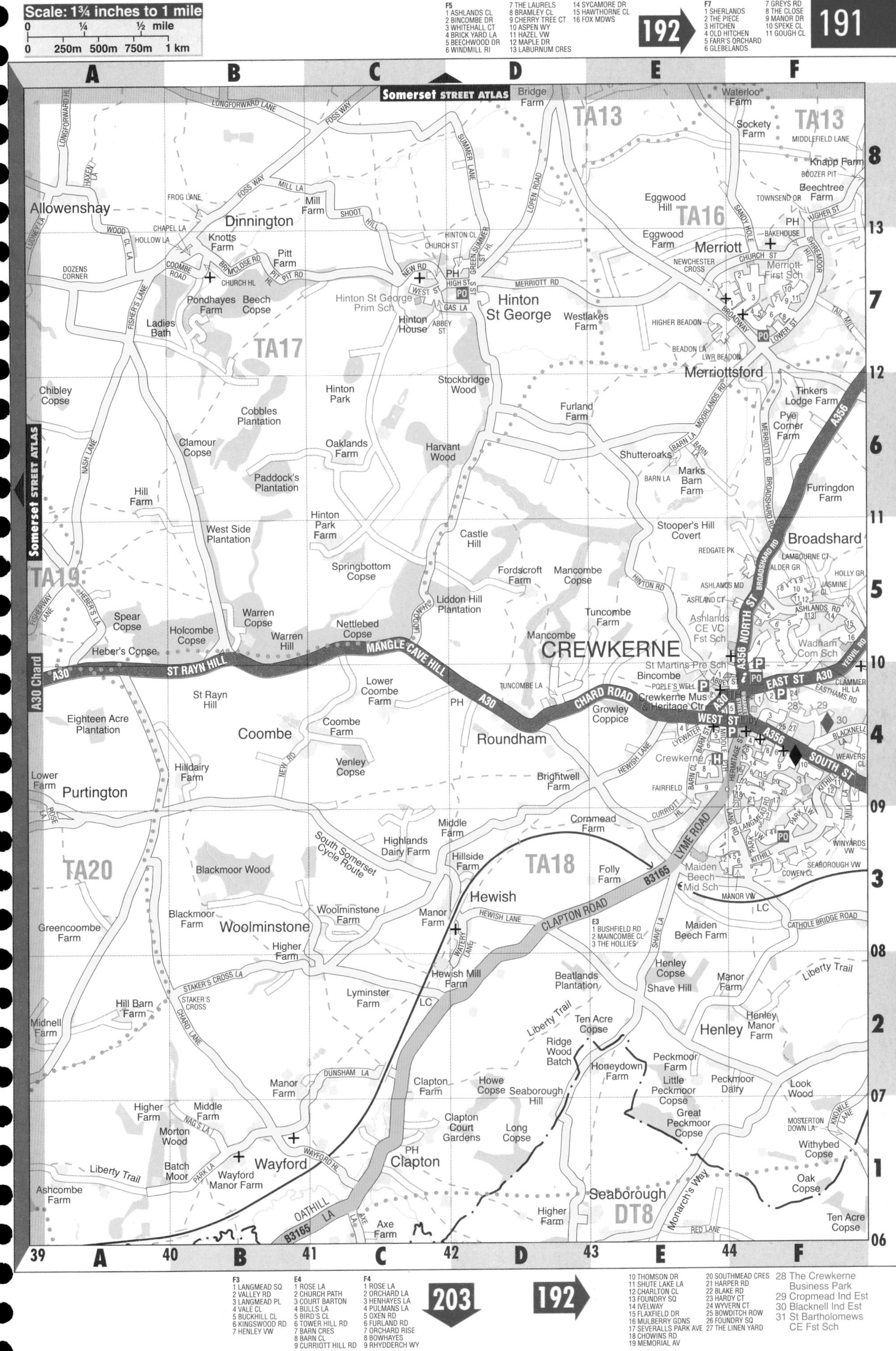

Scale: 1¾ inches to 1 mile
0 ¼ ½ mile
0 250m 500m 750m 1 km
F5
1 ASHLANDS CL
2 BINCOMBE DR
3 WHITEHALL CT
4 BRICK YARD LA
5 BEECHWOOD DR
6 WINDMILL RI
7 THE LAURELS
8 BRAMLEY CL
9 CHERRY TREE CT
10 ASPEN WY
11 HAZEL VW
12 MAPLE DR
13 LABURNUM CRES
14 SYCAMORE DR
15 HAWTHORNE CL
16 FOX MDWS
192
F7
1 SHERLANDS
2 THE PIECE
3 HITCHEN
4 OLD HITCHEN
5 FARR'S ORCHARD
6 GLEBELANDS
7 GREYS RD
8 THE CLOSE
9 MANOR DR
10 SPEKE CL
11 GOUGH CL
A B C D E F
Somerset STREET ATLAS
Bridge Farm
Waterloo Farm
TA13
Sockety Farm
TA13
MIDDLEFIELD LANE
Knapp Farm
BOOZER PIT
Beechtree Farm
TOWNSEND DR
8
13
7
12
6
11
5
10
4
09
3
08
2
07
1
06
LONGFORWARD HL
LONGFORWARD LANE
FOSS WAY
SUMMER LANE
LOPEN ROAD
Allowenshay
Dinnington
Mill Farm
Knotts Farm
Pitt Farm
FROG LANE
CHAPEL LA
HOLLOW LA
MILL LA
SHOOT HILL
WOOD CL LA
DOZENS CORNER
COOMBE ROAD
CHURCH HL
PIT RD
Pondhayes Farm
Beech Copse
Ladies Bath
TA17
FISHER'S LANE
Hinton St George Prim Sch
Hinton House
Hinton St George
HINTON CL
CHURCH ST
NEW RD
HIGH ST
WEST ST
GAS LA
ABBEY ST
GREEN
MERRIOTT RD
Westlakes Farm
Eggwood Hill
TA16
Eggwood Farm
Merriott
NEWCHESTER CROSS
CHURCH ST
Merriott First Sch
BAKEHOUSE
SANDY HOLE
SHIREMOOR HL
HIGHER ST
HIGHER BEADON
BEADON LA
LWR BEADON
BROADWAY
LOWER ST
TAIL MILL
Merriottsford
Chibley Copse
Hinton Park
Cobbles Plantation
Stockbridge Wood
Furland Farm
Tinkers Lodge Farm
Pye Corner Farm
A356
NASH LANE
Clamour Copse
Oaklands Farm
Harvant Wood
Shutteroaks
BARN LA
MOORLANDS RD
Marks Barn Farm
MERRIOTT RD
BROADSHARD RD
Furringdon Farm
Paddock's Plantation
Hill Farm
West Side Plantation
Hinton Park Farm
Castle Hill
Stooper's Hill Covert
Broadshard
REDGATE PK
LAMBOURNE CT
HOLLY GR
ALDER GR
JASMINE CL
ASHLANDS MD
ASHLAND CT
ASHLANDS RD
TA19
HEBER'S LA
FISHERWAY LANE
Springbottom Copse
Fordscroft Farm
Mancombe Copse
HINTON RD
Spear Copse
Warren Copse
Nettlebed Copse
Liddon Hill Plantation
LIDDON HL
Tuncombe Farm
Ashlands CE VC Fst Sch
NORTH ST
Wadham Com Sch
YEOVIL RD
Holcombe Copse
Warren Hill
Mancombe
Heber's Copse
CREWKERNE
A30 Chard
A30
ST RAYN HILL
MANGLE CAVE HILL
St Martins Pre Sch
Bincombe
POPLE'S WELL
ABBEY ST
EAST ST
CLAMMER HL LA
EASTHAMS RD
St Rayn Hill
Lower Coombe Farm
PH
TUNCOMBE LA
CHARD ROAD
Crewkerne Mus & Heritage Ctr
Growley Coppice
WEST ST
Liby
Eighteen Acre Plantation
Coombe
Coombe Farm
Roundham
LYEWATER
BARN CL
MIDDLE PATH
HERMITAGE ST
SOUTH ST
BLACKNELL LA
WEAVERS CL
Hilldairy Farm
Venley Copse
NEW RD
HEWISH LANE
Crewkerne
Brightwell Farm
FAIRFIELD
KITHILL
Lower Farm
Purtington
ROSE LA
CURRIOTT HL
LYME ROAD
LANG RD
LANGMEAD RD
PARK VW
MILL
Middle Farm
Cornmead Farm
Highlands Dairy Farm
South Somerset Cycle Route
WINYARDS VW
SEABOROUGH VW
TA20
Blackmoor Wood
Hillside Farm
TA18
Folly Farm
Maiden Beech Mid Sch
COWEN CL
MANOR VW
B3165
Hewish
Blackmoor Farm
Woolminstone
Woolminstone Farm
Manor Farm
HEWISH LANE
CLAPTON ROAD
E3
1 BUSHFIELD RD
2 MAINCOMBE CL
3 THE HOLLIES
SHAVE LA
Maiden Beech Farm
LC
CATHOLE BRIDGE ROAD
Greencoombe Farm
Higher Farm
WATERY LANE
Henley Copse
Manor Farm
Liberty Trail
STAKER'S CROSS LA
STAKER'S CROSS
Hewish Mill Farm
Beatlands Plantation
Shave Hill
Hill Barn Farm
Lyminster Farm
LC
CHARD LANE
Liberty Trail
Ten Acre Copse
Henley
Henley Manor Farm
Midnell Farm
Ridge Wood Batch
Honeydown Farm
Peckmoor Farm
Little Peckmoor Copse
Peckmoor Dairy
Look Wood
Manor Farm
DUNSHAM LA
Clapton Farm
Howe Copse
Seaborough Hill
Great Peckmoor Copse
MOSTERTON DOWN LA
KNOWLE LANE
Higher Farm
Middle Farm
NAG'S LA
Morton Wood
Clapton Court Gardens
Long Copse
Withybed Copse
Wayford
WAYFORD HL
PH
Clapton
Liberty Trail
Batch Moor
PARK LA
Wayford Manor Farm
Oak Copse
Ashcombe Farm
OATHILL LA
B3165
AXE LA
Axe Farm
Seaborough
Monarch's Way
Higher Farm
DT8
RED LANE
Ten Acre Copse
39 40 41 42 43 44
A B C D E F
F3
1 LANGMEAD SQ
2 VALLEY RD
3 LANGMEAD PL
4 VALE CL
5 BUCKHILL CL
6 KINGSWOOD RD
7 HENLEY VW
E4
1 ROSE LA
2 CHURCH PATH
3 COURT BARTON
4 BULLS LA
5 BIRD'S CL
6 TOWER HILL RD
7 BARN CRES
8 BARN CL
9 CURRIOTT HILL RD
F4
1 ROSE LA
2 ORCHARD LA
3 HENHAYES LA
4 PULMANS LA
5 OXEN RD
6 FURLAND RD
7 ORCHARD RISE
8 BOWHAYES
9 RHYDDERCH WY
203
192
10 THOMSON DR
11 SHUTE LAKE LA
12 CHARLTON CL
13 FOUNDRY SQ
14 IVELWAY
15 FLAXFIELD DR
16 MULBERRY GDNS
17 SEVERALLS PARK AVE
18 CHOWINS RD
19 MEMORIAL AV
20 SOUTHMEAD CRES
21 HARPER RD
22 BLAKE RD
23 HARDY CT
24 WYVERN CT
25 BOWDITCH ROW
26 FOUNDRY SQ
27 THE LINEN YARD
28 The Crewkerne Business Park
29 Cropmead Ind Est
30 Blacknell Ind Est
31 St Bartholomews CE Fst Sch

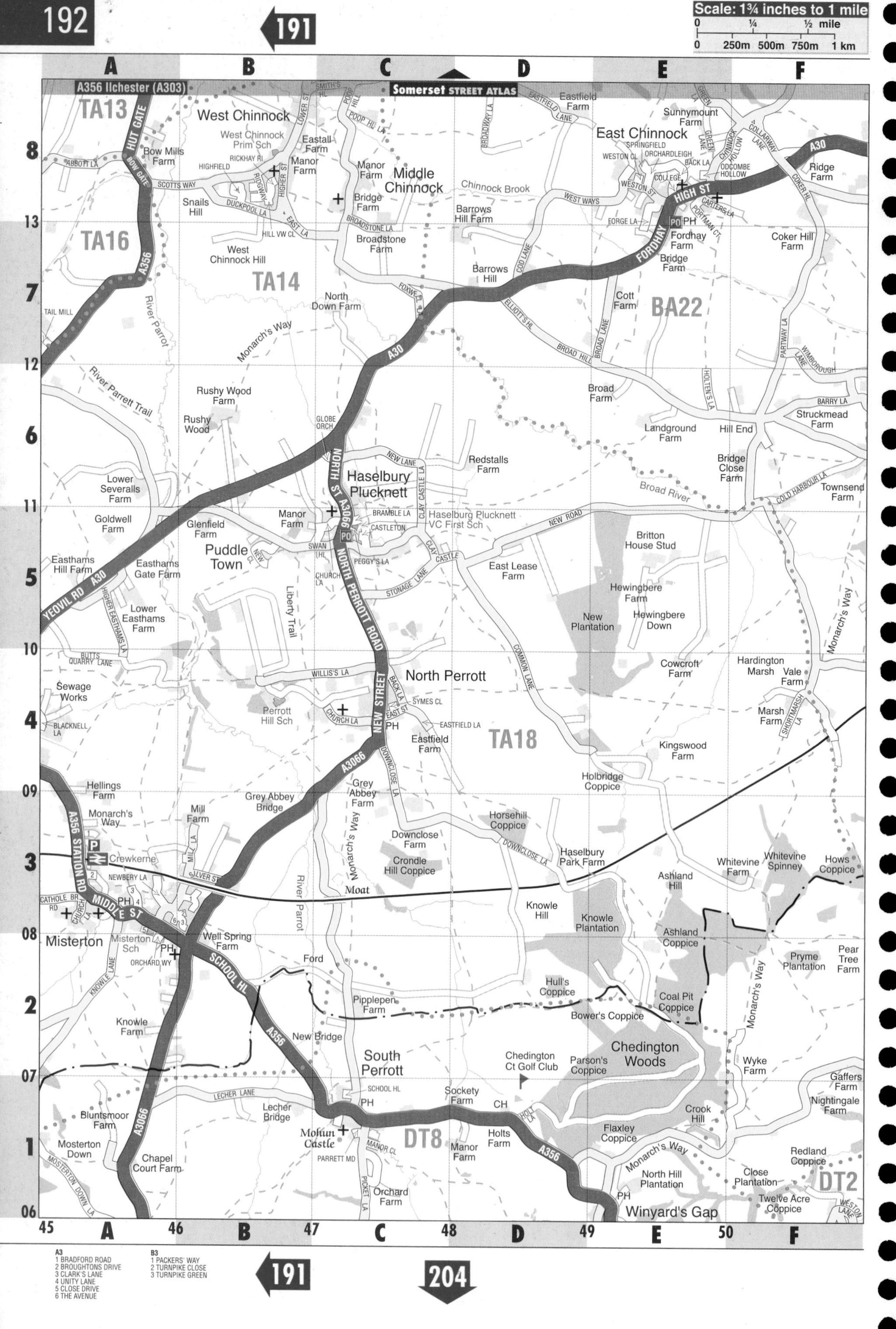

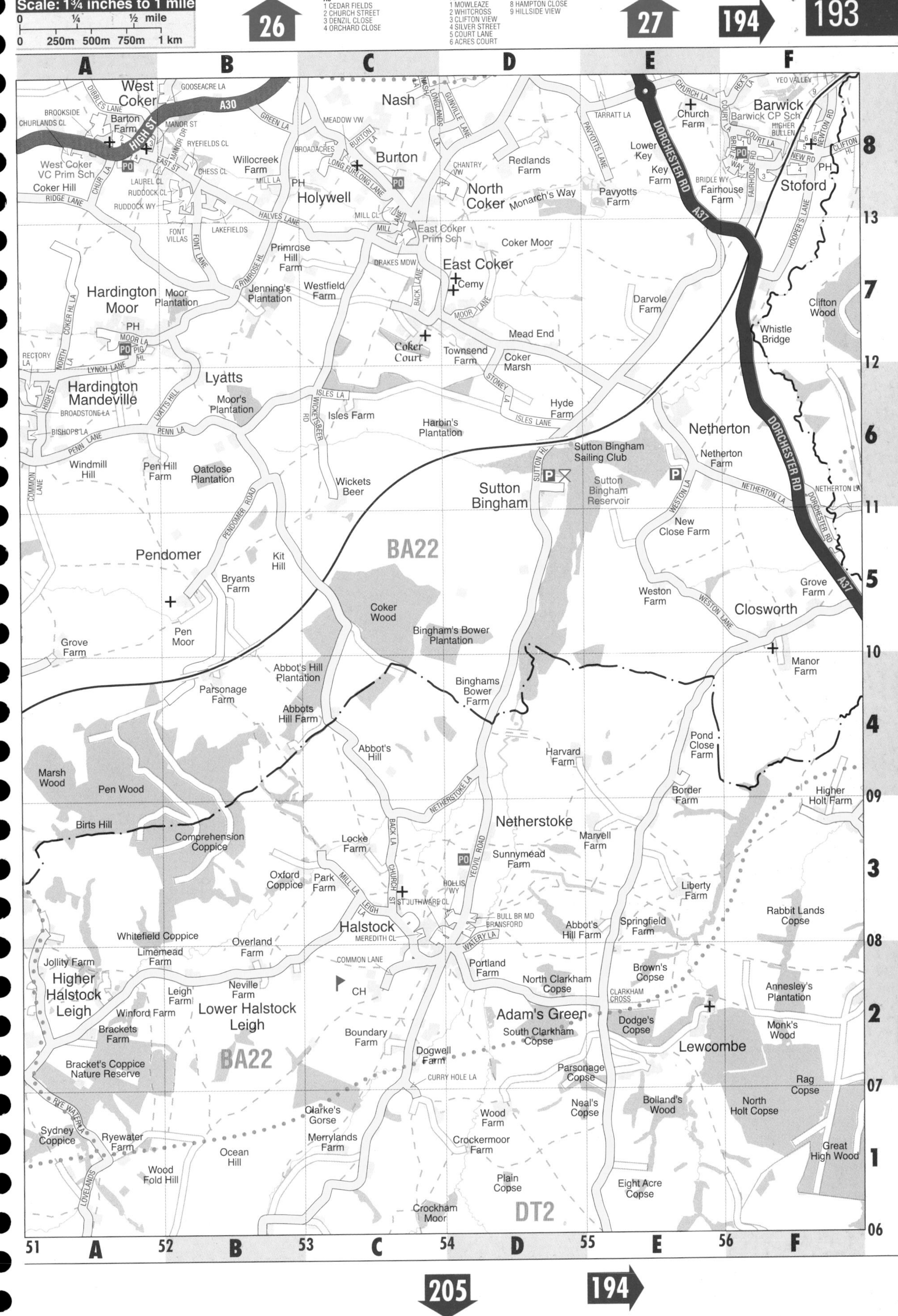
Scale: 1¾ inches to 1 mile
26
27
194
A8
1 CEDAR FIELDS
2 CHURCH STREET
3 DENZIL CLOSE
4 ORCHARD CLOSE
F8
1 MOWLEAZE
2 WHITCROSS
3 CLIFTON VIEW
4 SILVER STREET
5 COURT LANE
6 ACRES COURT
7 MEADOW VIEW
8 HAMPTON CLOSE
9 HILLSIDE VIEW
West Coker
Nash
Burton
Holywell
North Coker
East Coker
Barwick
Stoford
Hardington Moor
Hardington Mandeville
Lyatts
Pendomer
Sutton Bingham
Netherton
Closworth
BA22
Netherstoke
Halstock
Higher Halstock Leigh
Lower Halstock Leigh
Adam's Green
Lewcombe
DT2
Coker Wood
Marsh Wood
Pen Wood
DORCHESTER RD
A37
A30
205
194

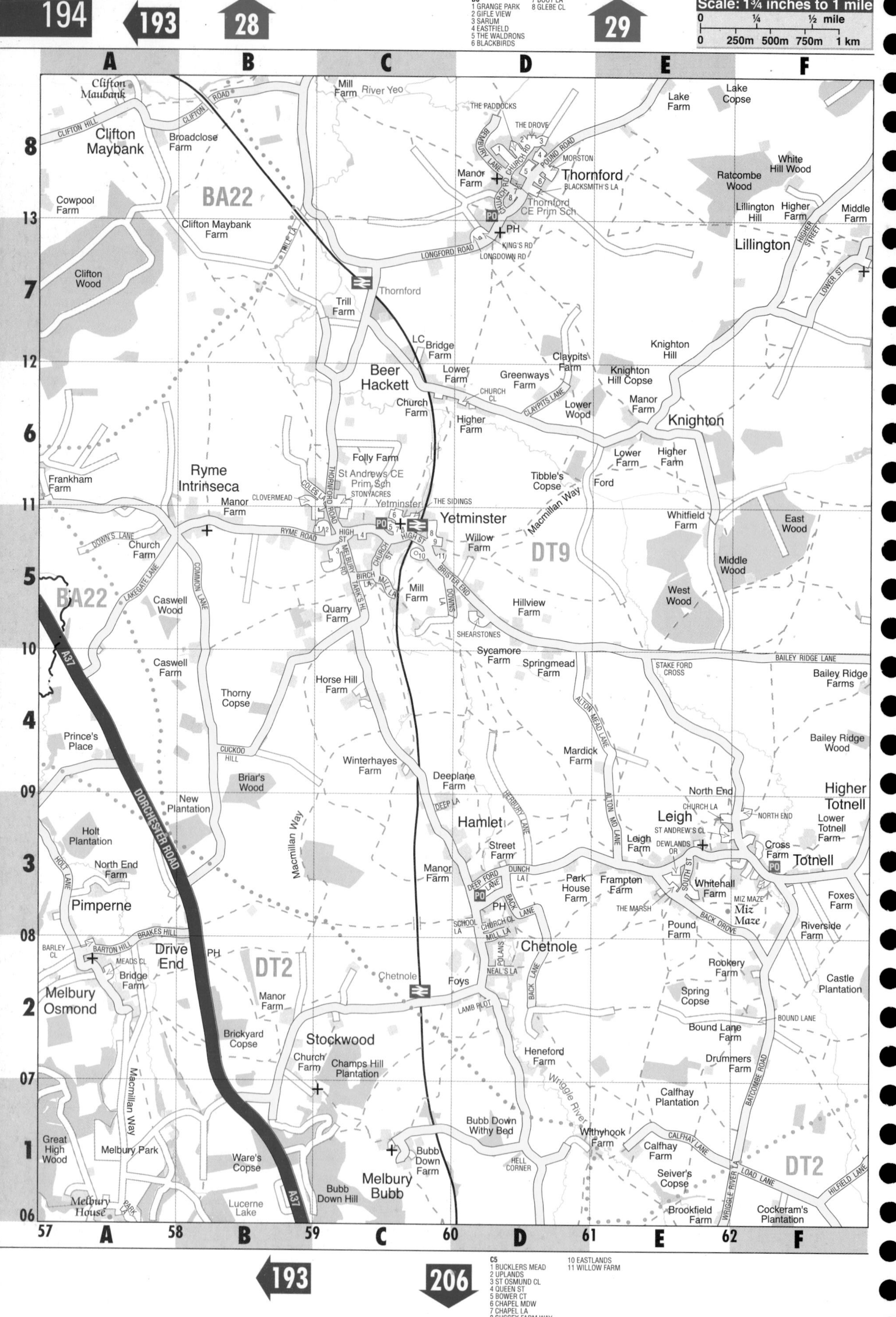

194

← 193

↑ 28

↑ 29

Scale: 1¾ inches to 1 mile
0   ¼   ½   mile
0   250m 500m 750m 1 km

D8
1 GRANGE PARK   7 BOOT LA
2 GIFLE VIEW   8 GLEBE CL
3 SARUM
4 EASTFIELD
5 THE WALDRONS
6 BLACKBIRDS

Clifton
Maubank
Clifton
Maybank
BA22
Broadclose
Farm
CLIFTON ROAD
CLIFTON HILL
Cowpool
Farm
Clifton Maybank
Farm
Clifton
Wood
Mill
Farm
River Yeo
THE PADDOCKS
THE DROVE
Lake
Farm
Lake
Copse
THE DROVE
MORSTON
Manor
Farm
Thornford
Blacksmith's La
Ratcombe
Wood
White
Hill Wood
Lillington
Hill
Higher
Farm
Middle
Farm
Thornford
CE Prim Sch
Lillington
HIGHER STREET
LOWER ST
PO
PH
Longford Road
King's Rd
Longdown Rd
Trill
Farm
Thornford
LC
Bridge
Farm
Beer
Hackett
Church
Farm
Lower
Farm
CHURCH CL
Greenways
Farm
Claypits
Farm
CLAYPITS LANE
Knighton
Hill
Knighton
Hill Copse
Higher
Farm
Lower
Wood
Lower
Farm
Manor
Farm
Knighton
Frankham
Farm
Ryme
Intrinseca
Manor
Farm
Clovermead
COLES LORD ROAD
Folly Farm
St Andrews CE
Prim Sch
STONYACRES
THE SIDINGS
Yetminster
Tibble's
Copse
Ford
Lower
Farm
Higher
Farm
Macmillan Way
Whitfield
Farm
East
Wood
BA22
Church
Farm
DOWN'S LANE
LANEGATE LANE
COMMON LANE
RYME ROAD
THORNFORD ROAD
MELBURY RD
HIGH ST
CHURCH ST
HIGH ST
BIRCH LA
BRISTER END LA
DEEP LANE
Yetminster
PO
Willow
Farm
DT9
Middle
Wood
West
Wood
Caswell
Wood
Quarry
Farm
Mill
Farm
Hillview
Farm
SHEARSTONES
Sycamore
Farm
Springmead
Farm
STAKE FORD
CROSS
BAILEY RIDGE LANE
Bailey Ridge
Farms
Caswell
Farm
Thorny
Copse
Horse Hill
Farm
Winterhayes
Farm
Deeplane
Farm
Mardick
Farm
ALTON MEAD LANE
ALTON MID LANE
Bailey Ridge
Wood
Prince's
Place
A37
DORCHESTER ROAD
CUCKOO
HILL
Briar's
Wood
Macmillan Way
North End
Leigh
St Andrew's Cl
DEWLANDS DR
NORTH END
CHURCH LA
Higher
Totnell
Lower
Totnell
Cross
Farm
Totnell
PO
Holt
Plantation
New
Plantation
DEEP LA
Hamlet
Street
Farm
Manor
Farm
DEEP FORD LANE
PO
DUNCH LA
BACK LANE
Park House
Farm
Frampton
Farm
SOUTH ST
Whitehall
Farm
MIZ MAZE
Miz
Maze
Foxes
Farm
North End
Farm
Pimperne
HOLT LANE
BARLEY CL
BRAKES HILL
BARTON HILL
MEADS CL
PH
SCHOOL LA
PH
CHURCH CL LANE
MILL LA
POLANS
NEAL'S LA
THE MARSH
Pound
Farm
BACK DROVE
Riverside
Farm
Castle
Plantation
Melbury
Osmond
Bridge
Farm
Drive
End
DT2
Manor
Farm
Chetnole
Foys
Chetnole
LAMB PLOT
Heneford
Farm
Rookery
Farm
Spring
Copse
Bound Lane
Farm
BOUND LANE
Drummers
Farm
Brickyard
Copse
Church
Farm
Champs Hill
Plantation
Stockwood
Wriddle River
Calfhay
Plantation
Great
High
Wood
Melbury Park
MACMILLAN WAY
PARK
Ware's
Copse
Lucerne
Lake
A37
Bubb
Down Hill
Melbury
Bubb
Bubb
Down
Farm
Bubb Down
Withy Bed
HELL
CORNER
Withyhook
Farm
Calfhay
Farm
CALFHAY LANE
Seiver's
Copse
Brookfield
Farm
WRIGGLE RIVER LA
LOAD LANE
BALCOMBE ROAD
HILFIELD LANE
Cockeram's
Plantation
DT2
Melbury
House

C5
1 BUCKLERS MEAD   10 EASTLANDS
2 UPLANDS   11 WILLOW FARM
3 ST OSMUND CL
4 QUEEN ST
5 BOWER CT
6 CHAPEL MDW
7 CHAPEL LA
8 SUSSEX FARM WAY
9 BRIERLEY HAY

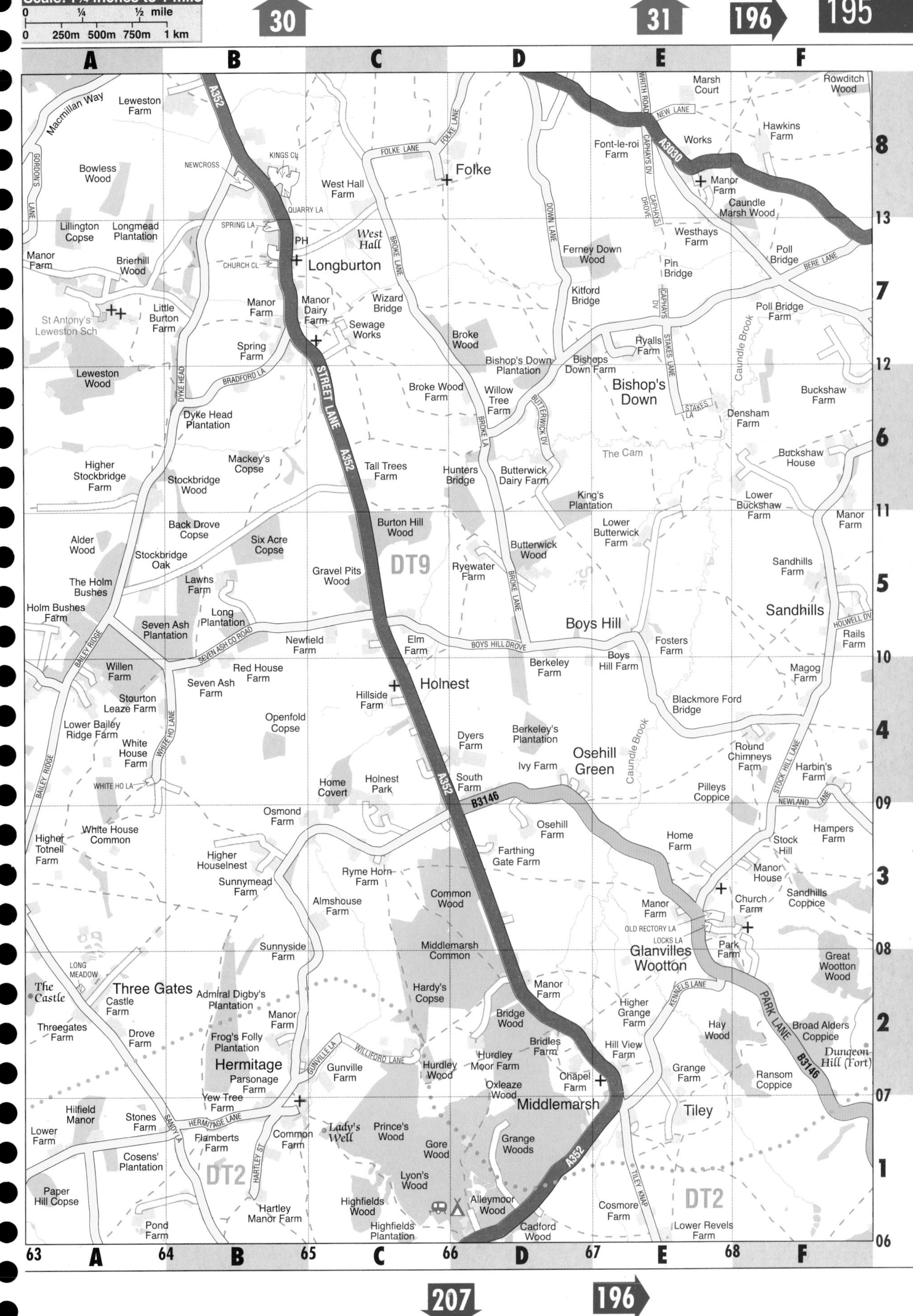
A
B
C
D
E
F
A352
Macmillan Way
Leweston Farm
Bowless Wood
NEWCROSS
KINGS CL
QUARRY LA
SPRING LA
CHURCH CL
PH
Longburton
West Hall Farm
West Hall
FOLKE LANE
Folke
Marsh Court
Rowditch Wood
NEW LANE
A3030
Works
Hawkins Farm
Font-le-roi Farm
Manor Farm
Caundle Marsh Wood
Lillington Copse
Longmead Plantation
Manor Farm
Brierhill Wood
Little Burton Farm
St Antony's Leweston Sch
Manor Farm
Manor Dairy Farm
Sewage Works
Wizard Bridge
Spring Farm
Leweston Wood
BRADFORD LA
DYKE HEAD
Dyke Head Plantation
STREET LANE
Broke Wood
Broke Wood Farm
Bishop's Down Plantation
Bishops Down Farm
Willow Tree Farm
Ferney Down Wood
Kitford Bridge
Westhays Farm
Pin Bridge
Poll Bridge
BERE LANE
Poll Bridge Farm
Ryalls Farm
Bishop's Down
STAKES LANE
Densham Farm
Buckshaw Farm
Caundle Brook
The Cam
Buckshaw House
Higher Stockbridge Farm
Mackey's Copse
Stockbridge Wood
Tall Trees Farm
Hunters Bridge
Butterwick Dairy Farm
King's Plantation
Lower Buckshaw Farm
Manor Farm
Back Drove Copse
Alder Wood
Stockbridge Oak
Six Acre Copse
Burton Hill Wood
DT9
Lower Butterwick Farm
Butterwick Wood
Ryewater Farm
Gravel Pits Wood
BROKE LANE
Sandhills Farm
Sandhills
The Holm Bushes
Lawns Farm
Holm Bushes Farm
Long Plantation
Seven Ash Plantation
SEVEN ASH CO ROAD
Newfield Farm
Elm Farm
BOYS HILL DROVE
Boys Hill
Boys Hill Farm
Fosters Farm
HOLWELL DV
Rails Farm
BAILEY RIDGE
Willen Farm
Red House Farm
Seven Ash Farm
Stourton Leaze Farm
Hillside Farm
Holnest
Berkeley Farm
Magog Farm
Blackmore Ford Bridge
Openfold Copse
Lower Bailey Ridge Farm
White House Farm
WHITE HO LANE
WHITE HO LA
Dyers Farm
Berkeley's Plantation
Osehill Green
Round Chimneys Farm
STOCK HILL LANE
Harbin's Farm
Ivy Farm
Home Covert
Holnest Park
South Farm
B3146
Pilleys Coppice
NEWLAND LANE
Osmond Farm
White House Common
Higher Totnell Farm
Osehill Farm
Home Farm
Hampers Farm
Stock Hill
Higher Houselnest
Farthing Gate Farm
Ryme Horn Farm
Manor House
Sunnymead Farm
Common Wood
Church Farm
Sandhills Coppice
Almshouse Farm
Manor Farm
OLD RECTORY LA
LOCKS LA
Park Farm
Middlemarsh Common
Sunnyside Farm
Glanvilles Wootton
Great Wootton Wood
LONG MEADOW
The Castle
Three Gates
Admiral Digby's Plantation
Castle Farm
Hardy's Copse
Manor Farm
KENNELS LANE
Higher Grange Farm
PARK LANE
Threegates Farm
Drove Farm
Manor Farm
Bridge Wood
Hay Wood
Broad Alders Coppice
Frog's Folly Plantation
Bridles Farm
Hill View Farm
Dungeon Hill (Fort)
GUNVILLE LA
WILLIFORD LANE
Hurdley Moor Farm
Hurdley Wood
Hermitage
Parsonage Farm
Gunville Farm
Grange Farm
Ransom Coppice
Oxleaze Wood
Chapel Farm
Yew Tree Farm
Middlemarsh
Tiley
Hilfield Manor
Stones Farm
HERMITAGE LANE
SANDY LA
Lower Farm
Flamberts Farm
Common Farm
Lady's Well
Prince's Wood
Gore Wood
Grange Woods
Cosens' Plantation
HARTLEY ST
DT2
Lyon's Wood
TILEY KNAP
DT2
Paper Hill Copse
Highfields Wood
Alleymoor Wood
Cosmore Farm
Hartley Manor Farm
Pond Farm
Highfields Plantation
Cadford Wood
Lower Revels Farm
63
64
65
66
67
68
13
12
11
10
09
08
07
06
8
7
6
5
4
3
2
1

195
32
33

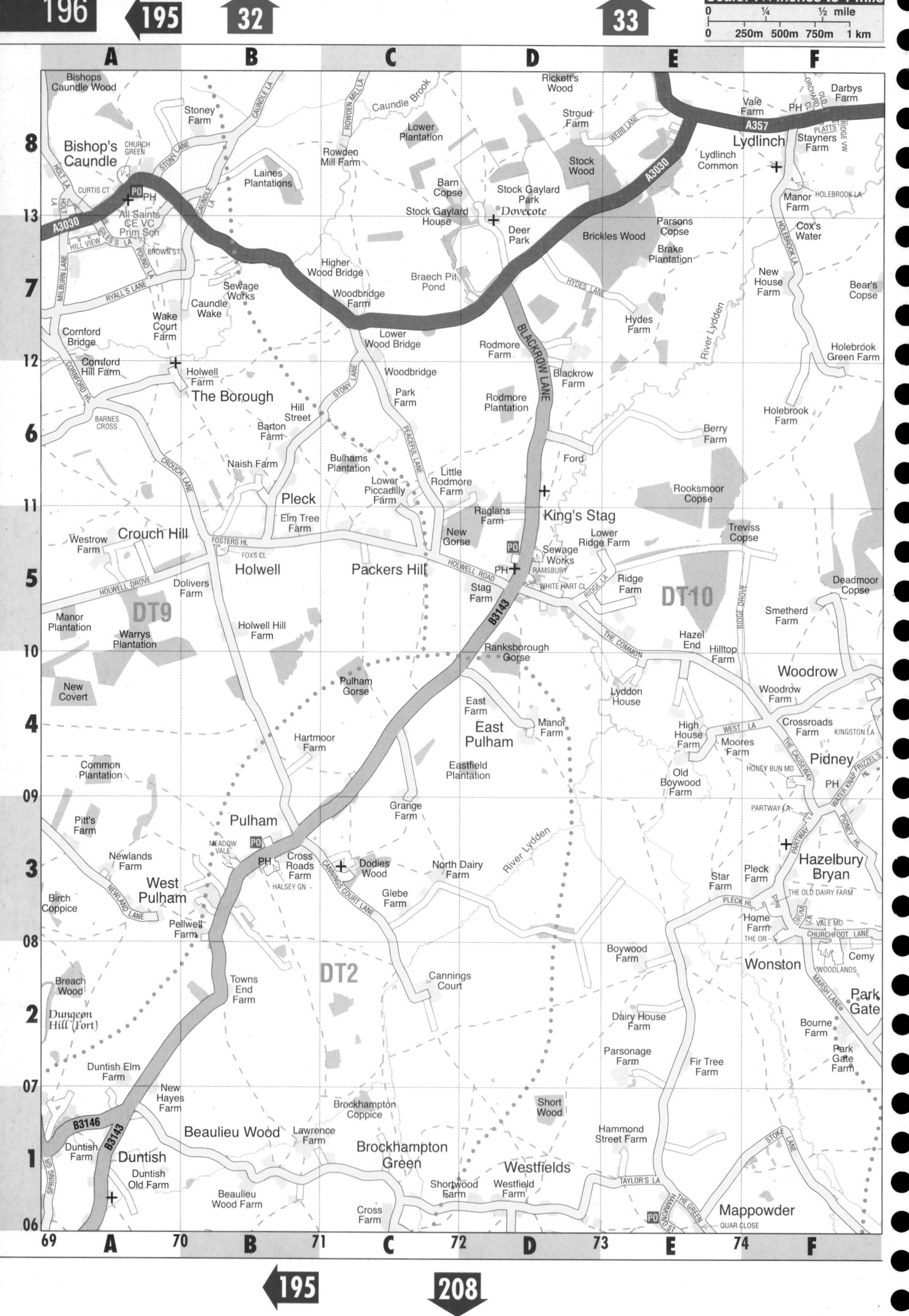

Scale: 1¾ inches to 1 mile
0 ¼ ½ mile
0 250m 500m 750m 1 km
A
B
C
D
E
F
8
13
7
12
6
11
5
10
4
09
3
08
2
07
1
06
69
70
71
72
73
74
Bishops Caundle Wood
Stoney Farm
Bishop's Caundle
CHURCH GREEN
CURTIS CT
PO
PH
All Saints CE VC Prim Sch
A3030
HILL VIEW
GILES'S LA
POUND LA
BROWN ST
HOLT LA
MILBURN LANE
RYALL'S LANE
STONY LANE
CAUNDLE LA
Laines Plantations
Rowden Mill Farm
ROWDEN MILL LA
Caundle Brook
Lower Plantation
Rickett's Wood
Stroud Farm
WEBB LANE
Stock Wood
Barn Copse
Stock Gaylard Park
Dovecote
Stock Gaylard House
Deer Park
Brickles Wood
Parsons Copse
Brake Plantation
Vale Farm
PH
Darbys Farm
A357
PLATTS
Lydlinch
Stayners Farm
Lydlinch Common
Manor Farm
HOLEBROOK LA
Cox's Water
New House Farm
Bear's Copse
Sewage Works
Caundle Wake
Wake Court Farm
Higher Wood Bridge
Woodbridge Farm
Braech Pit Pond
HYDES LANE
Hydes Farm
River Lydden
Cornford Bridge
Cornford Hill Farm
CORNFORD HL
Holwell Farm
The Borough
Lower Wood Bridge
Woodbridge
Park Farm
Rodmore Farm
BLACKROW LANE
Blackrow Farm
Holebrook Green Farm
Holebrook Farm
BARNES CROSS
Hill Street
Barton Farm
Rodmore Plantation
Berry Farm
CROUCH LANE
Naish Farm
Bulhams Plantation
PEACEFUL LANE
Little Rodmore Farm
Ford
Lower Piccadilly Farm
Rooksmoor Copse
Pleck
Elm Tree Farm
Raglans Farm
King's Stag
Westrow Farm
Crouch Hill
FOSTERS HL
FOXS CL
New Gorse
Lower Ridge Farm
Treviss Copse
Holwell
Packers Hill
HOLWELL ROAD
Sewage Works
RAMSBURY
WHITE HART CL
RIDGE LA
Ridge Farm
DT10
Deadmoor Copse
HOLWELL DROVE
Dolivers Farm
Stag Farm
B3143
RIDGE DROVE
Manor Plantation
DT9
Warrys Plantation
Holwell Hill Farm
Ranksborough Gorse
THE COMMON
Hazel End
Hilltop Farm
Smetherd Farm
Woodrow
New Covert
Pulham Gorse
East Farm
Lyddon House
Woodrow Farm
East Pulham
Manor Farm
High House Farm
WEST LA
Crossroads Farm
KINGSTON LA
Hartmoor Farm
Moores Farm
THE CAUSEWAY
Pidney
Common Plantation
Eastfield Plantation
Old Boywood Farm
HONEY BUN MD
FRIZZEL'S HL
WATER KNAP
Pitt's Farm
Grange Farm
PARTWAY LA
Pulham
PARTWAY
PIDNEY HL
MEADOW VALE
Newlands Farm
Cross Roads Farm
Dodies Wood
North Dairy Farm
Hazelbury Bryan
West Pulham
HALSEY GN
CANNINGS COURT LANE
Glebe Farm
Star Farm
Pleck Farm
THE OLD DAIRY FARM
Birch Coppice
NEWLAND LANE
Pellwell Farm
PLECK HL
Home Farm
DRUM LA
VALE MD
CHURCHFOOT LANE
THE OR
Boywood Farm
Cemy
Breach Wood
Towns End Farm
DT2
Cannings Court
Wonston
WOODLANDS
MARSH LANE
Park Gate
Dungeon Hill (Fort)
Dairy House Farm
Bourne Farm
Parsonage Farm
Fir Tree Farm
Park Gate Farm
Duntish Elm Farm
New Hayes Farm
Brockhampton Coppice
Short Wood
B3146
Beaulieu Wood
Lawrence Farm
Hammond Street Farm
STOKE LANE
Duntish Farm
Duntish
Brockhampton Green
Westfields
SPRING GR
Duntish Old Farm
Shortwood Farm
Westfield Farm
TAYLOR'S LA
Beaulieu Wood Farm
Cross Farm
HAMMOND ST
THE GREEN
Mappowder
QUAR CLOSE

195
208

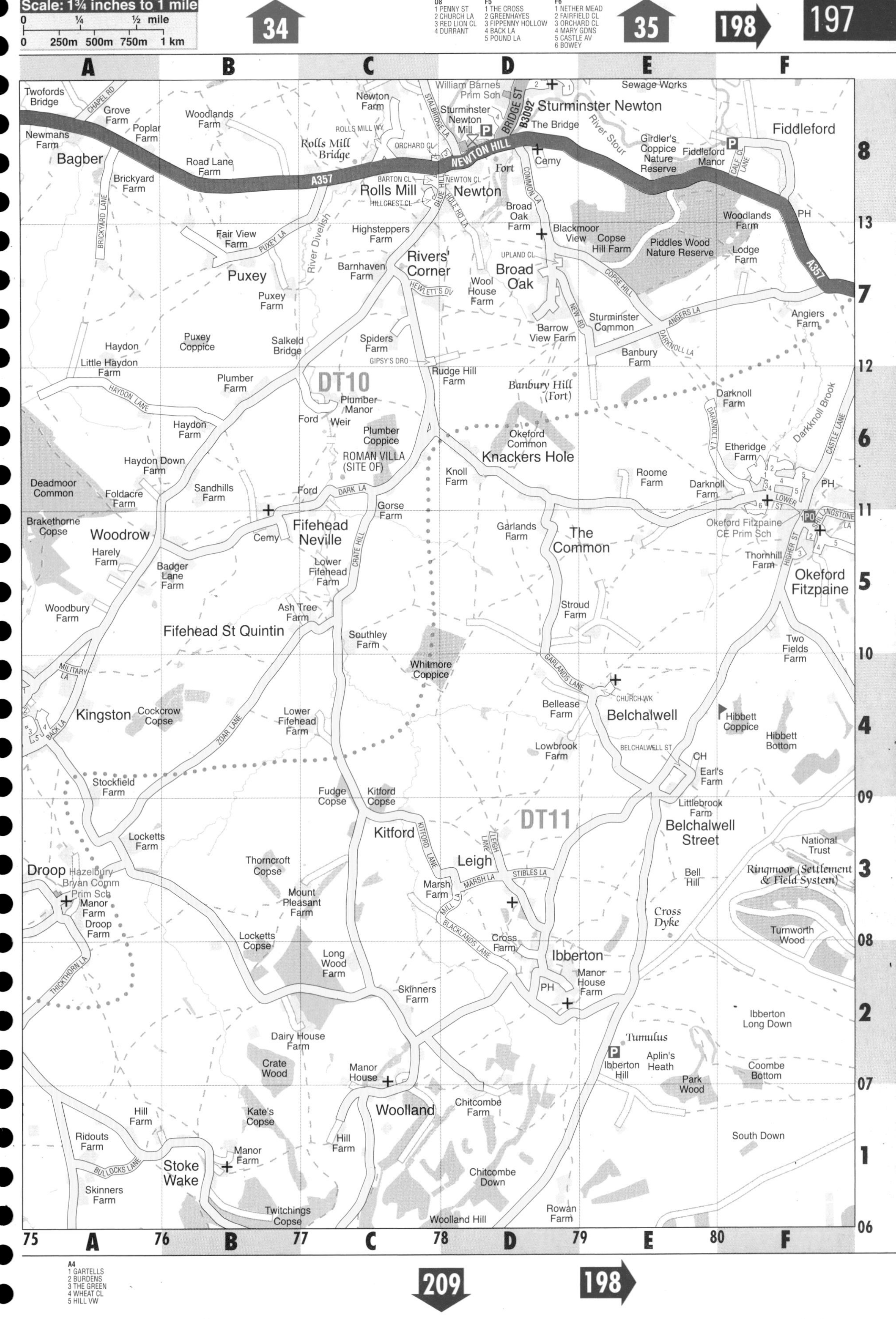
Scale: 1¾ inches to 1 mile
0 ¼ ½ mile
0 250m 500m 750m 1 km
34
35
198
D8
1 PENNY ST
2 CHURCH LA
3 RED LION CL
4 DURRANT
F5
1 THE CROSS
2 GREENHAYES
3 FIPPENNY HOLLOW
4 BACK LA
5 POUND LA
F6
1 NETHER MEAD
2 FAIRFIELD CL
3 ORCHARD CL
4 MARY GDNS
5 CASTLE AV
6 BOWEY
A B C D E F
8 13 7 12 6 11 5 10 4 09 3 08 2 07 1 06
75 76 77 78 79 80
Twofords Bridge
CHAPEL RD
Grove Farm
Newmans Farm
Poplar Farm
Woodlands Farm
Bagber
Road Lane Farm
Brickyard Farm
BRICKYARD LANE
A357
Newton Farm
William Barnes Prim Sch
STALBRIDGE LA
Sturminster Newton Mill
BRIDGE ST
B3092
Sturminster Newton
The Bridge
River Stour
Sewage Works
Girdler's Coppice Nature Reserve
Fiddleford Manor
Fiddleford
CALF CL LANE
ROLLS MILL WY
Rolls Mill Bridge
ORCHARD CL
NEWTON HILL
Fort
Cemy
BARTON CL
NEWTON CL
Rolls Mill
Newton
HILLCREST CL
BLUE HILL
HOLE HO LA
COMMON LA
Broad Oak Farm
Blackmoor View
Copse Hill Farm
Piddles Wood Nature Reserve
Woodlands Farm
PH
Lodge Farm
Fair View Farm
PUXEY LA
River Divelish
Highsteppers Farm
Rivers' Corner
Barnhaven Farm
UPLAND CL
Broad Oak
COPSE HILL
Puxey
Puxey Farm
HEWLETT'S DV
Wool House Farm
NEW RD
Sturminster Common
ANGERS LA
Angiers Farm
Haydon
Puxey Coppice
Salkeld Bridge
Spiders Farm
Barrow View Farm
DARKNOLL LA
Banbury Farm
Little Haydon Farm
GIPSY'S DRO
Rudge Hill Farm
Plumber Farm
DT10
Banbury Hill (Fort)
Darknoll Farm
HAYDON LANE
Plumber Manor
Ford
Weir
Darknoll Brook
Haydon Farm
Plumber Coppice
Okeford Common
CASTLE LANE
ROMAN VILLA (SITE OF)
Knackers Hole
Etheridge Farm
Haydon Down Farm
Knoll Farm
Roome Farm
Deadmoor Common
Sandhills Farm
Darknoll Farm
PH
Foldacre Farm
Ford
DARK LA
LOWER ST
Gorse Farm
Brakethorne Copse
Fifehead Neville
Garlands Farm
The Common
Okeford Fitzpaine CE Prim Sch
LINGSTONE LA
Woodrow
Cemy
CRATE HILL
Harely Farm
Lower Fifehead Farm
Thornhill Farm
HIGHER ST
Badger Lane Farm
Okeford Fitzpaine
Woodbury Farm
Ash Tree Farm
Stroud Farm
Fifehead St Quintin
Southley Farm
Two Fields Farm
MILITARY LA
Whitmore Coppice
GARLANDS LANE
CHURCH WK
Hibbett Coppice
Kingston
Cockcrow Copse
Lower Fifehead Farm
Bellease Farm
Belchalwell
ZOAR LANE
BACK LA
Hibbett Bottom
Lowbrook Farm
BELCHALWELL ST
CH
Earl's Farm
Stockfield Farm
Fudge Copse
Kitford Copse
Littlebrook Farm
DT11
Belchalwell Street
Locketts Farm
Kitford
KITFORD LANE
LEIGH LANE
National Trust
Leigh
Droop
Hazelbury Bryan Comm Prim Sch
Thorncroft Copse
STIBLES LA
MARSH LA
Bell Hill
Ringmoor (Settlement & Field System)
Manor Farm
Mount Pleasant Farm
Marsh Farm
MILL LA
Cross Dyke
Droop Farm
Turnworth Wood
BLACKLANDS LANE
Locketts Copse
Cross Farm
Ibberton
THICKTHORN LA
Long Wood Farm
Manor House Farm
Skinners Farm
PH
Ibberton Long Down
Dairy House Farm
Tumulus
Crate Wood
Ibberton Hill
Aplin's Heath
Coombe Bottom
Manor House
Park Wood
Hill Farm
Kate's Copse
Woolland
Chitcombe Farm
Ridouts Farm
Hill Farm
South Down
Manor Farm
BULLOCKS LANE
Stoke Wake
Chitcombe Down
Skinners Farm
Twitchings Copse
Woolland Hill
Rowan Farm
A4
1 GARTELLS
2 BURDENS
3 THE GREEN
4 WHEAT CL
5 HILL VW
209
198

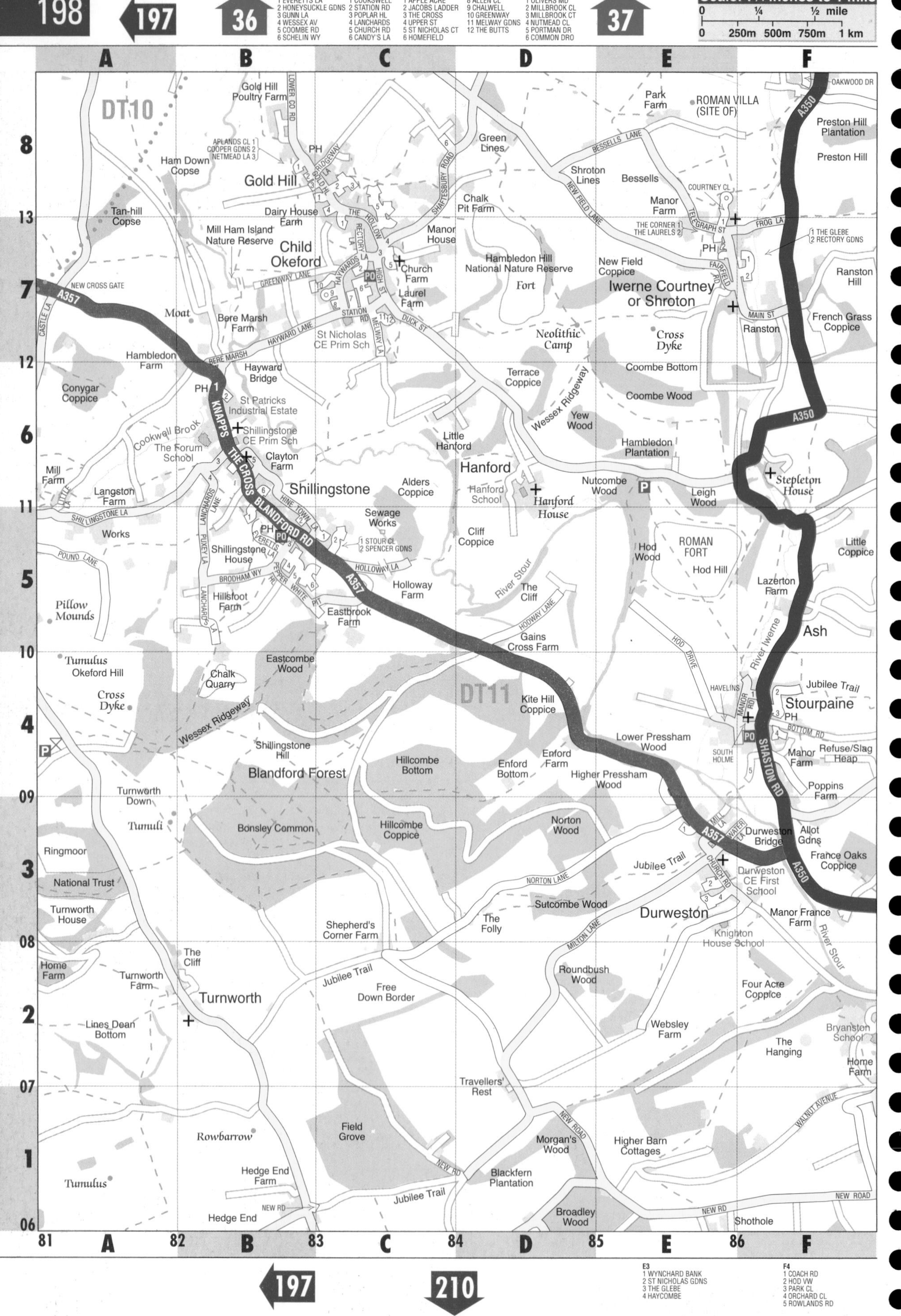
197
36
B5
1 EVERETTS LA
2 HONEYSUCKLE GDNS
3 GUNN LA
4 WESSEX AV
5 COOMBE RD
6 SCHELIN WY
B6
1 COOKSWELL
2 STATION RD
3 POPLAR HL
4 LANCHARDS
5 CHURCH RD
6 CANDY'S LA
C7
1 APPLE ACRE
2 JACOBS LADDER
3 THE CROSS
4 UPPER ST
5 ST NICHOLAS CT
6 HOMEFIELD
7 KNOTTS CL
8 ALLEN CL
9 CHALWELL
10 GREENWAY
11 MELWAY GDNS
12 THE BUTTS
C8
1 OLIVERS MD
2 MILLBROOK CL
3 MILLBROOK CT
4 NUTMEAD CL
5 PORTMAN DR
6 COMMON DRO
37
Scale: 1¾ inches to 1 mile
0 ¼ ½ mile
0 250m 500m 750m 1 km
A B C D E F
8 13 7 12 6 11 5 10 4 09 3 08 2 07 1 06
81 82 83 84 85 86
DT10
DT11
Gold Hill Poultry Farm
Ham Down Copse
Gold Hill
Tan-hill Copse
Dairy House Farm
Mill Ham Island Nature Reserve
Child Okeford
Church Farm
Laurel Farm
Manor House
Green Lines
Chalk Pit Farm
Hambledon Hill National Nature Reserve
Fort
Park Farm
ROMAN VILLA (SITE OF)
Preston Hill Plantation
Preston Hill
Shroton Lines
Bessells
Manor Farm
New Field Coppice
Iwerne Courtney or Shroton
Ranston Hill
Ranston
French Grass Coppice
Cross Dyke
Coombe Bottom
Coombe Wood
Neolithic Camp
Terrace Coppice
Wessex Ridgeway
Yew Wood
Hambledon Plantation
A357
A350
NEW CROSS GATE
Moat
Bere Marsh Farm
St Nicholas CE Prim Sch
Hambledon Farm
Conygar Coppice
Hayward Bridge
St Patricks Industrial Estate
Shillingstone CE Prim Sch
Cookwell Brook
The Forum School
Clayton Farm
Mill Farm
Langston Farm
Shillingstone
Alders Coppice
Little Hanford
Hanford
Hanford School
Hanford House
Nutcombe Wood
Leigh Wood
Stepleton House
Works
Sewage Works
Cliff Coppice
Shillingstone House
Hillsfoot Farm
Holloway Farm
Eastbrook Farm
Pillow Mounds
River Stour
The Cliff
Hod Wood
ROMAN FORT
Hod Hill
Little Coppice
Lazerton Farm
Ash
Gains Cross Farm
Tumulus
Okeford Hill
Cross Dyke
Chalk Quarry
Eastcombe Wood
Kite Hill Coppice
River Iwerne
Jubilee Trail
Stourpaine
Shillingstone Hill
Blandford Forest
Hillcombe Bottom
Enford Bottom
Enford Farm
Lower Pressham Wood
Higher Pressham Wood
Manor Farm
Refuse/Slag Heap
Poppins Farm
Turnworth Down
Tumuli
Ringmoor
National Trust
Bonsley Common
Hillcombe Coppice
Norton Wood
Durweston Bridge
Allot Gdns
France Oaks Coppice
Turnworth House
Shepherd's Corner Farm
The Folly
Sutcombe Wood
Durweston
Durweston CE First School
Manor France Farm
Knighton House School
Home Farm
The Cliff
Turnworth Farm
Turnworth
Free Down Border
Roundbush Wood
Four Acre Coppice
Lines Dean Bottom
Websley Farm
The Hanging
Bryanston School
Home Farm
Travellers' Rest
Rowbarrow
Field Grove
Morgan's Wood
Higher Barn Cottages
Tumulus
Hedge End Farm
Blackfern Plantation
Hedge End
Broadley Wood
Shothole
197
210
E3
1 WYNCHARD BANK
2 ST NICHOLAS GDNS
3 THE GLEBE
4 HAYCOMBE
F4
1 COACH RD
2 HOD VW
3 PARK CL
4 ORCHARD CL
5 ROWLANDS RD

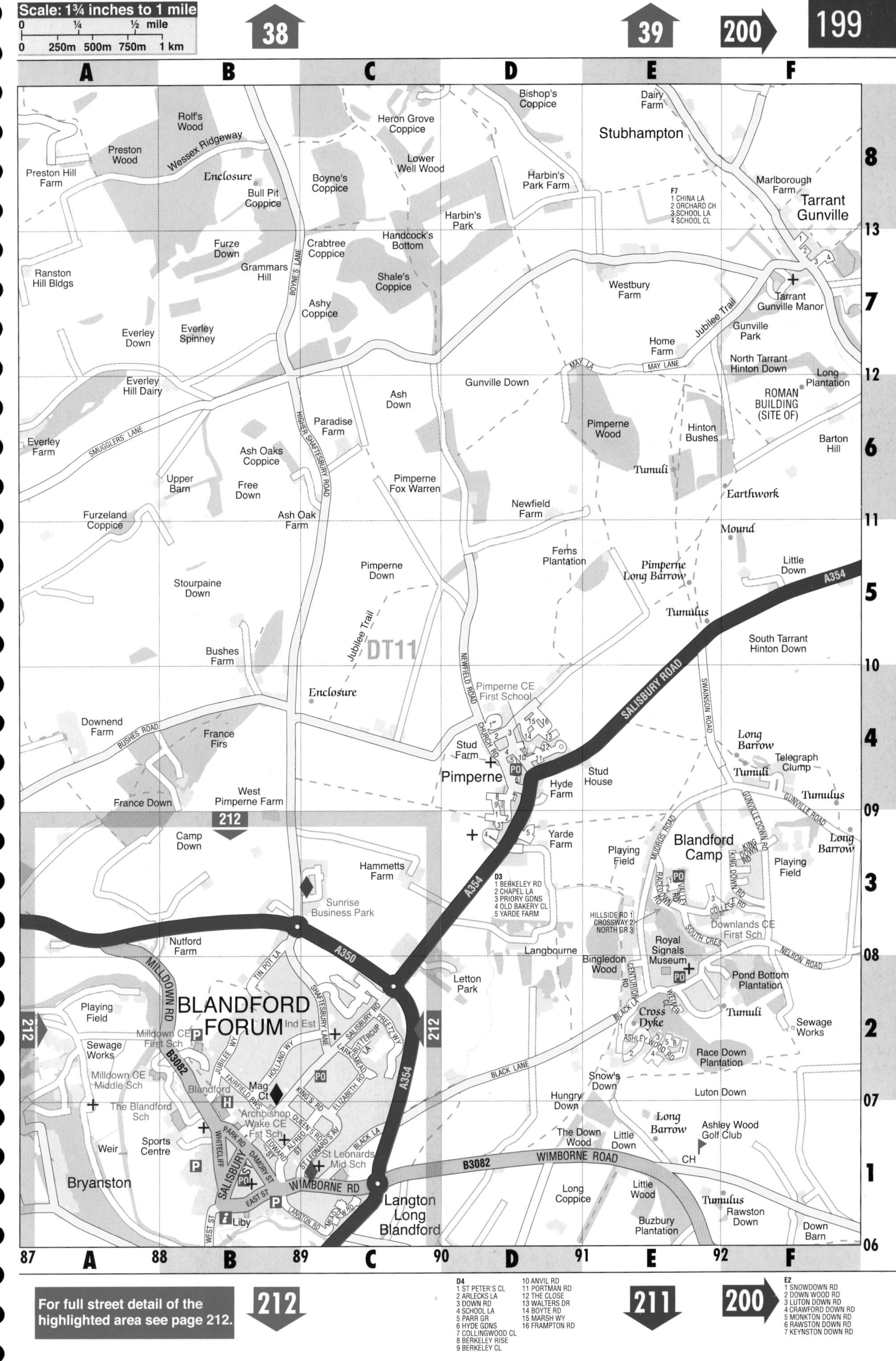

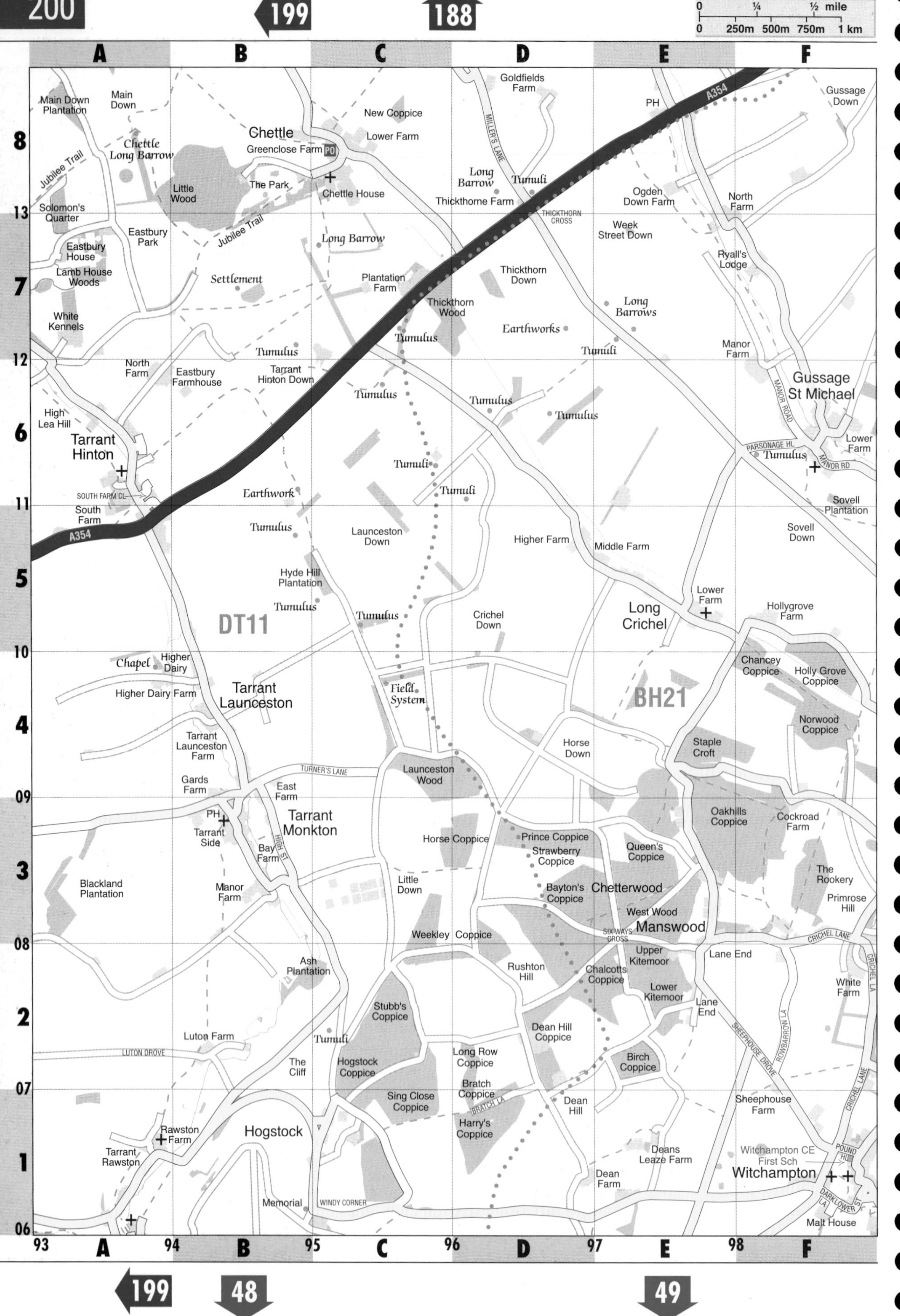

Scale: 1¾ inches to 1 mile

0   ¼   ½ mile
0   250m   500m   750m   1 km

Main Down Plantation
Main Down
Chettle Long Barrow
New Coppice
Lower Farm
Goldfields Farm
PH
A354
Gussage Down

Jubilee Trail
Chettle
Greenclose Farm PO
Long Barrow
Tumuli
Ogden Down Farm
North Farm

Solomon's Quarter
The Park
Chettle House
Thickthorne Farm
THICKTHORN CROSS
Week Street Down
Ryall's Lodge

Eastbury House
Eastbury Park
Long Barrow
Thickthorn Down
Manor Farm

Lamb House Woods
Settlement
Plantation Farm
Thickthorn Wood
Long Barrows
Gussage St Michael

White Kennels
Tumulus
Earthworks
Tumuli
PARSONAGE HL
Tumulus
MANOR ROAD
Lower Farm

North Farm
Eastbury Farmhouse
Tarrant Hinton Down
Tumulus
Tumulus
Tumulus
Sovell Plantation

High Lea Hill
Earthwork
Tumuli
Tumulus
Tumuli
Higher Farm
Middle Farm
Sovell Down
Hollygrove Farm

Tarrant Hinton
SOUTH FARM CL
South Farm
A354
Earthwork
Tumulus
Launceston Down
Long Crichel
Lower Farm

Hyde Hill Plantation
Tumulus
Crichel Down
Chancey Coppice
Holly Grove Coppice

DT11
Tumulus
Chapel
Higher Dairy
Field System
BH21
Norwood Coppice

Higher Dairy Farm
Tarrant Launceston
Launceston Wood
Horse Down
Staple Croft
Oakhills Coppice
Cockroad Farm

Gards Farm
East Farm
TURNER'S LANE
Queen's Coppice
The Rookery

PH
Tarrant Side
Tarrant Monkton
Bay Farm
Horse Coppice
Prince Coppice
Strawberry Coppice
Bayton's Coppice
Chetterwood
West Wood
Manswood
Primrose Hill

Blackland Plantation
Manor Farm
Little Down
Weekley Coppice
SIX-WAYS CROSS
Lane End
CRICHEL LANE
White Farm

Ash Plantation
Rushton Hill
Chalcotts Coppice
Upper Kitemoor
Lower Kitemoor
Lane End

Luton Farm
Stubb's Coppice
Dean Hill Coppice
Birch Coppice
SHEEPHOUSE DRIVE
ROWBARROW LA

LUTON DROVE
Tumuli
The Cliff
Hogstock Coppice
Long Row Coppice
Dean Hill
Sheephouse Farm
CRICHEL LANE

Rawston Farm
Hogstock
Sing Close Coppice
Bratch Coppice
BRATCH LA
Harry's Coppice
Dean Hill
Deans Leaze Farm
Witchampton CE First Sch
Witchampton
POUND HILL

Tarrant Rawston
Memorial
WINDY CORNER
Dean Farm
OAKLOWER LA
Malt House

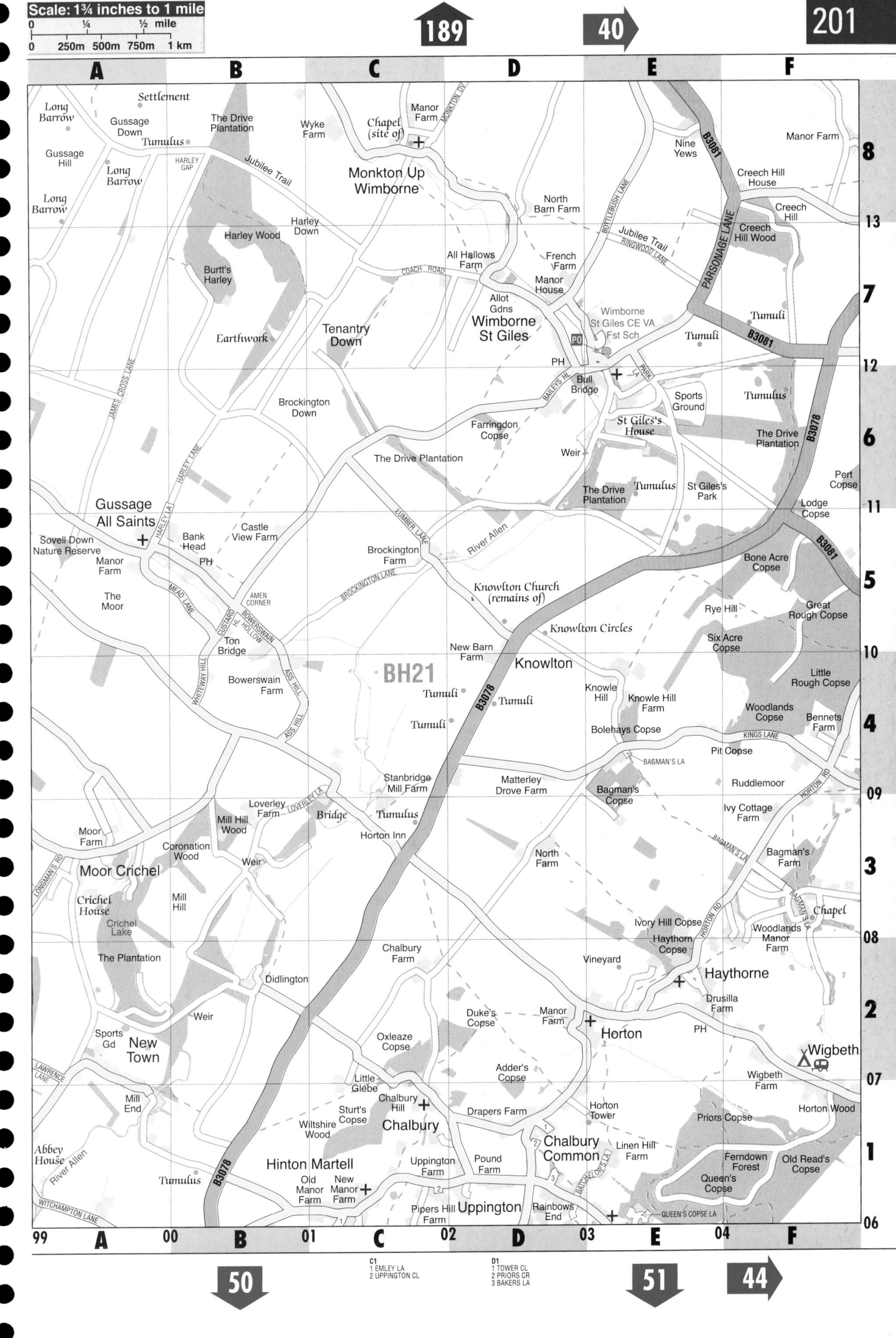
Scale: 1¾ inches to 1 mile
0 ¼ ½ mile
0 250m 500m 750m 1 km
189
40
A B C D E F
8
13
7
12
6
11
5
10
4
09
3
08
2
07
1
06
99 00 01 02 03 04
Long Barrow
Settlement
Gussage Down
Tumulus
The Drive Plantation
Wyke Farm
Chapel (site of)
Manor Farm
MONKTON DV
Nine Yews
B3081
Manor Farm
Gussage Hill
Long Barrow
HARLEY GAP
Jubilee Trail
Monkton Up Wimborne
Creech Hill House
Long Barrow
North Barn Farm
BOTTLEBUSH LANE
Creech Hill
Harley Down
Harley Wood
Jubilee Trail
RINGWOOD LANE
PARSONAGE LANE
Creech Hill Wood
Burtt's Harley
All Hallows Farm
COACH ROAD
French Farm
Manor House
Allot Gdns
Wimborne St Giles
Wimborne St Giles CE VA Fst Sch
Tumuli
Tenantry Down
Earthwork
PO
Tumuli
B3081
PH
PARK LA
JAMES CROSS LANE
Bull Bridge
BAILEYS HL
Brockington Down
Sports Ground
Tumulus
Farringdon Copse
St Giles's House
The Drive Plantation
B3078
The Drive Plantation
Weir
HARLEY LANE
The Drive Plantation
Tumulus
St Giles's Park
Pert Copse
Gussage All Saints
HARLEY LA
Lodge Copse
Castle View Farm
LUMBER LANE
River Allen
Sovell Down Nature Reserve
Bank Head
B3081
Brockington Farm
Manor Farm
PH
Bone Acre Copse
MEAD LANE
BROCKINGTON LANE
AMEN CORNER
Knowlton Church (remains of)
The Moor
Great Rough Copse
Rye Hill
CUSTARD HL
BOWERSWAIN HOLLOW
Knowlton Circles
Ton Bridge
Six Acre Copse
New Barn Farm
Knowlton
WHITEWAY HILL
BH21
Little Rough Copse
Bowerswain Farm
ASS HILL
Knowle Hill
Tumuli
B3078
Tumuli
Knowle Hill Farm
Woodlands Copse
Bennets Farm
Tumuli
ASS HILL
Bolehays Copse
KINGS LANE
Pit Copse
BAGMAN'S LA
Stanbridge Mill Farm
Matterley Drove Farm
Bagman's Copse
Ruddlemoor
HORTON RD
Loverley Farm
LOVERLEY LA
Mill Hill Wood
Bridge
Tumulus
Ivy Cottage Farm
Horton Inn
Moor Farm
Coronation Wood
BAGMAN'S LA
North Farm
Bagman's Farm
LONGMAN'S RD
Weir
Moor Crichel
Crichel House
Mill Hill
Ivory Hill Copse
HORTON RD
BAGMAN'S LA
Chapel
Crichel Lake
Haythorn Copse
Woodlands Manor Farm
Chalbury Farm
The Plantation
Vineyard
Haythorne
Didlington
Drusilla Farm
Weir
Duke's Copse
Manor Farm
Horton
PH
Sports Gd
New Town
Oxleaze Copse
Wigbeth
LAWRENCE LANE
Adder's Copse
Wigbeth Farm
Little Glebe
Mill End
Chalbury Hill
Horton Tower
Horton Wood
Sturt's Copse
Drapers Farm
Priors Copse
Wiltshire Wood
Chalbury
Abbey House
Chalbury Common
Linen Hill Farm
River Allen
Ferndown Forest
Old Read's Copse
Hinton Martell
Uppington Farm
Pound Farm
Queen's Copse
BATCHELOR'S LA
Tumulus
B3078
Old Manor Farm
New Manor Farm
WITCHAMPTON LANE
Pipers Hill Farm
Uppington
Rainbows End
QUEEN'S COPSE LA
50
C1
1 EMLEY LA
2 UPPINGTON CL
D1
1 TOWER CL
2 PRIORS CR
3 BAKERS LA
51
44

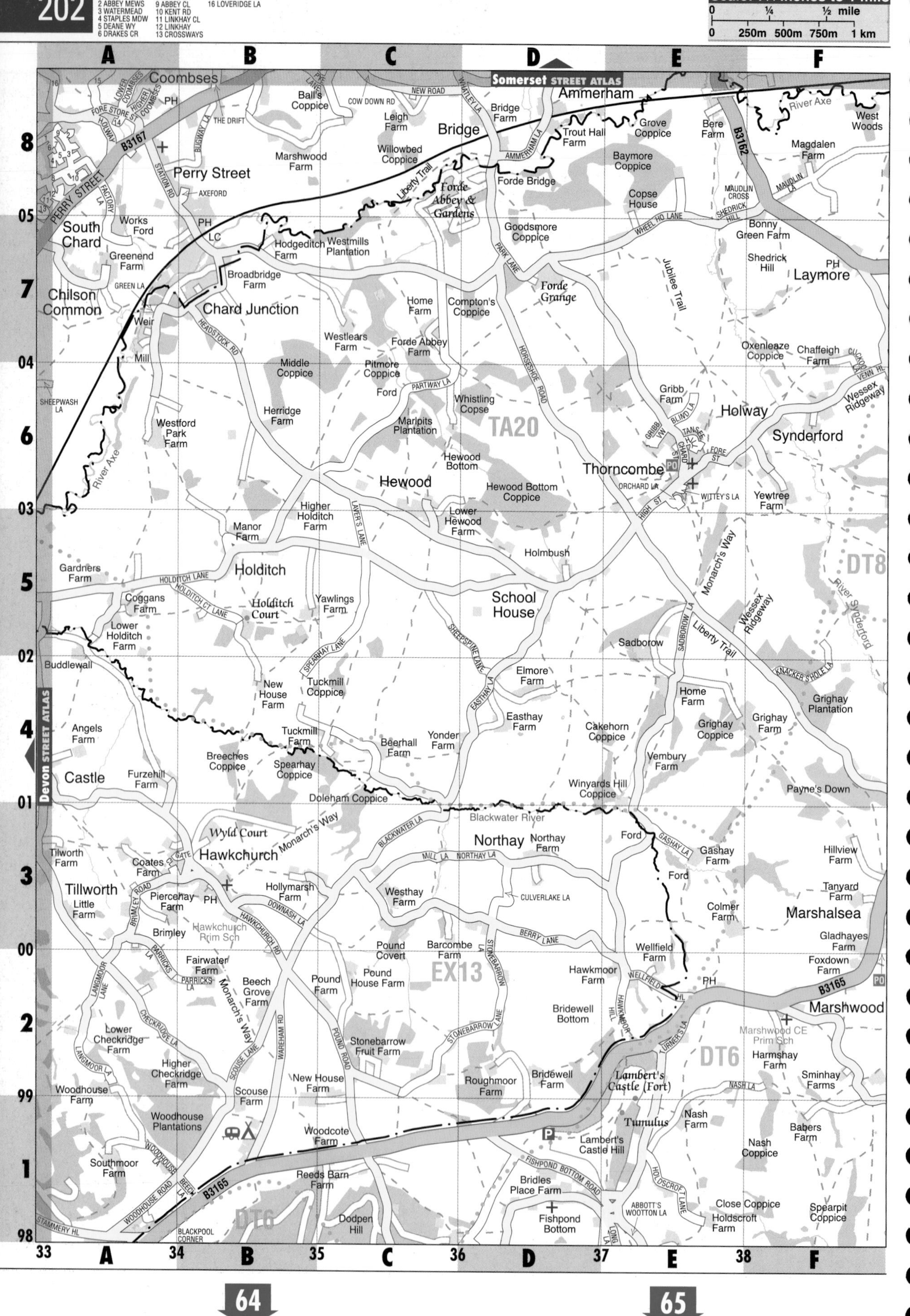

A8
1 LANGDONS WY
2 ABBEY MEWS
3 WATERMEAD
4 STAPLES MDW
5 DEANE WY
6 DRAKES CR
7 GULWAY MD
8 KENTS LA
9 ABBEY CL
10 KENT RD
11 LINKHAY CL
12 LINKHAY
13 CROSSWAYS
14 HOLLEYS CL
15 STOWELL LA
16 LOVERIDGE LA

Scale: 1¾ inches to 1 mile

0   ¼   ½ mile
0   250m   500m   750m   1 km

Somerset STREET ATLAS

Devon STREET ATLAS

Coombses
Ammerham
West Woods
Bridge
Perry Street
South Chard
Chilson Common
Chard Junction
Laymore
Holway
Synderford
Thorncombe
TA20
DT8
Hewood
Holditch
School House
Sadborow
EX13
Hawkchurch
Northay
Marshalsea
Tillworth
Castle
Marshwood
DT6
DT6
Lambert's Castle (Fort)
Marshwood

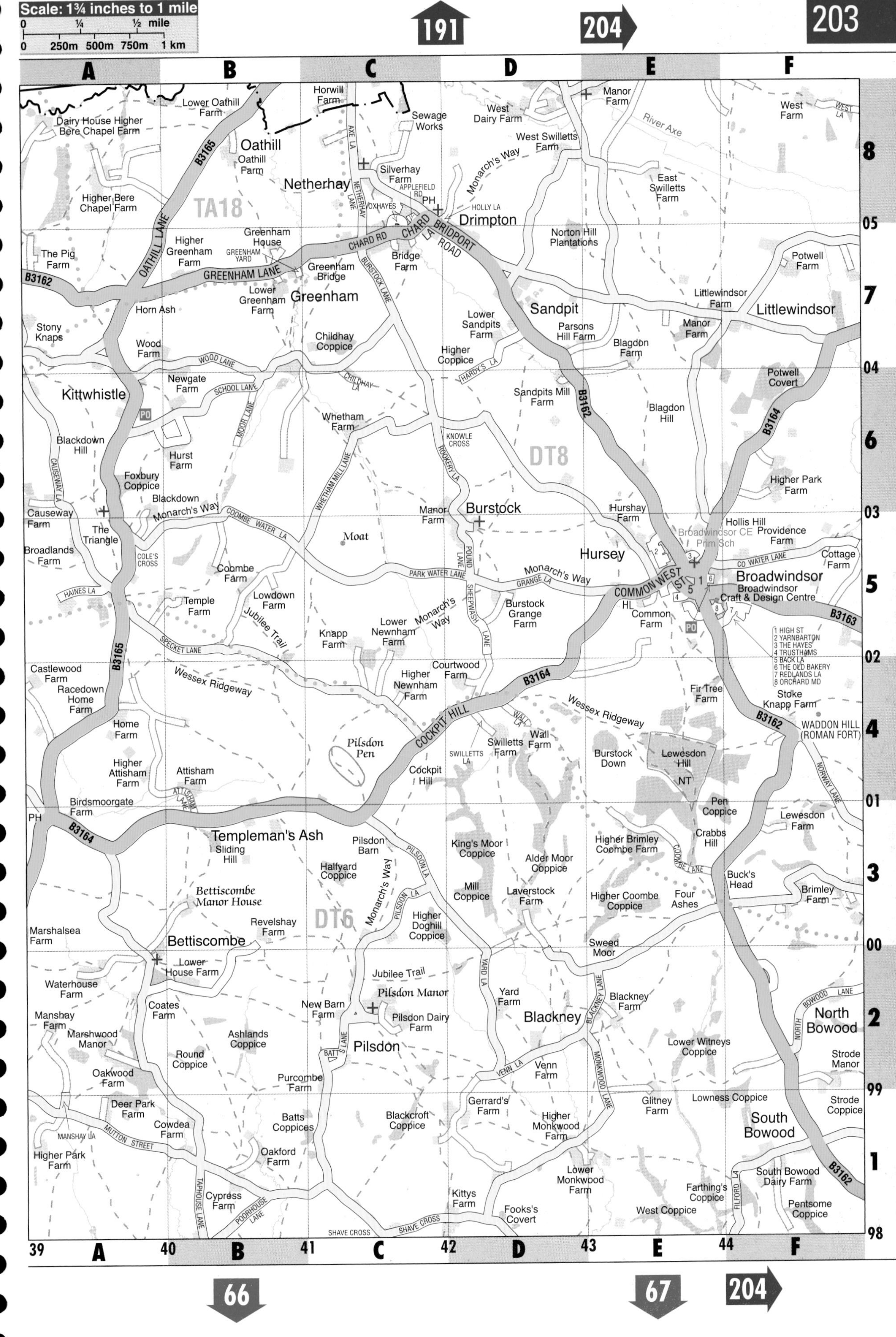
Scale: 1¾ inches to 1 mile
0 ¼ ½ mile
0 250m 500m 750m 1 km
191
204
A
B
C
D
E
F
8
05
7
04
6
03
5
02
4
01
3
00
2
99
1
98
39
40
41
42
43
44
66
67
204
Lower Oathill Farm
Horwill Farm
Sewage Works
Manor Farm
West Dairy Farm
West Farm
WEST LA
River Axe
Dairy House Higher Bere Chapel Farm
Oathill
Oathill Farm
B3165
AXE LA
West Swilletts Farm
Monarch's Way
Silverhay Farm
APPLEFIELD RD
PH
Netherhay
NETHERHAY LANE
OXHAYES
HOLLY LA
Drimpton
East Swilletts Farm
Higher Bere Chapel Farm
TA18
Greenham House
Higher Greenham Farm
GREENHAM YARD
CHARD RD
CHARD
BRIDPORT ROAD
LA
Norton Hill Plantations
The Pig Farm
OATHILL LANE
Bridge Farm
Potwell Farm
B3162
GREENHAM LANE
Greenham Bridge
BURSTOCK LANE
Lower Greenham Farm
Greenham
Littlewindsor Farm
Littlewindsor
Sandpit
Horn Ash
Lower Sandpits Farm
Parsons Hill Farm
Manor Farm
Stony Knaps
Childhay Coppice
Blagdon Farm
Wood Farm
WOOD LANE
Higher Coppice
HARDY'S LA
Newgate Farm
SCHOOL LANE
CHILDHAY LA
Potwell Covert
Kittwhistle
PO
MOOR LANE
Sandpits Mill Farm
Blagdon Hill
Whetham Farm
B3164
Blackdown Hill
KNOWLE CROSS
DT8
WHETHAM MILL LANE
ROOKERY LA
Hurst Farm
CAUSEWAY LA
Foxbury Coppice
Higher Park Farm
Blackdown
Monarch's Way
Manor Farm
Burstock
Causeway Farm
COOMBE WATER LA
Hurshay Farm
Hollis Hill
The Triangle
Moat
Broadwindsor CE Prim Sch
Providence Farm
Broadlands Farm
POUND LANE
Hursey
CO WATER LANE
Cottage Farm
COLE'S CROSS
Coombe Farm
PARK WATER LANE
Monarch's Way
GRANGE LA
COMMON WEST ST
Broadwindsor
Broadwindsor Craft & Design Centre
HAINES LA
Lowdown Farm
SHEEPWASH LANE
HL
Temple Farm
Jubilee Trail
Monarch's Way
Burstock Grange Farm
Common Farm
B3163
Lower Newnham Farm
Knapp Farm
1 HIGH ST
2 YARNBARTON
3 THE HAYES
4 TRUSTHAMS
5 BACK LA
6 THE OLD BAKERY
7 REDLANDS LA
8 ORCHARD MD
SPECKET LANE
Courtwood Farm
Castlewood Farm
Higher Newnham Farm
Wessex Ridgeway
Fir Tree Farm
Racedown Home Farm
Stoke Knapp Farm
Wessex Ridgeway
Home Farm
COCKPIT HILL
WALL LA
Pilsdon Pen
Swilletts Farm
Wall Farm
WADDON HILL (ROMAN FORT)
Burstock Down
Lewesdon Hill
SWILLETTS LA
NT
Higher Attisham Farm
Attisham Farm
Cockpit Hill
NORWAY LANE
ATTISHAM LANE
Birdsmoorgate Farm
Pen Coppice
PH
Lewesdon Farm
Templeman's Ash
Pilsdon Barn
Crabbs Hill
Sliding Hill
King's Moor Coppice
Higher Brimley Coombe Farm
PILSDON LA
COOMBE LANE
Halfyard Coppice
Alder Moor Coppice
Buck's Head
Bettiscombe Manor House
Monarch's Way
Mill Coppice
Laverstock Farm
Higher Coombe Coppice
Four Ashes
Brimley Farm
Revelshay Farm
Higher Doghill Coppice
DT6
Marshalsea Farm
Bettiscombe
Sweed Moor
YARD LA
Lower House Farm
Jubilee Trail
Waterhouse Farm
Yard Farm
BLACKNEY LANE
Blackney Farm
Pilsdon Manor
BOWOOD LANE
North Bowood
Coates Farm
New Barn Farm
Manshay Farm
Pilsdon Dairy Farm
Blackney
NORTH
Marshwood Manor
Ashlands Coppice
Lower Witneys Coppice
BATT'S LANE
Pilsdon
MONKWOOD LANE
Strode Manor
Round Coppice
VENN LA
Venn Farm
Oakwood Farm
Purcombe Farm
Gerrard's Farm
Glitney Farm
Lowness Coppice
Strode Coppice
Deer Park Farm
Batts Coppices
Blackcroft Coppice
Higher Monkwood Farm
South Bowood
Cowdea Farm
MANSHAY LA
MUTTON STREET
Higher Park Farm
Oakford Farm
Lower Monkwood Farm
South Bowood Dairy Farm
FILFORD LA
Farthing's Coppice
Cypress Farm
Kittys Farm
Pentsome Coppice
POORHOUSE LANE
TAPHOUSE LANE
Fooks's Covert
West Coppice
SHAVE CROSS
SHAVE CROSS

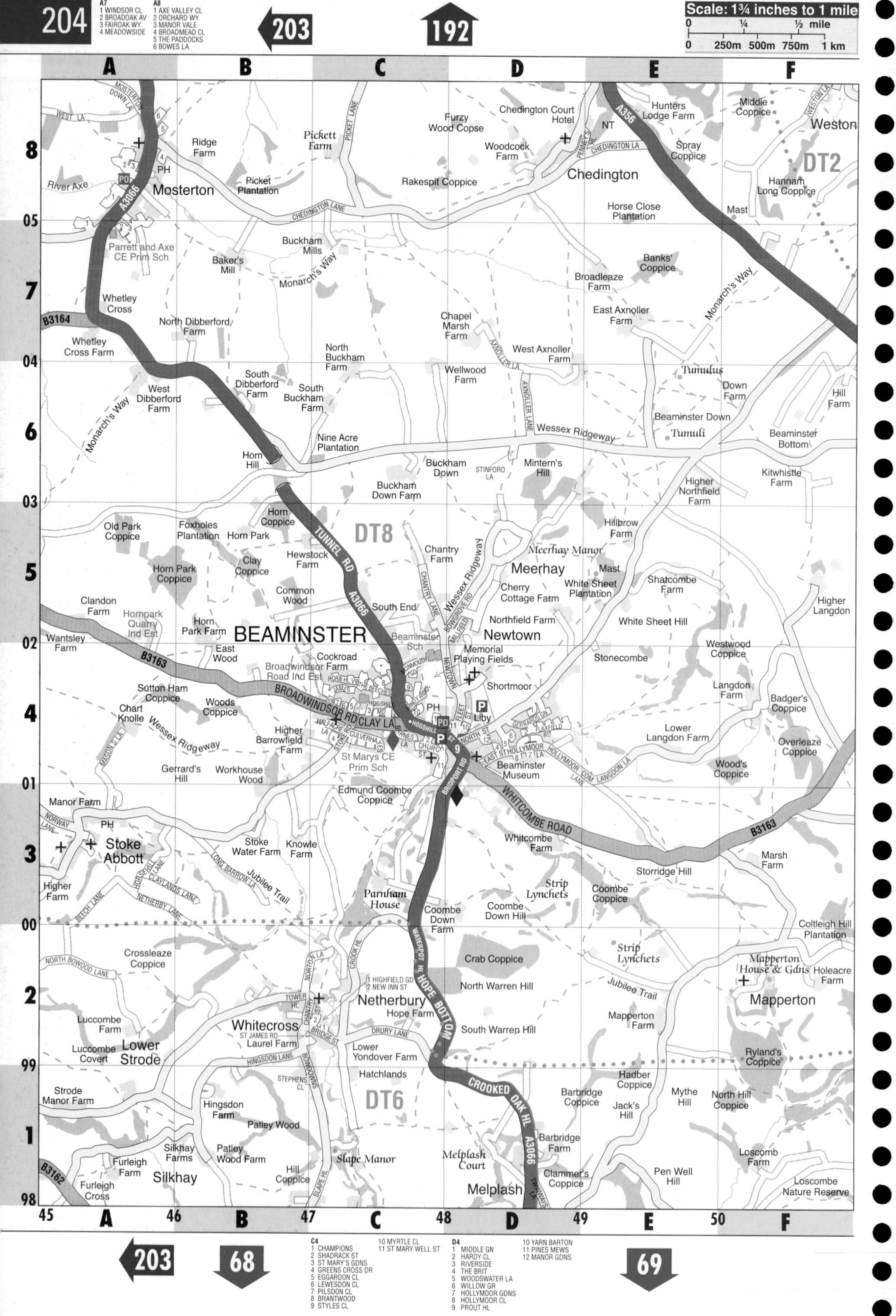

204
A7
1 WINDSOR CL
2 BROADOAK AV
3 FAIRDAK WY
4 MEADOWSIDE
A8
1 AXE VALLEY CL
2 ORCHARD WY
3 MANOR VALE
4 BROADMEAD CL
5 THE PADDOCKS
6 BOWES LA
203
192
Scale: 1¾ inches to 1 mile
0 ¼ ½ mile
0 250m 500m 750m 1 km
A B C D E F
8 05 7 04 6 03 5 02 4 01 3 00 2 99 1 98
45 46 47 48 49 50
Mosterton
River Axe
Parrett and Axe CE Prim Sch
Ridge Farm
Pickett Farm
Picket Plantation
Furzy Wood Copse
Chedington Court Hotel
Woodcock Farm
Rakespit Coppice
Chedington
Hunters Lodge Farm
Spray Coppice
Middle Coppice
Weston
DT2
Hannam Long Coppice
Mast
Horse Close Plantation
Buckham Mills
Baker's Mill
Monarch's Way
Banks' Coppice
Broadleaze Farm
Whetley Cross
B3164
Whetley Cross Farm
North Dibberford Farm
Chapel Marsh Farm
East Axnoller Farm
West Axnoller Farm
North Buckham Farm
South Dibberford Farm
South Buckham Farm
West Dibberford Farm
Wellwood Farm
Tumulus
Down Farm
Hill Farm
Beaminster Down
Tumuli
Beaminster Bottom
Wessex Ridgeway
Nine Acre Plantation
Horn Hill
Buckham Down
Mintern's Hill
Buckham Down Farm
Higher Northfield Farm
Kitwhistle Farm
Old Park Coppice
Foxholes Plantation
Horn Park
Horn Coppice
DT8
Hillbrow Farm
Chantry Farm
Meerhay Manor
Meerhay
Mast
Horn Park Coppice
Clay Coppice
Hewstock Farm
Cherry Cottage Farm
White Sheet Plantation
Shatcombe Farm
Clandon Farm
Hornpark Quarry Ind Est
Common Wood
South End
Northfield Farm
White Sheet Hill
Higher Langdon
Wantsley Farm
Horn Park Farm
BEAMINSTER
Beaminster Sch
Newtown
Memorial Playing Fields
Stonecombe
Westwood Coppice
East Wood
Cockroad Farm
Broadwindsor Road Ind Est
Shortmoor
Langdon Farm
Badger's Coppice
Sutton Ham Coppice
Woods Coppice
Chart Knolle
Higher Barrowfield Farm
Liby
Lower Langdon Farm
Overleaze Coppice
Gerrard's Hill
Workhouse Wood
St Marys CE Prim Sch
Beaminster Museum
Wood's Coppice
Manor Farm
Edmund Coombe Coppice
WHITCOMBE ROAD
B3163
Stoke Abbott
Stoke Water Farm
Knowle Farm
Whitcombe Farm
Marsh Farm
Storridge Hill
Higher Farm
Jubilee Trail
Parnham House
Strip Lynchets
Coombe Coppice
Coombe Down Farm
Coombe Down Hill
Coltleigh Hill Plantation
Crossleaze Coppice
Crab Coppice
Strip Lynchets
Mapperton House & Gdns
Holeacre Farm
North Warren Hill
Netherbury
Hope Farm
Mapperton
Mapperton Farm
Luccombe Farm
Whitecross
Laurel Farm
South Warren Hill
Luccombe Covert
Lower Strode
Lower Yondover Farm
Ryland's Coppice
Hatchlands
Hadber Coppice
Strode Manor Farm
DT6
Barbridge Coppice
Jack's Hill
Mythe Hill
North Hill Coppice
Hingsdon Farm
Patley Wood
Barbridge Farm
Silkhay Farms
Patley Wood Farm
Slape Manor
Melplash Court
Loscomb Farm
Furleigh Farm
Silkhay
Hill Coppice
Clammer's Coppice
Pen Well Hill
Furleigh Cross
Melplash
Loscombe Nature Reserve
B3162
A3066
A356
TUNNEL RD
BROADWINDSOR RD
CLAY LA
BRIDPORT RD
HOPE BOTTOM
CROOKED OAK HL
CHEDINGTON LANE
CHEDINGTON LA
AXNOLLER LA
AXNOLLER LANE
STINFORD LA
CHANTRY LANE
BOWGROVE RD
NEWTOWN
FLEET ST
NORTH ST
EAST ST
HOLLYMOOR LA
HOLLYMOOR COM LANE
LANGDON LA
GERRARDS GN
FAXFIELD RD
HOGSHILL ST
CHURCH ST
CULVERHAYES
HALFACRE RD
STONE LA
MASON'S LA
NORWAY LANE
HORSEHILL LANE
CLAYLANDS LANE
NETHERBY LANE
BEECH LANE
LONG BARROW LA
NORTH BOWOOD LANE
CROOK HL
NORTON LA
TOWER HL
CHANTRY ST
BRIDGE ST
DRURY LANE
WATERPOT HL
1 HIGHFIELD GD
2 NEW INN ST
HINGSDON LANE
BOWDOWNS
STEPHENS CL
ST JAMES RD
SLAPE HL
WEST LA
MOSTERTON DOWN LA
WESTON LA
NT
PH
PO
P
203
68
69
C4
1 CHAMPIONS
2 SHADRACK ST
3 ST MARY'S GDNS
4 GREENS CROSS DR
5 EGGARDON CL
6 LEWESDON CL
7 PILSDON CL
8 BRANTWOOD
9 STYLES CL
10 MYRTLE CL
11 ST MARY WELL ST
D4
1 MIDDLE GN
2 HARDY CL
3 RIVERSIDE
4 THE BRIT
5 WOODSWATER LA
6 WILLOW GR
7 HOLLYMOOR GDNS
8 HOLLYMOOR CL
9 PROUT HL
10 YARN BARTON
11 PINES MEWS
12 MANOR GDNS

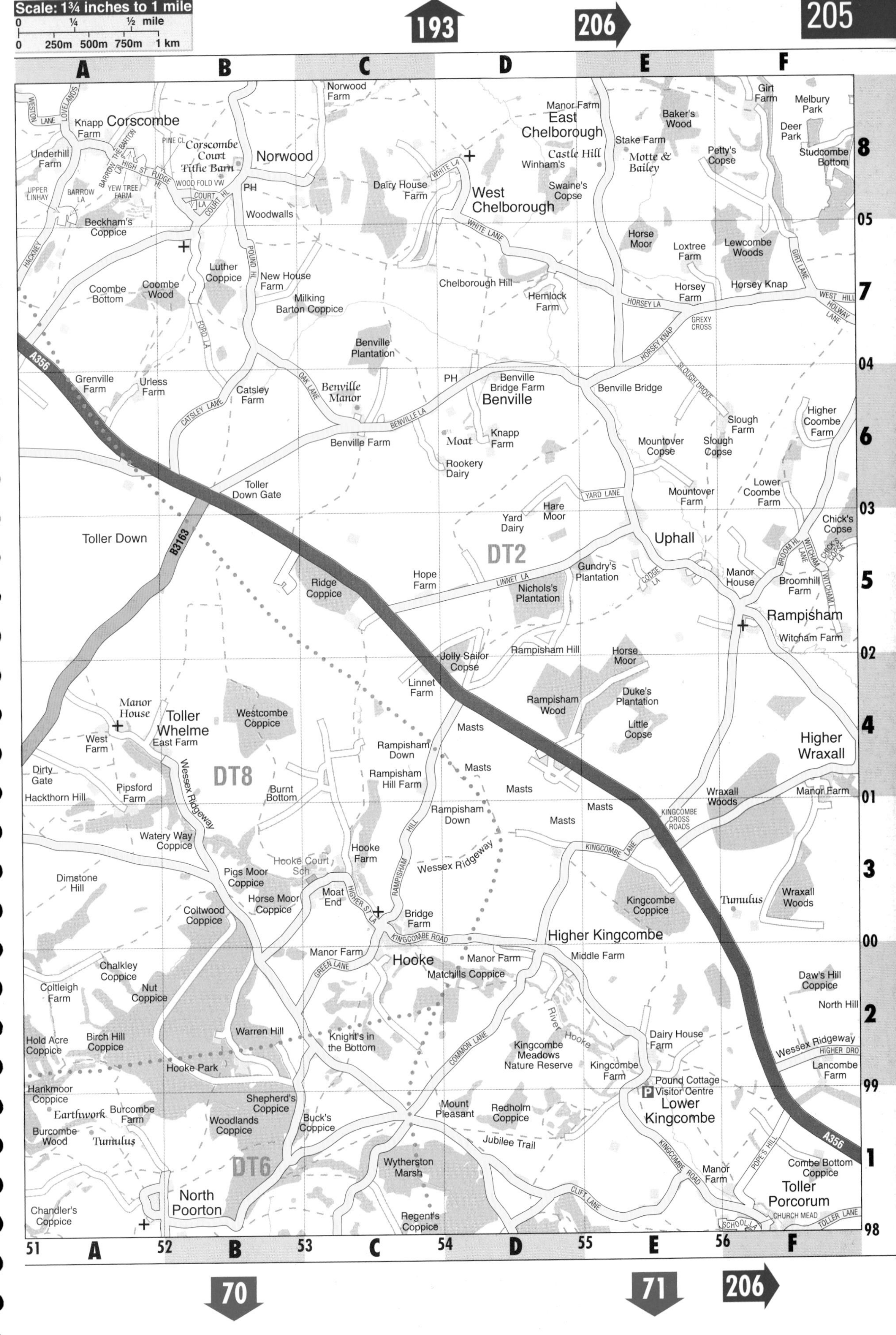
Scale: 1¾ inches to 1 mile
193
206
Corscombe
Norwood
East Chelborough
West Chelborough
Benville
Uphall
Rampisham
Toller Whelme
Higher Wraxall
Hooke
Higher Kingcombe
Lower Kingcombe
North Poorton
Toller Porcorum
Toller Down
DT2
DT8
DT6
A356
B3163
Wessex Ridgeway
Jubilee Trail
70
71
206

← 205
↑ 194

Scale: 1¾ inches to 1 mile

0 ¼ ½ mile
0 250m 500m 750m 1 km

A B C D E F

Melbury Sampford
Melbury Lake
Sares Wood
Bubb Down Plantation
Redford
Cockeram's Plantation
Lodge Farm
Melbury Park
Banger's Moor
Hazel Wood
Lower Woolcombe Farm
Redford Farm
Deansbrook Farm
Paradise Wood
Ash Copse
Hazel Farm
Higher Redford Farm
Newlands Farm
Parlour Moor
Evershot Plantation
Woolcombe Farm
Higher Woolcombe Farm
Baker's Moor
Dyers Farm
Highlands Farm
Great Head
05
TANYARD
PH.
BACK LA
THE COMMON
EAST HL
EAST HL
BLIND LA
BLIND LA
Holywell Farm
Spring Plantation
Alder Moor
Haydoh Wood
Harris Farm
Court Farm
Batcombe
Flower's Moor
WEST HILL
FORE ST
Sticklands VA Prim Sch
Burl Farm
Larkham Farm
Holywell
Horchester
HAYDON LANE
Hendover Coppice
Evershot
SUMMER LANE
Macmillan Way
Burl Farm
Horchester Farm
Horchester Copse
Batcombe Hill
East Hill
Batcombe Down
04
West Woods Farm
Dry Hill Moor
Burl Moor
CHANTMARLE LANE
LONG ASH LANE
STILE WY
STILE WY
West Woods Plantations
Fortunes Wood Farm
Chantmarle Moor
Wardon Hill Farm
White's Wood
Row Hill Coppice
03
HOLWAY LANE
Hillcrest Farm
SHORT CROSS
Frome Park Coppice
Brookway Farm
LONG ASH LANE
Sydling Woods
East Coppice
CHICK'S COPSE LA
Voss's Moor
Dawes Barton Farm
Park Farm
Manor Farm
Frome St Quintin
DT2
Clay Pigeon Raceway
Fisher's Bottom Coppice
Sydling Woods
Tumuli
Little Coppice
East Hill
02
Dudley Moor
Sewage Works
CHANTMARLE LA
CHANTMARLE LA
Chantmarle
Barnhayes Farm
Wardon Hill
Fisher's Bottom
Cross Hill
Inpark Farm
River Frome
Chantmarle Farm
Higher Chalmington
Old Wood
Ayles's Hill Bottom
01
West Holway
Macmillan Way
North Holway Farm
Holway Farm
Higher Chalmington Farm
Brookway Farm
Ayles's Hill
Stagg's Folly
North Field Hill
Lower Wraxall Farm
Lanes End
Chalmington Farm
Eweleaze Coppice
Loscombe Bottom
Tumulus
Chalkcombe Plantation
Lower Wraxall
WRAXALL LANE
Sandhills
Manor
Chalmington
Norton Plantation
Charity Bottom
00
South Wraxall Farm
Daw's Hill
Prospect Farm
Castle Hill
Tumulus
Castle Hill (Fort)
Castle Plantation
Lankham Bottom
Folly Hill
Peak End Hill
Grove Stall Farm
PO
PH
DUCK ST
Manor Farm
Lankham Bottom
The Coombe
99
Wessex Ridgeway
HIGHER DROVE
WRAXALL LA
ST HELEN'S LA
Cattistock
1 MEADOW CL
2 CAMPION WLK
3 BEECH TREE CL
Court House
Home Farm
Wallis Farm
Norden Hill
New Barn
Break Heart Hill
Half Moon Coppice
Chilfrome
Macmillan Way
Norden Farm
Combe Bottom
Wessex Ridgeway
Plain Bottom
Combe Hill
Fisher's Bottom
98
A356
TOLLER LA
Tumulus
Whitesheet Hill
WEBBERS PIECE
CATTISTOCK RD
A37

57 A 58 B 59 C 60 D 61 E 62 F

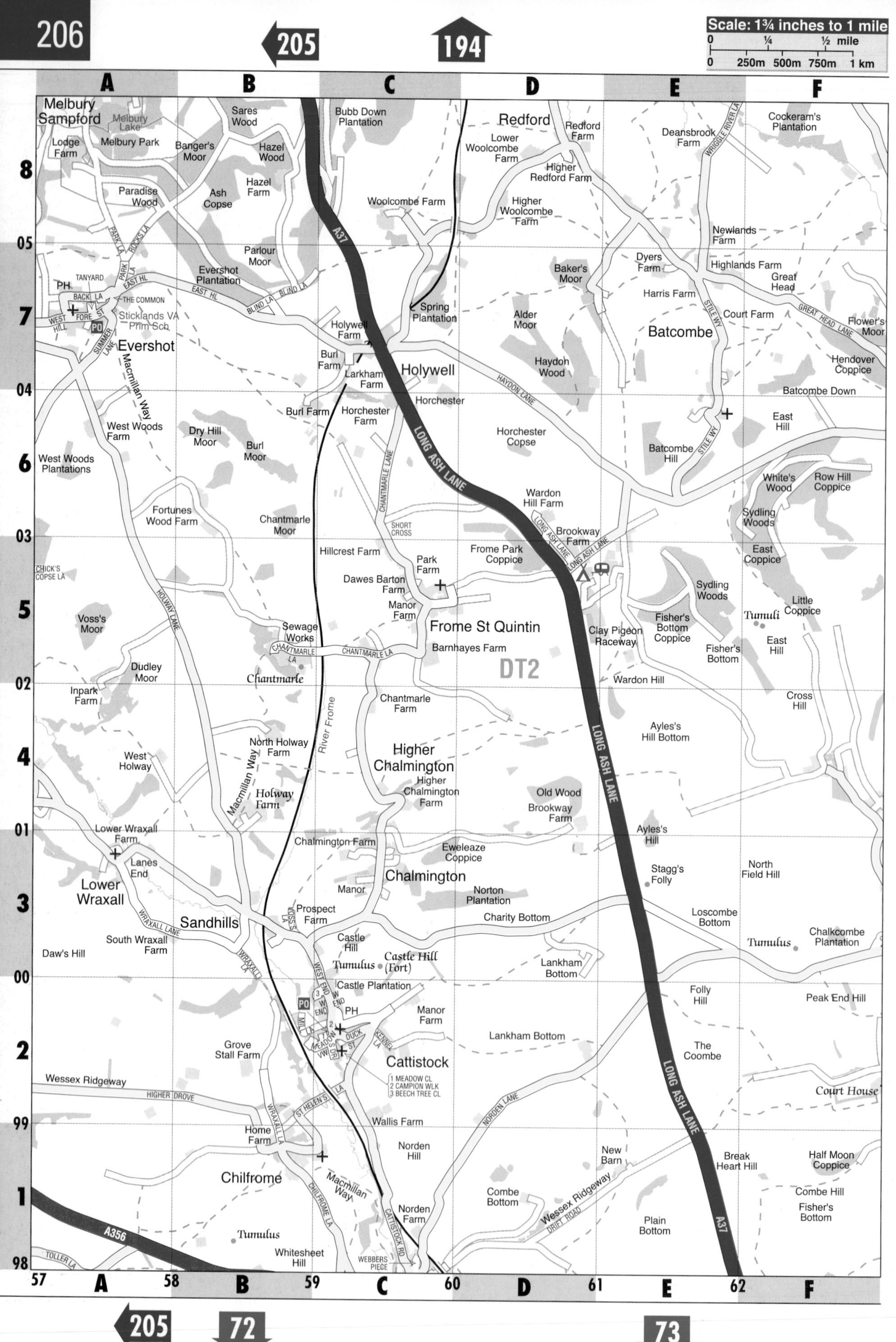

← 205
72
73 ↓

Scale: 1¾ inches to 1 mile

0   ¼   ½ mile
0 250m 500m 750m 1 km

195

208

207

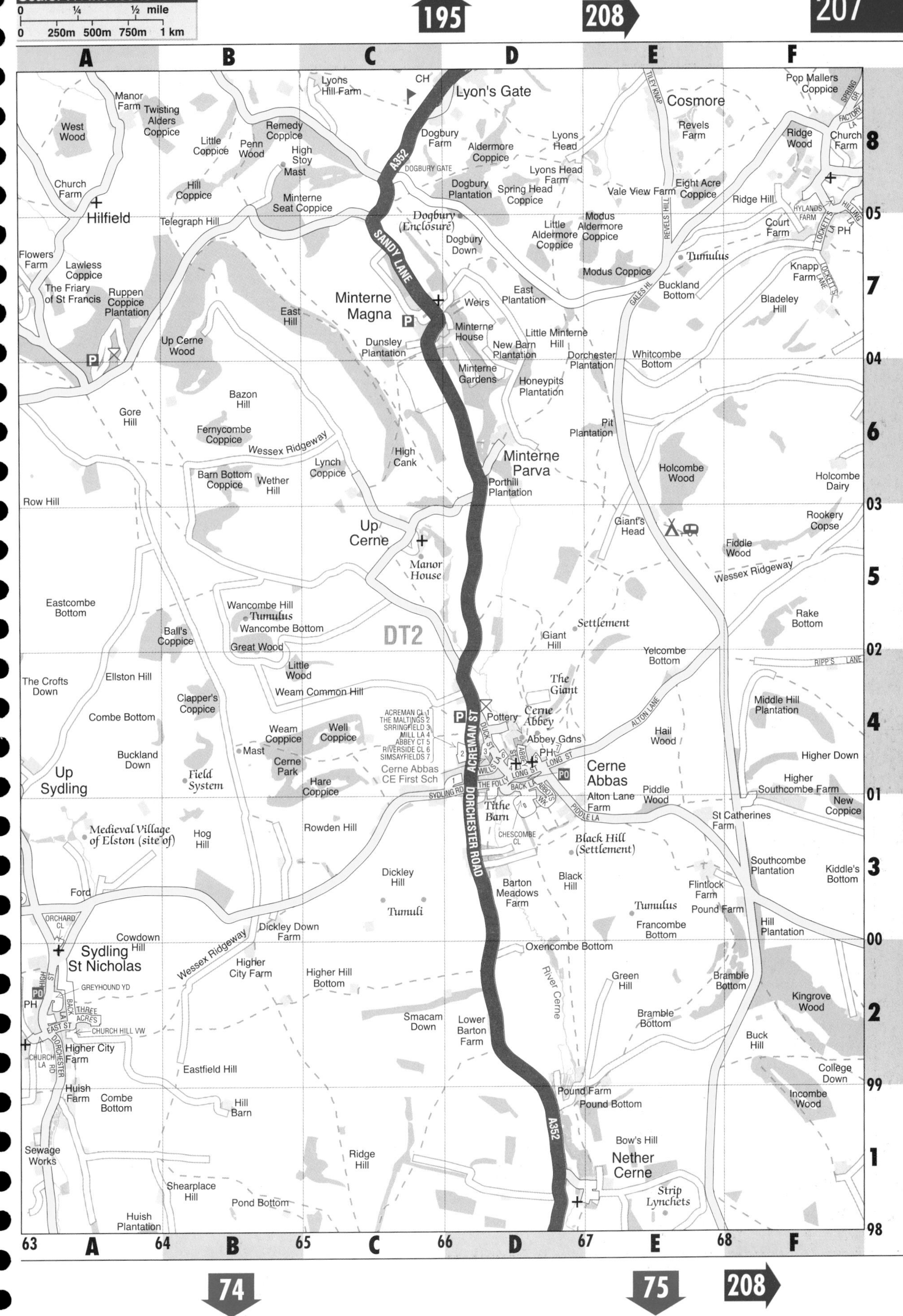

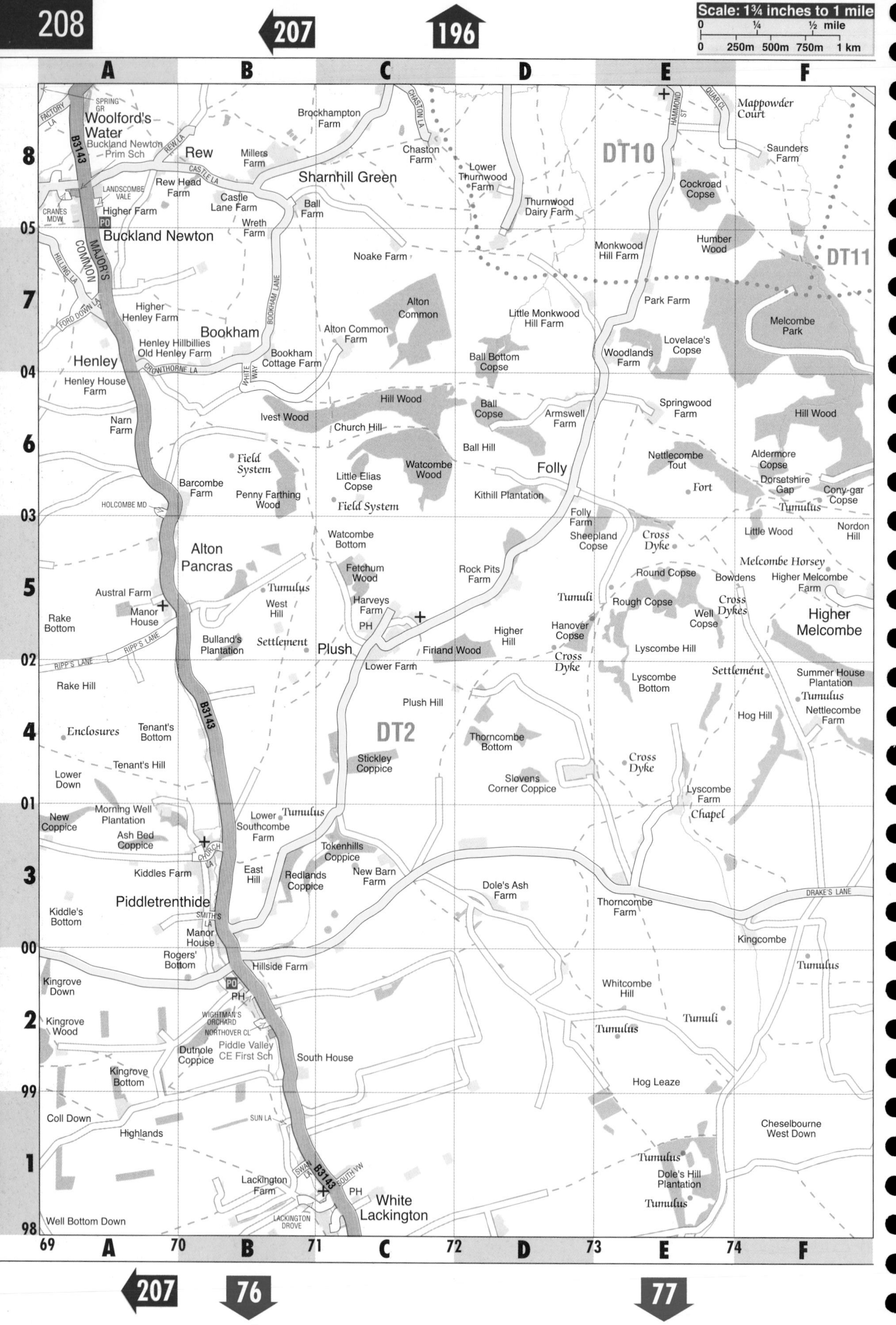
207
196
Scale: 1¾ inches to 1 mile
0 ¼ ½ mile
0 250m 500m 750m 1 km
A B C D E F
8
05
7
04
6
03
5
02
4
01
3
00
2
99
1
98
69 70 71 72 73 74
DT10
DT11
DT2
Woolford's Water
Buckland Newton Prim Sch
Rew
Millers Farm
Brockhampton Farm
Chaston Farm
Lower Thurnwood Farm
Mappowder Court
Saunders Farm
Rew Head Farm
Castle Lane Farm
Sharnhill Green
Ball Farm
Thurnwood Dairy Farm
Cockroad Copse
Higher Farm
Buckland Newton
Wreth Farm
Noake Farm
Monkwood Hill Farm
Humber Wood
Higher Henley Farm
Alton Common
Little Monkwood Hill Farm
Park Farm
Melcombe Park
Bookham
Henley Hillbillies Old Henley Farm
Alton Common Farm
Bookham Cottage Farm
Ball Bottom Copse
Woodlands Farm
Lovelace's Copse
Henley
Henley House Farm
Narn Farm
Ivest Wood
Hill Wood
Church Hill
Ball Copse
Armswell Farm
Springwood Farm
Hill Wood
Ball Hill
Field System
Barcombe Farm
Penny Farthing Wood
Little Elias Copse
Field System
Watcombe Wood
Folly
Kithill Plantation
Nettlecombe Tout
Fort
Aldermore Copse
Dorsetshire Gap
Tumulus
Cony-gar Copse
Alton Pancras
Watcombe Bottom
Folly Farm
Sheepland Copse
Cross Dyke
Little Wood
Nordon Hill
Melcombe Horsey
Fetchum Wood
Rock Pits Farm
Round Copse
Bowdens
Higher Melcombe Farm
Austral Farm
Tumulus
West Hill
Harveys Farm
Tumuli
Rough Copse
Cross Dykes
Well Copse
Higher Melcombe
Rake Bottom
Manor House
Bulland's Plantation
Settlement
Plush
PH
Firland Wood
Higher Hill
Hanover Copse
Lyscombe Hill
Cross Dyke
Rake Hill
Lower Farm
Lyscombe Bottom
Settlement
Summer House Plantation
Tumulus
Plush Hill
Nettlecombe Farm
Hog Hill
Enclosures
Tenant's Bottom
Thorncombe Bottom
Stickley Coppice
Tenant's Hill
Cross Dyke
Lower Down
Slovens Corner Coppice
Lyscombe Farm
Chapel
New Coppice
Morning Well Plantation
Lower Southcombe Farm
Tumulus
Ash Bed Coppice
Tokenhills Coppice
Kiddles Farm
East Hill
Redlands Coppice
New Barn Farm
Dole's Ash Farm
Piddletrenthide
Thorncombe Farm
Kiddle's Bottom
Manor House
Kingcombe
Rogers' Bottom
Hillside Farm
Tumulus
Kingrove Down
PO
PH
Whitcombe Hill
Kingrove Wood
Tumuli
Tumulus
Dutnole Coppice
Piddle Valley CE First Sch
South House
Kingrove Bottom
Hog Leaze
Coll Down
Highlands
Cheselbourne West Down
Tumulus
Lackington Farm
PH
White Lackington
Dole's Hill Plantation
Tumulus
Well Bottom Down
B3143
MAJOR'S COMMON
FACTORY LA
SPRING GR
REW LA
CASTLE LA
LANDSCOMBE VALE
CRANES MDW
HILLING LA
FORD DOWN LA
BOOKHAM LANE
CROWTHORNE LA
WHITE WAY
CHASTON LA
HAMMOND ST
QUAR CL
HOLCOMBE MD
RIPP'S LANE
CHURCH LA
SMITH'S LA
WIGHTMAN'S ORCHARD
NORTHOVER CL
SUN LA
SWAN LA
SOUTH VW
LACKINGTON DROVE
DRAKE'S LANE

Scale: 1¾ inches to 1 mile

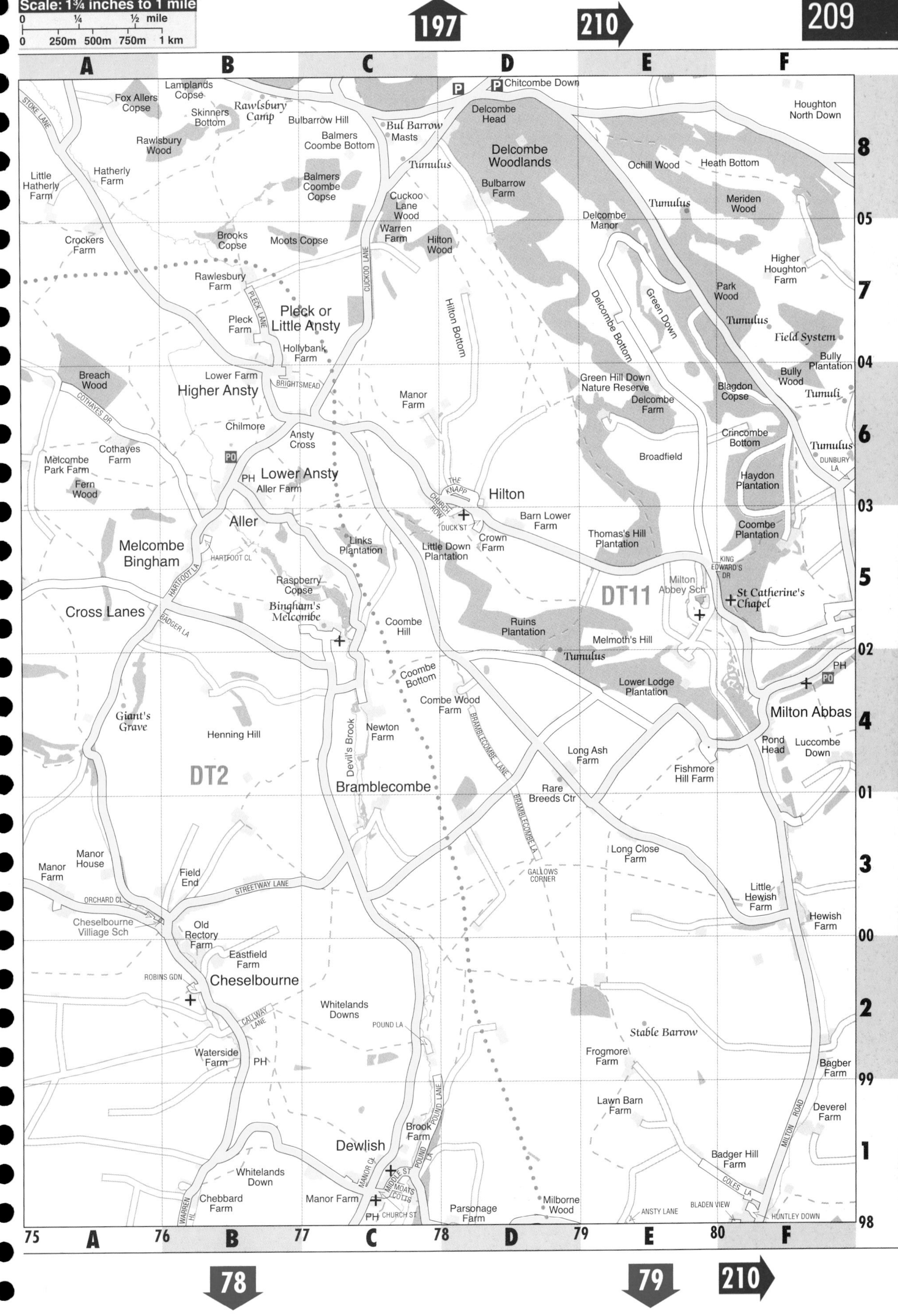

197
210
A
B
C
D
E
F
8
05
7
04
6
03
5
02
4
01
3
00
2
99
1
98
75
76
77
78
79
80
78
79
210
Lamplands Copse
Fox Allers Copse
Skinners Bottom
Rawlsbury Camp
Bulbarrow Hill
Balmers Coombe Bottom
Bul Barrow Masts
Chitcombe Down
Delcombe Head
Houghton North Down
Rawlsbury Wood
Delcombe Woodlands
Tumulus
Ochill Wood
Heath Bottom
Little Hatherly Farm
Hatherly Farm
Balmers Coombe Copse
Cuckoo Lane Wood
Bulbarrow Farm
Meriden Wood
Delcombe Manor
Crockers Farm
Brooks Copse
Moots Copse
Warren Farm
Hilton Wood
Higher Houghton Farm
Rawlesbury Farm
Park Wood
Pleck or Little Ansty
Hilton Bottom
Delcombe Bottom
Green Down
Field System
Pleck Farm
Hollybank Farm
Bully Plantation
Bully Wood
Breach Wood
Lower Farm
Higher Ansty
Green Hill Down Nature Reserve
Blagdon Copse
Tumuli
Manor Farm
Delcombe Farm
Chilmore
Ansty Cross
Crincombe Bottom
Melcombe Park Farm
Cothayes Farm
Broadfield
Tumulus
Lower Ansty
Aller Farm
Haydon Plantation
Fern Wood
Hilton
Barn Lower Farm
Aller
Coombe Plantation
Thomas's Hill Plantation
Melcombe Bingham
Links Plantation
Little Down Plantation
Crown Farm
Raspberry Copse
Milton Abbey Sch
St Catherine's Chapel
DT11
Cross Lanes
Bingham's Melcombe
Coombe Hill
Ruins Plantation
Melmoth's Hill
Coombe Bottom
Lower Lodge Plantation
Combe Wood Farm
Milton Abbas
Giant's Grave
Henning Hill
Newton Farm
Long Ash Farm
Pond Head
Luccombe Down
Devil's Brook
DT2
Fishmore Hill Farm
Bramblecombe
Rare Breeds Ctr
Manor House
Manor Farm
Long Close Farm
Field End
Little Hewish Farm
Cheselbourne Village Sch
Old Rectory Farm
Hewish Farm
Eastfield Farm
Cheselbourne
Whitelands Downs
Stable Barrow
Waterside Farm
Frogmore Farm
Bagber Farm
Lawn Barn Farm
Deverel Farm
Brook Farm
Dewlish
Badger Hill Farm
Whitelands Down
Chebbard Farm
Manor Farm
Parsonage Farm
Milborne Wood

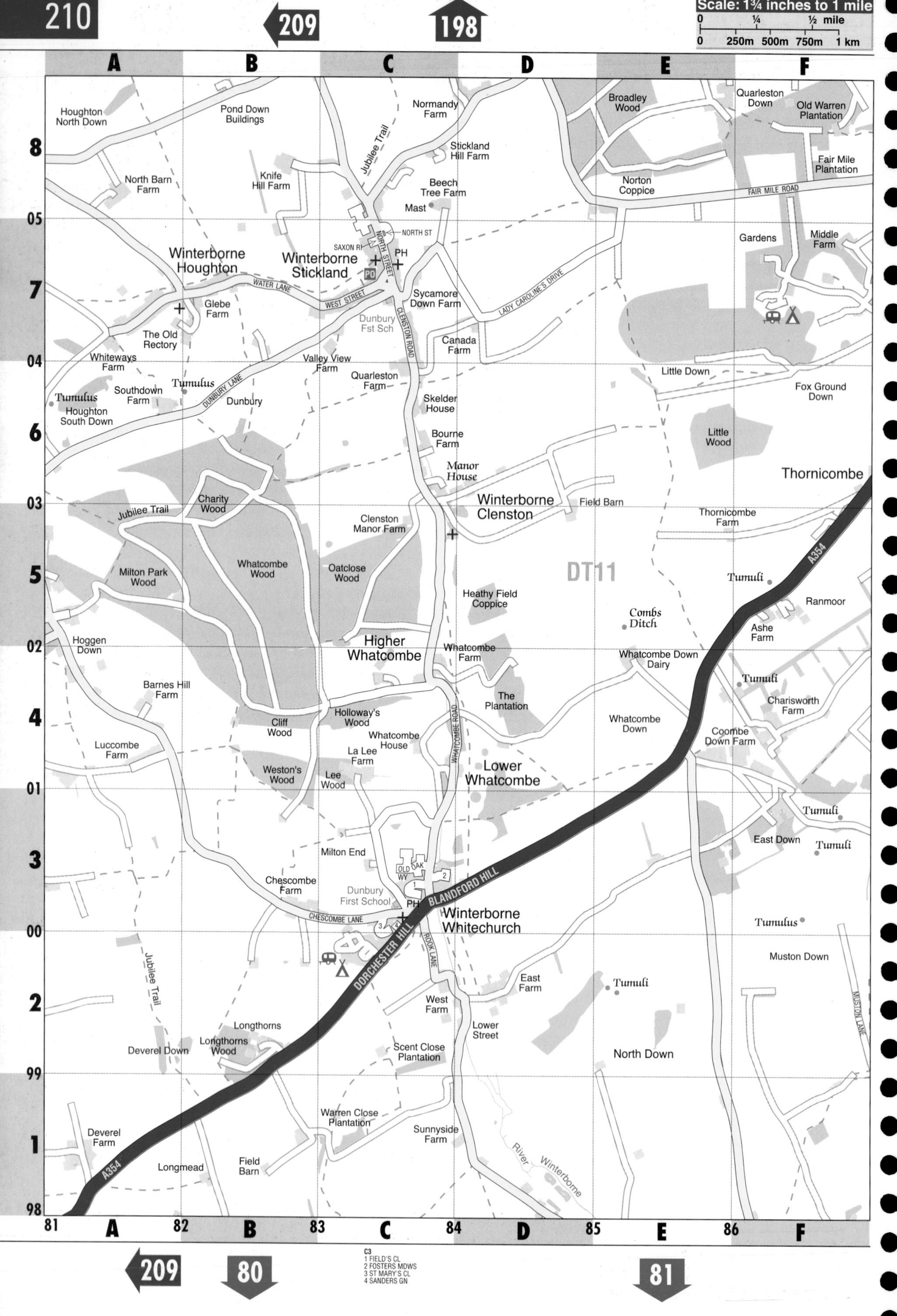

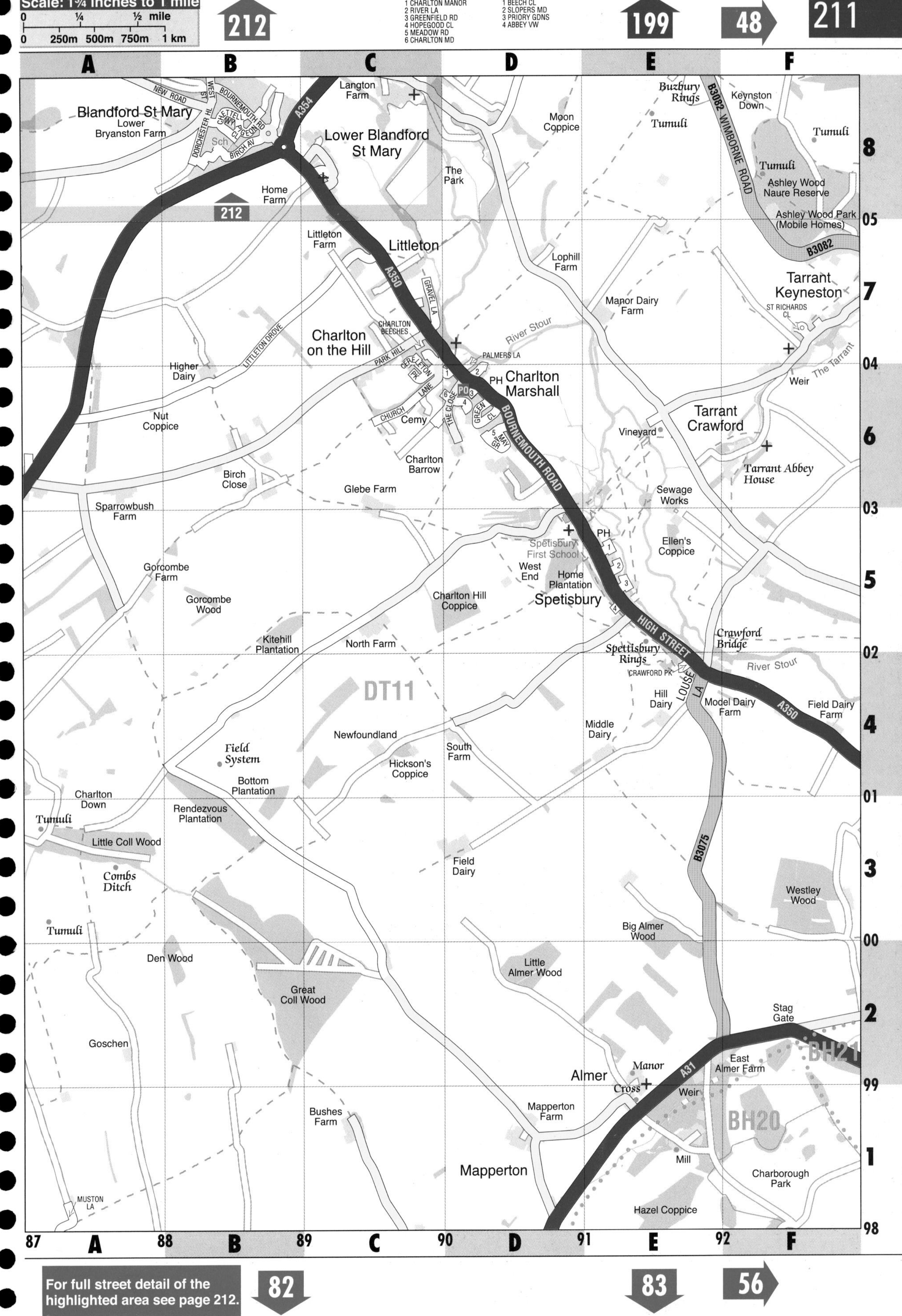

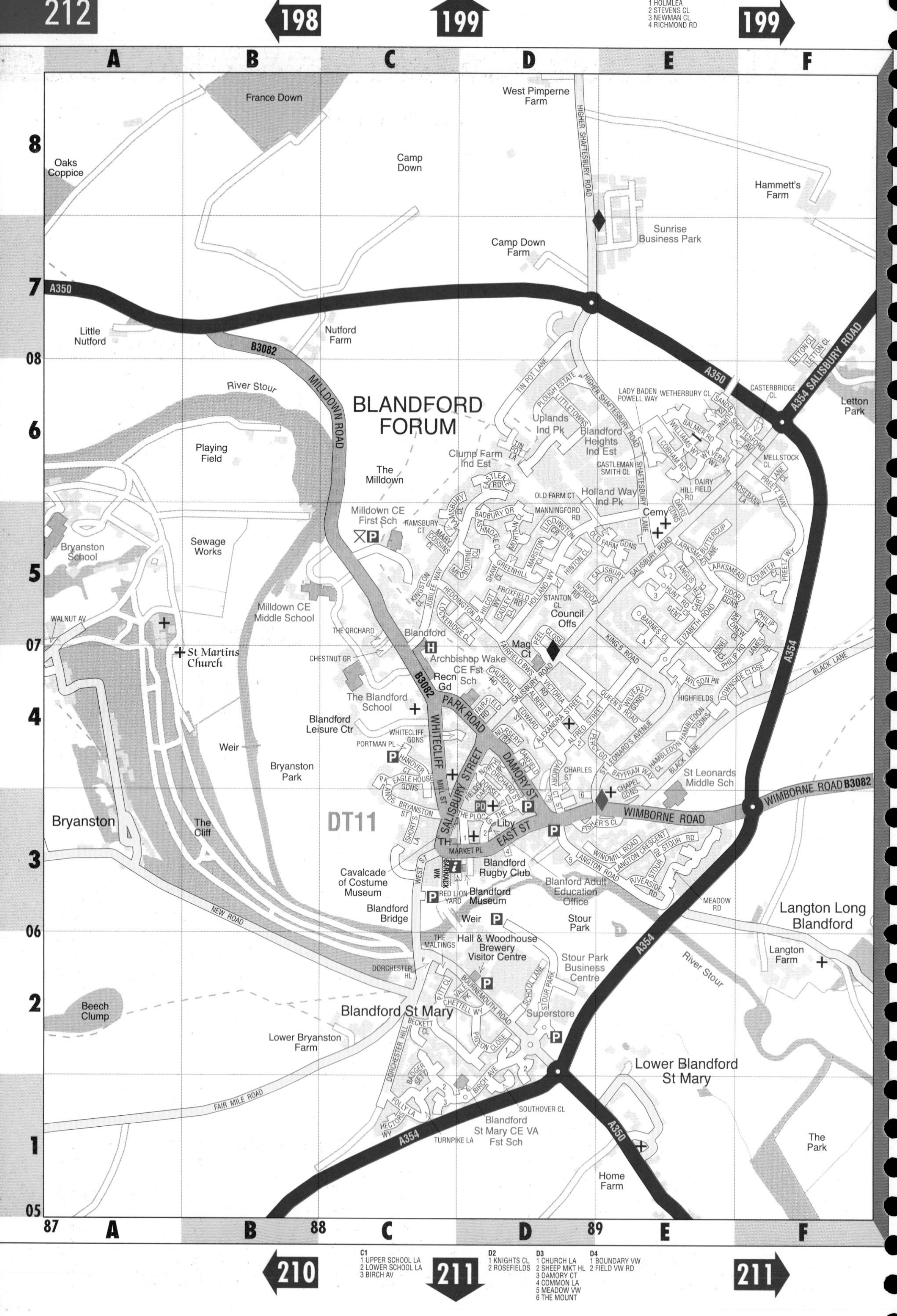
198
199
E5
1 HOLMLEA
2 STEVENS CL
3 NEWMAN CL
4 RICHMOND RD
199
A
B
C
D
E
F
8
7
08
6
5
07
4
3
06
2
1
05
87
88
89
France Down
West Pimperne Farm
HIGHER SHAFTESBURY ROAD
Oaks Coppice
Camp Down
Hammett's Farm
Sunrise Business Park
Camp Down Farm
A350
Little Nutford
Nutford Farm
B3082
MILLDOWN ROAD
River Stour
BLANDFORD FORUM
TIN POT LANE
PLOUGH ESTATE
LITTLETOWNS
LADY BADEN POWELL WAY
WETHERBURY CL
CASTERBRIDGE CL
LETTON CL
A354 SALISBURY ROAD
Letton Park
Uplands Ind Pk
Blandford Heights Ind Est
BALMER RD
WILLIAMS WY
CORBAM RD
SHOTTESFORD AV
MELLSTOCK
Playing Field
Clump Farm Ind Est
TIN POT LA
CASTLEMAN SMITH CL
DAIRY FIELD
HILL RD
PREETZ WAY
The Milldown
EASTLEAZE RD
OLD FARM CT
Holland Way Ind Pk
ROSEBANK LA
Milldown CE First Sch
RAMSBURY CT
BADBURY DR
MANNINGFORD RD
Cemy
DAVIS GDNS
SHAFTESBURY LANE
Bryanston School
Sewage Works
MARY COSSINS
OLD FARM GDNS
BUTTERCUP LANE
LARKSMEAD
HINTON CL
GREENHILL
SALISBURY ROAD
SALISBURY CR
KINGSTON
JUBILEE WAY
HEDDINGTON DR
HOLLAND WY
COUNTER CL
ANGUS
HUNT RD
TUDOR GDNS
GENT CL
CARTER CL
ELIZABETH ROAD
WALNUT AV
Milldown CE Middle School
FROXFIELD
STANTON CL
NORDON
Council Offs
BARNES CL
PHILIP RD
LOCKERIDGE CL
HILCOT WY
CADLEY RD
THE ORCHARD
Blandford
PEEL CLOSE
KING'S ROAD
DREW CL
ANNE CL
JAMES CL
St Martins Church
CHESTNUT GR
Mag Ct
Archbishop Wake CE Fst Sch
FAIRFIELD BWS
BLACK LANE
Recn Gd
WILSON PK
DOWNSIDE CLOSE
The Blandford School
CHURCHILL
SALISBURY ROAD
VICTORIA
WILVERLY GDNS
HIGHFIELDS
PARK ROAD
FAIRFIELD RD
EDWARD
ALBERT ST
ALEXANDRA STREET
ALFRED STREET
QUEEN'S ROAD
ST LEONARD'S AVENUE
HAMBLEDON GDNS
Blandford Leisure Ctr
WHITECLIFF GDNS
NURSERY RD
PERCY GD
PORTMAN PL
Weir
WHITECLIFF
OAKFIELD ST
HAMBLEDON CL
BLACK LANE
Bryanston Park
HANOVER
SALISBURY STREET
DAMORY ST
CHARLES ST
BAYFRAN WAY
St Leonards Middle Sch
EAGLE HOUSE GDNS
MILL ST
ORCHARD ST
DAMORY CT ST
CHAPEL GDNS
WIMBORNE ROAD B3082
BRYANSTON ST
PO
THE PLOCKS
WIMBORNE ROAD
Bryanston
DT11
Liby
FISHER'S CL
The Cliff
SHORTS LA
TH
EAST ST
MARKET PL
WINDMILL ROAD
LANGTON CRESCENT
STOUR RD
Blandford Rugby Club
LANGTON ROAD
STOUR RD
Cavalcade of Costume Museum
WEST ST
RED LION YARD
Blandford Museum
Blandford Adult Education Office
RIVERSIDE RD
MEADOW RD
Langton Long Blandford
NEW ROAD
Blandford Bridge
Weir
Stour Park
A354
THE MALTINGS
Hall & Woodhouse Brewery Visitor Centre
Langton Farm
Stour Park Business Centre
River Stour
DORCHESTER HL
PITT CL
VALE PK
BOURNEMOUTH ROAD
SCHOOL LANE
STOUR PARK
CHETTELL WY
Beech Clump
Blandford St Mary
Superstore
BECKETT CL
Lower Bryanston Farm
PIGEON CLOSE
DORCHESTER HILL
Lower Blandford St Mary
BADGER SETT
FAIR MILE ROAD
BIRCH AVE
FOLLY LA
SOUTHOVER CL
Blandford St Mary CE VA Fst Sch
HECTORS WY
A354
TURNPIKE LA
A350
The Park
Home Farm
210
211
C1
1 UPPER SCHOOL LA
2 LOWER SCHOOL LA
3 BIRCH AV
D2
1 KNIGHTS CL
2 ROSEFIELDS
D3
1 CHURCH LA
2 SHEEP MKT HL
3 DAMORY CT
4 COMMON LA
5 MEADOW VW
6 THE MOUNT
D4
1 BOUNDARY VW
2 FIELD VW RD
211

Index

Place name May be abbreviated on the map → **Church Rd 6 Beckenham BR2.........53 C6**

Location number Present when a number indicates the place's position in a crowded area of mapping

Locality, town or village Shown when more than one place has the same name

Postcode district District for the indexed place

Page and grid square Page number and grid reference for the standard mapping

Public and commercial buildings are highlighted in **magenta** **Places of interest** are highlighted in **blue** with a star★

Abbreviations used in the index

Acad	**Academy**	Comm	**Common**	Gd	**Ground**	L	**Leisure**	Prom	**Promenade**
App	**Approach**	Cott	**Cottage**	Gdn	**Garden**	La	**Lane**	Rd	**Road**
Arc	**Arcade**	Cres	**Crescent**	Gn	**Green**	Liby	**Library**	Recn	**Recreation**
Ave	**Avenue**	Cswy	**Causeway**	Gr	**Grove**	Mdw	**Meadow**	Ret	**Retail**
Bglw	**Bungalow**	Ct	**Court**	H	**Hall**	Meml	**Memorial**	Sh	**Shopping**
Bldg	**Building**	Ctr	**Centre**	Ho	**House**	Mkt	**Market**	Sq	**Square**
Bsns, Bus	**Business**	Ctry	**Country**	Hospl	**Hospital**	Mus	**Museum**	St	**Street**
Bvd	**Boulevard**	Cty	**County**	HQ	**Headquarters**	Orch	**Orchard**	Sta	**Station**
Cath	**Cathedral**	Dr	**Drive**	Hts	**Heights**	Pal	**Palace**	Terr	**Terrace**
Cir	**Circus**	Dro	**Drove**	Ind	**Industrial**	Par	**Parade**	TH	**Town Hall**
Cl	**Close**	Ed	**Education**	Inst	**Institute**	Pas	**Passage**	Univ	**University**
Cnr	**Corner**	Emb	**Embankment**	Int	**International**	Pk	**Park**	Wk, Wlk	**Walk**
Coll	**College**	Est	**Estate**	Intc	**Interchange**	Pl	**Place**	Wr	**Water**
Com	**Community**	Ex	**Exhibition**	Junc	**Junction**	Prec	**Precinct**	Yd	**Yard**

Index of localities, towns and villages

A

Abbotsbury . . . 149 B8
Acton . . . 177 F1
Adam's Green . . . 193 D2
Adber . . . 14 F5
Affpuddle . . . 111 F7
Alcester . . . 12 D2
Alderholt . . . 42 B6
Alderney . . . 88 C1
Aller . . . 209 B5
Allington . . . 100 B7
Allowenshay . . . 191 A8
Almer . . . 211 E2
Alton Pancras . . . 208 B5
Alvington . . . 26 D4
Alweston . . . 31 B1
Ameysford . . . 52 E1
Ammerham . . . 202 D8
Anderson . . . 82 B7
Arne . . . 144 C5
Ash
  Blandford Forum . . . 198 F5
  Bridport . . . 68 C5
Ashington . . . 59 A1
Ashley
  New Milton . . . 95 D3
  Ringwood . . . 54 F5
Ashley Heath . . . 54 B6
Ashmore . . . 39 C8
Askerswell . . . 102 D6
Athelhampton . . . 78 E1
Atrim . . . 68 A4
Avon . . . 63 F2

B

Bagber . . . 197 A8
Barrow Hill . . . 84 F4
Barrow Street . . . 3 F2
Barton on Sea . . . 126 F6
Barwick . . . 193 F8
Bashley . . . 95 A7
Batcombe . . . 206 E7
Bay . . . 6 A2
Beacon Hill . . . 86 A2
Beaminster . . . 204 B5
Bear Cross . . . 88 F5
Bearwood . . . 88 E6
Beaulieu Wood . . . 196 B1
Beckley . . . 94 C5
Bedchester . . . 37 C7
Beer Hackett . . . 194 C6
Belchalwell . . . 197 E4
Belchalwell Street . . . 197 E3
Benville . . . 205 D6
Bere Regis . . . 81 A2
Bettiscombe . . . 203 B3
Bickton . . . 43 B6
Bincombe . . . 152 E6
Binnegar . . . 141 B3
Bishop's Caundle . . . 196 A8
Bishop's Down . . . 195 E6
Bisterne . . . 63 F6
Bittles Green . . . 12 D7
Blackney . . . 203 D2
Blacknoll . . . 156 F8
Blackwater . . . 91 D4
Blandford Camp . . . 199 E3
Blandford Forum . . . 212 C6
Blandford St Mary . . . 212 C2
Blashford . . . 47 C2
Bleak Hill . . . 42 E3
Bloxworth . . . 82 B2
Bluntshay . . . 66 F7
Bookham . . . 208 B7
Boscombe . . . 122 E3
Bothenhampton . . . 100 E3
Bournemouth . . . 122 A2
Bourne Valley . . . 121 B6
Bourton . . . 1 E2
Boveridge . . . 190 B1
Bovington Camp . . . 139 D6
Bowden . . . 9 E4
Bowridge Hill . . . 6 B4
Boys Hill . . . 195 E5
Bradford Abbas . . . 28 D1
Bradford Peverell . . . 106 F6
Bradpole . . . 69 A1
Bramblecombe . . . 209 C4
Branksome . . . 120 F5
Branksome Park . . . 120 F1
Bransgore . . . 93 B8
Braytown . . . 140 A1
Briantspuddle . . . 112 B7
Bridge . . . 202 C8
Bridport . . . 100 B6
Broadmayne . . . 136 A1
Broadoak . . . 67 D5
Broad Oak . . . 197 D7
Broadshard . . . 191 F5
Broadstone . . . 87 B3
Broadwey . . . 152 A4
Broadwindsor . . . 203 F5
Brockhampton Green . . . 196 C1
Broom Hill . . . 51 D2
Bryanston . . . 212 A3
Brympton D'Evercy . . . 26 B3
Buckhorn Weston . . . 9 B6
Buckland Newton . . . 208 A7
Buckland Ripers . . . 151 D1
Bugley . . . 10 A6
Burleston . . . 78 F1
Burstock . . . 203 D6
Burton
  Christchurch . . . 92 D2
  Dorchester . . . 107 F4
  Mere . . . 3 D5
  Yeovil . . . 193 C8
Burton Bradstock . . . 128 B8
Bushey . . . 162 D3

C

Camel Green . . . 42 D6
Camesworth . . . 68 F7
Canford Cliffs . . . 147 E8
Canford Heath . . . 87 E1
Canford Magna . . . 60 A1
Cann . . . 24 A7
Cann Common . . . 24 D7
Castle . . . 202 A4
Castle Park . . . 134 D7
Castletown . . . 181 C1
Catherston Leweston . . . 65 C1
Cattistock . . . 206 C2
Cerne Abbas . . . 207 E4
Chalbury . . . 201 C1
Chalbury Common . . . 201 D1
Chaldon Herring or East Chaldon . . . 156 C3
Chalmington . . . 206 C3
Chard Junction . . . 202 B7
Charing Cross . . . 42 A5
Charlestown . . . 166 E2
Charlton Down . . . 75 D3
Charlton Marshall . . . 211 D6
Charlton on the Hill . . . 211 C7
Charminster
  Bournemouth . . . 90 C2
  Dorchester . . . 107 E5
Charmouth . . . 97 B7
Charnage . . . 3 F4
Chedington . . . 204 E8
Cheselbourne . . . 209 B2
Chesil . . . 186 E8
Chetnole . . . 194 D2
Chettle . . . 200 B8
Chickerell . . . 166 C5
Chideock . . . 99 A6
Chilbridge . . . 58 E7
Chilcombe . . . 102 D3
Child Okeford . . . 198 B7
Chilfrome . . . 206 B1
Chilson Common . . . 202 A7
Chilton Cantelo . . . 14 A8
Christchurch . . . 124 D5
Church Knowle . . . 176 C8
Clapgate . . . 50 E2
Clapton . . . 191 C1
Clifton Maybank . . . 194 A8
Closworth . . . 193 F5
Cobb . . . 96 B4
Cobley . . . 189 D7
Cocknowle . . . 161 A1
Coldharbour . . . 166 E7
Cold Harbour . . . 142 A8
Colehill . . . 60 B8
Colesbrook . . . 5 E4
Combe Almer . . . 84 D7
Compton Abbas . . . 24 A2
Compton Valence . . . 104 E7
Coneygar . . . 100 D7
Coombe
  Axminster . . . 65 B7
  Crewkerne . . . 191 B4
  Shaftesbury . . . 13 E2
Coombe Keynes . . . 158 A5
Coombses . . . 202 B8
Corfe Castle . . . 177 B8
Corfe Mullen . . . 86 C6
Corscombe . . . 205 A8
Coryates . . . 150 F7
Cosmore . . . 207 E8
Court Orchard . . . 100 C8
Cowgrove . . . 58 D4
Crab Orchard . . . 45 B2
Cranborne . . . 40 B7
Creech . . . 160 D3
Creekmoor . . . 118 F8
Crendell . . . 41 B7
Crewkerne . . . 191 E5
Cripplestyle . . . 41 B5
Crooked Withies . . . 51 F7
Cross Lanes . . . 209 A5
Crossways . . . 137 E5
Crouch Hill . . . 196 A5
Crow . . . 55 E4
Cruxton . . . 73 A5
Cucklington . . . 4 B4

D

Daggons . . . 41 E5
Damerham . . . 190 F2
Dean . . . 188 E2
Deanend . . . 188 E4
Deanland . . . 189 A5
Dean Park . . . 122 A4
Dewlands Common . . . 44 F6
Dewlish . . . 209 C1
Dinnington . . . 191 B8
Dorchester . . . 107 C2
Dottery . . . 68 B3
Downton . . . 127 F7
Drimpton . . . 203 D8
Drive End . . . 194 A2
Droop . . . 197 A3
Dudsbury . . . 61 C1
Duntish . . . 196 A1
Durweston . . . 198 E3

E

East Bloxworth . . . 82 E1
East Brook . . . 59 C5
East Burton . . . 139 E2
East Chelborough . . . 205 D8
East Chinnock . . . 192 E8
East Coker . . . 193 D7
East Compton . . . 24 A2
East Creech . . . 160 F2
East End . . . 58 E1
East Fleet . . . 166 B5
East Holme . . . 159 E8
East Holton . . . 117 A3
East Howe . . . 89 C3
East Knighton . . . 157 A8
East Lulworth . . . 173 D8
East Martin . . . 190 C6
East Melbury . . . 24 D5
East Morden . . . 83 D4
Easton . . . 187 B4
East Orchard . . . 36 E8
East Parley . . . 90 B8
East Pulham . . . 196 D4
East Stoke . . . 140 F1
East Stour . . . 10 E3
East Stour Common . . . 11 A3
Ebblake . . . 45 F4
Eccliffe . . . 10 D7
Edmondsham . . . 40 C3
Ellingham . . . 47 B5
Elm Hill . . . 7 B1
Elwell . . . 152 B6
Enmore Green . . . 12 D3
Ensbury . . . 89 F6
Ensbury Park . . . 89 C2
Evershot . . . 206 A7

F

Fairmile . . . 91 F1
Farnham . . . 188 C2
Farrington . . . 37 A3
Ferndown . . . 61 B5
Fiddleford . . . 197 F8
Fifehead Magdalen . . . 20 F7
Fifehead Neville . . . 197 C5

Fifehead St Quintin 197 B5
Filford.................. 67 E7
Fleet.................. 166 A5
Folke................. 195 D8
Folly................. 208 D6
Fontmell Magna 37 F7
Fontmell Parva 36 D2
Fordingbridge 43 B8
Forston 75 B4
Fortuneswell 186 E7
Foxholes 120 A6
Frampton 73 F3
Friars Cliff 125 D7
Frogham 43 F7
Frome St Quintin 206 D5
Furzebrook 161 A4
Furzehill 50 E1

G

Gannetts 21 C4
Gasper 1 C7
Gaunt's Common 51 B8
Giddy Green 139 E1
Gillingham 5 E1
Glanvilles Wootton ... 195 E2
Goathill 31 D7
Godmanstone 75 A7
God's Blessing Green .. 51 C3
Godwinscroft 93 C5
Gold Hill 198 B8
Gore 14 E3
Gotham 41 A3
Grange 50 F2
Grange Estate 62 F8
Greenham 203 C7
Grimstone 74 B1
Grove 187 B6
Gussage All Saints ... 201 A6
Gussage St Andrew ... 188 E1
Gussage St Michael ... 200 F6
Guy's Marsh 23 B6

H

Haddon Hill............ 90 E1
Hains................. 20 F4
Hale................... 4 A3
Halstock............. 193 C3
Ham Common............. 6 C1
Hamlet............... 194 D3
Hammoon............... 36 B2
Hampreston............ 60 E2
Hamworthy........... 118 C3
Hanford.............. 198 D6
Happy Bottom.......... 58 F1
Harbridge............. 43 B1
Harbridge Green....... 43 A2
Harcombe Bottom....... 64 A4
Hardington Mandeville. 193 A6
Hardington Moor...... 193 A7
Harman's Cross....... 177 F6
Hartgrove............. 22 F1
Haselbury Plucknett... 192 C6
Hawkchurch........... 202 B3
Haydon................ 31 C4
Haymoor Bottom........ 87 F1
Haythorne............ 201 F2
Hazelbury Bryan...... 196 F3
Hemsworth............. 49 C8
Henbury............... 56 E1
Henley
  Buckland Newton....208 A7
  Crewkerne..........191 E2
Henstridge............ 19 A4
Henstridge Ash........ 19 A5
Henstridge Bowden..... 18 A6
Henstridge Marsh...... 19 E5
Hermitage............ 195 B2
Herston.............. 178 F3
Hewish............... 191 B3
Hewood............... 202 C6
Highcliffe........... 125 E8
Higher Ansty......... 209 B6
Higher Bockhampton... 109 A5
Higher Chalmington... 206 C4
Higher Eype........... 99 F5
Higher Halstock Leigh. 193 A2
Higher Kingcombe..... 205 E3
Higher Melcombe...... 208 F5
Higher Nyland.......... 8 E1
Higher Row............ 51 F5
Higher Sandford....... 15 F5
Higher Totnell....... 194 F4
Higher Whatcombe..... 210 C5
Higher Woodsford..... 137 D7
Higher Wraxall....... 205 F4
Highlands............ 100 A4
Hightown............. 55 F6
Highwood............. 158 F8
Hilfield............. 207 A7
Hillbourne............ 87 A2
Hillbutts............. 58 F6
Hill View............. 86 D4
Hilton............... 209 D6
Hincknowle............ 69 B8
Hinton
  Christchurch....... 94 A3
  Yeovil............. 14 A6
Hinton Martell....... 201 B1
Hinton Parva.......... 50 B5
Hinton St George.... 191 D7
Hinton St Mary....... 35 B4
Hogstock............. 200 B1
Holdenhurst........... 91 B3
Holditch............. 202 B5

Hollands............. 27 C7
Hollow Oak........... 113 B8
Holmebridge.......... 141 E2
Holnest.............. 195 C4
Holt.................. 51 B4
Holt Heath........... 52 C6
Holton Heath......... 116 B3
Holt Wood............ 51 C8
Holway
  Chard.............. 202 E6
  Sherborne.......... 16 A5
Holwell
  Mere................ 3 C5
  Sturminster Newton 196 B5
Holywell
  Dorchester........ 206 C7
  Yeovil............ 193 C8
Hooke................ 205 C2
Hordle................ 95 F3
Horton............... 201 E2
Horton Common........ 44 F2
Horton Heath......... 44 C2
Hound Hill............ 58 E7
Houndstone........... 26 D6
Hummer............... 14 D4
Hungerford............ 43 F5
Hurn.................. 91 B7
Hursey............... 203 E5
Hurst................ 111 C1
Hyde
  Bridport.......... 100 F5
  Fordingbridge...... 43 F5

I

Ibberton............. 197 D2
Ibsley................ 47 C7
Iford................ 123 D7
Ivy Cross............ 13 A4
Iwerne Courtney or
  Shroton........... 198 E7
Iwerne Minster....... 37 F1

J

Jumpers Common 91 E1

K

Kimmeridge 175 D4
Kingsbury Regis 17 D3
Kingsland 68 A7
King's Stag 196 D5
Kingston
  Corfe Castle 176 F3
  Ringwood 55 B1
  Sturminster Newton 197 A4
Kingston Maurward ... 108 F2
Kingston Russell 104 C3
Kington Magna 9 C3
Kinson 89 B5
Kitford 197 C3
Kit Hill 23 A4
Kittwhistle 203 A6
Knackers Hole 197 D6
Knapp Hill 7 C2
Knighton
  Poole 88 D8
  Yetminster 194 E6
Knob's Crook 44 B4
Knowlton 201 D4

L

Lake 118 D1
Lambrook 68 E5
Lambs' Green 58 F2
Lane End 113 C6
Lanehouse 166 F2
Langham 9 E8
Langton Herring 150 C2
Langton Long
  Blandford 212 F3
Langton Matravers ... 178 A3
Laymore 202 F7
Leigh
  Sherborne 194 E3
  Sturminster Newton 197 D3
  Wimborne Minster .. 59 F4
Leigh Park 59 E4
Lewcombe 193 E2
Lillington 194 F7
Lilliput 147 C8
Limpers Hill 3 D4
Littlebredy 131 E7
Little Canford 60 D4
Littledown 123 A7
Littlemoor 152 F3
Little Pamphill 58 F5
Littleton 211 C7
Littlewindsor 203 F7
Little Woolgarston .. 177 D8
Litton Cheney 103 C1
Loders 69 D1
Lodmoor 167 E7
Long Bredy 103 F1
Longburton 195 C7
Long Crichel 200 E5
Long Cross 2 D5
Longfleet 119 D4
Longham 61 A1
Loscombe 69 E8
Lower Ansty 209 B6

Lower Blandford St
  Mary.............. 212 E1
Lower Bockhampton .. 109 A2
Lower Daggons 41 D8
Lower Eype........... 99 F3
Lower Halstock Leigh . 193 B2
Lower Hamworthy 119 A1
Lower Holwell 40 F6
Lower Kingcombe 205 E1
Lower Mannington 52 C7
Lower Marsh 19 F6
Lower Nyland 19 F8
Lower Odcombe 26 A4
Lower Parkstone 120 B3
Lower Row 51 F7
Lower Strode 204 A2
Lower Turmer 46 F7
Lower Whatcombe 210 D4
Lower Wraxall 206 A3
Lower Zeals 2 D5
Lufton 26 B6
Lulworth Camp 173 A7
Lyatts 193 B6
Lydlinch 196 F8
Lyme Regis 96 D5
Lyon's Gate 207 D8
Lytchett Matravers .. 84 D4
Lytchett Minster ... 116 F7

M

Madjeston 10 F7
Maiden Newton 73 A8
Mangerton 69 B4
Mannington 52 C8
Manston 36 A3
Manswood 200 E3
Mapperton
  Beaminster 204 F2
  Spetisbury 211 D1
Mappowder 196 F1
Margaret Marsh 22 C2
Marnhull 20 F2
Marshalsea 202 F3
Marshwood 202 F2
Martin 190 B6
Martin Drove End ... 190 A8
Martinstown or Winterbourne
  St Martin 133 D6
Meerhay 204 D5
Melbury Abbas 24 C5
Melbury Bubb 194 C1
Melbury Osmond 194 A2
Melbury Sampford ... 206 A8
Melcombe Bingham ... 209 A5
Melcombe Regis 167 B4
Melplash 204 D1
Mere 3 B5
Merley 59 D1
Merriott
  Beaminster 70 A4
  Crewkerne 191 E7
Merriottsford 191 E6
Merritown 90 E7
Middle Bockhampton .. 92 F6
Middle Chinnock 192 C8
Middlemarsh 195 D1
Milborne Port 17 C2
Milborne St Andrew .. 79 E7
Milborne Wick 17 B6
Miles Cross 99 E7
Milton Abbas 209 F4
Milton on Stour 5 D5
Minchington 188 D1
Minterne Magna 207 C7
Minterne Parva 207 D6
Misterton 192 A2
Mockbeggar 47 E7
Monkton Up Wimborne 201 C8
Monkton Wyld 64 B5
Moorbath 67 C3
Moordown 90 A2
Moorside 21 D3
Moortown 55 D5
Morcombelake 66 B1
Moreton 138 E7
Mosterton 204 E4
Motcombe 12 B8
Mounters 20 E1
Mount Pleasant 86 E7
Muckleford 106 B7
Mudeford 125 A5
Mudford 14 A4
Muscliffe 90 C4

N

Nash 193 C8
Neacroft 93 B6
Netherbury 204 C2
Nether Cerne 207 E1
Netherhay 203 C8
Netherstoke 193 D3
Netherton 193 E6
Nettlecombe 70 B3
New Milton 94 E5
Newport 82 C2
New Swanage 179 B6
Newton 197 D8
Newton Peveril 56 B4
Newtown
  Beaminster 204 D5
  Corfe Mullen 86 D7
  Poole 120 B7

New Town
  Gillingham 9 C2
  Milborne Port 17 B2
  Pimperne 188 C2
  Sixpenny Handley .. 188 F6
  Verwood 201 A2
  Yeovil 27 E6
Norden 161 C3
Northay 202 D3
North Bockhampton .. 92 F7
Northbourne 89 E4
North Bowood 203 F2
Northbrook 78 B2
North Chideock 99 A8
North Coker 193 D8
North End
  Fordingbridge 190 F3
  Gillingham 7 A3
North Gorley 43 D3
North Kingston 55 E2
North Perrott 192 C4
North Poorton 205 B1
Northport 142 E5
North Poulner 47 F2
North Wootton 30 F2
Norwood 205 B8
Nottington 152 A2
Notton 73 B4

O

Oakdale 119 D6
Oakley 59 E2
Oathill 203 B8
Oborne 16 E2
Okeford Fitzpaine .. 197 F5
Old Milton 94 E1
Old Town 119 C2
Organford 116 B6
Osehill Green 195 E4
Osmington 154 A3
Osmington Mills 169 C7
Ossemsley 94 E8
Ossessmley 94 E8
Overcombe 168 A7
Over Compton 28 E7
Owermoigne 155 E7
Oxbridge 68 F8

P

Packers Hill 196 C5
Pallington 111 C3
Pamphill 58 E6
Park Gate 196 F2
Parkway 14 F7
Parley Green 90 C7
Peacemarsh 5 E3
Pear Ash 1 C4
Pendomer 193 B5
Pen Mill 28 A6
Penn 64 C3
Penselwood 1 B4
Pentridge 189 E4
Perry Street 202 B8
Piddlehinton 76 F7
Piddletrenthide 208 A3
Pidney 196 F4
Pig Oak 51 A3
Pilford 60 A8
Pillwell 21 A3
Pilsdon 203 C2
Pimperne
  Blandford Forum .. 199 D4
  Yeovil 194 A3
Pinehurst Park 53 A1
Pleck
  Marnhull 34 B8
  Sturminster Newton 196 B6
Pleck or Little Ansty. 209 C7
Plush 208 C5
Pokesdown 123 A4
Poole 119 B3
Poolestown 33 E5
Portway 156 F7
Post Green 116 F7
Poulner 55 F8
Powerstock 70 B5
Poxwell 154 E5
Poyntington 16 D4
Preston 168 B8
Preston Plucknett ... 26 F4
Puddletown 78 A1
Puddle Town 192 B5
Pulham 196 B3
Puncknowle 129 F6
Purewell 124 D7
Purse Caundle 32 B8
Purtington 191 A4
Putton 166 E5
Puxey 197 B7
Pymore 68 D1

Q

Queen Oak 2 A3

R

Radipole 167 B7
Rampisham 205 F5
Redbridge 138 B5
Redford 206 D8
Red Hill 89 F5
Redlands 152 B1

Rew 208 B8
Ridge 143 B1
Rimpton 15 C8
Ringwood 47 D1
Rivers' Corner 197 C7
Rixon 35 C2
Rockford 47 E4
Rodden 150 C5
Rodgrove 8 C6
Rodwell 167 D1
Rolls Mill 197 C8
Romford 44 E7
Rook Street 3 A4
Rossmore 120 E7
Roundham 191 D4
Rowlands 59 C5
Rushton 141 B2
Ryall 66 D2
Ryme Intrinseca 194 B6

S

St Andrew's Well ... 100 E8
St Ives 54 C5
St James 12 E1
St Johns 59 C4
St Leonards 54 A2
Salwayash 68 B6
Sandbanks 147 C3
Sandford 142 F8
Sandford Orcas 15 F6
Sandhills
  Cattistock 206 B3
  Sherborne 195 F5
Sandpit 203 D7
School House 202 D5
Seaborough 191 E1
Seatown 99 A4
Sedgehill 7 F5
Shaftesbury 12 E4
Shaggs 158 C3
Shapwick 56 C8
Sharnhill Green 208 C8
Sherborne 30 A8
Sherford 115 D8
Shillingstone 198 C6
Shipton Gorge 101 C3
Silkhay 204 B1
Silton 5 A7
Sitterton 80 F3
Sixpenny Handley ... 189 A3
Skilling 100 B5
Sleight 58 D1
Slepe 115 F7
Somerford 124 E7
South Bockhampton .. 92 B7
Southbourne 123 F4
South Bowood 203 F1
Southbrook 3 B4
South Chard 202 A7
South End 190 F2
South Gorley 43 E2
Southill 167 A6
Southlands 180 E8
Southover
  Burton Bradstock . 128 B7
  Dorchester 73 D2
South Perrott 192 C2
South Poorton 70 C8
Southwell 186 F1
Spetisbury 211 D5
Springbourne 122 C5
Spyway 102 D7
Stafford's Green 16 A7
Stalbridge 33 E8
Stalbridge Weston ... 33 A6
Stallen 29 B6
Stanbridge 50 D4
Stanley Green 119 C6
Stanpit 124 C5
Stapehill 60 E5
Steeple 175 C6
Sterte 119 B3
Stinsford 108 E3
Stoborough 142 E1
Stoborough Green ... 161 A8
Stockwood 194 C2
Stoford 193 F8
Stoke Abbott 204 A3
Stokeford 140 F3
Stoke Wake 197 B1
Stone
  Bridport 101 A7
  Wimborne Minster . 59 A6
Stourpaine 198 F4
Stour Provost 21 D8
Stour Row 22 C7
Stourton Caundle 32 E3
Stratton 106 E8
Strouden 90 E1
Stubhampton 199 E8
Stuckton 43 E7
Studland 164 D1
Sturminster Marshall. 56 E4
Sturminster Newton .. 35 A1
Summerlands 27 B6
Sutton Bingham 193 D6
Sutton Holms 44 B8
Sutton Poyntz 153 D4
Sutton Waldron 37 E5
Swanage 179 C3
Swyre 129 D5
Sydling St Nicholas . 207 A2
Symondsbury 99 E8
Synderford 202 F6

T

Tadnoll 138 C2
Talbot Heath 121 B7
Talbot Village 89 C1
Talbot Woods 121 E7
Tarrant Crawford 211 E6
Tarrant Gunville 199 F8
Tarrant Hinton 200 A6
Tarrant Keyneston 48 A5
Tarrant Launceston . . . 200 B4
Tarrant Monkton 200 B3
Tarrant Rushton 48 B8
Templeman's Ash 203 B3
The Borough 196 B6
The Causeway 3 C4
The Common 197 E5
The Mount 69 A6
Thorncombe 202 E6
Thorne Coffin 26 C8
Thornford 194 D8
Thornicombe 210 F6
Three Gates 195 A2
Three Legged Cross 45 A1
Throop
  Bournemouth 90 E4
  Briantspuddle 112 D7
Tidpit 190 C6
Tiley 195 E1
Tillworth 202 A3
Tincleton 110 D4
Tiptoe 95 D8
Todber 21 D4
Tollard Farnham 188 B2
Tollard Royal 188 B4
Tollerford 72 E8
Toller Fratrum 72 C7
Toller Porcorum 71 E8
Toller Whelme 205 B4

Tolpuddle 79 D2
Totnell 194 F3
Towns End 19 B3
Town's End 81 C3
Trent 14 E2
Trickett's Cross 61 F7
Tuckton 123 F5
Turlin Moor 118 B4
Turmer 46 F8
Turners Puddle 112 D8
Turnworth 198 B2
Twyford 23 D2
Tyneham 174 C5

U

Ulwell 179 A6
Up Cerne 207 C5
Uphall 205 E5
Uploders 101 F8
Up Mudford 14 A2
Upper Parkstone 120 B5
Uppington 201 D1
Up Sydling 207 A4
Upton
  Poole 118 D7
  Preston 169 E8
Upwey 152 A6

V

Verwood 45 B6

W

Walditch 101 A6
Walkford 94 C1

Wallisdown 89 A2
Walton Elm 34 F8
Wareham 142 E5
Warmwell 137 A1
Warren 113 D3
Waterditch 93 B5
Waterloo 87 B1
Watton 100 B4
Wayford 191 B1
Waytown 68 E8
Well Bottom 39 D6
West Bay 100 C2
West Bexington 129 E2
Westbourne 121 C3
West Bourton 4 C7
West Chaldon 155 F2
West Chelborough 205 D8
West Chinnock 192 B8
West Cliff 121 C1
West Coker 193 A8
West Compton 71 E1
West End 29 E5
Westfields 196 D1
Westham 167 A3
West Holme 159 D8
West Howe 88 E4
West Hurn 90 F6
West Knighton 136 C3
West Lulworth 172 D6
West Melbury 24 A5
West Milton 69 E6
West Moors 53 B2
West Morden 83 B4
Weston
  Beaminster 204 F8
  Fortuneswell 186 E3
West Orchard 36 D6
West Parley 61 E1
West Pulham 196 A3
West Southbourne 123 D5

West Stafford 136 B8
West Stour 10 A2
Weymouth 167 E3
Whitchurch 19 A6
Whitchurch
  Canonicorum 66 A4
Whitcombe 135 F5
Whitecross 204 B2
White Cross 1 E5
Whitefield 83 A2
White Hill 3 C2
White Lackington 208 C1
Whitmore 44 B6
Wick 124 B4
Wigbeth 201 F2
Wimborne Minster 59 A6
Wimborne St Giles . . . 201 D7
Winfrith Newburgh . . . 156 F6
Winkton 92 C5
Winterborne Came 135 D5
Winterborne Clenston . . 210 D6
Winterborne
  Herringston 134 F5
Winterborne Houghton . 210 B7
Winterborne Kingston . . . 81 D8
Winterborne Monkton . . 134 C4
Winterborne Muston . . . 82 A7
Winterborne Stickland . . 210 C7
Winterborne Tomson . . . 82 D7
Winterborne
  Whitechurch 210 D3
Winterborne Zelston . . . 82 F7
Winterbourne Abbas . . . 105 C2
Winterbourne
  Steepleton 132 F8
Winton 121 F7
Winyard's Gap 192 E1
Witchampton 200 F1
Wolverton 2 B4
Wonston 196 F2

Woodbridge 23 B1
Woodcutts 188 D4
Woodlands 44 A6
Woodlands Common . . . 44 C6
Woodrow 196 F4
Woodsford 110 D2
Woodville 21 F8
Woodyates 189 D6
Wool 140 B2
Woolbridge Heath 140 A6
Woolford's Water 208 A8
Woolgarston 177 F8
Woolland 197 C1
Woolminstone 191 B3
Woolsbridge 53 D7
Wooth 68 E3
Wootton 95 B8
Wootton Fitzpaine 65 B4
Worgret 142 B2
Worth Matravers 183 D7
Wych 100 E2
Wyke 5 D1
Wyke Regis 180 D7
Wynford Eagle 72 D4

Y

Yenston 18 E7
Yeovil 27 A4
Yetminster 194 D5
Yondover 101 D8

Z

Zeals 2 A4

8th August Rd BH20 139 E7

A

Aaron Cl BH17 119 F7
Abbey Cl 9 TA20 202 A8
Abbey Ct 5 DT2 207 D4
Abbey Gdns
Cerne Abbas DT2 207 D4
Ferndown BH21 60 D5
Abbey Hill Cl SO23 126 E8
Abbey Hill Rd SO23 126 E8
Abbey Mews 2 TA20 202 A8
Abbey Pas SO23 126 E5
Abbey Prim Sch SP7 12 D1
Abbey Rd
Sherborne DT9 30 B6
West Moors BH22 62 A8
Yeovil BA21 26 F6
Abbey St
Cerne Abbas DT2 207 D4
Crewkerne TA18 191 E4
Hinton St George TA17 191 C7
Abbey View 4 DT11 211 E5
Abbey Wlk SP7 12 E2
Abbotsbury Castle (Hill Fort) DT3 130 D2
Abbotsbury Hill DT3 130 D1
Abbotsbury La DT2 130 F7
Abbotsbury Rd
Corfe Mullen BH18 86 F5
Weymouth DT4 167 B3
Abbotsbury Sub-Tropical Gdns DT3 148 E7
Abbotsbury Swannery DT3 149 B5
Abbots Cl BH23 125 F7
Abbots Meade BA21 26 F5
Abbots Quay 4 BH20 142 E3
Abbots Row 1 SO22 126 D6
Abbots Way
Sherborne DT9 29 F5
Yeovil BA21 26 F7
Abbots Wlk DT2 207 D4
Abbott Cl BH9 122 A8
Abbott La TA16 192 A8
Abbott Rd BH9 122 A8
Abbotts Cl SO23 126 E8
Abbotts Ct SO22 126 D8
Abbotts Mdw BH16 84 D3
Abbotts Rd SO23 126 E8
Abbott St BH21 58 D6
Abbotts Way BH22 62 A8
Abbott's Way SP8 5 F3
Abbott's Wootton La
Marshwood DT6 202 E1
Whitechurch Canonicorum DT6 65 D7
Abder Cross DT9 14 F4
Abels La DT9 14 E2
Aberdare Rd BH10 89 E3
Abingdon Dr BH23 126 C8
Abingdon Rd BH17 119 D8
Abinger Rd BH7 123 B6
Abney Rd BH10 89 D3
Acacia Ave BH31 45 E4
Acacia Cl DT4 167 B6
Acacia Rd SO41 95 F3
Acer Ave
Bridport DT6 100 F8
2 Bridport DT6 68 F1
Acer Dr BA21 26 E7
Ackerman Rd DT1 108 C1
Acland Rd
Bournemouth BH9 122 B8
7 Dorchester DT1 108 A2
Aconbury Ave 2 DT1 107 C1
Acorn Ave BH15 119 D2
Acorn Bsns Pk BH12 120 B8
Acorn Cl
Christchurch BH23 123 F8
New Milton BH25 95 C4
St Leonards BH24 54 A3
Winchester SO22 126 B8
Acorns The
West Moors BH24 62 B8
Wimborne Minster BH21 60 A4
Acorn Way BH31 45 C6
Acreman Cl 1 DT2 207 D4
Acreman Pl DT9 30 B5
Acreman St
Cerne Abbas DT2 207 D4
Sherborne DT9 30 B6
Acres Ct 6 BA22 193 F8
Acres Rd BH11 89 B2
Acton Rd BH10 89 B1
Adamsfield Gdns BH10 89 C2
Adastral Rd BH17 119 F8
Adastral Sq BH17 119 F8
Ad Astro Fst Sch BH17 87 F1
Adber Cl 2 BA21 28 A8
Addington Pl BH23 124 D6
Addiscombe Rd BH23 124 A7
Addison Cl
Gillingham SP8 6 A1
Winchester SO22 126 A3
Addison Sq BH24 55 D7
Addlewell La BA20 27 D4
Adelaide Cl BH23 123 F8
Adelaide Cres DT4 167 B3
Adelaide La 17 BH1 121 F3
Adeline Rd BH1,BH5 122 E4
Admirals Cl DT9 30 D8
Admirals Way BH20 142 E6
Admirals Wlk 13 BH2 121 D2
Admiralty Rd BH6 123 F3
Aerial Pk BH21 60 E6
Aggis Farm Rd BH31 45 A6
Agglestone Rd BH19 164 B1
Aigburth Rd BH19 178 F3
Airetons Cl BH18 87 C3
Airfield Cl DT2 137 D5
Airfield Ind Est
Christchurch BH23 124 F6
Christchurch BH23 125 A7
Airfield Rd BH23 124 F6
Airfield Way BH23 124 F7
Airlie Cnr SO22 126 C4
Airlie La SO22 126 C4
Airlie Rd SO22 126 C4
Airspeed Rd BH23 125 B7
Akeman Cl BA21 26 F7
Akeshill Cl BH25 95 B5
Alamein Rd BH20 139 F6
Alan Ct 10 BH23 126 B7
Alastair Cl BA21 27 B7
Alastair Dr BA21 27 B7
Albany BH1 122 C3
Albany Cl
Old Milton BH25 94 F1
Sherborne DT9 30 C8
Albany Ct 6 BH2 121 F4
Albany Dr BH21 45 A1
Albany Gdns BH15 118 F2
Albany Ho 17 BH13 121 A4
Albany Pk BH17 119 B8
Albany Rd DT4 166 E4
Albemarle Rd BH3 121 F7
Albert Cl BA21 27 A7
Albert Ct SO23 126 D7
Albert Rd
Bournemouth BH1 121 F3
Corfe Mullen BH21 86 D5
Dorchester DT1 107 F1
Ferndown BH22 61 D5
New Milton BH25 94 F2
Poole BH12 120 D6
Albert St
Blandford Forum DT11 212 D4
5 Radipole DT4 167 D3
Albert Terr DT5 186 E8
Albion Cl BH12 120 B7
Albion Pl 14 SO23 126 E6
Albion Rd BH23 91 F1
Albion Way BH31 44 F6
Alby Rd BH12 120 F5
Alcester Rd BH12 120 D6
Aldabrand Cl DT3 166 D4
Aldbury Ct BH25 127 A7
Alderbury Cl 5 BH19 178 F2
Alder Cl
Burton BH23 92 D1
3 Sandford BH20 116 A1
Sturminster Newton DT10 35 C2
Alder Cres BH12 120 F7
Alder Dr SP6 42 B5
Alder Gr
Crewkerne TA18 191 F5
Yeovil BA20 27 A2
Alder Hills BH12 121 A7
Alder Hills Ind Pk BH12 121 A7
Alder Hills Nature Reserve BH12 121 A7
Alderholt Pk SP6 42 A7
Alderholt Sports Club SP6 42 C5
Alder Hts BH12 121 A7
Alderley Rd BH10 89 D4
Alderney Ave BH12 88 D1
Alderney Hospl BH12 88 C2
Alderney Rdbt BH12 88 D2
Alder Rd
Poole BH12 120 F6
Poole BH12 121 A7
Sturminster Newton DT10 35 C2
Aldis Gdns BH15 118 E2
Aldondale Gdns BA20 27 C3
Aldridge Rd
Bournemouth BH10 89 C5
Ferndown BH22 61 E3
Aldridge Way BH22 61 F3
Alexander Cl BH23 124 E6
Alexandra Ct DT6 100 C5
Alexandra Lodge 8 BH1 122 A3
Alexandra Rd
Bournemouth BH6 123 C5
Bridport DT6 100 C6
Dorchester DT1 107 F1
Poole BH14 120 D5
Radipole DT4 167 D5
Weymouth DT4 166 E3
Yeovil BA21 27 F6
Alexandra St DT11 212 D4
Alexandra Terr
9 Dorchester DT1 108 A2
Winchester SO23 126 D5
Alexandria Ct BH22 61 E3
Alford Rd BH3 121 D7
Alfred Pl DT1 108 B1
Alfred Rd DT1 108 A1
Alfred St DT11 212 D4
Alice in Wonderland Family Fun Park BH23 90 E7
Alice Rd DT1 107 E1
Alington 22 BH4 121 C3
Alington Ave DT1 135 C8
Alington Cl BH14 147 C7
Alington Ho BH14 147 C7
Alington Rd
Bournemouth BH3 122 A6
Dorchester DT1 108 B1
Poole BH14 147 C7
Alington St 4 DT1 108 A2
Alington Terr 6 DT1 108 B2
Alipore Cl BH14 120 D3
Alipore Hts BH14 120 D3
Alisons The BH20 139 E2
Alison Way 6 SO22 126 D6
Allamanda Rd DT3 152 E2
Allberry Gdns DT3 168 A8
Allenbourn Mid Sch BH21 59 C5
Allenby Cl BH17 87 B2
Allenby Rd BH17 87 B2
Allen Cl 8 DT11 198 C7
Allen Ct BH21 59 C5
Allen Rd BH21 59 C4
Allens La BH16 118 D5
Allens Rd
Upton BH16 117 F6
Upton BH16 118 D6
Allenview Rd BH21 59 C5
Allingham Rd BA21 27 E7
Allington Gdns 3 DT6 100 B8
Allington Mead 3 DT6 100 C8
Allington Pk DT6 100 B7
All Saints CE Prim Sch SO23 126 F4
All Saints CE Sch DT4 180 D8
All Saints CE VC Prim Sch DT9 196 A7
All Saints' Rd
Dorchester DT1 108 B2
Weymouth DT4 180 C8
Alma Rd
Bournemouth BH9 121 F7
Bournemouth BH9 122 A7
Weymouth DT4 167 C3
Almer Rd BH15 118 E3
Almond Gr
Poole BH12 120 D7
Radipole DT4 167 B6
Almshouses BH10 89 C1
Alpha Ctr The BH17 119 B7
Alpha House Gall DT9 30 C5
Alpine Rd BH24 54 E2
Alswitha Terr 12 SO23 126 E7
Alton Ct 13 SO23 126 E8
Alton La DT2 207 E4
Alton Mead La DT9 194 E4
Alton Rd
Bournemouth BH10 89 B1
Poole BH14 120 C3
Alton Rd E BH14 120 D2
Alum Chine Rd BH4 121 B3
Alumdale Rd BH4 121 B2
Alumhurst Rd BH4 121 B2
Alvandi Gdns 2 BH25 95 B3
Alverton Ave BH15 119 F3
Alverton Hall 13 BH4 121 C2
Alvington La BA22 26 D4
Alyth Rd BH3 121 D6
Ambassador Cl BH23 125 A6
Ambassador Ind Est BH23 125 A6
Ambassador Trade Pk SP8 20 C7
Amberley Cl BH23 125 F8
Amberley Ct 10 BH1 122 A3
Amberley Ho BH22 61 D7
Amber Rd BH21 86 C4
Amberwood BH22 61 E7
Amberwood Dr BH23 93 F2
Amberwood Gdns BH23 94 A2
Amberwood Ho BH23 94 A2
Ambleside
Christchurch BH23 91 E3
Radipole DT4 167 B7
Ambrose Cl DT9 28 D2
Ambury La BH23 124 F8
Amelia Cl DT5 186 F8
Amen Cnr BH21 201 B5
Amersham Ct 37 BH4 121 C3
Amesbury Rd BH6 123 C6
Amethyst Rd BH23 124 F7
Ameysford Rd
Ferndown BH22 52 E1
Ferndown BH22 61 C7
Ameys La BH22 61 F7
Amiens Rd BH20 139 E7
Amira Ct 2 BH2 121 E3
Ammerham La TA20 202 D8
Ampfield Rd BH8 90 D3
Amsterdam Sq BH23 124 D6
Ancaster Rd BH19 178 F3
Anchor Cl
Bournemouth BH11 88 F6
Christchurch BH23 125 A5
Anchor Rd BH11 88 F5
Ancrum Lo 15 BH4 121 B3
Andbourne Ct BH6 123 F3
Andover Cl BH23 125 B7
Andover Gn BH20 139 C6
Andover Rd SO23 126 D8
Andover Road Ret Pk SO23 126 D7
Andre Ct BH23 126 B8
Andrew Cl DT11 212 E5
Andrew La BH25 95 D2
Andrews Cl BH11 89 A3
Angel Cl DT3 150 C1
Angeline Cl BH23 125 F8
Angel La
Barton on Sea BH25 127 D8
Ferndown BH22 61 B3
Langton Herring DT3 150 C2
Mere BA12 3 A5
Shaftesbury SP7 12 E3
Stour Provost SP8 10 F1
Angel Mews BH15 119 B2
Angers La DT10 197 E7
Anglebury Ave 2 BH19 179 B4
Anglebury Bsns Pk BH20 142 E5
Anglewood Mans 2 BH4 121 C3
Anglo-European Coll of Chiropractic BH5 123 A4
Angus Cl DT11 212 E5
Anjou Cl BH11 88 D5
Annandale Ct BH6 123 D4
Anncott Cl BH16 84 D3
Anne Cl
Blandford Forum DT11 212 E4
Christchurch BH23 92 A1
Annerley Rd BH1 122 C4
Annet Cl BH15 118 E2
Anning Rd DT7 96 C6
Annings La DT6 101 E1
Anson Cl
Christchurch BH23 124 F6
Ringwood BH24 55 E8
Anstey Cl BH11 89 A6
Anstey Rd BH11 89 A5
Ansty La DT11 79 C8
Antell's Way SP6 42 C6
Antelope Wlk 8 DT1 108 A2
Anthony's Ave BH14 120 C1
Antler Dr BH25 94 E4
Anvil Cl 1 BH19 178 E2
Anvil Cres BH18 86 F5
Anvil Rd 10 DT11 199 D4
Aplands Cl 1 DT11 198 B8
Apollo Cl
Dorchester DT1 134 F8
Poole BH12 120 D7
Apple Acre 1 DT11 198 C7
Applebee Way 2 DT7 96 C6
Apple Cl BH13 121 A4
Applefield Rd DT8 203 C8
Apple Gr BH23 91 E2
Appleslade Way BH25 95 B5
Appletree Cl
Bournemouth BH6 123 C5
New Milton BH25 95 A1
Radipole DT3 167 C8
Apple Tree Gr BH22 61 E6
Apple Tree Rd SP6 42 B5
Apple Trees La 2 DT6 99 A6
Approach Rd BH14 120 B3
April Cl BH11 89 A4
Apsley Cres BH17 87 C1
Apsley Ct 2 BH8 122 A5
Aragon Cl DT4 180 E8
Aragon Way BH9 90 B4
Arbour Ct 20 SO22 126 D6
Arbutus Cl DT1 108 A1
Arcade BH4 121 B3
Arcade The 14 BH1 121 F3
Arcadia Ave BH8 122 B7
Arcadia Rd BH23 91 F1
Archbishop Wake CE Fst Sch DT11 212 D4
Archdale Cl BH10 89 D2
Archery La SO23 126 D5
Archway Rd BH14 120 E4
Arden Rd BH9 89 F3
Arden Wlk BH25 95 B2
Ardmore Rd BH14 120 B4
Arena Bsns Ctr BH17 119 B8
Argyle Rd
Christchurch BH23 124 E5
Radipole DT4 167 D6
Swanage BH19 179 B2
Argyll Mans 8 BH5 122 E4
Argyll Rd
Bournemouth BH5 122 E4
Poole BH12 120 D6
Ariel Cl BH6 124 B4
Ariel Dr BH6 124 B4
Ark Dr BH22 61 F3
Arlecks La 2 DT11 199 D4
Arley Rd BH14 120 A2
Arlington DT4 167 A5
Arlington Cl BA21 26 E7
Arlington Ct BH25 127 B8
Arlington Pl 3 SO23 126 E6
Armada Way DT1 135 B8
Armoury Rd BA22 26 C6
Armoury Yd SP7 12 E3
Armstrong Rd DT6 100 C8
Arne Ave BH12 120 E7
Arne Cres BH12 120 F7
Arne Rd BH20 143 D1
Arne Reedbeds National Nature Reserve BH20 144 E6
Arnewood Ct BH2 121 E2
Arnewood Gdns BA20 27 B2
Arnewood Rd BH6 123 D5
Arnewood Sch The BH25 94 F2
Arnold Cl BH22 53 A3
Arnold Rd BH22 53 A3
Arnolds Cl BH25 126 F8
Arran Way BH23 94 B1
Arras Cres BH20 139 D7
Arras Rd BH20 139 D7
Arrowfield DT6 100 C6
Arrow Field DT6 100 C6
Arrowsmith Ct BH18 87 A4
Arrowsmith La BH21 87 E7
Arrowsmith Rd BH21 87 E7
Arthur Cl BH2 121 F5
Arthur La 3 BH23 124 A7
Arthur Rd
Christchurch BH23 124 A7
Winchester SO23 126 E7
Artillery Rd BA22 26 C6
Artist Row DT5 186 F7
Arts Inst of Bournemouth The BH12 121 C8
Arun Cl 2 SP8 5 F3
Arundel Cl BH25 94 E3
Arundel Rd BA21 28 A6
Arundel Way BH23 125 F7
Ascham Rd BH8 122 B5
Ascot Rd BH18 87 A4
Ash Ave BH20 116 B3
Ashbarn Cres SO22 126 C3
Ashbourne Ct 1 BH1 122 A3
Ashbourne Rd BH5 123 B5
Ashbrook Wlk BH16 117 A6
Ashburn Garth 2 BH24 55 F6
Ashburton Gdns BH10 89 D1
Ash Cl
Alderholt SP6 42 C5
Sandford BH20 143 A8
Shaftesbury SP7 13 A4
Swanage BH19 178 F2
Upton BH16 118 B8
Ashcombe La DT9 31 D3
Ashdene Cl BH21 59 D5
Ashdown
8 Bournemouth BH2 121 D2
Bournemouth BH2 121 D2
Ashdown Cl BH17 87 F1
Ashdown Tech Coll BH17 87 E1
Ashdown Wlk BH25 95 C2
Ash End BA8 19 A5
Ashford Gr BA21 27 D7
Ashford Rd
Bournemouth BH6 123 D7
Fordingbridge SP6 42 E8
Ash Gr BH24 55 E7
Ashgrove 1 BA12 3 B4
Ash Hill DT2 106 F8
Ashington Gdns BH21 86 F8
Ashington La BH21 59 A1
Ashington Pk BH25 95 B1
Ashington St 3 DT1 107 D1
Ash La DT6 68 D5
Ashland Ct TA18 191 E5
Ashlands CE VC Fst Sch TA18 191 E5
Ashlands Cl 1 TA18 191 F5
Ashlands Mdw TA18 191 F5
Ashlands Rd TA18 191 F5
Ashleigh Ave DT2 72 F8
Ashleigh Rise BH10 89 D2
Ashlet Gdns BH25 95 D4
Ashley Arnewood Ct 5 BH25 95 B2
Ashley Cl
Bournemouth BH1 122 E6
Ringwood BH24 55 F6
Ashley Common Rd BH25 95 C4
Ashley Cross BH14 120 A4
Ashley Ct BH22 62 A8
Ashley Dr BH24 46 E2
Ashley Dr N BH24 54 B5
Ashley Dr S BH24 54 B5
Ashley Dr W BH24 54 B5
Ashley Inf Sch BH25 95 D3
Ashley Jun Sch BH25 95 C3
Ashley La BH25,SO41 95 E4
Ashley Meads BH25 95 D4
Ashley Pk BH24 54 C6
Ashley Rd
Bournemouth BH1 122 E5
Dorchester DT1 135 A8
Marnhull DT10 21 A2
New Milton BH25 95 C3
Poole BH14 120 C5
Ashley Wood Golf Club DT11 199 E1
Ashley Wood Nature Reserve DT11 211 F8
Ashley Wood Park DT11 211 F8
Ashley Wood Rd DT11 199 E2
Ashling Cl BH8 122 C8
Ashling Cres BH8 122 B8
Ashmead
22 Bournemouth BH4 121 C2
Yeovil BA20 26 E2
Ashmeads Cl BH21 60 A6
Ashmeads Way BH21 60 A6
Ashmore BH21 59 D4
Ashmore Ave
Barton on Sea BH25 127 B8

Ashmore Ave *continued*
Hamworthy BH15 .... 118 F1
Ashmore Bottom DT11 ... 39 D1
Ashmore Cl DT11 .... 212 D5
Ashmore Cres BH15 ...... 118 F1
Ashmore Gr BH23 .... 93 E1
Ashmore Ho 39 BH4 ..... 121 C3
Ashmore Rd SO22 .... 126 B7
Ashridge Ave 1 BH10 .... 89 D5
Ashridge Gdns BH10 ..... 89 D5
Ashridge Par 2 BH10 .... 89 D5
Ashstead Gdns BH8 ...... 90 C3
Ashton Ct
3 New Milton BH25 ...... 95 B3
Poole BH13 .... 121 A2
Ashton Rd
Bournemouth BH9 .... 89 F2
1 Weymouth DT4 .... 167 C2
Ashtree Cl BH25 .... 95 D2
Ash Tree Cl 2 DT2 .... 78 B1
Ash Tree La SP7 .... 24 D6
Ashurst Rd
Bournemouth BH8 .... 90 D3
Ferndown BH22 .... 53 A3
Ashwell Ct BH23 .... 91 F1
Ash Wlk BA8 .... 19 A5
Ashwood Dr
Broadstone BH18 .... 87 C4
5 Yeovil without BA21 .... 28 A8
Asker Gdns DT6 .... 100 D6
Askwith Cl DT9 .... 29 F5
Aspen Dr BH31 .... 45 D6
Aspen Gdns BH12 .... 120 F7
Aspen Pl BH25 .... 95 B1
Aspen Rd
Charminster DT2 .... 75 D3
Poole BH12 .... 120 F7
Aspen Way
10 Crewkerne TA18 ...... 191 F5
Poole BH12 .... 120 F7
Asquith Cl BH23 .... 124 D6
Ass Hill BH21 .... 201 B4
Astbury Ave
Poole BH12 .... 121 A8
Poole BH12 .... 89 A1
Aston Mead BH23 .... 91 E4
Astrid Way 3 DT4 ...... 167 E4
Athelhampton House & Gdns
DT2 .... 78 E1
Athelhampton Rd DT2 .... 78 E1
Athelney Ct 7 BH1 ..... 122 B3
Athelney Way BA21 ...... 26 F6
Athelstan Rd
Bournemouth BH6 .... 123 E5
2 Dorchester DT1 ...... 108 B1
Atkinson Cl BH25 .... 127 B8
Atlantic Ct SO22 .... 126 A5
Atlantic Rd BH19 .... 179 B1
Atrium The
Ferndown BH22 .... 61 E7
29 Winchester SO23 .... 126 D6
Attisham La DT6 .... 203 B4
Attwood Cl SP6 .... 42 B5
Auburn Mans 5 BH13 ... 121 B4
Auckland Rd BH23 ...... 125 C7
Audemer Ct BH24 .... 55 E8
Audrayton Ct 8 BH6 .... 123 E3
Augusta Cl DT5 .... 187 B5
Augustan Cl 1 DT1 ..... 134 F7
Augusta Rd DT5 .... 187 B6
Austen Ave
Bournemouth BH10 ...... 89 E6
Winchester SO22 .... 126 A2
Austen Cl SO23 .... 126 E8
Auster Cl BH23 .... 125 B7
Austin Ave BH14 .... 120 B1
Austin Cl BH1 .... 122 D5
Australia Rd DT3 ...... 166 D3
Autumn Cl BH22 .... 61 B7
Autumn Copse BH25 ..... 95 D2
Autumn Rd BH11 .... 88 D3
Avalanche Rd DT5 ..... 186 E2
Avalon BH14 .... 147 C8
Avebury Ave BH10 ...... 89 E6
Avenue Ct BH13 .... 121 B3
Avenue La 13 BH2 ..... 121 E3
Avenue Rd
Bournemouth BH2 ...... 121 E3
Christchurch BH23 .... 123 F7
Christchurch BH23 .... 124 A8
Lyme Regis DT7 .... 96 B5
New Milton BH25 .... 95 A3
Radipole DT4 .... 167 D4
Walkford BH23 .... 94 C2
Wimborne Minster BH21 ... 59 D4
Winchester SO22 ...... 126 C6
Avenue Sh Ctr The 14
BH2 .... 121 E3
Avenue The
Bournemouth BH9 .... 89 F3
6 Crewkerne TA18 ..... 192 A3
Ferndown BH22 .... 53 A3
Poole BH13 .... 121 A2
Sherborne DT9 .... 30 C7
West Moors BH24 .... 62 B8
Yeovil BA21 .... 27 D6
Aviation Park W
East Parley BH23 ...... 90 C8
Hurn BH23 .... 62 D1
Avington Ct SO22 ..... 126 A5
Avlan Ct SO23 .... 126 D3
Avocet Cl
Chickerell DT3 .... 166 D5
2 Weymouth DT4 ...... 180 D6
Avon Ave BH24 .... 54 F3
Avon Bldgs BH23 ...... 124 B7
Avonbourne Sch BH7 ... 123 A7
Avon Castle BH24 ...... 54 F3

Avon Castle Dr BH24 ..... 54 F4
Avon Cl
Bournemouth BH8 .... 122 D6
Weymouth DT4 .... 166 E4
Yeovil BA21 .... 27 F6
Avoncliffe Rd BH6 ...... 123 E3
Avon Cotts BH23 .... 92 C5
Avon Cswy BH23 .... 91 C7
Avon Ct
Christchurch BH23 ..... 124 C6
7 Poole BH13 .... 121 A4
Avondale Gdns SP8 .... 5 F3
Avon Dr BH20 .... 142 E5
Avon Farm Cotts BH23 ... 63 E3
Avon Heath Ctry Pk BH24 . 54 D3
Avon Heath Ctry Pk (South
Pk) BH24 .... 63 B8
Avon Ho BH2 .... 121 E2
Avon Mews BH8 .... 122 C6
Avon Pk BH24 .... 54 F6
Avon Rd
Bournemouth BH8 .... 122 C6
Ferndown BH22 .... 53 A1
Avon Road E BH23 ...... 124 A8
Avon Road W BH23 ..... 123 F8
Avon Run Cl BH23 ...... 125 B5
Avon Run Rd BH23 ..... 125 B5
Avonsands BH23 .... 125 A5
Avon View Par BH23 ..... 92 C3
Avon View Rd BH23 ..... 92 C3
Avon Wharf BH23 ...... 124 C5
Award Rd
Ferndown BH21 .... 60 F5
Wimborne BH21 .... 61 A6
Axeford TA20 .... 202 B8
Axe La
Broadwindsor DT8 ...... 203 C8
West Crewkerne TA18 ... 191 C1
Axe Valley Cl 1 DT8 ... 204 A8
Axford Cl BH8 .... 90 D3
Axminster Rd DT6 .... 96 F8
Axnoller La DT8 .... 204 D6
Aylesbury Rd BH1 ...... 122 E4
Aynsley Ct 3 DT4 ...... 167 C4
Aysha Cl BH25 .... 95 B1
Azalea Cl BH24 .... 54 C5
Aztec Ctr BH17 .... 119 D8
Azura Cl BH21 .... 53 D6

B

Babwell Rd BA9 .... 4 B3
Babylon Hill DT9 .... 28 D5
Babylon View BA21 ...... 28 B7
Back Dro DT9 .... 194 E3
Back La
Bere Regis BH20 .... 81 A3
Bradford Abbas DT9 ..... 28 D1
5 Broadwindsor DT8 .... 203 E5
Cerne Abbas DT2 .... 207 D4
Chetnole DT9 .... 194 D3
East Chinnock BA22 .... 192 E8
East Coker BA22 .... 193 C7
Evershot DT2 .... 206 A7
Frome Vauchurch DT2 .... 72 F7
Gillingham SP8 .... 5 D5
Halstock BA22 .... 193 C3
Hazelbury Bryan DT10 .. 197 A4
Kington Magna SP8 .... 9 C3
North Perrott TA18 ..... 192 C4
4 Okeford Fitzpaine DT11 197 F5
Rimpton BA22 .... 15 B8
Sherborne DT9 .... 30 B6
Sixpenny Handley SP5 .. 189 A4
Sturminster Marshall BH21 . 56 D5
Swyre DT2 .... 129 D5
Sydling St Nicholas DT2 .. 207 A2
Back Rivers La DT6 .... 100 D6
Back St
Abbotsbury DT3 .... 149 B7
East Stour SP8 .... 10 E3
Portesham DT3 .... 132 A1
Winchester SO23 .... 126 D2
Backwater DT2 .... 78 B2
Badbury Cl BH18 .... 87 C3
Badbury Ct BH22 .... 61 F7
Badbury Dr DT11 .... 212 D5
Badbury Rings (Hill Fort)
DT11 .... 49 A2
Badbury View BH21 ...... 59 D5
Badbury View Rd BH21 ... 86 D8
Baden Cl BH25 .... 95 B1
Baden-Powell & St Peter's
CE Mid Sch BH14 ...... 120 B3
Bader Rd BH17 .... 119 E8
Badger Farm Rd SO22 ... 126 B1
Badger Hts BA22 .... 26 D5
Badger La DT2 .... 209 A5
Badgers Cl BH24 .... 54 B5
Badgers Copse BH25 ..... 95 C6
Badger Sett DT11 ...... 212 C2
Badgers Way DT10 .... 35 B2
Badgers Wlk BH22 .... 61 E7
Badger Way BH31 .... 45 B5
Baglake DT2 .... 103 C2
Bagman's La BH21 ..... 201 E3
Bagwood Rd DT11 .... 81 C7
Bailey Cl
New Milton BH25 .... 95 D4
Winchester SO22 .... 126 B4
Bailey Cres BH15 ...... 119 C7
Bailey Dr BH23 .... 123 F7
Bailey Hall BH23 ...... 123 F7
Bailey Ridge DT9 ...... 195 A4
Bailey Ridge La DT9 ... 194 F4
Bailey's Dro BH20 ..... 139 F2
Baileys Hill BH21 ..... 201 D6

Bailie Gate Ind Est BH21 . 56 E3
Baiter Gdns BH15 .... 119 C1
Bakehouse TA16 .... 191 F7
Bakehouse La 1 DT9 .... 28 D1
Baker Rd BH11 .... 89 A5
Baker's Cross DT6 .... 65 D4
Bakers Farm Rd BH31 .... 45 A7
Bakers La 3 BH21 ...... 201 D1
Bakers Paddock DT2 .... 136 C2
Bakers View BH21 .... 86 D6
Balaclava Rd
Bovington Camp BH20 ... 139 E7
Fortuneswell DT5 ...... 181 D1
Balcombe Rd BH13 ...... 121 A3
Baldwin Cl BH23 .... 124 D6
Balena Cl BH17 .... 119 A8
Balfour Cl BH23 .... 125 D8
Balfour Rd BH9 .... 89 F1
Ballam Cl BH16 .... 118 C7
Ballard Cl
Lytchett Matravers BH16 .. 84 D4
New Milton BH25 .... 95 B4
Poole BH15 .... 119 D1
Ballard Coll BH25 .... 95 A4
Ballard Lee BH19 ...... 179 C5
Ballard Rd
Poole BH15 .... 119 D1
Swanage BH19 .... 179 C5
Ballard Sch BH25 .... 95 A4
Ballard Way BH19 ...... 179 C5
Ball's Hill BA22 .... 26 A7
Ball's La BH21 .... 56 D5
Balmer Rd DT11 .... 212 E6
Balmoor Cl 5 BA12 .... 3 B3
Balmoral Ave BH8 .... 90 E1
Balmoral Cres DT1 ..... 135 C8
Balmoral Ct 3 BH23 .... 126 B7
Balmoral Ho BH2 .... 121 D3
Balmoral Rd
Poole BH14 .... 120 C3
Yeovil BA21 .... 28 A6
Balmoral Wlk BH25 ...... 94 F3
Balston Rd BH14 .... 120 A6
Balston Terr BH15 ..... 119 B2
Banbury Rd BH17 .... 119 C7
Bancroft Ct 1 BH15 .... 119 E4
Bank Chambers BH14 .... 120 E3
Bank Cl BH23 .... 124 B6
Bankside Ho 3 SO22 ... 126 C6
Bankside Rd BH9 .... 90 A3
Banks Rd BH13 .... 147 C4
Banstead Rd BH18 .... 87 A5
Banton Shard DT6 .... 68 F1
Barberry Way BH31 ...... 45 E5
Barbers Gate 9 BH15 ... 119 B1
Barbers Piles 1 BH15 .. 119 B1
Barbers Wharf 8 BH15 .. 119 B1
Barclay Mans BH2 ...... 121 F5
Barclay Rd DT4 .... 167 C3
Bardolfeston Village DT2 . 78 D2
Bar End Ind Est SO23 ... 126 F3
Bar End Rd SO23 .... 126 F4
Barfield Cl SO23 ...... 126 F4
Bargates BH23 .... 124 B7
Barges Cl DT2 .... 103 C2
Baring Rd
Bournemouth BH6 ...... 124 A3
Winchester SO23 ...... 126 F5
Barlake Ct 5 DT1 ..... 107 D1
Barlands Cl
Burton BH23 .... 92 C2
Portland DT5 .... 186 E1
Barley Cl DT2 .... 194 A2
Barleycroft Rd 1 DT5 .. 186 E3
Barley Down Dr SO22 ... 126 B2
Barleyfields 1 SP8 ...... 5 E4
Barley Way DT4 .... 167 E1
Barlynch Ct 1 BA21 ..... 26 F6
Barnaby Mead SP8 .... 5 F2
Barnack Wlk DT11 ..... 212 C3
Barn Cl
8 Crewkerne TA18 ..... 191 E4
Upton BH16 .... 118 A7
Barn Cres 7 TA18 ..... 191 E4
Barndale Dr BH20 ..... 143 A1
Barnes Cl
Blandford Forum DT11 ... 212 E5
Bournemouth BH10 ...... 89 D3
Marnhull DT10 .... 21 A2
Sturminster Newton DT10 .. 35 B1
Winchester SO23 ...... 126 D3
Barnes Cres
Bournemouth BH10 ...... 89 D3
Wimborne Minster BH21 ... 59 E4
Barnes Cross DT9 ..... 196 A6
Barnes Pl BA12 .... 3 A5
Barnes Rd
Bournemouth BH10 ...... 89 D3
Wareham Town BH20 .... 142 D2
Barnes Wallis Cl DT4 .. 166 E3
Barnes Way 5 DT1 ..... 108 B1
Barnet Cl BA21 .... 27 A7
Barney's Cl DT6 .... 97 B8
Barnfield BH23 .... 125 D8
Barnhaven Cl DT4 ..... 167 B1
Barnhill Rd BH20 ..... 143 A1
Barn La TA18 .... 191 E6
Barn Rd BH18 .... 87 B3
Barnsfield Rd BH24 .... 54 D2
Barnsley Dro BH21 ..... 50 A3
Barns Rd BH22 .... 62 A6
Barn St TA18 .... 191 E4
Barons Ct 7 BH12 ..... 121 B4
Baronsmede 2 BH2 .... 121 D4
Barons Rd BH11 .... 88 D6
Barrack La BH24 .... 55 F4
Barrack Rd
Christchurch BH23 .... 123 E8

Barrack Rd *continued*
Christchurch BH23 ...... 124 A6
Ferndown BH22 .... 62 A2
Weymouth DT4 .... 167 E2
Barracks Cl BA22 .... 26 D7
Barrack St DT6 .... 100 D7
Barrie Rd BH9 .... 89 F3
Barr La
Burton Bradstock DT6 ... 128 A8
Shipton Gorge DT6 ..... 101 D4
Barrow Cl DT1 .... 134 E7
Barrow Dr BH8 .... 90 F2
Barrowfield Cl DT6 .... 128 A8
Barrowgate Rd BH8 ...... 90 D3
Barrowgate Way BH8 .... 90 D3
Barrow Hill
Bere Regis BH20 .... 81 B3
Stalbridge DT10 .... 33 C8
Stourton Caundle DT10 .... 32 F2
Barrowland La DT2 ...... 71 B5
Barrow Rd BH8 .... 90 F2
Barrow Rise DT4 .... 180 B8
Barrow Street La BA12 ..... 3 F3
Barrow View BH22 .... 61 B6
Barrow Way BH8 .... 90 F2
Barrs Ave BH25 .... 95 B4
Barr's La DT6 .... 97 A8
Barrs Wood Dr BH25 ..... 95 B4
Barrs Wood Rd BH25 ..... 95 B4
Barry Gdns BH18 .... 86 F5
Barry La BA22 .... 192 F6
Barter Rd BH12 .... 121 A7
Barters La
Broadstone BH18 .... 86 F3
Donhead St Mary SP7 ..... 25 B8
Bartholomew Cl 7 SO23 126 E7
Bartlets Cl DT2 .... 133 C6
Bartlett Dr BH7 .... 123 B8
Bartletts Pl BA21 .... 26 F5
Bartletts The 4 BA12 ..... 3 B4
Bartley Ct 2 BH21 ...... 59 B5
Bartom's La BH16 .... 84 B2
Barton Chase BH25 ..... 126 F7
Barton Cl
Sturminster Newton
DT10 .... 197 C8
Toller Porcorum DT2 ..... 71 D8
West Stafford DT2 ..... 136 B8
Barton Common La
BH25 .... 127 B8
Barton Common Rd
BH25 .... 127 B7
Barton Court Ave BH25 .. 127 A8
Barton Court Rd BH25 .... 95 A1
Barton Croft BH25 ..... 127 A7
Barton Dr
Barton on Sea BH25 .... 126 F8
Overcombe/Preston DT3 .. 153 B1
Barton Gdns DT9 .... 29 F6
Barton Gn BH25 .... 127 B6
Barton Hill
Kington Magna SP8 .... 9 D4
Melbury Osmond DT2 .... 194 A2
Shaftesbury SP7 .... 12 E3
Barton Ho BH25 .... 126 E7
Barton La
Barton on Sea BH25 .... 126 E8
Mere BA12 .... 3 A5
Barton Lo BH12 .... 120 B5
Bartonside Rd BH25 ... 126 C7
Barton Way BH25 ...... 126 F8
Barton Wood Rd BH25 .. 126 E7
Barwick CP Sch BA22 ... 193 F8
Basan Hill DT2 .... 78 D5
Bascott Cl BH11 .... 89 A1
Bascott Rd BH11 .... 89 A1
Basepoint Bsns Ctr BH23 . 62 C1
Bashley Common Rd
BH25 .... 95 A8
Bashley Cross Rd BH25 ... 94 E5
Bashley Dr BH25 .... 95 B6
Bashley Rd BH25 .... 95 A6
Bassett Rd BH12 .... 120 B6
Bat Alley DT10 .... 20 E1
Batchelor Cres BH11 .... 88 F3
Batchelor Rd BH11 ...... 89 A3
Batchelor's La BH21 ... 201 D1
Batchpool La BA8 .... 8 A7
Batcombe Cl BH11 .... 88 E3
Batcombe Rd DT9 ...... 194 F1
Bath Hill Ct 11 BH1 ... 122 A3
Bath Hill Rdbt BH1 .... 122 A2
Bath Orch 6 DT6 .... 68 F1
Bath Rd
Bournemouth BH1 ...... 122 A3
Sturminster Newton DT10 .. 35 B2
Bathsheba Terr 8 DT1 .. 135 B8
Bath St DT4 .... 167 D3
Bathwell La DT9 .... 17 D2
Bats La DT2 .... 106 E1
Batstone Way BH22 ...... 61 B6
Batten Cl BH23 .... 124 D7
Batterley Dro BH21 ..... 41 B4
Battery Hill SO22 .... 126 A4
Battle Mead
Corfe Castle BH20 .... 177 A8
Swanage BH19 .... 179 B4
Batts La DT6 .... 203 C2
Bauntons Cl 1 DT9 ..... 17 C2
Baunton's Orch DT9 ..... 17 C2
Baverstock Rd BH12 ... 121 B8
Bayard Rd DT3 .... 152 E2
Bay Cl
Swanage BH19 .... 179 C5
Three Legged Cross BH21 .. 53 A8
Upton BH16 .... 118 B6
Baycliffe Rd DT4 ..... 167 B2
Bay Cres BH19 .... 179 B5

Baydon Cl DT3 .... 153 B1
Bay Fields SP8 .... 5 F2
Bayfran Way DT11 ...... 212 E4
Bay Hog La BH15 .... 119 B2
Bay La SP8 .... 6 A2
Baynard's Rd DT1 ...... 107 D1
Bay Rd SP8 .... 5 F2
Baytree Ho 24 SO23 .... 126 D6
Bay Tree Way BH23 ...... 93 D1
Bay View
Bournemouth BH2 .... 121 E2
3 Swanage BH19 .... 178 E2
Bayview Gdns BH2 ...... 121 E2
Bayview Mews BH2 ..... 121 E2
Bayview Rd DT7 .... 96 B6
Beach Ave BH25 .... 126 F7
Beach Cl BH13 .... 147 G8
Beachcroft BH13 ...... 121 A3
Beach Gdns BH19 ...... 179 B3
Beach Rd
Burton Bradstock DT6 ... 128 C7
Poole BH13 .... 147 G8
Studland BH19 .... 164 C2
Upton BH16 .... 118 A6
Beach View BH13 ..... 147 C4
Beachview Cl 1 DT4 ... 180 B8
Beacon Ct BH23 ...... 125 F7
Beacon Dr BH23 ...... 125 F7
Beaconfield Rd BA20 ..... 27 A1
Beacon Gdns BH18 ...... 86 E3
Beacon Hill La BH21 .... 86 B3
Beacon Park Cres BH16 . 118 A8
Beacon Park Rd BH16 ... 118 B7
Beacon Pk Cres BH16 ... 117 C7
Beacon Rd
Bournemouth BH2 ...... 121 F2
Broadstone BH18 .... 86 E3
Corfe Mullen BH18 ..... 85 F3
Upton BH16 .... 118 B7
Beaconsfield Rd
Christchurch BH23 .... 124 B7
Poole BH12 .... 120 D6
Beacon Way BH18 .... 86 E3
Beadon La TA16 ...... 191 E7
Beaminster Mus DT8 ... 204 D4
Beaminster Rd DT6 ..... 68 F1
Beaminster Sch DT8 ... 204 C5
Beamish Rd BH17 ..... 119 F8
Bear Cross Ave BH11 .... 88 F6
Bear Cross Rdbt BH11 .... 88 F6
Bearwood Prim Sch BH11 88 C6
Beatty Cl BH24 .... 55 E8
Beatty Rd BH9 .... 90 B1
Beauchamp Pl BH23 .... 124 A7
Beauchamps Gdns BH7 .. 123 A8
Beaucroft La BH21 ..... 59 E5
Beaucroft Rd BH21 ..... 59 E6
Beaucroft Sch BH21 .... 59 E6
Beau Ct
43 Bournemouth BH4 .... 121 C3
9 New Milton BH25 ..... 95 A3
Beaufort Cl BH23 ..... 125 B7
Beaufort Dr BH21 ...... 59 C5
Beaufort Ho 10 BH4 ... 121 C2
Beaufort Mews BH21 .... 59 B4
Beaufort Rd
Bournemouth BH6 ..... 123 D6
Winchester SO23 ..... 126 D4
Beaufoy Cl SP7 .... 13 A3
Beaufoys Ave BH22 ..... 61 D7
Beaufoys Cl BH22 ...... 61 C7
Beaufoys Ct BH22 ...... 61 C6
Beaulieu DT4 .... 167 A6
Beaulieu Ave BH23 .... 123 E7
Beaulieu Cl BH25 ...... 94 E3
Beaulieu Dr BA21 ...... 26 F6
Beaulieu Rd
Bournemouth BH4 ..... 121 B1
Christchurch BH23 ... 123 E7
Beaumond Gn 11 SO23 .. 126 D5
Beaumont Ave
Bridport DT6 .... 100 D8
Radipole DT4 .... 167 D6
Beaumont Rd BH13 .... 147 F7
Beaver Ind Est BH23 .. 125 A7
Beccles Cl BH15 ..... 118 F2
Becher Rd BH14 ...... 120 E4
Beckett Cl DT11 ..... 212 C2
Beckhampton Rd BH15 .. 118 E3
Becklands La DT6 ..... 65 E4
Beckley Copse BH23 ... 94 A2
Becton La BH25 ..... 127 B7
Becton Mead BH25 .... 95 B1
Bedale Way BH15 .... 119 F5
Bedford Cres BH7 ... 123 C7
Bedford Pl DT6 ..... 100 D7
Bedford Rd
Weymouth DT4 ...... 167 A3
Yeovil BA21 .... 27 F8
Bedford Rd N BH12 ... 88 C2
Bedford Rd S BH12 ... 88 C2
Bedford Terr DT6 ... 100 D7
Beech Ave
Bournemouth BH6 ... 123 C4
Christchurch BH23 .. 123 D8
Holton Heath BH20 .. 116 B3
Beechbank Ave BH17 .. 86 F1
Beech Cl
Alderholt SP6 .... 42 C5
Broadmayne DT2 .... 136 B1
Broadstone BH18 ..... 86 E4
1 Spetisbury DT11 .. 211 E5
Verwood BH31 .... 45 A5
West Lulworth BH20 .. 172 D6

Beechcroft
Bournemouth BH1 . . . . 121 F5
Bournemouth BH1 . . . . 122 A5
Beechcroft La 1 BH24 . . . 55 D8
Beechcroft Mews 2
BH24 . . . . 55 D8
Beechcroft St Pauls Prim
Sch DT4 . . . . 167 C4
Beech Ct BH21 . . . . 59 E4
Beeches The
Bournemouth BH7 . . . . 123 A8
1 Shaftesbury SP7 . . . . 12 E3
Wareham St Martin BH20 143 A8
Beechey Ct 6 BH8 . . . . 122 A5
Beechey Rd BH8 . . . . 122 A5
Beechfield 42 BH4 . . . . . . 121 C3
Beech La
Hawkchurch EX13 . . . . 202 B1
Netherbury DT8 . . . . 204 A3
St Leonards BH24 . . . . 54 A2
Beech Rd
Puddletown DT2 . . . . 78 B1
Puncknowle DT2 . . . . 129 E2
Radipole DT3 . . . . 152 B4
Beech Tree Cl 3 DT2 . . . 206 C2
Beechwood BA20 . . . . 27 A2
Beechwood Ave
Bournemouth BH5 . . . . 122 F4
Bournemouth BH5 . . . . 123 A4
New Milton BH25 . . . . 94 F4
Beech Wood Cl BH18 . . . . . 87 A3
Beechwood Ct BH2 . . . . . 121 E2
Beechwood Dr 5 TA18 . . 191 F5
Beechwood Gdns BH5 . . . 123 A4
Beechwood Lo 1 BH4 . . 121 C2
Beechwood Rd BH22 . . . . . 53 B1
Beel Cl 2 DT5 . . . . 181 B1
Beer St BA20 . . . . 27 B4
Beggar's La SO23 . . . . 126 F6
Belben Cl BH12 . . . . 88 D2
Belben Rd BH12 . . . . 88 C2
Belchalwell St DT11 . . . . . 197 E4
Belfield Park Ave DT4 . . . 167 B1
Belfield Rd BH6 . . . . 124 A4
Belgrave DT4 . . . . 167 B6
Belgrave Ct BH1 . . . . 122 D3
Belgrave Pl 3 DT5 . . . . . . 186 F8
Belgrave Rd BH13 . . . . 121 A2
Bellbury Cl 1 DT2 . . . . 78 B1
Bell Chase BA20 . . . . 26 F5
Belle Vue DT4 . . . . 167 E2
Belle Vue Cl BH6 . . . . 123 D4
Belle Vue Cres BH6 . . . . . 123 F4
Belle Vue Gdns 2 BH6 . . 123 F4
Belle Vue Gr BH22 . . . . 53 B2
Belle Vue Mans 6 BH6 . . 123 E3
Belle Vue Rd
Bournemouth BH6 . . . . 123 E3
Poole BH14 . . . . 120 C3
Swanage BH19 . . . . 179 C1
Weymouth DT4 . . . . 167 D1
Belle Vue Terr 6 DT5 . . . 186 F7
Belle Vue Wlk BH22 . . . . . . 61 E2
Bellflower Cl BH23 . . . . . . 125 B8
Bell Heather Cl BH16 . . . . 118 B8
Bellman's Cross BA8 . . . . . . 19 C6
Bellows Cross BH21 . . . . . . 40 D8
Bells Ho BH21 . . . . 59 D6
Bells La BA12 . . . . 2 A6
Bell's Orch La BH20 . . . . . 142 E4
Bell St
Shaftesbury SP7 . . . . 12 E3
Swanage BH19 . . . . 178 F2
Belmont Ave BH8 . . . . 90 C2
Belmont Cl
Shaftesbury SP7 . . . . 12 F2
Verwood BH31 . . . . 45 C5
Belmont Rd
New Milton BH25 . . . . 95 C4
Poole BH14 . . . . 120 C5
Belmour Lo 36 BH4 . . . . . 121 C3
Belvedere Rd
Bournemouth BH3 . . . . 122 A6
Christchurch BH23 . . . . . . 124 A7
3 Swanage BH19 . . . . 179 C1
Yeovil BA21 . . . . 28 B6
Belvoir Pk 8 BH13 . . . . . . 121 B3
Bembury La DT9 . . . . 194 D8
Bemister Rd BH9 . . . . 122 A8
Benbow Cres BH12 . . . . 88 E1
Benbridge Ave BH11 . . . . . . 88 F5
Bendigo Rd BH23 . . . . 123 E8
Benellen Ave BH4 . . . . 121 C4
Benellen Gdns BH4 . . . . . 121 D4
Benellen Rd BH4 . . . . 121 C5
Benellen Twrs 1 BH4 . . . 121 C4
Bengal Rd BH9 . . . . 121 E8
Beningfield Wood Nature
Reserve DT6 . . . . 69 F7
Benjamin Ct BH23 . . . . 123 F7
Benjamin Rd BH15 . . . . . . 118 D2
Benlease Way BH19 . . . . . 178 E2
Benmoor Rd BH17 . . . . . . 119 A8
Benmore Cl BH25 . . . . 95 C2
Benmore Rd BH9 . . . . 90 A1
Bennett Ho 4 BH4 . . . . . . 121 C4
Bennett Rd BH8 . . . . 122 C6
Bennetts Hill La DT6 . . . . 101 C2
Bennetts Water Gdns
DT3 . . . . 166 D4
Ben Nevis Rd DT4 . . . . 167 C1
Bennion Rd BH10 . . . . 89 C3
Benridge Bsns Pk BH17 . 119 B8
Benridge Cl BH18 . . . . 87 A3
Benson Rd BH17 . . . . 119 D7
Bentley Rd BH9 . . . . 89 F3
Benville La DT2 . . . . 205 C6
Benville Rd DT4 . . . . 166 F2
Bere Cl
Poole BH17 . . . . 87 D2
Winchester SO22 . . . . 126 B8
Bere Down La BH20 . . . . . . 80 F5
Bere La DT9 . . . . 195 F7
Bere Marsh DT11 . . . . 198 B7
Bere Rd
Northport BH20 . . . . 142 D5
Winterborne Kingston DT11 81 E8
Bere Regis Bsns Pk BH20 . 81 B2
Bere Regis Fst Sch BH20 . 81 B1
Bere Regis Sports Club
BH20 . . . . 81 C3
Beresford Cl BH12 . . . . . . 120 D6
Beresford Gdns BH23 . . . 124 E6
Beresford Rd
Bournemouth BH5 . . . . 123 B4
Poole BH12 . . . . 120 D6
Bereweeke Ave SO22 . . . . 126 C8
Bereweeke Cl SO22 . . . . . 126 C7
Bereweeke Ho SO22 . . . . 126 C7
Bereweeke Rd SO22 . . . . . 126 C7
Bereweeke Way SO22 . . . 126 C8
Berkeley Ave BH12 . . . . . . 120 D8
Berkeley Cl
9 Pimperne DT11 . . . . 199 D4
Verwood BH31 . . . . 45 A7
Berkeley Ct DT6 . . . . 100 D6
Berkeley Rd
Bournemouth BH3 . . . . 121 E7
1 Pimperne DT11 . . . . 199 D3
3 Yeovil BA20 . . . . 27 C4
Berkeley Rise 8 DT11 . . . 199 D4
Berkley Ave BH22 . . . . 61 D2
Berkley Manor 8 BH13 . . 121 B4
Bermuda Ct 5 BH23 . . . . 126 A7
Bernards Cl BH23 . . . . 123 E8
Berne Ct 15 BH1 . . . . 122 A3
Beron Ct BH15 . . . . 119 E6
Berrans Ave BH11 . . . . 89 B6
Berrans Ct BH11 . . . . 89 A6
Berry La EX13 . . . . 202 D3
Bertram Rd BH25 . . . . 95 C4
Berwick La DT6 . . . . 129 D6
Berwick Rd BH3 . . . . 121 E6
Bessborough Rd BH13 . . . 147 E7
Bessells La DT11 . . . . 198 D8
Bessemer Cl BH31 . . . . 45 E4
Bestwall Cres BH20 . . . . . 142 F3
Bestwall Rd BH20 . . . . 142 F3
Beswick Ave BH10 . . . . 89 D2
Bethany Ct BH12 . . . . 121 A7
Bethany Ho BH1 . . . . 122 D5
Bethany Jun CE Sch
BH1 . . . . 122 D5
Bethia Cl BH8 . . . . 122 D6
Bethia Rd BH8 . . . . 122 D6
Bettiscombe Cl BH17 . . . . . 87 E2
Beverley Gdns BH10 . . . . . 89 D3
Beverley Grange 50 BH4 . 121 C3
Beverley Rd DT3 . . . . 152 D3
Bexington Cl BH11 . . . . 88 E3
Bickerley Gdns BH24 . . . . . 55 B6
Bickerley Rd BH24 . . . . 55 B6
Bicknell Ct 5 BH4 . . . . . . 121 C4
Bicknell Gdns BA21 . . . . . . 27 D8
Bicknell Sch BH7 . . . . 123 A7
Bicton Rd BH11 . . . . 89 B3
Biddlecome Orch 5
DT6 . . . . 100 C8
Biddlesden Rd BA21 . . . . . . 26 E7
Big Ope DT5 . . . . 186 E7
Bilberry Ct 11 SO22 . . . . . 126 D6
Billingsmoor La 4 DT1 . . 107 C1
Bilshay La DT6 . . . . 68 A2
Bimport SP7 . . . . 12 D2
Bincleaves Rd DT4 . . . . . . 167 D1
Bincombe Dr 2 TA18 . . . . 191 F5
Bincombe Rise DT3 . . . . . 152 E3
Bindbarrow Rd DT6 . . . . . 128 C6
Bindells The DT3 . . . . 166 D5
Bindon Abbey BH20 . . . . . 140 D2
Bindon Cl
Poole BH12 . . . . 120 E7
West Lulworth BH20 . . . . . 172 E7
Bindon La BH20 . . . . 140 D1
Bindon Rd BH20 . . . . 172 C5
Bindon Way 2 BH20 . . . . 140 B2
Bingham Ave BH14 . . . . . . 147 D8
Bingham Cl
Christchurch BH23 . . . . . . 124 E7
Verwood BH31 . . . . 45 D4
Bingham Dr BH31 . . . . 45 C4
Bingham Rd
Bournemouth BH9 . . . . 122 A7
Christchurch BH23 . . . . . . 124 E7
Verwood BH31 . . . . 45 C4
Binghams Rd DT2 . . . . 137 D6
Binnegar La BH20 . . . . 141 C3
Binnie Rd BH12 . . . . 120 E5
Birch Ave
Beckley BH25 . . . . 94 D5
Blandford St Mary DT11 . . 212 D1
Burton BH23 . . . . 92 C3
Ferndown BH22 . . . . 61 F1
Holton Heath BH20 . . . . . . 116 B3
Birch Cl
Corfe Mullen BH21 . . . . 86 D6
Poole BH14 . . . . 120 E3
St Leonards BH24 . . . . 53 F3
Birch Copse BH17 . . . . 119 A8
Birch Ct 3 SO22 . . . . 126 A4
Birchdale 6 BA20 . . . . 26 F2
Birchdale Rd BH21 . . . . 59 D5
Birch Dr BH8 . . . . 91 A2
Birchfield Prim Sch BA21 27 F8
Birchfield Rd BA21 . . . . 27 F7
Birch Gr
Ferndown BH22 . . . . 52 F2
Old Milton BH25 . . . . 95 A1
Birch La
Puddletown DT2 . . . . 77 F3
Yetminster DT9 . . . . 194 C5
Birch Rd BH24 . . . . 54 D4
Birch Wlk BH22 . . . . 61 F3
Birchwood Cl BH23 . . . . . 125 E8
Birchwood Dr SP6 . . . . 42 C5
Birchwood Mews BH14 . . 120 D3
Birchwood Rd
Poole BH14 . . . . 120 D3
Upton BH16 . . . . 118 B6
Bird's Cl 5 TA18 . . . . 191 E4
Birds Hill Gdns 1 BH15 . 119 E3
Bird's Hill Rd BH15 . . . . . 119 E3
Birinus Rd SO23 . . . . 126 E7
Birkdale Ct BH18 . . . . 87 A5
Birkdale Rd BH18 . . . . 87 A5
Bishop Cl BH12 . . . . 121 C7
Bishop Ct BH24 . . . . 55 C7
Bishop of Winchester Comp
Sch The BH8 . . . . 90 D1
Bishop Rd BH9 . . . . 122 A8
Bishops Cl
Abbotsbury DT3 . . . . 149 B7
Bournemouth BH7 . . . . 122 F7
Mere BA12 . . . . 3 A6
Bishops Ct BH18 . . . . 87 A3
Bishops La BA22 . . . . 193 A6
Bishop's La DT9 . . . . 28 D2
Bishop's Rd
Abbotsbury DT3 . . . . 149 C8
Portesham DT3 . . . . 131 D1
Bishops Row 9 BH19 . . . . 179 A2
Bitchams Mead BH20 . . . . . 81 A2
Bitterne Way BH31 . . . . 45 C5
Blackberry La
Christchurch BH23 . . . . . . 124 F6
Radipole DT3 . . . . 152 C2
Sherborne DT9 . . . . 30 A7
Blackbird Cl BH17 . . . . 118 E8
Blackbirds 6 DT9 . . . . 194 D8
Blackbird Way BH23 . . . . . . 93 C8
Blackburn Rd BH12 . . . . . 120 B6
Blackers Hole (Cave)
BH19 . . . . 184 D6
Blackfield La BH22 . . . . 53 A3
Blackfield Rd BH8 . . . . 90 D3
Black Hill BH31 . . . . 45 C6
Blackhill Rd BH16 . . . . . . 116 D3
Blackhill Rd W BH16 . . . . 116 D2
Black La DT11 . . . . 212 E4
Blacklands La DT11 . . . . . 197 D3
Black Lawn SP8 . . . . 5 F4
Black Mere BA22 . . . . 26 C5
Blackmoor La BA8 . . . . 19 A4
Black Moor Rd BH31 . . . . . 45 E4
Blackmore Rd
Shaftesbury SP7 . . . . 13 A4
Stalbridge DT10 . . . . 33 D8
Blacknell Ind Est 30
TA18 . . . . 191 F4
Blacknell La TA18 . . . . 191 F4
Blackney La DT6 . . . . 203 E2
Blacknoll La DT2 . . . . 138 F1
Blacknor Rd DT5 . . . . 186 E3
Blackpool Cnr DT6 . . . . . . 202 B1
Blackrow La DT10 . . . . 196 D7
Blacksmith Cl BH21 . . . . . . 86 D5
Blacksmith's La DT9 . . . . 194 D8
Blacksmith's Piece DT2 . 105 E1
Black Swan Bldgs 16
SO22 . . . . 126 D6
Blackthorn Way
New Milton BH25 . . . . 95 D4
Verwood BH31 . . . . 45 D5
Blackwater BH23 . . . . 91 D4
Blackwater Dr BH21 . . . . . . 87 D7
Blackwater Gr SP6 . . . . 42 A5
Blackwater La EX13 . . . . . 202 C3
Bladen View DT11 . . . . 79 E8
Blagdon Cl DT2 . . . . 133 D6
Blagdon Rd DT1 . . . . 107 D1
Blair Ave BH14 . . . . 120 C4
Blair Cl BH25 . . . . 94 E3
Blake Dene Rd BH14 . . . . 120 B1
Blake Hill Ave BH14 . . . . . 120 D1
Blake Hill Cres BH14 . . . . 120 C1
Blake Rd 22 TA18 . . . . 191 F4
Blandford Cl BH15 . . . . . . 118 F2
Blandford Hill
Milborne St Andrew DT11 . . 79 E8
Winterborne Whitechurch
DT11 . . . . 210 C3
Blandford Hospl DT11 . . . 212 C5
Blandford Hts Ind Est
DT11 . . . . 212 E6
Blandford L Ctr DT11 . . . . 212 C4
Blandford Rd
Corfe Mullen BH21 . . . . 86 D8
Hamworthy BH16 . . . . 118 D4
Iwerne Minster DT11 . . . . . 37 F2
Pamphill BH21 . . . . 58 D7
Shapwick DT11 . . . . 48 F2
Shillingstone DT11 . . . . . . 198 B6
Sturminster Marshall BH21 . 56 C4
Blandford Rd N
Lytchett Minster & Upton
BH16 . . . . 85 B2
Upton BH16 . . . . 118 B7
Upton BH16 . . . . 118 B8
Blandford St Mary CE VA Fst
Sch DT11 . . . . 212 D1
Blandford Sch The DT11 212 C4
Blaney Way BH21 . . . . 86 C6
Blanford Adult Ed Office
DT11 . . . . 212 D3
Blashford Lakes Study Ctr
BH24 . . . . 47 C4
Bleak St BA9 . . . . 1 C3
Bleax Cl SP7 . . . . 22 E1
Bleet La SP8 . . . . 10 D6
Bleke St SP7 . . . . 12 E3
Blemheim Rd DT3 . . . . 152 B1
Blenheim 3 BH13 . . . . 121 B3
Blenheim Cres SO41 . . . . . 95 F4
Blenheim Ct
35 Bournemouth BH4 . . . . 121 C3
Christchurch BH23 . . . . . . 124 A8
Blenheim Dr BH23 . . . . . . 125 B6
Blenheim Mews 6 BH4 . 121 C4
Blenheim Rd BA21 . . . . 27 F7
Blind La
Berwick St John SP7 . . . . . 188 B8
Evershot DT2 . . . . 206 B7
Ringwood SP6 . . . . 43 E1
Thorncombe TA20 . . . . 202 E6
Wimborne Minster BH21 . . . 59 B5
Blind La Cl DT6 . . . . 68 F2
Blindmere Rd DT5 . . . . . . 186 E4
Blind St BH20 . . . . 81 B2
Blissford Hill SP6 . . . . 43 F5
Bloody Shard Gate DT11 . 188 A1
Bloomfield Ave BH9 . . . . . . 89 F2
Bloomfield Pl BH9 . . . . 89 F2
Bloxworth Rd
Poole BH12 . . . . 120 F8
Poole BH12 . . . . 121 A8
Blue Ball Hill SO23 . . . . . . 126 F6
Bluebell Cl BH23 . . . . 125 B8
Bluebell La BH17 . . . . 86 F1
Bluebell Rd BA22 . . . . 26 D5
Blue Pool BH20 . . . . 161 A3
Bluff The BH10 . . . . 89 F4
Bluntshay La DT6 . . . . 66 E8
Blyth Cl BH23 . . . . 91 D4
Blythe Rd BH21 . . . . 86 D6
Blythswood Ct BH25 . . . . 126 F7
Boar St BA12 . . . . 3 A5
Bob Hann Cl BH12 . . . . . . 120 D5
Bockhampton Cross
DT2 . . . . 109 A3
Bockhampton La DT2 . . . 109 A3
Bockhampton Rd BH23 . . . 92 E6
Bodkin La DT3 . . . . 168 A6
Bodley Rd BH13 . . . . 147 F7
Bodorgan Rd BH2 . . . . 121 F4
Bodowen Cl BH23 . . . . 92 D2
Bodowen Rd BH23 . . . . 92 D1
Bodsmarsh La DT10 . . . . . . 21 E1
Bognor Rd BH18 . . . . 86 F4
Bohay's Dr DT4 . . . . 180 C7
Bokerley Ditch SP6 . . . . . . 190 A5
Bokerley Junc SP5 . . . . . . 189 E6
Boldre Cl
Barton on Sea BH25 . . . . . 126 D8
Poole BH12 . . . . 120 D7
Boleyn Cres
Bournemouth BH9 . . . . 90 C4
Weymouth DT4 . . . . 180 E7
Bolton Cl BH6 . . . . 123 E3
Bolton Cres BH22 . . . . 62 A6
Bolton Ct 3 BH6 . . . . 123 E3
Bolton Rd BH6 . . . . 123 E3
Bon Accord Rd BH19 . . . . 179 B1
Bond Ave BH22 . . . . 52 F4
Bond Rd BH15 . . . . 119 F5
Bond St
Radipole DT4 . . . . 167 D3
4 Yeovil BA20 . . . . 27 D4
Yeovil BA22 . . . . 26 C5
Boney Rd BH20 . . . . 139 E7
Bonfields Ave BH19 . . . . . 179 B4
Bonham La BA12 . . . . 1 E7
Bonham Rd BH9 . . . . 121 F7
Bonhole La DT6 . . . . 101 E4
Bonington Cl BH23 . . . . . . 124 E8
Bonnett's La BH20 . . . . . . 142 E4
Bonscombe La DT6 . . . . . . 101 C5
Bonvils Rd BH19 . . . . 183 B7
Bookham La DT2 . . . . 208 B7
Boot La 7 DT9 . . . . 194 D8
Boozer Pit TA16 . . . . 191 F8
Border Dr BH16 . . . . 118 C5
Border Rd
Lytchett Minster & Upton
BH16 . . . . 117 E5
Upton BH16 . . . . 118 C5
Boreham Rd BH6 . . . . 123 D5
Borthwick Rd BH1 . . . . . . 122 E5
Boscobel Rd SO22 . . . . . . 126 D7
Boscombe Cliff Rd BH5 . 122 F3
Boscombe Grove Rd
BH1 . . . . 122 D5
Boscombe Overcliff Dr
Bournemouth BH5 . . . . 122 F3
Bournemouth BH5 . . . . 123 A3
Boscombe Spa Rd BH5 . . 122 D3
Bosley Cl BH23 . . . . 91 E2
Bosley Way BH23 . . . . 91 E2
Boston Lo 31 BH4 . . . . 121 C3
Boswell's Cl BH20 . . . . 81 B3
Bosworth Mews BH9 . . . . . 90 B4
Bothen Dr DT6 . . . . 100 E6
Bottlebush La BH21 . . . . . 189 E1
Bottom Rd DT11 . . . . 198 F4
Boulnois Ave BH14 . . . . . . 120 E3
Boulton Cl DT4 . . . . 180 D8
Boundary Ave BA22 . . . . . . 26 D7
Boundary Cl
Swanage BH19 . . . . 185 C8
Yeovil BA21 . . . . 27 A7
Boundary Dr BH21 . . . . 59 D6
Boundary La BH24 . . . . 53 F1
Boundary Rd
Bournemouth BH10 . . . . . . 121 D8
Bournemouth BH10 . . . . 89 E1
Yeovil BA22 . . . . 26 C5
Boundary Rdbt BH3,
BH10 . . . . 121 D8
Boundary View 1 DT11 . 212 D4
Boundary Way BA22 . . . . . 26 C7
Bound La DT9 . . . . 194 F2
Bountys La BH12 . . . . 120 E5
Bourne Ave BH2 . . . . 121 E3
Bourne Cl BH2 . . . . 121 D3
Bourne Ct
1 Bournemouth BH2 . . . . 121 F3
Wimborne Minster BH21 . . . 59 D5
Bourne Dr BH20 . . . . 142 D6
Bourne Dro DT2 . . . . 76 F6
Bournemouth Aviation Mus
BH23 . . . . 91 A8
Bournemouth Central Bsns
Pk BH1 . . . . 122 C5
Bournemouth Ho 2
BH1 . . . . 122 B3
Bournemouth Int Ctr
BH2 . . . . 121 F2
Bournemouth International
Airport BH23 . . . . 90 E8
Bournemouth Learning
Support Centre PRU
BH10 . . . . 89 D1
Bournemouth Memorial
Homes BH8 . . . . 90 F1
Bournemouth Nuffield
Derwent Suite BH7 . . . . . . 91 B1
Bournemouth Nuffield Hospl
The BH8 . . . . 122 A5
Bournemouth & Poole Coll
Annexe The BH1 . . . . 122 A3
Bournemouth & Poole Coll
(Constitution Hill Campus)
The BH14 . . . . 119 F5
Bournemouth & Poole Coll
(North Road Campus) The
BH14 . . . . 119 F4
Bournemouth & Poole Coll
The BH1 . . . . 122 B3
Bournemouth Rd
Blandford Forum DT11 . . . 212 D2
Charlton Marshall DT11 . . . 211 D6
Poole BH14 . . . . 120 D4
Bournemouth Sch BH8 . . . 90 C1
Bournemouth Sch for Girls
BH8 . . . . 90 C2
Bournemouth Sta BH8 . . 122 B4
Bournemouth Station Rdbt
BH8 . . . . 122 B4
Bournemouth Univ
(Lansdowne Campus)
BH1 . . . . 122 B3
Bournemouth Univ (Talbot
Campus) BH12 . . . . 121 C8
Bournemouth West Rdbt
BH2 . . . . 121 D3
Bourne Pines 4 BH2 . . . . 121 F4
Bourne Pk DT2 . . . . 77 B8
Bourne River Ct 9 BH4 . 121 D4
Bourne Valley Bsns Pk
BH12 . . . . 121 A5
Bourne Valley Rd BH12 . . 121 A5
Bourne Way SP8 . . . . 5 F3
Bournewood Dr BH4 . . . . 121 C4
Bourton Gdns BH7 . . . . . . 123 B8
Bouverie Cl 7 BH25 . . . . . 95 A1
Boveridge Gdns BH9 . . . . . 90 B4
Boveridge House Sch
BH21 . . . . 190 B1
Bovington Cl BH17 . . . . 87 F1
Bovington Fst Sch BH20 139 D6
Bovington La BH20 . . . . . . 139 E5
Bovington Mid Sch
BH20 . . . . 140 A5
Bowden La
Henstridge BA8 . . . . 18 C5
Milborne Port DT9 . . . . 17 F5
Bowden Rd
Abbas & Templecombe
BA8 . . . . 18 B8
Poole BH12 . . . . 88 C2
Bowditch Row 25 TA18 . . 191 F4
Bowdowns DT6 . . . . 204 B2
Bower Ct 5 DT9 . . . . 194 C5
Bower Rd BH8 . . . . 122 D8
Bowers Rd 4 DT5 . . . . 186 E3
Bowerswain Hollow
BH21 . . . . 201 B5
Bowerwood Rd SP6 . . . . . . 42 E8
Bowes La 6 DT8 . . . . 204 A8
Bowey 6 DT11 . . . . 197 F6
Bow Gate TA16 . . . . 192 A8
Bowgrove Rd DT8 . . . . 204 D5
Bowhayes
Bridport DT6 . . . . 100 E5
8 Crewkerne TA18 . . . . 191 F4
Bowland Rise BH25 . . . . . . 95 C2
Bowleaze BA21 . . . . 26 F6
Bowleaze Coveway DT3 . 168 B6
Bowling Green La SP5 . . . 189 D5
Bown Hill DT5 . . . . 186 E1
Bow The 3 DT1 . . . . 108 A2
Box Cl BH17 . . . . 119 B7
Boyd Rd BH12 . . . . 120 F6
Boyle Cl DT10 . . . . 33 D8
Boyne's La DT11 . . . . 38 D1
Boys Hill Dro DT9 . . . . 195 D5
Boyte Rd 14 DT11 . . . . 199 D4
Bozley Hill SP7 . . . . 24 A7

Brabazon Dr BH23 ...... 125 B7
Brabazon Rd BH21 ...... 59 F1
Brabourne Ave BH22 ..... 61 C4
Brackenbury Inf Sch DT5 ...... 186 E7
Bracken Cl BH24 .... 53 F4
Bracken Ct 10 BH4 ...... 121 D4
Brackendale Ct BH21 ..... 52 F8
Brackendale Rd BH8 .... 122 D8
Brackendown Ave DT3 .. 167 F8
Bracken Glen BH15 ..... 119 E5
Brackenhill BH13 .... 121 A1
Brackenhill Rd BH21 ..... 60 A7
Bracken Lodge 3 BH6 .. 123 F4
Bracken Rd
Bournemouth BH6 .... 123 C4
Ferndown BH22 .... 61 B7
Brackens Way 2 BH13 .. 147 F8
Bracken Way BH23 ...... 94 B1
Bracket's Coppice Nature Reserve BA22 .... 193 A2
Bracklesham Pl BH25 ... 126 F7
Brackley Cl BH23 .... 91 A8
Bradburne Rd BH2 ...... 121 E3
Bradbury Ho BH22 ...... 61 D7
Bradford La DT9 .... 195 B6
Bradford Rd
Bournemouth BH9 ...... 90 C4
1 Crewkerne TA18 ..... 192 A3
Sherborne DT9 .... 29 E5
Weymouth DT4 .... 167 B2
Bradley Peak SO22 ..... 126 A7
Bradpole Rd BH8 .... 90 E1
Bradstock Cl BH12 ..... 120 F8
Braemar Ave BH6 ...... 124 A4
Braemar Cl BH6 .... 124 A4
Braemar Dr BH23 ...... 93 F1
Braemar Rd DT1 ...... 135 C8
Braemore Ct SO22 ..... 126 A5
Braeside Bsns Pk BH15 .. 119 B4
Braeside Rd
Ferndown BH22 .... 53 B3
St Leonards BH24 ...... 54 A4
Braidley Rd BH2 ...... 121 E4
Brailswood Rd BH15 .... 119 E4
Braishfield Gdns BH8 .... 90 D2
Brakes Hill DT2 .... 194 A2
Bramar Ct 9 BH4 ...... 121 C2
Bramble Cl SP6 .... 42 C5
Bramblecombe La DT11 209 D4
Bramble Ct BH22 .... 53 A2
Bramble Dr DT6 .... 100 D2
Bramble Dro DT2 ...... 136 A2
Bramble Edge DT2 ..... 136 A2
Bramble La
Haselbury Plucknett TA18 .... 192 C5
Walkford BH23 .... 94 B1
Brambling Cl DT3 ...... 152 C4
Bramdon Cl 5 DT3 ..... 150 A8
Bramdon La DT3 ...... 150 C6
Bramley Cl 8 TA18 .... 191 F5
Bramley Ct BH22 ...... 61 C6
Bramley Hill
Bridport DT6 .... 100 E8
Mere BA12 .... 2 F5
Bramley Rd
Bournemouth BH10 ..... 89 C5
Ferndown BH22 .... 61 D6
Brampton Rd BH15 .... 119 D6
Bramshaw Gdns BH8 .... 90 D3
Bramshaw Way BH25 ... 126 D8
Branders Cl BH6 ...... 124 A4
Branders La BH6 ...... 124 B5
Brandon Ct 6 BH12 .... 121 B4
Brandwood Ct 4 BH14 .. 120 A3
Brandy La 2 DT5 ...... 186 E7
Brandy Row 1 DT5 ..... 186 E7
Branksea Ave BH15 .... 118 E1
Branksea Cl BH15 ..... 118 E1
Branksome Cl BH25 ..... 95 B2
Branksome Ct 4 BH13 .. 147 F8
Branksome Dene Rd BH4 .... 121 B2
Branksome Heath Mid Sch BH12 .... 120 C6
Branksome Hill Rd BH4 . 121 B5
Branksome Sta BH12 ... 120 F4
Branksome Twrs BH13 .. 147 H8
Branksome Wood Gdns BH2 .... 121 D4
Branksome Wood Rd BH2, BH4 .... 121 C4
Branscombe Cl 1 DT5 .. 186 E2
Bransford BA22 .... 193 D3
Bransgore CE Prim Sch BH23 .... 93 C8
Brantwood 8 DT8 ..... 204 C4
Branwell Cl BH23 ...... 92 A1
Brassey Cl BH9 .... 90 A1
Brassey Rd
Bournemouth BH9 ...... 90 A1
Winchester SO22 ..... 126 D7
Brassey Terr BH9 ..... 89 F1
Bratch La DT11 .... 200 D1
Breach Cl SP8 .... 1 E2
Breaches La BH20 ..... 163 A2
Breach Field 4 BH20 ... 140 A2
Breach La
Kington Magna SP8 ..... 9 C3
Shaftesbury SP7 ...... 12 D2
Breamore Cl BH25 ..... 94 E3
Brearley Ct BH23 ..... 126 B8
Brecon Cl
Bournemouth BH10 ..... 89 E6
New Milton BH25 ...... 95 C2
Bredy Cl BH17 .... 87 D1
Bredy La DT6 .... 101 F1
Bredy Rd DT6 .... 128 D7
Bremble Cl BH12 .... 88 C2
Breston Cl 2 DT5 ...... 186 E1
Brewers Quay Sh Village DT4 .... 167 E1
Brian Cl BH20 .... 143 A8
Briar Cl
Christchurch BH23 ..... 124 F6
Gillingham SP8 .... 5 E2
Mudford BA21 .... 28 A8
Poole BH15 .... 119 E5
Radipole DT4 .... 167 A5
Briarfield 49 BH4 ...... 121 C3
Briars End DT2 .... 137 E6
Briars The 3 BA20 ...... 26 F2
Briarswood Rd BH16 .... 118 C7
Briar Way BH21 .... 60 B5
Brickfields Ind Est SP8 ... 10 F8
Brickyard La
Bourton SP8 .... 1 E1
Corfe Mullen BH21 ..... 58 A1
Ferndown BH22 .... 61 A6
Gillingham SP8 .... 5 F1
Silton SP8 .... 4 E8
Sturminster Newton DT10 197 A7
Swanage BH19 .... 179 A5
Brick Yd La 4 TA18 ..... 191 F5
Bridewell Ct DT9 .... 30 C5
Bridewell La SP7 .... 7 A4
Bridge App BH15 .... 119 B1
Bridge Cl SP8 .... 6 A1
Bridge Inn La DT3 ..... 153 C1
Bridge Pl BH10 .... 89 D7
Bridge Rd DT6 .... 97 B8
Bridges Cl BH22 .... 53 A3
Bridge St
Bourton SP8 .... 1 E2
Christchurch BH23 ..... 124 C6
1 Lyme Regis DT7 ...... 96 C5
Netherbury DT6 .... 204 C2
Sturminster Marshall BH21. 56 D3
Sturminster Newton DT10 197 D8
7 Winchester SO23 ..... 126 F5
Bridges The BH24 ...... 55 A7
Bridgewater Rd BH12 ... 120 D6
Bridlebank Way DT3 .... 152 B3
Bridle Cl BH16 .... 118 D7
Bridle Cres BH7 .... 123 D7
Bridle Way
Barwick BA22 .... 193 E8
Wimborne Minster BH21 ... 60 C6
Bridleways BH31 .... 45 A6
Bridport Com Hospl DT6 100 B8
Bridport FC DT6 .... 100 C5
Bridport L Ctr DT6 ..... 100 C5
Bridport Prim Sch DT6 .. 100 E7
Bridport Rd
Beaminster DT8 .... 204 D3
Broadwindsor DT8 ..... 203 C8
Dorchester DT1 .... 107 C1
Poole BH12 .... 120 F8
Verwood BH31 .... 45 B6
Bridport & W Dorset Golf Club DT6 .... 100 D1
Brierley Ave BH22 ...... 61 E1
Brierley Cl BH10 .... 89 E5
Brierley Hay 9 DT9 .... 194 C5
Brierley Rd BH10 ...... 89 E4
Brigadier Cl 1 BA22 .... 26 C5
Brighthay La DT6 ...... 67 A1
Brightlands Ave BH6 ... 123 F5
Bright Rd BH15 .... 119 E6
Brightsmead DT2 ...... 209 B6
Brimclose Rd TA17 ..... 191 B7
Brimley Rd EX13 .... 202 A3
Brincombe Valley Prim Sch DT3 .... 152 E3
Brinscombe La 3 SP7 ... 13 A1
Brinsley Cl DT10 ...... 35 A1
Brinsons Cl BH23 ...... 92 C3
Brionne Way SP7 .... 13 A3
Brisbane Rd
Christchurch BH23 ..... 91 E1
Radipole DT3 .... 152 E2
Brister End DT9 .... 194 C5
Bristol Rd DT9 .... 30 B7
Briston Cl 6 DT1 ...... 107 C1
Britannia Ct BH12 ..... 120 B7
Britannia Rd BH14 ..... 120 A3
Britannia Way
Christchurch BH23 ..... 125 B7
Dorchester DT1 .... 134 E8
Britmore La SP7 .... 13 F8
Brit The 4 DT8 .... 204 D4
Brit View Rd DT6 ...... 100 B2
Britwell Dr BH20 ...... 172 C4
Brixey Cl BH12 .... 120 C7
Brixey Rd BH12 .... 120 C7
Brixey's La BH20 ...... 142 E4
Broadacres
East Coker BA22 ...... 193 C8
Gillingham SP8 .... 5 F3
Broad Ave BH8 .... 122 D8
Broad Chalke Down SO22 .... 126 A2
Broad Cl DT11 .... 81 E8
Broadcroft Gdns DT5 ... 187 A4
Broad Hill BA22 .... 192 D7
Broadhill La SP6 .... 43 F8
Broadhurst Ave BH10 .... 89 E4
Broad La
Bridport DT6 .... 100 B5
East Chinnock BA22 .... 192 E7
Broadlands 27 BH4 .... 121 C3
Broadlands Ave BH6 ... 123 F4
Broadlands Cl
Bournemouth BH8 ...... 90 D3
Walkford BH23 .... 94 B2
Broadlands Rd DT3 ..... 152 B2
Broadleaze BA21 .... 26 F6
Broadmayne Fst Sch DT2 .... 136 C3
Broadmayne Rd BH12 ... 121 A8
Broadmead DT2 .... 136 B2
Broadmead Ave DT6 .... 100 B7
Broadmead Cl 4 DT8 ... 204 A8
Broadmeadow Rd DT4 .. 180 D7
Broad Mead Rd BH21 .... 45 A1
Broadmoor Rd BH21 ..... 86 C7
Broadoak Ave 2 DT8 ... 204 A7
Broadoak Rd DT6 .... 67 E1
Broad Rd BH19 .... 179 C2
Broad Robin SP8 .... 5 E2
Broadshard La BH24 .... 47 C1
Broadshard Rd TA18 .... 191 F5
Broad St DT7 .... 96 C5
Broads The BH21 .... 58 F6
Broadstone Fst Sch BH18 87 B4
Broadstone La
Hardington Mandeville BA22 .... 193 A6
West Chinnock TA18 .... 192 C8
Broadstone Mid Sch BH18 .... 87 C5
Broadstone Way
Broadstone BH17 .... 86 F1
Poole BH17 .... 119 B7
Broadwater Ave BH14 ... 120 C2
Broadway
Merriott TA16 .... 191 E7
Southbourne BH6 ...... 124 B3
Broadway Ct BH12 ..... 121 A5
Broadway Gables BH14 .. 120 E4
Broadway Gdns 6 BH21 .. 59 C4
Broadway Ho BH18 ...... 87 B4
Broadway La
Bournemouth BH8 ...... 90 C4
West Chinnock BA22 ... 192 D8
Broadway Mews BH14 ... 119 F3
Broadway Pk 4 BH21 .... 59 C4
Broadway The
Bournemouth BH10 ..... 89 D6
Winchester SO23 ...... 126 E5
Broadwey Cl DT3 ...... 152 C4
Broadwindsor CE Prim Sch DT8 .... 203 E5
Broadwindsor Craft & Design Ctr DT8 .... 203 F5
Broadwindsor Rd DT8 ... 204 B4
Broadwindsor Road Ind Est DT8 .... 204 B4
Brockenhurst Rd BH9 .... 90 B2
Brockhills La BH25 ..... 95 C6
Brockington La BH21 ... 201 C5
Brockley Rd BH10 ...... 89 E4
Brocks Pine BH24 ...... 54 B3
Brockwood BH24 .... 53 F2
Brodham Way DT11 ..... 198 B5
Brog St BH21 .... 58 C1
Broke La DT9 .... 195 D6
Brombys The 11 BH15 ... 119 C2
Bromley Ho BH12 ...... 121 B5
Brompton Ct BH2 ...... 121 E3
Bronte Ave BH23 .... 92 A1
Brook Ave BH25 .... 95 B4
Brook Ave N BH25 ...... 95 B4
Brook Cl BH10 .... 89 C4
Brookdale Cl BH18 ..... 87 A4
Brookdale Farm BH18 ... 87 A4
Brook Dr BH31 .... 45 D4
Brook Ho BH25 .... 126 E7
Brookhouse St 8 DT1 ... 107 D1
Brook La
Bransgore BH23 .... 93 B7
Corfe Mullen BH21 ..... 86 C6
Henstridge BA8 .... 19 A4
Woodlands BH21 .... 44 B7
Brooklands
Bournemouth BH4 ..... 121 B3
Milborne St Andrew DT11 .. 79 E8
Brooklands Farm Conservation Ctr DT2 ... 75 B3
Brookland Way 4 BA8 ... 19 A4
Brooklyn Ct BH25 ...... 94 F3
Brookmead Cl DT3 ..... 153 D2
Brook Rd
Bournemouth BH10 ..... 89 C4
Poole BH12 .... 120 C5
Wimborne Minster BH21 ... 59 E4
Brook Road Depot BH21 .. 59 E3
Brooks Cl BH24 .... 55 D6
Brookside
8 Gillingham SP8 .... 5 F3
Milborne Port DT9 ..... 17 D1
Ringwood SP6 .... 43 E2
West Coker BA22 ...... 193 A8
Brookside Cl 2 DT3 .... 153 C2
Brookside Park Homes BH21 .... 86 B4
Brookside Rd
Bransgore BH23 .... 93 A8
Wimborne Minster BH21 ... 59 F4
Brookside Way BH23 .... 93 E1
Brooks Sh Ctr The SO23 . 126 E6
Brook St
Milborne Port DT9 ..... 17 D1
Shipton Gorge DT6 .... 101 D4
Brook Terr SP6 .... 43 B8
Brook Way BH23 ...... 125 C7
Broomfield Ct BH22 .... 61 E6
Broomfield Dr SP6 ..... 42 C5
Broom Hill DT2 .... 205 F5
Broom La BH6 .... 123 B4
Broom Rd BH12 .... 88 C1
Broom Road Bsns Pk BH12 .... 88 C1
Broughton Ave BH10 .... 89 E3
Broughton Cl BH10 ..... 89 E3
Broughton Cres DT4 .... 180 C7
Broughtons Dr 2 TA18 .. 192 A3
Brownen Rd BH9 ...... 122 B8
Brownes Pl DT2 .... 73 F3
Browning Ave
Bournemouth BH5 ..... 122 F4
Bournemouth BH5 ..... 123 A4
Browning Dr SO22 ..... 126 B6
Browning Rd BH12 ..... 120 D6
Brownlow Ct 33 BH4 ... 121 C3
Brownlow St DT4 ...... 167 D4
Brown's Cres DT3 ..... 166 E5
Brownsea Ave BH21 .... 86 D6
Brownsea Cl BH25 ..... 94 E3
Brownsea Ct BH14 .... 147 B8
Brownsea Island BH15 .. 146 D4
Brownsea Island Nature Reserve BH13 ..... 145 F5
Brownsea Rd BH13 .... 147 B3
Brownsea View Ave BH14 .... 120 C1
Brownsea View Cl BH14 . 120 C1
Browns La SP6 .... 190 E3
Brown's La SP8 .... 10 F3
Brown St DT9 .... 196 A7
Brudenell Ave BH13 ... 147 D7
Brudenell Rd BH13 .... 147 D6
Brunel Cl BH31 .... 45 E4
Brunel Dr DT3 .... 153 B1
Brune Way BH22 ...... 61 D3
Brunsell's Knap DT10 ... 33 A2
Brunstead Pl 1 BH12 .. 121 B4
Brunstead Rd BH12 ... 121 B4
Brunswick St BA20 .... 27 C4
Brushy Bush La SP5 ... 188 F3
Brutus Cl DT1 .... 134 E7
Bryanstone Rd BH3 ... 121 E7
Bryanston Sch DT11 ... 212 A5
Bryanston St DT11 .... 212 C3
Bryant Rd BH12 ...... 121 A8
Bryants La DT4 ...... 180 B8
Brymer Rd DT2 .... 110 B8
Brymers Ave 5 DT5 ... 186 F7
Brympton Ave BA22 .... 26 B4
Brympton Way BA20 ... 26 E3
Bryn Rd
Sandford BH20 .... 143 A8
Weymouth DT4 .... 167 B2
Bryony Cl BH18 .... 86 F3
Bryony Gdns SP8 .... 5 D2
Bub La BH23 .... 124 E6
Buccaneers Cl BH23 ... 124 E6
Buccleuch Rd BH13 ... 121 A1
Bucehayes Cl BH23 ... 126 A8
Buchanan Ave BH7 .... 122 E6
Buckbury Mews 13 DT1 . 135 B8
Buckhill Cl 5 TA18 ... 191 F3
Buckhorn Cl DT6 ...... 69 B8
Buckingham Ct
1 Christchurch BH23 ... 126 A7
Poole BH15 .... 119 D3
Buckingham Mans 5 BH1 .... 122 A3
Buckingham Rd
Gillingham SP8 .... 5 F1
Poole BH12 .... 120 D7
Buckingham Way DT1 .. 135 C8
Buckingham Wlk BH25 ... 94 E3
Buckland Gr BH23 ..... 93 E2
Buckland Newton Prim Sch DT2 .... 208 A8
Buckland Rd
Poole BH12 .... 120 C5
Yeovil BA21 .... 28 A6
Buckland Terr BH12 ... 120 C5
Buckle Pl BA22 .... 26 C6
Bucklers Mead 1 DT9 .. 194 C5
Bucklers Mead Rd BA21 .. 27 E8
Bucklers Mead Sch BA21 . 27 E8
Bucklers Way BH8 ..... 90 D3
Buckthorn Cl BH17 .... 86 F1
Buddens La SP7 .... 23 E4
Buddens Mdw BH21 .... 86 C4
Buddle Hill SP6 .... 43 E4
Buddleia Cl DT3 ...... 152 F2
Budmouth Ave DT3 .... 168 A6
Budmouth Com Sports Ctr DT4 .... 166 E3
Budmouth Tech Coll DT4 .... 166 E3
Buffalo Mews BH15 ... 119 B2
Buffetts Rd DT10 ...... 35 B2
Bugden's Copse Nature Reserve BH31 .... 45 B6
Bugdens La BH31 ...... 45 C6
Bugway La TA20 ...... 202 B8
Bulbury La BH16 ..... 115 F7
Bulbury Woods Golf Club BH16 .... 115 F8
Bull Bridge Mead BA22 .. 193 D3
Bull Cl 2 DT2 .... 106 E8
Bull Dro SO23 .... 126 F3
Buller Ave BA22 ...... 26 C6
Buller's Way DT3 .... 148 E6
Bullfinch Cl BH17 .... 86 F1
Bull Garden La DT10 ... 35 C1
Bull La
Maiden Newton DT2 .... 72 F8
Puncknowle DT2 ..... 129 E6
Bullocks La DT11 .... 197 A1
Bulls La 4 TA18 ..... 191 E4
Bumpers La DT5 ..... 187 B4
Bunford La BA20 ..... 26 E4
Bunting Rd BH22 ..... 61 B8
Burbidge Cl BH16 .... 84 C2
Burbitt La DT6 ...... 101 C4
Burbridge Cl BH17 ... 119 E8
Burcombe Rd BH10 .... 89 C5
Burdens 2 DT10 ..... 197 A4
Burdock Cl BH23 ..... 93 B1
Bure Cl BH23 .... 125 B6
Bure Haven Dr BH23 .. 125 A6
Bure Homage Gdns BH23 .... 125 B6
Bure Homage La BH23 .. 125 B6
Bure La BH23 .... 125 B6
Bure Pk BH23 .... 125 B6
Bure Rd BH23 .... 125 B6
Burford Cl BH23 ..... 91 D1
Burford Ct 4 BH1 ... 122 B3
Burges Cl DT10 ...... 20 E4
Burgess Cl BH11 ..... 88 F4
Burgess Field BH21 ... 44 C6
Burleigh Rd BH6 .... 123 D5
Burleston Dro DT2 ... 78 F2
Burley Cl
Barton on Sea BH25 .. 126 D8
Verwood BH31 .... 45 A5
Burley Rd
Bransgore BH23 ...... 93 A8
Poole BH12 .... 120 C6
Winkton BH23 .... 92 D6
Burling Terr 1 BH13 .. 121 A4
Burlington Arc 11 BH1 . 121 F3
Burlington Rd BH19 .. 179 C4
Burnaby Ct BH4 ..... 121 C1
Burnaby Rd BH4 ..... 121 C1
Burnage Ct 13 BH13 .. 147 F7
Burnbake Rd BH31 .... 45 B5
Burnbrae Rd BH22 .... 61 D1
Burn Cl BH31 .... 45 D4
Burnett Ave BH23 ... 123 E8
Burnett Cl SO22 .... 126 A8
Burnett Rd BH23 .... 123 F7
Burngate Rd BH15 ... 118 E2
Burnham Dr BH8 ..... 122 C7
Burnham Rd BH23 ..... 92 C2
Burnham's La BH19 .. 178 D5
Burnleigh Gdns BH25 ... 95 C4
Burnside
Christchurch BH23 ... 125 D8
Winterborne St Martin DT2 .... 133 C6
Burns Rd
Bournemouth BH6 .... 123 D7
Northport BH20 ..... 142 D6
Burn View DT2 ...... 107 F5
Burraton Sq 6 DT1 .. 107 D1
Burroughes Ave BA21 ... 27 A6
Burrows La BH31 ..... 45 B8
Burrywells DT2 ..... 102 D6
Bursledon Ho 4 BH25 ... 95 A2
Burstock La DT8 .... 203 C7
Burtley Rd BH6 ..... 123 F3
Burton Bradstock CE Prim Sch DT6 .... 128 C7
Burton CE Prim Sch BH23 92 C3
Burton Cl
Burton BH23 .... 92 C1
Shaftesbury SP7 ..... 13 A3
St Leonards BH24 .... 53 F5
Wool BH20 .... 139 F2
Burtoncroft BH23 .... 92 C3
Burton Cross BH20 .. 139 E1
Burton Hall BH23 .... 92 C3
Burton Hall Pl BH23 .. 92 D3
Burton Ho BH23 ..... 92 D1
Burton La BA22 .... 193 C8
Burton Rd
Abbotsbury DT3 .... 148 D6
Bothenhampton DT6 .. 100 E2
Burton Bradstock DT6 .. 128 A8
Christchurch BH23 .. 124 E7
Poole BH13 .... 121 A3
Puncknowle DT2 .... 129 E1
Wool BH20 .... 139 E1
Burton St DT10 ...... 20 E3
Burton Wood BH20 .. 139 F1
Burt's Hill BH21 ..... 59 D7
Burt's La BH21 ...... 52 C8
Burt's Pl 6 BH19 ... 179 C2
Bury Rd
Poole BH13 .... 120 F1
Poole BH13 .... 120 F2
Bushell Rd BH15 ... 119 C7
Bushes Hill SP8 ...... 5 A7
Bushes Rd DT11 .... 199 A4
Bushey La BH20 .... 162 D3
Bushey Rd BH8 ...... 90 C1
Bushfield Rd 1 TA18 .. 191 E3
Bushmead Dr BH24 ... 54 A5
Bush Pk DT11 .... 81 E8
Busket La SO23 .... 126 E5
Bute Dr BH23 ...... 126 B8
Butlers La BH24 ..... 47 E1
Butt Cl DT2 .... 78 B1
Buttercup Cl 2 SP8 ... 5 D2
Buttercup Dr BH23 ... 93 B1
Buttercup La DT11 .. 212 E5
Buttercup Way DT6 .. 100 D2
Butterwick Dro DT9 .. 195 D6
Buttery The BH23 ... 124 D7
Butt Farm Cl DT2 ... 105 D1
Butt La
Bere Regis BH20 ..... 81 B3
Whitechurch Canonicorum DT6 .... 66 D2
Butt La Hollow BH20 .. 81 B4
Butts Cl
Marnhull DT10 ...... 20 F2
Winchester SO22 ... 126 B7

Butts Cl *continued*
3 Winfrith Newburgh DT2 156 F6
Butts La SP8 21 C7
Butts Mead 1 SP7 13 A1
Butts Pond Ind Pk DT10 35 B2
Butts Quarry La TA18 192 A4
Butts The
12 Child Okeford DT11 198 C7
Shaftesbury SP7 12 C3
Buxton Cl 2 DT4 180 D8
Buxton Rd DT4 180 D8
Byron Ave SO22 126 B6
Byron Ct BH22 61 D5
Byron Ho 10 BH25 95 A2
Byron Rd
Barton on Sea BH25 126 E8
Bournemouth BH5 122 F3
Wimborne Minster BH21 59 C6

C

Cabot Bsns Village BH17 119 A7
Cabot La BH17 119 B8
Cabot Way BH25 94 F3
Cachy Rd BH20 139 E7
Caddy La BA12 2 F5
Cadhay Cl BH25 94 E3
Cadley Cl DT11 212 D5
Cadnam Way BH8 90 D3
Cadogan Rd BH24 55 D7
Caernarvon Cl 4 DT1 135 C8
Caesar Gn 2 DT1 134 E7
Caesar's Way BH18 86 E4
Caird Ave BH25 95 C2
Cairns Cl BH23 123 F8
Caister Cl BH22 61 C6
Calcraft Rd BH20 177 A8
Calder Rd BH17 119 F8
Caledonian Cl
Christchurch BH23 125 B7
Radipole DT4 167 D5
Caledon Rd BH14 120 E3
Cale Way SP8 11 B8
Caley Way DT6 69 A1
Calf Close La DT10 197 F8
Calfhay La DT9 194 E1
Calkin Cl BH23 92 A1
Calluna Rd BH12 120 B8
Callway La DT2 209 B2
Calmore Cl BH8 90 D3
Calves La SP7 12 B4
Calvin Rd BH9 121 F8
Camborne Pl BA21 28 A5
Camborne St BA21 28 A6
Cambridge Cl BA20 26 F5
Cambridge Gdns BH23 91 F2
Cambridge Rd
Bournemouth BH2 121 D3
Dorchester DT1 107 D1
Weymouth DT4 166 E3
Cambridge Wlk 1 DT1 107 D1
Camden Cl BH9 90 B1
Camden Way DT1 134 F7
Came Down Cl DT3 152 C3
Came Down Golf Club DT2 134 F2
Camel Green Rd 3 SP6 42 D6
Camellia Cl BH21 45 A1
Camellia Gdns BH25 95 B2
Camelot Way SP8 5 D1
Cameron Rd BH23 124 D7
Camesworth La DT6 69 A7
Came View Cl DT1 135 D8
Came View Rd DT1 135 C8
Camilla Ct BH13 121 B2
Cammel Rd BH22 61 D2
Campbell Rd
Bournemouth BH1 122 E5
Burton BH23 92 C3
Campion Cl
5 Gillingham SP8 5 D2
Radipole DT4 167 E7
Campion Dr BA22 26 D5
Campion Gr BH23 124 F6
Camp Rd
Chickerell DT4 180 B8
West Coker BA22 26 C1
Canberra Cres DT3 152 E3
Canberra Rd
Christchurch BH23 91 E1
Radipole DT3 152 E2
Candys Cl BH21 58 E2
Candys La BH21 58 E2
Candy's La 6 DT11 198 B6
Canford Ave BH11 89 A2
Canford Bottom BH21 60 C6
Canford Bottom Rdbt BH21 60 C5
Canford Cliffs Ave BH14 120 E2
Canford Cliffs Rd BH13 120 E2
Canford Cres BH13 147 E7
Canford Ct BH13 147 E6
Canford Gdns BH11 89 A1
Canford Heath Fst & Mid Schs BH17 119 D7
Canford Heath Nature Reserve BH11 88 B4
Canford Heath Rd BH17 87 E1
Canford Magna BH21 60 A1
Canford Park Events Arena & Sports Gd BH21 88 B7
Canford Pl 2 BH13 147 F7
Canford Rd
Bournemouth BH11 89 A1
Canford Rd *continued*
Poole BH15 119 D4
Canford Sch BH21 60 B2
Canford Summer Sch of Music DT9 30 B6
Canford View Dr BH21 60 B6
Canford Way BH12 88 C2
Cann Hill SP7 24 A5
Cannings Ct La DT2 196 C3
Cannington Coll BA20 26 E5
Cannon Cl BH18 87 A1
Cannon Ct Mews 1 DT9 17 D1
Cannon Hill Gdns BH21 60 B7
Cannon Hill Rd BH21 60 A7
Canon St SO23 126 E5
Canteen Rd DT5 181 D1
Canterbury Cl
Ferndown BH22 53 A1
Weymouth DT4 166 F3
Canute Rd 5 SO23 126 F4
Capella Ct BH2 121 F2
Capesthorne BH23 125 B5
Caphays Dro DT9 195 E7
Capital Ho 7 SO22 126 D6
Capitol Cl DT1 134 E8
Capper Rd E BH20 139 E6
Capper Rd W BH20 139 E6
Capstan Field BH19 178 A2
Capstans The BH14 147 B8
Capstone Pl BH8 122 D6
Capstone Rd BH8 122 B6
Captains Cove BH15 118 E3
Carbery Ave BH6 123 D5
Carbery Gdns BH6 123 E5
Carbery La 3 BH6 123 C4
Carbery Row 2 BH6 123 C4
Cardigan Rd
Bournemouth BH9 121 F8
Poole BH12 120 F4
Cards Mill La DT6 66 A7
Carent Cl DT10 21 A2
Carey App BH20 142 D5
Carey Cl BH20 142 D5
Carey Rd
Bournemouth BH9 89 F3
Northport BH20 142 D5
Careys Rd BH8 90 D4
Carina Ct BH13 147 C3
Carisbrooke
Poole BH13 147 E7
Radipole DT4 167 B6
Carisbrooke Cres BH15 118 D3
Carisbrooke Ct
1 Christchurch BH23 126 B7
New Milton BH25 94 F3
Carisbrooke Gdns BA20 27 B5
Carisbrooke Way BH23 93 E1
Carlinford 5 BH5 122 F3
Carlton Ave BH25 126 D8
Carlton Gr BH12 120 D5
Carlton Mount BH2 121 E2
Carlton Rd BH1 122 C4
Carlton Rd N DT4 167 D5
Carlton Rd S DT4 167 D5
Carlyle Rd BH6 123 D6
Carmel Cl BH15 118 D2
Carnarvon Rd 4 BH1 122 E4
Carnegie Cl BH12 120 D5
Caroline Ave BH23 124 F6
Caroline Pl 5 DT4 167 D3
Caroline Rd BH11 89 B2
Carpenters Cl 3 DT2 106 E8
Carradale BH23 125 B8
Carraway La DT10 20 F1
Carrbridge Cl BH3 121 D7
Carrbridge Gdns BH3 121 D7
Carrbridge Rd BH3 121 D7
Carrick Cl DT1 135 C8
Carrick Way BH25 95 C2
Carrington Cl 4 DT4 180 D8
Carrion La 4 BH20 142 E4
Carroll Ave BH22 61 E5
Carroll Cl BH12 121 A6
Carsworth Way BH17 88 A2
Carter Cl DT11 212 E5
Carter Com Sch BH15 118 F2
Carters Ave BH15 118 D4
Carters La BA22 192 E8
Carter's La
Chideock DT6 98 E8
9 Poole BH15 119 C2
Cartref Cl BH31 45 B6
Cartwright Cl BH10 89 C4
Carvers Ind Est BH24 55 C7
Carvers La BH24 55 C7
Carysfort Rd BH1 122 D4
Caseberry Ct 7 DT1 107 D1
Cashmoor Cl 4 BH12 120 F7
Caslake Cl BH25 94 F1
Cassel Ave BH13 121 B1
Casselles Ct 6 BH25 95 A2
Cassiobury Rd DT4 167 D4
Casterbridge Cl
Pimperne DT11 212 F6
4 Swanage BH19 178 E2
Casterbridge Ct 5 BH4 121 C3
Casterbridge Ind Est DT1 108 B2
Casterbridge Rd
Dorchester DT1 135 D8
Ferndown BH22 61 C3
Castle Ave
Christchurch BH23 125 E8
5 Okeford Fitzpaine DT11 197 F6
Winchester SO23 126 D6
Castle Cl
Cranborne BH21 40 B7
Dorchester DT1 107 D1
Castle Court Prep Sch BH21 86 B7
Castle Ct 2 BH23 126 A7
Castledene Cres BH14 120 A2
Castle Farm Rd BH16 84 C4
Castle Gate Cl BH8 90 C2
Castle Hill
Poole BH14 120 B4
Winchester SO22 126 D6
Castle Hill Cl SP7 12 D3
Castle Hill Cres BA12 3 A6
Castle Hill La
Cranborne BH21 40 B6
Mere BA12 3 A5
Castle Hill Rd DT4 180 B8
Castle La
Buckland Newton DT2 208 B8
Okeford Fitzpaine DT11 197 F6
Owermoigne DT2 155 D8
Castle Lane E BH7 123 C8
Castle La W BH9 90 C2
Castlemain Ave BH6 123 C5
Castlemaine Rd DT3 152 E2
Castleman Smith Cl DT11 212 E6
Castleman Way BH24 55 C6
Castlemews BH24 54 E5
Castle Par BH7 123 D7
Castlepoint
Bournemouth BH8 90 E1
Bournemouth BH8 90 E2
Castle Rd
Bournemouth BH9 90 A1
Fortuneswell DT5 181 A1
Sherborne DT9 30 D7
Castle Sq DT6 100 C5
Castle St
Christchurch BH23 124 B6
Cranborne BH21 40 B7
Mere BA12 2 F5
Poole BH15 119 C1
Castleton TA18 192 C5
Castleton Ave BH10 89 D6
Castleton Rd DT9 30 C6
Castleton Waterwheel Mus DT9 30 D6
Castletown DT5 181 B1
Castle Town Way DT9 30 C8
Castle View Dr BH16 84 C1
Castlewood BH24 54 F5
Catalina Cl BH23 125 A6
Catalina Dr BH15 119 E1
Caters Pl DT1 108 A2
Cathedral View 4 SO23 126 F4
Catherine Wheel Gdns BH23 91 E3
Cathole Bridge Rd TA18 191 F3
Cat La DT10 33 A2
Caton Cl BH12 121 B8
Catsley La DT2 205 B6
Cattistock Rd
Bournemouth BH8 90 E2
Maiden Newton DT2 72 F8
Cauldon Ave BH19 179 B4
Cauldron Barn Rd BH19 179 B4
Cauldron Cres BH19 179 B4
Cauldron Mdws 3 BH19 179 B4
Caundle La
Stalbridge DT10 33 A6
Stourton Caundle DT10 32 E1
Causeway Cl BH20 142 D5
Causeway La DT8 203 A6
Causeway The
Hazelbury Bryan DT10 196 F4
Milborne St Andrew DT11 79 E8
Cavalcade of Costume Mus DT11 212 C3
Cavalier Cl BA21 27 F8
Cavalier Way BA21 27 F8
Cavan Cres BH17 87 B1
Cave Hole DT5 186 F11
Cavendish Ct 9 BH4 121 C3
Cavendish Hall BH1 122 A5
Cavendish Pl BH1 122 A5
Cavendish Rd
Bournemouth BH1 121 F5
Bournemouth BH1 122 A5
Caversham Cl BH15 118 E3
Cawdor Rd BH3 121 D7
Caxton Cl BH23 125 A7
Cecil Ave BH8 122 C8
Cecil Cl BH21 86 E6
Cecil Ct BH8 122 B8
Cecil Hill BH8 122 B8
Cecil Rd
Bournemouth BH5 122 E4
Poole BH12 120 D6
Swanage BH19 179 A2
Cecil St BA20 27 D5
Cedar Ave
Bournemouth BH10 89 D6
Christchurch BH23 123 D8
St Leonards BH24 53 F3
Cedar Cl
Upton BH16 118 B8
1 Wool BH20 140 A2
Cedar Ct BH4 121 B2
Cedar Dr
2 Easton/Weston DT5 186 F1
Overcombe/Preston DT3 168 B8
Sandford BH20 116 A1
Wimborne Minster BH21 60 A5
Cedar Fields 1 BA22 193 A8
Cedar Gdns BH25 94 F1
Cedar Gr BA21 27 A6
Cedar Grange 18 BH13 121 A4
Cedar Manor BH4 121 C3
Cedar Rd
Charminster DT2 75 D2
Dorchester DT1 107 E2
Cedars The BH4 121 C4
Cedar Trad Pk BH21 60 F6
Cedar Way BH22 61 C8
Cedar Wlk SO22 126 C5
Celandine Cl
Christchurch BH23 125 B8
Radipole DT4 167 D6
Celandine Rd 3 BA22 26 C5
Cellars Farm Rd BH6 124 A3
Celtic Cres DT1 134 E7
Cemetery Ave BH15 119 F6
Cemetery Junc BH2 121 F5
Cemetery Rd
2 Gillingham SP8 5 F2
Portesham DT3 150 A8
Wimborne Minster BH21 59 B5
Centenary Gdns BA8 19 A4
Centenary Ho BH23 124 B7
Centenary Way BH1 122 E5
Central Acre 13 BA20 27 D4
Central Ave
Corfe Mullen BH21 86 D7
Poole BH12 120 E6
Central Dr
Bournemouth BH2 121 E5
West Moors BH24 62 B8
Central Rd BA20 27 D5
Centre Pl BH24 55 B7
Centurion Rd DT11 199 E2
Century Pk BA20 27 A5
Cereleton Pk DT11 211 C6
Cerne Abbas BH13 121 A1
Cerne Abbas CE Fst Sch DT2 207 C4
Cerne Abbas Giant DT2 207 D4
Cerne Abbas Tithe Barn DT2 207 D3
Cerne Abbey DT2 207 D4
Cerne Ave SP8 11 B8
Cerne Cl BH9 90 B4
Chaddesley Glen BH13 147 E6
Chaddesley Grange BH13 147 F6
Chaddesley Pines BH13 147 E6
Chaddesley Wood Rd BH13 147 E5
Chafeys Ave DT4 167 A5
Chaffey Cl BH24 55 E8
Chaffeymoor Hill SP8 1 B1
Chaffinch Cl
Broadstone BH17 86 F2
New Milton BH25 94 F2
Radipole DT3 152 D3
Chalbury Cl
Overcombe/Preston DT3 168 A8
Poole BH17 88 A2
Chalbury Ct 2 BH14 120 B4
Chalbury (Hill Fort) DT3 153 A4
Chalbury Lodge 1 DT3 153 B2
Chaldecott Gdns BH10 89 C4
Chaldon Rd BH17 87 F2
Chalfont Ave BH23 91 D3
Chalice Cl BH14 120 A4
Chalk Pit Cl BH20 81 B1
Chalk Pit La
Litton Cheney DT2 103 A2
Wool BH20 139 F1
Chalk The 2 DT11 37 F1
Chalky Rd DT2 136 A1
Challacombe St DT1 107 B2
Challenger Way BA22 26 C6
Chalwell 9 DT11 198 C7
Chalwyn Ind Est BH15, BH12 120 A7
Chamberlaine Rd DT4 180 C8
Champernhayes La DT6 64 E5
Champions 1 DT8 204 C4
Chancery La DT6 100 D6
Chander Cl BH22 61 E4
Chandler Cl DT3 167 D8
Chandlers DT9 30 C7
Chandlers Cl BH7 123 B8
Chandos Ave BH12 121 A8
Channel Ct
Barton on Sea BH25 126 E7
Bournemouth BH6 123 D3
Channel View Rd DT5 186 F4
Channons Ct 4 DT1 108 A2
Chant Cl BH23 124 D7
Chantmarle La DT2 206 B5
Chantry Cl BH23 93 F1
Chantry La DT8 204 C5
Chantry Mead SO22 126 C7
Chantry St DT6 204 C2
Chantry The
Bournemouth BH1 122 A4
Mere BA12 3 A5
Chantry View BA22 193 D8
Chapel Cl
Corfe Mullen BH21 86 C6
Langton Herring DT3 150 C1
Chapel Gate BH23 90 C8
Chapel Gdns DT11 212 E3
Chapelhay Hts 1 DT4 167 D2
Chapelhay St DT4 167 D2
Chapel Hill SP8 9 D2
Chapel La
Bransgore BH23 93 A8
Corfe Mullen BH21 86 C5
Dinnington TA17 191 B8
East Parley BH23 90 C8
Henstridge BA8 18 E7
Maiden Newton DT2 72 F8
7 Milborne Port DT9 17 D2
Chapel La *continued*
Osmington DT3 154 B1
Pen Selwood BA9 1 C3
2 Pimperne DT11 199 D3
Poole BH15 119 C2
Radipole DT3 152 C5
Wimborne Minster BH21 59 B5
Woodlands BH21 44 B7
7 Yetminster DT9 194 C5
Zennor BA12 1 E5
Chapel Mdw 6 DT9 194 C5
Chapel Rd
Poole BH14 120 A4
Sturminster Newton DT10 197 A8
Chapel Rise BH24 54 F2
Chapel St
Milborne St Andrew DT11 79 E7
Shipton Gorge DT6 101 D4
Chapel View 6 DT2 78 B1
Charberry Rise DT6 96 F7
Charborough Cl BH16 84 C4
Charborough House BH20 83 F8
Charborough Pk BH20 83 F8
Charborough Rd BH18 87 B3
Charborough Way 1 BH21 56 D4
Chard La
Broadwindsor DT8 203 C7
Wayford TA18 191 B2
Chard Rd
Broadwindsor DT8 203 C7
Crewkerne TA18 191 D4
Chards Mead Rd DT6 100 C7
Chard St TA20 202 E6
Charfield Cl SO22 126 C3
Charing Cl 2 BH24 55 C6
Charing Cross SP6 42 B5
Charlecote Mews 14 SO22 126 D6
Charles Cl SO23 126 F8
Charles Cres BH25 95 B5
Charles Garrett Cl 3 SP7 12 F3
Charles Gdns BH10 89 D2
Charles Keightley Ct BH21 59 D4
Charles Rd
Burton Bradstock DT6 128 B8
Christchurch BH23 124 F8
Poole BH15 119 D3
Yeovil BA21 27 F6
Charles's La BH24 55 E2
Charles St
Blandford Forum DT11 212 D4
Dorchester DT1 108 A1
Radipole DT4 167 D4
Charlotte Cl
Charminster DT2 107 E5
Christchurch BH23 125 A6
3 New Milton BH25 95 A2
Poole BH12 121 C7
Charlton Beeches DT11 211 C7
Charlton Cl
Bournemouth BH9 90 C4
12 Crewkerne TA18 191 F4
Hordle SO41 95 F3
Charlton La SP7 13 E1
Charlton Manor 1 DT11 211 D6
Charlton Mead 6 DT11 211 D6
Charltons The BH2 121 F5
Charminster Ave
Bournemouth BH9 122 B8
Bournemouth BH9 90 B1
Charminster Cl BH8 90 B2
Charminster Pl BH8 90 C2
Charminster Rd
Bournemouth BH8 122 B7
Bournemouth BH8 90 B1
Charmouth Cl DT7 96 C6
Charmouth Gr BH14 120 A4
Charmouth Heritage Coast Ctr DT6 97 A7
Charmouth Prim Sch DT6 97 A7
Charmouth Rd DT7 96 C6
Charnock Cl SO41 95 F3
Charnwood Ave BH9 90 B3
Charnwood Cl 1 BH22 53 A2
Chartcombe BH13 147 E8
Charter Rd BH11 88 D6
Chartwell
5 Poole BH13 121 B3
Radipole DT4 167 B6
Chaseborough Sq 4 DT1 107 D1
Chase Cres SP5 188 E4
Chaseside BH7 123 A8
Chase The
St Leonards BH24 54 F5
Verwood BH31 45 E5
Chaston La DT2 208 C8
Chatham Rd SO22 126 A3
Chatsworth Rd
Bournemouth BH8 122 C6
Poole BH14 120 B5
Yeovil BA21 27 F7
Chatsworth Way BH25 94 F3
Chaucer Cl BH21 59 C6
Chaucer Rd BH13 147 F8
Chaucombe Pl BH25 94 F1
Chaundler Rd SO23 126 E8
Cheam Rd BH18 86 F4
Cheap St DT9 30 B6
Checkridge La EX13 202 A2
Cheddington Rd BH9 90 A4
Chedington Cl BH17 87 E2
Chedington Court Golf Club DT8 192 D2
Chedington La DT8 204 B8
Cheese La DT3 150 E6

Chelmsford Rd BH16 . . . . 118 A7
Chelmsford St DT4 . . . . . 167 C4
Chelston Ave BA21 . . . . . . 27 D7
Cheltenham Rd BH12. . . 120 C5
Chelwood Gate DT4. . . . 166 E3
Chene Rd BH21 . . . . 59 D4
Cherford Rd BH11. . . . . . . 89 B2
Cherita Ct BH15. . . . . 119 F6
Cheriton 7 BH4 . . . . 121 C2
Cheriton Ave BH7. . . . . . 123 C8
Cheriton Cl SO22 . . . . . . 126 B7
Cheriton Rd SO22 . . . . . . 126 C6
Cheriton Way BH21 . . . . . 59 C6
Cherrett Cl BH11. . . . . 88 F4
Cherries Dr BH9 . . . . 89 E2
Cherry Cl
  Poole BH14 . . . . 120 B4
  Sandford BH20 . . . . 143 B8
Cherry Ct BH14 . . . . 120 B5
Cherryfields SP8 . . . . 5 F4
Cherry Gr BH22. . . . . 61 C6
Cherry Hill Gdns BH16. . 118 B6
Cherry Hill Gr
  Upton BH16 . . . . 117 D6
  Upton BH16 . . . . 118 B6
Cherry Orch La
  Cann SP7 . . . . 11 F2
  Gillingham SP8 . . . . 5 C2
Cherry Tree DT6 . . . . 100 B8
Cherry Tree BH24 . . . . . . 53 F3
Cherry Tree Ct
  9 Crewkerne TA18. . . . . 191 F5
  4 New Milton BH25. . . . 95 B1
Cherry Tree Dr
  Beckley BH25. . . . . 94 E5
  Yeovil BA20 . . . . 26 F2
Chescombe Rd DT2. . . . . 207 D3
Chescombe La DT11 . . . . 210 B3
Cheselbourne Villiage Sch
  DT2. . . . . 209 A3
Cheshire Dr BH8 . . . . 91 A2
Chesil Beach DT3 . . . . . . 149 C2
Chesil Beach Holiday Village
  DT4 . . . . 180 C5
Chesil Beach Visitor Ctr
  DT4. . . . . 180 D4
Chesilbourne Gr BH8 . . . . 90 D3
Chesildene Ave BH8 . . . . . 90 D3
Chesildene Dr BH8. . . . . . 90 D3
Chesil Gdns BH12. . . . . . 120 B8
Chesil St SO23 . . . . 126 F5
Chesil Terr SO23 . . . . 126 F5
Chesil View DT4 . . . . 180 C7
Chessel Ave BH5. . . . . . . 122 F4
Chessels Cl BA22 . . . . . . 193 B8
Chester Cl DT1 . . . . 135 C8
Chesterfield Cl BH13 . . . . 147 F8
Chesterfield Ct BH1. . . . . 122 C3
Chester Rd
  Poole BH13 . . . . 121 A2
  Winchester SO23. . . . . . 126 F6
Chestnut Ave
  Barton on Sea BH25 . . . 127 A8
  Bournemouth BH6. . . . . 123 C4
  Christchurch BH23 . . . . 123 D8
  Verwood BH24. . . . . 46 D6
  Wareham St Martin BH20 116 B3
Chestnut Cl BH20 . . . . . . 143 B8
Chestnut Dr BA20 . . . . . . 27 B3
Chestnut Gr
  Blandford Forum DT11 . . 212 B4
  Ferndown BH22. . . . . . . 60 E6
Chestnut Pl DT3 . . . . 167 C7
Chestnut Rd
  Bridport DT6 . . . . 100 D4
  Charminster DT2. . . . . . 75 D2
Chestnut Way
  Burton BH23 . . . . 92 C3
  Dorchester DT1 . . . . . . 107 D2
  Gillingham SP8 . . . . 5 D1
Chetcombe Rd BA12. . . . . . 3 B6
Chetnole Cl BH17 . . . . 88 A1
Chetnole Sta DT9 . . . . . . 194 C2
Chettell Way DT11 . . . . . 212 D2
Chetwode Way BH17. . . . . 87 B2
Cheviot Court Flats
  BH23 . . . . 124 F8
Cheviots The BH14. . . . . 120 C3
Cheviot Way BH31 . . . . . . 45 B5
Chewton Common Rd
  BH23 . . . . 124 B8
Chewton Farm Rd BH23 . 94 C1
Chewton Lodge BH23 . . . 126 B8
Chewton Mews BH23. . . . 94 A2
Chewton Way BH23 . . . . . 94 B1
Cheyne 1 DT5 . . . . 186 E1
Cheyne Gdns BH4. . . . . . 121 C2
Chichester Rd 1 BH24 . . 47 E1
Chichester Way BH23 . . . 125 A5
Chichester Wlk BH21. . . . 59 E1
Chickerell Cl BH9. . . . . . . 90 B3
Chickerell Hill DT3. . . . . 166 B6
Chickerell Prim Sch
  DT3. . . . . 166 D5
Chickerell Rd DT3 . . . . . 166 D4
Chick's Copse La DT2 . . 205 F5
Chideock Cl BH12. . . . . . 120 E6
Chideock Hill DT6. . . . . . . 98 E7
Chigwell Rd BH8. . . . . 90 B1
Chilbolton Ave SO22 . . . 126 B6
Chilbolton Ct SO22. . . . . 126 A5
Chilbury Gdns DT2. . . . . 155 D7
Chilcombe Hts SO23 . . . 126 F5
Chilcombe La DT6 . . . . . 102 D3
Chilcombe Rd BH6. . . . . 123 B5
Childhay La DT8 . . . . 203 C6
Chilfrome Cl BH17. . . . . . . 87 C1

Chilfrome La
  Chilfrome DT2 . . . . 206 B1
  Maiden Newton DT2 . . . . 72 E8
Chiltern Cl
  Old Milton BH25 . . . . . . 94 F1
  Poole BH4 . . . . 121 B5
Chiltern Ct 5 BH23 . . . . 124 F8
Chiltern Dr
  Barton on Sea BH25 . . . 126 E8
  Verwood BH31. . . . . 45 B6
Chilton Gr BA21. . . . . 27 C7
Chimes The BH4 . . . . 121 B3
China La 1 DT11 . . . . . . 199 F7
Chine Cres BH2 . . . . 121 D2
Chine Crescent Rd BH2 . 121 D2
Chine Wlk BH22. . . . . 61 E1
Chinnock Hollow BA22 . 192 E8
Chippel La DT10 . . . . 20 F1
Chisels La BH23. . . . . 93 B6
Chislehurst 16 BH4. . . . . 121 C3
Chiswell DT5 . . . . 186 E8
Chiswell Rd BH17. . . . . . . 87 D1
Chitten Hill BH20 . . . . . . 115 C7
Chivrick Cl DT10 . . . . 35 C3
Chloe Gdns BH12. . . . . . 120 D7
Chorley Cl BH15. . . . . . . 119 C6
Chowins Rd 18 TA18. . . . 191 F4
Chris Cres BH11 . . . . 118 C7
Christchurch Bay Rd
  BH25 . . . . 126 F7
Christchurch By-Pass
  BH23. . . . . 124 D8
Christchurch Castle
  BH23. . . . . 124 B6
Christchurch Gdns 1
  SO23 . . . . 126 D3
Christchurch Hospl
  BH23. . . . . 123 F8
Christchurch Jun Sch
  BH23. . . . . 124 A7
Christchurch Prim Sch
  BH23. . . . . 124 A7
Christchurch Priory
  BH23. . . . . 124 C6
Christchurch Rd
  Barton on Sea BH25 . . . 126 D8
  Bournemouth BH1,BH7 . . 122 D4
  Bournemouth BH7. . . . . 123 B6
  Ferndown BH22. . . . . . . 61 C1
  Hurn BH23. . . . . 91 C5
  Ringwood BH24 . . . . 55 C4
  Winchester SO23. . . . . . 126 D3
  Winchester SO23. . . . . . 126 D5
Christchurch Sta BH23 . 124 A7
Christopher Cl BA20 . . . . 27 A5
Christopher Cres BH15 . 119 C6
Christ's Hospital 13
  SO23 . . . . 126 D3
Christ the King RC Prim Sch
  BH11. . . . . 89 A5
Christy's Gdns SP7 . . . . . 12 F3
Christy's La SP7. . . . . 12 F3
Church Acre 3 DT1. . . . . 108 B2
Church Cl
  Beer Hackett DT9 . . . . . 194 D6
  2 Bourton SP8. . . . . 1 D1
  Bridport DT6 . . . . 69 A1
  Chetnole DT9. . . . . 194 D3
  6 Dorchester DT1 . . . . . 108 A2
  Fontmell Magna SP7 . . . 37 E7
  Longburton DT9 . . . . . . 195 B7
  Stour Provost SP7 . . . . . 22 C7
  3 Swanage BH19. . . . . 179 B2
  Todber DT10 . . . . 21 D4
Churchfield BH31. . . . . . . 45 A6
Churchfield Cres BH15 . 119 E4
Churchfield Ct 2 BH15. . 119 E3
Churchfield La BH24 . . . . 43 A1
Churchfield Rd BH15. . . . 119 E3
Churchfoot La DT10. . . . 196 F3
Church Gn
  Bishop's Caundle DT9 . . 196 A8
  2 Wareham BH20 . . . . . 142 E3
Church Hill
  Buckhorn Weston SP8 . . . . 9 B6
  Dinnington TA17. . . . . . 191 B7
  Iwerne Minster DT11 . . . 37 F2
  Kington Magna SP8 . . . . . 9 D3
  Langton Herring DT3 . . . 150 C1
  Marnhull DT10 . . . . 21 A3
  Milborne St Andrew DT11 . 79 E7
  Piddlehinton DT2. . . . . . 76 F7
  Shaftesbury SP7 . . . . . . 12 D3
  Stalbridge DT10. . . . . . . 19 C1
  2 Swanage BH19. . . . . 179 B2
  Verwood BH31. . . . . 45 A6
  West Stour SP8 . . . . 10 A3
  Woodlands BH21. . . . . . 44 B7
Church Hill La DT2. . . . . 104 D7
Church Hill View DT2 . . . 207 A2
Churchill Cl
  Alderholt SP6. . . . . 42 A5
  Sturminster Marshall BH21. 56 D4
  4 Weymouth DT4. . . . . 180 C8
Churchill Cres BH12. . . . 120 C6
Churchill Ct BH25. . . . . . . 94 F2
Churchill Dro BH21 . . . . . 40 E7
Churchill Gdns BH12. . . . 120 C5
Churchill Rd
  Blandford Forum DT11 . . 212 D4
  Bournemouth BH1. . . . . 122 E5
  Bovington Camp BH20. . . 139 C7
  Poole BH12 . . . . 120 D6
  Wimborne Minster BH21. . 59 E3
Church Knap DT4. . . . . . 180 C8
Church Knowle Animal
  Sanctuary BH20. . . . . . 176 B7

Church La
  Barwick BA22 . . . . 193 E8
  Bere Regis BH20 . . . . . . 81 B2
  1 Blandford Forum DT11 212 D3
  Charlton Marshall DT11. . 211 C6
  Chickerell DT3 . . . . 151 D2
  Coombe Keynes BH20 . . 158 A5
  Crewkerne TA18 . . . . . . 192 A3
  Damerham SP6 . . . . . . 190 F2
  Easton/Weston DT5 . . . . 186 F1
  East Orchard SP7 . . . . . . 36 F7
  Ferndown BH22. . . . . . . 89 F7
  Frampton DT2 . . . . 73 F3
  Godmanstone DT2. . . . . 75 B7
  Haselbury Plucknett TA18 . 192 E5
  Leigh DT9. . . . . 194 E3
  Margaret Marsh SP7 . . . . 22 C2
  Old Milton BH25 . . . . . . 94 F1
  Osmington DT3 . . . . . . 154 A1
  Overcombe/Preston DT3. . 169 A8
  Owermoigne DT2. . . . . . 155 D7
  Piddletrenthide DT2 . . . 208 B3
  Portesham DT3 . . . . . . 150 A8
  Rimpton BA22 . . . . 15 B8
  Shaftesbury SP7 . . . . . . 12 C2
  Stinsford DT2 . . . . 108 E3
  Stour Provost SP7 . . . . . 21 C7
  2 Sturminster Newton
    DT10. . . . . 197 D8
  Sutton Waldron DT11 . . . 37 E4
  Sydling St Nicholas DT2 . 207 A2
  Wareham BH20 . . . . . . 142 F3
  Wool BH20. . . . . 140 B2
Churchmoor Rd BH21 . . . 60 A5
Church Ope DT5 . . . . 187 B3
Church Path
  2 Crewkerne TA18. . . . . 191 E4
  Litton Cheney DT2 . . . . 103 C2
  Yeovil BA22 . . . . 27 D5
Church Rd
  Bournemouth BH6. . . . . 123 F3
  Bradford Abbas DT9 . . . 28 D1
  Durweston DT11 . . . . . . 198 E3
  Ferndown BH22. . . . . . . 61 C5
  Iwerne Minster DT11 . . . 37 F1
  Maiden Newton DT2 . . . . 72 F8
  Overcombe/Preston DT3. . 168 D3
  Pimperne DT11 . . . . . . 199 D4
  Poole BH14 . . . . 120 A4
  5 Shillingstone DT11 . . . 198 B6
  Silton SP8 . . . . 2 A1
  Studland BH19. . . . . . . 164 D2
  Thornford DT9 . . . . 194 D8
  Three Legged Cross BH21. . 45 A1
  West Lulworth BH20 . . . 172 C6
  West Stour SP8 . . . . 10 A3
Church Row DT11. . . . . . 209 C6
Church St
  Bridport DT6 . . . . 100 D6
  Burton Bradstock DT6. . . 128 B8
  Christchurch BH23 . . . . 124 B6
  Cranborne BH21 . . . . . . 40 A7
  Dewlish DT2 . . . . 209 C1
  5 Dorchester DT1 . . . . . 108 A2
  Fontmell Magna SP7 . . . 37 F7
  Fordingbridge SP6. . . . . 43 A8
  Halstock BA22 . . . . 193 C3
  Henstridge BA8 . . . . 19 A4
  Hinton St George TA17 . . 191 E6
  Kington Magna SP8 . . . . . 9 C3
  Lyme Regis DT7 . . . . 96 C5
  Mere BA12 . . . . 3 A5
  Merriott TA16. . . . . 191 F7
  Milborne Port DT9. . . . . 17 D2
  Poole BH15 . . . . 119 B1
  Puncknowle DT2 . . . . . . 129 E6
  Shapwick DT11 . . . . 56 B8
  Sturminster Marshall BH21. 56 E5
  Sturminster Newton DT10. . 35 B1
  Upwey DT3 . . . . 152 A7
  Wareham BH20 . . . . . . 142 E3
  2 West Coker BA22 . . . . 193 A8
  West Stour SP8 . . . . 10 A3
  6 Wimborne Minster BH21 59 B5
  Winterborne Kingston BH20 81 E8
  Yeovil BA20 . . . . 27 D5
  Yetminster DT9 . . . . . . 194 C5
Church Track SP8. . . . . . . 1 D1
Church View SP8 . . . . .5 E1
Churchward Ave DT3. . . . 153 B1
Churchwell Cl 3 DT9 . . . 28 C1
Churchwell St DT9 . . . . . 28 C1
Church Wlk
  Littlebredy DT2 . . . . 131 D7
  Motcombe SP7. . . . . 12 B7
  Okeford Fitzpaine DT11. . 197 E4
Chur La BA22 . . . . 193 A8
Churlands Cl BA22 . . . . . 193 A8
Chydyok Rd DT2 . . . . . . 156 C3
Cinnamon La 7 BH15 . . . 119 B1
Circle The
  3 Bournemouth BH9 . . . . 90 A4
  Poole BH13 . . . . 147 E7
City Bsns Ctr SO23 . . . . . 126 E6
City Rd SO23 . . . . 126 E6
Claire Ct 6 BH23 . . . . . . 124 A7
Clammer Hill La TA18 . . . 191 F4
Clanfield DT9. . . . . 29 F4
Clap La SP5 . . . . 188 B4
Clappentail La DT7. . . . . . 96 A5
Clappentail Pk DT7 . . . . . 96 A5
Clapton Court Gdns
  TA18. . . . . 191 D1
Clapton Rd TA18 . . . . . . 191 D3
Clare Ave DT4 . . . . 166 E2
Claremont Ave
  Bournemouth BH9 . . . . . 90 A3
  Gillingham SP8 . . . . 5 F3

Claremont Gdns DT6 . . . . 100 D8
Claremont Rd
  Bournemouth BH9 . . . . . 90 B2
  Bridport DT6 . . . . 100 D8
Clarence Cl 2 DT5. . . . . 186 F4
Clarence Ct BA20 . . . . . . 27 C5
Clarence Park Rd BH7. . . 123 A6
Clarence Pl BH23 . . . . . . 123 F8
Clarence Rd
  Dorchester DT1 . . . . . . 134 F8
  Easton/Weston DT5 . . . . 186 F4
  3 Poole BH14 . . . . 120 A3
  Weymouth DT4 . . . . . . 166 F1
Clarence St BA20 . . . . . . 27 C4
Clarence Terr 14 BA20 . . 27 C4
Clarendon Ave DT3 . . . . . 152 C1
Clarendon Cl
  Broadstone BH18 . . . . . . 87 A4
  Gillingham SP8 . . . . 5 D2
Clarendon Ct 3 BH2. . . . 121 D2
Clarendon Rd
  Bournemouth BH4 . . . . . 121 D3
  Broadstone BH18 . . . . . . 86 F4
  Christchurch BH23 . . . . 124 A7
Clarkham Cross BA22 . . 193 E2
Clarks Cl BA22 . . . . 26 C5
Clark's Cl BH24 . . . . 55 C7
Clark's La TA18 . . . . 192 A3
Clatcombe La DT9 . . . . . . 15 F3
Claudius Cl DT1. . . . . . . 134 E7
Clausentum Rd SO23 . . . 126 D3
Clay Castle TA18 . . . . . . 192 C5
Clay Castle La TA18 . . . . 192 C5
Clayesmore Prep Sch
  DT11. . . . . 37 E2
Clayesmore Sch DT11. . . 37 E2
Clayford Ave BH22 . . . . . . 61 B7
Clayford Cl BH17. . . . . . . 87 D2
Clay La
  Beaminster DT8. . . . . . 204 C4
  Puncknowle DT2 . . . . . . 129 F4
Claylake Dr BH31 . . . . . . 45 C5
Claylands La DT8 . . . . . . 204 A3
Clay Pigeon Raceway
  DT2. . . . . 206 E5
Claypits La
  Beer Hackett DT9 . . . . . 194 D6
  Winfrith Newburgh DT2. . 157 A6
Clayton Cl
  Radipole DT3 . . . . 152 D3
  Yeovil BA22 . . . . 26 C6
Clearmount Rd DT4 . . . . 180 E8
Cleasby Grange 2 BH5. . 122 F3
Cleeve Ho BH25. . . . . . . 126 F7
Cleeves Cl BH12 . . . . 88 D2
Clematis Cl BH23 . . . . . . 125 C8
Clement Mews BH4 . . . . 121 B3
Clements La DT5. . . . . . . 186 E8
Clement's La BA12 . . . . . . 3 B4
Clenston Rd DT11 . . . . . . 210 C2
Cleveland Ave DT4 . . . . . 167 D7
Cleveland Cl BH25 . . . . . 126 D7
Cleveland Ct 4 BH4. . . . 121 D2
Cleveland Gdns BH1 . . . . 122 C5
Cleveland Rd BH1. . . . . . 122 D5
Cleverlawns DT3. . . . . . . 148 F7
Cleves Cl DT4 . . . . 180 E7
Cleve The BA21 . . . . 26 E6
Cliff Ave BH19 . . . . 179 C4
Cliff Cres BH25 . . . . 126 F7
Cliff Dr
  Christchurch BH23 . . . . 125 C6
  Poole BH13 . . . . 147 E6
Cliffe Rd BH25 . . . . 126 E7
Clifford Rd BH9. . . . . 90 A1
Cliff Rd DT6 . . . . 128 B7
Cliff Way DT5 . . . . 186 D1
Cliff Wlk 17 BH4 . . . . . . 121 C2
Clift La DT2. . . . . 205 D1
Clifton Cl
  Swanage BH19 . . . . 179 C4
  Yeovil BA21 . . . . 28 A6
Clifton Ct
  1 Bournemouth BH7 . . . 122 F4
  Hamworthy BH15 . . . . . 118 D4
  3 New Milton BH25. . . . 95 A1
Clifton Gdns BH22 . . . . . . 61 C4
Clifton Hill
  Clifton Maybank BA22 . . 193 F8
  Winchester SO22. . . . . . 126 D6
Clifton Lodge No 1 18
  SO22 . . . . 126 D6
Clifton Lodge No 2 19
  SO22 . . . . 126 D6
Clifton Pl 1 DT4. . . . . . . 167 D7
Clifton Rd
  Bournemouth BH6. . . . . 123 D3
  Clifton Maybank BA22 . . 194 B8
  Poole BH14 . . . . 120 E2
  Swanage BH19 . . . . 179 B4
  Winchester SO22. . . . . . 126 D6
Clifton Terr SO22 . . . . . . 126 D6
Clifton View 3 BA22 . . . 193 F8
Clingan Rd BH6. . . . . 123 D7
Clinton Cl DT3 . . . . 94 B2
Clive Ct 23 BH4 . . . . 121 C3
Cliveden Cl BH22 . . . . 61 C7
Clive Rd
  Bournemouth BH9 . . . . . 89 F1
  Christchurch BH23 . . . . 93 E2
Clivia Cl DT3. . . . . 152 E2
Cloisters The
  3 Christchurch BH23. . . 124 B6
  2 Ringwood BH24 . . . . . 55 C6
Close Dr 5 TA18. . . . . . . 192 A3
Close The
  Barton on Sea BH25 . . . 127 B8
  Blandford Forum DT11 . . 212 D3

Che–Col 221

Close The continued
  Broadstone BH18 . . . . . . 86 E3
  Charlton Marshall DT11. . 211 D6
  8 Merriott TA16. . . . . . . 191 F7
  12 Pimperne DT11 . . . . . 199 D4
  Ringwood BH24 . . . . 55 B7
  St Leonards BH24 . . . . . 54 C4
Clouds Hill BH20 . . . . . . 112 C2
Clough's Rd BH24 . . . . . . 55 D7
Clovens Rd DT5. . . . . . . 186 F7
Clover Cl BH23. . . . . 125 E8
Clover Ct BH25 . . . . 95 D4
Clover Dr BH17 . . . . 86 F1
Cloverfields SP8 . . . . .5 E4
Clovermead DT9 . . . . . . 194 B6
Clovers The BH12 . . . . . . 121 A8
Clovers Wlk 5 BA20 . . . . 27 D4
Clowes Ave BH24 . . . . . . 124 B3
Clump Farm Ind Est
  DT11. . . . . 212 C6
Clump Hill BH21 . . . . 44 C1
Cluny Cres BH19 . . . . . . 179 C2
Clyde Rd BH17. . . . . 87 B2
Clyffe View DT2 . . . . 137 D6
Clyppetts 2 DT11 . . . . . . 81 E8
Coach House Mews BH22. . 61 F7
Coach House Pl BH1 . . . . 122 A5
Coach Rd
  1 Stourpaine DT11 . . . . 198 F4
  Wimborne St Giles BH21. . 201 C7
Coach Rd The DT7 . . . . . . 64 A2
Coastguard Cotts BH25. . 126 E8
Coastguard Rd
  5 Fortuneswell DT5. . . . 186 F8
  Langton Herring DT3. . . 150 B1
Coastguard Way BH23. . . 124 F5
Cobbett Cl SO22 . . . . . . 126 A3
Cobb Rd DT7 . . . . 96 B4
Cobbs La BH15. . . . . 119 E6
Cobb's Rd BH21. . . . . 59 E6
Cobham Dr DT4. . . . . . . 166 F3
Cobham Rd
  Blandford Forum DT11 . . 212 E6
  Bournemouth BH9 . . . . . 90 A3
  Ferndown BH21. . . . . . . 61 A8
  Ferndown Town BH22 . . . 52 D1
Cobham Way BH21. . . . . . 59 E1
Cobley Cl SP5 . . . . 189 D6
Coburg Rd DT1 . . . . 107 E1
Cockerell Cl BH21. . . . . . 59 F1
Cocklands DT2 . . . . 107 E6
Cockles La DT4 . . . . 167 A1
Cockpit Hill DT6 . . . . 203 C4
Codge La DT2 . . . . 205 E5
Cod La BA22 . . . . 192 D7
Codogan Ct 3 BH1 . . . . . 122 B3
Cogdean Cl BH21 . . . . . . 86 E8
Cogdean Rd BH17 . . . . . . 87 D2
Cogdeane Rd BH17. . . . . 87 D2
Cogdean Way BH21. . . . . 86 E8
Cogdean Wlk BH21. . . . . 86 E8
Coker Cl SO22 . . . . 126 C6
Coker Hill BA22 . . . . 192 F8
Coker Hill La BA22 . . . . . 193 A7
Colber Medieval Village of
  DT10. . . . . 34 F1
Colborne Ave BH21 . . . . . 59 F6
Colborne Cl BH15. . . . . . 119 D1
Colbourne Cl BH23 . . . . . 93 A8
Colbourne Ct 7 SO23 . . . 126 E8
Coldharbour SP8 . . . . .5 E2
Cold Harbour
  Milborne Port DT9 . . . . . 17 D2
  Sherborne DT9 . . . . 30 C7
Cold Harbour Bsns Pk
  DT9. . . . . 30 D8
Cold Harbour La BA22. . . 192 F6
Colebrook Pl SO23 . . . . . 126 F5
Colebrook St SO23 . . . . . 126 E5
Colehill Cres BH9 . . . . . . 90 B3
Colehill Dro DT2 . . . . . . 156 D6
Colehill Fst Sch BH21 . . . 60 A7
Colehill
  Colehill BH21. . . . . 59 F8
  Holt BH21 . . . . 51 C1
  Wimborne Minster BH21. . 60 A8
Colehill Rd BH20. . . . . . . 83 F6
Coleman Rd BH11. . . . . . 89 A3
Colemere Gdns BH23. . . 125 F8
Colemore Rd BH7. . . . . . 123 C7
Coleridge Gn BH23. . . . . 124 F8
Cole St La SP8 . . . . 11 B6
Coles Ave BH15 . . . . 118 E2
Coles Cl DT10. . . . . 35 C1
Coles Gdns BH15. . . . . . 118 E2
Coles La
  Milborne St Andrew
    DT11. . . . . 209 F1
  Yetminster DT9 . . . . . . 194 B6
Cole's La SP7 . . . . 12 A1
Colin Cl BH21. . . . . 86 D5
Collarway La BA22 . . . . . 192 F8
College BA22 . . . . 192 E8
College Arms SP7 . . . . . . 22 B7
College Gn BA21. . . . . . . 27 C6
College Rd
  Blandford Camp DT11 . . 199 E3
  Bournemouth BH5 . . . . . 123 A4
  Ringwood BH24 . . . . 55 C7
College St SO23 . . . . 126 E5
College Wlk SO23 . . . . . . 126 E4
Collett Cl DT3 . . . . 153 B1
Colletts Ct BH20. . . . . . . 177 A7
Collier's La BH20. . . . . . . 139 C7
Collingbourne Ave BH6 . 123 D7

Collingwood Cl **7** DT11 . 199 D4
Collingwood Rd BH21 . . . 53 A6
Collins La
  Ringwood BH24 . . . . 55 C7
  Weymouth DT4 . . . . 180 C7
Colliton St DT1 . . . . 108 A2
Coll of Air Traffic Control
  BH23 . . . . 90 F7
Collwood Cl BH15 . . . . . . 119 C7
Collyer's Rise SP7 . . . . 37 F6
Colman Ct BH1 . . . . 122 C3
Colmer Rd BA21 . . . . 27 D5
Cologne Rd BH20 . . . . . . 140 A6
Colonnade Rd **3** BH5 . . . 123 A5
Colonnade Road W **2**
  BH5 . . . . 123 A5
Colson Cl SO23 . . . . 126 F6
Colson Rd SO23 . . . . 126 F6
Colt Cl BH21 . . . . 60 B6
Columbian Way BH10 . . . 89 C2
Columbia Rd BH10 . . . . . . 89 C2
Columbia Trees La BH10 . 89 C1
Columbine Cl BH23 . . . . . . 93 B1
Colville Cl **4** BH5 . . . . . . 123 A5
Colville Rd **5** BH5 . . . . . 123 A5
Colway Cl DT7 . . . . 96 B7
Colway La DT7 . . . . 96 B6
Colwell Sh Ctr DT4 . . . . . 167 D3
Combe Hill
  Milborne Port DT9 . . . . . . 17 B3
  Templecombe BA8 . . . . . . 18 E8
Combe Pk BA21 . . . . 27 B7
Comber Rd **1** BH9 . . . . . . 90 A3
Combe Way DT2 . . . . 137 D5
Comet Cl DT4 . . . . 166 F1
Comet Way BH23 . . . . . . 125 A6
Comley Rd BH9 . . . . 89 F2
Commercial Rd
  Bournemouth BH2 . . . . . 121 E3
  Poole BH14 . . . . 120 A4
  Radipole DT4 . . . . 167 D2
  1 Swanage BH19 . . . . . 179 C2
Common Dro
  6 Child Okeford DT11 . 198 C8
  Farnham DT11 . . . . 188 B3
Common Hill DT8 . . . . . . 203 E5
Common La
  4 Blandford Forum
    DT11 . . . . 212 D3
  Burton Bradstock DT6 . . 128 C7
  East Stour SP8 . . . . 11 A3
  Halstock BA22 . . . . 193 C2
  Hardington Mandeville
    BA22 . . . . 193 A6
  Haselbury Plucknett TA18 . 192 D5
  Henstridge BA8 . . . . 18 F8
  Kington Magna SP8 . . . . . 9 C1
  Marnhull DT10 . . . . 34 D8
  Ryme Intrinseca DT9 . . . . 194 B5
  Sturminster Newton DT10 197 D8
  Toller Porcorum DT2 . . . . 205 D2
Common Mead Ave SP8 . . 5 E1
Common Mead La SP8 . . . 5 D1
Common Rd SP5 . . . . 188 F4
Common The
  Evershot DT2 . . . . 206 A7
  Hazelbury Bryan DT10 . . 196 E5
  Moreton DT2 . . . . 138 C8
Common Water La DT8 . . 203 F5
Compton Abbas Airfield
  SP5 . . . . 24 E2
Compton Acres Gdns
  BH13 . . . . 147 E7
Compton Ave BH14 . . . . . 120 B4
Compton Beeches BH24 . . 54 C5
Compton Cl
  Verwood BH31 . . . . 45 B6
  3 Yeovil BA21 . . . . 28 A8
Compton Cres BH22 . . . . . 53 C1
Compton Ct
  4 Bournemouth BH6 . . 123 F4
  Poole BH14 . . . . 120 D3
Compton Dr BH14 . . . . . . 120 C2
Compton Gdns BH14 . . . . 120 C2
Compton Lo **28** BH4 . . . . 121 C3
Compton Rd
  New Milton BH25 . . . . . . 95 A2
  Over Compton DT9 . . . . . 28 C5
  Winchester SO23 . . . . . . 126 D5
Concorde Cl DT4 . . . . 166 F1
Condor Cl BH21 . . . . 53 D6
Coneygar Cl DT6 . . . . 100 D8
Coneygar La
  Bridport DT6 . . . . 100 D8
  Ferndown BH22 . . . . 61 B3
Coneygar Rd DT6 . . . . . . 100 D8
Coney Gn **5** SO23 . . . . . 126 E8
Conifer Ave BH14 . . . . . . 120 B2
Conifer Cl
  Christchurch BH23 . . . . . . 91 D3
  Ferndown BH22 . . . . 61 F1
  St Leonards BH24 . . . . . . 53 F4
  Winchester SO22 . . . . . . 126 D7
Conifers **4** BH13 . . . . . . 147 E7
Conifers Prim Sch DT4 . . 167 A3
Coniston Ave BH11 . . . . . . 88 F6
Coniston Cl BH31 . . . . 45 A5
Coniston Cres DT3 . . . . . . 167 C7
Coniston Gdns BA21 . . . . . 27 B7
Coniston Rd BH24 . . . . 55 D6
Connaught Cl BH21 . . . . . . 94 E1
Connaught Cres BH12 . . . 120 E6
Connaught Gdns DT4 . . . 167 B1
Connaught Rd
  Bournemouth BH5 . . . . . 123 B5

Connaught Rd continued
  2 Weymouth DT4 . . . . . 180 E8
Connell Rd BH15 . . . . 119 C5
Conniger La BH20 . . . . . . 142 F3
Conservatory The **6**
  SO23 . . . . 126 F5
Consort Cl BH12 . . . . 120 C5
Consort Ho BH22 . . . . 61 D6
Constable Cl
  Ferndown BH22 . . . . 61 C4
  Yeovil BA21 . . . . 28 A8
Constable's Gate **10**
  SO23 . . . . 126 D5
Constitution Hill Gdns
  BH14 . . . . 120 A5
Constitution Hill Rd
  BH14 . . . . 120 A5
Convent Meadow Mobile
  Home Site BH23 . . . . . . 124 C5
Conway Cl BH25 . . . . 95 B3
Conway Ct **10** BH25 . . . . . 95 B3
Conway Dr DT2 . . . . 136 B2
Conways Dr BH14 . . . . . . 120 A4
Conway Wlk **7** DT1 . . . . . 135 C8
Cook Cl BH24 . . . . 55 C8
Cooke Gdns BH12 . . . . . . 120 F6
Cooke Rd BH12 . . . . 120 F6
Cook Row BH21 . . . . 59 B4
Cooks La DT9 . . . . 30 B5
Cook's La DT10 . . . . 33 C3
Cookswell **1** DT11 . . . . . 198 B6
Coolhurst BH14 . . . . 147 C7
Coombe DT9 . . . . 30 A7
Coombe Ave
  Bournemouth BH10 . . . . . 89 C3
  Radipole DT4 . . . . 167 E6
Coombe Cl BA21 . . . . 27 C8
Coombe Gdns BH10 . . . . . 89 C2
Coombe Heath Nature
  Reserve BH20 . . . . 158 E6
Coombe Hill BH19 . . . . . . 178 C2
Coombe La
  Castleton DT9 . . . . 15 D1
  Stoke Abbott DT8 . . . . . . 203 E3
Coombe Rd
  Dinnington TA17 . . . . 191 B7
  Puddletown DT2 . . . . 78 B1
  5 Shillingstone DT11 . . 198 B5
  Winterbourne Steepleton
    DT2 . . . . 105 E1
Coombe St La BA21 . . . . . 27 C8
Coombes Cl DT2 . . . . 103 C2
Coombe St
  Lyme Regis DT7 . . . . 96 C5
  Pen Selwood BA9 . . . . . . 1 D1
Coombe Valley Rd DT3 . . 153 A2
Coombe Wr La DT8 . . . . . 203 B6
Cooper Dean Dr BH8 . . . . 90 F1
Cooper Dean Rdbt The BH7,
  BH8 . . . . 91 A1
Cooper Gdns **2** DT11 . . 198 B8
Cooper's Cl **3** BH20 . . . 142 E4
Coopers Dr DT6 . . . . 100 D3
Coopers La BH31 . . . . 45 B8
Copeland Dr BH14 . . . . . . 120 B2
Copper Beech Cl BH13 . . 121 A4
Copper Beeches **2** BH2 . 121 F4
Copper Beech Gdns BH10 89 D2
Coppercourt Leaze **5**
  BH21 . . . . 59 C4
Coppern Way DT10 . . . . . . 33 D8
Coppers Cl SP6 . . . . 42 C6
Coppice Ave BH22 . . . . . . 61 B7
Coppice Cl
  New Milton BH25 . . . . . . 95 A4
  St Leonards BH24 . . . . . . 54 B4
  West Coker BA20 . . . . . . 26 F2
  Winchester SO22 . . . . . . 126 A7
Coppice St SP7 . . . . 12 F2
Coppice The
  Chickerell DT3 . . . . 166 E5
  Christchurch BH23 . . . . . 125 B6
Coppice View BH10 . . . . . 89 E3
Copse Ave BH25 . . . . 95 B2
Copse Cl BH14 . . . . 119 F3
Copse Hill DT10 . . . . 197 E7
Copse Rd
  Brympton BA22 . . . . 26 D7
  New Milton BH25 . . . . . . 95 B2
  Verwood BH31 . . . . 45 B6
Copse The BH24 . . . . 62 C8
Copse Way BH23 . . . . 125 E8
Copsewood Ave BH8 . . . . 90 E1
Copythorne Cl BH8. . . . . . 90 D2
Coral Ct **2** BH13 . . . . . . 121 A4
Coram Ave DT7 . . . . 96 B4
Coram Cl **3** SO23 . . . . . 126 E8
Corbar Rd BH13 . . . . 123 E8
Corbiere Ave BH12 . . . . . . 88 C1
Corbin Ave BH22 . . . . 62 A6
Corbin Way DT6 . . . . 68 E2
Cordery Gdns SP8 . . . . . . 5 F3
Cordova Gdns DT6 . . . . . 100 D7
Corfe Castle BH20 . . . . . . 161 F1
Corfe Castle Fst Sch
  BH20 . . . . 177 A8
Corfe Castle Model Village &
  Gdns BH20 . . . . 177 A8
Corfe Castle Mus **3**
  BH20 . . . . 162 A1
Corfe Castle Sta BH20. . . 162 A1
Corfe Halt Cl BH21 . . . . . . 58 E1
Corfe Hills Sch BH18 . . . . 86 F6
Corfe Lodge Rd BH18 . . . 86 D3
Corfe Mews BH15 . . . . . . 119 D4
Corfe Mullen Mdw Nature
  Reserve BH21 . . . . 85 D6

Corfe Rd
  Arne BH20 . . . . 160 F8
  Radipole DT4 . . . . 167 E6
  Stoborough Green BH20 . 142 E1
Corfe View Rd
  Corfe Mullen BH21 . . . . . 86 C5
  Poole BH14 . . . . 120 A5
Corfe Way BH18 . . . . 86 E3
Corfu BH13 . . . . 147 E6
Corhampton Rd BH6 . . . . 123 C6
Cornelia Cres BH12 . . . . . 121 A6
Corner La SP7 . . . . 7 C2
Corner The
  1 Iwerne Courtney or Shroton
    DT11 . . . . 198 E7
  Winchester SO22 . . . . . . 126 C7
Cornerways Ct **3** BH25. . . 95 B2
Cornes Cl SO23 . . . . 126 B5
Cornflower Cl DT3 . . . . . . 152 F2
Cornflower Dr BH23 . . . . . 125 C8
Cornford Hill DT9 . . . . . . 196 A6
Cornford Way BH23 . . . . . 125 D8
Cornhill DT9 . . . . 30 A6
Cornhill Way DT3 . . . . . . 153 C2
Cornish Gdns BH10 . . . . . 89 D1
Cornmarket Cl **7** BH21. . . 59 B5
Cornpits La SP6 . . . . 190 E2
Cornwall Cl DT4 . . . . 167 A3
Cornwall Rd
  1 Dorchester DT1 . . . . 107 F2
  2 Swanage BH19 . . . . 179 C2
Coronation Ave
  Bournemouth BH9 . . . . . 89 F2
  Upton BH16 . . . . 118 B7
  Yeovil BA21 . . . . 27 A7
Coronation Cl BH31 . . . . . 45 B7
Coronation Rd
  Bridport DT6 . . . . 100 C5
  1 Fortuneswell DT5 . . . 186 F8
  Gillingham SP8 . . . . 5 E2
  Radipole DT3 . . . . 167 C2
  Verwood BH31 . . . . 45 B7
Corporation Rd
  Bournemouth BH1 . . . . . 122 C5
  Weymouth DT4 . . . . 167 B3
Corpus Christi RC Prim Sch
  BH5 . . . . 123 A5
Corscombe Cl
  Poole BH17 . . . . 87 E2
  Radipole DT4 . . . . 167 D3
Cortmerron **20** BH4 . . . . 121 C2
Corton Cl **1** BA21 . . . . . . 28 A8
Cortry Cl BH12 . . . . 121 A7
Corvette Cl BH23 . . . . 125 C7
Cossack La BH14 . . . . 120 A5
Cossack Lane Ho **26**
  SO23 . . . . 126 E6
Cossins La **1** TA18 . . . . . 191 F4
Cotes Ave BH14 . . . . 120 A5
Cotes Ct BH14 . . . . 120 A5
Cothayes Dro DT2 . . . . . . 209 A6
Cotlands Rd BH8 . . . . 122 B4
Cotswold Cl BH31 . . . . 45 B6
Cotswold Ct **6** BH23 . . . 124 F8
Cottage Cl **2** BH20 . . . . 140 A2
Cottage Gdns BH12 . . . . . 121 A7
Cottage Mews **5** BH24 . . 55 B7
Cotton Cl BH18 . . . . 86 F5
Council Hos BH23 . . . . 63 F2
Counter Cl DT11 . . . . 212 F5
Countess Cl 87 E8
Countess Gdns BH7 . . . . . 122 F8
County Gates La **10** BH4. 121 B4
County Hall DT1 . . . . 107 F2
County Mus DT1 . . . . 108 A2
County Records Office
  DT1 . . . . 107 F2
Court Ash BA20 . . . . 27 D5
Courtauld Dr DT4 . . . . . . 180 D8
Court Barton
  3 Crewkerne TA18 . . . 191 E4
  Easton/Weston DT5 . . . . 186 E4
Court Cl
  Bridport DT6 . . . . 68 F1
  3 Christchurch BH23 . . 124 E7
Courtenay Cl BH20 . . . . . 142 F6
Courtenay Dr BH21 . . . . . 59 C6
Courtenay Rd BH14 . . . . . 120 B4
Court Gdns BA21 . . . . 27 A8
Court Hill
  Corscombe DT2 . . . . 205 B8
  Damerham SP6 . . . . 190 F2
Courthill Fst Sch BH14 . . 120 D4
Courthill Rd BH14 . . . . . . 120 C4
Court La
  Corscombe DT2 . . . . 205 B8
  Milborne Port DT9 . . . . . 17 C3
  5 Stofold BA22 . . . . . . 193 F8
Courtlands Rd DT5 . . . . . . 186 E3
Courtleigh Manor **6**
  BH5 . . . . 122 D4
Courtney Cl DT11 . . . . . . 198 E8
Courtney Pl BH21 . . . . 86 C5
Court Orchard Rd DT6 . . 100 C8
Court Rd
  Bournemouth BH9 . . . . . 90 B1
  Radipole DT3 . . . . 152 B2
  Swanage BH19 . . . . 179 A2
Courtyard The
  Christchurch BH23 . . . . . 124 D6
  Poole BH12 . . . . 88 C1
  Wimborne Minster BH21. . 60 A4
Covena Rd BH6 . . . . 123 E6
Coventry Cl BH21 . . . . 86 C4
Coventry Cres BH17 . . . . . 87 A1
Coventry Ct **8** SO23 . . . 126 E8
Cove Rd BH10 . . . . 89 C2
Cove Row **5** DT3 . . . . . . 167 E2

Cove St DT4 . . . . 167 E2
Cowards La DT3 . . . . 149 A7
Cow Down Rd TA20 . . . . . 202 C8
Cowdray Ho **25** SO23 . . . 126 D6
Cowdrey Gdns BH8 . . . . . 90 F2
Cow Dro BH20 . . . . 81 C2
Cowdrys Field **2** BH21 . . 59 B6
Cowell Cl TA18 . . . . 191 F3
Cowen Cl TA18 . . . . 191 F3
Cowgrove Rd BH21 . . . . . . 58 F5
Cow La
  Long Bredy DT2 . . . . . . 103 C1
  Swanage BH19 . . . . 179 A2
  Wareham BH20 . . . . 142 E3
Cowlease **1** BH19 . . . . . 179 A2
Cowleaze DT2 . . . . 133 D6
Cowleaze Rd DT2 . . . . . . 136 B1
Cowley Cl **2** DT1 . . . . . . 107 E1
Cowley Rd BH17 . . . . 119 D8
Cowleys Rd BH23 . . . . 92 C2
Cowper Ave BH25 . . . . 95 A1
Cowper Rd BH9 . . . . 89 F2
Cowpitts La BH24 . . . . 47 F2
Cowslip Rd BH18 . . . . 86 F2
Cox Ave BH9 . . . . 90 B4
Cox Cl BH9 . . . . 90 B4
Cox Hill DT10 . . . . 34 D7
Cox's La
  Litton Cheney DT2 . . . . . 103 B1
  Long Bredy DT2 . . . . 130 D8
Coxstone La BH24 . . . . . . 55 B6
Coy Pond Rd BH12 . . . . . 121 B5
Crabbswood La SO41. . . . . 95 E8
Crab La BA12 . . . . 2 B6
Crab Orchard Way BH21 . . 45 A2
Crabton Close Rd BH5. . . 122 F4
Crabtree Cl BH23 . . . . 92 C2
Crack La DT9 . . . . 178 C3
Crackmore DT9 . . . . 17 C1
Craigmoor Ave BH8 . . . . . 90 F1
Craigmoor Cl BH8 . . . . . . 90 F1
Craigmoor Way BH8 . . . . 90 E2
Craigside Rd BH24 . . . . . . 53 F4
Craigwood Dr BH22 . . . . . 61 E4
Cranborne CE VA Fst Sch
  BH21 . . . . 40 B7
Cranborne Cres BH12 . . . 120 B6
Cranborne Ct
  17 Bournemouth BH4 . . 121 C3
  Bournemouth BH9 . . . . . 122 B8
Cranborne Dr **1** SP7. . . . 12 F4
Cranborne Manor BH21 . . 40 B8
Cranborne Mid Sch BH21 . 40 B8
Cranborne Pl BH25 . . . . . . 94 E3
Cranborne Rd
  Alderholt SP6 . . . . 41 C5
  Bournemouth BH2 . . . . . 121 E3
  Hinton Parva BH21 . . . . . 50 C5
  Swanage BH19 . . . . 179 B3
  Wimborne Minster BH21. . 59 C4
Cranbourne Ct BH17 . . . . 88 A2
Cranbrook Mews BH12 . . 120 B6
Cranbrook Rd BH12 . . . . 120 B6
Crane Cl BH31 . . . . 45 A7
Crane Dr BH31 . . . . 45 A6
Cranemoor Ave BH23 . . . . 93 E2
Cranemoor Cl BH23 . . . . . 93 E2
Cranemoor Gdns BH23 . . 93 F2
Cranes Mdw DT2 . . . . . . 208 A8
Cranes Mews BH15 . . . . . 119 D3
Cranesmoor Cl BH20 . . . 139 C6
Crane St BH21 . . . . 40 B7
Crane Valley Golf Club
  BH21 . . . . 44 D6
Crane Way BH21 . . . . 53 D6
Cranford Ave BH21 . . . . . . 59 D5
Cranford Ave DT4 . . . . . . 167 E5
Cranleigh Ct BH6 . . . . . . 123 E5
Cranleigh Gdns BH6 . . . . 123 E5
Cranleigh Rd BH6 . . . . . . 123 D5
Cranmer Rd BH9 . . . . 121 F8
Cransley Ct
  Bournemouth BH4 . . . . . 121 C2
  4 Bournemouth BH4 . . 121 C2
Crantock Gr BH8 . . . . 90 F2
Cranwell Cl BH11 . . . . 88 E4
Cranworth Rd SO22 . . . . 126 D7
Crate Hill DT10 . . . . 197 C5
Crate La SP7 . . . . 7 F5
Crawford Bridge DT11 . . . 211 E5
Crawford Down Rd **4**
  DT11 . . . . 199 E2
Crawford Pk DT11 . . . . . . 211 E4
Crawshaw Rd BH14 . . . . . 120 B2
Creasey Rd BH11 . . . . 89 A5
Creech Grange BH20 . . . . 160 C1
Creech Rd BH12 . . . . 120 C5
Creech Way DT3 . . . . 167 B8
Creedy Dr BH23 . . . . 124 B5
Creekmoor La BH17 . . . . . 119 A8
Crescent Ct
  Barton on Sea BH25 . . . 126 C7
  14 Bournemouth BH2 . . 121 D2
Crescent Dr BH25 . . . . . . 126 F7
Crescent Rd
  Bournemouth BH2 . . . . . 121 E3
  Poole BH14 . . . . 120 A4
  Verwood BH31 . . . . 45 C6
  Wimborne Minster BH21. . 59 C4
Crescent St DT4 . . . . 167 E4
Crescent The
  Barton on Sea BH25 . . . 126 D8
  3 Bournemouth BH1 . . 122 F4
  West Moors BH24 . . . . . . 62 B8
  1 Yeovil BA20 . . . . 27 C4
Crescent Wlk BH22 . . . . . . 61 E2
Cresta Gdns BH22 . . . . . . 61 E2
Crest Rd BH12 . . . . 120 C6

Crewkerne Bsns Pk The **28**
  TA18 . . . . 191 F4
Crewkerne Hospl TA18 . . 191 E4
Crewkerne Mus & Heritage
  Ctr TA18 . . . . 191 E4
Crewkerne Sta TA18. . . . . 192 A3
Cribb Cl BH17 . . . . 119 E7
Crichel House BH21 . . . . . 201 A3
Crichel La BH21 . . . . 200 F1
Crichel Mount Rd BH14 . 147 C2
Crichel Rd BH9 . . . . 122 A8
Cricket Chambers BH1 . . 122 A4
Cricket Cl DT3 . . . . 124 F5
Crimea Rd BH9 . . . . 121 F7
Cringle Ave BH6 . . . . 124 A4
Crispin Cl BH23 . . . . 125 F8
Crispstead La SO23 . . . . . 126 D3
Criterion Arc **16** BH1 . . . 121 F3
Crockford Cl BH25 . . . . . . 95 B5
Crock La DT6 . . . . 100 E6
Croft Cl BH21 . . . . 86 D7
Crofton Ave BA21 . . . . 27 D5
Crofton Cl BH23 . . . . 91 E1
Crofton Pk BA21 . . . . 27 D5
Crofton Rd BA21 . . . . 27 D6
Croft Rd
  Bournemouth BH9 . . . . . 89 F2
  Bransgore BH23 . . . . 93 B6
  Christchurch BH23 . . . . . 124 F7
  Easton/Weston DT5 . . . . 186 E4
  Poole BH12 . . . . 120 B6
  Ringwood BH24 . . . . 47 E1
Croft The
  Wareham BH20 . . . . 142 F4
  3 Yeovil BA20 . . . . 26 E2
Cromer Gdns BH12 . . . . . 120 F5
Cromer Rd
  Bournemouth BH8 . . . . . 122 D7
  Poole BH12 . . . . 120 F5
Cromwell Pl **2** BH5 . . . . 123 B5
Cromwell Rd
  Bournemouth BH5 . . . . . 123 B5
  Dorchester DT1 . . . . 135 A8
  Poole BH12 . . . . 120 D5
  Weymouth DT4 . . . . 167 B3
  4 Wimborne Minster BH21 59 D4
  Winchester SO22 . . . . . . 126 C4
  Yeovil BA21 . . . . 27 F6
Crooked La BA9 . . . . 4 C3
Crooked Oak Hill DT6 . . 204 D1
Crookhays SP7 . . . . 12 F4
Crook Hill DT6 . . . . 204 C2
Cropmead Ind Est **29**
  TA18 . . . . 191 F4
Crosby Rd BH4 . . . . 121 C1
Crossfields DT9 . . . . 28 F8
Cross & Hand Stone DT2 206 F6
Cross Keys Pas **6** SO23 . 126 E5
Cross La SP8 . . . . 5 E7
Crossmead Ave BH25 . . . . 95 A2
Cross Rd
  Bradford Abbas DT9 . . . . 28 D2
  1 Weymouth DT4 . . . . 180 E8
Cross St SO23 . . . . 126 D6
Cross The
  2 Bradford Abbas DT9 . . 28 D1
  3 Child Okeford DT11 . 198 C7
  1 Okeford Fitzpaine DT11 197 F5
  Shillingstone DT11 . . . . . 198 B6
  3 Wool BH20 . . . . 140 B2
Crosstree Cl DT2 . . . . 136 B1
Crossway **2** DT11 . . . . . 199 E3
Cross Way
  Bradford Abbas DT9 . . . . 28 D2
  Christchurch BH23 . . . . . 91 D1
Crossways **13** TA20 . . . . 202 A8
Crossways The BH16 . . . . 118 C2
Croucher's Croft SO22 . . 126 A7
Crouch La DT9 . . . . 196 A6
Crow Arch La **1** BH24. . . 55 D6
Crow Arch Lane Ind Est
  BH24 . . . . 55 D6
Crowder Terr SO22 . . . . . 126 D5
Crowe Hill Ct **2** BH15 . . 119 E4
Crow La BH24 . . . . 55 E6
Crown Cl BH12 . . . . 120 C5
Crown Ct
  Milborne St Andrew DT11. . 79 E8
  4 Wimborne Minster BH21 59 B5
Crown Farm Terr DT5 . . . 187 A5
Crown Mead BH21 . . . . . . 59 C4
Crown Rd DT10 . . . . 21 A2
Crown Yd **2** DT2 . . . . . . 156 F2
Crowthorne La DT2 . . . . . 208 A7
Crumpets Dr BH16 . . . . . . 84 F5
Crumplers Cl BH16 . . . . . . 84 B3
Crusader Ct **3** BH4 . . . . 121 B4
Crusader Rd BH11 . . . . 88 D4
Cruxton Farm Ctyd BH21 . 59 D2
Cruxton La DT2 . . . . 73 A6
Cucklington Gdns BH9 . . . 90 B4
Cuckoo Hill DT9 . . . . 194 B4
Cuckoo La
  Broadwindsor TA20 . . . . 202 F7
  Hilton DT11 . . . . 209 C2
  Stinsford DT2 . . . . 109 A6
Cuckoo Rd BH12 . . . . 120 A8
Cudnell Ave BH11 . . . . 89 A6
Cuffnells Cl BH24 . . . . 47 D8
Cul-de-Sac BH25 . . . . 126 C8
Culford Cl BH8 . . . . 90 F2
Culford Ct **1** BH8. . . . . . 122 A5
Cull Cl BH12 . . . . 121 C8
Culliford Rd DT1 . . . . 135 B8
Culliford Rd N **6** DT1 . . . 108 B1
Culliford Rd S **11** DT1 . . 135 B8
Culliford Way DT3 . . . . . . 152 E3

Cull La BH25 95 B5
Cull Peppers Dish (Sink Hole) DT2 112 A6
Cullwood La BH25 95 B5
Culverhayes Cl [5] BH21 59 B6
Culverhayes Pl BH21 59 B6
Culverhayes Rd BH21 59 B6
Culverlake La EX13 202 D3
Culver Mews SO23 126 E5
Culver Rd
New Milton BH25 94 F2
Winchester SO23 126 D4
Culvers Cl DT9 30 A6
Culvers La SP8 5 C1
Culverwell Gdns [6] SO23 126 D5
Cumberland Dr DT4 166 F4
Cumnor Rd BH1 122 A3
Cunnage La BA12 3 F1
Cunningham Cl
Bournemouth BH11 89 A3
Bovington Camp BH20 139 F6
Christchurch BH23 125 A6
[4] Ringwood BH24 55 E8
[3] Weymouth DT4 180 B8
Cunningham Cres BH11 89 B3
Cunningham Ct BH25 94 F3
Cunningham Pl BH11 89 A3
Cunnington Cl DT1 134 E7
Curlew Cl
[1] Chickerell DT3 166 D5
Ferndown BH22 61 B7
Curlew Rd
Bournemouth BH8 90 D2
Christchurch BH23 125 A6
Curlews The BH31 45 C5
Curlieu Rd BH15 119 E6
Curriott Hill TA18 191 E3
Curriott Hill Rd [9] TA18 191 E4
Curry Hole La DT2 193 D2
Curtis Ct DT9 196 A8
Curtis Rd BH12 120 C5
Curzon Ct [46] BH4 121 C3
Curzon Rd
Bournemouth BH1 122 D6
Poole BH14 120 A3
Curzon Way BH23 125 D8
Custard Hill BH21 201 B5
Custom House Quay DT4 167 D2
Cuthburga Rd BH21 59 C4
Cuthbury Cl BH21 59 A4
Cuthbury Gdns BH21 59 A5
Cutler Cl
New Milton BH25 95 C3
Poole BH12 121 C7
Cutlers Pl BH21 60 A5
Cutt Mill La DT10 34 F6
Cynthia Cl BH12 120 B7
Cynthia Ho BH12 120 B7
Cynthia Rd BH12 120 B7
Cypress Dr BA20 27 A2
Cypress Rd DT2 75 D3
Cypress Way [1] SP8 5 F2
Cyril Rd BH8 122 C6

D

Dacombe Cl BH16 118 C7
Dacombe Dr
Upton BH16 117 E7
Upton BH16 118 C7
Daggons Rd SP6 41 F6
Dagmar Rd DT1 107 F1
Dahlia Cl DT3 152 F2
Dahlia Ct BH15 119 E6
Dairy Cl
Christchurch BH23 124 D7
Corfe Mullen BH21 86 B4
Dairy Field DT11 212 E6
Daisy Cl BH15 119 D6
Dakota Cl BH23 125 B7
Dale Ave DT4 167 D6
Dale Cl BH15 119 F6
Daler Ct [1] BH20 142 F3
Dale Rd BH15 119 F6
Dales Cl BH21 60 C6
Dales Dr BH21 60 B5
Dales La BH23 90 E7
Dale Valley Rd BH15 119 F7
Dalewood Ave BH11 88 E5
Dalkeith Arc BH1 121 F3
Dalkeith Rd
Corfe Mullen BH21 86 D4
Poole BH13 121 A1
Dalling Rd BH12 121 A5
Dalmeny Rd BH6 124 A3
Dalwoods DT9 30 B5
Dalzell [19] SO23 126 E8
Damerham Rd BH8 90 D3
Damers Fst Sch DT1 107 F1
Damer's Rd DT1 107 D1
Damory Court St DT11 212 D4
Damory Ct [3] DT11 212 D3
Damory St DT11 212 D4
Dampier Pl [2] BA21 27 E5
Dampier St [3] BA21 27 E5
Danecourt Cl BH14 119 F4
Danecourt Rd BH14 119 F4
Danecrest Rd SO41 95 F3
Dane Ct BH14 120 A4
Dane Dr BH22 61 E3
Danehurst New Rd SO41 95 C8
Danemark Ct [5] SO23 126 E6
Danesbury Ave BH6 123 F4
Danesbury Mdws BH25 95 C5
Danes Cl BH25 127 A7
Danes Rd [4] SO23 126 E7
Danestead Ho [3] BH25 95 A3
Daneswood Rd BH25 95 C3
Daniel Dr BH20 142 D5
Daniel Gdns [2] BH15 119 C1
Danielsfield Rd BA20 27 B2
Dansie Cl BH14 120 B4
Darby La [6] DT6 128 B8
Darby's Cl BH15 119 D6
Darby's Cnr BH17 87 C2
Darby's La BH15 119 D6
Darby's La N BH17 119 D8
Darkie La BH19 179 A6
Dark La
Fifehead Neville DT10 197 C6
Hinton BH23 94 A4
Mere BA12 3 A5
Sandford Orcas DT9 15 D6
Tincleton DT2 110 D5
Witchampton BH21 200 F1
Darknoll La DT11 197 E6
Darley Rd BH22 61 C3
Darracott Rd BH5 123 B5
Darrian Ct BH16 118 B7
Darwin Ave BH23 91 E1
Darwin Cl DT3 152 D3
Darwin Ct [4] BH13 121 A4
Dashwood Cl DT10 35 C2
Davenant Cl [5] SP8 5 E1
Davenport Cl BH16 118 C7
David Cowan Ho [23] SO23 126 D6
David's La BH24 54 E5
David Way
Poole BH15 118 D2
Upton BH15 117 F2
Davis Ct BH12 120 E5
Davis Field BH25 94 F2
Davis Gdns DT11 212 E6
Davis Rd BH12 120 E5
Dawkins Bsns Ctr BH15 118 D3
Dawkins Rd BH15 118 D3
Dawkins Way BH25 95 A2
Dawlish Cres DT4 180 D7
Dawn Cl BH10 89 C2
Dawn Gdns SO22 126 A4
Daws Ave BH11 89 B2
Daylesford Cl BH14 120 A2
Day's Ct BH21 59 D4
Day's Rd BH19 178 E2
Daytona BH14 147 C7
Deacon Gdns BH11 89 A5
Deacon Rd BH11 89 A5
Dean Cl
Hamworthy BH15 118 E3
Winchester SO22 126 A8
Dean Court (Bournemouth FC) BH7 122 F6
Deane Ave SP8 5 E1
Deane Way [5] TA20 202 A8
Dean La SP5 188 F6
Dean La Dro SP5 188 F4
Dean Park Cres BH1 121 F3
Dean Park Rd BH1 121 F4
Deans Court La BH21 59 C4
Deanscroft Rd BH10 89 E4
Deans Dro BH16 84 D2
Deans Gr BH21 59 D7
Deansleigh Cl [6] DT3 168 B8
Deansleigh Rd BH7 91 B1
Dean's Rd [6] BH5 123 B5
Deans The BH1 121 F4
Dean Swift Cres BH14 147 C8
Dear Hay La BH15 119 C2
Decies Rd BH14 120 B5
De Courtenai Cl BH11 88 E5
Deepdene La BH11 88 E5
Deep Ford La DT9 194 D3
Deep La DT9 194 C3
Deerleap Way BH25 95 B5
Deer Park Cl BH25 94 F4
Dee Way BH15 119 B1
De Haviland Cl BH21 59 F2
De Havilland Ho BH23 125 A6
De Havilland Way BH23 125 A6
Delamere Gdns BH10 89 E3
Delft Mews BH23 124 D6
Delhi Cl BH14 120 D3
Delhi La DT5 187 A4
Delhi Rd BH9 89 F2
Delilah Rd BH15 118 D2
De Lisle Rd BH3 121 F7
Delkeith Ct BH22 61 D4
Dell Cl BH18 86 E4
Dell The BH23 126 C8
Delph Rd BH21 87 D8
Delph Woods Woodland Trail BH18,BH21 87 C7
Delta Cl BH23 125 A7
De Lunn Bldgs [8] SO23 126 E6
De Mauley Ct BH13 147 E8
De Mauley Rd BH13 147 E8
De Montfort Rd BH21 59 D1
De Moulham Rd BH19 179 B4
Denby Rd BH15 119 E4
Dene Cl BH24 47 E1
Denecote Lodge BH13 147 H8
Denes Ave BA12 3 A6
Dene The BH13 121 A2
Deneve Ave BH17 87 C1
Dene Wlk BH22 61 E1
Denewood Copse BH22 52 F4
Denewood Rd
Bournemouth BH4 121 B3
Ferndown BH22 52 F4
Denhall Cl DT10 35 A2
Denham Cl
Poole BH17 87 E3
Denham Cl *continued*
Winchester SO23 126 D8
Denham Dr
Cann SP7 23 A5
Christchurch BH23 93 F1
Denhay La DT6 67 B5
Denholm Cl BH24 47 E1
Denison Rd BH17 87 C1
Denmark La BH15 119 D3
Denmark Rd
Bournemouth BH9 89 F1
Poole BH15 119 D3
Denmark Terr BH1 122 E6
Denmead BH25 95 D4
Denmead Rd BH6 123 D7
Dennis Rd
Corfe Mullen BH21 86 D5
Weymouth DT4 167 B2
Dennistoun Ave BH23 124 F7
Denzil Cl [3] BA22 193 A8
Derby Rd BH1 122 C4
Derby St DT4 167 D4
De Redvers Rd BH14 120 C2
Dereham Way BH12 120 F6
Derritt La BH23 92 D8
Derrybrian Gdns BH25 95 A2
Derwent Cl
Bournemouth BH9 90 A2
Ferndown BH22 62 A6
Derwent Gdns BA21 27 F6
Derwent Rd
New Milton BH25 95 B5
Weymouth DT4 180 D6
Derwentwater Rd BH21 59 C2
Derwent Way [3] BA21 26 E6
Deverel Cl BH23 124 A8
Deverel Rd DT2 75 D2
Devonedge La DT6 97 B8
Devon Rd
Christchurch BH23 123 E8
Poole BH15 119 E5
Weymouth DT4 167 B4
Deweys La [8] BH24 55 B7
Dewey's Way SP8 5 F2
Dewlands Orch DT9 194 E3
Dewlands Rd BH31 44 F6
Dewlands Way BH31 45 A6
Dewlish Cl BH17 88 A2
Diamond Cl SP6 43 A8
Diana Cl
Dorchester DT1 134 F7
Ferndown BH22 61 D6
Diana Ct [7] BH23 126 A7
Diana Way BH21 86 E7
Dibbles La BA22 193 A8
Dibden Cl BH8 90 D3
Dickens Rd BH6 123 D7
Dick o' Th' Banks Cl DT2 137 D6
Dick o' Th' Banks Rd DT2 137 D6
Didcot Rd BH17 119 D7
Digby Rd DT9 30 B5
Diggory Cres DT1 135 B8
Dillons Gdns BH16 84 C2
Dilly La BH25 127 A7
Diments Gdns [2] DT6 100 C8
Dinah's Hollow SP7 24 C6
Dingle Rd BH5 123 B4
Dingley Rd BH15 119 D6
Dinham Ct BH25 95 D4
Dinham Rd BH25 95 D4
Dinhay DT10 20 E4
Dinosaur Experience The BH19 177 F1
Dinosaur Mus DT1 108 A2
Diprose Rd BH21 86 E7
Discovery Court Bsns Ctr BH12 88 E2
Discovery (Interactive Science Ctr) DT4 167 E1
Disraeli Rd BH23 124 D6
Dock Rd DT5 181 C2
Doctor Roberts Cl DT6 100 C5
Dodham Cres BA20 27 B4
Dodhams Farm Cl DT6 68 F1
Doe Copse Way BH25 94 E4
Does La BH31 44 F6
Dogbury Gate DT2 207 C8
Dogdean BH21 59 C8
Dogwood Rd BH18 86 E2
Dolbery Rd N BH12 88 D2
Dolbery Rd S BH12 88 C1
Dollings The [1] BH20 177 A7
Dollin's La [3] BH20 142 E4
Dolmans Hill BH16 84 A1
Dolphin Ave BH10 89 E5
Dolphin Cl [2] DT7 96 C5
Dolphin Ct BH13 121 B2
Dolphin Ctr [3] BH15 119 C2
Dolphin La SP8 5 E4
Dolphin Mans BH25 127 A6
Dolphin Pl BH25 127 A7
Dolphin Quays [10] BH15 119 C1
Dome Alley SO23 126 E5
Dominion Ctr BH11 88 E3
Dominion Rd BH11 88 E3
Domum Rd SO23 126 F4
Doncaster Rd DT4 180 D6
Donhead Hollow SP7 25 D7
Donkey La
Bere Regis BH20 113 B6
Bridport DT6 100 C8
[5] Burton Bradstock DT6 128 B8
Donnelly Rd BH6 123 F5
Donnington Ct [2] SO23 126 E7
Donnington Dr BH23 125 B7
Donoughmore Rd [1] BH1 122 E4
Dorcester Mkt DT1 108 A1
Dorchester Adult Ed Ctr DT1 108 B1
Dorchester Gdns BH15 119 E5
Dorchester Hill
Blandford Forum DT11 212 C2
Milborne St Andrew DT11 79 E8
Winterborne Whitechurch DT11 210 C2
Dorchester Mans BH1 122 D3
Dorchester Mid Sch DT1 134 E8
Dorchester Prep Sch DT1 108 B1
Dorchester Rd
Askerswell DT2 103 A4
Bincombe DT3 134 C1
Cerne Abbas DT2 207 D4
Closworth BA22 193 F6
Loders DT6 101 C6
Maiden Newton DT2 73 A7
Poole BH15 119 E6
Radipole DT3 152 B2
Stratton DT2 106 C8
Sydling St Nicholas DT2 207 A2
Tolpuddle DT2 79 B2
Upton BH16 118 A7
Wool BH20 139 E1
Yeovil BA20 27 C2
Dorchester South Sta DT1 108 A1
Dorchester Town Football Club DT2 134 F6
Dorchester W Sta DT1 107 F1
Dore Cl BA21 26 E7
Dormers The BH25 94 F1
Dornie Rd BH13 147 E7
Dorset Ave BH22 61 D3
Dorset Cl DT4 167 A3
Dorset Cty Hospl DT1 107 E1
Dorset Fire & Rescue Service HQ DT1 108 A3
Dorset Grange BH23 123 F7
Dorset Heavy Horse Ctr BH21 40 F2
Dorset Ho BH13 121 A2
Dorset Lake Ave BH14 147 B8
Dorset Lake Manor BH14 120 A2
Dorset Police HQ DT2 139 D2
Dorset Rd
Bournemouth BH4 121 C5
Christchurch BH23 124 F8
Dorset St DT11 212 D4
Dorset Teddy Bear Mus DT1 108 A2
Dorset Terr [8] DT4 167 D2
Dorset Way BH17 119 E7
Dottery Rd DT6 68 B2
Double Comm DT6 97 A7
Douglas Ave BH23 124 A6
Douglas Cl BH16 118 C7
Douglas Gdns BH12 120 E5
Douglas Mews
Bournemouth BH6 123 C5
Upton BH16 118 C8
Douglas Rd
Bournemouth BH6 123 E4
Poole BH12 120 E5
Weymouth DT4 180 D6
Doulton Cl [5] DT4 167 C3
Doulton Gdns BH14 120 B2
Doussie Cl BH16 118 B8
Dover Cl BH13 121 A3
Dover Rd
Poole BH13 121 A3
Weymouth DT4 180 D6
Dover St SP7 21 F5
Doveshill Cres BH10 89 D3
Doveshill Gdns BH10 89 D3
Doveshill Mobile Home Pk BH10 89 D3
Doves The DT3 152 D3
Dowlands Cl BH10 89 D4
Dowlands Rd BH10 89 D4
Dowman Pl DT4 180 D5
Downash La EX13 202 B3
Downclose [2] DT4 180 D7
Downclose La TA18 192 C4
Down End DT2 107 E6
Downes St DT6 100 D6
Downey Cl BH11 88 F2
Down House La DT6 99 E4
Down La
Folke DT9 195 D8
Trent DT9 14 F2
Downlands CE Fst Sch DT11 199 F3
Downlands Pl BH17 119 F8
Downleaze [1] BA20 26 F2
Down Lodge Cl SP6 42 C6
Down Rd
[3] Pimperne DT11 199 D4
Weymouth DT4 167 C1
Downside Cl
Blandford Forum DT11 212 E4
Charmouth DT6 97 A7
Mere BA12 3 A6
Downside La DT11 107 C1
Downs La DT9 194 C5
Down's La DT9 194 A5
Downsview Dr SP8 5 F3
Downton Cl BH8 90 D3
Downton La SO41 127 F7
Downview Rd SP6 190 B6
Down Wood Rd [2] DT11 199 E2
Doyne Rd BH14 120 E4
Dozens Cnr TA17 191 A7
Dragons Hill DT7 96 C7
Dragoon Way BH23 123 F7
Drake Ave DT3 166 D5
Drake Cl
Christchurch BH23 124 F6
New Milton BH25 94 F3
Ringwood BH24 47 E1
Drake Ct [4] BH15 119 C1
Drake Rd BH15 119 C1
Drakes Cres [6] TA20 202 A8
Drake's La DT2 208 F3
Drakes Mdw BA22 193 C7
Drakes Rd BH22 61 F3
Draper Rd
Bournemouth BH11 89 A4
Christchurch BH23 124 E7
Drax Ave BH20 142 E5
Draycott Rd BH10 89 D2
Drayton St SO22 126 A4
Dreadnought Trad Est DT6 100 B6
Dreswick Cl BH23 91 D4
Drew Cl
Bridport DT6 68 F1
Poole BH12 121 C7
Drew Grange BH15 118 E4
Drewitt Ind Est BH11 88 E3
Drew's La DT10 19 C1
Drift Rd DT2 72 F8
Drift The TA20 202 B8
Drive The
Poole BH12 120 D5
Poole BH13 147 D7
Drones La SP7 23 D2
Drove Cl DT10 32 F3
Drove La SP7 36 F6
Drove Rd DT10 32 F3
Droves The SP5 188 E4
Drove The
Arne BH20 160 F8
Shapwick DT11 56 E7
Thornford DT9 194 D8
Winfrith Newburgh DT2 156 E8
Droveway La BA21 14 A5
Droxford Rd BH6 123 B6
Druce La DT2 77 F3
Druids Cl BH22 61 D2
Druitt Rd BH23 124 F8
Drum La DT10 196 F3
Drummond Cl SO22 126 C3
Drummond Rd
Bournemouth BH1 122 D4
Swanage BH19 179 C1
Drury La DT6 204 C2
Drury Rd BH4 121 B2
Dryden Cl BH24 54 A5
Dry La SP8 5 C1
Duart Ct BH25 95 C3
Duchy Cl DT1 135 C8
Ducking Stool La BH23 124 B6
Duck Island La BH24 55 B6
Duck La
Bournemouth BH11 88 F4
Stalbridge DT10 19 D1
Duckpool La TA18 192 B8
Duck St
Bridport DT6 100 E4
Cattistock DT2 206 C2
Cerne Abbas DT2 207 D4
Chideock DT6 99 A6
Child Okeford DT11 198 C7
Hilton DT11 209 D5
Symondsbury DT6 99 F7
Winterborne Kingston DT11 81 E7
Wool BH20 140 B1
Dudley Ave SO41 95 F3
Dudley Gdns BH10 89 D5
Dudley Pl [3] BH25 95 B1
Dudley Rd BH10 89 D5
Dudmoor Farm Rd BH23 91 F4
Dudmoor La BH23 91 F3
Dudsbury Ave BH22 61 D4
Dudsbury Cres BH22 61 E4
Dudsbury Gdns BH22 89 E8
Dudsbury Rd BH22 61 D1
Dudsway Ct BH22 61 D4
Dugberry Hill DT6 70 B6
Dugdell Cl BH22 61 F6
Duke's Ave DT1 108 B1
Dukes Cl
Bournemouth BH6 123 D6
Martinstown DT2 133 C6
Dukes Dr BH11 88 E5
Dukesfield BH23 91 D2
Dullar La
Lytchett Matravers BH20 84 B6
Sturminster Marshall BH21 56 C2
Dulsie Rd BH3 121 C7
Dumbarton Rd DT4 180 D6
Dummer Mews [5] SO23 126 D5
Dumpton Sch BH21 59 D8
Dunbar Cres BH23 93 F2
Dunbar Rd BH3 121 E6
Dunbury Fst Sch
Winterborne Stickland DT11 210 C7
Winterborne Whitechurch DT11 210 C3
Dunbury La DT11 209 F6
Duncan Cres BH20 139 F6
Duncan Pl BH20 139 F6
Duncan Rd BH25 95 D4
Dunch La DT9 194 D3
Duncliffe Cl DT10 33 E8
Duncliffe View SP8 10 E3
Duncliff Rd BH6 124 A4

Duncombe Dr BH24 46 E3
Dundas Rd BH17 119 E8
Dundee Rd DT4 180 D6
Dune Crest BH13 147 C3
Dunedin Cl BH22 61 B3
Dunedin Dr BH22 61 B3
Dunedin Gdns BH22 61 B3
Dunedin Gr BH23 125 C7
Dunford Cl
Barton on Sea BH25 126 E8
Old Milton BH25 94 E1
Dunford Pl 7 BH19 179 B2
Dunford Rd BH12 120 D5
Dunkeld Rd BH3 121 E6
Dunlin Cl BH23 125 B5
Dunnock Cl BH22 61 B8
Dunn's La
Iwerne Minster DT11 37 F2
Silton SP8 2 A1
Dunsham La TA18 191 C2
Dunspit La DT11 188 B1
Dunstans La BH15 120 A6
Dunyeats Rd BH18 87 B4
Dunyeats Rdbt BH18 87 D5
Duplock Ho BH25 95 A3
D'Urberville Cl 4 DT1 134 F7
D'Urberville Dr BH19 179 B4
Durdells Ave BH11 89 A5
Durdells Gdns BH11 89 A5
Durland Cl BH25 95 A1
Durley Chine Ct 12 BH2 121 D2
Durley Chine Rd BH2 121 D2
Durley Chine Rd S BH2 121 D2
Durley Gdns BH2 121 D2
Durley Rd BH2 121 E2
Durley Rdbt BH2 121 E2
Durlston Court Sch BH25 127 A8
Durlston Cres BH23 91 D4
Durlston Ctry Pk BH19 185 B7
Durlston Rd
Poole BH14 120 C2
Swanage BH19 179 C1
Durnford Dro BH19 178 B1
Durngate Pl SO23 126 F6
Durngate St DT1 108 A2
Durngate Terr 5 SO23 126 F6
Durnover Ct DT1 108 B2
Durrant 4 DT10 197 D8
Durrant Cl DT9 30 B5
Durrant Rd
Bournemouth BH2 121 E4
Poole BH14 120 C3
Durrington Pl BH7 123 B6
Durrington Rd BH7 123 B7
Durweston CE Fst Sch DT11 198 F3
Durweston Cl BH9 90 B3
Dyke Head DT9 195 B6
Dymewood Rd BH21 53 A7
Dyson Dr SO23 126 E8

E

Eadon Cl DT3 168 A7
Eagle Ct 8 SO23 126 D6
Eagle House Gdns DT11 212 C4
Eagle Rd BH13 121 A4
Eagle Rise BH8 90 D1
Eaglhurst 5 BH13 121 A4
Earl Cl 1 DT1 108 B1
Earle Rd BH4 121 C1
Earle St BA20 27 E4
Earlham Dr BH14 120 C4
Earls Cl DT9 30 C7
Earlsdon Way BH23 125 F8
Earlsdown 9 SO23 126 F5
Earlswood 16 BH4 121 C2
Earlswood Dr SP6 42 B5
Earlswood Pk BH25 95 C4
Earthpits La SP5 189 E4
Eastacre SO22 126 C7
East Ave
Barton on Sea BH25 126 C7
Bournemouth BH3 121 D6
East Avenue Rdbt BH3 121 E6
East Borough BH21 59 B5
Eastbrook Row BH21 59 C4
East Burton Rd BH20 139 F2
Eastbury Ct BH23 124 F4
East Cl BH25 126 D8
East Cliff
8 Bournemouth BH2 121 F4
Lyme Regis DT7 96 C5
East Cliff Way BH23 125 C7
East Coker Prim Sch BA22 193 D7
East Coker Rd BA20 27 B1
Eastcott Cl BH7 123 A8
East Dorset Trade Pk BH21 60 F6
Eastdown Ave DT3 167 F8
Eastdown Gdns 3 DT3 168 A6
East Dr BH24 62 B7
East Dro BH19 178 B2
Easter Rd BH9 90 A2
East Farm La DT2 155 D7
Eastfield 4 DT9 194 D8
Eastfield Ct BH24 55 E7
Eastfield La
North Perrott TA18 192 C4
Ringwood BH24 55 E7
West Chinnock BA22 192 D8
Eastgate St SO23 126 F5
Easthams Rd TA18 191 F4
Easthay La TA20 202 D4
East Hill
Charminster DT2 107 D6
Evershot DT2 206 A7
Winchester SO23 126 F4
East Howe La BH10 89 C4
East Knighton La DT2 157 A7
East La TA18 192 B8
Eastlake Ave BH12 120 C6
Eastland Rd BA21 27 E5
Eastlands
New Milton BH25 95 B1
10 Yetminster DT9 194 C5
Eastleaze Rd DT11 212 D6
East Mill La DT9 30 C6
East Morden Dro BH20 83 D6
Easton Hollow SP5 188 B7
Easton La DT5 187 A5
Easton Lane Bsns Ctr SO23 126 F6
Easton Sq 4 DT5 187 A4
Easton St DT5 187 A4
Eastop La DT10 33 B5
East Overcliff Dr BH1 122 C3
East Quay 11 BH15 119 C1
East Quay Rd BH15 119 C1
East Rd DT6 100 E6
East St
Beaminster DT8 204 D4
Blandford Forum DT11 212 D3
4 Bourton SP8 1 E1
Bridport DT6 100 D6
Chickerell DT3 166 C6
Corfe Castle BH20 162 A1
Crewkerne TA18 191 F4
Fortuneswell DT5 186 F7
Milborne Port DT9 17 D2
North Perrott TA18 192 C4
Poole BH15 119 C1
Radipole DT4 167 E2
Sydling St Nicholas DT2 207 A2
Wareham BH20 142 E3
West Coker BA22 193 A8
Wimborne Minster BH21 59 C4
9 Winterborne Kingston DT11 81 E8
East Stoke Fen Nature Reserve BH20 140 E2
East View Rd BH24 55 D7
Eastville BA21 27 E5
East Walls BH20 142 F3
East Way
Bournemouth BH8 90 C1
Corfe Mullen BH21 86 D5
East Weare Rd DT5 181 B1
Eastwell La DT10 35 A8
Eastwood Ave BH22 61 E6
Eastworth Rd BH31 45 A7
East Wyld Rd DT4 167 A3
Eaton Rd BH13 121 A2
Ebblake Ind Est BH31 45 E4
Ebden Rd SO23 126 F6
Ebenezer La 6 BH24 55 B7
Ebor Cl BH22 61 E2
Ebor Rd
Poole BH12 120 D6
Weymouth DT4 180 C8
Ebury Ct 7 BH4 121 C3
Eccles Rd BH15 119 A2
Eddison Ave DT1 108 C1
Eddy Green Rd BH16 84 B2
Eden Ct
9 Bournemouth BH1 122 B3
11 Bournemouth BH4 121 C2
Eden Gr BH21 59 D3
Edenhurst 12 BH4 121 C3
Edgar Rd SO23 126 D4
Edgarton Rd BH17 87 D3
Edgar Villas SO23 126 D4
Edgehill Rd
Bournemouth BH9 121 E8
Bournemouth BH9 89 F1
Bridport DT6 100 B5
Edgemoor Rd BH22 53 C1
Edifred Rd BH9 90 A4
Edinburgh Ho 4 SO22 126 D6
Edington Rd SO23 126 E7
Edith Ct 2 SP8 5 E1
Edmondsham Ho 16 BH2 121 E3
Edmondsham House & Gdns BH21 40 C4
Edmondsham Rd BH31 45 A7
Edmunds Cl 8 BH25 95 A1
Edward Cl BA22 26 D6
Edward Cres BH20 142 E4
Edward May Ct BH11 89 A4
Edward Rd
Bournemouth BH11 89 B3
Christchurch BH23 124 F8
Dorchester DT1 107 F1
Poole BH14 120 C5
Winchester SO23 126 D3
Edwards Ct BH23 126 A8
Edward St
Blandford Forum DT11 212 D4
4 Radipole DT4 167 D4
Edwina Cl BH24 47 E1
Edwina Dr BH17 87 B2
Egbert Rd SO23 126 E7
Egdon Cl
Bere Regis BH20 81 B2
Ferndown BH22 61 B3
Egdon Ct BH16 118 B7
Egdon Dr BH21 87 E8
Egdon Glen DT2 137 E6
Egdon Rd
Dorchester DT1 135 B7
Egdon Rd *continued*
Northport BH20 142 D5
Egerton Ct BH8 122 D6
Egerton Gdns BH8 122 D6
Egerton Rd BH8 122 D6
Eggardon Cl 5 DT8 204 C4
Eggardon Hill (Fort) DT6 71 A2
Egmont Cl BH24 54 E2
Egmont Dr BH24 54 F2
Egmont Gdns BH24 54 E2
Egmont Rd BH16 118 B4
Elbury View SP7 37 E7
Elderberry La BH23 124 F6
Elder Cl SO22 126 A2
Elder Rd BH20 81 A2
Eldon Ave BH25 126 E8
Eldon Cl BH25 126 E8
Eldon Ct 5 BH14 120 A4
Eldon Pl BH4 121 B3
Eldon Rd BH9 89 E1
Eldons Dro BH16 84 C3
Eldon Terr 5 BH19 179 B2
Eldridge Cl 3 DT1 134 F7
Eleanor Ct BH25 94 F1
Eleanor Dr BH11 88 D5
Eleanor Gdns BH23 123 E8
Elfin Dr BH22 61 C7
Elgar Rd BH10 89 D4
Elgin Rd
Bournemouth BH4 121 D6
Poole BH14 120 C2
Elijah Cl BH15 118 E2
Eliot Ho 8 BH25 95 A2
Eliotts Dr BA21 27 A7
Elise Cl BH7 123 B8
Elizabeth Ave
Bridport DT6 100 C5
Christchurch BH23 123 F8
Elizabeth Cl 1 DT7 96 C6
Elizabeth Ct
1 Bournemouth BH1 122 B3
Ferndown BH22 61 D6
8 New Milton BH25 95 B2
Elizabeth Gdns BH23 125 D7
Elizabeth Pl DT1 107 D1
Elizabeth Rd
Blandford Forum DT11 212 E5
Poole BH15 119 D3
Upton BH16 118 C7
Wimborne Minster BH21 59 C5
Elizabeth Way DT3 166 E3
Ellerslie Cl DT2 107 E6
Ellesdon DT6 97 B8
Ellesfield Dr BH22 61 D2
Elles Rd BH20 139 D7
Ellingham Dr BH24 46 E4
Ellingham Dro BH24 47 E5
Ellingham Rd BH25 126 D8
Elliott Rd BH11 88 F3
Elliott's Hill BA22 192 D7
Elm Ave
Christchurch BH23 91 E1
Holton Heath BH20 116 B3
New Milton BH25 95 A2
Elm Cl
Motcombe SP7 7 B1
Overcombe/Preston DT3 168 A6
Sturminster Newton DT10 35 C1
Elm Ct
5 New Milton BH25 95 A2
Winchester SO22 126 C6
Elmes Rd BH9 89 F2
Elmgate Dr
Bournemouth BH7 122 F7
Bournemouth BH7 123 A7
Elm Gdns BH4 121 C5
Elmhurst Ave BA21 27 D7
Elmhurst Rd
Bournemouth BH11 89 A5
Ferndown BH22 53 B1
Elmhurst Way BH22 53 B1
Elm La DT2 75 D2
Elmleigh BA21 26 E7
Elmore Dr BH24 54 A6
Elm Rd SO22 126 C6
Elmrise Prim Sch BH11 89 A4
Elms Ave BH14 120 A1
Elms Cl BH14 120 A1
Elmstead Rd BH13 147 F8
Elms Way BH6 123 E4
Elm Tree Wlk BH22 89 E8
Elmwood Way BH23 126 A7
Elphinstone Rd BH23 94 B1
Elsdon's La DT6 64 B4
Elston Medieval Village of DT2 207 A3
Eltham Cl BH7 123 B8
Elvastone St 1 DT1 107 C1
Elveroakes Way DT4 180 C6
Elvin Cl SO41 95 F3
Elwell DT6 100 E5
Elwell Manor Gdns DT4 167 D1
Elwell St DT3 152 B6
Elwood Cl BH20 142 F8
Elwyn Rd BH1,BH8 122 C5
Elysium Ct BH22 61 E3
Elziver Cl DT3 166 D5
Embankment Way BH24 55 D6
Emberley Cl BH22 62 A6
Emerald Cl BH24 54 A6
Emerson Cl 12 BH15 119 C2
Emerson Rd
Poole BH15 119 D2
Weymouth DT4 167 B2
Emily Cl BH23 92 A1
Emily Ct BH14 120 E5
Emley La 1 BH21 201 C1
Emmadale Rd DT4 167 B3
Emmanuel CE VC Mid Sch The BH31 45 A4
Emminster Cl DT3 168 A8
Empool Cl DT2 137 D5
Emsbury Rd DT10 35 C3
Encombe Cl BH12 120 F8
Encombe Rd BH20 142 D3
Endeavour Ind Pk BH24 55 D6
Endfield Cl BH23 91 F1
Endfield Rd
Bournemouth BH9 90 A2
Christchurch BH23 91 E1
Enfield Ave BH15 119 E6
Enfield Cres BH15 119 E6
Enfield Rd BH15 119 E6
Englands Way BH11 88 D4
English Ct 15 BH2 121 D4
Enkworth Rd DT3 168 A7
Ensbury Ave BH10 89 D1
Ensbury Cl BH10 89 D1
Ensbury Ct BH10 89 E2
Ensbury Park Rd BH9 89 E2
Enterprise Way BH23 90 C8
Epiphany CE Prim Sch The BH9 90 B4
Erica Dr BH21 86 D6
Ericksen Rd BH11 89 C3
Erinbank Mans BH1 122 C3
Erin Rd BH20 139 E7
Ermine St BA21 26 F7
Erpingham Rd BH12 121 A5
Erskine Rd SO22 126 C5
Esmonde Way BH17 119 F8
Esplanade
Bridport DT6 100 B1
Poole BH13 147 F7
Portland DT5 186 E8
Radipole DT4 167 E2
Essex Ave BH23 91 F1
Essex Rd DT4 167 C3
Ethelbert Rd BH21 59 D4
Eton Gdns BH4 121 C4
Eton Mans 2 BH6 123 E3
Ettrick Rd BH13 121 A1
Eucalyptus Ave BH24 54 C2
Euston Gr BH24 55 C6
Evans Cl
Bournemouth BH11 88 F1
St Leonards BH24 54 A6
Evelyn Mews 1 BH9 89 F1
Evelyn Rd BH9 90 A2
Evening Glade BH22 61 E4
Eventide Homes BH8 90 E2
Everdene Cl BH22 61 C2
Everdene Dr DT4 166 E3
Everdene Rd 2 DT1 135 B8
Everest Rd
Christchurch BH23 124 E8
Weymouth DT4 167 C1
Everetts La 1 DT11 198 B5
Everglades Cl BH22 61 D7
Evergreen Cl BH21 53 A8
Evergreens BH24 54 A6
Evering Ave BH12 88 D1
Evering Gdns BH12 88 C1
Everon Gdns BH25 95 B1
Evershot Rd BH8 90 E2
Evershot Wlk 19 DT1 107 D1
Eversleigh 10 BH2 121 D2
Eversley Pl SO22 126 B3
Everton Rd 2 BA20 27 C4
Evesham Ave BA21 26 E6
Evesham Cl BH7 123 B8
Evesham Ct BH13 121 A1
Exbourne Manor BH1 122 C3
Exbury Dr BH11 88 F5
Excelsior Rd BH14 120 C3
Exeter Cres BH2 121 F3
Exeter Ct 5 BH23 126 B7
Exeter La BH2 121 F2
Exeter Park Mans BH2 121 F2
Exeter Park Rd BH2 121 F2
Exeter Rd
Bournemouth BH2 121 F3
4 Swanage BH19 179 C2
Exton Rd BH6 123 D7
Eynon Mews BH24 55 B6
Eype Down Rd DT6 99 E5

F

Fabers Yd 12 SO22 126 D6
Factory Hill SP8 1 F3
Factory La
Buckland Newton DT2 207 F8
Tatworth & Forton TA20 202 A8
Factory Rd BH16 118 C6
Fairclose DT4 167 B1
Faircourt 8 BH25 95 B3
Faircross Ave DT4 167 C1
Fairey Cl SP8 5 F3
Fairey Cres SP8 5 F3
Fairfax 1 DT6 99 A6
Fairfield
Christchurch BH23 124 B7
Crewkerne TA18 191 E4
Sherborne DT9 30 B7
Fairfield Bglws DT11 212 D5
Fairfield Cl
Christchurch BH23 124 B7
2 Okeford Fitzpaine DT11 197 F6
Wimborne Minster BH21 59 F5
Fairfield Hts DT9 30 B7
Fairfield Pk DT7 96 C6
Fairfield Rd
Barton on Sea BH25 126 E7
Blandford Forum DT11 212 D4
Fairfield Rd *continued*
2 Dorchester DT1 107 F1
Iwerne Courtney or Shroton DT11 198 E7
Wimborne Minster BH21 59 D4
Winchester SO22 126 D7
Fairhaven Ct 9 BH5 122 E4
Fairhouse Rd BA22 193 F8
Fairies Dr BH22 61 F3
Fairlane SP7 13 A2
Fairlawn BH22 61 D5
Fairlawn Ho 9 SO22 126 D5
Fair Lea BH2 121 E2
Fairlie BH24 47 E1
Fairlie Pk BH24 47 D1
Fairlight La SO41 95 D8
Fairmead Rd BA21 27 E8
Fairmead Sch BA21 27 E8
Fairmile Par BH23 91 F1
Fairmile Rd BH23 91 F1
Fair Mile Rd DT11 210 F8
Fairoak Way 3 DT8 204 A7
Fairthorn Ct 3 BH2 121 F4
Fairview Cres BH18 87 A5
Fairview Dr BH18 87 A5
Fairview Pk BH14 120 C3
Fairview Rd
Broadstone BH18 87 A5
Weymouth DT4 180 D7
Fairway Dr
Christchurch BH23 123 F6
Wareham Town BH20 142 C6
Fairway Rd BH14 147 C8
Fairways BH22 61 F6
Fairway The BH25 127 B7
Fairway View BA21 27 F6
Fairwinds BH13 147 B3
Fairwood Rd BH31 45 E5
Fairy Bridge Wlk 1 SP8 5 F3
Falcon Dr BH23 125 A5
Falconer Dr BH15 118 E4
Falcon View SO22 126 A2
Falkland Sq 2 BH15 119 C2
Fallow Field SO22 126 B2
Fallows The BH25 95 B5
Fancy Rd BH12 120 B8
Fancys Cl DT5 187 A4
Fancy's Row BH20 116 B4
Fantley La SP8 2 B1
Farcroft Rd BH12 120 B5
Far Ends 4 BH14 120 B4
Farfrae Cres DT1 135 B8
Faringdon Ct 17 SO23 126 E8
Farm Cl
Radipole DT4 167 A5
Ringwood BH24 55 C8
Farm Ct BH21 60 A4
Farmdene Cl BH23 125 D8
Farmer Palmer's Farm Pk BH16 116 B5
Farmers Wlk 1 BH21 59 B6
Farm La
Christchurch BH23 125 A5
West Lulworth BH20 172 D6
Farm La N BH25 127 A8
Farm La S BH25 127 A8
Farm Rd
Bradford Abbas DT9 28 C2
Ferndown BH22 52 F2
Farnham Rd BH12 121 A7
Farriers Cl BH21 60 B6
Farringdon Cl 2 DT1 134 F7
Farrington
24 Bournemouth BH4 121 C2
Bournemouth BH4 121 C2
Farr's Orch 5 TA16 191 F7
Farthings Ct The 13 BH1 122 A3
Farwell Cl BH23 92 C3
Farwell Rd BH12 88 C2
Faversham
9 Bournemouth BH2 121 D2
Radipole DT4 167 A6
Fawcett Rd BH25 94 F2
Fawley Gn BH8 90 D3
Fawn Gdns BH25 94 F4
Fellowsmead DT10 20 F2
Felton Cres BH23 125 F8
Felton Ct BH14 119 F5
Felton Rd BH14 119 F5
Fenleigh Cl BH25 95 B1
Fennel Rd BA12 3 B6
Fennel Way BA22 26 C5
Fenton Rd BH6 123 C5
Fenway Cl DT1 108 D1
Fenwick Ct BH8 122 B5
Fern Bank
5 Bournemouth BH2 121 F3
Three Legged Cross BH21 53 A7
Fern Barrow BH12 121 B7
Fern Brook La SP8 6 B1
Fern Cl
Alderholt SP6 42 C5
Burton BH23 92 C2
Ferncroft Gdns BH10 89 D5
Ferncroft Rd BH10 89 D5
Ferndale Gdns BA21 27 A6
Ferndale Rd
New Milton BH25 95 B4
Radipole DT4 167 D6
Ferndown Forest Golf Club BH22 52 E1
Ferndown Fst Sch BH22 61 C5
Ferndown Ind Est BH21 60 F7
Ferndown Mid Sch BH22 61 C5
Ferndown Rd DT7 96 C5
Ferndown Upper Sch BH22 61 B6
Ferne Hollow SP5 188 A8

Ferney Way SP5 188 C4
Fernglade BH25 95 A3
Fernheath Cl BH11 89 A3
Fernheath Rd BH11 89 A3
Fern Hill SP8 11 A3
Fernhill Ave DT4 167 D6
Fernhill Cl BH17 88 A2
Fernhill Flats 6 BH2 121 F3
Fernhill Gate BH25 95 A5
Fernhill La BH25 95 A4
Fernhill Rd BH25 95 A3
Fernlea BH23 124 D6
Fernlea Ave BH22 61 D4
Fernlea Cl
Ferndown BH22 61 D4
St Leonards BH24 54 A4
Fernlea Gdns BH22 61 D4
Fernside Ave BH14 119 F4
Fernside Bsns Pk BH22 61 A7
Fernside Ct BH15 119 E4
Fernside Rd
Bournemouth BH9 121 E8
Ferndown BH22 53 A2
Poole BH15 119 E4
Fernway Cl BH21 60 B4
Fernwood Cl BH24 54 D5
Ferris Ave BH8 90 D2
Ferris Cl BH8 90 D2
Ferris Pl BH8 90 D2
Ferrymans Way 5 DT4 180 D5
Ferry Rd
Bournemouth BH6 123 F3
Poole BH15 119 B1
Poole BH19 147 A1
Studland BH19 164 C3
Ferry Way BH13 147 B3
Feversham Ave BH8 90 E1
Fiddleford Manor DT10 197 F8
Field Barn Dr DT4 167 B5
Field Cl DT10 35 C2
Fieldfare Cl DT3 152 D3
Fielding Rd BA21 27 E6
Fieldings The SP8 10 D3
Field La
Gillingham SP8 5 B4
Kington Magna SP8 9 D2
Pen Selwood BA9 1 B3
Field Pl
Barton on Sea BH25 126 D8
Verwood BH31 45 A7
Fields Barn DT2 156 E5
Field's Cl 1 DT11 210 C3
Fields Oak DT11 212 D4
Fields The BA12 3 B6
Field View Rd 2 DT11 212 D4
Fieldway BH24 55 D8
Field Way
Christchurch BH23 93 D1
Corfe Mullen BH21 86 E8
Fifehead Hill SP8 20 F7
Fifehead Wood Nature
Reserve SP8 20 E8
Filbridge Rise DT10 35 C2
Filford La DT6 67 E8
Filleul Rd BH20 115 F1
Fillybrook Bsns Pk SP8 9 B5
Finches The DT3 152 C3
Finchfield Ave BH11 88 F6
Findlay Pl BH19 178 F3
Fineshade 7 BH13 147 F7
Fippenny Hollow 3
DT11 197 F5
Fir Ave
Holton Heath BH20 116 B3
New Milton BH25 95 B2
Firbank Rd BH9 122 B8
Firch La DT6 101 B6
Fir Cl BH22 53 A3
Fir Dr DT3 153 C1
Firecrest Cl DT3 152 C4
Firmain Rd BH12 88 D1
Firs Glen Rd
Bournemouth BH9 121 E8
Ferndown BH22 53 A2
Verwood BH31 45 B5
Firshill BH23 125 E8
Firside Rd BH21 86 C4
Firs La BH14 147 B8
First Cliff Wlk 1 DT6 100 B2
Firs The
Bournemouth BH1 122 A4
Winchester SO22 126 C7
First Marine Ave BH25 126 F7
Firsway BH16 118 C7
Fir Tree Cl
Dorchester DT1 107 D2
Netherbury DT6 68 B6
St Leonards BH24 53 F2
Firtree Cres SO41 95 F3
Fir Tree Hill SP6 42 C6
Fir Tree La BH23 93 D1
Fir Vale Rd BH1 121 F3
Fisherbridge Rd DT3 168 C8
Fisherman's Ave BH5 123 B4
Fisherman's Bank BH23 124 E5
Fishermans Cl DT3 166 D6
Fishermans Rd BH15 119 C1
Fisherman's Wlk BH5 123 B4
Fishers Cl DT9 14 E2
Fisher's Cl DT11 212 D3
Fisher's La TA17 191 A7
Fishers Pl DT2 170 A7
Fisherway La TA19 191 A5
Fishey La SP7 36 E5
Fishpond Bottom Rd
DT6 202 D1
Fishweir Fields 1 DT6 68 F1
Fishweir La DT6 68 F1
Fitzharris Ave BH9 122 A7
Fitzmaurice Rd BH23 123 E8
Fitzpain Cl BH22 61 D2
Fitzpain Rd BH22 61 D2
Fitzwilliam Cl BH11 88 E5
Fitzworth Ave BH16 118 C4
Five Acres DT6 97 A7
Five Bridges Rd SO23 126 C1
Fiveways Specl Sch BA21 27 F6
Flaghead BH13 147 E6
Flaghead Chine Rd BH13 147 E6
Flaghead Rd BH13 147 E7
Flambard Ave BH23 92 A1
Flambard Rd BH14 120 C2
Flanders Cl DT10 21 A2
Flaxfield Dr 15 TA18 191 F4
Flax La DT9 28 F7
Flax Way BA21 26 E6
Flazen Cl BH11 88 D3
Fleet Ct DT3 166 E3
Fleet Rd DT3 166 A5
Fleetsbridge Bsns Ctr
BH17 119 B7
Fleet's Cnr BH17 119 B7
Fleets Est BH15 119 B6
Fleets La BH15 119 C6
Fleetspoint Bsns Ctr
BH15 119 B5
Fleet St DT8 204 D4
Fleet View DT4 180 C7
Fleetwood Ct BH15 119 C7
Fletcher Cl BH10 89 D3
Fletcher Rd BH10 89 D3
Flood La DT6 100 D4
Floral Farm BH21 60 A2
Florence Rd
Bournemouth BH5 122 F4
Dorchester DT1 134 E8
Poole BH14 120 D4
Floriston Gdns BH25 95 D3
Flower Ct BH21 59 D3
Flowers Dro BH16 84 D4
Flushing Mdw BA21 28 A5
Folke La DT9 31 A1
Folly Farm La BH24 54 E6
Folly Fields BA21 27 D7
Folly La
Blandford St Mary DT11 212 C1
Gillingham SP8 10 D5
Kington Magna SP8 9 E4
Nether Compton DT9 28 F8
Wareham BH20 142 E4
Wool BH20 140 A2
Folly Mill Gdns DT6 100 D6
Folly Mill La DT6 100 D6
Folly The DT2 207 D4
Font La BA22 193 B7
Fontmell Down Nature
Reserve SP5 24 D1
Fontmell Rd BH18 87 C3
Font Villas BA22 193 B7
Footners La BH23 92 C2
Foot's Hill SP7 24 B7
Ford Cl BH22 61 F7
Ford Down La DT2 208 A7
Forde Abbey & Gdns
TA20 202 C8
Forde Pk BA21 26 E7
Fordhay BA22 192 E7
Fordingbridge Rd SP6 42 C7
Fordington Ave SO22 126 C6
Fordington Gdns 3 DT1 108 B1
Fordington Gn 5 DT1 108 B2
Fordington Rd SO22 126 C7
Ford La
Corscombe DT2 205 B7
Ferndown BH22 62 A7
Forehill Cl DT3 168 B8
Foreland Cl BH23 91 D4
Foreland Rd BH16 118 C4
Fore St
Evershot DT2 206 A7
Thorncombe TA20 202 E6
Forest Cl
Christchurch BH23 93 D1
Verwood BH24 45 F4
Forest Ct BH25 95 B2
Forest Ct Hills 3 BH24 55 F6
Forest Edge BH25 95 C4
Forest Edge Dr BH24 53 F5
Forest Edge Rd BH20 142 F7
Forest Hill BA20 27 A2
Forest Ho 14 BH1 122 A3
Forest La
Corfe Castle BH20 162 F1
Verwood BH31 45 A7
Forestlake Ave BH24 55 F6
Forest Links Rd BH21 52 D1
Forest Oak Dr BH25 95 A5
Fore Store St TA20 202 A8
Forest Pines BH25 95 A4
Forest Rd
Ferndown BH22 53 B3
Poole BH13 121 A2
Forest Rise BH23 93 D2
Forestside Gdns BH24 47 E1
Forestside The BH31 45 F5
Forest View
Beckley BH25 94 D5
Crossways DT2 137 D6
Forest View Cl BH9 90 A2
Forest View Dr BH21 61 A5
Forest View Rd BH9 90 A3
Forest Way
Christchurch BH23 93 D1
Ferndown BH21 61 A5
Forge End 2 SP8 10 D2
Forge La
East Chinnock BA22 192 E8
Verwood BH31 44 F5
Zeale SP8 1 F3
Forsters La DT6 69 A1
Forsyth Gdns BH10 89 C1
Fort Cumberland Cl
BH15 118 D2
Fortescue Rd
Bournemouth BH3 122 A6
Poole BH12 120 D6
Forton Cl BH10 89 E4
Fortress Gn 5 DT1 134 E7
Fortuneswell DT5 186 E8
Forty Foot Way DT6 100 B2
Forum Gn 1 DT1 134 E7
Forum Sch The DT11 198 B6
Fosse Cl BA21 26 F7
Fosse Gn 7 DT1 134 E7
Fossett Way 4 DT4 180 B8
Fosse Way 1 BA21 26 F7
Foss Orch DT6 99 A6
Foss Way TA17 191 C8
Fosters Hill DT9 196 B5
Fosters Mdws 2 DT11 210 C3
Fosters Spring 1 BH16 84 D2
Foundry Cl DT6 100 A7
Foundry Knapp DT6 100 A7
Foundry La DT6 100 C6
Foundry Sq 13 TA18 191 F4
Fountain Ct BH13 121 B2
Fountain Mead 3 SP7 12 F4
Fountain Rdbt BH23 124 B6
Fountains Cl BA21 26 E7
Fountain Way BH23 124 B6
Fouracre Cl DT6 100 D8
Four Acres DT5 186 E3
Fourgates Rd 1 DT1 107 E1
Fourth Cliff Wlk DT6 100 B2
Four Wells Rd BH21 60 A7
Foxbury BH20 139 C7
Foxbury Rd
St Leonards BH24 54 B1
St Leonards BH24 62 F8
Fox Cl DT6 69 A1
Foxcote 1 BA20 26 E2
Foxcote Gdns BH25 94 F3
Foxcroft Dr BH21 60 B5
Foxdale Ct 17 BH2 121 E3
Foxes Cl BH31 45 B5
Foxglove Cl
Christchurch BH23 125 C8
Gillingham SP8 5 E2
Foxglove Pl BH25 95 D4
Foxgloves BH16 118 B7
Foxglove Way
Bridport DT6 100 D3
Radipole DT3 152 F2
Yeovil BA22 26 C5
Foxhill Cl 8 BH19 179 A2
Foxhills BH31 45 D6
Foxhills Cres BH16 84 D3
Foxhills Dr BH16 84 D3
Foxhills La BH16 84 D1
Foxhills Rd BH16 84 D3
Foxholes 1 BH6 123 F4
Foxholes Rd
Bournemouth BH6 123 F4
Poole BH15 119 F6
Fox La
Wimborne Minster BH21 60 C5
Winchester SO22 126 A3
Fox La Terr DT10 35 B1
Fox Mdws 16 TA18 191 F5
Foxs Cl DT9 196 B5
Foxwell La TA18 192 C7
Foxwood Ave BH23 124 F5
Foyle Hill SP7 12 C1
Framerville Rd BH20 139 E7
Frampton Cl BH25 95 C5
Frampton Pl BH24 55 C7
Frampton Rd
Bournemouth BH9 122 A8
16 Pimperne DT11 199 D4
Francesca Ct 5 BH23 124 E7
Francesca Grange 4
BH23 124 E7
Francesca Lo 1 BH23 124 E6
Frances Ct 7 BH23 126 B7
Frances Rd BH1 122 C4
Frances Sheldon Ct
SO22 126 C5
Franchise St DT4 167 D2
Francis Ave BH11 88 D3
Francis Avenue Ind Est
BH11 88 D3
Francis Rd
Poole BH12 120 E5
Weymouth DT4 167 B2
Frankland Cres BH14 120 E3
Franklin Cl DT4 167 B2
Franklin Rd
Bournemouth BH9 90 A3
New Milton BH25 95 C4
Weymouth DT4 167 B3
Franklyn Cl BH16 118 B7
Frankston Rd BH6 123 C4
Franks Way BH12 120 B7
Frank Wareham Cottage
Homes The BH9 90 A4
Fraser Ave DT4 166 F1
Fraser Ct BH25 94 F3
Fraser Rd BH12 120 F8
Freame Way SP8 5 D1
Freda Rd BH23 123 F6
Frederica Rd BH9 121 E8
Freedom Ave BA21 27 A6
Freemans Cl BH21 60 B6
Freemans La BH21 60 B5
Freemantle Rd DT4 166 F1
Freesia Cl DT3 152 E2
Fremington Ct 6 BH25 95 B3
French Hill La SP7 23 F4
French Mill La SP7 23 F7
French Mill Rise SP7 12 F1
French Rd BH17 87 B1
French's Farm Rd
Upton BH16 117 B7
Upton BH16 118 A7
Frensham Cl BH10 89 E3
Freshwater Cl 4 DT5 186 E1
Freshwater Dr BH15 118 D3
Freshwater Rd BH23 125 C6
Friars Ave BA21 26 F6
Friars Cl 2 DT1 135 C8
Friarsgate SO23 126 E6
Friars Gate BH23 125 C6
Friars Moor DT10 35 C1
Friars Rd BH23 125 B6
Friars Wlk BH25 127 A8
Friar Waddon Rd DT3 151 F8
Friary Gdns 7 SO23 126 D5
Friary Hill DT1 108 A2
Friary La DT1 108 A2
Friday's Heron BH21 40 B7
Frinton Ct 2 BH14 120 A4
Fritham Gdns BH8 90 D3
Frizzel's Hill DT10 196 F4
Frobisher Ave BH12 88 F1
Frobisher Cl
Christchurch BH23 124 F6
3 Ringwood BH24 47 E1
Frogham Hill SP6 43 F6
Frog La
Dinnington TA17 191 B8
Fordingbridge SP6 43 A7
Iwerne Courtney or Shroton
DT11 198 F7
Motcombe SP7 12 C7
Frogmore La DT2 71 E8
Frome Ave BH20 139 F2
Frome La DT2 72 F7
Frome Rd BH20 142 D3
Frome Terr DT1 108 A2
Frome Valley Rd DT2 137 C6
Frome View
Bradford Peverell DT2 107 A6
Maiden Newton DT2 73 A8
Front La BH21 56 D5
Front St
East Stour SP8 10 F3
Portesham DT3 132 A1
Froom's La BH20 81 C1
Frost Rd BH11 88 F3
Froud Way BH21 86 C4
Froxfield Rd DT11 212 D5
Fryer Cl BH11 89 B5
Fryers Copse BH21 60 C6
Fryers Rd BH21 53 A8
Frys Cl BH16 84 C4
Fry's Cl DT3 150 A8
Fry's La DT2 75 A7
Fudge Hill DT2 205 A8
Fulbrooks Cl DT6 100 C7
Fulbrooks La DT6 100 C7
Fulcrum Ctr The BH12 88 C2
Fulflood Ct 2 SO22 126 C6
Fulmar Rd BH23 125 A5
Fulwood Ave BH11 88 E5
Furge Gr BA8 19 A4
Furge La BA8 19 A3
Furland Rd 6 TA18 191 F4
Furlands DT5 186 F3
Furley Cl 8 SO23 126 F6
Furlong La DT9 17 B3
Furlong Mews 3 BH24 55 B7
Furlong Sh Ctr BH24 55 B8
Furlongs The DT9 30 B7
Furlong The BH24 55 B7
Furnell Rd BH15 119 D1
Furzebrook Cl BH17 87 E3
Furzebrook Rd BH20 161 A4
Furze Croft BH25 95 A2
Furzehill
Colehill BH21 59 C8
Holt BH21 50 F1
Furze Hill Dr BH14 120 C1
Furzelands Rd BH21 53 A8
Furze The 2 BA20 26 E2
Furzey Rd BH16 118 B6
Furzy Cl DT3 168 B7

G

Gablehurst BH16 118 C7
Gabriel Gn 1 DT1 135 B8
Gadbridge Ct 14 BH4 121 C2
Gainsborough DT9 17 C2
Gainsborough Ave BH25 95 B5
Gainsborough Ct 4 BH5 123 B5
Gainsborough Dr DT9 29 E5
Gainsborough Hill DT9 30 C4
Gainsborough Ho BH25 127 A6
Gainsborough Rd
Bournemouth BH7 122 F7
St Leonards BH24 54 A5
Gainsborough Way BA21 28 A8
Gale Cres DT6 100 C5
Gales Hill DT2 207 E7
Gallop's La BH20 83 C2
Gallop Way BH12 121 C7
Galloway Rd BH15 118 D4
Gallows Cnr
Iwerne Courtney or Shroton
DT11 36 F1
Gallows Cnr *continued*
Milton Abbas DT11 209 D3
Gallows Dr BH22 61 E1
Gallows Hill
Arne BH20 161 C4
Owermoigne DT2 155 D6
Gallwey Rd DT4 180 C7
Galton Ave BH23 123 F6
Gannetts Pk BH19 179 B3
Garden Cl
Bridport DT6 100 D7
Litton Cheney DT2 103 B2
New Milton BH25 95 A1
Garden Ct BH1 122 D6
Garden Ho 6 BH1 122 B3
Garden La
St Leonards BH24 54 A3
25 Winchester SO23 126 E6
Gardens Cres BH14 147 B8
Gardens Ct 5 BH15 119 E3
Gardenside 1 DT6 97 A7
Gardens Rd BH14 147 B8
Garden Wlk BH22 61 E7
Gardner Ct BH23 123 E8
Gardner Rd
Christchurch BH23 123 E8
Ringwood BH24 55 D6
Garfield Ave
Bournemouth BH1 122 D5
Dorchester DT1 134 E8
Garland Cres DT1 135 B8
Garland Rd BH15 119 D4
Garlands La DT11 197 D4
Garnier Rd SO23 126 E3
Garrett Rd BA20 26 F3
Garsdale Cl BH11 89 A6
Gar St SO23 126 D5
Garston Hill DT3 166 C6
Garston Wood Nature
Reserve SP5 189 B6
Gartells 1 DT10 197 A4
Garth Cl BH24 53 F4
Garth Rd BH9 90 A1
Gascoigne's La SP7 23 E8
Gascoyne La DT2 107 B6
Gashay La EX13 202 E3
Gas House Hill DT9 30 C5
Gas La TA17 191 C7
Gasper St BA12 1 C6
Gassons La DT6 66 A4
Gate Cl EX13 202 A3
Gatemore Rd DT2 138 E1
Gateway The BH13 120 F4
Gaydon Rise BH11 88 E4
Gaza Rd BH20 139 D7
Gazelle Rd BA20 26 F3
Geelong Cl DT3 152 E2
General Johnson Ct 4
SO22 126 A4
Geneva Ave BH6 123 D5
Gent Cl DT11 212 E5
George Eyston Dr SO22 126 B4
George Rdbt The BH15 119 C3
Georges Cl DT6 97 B8
Georges Mews BH21 86 D7
George Smith Way BA22 26 C6
George St
Bridport DT6 100 C2
Sherborne DT9 30 B6
Georgian Cl BH24 55 C8
Georgian Way BH10 89 F4
Georgina Cl BH12 121 C8
Georgina Talbot Ho
BH12 121 B8
Gerald Rd BH3 122 A6
Germaine Cl BH23 125 F8
Gervis Cres BH14 120 A4
Gervis Pl BH1 121 F3
Gervis Rd BH1 122 B3
Giant's Grave DT2 209 A4
Gibbs Gn BH16 84 D2
Gibbs La DT6 66 C1
Gibbs Marsh Trading Est
DT10 20 A4
Gibson Rd BH17 119 E7
Giddy Gn La BH20 139 E2
Giddy Gn Rd BH20 139 E2
Giddylake BH21 59 D6
Gifle View 2 DT9 194 D8
Gigg La SP8 8 E4
Gilbert Cl SP6 42 D6
Gilbert Rd
Bournemouth BH8 122 D6
Swanage BH19 179 B2
Giles Cl DT2 107 A6
Giles's La
Bishop's Caundle DT9 196 A7
Morden BH20 83 D3
Gillam Rd BH10 89 D5
Gillett Rd BH12 121 C7
Gillingham Adult Ed Ctr
Gillingham SP8 5 F2
Shaftesbury SP7 12 D3
Gillingham Cl BH9 90 C4
Gillingham L Ctr SP8 6 A2
Gillingham Mus SP8 5 F1
Gillingham Prim Sch SP8 5 A2
Gillingham Sch SP8 6 A2
Gillingham Sta SP8 5 F1
Gillion Ct 2 BH23 124 E6
Gipsy La DT6 68 E1
Gipsy's Dro DT10 197 C7
Girt La DT2 205 F7
Glacis DT5 187 A7
Gladdis Rd BH11 88 F3

Gladelands Cl BH18 86 E4
Gladelands Pk BH22 61 F7
Gladelands Way BH18 86 E4
Glade The
Christchurch BH23 91 E1
St Leonards BH24 54 A5
Gladiator Gn 3 DT1 134 E7
Gladstone Cl
Bridport DT6 100 E7
Christchurch BH23 124 D6
2 Radipole DT3 152 E2
Gladstone Rd
Bournemouth BH7 122 F5
Poole BH12 120 C5
Gladstone Rd E BH7 122 F5
Gladstone Rd W BH1 122 F5
Gladstone St SO23 126 D6
Glamis Ave BH10 89 E5
Glastonbury Ct BA21 26 F6
Gleadowe Ave BH23 124 A6
Glebe Cl
Abbotsbury DT3 149 C7
Bridport DT6 100 D5
Maiden Newton DT2 72 F8
Overcombe/Preston DT3 169 A8
8 Thornford DT9 194 D8
Weymouth DT4 167 C1
Glebe Ct 4 DT11 37 F1
Glebefields DT2 106 F7
Glebeford Cl DT2 155 E7
Glebe Gdns SP7 12 B8
Glebeland Cl DT2 136 A7
Glebeland La DT6 65 F7
Glebelands 6 TA16 191 F7
Glebe Rd BH16 84 C1
Glebe The
3 Durweston DT11 198 E3
1 Iwerne Courtney or Shroton DT11 198 F7
3 Iwerne Minster DT11 37 F1
Glebe Way DT2 136 C3
Glenair Ave BH14 120 A3
Glenair Cres BH14 120 A3
Glenair Rd BH14 120 A3
Glen Ave DT4 167 C2
Glenavon BH25 95 C2
Glenavon Rd BH23 93 F1
Glen Cl BH25 126 D8
Glencoe Rd
Bournemouth BH7 122 F7
Poole BH12 120 D5
Glendale Ave BH22 61 E6
Glendale Cl
Christchurch BH23 91 D3
Wimborne Minster BH21 59 C5
Glendale Ct BH23 91 D3
Glendale Rd BH6 124 A4
Glendinning Ave DT4 167 D5
Glendon Ave BH10 89 C6
Glendrive BH25 126 C8
Gleneagles
Christchurch BH23 123 F6
Poole BH13 121 B2
Gleneagles Ave BH14 120 D2
Gleneagles Cl BH22 61 F6
Glenferness Ave BH4 121 D5
Glen Fern Rd BH1 122 A3
Glengariff Rd BH14 120 C2
Glengarry BH25 95 C2
Glengarry Way BH23 125 C6
Glenives Cl BH24 54 B4
Glenmeadows Dr BH10 89 B5
Glenmoor Cl BH10 89 D1
Glenmoor Rd
Bournemouth BH9 121 E8
Ferndown BH22 61 D3
Glenmoor Sch BH10 89 D1
Glenmore Rd DT4 167 B4
Glenmount Dr BH14 120 B4
Glennie Way DT3 166 D4
Glen Rd
Bournemouth BH5 122 F4
Poole BH14 120 B4
Glenroyd Gdns BH6 123 E4
Glenside BH23,BH25 126 B7
Glen Spey BH25 95 D2
Glen The
Poole BH12 120 D6
Poole, Canford Cliffs BH13 147 E8
Glenthorne Ave BA21 27 D7
Glenville Cl BH23 94 B2
Glenville Gdns BH10 89 C2
Glenville Rd
Bournemouth BH10 89 C2
Walkford BH23 94 B2
Yeovil BA21 27 F6
Glenwood Cl BH22 53 A2
Glenwood La BH22 53 A2
Glenwood Rd
Ferndown BH22 53 A2
Verwood BH31 45 A5
Glenwood Way 2 BH22 53 A2
Glissons BH22 61 A2
Globe Cl 3 BH19 178 F2
Globe La BH15 119 C2
Globe Orch TA18 192 C6
Gloucester Cl DT3 166 E3
Gloucester Mews DT4 167 D3
Gloucester Rd
Bournemouth BH7 122 F5
3 Dorchester DT1 107 E1
Poole BH12 120 E5
Gloucester St DT4 167 D3
Glovers Cl 2 DT9 17 D2
Glovers Walk Sh Ctr BA20 27 E4
Glovers Wlk 16 BA20 27 D4
Glue Hill DT10 197 C8
Glyde Path Rd DT1 108 A2
Glyn Pl SP7 24 D6
Glynville Cl BH21 60 A7
Glynville Ct BH21 60 A7
Glynville Rd BH21 60 A7
Goathill Rd
Goathill DT9 31 D6
Milborne Port DT9 17 C1
Goathorn Cl BH16 118 D4
Godlingston Manor BH19 178 E5
Godmanston Cl BH17 88 A1
God's Blessing La BH21 51 B3
Godshill Cl BH8 90 D3
Godson Ho 27 SO23 126 E6
Goldcrest Cl DT3 152 C4
Goldcroft BA21 27 D5
Goldcroft Ave DT4 167 C5
Goldcroft Rd DT4 167 C5
Golden Gates BH13 147 B3
Golden Hill DT10 32 F2
Goldenleas Ct BH11 88 D3
Goldenleas Dr BH11 88 D3
Golden Sands BH13 147 B3
Goldenstones Pool & L Ctr BA20 27 C3
Goldfinch Cl BH25 94 F2
Goldfinch Rd BH17 118 E8
Gold Hill
Child Okeford DT11 198 B8
Shaftesbury SP7 12 E2
Golding's La DT9 17 C1
Gold St DT10 33 C8
Golf Links Rd
Broadstone BH18 87 B5
Ferndown BH22 61 E4
Goliath Rd BH15 118 D2
Good Rd BH12 120 C7
Goodwin's La BH20 83 D2
Gooseacre La BA22 26 C1
Gooseberry La 7 BH24 55 B7
Goose Hill DT3 149 F7
Gordon Cres 1 DT4 166 F2
Gordon Ct 7 BH4 121 C4
Gordon Mount BH23 126 B8
Gordon Rd
Bournemouth BH1 122 D4
Christchurch BH23 126 A8
Poole BH12 121 A5
6 Swanage BH19 179 A2
Wimborne Minster BH21 59 E4
Winchester SO23 126 E6
Yeovil BA21 27 E6
Gordon Rd S BH12 121 A5
Gordon's La DT9 195 A8
Gordon Watson Ho SO23 126 D3
Gordon Way BH23 92 D1
Gore Cross DT6 68 F2
Gore Cross Bsns Pk DT6 68 E2
Gore Cross Way 5 DT6 68 F1
Gore Grange BH25 94 F2
Gore Hill BH20 142 F7
Gore La DT6 68 F2
Gore Rd BH25 94 E2
Gore Rd Ind Est BH25 94 F2
Gorey Rd BH12 88 D1
Goring Field SO22 126 A7
Gorleston Rd BH12 120 F5
Gorley Lynch SP6 43 F4
Gorley Rd BH24 47 E1
Gorse Cl
New Milton BH25 95 D4
St Leonards BH24 53 F4
Gorsecliff Ct 7 BH5 122 D4
Gorsecliff Rd BH10 89 D1
Gorsefield Rd BH25 95 B4
Gorse Hill Cl BH15 119 F5
Gorse Hill Cres BH15 119 E5
Gorse Hill Rd BH15 119 F5
Gorse Knoll Dr BH31 45 A7
Gorse La BH16 118 D7
Gorseland Ct BH22 61 E3
Gorse Rd
Corfe Mullen BH21 86 C5
Poole BH21 85 E5
Gort Rd
Bournemouth BH11 89 B3
Poole BH17 87 A1
Gosling Cl BH17 119 F7
Goss Pl 2 DT4 167 C4
Gough Cl 11 TA16 191 F7
Gough Cres BH17 87 B2
Goughs Cl DT10 35 A1
Gould's Hill
Upwey DT3 152 A7
Winterborne St Martin DT2 133 F3
Goulds Hill Cl DT3 152 A7
Gover Cl BH20 143 B1
Gower Rd SP7 13 A2
Grace Darling Ho BH15 119 D1
Grafton Ave DT4 167 A6
Grafton Cl
Bournemouth BH3 122 A7
Christchurch BH23 124 D6
Grafton Rd
Bournemouth BH3 122 A6
Winchester SO23 126 D4
Grammar School La BH21 59 B4
Granby Cl DT4 166 F3
Granby Ind Est DT4 166 E4
Granby Rd BH9 90 A4
Granby Way DT4 167 A5
Grand Ave BH6 123 C4
Grand Par 13 BH15 119 B1
Grange BH21 50 E1
Grange Arch (Folly) BH20 175 C8
Grange Cl SO23 126 C2
Grangecroft Rd 3 DT5 186 E3
Grange Ct 5 BH1 122 B3
Grange Gdns BH12 120 E8
Grange Hill BH20 160 C1
Grange La DT8 203 D5
Grange Pk 1 DT9 194 D8
Grange Rd
Bournemouth BH6 123 D3
Broadstone BH18 87 A4
Christchurch BH23 125 B7
Church Knowle BH20 160 D4
Radipole DT4 167 E5
St Leonards BH24 53 F2
Winchester SO23 126 C1
Grange Road Bsns Ctr BH23 125 A7
Grange Sch The BH23 124 E7
Grangewood Hall BH21 59 D5
Grans Barrow (Long Barrow) SP6 190 E6
Grantham Rd BH1 122 E5
Grantley Rd 3 BH5 122 F4
Grant's Ave BH1 122 D6
Grants Cl BH1 122 E6
Granville Gdns 2 SP7 12 F3
Granville Pl
9 Bournemouth BH1 121 F3
Winchester SO23 126 F4
Granville Rd
Bournemouth BH5 123 A5
Poole BH12 120 B5
Weymouth DT4 167 C2
Granville Way DT9 30 C8
Grasmere Cl BH23 91 D3
Grasmere Gdns BH25 95 B5
Grasmere Rd
Bournemouth BH5 123 A4
Poole BH13 147 B3
Radipole DT3 167 C6
Grass Royal BA21 27 E6
Grass Royal Jun Sch BA21 27 E6
Gravel Hill BH17,BH18, BH21 87 D5
Gravel La
Charlton Marshall DT11 211 C7
Ringwood BH24 55 C8
Gray Cl BH17 119 F8
Graycot Cl BH10 89 C5
Grays DT4 167 B6
Grays Cl SP7 12 B8
Gray's Yd 5 BH15 119 C1
Great Cnr BA21 26 E6
Great Dorset Maize Maze & Farm Pk The DT3 150 B4
Great Down La DT10 21 B4
Great Gd SP7 13 A4
Great George St DT4 167 D3
Great Head La DT2 206 F7
Great Hill BA9 1 B3
Great La SP7 12 F2
Great Minster St 2 SO23 126 E5
Great Owens Dr BH20 142 D6
Great Pit La BA22 15 B5
Great Western Rd DT1 108 A1
Great Western Terr
Radipole DT4 167 D6
Yeovil BA21 27 F5
Greaves Cl BH10 89 C3
Grebe Cl
Broadstone BH17 118 E8
2 Chickerell DT3 166 D5
Christchurch BH23 125 A6
Greenacre
Barton on Sea BH25 127 A8
Charminster DT2 107 E6
Greenacre Cl BH16 118 C6
Greenacres
32 Bournemouth BH4 121 C3
Puddletown DT2 78 A1
Green Acres BH23 124 F7
Greenacres Cl BH10 89 E6
Green Acres Cl BH24 54 F5
Green Bottom BH21 60 A7
Green Cl
Bere Regis BH20 81 B1
Bradpole DT6 100 F8
Charlton Marshall DT11 211 D6
Poole BH15 119 D1
Sturminster Newton DT10 35 C2
Greenclose La BH21 59 D4
Green Dr 1 SP6 42 D6
Greenfield Gdns BH25 127 B8
Greenfield Rd
3 Charlton Marshall DT11 211 D6
Poole BH15 119 E7
Greenfields 1 BH12 120 F7
Greenfinch Cl BH17 86 F1
Greenfinch Wlk BH24 55 E5
Greenford CE Prim Sch DT2 72 E8
Greenford La
Compton Valence DT2 104 C8
Maiden Newton DT2 72 D4
Green Gdns BH15 119 D1
Greenham La TA18 203 B7
Greenham Yd TA18 203 B7
Greenhayes
Broadstone BH18 87 C2
Charmouth DT6 96 F7
2 Okeford Fitzpaine DT11 197 F5
Greenhays Rise BH21 59 C5
Greenhill
Blandford Forum DT11 212 D5
Radipole DT4 167 E5
Sherborne DT9 30 B6
Greenhill Ave SO22 126 C6
Greenhill Cl
Wimborne Minster BH21 59 D6
Winchester SO22 126 C6
Greenhill La BH21 59 D6
Greenhill Rd
Wimborne Minster BH21 59 D6
Winchester SO22 126 B6
Yeovil BA21 27 E7
Greenhill Terr
4 Fortuneswell DT5 186 F8
Winchester SO22 126 C6
Greenings Ct 7 DT1 108 B2
Green Jacket Cl SO22 126 C3
Green La
Ashmore SP5 39 C8
Barton on Sea BH25 127 B8
Bournemouth BH10 89 D3
Bradpole DT6 101 A7
Bridport DT6 100 E5
Chickerell DT3 166 E5
Crossways DT2 137 D6
East Chinnock BA22 192 E8
Ferndown BH22 61 A1
Hooke DT8 205 C2
Kington Magna SP8 9 C3
Ossemsley BH25 94 E8
Ringwood BH24 55 D3
Ringwood BH24 55 D7
Sixpenny Handley SP5 188 E4
Stour Provost SP7 22 D4
Sturminster Marshall DT11 56 B5
Tatworth & Forton TA20 202 A7
West Coker BA22 193 B8
Weymouth DT4 180 E8
Green Loaning BH23 124 F5
Green Mead BA21 26 E6
Green Park Cl SO23 126 F8
Green Pit Knapp DT6 65 B2
Green Pk BH1 122 D3
Green Rd
Bournemouth BH9 122 A8
Poole BH15 119 D1
Greens Cross Dr 4 DT8 204 C4
Greenside Ct BH25 127 B6
Greensleeves Ave BH18 87 B6
Greensome Dr BH22 61 F6
Green St TA17 191 D7
Green The
Burton BH23 92 D2
3 Hazelbury Bryan DT10 197 A4
Mappowder DT10 196 E1
Puddletown DT2 78 B1
Sherborne DT9 30 B6
Stratton DT2 106 D8
Greenway
10 Child Okeford DT11 198 C7
Lyme Regis DT7 96 A5
Greenway Cl DT3 167 C8
Greenway Cres BH16 118 A7
Greenway La DT11 198 B7
Greenway Rd DT3 152 C1
Greenways
Christchurch BH23 125 F8
Easton/Weston DT5 186 F3
Greenways Ave BH8 90 C3
Greenways Ct BH22 61 E3
Greenwood Ave
Ferndown BH22 61 E6
Poole BH14 147 C8
Greenwood Copse BH24 54 B4
Greenwood Rd
Bournemouth BH9 121 E8
Yeovil BA21 26 F7
Greenwoods 6 BH25 95 B1
Greenwood Way BH24 54 B4
Grenfell Rd BH9 89 F3
Grenville Cl BH24 47 E1
Grenville Ct
11 Bournemouth BH4 121 D4
15 Poole BH15 119 C2
Grenville Rd BH21 59 D4
Gresham Rd BH9 90 B1
Grexy Cross DT2 205 E7
Greyfriars 2 SO23 126 F6
Greyhound Yd DT2 207 A2
Grey Mare & Her Colts (Long Barrow) DT3 131 C3
Greys Rd 7 TA16 191 F7
Greystoke Ave BH11 88 F5
Greystones Cl DT2 137 D6
Gribb View TA20 202 E6
Griffin Ct BH21 59 D3
Griffiths Gdns BH10 89 B5
Grim's Ditch SP5 189 D7
Grimsey La SP8 4 F8
Grosvenor Cl BH24 53 F5
Grosvenor Cres DT1 135 A8
Grosvenor Ct
8 Bournemouth BH1 122 B3
2 Bournemouth BH1 122 D4
Christchurch BH23 126 B8
Grosvenor Dr SO23 126 F8
Grosvenor Gdns BH1 122 E4
Grosvenor Ho 6 BH4 121 C3
Grosvenor Lo 8 BH4 121 C3
Grosvenor Pines 13 BH4 121 C3
Grosvenor Rd
Bournemouth BH4 121 C3
Dorchester DT1 135 A8
Easton/Weston DT5 186 F4
Radipole DT4 167 D6
Shaftesbury SP7 12 F4
Stalbridge DT10 33 C8
Grosvenor Rd *continued*
Swanage BH19 179 C1
Grove Ave
Radipole DT4 167 D6
Yeovil BA20 27 B5
Grove Gdns BH25 127 A7
Grove Inf Sch DT5 187 C6
Grove La
Abbotsbury DT3 149 B6
Bothenhampton DT6 101 B6
Portesham DT3 150 E5
Stalbridge DT10 33 C8
Grove La Cl DT10 33 C8
Groveley Bsns Ctr BH23 124 E6
Groveley Rd
Bournemouth BH4 121 B2
Christchurch BH23 124 E6
Grovely Ave BH5 122 F3
Grove Mans 10 BH1 122 B3
Grove Orch 3 DT6 128 B8
Grove Rd
Barton on Sea BH25 127 A7
Bournemouth BH1 122 B3
Burton Bradstock DT6 128 B8
Easton/Weston DT5 187 B5
Poole BH12 120 B6
Wimborne Minster BH21 59 D4
Grove Road E BH23 124 A8
Grove Road W BH23 123 F8
Grove The
Bournemouth BH9 89 F3
Bournemouth BH9 90 A4
Christchurch BH23 91 E1
Dorchester DT1 107 F2
Ferndown BH22 61 C4
Verwood BH31 45 C5
Grove Trading Est The DT1 107 F3
Grower Gdns BH11 89 A4
Grugs La BH21 40 A7
Gryphon L Ctr DT9 30 C8
Gryphon Sch The DT9 30 B8
Guard Ave BA22 26 D6
Guernsey Rd BH12 88 D1
Guernsey St 2 DT5 186 F7
Guest Ave BH12 121 A6
Guest Cl BH12 121 A6
Guest Rd BH16 118 B7
Guildford Ct 2 BH4 121 C4
Guildhall Ct BH15 119 B2
Guildhall Mus BH15 119 B2
Guildhill Rd BH6 123 E4
Guinevere Cl BA21 26 F7
Gulliver Cl BH14 147 C8
Gulliver Ct 1 BH21 59 C5
Gullivers Orch 1 DT6 101 D4
Gulway Mead 7 TA20 202 A8
Gundry La DT6 100 C6
Gundry Moor Trading Est BH21 53 B6
Gundry Rd DT6 100 F7
Gunners La BA22 26 C5
Gunn La 3 DT11 198 B5
Gunville Cres BH9 90 B3
Gunville Down Rd DT11 199 F4
Gunville La
East Coker BA22 193 D8
Hermitage DT2 195 C2
Gunville Rd DT11 199 F4
Gurjun Cl BH16 118 A8
Gurkha Mus The SO23 126 D5
Gurney Rd BH21 86 E6
Gussage Rd BH12 120 F8
Gwenlyn Rd
Upton BH16 117 E6
Upton BH16 118 C6
Gwynne Rd BH12 120 E5
Gyllas Way SP8 5 F4
Gypshayes BH19 178 B2
Gypsy La
Easton/Weston DT5 186 F3
Ringwood BH24 55 D8
2 Weymouth DT4 167 C2

H

Haarlem Mews BH23 124 D7
Hackney DT2 205 A7
Hadden Rd BH8 122 D8
Haddon La DT10 19 E2
Haddons Dr BH21 52 F6
Hadley Way BH18 86 E3
Hadow Rd BH10 89 C3
Hadrian Cl BH22 61 D2
Hadrian Way BH21 86 E8
Hahnemann Rd BH2 121 E2
Haig Ave BH13 120 E1
Haimes La SP7 12 E3
Hainault Dr BH31 45 C6
Haines La DT8 203 A5
Hains La DT10 20 E5
Haking Rd BH23 124 D7
Halcyon Ct BH15 119 C6
Hale Ave BH25 95 B2
Hale Gdns BH25 95 B2
Hales Mdw BA21 14 A3
Halewood Way BH23 123 F8
Half Acres DT9 30 A5
Half Hide Down SP5 188 B3
Half Moon St DT9 30 B5
Halfpenny La SP5 39 C7
Halifax Way BH23 125 B7
Hallet Ct DT7 96 B6
Hallet Gdns BA20 27 C4
Hall Rd BH11 88 F3
Halls Cnr BH16 84 C1
Halls Rd BH16 84 B1

Hall & Woodhouse Brewery
Visitor Ctr DT11........212 D2
Halsey Gn DT2.......... 196 B3
Halstock Cl 1 DT3......153 C2
Halstock Cres BH17......87 D2
Halter Path BH15.......118 E3
Halter Rise BH21.........60 C6
Halton Cl BH23..........93 B8
Halves Cotts BH20......177 A7
Halves La BA22.........193 B8
Hambledon Cl
Blandford Forum DT11...212 E4
Todber DT10............21 D4
Hambledon Gdns
Blandford Forum DT11...212 E4
Bournemouth BH6........123 C6
Hambledon Hill National
Nature Reserve DT11...198 D7
Hambledon Rd
Bournemouth BH7.......123 B7
Bournemouth,West Southbourne
BH6................123 C6
Hambledon View DT10...35 C2
Hamble Rd BH15........120 A6
Hamblin Way BH8........90 E2
Hambro Rd DT5.........186 F7
Hamcroft DT5..........186 F4
Hamilton Bsns Pk BH25..94 E2
Hamilton Cl
Bournemouth BH1.......122 D5
Christchurch BH23......124 F4
Hamworthy BH15.......118 E2
Radipole DT3...........152 E2
Hamilton Cres BH15.....118 E2
Hamilton Ct
1 Bournemouth BH8....122 B5
1 Wimborne Minster BH21 59 B5
Hamilton Mews BH23....93 B8
Hamilton Rd
Bournemouth BH1.......122 D4
Corfe Mullen BH21.......86 E5
Hamworthy BH15.......118 E2
Hamilton Way BH25......94 E2
Ham La
1 Gillingham SP8.........6 B1
Hampreston BH21........60 E3
Marnhull DT10...........20 D4
Trent DT9...............15 A2
Wimborne Minster BH21...60 C5
Hamlands DT2..........105 E1
Ham Mdw DT10..........20 D4
Hammett Cl DT2.........79 D1
Hammond Ave DT4.....167 A6
Hammonds Mead DT6....97 A7
Hammond St DT10......196 E1
Hampden La BH6.......123 B5
Hampreston CE Fst Sch
BH21..................60 E3
Hampshire Cl BH23......91 F2
Hampshire Ct 3 BH2...121 F3
Hampshire Hatches La
BH24...................55 B4
Hampshire Ho 2 BH2...121 F3
Hampshire Rd DT4......166 F4
Hampton DT3...........132 A1
Hampton Cl 8 BA22....193 F8
Hampton Ct 5 BH2.....121 D4
Hampton Dr BH24.......47 D1
Hampton La SO22.......126 A7
Hamworthy Fst Sch
BH15..................118 F1
Hamworthy LODGE BH15 118 F2
Hamworthy Mid Sch
BH15..................118 F1
Hamworthy Sta BH16...118 D4
Hanbury Rd 7 BH19....179 A2
Handley Ct BH24.........55 B7
Handley Lodge 2 BH12.120 F7
Hands La DT3...........149 B7
Handy Villas 22 SO23....126 E6
Hanford Sch DT11......198 D6
Hanham Ct BH12........121 B8
Hanham Rd
Corfe Mullen BH21.......86 D5
Wimborne Minster BH21...59 C5
Hankinson Rd BH9......122 A8
Hanlon Cl BH11..........89 B4
Hannam's Cl BH16.......84 D3
Hannington Pl BH7.....123 A5
Hannington Rd BH7....123 A5
Hanover Cl DT10.........35 A2
Hanover Ct DT11.......212 C4
Hanover Gn BH17.......119 F7
Hanover Ho BH15......119 D3
Hanover La SP8...........5 D1
Hanover Lodge SO23....126 D4
Hanover Rd DT4........167 D5
Happy Island Way DT6..100 F7
Harbeck Rd BH8..........90 C3
Harbour BA21............26 E5
Harbour Cl BH13........147 D6
Harbour Cres BH23.....124 E5
Harbour Ct
Barton on Sea BH25.....126 E7
Christchurch BH23......124 E6
Poole BH13............147 E6
Harbour Hill DT3........166 F8
Harbour Hill Cres BH15..119 E5
Harbour Hill Rd BH15...119 E5
Harbour Hospl The
BH15..................119 D3
Harbour Lights BH15....119 E4
Harbour Prospect BH14.147 C8
Harbour Rd
Bournemouth BH6.......124 A3
Sherborne DT9...........30 C7
Harbour View Cl BH14...120 A5
Harbour View Ct BH23..124 B5
Harbour View Rd
Fortuneswell DT5.......186 F8
Poole BH14............120 A5
Harbour Watch BH14....147 C7
Harbour Way DT9........30 B7
Harbridge Dro BH24......42 E3
Harbridge Sch BH24.....46 F8
Harcombe Cl BH17.......87 E3
Harcombe Rd DT7........64 A3
Harcourt Mews 6 BH5..123 A5
Harcourt Rd BH5.......123 A5
Harding's La SP8..........6 A1
Hardwick St 2 DT4.....167 E4
Hardy Ave DT4.........167 B2
Hardy Cl
2 Beaminster DT8......204 D4
Ferndown BH22..........53 B1
Marnhull DT10...........21 A3
Martinstown DT2........133 D6
New Milton BH25........94 F3
Hardy Cres
Stalbridge DT10..........33 D8
Wimborne Minster BH21...59 D4
Hardy Ct 23 TA18.......191 F3
Hardy Mon DT2.........132 C4
Hardy Rd
Bridport DT6...........100 E7
Ferndown BH22..........53 B1
Poole BH14............120 D4
Wareham BH20.........142 D2
Hardy's Birthplace DT2..109 B5
Hardy's La DT8.........203 D6
Hare La
Cranborne BH21.........40 F5
New Milton BH25,SO41....95 E3
Hares Gn BH7..........123 A8
Harewood Ave
Bournemouth BH7.......122 F7
Bournemouth BH7.......123 A6
Harewood Cres BH7....122 F8
Harewood Gdns BH7....122 F7
Harewood Pl BH7.......123 B6
Harewood Rd DT1......107 C1
Harford Rd BH12........120 C8
Hargrove La DT10........33 F4
Harkwood Dr BH15.....118 E4
Harland Rd BH6........124 A3
Harleston Villas 5 BH21..59 D4
Harley Gap BH21.......201 B8
Harley La BH21.........201 A5
Harman's Cross Sta
BH19..................177 E5
Harness Cl BH21.........60 B6
Harper Rd 21 TA18......191 F4
Harpitts La SP8............9 E4
Harpway La BH23........92 C6
Harraby Gn BH18........87 A3
Harrier Dr BH21.........59 D2
Harriers Cl BH23.......125 D8
Harrington Ct BH23.....125 F7
Harrison Ave BH1.......122 D6
Harrison Cl BH23........92 C3
Harrison Way BH22......53 A3
Harris Way BH25.........95 B6
Harrow Cl BH23..........93 B7
Harrow Down SO22.....126 B2
Harrow Rd BH23.........93 B6
Harry Barrow Cl 1 BH24.55 C6
Harry Lodge's La SP8.....5 A1
Hart Cl BH25............94 F4
Hartfoot Cl DT2........209 B5
Hartfoot La DT2........209 B5
Harting Rd BH6........123 D7
Hartland Moor National
Nature Reserve BH20...161 E7
Hartlebury Terr 2 DT4..167 D2
Hartley St DT2.........195 B1
Hartmoor Hill SP8.........9 D5
Hartnell Ct BH21.........86 D5
Hartsbourne Dr BH7....123 B8
Hart's La
Holt BH21...............51 C3
Nether Compton DT9......29 B6
Harvest Cl SO22.......126 B2
Harvey Rd
Bournemouth BH5.......123 A5
Oakley BH21............87 E8
Harveys Cl DT2..........73 A8
Harwell Rd BH17.......119 D7
Harwood Ct BH25........94 F3
Haselbury Plucknett VC Fst
Sch TA18..............192 C5
Haskells Rd BH12......120 B7
Haslemere Ave BH23....126 A8
Haslemere Pl BH23.....126 A8
Hasler Rd BH17..........87 D2
Haslop Rd BH21..........60 A7
Hastings Rd
Bournemouth BH8........90 F2
Poole BH17..............87 B2
Hatch Pond Rd BH17....119 C8
Hatfield Ct BH25.........94 E3
Hatfield Gdns BH7......123 B8
Hathaway Rd BH6......123 D4
Hatherden Ave BH14....119 F5
Hatherley Rd SO22.....126 D7
Hathermead Gdns BA21..27 F7
Havelins DT11..........198 E4
Havelock Rd BH12......121 A5
Havelock Way BH23.....93 D2
Haven Cotts BH23.......125 A4
Haven Ct BH13.........147 B3
Haven Gdns BH25........95 B2
Havenhurst BH13.......147 E6
Haven Rd
Corfe Mullen BH21.......86 C6
Poole BH13............147 E7
Haverstock Rd BH9......90 B2
Haviland Mews BH7.....122 F5
Haviland Rd
Bournemouth BH7.......122 F5
Ferndown BH21..........61 A7
Haviland Rd E BH7......122 F5
Haviland Rd W BH1.....122 F5
Hawden Rd BH11.........89 A1
Hawkchurch Gdns BH17..87 E2
Hawkchurch Prim Sch
EX13..................202 B3
Hawkchurch Rd EX13...202 B3
Hawk Cl BH21............60 A7
Hawkcombe La SP7......23 E1
Hawker Cl BH21..........59 F1
Hawker's La SP7.........22 B8
Hawkesdene SP7.........12 F1
Hawkesdene La SP7......12 F2
Hawkesworth Cl DT3....153 B1
Hawkins Cl 2 BH24......47 E1
Hawkins Rd BH12........88 F1
Hawkins Way BA21.......26 E6
Hawkmoor Hill EX13....202 E2
Hawkwood Rd BH1,BH5..122 F4
Haworth Cl BH23.........92 A1
Hawthorn Ave SP8.........5 E2
Hawthorn Cl
5 Dorchester DT1......107 E2
New Milton BH25.........95 C4
Radipole DT4...........167 A6
1 Shaftesbury SP7.......13 A4
Hawthorn Dr BH17.......86 F1
Hawthorne Cl 15 TA18...191 F5
Hawthorne Rd DT1......107 E2
Hawthorn Rd
Bournemouth BH9.......121 F8
Burton BH23.............92 E4
Charminster DT2.........75 D2
Yeovil BA21.............27 F7
Hawthorns The
Christchurch BH23......124 F6
Stalbridge DT10..........33 E7
Haxen La TA17..........191 A8
Haycock Way 2 BH21....56 D4
Haycombe 4 DT11......198 E3
Haycrafts La BH19......177 E3
Haydon Hill Nature Reserve
DT2.....................75 B1
Haydon Hollow DT9......31 C5
Haydon La
Frome St Quintin DT2....206 D7
Lydlinch DT10..........197 A6
Haydon Rd BH13.......121 B1
Haye Cl DT7.............96 A6
Haye La DT7.............96 A6
Hayes Ave BH7.........122 E6
Hayes Cl BH21...........60 A4
Hayes La BH21...........60 B5
Hayes The 3 DT8.......203 E5
Hayeswood Fst Sch BH21. 60 B6
Hayeswood Rd BH21.....60 A6
Haylands DT5...........186 F3
Haymoor Ave DT3.......167 F8
Haymoor Mid Sch BH17..87 E1
Haymoor Rd BH15......120 A7
Haynes Ave BH15......119 D4
Haysoms Cl BH25........95 B1
Hayters Way SP6.........42 C6
Hayward Cres BH31......45 A5
Hayward La DT11.......198 B7
Haywards Ave DT3......167 D7
Haywards Farm Cl BH31..45 A5
Haywards La
Child Okeford DT11....198 C7
Corfe Mullen BH21.......86 C7
Hayward Way BH31.......44 F5
Hazelbury Bryan Com Prim
Sch DT10..............197 A3
Hazel Cl
Alderholt SP6............42 C5
Christchurch BH23.......93 C1
Hazel Ct
Bournemouth BH9........90 C4
1 New Milton BH25.......95 B1
Winchester SO22.......126 A8
Hazeldown Ave DT3.....167 F8
Hazel Dr
Ferndown BH22..........61 D8
2 Overcombe/Preston
DT3...................153 B2
Hazel Gr SO22.........126 B3
Hazel La DT2...........129 E7
Hazell Ave BH10.........89 B2
Hazelton Cl BH7........123 A8
Hazel View 11 TA18.....191 F5
Hazelwood Ave BH25.....94 F4
Hazelwood Dr BH31......45 D4
Hazlebury Rd BH17.....119 A7
Hazlemere Dr BH24.......54 A3
Hazzard's Hill BA12.......3 B5
Headinglea 9 BH13.....121 B3
Head La SP8.............10 D3
Headland Cl 3 DT5......186 E1
Headlands Bsns Pk BH24. 47 C2
Headless Cross BH10.....89 D5
Heads Farm Cl BH10.....89 E5
Head's La BH10..........89 E5
Headstock Rd TA20.....202 B7
Headswell Ave BH10.....89 E4
Headswell Cres BH10....89 E4
Headswell Gdns BH10....89 E4
Heanor Cl BH10..........89 C2
Heath Ave BH15........119 D6
Heath Cl
Bovington Camp BH20...139 C7
Wimborne Minster BH21...60 B7
Heathcote Cl DT1.......108 B1
Heathcote Ct 2 BH7....122 F4
Heathcote Rd BH5,BH7..122 F4
Heatherbank Rd BH4....121 C3
Heatherbrae La BH16...118 B6
Heather Cl
Bournemouth BH8........90 D4
Corfe Mullen BH21.......86 E6
St Leonards BH24........54 A3
Walkford BH23...........94 A2
Heatherdell
Upton BH16............117 D6
Upton BH16............118 B6
Heatherdown Rd 1 BH22 53 C1
Heatherdown Way 2
BH22....................53 C1
Heather Dr BH22.........61 D7
Heather Fields 2 SP8.....5 F4
Heatherlands Fst Sch
BH12..................120 E5
Heatherlands Rise BH12 120 D5
Heatherlea Rd BH6.....123 D4
Heather Lo 1 BH25......95 A3
Heather Rd
Bournemouth BH10.......89 D3
Yeovil BA21.............27 E7
Heather View Rd BH12..120 F7
Heather Way
Ferndown BH22..........61 D7
Yeovil BA22.............26 C5
Heath Farm Cl BH22.....61 C3
Heath Farm Rd BH22.....61 C3
Heath Farm Way BH22...61 C3
Heathfield Ave BH12....121 A8
Heathfield Rd BH22......53 C1
Heathfields Way SP7.....12 F4
Heathfield Way BH22.....53 B1
Heath Green Rd BH19...164 B1
Heathland Cl DT2.......137 D5
Heathlands Ave BH22....61 D2
Heathlands Cl
Burton BH23.............92 C3
Verwood BH31...........45 C6
Heathlands Prim Sch
BH11....................89 A3
Heath Rd
Hordle SO41.............95 F3
St Leonards BH24........53 F4
Walkford BH23...........94 B1
Heathwood Ave BH25....126 E8
Heathwood Rd
Bournemouth BH9.......121 E8
Weymouth DT4..........167 B4
Heathy Cl BH25.........126 F8
Heaton Rd BH10.........89 B2
Heavytree Rd BH14.....120 B4
Heber's La TA17........191 A5
Heckford La BH15......119 D3
Heckford Rd
Corfe Mullen BH21.......86 C5
Poole BH15............119 D4
Hectors Way DT11......212 C1
Heddington Dr DT11....212 C5
Hedgerley BH25........127 B8
Heights App BH16......118 C7
Heights Rd BH16.......118 C8
Helena Rd BA20..........26 F1
Helen La 2 DT4........167 E2
Helic Ho 2 BH21.........59 C5
Hell Cnr DT2...........194 D1
Hell La DT6.............99 A8
Hell Stone (Long Barrow)
DT3...................132 A2
Helston Cl DT3.........132 A1
Helyar Rd BH8...........90 F2
Hembury Rd DT2.......102 C7
Hemlet's Cl DT6.........68 F1
Hemsbach Ct 1 BH20...142 E3
Henbest Cl BH21.........60 C5
Henbury Cl
Corfe Mullen BH21.......86 D6
Poole BH17..............88 A2
Henbury Rise BH21......86 D6
Henbury View Fst Sch
Corfe Mullen BH21.......86 C6
Poole BH21..............85 E6
Henbury View Rd BH21...86 D6
Henchard Cl BH22.......61 C2
Hendford 6 BA20........27 D4
Hendford Gdns BH10.....89 D2
Hendford Gr BA20........27 C4
Hendford Hill BA20......27 B3
Hendford Rd BH10.......89 D2
Hendrie Cl BH19........178 F2
Hengistbury Head Nature
Reserve BH6...........124 E2
Hengistbury Head Nature
Trail BH6.............124 C3
Hengistbury Rd
Barton on Sea BH25.....126 E8
Bournemouth BH6.......124 A3
Hengist Cvn Pk BH6....124 B4
Hengist Rd BH1........122 D4
Henhayes La 3 TA18....191 F4
Henley Gdns BH7.......123 A7
Henley View 7 TA18....191 F3
Henning's Park Rd BH15. 119 E5
Henning Way DT9........17 D3
Henry Cl DT4...........180 E7
Henry's Way DT7.........96 C6
Henstridge Trad Est BA8..20 A5
Henville Rd 6 BH8......122 C5
Herbert Ave BH12.......120 D7
Herbert Ct BH12........120 D7
Herbert Hospl BH4......121 B2
Herberton Rd BH6......123 C5
Herbert Rd
New Milton BH25.........95 B3
Poole BH4..............121 B2
Herblay Cl BA21.........28 A6
Herbury La DT9.........194 D4
Hercules Rd BH15......118 D3
Hereford Cres DT4.....167 A3
Hereford Rd DT4.......167 A3
Heritage Ct BH13.......147 F7
Hermitage Ct 8 DT1....107 C1
Hermitage La DT2......195 B1
Hermitage Rd BH14.....120 A5
Hermitage St TA18......191 F4
Hermitage The BH14....120 A5
Herm Rd BH12...........88 D1
Heron Cl
3 Chickerell DT3......166 D5
Overcombe/Preston DT3..168 A6
Heron Court Rd BH3,BH9 122 A7
Heron Dr BH21...........60 A8
Herringston Rd DT1.....135 A7
Herrison Rd DT2.........75 E2
Herstone Cl BH17........87 F1
Herston Halt Sta BH19..178 E3
Hertford Ct 6 BH23.....126 B7
Hertford Rd BA21.........28 A8
Hesketh Cl BH24.........54 C5
Hessary St 9 DT1.......107 C1
Hestan Cl BH23..........91 D4
Heston Way BH22........52 F3
Hetherly Rd DT3........167 C7
Hewish La TA18........191 D3
Hewitt Rd BH15........118 E4
Hewlett's Dro DT10.....197 C7
Heysham Rd BH18........87 A3
Heytesbury Rd BH6.....123 D5
Hibbard Ct BH10.........89 D1
Hibberds Field BH21.....40 B7
Hibberd Way BH10.......89 D1
Hibbs Cl
Northport BH20........142 E5
Upton BH16............118 C7
Hickes Cl BH11..........88 F4
Hickory Cl
1 Upton BH16..........117 C8
Upton BH16............118 A8
Highacres DT6...........69 D1
Highbridge Rd BH14....120 C3
High Brow BH22.........61 D5
Highbury Cl BH25........95 B2
High Cl BH21............56 D4
Highcliffe Castle BH23..125 E7
Highcliffe Cnr BH23.....126 B8
Highcliffe Rd
Christchurch BH23......125 C7
1 Swanage BH19.......179 C4
Winchester SO23.......126 F4
Highcliffe St Marks's Prim
Sch BH23................93 F1
Highcliffe Sch BH23......93 D1
Highcliff Rd DT7.........96 A5
Highdown DT3..........167 F8
Highdown Ave DT1......107 D1
Higher Barn Cl SP7......24 C6
Higher Beadon TA16....191 E7
Higher Blandford Rd
Corfe Mullen BH18,BH21...86 F6
Shaftesbury SP7.........13 A1
Higher Bullen BA22.....193 F8
Higher Cheap St DT9.....30 B6
Higher Coombses TA20..202 A8
Higher Day's Rd BH19...178 E2
Higher Dro DT2.........205 F2
Higher Easthams La
TA18..................192 A5
Higher End DT3.........166 C5
Higher Eype Rd DT6......99 F5
Higher Filbank BH20....177 A7
Higher Gdns BH20......177 A8
Higher Gunville 5 DT9...17 D2
Higher Kingsbury DT9....17 D3
Higher Kingsbury Cl DT9.17 C3
Higher Kingston BA21....27 D5
Higher Merley La BH21...86 E8
Higher Ream BA21........26 E6
Higher St La DT8.......205 C3
Higher Sea La DT6.......97 A8
Higher Shaftesbury Rd
DT11..................212 D8
Higher St
Bridport DT6............69 A1
Iwerne Minster DT11.....37 F2
Lillington DT9..........194 F7
Merriott TA16..........191 F8
Morden BH20.............83 D4
Okeford Fitzpaine DT11..197 F5
West Chinnock TA18.....192 B8
Higher Westbury DT9....28 D1
High E St DT1..........108 A2
Highfield Ave BH24......55 C8
Highfield Cl
Charminster DT2.......107 D7
Corfe Mullen BH21.......86 E5
Highfield Dr BH24.......47 C1
Highfield Gdns 1 DT6..204 C2
Highfield Ho 3 BH14...120 B4
Highfield Rd
Bournemouth BH9........89 E2
Corfe Mullen BH21.......86 E5
Ferndown BH22..........53 A4
Ringwood BH24..........55 C8
Yeovil BA21.............27 E6
Highfields
Blandford Forum DT11...212 E4
West Chinnock TA18.....192 B8
Highfield Terr 1 SO22..126 D5
Highgate La DT2.......136 D6
Highgrove SP8.............5 F4
Highgrove Cl 5 DT1....135 B8
High Howe Cl BH11......88 E4

High Howe Gdns BH11 88 E4
High Howe La BH11 88 E4
Highland Ave BH23 94 B1
Highland Rd
Poole BH14 120 B5
Weymouth DT4 167 C3
Wimborne Minster BH21 59 D6
Highlands Cres BH10 89 C4
Highlands Rd BH25 127 A8
Highland View Cl BH21 59 D5
High Lea BA21 27 D8
High Marryats BH25 127 A7
High Mead BH22 61 A2
High Mead La BH22 61 A1
Highmoor Cl
Corfe Mullen BH21 86 D5
Poole BH14 120 B3
Highmoor Rd
Bournemouth BH11 89 A1
Corfe Mullen BH21 86 D5
Poole BH14 120 B3
Poole BH21 85 F5
High Oaks Gdns BH11 88 E4
High Park Rd BH18 86 E4
High Pines BH23 125 D7
High Ridge Cres BH25 95 C2
High St Cl BH20 140 A2
High St Fordington DT1 108 B2
High St N BH15 119 D3
High St
Ashmore SP5 39 C8
[1] Broadwindsor DT8 203 E5
Burton Bradstock DT6 128 B7
Child Okeford DT11 198 C7
Christchurch BH23 124 B6
Corscombe DT2 205 A8
Cranborne BH21 40 A7
Damerham SP6 190 F3
East Chinnock BA22 192 E8
[3] Easton/Weston DT5 186 F1
Fortuneswell DT5 186 E7
Gillingham SP8 5 F2
Hardington Mandeville BA22 193 A6
Henstridge BA8 19 A4
Hinton St George TA17 191 C7
Lytchett Matravers BH16 84 C3
Milborne Port DT9 17 D2
Piddlehinton DT2 76 E8
Poole BH15 119 C2
Puddletown DT2 78 B1
Rimpton BA22 15 B8
Ringwood BH24 55 B7
Shaftesbury SP7 12 E2
Shapwick DT11 48 C1
Sixpenny Handley SP5 189 A4
Spetisbury DT11 211 E5
Stalbridge DT10 33 C8
St Leonards BH24 54 A6
Stourton with Gasper BA12 1 E8
Sturminster Marshall BH21 56 D4
Swanage BH19 178 B2
Sydling St Nicholas DT2 207 A2
Tarrant Monkton DT11 200 B3
Thorncombe TA20 202 E5
Toller Porcorum DT2 71 D8
Weymouth DT4 180 C7
Wimborne Minster BH21 59 B4
Winchester SO23 126 D6
Winchester SO23 126 E5
Winchester SO23 126 F5
Winfrith Newburgh DT2 156 F5
Wool BH20 140 B2
Yeovil BA20 27 D4
Yetminster DT9 194 C5
Zeale SP8 1 F3
Hightown Gdns BH24 55 D6
Hightown Ind Est BH24 55 D6
Hightown Rd BH24 55 C6
High Trees
Broadmayne DT2 136 C1
Poole BH13 147 G8
Hightrees Ave BH8 90 F1
High Trees Dr SO22 126 C8
High Trees Wlk BH22 61 D7
Highview Cl BH23 91 E3
Highview Gdns BH12 120 C7
High Way BH18 86 F3
Highwood Cl SP6 41 F6
Highwood La BH24 47 E4
Highwood Rd BH14 120 E4
High W St
Dorchester DT1 108 A2
Weymouth DT4 167 D2
Hilary Rd BH17 87 C1
Hilcot Way DT11 212 D5
Hilda Rd BH12 120 E7
Hiley Rd BH15 119 C6
Hilfield La DT2 194 F1
Hillard Ct [7] BH20 142 E3
Hillary Rd BH23 124 E8
Hillborne Gdns [1] BA21 26 E5
Hillbourne Com Fst & Mid Schs BH17 87 B2
Hillbourne Rd
Poole BH17 87 A2
[1] Weymouth DT4 180 D7
Hill Brow DT9 29 F4
Hillbrow Rd BH6 123 B6
Hillbury Rd SP6 42 D6
Hill Cl
Bransgore BH23 93 A8
[5] Bridport DT6 100 B2
Hillcrest Ave BH22 61 C8
Hillcrest Cl
Bournemouth BH9 90 A3
Sturminster Newton DT10 197 C8
Hillcrest Hospl BH10 89 D1
Hillcrest Rd
Bournemouth BH9 90 A3
Corfe Mullen BH21 86 C5
Poole BH12 120 A5
Weymouth DT4 180 E7
Hill Crest Rd BA21 27 E6
Hillfield Cl DT3 152 B4
Hillfort Cl DT1 134 E7
Hillfort Mews [6] DT1 134 E7
Hillgrove Ave BA20 27 B2
Hill House Cl DT9 30 C7
Hillier Way SO23 126 E8
Hillingdon DT6 100 E8
Hillingdon Ct BA21 26 E6
Hilling La DT2 208 A7
Hill La
Bransgore BH23 93 A8
Burton BH23 92 F2
Hillman Rd BH14 120 D5
Hillmeadow BH31 45 C4
Hill Rd
Blandford Forum DT11 212 E6
Lyme Regis DT7 96 B5
Swanage BH19 179 B5
Hill Rise DT6 100 B2
Hill Rise Rd DT7 96 B5
Hillsea Rd BH19 179 A2
Hillside Cl
Mere BA12 2 E5
Winchester SO22 126 A8
Hillside Dr BH23 91 D3
Hillside Fst Sch BH31 45 B7
Hillside Gdns BH21 86 C4
Hillside Mews
Corfe Mullen BH21 86 C4
[2] Poole BH21 85 E4
Hillside Rd
[1] Blandford Camp DT11 199 E3
Corfe Mullen BH21 86 C5
Poole BH12 88 F1
Verwood BH31 45 C7
Winchester SO22 126 A7
Woodlands BH21 44 C6
[3] Wool BH20 140 A1
Hillside Terr [4] BA20 27 E5
Hillside View [9] BA22 193 F8
Hill St BH15 119 C2
Hill Terr BH21 60 A2
Hilltop Cl BH22 61 B7
Hilltop Rd
Corfe Mullen BH21 86 E5
Ferndown BH22 61 B7
Hillview DT6 68 F1
Hill View
Bishop's Caundle DT9 196 A7
Charminster DT2 107 C6
[5] Hazelbury Bryan DT10 197 A4
Maiden Newton DT2 73 A7
Mudford BA21 14 A3
Overcombe/Preston DT3 169 A8
Yeovil BA20 27 E5
Hill View Cl TA18 192 B7
Hillview Est [1] DT6 100 C8
Hill View Prim Sch BH10 89 E3
Hillview Rd
Bournemouth BH10 89 D3
Swanage BH19 179 A2
Hill View Rd BH22 61 C7
Hill Way BH24 54 A5
Hilmar Dr SP8 5 E2
Hiltom Rd BH24 55 D7
Hilton Cl BH15 120 A6
Hilton Rd BH25 95 B4
Hilton Rd Cl DT11 79 E8
Hinchcliffe Cl BH15 118 F2
Hinchcliffe Rd BH15 118 F2
Hine Cl SP8 11 B8
Hine's Mead La DT2 103 C1
Hine Town La DT11 198 B6
Hingsdon La DT6 204 B2
Hintock St DT1 107 D1
Hinton Admiral Mews BH23 93 E2
Hinton Admiral Sta BH23 93 E2
Hinton Cl
Blandford Forum DT11 212 D5
Hinton St George TA17 191 C7
Hinton Cross BA22 14 B5
Hinton La DT10 35 C7
Hinton Rd
Bournemouth BH1 121 F3
West Crewkerne TA18 191 E5
Hinton St George Prim Sch TA17 191 C7
Hinton St Mary Roman Villa DT10 35 B4
Hinton View DT10 35 B2
Hinton Wood BH1 122 A2
Hinton Wood Ave BH23 93 E1
Hintonwood La BH23 93 E2
Hitchen [3] TA16 191 F7
Hive Cl DT6 128 C7
Hive Gdns BH13 147 D6
Hobart Rd BH25 94 F2
Hobbs Pk BH24 54 B4
Hobbs Rd BH12 120 C8
Hobgoblin DT11 37 F1
Hoburne Ct BH23 93 C1
Hoburne Cvn Pk BH23 125 C8
Hoburne Gdns BH23 93 C1
Hoburne La BH23 125 C8
Hoburne Rd BH19 179 A2
Hodder's La DT7 64 A2
Hod Dr DT11 198 E5
Hodges Cl BH17 119 E7
Hod Hill (Hill Fort & Roman Fort) DT11 198 E5
Hod View [2] DT11 198 F4
Hodway La DT11 198 D5
Hogarth Way BH8 91 A2
Hog Cliff National Nature Reserve DT2 73 D7
Hogshill St DT8 204 C4
Hogue Ave BH10 89 D5
Holbaek Cl DT1 135 B7
Holburne Naish BH25 126 D8
Holbury Cl BH8 90 E3
Holcombe Cl DT3 168 D8
Holcombe Mead DT2 208 A6
Holcombe Rd BH16 118 B6
Holdenhurst Ave BH7 123 C7
Holdenhurst Rd
Bournemouth BH8 122 C5
Bournemouth, Holdenhurst BH8 91 B3
Holditch Ct La TA20 202 A5
Holditch La TA20 202 A5
Holdscroft La DT6 202 E1
Holebrook La DT10 196 F7
Hole House La DT10 197 D8
Holes Bay North Rdbt BH17 119 A6
Holes Bay Pk BH15 119 B4
Holes Bay Rd BH15 119 B4
Holes Bay Rdbt BH15 119 B5
Holes Cl SO41 95 F4
Holland Rd DT4 167 C3
Hollands Cl BH20 176 F8
Hollands Mead Ave DT2 155 D7
Hollands Wood Dr BH25 95 B5
Holland Way
Blandford Forum DT11 212 D5
Corfe Mullen BH18 86 F5
Holland Way Ind Pk DT11 212 E6
Hollenden [9] BH13 121 A4
Holleys Cl [14] TA20 202 A8
Hollies The
[3] Crewkerne TA18 191 E3
Yeovil BA21 27 E7
Hollis Way BA22 193 D3
Holloway Ave BH11 88 F5
Holloway La DT11 198 C5
Holloway Rd DT1 108 B2
Hollow Hill DT2 108 F4
Hollow La TA17 191 B7
Hollow Oak BH20 113 B8
Hollow Oak Rd BH20 142 E1
Hollow The
Affpuddle DT2 112 B6
Child Okeford DT11 198 C8
[4] Sixpenny Handley SP5 189 A4
Hollow Way DT6 100 D4
Holly Cl
[3] Dorchester DT1 107 E2
Ferndown BH22 52 F2
[2] Sandford BH20 116 A1
[1] St Leonards BH24 53 F4
Upton BH16 118 A7
Holly Ct BH15 119 D4
Holly Gdns BH23 92 D1
Holly Gr
Merriott TA18 191 F5
Verwood BH31 45 A5
Holly Green Rise BH11 88 E4
Holly Hedge La BH17 119 C8
Holly La
Broadwindsor DT8 203 D8
New Milton BH25 95 C4
Walkford BH23 94 C2
Holly Lo [13] BH13 121 A4
Holly Mdws SO22 126 A8
Hollymoor Cl [8] DT8 204 D4
Hollymoor Common La DT8 204 D4
Hollymoor Gdns [7] DT8 204 D4
Hollymoor La DT8 204 D4
Holly Rd DT4 167 C3
Holm Cl BH24 47 E1
Holmead Wlk DT1 107 D1
Holme Cl DT3 167 B8
Holme La
East Holme BH20 160 B7
East Stoke BH20 141 A1
Holme Rd BH23 126 B8
Holmes Rd BH19 178 E2
Holmfield Ave BH7 123 C7
Holm Hill La BH23,BH25 94 B7
Holmhurst Ave BH23 93 F1
Holmlea [1] DT11 212 E5
Holm Oak Cl BH31 45 A8
Holmwood Garth [1] BH24 55 F6
Holnest Rd BH17 87 D1
Holten's La BA22 192 E6
Holt Heath National Nature Reserve BH21 51 E8
Holt Hill DT9 31 F1
Holt Ho BH8 122 D5
Holt La
Bishop's Caundle DT9 196 A8
Holt BH21 51 B4
Melbury Osmond DT2 194 A3
South Perrott DT8 192 D1
Stourton Caundle DT10 32 B2
Holton Heath Ind Est BH16 116 D2
Holton Heath Sta BH16 116 D1
Holton Rd BH16 116 D2
Holt Pl BH22 61 F7
Holt Rd
Holt BH21 51 D5
Holt Rd *continued*
Horton BH21 52 F8
Poole BH12 120 F6
Wool BH20 139 D6
Holway TA20 202 A8
Holway La DT2 206 A5
Holway Woods Nature Reserve DT9 16 A5
Holwell Dro DT9 195 F5
Holwell Rd DT10 196 C5
Holworth Cl BH11 88 E3
Holyrood Cl BH17 119 A8
Holy Trinity CE Inf Sch [1] DT4 167 C1
Holy Trinity CE Jun Sch [2] DT4 167 C1
Holy Trintiy CE VA Prim Sch BA20 27 A3
Holywell Cl BH17 87 D3
Homecliffe Ho BH23 126 B8
Homecorfe Ho BH18 87 B5
Homedale Ho BH2 121 F5
Homedene Ho BH15 119 D3
Home Dr BA21 27 A6
Home Farm BH25 127 E8
Home Farm Cl DT6 101 E8
Home Farm La BA22 15 A8
Home Farm Way
Shipton Gorge DT6 101 D3
Verwood BH31 45 A7
Homefield
[6] Child Okeford DT11 198 C7
Mere BA12 2 F5
Milborne St Andrew DT11 79 F7
Shaftesbury SP7 12 F4
Homefield Ho [7] BH25 95 A2
Homefield Ind Prep Sch BH6 123 F5
Homelake Ho BH14 120 B3
Homelands Est BH23 123 F6
Homelands Ho BH22 61 D5
Homeleigh Ho [5] BH8 122 A5
Homelife Ho BH8 122 B4
Homemill Ho [5] BH25 95 A3
Homeoaks Ho BH2 121 F5
Home Rd BH11 89 B6
Homerise Ho [1] SO23 126 E6
Homeside Rd BH9 90 A2
Homestour Ho [1] BH23 124 A6
Homeview Ho BH15 119 D3
Homewood Cl BH25 95 C3
Honeybourne Cres BH6 124 A4
Honeybrook Victorian Farm & Ctry Pk BH21 50 D2
Honey Bun Mdw DT10 196 F4
Honeycombe Rise DT9 29 F4
Honeyfields [3] SP8 5 F4
Honeymead La DT10 35 B2
Honeysuckle Cl
Radipole DT3 152 F2
Winchester SO22 126 C2
Honeysuckle Gdns [2] DT11 198 B5
Honeysuckle La BH17 86 F1
Honeysuckle Way BH23 125 B8
Honeywood Ho BH14 147 C7
Hood Cl BH10 89 B1
Hood Cres BH10 89 B1
Hooke Cl BH17 88 A2
Hooke Ct Sch DT8 205 B3
Hooper's La
Barwick BA22 193 F7
Puncknowle DT2 129 F6
Hop Cl
Upton BH16 117 B7
Upton BH16 118 A7
Hope Bottom DT6 204 C2
Hope Cl DT2 137 D5
Hope Cross SP8 9 A6
Hopegood Cl [4] DT11 211 D6
Hope Sq [9] DT4 167 E1
Hope Terr DT2 133 D6
Hopkins Cl BH8 91 A2
Hopmans Cl BH16 84 B4
Hopsfield DT11 79 E8
Horace Rd [7] BH5 122 E4
Hornbeam Cl DT4 167 B6
Hornbeam Rd DT2 75 D3
Hornbeam Sq BH15 119 D2
Hornbeam Way BH21 59 E5
Horncastles La DT9 29 F6
Horning Rd BH12 120 F5
Hornpark Quarry Ind Est DT8 204 A5
Horn Pk DT8 204 B5
Horsa Cl BH6 123 E4
Horsa Ct BH6 123 E4
Horsa Rd BH6 123 E4
Horsecastles DT9 30 A5
Horsecliffe La BH19 179 C3
Horsefields SP8 5 E4
Horsehill La DT8 204 A3
Horseponds SP7 12 D3
Horseshoe Cl BH21 60 B6
Horseshoe Common Rdbt BH1 121 F3
Horseshoe Ct [5] BH1 121 F4
Horseshoe Rd TA20 202 D7
Horseshoe The BH13 147 C4
Horsey Knap DT2 205 E7
Horsey La
East Chelborough DT2 205 E7
Yeovil BA20 27 C4
Horsford St DT4 167 E1
Horsham Ave BH10 89 C6
Horton Cl
Bournemouth BH9 90 C3
Yeovil BA21 26 F6
Horton Ho BH22 61 F7
Horton Rd
Horton BH21 44 D1
St Leonards BH24 54 C6
St Leonards & St Ives BH24 53 E6
Woodlands BH21 201 F3
Horton Twr (Folly) BH21 201 E1
Horton Way BH31 44 F5
Horyford Cl [3] DT3 153 C2
Hosey Rd DT10 35 C3
Hosker Rd BH5 123 B5
Hospital La
Allington DT6 100 B8
Sherborne DT9 30 B6
Hotton Heath National Nature Reserve BH16 116 F3
Houlton Rd BH15 119 E4
Hound St DT9 30 B6
Houndstone Cl BA21 26 E5
Houndstone Ct [2] BA22 26 C5
Hounds Way BH21 60 B5
Hounslow Cl BH15 118 F1
Howard Cl
Bothenhampton DT6 101 A7
Christchurch BH23 124 F6
Weymouth DT4 180 E7
Howard Rd
Bournemouth BH8 122 C8
Bridport DT6 100 F6
[5] Swanage BH19 179 A2
Verwood BH31 45 B6
Yeovil BA21 28 A6
Howard's La BH20 142 E3
Howarth Cl [1] DT6 128 B8
Howe Cl
Christchurch BH23 124 F5
New Milton BH25 94 F3
Howe La BH31 45 A5
Howell Ho BH21 59 F7
Howe's Eype La DT6 99 E5
Howeth Cl BH10 89 D3
Howeth Rd BH10 89 D3
Howton Cl BH10 89 C5
Howton Rd BH10 89 C5
Hoxley Rd BH10 89 D4
Hoyal Rd BH15 118 D3
Hubert Rd SO23 126 C2
Hudson Cl
Poole BH12 88 C2
Ringwood BH24 55 E8
Hughes Bsns Ctr BH23 125 A7
Huish BA20 27 C4
Huish CP Sch BA20 27 C5
Huish La DT9 31 E4
Hull Cres BH11 88 D4
Hull Rd BH11 88 E4
Hull Way BH11 88 E4
Humber Chase BH20 142 C5
Humber Rd BH22 62 A6
Humpy La DT9 31 B1
Hundred Stone BA21 27 D8
Hundredstone Cl BA21 27 D8
Hungerford Hill SP6 43 D6
Hungerford Rd BH8 90 D3
Hunger Hill BH15 119 C2
Hunter Cl
Christchurch BH23 125 A7
Wimborne Minster BH21 60 C6
Hunters Cl BH31 45 E5
Hunters Mead SP7 7 B1
Huntfield Rd BH9 90 B2
Huntick Est BH16 84 D3
Huntick Rd BH16 84 F3
Huntingdon Dr BH21 55 E1
Huntingdon Gdns BH23 92 A2
Huntley Down DT11 209 F1
Huntly Rd BH3 121 D7
Hunt Rd
Blandford Forum DT11 212 E5
Christchurch BH23 124 F8
Poole BH15 119 E4
Hunt's Hill DT10 21 E5
Hunts Mead DT9 29 F4
Huntvale Rd BH9 90 B3
Hurdles The BH23 123 E8
Hurn Cl BH24 54 F6
Hurn Court La BH23 90 F6
Hurn Ct BH8 91 A4
Hurn La BH24 54 F6
Hurn Rd
Christchurch BH23 91 D3
St Leonards & St Ives BH24 54 F4
Hurn Way BH23 91 D1
Hurricane Cl DT2 137 D6
Hursley Cl BH7 123 C8
Hurstbourne Ave BH23 93 E1
Hurst Cl
Barton on Sea BH25 126 D8
Walkford BH23 94 C2
Hurst Ct [4] BH23 126 A7
Hurstdene Rd BH8 90 C2
Hurst Hill BH14 147 C8
Hurst Rd
Moreton DT2 111 C1
Ringwood BH24 47 C1
Hussar Cl BH23 123 F7
Hussey Cl [2] SO23 126 E8
Hussey's DT10 20 E1
Hutchins Cl DT1 134 E7
Hut Gate TA13 192 A8
Hyacinth Cl BH17 86 F1
Hybris Bsns Pk DT2 137 E6
Hyde Abbey Rd SO23 126 E6
Hyde CE Prim Sch SP6 43 F5
Hyde Church La SO23 126 E7
Hyde Church Path [6] SO23 126 E7
Hyde Cl SO23 126 E7

Hyde Ct BA21 26 E6
Hyde Gate 10 SO23 126 E7
Hyde Gdns 6 DT11 199 D4
Hyde House Gdns 5
SO23 126 E7
Hyde La SP6 43 E6
Hyde Lodge SO23 126 D7
Hyde Rd
Bournemouth BH10 89 C5
Gillingham SP8 5 E3
Wool BH20 140 A2
Hydes La DT10 196 D7
Hyde St SO23 126 E7
Hyde The
New Milton BH25 94 E4
Swanage BH19 178 C2
Hynesbury Rd BH23 125 C6
Hythe Rd BH15 120 A7
Hythe The DT3 166 D5

I

Ibbertson Cl BH8 90 F2
Ibbertson Rd BH8 90 F2
Ibbertson Way BH8 90 F2
Ibbett Rd BH10 89 C3
Ibsley Cl BH8 122 C6
Ibsley Dro BH24 43 D1
Icen La
Bincombe DT3 152 C4
Shipton Gorge DT6 101 E4
Icen Rd DT3 167 C7
Icen Way DT1 108 A2
Iddesleigh Rd
Bournemouth BH3 121 F6
Bournemouth BH3 122 A6
Iford Bridge Home Pk
BH6 123 D7
Iford Gdns BH7 123 C7
Iford La BH6 123 E6
Ilchester Rd
Weymouth DT4 167 C3
Yeovil BA21 27 B7
Ilford Cl BH6 123 F5
Ilminster Rd BH19 179 B2
Ilsington House DT2 78 C1
Ilsington Rd DT2 109 F4
Imber Dr BH23 125 F8
Imber Rd SP7 13 A3
Imbrecourt BH13 147 E7
Imperial Ct 4 BH13 147 F7
Incline Rd DT5 187 B6
Ingarth 7 BH6 123 E3
Inglegreen Cl BH25 94 F1
Inglesham Way BH15 118 E4
Inglewood Ave BH8 90 F1
Inglewood Dr BH25 95 B2
Ingram Wlk 1 BH21 59 D4
Ingworth Rd BH12 121 A5
Inmosthay DT5 187 A5
Inner Breakwater Rd
DT5 181 D1
Insley Cres BH18 86 E5
Institute Rd BH19 179 C2
Inveravon BH23 124 F4
Inverclyde Ho BH14 120 B4
Inverclyde Rd BH14 120 C4
Inverleigh Rd BH6 123 C6
Inverness Rd BH13 147 E7
Ipswich Rd BH12 121 B4
Iris Gdns 6 SP8 5 E1
Iris Rd BH9 89 F1
Irvine Way BH23 124 E8
Irving La BH6 123 D5
Irving Rd BH6 123 D5
Isaacs Cl BH12 121 B7
Island View Ave BH23 125 B5
Island View Rd BH25 126 C7
Isle of Purbeck Golf Club
BH19 178 E8
Isle Rd DT5 186 E3
Isles La BA22 193 D6
Itchen Ct 3 SO23 126 F6
Ivamy Pl BH11 88 F2
Ivel Cl DT1 135 B8
Ivel Ct BA20 27 E4
Ivelway 14 TA18 191 F4
Ivor Rd
Corfe Mullen BH21 86 D4
Poole BH15 119 A1
Ivy Cl
4 Gillingham SP8 5 D2
St Leonards BH24 53 F4
Winchester SO22 126 C3
Ivy La BH24 47 D4
Ivy Mead BA12 3 B5
Ivy Rd BH21 87 D8
Iwerne Cl BH9 90 B4

J

Jacey Ho 6 BH1 122 A3
Jacklin Ct BH18 87 B5
Jack Paul Cl BA12 3 A6
Jack's Hedge Cnr BH21 189 F2
Jackson Gdns BH12 120 C6
Jackson Rd BH12 120 C6
Jack the Treacle Eater
(Folly) BA22 27 E1
Jacmar Ct 4 BH25 95 B2
Jacobean Cl BH23 94 B1
Jacobs Ladder 2 DT11 198 C7
Jacobs Rd BH15 118 E2
Jacqueline Rd BH12 120 C7
James Cl DT11 212 F5
James Cross La BH21 201 A6
James Day Mead 2
BH19 179 B5
Jameson Rd BH9 89 F1
James Rd
Dorchester DT1 134 E8
Poole BH12 121 A5
James St DT4 167 D2
Janred Ct BH25 126 E7
Jarvis Cl DT10 33 D7
Jarvis Way DT10 33 D8
Jasmine Cl
Crewkerne TA18 191 F5
Yeovil BA22 26 D5
Jasmine Way 2 DT4 180 B8
Jaundrells Cl BH25 95 C3
Jay's Ct BH23 126 B8
Jeanneau Cl 4 SP7 12 F3
Jefferson Ave BH1 122 D6
Jellicoe Cl BH14 119 F5
Jellicoe Dr BH23 124 F6
Jenner Cl BH31 45 A7
Jenner Way DT3 152 D3
Jennings Rd BH14 120 C2
Jennys La BH16 84 B4
Jephcote Rd BH11 88 F4
Jeremy Cl 1 BH20 140 B2
Jersey Cl BH12 88 D1
Jersey Rd BH12 88 D1
Jesmond Ave BH23 125 F8
Jesop Cl 1 SP8 5 E1
Jessica Ave BH31 44 F7
Jessopp Ave DT6 100 F7
Jessopp Cl BH10 89 F4
Jessopp Ho 6 BH21 59 C5
Jessopp Rd BH21 60 B6
Jesty's Ave DT3 152 C4
Jewell Rd BH8 91 A2
Jewry St SO23 126 E6
Jimmy Brown Ave BH21 53 A5
Jock's Hill DT2 78 E6
Johnson Rd BH21 61 A8
Johnson's Ctyd DT9 30 C5
Johns Rd BH20 142 D5
Johnstone Rd BH23 124 E6
Johnston Rd BH15 119 D7
Jolliffe Ave BH15 119 D4
Jolliffe Rd BH15 119 D4
Jopps Cnr BH23 92 C4
Jordan Hill Roman Temple
DT3 168 B7
Jordan Way 5 DT3 152 C4
Joshua Cl BH15 118 E2
Journeys End DT6 100 B6
Jowitt Dr BH25 94 F2
Joyce Dickson Cl 2
BH24 55 D6
Joys Rd BH21 53 A8
Juan's La SP8 9 D2
Jubilee Cl
Corfe Mullen BH21 86 E7
Radipole DT4 167 D4
Ringwood BH24 55 E8
Jubilee Cres BH12 120 D5
Jubilee Cross BH16 85 A4
Jubilee Ent Ctr DT4 167 D4
Jubilee Gdns
Bournemouth BH10 89 D2
3 Corfe Castle BH20 177 A7
Jubilee Rd
Corfe Mullen BH21 86 E7
Poole BH12 120 D5
Swanage BH19 178 F2
Jubilee Trail DT2 135 C4
Jubilee Way DT11 212 C5
Julia Cl BH23 125 F8
Julian's Rd BH21 59 A4
Julyan Ave BH12 121 A8
Jumpers Ave BH23 123 E8
Jumpers Rd BH23 123 F8
Junction Rd
Bournemouth BH9 121 F8
Hamworthy BH16 118 D4
Juniper Cl
Ferndown BH22 61 C8
Three Legged Cross BH21 53 A8
Winchester SO22 126 B3
Yeovil BA20 27 B3
Juniper Flats BH23 123 E8
Juniper Gdns 7 SP8 5 E1
Juniper Way DT3 152 C3
Jupiter Way BH21 86 E8
Justin Bsns Pk BH20 142 F5
Justin Gdns BH10 89 E4

K

Kamptee Copse BH25 95 B6
Kangaw Pl BH15 118 D2
Katherine Chance Cl
BH23 92 C3
Katterns Cl BH23 91 E2
Kay Cl BH23 124 E6
Kayes Cl DT4 180 C8
K&B Est BH17 119 B8
Keats Cl SO22 126 A2
Keats Ho 1 BH25 95 A1
Keble St SO22 126 A4
Keeble Cl BH10 89 D6
Keeble Cres BH10 89 D6
Keeble Rd BH10 89 D6
Keepers La BH21 60 F4
Keep Military Mus The
DT1 107 F2
Keighley Ave BH18 86 F1
Keith Rd BH3 121 D7
Kellaway Ct 10 DT4 167 E2
Kellaway Rd BH17 119 F8
Kellaway Terr DT4 167 C3
Kelly Cl BH17 119 F8
Kelsall Gdns BH25 95 A3
Kemp Rd BH9 121 F8
Kempston Rd DT4 167 D1
Kemp Welch Ct BH12 121 B8
Kendalls La SP8 5 E5
Kenilworth DT4 167 B6
Kenilworth Cl BH25 95 B3
Kenilworth Ct
2 Christchurch BH23 124 A7
1 Poole BH13 147 F8
9 Winchester SO23 126 E8
Kenmoor Cl DT3 167 F8
Kenmore Dr BA21 27 D6
Kennard Ct BH25 94 F3
Kennard Rd BH25 94 F3
Kennart Rd BH17 119 B7
Kennel La DT2 206 C2
Kennels La DT9 195 E2
Kenneth Ct 9 BH23 126 B7
Kennington Rd BH17 119 D8
Kennington Sq 5 BH20 142 E4
Ken Rd BH6 123 E4
Kensington Ct 14 BH13 121 B3
Kensington Dr 1 BH2 121 D4
Kensington Wlk 8 DT1 135 C8
Kent Cl DT4 166 F3
Kent Ho 28 BH4 121 C3
Kentisworth Rd DT10 20 F1
Kent La BH24 43 A1
Kent Rd
Poole BH12 120 E6
10 Tatworth TA20 202 A8
Kents La 8 TA20 202 A8
Kenwyn Rd DT6 100 E7
Kenyon Cl BH15 119 E7
Kenyon Rd BH15 119 E7
Keppel Cl BH24 55 D7
Kerley Rd BH2 121 E2
Kernells Ct 2 BH4 121 B4
Kerrfield SO22 126 B5
Kerrfield Mews SO22 126 B5
Kestrel Cl
Ferndown BH22 61 B7
Upton BH16 118 B8
Winchester SO22 126 B2
Kestrel Ct BH24 55 C8
Kestrel Dr BH23 125 A6
Kestrel View DT3 152 C3
Kestrel Way SP6 42 D5
Keswick Ct BH25 95 B5
Keswick Rd
Bournemouth BH5 122 F4
Bournemouth BH5 123 A4
New Milton BH25 95 B5
Keswick Way BH31 45 A5
Keverstone Ct BH1 122 D3
Keyes Cl
Christchurch BH23 124 F6
Poole BH12 88 F1
Keynston Down Rd 7
DT11 199 E2
Keysworth Ave BH25 126 F8
Keysworth Dr BH20 143 A8
Keysworth Rd BH16 118 C4
Khartoum Rd DT4 180 E8
Khyber Rd BH12 120 D5
Kiddles BA21 27 E5
Kidmore Cl 2 DT6 97 A7
Killicks Hill DT5 186 F7
Killock 6 BH13 147 F7
Kilmarnock Rd BH9 89 F1
Kilmington Way BH23 125 F8
Kiln Cl BH21 86 C4
Kiln Way BH31 45 E4
Kilwood Coppice & Meadows
Nature Reserve BH20 161 B2
Kimberley Cl
Christchurch BH23 123 F8
1 Radipole DT3 152 E2
Kimberley Rd
Bournemouth BH6 123 C5
Poole BH14 120 B3
Kimber Rd BH11 88 F3
Kimmeridge Ave BH12 120 C8
Kimmeridge Cl DT3 167 B8
Kine Bush La SP8 10 B7
King Alfred Pl SO23 126 E7
King Alfred's Way SP7 12 F3
King Alfred Terr 13
SO23 126 E7
King Arthur Dr BA21 26 F7
King Charles Way DT6 100 F7
King Cl BH24 54 B4
Kingcombe Cross Roads
DT2 205 E3
Kingcombe La DT2 205 E3
Kingcombe Meadows Nature
Reserve DT2 205 D2
Kingcombe Rd DT8 205 C3
Kingcup Cl BH18 86 E2
King Down Dro BH21 49 C3
King Down Rd DT11 199 F3
King Edmund Ct SP8 5 E2
King Edward Ave BH9 90 A2
King Edward Ct BH9 89 F2
King Edward's Dr DT11 209 F5
Kingfisher Cl
Bournemouth BH6 123 E6
Ferndown BH22 53 B2
1 Weymouth DT4 180 D6
Kingfisher Ct BH8 122 D6
Kingfisher Park Homes 3
BH10 89 F4
Kingfishers 4 BH23 124 A5
Kingfishers The BH31 45 C5
Kingfisher Way
Christchurch BH23 125 A5
Ringwood BH24 47 D1
King George Ave BH9 89 F2
King George Mobile Home
Pk BH25 94 F1
King George St 7 BA20 27 D4
King George V Rd BH20 139 E7
King Harold Ct SO23 126 D4
King John Ave BH11 88 D5
King John Cl BH11 88 D6
King John Rd SP8 6 A1
Kingland Cres 4 BH15 119 C2
Kingland Rd BH15 119 D2
King Richard Dr BH11 88 D5
Kings Arms La BH24 55 B7
Kings Arms Row BH24 55 B7
Kings Ave
Poole BH14 120 D2
Winchester SO22 126 C3
King's Ave BH23 123 F6
Kingsbere Ave BH10 89 B2
Kingsbere Cres DT1 135 A7
Kingsbere Gdns BH23 126 A8
Kingsbere La SP7 13 A4
Kingsbere Rd
Overcombe/Preston
DT3 168 A7
Poole BH15 119 E5
Kingsbridge Rd BH14 120 C3
Kingsbury's La BH24 55 B7
Kings Cl
Ferndown BH22 53 A1
Longburton DT9 195 B8
Poole BH15 119 D5
Kingscourt Cl 2 SP8 6 B1
Kingscourt Rd SP8 6 B1
Kings Cres DT9 30 B7
King's Cres BH14 120 E2
King's Ct Pal SP8 6 B1
Kingsdale Ct 9 SO22 126 D6
Kingsfield BH24 55 C7
Kingsgate 10 BH13 121 B3
Kingsgate Rd SO23 126 D4
Kingsgate St SO23 126 E4
Kings Grange 11 BH4 121 D2
Kings Head Yd 1 SO23 126 E5
Kings High Sch BH10 89 C3
Kings Hill 2 SP7 12 E3
Kings La BH21 201 F4
King's La DT6 70 D5
Kingsland Ct BH13 147 F7
Kingsleigh Prim Sch
BH10 89 C3
Kingsley Ave BH6 124 A4
Kingsley Cl BH6 124 A4
Kingsley Paddock DT2 72 F7
Kingsley Pl SO22 126 C3
Kingsman La SP7 12 E2
Kings Mead DT2 78 B1
Kingsmead Ct 5 BH21 59 B5
Kingsmill Rd BH17 119 E7
King's Mill Rd DT10 34 B6
Kingsnorth Cl DT6 100 E7
Kings Park Com Hospl
BH7 122 F5
King's Park Dr BH7,BH1 122 E6
King's Park Prim Sch
BH1 122 E5
King's Park Rd BH7 122 E6
King's Pitt 3 DT1 107 C1
Kings Rd
Dorchester DT1 108 B1
New Milton BH25 95 C3
Radipole DT3 167 C7
Sherborne DT9 30 B7
Winchester SO22 126 A4
King's Rd
Blandford Forum DT11 212 E5
Bournemouth BH3 122 A7
Thornford DT9 194 D7
Kings Rd E BH19 179 B2
Kings Rd W BH19 179 A2
Kings Row 3 SO22 126 D6
King's Royal Hussars Mus
The SO23 126 D5
King's St BH21 56 D5
King St
Bridport DT6 100 D6
Fortuneswell DT5 186 F7
Radipole DT4 167 D4
Wimborne Minster BH21 59 B4
Yeovil BA21 27 D6
Kingsthorn Rd 1 DT1 107 C2
Kingston BA20 27 C5
Kingston Cl DT11 212 C5
Kingston Hill BH20 176 F4
Kingston La DT10 196 F4
Kingston Lacy House
BH21 58 B7
Kingston Maurward Coll
DT2 108 F3
Kingston Maurward Gdns &
Animal Pk DT2 108 E3
Kingston Rd BH15 119 D4
Kingston View BA21 27 D6
Kingsway
Ferndown BH22 61 B8
Lyme Regis DT7 96 C6
Kingsway Cl BH23 91 F1
Kingswell Cl BH10 89 D2
Kingswell Gdns BH10 89 B2
Kingswell Gr BH10 89 B2
Kingswell Rd BH10 89 C2
King's Wlk 8 SO23 126 E5
Kingswood 15 BH4 121 C2
Kingswood Cl 2 BH19 178 E2
Kingswood Rd 6 TA18 191 F3
Kinross Rd BH3 121 E6
Kinsbourne Ave BH10 89 D2
Kinson Ave BH15 120 A7
Kinson Gr BH10 89 C6
Kinson Park Rd BH10 89 D6
Kinson Pottery Ind Est
BH14 120 A6
Kinson Prim Sch BH11 89 B5
Kinson Rd BH10 89 C3
Kiosks The 9 BH15 119 C1
Kipling Rd BH14 120 B5
Kirby Cl BH15 119 F6
Kirby Way BH6 123 D4
Kirkham Ave BH23 92 C3
Kirkleton Ave DT4 167 D5
Kirkway BH18 87 B4
Kitchener Cres BH17 87 B2
Kitchener Rd DT4 167 B3
Kite's Nest La SP8 1 E2
Kitford La DT11 197 C3
Kithill TA18 191 F3
Kit La DT2 155 D7
Kitscroft Rd BH10 89 C5
Kitt Hill DT9 30 A6
Kittiwake Cl BH6 123 D6
Kiwi Cl BH15 119 E3
Knacker's Hole La TA20 202 F4
Knap Barrow (Long Barrow)
SP6 190 D6
Knapp Cl BH23 124 A8
Knapp Mill Ave BH23 124 A8
Knapps DT11 198 B6
Knapp The
Chickerell DT3 166 C6
Fontmell Magna SP7 37 F6
Hilton DT11 209 D6
Shaftesbury SP7 12 D3
Knapwater Wlk 12 DT1 135 B8
Knight Cl SO23 126 E8
Knighton Heath Cl BH11 88 E4
Knighton Heath Ind Est
BH11 88 E2
Knighton Heath Rd BH11 88 E4
Knighton House Sch
DT11 198 E3
Knighton La
Bournemouth BH21 88 D7
Broadmayne DT2 136 C2
Knighton Pk BH25 126 E8
Knightsbridge Ct BH2 121 E2
Knights Cl 1 DT11 212 D2
Knightsdale Rd DT4 167 B2
Knightsdale Road Swimming
Pool DT4 167 B2
Knights Rd BH11 88 D5
Knightstone Ct 2 BH20 142 F3
Knightstone Rise DT6 68 F1
Knightwood Cl BH23 125 D8
Knobcrook Rd 3 BH21 59 B6
Knole Ct 5 BH1 122 D4
Knole Gdns BH1 122 D4
Knole Rd BH1 122 D4
Knoll Gdns
Ferndown BH21 60 F4
St Leonards BH24 54 B4
Knoll La BH21 86 B7
Knoll Manor BH2 121 F5
Knoll Pl SP8 5 E3
Knoll Rise DT3 152 E2
Knollsea Cl 1 BH19 179 C1
Knotts Cl 7 DT11 198 C7
Knotts Paddock DT9 30 C6
Knowle Cross DT8 203 D6
Knowle Hill BH20 140 A1
Knowle La TA18 191 F1
Knowles Cl BH23 124 E7
Knowle Wood Knap 1
BH20 140 A1
Knowl La DT6 101 D7
Knowlton Church BH21 201 D5
Knowlton Circles BH21 201 D5
Knowlton Gdns BH9 90 B3
Knowlton Rd BH17 87 F2
Knyveton Ho BH1 122 B4
Knyveton Rd BH1 122 C4
Kynegils Rd SO22 126 B8
Kyrchil La BH21 59 F6
Kyrchil Way BH21 59 F7

L

Labrador Dr BH15 119 D1
Laburnam Way SP8 5 D1
Laburnum Cl
Ferndown BH22 61 B6
Radipole DT4 167 B6
1 Sandford BH20 116 A1
Verwood BH31 45 E5
Laburnum Cres 13 TA18 191 F5
Laburnum Ho 8 BH10 89 F4
Laburnum Rd DT2 75 D3
Laburnum Way BA20 26 F2
Lacey Cres BH15 120 A6
Lackington Dro DT2 208 B1
Lacy Cl BH21 59 C6
Lacy Dr BH21 59 C6
Lady Baden Powell Way
DT11 212 E6
Lady Caroline's Dr DT11 210 D7
Lady Mead Cl 3 DT5 187 A4
Lady St Mary CE Fst Sch The
BH20 142 D3
Ladysmith Cl BH23 124 E7
Lagado Cl BH14 147 C8

Lagland Ct **14** BH15 . . . . 119 C2
Lagland St BH15 . . . . 119 C2
Lagoon Cl BH14 . . . . 147 B8
Lagoon Rd BH14 . . . . 147 B8
Laidlaw Cl BH12 . . . . 121 B8
Lainston Cl SO22 . . . . 126 A8
Lake Ave BH15 . . . . 118 D1
Lake Cres BH15 . . . . 118 E3
Lake Dr
 Hamworthy BH15 . . . . . 118 D1
 Poole BH15 . . . . 118 D2
 Upton BH15 . . . . 117 F1
Lake Farm Cl BH21 . . . . 89 B8
Lakefields BA22 . . . . 193 B7
Lakegate La DT9 . . . . 194 A5
Lake Grove Rd BH25 . . . . . . 95 A4
Lake La DT6 . . . . 100 D4
Lake Rd
 Bournemouth BH11 . . . . . 89 C6
 Hamworthy BH15 . . . . . 118 E2
 Verwood BH31 . . . . 45 C4
Lakeside BH24 . . . . 55 E6
Lakeside Gdns DT3 . . . . . . 167 B7
Lakeside Pines BH25 . . . . . 95 A4
Lakeside Rd BH13 . . . . . . 121 A1
Lakeview Dr BH24 . . . . 55 E6
Lake View Manor BH25 . . . . 95 A3
Lakewood Rd BH23 . . . . . . 93 F1
Lambert Cl **4** DT9 . . . . . 17 C2
Lambert's Castle (Fort)
 DT6 . . . . 202 E2
Lambourne Ct TA18 . . . . . . 191 F5
Lamb Plot DT9 . . . . 194 D2
Lambs Cl BH17 . . . . 87 C1
Lambsfield DT9 . . . . 30 C7
Lambsgreen La BH21 . . . . . 58 F2
Lambs La BH21 . . . . 56 D3
Lammas Cl SP8 . . . . 5 F3
Lampton Cl BH20 . . . . 139 F2
Lampton Gdns **5** BH9 . . . . 89 F1
Lanark Cl BH15 . . . . 118 E2
Lancaster Cl
 Christchurch BH23 . . . . . 125 C7
 Corfe Mullen BH18 . . . . . . 86 F5
Lancaster Dr
 Corfe Mullen BH18 . . . . . . 86 F5
 Verwood BH31 . . . . 45 A5
Lancaster Rd
 Dorchester DT1 . . . . 108 B1
 Ferndown BH21 . . . . 61 A8
 Radipole DT3 . . . . 152 B1
Lancer Cl BH23 . . . . 123 F7
Lanchards **4** DT11 . . . . . 198 B6
Lanchards La DT11 . . . . . . 198 B5
Lander Cl BH11 . . . . 119 D1
Landers Reach **3** BH16 . . 84 D2
Landford Gdns BH8 . . . . . . 90 D2
Landford Way BH8 . . . . 90 D2
Landscombe Vale DT2 . . . . 208 A8
Landseer Rd **1** BH4 . . . . 121 C3
Landshire La
 Fifehead Magdalen SP8 . . . 20 C5
 Stalbridge BA8 . . . . 19 D3
Lane Cl DT11 . . . . 212 F6
Lane End DT6 . . . . 79 F7
Lanehouse Rocks Rd **1**
 DT4 . . . . 180 C8
Lane Lowther Gdns The **4**
 BH8 . . . . 122 C5
Lane-side SP7 . . . . 12 F4
Lanes The BH25 . . . . 95 A5
Lane The BH20 . . . . 176 F4
Langdon Ct BH14 . . . . 120 D4
Langdon La
 Beaminster DT8 . . . . . . 204 E4
 Chideock DT6 . . . . 98 E7
Langdon Rd BH14 . . . . . . 120 D4
Langdons DT9 . . . . 30 C7
Langdons Way **1** TA20 . . 202 A8
Langfords La **2** SP7 . . . . 12 D2
Langham Ct BH21 . . . . 91 F1
Langham La SP8 . . . . 4 F1
Langley Chase BH24 . . . . . 54 B5
Langley Rd
 Christchurch BH23 . . . . . . 93 E1
 Poole BH14 . . . . 120 F4
Langmead Pl **3** TA18 . . . 191 F5
Langmead Rd TA18 . . . . . . 191 F3
Langmead Sq **1** TA18 . . . 191 F5
Langmoor La EX13 . . . . . . 202 A2
Lang Rd TA18 . . . . 191 F3
Langside Ave BH12 . . . . . . 121 A4
Langside Sch BH12 . . . . . . 121 A8
Langton Ave DT4 . . . . 180 C6
Langton Cl
 Barton on Sea BH25 . . . . 127 B8
 Winchester SO22 . . . . . . 126 C7
Langton Cres DT11 . . . . . . 212 E3
Langton Matravers Mus
 BH19 . . . . 178 B3
Langton Rd
 Blandford Forum DT11 . . . 212 D3
 Bournemouth BH7 . . . . . 122 F5
Lankhills Rd SO22 . . . . . . 126 E7
Lansdell **4** BH15 . . . . . . 119 E3
Lansdowne Ave SO23 . . . . 126 D3
Lansdowne Cres BH1 . . . . . 122 B3
Lansdowne Ct **3** SO23 . . . 126 D3
Lansdowne Gdns BH1 . . . . 122 A4
Lansdowne Rd
 Bournemouth BH1 . . . . . 122 A5
 Bridport DT6 . . . . 100 D4
Lansdowne Rdbt The
 BH1 . . . . 122 A3
Lansdowne Sq DT4 . . . . . . 167 C1

Lantern Ct SO23 . . . . 126 C4
Lapwing Rd BH21 . . . . 60 A7
Lara Cl BH8 . . . . 90 D3
Larch Cl
 Broadstone BH17 . . . . . . 86 C1
 Hordle SO41 . . . . 95 F3
 Sandford BH20 . . . . 143 B8
 St Leonards BH24 . . . . . . 54 C4
Larch Way BH22 . . . . 61 C7
Larcombe La DT6 . . . . 69 D5
Larkhill Rd BA21 . . . . 27 A6
Lark Hill Rise SO22 . . . . . . 126 B2
Lark Rd BH23 . . . . 125 A6
Larks Cl BH22 . . . . 61 B7
Larksfield Ave BH9 . . . . . . 90 C3
Larkshill Cl BH25 . . . . 95 B4
Larks Mdw DT10 . . . . 33 E8
Larksmead DT11 . . . . 212 E5
Larkspur Cl DT4 . . . . 167 E6
Larkspur Cres BA21 . . . . . 26 F7
Larks Rise BH22 . . . . 61 B7
Larmer Tree Gdns SP5 . . . 188 B4
Lascelles Ct **1** BH7 . . . . 123 B6
Lascelles Rd BH7 . . . . 123 B6
Latch Farm Ave BH23 . . . . 124 A8
Latimer Rd BH9 . . . . 121 F8
Latimers Cl BH23 . . . . 93 F1
Launches The BH20 . . . . . 172 C6
Laundry La **3** SP7 . . . . . 12 D2
Laurel Ave BH20 . . . . 116 B2
Laurel Cl
 1 Bridport DT6 . . . . . 100 B8
 Christchurch BH23 . . . . . 93 D1
 Corfe Mullen BH21 . . . . . 86 D6
 Hordle SO41 . . . . 95 E4
 St Leonards BH24 . . . . . . 54 A4
 West Coker BA22 . . . . . . 193 B8
Laurel Dr BH18 . . . . 87 C4
Laurel Gdns BH18 . . . . 87 C4
Laurel La BH24 . . . . 54 A3
Laurels The
 Broadstone BH18 . . . . . . 87 B4
 7 Crewkerne TA18 . . . 191 F5
 Ferndown BH21 . . . . 61 C7
 8 Gillingham SP8 . . . . 5 E1
 2 Iwerne Courtney or Shroton
 DT11 . . . . 198 E7
Lavender Cl BH31 . . . . 45 E5
Lavender Rd
 Bournemouth BH8 . . . . . . 90 A4
 Hordle SO41 . . . . 95 E3
Lavender Villas BH23 . . . . 126 A8
Lavender Way BH18 . . . . . . 86 D3
Lavender Wlk BH8 . . . . 90 A4
Laver's La TA20 . . . . 202 C6
Laverstock **3** BH5 . . . . . 122 F3
Lavinia Rd BH12 . . . . 120 C7
Lawford Rd BH9 . . . . 90 A4
Lawn Ct **13** BH2 . . . . . . 121 D4
Lawn Ho **24** SO23 . . . . . 126 E6
Lawns Cl BH21 . . . . 60 C6
Lawns Rd BH21 . . . . 60 B6
Lawn St SO23 . . . . 126 E6
Lawns The
 Charmouth DT6 . . . . 97 B7
 Christchurch BH23 . . . . . 126 B8
Lawn View BH25 . . . . 94 D5
Lawrence Ct BH8 . . . . 122 C6
Lawrence Dr
 Crossways DT2 . . . . 137 D5
 Poole BH13 . . . . 120 E1
Lawrence La
 Hyde SP6 . . . . 43 D4
 Witchampton BH21 . . . . 201 A2
Lawrence of Arabia's Cottage
 BH20 . . . . 112 C2
Lawrence of Arabia's Grave
 DT2 . . . . 138 E7
Lawrence Rd BH24 . . . . . . 47 E2
Lawrence Way **4** SO23 . . 126 E8
Lawson Rd BH12 . . . . 120 B6
Layard Dr BH21 . . . . 59 D1
Laymoor La BH21 . . . . 60 D5
Layton Ct BH12 . . . . 120 D5
Layton La SP7 . . . . 12 E2
Layton Rd BH12 . . . . 120 D5
Lea Cl BA21 . . . . 27 D8
Leamington Rd
 Bournemouth BH9 . . . . . 122 A7
 Weymouth DT4 . . . . 166 F2
Leanne Bsns Pk BH20 . . . . 142 E5
Leaphill Rd BH7 . . . . 123 B6
Lea Rd DT4 . . . . 180 B8
Learoyd Rd BH17 . . . . 119 E7
Lea The BH31 . . . . 45 C5
Lea Way BH11 . . . . 88 E6
Leaze La BA21 . . . . 28 A4
Lecher La DT8 . . . . 192 B1
Lechlade Gdns BH7 . . . . . 123 B8
Ledbury Rd BH23 . . . . 124 F5
Leddington Way SP8 . . . . . 5 E4
Ledgard Cl BH14 . . . . 120 B4
Lee Ct BH21 . . . . 61 D4
Leedam Rd BH10 . . . . 89 D4
Leeds Cres DT4 . . . . 166 F2
Lee La DT6 . . . . 101 A7
Lees Cl BH23 . . . . 91 D4
Leeson Cl **2** BH19 . . . . . 178 F2
Leeson Dr BH22 . . . . 61 B8
Leeson House Field Studies
 Ctr BH19 . . . . 178 C2
Leeson Rd BH7 . . . . 122 F7
Leet Cl **1** DT5 . . . . 181 B1
Leet Ct DT9 . . . . 29 F4
Legg La DT9 . . . . 59 D4
Legion Cl
 Dorchester DT1 . . . . 134 E7
 Hamworthy BH15 . . . . . 118 E2

Legion Rd
 Hamworthy BH15 . . . . . . 118 E2
 Yeovil BA21 . . . . 27 B6
Leicester Rd BH13 . . . . . . 120 F3
Leigham Vale Rd BH6 . . . . 123 D4
Leigh Cl BH21 . . . . 59 E4
Leigh Comm BH21 . . . . . . 59 E5
Leigh Gdns BH21 . . . . 59 D4
Leigh La
 Halstock BA22 . . . . 193 C3
 Ibberton DT11 . . . . 197 D3
 Wimborne Minster BH21 . . 59 F5
Leigh Rd
 New Milton BH25 . . . . . . 95 A3
 Wimborne Minster BH21 . . 59 E4
 Wimborne Minster BH21 . . 60 A4
Leighton Lo **3** BH2 . . . . 121 D4
Le Neubourg Way SP8 . . . . . 5 F1
Lennox St DT4 . . . . 167 D4
Lentham Cl BH17 . . . . 87 D1
Lenthay Cl DT9 . . . . 29 F4
Lenthay Rd DT9 . . . . 29 F4
Lent Hill Ct SO22 . . . . 126 B4
Le Patourel Cl BH23 . . . . . 124 D7
Lerrett Cl DT3 . . . . 166 D6
Leslie Rd
 Bournemouth BH9 . . . . . 121 F7
 Poole BH12 . . . . 120 A3
Lessingham Ave DT4 . . . . 180 C6
Letton Cl DT11 . . . . 212 F6
Leven Ave BH4 . . . . 121 D5
Leven Cl BH4 . . . . 121 D4
Levet's La **4** BH15 . . . . 119 B1
Lewell Way DT2 . . . . 136 C3
Lewens Cl BH21 . . . . 59 C4
Lewens La BH21 . . . . 59 C4
Lewesdon Cl **6** DT8 . . . . 204 C4
Lewesdon Dr BH18 . . . . . . 86 F4
Lewesdon Hill DT8 . . . . . . 203 E4
Leybourne Ave BH10 . . . . . 89 D4
Leybourne Cl BH10 . . . . . . 89 C5
Leydene Ave BH8 . . . . 90 F1
Leydene Cl BH8 . . . . 90 F1
Leyland Rd BH12 . . . . 88 E2
Leyside BH23 . . . . 124 C6
Leyton Conyers **11** BH13 . 147 F7
Liberty **11** BH21 . . . . . . 53 D6
Liberty Ct BH23 . . . . 123 F7
Liberty's Raptor & Reptile Ctr
 BH24 . . . . 55 E5
Library Mews BH12 . . . . . 120 D5
Library Rd
 Bournemouth BH9 . . . . . . 89 F1
 Ferndown BH22 . . . . 61 D5
 Poole BH12 . . . . 120 E5
Lichfield Rd DT4 . . . . 167 A2
Liddington Cres DT11 . . . . 212 D5
Liddon Hill TA18 . . . . 191 C5
Liederbach Dr BH31 . . . . . 45 E3
Lighthouse Rd BH19 . . . . . 185 C7
Lights Cl BH23 . . . . 124 B7
Lilac Cl BH24 . . . . 55 B8
Lilliput CE Fst Sch BH14 . . 147 C8
Lilliput Rd BH14 . . . . 120 B3
Lilliput Rd BH14 . . . . 147 D8
Limber Rd BA22 . . . . 26 C6
Lime Cl
 Dorchester DT1 . . . . 134 C8
 Poole BH15 . . . . 119 F6
Lime Hill DT6 . . . . 70 B7
Lime Kiln BA21 . . . . 26 E5
Limekiln Cl **2** DT5 . . . . 186 E2
Lime Kiln La BA8 . . . . 19 A3
Lime Kiln Rd BH16 . . . . . . 84 C4
Limerick Cl **3** DT9 . . . . . 17 D2
Limes The BA20 . . . . 27 A2
Lime Tree Ave BH24 . . . . . 54 A2
Lime Tree Cl SP6 . . . . 42 B6
Limited Rd BH9 . . . . 90 A1
Lin Brook Dr BH24 . . . . . . 47 E2
Linclieth Rd **3** BH20 . . . 140 A2
Lincoln Ave
 Bournemouth BH1 . . . . . 122 D5
 Christchurch BH23 . . . . . 91 F2
Lincoln Rd
 Poole BH12 . . . . 120 D7
 2 Weymouth DT4 . . . . 166 F2
Lindbergh Rd BH21 . . . . . . 61 A8
Linden Ave DT1 . . . . 108 A1
Linden Cl BH22 . . . . 61 D1
Linden Gdns **1** BH24 . . . 55 B8
Linden Pk SP7 . . . . 13 A2
Linden Rd
 Bournemouth BH9 . . . . . . 90 A3
 Ferndown BH22 . . . . 61 D1
 Poole BH12 . . . . 120 C6
 Swanage BH19 . . . . 179 A2
Lindens The BH23 . . . . 92 D3
Lindford Rd BH24 . . . . 47 F1
Lindlar Cl SP7 . . . . 12 F4
Lindsay Ct **19** BH13 . . . . 121 A4
Lindsay Manor **11** BH13 . 121 A4
Lindsay Pk **15** BH13 . . . . 121 A4
Lindsay Rd
 Poole BH13 . . . . 120 F4
 Poole BH13 . . . . 121 A4
Lindum Ct **3** BH13 . . . . 121 A4
Linen Yard The **27** TA18 . 191 F4
Lineside BH23 . . . . 124 C8
Linford Cl BH25 . . . . 95 B4
Linford Rd BH24 . . . . 47 F1
Lingdale Rd BH6 . . . . 123 D6
Lingfield Ave BA21 . . . . . . 27 F7
Lingfield Grange **11**
 BH13 . . . . 121 B3
Ling Rd BH12 . . . . 88 B1
Lington Cl DT2 . . . . 137 D6

Lingwood Ave BH23 . . . . . 124 F6
Linhorns La BH25 . . . . 95 A5
Linkhay **12** TA20 . . . . . . 202 A8
Linkhay Cl **11** TA20 . . . . 202 A8
Link Rd BH24 . . . . 47 E1
Link Rise BH21 . . . . 86 E6
Links Dr BH23 . . . . 91 D1
Linkside Ave BH7 . . . . 122 F8
Links Rd
 Poole BH14 . . . . 120 D2
 Weymouth DT4 . . . . 167 B4
 Winchester SO22 . . . . . . 126 B7
Links View Ave BH14 . . . . 120 E2
Linmead Dr BH11 . . . . 89 A6
Linnet Cl
 Radipole DT3 . . . . 152 C4
 Ringwood BH24 . . . . 55 E6
Linnet Dr BH25 . . . . 94 F3
Linnet La DT2 . . . . 205 D5
Linnet Rd BH17 . . . . 118 F8
Linsay Rd BH20 . . . . 139 E5
Lintern La SP8 . . . . 11 A5
Linthorpe Rd BH15 . . . . . . 119 E4
Linton Lawns BH22 . . . . . . 61 E3
Linwood Rd BH9 . . . . 122 B7
Linwood Rd BH9 . . . . 122 A7
Lionheart Cl BH11 . . . . 88 D5
Lions Hall **4** SO22 . . . . . 126 D5
Lions Hill Way BH24 . . . . . 53 E4
Lions La BH24 . . . . 53 F4
Lions Wood BH24 . . . . 54 A4
Liscombe Cl DT1 . . . . 107 D2
Lisle Cl SO22 . . . . 126 C4
Lissenden **1** BH13 . . . . . 121 B3
Litchford Rd BH25 . . . . . . 95 C3
Little Barrs Dr BH25 . . . . . 95 B4
Little Britain DT1 . . . . 108 C1
Little Content La SP7 . . . . 12 F3
Littlecroft Ave BH9 . . . . . . 90 B3
Little Croft Rd BH12 . . . . . 120 B6
Little Cl
 Poole BH14 . . . . 147 C2
 Poole, Canford Cliffs BH13 . 147 F8
Little Dewlands BH31 . . . . . 44 F6
Littledown SP7 . . . . 12 F5
Littledown Ave BH7 . . . . . 122 F7
Littledown Dr BH7 . . . . . . 122 F7
Little England DT11 . . . . . . 79 E7
Littlefield DT9 . . . . 29 F4
Littlefield La **8** SP5 . . . . 189 A4
Little Forest Mans **12**
 BH1 . . . . 122 A3
Little Forest Rd BH4 . . . . . 121 E5
Little Fosters BH13 . . . . . 147 E6
Little Lane DT11 . . . . 198 A6
Little Lonnen
 Colehill BH21 . . . . 59 F8
 Wimborne Minster BH21 . . 60 A8
Littlemead
 Broadmayne DT2 . . . . . . 136 B1
 Radipole DT3 . . . . 152 B3
Littlemead Cl BH17 . . . . . 119 A7
Littlemill La SP5 . . . . 190 F3
Little Minster St SO23 . . . . 126 E5
Littlemoor Ave BH11 . . . . . 88 D4
Littlemoor Rd
 Overcombe/Preston
 DT3 . . . . 168 A8
 Radipole DT3 . . . . 152 C4
Littleton Dro DT11 . . . . . . 211 B6
Littletowns DT11 . . . . 212 D6
Littleview Rd DT4 . . . . . . 166 F2
Litton Hill DT2 . . . . 103 B2
Litton La
 Askerswell DT2 . . . . 102 E5
 Litton Cheney DT2 . . . . . 103 B1
 Puncknowle DT2 . . . . . . 129 E7
Liverpool Rd **3** DT4 . . . . 166 F2
Livingstone Rd
 Bournemouth BH5 . . . . . 123 B5
 Christchurch BH23 . . . . . 124 D7
 Poole BH12 . . . . 120 C6
 Wimborne Minster BH21 . . 59 E4
Llewellin Ct
 6 Upton BH16 . . . . . . 117 E7
 Upton BH16 . . . . 118 C7
Llewelyn Cl BH16 . . . . 118 C7
Loaders Cl BH9 . . . . 122 A8
Load La DT2 . . . . 194 F1
Locarno Rd BH19 . . . . 179 B2
Loch Rd BH14 . . . . 120 E5
Lockeridge Cl DT11 . . . . . 212 C5
Lockett's La DT2 . . . . 207 F2
Locks La
 Glanvilles Wootton DT9 . . 195 E3
 Loders DT6 . . . . 101 F6
 Stratton DT2 . . . . 106 E8
Locksley Dr BH22 . . . . 61 C3
Locks Piece **5** BH20 . . . 140 A2
Lockwood Terr SP8 . . . . . . 11 B8
Lockyers Dr BH22 . . . . 61 F6
Lockyer's Mid Sch BH21 . . 86 D8
Lockyers Rd BH21 . . . . 86 E8
Lockyer's Way BH16 . . . . . 84 D3
Lodbourne Gdns SP8 . . . . . 5 F3
Lodbourne Gn **7** SP8 . . . . 5 F3
Lodbourne Terr **5** SP8 . . . 5 F3
Lodden View **2** SP8 . . . . 11 A8
Loders CE Prim Sch DT6 . . 69 C1
Loders Cl BH17 . . . . 87 D3
Loders La DT6 . . . . 101 E4
Lodge Cl BH14 . . . . 120 E4
Lodge La DT6 . . . . 100 B7
Lodge Rd
 Christchurch BH23 . . . . . 123 E8
 Holt BH21 . . . . 51 B6
Lodge The BH2 . . . . 121 E4

Lodge Way DT4 . . . . 180 D8
Lodmoor Ave DT3 . . . . . . 167 D7
Lodmoor Ctry Pk DT3 . . . . 167 F6
Loewy Cres BH12 . . . . 88 D2
Lombard Ave BH6 . . . . . . 123 D5
Lombardy Cl BH31 . . . . . . 45 D5
Lomer La SP6 . . . . 42 E4
Lomond Dr DT4 . . . . 167 C1
London Cl
 1 Dorchester DT1 . . . 108 B2
 Piddlehinton DT2 . . . . . . 76 F7
London La BH23 . . . . 63 F2
London Rd
 Dorchester DT1 . . . . 108 B2
 Milborne Port DT9 . . . . . . 17 E1
London Row DT2 . . . . 76 F7
Lone Pine Dr BH22 . . . . . . 61 E3
Lone Pine Pk BH22 . . . . . . 61 F3
Lone Pine Way BH22 . . . . . 61 F2
Long Acre DT5 . . . . 187 A4
Longacre Dr BH22 . . . . . . 61 C4
Long Ash La
 Frampton DT2 . . . . 74 A3
 Frome St Quintin DT2 . . . 206 D6
Longbarrow Cl BH8 . . . . . . 91 A1
Long Barrow La DT8 . . . . . 204 B3
Long Bredy Hut La DT2 . . . 103 F2
Longbury Hill La SP8 . . . . . 5 B4
Long Cl
 Winchester SO23 . . . . . . 126 C3
 Yeovil BA21 . . . . 26 E5
Longcroft Rd
 Weymouth DT4 . . . . 167 B3
 Yeovil BA21 . . . . 27 D6
Long Cross SP7 . . . . 12 E3
Longdown Rd DT9 . . . . . . 194 D7
Long Entry DT7 . . . . 96 C5
Longespee Rd BH21 . . . . . 87 E8
Longfield Dr
 Bournemouth BH11 . . . . . 89 A6
 Ferndown BH22 . . . . 89 E8
Longfield Rd DT4 . . . . . . 167 D1
Longfleet CE Comb Sch
 BH15 . . . . 119 D4
Longfleet Rd BH15 . . . . . . 119 E4
Longford Rd DT9 . . . . 194 C7
Longforward Hill TA17 . . . 191 A8
Longforward La TA17 . . . . 191 B8
Long Furlong La BA22 . . . . 193 C8
Longham Bsns Ctr BH22 . . 61 B2
Longhayes Ave DT6 . . . . . 100 B8
Long Hill BA12 . . . . 2 F5
Long La
 Bothenhampton DT6 . . . . 100 F4
 Bourton SP8 . . . . 1 B1
 Cann SP7 . . . . 24 A7
 Colehill BH21 . . . . 51 B1
 Colehill BH21 . . . . 59 E8
 Cucklington BA9 . . . . 4 A1
 Puddletown DT2 . . . . 78 B2
 Ringwood BH24 . . . . 55 D4
 Whitechurch Canonicorum
 DT6 . . . . 65 C7
Longlands La BA22 . . . . . 193 C8
Longland's La
 Littlebredy DT2 . . . . 131 F7
 Winterbourne Abbas DT2 . 105 B1
Longleat Gdns BH25 . . . . . 94 E3
Longman's Rd BH21 . . . . . 201 A3
Long Mdw DT9 . . . . 195 A2
Longmead SP7 . . . . 12 F3
Long Mead BA21 . . . . 26 E5
Longmead Ind Est SP7 . . . . 12 F3
Longmeadow La BH17 . . . 118 E8
Long Rd BH10 . . . . 89 C5
Long's La DT6 . . . . 100 E7
Longspee Sch BH17 . . . . . 119 D7
Long St
 Cerne Abbas DT2 . . . . . 207 D4
 Sherborne DT9 . . . . 30 C6
Longstone Cl DT5 . . . . . . 186 E1
Lonnen Rd
 Wimborne Minster BH21 . . 51 D1
 Wimborne Minster BH21 . . 60 A8
Lonnen Wood Cl BH21 . . . . 60 A8
Lonsdale Rd BH3 . . . . 121 F6
Looke La DT2 . . . . 129 F6
Lopen Rd TA17 . . . . 191 D8
Loraine Ave BH23 . . . . . . 126 C8
Lord Cl BH17 . . . . 119 F7
Lordsmead Rd BA12 . . . . . . 3 B4
Lorne Park Rd BH1 . . . . . . 122 A3
Lorne Rd DT1 . . . . 107 E1
Lornton Wlk **10** DT1 . . . . 135 B8
Lorton La DT3 . . . . 152 B3
Lorton Mdws Nature Reserve
 DT3 . . . . 152 F3
Loscombe Nature Reserve
 DT6 . . . . 204 F1
Lotmoor Hill SP8 . . . . 10 C2
Louise Rd DT1 . . . . 107 E1
Louse La DT11 . . . . 211 E4
Louviers Rd DT3 . . . . 152 E2
Lovage Way **6** BA12 . . . . 3 B6
Love La
 Marnhull DT10 . . . . 21 A4
 Shaftesbury SP7 . . . . 12 D2
Lovelands DT2 . . . . 193 A1
Lovells Mead DT10 . . . . . . 20 E3
Loveridge La **16** TA20 . . 202 A8
Loverley La BH21 . . . . 201 B3
Love's La DT5 . . . . 66 C1
Lowden Cl SO22 . . . . 126 B2
Lower Acreman St DT9 . . . . 30 B5
Lower Ashley Rd BH25 . . . . 95 D2
Lower Beadon TA16 . . . . . 191 E7
Lower Blandford Rd
 Broadstone BH18 . . . . . . 87 B3

Lower Blandford Rd *continued*
Cann SP7 ... 24 A7
Lower Boyston La DT9 ... 16 E3
Lower Brook St SO23 ... 126 E6
Lower Catherston Rd DT6 65 B1
Lower Comm La BH21 ... 53 C7
Lower Comm Rd DT11 ... 36 D1
Lower Coombses TA20 . 202 A8
Lower E Coker Rd BA20 .. 27 B1
Lower Fairmead Rd BA21. 27 F8
Lower Golf Links Rd BH18 87 B5
Lower Gunville [4] DT9 ... 17 D2
Lower Hillside Rd BH20 . 140 A1
Lower Kingsbury DT9 ... 17 D3
Lower North Rd SP5 ... 188 C5
Lower Odcombe BA22 ... 26 A4
Lower Putton La DT3 ... 166 D6
Lower Rd
Stalbridge DT10 ... 33 E7
Toller Porcorum DT2 ... 71 E8
Lower Ream BA21 ... 26 E5
Lower St Alban St [4]
DT4 ... 167 D2
Lower St Edmund St [5]
DT4 ... 167 D2
Lower Sch La [2] DT11 ... 212 C1
Lower Sea La DT6 ... 97 A7
Lower South Rd SP5 ... 188 C4
Lower St
Lillington DT9 ... 194 F7
Merriott TA16 ... 191 F7
Morden BH20 ... 83 C2
Okeford Fitzpaine DT11 ... 197 F6
West Chinnock TA18 ... 192 B8
Witchampton BH21 ... 200 F1
Lower Stanmore La
SO23 ... 126 C3
Lower Steppes BH19 ... 178 C2
Lower Townsend DT6 ... 128 B8
Lower Turners Barn La
BA20 ... 27 B1
Lower Walditch La DT6 .. 100 F6
Lower Way DT3 ... 166 D6
Lower Wraxhill Rd BA20 .. 27 A1
Lowesmore Ct BH14 ... 120 C4
Low's Hill La DT9 ... 29 C5
Lowther Gdns [3] BH8 ... 122 C5
Lowther Rd
Bournemouth BH8 ... 122 B6
Yeovil BA21 ... 28 A7
Lox La SP7 ... 11 E4
Loyd-Lindsay Sq SO22 .. 126 B8
Lubbecke Way DT1 ... 108 C1
Lucas Rd
Poole BH15 ... 119 B1
Poole, Upper Parkstone
BH12 ... 120 C6
Lucerne Ave BH6 ... 123 D5
Lucetta La DT1 ... 135 B8
Luckham Cl BH9 ... 90 B2
Luckham Gdns BH9 ... 90 C2
Luckham Pl BH9 ... 90 B2
Luckham Rd BH9 ... 90 B2
Luckham Rd E BH9 ... 90 B2
Ludbourne Rd DT9 ... 30 C5
Ludlow Rd DT4 ... 166 F2
Ludney La TA17 ... 191 A7
Lufton Manor Coll BA22 .. 26 B7
Lufton Trad Est BA22 ... 26 C7
Lufton Way BA22 ... 26 D6
Lugger Cl DT3 ... 166 C6
Luke St SP7 ... 188 B8
Lulworth Ave BH15 ... 118 E1
Lulworth Castle BH20 ... 158 C1
Lulworth Cl BH15 ... 118 E1
Lulworth Cres BH15 ... 118 E1
Lulworth Ct BH15 ... 118 E2
Lulworth Her Ctr BH20 .. 172 C5
Lulworth Rd BH20 ... 140 B1
Lumber La BH21 ... 201 C5
Lumby Dr BH24 ... 55 D8
Lumby Drive Pk BH24 ... 55 D8
Lupin Way BA22 ... 26 D5
Lurmer St SP7 ... 37 F6
Luscombe Rd BH14 ... 120 C2
Luther Rd BH9 ... 121 F8
Luton Down Rd [3] DT11 . 199 E2
Luton Dro DT11 ... 200 A2
Lyatts Hill BA22 ... 193 A6
Lych Gate Ct BH24 ... 55 E6
Lyde La BA21 ... 28 B6
Lyde Rd BA21 ... 27 F5
Lydford Gdns BH11 ... 89 A2
Lydford Rd BH11 ... 89 A2
Lydfords La SP8 ... 5 D2
Lydgate St [7] DT1 ... 107 C1
Lydlinch Cl BH22 ... 61 D1
Lydwell Cl
Bournemouth BH11 ... 88 F5
Weymouth DT4 ... 180 E8
Lyell Rd BH12 ... 120 C6
Lyewater TA18 ... 191 E4
Lym Cl DT7 ... 96 C5
Lyme Cres BH23 ... 125 F8
Lyme Rd
Crewkerne TA18 ... 191 E3
Lyme Regis DT7 ... 96 A7
Lyme Regis Golf Club
DT7 ... 96 D8
Lyme Regis L Ctr DT7 ... 96 B5
Lyme Regis Marine Aquarium
DT8 ... 96 C4
Lymes Cl [3] DT4 ... 180 C8
Lymington Rd
Christchurch BH23 ... 125 F7
New Milton BH25 ... 95 C1
Lynch Cl
Mere BA12 ... 3 B5

Lynch Cl *continued*
Milborne St Andrew DT11 .. 79 D8
Winchester SO22 ... 126 C8
Lynch La
Hardington Mandeville
BA22 ... 193 A6
Weymouth DT4 ... 166 F2
Lynch La Ind Est DT4 ... 166 E2
Lynch Rd DT4 ... 166 F2
Lyndale Rd DT4 ... 180 D6
Lyndhurst Rd
Bransgore BH23 ... 93 D6
Christchurch BH23 ... 93 D2
Lyndon Ct BH23 ... 91 F1
Lynes La BH24 ... 55 B7
Lynford Ave SO22 ... 126 C8
Lynford Way SO22 ... 126 C8
Lynmoor Rd DT4 ... 167 E6
Lynn Rd BH17 ... 87 F1
Lynric Cl BH25 ... 127 A7
Lynton Cres BH23 ... 91 D3
Lynwood Cl BH22 ... 61 D7
Lynwood Ct SO22 ... 126 D8
Lynwood Dr BH21 ... 87 E8
Lynx Trad Est BA20 ... 26 F3
Lynx West Trading Est
BA20 ... 26 E3
Lyon Ave BH25 ... 95 B3
Lyon Rd BH12 ... 88 E2
Lysander Cl BH23 ... 125 C7
Lysander Rd BA20 ... 26 F3
Lystra Rd BH9 ... 90 A3
Lytchett Dr BH18 ... 86 F2
Lytchett La BH20 ... 140 A4
Lytchett Matravers Prim Sch
BH16 ... 84 C2
Lytchett Minster Sch
BH16 ... 116 F8
Lytchett Way BH16 ... 118 B6
Lytham Rd BH18 ... 87 A3
Lytton Rd BH1,BH8 ... 122 C5

M

Mabey Ave BH10 ... 89 D2
MacAndrew Rd BH13 ... 147 F7
MacAulay Rd BH18 ... 87 A4
McCreery Rd DT9 ... 30 B7
McIntyre Rd BH23 ... 91 A8
McKay Way DT4 ... 166 E2
McKinley Rd BH4 ... 121 C2
Macklin Ho [21] SO22 ... 126 D6
MacLaren Rd BH9 ... 89 F3
Maclean Rd BH11 ... 88 F3
Macville Ave BH20 ... 140 B1
McWilliam Cl BH12 ... 121 C8
McWilliam Rd [2] BH9 ... 90 A2
Madeira Rd
Bournemouth BH1 ... 122 A4
Poole BH14 ... 120 D5
Madeline Cl BH12 ... 120 B7
Madeline Cres BH12 ... 120 B7
Madison Ave BH1 ... 122 D6
Maen Gdns DT1 ... 108 B1
Magdalen Hill SO23 ... 126 F5
Magdalen La
Bridport DT6 ... 100 B6
Christchurch BH23 ... 124 A6
Magdalen Mews [8]
SO23 ... 126 F5
Magiston St DT2 ... 106 D8
Magna Cl
Bournemouth BH11 ... 88 F6
Yeovil BA21 ... 27 F8
Magna Gdns BH11 ... 88 F6
Magna Rd BH21 ... 88 C7
Magnolia Cl
Bournemouth BH6 ... 124 A5
[3] Radipole DT3 ... 152 E2
Verwood BH31 ... 45 E4
Magnolia Dr DT2 ... 75 E3
Magnolia Ho [6] BH10 ... 89 F4
Magpie Cl BH8 ... 90 C3
Magpie Gr BH25 ... 94 F2
Mag's Barrow BH22 ... 61 E2
Maiden Beech Mid Sch
TA18 ... 191 E3
Maiden Castle (Hill Fort)
DT2 ... 134 B6
Maiden Castle Rd DT2 ... 134 C7
Maiden Newton Sta DT2 . 73 A8
Maiden St DT4 ... 167 E2
Maidment Cl BH11 ... 88 E4
Maincombe Cl [2] TA18 .. 191 E3
Main Rd
Fortuneswell DT5 ... 181 C1
Tolpuddle DT2 ... 79 D1
West Lulworth BH20 ... 172 C4
Main St
Bridport DT6 ... 100 E4
Broadmayne DT2 ... 136 B2
Chideock DT6 ... 99 A6
Iwerne Courtney or Shroton
DT11 ... 198 F7
Maitlands The [2] BH2 ... 121 D2
Majorca Mans [4] BH2 ... 121 E3
Major's Comm DT2 ... 208 A7
Malan Cl BH17 ... 119 E8
Malcomb Cl BH6 ... 124 A3
Mallams DT5 ... 186 E7
Mallard Bldgs [6] BH25 ... 95 A3
Mallard Cl
Bournemouth BH8 ... 90 C1
Christchurch BH23 ... 125 A6
Mallard Rd
Bournemouth BH8 ... 90 D1
Wimborne Minster BH21 ... 60 A7

Mallards Gn DT2 ... 133 F7
Mallory Cl BH23 ... 124 F8
Mallow Cl
Broadstone BH18 ... 86 E3
Christchurch BH23 ... 125 C8
Mallows The BH25 ... 95 D4
Malmesbury Ct BH8 ... 122 C6
Malmesbury Gdns SO22 . 126 B8
Malmesbury Park Pl [7]
BH8 ... 122 C5
Malmesbury Park Prim Sch
BH8 ... 122 B5
Malmesbury Park Rd
BH8 ... 122 B6
Malmesbury Rd BH24 ... 54 A3
Malmesbury Way BA21 ... 26 E6
Malmsbury Cl [6] BH23 ... 124 A5
Maloren Way BH22 ... 53 C1
Malta Cl [2] DT1 ... 107 E2
Malthouse [7] BH15 ... 119 C2
Malthouse La DT9 ... 14 F2
Malthouse Mdw DT3 ... 149 F8
Maltings The
Blandford Forum DT11 ... 212 C2
Bournemouth BH11 ... 88 F6
[2] Cerne Abbas DT2 ... 207 D4
[3] Poole BH15 ... 119 E3
Weymouth DT4 ... 167 D1
Malvern Cl BH9 ... 90 A3
Malvern Ct
[4] Bournemouth BH9 ... 90 A2
[2] Christchurch BH23 ... 124 F8
[2] Yeovil BA21 ... 26 F6
Malvern Rd BH9 ... 90 A2
Malvern Terr DT4 ... 167 B2
Mampitts La SP7 ... 13 A2
Mampitts Rd SP7 ... 13 A2
Mandalay Cl BH31 ... 45 A5
Mandale Cl BH11 ... 89 A4
Mandale Rd BH11 ... 88 F3
Mandeville Cl DT4 ... 180 B8
Mandeville Rd DT4 ... 180 B8
Mandeville Stoke La DT6 . 66 B7
Mangerton La DT6 ... 69 A3
Mangerton Water Mill
DT6 ... 69 C4
Mangle Cave Hill TA18 .. 191 C5
Manington Hall [5] BH4 .. 121 C2
Manning Ave BH23 ... 93 C1
Manningford Rd DT11 ... 212 D5
Mannings Heath Rd BH12 88 B1
Mannings Heath Rdbt
BH17 ... 88 B2
Mannings Heath Ret Pk
BH12 ... 120 A8
Mannington Pl [12] BH2 .. 121 E3
Mannington Way BH22 ... 52 F2
Manor Ave
Lyme Regis DT7 ... 96 B6
Poole BH12 ... 88 C1
Manor Cl
Bradford Abbas DT9 ... 28 C2
Dewlish DT2 ... 209 C1
Ferndown BH22 ... 61 E5
[1] Portesham DT3 ... 150 A8
South Perrott DT8 ... 192 C1
Stratton DT2 ... 106 E8
Templecombe BA8 ... 18 D8
[7] Winchester SO23 ... 126 F6
Manor Ct
Ringwood BH24 ... 55 C8
Verwood BH31 ... 45 B6
Manor Dr
[9] Merriott TA16 ... 191 F7
West Coker BA22 ... 193 B8
Manor Farm Cl
Litton Cheney DT2 ... 103 C2
Old Milton BH25 ... 94 F1
Manor Farm Ct DT2 ... 133 D6
Manor Farm Rd
Bere Regis BH20 ... 81 B2
Bournemouth BH10 ... 89 C7
Manor Farmyard BH8 ... 91 B3
Manor Fields DT6 ... 100 E6
Manor Gdns
[12] Beaminster DT8 ... 204 D4
[2] Ringwood BH24 ... 55 B8
Verwood BH31 ... 45 B6
Manor Gr DT2 ... 133 D6
Manor Ho BH18 ... 87 A4
Manor La
Bradford Peverell DT2 ... 106 F5
Verwood BH31 ... 45 B5
Manor Park CE Fst Sch
DT1 ... 135 B8
Manor Pk BH15 ... 119 B5
Manor Rd
Bournemouth BH1 ... 122 C3
Christchurch BH23 ... 124 A6
Dorchester DT1 ... 135 A8
Gussage St Michael BH21 . 200 F6
Mere BA12 ... 2 F7
Milborne Port DT9 ... 17 C3
New Milton BH25 ... 95 B3
Radipole DT3 ... 167 B8
Ringwood BH24 ... 55 C7
Stourpaine DT11 ... 198 F4
Studland BH19 ... 164 D2
Swanage BH19 ... 179 B2
Verwood BH31 ... 45 B6
Yeovil BA20 ... 27 C4
Manorside Comb Sch
BH12 ... 88 D1
Manor St BA22 ... 193 B8
Manor Vale [3] DT8 ... 204 A8
Manor View TA18 ... 191 E3
Manor Way BH31 ... 45 B7
Mansard Ct BH13 ... 147 B3

Manscombe Abbey DT6 .. 66 B2
Mansel Cl BH12 ... 121 C7
Mansfield Ave BH14 ... 120 C4
Mansfield Cl
Ferndown BH22 ... 61 D2
Poole BH14 ... 120 C4
Mansfield Rd
Bournemouth BH9 ... 89 E1
Poole BH14 ... 120 C4
Ringwood BH24 ... 55 B7
Manshay La DT6 ... 203 A1
Manston Rd DT10 ... 35 C2
Manton Cl BH15 ... 118 E3
Manton Rd BH15 ... 118 E3
Manwell Dr BH19 ... 179 A1
Manwell Rd BH19 ... 179 B1
Manwell's La [6] BH19 ... 179 B2
Maple Bsns Pk BH21 ... 60 F7
Maple Cl
Barton on Sea BH25 ... 127 B7
Christchurch BH23 ... 125 F7
[4] Overcombe/Preston
DT3 ... 153 B2
Sandford BH20 ... 143 A8
Shaftesbury SP7 ... 12 F4
Maple Dr
[12] Crewkerne TA18 ... 191 F5
Ferndown BH22 ... 61 C8
Yeovil BA20 ... 27 B3
Maple Gdns DT6 ... 100 D5
Maple Lo BH16 ... 118 C7
Maple Rd
Bournemouth BH9 ... 121 F8
Charminster DT2 ... 75 D2
Poole BH15 ... 119 D3
Maple Way SP8 ... 5 D1
Mapperton Cl BH17 ... 87 F2
Mapperton Hill SP8 ... 2 E1
Mapperton House & Gdns
DT8 ... 204 F2
Mapperton La DT6 ... 69 B8
Mappowder Ct DT10 ... 208 F8
Marabout Cl BH23 ... 124 D7
Marabout Ind Est DT1 ... 107 F2
Marchwood Rd BH10 ... 89 C3
Margards La BH31 ... 45 A5
Margaret Pl DT1 ... 107 E1
Marian Cl BH21 ... 86 C4
Marianne Rd
Poole BH12 ... 121 C8
Wimborne Minster BH21 ... 60 A7
Marian Rd
Corfe Mullen BH21 ... 86 C4
Poole BH21 ... 85 E4
Marie Cl BH12 ... 120 D7
Marie Rd DT1 ... 107 E1
Marina Ct
[2] Bournemouth BH5 ... 122 E3
Christchurch BH23 ... 126 A7
Marina Dr BH14 ... 120 B1
Marina Gdns DT4 ... 167 B1
Marina The BH5 ... 122 E3
Marina Twrs [5] BH5 ... 122 E3
Marina View [1] BH23 ... 124 A5
Marine Ct BH25 ... 126 D7
Marine Dr BH25 ... 126 E7
Marine Dr E BH25 ... 127 A6
Marine Drive W BH25 ... 126 E7
Marine Par DT7 ... 96 B4
Marine Point BH25 ... 126 F7
Marine Prospect BH25 .. 126 F7
Marine Rd BH6 ... 123 D3
Mariners Ct BH23 ... 125 A6
Mariners Dr BH19 ... 179 A2
Mariners Reach BH25 ... 127 A6
Mariners Way DT3 ... 166 D6
Market Cl BH15 ... 119 C2
Market La SO23 ... 126 E5
Market Pl
Blandford Forum DT11 ... 212 D3
Ringwood BH24 ... 55 B7
Sturminster Newton DT10 .. 35 B1
Markets La DT6 ... 101 E3
Market St
Abbotsbury DT3 ... 149 B7
Poole BH15 ... 119 B2
Radipole DT4 ... 167 D2
Winchester SO23 ... 126 E5
Yeovil BA20 ... 27 D5
Market Way BH21 ... 59 D4
Markham Ave
Bournemouth BH10 ... 89 D7
Weymouth DT4 ... 167 B2
Markham Cl BH10 ... 89 D6
Markham Rd BH9 ... 122 A8
Mark's La BH25 ... 95 A6
Marks Rd BH9 ... 89 F3
Marlborough Ave DT4 ... 180 C7
Marlborough Ct
[30] Bournemouth BH4 ... 121 C3
[3] Wimborne Minster BH21 59 C5
Marlborough Mans [2]
BH7 ... 123 B6
Marlborough Pines [25]
BH4 ... 121 C3
Marlborough Pl BH21 ... 59 D5
Marlborough Rd
Bournemouth BH4 ... 121 C3
Poole BH14 ... 120 C4
Yeovil BA21 ... 28 A6
Marl Cl BA21 ... 27 A7
Marler Ho [9] BH4 ... 121 B4
Marley Ave BH25 ... 94 F3
Marley Cl
New Milton BH25 ... 94 F3
Overcombe/Preston DT3 . 153 C1
Marline Rd BH12 ... 120 D6
Marl La DT9 ... 28 D6

Marlott Rd
Gillingham SP8 ... 5 E4
Poole BH15 ... 119 C5
Marlow Dr BH23 ... 91 E3
Marlow Rd DT4 ... 167 D1
Marlpit Dr BH23 ... 94 A2
Marlpit La BH25 ... 95 A8
Marmion Gn BH23 ... 124 F7
Marnhull Rd
Hinton St Mary DT10 ... 35 A5
Poole BH15 ... 119 D4
Marnhull Rise SO22 ... 126 A5
Marpet Cl BH11 ... 88 F6
Marquis Cl DT4 ... 166 F2
Marquis Way BH11 ... 88 D5
Marriage La DT10 ... 35 A6
Marrowbone La DT6 ... 100 E4
Marryat Ct
Christchurch BH23 ... 126 B7
New Milton BH25 ... 94 F3
Marryat Rd BH25 ... 94 F3
Marshall Row [5] BH19 .. 179 C2
Marshallsay Rd DT3 ... 166 D6
Marshal Rd BH17 ... 87 B1
Marsh Athletics Ctr The
DT4 ... 167 B2
Marshfield BH21 ... 59 F7
Marsh Gate DT6 ... 100 D3
Marsh La
Christchurch BH23 ... 91 F2
Hazelbury Bryan DT10 ... 196 F2
Henstridge BA8 ... 19 D5
Ibberton DT11 ... 197 D3
Pen Selwood BA9 ... 1 A4
Upton BH16 ... 118 A7
Wincanton BA9 ... 8 E8
Winterborne Kingston DT11 81 F7
Yeovil BA21 ... 27 E7
Marshlands Cl BH23 ... 124 D6
Marsh Rd DT4 ... 167 C2
Marsh The DT9 ... 194 E3
Marsh Way
[15] Pimperne DT11 ... 199 D4
Swanage BH19 ... 178 F2
Marshwood Ave BH17 ... 87 F3
Marshwood CE Prim Sch
DT6 ... 202 F2
Marshwood Rd [14] DT1 .. 135 B8
Marston Cl
Blandford Forum DT11 ... 212 D5
New Milton BH25 ... 95 B5
Marston Gate [6] SO23 ... 126 E6
Marston Gr BH23 ... 93 E1
Marston Rd
New Milton BH25 ... 95 B5
Poole BH15 ... 119 B2
Sherborne DT9 ... 30 A7
Martel Cl DT2 ... 136 A1
Martello Ho [5] BH13 ... 147 F8
Martello Pk BH13 ... 147 F7
Martello Rd BH13 ... 120 F1
Martello Rd S BH13 ... 147 F8
Martello Twrs BH13 ... 147 F7
Martells The BH25 ... 127 B7
Martin Cl BH17 ... 118 F8
Martindale Ave BH21 ... 60 B5
Martin Down National Nature
Reserve SP5 ... 189 F6
Martin Drove End SP6 .. 190 A7
Martingale Cl BH16 ... 118 D7
Martins Cl BH22 ... 61 E7
Martinscroft Rd [2] DT5 .. 186 E3
Martins Dr BH22 ... 61 E7
Martins Hill Cl BH23 ... 92 C1
Martins Hill La BH23 ... 92 C1
Martin's La SP8 ... 5 C8
Martins Way BH22 ... 61 E7
Martleaves Cl [6] DT4 ... 180 C8
Martyr Cl DT1 ... 134 E7
Marwell Cl BH7 ... 123 A7
Mary Cossins Cl DT11 ... 212 C5
Mary Gdns [4] DT11 ... 197 F6
Mary La BH22 ... 52 F2
Maryland Rd BH16 ... 118 C4
Mary St BA21 ... 27 D5
Maskew Cl DT3 ... 166 D5
Mason's La DT8 ... 204 A4
Masters Ct BH4 ... 121 D3
Masterson Cl BH23 ... 124 D7
Matchams Cl BH24 ... 63 B7
Matchams La BH23 ... 63 B4
Matchams L Pk BH24 ... 54 D2
Matilda Pl [4] SO23 ... 126 E6
Matlock Rd BH22 ... 61 C3
Matthews Rd BA21 ... 27 E5
Maudlin Cross TA20 ... 202 E8
Maudlin La TA20 ... 202 F8
Maud Rd DT1 ... 107 F1
Maumbury Rd DT1 ... 107 F1
Maumbury Rings DT1 ... 135 A8
Maundeville Cres BH23 .. 123 E8
Maundeville Rd BH23 ... 123 E8
Maunsell Ave DT3 ... 153 B1
Maureen Cl BH12 ... 120 B8
Maurice Rd BH8 ... 122 D8
Mavis Rd BH9 ... 90 B1
Max Gate DT1 ... 135 D8
Maxwell Rd
Bournemouth BH9 ... 122 A7
Broadstone BH18 ... 86 E3
Poole BH13 ... 147 F7
Maycroft Rd DT4 ... 167 D1
Mayfair BH4 ... 121 C2
Mayfair Ct BH13 ... 121 B2
Mayfair Gdns BH11 ... 89 A4

Mayfield DT2 . . . . 133 E7
Mayfield Ave BH14 . . . . . 120 E3
Mayfield Cl
  Ferndown BH22 . . . . 61 C6
  Radipole DT4 . . . . 167 A6
Mayfield Dr BH22 . . . . 61 C6
Mayfield Rd
  Bournemouth BH9 . . . . . . 90 A2
  Yeovil BA21 . . . . 27 F6
Mayfield Way BH22 . . . . . 121 C6
Mayford BH12 . . . . 121 B6
May Gdns
  Bournemouth BH11 . . . . . . 88 E4
  Walkford BH23 . . . . 94 B2
May Gr DT11 . . . . 211 D6
May La DT11 . . . . 199 D7
Maylyn Rd
  Beacon Hill BH16 . . . . 86 A2
  Lytchett Minster & Upton
  BH16 . . . . 85 B2
May Terrace Gdns DT3 . 166 D6
May Tree Cl SO22 . . . . . . 126 A2
Mead Ave BA22 . . . . 26 D6
Mead Bower DT5 . . . . 186 E1
Mead Cl BH18 . . . . 87 A1
Mead Fields DT6 . . . . 100 B8
Mead La
  Allington DT6 . . . . 100 A8
  Gussage All Saints BH21 . . . 201 A5
Meadowbank BH16 . . . . . 118 C8
Meadow Bottom DT2 . . . . 106 D8
Meadow Cl
  Bransgore BH23 . . . . 93 A8
  1 Cattistock DT2 . . . . . . 206 C2
  Chickerell DT3 . . . . 166 C5
  Ferndown BH22 . . . . 61 D1
  Henstridge BA8 . . . . 19 A5
  Ringwood BH24 . . . . 55 D8
  Sopley BH23 . . . . 92 B7
  Stalbridge DT10 . . . . 33 D8
Meadow Court Cl BH9 . . . . 90 A3
Meadowcroft **4** SP8 . . . . . 11 A8
Meadow Ct
  2 Bournemouth BH9 . . . . 90 A3
  3 Wimborne Minster BH21 . 59 D4
Meadow Farm La BH21 . . . 86 D8
Meadow Gr BH31 . . . . 45 D5
Meadow La
  Burton BH23 . . . . 92 C2
  Wool BH20 . . . . 140 A2
Meadowland BH23 . . . . . 124 F6
Meadowlands DT6 . . . . . . 100 D2
Meadow Rd
  5 Charlton Marshall
  DT11 . . . . 211 D6
  Langton Long Blandford
  DT11 . . . . 212 E3
  New Milton BH25 . . . . 95 B4
  Ringwood BH24 . . . . 55 D8
  Yeovil BA21 . . . . 27 F7
Meadow Rise BH18 . . . . . . 86 F5
Meadows Cl BH16 . . . . . . 118 C7
Meadows Dr
  8 Upton BH16 . . . . 117 E7
  Upton BH16 . . . . 118 C7
Meadowside **4** DT8 . . . . 204 A7
Meadows The
  Bourton SP8 . . . . 1 F2
  3 Gillingham SP8 . . . . . . 11 A8
Meadowsweet Rd BH17 . . 118 E8
Meadow Vale DT2 . . . . . . 196 B3
Meadow View
  5 Blandford Forum
  DT11 . . . . 212 D3
  Bradford Peverell DT2 . . . 107 A6
  Cattistock DT2 . . . . 206 B2
  Charminster DT2 . . . . 107 D6
  East Coker BA22 . . . . 193 C8
  7 Stofold BA22 . . . . 193 F8
Meadow View Cl BH20 . . 142 F3
Meadow View Rd
  Bournemouth BH11 . . . . . . 88 E4
  Radipole DT4 . . . . 152 C4
Meadow Way
  Barton on Sea BH25 . . . . 127 A7
  Charmouth DT6 . . . . 97 B7
  Ringwood BH24 . . . . 55 D8
  Verwood BH31 . . . . 45 C4
  Winchester SO22 . . . . . . 126 A2
Mead Rd
  Corfe Castle BH20 . . . . . 177 A7
  Radipole DT4 . . . . 167 A6
  Winchester SO23 . . . . . . 126 C2
Meads Cl DT2 . . . . 194 A2
Meads The DT9 . . . . 17 D2
Mead The BA8 . . . . 19 B3
Meadus's La BH20 . . . . . . 162 D3
Meadway **4** DT6 . . . . . . 100 B2
Meadway The BH23 . . . . . . 93 D2
Medbourne Cl DT11 . . . . 212 C5
Medina Way BH23 . . . . . . 125 C6
Medlar Cl BH23 . . . . 92 D1
Medway Dr DT3 . . . . 168 B8
Medway Rd BH22 . . . . 62 A6
Meech Cl DT6 . . . . 100 D4
Meech Way DT2 . . . . 75 E2
Meerhay La DT6 . . . . 65 A4
Meerhay Manor DT8 . . . . 204 D5
Meeting House La BH24 . . 55 B7
Melancholy La BH20 . . . . 142 E1
Melbourne Rd
  Bournemouth BH8 . . . . . . 122 C6
  Christchurch BH23 . . . . . . 91 E1
Melbourne St DT4 . . . . . . 167 B3
Melbury Abbas Mill SP7 . . 24 B6

Melbury Ave BH12 . . . . . 120 E7
Melbury Cl BH22 . . . . 61 D4
Melbury House DT2 . . . . . 194 A1
Melbury Pk DT2 . . . . 194 A1
Melbury Rd
  Weymouth DT4 . . . . 167 C3
  Yetminster DT9 . . . . 194 C5
Melbury St SP7 . . . . 24 C4
Melbury Way SP7 . . . . 13 A3
Melchester Cl **2** SP8 . . . . 5 E4
Melcombe Ave DT4 . . . . . 167 E5
Melcombe Horsey DT2 . . 208 F5
Melford St BH1 . . . . 122 A3
Mellstock Ave DT1 . . . . . 135 A7
Mellstock Cl DT11 . . . . . 212 F6
Mellstock Cres BH20 . . . 142 D5
Mellstock Rd BH15 . . . . . 119 D5
Melplash Ct DT6 . . . . 204 D1
Melrose Ct BH25 . . . . 95 C3
Melrose Rd BA21 . . . . 27 D6
Melstock Ave DT3 . . . . . . 168 A7
Melstock Rd SP8 . . . . 5 E4
Melton Ct
  Poole BH13 . . . . 120 F4
  14 Poole BH13 . . . . 121 A4
Melverley Gdns BH21 . . . . 59 D5
Melville Rd BH9 . . . . 121 E8
Melway Gdns **11** DT11 . . 198 C7
Melway La DT11 . . . . 198 C7
Memorial Ave **19** TA18 . . 191 F4
Memorial Rd BA22 . . . . . . 26 D6
Mendip Cl
  New Milton BH25 . . . . 95 B2
  Verwood BH31 . . . . 45 B5
Mendip Ct **4** BH23 . . . . 124 F8
Mendip Rd BH31 . . . . 45 B6
Menin Rd BH20 . . . . 139 C6
Mentone Rd **2** BH14 . . . 120 A3
Meon Ho SO23 . . . . 126 F4
Meon Rd BH7 . . . . 123 B7
Mercery Rd DT3 . . . . 167 C7
Merchants Pl **19** SO23 . . 126 E6
Mere By-pass BA12 . . . . 2 F6
Mere Castle BA12 . . . . 2 F6
Meredith Cl
  Christchurch BH23 . . . . . 124 D7
  Halstock BA22 . . . . 193 C3
Mere Sch BA12 . . . . 3 B5
Merevale Way BA21 . . . . . 26 E7
Meriden Cl BH31 . . . . 147 F7
Meriden St **11** SO23 . . . 126 E8
Meridians The BH23 . . . . 123 F6
Merino Way BH22 . . . . 53 B1
Merlewood Cl BH2 . . . . . 121 F4
Merlewood Ct **9** BH25 . . 95 B3
Merley Court Touring Pk
  BH21 . . . . 59 C1
Merley Dr BH23 . . . . 126 A8
Merley Fst Sch BH21 . . . . . 59 D1
Merley Gdns BH21 . . . . . . 59 E1
Merley Ho BH21 . . . . 59 B1
Merley House Holiday Pk
  BH21 . . . . 59 B1
Merley House La BH21 . . . 59 C1
Merley La BH21 . . . . 59 E1
Merley Park Rd
  Ashington BH21 . . . . 87 B8
  Corfe Mullen BH21 . . . . . . 86 F8
  Merley BH21 . . . . 59 C1
Merley Rd DT4 . . . . 180 E4
Merley Ways BH21 . . . . . . 59 D2
Merlin Ave N DT3 . . . . . . 152 B3
Merlin Ave S DT3 . . . . . . 152 B3
Merlin Cl BH24 . . . . 55 E6
Merlin Way BH23 . . . . . . 125 A5
Mermaid Ct **3** BH5 . . . . 122 E3
Mermond Pl BH19 . . . . . . 179 C2
Merredin Cl DT3 . . . . 152 D3
Merriefield Ave BH18 . . . . 87 B5
Merriefield Cl BH18 . . . . . 87 B6
Merriefield Dr BH18 . . . . . 87 B6
Merrifield BH21 . . . . 59 E8
Merriott Fst Sch TA16 . . . 191 F7
Merriott Rd
  Hinton St George TA17 . . 191 D7
  Merriott TA18 . . . . 191 F6
Merritown La BH23 . . . . . . 90 D7
Merrivale Ave BH6 . . . . . 123 E5
Merrow Ave BH12 . . . . . . 121 B7
Merrow Chase **1** BH13 . . 147 F7
Merryfield Cl
  Bransgore BH23 . . . . 93 A8
  Verwood BH31 . . . . 45 B7
Merryfield La BH10 . . . . . . 89 C4
Merryfield La BH10 . . . . . . 89 C4
Merryweather Est **6**
  BH24 . . . . 55 E8
Merton Ct
  2 Christchurch BH23 . . 126 E7
  3 Poole BH15 . . . . 119 E4
Merville Gdns BH9 . . . . . 121 F8
Methuen Cl **2** BH8 . . . . 122 C5
Methuen Rd
  Bournemouth BH8 . . . . . . 122 B5
  Poole BH17 . . . . 87 B2
Mews La SO22 . . . . 126 D5
Mews The
  Bournemouth BH2 . . . . . 121 D3
  Verwood BH31 . . . . 45 C4
Meyrick Cl BH23 . . . . 93 A7
Meyrick Park Cres BH3 . . 121 F6
Meyrick Park Mans **7**
  BH2 . . . . 121 F4
Meyrick Rd BH1 . . . . 122 B5
Michelgrove Rd BH5 . . . . 122 E3
Michelmersh Gn BH8 . . . . 90 D2
Mickleham Cl BH12 . . . . . 121 B8

Middlebere Cres BH16 . . 118 C4
Middlebere Dr BH20 . . . . 142 D6
Middle Brook BH11 . . . . . . 89 A6
Middle Brook St SO23 . . . 126 E6
Middle Farm Way DT1 . . . 107 D1
Middlefield BH20 . . . . . . 141 B8
Middlefield La TA13 . . . . 191 F8
Middle Field La DT9 . . . . . 15 D5
Middle Gn **1** DT8 . . . . . 204 D4
Middlehill Dr BH21 . . . . . . 60 B6
Middlehill Rd BH21 . . . . . . 60 A6
Middle La
  Martin SP6 . . . . 190 A7
  Ringwood BH24 . . . . 55 C7
Middlemarsh St DT1 . . . . 107 D1
Middle Path TA18 . . . . . . 191 E4
Middle Rd
  Bournemouth BH10 . . . . . . 89 C5
  Lytchett Matravers BH16 . . 84 B2
  Poole BH15 . . . . 119 E6
  Sturminster Marshall BH21 . 56 E3
  Tiptoe SO41 . . . . 95 E8
  Winchester SO22 . . . . . . 126 C6
Middle St
  Bridport DT6 . . . . 69 A1
  Burton Bradstock DT6 . . . 128 B8
  Crewkerne TA18 . . . . 192 A3
  Dewlish DT2 . . . . 209 C1
  Rimpton BA22 . . . . 15 B8
  Yeovil BA20 . . . . 27 D4
Middleton Mews BH25 . . . 94 F1
Middleton Rd
  Bournemouth BH9 . . . . . . 89 C2
  Ringwood BH24 . . . . 55 C8
Midland Rd BH9 . . . . 89 F1
Midleaze DT9 . . . . 29 E5
Midney La BH20 . . . . 4 B8
Midway Path BH13 . . . . . 147 C3
Midwood Ave BH8 . . . . . . 90 F1
Milborne Cres BH12 . . . . 120 E8
Milborne Fst Sch DT11 . . . 79 E8
Milborne Port Prim Sch
  DT9 . . . . 17 D2
Milbourne Rd BH20 . . . . . 61 C6
Milburn Cl **3** BH4 . . . . 121 C4
Milburn La DT9 . . . . 196 A7
Milburn Rd BH4 . . . . 121 B4
Mildenhall **5** BH2 . . . . 121 D2
Mildmay Ct **2** SO23 . . . 126 F5
Mildmay St SO22 . . . . . . 126 B3
Miles Ave BH20 . . . . 142 F8
Miles Gdns DT3 . . . . 152 B5
Milestone Rd BH15 . . . . . 119 D5
Milestone Way SP8 . . . . . . 5 D1
Military La DT10 . . . . . . 197 A4
Milland Rd SO23 . . . . . . 126 F4
Millbank Ho **5** BH21 . . . 59 C5
Millbrook BA20 . . . . 27 C4
Millbrook Cl **2** DT11 . . 198 C8
Millbrook Ct **3** DT11 . . 198 C8
Mill Cl BH22 . . . . 193 C8
Milldown CE Fst Sch
  DT11 . . . . 212 C5
Milldown CE Mid Sch
  DT11 . . . . 212 B5
Milldown Rd DT11 . . . . . 212 B6
Mill End SP6 . . . . 190 F2
Miller Cl BH25 . . . . 95 C4
Miller Rd BH23 . . . . 124 D7
Millers Ct DT3 . . . . 153 C1
Miller's Cl DT1 . . . . 107 E3
Miller's Hill DT9 . . . . 17 A5
Miller's La
  Farnham DT11 . . . . 200 D8
  Sixpenny Handley DT11 . . 188 D1
Millfield
  New Milton BH25 . . . . 94 E3
  Poole BH17 . . . . 119 A7
Mill Gn DT7 . . . . 96 C5
Mill Ham Island Nature
  Reserve DT11 . . . . 198 B7
Millhams Cl BH10 . . . . . . 89 B6
Millhams Dr BH10 . . . . . . 89 B6
Millhams Rd BH10 . . . . . . 89 B6
Millhams St BH23 . . . . . . 124 B6
Millhams Street N **2**
  BH23 . . . . 124 B6
Mill Hill Cl BH14 . . . . . . 120 B3
Mill Hollow La SP7 . . . . . . 24 B6
Mill House Cider Mus
  DT2 . . . . 137 C3
Mill La
  Bourton SP8 . . . . 1 E2
  Bradford Abbas DT9 . . . . . 28 D1
  Cann SP7 . . . . 24 A6
  Cattistock DT2 . . . . 206 B2
  4 Cerne Abbas DT2 . . . 207 D4
  Charminster DT2 . . . . . . 107 D7
  Chetnole DT9 . . . . 194 D4
  Chideock DT6 . . . . 99 A4
  Christchurch BH23 . . . . . 126 B8
  Cranborne BH21 . . . . 40 C6
  Crewkerne TA18 . . . . 191 F3
  Durweston DT11 . . . . . . 198 E3
  East Coker BA22 . . . . . . 193 C7
  Halstock BA22 . . . . 193 C3
  Hawkchurch EX13 . . . . . . 202 C3
  Hurn BH23 . . . . 91 B6
  Ibberton DT11 . . . . 197 D3

Mill La continued
  Kingstone LA17 . . . . 191 B3
  Lyme Regis DT7 . . . . 96 A7
  Lyme Regis DT7 . . . . 96 C5
  Marnhull DT10 . . . . 20 E4
  Mere BA12 . . . . 3 B5
  Misterton TA18 . . . . 192 B3
  Poole BH14 . . . . 120 B3
  Shapwick DT11 . . . . 56 E6
  Silton SP8 . . . . 1 F2
  Stour Provost SP8 . . . . . . 21 C7
  Stratton DT2 . . . . 106 E8
  Symondsbury DT6 . . . . . . 99 F8
  Trent DT9 . . . . 14 E1
  Wareham BH20 . . . . 142 E4
  West Coker BA22 . . . . . . 193 B8
  Wimborne Minster BH21 . . 59 C5
  Winterbourne Abbas DT2 . 132 F8
  Wootton Fitzpaine DT6 . . . 64 D4
  Yeovil BA20 . . . . 27 D4
  Yetminster DT9 . . . . 194 C5
Mill Rd
  Bournemouth BH8 . . . . . . 122 A6
  Milborne St Andrew DT11 . 79 E8
  Poole BH14 . . . . 120 D3
  Weymouth DT4 . . . . 167 C3
  Wimborne Minster BH21 . . 59 C6
Mill Rd BH8 . . . . 90 E3
Mill Rd S BH8 . . . . 90 D3
Mill Rise SP8 . . . . 1 E2
Mills Rd DT3 . . . . 169 C8
Mill St
  Blandford Forum DT11 . . 212 C3
  Burton Bradstock DT6 . . . 128 B7
  Dorchester DT1 . . . . 108 B2
  Fontmell Magna SP7 . . . . . 37 F6
  Puddletown DT2 . . . . 78 B1
  Radipole DT3 . . . . 152 B4
  Rimpton BA22 . . . . 15 B8
  Sleight BA21 . . . . 58 A1
Mills The BH12 . . . . 120 E7
Millstream Cl
  Poole BH17 . . . . 119 A7
  Wimborne Minster BH21 . . 59 C4
Millstream Trad Est BH24 . 55 D5
Millyford Cl BH25 . . . . . . 126 D8
Milman Ct **12** SO23 . . . 126 E6
Milne Rd BH17 . . . . 87 B1
Milner Pl SO22 . . . . 126 C4
Milner Rd BH4 . . . . 121 C1
Milnthorpe La SO22 . . . . 126 C5
Milom La DT6 . . . . 67 B1
Milton Abbey Sch DT11 . 209 E5
Milton Bsns Ctr BH25 . . . . 94 E2
Milton Cl
  Poole BH14 . . . . 120 D3
  Radipole DT4 . . . . 167 D6
  Yeovil BA21 . . . . 26 E6
Milton Cres DT3 . . . . 167 C6
Milton Ct BH22 . . . . 61 D5
Milton Gr BH25 . . . . 95 B2
Milton House BA21 . . . . . 14 B3
Milton La DT11 . . . . 198 D2
Milton Mead BH25 . . . . . . 94 F2
Milton on Stour CE Prim Sch
  SP8 . . . . 5 E6
Milton Rd
  Bournemouth BH8 . . . . . . 122 A6
  Poole BH14 . . . . 120 D3
  Weymouth DT4 . . . . 167 C3
  Wimborne Minster BH21 . . 59 C6
Milton Terr DT4 . . . . 167 D6
Milton Villas BH8 . . . . . . 122 A5
Milvers La DT6 . . . . 101 B3
Milverton Cl BH23 . . . . . . 93 E1
Milverton Rd SO22 . . . . . 126 C6
Mimosa Ave BH21 . . . . . . 87 E8
Minden Way SO22 . . . . . 126 A3
Minerva Cl SO22 . . . . . . 126 A3
Minstead Rd BH10 . . . . . . 89 C3
Minster La **3** SO23 . . . 126 E5
Minster The BH21 . . . . . . 59 B4
Minster View BH21 . . . . . . 59 C5
Minster Way BH16 . . . . . 118 B7
Minterne Gdns DT2 . . . . 207 D6
Minterne Grange BH14 . . 147 C7
Minterne Rd
  3 Bournemouth BH9 . . . 90 A2
  Christchurch BH23 . . . . . 124 E5
  Poole BH14 . . . . 147 C7
Minters Ct **28** SO23 . . . 126 D6
Minton Mews BH2 . . . . . 121 F5
Minton Pl **1** DT4 . . . . . 167 C4
Mission Hall La DT3 . . . . 153 D2
Mission La BH18 . . . . 87 A2
Mission Rd BH18 . . . . 87 A2
Misterton Sch TA18 . . . . 192 A4
Mistover Cl DT1 . . . . 135 A7
Mistover Rd BH20 . . . . . . 142 D5
Mitchell Cl BH25 . . . . . . 127 A7
Mitchell Rd
  Ferndown BH21 . . . . 61 A7
  Poole BH17 . . . . 119 F8
Mitchell St **1** DT7 . . . . 167 E2
Mitchelmore Rd BA21 . . . 27 D6
Mithras DT11 . . . . 134 E8
Mitre Ct **5** BH23 . . . . . 124 A7
Mixen La **15** DT1 . . . . . 135 B8
Miz Maze DT9 . . . . 194 F3
Moat Ct BH4 . . . . 121 C5
Moat La BH25 . . . . 126 F8
Moats Cotts DT2 . . . . . . 209 C1
Mockbeggar La BH24 . . . . 47 C7
Moffat Rd BH23 . . . . 124 D7
Mohune Way DT3 . . . . . . 166 D5
Mohuns Pk BA8 . . . . 19 C7
Molyneux Rd BH25 . . . . . . 95 D3
Monaco Ct BH9 . . . . 122 B8
Monarch Cl **29** BH4 . . . 121 C3
Monarch Way SO22 . . . . 126 A4
Moneyfly Rd BH31 . . . . . . 45 D5
Monk Barton Cl BA21 . . . . 26 E7

Monkey World Ape Rescue
  Ctr BH20 . . . . 140 B6
Monks Cl BH22 . . . . 62 A8
Monks Dale BA21 . . . . 26 F7
Monkshood Cl BH23 . . . . . 93 B1
Monks Rd SO23 . . . . 126 E7
Monks Way BH11 . . . . 88 D5
Monkswell Gn BH23 . . . . 124 D6
Monkton Cl BH22 . . . . 61 D6
Monkton Cres BH12 . . . . 120 E8
Monkton Down Rd **5**
  DT11 . . . . 199 E2
Monkton Hill DT2 . . . . . . 134 E5
Monkton Wyld Cross DT6 . 64 A7
Monkton Wyld La DT6 . . . 64 C5
Monkwood La DT6 . . . . . 203 E2
Monkworthy Dr BH24 . . . . 54 B5
Monmouth Ave DT3 . . . . 167 D7
Monmouth Cl BH31 . . . . . 45 D4
Monmouth Dr BH31 . . . . . 45 D4
Monmouth Rd
  Dorchester DT1 . . . . 108 B1
  Wareham BH20 . . . . 142 D3
  Yeovil BA21 . . . . 27 F7
Monmouth St **5** DT7 . . . 96 C5
Monnington La **6** DT1 . . 107 C2
Monsal Ave BH22 . . . . 61 C3
Mons The **17** SO23 . . . . 126 D6
Montacute Sch BH17 . . . . 87 C2
Montacute Way DT1 . . . . . 87 E8
Montague Rd BH5 . . . . . . 123 B4
Montagu Pk BH23 . . . . . . 126 A7
Montagu Rd BH23 . . . . . . 126 B8
Monteray Dr SO41 . . . . . . 95 F4
Montgomery Ave BH11 . . . 89 B3
Montgomery Cl SO22 . . . 126 A3
Montrose Cl
  1 Easton/Weston DT5 . . 186 F4
  Verwood BH31 . . . . 45 B6
Montrose Dr BH10 . . . . . . 89 B2
Montrose Rd BA21 . . . . . . 28 A7
Moonrakers Way BH23 . . . 93 E1
Moorcombe Dr DT3 . . . . 153 B1
Moorcroft Ave BH23 . . . . 92 C2
Moordown Ave DT3 . . . . 167 F8
Moordown Cl BH9 . . . . 90 A4
Moordown St John's CE Prim
  Sch BH9 . . . . 89 F1
Moore Ave BH11 . . . . 89 A4
Moore Cl BH25 . . . . 94 F1
Moorfield Gr BH9 . . . . 89 F2
Moorfield Rd DT5 . . . . . . 187 A4
Moorfields Rd BH13 . . . . 147 F8
Moorhaven BH22 . . . . 61 D6
Moorhills **2** BH21 . . . . . 59 D4
Moorings Cl BH15 . . . . . . 118 F1
Moorings The **2** BH23 . . 124 A5
Moor La
  Broadwindsor DT8 . . . . . 203 B6
  Buckhorn Weston SP8 . . . . 4 D1
  East Coker BA22 . . . . . . 193 D7
  Hardington Mandeville
  BA22 . . . . 193 A7
  Sturminster Marshall BH21 . 56 E3
Moorland Ave BH25 . . . . 126 F8
Moorland Cres BH16 . . . . 118 B7
Moorland Gate BH24 . . . . 55 C5
Moorland Par BH16 . . . . . 118 B7
Moorland Rd BH1 . . . . . . 122 D4
Moorlands Coll BH23 . . . . 92 B6
Moorlands Rd
  Ferndown BH22 . . . . 53 A3
  Merriott TA18 . . . . 191 E6
  Verwood BH31 . . . . 45 B7
Moorlands Rise BH22 . . . . 53 B3
Moorland Way BH16 . . . . 118 B7
Moorlea **2** BH8 . . . . . . 122 B6
Moor Rd
  Broadstone BH18 . . . . 87 B5
  Swanage BH19 . . . . 179 B5
Moors Cl BH23 . . . . 91 B7
Moor Side BH24 . . . . 62 B8
Moorside Ave DT4 . . . . . 167 E7
Moorside Cl BH11 . . . . . . 89 B3
Moorside Gdns BH11 . . . . 89 B3
Moorside Rd
  Bournemouth BH11 . . . . . 89 B3
  Corfe Mullen BH21 . . . . . 86 D5
  Ferndown BH22 . . . . 53 A2
Moors Valley Ctry Pk
  BH24 . . . . 46 B1
Moor The DT2 . . . . 78 B2
Moortown Dr
  Bournemouth BH21 . . . . . 88 B8
  Wimborne Minster BH21 . . 60 B1
Moortown Farm BH21 . . . . 88 B8
Moortown House BH24 . . . 55 C5
Moortown La BH24 . . . . . . 55 D4
Moorvale Rd BH9 . . . . 90 A2
Moor View Rd BH15 . . . . 119 E6
Moorway La DT9 . . . . 15 E4
Morant Ct **4** BH25 . . . . 95 B3
Moraston St **4** DT1 . . . 107 C2
Moray Ct **11** BH21 . . . . . 59 B5
Morden Ave BH22 . . . . . . 61 C4
Morden Bog National Nature
  Reserve BH20 . . . . 115 D2
Morden La BH20 . . . . 82 D3
Morden Park Cnr BH20 . . 115 C8
Morden Rd
  Bournemouth BH9 . . . . . . 89 E1
  Wareham St Martin BH20 . 115 D3
Morestead Rd SO23 . . . . 126 F2
Moreton Dr
  Moreton DT2 . . . . 138 F8
  Turners Puddle DT2 . . . . 112 B2

Moreton House Gdns DT2 . . . 138 F7
Moreton Rd
Bournemouth BH9 . . . 90 B4
Crossways DT2 . . . 137 E5
Moreton Sta DT2 . . . 137 F7
Morgan's La SP5 . . . 189 E5
Moriconium Quay BH15 . 118 D1
Morington Ct 8 BH8 . . . 122 A5
Morley Cl
Bournemouth BH5 . . . 123 A5
Burton BH23 . . . 92 C3
Morley Rd BH5 . . . 123 A5
Morley Way BH22 . . . 61 F3
Mornington Dr SO22 . . . 126 A8
Mornish Rd BH13 . . . 120 F2
Morrison Ave BH12 . . . 120 F6
Morrison Rd BH19 . . . 179 A2
Morris Rd
Poole BH17 . . . 119 D8
Wool BH20 . . . 139 F6
Morston DT9 . . . 194 D8
Mortain Cl DT11 . . . 212 D5
Mortimer Cl BH23 . . . 125 A6
Mortimer Rd BH8 . . . 90 B1
Mossley Ave
Poole BH12 . . . 121 A8
Poole BH12 . . . 89 A1
Moss Rd SO23 . . . 126 F6
Mosterton Down La DT8 . 192 A1
Motcombe CE VA Prim Sch SP7 . . . 12 B7
Motcombe Park Sports Ctr SP7 . . . 12 B6
Motcombe Rd
Poole BH13 . . . 121 A2
Shaftesbury SP7 . . . 12 E3
Mountain Ash Rd 4 DT1 107 E2
Mount Ave BH25 . . . 95 A1
Mountbatten Cl
Christchurch BH23 . . . 125 A5
Weymouth DT4 . . . 180 B8
Mountbatten Ct BH25 . . . 94 F3
Mountbatten Dr BH22 . . . 61 C5
Mountbatten Gdns BH8 . . 90 F2
Mountbatten Rd BH13 . . . 121 B1
Mount Cl BH25 . . . 95 A1
Mounters Cl DT10 . . . 20 E1
Mount Grace Dr BH14 . . . 147 D7
Mount Heatherbank 7 BH1 . . . 121 F3
Mount Joy DT6 . . . 100 D3
Mountjoy Cl BH21 . . . 59 F2
Mountjoy Specl Sch DT6 . . . 100 D4
Mount La DT6 . . . 99 F3
Mount Pleasant
Bridport DT6 . . . 100 C7
Christchurch BH23 . . . 125 A5
East Lulworth BH20 . . . 158 E1
Ringwood BH24 . . . 55 C7
Wareham Town BH20 . . . 142 E4
Yeovil BA21 . . . 27 E5
Mount Pleasant Ave N DT3 . . . 167 B8
Mount Pleasant Ave S DT3 . . . 167 C7
Mount Pleasant Bsns Pk DT3 . . . 167 C8
Mount Pleasant Dr BH8 . . 90 F1
Mount Pleasant La 3 BH19 . . . 179 C2
Mount Pleasant Rd BH15 . . . 119 D3
Mount Rd
Bournemouth BH11 . . . 89 B4
Poole BH14 . . . 120 B5
Mount Scar BH19 . . . 179 B1
Mount Skippet Way DT2 137 D5
Mount The
6 Blandford Forum DT11 . . . 212 D3
Ringwood BH24 . . . 55 E8
Mower La DT11 . . . 37 A5
Mowes La DT10 . . . 34 F8
Mowleaze 1 BA22 . . . 193 F8
Mowlem Theatre BH19 . . 179 C2
Moyles Court Sch BH24 . . 47 E6
Moynton Cl DT2 . . . 137 D6
Moynton Rd 6 DT1 . . . 135 B8
Muchelney Way BA21 . . . 26 E7
Muckleford Nature Reserve DT2 . . . 106 C7
Muddox Barrow La BH20 . 81 B5
Muddyford La DT6 . . . 98 D7
Mudeford Com Inf Sch BH23 . . . 124 E6
Mudeford Green Cl BH23 . . . 124 F5
Mudeford Jun Sch BH23 124 F6
Mudeford La BH23 . . . 124 F6
Mude Gdns BH23 . . . 125 A5
Mudford Rd BA21 . . . 27 D7
Mudros Rd DT11 . . . 199 E3
Mulberry Cl SP8 . . . 5 F2
Mulberry Ct
4 Christchurch BH23 . . . 124 A7
1 Sixpenny Handley SP5 . 189 B4
Mulberry Gdns
Charminster DT2 . . . 75 D2
16 Crewkerne TA18 . . . 191 F4
Fordingbridge SP6 . . . 43 A8
Mullins Cl BH12 . . . 121 C8
Munden's La DT9 . . . 31 B1
Munster Rd BH14 . . . 120 D3
Murley Rd BH9 . . . 122 A8
Murray-Smith Dr BA22 . . . 26 C6
Musbury Cl DT10 . . . 20 E4
Musbury La DT10 . . . 20 E4
Muscliffe La BH9 . . . 90 B5
Muscliffe Rd
Bournemouth BH9 . . . 121 F8
Bournemouth BH9 . . . 89 F1
Muscliff Prim Sch BH9 . . . 90 C4
Musgrave Pl 4 DT4 . . . 167 E4
Mus of Electricity BH23 . 124 B7
Muston La DT11 . . . 82 A8
Mustons La 4 SP7 . . . 12 E3
Mutton St DT6 . . . 203 A1
Myrtle Cl
10 Beaminster DT8 . . . 204 C4
Hordle SO41 . . . 95 F4
Myrtle Rd BH8 . . . 122 C6

N

Nada Rd BH23 . . . 93 D1
Nag's La TA18 . . . 191 B1
Nairn Ct BH3 . . . 121 E7
Nairn Rd
Bournemouth BH3 . . . 121 E6
Poole BH13 . . . 147 E7
Naish Rd BH25 . . . 126 E7
Nallers La DT2 . . . 102 E6
Namu Rd BH9 . . . 89 E1
Nansen Ave BH15 . . . 119 D5
Nantillo St 11 DT1 . . . 107 D1
Napier Rd BH15 . . . 118 C3
Napiers Way DT11 . . . 37 E4
Narrow La BH24 . . . 47 F1
Naseby Rd BH9 . . . 90 A2
Nash La
Chillington TA17 . . . 191 A6
Marnhull DT10 . . . 21 A3
Marshwood DT6 . . . 202 E2
Yeovil BA20 . . . 26 F1
Nathan Cl BA20 . . . 26 F2
Nathen Gdns BH15 . . . 118 D3
Nations Rd SP8 . . . 10 B6
Navarac Ct BH14 . . . 120 C3
Nea Cl BH23 . . . 125 D8
Neacroft Cl BH25 . . . 126 D8
Nea Dr BH24 . . . 46 E4
Neal's La DT9 . . . 194 D2
Nea Rd BH23 . . . 125 E8
Neathem Rd BA21 . . . 27 E7
Neighbourhood Ctr BH17. 87 E2
Nelson Cl BH25 . . . 94 F3
Nelson Ct 13 BH15 . . . 119 C2
Nelson Dr BH23 . . . 124 F6
Nelson Rd
Poole BH4,BH12 . . . 121 B4
Tarrant Monkton DT11 . . . 199 F3
Nether Abber Village BA22 . . . 14 D7
Netherby La DT8 . . . 204 A3
Nethercliffe Sch SO22 . . . 126 C7
Nethercoombe La DT9 . . . 30 A7
Netherhall Gdns BH4 . . . 121 C3
Netherhay La DT8 . . . 203 C8
Nether Mead 1 DT11 . . . 197 F6
Netherstoke La BA22 . . . 193 C3
Netherton La BA22 . . . 193 F6
Netherton Rd
Weymouth DT4 . . . 167 D1
Yeovil BA21 . . . 27 F7
Netherton St 5 DT1 . . . 107 C1
Netherwood Pl BH21 . . . 59 A5
Netley 3 BA21 . . . 26 F6
Netley Cl BH15 . . . 120 A7
Netmead La 3 DT11 . . . 198 B8
Nettlebed Nursery SP7 . . . 12 E3
Nettlecombe SP7 . . . 13 A3
Nettleton Cl BH17 . . . 119 E7
New Barn Rd DT3 . . . 149 D4
Newberry Gdns 8 DT4 . . 167 E2
Newberry Rd DT4 . . . 167 D2
Newbery La TA18 . . . 192 A3
New Bond St DT4 . . . 167 D3
New Borough Rd BH21 . . . 59 D3
Newburgh St SO23 . . . 126 D6
Newbury SP8 . . . 6 A1
Newbury Dr BH10 . . . 89 D1
Newchester Cross TA16 . 191 E7
New Cl
Bourton SP8 . . . 1 E2
Haselbury Plucknett TA18 . 192 B5
New Close Gdns DT4 . . . 167 D1
Newcombe La DT2 . . . 108 E3
Newcombe Rd
Bournemouth BH6 . . . 123 E5
Ferndown BH22 . . . 53 A3
New Cotts BH21 . . . 60 E2
Newcroft Gdns BH23 . . . 124 A8
Newcross DT9 . . . 195 B8
New Cross Gate DT11 . . . 198 A7
New Cut BA12 . . . 3 A6
Newell DT9 . . . 30 A6
New Field La DT11 . . . 198 D8
Newfield Rd DT11 . . . 199 D5
New Fields Bsns Pk BH17 . . . 119 D8
Newfoundland Cl BH19 . . 183 D8
Newfoundland Dr BH15 . 119 D2
Newfoundland Drive Rdbt BH15 . . . 119 D1
New Gd DT5 . . . 187 A7
New Harbour Rd BH15 . . 119 B1
New Harbour Rd S
Poole BH15 . . . 146 B8
Upton BH15 . . . 145 D8
New Harbour Road W BH15 . . . 119 A1
Newhaven DT2 . . . 105 E1
New Inn St 2 DT6 . . . 204 C2
New La
Bashley BH25 . . . 94 F6
Cann SP7 . . . 13 B1
Caundle Marsh DT9 . . . 195 E8
Haselbury Plucknett TA18 . 192 C6
Morden BH20 . . . 83 C3
Motcombe SP7 . . . 12 B8
Stour Provost SP8 . . . 11 B2
Newland DT9 . . . 30 C6
Newland Gdn DT9 . . . 30 C6
Newland La DT9 . . . 195 F3
Newlands Rd
Bournemouth BH7 . . . 123 A6
Christchurch BH23 . . . 124 F7
New Milton BH25 . . . 95 B1
Newlands Way BH18 . . . 86 D3
New Line BH20 . . . 161 D3
Newlyn Way BH12 . . . 120 E7
Newman Cl 3 DT11 . . . 212 E5
Newmans Cl
West Moors BH22 . . . 53 A5
Wimborne Minster BH21 . . . 59 D3
Newman's La BH22 . . . 52 E5
New Merrifield BH21 . . . 59 F7
New Milton Inf Sch BH25. 95 A1
New Milton Jun Sch BH25 . . . 95 A1
New Milton Sta BH25 . . . 95 A3
Newmorton Rd BH9 . . . 90 A4
New Orchard BH15 . . . 119 B2
New Par BH10 . . . 89 E3
New Park Rd BH6 . . . 123 C4
Newport La BH20 . . . 82 C2
New Quay Rd BH15 . . . 119 B1
New Rd
Arne BH20 . . . 143 A1
Bournemouth BH10 . . . 89 E7
Bourton SP8 . . . 1 E2
Bovington Camp BH20 . . . 139 D7
Brympton BA22 . . . 26 C5
Castleton DT9 . . . 30 B4
Corfe Castle BH20 . . . 162 E1
Ferndown BH22 . . . 61 E3
Gillingham SP8 . . . 6 A1
Haselbury Plucknett TA18 . 192 D5
Hinton St George TA17 . . . 191 C7
Loders DT6 . . . 101 E7
Lytchett Minster & Upton BH16 . . . 116 F7
Poole BH12 . . . 120 D6
Portesham DT3 . . . 150 A8
Portland DT5 . . . 186 F6
Radipole DT4 . . . 167 D4
Ringwood BH24 . . . 47 D8
Ringwood BH24 . . . 55 C4
Shaftesbury SP7 . . . 12 D3
Shapwick DT11 . . . 48 D1
Stalbridge DT10 . . . 33 D8
Stoborough Green BH20 . . 160 F8
Stofold BA22 . . . 193 F8
Sturminster Newton DT10 197 D7
West Crewkerne TA18 . . . 191 B4
Weymouth DT4 . . . 167 D2
Winsham TA20 . . . 202 C8
Winterborne Stickland DT11 . . . 198 B1
Woodlands BH21 . . . 44 C7
Wool BH20 . . . 139 F1
Zeale SP8 . . . 2 A3
New St La
Loders DT6 . . . 69 D1
Symondsbury DT6 . . . 99 F6
New St
2 Dorchester DT1 . . . 108 A1
Easton/Weston DT5 . . . 187 A4
Marnhull DT10 . . . 20 F2
North Perrott TA18 . . . 192 C4
5 Poole BH15 . . . 119 B1
Puddletown DT2 . . . 78 B1
Radipole DT4 . . . 167 E2
Ringwood BH24 . . . 55 C6
Wareham BH20 . . . 142 E3
Newstead Rd
Bournemouth BH6 . . . 123 D4
Weymouth DT4 . . . 167 C2
Newton Cl
Gillingham SP8 . . . 5 E1
Sturminster Newton DT10 197 D8
Newton Hill DT10 . . . 197 D8
Newton Manor Cl 2 BH19 . . . 179 A2
Newton Morrell BH14 . . . 120 D3
Newton Rd
Barton on Sea BH25 . . . 127 B8
Maiden Newton DT2 . . . 73 A8
Poole BH13 . . . 147 F8
Stofold BA22 . . . 193 F8
Sturminster Marshall BH21. 56 C4
Swanage BH19 . . . 179 C1
Yeovil BA20 . . . 27 E3
Newton Rise 4 BH19 . . . 179 A2
Newton's Rd DT4 . . . 167 E1
Newton Surmaville BA20 . 27 F3
Newtown DT8 . . . 204 C4
Newtown Bsns Ctr BH12 120 A7
Newtown Hill BH20 . . . 157 F4
Newtown La
Corfe Mullen BH21 . . . 86 D8
Ringwood BH24 . . . 43 E1
Verwood BH31 . . . 45 C5
Newtown Rd BH31 . . . 45 C5
Nichola Ct BH12 . . . 120 B7
Nicholas Cl BH23 . . . 94 B2
Nicholas Gdns BH10 . . . 89 C2
Nicholson Cl BH17 . . . 119 E8
Nickel Cl SO23 . . . 126 F6
Nightingale Cl
Verwood BH31 . . . 45 C5
Nightingale Cl *continued*
5 Winchester SO22 . . . 126 A4
Nightingale Dr DT3 . . . 152 C4
Nightjar Cl BH17 . . . 118 F8
Nimrod Way BH21 . . . 60 F6
Nine Stones (Stone Circle) DT2 . . . 105 C1
Noade St SP5 . . . 25 C1
Noah Henville Cnr 4 DT11 . . . 81 E8
Noake Rd DT9 . . . 29 F5
Noble Cl BH11 . . . 88 F1
Noel Rd BH10 . . . 89 B2
Noel The BH25 . . . 95 C3
Nonesuch Cl 3 DT1 . . . 135 B8
Noon Gdns BH31 . . . 45 D6
Noon Hill Dr BH31 . . . 45 D6
Noon Hill Rd BH31 . . . 45 D6
Norburton DT6 . . . 128 B8
Norcliffe Cl BH11 . . . 89 B3
Norden Dr BH20 . . . 142 C6
Norden La DT2 . . . 72 F8
Norden Sta BH20 . . . 161 F2
Nordon Rd DT11 . . . 212 D5
Nordons DT6 . . . 100 E5
Norfolk Ave BH23 . . . 91 F2
Norfolk Rd DT4 . . . 167 A4
Norleywood BH23 . . . 125 F8
Norman Ave BH12 . . . 121 A6
Norman Cl DT6 . . . 100 F7
Normandy Dr BH23 . . . 124 D7
Normandy Way
Bridport DT6 . . . 100 D5
Dorchester DT1 . . . 107 E2
Hamworthy BH15 . . . 118 D2
Norman Gdns BH12 . . . 121 A6
Normanhurst Ave BH8 . . 90 E1
Norman Rd SO23 . . . 126 D4
Normans SO23 . . . 126 D4
Normanton Cl BH23 . . . 91 F1
Norris Cl BH24 . . . 54 A4
Norris Gdns BH25 . . . 95 A1
Norrish Rd BH12 . . . 120 C5
North Allington DT6 . . . 100 C7
North Ave
Bournemouth BH10 . . . 89 D6
Lyme Regis DT7 . . . 96 B6
Northay La EX13 . . . 202 C3
North Bestwall Rd BH20 . 142 F4
Northbourne Ave BH10 . . 89 D5
Northbourne Gdns BH10 . 89 E5
Northbourne Pl 3 BH10 . 89 D5
Northbourne Rdbt BH10 . . 89 E5
North Bowood La DT6 . . 203 F2
Northbrook Rd
Broadstone BH18 . . . 87 A2
Swanage BH19 . . . 179 A5
Yeovil BA21 . . . 27 E7
Northcote Rd BH1 . . . 122 C4
North Cres DT9 . . . 17 D4
North Cswy BH20 . . . 142 E5
North Dr
Ossemsley BH25 . . . 94 E8
West Moors BH24 . . . 62 B8
North End DT9 . . . 194 F3
North End La SP6 . . . 42 F4
Northernhay 1 DT1 . . . 108 A2
Northey Rd BH6 . . . 123 E6
Northfield Rd BH24 . . . 47 D1
Northgate Chambers 10 SO23 . . . 126 E6
Northgate Lodge 2 SO23 . . . 126 E6
North Gr 3 DT11 . . . 199 E3
North Hill Cl
Burton Bradstock DT6 . . . 128 B8
Winchester SO22 . . . 126 D8
North Hill Ct SO22 . . . 126 D7
North Hill Way DT6 . . . 100 D4
North Instow BH19 . . . 177 F5
North La
Hardington Mandeville BA22 . . . 193 A7
Yeovil BA20 . . . 27 D5
Northlands Dr SO23 . . . 126 E8
Northleigh La BH21 . . . 59 E6
North Lodge Rd BH14 . . . 120 E4
Northmead Dr BH17 . . . 118 F8
Northmere Dr BH12 . . . 120 F7
Northmere Rd BH12 . . . 120 F7
North Mills Rd DT6 . . . 100 D7
North Mills Trading Est DT6 . . . 100 D8
Northmoor Way BH20 . . . 142 D6
Northover BH3 . . . 121 F6
Northover Cl
Burton Bradstock DT6 . . . 128 C8
Piddletrenthide DT2 . . . 208 B2
Northover La SO41 . . . 95 E7
North Perrott Rd TA18 . . 192 C5
North Pk DT2 . . . 73 F3
North Pl DT11 . . . 212 D4
Northport Dr BH20 . . . 142 E6
North Poulner Rd BH24 . . 47 D2
North Quay DT4 . . . 167 D2
North Rd
Ashmore SP5 . . . 25 C1
Bournemouth BH7 . . . 122 E5
Chideock DT6 . . . 99 A7
Mere BA12 . . . 3 A6
Poole BH14 . . . 120 A4
Sherborne DT9 . . . 30 C7
Weymouth DT4 . . . 180 B8
North Rew La DT2 . . . 106 B1
Northshore BH13 . . . 147 C4
North Sq
Chickerell DT3 . . . 166 C6
2 Dorchester DT1 . . . 108 A2
North St
Beaminster DT8 . . . 204 D4
Bere Regis BH20 . . . 81 B2
Bradford Abbas DT9 . . . 28 D2
Bridport DT6 . . . 100 D7
Charminster DT2 . . . 75 D1
Crewkerne TA18 . . . 191 F5
Fontmell Magna SP7 . . . 37 F7
Haselbury Plucknett TA18 . 192 C6
Langton Matravers BH19 . 178 A2
Mere BA12 . . . 3 A5
Milborne Port DT9 . . . 17 D2
Poole BH15 . . . 119 C2
Wareham BH20 . . . 142 E4
Winterborne Kingston DT11 81 E8
Winterborne Stickland DT11 . . . 210 C7
North Terr BA21 . . . 27 E6
North View SO22 . . . 126 C6
North Walls
Wareham BH20 . . . 142 D4
Winchester SO23 . . . 126 E6
Nortoft Rd BH8 . . . 122 B6
Norton Cl BH23 . . . 124 D7
Norton Gdns BH9 . . . 89 E1
Norton La DT11 . . . 198 D3
Norton Rd
Bournemouth BH9 . . . 121 E8
Bournemouth BH9 . . . 89 E1
Norton Way BH15 . . . 119 A1
Norway Cl 3 BH9 . . . 89 F1
Norway La DT8 . . . 203 F4
Norwich Ave BH2 . . . 121 D3
Norwich Ave W BH2 . . . 121 D3
Norwich Ct 5 BH2 . . . 121 E3
Norwich Mans BH2 . . . 121 D3
Norwich Rd
Bournemouth BH2 . . . 121 E3
Weymouth DT4 . . . 167 D1
Norwood Pl BH5 . . . 123 B5
Nothe Fort DT4 . . . 167 F2
Nothe Par DT4 . . . 167 E2
Nottington La
Chickerell DT3 . . . 151 C2
Radipole DT3 . . . 152 A2
Nouale La BH24 . . . 55 F7
Noyce Gdns BH8 . . . 91 B2
Nuffield Ind Est BH17 . . . 119 D8
Nuffield Rd BH17 . . . 119 D7
Nugent Rd BH6 . . . 124 A4
Nundico BH20 . . . 142 E4
Nunnery Mead Nature Reserve DT2 . . . 73 D3
Nuns Rd SO23 . . . 126 E7
Nuns Wlk SO23 . . . 126 F8
Nursery Gdns
Bridport DT6 . . . 100 E7
3 Mere BA12 . . . 3 A5
Winchester SO22 . . . 126 B6
Nursery Rd
Blandford Forum DT11 . . . 212 D4
Bournemouth BH9 . . . 90 A3
Ringwood BH24 . . . 55 C6
Yeovil BA20 . . . 27 C3
Nursling Gn BH8 . . . 90 D2
Nutcombe Cl DT6 . . . 97 A8
Nutcrack La BH20 . . . 142 F1
Nutgrove Ave DT4 . . . 166 F1
Nuthatch Cl
Broadstone BH17 . . . 118 F8
Ferndown BH22 . . . 61 B8
Radipole DT3 . . . 152 D3
Nutley Cl BH11 . . . 88 F4
Nutley Way BH11 . . . 88 F4
Nutmead Cl 4 DT11 . . . 198 C8
Nyland La SP8 . . . 8 D1

O

Oak Ave
Christchurch BH23 . . . 123 D8
Holton Heath BH20 . . . 116 B3
Oakbury Dr DT3 . . . 168 A7
Oak Cl
Corfe Mullen BH21 . . . 86 C5
Ferndown BH22 . . . 61 E1
Oakdale Rd BH15 . . . 119 E6
Oakdale South Road Mid Sch BH15 . . . 119 C5
Oakdene Cl BH21 . . . 59 D5
Oakdene Rd BH20 . . . 139 F1
Oak Dr BH15 . . . 119 D2
Oakfield Rd BH15 . . . 119 C6
Oakfield St DT11 . . . 212 D4
Oakford Ct BH8 . . . 90 D3
Oak Gdns BH11 . . . 89 B1
Oakham Grange BH22 . . . 61 E5
Oakhurst BH23 . . . 124 F7
Oakhurst Cl BH22 . . . 53 B2
Oakhurst Fst Sch BH22 . . . 53 B2
Oakhurst La BH22 . . . 53 B2
Oakhurst Rd BH22 . . . 53 B2
Oak La
Corscombe DT2 . . . 205 C6
Mere BA12 . . . 3 B4
Ringwood BH24 . . . 55 D8
Oaklands Cl
Verwood BH31 . . . 45 A6
6 Winchester SO22 . . . 126 A4
Oaklands Rd BA21 . . . 27 F7
Oakland Wlk BH22 . . . 61 F1
Oakleigh 4 BA20 . . . 26 F2
Oakleigh Way BH23 . . . 125 F7
Oakley Gdns BH16 . . . 118 A7

Oakley Hill BH21..........59 D2
Oakley La
  Farnham DT11..........188 C2
  Merley BH21..........59 E2
  Wimborne Minster BH21.....60 A2
Oakley Pl DT4..........167 D2
Oakley Rd BH21..........59 D2
Oakley Sh Ctr BH21..........59 E1
Oakley Straight BH21.....59 D2
Oakmead Coll of Tech
  BH11..........88 F4
Oakmead Gdns BH11.....88 F4
Oakmead Rd BH17.....118 F7
Oak Mews BH12.....120 C5
Oak Rd
  Alderholt SP6..........42 B5
  Bournemouth BH8.....122 C6
  Charminster DT2.......75 D2
  New Milton BH25.......95 C3
  Upton BH16..........118 C6
Oaks Dr BH24..........53 F3
Oaks Mead BH31.....45 B6
Oaks The
  Gillingham SP8..........5 E1
  Verwood BH31..........45 A7
Oaktree Cl BH20.....142 C1
Oak Vale La BA8.....19 B4
Oak Way BA22.....26 C7
Oakwood
  Bournemouth BH3.....121 E7
  West Knighton DT2.....136 C3
Oakwood Ave BH25.....95 C4
Oakwood Cl BH9.....90 B2
Oakwood Ct BH25.....95 B3
Oakwood Dr 5 DT11...37 F1
Oakwood Rd
  Bournemouth BH9.....90 B2
  Christchurch BH23.....93 E1
Oasis Mews BH16.....118 A7
Oasis The 12 BH13...121 A4
Oates Rd BH9..........89 E1
Oathill La
  Broadwindsor TA18.....203 A7
  West Crewkerne TA18...191 B1
Oban Rd BH3..........121 E7
Oborne Rd DT9..........30 D7
Oceanarium BH2.....121 E7
Ocean Hts 4 BH5.....122 F3
Octagon Theatre BA20...27 C4
Octavia Hill SO22.....126 B4
Odcombe Hollow BA22..192 E8
Oglander Rd SO23.....126 E8
Okeford Fitzpaine CE Prim
  Sch DT11..........197 F5
Okeford Rd BH18.....87 C2
OK Mobile Home Pk
  BH23..........125 B8
Old Bakery Cl 4 DT11..199 D3
Old Bakery The 6 DT8..203 E5
Old Barn Cl
  Christchurch BH23.....91 D2
  Ringwood BH24..........55 D7
Old Barn Farm Rd BH21..53 C6
Old Barn Rd
  Bere Regis BH20.....81 A2
  Christchurch BH23.....91 D2
Old Barn Way BA20.....27 A2
Old Bincombe La DT3...153 C2
Old Boundary Rd SP7...12 F2
Old Bound Rd BH16.....118 C6
Old Bowden Way DT9...17 D4
Old Brewery The 10
  BH15..........119 C2
Old Brickfields DT2.....136 C3
Old Bridge Rd BH6.....123 D7
Old Castle Rd DT4.....180 E7
Old Chalk Pit BH20.....81 B1
Old Chapel Dr BH16.....84 C4
Old Christchurch La 12
  BH1..........121 F3
Old Christchurch Rd
  BH1..........121 F3
Old Church Rd DT6.....100 E4
Old Coach Mews BH14..120 A4
Old Coastguard Rd BH13 147 B4
Old Dairy Farm The
  DT10..........196 F3
Old Depot Rd SP1.....181 C1
Old Farm Cl BH24.....47 E2
Old Farm Ct DT11.....212 D6
Old Farm Rd BH15.....119 E6
Old Farm Way DT2.....137 D5
Old Forge Cl BH16.....116 F6
Old Forge Rd BH21.....60 F6
Old Furzebrook Rd BH20 160 F8
Old Gdns SO22..........126 D8
Old Generator Ho The
  BH12..........121 A5
Old Granary Cl DT3.....153 C1
Old Ham La BH21.....60 D4
Old Highway Mews BH21.59 D4
Old Hillside Rd SO22...126 A8
Old Hitchen 4 TA16...191 F7
Old Hollow BA12..........3 B6
Old Kiln Rd
  Ridge BH20..........143 B1
  Upton BH16..........118 D6
Old Lifeboat House
  BH15..........119 C1
Old Lyme Hill DT6.....96 F8
Old Lyme Rd DT6.....96 F7
Old Malthouse Sch The
  BH19..........178 B2
Old Manor Cl BH21.....59 D4

Old Market Rd BH21.....86 A8
Old Mill La DT11.....21 A4
Old Mills DT2..........71 E8
Old Milton Gn BH25.....94 F1
Old Milton Rd BH25.....95 A2
Old Mkt Rd BH21.....85 B7
Old Mulberry Cl BH10...89 A1
Old Oak Way DT11.....210 C3
Old Orchard BH15.....119 C1
Old Orchard Cl DT10...196 F8
Old Parish La DT4.....167 B3
Old Pines BH25.....61 E4
Old Pound Cl BH16.....84 C3
Old Pound Ct 3 SP8.....1 D1
Old Priory Rd BH23.....123 F4
Old Rd
  Odcombe BA22..........26 A3
  Wimborne Minster BH21...59 B5
Old Rd The DT9..........18 B2
Old Rectory Cl
  4 Charmouth DT6.......97 A7
  Corfe Mullen BH21.....86 D8
Old Rectory La DT9.....195 E3
Old Ropewalk BH15.....119 A1
Old Rope Wlk The BH15..118 F1
Old St John's Mews BH9..89 F3
Old Sandpit La BH16...86 A2
Old Sawmill Cl BH31...45 A7
Old Sch Cl DT9..........31 B1
Old Sch La
  Hinton St Mary DT10...35 A5
  Iwerne Minster DT11...37 F1
Old School Cl
  Ferndown BH22..........61 C5
  Poole BH14..........120 A4
Old Sch Pl DT9..........30 A5
Old St BH21..........56 E3
Old Stacks Gdns 1 BH24.55 E6
Old Station App SO23..126 F5
Old Station Gdns BA8...19 B5
Old Station Rd
  Radipole DT4..........152 B4
  4 Yeovil BA20..........27 E4
Old Station Way BA20...27 E4
Old Town Mews 8
  BH15..........119 C2
Old Vicarage Cl BH10...89 E6
Old Vicarage Gdn DT7...96 B5
Old Wareham Rd
  Corfe Mullen BH16,BH21..86 A3
  Poole BH12..........120 A7
Olga Rd DT1..........107 F1
Oliver's Battery Prim Sch
  SO22..........126 A1
Olivers Mead 1 DT11...198 C8
Olivers Rd BH21.....60 A6
Olivers Way BH21.....60 A6
Onslow Gdns BH21.....59 D6
Onslow Rd BH21.....59 D6
Ophir Gdns 1 BH8.....122 C5
Ophir Rd BH8..........122 B5
Oratory Gdns BH13.....147 F8
Orchard Ave
  Bridport DT6..........100 C8
  Poole BH14..........119 F2
Orchard Chase 2 DT11.199 F7
Orchard Cl
  3 Charmouth DT6.......97 A7
  Cheselbourne DT2.....209 A3
  Christchurch BH23.....124 A6
  Corfe Mullen BH21.....86 D7
  Ferndown BH22..........61 E5
  Fontmell Magna SP7...37 E6
  Lytchett Minster & Upton
    BH16..........116 F6
  3 Okeford Fitzpaine DT11 197 F6
  Ringwood BH24..........55 C8
  4 Stourpaine DT11.....198 F4
  Sturminster Newton DT10 197 C8
  Sydling St Nicholas DT2..207 A3
  4 West Coker BA22.....193 A8
Orchard Cres DT6.....100 C8
Orchard Ct BH31.....45 C5
Orchard Dr DT3.....168 B7
Orchard Gr BH25.....95 A1
Orchard Ho SO22.....126 C5
Orchard La
  Corfe Mullen BH21.....86 D7
  2 Crewkerne TA18.....191 F4
  Thorncombe TA20.....202 E6
  7 Winterborne Kingston
    DT11..........81 E8
Orchardleigh BA22.....192 E8
Orchard Leigh BH25...95 B2
Orchard Mead
  8 Broadwindsor DT8.....203 E5
  3 Ringwood BH24.....55 B8
Orchard Mews
  Christchurch BH23.....124 A6
  7 Gillingham SP8.....5 D2
Orchard Rd
  Gillingham SP8..........5 E2
  Milborne Port DT9.....17 C2
Orchard Rise
  7 Crewkerne TA18.....191 F4
  Milborne St Andrew DT11..79 E7
Orchard St
  Blandford Forum DT11...212 D4
  Bournemouth BH2.....121 E3
  Dorchester DT1.....108 A2
  Yeovil BA20..........27 B4
Orchard The
  Blandford Forum DT11..212 C5
  Bournemouth BH11.....88 D6
  Bransgore BH23.....93 C8
  Hazelbury Bryan DT10...196 F3
  Radipole DT3..........152 B3
  2 Sixpenny Handley SP5..189 B4

Orchard The continued
  Winfrith Newburgh DT2..156 F6
Orchard Way
  Misterton TA18.....192 A2
  2 Mosterton DT8.....204 A8
Orchard Wlk
  15 Bournemouth BH2...121 E3
  Milbourne Port DT9...17 C2
  Winchester SO22.....126 B8
Orcheston Rd BH8.....122 C6
Orchid Way BH23.....124 C7
Orestes Gate BH23...125 A5
Orford Cl BH23.....91 D4
Orford St DT7..........78 B1
Organford Rd BH16.....116 C4
Orion Rd DT4..........167 D1
Ormonde Rd BH13.....121 A2
Osborne Cl 5 DT1.....135 C8
Osborne Rd
  Bournemouth BH9.....121 E8
  New Milton BH25.......95 B3
  Poole BH14..........120 B3
  Swanage BH19.....179 B2
  Wimborne Minster BH21..59 D4
  Yeovil BA20..........27 C5
Osborne Sch SO23.....126 D7
Osborne Ho 4 BH25...95 A3
Osbourne Rd DT6.....100 D7
Osmay Rd BH19.....185 C3
Osmington Dro DT2.....136 B1
Osmington White Horse
  DT3..........153 F5
Osprey Cl BH23.....125 A5
Osprey Quay Bsns
  Development DT5.....180 F1
Osprey Rd DT4..........180 D5
Ossemsley Manor Ho
  BH23..........94 D6
Ossemsley South Dr BH25 94 F8
Osterley Cl BH23.....124 A8
Oswald Cl BH9..........89 E2
Oswald Rd BH9..........89 F2
Otterbourne 14 BH2...121 D4
Otter Cl
  Upton BH16..........118 B6
  Verwood BH31..........45 C5
Otter Rd BH15.....119 F6
Otters Wlk BH25.....95 C5
Ottery La DT9..........30 A5
Oval Gdn BH20.....160 F8
Oval The BH20.....172 E8
Overbury Cl DT4.....166 F2
Overbury Manor BH12...121 B5
Overbury Rd BH14.....120 C3
Overcliffe Mans BH1...122 C3
Overcombe BA8.....18 D8
Overcombe Cl BH17.....87 E2
Overcombe Dr DT3.....168 B7
Overlands Rd DT4.....180 B8
Over Links Dr BH14.....120 D2
Overton Cl DT7.....96 C7
Ovington Ave BH7.....123 C7
Ovington Gdns BH7.....123 C7
Owen's Rd SO22.....126 D7
Owermoigne CE Fst Sch
  DT2..........155 E7
Owlshotts BH13.....147 F7
Owls Rd
  Bournemouth BH5.....122 E3
  Verwood BH31..........45 C5
Ox Dro
  Berwick St John SP5...188 B7
  Bower Chalke SP5.....189 A8
Oxencroft 4 SP7.....12 F4
Oxen Rd 6 TA18.....191 F4
Oxey Cl BH25.....95 A1
Oxford Ave BH6.....123 B5
Oxford La BH11.....89 B6
Oxford Rd
  Bournemouth BH8.....122 B4
  Yeovil BA20..........28 B7
Oxhayes DT8.....203 C8
Ozone Terr DT7.....96 B4

P

Paceycombe Way DT1...107 C2
Packers' Way 1 TA18..192 B3
Paddington Cl BH11.....88 D4
Paddington Gn BH11...88 D3
Paddock Cl
  Ferndown BH21..........61 A5
  Lytchett Matravers BH16..84 A5
  Poole BH12..........120 B7
  Shaftesbury SP7.....13 A1
  10 Sixpenny Handley SP5.189 A3
  St Leonards BH24.....54 B4
Paddock Gr BH31.....45 C5
Paddock's Cross DT6...67 B8
Paddock's La DT6.....67 B8
Paddocks The
  Bournemouth BH10.....89 D4
  1 Iwerne Minster DT11..37 F1
  Mere BH12..........3 A5
  5 Mosterton DT8.....204 A8
  Thornford DT9.....194 D8
Paddock The
  West Moors BH24.....62 C8
  West Stafford DT2.....136 B8
Paddock Wlk DT9.....17 C2
Padfield Cl BH26.....123 E6
Padget Rd BH24.....47 E1
Padstow Pl SP6.....43 A8
Pageant Dr DT5.....30 B5
Pageants Cft BH16.....68 F1
Page Dr 1 DT5.....186 F1
Paget Cl BH21.....60 A7

Paget Rd BH11..........89 A4
Painters Field SO23...126 C2
Paisley Rd BH6.....123 C5
Palace Rd SP8..........6 A1
Palfrey Rd BH10.....89 D5
Palma Ct BH23.....126 A7
Palmer Pl BH25.....95 A4
Palmer Rd BH15.....119 C5
Palmers Brewery DT6..100 C5
Palmers Orch BH16.....84 C3
Palmerston Ave BH23..124 D6
Palmerston Cl BH16...118 D7
Palmerston Ct 2 SO23.126 D3
Palmerston Rd
  Bournemouth BH1.....122 E5
  Poole BH14..........120 D4
  Upton BH16..........117 E7
  Upton BH16..........118 C7
Palm Hall Cl SO23.....126 F5
Pamphill CE Fst Sch BH21 58 E5
Panorama Rd
  Poole BH13..........147 B3
  Swanage BH19.....179 A6
Pans Cnr BH22.....61 F3
Parade The
  4 Bournemouth BH6...123 E3
  New Milton BH25.......95 D4
  Old Milton BH25.......94 F1
  Poole BH7..........87 B1
Paradise La BH20.....83 C4
Paradise Rd BH21.....51 F7
Paradise St 14 BH15...119 B1
Parchment St SO23.....126 E6
Parcroft Gdns BA20...27 B5
Parcroft Jun Sch BA20..27 B5
Pardys Hill BH21.....86 D8
Parfields BA20.....27 B5
Parham Cl BH25.....94 E3
Parham Rd BH10.....89 C2
Paris Ct SP8.....5 E1
Parish Mews 3 BA21...26 E5
Parish Rd BH15.....119 E3
Park Ave
  Bournemouth BH10.....89 C6
  Winchester SO23.....126 E6
Park Cl
  Burton BH23..........92 C3
  New Milton BH25.......95 C5
  3 Stourpaine DT11...198 F4
  Winchester SO23.....126 E6
Park Ct
  12 Poole BH13.....121 B3
  1 Winchester SO23...126 E8
Park Dr
  Holton Heath BH16.....116 B3
  Verwood BH31..........45 A7
Parkelea BH21.....56 D4
Parker Rd BH9.....121 F7
Parkers Cl BH24.....47 E1
Park Est Rd DT5.....186 F4
Park Gate BH25.....95 A2
Park Gate Mews 7 BH2.121 E3
Park Gdns
  Christchurch BH23.....124 E7
  Yeovil BA20..........27 C5
Park Gr DT10.....33 C8
Park Hill DT11.....211 C6
Park Ho SO23.....126 E6
Park Homer Dr BH21...60 A6
Park Homer Rd BH21...59 F6
Park La
  Alderholt SP6.....42 B6
  Bournemouth BH10.....89 F4
  Evershot DT2.....206 A7
  Glanvilles Wootton DT9..195 F2
  Henstridge BA8.....19 B7
  Radipole DT4.....167 D3
  Shapwick DT11.....48 C1
  Thorncombe TA20.....202 D7
  Wayford TA18.....191 B1
  Wimborne Minster BH21..59 C4
  Wimborne St Giles BH21.201 E5
  Woodlands BH21.....44 B6
Park Lake Rd BH15.....119 E2
Parkland Cl BH24.....45 F4
Parkland Dr BH25.....126 F8
Parkland Pl BH25.....95 A2
Parklands 11 BH4.....121 C3
Park Mead Rd DT4.....180 C7
Park Pl BH14.....119 F4
Park Rd
  Blandford Forum DT11...212 C4
  Bournemouth BH8.....122 A5
  Bridport DT6.....100 C7
  Easton/Weston DT5...187 A4
  Henstridge BA8.....19 A4
  New Milton BH25.......95 C5
  Old Milton BH25.......94 F1
  Poole BH15,BH14.....119 F3
  Stalbridge DT10.....33 C8
  Swanage BH19.....179 C2
  Winchester SO22,SO23..126 D8
  Yeovil BA20..........27 D5
Park Sch The BA20.....27 C5
Parkside
  Christchurch BH23.....93 D1
  Ringwood BH24.....55 B6
Parkside Gdns
  Bournemouth BH10.....89 E2
  Winchester SO22.....126 A8
Parkside Ind Est BH24..55 C5
Parkside Rd BH14.....120 C4
Park's La DT2.....130 D7
Park St
  Radipole DT4.....167 D3
  Yeovil BA20..........27 D3

Parkstone Ave BH14...120 D4
Parkstone Gram Sch
  BH17..........87 B1
Parkstone Hts
  Poole BH14..........119 F5
  Poole BH14..........120 A5
Parkstone Rd BH15.....119 E3
Parkstone Sta BH14...120 B3
Park The
  Barton on Sea BH25...126 C7
  Wimborne Minster BH21..60 A1
  Yeovil BA20..........27 C5
Parkview BH2.....121 E4
Park View
  Crewkerne TA18.....191 F3
  New Milton BH25.......95 A2
  7 Poole BH15.....119 E3
  Winchester SO22.....126 A8
Park View Ct BH8.....122 C7
Park View Mews BH25...95 A2
Park Water La DT8.....203 C5
Parkway DT6.....97 B7
Park Way BH22.....53 A2
Parkway Dr BH8.....122 E8
Parkwood La 7 BH5...123 B5
Parkwood Rd
  Bournemouth BH5.....123 A4
  Wimborne Minster BH21..59 C4
Parley Cl BH22.....61 F1
Parley Cross BH22.....89 E8
Parley Fst Sch BH22...61 D3
Parley Green La BH23...90 B7
Parley La BH23.....90 D7
Parley Rd BH9.....90 A2
Parliament Pl SO22.....126 A2
Parmiter Dr BH21.....59 E4
Parmiter Ho 6 SO23...126 F6
Parmiter Rd BH21.....59 E4
Parmiter Way BH21.....59 E4
Parnham House DT8...204 C3
Parrett & Axe CE Prim Sch
  DT8..........204 A7
Parrett Mead DT8.....192 C1
Parr Gr 5 DT11.....199 D4
Parr Ho 1 BH14.....120 A4
Parricks La EX13.....202 A3
Parr St BH14.....120 A4
Parsonage Barn La BH24..55 C7
Parsonage Ct 9 BH8...122 A5
Parsonage Hill DT11...200 F6
Parsonage La BH21...201 E7
Parsonage Rd
  Bournemouth BH1.....122 A3
  Bridport DT6.....100 C8
Parsonage St SP7.....37 F6
Parsonage The 3 SP5...189 B4
Parsons Cl 1 BH19...179 B3
Parsons La DT2.....102 E6
Parsons Pool 3 SP7...12 E3
Partridge Cl BH23.....125 A5
Partridge Dr BH14.....120 C1
Partridge Gn BH25.....95 B6
Partridge Wlk BH14...120 B1
Partway DT10.....196 F3
Partway La
  Hardington Mandeville
    BA22..........192 F7
  Hazelbury Bryan DT10...196 F3
  Thorncombe TA20.....202 C6
Pascoe Cl BH14.....120 A4
Pasture Way DT6.....100 D5
Patchins Rd BH16.....118 B4
Patchins The BH14.....147 E6
Paternoster Ho 4 SO23 126 E5
Paternoster Row 5
  SO23..........126 E5
Patson Hill La DT9.....15 C2
Pattinson Ct BA21.....27 F6
Paulet Pl SO22.....126 C3
Paul's Mead DT5.....186 F7
Pauls Way DT2.....137 D6
Pauncefote Rd BH5.....123 A5
Pauntley Rd BH23.....124 E5
Pavan Gdns BH10.....89 C2
Pavilion The 23 BH4...121 C2
Pavilion Theatre BH1...167 E3
Pavyotts La BA22.....193 E8
Payne Cl BH21.....53 A5
Paynes Cl DT2.....76 E7
Peace Cl BH23.....93 A8
Peaceful La DT10.....196 C6
Peacemarsh Farm Cl 3
  SP8..........5 E4
Pear Ash La BA9.....1 C4
Pearce Ave BH14.....120 A1
Pearce Gdns BH14.....120 A1
Pearce Rd BH16.....118 B6
Pearce-Smith Ct BH25..126 E7
Pear Cl BH12.....121 B4
Pearl Gdns BH10.....89 C4
Pearl Rd BH10.....89 C4
Pearson Ave BH14.....120 B5
Pearson Gdns BH10...89 D6
Pear Tree Cl
  Alderholt SP6.....42 B5
  Bransgore BH23.....93 B8
Peascombe Nature Reserve
  ....69 E1
Peatons La BH16.....84 B4
Peckham Ave BH25.....95 A2
Peddlars Wlk 4 BH24...55 B7
Peeks Mews BH6.....123 F5
Peel Cl
  Blandford Forum DT11...212 D5
  Poole BH12.....120 C5
Peelers Ct DT6.....100 D7
Pegasus Ct
  Bournemouth BH1.....122 A5

Pegasus Ct *continued*
8 New Milton BH25 ... 95 A3
Pegasus Lodge BH22 ... 61 D5
Peggy's La TA18 ... 192 C5
Pelham 21 BH13 ... 121 A4
Pelham Cl BH23 ... 124 D6
Pelican Mead BH24 ... 55 E5
Pemberton Cl DT3 ... 152 D3
Pembroke Cl BA21 ... 28 A7
Pembroke Ct 4 BH23 ... 126 B7
Pembroke Rd
Bournemouth BH4 ... 121 B2
Poole BH12 ... 120 D7
Penbugle Yd 14 DT1 ... 107 D1
Pen Craig 2 BH13 ... 121 B3
Pendomer Rd BA22 ... 193 B5
Pendruffle La 12 DT1 ... 107 D1
Penelope Ct 12 BH23 ... 126 B7
Pengelly Ave BH10 ... 89 E5
Penhale Wlk 17 DT1 ... 107 D1
Peninsula Rd SO22 ... 126 C5
Peninsula Sq SO23 ... 126 D5
Pen Mill Hill BA9 ... 1 E3
Pen Mill Inf Sch BA21 ... 27 F6
Pen Mill Trading Est BA21 ... 28 B6
Penmore Rd DT9 ... 15 C5
Pennant Way BH23 ... 124 F7
Penn Cl BH25 ... 94 E1
Penn Cross DT6 ... 64 D1
Penn Hill BA20 ... 27 D4
Penn Hill Ave BH14 ... 120 D3
Penn Hill Pk BA20 ... 27 D4
Penn Hill View DT2 ... 106 D8
Pennine Ct 8 BH23 ... 124 F8
Pennine Way BH31 ... 45 B5
Pennington Cl BH22 ... 52 F1
Pennington Cres BH22 ... 52 F2
Pennington Ho 6 BH4 ... 121 C2
Pennington Rd BH22 ... 52 F2
Penn La BA22 ... 193 A6
Pennsylvania Rd DT5 ... 187 B3
Penny Hedge BH25 ... 127 B8
Penny Plot DT7 ... 96 A6
Penny's Cnr SO41 ... 95 F4
Penny's Ct BH22 ... 61 D5
Penny's La BH21 ... 40 B7
Penny's Mead BH21 ... 40 B7
Penny St
Radipole DT4 ... 167 D4
Sturminster Newton DT10 ... 35 B1
Penny's Wlk BH22 ... 61 D5
Penny Way BH23 ... 125 C6
Pennywell Gdns BH25 ... 95 D4
Penrith Cl BH31 ... 45 A5
Penrith Rd BH5 ... 123 A4
Penrose Cl BH16 ... 84 C2
Penrose Rd BH22 ... 61 D6
Penton Pl 8 SO23 ... 126 F4
Pentons Hill SP6 ... 43 F6
Pentridge La DT10 ... 34 D4
Penwithen Sch DT2 ... 134 E5
Peppercorn Cl BH23 ... 124 E8
Pepper Hill DT11 ... 198 B5
Percy Gdns DT11 ... 212 D4
Percy Rd
Bournemouth BH5 ... 122 F4
Yeovil BA21 ... 27 F6
Peregrine Rd BH23 ... 125 A5
Pergin Cres BH17 ... 119 B7
Pergin Way BH17 ... 119 B7
Perrott Hill Sch TA18 ... 192 B4
Perryfield Gdns BH7 ... 123 B8
Perry Gdns BH15 ... 119 C1
Perry St TA20 ... 202 A7
Persley Rd BH10 ... 89 E4
Perth Cl BH23 ... 91 E1
Perth St DT4 ... 167 B3
Peter Grant Way BH22 ... 61 C5
Peters Cl BH16 ... 118 C6
Petersfield Pl BH7 ... 123 B7
Petersfield Rd BH7 ... 123 B7
Petersham La BH21 ... 51 A4
Petersham Rd BH17 ... 119 A8
Peters Rd BH22 ... 61 F3
Peter St 3 BA20 ... 27 D4
Peter Symonds Coll SO22 ... 126 D7
Petit Rd BH9 ... 90 A3
Petter's Way BA20 ... 27 D4
Pettitts Cl DT9 ... 28 C2
Pettridge La BA12 ... 3 A5
Pettycrate La DT6 ... 98 E5
Petwyn Cl BH22 ... 62 A6
Peverell Ave E DT1 ... 107 B2
Peverell Rd BH16 ... 118 B4
Peveril Cl BH24 ... 54 B6
Peveril Point Rd BH19 ... 179 D2
Peveril Rd BH19 ... 179 C1
Phelipps Rd
Corfe Mullen BH21 ... 86 E6
2 Poole BH21 ... 85 F6
Philip Green Meml Sch BH21 ... 190 C1
Philip Rd DT11 ... 212 E4
Phillips Rd DT10 ... 21 A2
Philpot Mus The DT7 ... 96 C5
Phyldon Cl BH12 ... 120 B5
Phyldon Rd BH12 ... 120 B6
Piccadilly La DT11 ... 56 C8
Pickard Rd BH22 ... 61 F7
Pickering Cl BH18 ... 87 A2
Picket La DT8 ... 192 C1
Pickett La BA21 ... 27 C7
Picketts Cross DT2 ... 74 A4
Pickford Rd BH9 ... 89 E1
Piddlehinton Ent Pk DT2 ... 77 A6
Piddle La DT2 ... 207 D3
Piddles Wood Nature Reserve DT10 ... 197 E7
Piddle Valley CE Fst Sch DT2 ... 208 B2
Pidney Hill DT10 ... 196 F3
Piece Rd DT9 ... 17 C3
Piece The 2 TA16 ... 191 F7
Pierston Fields SP8 ... 5 C6
Pigeon Cl
Blandford Forum DT11 ... 212 D2
Winfrith Newburgh DT2 ... 156 F5
Pig Hill BA22 ... 193 A7
Pig Shoot La BH23 ... 90 F5
Pikes La BH19 ... 183 C7
Pile La DT10 ... 32 F5
Pilford Heath Rd BH21 ... 60 B7
Pilford La BH21 ... 51 D2
Pilgrim Pk BH24 ... 55 E8
Pilgrim's Cl BH25 ... 95 C3
Pilgrims Gate SO22 ... 126 C7
Pilgrims Sch The SO23 ... 126 E5
Pilgrims Way
Poole BH17 ... 119 A7
4 Radipole DT4 ... 167 E2
Pill Mdw SP8 ... 9 C3
Pilot Hight Rd BH11 ... 89 A4
Pilsdon Cl 7 DT8 ... 204 C4
Pilsdon Dr BH17 ... 87 E3
Pilsdon La DT6 ... 203 C3
Pilsdon Pen DT6 ... 203 C4
Pilwell DT10 ... 21 A3
Pimperleaze Rd BA12 ... 3 F1
Pimpern Cl BH17 ... 87 F2
Pimperne CE Fst Sch DT11 ... 199 D4
Pimpernel Ct 6 SP8 ... 5 D2
Pimperne Long Barrow DT11 ... 199 E5
Pineapple Bsns Pk DT6 ... 68 D6
Pineapple La DT6 ... 68 C6
Pine Ave
Bournemouth BH6 ... 123 C4
Poole BH12 ... 120 F6
Pinebeach Ct BH13 ... 147 G8
Pine Cl
Barton on Sea BH25 ... 126 E8
Ferndown BH22 ... 61 C7
Pinecliffe Ave BH6 ... 123 C4
Pinecliffe Rd BH25 ... 126 C7
Pinecliff Rd BH13 ... 147 G8
Pine Cres
Christchurch BH23 ... 125 E8
Holton Heath BH20 ... 116 B3
Pine Dr
Poole BH13 ... 120 F3
Poole BH13 ... 121 A2
St Leonards BH24 ... 54 B4
Pine End BH22 ... 61 F3
Pine Glen Ave BH22 ... 61 C8
Pine Grange 4 BH1 ... 122 A3
Pine Ho BH25 ... 95 A3
Pineholt Cl BH24 ... 54 C5
Pinehurst Ave BH23 ... 124 F5
Pinehurst Pk BH22 ... 61 F8
Pinehurst Rd BH22 ... 53 A1
Pine Lodge 10 BH13 ... 147 F7
Pine Manor Rd BH24 ... 53 F5
Pine Mans 3 BH1 ... 122 D4
Pinemoor Cl DT3 ... 167 F8
Pine Park Mans 16 BH13 ... 121 A4
Pine Rd
Alderholt SP6 ... 42 B5
Bournemouth BH9 ... 122 A8
East End BH21 ... 58 F1
Pine Ridge DT7 ... 96 C7
Pineside BH9 ... 122 A8
Pines Mews 11 DT8 ... 204 D4
Pinesprings Dr BH18 ... 86 E2
Pines The BH13 ... 121 A2
Pine Tree Ave BA20 ... 27 B3
Pine Tree Cl BH21 ... 59 D5
Pine Tree Glen BH4 ... 121 C3
Pinetree Wlk BH17 ... 118 F8
Pine Vale Cres BH10 ... 89 F3
Pine View DT6 ... 100 B6
Pine View Cl
Upton BH16 ... 118 C6
Verwood BH31 ... 44 F7
Pine View Rd BH31 ... 44 F7
Pine Wlk
Lyme Regis DT7 ... 96 B4
Verwood BH31 ... 45 D5
Pinewood Ave BH10 ... 89 D5
Pinewood Cl
Bournemouth BH10 ... 89 D5
Upton BH16 ... 118 A7
Walkford BH23 ... 94 A2
Pinewood Gdns BH22 ... 61 D7
Pinewood Rd
Christchurch BH23 ... 93 F1
Ferndown BH22 ... 61 C7
Hordle SO41 ... 95 F3
Poole BH13 ... 121 B1
St Leonards BH24 ... 54 B4
Upton BH16 ... 118 B7
Pinford La DT9 ... 30 E6
Pink Knoll Hollow DT9 ... 15 E8
Pinnacle The 7 BH1 ... 122 A3
Pipers Ash 2 BH24 ... 55 E8
Pipers Dr BH23 ... 125 A7
Pipit Cl DT3 ... 152 D3
Pippin Cl BH23 ... 91 E2
Pirates La DT4 ... 180 B7
Pitcher Cl 3 DT11 ... 81 E8
Pitchers DT6 ... 68 B6
Pitcote La 15 DT1 ... 107 D1
Pitfield Cnr BA22 ... 15 A6
Pit Hill TA17 ... 191 B7
Pitman's La DT6 ... 66 B1
Pit Rd TA17 ... 191 B7
Pitt Cl DT11 ... 212 C2
Pitthouse La BH23 ... 91 D8
Pitt La DT6 ... 65 E3
Pittmore Rd BH23 ... 92 C2
Pitt's Dro BH21 ... 49 E1
Pitts La
Melbury Abbas SP7 ... 23 F5
Sedgehill & Semley SP7 ... 7 C5
Pitts Orch DT10 ... 35 B1
Pitts Pl BH25 ... 95 D2
Pitwines Cl BH15 ... 119 D2
Pix Mead Gdns SP7 ... 13 A2
Placket La BA20 ... 27 A1
Plain The DT2 ... 109 A6
Plaisters La DT3 ... 153 C5
Plantagenet Chase BA20 ... 27 A2
Plantagenet Cres BH11 ... 88 D5
Plantagenet Pk BA20 ... 27 A3
Plantagenet Way 8 SP8 ... 5 D2
Plantation Ct BH17 ... 87 C1
Plantation Dr BH23 ... 94 A2
Plantation Rd BH17 ... 87 C1
Plant Park Rd BH24 ... 54 E2
Plassey Cl DT1 ... 107 E2
Plassey Cres BH10 ... 89 C5
Platts DT10 ... 196 F8
Playfield Cl 2 BA8 ... 19 A4
Playfields Dr BH12 ... 120 E6
Pleasance Way BH25 ... 94 F3
Pleck Hill DT10 ... 196 E3
Pleck La DT2 ... 209 B7
Plecy Cl BH22 ... 61 D2
Plemont Cl BH12 ... 88 E1
Plocks The DT11 ... 212 D3
Plot La DT9 ... 14 F1
Plott La BA8 ... 19 C5
Plough Est DT11 ... 212 D6
Plough Way SO22 ... 126 B2
Plover Cl 2 DT9 ... 17 C2
Plover Ct BA21 ... 26 F6
Plover Dr DT3 ... 166 D5
Plover Rd DT9 ... 17 C2
Plover Wlk 6 DT4 ... 180 D6
Plowman Cl DT10 ... 21 A3
Plucknett Row BA20 ... 26 E5
Plumbley Mdws 6 DT11 ... 81 E8
Plumbtree Gdns DT6 ... 100 E5
Plumer Rd BH17 ... 87 A1
Plum Orch DT9 ... 28 F7
Podington Mdws DT3 ... 166 D5
Poets Way SO22 ... 126 B6
Point The BH5 ... 122 E3
Pokesdown Com Prim Sch BH5 ... 123 B5
Pokesdown Sta BH7 ... 123 A5
Polans DT9 ... 194 D2
Policemans La BH16 ... 117 B7
Pollards La DT2 ... 155 D7
Pomona Cl BH22 ... 61 D6
Pompey's Cnr BH21 ... 61 A4
Pompey's La BH22 ... 61 B2
Pond Cl
Henstridge BA8 ... 19 A4
New Milton BH25 ... 95 A3
Pond Head BH21 ... 51 C6
Pond Wlk DT10 ... 33 C8
Ponsonby Rd BH14 ... 120 D4
Pony Dr BH16 ... 118 D7
Poole Aquarium & Serpentarium BH15 ... 119 C1
Poole Commerce Ctr BH12 ... 120 F5
Poole Gram Sch BH17 ... 87 D2
Poole High Sch BH15 ... 119 C4
Poole Hill BH2 ... 121 D3
Poole Hospl BH15 ... 119 D3
Poole La BH11 ... 89 B5
Poole Rd
Bournemouth BH4 ... 121 C3
Lytchett Matravers BH16 ... 84 F5
Poole BH13 ... 121 A4
Sturminster Marshall BH21 ... 56 D2
Upton BH16 ... 118 D7
Wimborne Minster BH21 ... 59 C4
Poole's Ct 4 DT7 ... 96 C5
Poole Sta BH15 ... 119 C3
Pool Lane Rdbt BH11 ... 88 E4
Poop Hill TA18 ... 192 C8
Poop Hill La TA18 ... 192 C8
Poorhouse La DT6 ... 66 C8
Pope's La DT9 ... 17 D2
Popes Rd BH15 ... 119 D6
Poplar Cl
Bransgore BH23 ... 93 C8
Christchurch BH23 ... 126 B8
3 Poole BH15 ... 119 B1
Radipole DT4 ... 167 A6
Wimborne Minster BH21 ... 59 D5
Poplar Cres BH24 ... 55 D7
Poplar Dr BA21 ... 26 E7
Poplar Hill 3 DT11 ... 198 B6
Poplar La BH23 ... 93 C8
Poplar Rd BH25 ... 95 D4
Poplar Way BH24 ... 55 D7
Pople's Well TA18 ... 191 E4
Poppy Cl
Christchurch BH23 ... 125 C8
Upton BH16 ... 117 B7
Yeovil BA22 ... 26 D5
Poppyfields SP8 ... 5 F4
Portadene 1 BH4 ... 121 D2
Portal Rd SO23 ... 126 F4
Portarlington Cl BH4 ... 121 D2
Portarlington Ct 24 BH4 ... 121 C3
Portarlington Rd BH4 ... 121 C2
Portchester Ct 3 BH8 ... 122 B5
Portchester Pl BH8 ... 122 B5
Portchester Rd BH8 ... 122 A5
Portchester Sch BH7 ... 123 A7
Portelet Cl BH12 ... 88 D2
Porter Rd BH17 ... 119 B7
Porters La BH21 ... 60 C6
Portesham CE Prim Sch DT3 ... 150 A8
Portesham Gdns BH9 ... 90 B4
Portesham Hill DT3 ... 132 A1
Portesham Way BH17 ... 87 E3
Portfield Cl BH23 ... 124 A7
Portfield Rd BH23 ... 124 A7
Portfield Sch
Christchurch BH23 ... 124 A6
East Parley BH23 ... 90 B8
Portiere Ho BH11 ... 89 A4
Port La DT6 ... 101 D3
Portland Beach Rd DT4 ... 180 E3
Portland Bird Obsy DT5 ... 186 E10
Portland Castle DT5 ... 181 A1
Portland Cres DT4 ... 167 B2
Portland Ct DT7 ... 96 A5
Portland Hospl DT5 ... 181 B1
Portland Mus DT5 ... 187 B3
Portland Pl BH2 ... 121 F4
Portland Port DT5 ... 181 C2
Portland Rd
Bournemouth BH9 ... 122 A8
Weymouth DT4 ... 180 C7
Portman Cres BH5 ... 123 B4
Portman Ct BA22 ... 192 E8
Portman Dr 5 DT11 ... 198 C8
Portman Pl DT11 ... 212 C4
Portman Rd
Bournemouth BH7 ... 122 F5
11 Pimperne DT11 ... 199 D4
Portman Terr BH5 ... 123 B4
Portmore Cl BH18 ... 87 C6
Portmore Gdns DT4 ... 167 C1
Portnell's La BA12 ... 1 F4
Portreeve Dr BA21 ... 27 D6
Port Regis Sch SP7 ... 12 B5
Portswood Dr 2 BH10 ... 90 A4
Portway DT2 ... 102 C6
Portwey Cl DT4 ... 167 C1
Possessions Cnr SP5 ... 25 B3
Post Green Rd BH16 ... 116 F7
Post Office Bldgs BH9 ... 121 F8
Post Office La BH24 ... 54 C5
Post Office Rd
18 Bournemouth BH1 ... 121 F3
Gillingham SP8 ... 5 D6
Potterne Way BH21 ... 45 D4
Potterne Wood Cl BH31 ... 45 E4
Potters Way BH14 ... 120 C2
Pottery Junc BH14 ... 120 E5
Pottery La DT4 ... 167 C4
Pottery Lines BH20 ... 142 F7
Pottery Rd BH14 ... 120 B2
Poulner Hill BH24 ... 55 F8
Poulner Jun & Inf Sch BH24 ... 47 E2
Poulner Pk BH24 ... 47 E1
Poundbury Cres DT1 ... 107 E2
Poundbury Rd DT1 ... 107 E3
Poundbury Trad Est DT1 ... 107 E2
Pound Cl
Charminster DT2 ... 107 D6
Poole BH15 ... 119 F5
Ringwood BH24 ... 55 C8
Stalbridge DT10 ... 33 C8
Yeovil BA21 ... 26 E5
Pound Cottage Visitor Ctr DT2 ... 205 E2
Pound Hill
Corscombe DT2 ... 205 B7
Witchampton BH21 ... 200 F1
Pound La
Bishop's Caundle DT9 ... 196 A7
Burstock DT8 ... 203 D5
1 Christchurch BH23 ... 124 B6
Damerham SP6 ... 190 E3
Dewlish DT2 ... 209 C1
2 Dorchester DT1 ... 108 B2
Gillingham SP8 ... 5 D2
Okeford Fitzpaine DT11 ... 198 A5
Poole BH15 ... 119 E5
Shaftesbury SP7 ... 13 A3
Wareham BH20 ... 142 E3
Wootton Fitzpaine DT6 ... 64 B6
Pound Piece
Easton/Weston DT5 ... 186 F4
Maiden Newton DT2 ... 72 F8
Pound Rd
Hawkchurch EX13 ... 202 C2
Lyme Regis DT7 ... 96 B5
Thornford DT9 ... 194 D8
Pound St DT7 ... 96 B5
Pound The BA12 ... 3 B5
Powell Rd BH14 ... 120 B3
Powell Theatre DT9 ... 30 B6
Powerscourt Rd BH25 ... 126 E7
Powerstock CE Prim Sch DT6 ... 70 A5
Powerstock Comm Nature Reserve DT6 ... 70 F6
Powis Cl BH25 ... 95 B3
Powys Cl DT1 ... 134 E8
Powys Gn DT9 ... 30 A6
Poxwell Cairn Circ DT2 ... 154 F2
Poxwell Dro DT2 ... 154 B4
Prankerds Rd 3 DT9 ... 17 C2
Preetz Way DT11 ... 212 F6
Preston Cl BH16 ... 118 C7
Preston Ct BH20 ... 142 E5
Preston Cty Comp Sch BA21 ... 26 F5
Preston Gr BA20 ... 27 A5
Preston La BH23 ... 92 D3
Preston Rd
Overcombe/Preston DT3 ... 153 C1
Poole BH15 ... 119 C6
Weymouth DT3 ... 167 F6
Yeovil BA22 ... 26 C5
Preston VC Prim Sch BA21 ... 27 A5
Preston Way BH23 ... 125 D8
Preston Wildlife Gdn DT3 ... 152 D2
Prestwood Cl BH25 ... 94 F1
Pretoria Terr DT4 ... 167 C2
Priest La BH23 ... 92 B7
Priestlands DT9 ... 30 B7
Priestlands La DT9 ... 30 B7
Priestley Rd BH10 ... 89 B1
Priest's House Mus & Gdns BH21 ... 59 B4
Priest's Rd BH19 ... 179 A2
Priest's Way BH19 ... 178 F2
Prime La DT6 ... 65 F7
Primrose Cl 3 SP8 ... 5 D2
Primrose Gdns BH17 ... 86 F1
Primrose Hill BA22 ... 193 B7
Primrose La BA21 ... 14 A1
Primrose Way
Christchurch BH23 ... 125 C8
Corfe Mullen BH21 ... 86 E7
Primula Cl DT3 ... 152 F2
Prince Of Wales Rd
Bournemouth BH4 ... 121 C4
Dorchester DT1 ... 108 A1
3 Weymouth DT4 ... 167 C2
Prince of Wales Sch The DT1 ... 134 D8
Prince's Bldgs 21 SO23 ... 126 E6
Princes Ct 8 BH13 ... 121 A4
Prince's Ct BH22 ... 61 D5
Prince's Dr DT4 ... 167 D6
Princes Pl SO22 ... 126 C3
Prince's Pl BH25 ... 95 C3
Princes Rd BH22 ... 61 D5
Princess Ave BH23 ... 124 B6
Princess Ct 11 SO23 ... 126 E6
Princess Rd
Bournemouth BH4 ... 121 B4
Bridport DT6 ... 100 C5
Poole BH13 ... 121 A4
Swanage BH19 ... 179 A2
Princes St BA20 ... 27 D4
Prince's St DT1 ... 108 A2
Pringles Cl BH22 ... 61 E5
Pringles Dr BH22 ... 61 E5
Prinstead Cl 6 SO23 ... 126 F4
Printers Row 13 SO23 ... 126 D6
Priors Barton SO23 ... 126 D3
Priors Cl BH23 ... 125 C7
Priors Cnr 2 BH21 ... 201 D1
Priors Rd BH17 ... 119 A8
Priors Wlk 3 BH21 ... 59 B5
Priory CE Prim Sch The BH23 ... 124 B6
Priory Cl BA20 ... 26 F1
Priory Gdns
3 Pimperne DT11 ... 199 D3
3 Spetisbury DT11 ... 211 E5
West Moors BH22 ... 62 A8
13 Winchester SO23 ... 126 E6
Priory Glade BA21 ... 26 E6
Priory Ho BH23 ... 124 C5
Priory Ind Pk BH23 ... 125 B7
Priory La DT6 ... 100 C6
Priory Quay BH23 ... 124 C5
Priory Rd
Bournemouth BH2 ... 121 E2
Portland DT5 ... 186 F6
West Moors BH22 ... 62 A8
Priory View Ct 4 BH23 ... 124 B6
Priory View Pl 3 BH9 ... 90 A3
Priory View Rd
Bournemouth BH9 ... 90 A3
Burton BH23 ... 92 C2
Privet Rd BH9 ... 121 F8
Promenade BH23 ... 125 B5
Prospect Cl 2 SP8 ... 6 A1
Prospect Cres BH19 ... 179 A3
Prospect Pl
Mere BA12 ... 2 F5
9 Weymouth DT4 ... 167 D2
Prospect Rd
Dorchester DT1 ... 107 E2
Lytchett Matravers BH16 ... 84 D3
Prosperous St 1 BH15 ... 119 C1
Prout Hill 9 DT8 ... 204 D4
Prunus Cl BH22 ... 61 B7
Prunus Dr BH22 ... 61 B7
Pryors Wlk 2 BH16 ... 84 D2
Pud Brook 2 DT9 ... 17 D1
Puddledock La DT3 ... 153 C1
Puddletown CE Fst Sch DT2 ... 78 B1
Puddletown Cres BH17 ... 87 F2
Puddletown Rd
Arne BH20 ... 142 A3
Bere Regis BH20 ... 140 E7
East Stoke BH20 ... 113 B1
Pugmill La DT3 ... 166 D5
Pullman Way BH24 ... 55 C6
Pulmans La 4 TA18 ... 191 F4
Purbeck Adult Ed Ctr BH20 ... 142 D3
Purbeck Ave BH15 ... 118 E1

Purbeck Cl
  Loders DT6 . . . . **101** F8
  Lytchett Matravers BH16 . . **84** D3
  Upton BH16 . . . . **118** B7
  Weymouth DT4 . . . . **167** B1
Purbeck Ct
  Bournemouth BH5 . . . . . . **123** B3
  3 Christchurch BH23 . . . . **124** F8
Purbeck Dr BH31 . . . . **45** B5
Purbeck Gdns BH14 . . . . . **119** F5
Purbeck Hts BH14. . . . . . . **120** B5
Purbeck Marine Wildlife
  Reserve BH20 . . . . **175** B2
Purbeck Rd
  Barton on Sea BH25 . . . . **126** D7
  Bournemouth BH2 . . . . . . **121** E2
  Lytchett Matravers BH16 . . **84** D4
Purbeck Sch The BH20 . . . **142** C2
Purbeck Sports Ctr &
  Swimming Pool BH20 . . . **142** C2
Purbeck Terr Rd BH19 . . . **179** C1
Purbeck Toy & Musical Box
  Mus BH20 . . . . **144** C4
Purbeck View 9 BH19 . . . **178** B2
Purbeck View Sch BH19 . . **179** B3
Purchase Rd BH12 . . . . . . **121** C7
Purdy Ho BH11 . . . . **89** A4
Purewell BH23 . . . . **124** D6
Purewell Cl BH23 . . . . **124** E6
Purewell Cross BH23 . . . . **124** E6
Purewell Cross BH23 . . . . **124** D7
Purewell Ct 2 BH23 . . . . **124** E7
Purewell Rdbt BH23 . . . . . **124** E6
Purns Mill La SP8 . . . . **5** F5
Pussex La BH23 . . . . **91** A7
Putton La DT3 . . . . **166** D5
Putt's La DT9 . . . . **16** B8
Puxey La
  Shillingstone DT11 . . . . . . **198** B5
  Sturminster Newton DT10 . **197** B7
Pye Cl BH21 . . . . **86** E7
Pye Cnr BH21 . . . . **59** B4
Pye La
  Cranborne BH21 . . . . **41** A6
  Tatworth & Forton TA20 . . **202** A8
  Wimborne Minster BH21 . . **59** B4
Pymore La DT6 . . . . **68** C3
Pymore Rd DT6 . . . . **68** E1

Q

Quadrant Ctr The BH1 . . . **121** F3
Quantock Ct 7 BH23 . . . . **124** F8
Quar Cl DT10 . . . . **196** E1
Quarr Dr DT9 . . . . **30** B8
Quarr Hill
  Morden BH20. . . . . **83** C1
  Wool BH20. . . . . **140** B1
Quarr La
  Lytchett Matravers BH16 . . **84** A1
  Sherborne DT9 . . . . **30** B8
  Symondsbury DT6 . . . . **99** D6
Quarry Chase 4 BH4. . . . **121** C3
Quarry Cl
  2 Shipton Gorge DT6. . . **101** D4
  Stour Provost SP8 . . . . **21** D8
  Sturminster Newton DT10. . **35** B2
  8 Swanage BH19. . . . . . **178** F2
  Wimborne Minster BH21. . . **60** B7
Quarry Dr BH21 . . . . **60** B7
Quarry Fields Ind Est BA12 . **2** E5
Quarry La
  Bothenhampton DT6 . . . . **100** E4
  Bradford Abbas DT9 . . . . . **28** C3
  Longburton DT9 . . . . **195** B8
  Melbury Abbas SP7 . . . . . . **24** B5
Quarry Rd BH21. . . . . **60** B7
Quarterjack Mews 1
  BH21 . . . . **59** C4
Quayle Dr BH11 . . . . **88** F6
Quay Point 8 BH15 . . . . **119** C1
Quay Rd BH23 . . . . **124** B6
Quayside DT6. . . . . **100** C1
Quay The
  Poole BH15 . . . . **119** C1
  3 Wareham Town BH20 . . **142** E3
Quebec Pl 2 DT4 . . . . . . **167** D3
Queen Anne Dr
  Oakley BH21 . . . . **87** E8
  Wimborne Minster BH21 . . . **60** A1
Queen Eleanor Rd SP8 . . . . **6** A1
Queen Elizabeth Ct BH21 . **59** B4
Queen Elizabeth's Sch
  BH21. . . . . **58** F6
Queen Mary Ave BH9 . . . . **89** F2
Queen's Ave
  Christchurch BH23 . . . . . **124** B5
  Dorchester DT1 . . . . **134** E8
Queensbury Mans 9
  BH1 . . . . **122** A3
Queens Cl BH22. . . . . **52** F1
Queen's Copse La BH21 . . **51** C8
Queens Ct
  16 Bournemouth BH4 . . . **121** D4
  Bournemouth, Charminster
    BH8. . . . . **122** B8
  New Milton BH25. . . . . **95** D3
  12 Winchester SO23 . . . . **126** D5
Queens Gdns BH21 . . . . . **121** D4
Queens Gr
  New Milton BH25. . . . . **95** C4
  Pen Selwood BA9 . . . . **1** C3
Queensland Rd
  Bournemouth BH5 . . . . . . **123** A5

Queensland Rd *continued*
  Weymouth DT4 . . . . **167** B3
Queensmead
  Burton BH23 . . . . **92** A1
  4 Wimborne Minster BH21 **59** C5
Queens Mead
  8 Swanage BH19. . . . . . **179** B2
  Winchester SO22. . . . . . . **126** A4
Queen's Park Ave BH8. . . . **122** D8
Queen's Park Gdns BH8 . . **122** D7
Queen's Park Inf Sch BH8 **90** C1
Queen's Park Jun Sch
  BH8. . . . . **90** B1
Queen's Park Rd BH8. . . . **122** D7
Queen's Park South Dr
  BH8 . . . . **122** D7
Queen's Park West Dr
  BH8 . . . . **122** D7
Queens Rd
  Bradford Abbas DT9 . . . . . **28** D2
  Bridport DT6 . . . . **100** C6
  Ferndown BH22 . . . . **61** D7
  Fortuneswell DT5 . . . . . . **186** E8
  1 Mere BA12. . . . . **3** B6
  Radipole DT3 . . . . **167** C7
Queen's Rd
  Blandford Forum DT11 . . . **212** E4
  Bournemouth BH3 . . . . . . **121** D4
  Christchurch BH23 . . . . . **124** E6
  Corfe Mullen BH21 . . . . . . **86** D5
  Poole BH14 . . . . **120** D4
  Swanage BH19 . . . . **179** B1
  Winchester SO22 . . . . . . **126** B5
Queensway
  New Milton BH25. . . . . **94** E3
  Ringwood BH24 . . . . **55** D7
  Yeovil BA20 . . . . **27** C5
Queensway Pl BA20 . . . . . . **27** C4
Queens Wlk
  Charmouth DT6 . . . . **97** B7
  Lyme Regis DT7 . . . . **96** B6
Queenswood Ave BH8. . . . **90** E1
Queenswood Dr BH22 . . . . **61** D7
Queenwell DT6 . . . . **68** E1
Quibo La DT4. . . . . **167** A3
Quince La BH21. . . . . **59** E6
Quintin Cl BH23. . . . . **125** F8
Quomp The BH24 . . . . **55** C7

R

Rabin Hill DT10 . . . . **35** B2
Rabling La BH19 . . . . **179** B3
Rabling Rd BH19 . . . . **179** B3
Racedown Rd DT11 . . . . . **199** E3
Rachel Cl BH12 . . . . **120** C7
Radipole La
  Radipole DT4 . . . . **167** A5
  Weymouth DT4 . . . . **166** F4
Radipole Lake Visitor Ctr
  DT4 . . . . **167** D4
Radipole Park Dr DT4 . . . **167** D5
Radipole Prim Sch DT3 . . **167** B8
Radipole Rd BH17 . . . . **88** A2
Raglan Gdns BH11 . . . . . . **89** A2
Raglan Terr BA21 . . . . **27** A7
Railway Dr BH21 . . . . **56** D4
Railway Terr 4 SP8 . . . . **6** A1
Raleigh Cl
  Christchurch BH23 . . . . . **124** F5
  New Milton BH25. . . . . **94** F3
  3 Ringwood BH24 . . . . . **55** E8
Raleigh Rd
  Poole BH12 . . . . **88** E1
  Stalbridge DT10. . . . . **33** E8
Ralph Jessop Ct BH12 . . . **120** D7
Ralph Rd BH21. . . . . **86** E7
Ram La DT11 . . . . **48** C1
Rampart Wlk 4 DT1 . . . . **134** E7
Rampisham Hill DT8 . . . . **205** C3
Ramsbury DT10 . . . . **196** D5
Ramsbury Cl DT11 . . . . . . **212** D5
Ramsbury Ct DT11 . . . . . **212** C5
Ramsey Ct BH25 . . . . **94** F3
Ram's Hill DT10 . . . . **21** F2
Rances Way SO22 . . . . . . **126** C3
Randall Cl DT3. . . . . **166** D5
Randalls Hill BH16. . . . . . . **85** B1
Randolph Rd
  2 Bournemouth BH1 . . . **122** E4
  Poole BH14 . . . . **120** C5
Ranelagh Rd
  Christchurch BH23 . . . . . **125** F7
  Radipole DT4 . . . . **167** D4
  Winchester SO23 . . . . . . **126** D4
Rare Breeds Ctr DT11 . . . **209** D4
Rashley Rd DT3 . . . . **166** D5
Raspberry La SP7 . . . . **12** D2
Ratcliff's Gdn SP7 . . . . **12** D2
Ratleigh La DT9 . . . . **29** B6
Ravana Ct 4 BH8 . . . . . . **122** A5
Ravenscourt Rd BH6 . . . . **123** C5
Ravensdale BH12. . . . . . . **120** C6
Ravenshall 7 BH2 . . . . . . **121** D2
Raven Way BH23 . . . . **124** A5
Ravine Cl BH13 . . . . **147** F7
Ravine Gdns 5 BH13. . . . **147** F7
Ravine Rd
  Bournemouth BH5 . . . . . . **123** B4
  Poole BH13 . . . . **147** F7
Rawles Way DT6 . . . . **100** D7
Rawston Down Rd 6
  DT11 . . . . **199** E2

Rax La DT6 . . . . **100** D7
Raymond Cl BH31 . . . . **45** D6
Raymond Rd DT4 . . . . **166** F2
Rayners Dr BH12 . . . . **120** D6
Rayscliff 21 BH4 . . . . **121** C2
Reap La DT5 . . . . **186** E2
Rebbeck Rd BH7 . . . . **123** A6
Reckford Rd BH23 . . . . . . **124** C2
Reckleford Inf Sch BA21 . . **27** E5
Recreation Rd BH12. . . . . **120** E6
Rectory Ave BH21. . . . . . . **58** D1
Rectory Cl DT2 . . . . **136** B1
Rectory Gdns 2 DT11 . . . **198** F7
Rectory La
  Child Okeford DT11 . . . . . **198** C7
  Hardington Mandeville
    BA22. . . . . **193** A7
  Puncknowle DT2 . . . . **129** E6
  Studland BH19. . . . . **164** C2
  West Stafford DT2. . . . . . **136** A8
Rectory Rd
  Broadmayne DT2 . . . . . . **136** B2
  Piddlehinton DT2 . . . . **76** E7
  Poole BH15 . . . . **119** C6
Rectory Way DT4 . . . . **167** C1
Redan Cl DT3 . . . . **125** F7
Redbreast Rd BH9 . . . . **90** A3
Redbreast Rd N BH9 . . . . . **90** A3
Redbridge Cl DT2. . . . . . . **137** F5
Redbridge Rd DT2 . . . . . . **137** F6
Redcliffe Cl BH23 . . . . **92** C3
Redcliffe Rd BH19 . . . . . . **179** B5
Redcliff View DT11 . . . . . **167** E1
Redcotts La BH21 . . . . **59** B5
Redcotts Rd BH21 . . . . . . **59** B5
Red Deer Ct 4 SO22 . . . . **126** C6
Redgate Pk TA18 . . . . **191** E5
Redhill Ave BH9 . . . . **89** F3
Redhill Cl BH10 . . . . **89** F3
Redhill Cres BH9. . . . . **89** F3
Redhill Ct 1 BH10 . . . . . . **90** A4
Redhill Dr BH10. . . . . **89** E3
Redhill Park Homes 1
  BH10 . . . . **89** F4
Redhill Rdbt BH10 . . . . **89** F4
Redhoave Rd BH17. . . . . . **87** E2
Redhole La DT9 . . . . **16** B2
Red Horn Cl BH16 . . . . . . **118** C4
Red House Mus & Gdns
  BH23. . . . . **124** B6
Red La
  Corfe Mullen BH21 . . . . . . **86** A8
  Seaborough DT8 . . . . **191** E1
  Sixpenny Handley SP5 . . . **189** A3
  Todber DT10 . . . . **21** D4
Redlands
  Christchurch BH23 . . . . . **125** A7
  Poole BH12 . . . . **120** F5
Redlands La 7 DT8 . . . . . **203** F5
Red Lion Cl 3 DT10. . . . . **197** D8
Red Lion Yd DT11 . . . . . . **212** C3
Redmans La SP7 . . . . **24** B6
Redmans View BH31 . . . . . **45** A6
Red Oaks Cl BH22. . . . . . . **61** B7
Redpoll Cl 1 DT3 . . . . . . **152** C4
Red Post
  Bloxworth DT11 . . . . **82** C7
  Poyntington DT9 . . . . **16** C4
Redsails BH13 . . . . **147** B3
Redshank Cl BH17 . . . . **86** F1
Redvers Rd BH23 . . . . **124** E7
Red Wing Rd DT9 . . . . **17** C2
Redwood Cl BH24. . . . . . . **55** D7
Redwood Dr BH22 . . . . **61** C8
Redwood Rd
  Upton BH16. . . . . **118** A8
  Yeovil BA21 . . . . **28** A8
Reedling Ct DT3 . . . . **152** C3
Reed View Cl DT4. . . . . . . **167** A5
Reeves Orch BH21 . . . . . . **56** D5
Reforne DT5. . . . . **186** F4
Reforne Cl 1 DT5 . . . . . . **187** A4
Regency Cres BH23 . . . . . **123** F8
Regency Ct 9 BH8 . . . . **5** D1
Regency Dr 7 DT3. . . . . . **152** C4
Regent Ct 18 SO23 . . . . . **126** E8
Regent Dr BH7. . . . . **122** F8
Regents The 2 BA21. . . . . **26** E6
Regent Way BH23 . . . . . . **124** B6
Reid St BH23 . . . . **124** A8
Rempstone Rd
  Oakley BH21 . . . . **87** D8
  Swanage BH19 . . . . **179** B2
Rempstone Sh Arc 8
  BH20 . . . . **142** E3
Remus Cl DT1 . . . . **134** E7
Renault Dr BH18 . . . . **87** A1
Rendalls Wlk DT6 . . . . . . **100** B6
Renfrew Cl DT1. . . . . **135** C8
Renscombe Rd BH19 . . . . **183** B8
Restharrow BH1 . . . . **122** A4
Retreat Rd BH21 . . . . **59** D4
Revels Hill DT2 . . . . **207** E7
Rew La DT2. . . . . **208** A8
Rex La DT3 . . . . **166** D5
Rex's La BA22. . . . . **27** F1
Reynard Ct BH15. . . . . . . **119** F3
Reynards Way DT3 . . . . . **153** C1
Rhine Rd BH20. . . . . **139** E6
Rhode La DT7 . . . . **64** A1
Rhosewood Dr DT3 . . . . . **153** B1
Rhydderch Way 9 TA18. **191** F4
Ribble Cl BH18 . . . . **87** A2
Ribbonwood Hts BH14 . . **120** B4
Ricardo Cres BH23 . . . . . **125** A6
Rice Gdns BH16. . . . . **118** D4
Rice Terr BH16 . . . . **118** D4

Richard Cl
  2 Upton BH16 . . . . **117** D8
  Upton BH16 . . . . **118** B8
Richard Moss Ho 9
  SO23 . . . . **126** E6
Richmond Cl DT9 . . . . **30** A5
Richmond Ct 7 BH25 . . . . **95** A3
Richmond Gdns BH11 . . . **121** F3
Richmond Gn DT9 . . . . **30** A6
Richmond Hill BH2. . . . . . **121** F3
Richmond Hill Dr BH2. . . **121** F3
Richmond Ho 5 SO22. . . **126** D6
Richmond Park Ave BH8 . **122** C7
Richmond Park Cl BH8. . . **122** D6
Richmond Park Cres
  BH8 . . . . **122** C7
Richmond Park Rd BH8 . **122** C7
Richmond Rd
  4 Blandford Forum
    DT11 . . . . **212** E5
  Poole BH14 . . . . **120** C4
  Sherborne DT9 . . . . **30** A5
  Swanage BH19 . . . . **179** B2
  Wimborne Minster BH21. . . **59** D4
  Yeovil BA20 . . . . **27** C4
Richmond Rise BH22 . . . . **122** D6
Richmond Way BA21 . . . . . **26** E6
Richmond Wood Rd
  BH8 . . . . **122** C7
Ricketts La DT10 . . . . **35** B1
Rickhay Rise DT10 . . . . . **192** B8
Ridgeback La DT6 . . . . **69** E8
Ridge Dro DT10. . . . . **196** F5
Ridgefield Gdns BH23 . . . **125** D8
Ridge La
  Hazelbury Bryan DT10 . . . **196** D5
  West Coker BA22 . . . . **193** A6
Ridgemead 5 BA20. . . . . . **26** F2
Ridgemount Gdns BH15 . **118** E3
Ridge The DT9. . . . . **16** E5
Ridge View DT10. . . . . . . **196** F8
Ridgeway
  Bradpole DT6. . . . . **68** F1
  Broadstone BH18 . . . . **87** B4
  Corfe Mullen BH21 . . . . . . **86** D8
  Ferndown BH22. . . . . **89** E8
  Sherborne DT9 . . . . **29** F5
  Winchester SO22. . . . . . . **126** A3
Ridge Way
  Puddletown DT2 . . . . **76** F1
  Shaftesbury SP7 . . . . **12** F4
Ridgeway La
  Child Okeford DT11 . . . . . **198** C8
  Hinton St Mary DT10 . . . . . **35** B4
Ridgeway Rd SP8 . . . . **5** E3
Ridgway TA18 . . . . **192** B8
Ridley Rd BH9 . . . . **121** F8
Ridout Cl BH10 . . . . **89** B1
Ridwood DT6 . . . . **99** A6
Rigg La DT9 . . . . **14** F2
Riggs Gdns BH11 . . . . **88** F2
Rigler Rd BH15 . . . . **119** A2
Rimbrow Cl DT3 . . . . **153** C1
Rimbury Way BH23. . . . . **124** A8
Rimpton Hill BA22 . . . . . . **15** A7
Ring St DT10 . . . . **33** D8
Ringstead Cres DT3 . . . . **168** B6
Rings The DT3 . . . . **79** F8
Ringwood Inf Sch BH24 . . **55** C6
Ringwood Jun Sch BH24 . . **55** C6
Ringwood La BH24 . . . . . . **201** E7
Ringwood L Ctr BH24 . . . . **55** C7
Ringwood Rd
  Alderholt SP6. . . . . **42** C5
  Bournemouth BH11 . . . . . **88** E4
  Bransgore BH23 . . . . **93** D5
  Ferndown BH22. . . . . **61** C4
  Fordingbridge SP6. . . . . . **43** C5
  Hyde SP6 . . . . **43** E4
  Poole BH12 . . . . **120** B7
  Sopley BH23 . . . . **92** A7
  St Leonards BH24 . . . . **53** F2
  Three Legged Cross BH21. . **52** F8
  Verwood BH31. . . . . **45** D6
  Walkford BH23 . . . . **94** B1
  West Moors BH22 . . . . **62** A8
Ringwood Rd Nature Reserve
  BH11 . . . . **88** E5
Ringwood Road Ret Pk
  BH11 . . . . **88** E5
Ringwood Sch BH24 . . . . . **55** C7
Ringwood Trad Est BH24 . **55** C6
Rip Croft DT5 . . . . **186** E2
Ripley Ct BH22 . . . . **61** F7
Ripon Rd BH9 . . . . **90** A1
Ripp's La DT2 . . . . **207** F4
Rise The
  Radipole DT4 . . . . **167** A5
  Stratton DT2 . . . . **106** D8
Ritchie Pl BH22 . . . . **52** F3
Ritchie Rd
  Bournemouth BH11 . . . . . **89** B4
  Yeovil BA21 . . . . **26** C5
River Cl BH21. . . . . **59** C6
Riverdale La BH23 . . . . . . **124** A6
River La 2 DT11 . . . . **211** D6
Riverland Ct 4 BH23 . . . . **124** A6
Riverlea Rd BH23 . . . . . . **124** A6
Rivermead Gdns BH23. . . . **91** E2
River Pk BH6 . . . . **123** F6
Riversdale 8 BH21 . . . . . . **59** C4
Riversdale Rd BH6 . . . . . . **124** A4
Riversdene DT11 . . . . **48** A6
Riverside
  3 Beaminster DT8 . . . . . **204** D4
  4 Bournemouth BH10 . . . . **89** D4
  Ringwood BH24 . . . . **55** B6
Riverside Ave BH7 . . . . **91** C1

Riverside Cl 6 DT2 . . . . . **207** D8
Riverside Ct 7 BH4 . . . . **121** D4
Riverside Ho 4 SO23 . . . **126** F6
Riverside La BH6 . . . . **123** F5
Riverside Pk BH23 . . . . . **124** A5
Riverside Pk Ind Est BH21 **59** D3
Riverside Rd
  Blandford Forum DT11 . . . **212** E3
  Bournemouth BH6 . . . . . . **123** F5
  Ferndown BH22. . . . . **52** F2
Riverslea Mews BH23 . . . **124** D6
Rivers Mead DT10. . . . . . . **35** C2
Riversmeet Ct BH23. . . . . **124** D6
Rivers Rd BA21 . . . . **27** F8
Rivervale DT6 . . . . **100** C8
River View SP8 . . . . **5** E2
River Way
  Charmouth DT6 . . . . **97** B7
  Christchurch BH23 . . . . . . **91** D2
Riviera 11 BH1. . . . . **122** B3
Riviera Ct
  Bournemouth BH2 . . . . . . **121** D3
  3 Poole BH13 . . . . **147** F7
Rixon Cl DT10 . . . . **35** C1
Rixon Hill DT10 . . . . **35** C1
R L Stevenson Ave BH4. . **121** B3
RNLI Mus BH15 . . . . **119** C2
Roberts La
  Poole BH17 . . . . **118** F7
  Poole BH17 . . . . **119** A7
Robertson Rd BH20 . . . . . **139** D7
Roberts Pl DT1 . . . . **107** C1
Roberts Rd
  Bournemouth BH7 . . . . . . **123** A6
  Poole BH17 . . . . **87** B1
Robin Cl 2 DT3. . . . . **152** C4
Robin Cres BH25 . . . . **94** D5
Robin Gdns BH23 . . . . . . **124** A8
Robin Gr BH25 . . . . **94** F2
Robins Ct 7 BH21 . . . . . . **59** C4
Robins Garth DT1. . . . . . . **108** A3
Robins Gdn DT2 . . . . **209** A2
Robinson Hts DT10 . . . . . . **33** D8
Robins Way BH23 . . . . . . **125** B5
Robinswood Dr BH22. . . . . **61** D7
Robsall Cl BH12. . . . . **120** C7
Robville Ct 3 BH7 . . . . . . **123** B6
Rochester Rd BH11 . . . . . . **89** B4
Rockbourne Gdns BH25 . **126** D8
Rockbourne La SP6 . . . . . **190** F3
Rockford Cl BH6. . . . . **123** F3
Rockhampton Cl DT3 . . . . **152** D3
Rockley Mews BH15. . . . . **118** E2
Rockley Pk Cvn Est BH15,
  BH16 . . . . **118** B3
Rockley Rd BH15. . . . . . . **118** E1
Rocks La DT2 . . . . **206** A7
Rockway DT6 . . . . **101** C4
Rocky Knap DT3 . . . . **167** C7
Rodden Cl DT4. . . . . **180** C8
Rodden La DT3 . . . . **150** C5
Rodden Row DT3 . . . . **149** B7
Rodgett Cres BH20 . . . . . **142** F8
Rod Hill La DT2 . . . . **78** B1
Rodney Cl BH12. . . . . **121** A8
Rodney Ct
  Christchurch BH23 . . . . . **125** A6
  7 Poole BH15 . . . . **119** C1
Rodney Dr BH23 . . . . **124** F6
Rodway BH21 . . . . **59** C4
Rodwell Ave DT4. . . . . . . **167** D1
Rodwell Cl BH10 . . . . **89** C6
Rodwell Rd DT4 . . . . **167** D1
Rodwell St DT4 . . . . **167** D1
Roe Ave BA22 . . . . **26** C5
Roebuck Cl BH25 . . . . **95** B3
Roe La BA22 . . . . **15** B8
Roeshot Cres BH23 . . . . . . **93** E1
Roeshot Hill BH23. . . . . . . **93** C2
Roi-mar Home Pk BH8 . . . **90** D4
Roke Rd BH20 . . . . **80** F4
Rolfe Cres DT3 . . . . **166** D6
Rolls Bridge La SP8 . . . . . . **5** E2
Rolls Bridge Way SP8 . . . . **5** D2
Rolls Dr BH6. . . . . **124** B3
Rolls Mill Way DT10. . . . . **197** C8
Roman Cl DT3 . . . . **167** C7
Roman Hill Trading Est
  DT2 . . . . **154** D6
Roman Hts BH21 . . . . **86** E3
Roman Rd
  Corfe Mullen BH18 . . . . . . **86** E5
  Dorchester DT1 . . . . **134** F8
  Osmington DT3 . . . . **154** A1
  Radipole DT3 . . . . **167** C7
Romans' Rd SO23 . . . . . . **126** D4
Roman Way BH21 . . . . **58** C5
Romney Cl BH10 . . . . **89** E3
Romney Ct 51 BH4 . . . . . **121** C3
Romney Rd BH10 . . . . **89** E4
Romsey Rd
  Winchester SO22. . . . . . . **126** A4
  Yeovil BA21 . . . . **28** A7
Romulus Cl DT1 . . . . **134** E7
Ronald Bowker Ct 1
  SO22 . . . . **126** C6
Rookery Cl SP8 . . . . **11** B8
Rookery La
  Burstock DT8. . . . . **203** C6
  Uplyme DT7 . . . . **64** A2
Rookery The DT2 . . . . **130** F8
Rook Hill Rd BH23 . . . . . . **125** B6
Rook La DT11 . . . . **210** C2
Rooks Down Rd SO22 . . . **126** B3
Rook St BA12 . . . . **3** A4
Roosevelt Cres BH11. . . . . **89** B6
Ropers La BH16 . . . . **118** D7
Roper's La BH20 . . . . **142** E4

Ropewalk Ho 7 SO23 126 E6
Rope Walks DT6 100 C6
Roping Rd BA21 27 C6
Ropley Rd BH7 123 C7
Rosamond Ave DT6 101 D4
Rosamund Ave BH21 59 E1
Roscrea Cl BH6 124 B4
Roscrea Dr BH6 124 B4
Rosebank La DT11 212 F6
Roseberry Gdns 3 SP8 5 F3
Rosebery Ave BA21 27 F6
Rosebery Cl BH31 45 E5
Rosebery Rd BH5 123 A5
Rosebud Ave 1 BH9 90 A2
Rosecrae Cl BH25 94 F4
Rose Cres BH15 119 F6
Rosecroft Rd DT4 166 F1
Rose Ct
3 Gillingham SP8 6 A1
Poole BH15 119 E3
Rosedale Cl 3 BH23 124 E6
Rose Farm Cl BH22 61 B3
Rosefields 2 DT11 212 D2
Rose Gdns BH9 90 A3
Rose Gdn The BH23 91 D1
Rose La
1 Crewkerne TA18 191 E4
Winsham TA20 191 A4
Roselyn Cres DT9 31 B1
Rosemary Ct 8 BH23 126 B7
Rosemary Gdns BH12 120 B7
Rosemary La DT3 149 B7
Rosemary Rd BH12 120 C7
Rosemary St DT9 17 C2
Rosemount Rd BH4 121 B2
Rose's La DT3 150 C2
Rosewarne Ct 9 SO23 126 E7
Rosewood Gdns BH25 94 F4
Roslin Gdns BH3 121 D7
Roslin Rd BH3 121 E7
Roslin Rd S BH3 121 E7
Ross Cl BH20 139 F6
Ross Gdns BH11 88 C5
Ross Glades BH3 121 E6
Rossiters Quay BH23 124 C6
Rossley Cl BH23 93 E2
Rossmore Com Coll BH12 120 D8
Rossmore Par BH12 120 B8
Rossmore Rd BH12 120 D7
Ross Rd BH24 47 E1
Rotary Cl BH21 59 F7
Rothbury Pk BH25 95 B2
Rotherfield Rd
Bournemouth BH5 123 B3
Walkford BH23 94 A1
Rotherham Rd DT5 181 C1
Rothesay Dr BH23 125 E7
Rothesay Rd
Bournemouth BH4 121 C5
Dorchester DT1 135 A8
Rotterdam Dr BH23 124 D7
Rough Down La DT6 65 B2
Rough Height BH19 179 B1
Roumelia La BH1,BH5 122 E4
Roundham Gdns
Bridport DT6 100 D3
Weymouth DT4 167 A2
Roundhaye Gdns BH11 88 F6
Roundhaye Rd BH11 88 F6
Roundhayes Cl DT4 167 A2
Roundways BH11 88 F3
Rowan Cl
Christchurch BH23 125 D8
Radipole DT4 167 A6
Sandford BH20 143 A8
St Leonards & St Ives BH24 53 F4
Rowan Dr
Broadstone BH17 86 E1
Christchurch BH23 125 D8
Verwood BH31 45 D4
Rowan Way BA20 27 A3
Rowbarrow Cl BH17 87 E2
Rowbarrow Hill DT9 19 F4
Rowbarrow La BH21 200 F2
Rowden Mill La DT10 32 E1
Rowe Gdns 6 BH12 120 F7
Rowena Rd BH6 123 F5
Rowland Ave BH15 119 E6
Rowlands Hill BH21 59 D6
Rowlands Rd 5 DT11 198 F4
Rowls La BA9 4 B3
Rownhams Rd BH8 90 D3
Row The DT10 35 A1
Roxborough 47 BH4 121 C3
Royal Arc 5 BH1 122 E4
Royal Bournemouth Gen Hospl The BH7 91 B1
Royal Cl BA21 27 E6
Royal Greenjackets Mus SO23 126 D5
Royal Hampshire Cty Hospl SO22 126 C5
Royal Hampshire Regiment Mus SO23 126 D5
Royal Manor Sch The DT5 186 F4
Royal Oak Rd BH10 89 C5
Royal Signals Mus DT11 199 E3
Royal Victoria Mews BH4 121 D3
Royal Winchester Mews SO22 126 A5
Roydon Cl SO22 126 C3
Royster Cl BH17 87 C1
Royston Dr BH21 59 D5
Royston Pl BH25 127 B8
Rozelle Rd BH14 120 C4
Rozel Manor BH13 121 B2
Ruben Dr BH15 118 D2
Rubens Cl BH25 95 B3
Ruddock Cl BA22 193 B8
Ruddock Way BA22 193 A8
Rue La DT9 31 F4
Ruffield Cl SO22 126 A8
Rufford Gdns BH6 123 E5
Rufus Castle DT5 187 B3
Rufus Way DT5 187 B5
Rugby Rd BH17 87 A1
Ruins La DT6 99 A6
Rundlestone Ct DT1 107 B2
Runnymede Ave BH11 88 E6
Runnymede Rd BA21 27 F8
Runton Rd BH12 120 F5
Runway The BH23 125 B7
Rural La DT2 73 F3
Ruscombe La DT6 69 E6
Rushall La BH21 86 A5
Rushcombe Fst Sch
Corfe Mullen BH21 86 D5
Poole BH21 85 F6
Rushcombe Way BH21 86 E6
Rushetts Cl 4 DT5 186 F1
Rushford Warren BH23 124 F5
Rushmere Rd BH6 123 D7
Rushmore Golf Club SP5 188 C5
Rushton Cres BH3 121 F6
Ruskin Ave BH9 90 B3
Russell Ave
Swanage BH19 179 B1
Weymouth DT4 167 B1
Russell Cotes Art Gall & Mus BH1 122 A2
Russell Cotes Rd BH1 122 A2
Russell Ct 2 BH25 95 A3
Russell Dr
Christchurch BH23 124 D6
Swanage BH19 179 B1
Russell Gdns
Hamworthy BH16 118 C4
St Leonards BH24 54 D5
Russell Rd SO23 126 E8
Russel Rd BH10 89 C6
Russet Cl BH22 61 D6
Russet Way BA20 26 F2
Rutland Manor 10 BH13 121 A4
Rutland Rd
Bournemouth BH9 122 B8
Christchurch BH23 91 F1
Weymouth DT4 167 B4
Ryall Rd
Poole BH17 87 D1
Whitechurch Canonicorum DT6 66 D2
Ryall's La DT9 196 A7
Ryan Cl
Ferndown BH22 61 C7
Northport BH20 142 E5
Ryan Gdns
Bournemouth BH11 89 B6
Ferndown BH22 61 C7
Rydal Cl BH23 91 D4
Rydal Ho 2 BH4 121 C2
Rydal Mews BH21 59 D5
Ryecroft Ave BH11 88 E5
Ryefields Cl BA22 193 B8
Rye Gdns BA20 26 F2
Rye Hill BH20 81 B1
Rye Hill Cl BH20 81 B1
Ryemead La DT4 180 C6
Rye Wr La TA18 193 A1
Ryland's La DT4 180 D8
Rymbury DT3 153 C1
Ryme Rd DT9 194 B5

S

Sackmore Gn DT10 20 F3
Sackmore La DT10 20 F3
Sackville St DT11 81 E8
Sadborow La TA20 202 E5
Saddle Cl BH21 60 C6
Saffron Ct BH11 88 D3
Saffron Dr BH23 125 B8
Saffron Way BH11 88 D3
St Adlem's CE Comb Sch BH12 121 A6
St Alban's Ave BH8 122 C7
St Alban's Cres BH8 122 B8
St Alban's Rd BH8 122 B7
St Alban St DT4 167 D2
St Aldhelm's BH14 120 F4
St Aldhelm's Cl BH13 120 F3
St Aldhelm's Pl BH13 120 F4
St Aldhelm's Rd
Poole BH13 120 F4
Sherborne DT9 30 B8
St Andrews 3 BH23 124 A6
St Andrews Ave DT3 167 D7
St Andrews CE Prim Sch
Overcombe/Preston DT3 153 A2
Yetminster DT9 194 C6
St Andrews Cl 4 DT1 135 B8
St Andrew's Cl DT9 194 E3
St Andrews Dr DT6 97 A8
St Andrews Ind Est DT6 100 F8
St Andrews Mdw DT7 96 B6
St Andrews Rd
Broadstone BH18 87 A5
Yeovil BA20 27 A5
St Andrew's Rd DT6 68 F1
St Andrews View SP7 37 E7
St Anne's Ave BH6 123 E5
St Annes Cl
Cann SP7 23 B6
Winchester SO22 126 A2
St Anne's Gdns BA21 27 A6
St Anne's Rd
Upton BH16 118 B7
Weymouth DT4 180 E7
St Ann's Ct 1 BH1 122 E5
St Ann's Hospl BH13 147 E6
St Anthony's Rd BH2 121 F5
St Antony's 6 BH4 121 D2
St Antony's Leweston Sch DT9 195 A7
St Aubyns Ct BH15 119 B2
St Augustines RC Prim Sch DT4 167 B1
St Augustin's Rd BH2 121 F5
St Bartholomews CE Fst Sch 31 TA18 191 F4
St Bede CE Prim Sch SO23 126 E6
St Bede's Ct 8 SO23 126 E7
St Brelades Ave BH12 88 D1
St Catharines Rd BH19 185 C7
St Catherines BH21 59 C4
St Catherines Chapel DT3 149 A6
St Catherine's Cres 2 DT9 30 A5
St Catherine's Par BH23 91 F1
St Catherines RC Prim Sch DT6 100 D8
St Catherine's RC Prim Sch BH21 60 B6
St Catherine's Rd
Bournemouth BH6 123 F3
Winchester SO23 126 F4
St Catherine's Way BH23 91 D3
St Cecilia's Gdns DT6 100 D8
St Clair Rd BH13 147 F7
St Cleeve Way BH22 61 C3
St Clement's Gdns BH1 122 D5
St Clements Rd BH15 120 A7
St Clement's Rd BH1 122 D5
St Clement's & St John's CE Inf Sch BH1 122 D5
St Clement St 2 SO23 126 D5
St Cross Ct 4 SO23 126 D3
St Cross Hospital SO23 126 D2
St Cross Mede SO23 126 C2
St Cross Rd SO23 126 D3
St Davids Cl 9 DT1 135 B8
St David's Cres BA21 27 D7
St David's Ct 3 BH1 122 E5
St David's Rd
Upton BH16 118 B7
Weymouth DT4 180 D7
St Denys 2 BH25 95 B1
St Edmund St 6 DT4 167 D2
St Edwards 1 SP7 12 F3
St Edwards Cl BH20 177 A8
St Edward's RC/CE Sch BH15 119 F7
St Faith's CE Prim Sch SO22 126 D3
St Faith's Rd SO23 126 D3
St George's Almshos 6 BH15 119 B1
St George's Ave
Bournemouth BH8 122 C8
Poole BH12 120 B8
Radipole DT4 167 E6
Yeovil BA21 27 D7
St Georges CE Fst Sch BH19 178 B3
St Georges Cl DT1 108 D1
St George's Cl
Bournemouth BH8 122 C8
Christchurch BH23 125 D8
Swanage BH19 178 B2
St Georges Ct BH22 61 E5
St George's Ct 2 BH1 122 E5
St George's Ct BH12 120 B8
St Georges Dr
Bournemouth BH11 88 D3
Bransgore BH23 93 B8
St George's Dr BH22 61 C4
St Georges Est Rd DT5 186 F4
St Georges Hill DT7 96 A6
St George's Ho 16 SO23 126 E6
St Georges Inf Sch DT5 186 F3
St Georges Mans 5 BH5 122 F4
St Georges Rd DT1 108 C1
St George's Rd
Portland DT5 186 F4
Shaftesbury SP7 12 F2
St George's Sch SP8 1 D1
St George's St SO23 126 E6
St Gildas Cath Sch BA21 27 D5
St Giles Cl
Chideock DT6 99 A7
Winchester SO23 126 F5
St Giles Hill SO23 126 F5
St Giles's House BH21 201 E6
St Gregory CE Prim Sch DT10 20 F2
St Helen's La DT2 206 B2
St Helen's Rd
Dorchester DT1 107 F2
Sandford BH20 143 A8
Weymouth DT4 166 F2
St Helier Ave DT3 152 B4
St Helier Rd BH12 88 D1
St Ives End La BH24 54 C4
St Ives Gdns BH2 121 F5
St Ives Pk BH24 54 C5
St Ives Wood BH24 54 D5
St James CE Fst Sch
Alderholt SP6 42 C6
Holt BH21 51 A6
St James' CE Prim Sch BH7 123 B6
St James Cl 2 BH15 119 B1
St James' La SO22,SO23 126 D5
Saint James Pk DT6 69 A1
St James Rd BH22 61 A6
St James's 1 BH5 122 E3
St James's Cl BA21 26 F5
St James's Pk BA21 26 E5
St James's Sq BH5 123 A5
St James St SP7 12 E2
St James' Terr SO22, SO23 126 D5
St James' Villas SO23 126 D5
St Johns CE Aided Prim Sch DT4 167 E6
St Johns CE Fst Sch BH21 59 D4
St John's Cl BH21 59 D4
St John's Ct 4 BH1 122 E5
St John's Gdns 2 BH9 89 F1
St John's Hill
Shaftesbury SP7 12 D2
Wareham BH20 142 E3
Wimborne Minster BH21 59 D5
St John's Hospital (Almshouses)(N) 1 SO23 126 F5
St John's Hospital (Almshouses)(S) 3 SO23 126 F5
St Johns Rd BH25 95 A7
St John's Rd
Bournemouth BH5 122 E4
Christchurch BH23 124 A6
Poole BH15 119 D4
Winchester SO23 126 F6
Yeovil BA21 27 E7
St John's St SO23 126 F5
St Joseph's RC Comb Sch BH12 120 E7
St Joseph's RC Prim Sch BH23 125 A8
St Julien Cres DT3 152 B3
St Julien Rd 1 BH20 139 D7
St Just Cl BH22 61 C3
St Juthware Cl BA22 193 C3
St Katharine's CE Prim Sch BH6 124 B4
St Katherine's Ave DT6 100 F7
St Katherine's Dr DT6 100 E8
St Lawrence 4 DT6 128 B8
St Lawrence Cres SP7 12 F4
St Lawrence Rd DT3 152 C5
St Ledger's Pl BH8 122 D6
St Ledger's Rd BH8 122 D6
St Leonard's Ave DT11 212 E4
St Leonards Farm Pk BH22 62 A8
St Leonards Hospl BH24 53 E1
St Leonards Mid Sch DT11 212 E4
St Leonard's Rd
Bournemouth BH8 122 B6
Weymouth DT4 167 D1
St Leonards Way BH24 53 F5
St Luke's CE Prim Sch BH9 121 F8
St Luke's Ct 2 DT6 100 B8
St Luke's Rd
Bournemouth BH3 121 F7
Bournemouth BH3 122 A7
St Maradox La BH9 89 F2
St Margarets BH2 121 F5
St Margaret's Almshouses BH21 59 A5
St Margaret's Ave BH23 124 B5
St Margarets Cl BH21 59 A5
St Margarets Hill BH21 59 A5
St Margaret's Hill BH21 59 A6
St Margaret's Rd
Bournemouth BH10 89 C2
Poole BH15 119 D4
St Mark's CE Prim Sch BH10 89 C1
St Marks CE VA Fst Sch BH19 178 F2
St Mark's Rd BH11 89 B3
St Martins Church DT11 212 B4
St Martins Cl DT2 136 B2
St Martin's Cl
1 Wareham BH20 142 E4
Winchester SO23 126 F6
St Martins Field DT2 133 D7
St Martin's La BH20 142 E4
St Martins Pre Sch TA18 191 E4
St Martins Rd BH16 118 A7
St Martin's Rd
3 Fortuneswell DT5 186 F7
Sandford BH20 143 A8
Shaftesbury SP7 12 F2
Weymouth DT4 180 E8
St Martin's Sq SP8 5 F2
St Martins Trad Pk SO23 126 F6
St Martins Way BA20 26 F2
St Mary Cath Prim Sch DT10 21 A5
St Mary CE Prim Sch DT9 28 D1
St Mary Magdalen Almshouses 4 SO23 126 F5
St Marys Cath Prim Sch DT1 135 B8
St Marys CE Fst Sch
Charminster DT2 107 D6
Ferndown BH22 52 F3
St Marys CE Mid Sch DT2 110 A8
St Marys CE Prim Sch DT8 204 C4
St Marys Cl BH23 93 C8
St Mary's Cl
Northport BH20 142 C5
7 Sixpenny Handley SP5 189 A4
3 Winterborne Whitechurch DT11 210 C3
St Mary's Cres BA21 27 E8
St Mary's Ct BH6 123 E3
St Mary's Gdns 3 DT8 204 C4
St Mary's Maternity Hospl BH15 119 D3
St Mary's Mews BH22 61 D4
St Mary's RC Comb Sch BH15 119 E5
St Marys RC Fst Sch
Swanage BH19 179 B2
Wool BH20 140 A2
St Mary's Rd
Bournemouth BH1 122 D6
Ferndown BH22 61 D5
Poole BH15 119 E4
Sherborne DT9 29 F5
St Marys Sch
Bridport DT6 100 C5
Donhead St Mary SP7 13 D3
St Mary St
7 Radipole DT4 167 D2
Winchester SO22 126 B3
St Mary the Virgin Prim Sch SP8 11 B8
St Mary Well St 11 DT8 204 C4
St Mathews Rd SO22 126 B8
St Merrin's Cl BH10 89 C4
St Michaels DT7 96 C6
St Michael's BH2 121 D3
St Michael's Ave BA21 27 E7
St Michael's CE Mid Sch BH21 59 E7
St Michael's CE Prim Sch BH2 121 D3
St Michaels Cl
Hamworthy BH15 118 E3
Over Compton DT9 28 E7
Verwood BH31 45 B5
St Michaels Ct
1 Bournemouth BH6 123 C4
Weymouth DT4 167 C1
St Michael's Gdns 8 SO23 126 D5
St Michael's La DT6 100 C6
St Michael's Mews 9 BH2 121 E3
St Michael's Pas SO23 126 E4
St Michael's Pl 11 BH2 121 E3
St Michaels Prim Sch DT7 96 C6
St Michaels Rd BH31 45 B4
St Michael's Rd
Bournemouth BH2 121 E2
6 Wareham BH20 142 E3
Winchester SO23 126 D4
Yeovil BA21 27 F6
St Michael's Rdbt BH4 121 D3
St Michaels Trading Est DT6 100 C6
St Nicholas CE Prim Sch DT11 198 C7
St Nicholas Cl
3 Henstridge BA8 19 A4
11 Yeovil BA20 27 D4
St Nicholas Ct 5 DT11 198 C7
St Nicholas Gdns 2 DT11 198 E3
St Nicholas & Lawrence CE Prim Sch DT3 152 C2
St Nicholas St DT4 167 D2
St Osmund Cl 3 DT9 194 C5
St Osmunds CE Mid Sch DT1 135 B8
St Osmunds Com Sports Ctr DT1 135 A8
St Osmund's Rd BH14 120 D3
St Patricks Ave DT4 166 F1
St Patricks Ind Est DT11 198 B6
St Patrick's Rd 2 BA21 26 F7
St Paul's Cl DT9 30 C7
St Pauls Ct 15 SO22 126 D6
St Paul's Gn DT9 30 C8
St Paul's Hill SO22 126 D6
St Paul's La BH8 122 B4
St Pauls Pl 26 SO23 126 D6
St Paul's Pl BH8 122 B4
St Paul's Rd
Bournemouth BH8 122 B4
4 Fortuneswell DT5 186 F7
St Peter's Cl 1 DT11 199 D4
St Peters Ct 3 BH1 122 A3
St Peter's Ct 3 BH14 120 A4
St Peter's Gate 13 BH1 121 F3
St Peter's RC Comp Sch BH6 123 F4
St Peter's RC Sch BH7 123 B8
St Peter's Rd
Bournemouth BH1 121 F3
Bournemouth BH1 122 A3
Poole BH14 120 A4
St Peter's Rdbt BH1 122 A3
St Peter St SO23 126 E6
St Peter's Wlk 15 BH1 121 F3
St Rayn Hill TA18 191 A4
St Richards Cl DT11 211 F7

St Rumbold's Rd SP7 ..... 12 F2
St Saviours Cl BH7 ..... 123 C7
St Stephen's Ct BH2 ..... 121 E4
St Stephens La BH31 ..... 45 C6
St Stephen's Rd
Bournemouth BH2 ..... 121 E3
Winchester SO22 ..... 126 B8
St Stephen's Way 4
BH2 ..... 121 F3
St Swithuns Ave DT6 ..... 100 C7
St Swithins Cl DT9 ..... 30 C6
St Swithins Rd DT6 ..... 100 C7
St Swithin's Rd DT9 ..... 30 C6
St Swithun's Rd BH1 ..... 122 B4
St Swithun's Rdbt BH1 ..... 122 B3
St Swithun's Rd S BH1 ..... 122 B4
St Swithun St SO23 ..... 126 E5
St Thomas Cl BH10 ..... 89 D2
St Thomas Cross 1 BA21. 27 E5
St Thomas Garnet's RC Sch
BH5 ..... 123 A5
St Thomas Mews 3
SO23 ..... 126 D5
St Thomas Rd DT1 ..... 107 F2
St Thomas St
Radipole DT4 ..... 167 D2
Winchester SO23 ..... 126 D5
St Valerie Rd BH2 ..... 121 F5
St Vast's Rd BH19 ..... 179 C1
St Walburga's RC Prim Sch
BH9 ..... 90 B1
St Winifred's Rd BH2 ..... 121 F5
Salcot Rd SO23 ..... 126 E8
Salerno Pl BH15 ..... 118 D2
Salisbury Cres DT11 ..... 212 D5
Salisbury Rd
Blandford Forum DT11 ... 212 D4
Bournemouth BH1 ..... 122 E4
Burton BH23 ..... 92 D2
Donhead St Mary SP7 ..... 13 D1
Pimperne DT11 ..... 199 E4
Poole BH14 ..... 120 C5
Ringwood BH24 ..... 47 B7
Ringwood SP6 ..... 43 C1
Shaftesbury SP7 ..... 12 F2
Sopley, Winkton BH23 ..... 92 B5
2 Swanage BH19 ..... 179 C1
Weymouth DT4 ..... 167 C3
Salisbury St
Blandford Forum DT11 ... 212 C3
Cranborne BH21 ..... 40 A8
Dorchester DT1 ..... 108 B2
Marnhull DT10 ..... 21 B2
Mere BA12 ..... 3 A5
Shaftesbury SP7 ..... 12 F2
Sally Kings La SP7 ..... 12 D3
Sally Lovell's La BA8 ..... 18 E7
Salterns Ct BH14 ..... 147 B8
Salterns Point BH14 ..... 147 B8
Salterns Quay BH14 ..... 147 B8
Salterns Rd BH14 ..... 120 A3
Salterns Way BH14 ..... 147 B8
Salter Rd BH13 ..... 147 C3
Salthouse La BA20 ..... 27 C4
Saltings Rd BH16 ..... 118 B6
Salway Ash CE Prim Sch
DT6 ..... 68 B8
Salway Dr DT6 ..... 68 B6
Samantha Cl BH10 ..... 89 E3
Samarate Way BA20 ..... 26 F5
Sammy Miller Motorcycle
Mus BH25 ..... 94 E5
Samphire Cl DT4 ..... 167 D6
Samples Way BH17 ..... 119 F8
Samson Rd BH15 ..... 118 D2
Samways Cl BA22 ..... 26 D5
Sancreed Rd BH12 ..... 120 E7
Sancroft Ho BH21 ..... 60 A1
Sandbanks Bsns Ctr
BH13 ..... 147 B3
Sandbanks Rd
Poole BH14 ..... 120 A2
Poole BH15,BH14 ..... 119 F3
Sandbourne Ave DT11 ... 212 E6
Sandbourne Cl 6 BH19 . 178 F2
Sandbourne Rd
Bournemouth BH4 ..... 121 C1
Overcombe/Preston DT3 .. 168 B7
Poole BH15 ..... 119 D4
Sandecotes Rd BH14 ..... 120 C3
Sanderling Cl 6 DT3 ..... 152 C4
Sanderlings 3 BH24 ..... 55 E6
Sanders Gn 4 DT11 ..... 210 C3
Sandford Cl BH9 ..... 90 C3
Sandford Dr BH20 ..... 116 B2
Sandford La BH20 ..... 142 E5
Sandford Lane Ind Est
BH20 ..... 142 F5
Sandford Mid Sch BH20 116 A1
Sandford Orcas Manor
House DT9 ..... 15 E6
Sandford Orcas Rd DT9 .. 15 F4
Sandford Rd
Northport BH20 ..... 142 E5
Sandford BH20 ..... 142 F7
Wareham St Martin BH20 . 116 B2
Sandford St Martin Fst Sch
BH20 ..... 143 A8
Sandford Way BH18 ..... 86 F2
Sandhills Cl BH17 ..... 87 D2
Sandhills Cres BH20 ..... 139 E2
Sandhurst Dr BH21 ..... 53 C7
Sandhurst Rd BA20 ..... 27 B2
Sandilands Cl SP8 ..... 10 E3
Sandleheath Rd SP6 ..... 42 B7
Sandlewood Cl 4 BA21 .. 28 A8
Sandmartin Cl BH25 ..... 126 F7
Sandown Cl BA20 ..... 27 C5
Sandown Rd BH23 ..... 124 E6
Sandpiper Cl BH17 ..... 86 F1
Sandpiper Way DT4 ..... 180 D6
Sandringham Cl BH9 ..... 90 B4
Sandringham Ct
Bournemouth BH8 ..... 122 C6
1 Dorchester DT1 ..... 135 C8
Sandringham Gdns BH9 ... 90 B4
Sandringham Rd
Poole BH14 ..... 120 C3
Yeovil BA21 ..... 28 A6
Sandringham Sports Ctr
DT1 ..... 108 B1
Sandroyd Sch SP5 ..... 188 C5
Sandsfoot Castle DT4 ... 180 E7
Sandy Cl BH21 ..... 60 A8
Sandy Hill La BH20 ..... 177 C8
Sandy Hole TA16 ..... 191 F8
Sandyhurst Cl BH17 ..... 87 C1
Sandy La
Bournemouth BH6 ..... 123 B5
Christchurch BH23 ..... 91 E2
Hilfield DT2 ..... 195 A1
Lytchett Matravers BH16 .. 84 E6
Minterne Magna DT2 ..... 207 C7
Pamphill BH21 ..... 58 B5
St Leonards BH24 ..... 54 C5
Upton BH16 ..... 118 B6
Verwood BH21 ..... 45 A2
Verwood BH31 ..... 45 C6
Whitechurch Canonicorum
DT6 ..... 65 A8
Wimborne Minster BH21 ... 60 A8
Sandy Mead Rd BH8 ..... 90 F1
Sandy Plot BH23 ..... 124 C8
Sandy Way BH10 ..... 89 E4
San Remo Twrs 4 BH5 .. 122 E3
Santoy BH13 ..... 147 D5
Sarah Cl BH7 ..... 123 B8
Sarah Sands Cl BH23 ..... 124 D8
Sark Rd BH12 ..... 120 D8
Sarum 3 DT9 ..... 194 D8
Sarum Ave BH22 ..... 53 A4
Sarum Cl SO22 ..... 126 A5
Sarum Ct
Poole BH14 ..... 120 C4
Winchester SO22 ..... 126 B5
Sarum Road Hospl SO22 126 A5
Sarum St 12 BH15 ..... 119 B1
Saulfland Dr BH23 ..... 125 D8
Saulfland Ho BH23 ..... 125 D8
Saulfland Pl BH23 ..... 125 D8
Saville Ct BH21 ..... 59 D3
Sawyers La 1 DT2 ..... 106 E8
Saxonbury Rd BH6 ..... 123 E5
Saxon Ct 17 SO23 ..... 126 E6
Saxonford Rd BH23 ..... 125 C7
Saxon Hts BH6 ..... 123 E5
Saxonhurst Cl BH10 ..... 89 E5
Saxonhurst Gdns BH10 ... 89 E4
Saxonhurst Rd BH10 ..... 89 E4
Saxon King Gdns BH6 ... 124 B4
Saxon Mead Cl SP8 ..... 5 E3
Saxon Rd SO23 ..... 126 E7
Saxon Rise DT11 ..... 210 C7
Saxon Spur SP7 ..... 12 F4
Saxon Sq Sh Ctr BH23 ... 124 B6
Saxon Way SP6 ..... 42 C5
Scadden's Cnr DT6 ..... 66 B8
Scarf Rd BH17 ..... 119 F7
Schelin Way 6 DT11 ..... 198 B5
School Cl
Chickerell DT3 ..... 166 D6
4 Tarrant Gunville DT11 . 199 F7
Verwood BH31 ..... 45 C7
School Hill
Chickerell DT3 ..... 166 D6
Cucklington BA9 ..... 4 A3
Powerstock DT6 ..... 70 B5
South Perrott DT8 ..... 192 C1
Schoolhouse La DT10 ..... 21 A2
School House La DT2 ... 103 B1
School La
Askerswell DT2 ..... 102 D7
Blandford Forum DT11 ... 212 D2
Bournemouth BH11 ..... 89 B6
Broadwindsor DT8 ..... 203 B6
Chetnole DT9 ..... 194 D3
1 Dorchester DT1 ..... 107 F2
Gillingham SP8 ..... 6 A2
4 Pimperne DT11 ..... 199 D4
Poole BH15 ..... 119 C5
Ringwood BH24 ..... 55 C7
St Leonards BH24 ..... 54 C5
Studland BH19 ..... 164 C1
3 Tarrant Gunville DT11 . 199 F7
Toller Porcorum DT2 ..... 71 E8
Verwood BH21 ..... 53 B7
West Lulworth BH20 ..... 172 D6
Wimborne Minster BH21 ... 59 B5
Winfrith Newburgh DT2 ... 156 F6
Woodsford DT2 ..... 110 C1
School Rd SP8 ..... 5 F1
School St 6 DT4 ..... 167 D3
Scimitar Rd BA22 ..... 26 D6
Scotchey Hill SP8 ..... 10 D1
Scotchey La SP8 ..... 10 F1
Scott Cl
Poole BH12 ..... 88 F1
Stoborough Green BH20 .. 160 E8
Scotter Rd BH7 ..... 123 B6
Scotton Way The DT2 ... 137 D5
Scott Rd
Poole BH12 ..... 120 F8
Poole BH12 ..... 88 F1
Scott's Gn BH23 ..... 124 F8
Scotts Hill La BH23 ..... 124 D7
Scott's La DT6 ..... 64 A5
Scotts Way TA18 ..... 192 A8
Scouse La EX13 ..... 202 B2
Scutts Cl BH16 ..... 84 C4
Seabank Cl
4 Upton BH16 ..... 117 C7
Upton BH16 ..... 118 A7
Seaborough View TA18 .. 191 F3
Seabourne Pl 5 BH5 ... 123 B5
Seabourne Rd BH5 ..... 123 B5
Seacliff Ct BH6 ..... 123 D3
Seacombe Rd BH13 ..... 147 B3
Seacroft Ave BH25 ..... 126 E8
Seafield Cl BH25 ..... 126 F7
Seafield Dr BH6 ..... 123 E5
Seafield Rd
Barton on Sea BH25 ..... 126 E8
Bournemouth BH6 ..... 123 D4
Christchurch BH23 ..... 125 C7
Seagrim Rd BH8 ..... 90 C3
Seagull Rd BH8 ..... 90 C1
Sea Hill La DT6 ..... 99 A5
Sea King Rd BA20 ..... 26 F3
Seamoor Cl DT3 ..... 167 F8
Seamoor La BH4 ..... 121 B3
Seamoor Rd BH4 ..... 121 B3
Sea Point 8 BH13 ..... 147 F7
Sea Rd
Barton on Sea BH25 ..... 126 E8
Bournemouthe BH5 ..... 122 E4
Bournemouth, Southbourne
BH6 ..... 123 F3
Sea Rd N DT6 ..... 100 E7
Sea Rd S DT6 ..... 100 D5
Seaton Cl BH23 ..... 126 B8
Seaton Rd
Christchurch BH23 ..... 126 B8
Yeovil BA20 ..... 27 B4
Seatown Cl BH17 ..... 88 A1
Sea View 6 DT5 ..... 186 F8
Seaview Rd
Barton on Sea BH25 ..... 126 D7
Walkford BH23 ..... 94 C1
Sea View Rd
Poole BH15 ..... 120 A6
Upton BH16 ..... 118 A7
Sea Vixen Ind Est BH23 .. 125 A8
Seaward Ave
Barton on Sea BH25 ..... 126 F7
Bournemouth BH6 ..... 123 B4
Seaward Gdns DT6 ..... 100 D2
Seaward Rd BH19 ..... 179 B4
Seaway BH25 ..... 127 B8
Seaway Ave BH23 ..... 125 C7
Second Cliff Wlk 2 DT6 . 100 B2
Second Marine Ave
BH25 ..... 127 A6
Seddon Cl BH25 ..... 127 B8
Sedgefield Cl DT4 ..... 167 C3
Sedgemoor Cl BA21 ..... 27 F6
Sedgley Rd BH9 ..... 121 E8
Seed Warehouse The 3
BH15 ..... 119 C1
Selborne Pl SO22 ..... 126 B3
Selby Cl BH18 ..... 87 A3
Seldown BH15 ..... 119 D3
Seldown Bridge BH15 ... 119 D2
Seldown La BH15 ..... 119 D3
Seldown Rd BH15 ..... 119 D3
Self Rd BH15 ..... 119 A2
Selfridge Ave BH6 ..... 124 B3
Selfridge Cl BH6 ..... 124 B3
Seliot Cl BH15 ..... 119 D5
Selkirk Cl BH21 ..... 59 E1
Selle Rd BH20 ..... 139 F6
Sellwood Way BH25 ..... 126 D8
Selwood Cl DT10 ..... 35 C2
Selwood Pk BH10 ..... 89 C7
Selworthy Cl BH14 ..... 120 A2
Selwyn Cl DT3 ..... 152 D3
Sentinal Ct BH15 ..... 119 E3
Sentry Rd BH19 ..... 179 C2
Sermon Rd SO22 ..... 126 A7
Serpentine Rd BH15 ..... 119 C3
Serrells Mead BH19 ..... 178 C2
Setley Gdns BH8 ..... 90 E3
Seven Acres 5 DT5 ..... 186 E1
Seven Acres Rd DT3 ..... 153 C1
Seven Ash Comm Rd
DT9 ..... 195 B4
Seven Barrows Rd BH20 142 D6
Sevenoaks Dr BH7 ..... 123 A8
Severalls Park Ave 17
TA18 ..... 191 F4
Severn Rd BH22 ..... 62 A5
Sewell Rd BH20 ..... 139 D7
Seymer Rd BH19 ..... 179 C2
Seymour Rd BH24 ..... 47 D1
Shadrack DT6 ..... 128 B8
Shadrack St 2 DT8 ..... 204 C4
Shaftesbury Abbey Mus &
Gdn SP7 ..... 12 D2
Shaftesbury Arts Ctr SP7 . 12 E2
Shaftesbury Cl BH22 ..... 53 B1
Shaftesbury Ct BH3 ..... 121 F6
Shaftesbury La DT11 ..... 212 E6
Shaftesbury L Ctr SP7 ..... 12 F2
Shaftesbury Prim Sch
SP7 ..... 13 A2
Shaftesbury Rd
Bournemouth BH8 ..... 122 C6
Child Okeford DT11 ..... 198 C8
Ferndown BH22 ..... 53 A1
Gillingham SP8 ..... 11 C7
Henstridge BA8 ..... 19 D6
Kington Magna SP8 ..... 20 A7
Shaftesbury Rd *continued*
Mere BA12 ..... 3 B4
Poole BH15 ..... 119 D3
Shaftesbury Sch SP7 ..... 12 F1
Shaftesbury Town Mus
SP7 ..... 12 E2
Shakespeare Rd
Bournemouth BH6 ..... 123 D7
Wimborne Minster BH21 .. 59 C6
Shamrock Ct 2 BH21 ..... 59 C4
Shapland Ave BH11 ..... 88 E5
Shapwick Rd BH15 ..... 119 A1
Shard Cl BH31 ..... 45 C6
Sharlands Cl BH18 ..... 87 B3
Sharp Rd BH12 ..... 121 A7
Shaston Cl 4 BH19 ..... 178 F2
Shaston Cres DT1 ..... 135 B7
Shaston Rd DT11 ..... 198 F4
Shatcombe La DT2 ..... 71 D3
Shatter's Hill BH20 ..... 142 E4
Shave Cross DT6 ..... 203 C1
Shave Hill SP8 ..... 9 B7
Shave La
Todber DT10 ..... 21 D5
West Crewkerne TA18 ..... 191 E3
Shaves La BH25 ..... 95 A5
Shaw Cl DT11 ..... 212 D5
Shaw Dr BH20 ..... 142 F8
Shawford Gdns BH8 ..... 90 D2
Shawford Rd BH8 ..... 90 D3
Shaw Rd BH24 ..... 47 E2
Shear Plot DT6 ..... 99 F8
Shears Rd DT4 ..... 167 D7
Shearstones DT9 ..... 194 D5
Sheasby Cl 9 SP5 ..... 189 A3
Shedbush La DT6 ..... 98 C8
Shedrick Hill TA20 ..... 202 E8
Sheepcroft La BH21 ..... 51 D3
Sheepdown Rd 3 DT1 .. 107 C2
Sheephouse Dro BH21 .. 200 E2
Sheeplands La DT9 ..... 29 F6
Sheeplands The DT9 ..... 29 F7
Sheep Market Hill 2
DT11 ..... 212 D3
Sheepspine La TA20 ..... 202 C5
Sheepwash La
Burstock DT8 ..... 203 D5
Tatworth & Forton TA20 .. 202 A6
Shelbourne Cl BH8 ..... 122 D6
Shelbourne Rd BH8 ..... 122 B6
Sheldrake Rd BH23 ..... 125 A5
Shell Bay Sailing Ctr
BH19 ..... 147 A1
Shelley Cl
Bournemouth BH1 ..... 122 E5
Christchurch BH23 ..... 125 C7
St Leonards BH24 ..... 54 A5
Winchester SO22 ..... 126 B6
Yeovil BA21 ..... 26 F6
Shelley Ct
10 Bournemouth BH4 ..... 121 C3
Ferndown BH22 ..... 61 D5
Shelley Gdns BH1 ..... 122 E5
Shelley Hamlets BH23 ... 125 D7
Shelley Hill BH23 ..... 125 D7
Shelley Ho 9 BH25 ..... 95 A2
Shelley Rd
Bournemouth BH1 ..... 122 E5
Poole BH12 ..... 120 D5
Shelley Rd E BH7 ..... 122 F5
Shelton Rd BH6 ..... 123 C6
Shenstone Ct 2 BH25 ..... 95 A1
Shepherd Cl BH23 ..... 93 F1
Shepherds Croft DT5 ..... 187 C5
Shepherds Hill BH24 ..... 46 E6
Shepherd's Hill SP8 ..... 9 C7
Shepherds La BH24 ..... 46 C6
Shepherds Way
Bournemouth BH7 ..... 123 A7
West Lulworth BH20 ..... 172 D6
Sheppards Field 4 BH21 . 59 B6
Sherborn Cres BH17 ..... 88 A2
Sherborne Abbey DT9 ..... 30 B6
Sherborne Abbey CE Prim
Sch DT9 ..... 29 F4
Sherborne Cswy SP7 ..... 11 E3
Sherborne Dr BH22 ..... 61 D4
Sherborne Golf Club DT9. 16 A3
Sherborne Hill DT9 ..... 30 C3
Sherborne House DT9 ..... 30 B6
Sherborne Mus DT9 ..... 30 C5
Sherborne New Castle
DT9 ..... 30 D5
Sherborne Prep Sch DT9. 30 B5
Sherborne Prim Sch DT9. 30 C7
Sherborne Rd
Henstridge BA8 ..... 18 F4
Milborne Port DT9 ..... 17 C2
Yeovil BA20 ..... 27 E5
Sherborne Sch DT9 ..... 30 B6
Sherborne Sch for Girls
DT9 ..... 30 A6
Sherborne Sch Int Coll
DT9 ..... 30 A6
Sherborne Sta DT9 ..... 30 B5
Sherbourne La 5 DT7 ..... 96 C5
Sherbourne Old Castle
DT9 ..... 30 D6
Sherfield Cl BH8 ..... 90 D2
Sherford Cl BH20 ..... 142 D6
Sherford Dr BH20 ..... 142 E6
Sheridan Cl
Frampton DT2 ..... 73 F3
Winchester SO22 ..... 126 A3
Sheriden Way 5 BH21 ..... 56 D4
Sheringham Rd BH12 ..... 120 F5
Sherlands 1 TA16 ..... 191 F7
Sherren Ave DT2 ..... 75 E2
Sherrin Cl BH15 ..... 119 D5
Sherwood Ave
Ferndown BH22 ..... 61 C3
Poole BH14 ..... 120 A3
Sherwood Cl BH23 ..... 123 F7
Sherwood Dr BH31 ..... 45 D6
Shetland View BH31 ..... 45 C6
Shiller's La DT9 ..... 15 F6
Shillingstone CE Prim Sch
DT11 ..... 198 B6
Shillingstone Dr BH9 ..... 90 B3
Shillingstone Gdns 3
BH12 ..... 120 F7
Shillingstone La DT11 ... 198 A5
Shillito Rd BH12 ..... 120 E5
Ship Knapp DT6 ..... 98 B8
Shipney La DT10 ..... 19 E2
Shipstal Cl BH16 ..... 118 C4
Shipstal Nature Trail
BH20 ..... 144 D4
Shipton La
Burton Bradstock DT6 ... 101 C1
Loders DT6 ..... 101 E5
Shipton Rd DT6 ..... 101 D3
Shirecroft Rd DT4 ..... 167 A3
Shiremoor Hill TA16 ..... 191 F7
Shires Cl BH24 ..... 55 C4
Shires Copse BH6 ..... 123 F3
Shires Mead BH31 ..... 45 C6
Shirley Cl
Ferndown BH22 ..... 53 A2
Swanage BH19 ..... 178 F2
Shirley Rd
Bournemouth BH9 ..... 90 A1
Poole BH12 ..... 120 B6
Upton BH16 ..... 118 C7
Wareham BH20 ..... 142 D3
Shoe La DT6 ..... 100 F8
Shoot Hill TA17 ..... 191 C8
Shop La DT3 ..... 150 C1
Shoreacres BH13 ..... 147 C3
Shore Ave BH16 ..... 118 C6
Shore Cl
3 Upton BH16 ..... 117 E6
Upton BH16 ..... 118 C6
Shoredown La DT9 ..... 17 D6
Shore Gdns BH16 ..... 118 B6
Shore La
Lytchett Minster & Upton
BH16 ..... 117 E5
Upton BH16 ..... 118 C6
Shore Rd
Poole BH13 ..... 147 D5
Poole BH13 ..... 147 D6
Swanage BH19 ..... 179 C3
Short Cl BH12 ..... 121 A8
Short Cross DT2 ..... 206 C6
Shortedge DT10 ..... 35 C2
Shortlake La DT3 ..... 169 A8
Shortlands DT5 ..... 186 F3
Shortlands Rd DT3 ..... 152 B5
Shortmarsh La TA18 ..... 192 F4
Short Rd DT4 ..... 167 B3
Shorts Cl BH23 ..... 92 C1
Shorts Green La SP7 ..... 12 B8
Short's La DT11 ..... 212 C3
Shottesford Ave DT11 ... 212 E6
Shottsford Cl 7 BH19 ... 178 F2
Shottsford Rd BH15 ..... 119 C5
Shreen Cl 9 SP8 ..... 5 F3
Shreen Way SP8 ..... 5 F3
Shrewsbury Rd BA21 ..... 26 D7
Shrubbery La DT4 ..... 180 C8
Shute La DT11 ..... 37 F1
Shute Lake La 11 TA18 .. 191 F4
Shute's La SP8 ..... 9 C8
Sidings The DT9 ..... 194 C6
Sidmouth Rd DT7 ..... 96 A5
Sidney Gdns 2 BH9 ..... 90 B4
Sidney Smith Ct BH17 ..... 87 E2
Silchester Cl BH2 ..... 121 F5
Silchester Pl 11 SO23 ..... 126 F7
Silk House Barton DT10 .. 33 C8
Sillen La SP6 ..... 190 B6
Silton Rd SP8 ..... 1 F2
Silver Birch Cl BH13 ..... 121 A4
Silver Bsns Pk BH23 ..... 124 F7
Silverdale BH25 ..... 127 B7
Silverdale Cl BH18 ..... 86 E4
Silverdale Cres 2 SP6 ... 42 C6
Silver Hill SO23 ..... 126 E5
Silver St
5 Christchurch BH23 ..... 124 B6
Crewkerne TA18 ..... 192 B3
Lyme Regis DT7 ..... 96 B5
Overcombe/Preston DT3 .. 153 D2
4 Stofold BA22 ..... 193 F8
Yeovil BA20 ..... 27 D5
Silver Way BH23 ..... 125 E7
Silverwood Cl
Merley BH21 ..... 59 D2
Winchester SO22 ..... 126 B3
Silwood Cl SO22 ..... 126 C7
Simmonds Cl BH15 ..... 119 D5
Simonds Ct 6 SO23 ..... 126 E8
Simons Rd DT9 ..... 30 B7
Simsay Fields 7 DT2 ..... 207 D4
Sinclair Ct 4 BH14 ..... 120 A4
Singleton Dr BH10 ..... 89 C2
Sir John Colfox Sch The
DT6 ..... 68 E1
Sir Richard Hull Rd
BH20 ..... 139 D6
Siskin Cl BH22 ..... 61 B7
Sitterton Cl BH20 ..... 81 A3
Sixpenny Cl BH12 ..... 120 F7
Sixpenny Handley Fst Sch
SP5 ..... 189 A4

Six Ways Cross BH21 200 E3
Skilling Hill Rd DT6 100 C5
Skilling La DT6 100 B5
Skinner St BH15 119 C1
Skipton Cl BH18 87 A2
Slade La BA22 15 B6
Slader Bsns Pk BH17 87 E1
Slades Farm Rd BH10 89 D2
Slades Gn DT6 100 E5
Slade's La BH10 121 C8
Slape Hill DT6 68 D8
Sleepbrook Cl BH31 45 A6
Sleepers Delle Gdns
SO22 126 C4
Sleeper's Hill SO22 126 B4
Sleepers Hill Gdns SO22 126 B4
Sleeper's Hill Ho SO22 126 B4
Sleight Cl BA21 26 E6
Sleight La
Corfe Mullen BH21 86 C8
Poole BH21 85 E8
Slepe Cres BH12 120 F8
Slinn Rd BH23 124 E7
Slip Way BH15 119 B2
Slodbrook La SP8 2 D1
Slopers Mead 2 DT11 211 E5
Slough Dro DT2 205 E7
Slough La
Horton BH21 44 A2
Lytchett Minster & Upton
BH16 117 B6
Upton BH16 118 A6
Slyer's La
Puddletown DT2 76 F1
Stinsford DT2 108 D6
Smacombe La DT6 101 D4
Smallmouth Cl 4 DT4 180 D5
Smishops La DT6 69 D1
Smithfield Pl BH9 89 F1
Smith's Hill TA18 192 B8
Smith's La DT2 208 B3
Smithson Cl BH12 121 C8
Smith's Terr BA21 27 E6
Smithy La BH25 94 F6
Smokey Hole La DT1 108 C1
Smugglers La BH21 59 E7
Smugglers' La
Colehill BH21 50 F1
Stourpaine DT11 199 A6
Smugglers La N BH23 93 E1
Smugglers La S BH23 125 E8
Smugglers Reach BH23 125 A5
Smugglers Wood Rd
BH23 93 D1
Snag La DT11 79 E6
Snail's La BH24 47 D3
Snowdon Rd BH4 121 C4
Snow Down Rd 1 DT11 199 E2
Snowdrop Gdns BH23 93 B1
Snow Hill BH20 81 B2
Snow Hill La BH20 81 B2
Soberton Rd BH8 122 D6
Sodern La DT2 107 C7
Sodom La DT10 21 B3
Solar Ct BH13 121 A2
Soldiers Rd BH20 161 C7
Soldier's Ring SP6 190 D4
Solent Dr BH25 127 A7
Solent Lo 5 BH25 95 A1
Solent Rd
Barton on Sea BH25 126 D7
Bournemouth BH6 124 A3
Swanage BH19 185 C8
Walkford BH23 94 B2
Solent View BH6 124 A3
Solly Cl BH12 120 E7
Solomon Way BH15 118 D2
Somerby Rd BH15 119 D6
Somerfields DT7 96 A5
Somerford Ave BH23 125 B8
Somerford Bsns Pk
BH23 125 A7
Somerford Ct BH23 125 E7
Somerford Prim Com Sch
BH23 124 E7
Somerford Rd BH23 124 F7
Somerford Rdbt BH23 125 A8
Somerford Way BH23 124 E6
Somerleigh Rd DT1 108 A1
Somerley Pk BH24 46 E5
Somerley Rd BH9 122 A8
Somerley View BH24 55 B8
Somers Cl SO22 126 B3
Somerset Cl SP8 5 E3
Somerset Rd
Bournemouth BH7 122 F5
Bournemouth BH7 123 A5
Christchurch BH23 123 E8
Weymouth DT4 167 A4
Somers Rd DT7 96 A5
Somerton Cl BH25 95 D3
Somerville Ct BH25 94 F3
Somerville Rd
Bournemouth BH2 121 D3
Ringwood BH24 55 E8
Sonning Way BH8 90 B2
Sopers La
Christchurch BH23 124 A6
Poole BH17 87 B1
Sopley Cl BH25 126 D8
Sopley Common Nature
Reserve BH23 91 C8
Sopley Farm Bldgs BH23 92 B6
Sopwith Cl BH23 125 B6
Sopwith Cres
Merley BH21 59 E2
Merley BH21 59 F1
Sorrel Cl DT4 167 E6
Sorrel Gdns BH18 86 F2
Sorrell Ct BH23 125 B8
Sorrell Way BH23 125 B8
Sorrel Way SP8 5 D2
Souter Way DT3 167 D8
Southampton Rd BH24 55 D8
South Annings 2 DT6 128 B8
South Ave
Lyme Regis DT7 96 B6
New Milton BH25 95 B2
Sherborne DT9 29 F4
Southbourne Coast Rd
BH6 123 F3
Southbourne Cross Roads 5
BH6 123 E3
Southbourne Gr BH6 123 C4
Southbourne Lane Central 6
BH6 123 C4
Southbourne Lane E 5
BH6 123 C4
Southbourne Lane W
BH6 123 B4
Southbourne Overcliff Dr
BH6 123 D3
Southbourne Rd BH6 123 C4
Southbourne Sands BH6 123 D3
Southbrook
Bere Regis BH20 81 B2
Mere BA12 3 C4
Southbrook Cl BH17 88 A2
Southbrook Gdns 2 BA12 3 B4
Southcliffe Rd
Barton on Sea BH25 126 D7
Christchurch BH23 125 C6
South Cliff Rd
Bournemouth BH2 121 F2
Swanage BH19 179 C1
Southcote Rd BH1 122 C4
South Cres DT11 199 E3
Southcroft Rd DT4 166 F1
South Cswy BH20 142 E2
South Ct DT9 29 F4
South Ct Ave DT1 135 A8
Southdown Ave DT3 168 A6
Southdown Ct 1 BH23 124 F8
Southdown Rd DT4 180 E8
Southdown Way BH22 53 A1
South Dr
Cattistock DT2 206 C2
West Moors BH24 62 B7
South Dro DT2 135 F1
Southern Ave BH22 53 C1
Southernhay Rd BH31 45 D6
Southern La
Barton on Sea BH25 126 F8
Old Milton BH25 94 F1
Southern Oaks BH25 94 F1
Southern Rd BH6 123 C4
Southey Rd BH23 124 F7
South Farm Cl DT11 200 A6
Southfield Ave DT4 167 D6
Southfield Mews 4 BH24 55 C6
Southgate St SO23 126 D5
Southgate Villas SO23 126 D5
South Haven Cl BH16 118 B3
South Hill SP6 42 C6
South Holme DT11 198 E4
Southill Ave BH12 120 C6
Southill Garden Dr DT4 167 B6
Southill Gdns BH9 90 A1
Southill Prim Sch DT4 167 A7
Southill Rd
Bournemouth BH9 90 A1
Poole BH12 120 D7
South Instow BH19 177 F5
South Kinson Dr BH11 89 B4
Southlands Ave
Bournemouth BH6 123 F4
Corfe Mullen BH21 86 D6
Southlands Cl
Corfe Mullen BH21 86 D6
Poole BH21 85 F6
Southlands Ct BH18 87 A3
Southlands Rd DT4 180 E8
South Lawns DT6 100 D5
Southlawns Wlk BH25 94 F1
Southlea Ave BH6 123 F4
South Lodge BH13 147 G7
South Mead BH20 81 A2
Southmead Cres 20
TA18 191 F4
Southmead La BA8 19 B3
South Mill La DT6 100 D5
Southover DT6 128 B7
Southover Cl DT11 212 D1
Southover La DT2 79 C1
South Par 3 DT4 167 E2
South Park Rd BH12 121 A8
South Poorton Nature
Reserve DT6 70 A8
South Rd
Bournemouth BH1 122 E5
Corfe Mullen BH21 86 E6
Poole BH15 119 C2
Swanage BH19 179 A2
Weymouth DT4 180 C6
South Road Comb Sch
BH15 119 C2
South Somerset Mus of
BA20 27 C4
South St
Arne BH20 142 E3
Bridport DT6 100 D6
Corfe Castle BH20 176 F3
Crewkerne TA18 191 F4
Dorchester DT1 108 A1
4 Gillingham SP8 5 F1
Hinton St George TA17 191 D7
South St *continued*
Kington Magna SP8 9 C2
Leigh DT9 194 E3
Milborne Port DT9 17 D2
Sherborne DT9 30 B5
Yeovil BA20 27 D4
South View
Bournemouth BH2 121 F5
Bradford Abbas DT9 28 D2
Piddletrenthide DT2 208 C1
Winchester SO22 126 C6
South View Park Homes
SO22 126 A1
South View Pl 10 BH2 121 E3
Southview Rd DT4 167 B3
South View Rd
Christchurch BH23 124 A6
Milborne Port DT9 17 C2
Southville BA21 27 E5
Southville Rd BH5 123 B5
South Walks Rd DT1 108 A1
South Way DT5 186 D1
Southway Cl BA21 27 B7
Southway Cres BA21 27 B6
Southway Dr BA21 27 C6
Southwell Prim Sch DT5 186 E1
Southwell Rd DT5 187 A2
South Western Bsns Pk
DT9 30 B5
South Western Cres
BH14 120 B2
Southwick Pl BH6 123 C7
Southwick Rd BH6 123 C6
South Wlk DT6 100 C6
Southwood Ave
Bournemouth BH6 123 C4
Walkford BH23 94 B1
Southwood Cl
Ferndown BH22 61 C6
Walkford BH23 94 A1
Southwoods BA20 27 C3
Sovell Down Nature Reserve
BH21 201 A5
Sovereign Bsns Ctr
BH15 119 B6
Sovereign Cl BH7 122 F8
Sovereign Ctr 6 BH1 122 E4
Spa Ave DT3 167 C7
Spadger La DT2 136 A8
Sparacre Gdns DT6 100 D7
Spa Rd DT3 167 B7
Sparkford Cl
Bournemouth BH7 123 B8
Winchester SO22 126 C4
Sparkford Rd SO22 126 C5
Sparrow Croft SP8 11 B8
Sparrow Rd BA21 27 D6
Spearhay La TA20 202 B4
Specket La DT6 203 A5
Speedwell Dr BH23 125 B8
Speke Cl 10 TA16 191 F7
Spence La DT6 64 F5
Spencer Ct 1 BH25 95 B2
Spencer Gdns 2 DT11 198 C5
Spencer Rd
Bournemouth BH1 122 C4
New Milton BH25 95 B2
Poole BH13 147 F8
Spetisbury Cl BH9 90 B3
Spetisbury Fst Sch DT11 211 D5
Spettisbury Rings (Hill Fort)
DT11 211 E5
Spicer La BH11 88 E5
Spicers Ct 2 SO22 126 D6
Spiller Rd DT3 166 D5
Spinacre BH25 127 B8
Spindle Cl BH18 86 F2
Spindlewood Cl 10 BH25 95 A1
Spingfield Rd BA12 3 B5
Spinners Cl BH22 53 A1
Spinners' La DT6 101 A6
Spinners Way 2 BA12 3 B6
Spinney Cl 2 BH24 53 F4
Spinneys La BH22 61 D5
Spinney The
Broadmayne DT2 136 B1
Lytchett Matravers BH16 84 D2
Radipole DT3 152 B2
St Leonards BH24 54 B6
7 Yeovil BA20 26 F2
Spinney Way BH25 95 B6
Spitfire Cl DT2 137 D5
Spittlefields BH24 55 D7
Spittles La DT7 96 C6
Spread Eagle Hill SP7 24 C3
Spring Ave DT4 167 D1
Springbank Rd BH7 122 F8
Springbourne Ct BH1 122 D5
Springbourne Mews
BH1 122 C5
Springbrook Cl BH20 177 E6
Spring Cl
4 Bridport DT6 68 F1
Verwood BH31 45 B5
Spring Ct BH12 120 D5
Springdale Ave BH18 86 F5
Springdale Fst Sch BH18 86 E4
Springdale Gr BH21 86 E4
Springdale Rd BH18,BH21 86 E4
Springfield
3 Cerne Abbas DT2 207 D4
East Chinnock BA22 192 E8
Puncknowle DT2 129 F6
Springfield Ave
Bournemouth BH6 124 A4
Christchurch BH23 91 D2
Springfield Cl
2 Shaftesbury SP7 13 A4
Springfield Cl *continued*
Verwood BH31 45 B5
Springfield Cres
Poole BH14 120 B4
Radipole DT3 152 B3
5 Sherborne DT9 30 A5
Springfield Gdns BH25 95 D2
Springfield Pl BA21 27 A7
Springfield Rd
Milborne Port DT9 17 D3
Poole BH14 120 A4
Radipole DT3 152 B3
4 Swanage BH19 179 B2
Verwood BH31 45 B5
Yeovil BA21 27 A7
Springfields
Holt BH21 51 B4
Stalbridge DT10 33 E8
Spring Gdns
1 Fortuneswell DT5 186 F7
Poole BH12 120 D5
West Knighton DT2 136 C3
Weymouth DT4 167 D1
Spring Gr DT2 196 A1
Springham Wlk 18 DT1 107 D1
Springhill Gdns DT7 96 B6
Spring La
Longburton DT9 195 B7
New Milton BH25 95 D2
Sandford Orcas DT9 15 F5
3 Weymouth DT4 167 D1
Spring Rd
Bournemouth BH1 122 D5
Weymouth DT4 167 D1
6 Weymouth DT4 167 E2
Spring St BH20 140 B2
Springvale Ave
Bournemouth BH7 122 F8
Bournemouth BH7 123 A8
Springwater Cl BH11 89 A3
Springwater Ct BH23 124 D6
Springwater Dr BH23 124 D6
Springwater Rd BH11 89 A3
Springwell Cl BH20 177 A8
Spruce Cl BH17 86 E1
Spur Cl BH21 60 C6
Spurgeon Rd BH7 123 B6
Spur Hill Ave BH14 120 D3
Spur Rd BH14 120 D3
Spy Cl BH16 84 C3
Spyway Rd DT2 102 C7
Square Cl BH21 60 F3
Square The
Bournemouth BH2 121 F3
2 Cattistock DT2 206 C2
1 Corfe Castle BH20 162 A1
Cranborne BH21 40 B7
3 Gillingham SP8 5 F1
Langton Herring DT3 150 C1
Mere BA12 3 A5
Milborne St Andrew DT11 79 E8
Powerstock DT6 70 B4
Puddletown DT2 78 B1
West Moors BH24 62 B8
Wimborne Minster BH21 59 B5
Winchester SO23 126 E5
Squirrel's Cl BH23 91 D2
Squirrel's Cnr BH21 189 D1
Squirrel Wlk BH31 45 B5
Stables The BH23 123 F7
Stacey Cl BH12 120 C7
Stacey Gdns BH8 90 F2
Stadium Way BH15 119 C3
Stafford Cl DT2 136 C4
Stafford Gdns DT2 136 A8
Stafford Rd
Bournemouth BH1 122 A4
Swanage BH19 179 C2
Stag Cl BH25 94 E4
Stagswood BH31 44 F6
Stainers Mead SP7 7 B1
Stainforth Cl DT4 166 F3
Stake Ford Cross DT9 194 E4
Staker's Cross TA18 191 B2
Staker's Cross La TA18 191 B2
Stakes La DT9 195 E6
Stalbridge CE Prim Sch
DT10 19 D1
Stalbridge Cl DT10 33 D8
Stalbridge Dr BH22 61 D4
Stalbridge La DT10 34 F2
Stalbridge Pk DT10 19 B1
Stalbridge Rd
Henstridge BA8 19 B3
Poole BH17 119 A7
Stalbridge DT10 32 F4
Stalbridge Trad Est DT10 33 D8
Stalham Rd BH12 120 F6
Stallards La BH24 55 B7
Stamford Rd BH6 123 D5
Stammery Hill EX13 202 A1
Stanbarrow Cl BH20 81 A2
Standfast Wlk 16 DT1 135 B8
Standpitts La SP8 10 E6
Stanfield Cl BH12 120 D7
Stanfield Rd
Bournemouth BH9 121 E8
Ferndown BH22 61 C6
Poole BH12 120 D7
Stanier Rd DT3 153 B1
Staniforth Ct BH23 124 D6
Stanley Cl BH31 45 C5
Stanley Ct
Bournemouth BH1 122 C5
Poole BH15 119 C6
Stanley Green Cres
BH15 119 C5
Stanley Green Fst Sch
BH15 119 C6
Stanley Green Ind Est
BH15 119 B5
Stanley Green Rd
Poole BH15 119 C5
Poole BH15 119 C6
Stanley Pearce Ho BH17 87 C1
Stanley Pk (Cvn & Chalet
Site) BH25 95 C6
Stanley Rd
Bournemouth BH1 122 C5
Christchurch BH23 126 A8
Poole BH15 119 C1
Stanley St 1 DT4 167 D4
Stanmore La SO22 126 B3
Stanmore Prim Sch
SO22 126 C3
Stannington Cl BH25 95 B2
Stanpit BH23 124 E5
Stanstead Rd DT2 73 A8
Stanton Cl DT11 212 D5
Stanton Lacy 12 BH13 147 F7
Stanton Rd BH10 89 C2
Stapehill Cres BH21 60 C5
Stapehill Mus & Gdns
BH21 60 E5
Stapehill Rd BH21 60 F4
Staple Close La BH15 119 C6
Staple Cross BH23 124 E8
Staplecross La BH23 124 D8
Stapleford Ave BH22 61 F6
Staple Gdns 31 SO23 126 D6
Staples Mdw 4 TA20 202 A8
Staples Terr DT7 96 C6
Star La
2 Ringwood BH24 55 B7
Whitechurch Canonicorum
DT6 98 D8
Starlight Farm Cl BH31 45 C7
Stars La BA20 27 D4
Station App
Broadstone BH18 87 A4
Dorchester DT1 108 A1
Station Hill SO23 126 D6
Station Pl 1 BH19 179 B2
Station Rd
Alderholt SP6 42 B6
Child Okeford DT11 198 C7
Christchurch BH23 124 A7
Christchurch, Highcliffe
BH23 93 E2
2 Easton/Weston DT5 187 A4
Ferndown BH22 53 A2
Gillingham SP8 5 F1
Henstridge BA8 19 B5
Holton Heath BH20 116 C3
Maiden Newton DT2 72 F8
Milborne Port DT9 17 D4
Misterton TA18 192 A3
Moreton DT2 138 A7
New Milton BH25 95 A2
Poole BH14 120 B4
Poole BH15 119 A1
Sherborne DT9 30 B5
2 Shillingstone DT11 198 B6
Stalbridge DT10 19 D1
Sturminster Marshall BH21 56 D3
Sturminster Newton DT10 35 B1
Swanage BH19 179 B2
Tatworth & Forton TA20 202 A8
Verwood BH31 45 A7
Wareham St Martin BH16 116 C1
Wimborne Minster BH21 59 D3
32 Winchester SO23 126 D6
Wool BH20 140 A2
Station Rd Ind Est
Gillingham SP8 5 F1
Maiden Newton DT2 72 F8
Station Terr BH21 59 D4
Station Yd SP6 42 A6
Staunton BH2 121 F2
Stavordale Rd DT4 167 C3
Stearts La DT10 35 B5
Stedman Rd BH5 123 B5
Steels La SP6 190 F2
Steel's La BA9 1 A3
Steel Well La BA8 19 B4
Steepdene BH14 120 B3
Steeple Cl
Poole BH17 87 D3
Radipole DT3 167 B8
Steepleton Rd BH18 87 C3
Steep St BA12 3 A6
Steer Rd BH19 178 F2
Stella Ct 13 BH23 126 B7
Stem La BH25 94 E4
Stenhurst Rd BH15 119 E6
Stephen Langton Dr
BH11 88 D5
Stephen's Castle Nature
Reserve BH31 45 C8
Stepnell Reach BH16 118 D5
Steppes BH19 178 C3
Steppes Hill BH19 178 C2
Step Terr SO22 126 C6
Sterte Ave BH15 119 B4
Sterte Avenue W BH15 119 B4
Sterte Cl BH15 119 C4
Sterte Ct BH15 119 C4
Sterte Espl BH15 119 C3
Sterte Ind Est BH15 119 B4
Sterte Rd BH15 119 C4
Stevens Cl 2 DT11 212 E5
Stevenson Cres BH14 120 E3

Stevenson Rd BH6 . . . . . . 124 A3
Stevensons Cl **3** BH21 . . 59 C4
Steward's La DT11 . . . . 56 B8
Stewart Cl **5** BH8 . . . . 122 C5
Stewart Rd BH6 . . . . 122 B6
Stewarts Way BH22 . . . . . . 61 E7
Stibles La DT11 . . . . 197 D3
Stiby Rd BA21 . . . . 27 A7
Sticklands VA Prim Sch
DT2 . . . . 206 A7
Stileham Bank DT11 . . . . . 79 C4
Stile La DT7 . . . . 96 B4
Stile Way DT2 . . . . 206 E6
Stillmore Rd BH11 . . . . 88 D3
Stinsford Cl BH9 . . . . 90 B4
Stinsford Hill DT2 . . . . 108 D3
Stinsford Rd BH17 . . . . 87 D1
Stinsford View DT1 . . . . . . 108 C1
Stirling Bsns Pk BH21 . . . . 60 F7
Stirling Cl BH25 . . . . 95 B3
Stirling Ct
  3 Bournemouth BH4 . . . . 121 C2
  11 New Milton BH25 . . . . 95 B3
Stirling Rd
  Bournemouth BH3 . . . . . 121 E7
  Radipole DT3 . . . . 167 C8
Stirling Way BH23 . . . . . . 125 B6
Stirrup Cl
  Upton BH16 . . . . 118 D7
  Wimborne Minster BH21 . 60 C6
Stoborough CE Fst Sch
BH20 . . . . 142 E1
Stoborough Cl DT3 . . . . . . 167 B8
Stoborough Dr BH18 . . . . . 87 A2
Stoborough Heath National
  Nature Reserve BH20 . . 143 B1
Stoborough Mdw BH20 . . 160 F8
Stockbridge Cl BH17 . . . . . 88 B2
Stockbridge Rd SO22 . . . . 126 B7
Stockers Ave SO22 . . . . . . 126 B7
Stock Hill La DT9 . . . . 195 F4
Stockley Rd BH20 . . . . 142 D6
Stokehouse St DT1 . . . . . . 107 D1
Stoke La DT10 . . . . 196 F1
Stoke Mill La DT6 . . . . 67 A8
Stoke Rd
  Beaminster DT8 . . . . 204 C4
  Weymouth DT4 . . . . 180 D7
Stokes Ave BH15 . . . . 119 D4
Stokes La DT10 . . . . 32 F3
Stoke Wood Rd
  Bournemouth BH3 . . . . . 121 F6
  Bournemouth BH3 . . . . . 122 A7
Stonage La TA18 . . . . 192 C5
Stonebarrow La
  Charmouth DT6 . . . . 97 C7
  Hawkchurch EX13 . . . . . 202 D3
  Stanton St Gabriel DT6 . 97 E7
Stonechat Cl
  Ferndown BH22 . . . . 61 B8
  3 Radipole DT3 . . . . . . 152 C4
Stonechat Ct BH23 . . . . . . 124 F7
Stonecrop Cl BH18 . . . . . . 86 E2
Stonedene DT9 . . . . 30 B8
Stone Gdns BH8 . . . . 91 A2
Stonehill Down Nature
  Reserve BH20 . . . . 160 E1
Stone La
  Wimborne Minster BH21 . 59 A6
  Yeovil BA21 . . . . 27 C8
Stone Lane Ind Est BH21 . 59 B6
Stoneleigh **8** BH13 . . . . . . 147 F8
Stoneleigh Ave SO41 . . . . 95 F4
Stoney Ct SO22 . . . . 126 C8
Stoney La
  East Coker BA22 . . . . . . 193 D6
  Winchester SO22 . . . . . . 126 C8
Stoneylawn DT10 . . . . 21 B2
Stoney Lawn DT11 . . . . . . 81 D8
Stonyacres DT9 . . . . 194 C6
Stony Down La DT6 . . . . . . 65 B4
Stony La
  Bishop's Caundle DT9 . . 196 A8
  Burton BH23 . . . . 92 C2
  Christchurch BH23 . . . . . 124 C7
  Damerham SP6 . . . . 190 E2
  Holwell DT10 . . . . 196 C6
Stony Lane S BH23 . . . . . . 124 D6
Stopples La SO41 . . . . 95 F3
Story La BH18 . . . . 87 B4
Stottingway St DT3 . . . . . . 152 B5
Stourbank Rd BH23 . . . . . 124 A6
Stourcastle Cl **4** SP8 . . . . 5 E4
Stour Cl
  1 East Stour SP8 . . . . . . 10 D2
  Ferndown BH21 . . . . 60 D4
  1 Shillingstone DT11 . . 198 C5
Stourcliffe Ave BH6 . . . . . 123 C4
Stourcroft Dr BH23 . . . . . . 91 E1
Stour Ct **6** BH13 . . . . 121 A4
Stour Dr BH20 . . . . 142 D6
Stourfield Inf & Jun Schs
BH6 . . . . 123 D6
Stourfield Rd BH5 . . . . 123 B4
Stour Gdns SP8 . . . . 5 E1
Stour Hill SP8 . . . . 9 E1
Stour Hill Pk SP8 . . . . 9 E1
Stour La SP8 . . . . 21 E8
Stour Mdws SP8 . . . . 5 E1
Stourpaine Rd BH17 . . . . . 87 D2
Stour Park Bsns Ctr
DT11 . . . . 212 D2
Stour Pk
  Blandford Forum DT11 . . 212 D2

Stour Pk *continued*
  Bournemouth BH10 . . . . 89 E6
Stour Rd
  Blandford Forum DT11 . . 212 E3
  Bournemouth BH8 . . . . . 122 D6
  Christchurch BH23 . . . . . 124 A6
Stour Rdbt BH23 . . . . 123 F5
Stourton Ct **21** BH4 . . . . . 121 C3
Stourton Way BA21 . . . . . . 26 E7
Stourvale Ave BH23 . . . . . 123 D8
Stourvale Pl **3** BH5 . . . . . 123 B5
Stourvale Rd BH23 . . . . . . 123 C6
Stour View Cl DT10 . . . . . . 35 B2
Stour View Gdns BH21 . . . 58 E1
Stour Way BH23 . . . . 91 D1
Stour Wlk
  Bournemouth BH8 . . . . . 90 D4
  Wimborne Minster BH21 . 59 D3
Stourwood Ave BH6 . . . . . 123 D4
Stourwood Mans **4** BH6 123 C4
Stourwood Rd BH6 . . . . . . 123 D4
Stowcastle St **9** DT1 . . . . 107 D1
Stowell Cres BH20 . . . . . . 142 D2
Stowell La **15** TA20 . . . . . 202 A8
Stower Provost Prim Sch
SP8 . . . . 21 F8
Stowey St DT1 . . . . 107 C1
Straight La SP5 . . . . 188 E3
Straits DT5 . . . . 187 A4
Strand St BH15 . . . . 119 C1
Stratfield Pl BH25 . . . . 94 E3
Stratford Ct **10** SO23 . . . . 126 E8
Stratford Rd 26 F5
Strathmore Dr BH31 . . . . . 45 C6
Strathmore Rd BH9 . . . . . . 90 A4
Stratton Rd BH9 . . . . 90 C3
Streche Rd
  Swanage BH19 . . . . 179 C5
  Wareham BH20 . . . . 142 D3
Street La
  Longburton DT9 . . . . 195 C6
  Sedgehill & Semley SP7 . 7 A4
Streets La BH24 . . . . 55 E4
Street The
  Charmouth DT6 . . . . 97 B8
  Moreton DT2 . . . . 138 E7
  Motcombe SP7 . . . . 7 B1
  Sutton Waldron DT11 . . . 37 D5
  Winterborne Zelston DT11 . 82 F7
Streetway La DT2 . . . . 209 B3
Strete Mount **1** BH23 . . . 124 E7
Stretton Rd BH14 . . . . 120 B4
Strides La BH24 . . . . 55 A7
Strode Gdns BH24 . . . . 54 D5
Strodes La DT2 . . . . 75 D2
Strongate La DT6 . . . . 68 A7
Strouden Ave BH8 . . . . . . 122 C8
Strouden Rd BH9 . . . . 90 A1
Stroud Gdns BH23 . . . . . . 124 E6
Stroud La BH23 . . . . 124 F6
Stroud Park Ave BH23 . . . 124 E6
Stroudley Cres DT3 . . . . . . 153 C1
Struan Ct BH24 . . . . 54 C6
Struan Dr BH24 . . . . 54 C6
Struan Gdns BH24 . . . . 54 B6
Stuart Cl BH16 . . . . 118 B7
Stuart Cres SO22 . . . . 126 C3
Stuart La SP8 . . . . 5 D2
Stuart Rd BH23 . . . . 126 B8
Stuart Way DT6 . . . . 100 B7
Stubhampton Bottom
  DT11 . . . . 38 E5
Stuckton Rd SP6 . . . . 43 D8
Student Village BH12 . . . . 121 D8
Studland Beach & Nature
  Reserve BH19 . . . . 164 C3
Studland & **20** BH4 . . . . . 121 C3
Studland & Godlingston
  Heath National Nature
  Reserve BH19 . . . . 164 B6
Studland Rd BH4 . . . . 121 C1
Studland Way DT3 . . . . . . 167 B8
Studley Cl BH25 . . . . 126 C8
Studley Ct BH25 . . . . 126 D8
Sturminster L Ctr DT10 . . . 35 B3
Sturminster Marshall Fst Sch
  BH21 . . . . 56 E4
Sturminster Newton High
  Sch DT10 . . . . 35 B3
Sturminster Newton Mus
  DT10 . . . . 35 B2
Sturminster Rd **1** BH9 . . . 90 B4
Sturt La BH20 . . . . 81 D4
Styles Cl **9** DT8 . . . . 204 C4
Styles La DT1 . . . . 78 B1
Sudan Rd DT4 . . . . 180 E8
Suffolk Ave BH23 . . . . 91 F2
Suffolk Cl BH21 . . . . 60 A4
Suffolk Rd BH2 . . . . 121 E3
Suffolk Rd S BH2 . . . . 121 D3
Sugar Hill BH20 . . . . 114 B6
Summercroft Way **4**
  BH22 . . . . 53 A3
Summerfield Cl BH23 . . . . 92 C2
Summer Field Cl BH21 . . . 60 A4
Summerfields
  Bournemouth BH7 . . . . . 122 F7
  Henstridge BA8 . . . . 19 B5
Summer Fields BH31 . . . . . 45 A4
Summer Hill TA17 . . . . 191 D7
Summerhill Rd DT7 . . . . . . 96 C6
Summer House Terr
  BA20 . . . . 27 D4
Summerhouse View BA22 . 27 E6
Summer La
  Evershot DT2 . . . . 206 A7
  Hinton St George TA17 . 191 D8

Summerlands
  Ferndown BH22 . . . . 61 D6
  Yeovil BA21 . . . . 27 A6
Summerlands Hospl BA21 27 B5
Summerleaze Pk BA20 . . . 27 B5
Summers Ave BH11 . . . . . . 89 B6
Summers La BH23 . . . . 92 D1
Summertrees Ct BH25 . . . . 95 D4
Sunbury Cl BH11 . . . . 89 A6
Sunbury Ct **24** BH4 . . . . . 121 C3
Sunderland Dr BH23 . . . . . 125 B7
Sundew Cl
  Christchurch BH23 . . . . . 93 C1
  New Milton BH25 . . . . . . 95 D4
  Radipole DT4 . . . . 167 E7
Sundew Rd BH18 . . . . 86 E2
Sun La
  Piddletrenthide DT2 . . . . 208 B1
  Whitchurch Canonicorum
  DT6 . . . . 98 D8
Sunningdale
  41 Bournemouth BH4 . . 121 C3
  Christchurch BH23 . . . . . 123 F6
  6 Poole BH15 . . . . 119 C3
Sunningdale Cres BH10 . . 89 C4
Sunningdale Gdns BH18 . . 87 A5
Sunningdale Rd BA21 . . . . 27 C6
Sunningdale Rise DT3 . . . . 153 B1
Sunninghill Prep Sch
  DT1 . . . . 108 A1
Sunnybank Dr BH21 . . . . . 60 B5
Sunnybank Rd BH21 . . . . . 60 B5
Sunnybank Way BH21 . . . . 60 B6
Sunnyfield Rd BH25 . . . . . 127 A8
Sunnyfields DT3 . . . . 153 C1
Sunny Hill Ct DT3 . . . . 120 D5
Sunny Hill Rd BH12 . . . . . 120 D5
Sunnyhill Rd BH6 . . . . 123 C5
Sunnylands Ave BH6 . . . . 123 F4
Sunnymoor Rd BH11 . . . . . 89 A1
Sunnyside
  Ridge BH20 . . . . 143 B1
  West Lulworth BH20 . . . 172 A5
Sunnyside Rd
  Poole BH12 . . . . 120 D6
  Weymouth DT4 . . . . 180 C7
Sunridge Cl
  Poole BH12 . . . . 121 A6
  Swanage BH19 . . . . 179 B1
Sunrise Bsns Pk DT11 . . . 212 F2
Sunrise Ct BH22 . . . . 61 D5
Sunset Lo BH13 . . . . 121 A2
Surrey Cl
  Christchurch BH23 . . . . . 91 F2
  Weymouth DT4 . . . . 166 F4
Surrey Gdns BH4 . . . . 121 C4
Surrey Lo **8** BH4 . . . . . . 121 C4
Surrey Rd
  Bournemouth BH2 . . . . . 121 D4
  Bournemouth BH4,BH12 . 121 C4
Surrey Rd S BH4 . . . . 121 C4
Sussex Cl BH9 . . . . 90 B4
Sussex Farm Way **8**
  DT9 . . . . 194 C5
Sussex Rd BH23 . . . . 167 B3
Sussex St SO23 . . . . 126 C6
Sutcliffe Ave DT4 . . . . 167 A6
Sutherland Ave BH18 . . . . 86 E5
Suttil Cres DT6 . . . . 68 E2
Sutton Cl
  4 Gillingham SP8 . . . . . . 5 E1
  Overcombe/Preston DT3. 153 C2
  Poole BH17 . . . . 88 B2
Sutton Court Lawns DT3 . 153 C2
Sutton Gdns SO23 . . . . . . 126 E6
Sutton Grange BA21 . . . . . 26 E6
Sutton Hill BA22 . . . . 193 D6
Sutton Holms Nature
  Reserve BH21 . . . . 40 B1
Sutton Pk DT3 . . . . 153 D1
Sutton Rd
  Bournemouth BH9 . . . . . 90 B1
  Overcombe/Preston DT3. 153 D4
Swaffield Gdns **5** DT4 . . 180 C8
Swainson Rd DT1 . . . . 199 E4
Swallow Cl BH17 . . . . 87 B2
Swallowcliffe Gdns BA20 . 27 C5
Swallowfields **1** SP8 . . . . . 5 F4
Swallow Way BH21 . . . . . . 60 A7
Swanage Fst Sch BH19 . . 179 B1
Swanage Her Ctr BH19 . . 179 C2
Swanage Hospl BH19 . . . 179 C1
Swanage Mid Sch BH19 . 178 E3
Swanage Rd BH19 . . . . . . 164 C1
Swanage Rly BH19 . . . . . . 177 D5
Swan Gn **3** BH23 . . . . . . 124 A5
Swan Hill TA18 . . . . 192 B5
Swan La
  Piddletrenthide DT2 . . . . 208 B1
  Winchester SO23 . . . . . . 126 C6
Swan Mead BH24 . . . . 55 E6
Swanmore Cl BH7 . . . . . . 123 B7
Swanmore Rd BH7 . . . . . . 123 B7
Swansbury Dr BH8 . . . . . . 91 B2
Swan St BH21 . . . . 40 A7
Swan Theatre BA20 . . . . . 27 D3
Sway Gdns BH8 . . . . 90 D2
Sway Rd BH25,SO41 . . . . . 95 C6
Sweep The **1** BH24 . . . . . 55 B7
Sweet Hill La DT5 . . . . 186 E1
Sweet Hill Rd DT5 . . . . . . 186 E1
Sweetmans Rd SP7 . . . . . . 12 F4
Swift Cl
  Broadstone BH17 . . . . . . 118 F8
  Winchester SO22 . . . . . . 126 B3
Swilletts La DT6 . . . . 203 D4
Swinton Ave **4** BH20 . . . 139 D7
Swordfish Dr BH23 . . . . . . 125 B7

Swyre Rd DT2 . . . . 129 E3
Sycamore Ave BH20 . . . . . 116 B3
Sycamore Cl
  Broadstone BH17 . . . . . . 86 F1
  Christchurch BH23 . . . . . 123 D8
  Sandford BH20 . . . . 143 B8
  5 Sixpenny Handley SP5 . 189 A4
Sycamore Dr
  14 Crewkerne TA18 . . . . 191 F5
  Yeovil BA22 . . . . 27 B2
Sycamore Pl BH21 . . . . 60 D5
Sycamore Rd
  Hordle SO41 . . . . 95 F4
  Radipole DT4 . . . . 167 A6
Sycamore Way SP8 . . . . . . 5 D1
Sydenham Cres BH20 . . . 139 F2
Sydenham Rd BH19 . . . . . 178 E2
Sydenham Way **4** DT1 . . 108 B1
Sydling Cl BH17 . . . . 88 B2
Sydling Rd
  Cerne Abbas DT2 . . . . . 207 C3
  Yeovil BA21 . . . . 27 F6
Sydney Pl **3** SP8 . . . . 5 E1
Sydney Rd
  Broadstone BH18 . . . . . . 87 A3
  Christchurch BH23 . . . . . 91 E1
Sydney St DT4 . . . . 167 B3
Sylmor Gdns BH9 . . . . 90 A2
Sylvan Cl
  4 Gillingham SP8 . . . . . . 5 F3
  St Leonards BH24 . . . . . 53 F4
Sylvan Fst Sch BH12 . . . . 120 B6
Sylvan Rd BH12 . . . . 120 B6
Sylvan Way SP8 . . . . 5 F3
Symes Cl TA18 . . . . 192 C4
Symes Rd BH15 . . . . 118 E4
Symondsbury CE Prim Sch
  DT6 . . . . 99 F8
Symonds Cl DT3 . . . . 167 D7
Symonds St SO23 . . . . 126 E5
Syward Cl DT1 . . . . 108 C1
Syward Rd DT1 . . . . 135 C8

T

Tabbit's Hill La BH20 . . . . 177 F6
Tabernacle La **8** BA20 . . . 27 D4
Tadden Cotts BH21 . . . . . . 58 D7
Tadden Wlk BH18 . . . . 86 F2
Tadnoll Nature Reserve
  DT2 . . . . 138 C3
Tail Mill TA16 . . . . 191 F7
Tait Cl BH17 . . . . 119 E7
Talbot Ave BH3 . . . . 121 E7
Talbot Comb Sch BH12 . . 121 B8
Talbot Cl BH9 . . . . 89 F1
Talbot Dr
  Christchurch BH23 . . . . . 93 F2
  Poole BH12 . . . . 121 B8
Talbothays Rd **17** DT1 . . . 135 B8
Talbot Heath Sch BH4 . . . 121 C5
Talbot Hill Rd BH9 . . . . . . 121 D8
Talbot House Prep Sch
  BH9 . . . . 121 E7
Talbot Manor BH3 . . . . . . 121 D8
Talbot Mdws BH12 . . . . . . 121 B8
Talbot Mews BH10 . . . . . . 89 B1
Talbot Rd
  Bournemouth BH9 . . . . . 121 D8
  Bournemouth BH9 . . . . . 121 D8
  Lyme Regis DT7 . . . . 96 B7
Talbot Rdbt BH3 . . . . 121 D7
Talbot Rise BH10 . . . . 89 C2
Tallidge Cl DT3 . . . . 153 C2
Tamar Cl BH22 . . . . 62 A5
Tamlin St BH20 . . . . 143 A8
Tamworth Rd BH7 . . . . . . 122 F5
Tanglewood Ct **1** BH25 . . 95 B3
Tanglewood Lo BH17 . . . . 118 F3
Tangmere Cl BH23 . . . . . . 125 B6
Tangmere Pl BH17 . . . . . . 119 E7
Tan Howse Cl BH7 . . . . . . 123 B8
Tank Mus The BH20 . . . . . 139 D5
Tan La SP8 . . . . 2 A5
Tanner's La **5** BH20 . . . . . 142 E3
Tanner St **7** SO23 . . . . . . 126 C6
Tannery Rd DT6 . . . . 100 C6
Tansee Hill TA20 . . . . 202 E6
Tantinoby La BH20 . . . . . . 142 D5
Tanyard DT2 . . . . 206 A7
Tanyard La SP7 . . . . 12 C2
Tanzey La DT11 . . . . 21 B3
Taphouse La DT6 . . . . 203 B1
Tapper Ct BH21 . . . . 59 E4
Tark's Hill DT9 . . . . 194 C5
Tarn Dr BH17 . . . . 118 F3
Tarrant Cl BH17 . . . . 87 E2
Tarrant Dr BH20 . . . . 142 D6
Tarrant Rd BH9 . . . . 90 B3
Tarrants The **12** BH2 . . . . 121 D4
Tarratt La BA20 . . . . 27 B1
Tarratt Rd BA20 . . . . 27 B1
Tasman Cl BH23 . . . . 123 F6
Tatnam Cres BH15 . . . . . . 119 C3
Tatnam Rd BH15 . . . . 119 C4
Tattershall Gdns **4** BH21. 56 D4
Taunton Rd BH19 . . . . 179 C2
Taverner Cl BH15 . . . . 119 D2
Taylor Dr BH8 . . . . 90 D4
Taylor's Bldgs **6** BH15 . . 119 C1
Taylor's La
  Mappowder DT10 . . . . . . 196 E1
  Whitchurch Canonicorum
  DT6 . . . . 66 B2
Taylor Way BH31 . . . . 45 C6
Teak Cl BH13 . . . . 147 H8
Teal Ave DT3 . . . . 166 D5

Teasel Way BH22 . . . . 53 A1
Tecan Way DT4 . . . . 166 F3
Technology Rd BH17 . . . . . 119 A8
Tedder Cl BH11 . . . . 89 B3
Tedder Gdns BH11 . . . . . . 89 B3
Tedder Rd BH11 . . . . 89 B3
Teeling Rd DT3 . . . . 167 D7
Teg Down Meads SO22 . . 126 A7
Telegraph St DT11 . . . . . . 198 E8
Telford Cl DT3 . . . . 153 B2
Telford Rd BH21 . . . . 61 A8
Temple Cl DT1 . . . . 134 F8
Templecombe La SP8 . . . . . 8 F5
Temple La BA8 . . . . 8 B2
Temple Mews BH1 . . . . . . 122 D6
Templer Cl BH11 . . . . 88 F1
Temple Trees **45** BH4 . . . 121 C3
Ten Acres SP7 . . . . 13 A3
Tennyson Rd
  Bournemouth BH9 . . . . . 89 F2
  1 Poole BH14 . . . . 120 A3
  Weymouth DT4 . . . . 167 C2
  Wimborne Minster BH21. . 59 C6
Tenon Ct BH23 . . . . 124 B7
Tensing Rd BH23 . . . . 124 E8
Terence Ave BH17 . . . . . . 87 C1
Terence Rd BH21 . . . . 86 C5
Termare Ct BA22 . . . . 26 D6
Terminus St **3** DT4 . . . . . 167 D4
Tern Ct BH6 . . . . 123 D6
Terrace Rd BH2 . . . . 121 E3
Terrace The DT2 . . . . 133 D7
Terracotta Warriors Mus
  DT1 . . . . 108 B2
Terrington Ave BH23 . . . . 93 C1
Test Ho SO23 . . . . 126 F4
Tewkesbury **4** BA21 . . . . . 26 F6
Thames Cl BH22 . . . . 62 A6
Thames Mews **11** BH15 . . 119 B1
Thames St BH15 . . . . 119 B1
Thatcham Ct BA21 . . . . . . 27 B7
Thatcham Pk BA21 . . . . . . 27 B7
Thatcham Pk Cl BA21 . . . . 27 B7
Theobold Rd BH23 . . . . . . 91 A8
Thessaly Ct **4** BH5 . . . . . 122 F4
Thetchers Cl BH25 . . . . . . 95 B5
Thetford Rd BH12 . . . . 120 F5
Thickthorn Cross BH21 . . 200 D7
Thickthorn La DT11 . . . . . 197 A2
Third Cliff Wlk **3** DT6 . . . 100 B3
Thistlebarrow Rd BH7 . . . 122 E6
Thistle Cl DT3 . . . . 125 C8
Thomas Hardy Cl DT10 . . . 35 B2
Thomas Hardy Dr SP7 . . . 13 A3
Thomas Hardye L Ctr
  DT1 . . . . 134 D8
Thomas Hardye Sch The
  DT1 . . . . 134 E8
Thomas Lockyer Cl BH31 . 45 C5
Thompson Cl
  Allington DT6 . . . . 100 B7
  Puddletown DT2 . . . . 78 A2
Thomson Dr **10** TA18 . . . 191 F4
Thoresby Ct BH25 . . . . . . 94 E3
Thornbury **18** BH4 . . . . . . 121 C3
Thornbury Rd BH6 . . . . . . 124 A4
Thorncombe Beacon DT6. 99 D4
Thorncombe Cl
  Bournemouth BH9 . . . . . 90 B4
  Poole BH17 . . . . 87 E2
Thorncombe Wood Nature
  Reserve DT2 . . . . 109 B5
Thorne Cl BH31 . . . . 45 A7
Thorne Gdns BA21 . . . . . . 26 E7
Thorne La BA21 . . . . 26 E7
Thorners CE Prim Sch
  DT2 . . . . 103 C1
Thornfield Dr BH23 . . . . . . 93 C1
Thornford CE Prim Sch
  DT9 . . . . 194 D8
Thornford Rd DT9 . . . . . . 194 C6
Thornford Sta DT9 . . . . . . 194 C7
Thornham Rd BH25 . . . . . 95 D3
Thornhill Cl **8** DT1 . . . . . 134 E7
Thornhill Cres DT4 . . . . . . 167 C4
Thornhill Rd DT10 . . . . 33 D8
Thornicks DT2 . . . . 156 F6
Thornley Rd BH10 . . . . 89 D4
Thornlow Cl DT4 . . . . 180 D8
Thornlow Prep Sch **3**
  DT4 . . . . 167 C1
Thorn Rd BH17 . . . . 87 D3
Thornton Cl BH21 . . . . 86 C5
Thornton Rd BA21 . . . . . . 26 F8
Thorny La BA22 . . . . 14 D6
Thorogood Ct **4** BH15 . . 119 E4
Thrasher's La BH20 . . . . . 162 B3
Thread Mill La DT6 . . . . . . 68 D2
Three Acre Dr BH25 . . . . . 126 F8
Three Acre La BH19 . . . . . 178 D2
Three Acres DT2 . . . . 207 A2
Three Corner Mead **2**
  BA21 . . . . 26 E5
Three Cross Rd BH21 . . . . 53 B5
Three Lanes Way DT2 . . . . 78 A2
Three Legged Cross Fst Sch
  BH21 . . . . 45 A1
Three Lions Cl **9** BH21 . . 59 B5
Three Yards Cl DT5 . . . . . 186 F1
Thrift Cl DT10 . . . . 33 E8
Throop Cl BH8 . . . . 91 B4
Throop Hollow DT2 . . . . . 112 D6
Throop Rd
  Abbas & Templecombe BA8. . 8 A3
  Bournemouth BH8 . . . . . 90 A4
  Bournemouth BH8 . . . . . 91 A2
  Throopside Ave BH9 . . . . 90 D4
  Thrush Rd BH12 . . . . 88 C1

Thurmond Cres SO22 ... 126 A4
Thurmond Rd SO22 ... 126 A4
Thursby Rd BH23 ... 93 F1
Thurstin Way SP8 ... 5 F3
Thwaite Rd BH12 ... 121 B5
Tidemill Cl BH23 ... 124 A8
Tiffany Cl SO41 ... 95 F4
Tilburg Rd BH23 ... 124 D7
Tilbury Mead 2 BH20 ... 177 A7
Tiley Knap DT2 ... 195 E1
Tiller Gdns BH11 ... 89 A5
Tillycombe Rd DT5 ... 187 A7
Tilly Whim Caves BH19 .. 185 C6
Tilly Whim La DT2 ... 106 F3
Timber Hill DT7 ... 96 C7
Timewalk Journey DT4 .. 167 E1
Timothy Cl BH10 ... 89 D5
Tincleton Cross DT2 ... 110 D5
Tincleton Gdns BH9 ... 90 B4
Tinker's La
Cucklington BA9 ... 4 B5
Wareham BH20 ... 142 E4
Tinneys La DT9 ... 30 C6
Tin Pot La DT11 ... 212 D6
Tintagel Rd BA21 ... 26 F7
Tintern BA21 ... 26 E6
Tintern La 16 DT1 ... 107 C1
Tintinhull Rd BA21 ... 27 A8
Tiptoe Prim Sch SO41 ... 95 D8
Tithe Barn Mus BH19 ... 179 B2
Tiverton Ct 34 BH4 ... 121 C3
Tizard's Knap DT6 ... 66 B1
Toby's Cl DT5 ... 186 F3
Tobys Ct SP7 ... 12 E3
Todber Cl BH11 ... 88 D3
Tollard Cl BH12 ... 120 E8
Tollerdown Rd 4 DT4 ... 166 F2
Tollerford Rd BH17 ... 87 D2
Toller La DT2 ... 206 A1
Tollgate Pk SP7 ... 12 F5
Tollgate The 3 SO23 ... 126 E7
Tolpuddle Gdns BH9 ... 90 B4
Tolstoi Rd BH14 ... 120 A6
Tomlins La SP8 ... 5 E2
Tomlins La Ind Est SP8 ... 5 E2
Toms Field Rd BH19 ... 178 B2
Tonge Rd BH11 ... 89 B6
Toose The BA21 ... 26 E6
Tophill Jun Sch DT5 ... 187 A4
Topiary The
Poole BH14 ... 119 F5
Poole BH15 ... 120 A5
Top La
Ringwood BH24 ... 55 C7
Stourton with Gasper BA12 .. 1 D7
Torbay Rd BH14 ... 120 C3
Torre The BA21 ... 26 E6
Torvain Pk BH14 ... 120 A5
Totmel Rd BH17 ... 88 A2
Tourney Rd BH11 ... 88 E6
Tout Hill
East Stoke BH20 ... 140 B4
Shaftesbury SP7 ... 12 D3
Tout Hill La DT2 ... 104 E6
Tout Quarry Nature Reserve
DT5 ... 186 F6
Tout Quarry Sculpture Pk
DT5 ... 186 F5
Towans The BH13 ... 147 C3
Tower Cl 1 BH21 ... 201 D1
Tower Ct
Bournemouth BH2 ... 121 E2
10 Winchester SO22 ... 126 D6
Tower Hill
Bere Regis BH20 ... 81 B2
Iwerne Minster DT11 ... 38 C2
Netherbury DT6 ... 204 B2
Tower Hill Rd 6 TA18 ... 191 E4
Tower La BH21 ... 59 D6
Tower Park Rdbt BH15 .. 119 F7
Tower Rd
Bournemouth BH1 ... 122 E5
Poole BH13 ... 121 B2
Winchester SO23 ... 126 D6
Yeovil BA21 ... 27 D8
Tower Rd W BH13 ... 121 A1
Towers Farm BH21 ... 86 D7
Tower St SO23 ... 126 D6
Towers Way BH21 ... 86 D7
Town Farm Pl 6 SP5 ... 189 B4
Towngate Bridge BH15 .. 119 C3
Towngate Mews BH24 ... 55 C6
Towngate Sh Ctr 1
BH15 ... 119 C2
Town Hall La BH19 ... 179 B2
Townsend BH21 ... 56 D4
Townsend Cl
Bournemouth BH11 ... 89 B6
Mere BA12 ... 2 F5
Townsend Gn BA8 ... 19 B4
Townsend La SP6 ... 190 A6
Townsend Mead BH20 ... 177 A7
Townsend Nature Reserve
BH19 ... 179 A1
Townsend Orch TA16 ... 191 F8
Townsend Prim Sch BH8 . 91 A2
Townsend Rd
Corfe Castle BH20 ... 177 A7
Swanage BH19 ... 179 B1
Townsend Way DT6 ... 68 F2
Townsville Rd BH9 ... 90 B2
Tozer Cl BH11 ... 88 F2
Tracey Ct 8 BH23 ... 126 A7
Tradecroft DT5 ... 186 E5
Tradecroft Ind Est DT5 .. 186 F5
Trafalgar Ct BH23 ... 124 F5
Trafalgar Rd BH9 ... 121 F7
Trafalgar St SO23 ... 126 D6
Treasury Ct 27 SO23 ... 126 D6
Treebys Cl BH23 ... 92 D1
Tree Hamlets BH16 ... 118 C5
Treeside BH23 ... 93 C2
Treetops 9 BH13 ... 147 F7
Trefoil Way BH23 ... 125 C8
Tregonwell Ct 18 BH2 ... 121 E3
Tregonwell Rd BH2 ... 121 E2
Trellech Ct 1 BA22 ... 26 E6
Treloen Ct 3 BH8 ... 122 A5
Trenchard Mdw BH16 ... 84 D3
Trenchard Way DT3 ... 166 D5
Trendle St DT9 ... 30 B5
Trent Cl
Tolpuddle DT2 ... 79 D1
Yeovil BA21 ... 28 A8
Trent Dr BH20 ... 142 D5
Trentham Ave BH7 ... 123 B8
Trentham Cl BH7 ... 123 B8
Trent Path La DT9 ... 29 E7
Trent Way BH22 ... 62 A6
Tresco Spinney BA21 ... 26 E6
Tresillian Cl BH23 ... 94 B2
Tresillian Way BH23 ... 94 B2
Treves Rd DT1 ... 134 E8
Trevone 5 BH25 ... 95 B3
Triangle The
Bournemouth BH2 ... 121 E3
Upton BH16 ... 118 B7
Tricketts La BH22 ... 61 F6
Trigon Rd BH15 ... 119 D7
Trill La DT9 ... 194 B7
Trinidad Cres BH12 ... 120 C8
Trinidad Ho BH12 ... 120 C8
Trinity 2 BH1 ... 122 A3
Trinity CE VA Fst Sch
BH31 ... 45 B8
Trinity Ct 10 DT4 ... 167 D2
Trinity Gdns 20 SO23 ... 126 E6
Trinity House Lighthouse
DT5 ... 186 D9
Trinity Ind Est BH21 ... 59 E3
Trinity La BH20 ... 142 E3
Trinity Rd
Bournemouth BH1 ... 122 A4
Weymouth DT4 ... 167 D2
Trinity St
Dorchester DT1 ... 108 A2
7 Weymouth DT4 ... 167 E2
Trinity Terr DT4 ... 167 D2
Trinity Way DT6 ... 68 F1
Troak Cl BH23 ... 124 E8
Troon Rd BH18 ... 87 A5
Trotters La BH21 ... 60 B6
Troublefield Nature Reserve
BH23 ... 91 A8
Trowbridge Ct 18 SO23 .. 126 E6
Truman Rd BH11 ... 89 B6
Truscott Ave BH9 ... 122 A7
Trusthams 4 DT8 ... 203 E5
Trustin Cl 6 DT6 ... 100 C8
Trystworthy 3 BH2 ... 121 E3
Tuckers La BH15 ... 118 F1
Tuckers Mill Cl BH20 ... 160 F8
Tucks Cl BH23 ... 93 A8
Tuckton Cl BH6 ... 123 D4
Tuckton Rd
Bournemouth,Southbourne
BH6 ... 123 F5
Bournemouth,West Southbourne
BH6 ... 123 E4
Tuckton Rdbt BH6 ... 123 F5
TUC Mml Cottage &
Tolpuddle Martyrs Mus
DT2 ... 79 B2
Tudor Arc Sh Ctr DT1 ... 108 A1
Tudor Cl SP6 ... 42 C5
Tudor Ct
Bournemouth BH1 ... 122 A5
Poole BH15 ... 119 E6
Tudor Gdns DT11 ... 212 E5
Tudor Rd BH18 ... 87 B4
Tulse Hill BA12 ... 1 F3
Tuncombe La TA18 ... 191 D4
Tunnel Rd DT8 ... 204 C5
Turbary Cl BH12 ... 120 D8
Turbary Ct
Bournemouth BH12 ... 89 A1
Ferndown BH22 ... 61 F6
Upton BH16 ... 118 C8
Turbary Hts BH11 ... 88 F1
Turbary Park Ave BH11 ... 89 A2
Turbary Rd
Ferndown BH22 ... 61 F6
Poole BH12 ... 120 D8
Turbary Ret Pk BH11 ... 88 E3
Turberville Rd BH20 ... 81 B2
Turbetts Cl BH16 ... 84 C4
Turf Croft Ct BH23 ... 94 B2
Turk's La BH14 ... 120 A1
Turlin Moor Com Fst Sch
BH16 ... 118 C4
Turlin Moor Com Mid Sch
BH16 ... 118 C4
Turlin Moor Mid Sch
BH16 ... 117 E4
Turlin Rd BH16 ... 118 C4
Turnberry Cl BH23 ... 123 F6
Turner's Barn La BA20 ... 27 B2
Turners La SP8 ... 5 E2
Turner's La
Marshwood DT6 ... 202 E2
Tarrant Monkton DT11 ... 200 B4
Turnpike Cl 2 TA18 ... 192 B3
Turnpike Gn 3 TA18 ... 192 B3
Turnpike La DT11 ... 212 C1
Turnstone Cl DT3 ... 152 D4
Turnworth Cl BH18 ... 87 C3
Turton St 3 DT4 ... 167 D3
Tut Hill DT9 ... 31 E1
Tweedale Rd BH9 ... 90 C3
Twemlow Ave BH14 ... 119 F3
Twin Oak Pk BH23 ... 92 D6
Twin Oaks Cl BH18 ... 87 A3
Twinways La DT6 ... 69 B8
Two Droves DT2 ... 109 F8
Two Elms BA22 ... 14 C8
Two Tower La BA20 ... 27 D2
Twyford Cl BH8 ... 90 D2
Twyford Ct 16 SO23 ... 126 E8
Twyford Ho BH22 ... 61 F6
Twyford Way BH17 ... 88 A2
Twynham Ave BH23 ... 124 A7
Twynham Rd BH6 ... 123 F4
Twynham Sch BH23 ... 124 A6
Tyberton St 5 DT1 ... 107 C1
Tynedale Cl BH9 ... 90 B4
Tyneham Ave BH12 ... 120 C8
Tyneham Cl
Radipole DT3 ... 167 B8
Sandford BH20 ... 143 A8
Tyneham Mus BH20 ... 174 C5
Tynham Ct BH23 ... 124 C6
Tyrrell Gdns BH8 ... 91 A2
Tytherley Gn BH8 ... 90 D2

U

Ubsdell Cl BH25 ... 95 A3
Uddens Dr
Ferndown Town BH21 ... 51 F1
Wimborne Minster BH21 ... 60 D7
Uddens Trad Est BH21 ... 60 E6
Ullswater Cres DT3 ... 167 B7
Ullswater Rd BH21 ... 59 C2
Ulwell Rd BH19 ... 179 C4
Umbers Hill 1 SP7 ... 12 D2
Undercliff Dr
Bournemouth BH1 ... 121 F2
Bournemouth BH1 ... 122 C2
Undercliff Rd BH5 ... 122 E3
Underdown Hollow DT9 .. 28 C3
Underhedge Gdns DT5 .. 186 E1
Underhill
Mere BA12 ... 2 F5
Pen Selwood BA9 ... 1 B2
Underhill Jun Sch DT5 .. 186 E7
Underwood Cl BH17 ... 87 B1
Union St
Winchester SO23 ... 126 F6
2 Yeovil BA20 ... 27 D4
Unity La 4 TA18 ... 192 A3
Univ Coll Winchester
SO22 ... 126 C5
University Rdbt BH10 ... 121 C8
Upland Cl DT10 ... 197 D7
Uplands
Bothenhampton DT6 ... 101 A6
2 Yetminster DT9 ... 194 C5
Uplands Ave BH25 ... 127 A8
Uplands Cl BH22 ... 62 A8
Uplands Gdns BH8 ... 90 C2
Uplands Ind Pk DT11 ... 212 D6
Uplands Rd
Bournemouth BH8 ... 90 C2
Ferndown BH22 ... 53 C1
Uplands Sch BH14 ... 120 C3
Uplyme Cl BH17 ... 88 A2
Uplyme Rd DT7 ... 96 A6
Upper Brook St SO23 ... 126 E6
Upper Fairfield Rd 3
DT1 ... 107 F1
Upper Golf Links Rd BH18 87 B5
Upper Gordon Rd BH23 ... 94 A1
Upper High St SO23 ... 126 D6
Upper Hinton Rd BH1 ... 121 F3
Upper Norwich Rd 6
BH2 ... 121 E3
Upper N Rd SP5 ... 188 C5
Upper Rd BH12 ... 120 C6
Upper Sch La 1 DT11 ... 212 C1
Upper St 4 DT11 ... 198 C7
Upper Terrace Rd BH2 .. 121 E3
Upper Water St 4 BA12 ... 3 B5
Upper Westhill Rd DT7 ... 96 A5
Uppington Cl 2 BH21 ... 201 C1
Uppleby Rd BH12 ... 120 C6
Upton Cl BH16 ... 118 B7
Upton Cross Mobile Home Pk
2 Upton BH16 ... 117 E7
Upton BH16 ... 118 C7
Upton Ct BH16 ... 118 C7
Upton Ctry Pk BH17 ... 118 F6
Upton Heath Est
Upton BH16 ... 117 F7
Upton BH16 ... 118 D7
Upton Ind Est
Upton BH16 ... 117 F6
Upton BH16 ... 118 D6
Upton Inf Sch BH16 ... 118 A7
Upton Jun Sch
Upton BH16 ... 117 C7
Upton BH16 ... 118 A7
Upton Rd
Poole BH17 ... 118 F7
Poole BH17 ... 119 B7
Upton Way BH18 ... 86 F3
Upway St 2 DT4 ... 167 D4
Upwey Ave BH15 ... 118 E3
Upwey Sta DT3 ... 152 C3
Utrecht Ct BH23 ... 124 D7

V

Vaggs La SO41 ... 95 E6
Vale Cl
4 Crewkerne TA18 ... 191 F3
Poole BH14 ... 120 E4
Vale Lodge BH1 ... 122 D5
Vale Mans 4 BH1 ... 122 D4
Vale Mead DT10 ... 196 F3
Valencia Cl BH23 ... 91 D4
Vale Pk DT11 ... 212 D2
Vale Rd
Bournemouth BH1 ... 122 D4
Poole BH14 ... 120 E4
Stalbridge DT10 ... 33 D8
West Lulworth BH20 ... 172 E6
Yeovil BA21 ... 28 A6
Vale St BA8 ... 19 A4
Valette Rd BH9 ... 90 A3
Vale View BA8 ... 19 A5
Vale View Pk SO41 ... 95 F7
Valiant Way BH23 ... 125 B7
Valley Bladen DT2 ... 112 A7
Valley Cl
Christchurch BH23 ... 91 E3
Overcombe/Preston DT3 .. 153 D1
Yeovil BA21 ... 27 D6
Valley Ct The SO22 ... 126 B4
Valley of Stones National
Nature Reserve DT2 ... 131 F4
Valley Rd
Blandford Camp DT11 ... 199 E3
Bournemouth BH8 ... 90 F3
Bridport DT6 ... 100 D4
2 Crewkerne TA18 ... 191 F3
Langton Matravers BH19 . 178 C3
Worth Matravers BH20 ... 177 D6
Valley The SO22 ... 126 B4
Valley View BH12 ... 121 B7
Vallis Cl BH15 ... 119 D1
Vanguard Ave DT4 ... 166 F1
Vanguard Rd
Bournemouth BH8 ... 90 E1
6 Poole BH15 ... 119 C2
Vantage Way BH12 ... 88 B2
Veals La DT10 ... 35 A5
Vearse Cl DT6 ... 100 B5
Vecta Cl BH23 ... 125 C6
Vectis Rd BH25 ... 126 D7
Velvet Lawn Rd BH25 ... 94 F4
Venator Pl BH21 ... 59 C6
Venn Hill TA20 ... 202 F6
Venning Ave BH11 ... 88 E5
Venn La
Chideock DT6 ... 66 F2
Stoke Abbott DT6 ... 203 D2
Venn The SP7 ... 12 F3
Ventnor Rd DT5 ... 186 F8
Ventry Cl BH13 ... 120 F4
Ventura Ctr The BH16 ... 118 D6
Ventura Pl BH16 ... 118 D6
Verity Cres BH17 ... 88 A1
Verlands Rd DT3 ... 153 D1
Vermin La BH20 ... 83 B7
Vernalls Cl BH10 ... 89 D6
Vernalls Ct BH25 ... 95 C5
Vernalls Gdns BH10 ... 89 D5
Vernalls Rd DT9 ... 30 B7
Verne Cl DT4 ... 167 C1
Verne Common Rd DT5 . 186 F8
Verne Hill Rd DT5 ... 187 A7
Verne Rd
Verwood BH31 ... 45 C5
Weymouth DT4 ... 167 C1
Verne Way DT4 ... 167 C1
Verney Cl BH11 ... 89 B3
Verney Rd BH11 ... 89 A3
Vernham Rd SO22 ... 126 C8
Verno La BH23 ... 93 C1
Verona Ave BH6 ... 123 D5
Verriott's La DT6 ... 66 C1
Verulam Pl 8 BH1 ... 121 F3
Verulam Rd BH14 ... 119 F4
Verwood CE Fst Sch
BH31 ... 45 A5
Verwood Cres BH6 ... 124 B4
Verwood Ind Est BH31 ... 45 D6
Verwood L Ctr BH31 ... 45 B6
Verwood Rd
St Leonards & St Ives
BH24 ... 46 C2
Three Legged Cross BH21 .. 45 B1
Verwood BH21 ... 53 A8
Woodlands BH21 ... 44 C7
Verwood Sports Ctr BH31 45 D6
Vespasian Way DT1 ... 134 E7
Vetch Cl BH23 ... 125 C8
Vian Ct BH25 ... 94 F3
Vicarage Cl 2 BH20 ... 140 A1
Vicarage Cotts BH8 ... 90 F3
Vicarage Ct 4 DT6 ... 100 C8
Vicarage La DT2 ... 107 E6
Vicarage Rd
Bournemouth BH9 ... 89 F1
Poole BH15 ... 119 C6
Verwood BH31 ... 45 B6
Vicarage St 9 BA20 ... 27 D4
Vicarage Way BH23 ... 92 D2
Vickers Cl BH8 ... 91 B2
Vickery Way BH23 ... 124 D8
Victoria Ave
Bournemouth BH9 ... 89 E1
Radipole DT3 ... 152 B5
Swanage BH19 ... 179 A3
Victoria Ave Ind Est
BH19 ... 178 F3
Victoria Cl
Corfe Mullen BH21 ... 86 D5
Wool BH20 ... 139 D6
Yeovil BA21 ... 27 F6
Victoria Cres BH12 ... 120 D6
Victoria Gdns
Ferndown BH22 ... 61 D6
Ringwood BH24 ... 55 C6
Victoria Gr DT6 ... 100 D7
Victoria Ho 33 SO23 ... 126 D6
Victoria Hospl BH21 ... 59 A5
Victoria Park Pl 4 BH9 .. 89 F1
Victoria Park Rd BH9 ... 89 E1
Victoria Pl
Bournemouth BH1,BH8 .. 122 C5
Easton/Weston DT5 ... 187 A5
Wimborne Minster BH21 ... 59 B5
Victoria Rd
Blandford Forum DT11 ... 212 D4
Bournemouth BH1 ... 122 C5
Christchurch BH23 ... 124 E5
Dorchester DT1 ... 107 F1
Easton/Weston DT5 ... 187 B5
Ferndown BH22 ... 61 D6
Gillingham SP8 ... 6 A1
Poole BH12 ... 120 C6
Swanage BH19 ... 179 C5
Weymouth DT4 ... 180 C7
Wimborne Minster BH21 ... 59 B5
Winchester SO23 ... 126 D7
Yeovil BA21 ... 27 F6
Victoria Sch BH13 ... 120 F4
Victoria Sq DT5 ... 186 E8
Victoria St
Radipole DT4 ... 167 E4
Shaftesbury SP7 ... 12 E3
Victor Jackson Ave DT1 . 107 C1
Victory Cl BH21 ... 53 D6
Victory Rd DT5 ... 186 E8
View Rd DT7 ... 96 B5
Viewside Cl BH21 ... 86 C5
Viking Cl BH6 ... 124 A4
Viking Way
Bournemouth BH6 ... 124 A4
Christchurch BH23 ... 125 A5
Village Rd DT6 ... 68 F1
Villas The BH25 ... 94 E5
Villette Cl BH23 ... 92 A1
Villiers Ct SO23 ... 126 D5
Vince Cl BH11 ... 89 B5
Vincent Cl 2 BH25 ... 95 A2
Vincent Pl BA20 ... 27 D5
Vincent Rd 1 BH25 ... 95 A2
Vincents Cl DT9 ... 31 A1
Vine Cl BH7 ... 123 A7
Vine Farm Cl BH12 ... 121 C8
Vine Farm Rd BH12 ... 121 B8
Vine Hill BH21 ... 58 E5
Vineries Cl BH21 ... 59 F6
Vineries The BH21 ... 59 F6
Vinery The BH25 ... 95 B2
Vineyard Cl BH16 ... 84 C3
Vinney Cross DT6 ... 102 A6
Vinneys Cl BH23 ... 92 C2
Violet Farm Cl BH21 ... 86 D8
Violet La BH25 ... 95 A4
Virginia Cl
1 Henstridge BA8 ... 19 A4
Poole BH12 ... 120 C7
Viscount Cl BH11 ... 88 D5
Viscount Ct BH11 ... 88 D5
Viscount Dr BH23 ... 125 B7
Viscount Rd DT4 ... 166 F1
Viscount Wlk BH11 ... 88 D5
Vista Marina BH13 ... 147 D6
Vivian Pk BH19 ... 179 B4
Vixen Wlk BH25 ... 95 B5
Voss's La DT2 ... 206 B3
Vulcan Cl DT4 ... 166 F1
Vulcan Way BH23 ... 125 B7

W

Waddock Dro DT2 ... 111 E3
Waddon Hill (Roman Fort)
DT8 ... 203 F4
Waddon Way DT6 ... 69 D2
Wadham Com Sch TA18 . 191 F5
Wadmore La BH19 ... 164 C2
Wagtail Dr BH25 ... 94 F2
Wain Rd BH20 ... 139 D7
Wainwright Cl DT3 ... 153 B1
Wakefield Ave BH10 ... 89 E5
Wakeham DT5 ... 187 A4
Wakely Gdns BH11 ... 89 A5
Wakely Rd BH11 ... 89 B5
Walcheren Pl BH15 ... 118 C3
Walcote Pl 30 SO23 ... 126 D6
Walcott Ave BH23 ... 91 F1
Walditch Gdns BH17 ... 87 E2
Walditch Rd DT6 ... 100 F6
Waldren Cl BH15 ... 119 E2
Waldrons The 5 DT9 ... 194 D8
Wales St SO23 ... 126 F6
Walford Cl BH21 ... 59 C6
Walford Gdns BH21 ... 59 B6
Walford Mill Craft Ctr
BH21 ... 59 B6
Walker Cres DT4 ... 180 C6
Walkford La BH25 ... 94 D3
Walkford Rd BH23 ... 94 C2
Walkford Way BH23 ... 94 B1
Walking Field La BH15 . 119 D2
Walkwood Ave BH7 ... 123 B8

Wallace Ct BH18 87 A3
Wallace Rd BH18 87 A3
Walliscott Rd BH11 89 A1
Wallisdown Rd BH10 121 C8
Wallisdown Rdbt BH12 89 A1
Wallis Rd BH10 89 B1
Wall La DT6 203 D4
Wallsend Cl 3 DT5 186 E2
Walls View Rd BH20 142 D5
Walnut Ave DT11 198 F1
Walnut Cl BH25 94 F3
Walnut Gr SO22 126 B7
Walnut Orch 3 DT3 150 A8
Walnut Rd BA12 3 B4
Walnut Tree Field Nature Reserve DT11 56 D5
Walpole Rd
  Bournemouth BH1 122 E5
  Winchester SO22 126 A3
Walpole St DT4 167 D4
Walrond Rd BH19 179 B3
Walsford Rd BH4 121 C5
Walsingham Dene BH7 122 F8
Walters Dr 13 DT11 199 D4
Waltham Rd BH7 123 B6
Walton Elm Hill DT10 35 A8
Walton Pl SO22 126 B3
Walton Rd
  Bournemouth BH10 89 C2
  Poole BH15 120 A6
Wanchard La DT2 107 C7
Wanderwell DT6 100 D3
Wanderwell Farm La DT6 100 D4
Wanstead Cl BH24 47 D1
Warbler Cl BH16 118 B8
Warburton Rd BH17 119 E8
Wardcliffe Rd DT4 167 C3
Wareham Ct
  Bournemouth BH7 123 B6
  Hamworthy BH15 118 E2
Wareham Golf Club BH20 142 E6
Wareham Hospl BH20 142 D4
Wareham Mid Sch BH20 142 D3
Wareham Rd
  Corfe Mullen BH21 86 D5
  Hawkchurch EX13 202 B2
  Lytchett Matravers BH16 84 D3
  Lytchett Minster & Upton BH16 116 B6
  Owermoigne DT2 155 E7
  Wareham St Martin BH16 116 D4
  Warmwell DT2 155 B7
Wareham Sta BH20 142 D5
Wareham Town Mus BH20 142 E3
Ware La DT7 96 A4
Wares Cl 5 DT11 81 E8
Warland Way BH21 86 E7
Warmwell Cl
  Bournemouth BH9 90 B4
  Poole BH17 87 F2
Warmwell Dro DT2 154 D6
Warmwell Rd DT2 137 D5
Warne Hill DT6 100 F7
Warner Ct 12 SO23 126 E8
Warnford Rd BH7 123 B7
Warren Ave BH23 124 F5
Warren Cl
  St Leonards BH24 54 F5
  Weymouth DT4 166 F2
Warren Dr BH24 54 F5
Warren Edge Cl BH6 123 F3
Warren Edge Ct BH6 123 F3
Warren Edge Rd BH6 123 F3
Warren Hill DT2 78 C7
Warren La BH24 54 F5
Warren Rd
  Bere Regis BH20 113 C4
  Bournemouth BH4 121 B2
  Poole BH14 120 D4
  Puddletown DT2 78 B5
Warren Way BH16 116 D2
Warren Wlk BH22 61 B7
Warrior Ave BA22 26 C6
Warrior Rd BA22 26 D6
Warwick Ave BH25 95 B3
Warwick Cl 14 SO23 126 E8
Warwick Ct 15 SO23 126 E8
Warwick Pl 1 BH7 123 A5
Warwick Rd
  Bournemouth BH7 123 A5
  Poole BH14 120 C3
Washington Ave BH1 122 D6
Washpond La BH19 178 F5
Watcombe Rd BH6 123 D5
Water Cl SO23 126 E5
Watercombe Hts BA20 26 F2
Watercombe La BA20 26 E3
Watercombe Pk BA20 26 F3
Waterditch Rd BH23 93 A4
Waterford Cl BH14 120 A2
Waterford Gdns BH23 126 A7
Waterford Lodge BH23 125 B6
Waterford Pl BH23 126 B7
Waterford Rd
  Christchurch BH23 126 B7
  New Milton BH25 95 C3
Waterfront Mus BH15 119 B1
Watergardens BH8 122 A5
Watergates La DT2 136 C3
Water Knap DT10 196 F3
Water La
  Bournemouth BH6 123 D7

Water La *continued*
  Durweston DT11 198 E3
  Swyre DT6 129 C8
  Winchester SO23 126 F5
  Winfrith Newburgh DT2 156 F7
  Winterborne Stickland DT11 210 B7
Water Lane Farm BH10 89 E6
Waterloo Ho BH17 87 B1
Waterloo La
  Silton SP8 5 B7
  Stourton Caundle DT10 33 A3
Waterloo Rd
  Bournemouth BH9 121 F7
  Corfe Mullen BH21 86 B5
  Poole BH17 119 C8
Waterloo Way 3 BH24 55 C6
Watermead
  5 Christchurch BH23 124 A5
  3 Tatworth TA20 202 A8
Water Meadow La BH20 139 E2
Watermill Rd BH23 124 A8
Waterpot Hill DT6 204 C2
Waters Edge BH13 147 D6
Watership Dr BH24 55 F5
Waterside BH23 124 F4
Waterside Cl BH24 47 D1
Watersmead SO23 126 D3
Watersmeet 5 SO23 126 F5
Watersmeet Ct BH23 124 B5
Water St
  Berwick St John SP7 188 B8
  Cranborne BH21 40 B7
  Mere BA12 3 B5
Waterston Cl BH17 87 D1
Waterston La DT2 77 D3
Waterston Manor DT2 77 D3
Water Tower Rd BH18 87 C4
Watery La
  Christchurch BH23 125 A8
  Donhead St Mary SP7 24 F8
  Halstock BA22 193 D2
  Iwerne Minster DT11 37 F1
  Lytchett Minster & Upton BH16 117 B7
  Radipole DT3 152 B4
  Shaftesbury SP7 12 E2
  Studland BH19 164 D1
  Tincleton DT2 110 D3
  Upton BH16 118 A7
  West Crewkerne TA18 191 D2
Watford La DT6 68 E2
Watkin Rd 6 BH5 122 F4
Watling St BA21 26 F7
Watton Cl BH8 91 A2
Watton Cross DT6 100 B5
Watton Gdns DT6 100 E8
Watton La DT6 100 B5
Watton Pk DT6 100 C5
Wavell Ave BH17 87 A1
Wavell Rd BH11 89 B4
Wavell Way SO22 126 A3
Wavendon Ave BH25 126 E8
Wavering La SP8 5 C2
Waverley 14 BH4 121 C3
Waverley Cres BH15 119 D6
Waverley Ho 9 BH25 95 B2
Waverley Rd
  New Milton BH25 95 B2
  Radipole DT3 167 C6
Wayclose La
  Buckhorn Weston SP8 9 B8
  Cucklington SP8 4 B2
Wayford Hill TA18 191 B1
Wayground Rd BH21 58 E1
Wayman Rd BH21 86 E6
Wayne Rd BH12 120 B6
Waynflete Pl SO22 126 A4
Wayside Rd
  Bournemouth BH6 123 E4
  St Leonards BH24 54 A1
  St Leonards BH24 62 F8
Waytown Cl BH17 87 D1
Weare Cl DT5 186 F7
Weatherbury Rd SP8 5 E3
Weatherbury Way DT1 135 A7
Weatherby Castle (Obelisk & Hill Fort)) BH20 79 F5
Weavers Cl
  Crewkerne TA18 191 F4
  Ferndown BH22 53 A1
Webbers Cl BH20 176 F8
Webbers Piece DT2 206 C1
Webb La DT10 196 E8
Webbs Cl BH24 53 F6
Webb's Way BH11 88 F1
Webster Rd
  Bournemouth BH9 90 A3
  Winchester SO22 126 A7
Wedgewood Rd 4 DT4 167 C3
Wedgwood Dr BH14 120 A2
Weeke Manor Cl SO22 126 B8
Weeke Prim Sch SO22 126 B8
Weiner Cl DT11 199 E2
Weir End Rd 2 DT1 107 C2
Weirs The 3 SO23 126 F4
Weir The DT3 153 C1
Weir View DT2 107 C6
Welbeck Rd BA21 28 A7
Weldon Ave BH11 88 E5
Welland Ct 10 DT1 107 D1
Welland Rd
  Wimborne Minster BH21 59 D4
  Yeovil BA21 27 F7
Wellbridge Cl DT1 135 A7
Well Cl BH25 94 F2
Wellesley Ave BH23 125 C7
Wellfield Hill EX13 202 E2

Wellfields Dr DT6 100 F8
Wellington Ave BH23 125 C7
Wellington Ct
  Bournemouth BH2 121 D3
  7 Bournemouth BH8 122 A5
  New Milton BH25 95 A3
Wellingtonia Gdns SO41 95 F4
Wellington Rd
  Bournemouth BH8 122 A5
  Poole BH14 120 C3
Well La
  Poole BH15 119 C4
  Powerstock DT6 70 B4
  Shaftesbury SP7 12 D3
Well Plot DT6 101 D8
Wellstead Rd BH20 142 D6
Wendover Cl BH25 94 F1
Wendy Cres BH22 61 F3
Wenlock Ct 9 BH23 124 F8
Wentwood Gdns BH25 95 D2
Wentworth BH14 147 C7
Wentworth Ave BH5 123 B4
Wentworth Cl
  Bournemouth BH5 123 B3
  Radipole DT3 152 E2
Wentworth Coll BH5 123 A4
Wentworth Dr
  Broadstone BH18 87 B5
  Christchurch BH23 123 F6
Wentworth Grange
  Ferndown BH22 61 D7
  Winchester SO22 126 C4
Wentworth Rd BA21 28 A7
Wescott Way BH11 88 E4
Wesley Cl
  8 Bournemouth BH8 122 C5
  Charmouth DT6 97 B8
Wesley Grange 48 BH4 121 C3
Wesley Ho
  Trickett's Cross BH22 61 F6
  15 Winchester SO23 126 E6
Wesley Rd
  Poole BH12 120 C5
  Wimborne Minster BH21 59 E5
Wessex Ave
  New Milton BH25 95 A2
  4 Shillingstone DT11 198 B5
Wessex Cl BH23 125 C7
Wessex Ct 22 SO23 126 D6
Wessex Dr
  Bradford Abbas DT9 28 D1
  Winchester SO22 126 C8
Wessex Est BH24 55 D8
Wessex Gate BH8 122 C6
Wessex Gate Ret Pk BH15 119 B6
Wessex Golf Ctr DT4 166 F5
Wessex Oval BH20 142 C5
Wessex Rd
  Dorchester DT1 107 D2
  Poole BH14 120 A3
  Ringwood BH24 55 D8
  Stalbridge DT10 33 E8
  Weymouth DT4 167 B3
  Yeovil BA21 27 A8
Wessex Ridgeway DT11 39 C5
Wessex Trade Ctr BH12 120 A7
Wessex Way
  Bournemouth BH2,BH4 121 C3
  Bournemouth BH8 122 C5
  Dorchester DT1 107 D2
  Gillingham SP8 5 E3
  1 Swanage BH19 179 B4
West Allington DT6 100 B7
West Ave BH21 53 A8
West Bay Cres DT4 180 C7
West Bay Rd DT6 100 D2
West Bexington Nature Reserve DT2 129 D2
West Borough BH21 59 B5
Westbourne Cl
  Bournemouth BH4 121 C3
  Yeovil BA20 27 A5
Westbourne Gate 15 BH4 121 C3
Westbourne Gr BA20 27 A5
Westbourne Park Rd BH4 121 B2
Westbourne Rd DT4 167 D5
West Bourton Rd SP8 1 D1
Westbridge Pk DT9 29 F4
West Brook BA21 26 F6
Westbrook Cl BH10 89 D2
Westbrook Rd SP8 10 A8
Westbury
  Bradford Abbas DT9 28 D2
  Sherborne DT9 30 B4
Westbury Cl
  Barton on Sea BH25 127 B8
  Bransgore BH23 93 A7
  Christchurch BH23 93 D1
Westbury Ct 1 BH14 120 B4
Westbury Rd BH24 55 D7
Westby Rd BH5 122 F4
West Chinnock Prim Sch TA18 192 B8
West Cl
  Chickerell DT3 166 C6
  Verwood BH31 44 F6
West Cliff 9 BH2 121 F4
West Cliff Cotts BH2 121 E2
West Cliff Ct 40 BH4 121 C3
West Cliff Gdns BH2 121 E2
Westcliff Ho 8 BH4 121 C2
West Cliff Mews BH2 121 E2
Westcliff Palms 18 BH4 121 C2
Westcliff Rd
  Charmouth DT6 96 F7

Westcliff Rd *continued*
  Easton/Weston DT5 186 E3
West Cliff Rd
  Bournemouth BH4 121 C2
  Bridport DT6 100 B2
West Close Ho BH6 124 A4
West Coker Rd
  East Coker BA20 26 E1
  Yeovil BA20 27 A2
West Coker VC Prim Sch BA22 193 A8
Westcroft Par 7 BH25 95 B2
Westcroft Pk BH18 87 C4
Westdowne Cl DT4 167 A2
Westdown Rd BH11 89 A5
West Downs Student Village SO22 126 B5
West Dr
  3 Swanage BH19 179 A2
  West Moors BH24 62 B8
West Durlston La BH19 179 B1
West End DT2 206 C2
West End Cl SO22 126 C6
West End Terr SO22 126 C6
Westerhall Rd DT4 167 E5
Westerham 7 BH13 121 B3
Westerham Rd BH4 121 B3
Westerleigh 12 BH4 121 C2
Western Ave
  Barton on Sea BH25 126 D8
  Bournemouth BH10 89 D4
  Poole BH13 120 F2
  Yeovil BA22 26 D7
Western CE Prim Sch SO22 126 B6
Western Cl BH10 89 D5
Western Downland Prim Sch SP6 190 F2
Westerngate 13 BH13 121 B3
Western Rd
  Poole BH13 121 A2
  Poole, Canford Cliffs BH13 147 F8
  Winchester SO22 126 C6
Western St DT9 28 D7
Westfield
  2 Portesham DT3 150 A8
  Sherborne DT9 29 F4
  10 Wimborne Minster BH21 59 B5
Westfield Ave BA21 27 A6
Westfield Cl BH21 59 B5
Westfield Com Sch BA21 27 A6
Westfield Cres BA21 27 B6
Westfield Est BA12 1 F4
Westfield Gr BA21 27 B7
Westfield Inf Sch BA21 27 A6
Westfield Pl BA21 27 A7
Westfield Rd
  Bournemouth BH6 123 E4
  Yeovil BA21 27 B6
Westfield Tech Coll DT3 153 A1
West Gables Cl DT6 100 B7
Westgate Mus SO23 126 D6
Westgate Pk BH4 121 B3
Westgate Sch The SO22 126 C7
Westham Cl BH17 87 E3
Westham Rd DT4 167 D3
Westhaven DT4 167 A2
Westhaven Hospl DT4 167 A4
West Hayes SO22 126 B5
Westheath Rd BH18 87 B4
West Hendford BA20 27 C4
West Hill
  Charminster DT2 107 D6
  Evershot DT2 206 A7
  Milborne Port DT9 17 D2
Westhill Cl 5 DT4 180 B8
West Hill Dr SO22 126 C6
West Hill Pk SO22 126 B6
West Hill Pl 2 BH2 121 E3
Westhill Rd DT4 180 C7
West Hill Rd
  Bournemouth BH2 121 E2
  Lyme Regis DT7 96 B5
West Howe Cl BH11 89 A4
West Howe Ind Est BH11 88 E3
West La
  Arne BH20 142 E1
  Hazelbury Bryan DT10 196 E4
  Melbury Abbas SP7 24 B6
  Mosterton DT8 204 A8
  North Wootton DT9 31 A3
Westlake Cl DT3 152 B4
Westland Rd BA20 27 B4
Westlands Ct BH23 93 A8
Westlands Dr BH13 147 F8
Westleaze DT2 107 E5
Westleaze Cl DT2 107 E5
Westley Cl SO22 126 B7
West Lulworth CE Fst Sch BH20 172 E6
West Mans 3 BH4 121 C3
West Mead DT6 100 B7
West Mill Cres BH20 142 D5
West Mill La
  Castleton DT9 30 A3
  Stalbridge DT10 20 A3
West Mills Rd DT1 107 F2
Westminster BA22 26 D6
Westminster Cl 2 SP7 12 F4
Westminster Ct BH25 126 F7
Westminster Meml Hospl SP7 12 E2
Westminster Rd
  Northport BH20 142 C5
  Poole BH13 121 B1
Westminster Rd E BH13 121 B1
Westminster Rd Ind Est BH20 142 C5

Westminster St 10 BA20 27 D4
West Moors Mid Sch BH22 53 B1
West Moors Rd
  Ferndown BH22 61 D7
  Three Legged Cross BH21 53 A7
  West Moors BH22 52 F4
Westmoreland Ct SO41 95 F3
Weston Cl BA22 192 E8
Weston Dr BH1 122 B3
Weston Hill SP8 9 B6
Weston La
  Closworth BA22 193 E5
  Corscombe DT2 205 A8
Weston Rd
  Colehill BH21 59 F7
  Easton/Weston DT5 186 F4
  Weymouth DT4 167 C2
  Worth Matravers BH19 183 C7
Weston St
  East Chinnock BA22 192 E8
  Easton/Weston DT5 187 A2
West Overcliff Dr BH4 121 D1
Westover Hill DT6 64 F2
Westover La BH24 54 F6
Westover Rd
  Bournemouth BH1 121 F3
  4 Dorchester DT1 107 F1
Westover Retail Pk BH9 90 A4
West Pk BA20 27 B5
West Pk Dr SP6 190 F3
West Pk La SP6 190 F3
Westport Rd BH20 142 D3
West Quay Rd BH15 119 B2
Westray Hall BH4 121 C1
West Rd
  Bournemouth BH5 123 B4
  Bransgore BH23 93 A8
  Symondsbury DT6 100 A7
  West Lulworth BH20 172 C6
Westridge 6 DT9 30 A5
West Row BH21 59 B4
West Row Mews BH21 59 B4
West St
  Abbas & Templecombe BA8 18 C8
  Abbotsbury DT3 149 A7
  Bere Regis BH20 81 A3
  Blandford Forum DT11 212 C3
  Bridport DT6 100 C6
  Broadwindsor DT8 203 E5
  Chickerell DT3 166 C6
  2 Corfe Castle BH20 162 A1
  Corfe Castle BH20 176 E4
  Crewkerne TA18 191 E4
  Fontmell Magna SP7 37 E6
  Hinton St George TA17 191 C7
  Kingston Magna SP8 9 C2
  Poole BH15 119 B2
  Radipole DT4 167 D2
  Ringwood BH24 55 A7
  Shapwick DT11 56 B8
  Wareham BH20 142 E3
  Wimborne Minster BH21 59 B5
  Winterborne Kingston DT11 81 D8
  Winterbourne Stickland DT11 210 C7
  Yeovil BA20 27 B4
West Station Terr BH4 121 D3
West Street Ct 8 BH21 59 B5
West Undercliff Prom BH2 121 D1
West View SP7 37 E7
West View Rd
  Christchurch BH23 124 E6
  Poole BH15 119 C4
Westville BA21 27 E5
West Walks Rd DT1 107 F2
West Walls BH20 142 D3
West Way
  Bournemouth BH9 90 B2
  Broadstone BH18 86 F3
  Easton/Weston DT5 186 E1
  Winterbourne Abbas DT2 105 D2
West Way Cl BH9 90 B1
West Ways BA22 192 D8
Westwey Rd DT4 167 D2
West Wlk DT6 100 B2
Westwood Ave BH22 61 D6
Westwoods & Glendene Pk BH25 94 D6
West Wools DT5 186 E1
Wetherbury Cl DT11 212 E6
Wetherby Cl
  Broadstone BH18 87 A2
  Milborne St Andrew DT11 79 F7
Wet La BA12 3 D2
Weyman's Ave BH10 89 C6
Weymans Dr BH10 89 C6
Weymouth Ave DT1 134 F8
Weymouth Bay Ave DT4 167 D7
Weymouth Coll DT4 167 E5
Weymouth Com Hospl DT4 167 E5
Weymouth Golf Club DT4 167 B4
Weymouth Marina DT4 167 D2
Weymouth Mus DT4 167 E1
Weymouth & Portland Sailing Acad DT6 181 A2
Weymouth Rd
  Dorchester DT1 134 F7
  Poole BH14 120 C5
Weymouth Rugby Football Club DT3 167 E8
Weymouth Sealife Pk DT4 167 F6

Weymouth Sports Club DT3 ... 152 B1
Weymouth Sta DT4 ... 167 D4
Weymouth Tennis Club DT4 ... 167 C5
Weymouth Way DT4 ... 167 B6
Wey Valley Sch & Sports Coll The DT3 ... 152 C2
Weyview Cres DT3 ... 152 B4
Wharf Cl BH12 ... 120 E6
Wharfdale Rd
Bournemouth BH4 ... 121 D4
Poole BH12 ... 120 E6
Wharf Hill SO23 ... 126 F4
Wharf Mill 1 SO23 ... 126 F4
Wharncliffe Ct BH23 ... 125 F7
Wharncliffe Gdns BH23 .. 126 A7
Wharncliffe Rd
Bournemouth BH5 ... 122 D4
Christchurch BH23 ... 126 A7
Whatcombe Rd DT11 ... 210 D4
Whatleigh Cl BH15 ... 119 C1
Whatley La TA20 ... 202 C8
Wheat Cl 4 DT10 ... 197 A4
Wheatear Cl 4 DT3 ... 152 C4
Wheat Farland DT3 ... 166 D6
Wheathill Cl 1 DT9 ... 17 D2
Wheathill La DT9 ... 17 E3
Wheathill Way DT9 ... 17 D2
Wheatland Cl SO22 ... 126 B3
Wheatlands DT5 ... 186 E1
Wheaton Grange 4 BH4 ... 121 D4
Wheaton Rd BH7 ... 123 A5
Wheatplot Park Homes 2 BH10 ... 89 F4
Wheelers La BH11 ... 88 D6
Wheel House La TA20 ... 202 E7
Wheelwright's Cl SP5 ... 189 A4
Whetham Mill La DT8 ... 203 C6
Whetland's La DT6 ... 69 D1
Whimbrel Ct BH23 ... 125 A6
Whincroft Cl BH22 ... 61 E7
Whincroft Dr BH22 ... 61 E6
Whitby Ave BH18 ... 87 A2
Whitby Cl BH23 ... 91 D4
Whitby Cres BH18 ... 87 A2
Whitchurch Ave BH18 ... 87 C3
Whitchurch La BA8 ... 19 A6
Whitcombe Rd DT8 ... 204 D3
Whitebeam Way BH31 ... 45 D5
White Cl
3 Bridport DT6 ... 68 F1
Poole BH15 ... 120 A7
Whitecliff DT11 ... 212 C4
Whitecliff Cres BH14 ... 120 A2
Whitecliff Gdns DT11 ... 212 C4
Whitecliff Rd
Poole BH14 ... 119 F2
Sw ... 179 B5
Wh ... 87 E3
Wh ... 180 E8
W ... 21 D8
W
W
Wh
White Knig
White La DT2 ...
White Lane Cl DT10 ...
Whitelegg Way BH10 ... 89
White Lovington BH20 ... 81 B1
Whitemarsh 3 BA12 ... 3 B4
White Mead BA21 ... 26 E6
White Mill DT11 ... 56 F6
White Mill Bridge BH21 .. 56 F5
White Pit DT11 ... 198 B5
White Pit La SP7 ... 24 D4
White Rd BA12 ... 3 B6
Whites Cl DT2 ... 76 E8
Whitesheets Prim Sch BA12 ... 2 A4
Whiteshute La SO23 ... 126 C3
White Way
Buckland Newton DT2 ... 208 B6
Litton Cheney DT2 ... 103 C3
Whiteway Hill BH21 ... 201 B4
White Way La DT10 ... 21 E1
Whiteways BH21 ... 59 E6
Whitfield Pk BH24 ... 54 D5
Whitfield Rd DT1 ... 107 D1
Whithay La DT6 ... 68 B7
Whitingham Ct 1 BH5 ... 123 B5
Whitley Way BH25 ... 95 B5
Whitmore La BH21 ... 44 B7
Whitsbury Cl BH8 ... 90 D2
Whittle Rd BH21 ... 60 F7
Whittles Way BH15 ... 119 B2
Whynot Way DT3 ... 166 D4
Wick 1 Ind Est BH25 ... 94 E2
Wick 2 Ind Est BH25 ... 94 E2
Wick Cl BH25 ... 94 E2
Wick Dr BH25 ... 94 E2
Wicket Rd BH10 ... 89 C5
Wicketsbeer Rd BA22 ... 193 C6
Wick Farm BH6 ... 124 B5
Wickfield Ave BH23 ... 124 B6
Wickfield Cl BH23 ... 124 B6
Wickford Ho BH23 ... 124 A6
Wickham Ct BH22 ... 61 E6
Wickham Dr BH21 ... 86 D4
Wickham Rd BH7 ... 123 A5
Wick Hill DT9 ... 17 B6
Wick La
Bournemouth BH6 ... 124 A5
Christchurch BH23 ... 124 B6
Wicklea Rd BH6 ... 124 B4
Wickmeads Rd BH6 ... 124 A5
Wick Point Mews BH23 .. 124 B5
Wick Rd DT9 ... 17 C4
Widdicombe Ave BH14 .. 120 E2
Wide St DT5 ... 186 F5
Widget Cl BH11 ... 89 B2
Widworthy Dr BH18 ... 86 F5
Wightman's Orch DT2 ... 208 B2
Wight Wlk BH22 ... 61 E2
Wilberforce Cl 2 SO22 .. 126 A4
Wilderness The DT9 ... 30 C6
Wilderton Rd
Poole BH13 ... 120 F3
Poole BH13 ... 121 A4
Wilderton Rd W BH13 ... 121 A4
Wildfell Cl BH23 ... 92 A1
Wildown Gdns BH6 ... 124 A3
Wildown Rd BH6 ... 124 A3
Wilfred Rd BH5 ... 122 F4
Wilkinson Dr BH8 ... 91 B2
Wilkins Way BH15 ... 119 B2
Willett Rd BH21 ... 59 A2
William Barnes Prim Sch DT10 ... 197 D8
William Cl BH23 ... 94 A2
William Ct 11 BH23 ... 126 B7
William Rd BH7 ... 122 F7
Williams Ave DT1 ... 107 F2
Williams' Ave DT4 ... 180 C7
William's Ind Pk BH25 ... 94 E2
William St DT4 ... 167 E4
Williams Way DT11 ... 212 E6
Williford La DT2 ... 195 C2
Willis's La TA18 ... 192 B4
Willis Way BH15 ... 119 B6
Willoughby Cl 3 DT2 ... 78 B1
Willow Cl
Bournemouth BH4 ... 121 B5
St Leonards BH24 ... 53 F4
Upton BH16 ... 118 D5
Willow Cres
Holton Heath BH20 ... 116 B2
Overcombe/Preston DT3 .. 153 B2
Willow Ct BH7 ... 123 C6
llowdene Cl BH25 ... 95 C3
... 124 A5
... 55 C5
... C6
Wilmsl
Wilmur Cres
Wilson Pk DT11 ...
Wilson Rd
Bournemouth BH1 ... 122 E6
Dorchester DT1 ... 108 C1
Poole BH14 ... 120 C4
Wilton Cl BH23 ... 91 D1
Wilton Dr DT4 ... 167 B1
Wilton Gdns BH25 ... 94 F3
Wilton Pl 19 BH4 ... 121 C2
Wilton Rd
Bournemouth BH7 ... 122 F5
Yeovil BA21 ... 28 A8
Wiltshire Ave DT4 ... 167 A3
Wiltshire Cl SP8 ... 5 E3
Wiltshire Gdns BH23 ... 92 F8
Wiltshire Rd BH23 ... 92 F8
Wilverley Ave BH8 ... 90 F2
Wilverley Rd BH23 ... 125 A7
Wilverly Gdns DT11 ... 212 E4
Wimborne Fst Sch BH21 .. 59 B5
Wimborne Ho BH22 ... 61 F7
Wimborne Minster Model Town & Gdns BH21 ... 59 B4
Wimborne Rd
Blandford Forum DT11 ... 212 E3
Bournemouth BH11 ... 89 C6
Bournemouth BH9 ... 121 F5
Bournemouth BH9 ... 121 F8
East End BH21 ... 58 F1
Langton Long Blandford DT11 ... 199 D1
Lytchett Matravers BH16 .. 84 E4
Poole BH15 ... 119 D4
Poole BH15 ... 119 D6
Tarrant Rushton DT11 ... 48 A6
Wimborne Minster BH21 ... 59 E6
Wimborne Rd E
Ferndown BH22 ... 61 B6
Ferndown BH22 ... 61 E7
Wimborne Rd W
Ferndown BH21 ... 60 E6
Wimborne Minster BH21 ... 60 B4
Wimborne St Giles CE VA Fst Sch BH21 ... 201 E7
Wimborne St BH21 ... 40 A7
Wimborough La BA22 ... 192 F7
Winbrook Fold 1 DT2 .. 156 F6
Winchelsea Specl Sch BH12 ... 88 D1
Winchester Cath SO23 ... 126 E5
Winchester Christian Sch SO22 ... 126 B3
Winchester City Mill SO23 ... 126 F5
Winchester Cl DT4 ... 166 F3
Winchester Coll SO23 ... 126 E4
Winchester Cty Mus SO23 ... 126 E5
Winchester Gdns BA21 ... 27 E7
Winchester Pl 5 BH15 .. 119 C2
Winchester Rd BH25 ... 95 C4
Winchester Sch of Art SO23 ... 126 F6
Winchester Sta SO22 ... 126 D6
Wincombe Bsns Pk SP7 .. 13 A5
Wincombe Cl BH22 ... 61 D3
Wincombe Dr BH22 ... 61 D4
Wincombe La SP7 ... 12 F3
Wincombe Pk SP7 ... 13 C5
Windermere Cl BA20 ... 27 B2
Windermere Cres DT3 .. 167 B6
Windermere Rd BH3 ... 122 A7
Windgreen Est BH21 ... 86 E7
Windham Mews BH1 ... 122 D5
Windham Rd BH1 ... 122 D5
Windmill Cl
Shaftesbury SP7 ... 12 F4
St Leonards BH24 ... 54 F4
Windmill La BH24 ... 54 F4
Windmill Rd DT11 ... 212 D3
Windmill Rise 6 TA18 .. 191 F5
Windslade St 13 DT1 ... 107 D1
Windsor Cl
Bovington Camp BH20 ... 139 E6
Hordle SO41 ... 95 E4
1 Mosterton DT8 ... 204 A7
St Leonards BH24 ... 54 B5
Windsor Ct
3 Christchurch BH23 ... 126 A7
Poole BH14 ... 120 B3
Windsor Ho 1 SO23 ... 126 F6
Windsor La SP8 ... 5 D1
Windsor Mans 1 BH6 ... 123 E3
or Rd
BH5 ... 122 E4
... 123 E7
... 107 E1
... 2
... F6
... B2
... 7 E7
... 93 D1
... 119 D6
... 122 C3
... 30 A5
... 153 B2
... 13 A3
... 119 E5
Wim ... 92 C3
Winkton ... 92 C5
Winkton Ho BH23 ... 92 C4
Winnards Cl BH22 ... 61 E2
Winniford Cl 3 DT6 ... 99 A7
Winsford Cl BH23 ... 93 D1
Winsley Ave BH6 ... 123 C4
Winslow Rd DT3 ... 153 D1
Winspit Cl BH15 ... 118 E3
Winspit Rd BH19 ... 183 C7
Winston Ave BH12 ... 121 A6
Winston Ct
1 Christchurch BH23 ... 124 A7
4 Old Milton BH25 ... 95 A1
Winston Dr BA21 ... 27 B8
Winston Gdns BH12 ... 121 A6
Winston Par 6 BH25 ... 95 A1
Winston Pk BH12 ... 121 A6
Winston Rd BH9 ... 90 A3
Winston Way BH24 ... 55 D8
Winterborne La BH20 ... 82 F5
Winterbourne Cl BH15 ... 119 D4
Winterbourne Copse DT4 ... 180 D8
Winterbourne Hospl DT1 ... 134 F7
Winterbourne Rd BH15 .. 119 D5
Winterbourne Valley CE Fst Sch DT2 ... 105 D1
Winterhayes Cl BH17 ... 87 E3
Winter La DT9 ... 15 F6
Winters Cl 6 DT3 ... 150 A8
Winter's La DT3 ... 150 D8
Winton Boys' Sch BH10 ... 89 D1
Winton Cl SO22 ... 126 D8
Winton Prim Sch BH9 ... 89 E2
Winton Way
Bournemouth BH10 ... 89 D1
New Milton BH25 ... 95 B5
Winyards View TA18 ... 191 F3
Wisbech Way SO41 ... 95 F3
Wishart Gdns BH9 ... 90 B5
Wishay St 2 DT1 ... 107 D1
Wistaria Ho 7 BH10 ... 89 F4
Wisteria Cl BA22 ... 26 D5
Wisteria Dr BH31 ... 45 E4
Witcham La DT2 ... 205 F5
Witchampton CE Fst Sch BH21 ... 200 F1
Witchampton La BH21 ... 50 B8
Witchampton Rd BH18 ... 86 F2
Witch Cl SP8 ... 10 D3
Witch La SP8 ... 10 D4
Withermoor Rd BH9 ... 121 E8
Withies Croft DT5 ... 187 C5
Withingham Rd BH13 ... 120 F3
Withybed La BA9 ... 4 C3
Witley BH14 ... 147 C7
Witney Rd BH17 ... 87 D1
Wittey's La TA20 ... 202 E6
Wivenhoe Ho BH22 ... 61 F6
Woburn Rd BA21 ... 28 A7
Woking Rd BH14 ... 120 C4
Wolfe Cl
Christchurch BH23 ... 124 D7
Winchester SO22 ... 126 A3
Wolfeton House DT2 ... 107 D5
Wollaston Rd
Bournemouth BH6 ... 123 F3
Dorchester DT1 ... 108 A1
Wollaton Cres BH22 ... 61 C3
Wollaton Rd BH22 ... 61 C3
Wollstonecraft Rd 1 BH5 ... 122 F3
Wolseley Rd BH12 ... 120 D6
Wolterton Rd BH12 ... 121 A5
Wolverley Ct 19 BH4 ... 121 C3
Wolverton Rd BH7 ... 122 F5
Wolvesey Castle (Old Bishop's Palace) SO23 .. 126 E5
Wolvesey Terr 2 SO23 .. 126 F4
Wonderholm Par BH11 ... 89 B2
Woodacre Gdns BH22 ... 61 E4
Woodbury BH1 ... 122 A2
Woodbury Ave BH8 ... 90 F2
Woodbury Cl BH23 ... 91 E3
Woodbury Dro DT2 ... 137 C6
Woodbury Hill (Hill Fort) BH20 ... 81 C2
Wood Cl La TA17 ... 191 A8
Woodcocks Cres BH7 ... 123 A8
Woodcote 2 BA20 ... 26 F2
Woodcote Dr BH16 ... 118 B6
Woodcutts La BH21 ... 50 D7
Woodend Rd BH9 ... 121 E8
odfield Gdns BH23 ... 93 D1
odfield Rd BH11 ... 89 A5
oodford Cl BH24 ... 55 D7
oodford Rd BH1 ... 122 C4
Woodgreen Dr BH11 ... 88 D4
Woodhayes BA8 ... 19 A3
Woodhayes Ave BH23 ... 93 E2
Woodhenge BA22 ... 26 D5
Wood Ho 6 BH13 ... 121 B3
Woodhouse Cross SP8 ... 4 F3
Woodhouse La EX13 ... 202 A1
Woodhouse Rd EX13 ... 202 A1
Wood La
Bournemouth BH11 ... 88 E6
Broadwindsor DT8 ... 203 B7
Hinton St Mary DT10 ... 35 A4
Stalbridge DT10 ... 33 C7
Symondsbury DT6 ... 67 D5
Woodlake Cl BH17 ... 87 D1
Woodland Ave BH5 ... 123 A4
Woodland Cl BH31 ... 45 A7
Woodland Ct BH7 ... 122 F5
Woodland Gr 12 BA20 ... 27 D4
Woodland Mans BH14 ... 120 B5
Woodlands
Broadmayne DT2 ... 136 B1
Hazelbury Bryan DT10 ... 196 F2
20 Poole BH13 ... 121 A4
Woodlands Ave BH15 ... 118 F3
Woodlands Cl BH23 ... 93 A8
Woodlands Cres
Dorchester DT1 ... 107 C2
Hamworthy BH15 ... 118 F3
Woodlands Ct
Poole BH12 ... 121 B5
Winchester SO22 ... 126 A8
1 Winchester SO23 ... 126 E7
Woodlands Dr BH20 ... 143 B8
Woodlands Manor BA12 ... 3 A3
Woodlands Mead DT10 ... 20 E4
Woodlands Rd
Barton on Sea BH25 ... 126 E7
Mere BA12 ... 3 B2
Woodlands Rd Ind Est BA12 ... 3 B4
Woodlands Way
New Milton BH25 ... 95 B5
St Leonards BH24 ... 54 B4
Woodland Way BH23 ... 125 D8
Woodland Wlk
Bournemouth BH5 ... 123 A4
Ferndown BH22 ... 61 F7
Wood Lawn Cl BH25 ... 126 F8
Woodlea Cl SO22 ... 126 C8
Woodleaze Cl BH18 ... 87 B6
Woodlinken Cl BH31 ... 45 D4
Woodlinken Dr BH31 ... 45 D4
Woodlinken Way BH31 ... 45 E4
Woodmead Rd DT7 ... 96 B5
Woodmill Cl DT10 ... 19 D1
Woodpecker Cl BH31 ... 45 B5
Woodpecker Dr BH17 ... 118 F8
Woodpecker Mdw SP8 ... 11 A8
Woodpeckers SO23 ... 126 E8
Woodpeckers Dr SO22 .. 126 A8
Woodpeckers The DT3 .. 152 D4
Woodrising BH13 ... 147 B3
Woodrisings The 6 BH2 ... 121 D4
Woodroffe Mdw DT7 ... 96 A6
Woodroffe Sch The DT7 .. 96 A6
Wood Row BH9 ... 90 E4
Woodruff Cl BH23 ... 125 C8
Woodsage Dr SP8 ... 5 D2
Woods Edge BH18 ... 87 A2
Woodsford Castle DT2 ... 110 B1
Woodsford Cl DT2 ... 137 D6
Woodsford La DT2 ... 138 A7
Woodsford Rd DT2 ... 137 D7
Woodside Cl BH22 ... 61 E6
Woodside Rd
Bournemouth BH5 ... 123 B4
Ferndown BH22 ... 52 F4
Ferndown BH22 ... 61 E6
Poole BH14 ... 120 C3
Woodstock Cl BH14 ... 120 B2
Woodstock La BH24 ... 55 C7
Woodstock Rd
Burton BH23 ... 92 D2
Poole BH14 ... 120 A2
Yeovil BA21 ... 27 E7
Woods View Rd BH9 ... 121 D8
Woodswater La 5 DT8 .. 204 D4
Woodvale Gdns BH25 ... 95 C4
Wood View BH21 ... 60 A8
Woodward Pl DT4 ... 167 E6
Wooland Gdns DT4 ... 180 C8
Woolands La SP7 ... 12 D4
Wool CE Fst Sch BH20 .. 140 B1
Woolcombe Rd DT5 ... 186 E3
Woolcott La 1 SP8 ... 1 D1
Woolford Cl 1 SO22 ... 126 A4
Woolmer La BH24 ... 47 C2
Wool Rd BH12 ... 120 B8
Woolsbridge Ind Est BH21 ... 53 D6
Woolsbridge Rd BH24 ... 54 A4
Woolslope Cl BH22 ... 53 A1
Woolslope Gdns BH22 ... 53 B1
Woolslope Rd BH22 ... 53 A1
Wool Sta BH20 ... 140 B2
Woolven Cl BH14 ... 120 A5
Woolverston SO22 ... 126 C7
Wooperton St 4 DT4 ... 167 D3
Wootton Cross DT6 ... 65 C4
Wootton Gdns BH1 ... 122 A3
Wootton Gr DT9 ... 30 B7
Wootton La DT6 ... 65 B4
Wootton Mount BH1 ... 122 A3
Wootton Rd BH25 ... 95 D7
Wootton Rough BH25 ... 95 B8
Worbarrow Gdns BH12 .. 120 C8
Wordsworth Ave BH8 ... 90 E1
Wordsworth Cl SO22 ... 126 B6
Worgret Hill BH20 ... 141 F2
Worgret Rd
Poole BH15 ... 119 D7
Wareham BH20 ... 142 C3
Worrell Dr BH12 ... 120 C8
Worthington Cres BH14 . 120 A3
Worthy La SO23 ... 126 E7
Worthy Rd
New Milton BH25 ... 95 A3
Winchester SO23 ... 126 E8
Wortley Rd BH23 ... 126 A7
Wrackle Cl DT2 ... 106 E8
Wraxall Cl BH17 ... 87 D1
Wraxall La
Chilfrome DT2 ... 206 B2
Wraxall DT2 ... 206 A3
Wraxhill Rd BA20 ... 27 A1
Wren Cl
Christchurch BH23 ... 125 B5
New Milton BH25 ... 94 F2
Ringwood BH24 ... 55 E6
Winchester SO22 ... 126 B3
Wren Cres BH12 ... 121 B5
Wren Gdns SP6 ... 42 D5
Wriggle River La DT2 ... 194 E1
Writh Rd DT9 ... 31 C1
Wroxham Rd
Poole BH12 ... 120 F5
Poole BH12 ... 121 A5
Wyatts Cl BH21 ... 86 D6
Wyatts La BH21 ... 86 C6
Wyatt's La BH20 ... 142 F3
Wych Hill DT6 ... 100 D3
Wych Ridge DT6 ... 100 D3

Wychside Cl DT6 .... 100 D3
Wychwood 38 BH4 ...... 121 C3
Wychwood Cl BH2 ...... 121 F4
Wychwood Dr BH2 ...... 121 F4
Wychwood Grange 1
BH2 .... 121 F4
Wycliffe Rd BH9 .... 121 F8
Wydford Cl DT9 .... 29 F5
Wyelands Ave BH21 ...... 60 D5
Wykeham Cl BH17 ...... 119 E8
Wykeham Pl SO22 ...... 126 B4
Wykeham Terr 7
SO23 .... 126 F4
Wyke Mark SO22 .... 126 A8
Wyke Oliver Rd DT3 ..... 153 A1
Wyke Prim Sch SP8 .... 5 D1
Wyke Rd
Gillingham SP8 .... 5 E2
Weymouth DT4 .... 167 B1
Wyke Regis CE Jun Sch
DT4 .... 180 C7
Wyke Regis Com & Sports
Ctr DT4 .... 180 C6
Wyke Regis Inf Sch DT4 . 180 B7
Wyke Sq 7 DT4 .... 180 C8
Wynchard Bank 1 DT11 . 198 E3
Wyncombe Rd BH5 ..... 123 B5
Wyndham Cl BH23 .... 94 B2
Wyndham Rd
Poole BH14 .... 120 B3
Walkford BH23 .... 94 B2
Wyndham St BA20 .... 27 E5
Wyndham View BA21 ..... 27 F5
Wynford Rd
Bournemouth BH9 .... 90 B4
Poole BH14 .... 120 C4
Wynne Cl BH18 .... 86 F4
Wynnes Cl 4 DT9 .... 30 A5
Wynnes Rise DT9 .... 30 A5
Wynter Cl BH7 .... 122 F7
Wytch Pas BH20 .... 162 D8
Wyvern Cl
East Coker BA20 .... 26 E1
Poole BH12 .... 120 D7
Wyvern Ct 24 TA18 ...... 191 F4
Wyvern Rd 1 DT1 ...... 107 E2
Wyvern Specl Sch DT4 .. 167 A2
Wyvern Way DT11 .... 212 E6

Y

Yalbury La DT2 .... 137 C6
Yalbury Wood SP8 .... 5 E3
Yard La DT6 .... 203 D2
Yarmouth Cl BH12 ...... 121 A5
Yarmouth Rd
Poole BH12 .... 120 F6
Poole BH12 .... 121 A5
Yarnbarton 2 DT8 ...... 203 E5
Yarn Barton
10 Beaminster DT8 ...... 204 D4
5 Yeovil BA20 .... 27 C4
Yarrells Cl BH16 .... 118 C6
Yarrells Dr
Upton BH16 .... 117 D7
Upton BH16 .... 118 B7
Yarrells La BH16 .... 118 C6
Yarrells Prep Sch BH16 .. 117 D7
Yarrells Sch BH16 ...... 118 B7
Yarrow Cl BH23 .... 125 B8
Yarrow Ct 1 SP8 .... 5 D2
Yarrow Rd BH12 .... 120 A8
Yearlings' Dro BH20 ..... 113 A7
Yeates Rd DT5 .... 186 F6
Yeatman Hospl DT9 ...... 30 B6
Yeatmans Cl SP7 .... 12 D3
Yeatmans La SP7 .... 12 D3
Yeatmans Old Mill 10
BH15 .... 119 B1
Yeatminster Rd BH17 .... 87 F2
Yellowham Hill DT2 ..... 109 C8
Yellow La DT6 .... 69 C2
Yelverton Rd 10 BH1 .... 121 F3
Yenston Hill BA8 .... 18 E8
Yeolands Rd 5 DT5 ..... 186 E3
Yeo L Pk BA20 .... 27 E4
Yeomans Ind Pk BH8 ..... 90 F2
Yeomans Lodge 6 BH25 . 95 B2
Yeomans Rd BH8 .... 90 E3
Yeomans Way BH8 .... 90 E2
Yeo Valley BA22 .... 27 F1
Yeovil Airfield BA20 ...... 27 A4
Yeovil Coll BA21 .... 28 A6
Yeovil Coll IT Ctr BA20 ... 27 E4
Yeovil District Hospl
BA21 .... 27 C6
Yeovil Golf Club BA21 .... 28 A4
Yeovil Junction Sta BA22 . 28 A1
Yeovil Pen Mill Sta BA21 . 28 A5
Yeovil Rd
Crewkerne TA18 .... 192 A5
Halstock BA22 .... 193 D3
Sherborne DT9 .... 30 A6
Yeovil BA20 .... 27 B1
Yeovil Ski Activity Ctr
BA20 .... 27 E4
Yeovil Sports Club
BA21 .... 27 A7
Yerville Gdns SO41 .... 95 F3
Yetminster Sta DT9 ..... 194 C5
Yew La BH25 .... 95 C4
Yews The BA12 .... 3 A6
Yewstock Specl Sch
DT10 .... 35 B2
Yew Tree Cl
Wimborne Minster BH21 ... 59 D5
Yeovil BA20 .... 27 A2
Yew Tree Ct 5 BH25 ..... 95 B1
Yew Tree La DT2 .... 106 F6
York Ave BH25 .... 95 B3
York Cl
Broadstone BH18 .... 87 A2
Charminster DT2 .... 107 E6
Christchurch BH23 ..... 123 F7
York Ho 20 SO23 .... 126 E8
York Pl
Bournemouth BH7 ...... 123 A5
7 New Milton BH25 ...... 95 B3
Yeovil BA20 .... 27 C5
York Rd
Bournemouth BH1 ...... 122 B4
Broadstone BH18 .... 87 A2
Dorchester DT1 .... 108 B1
York Terr 7 DT1 .... 135 B8
Youngs Endowed Prim Sch
DT9 .... 14 E2
Youngs Rd BH11 .... 89 A5

Z

Zamek Cl BH11 .... 89 A5
Zeals Green Dr BA12 ...... 2 A4
Zeals Rise BA12 .... 1 F4
Zetland Ct BH4 .... 121 B1
Zig Zag Hill SP7 .... 24 E6
Zinnia Cl BH10 .... 89 E2
Zoar La DT10 .... 197 B4

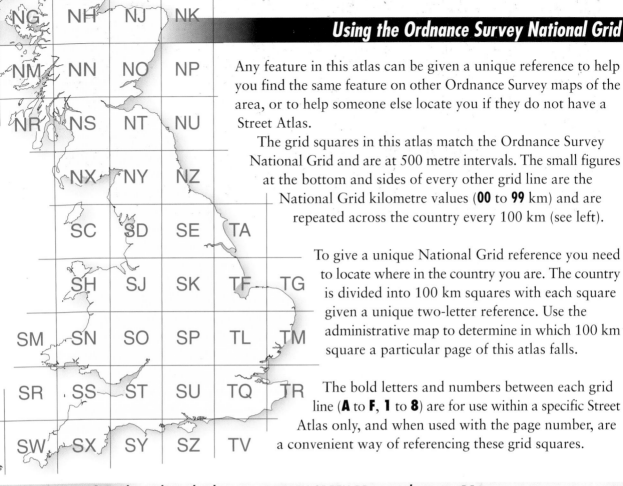

Any feature in this atlas can be given a unique reference to help you find the same feature on other Ordnance Survey maps of the area, or to help someone else locate you if they do not have a Street Atlas.

The grid squares in this atlas match the Ordnance Survey National Grid and are at 500 metre intervals. The small figures at the bottom and sides of every other grid line are the National Grid kilometre values (**00** to **99** km) and are repeated across the country every 100 km (see left).

To give a unique National Grid reference you need to locate where in the country you are. The country is divided into 100 km squares with each square given a unique two-letter reference. Use the administrative map to determine in which 100 km square a particular page of this atlas falls.

The bold letters and numbers between each grid line (**A** to **F**, **1** to **8**) are for use within a specific Street Atlas only, and when used with the page number, are a convenient way of referencing these grid squares.

Example   The railway bridge over DARLEY GREEN RD in grid square B1

Step 1: Identify the two-letter reference, in this example the page is in **SP**

Step 2: Identify the 1 km square in which the railway bridge falls. Use the figures in the southwest corner of this square: Eastings **17**, Northings **74**. This gives a unique reference: **SP 17 74**, accurate to 1 km.

Step 3: To give a more precise reference accurate to 100 m you need to estimate how many tenths along and how many tenths up this 1 km square the feature is (to help with this the 1 km square is divided into four 500 m squares). This makes the bridge about **8** tenths along and about **1** tenth up from the southwest corner.

This gives a unique reference: **SP 178 741**, accurate to 100 m.

Eastings (read from left to right along the bottom) come before Northings (read from bottom to top). If you have trouble remembering say to yourself "Along the hall, THEN up the stairs"!

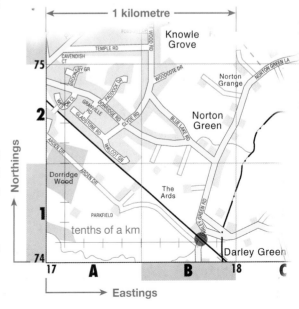

PHILIP'S MAPS

the Gold Standard for drivers

◆ **Philip's street atlases cover every county in England, Wales, Northern Ireland and much of Scotland**

◆ Every named street is shown, including alleys, lanes and walkways

◆ Thousands of additional features marked: stations, public buildings, car parks, places of interest

◆ Route-planning maps to get you close to your destination

◆ Postcodes on the maps and in the index

◆ Widely used by the emergency services, transport companies and local authorities

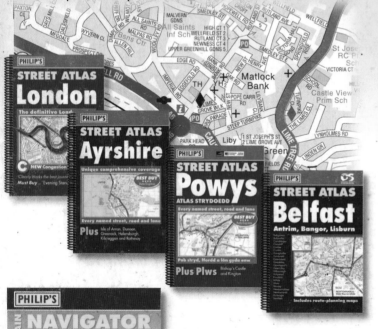

For national mapping, choose **Philip's Navigator Britain** the most detailed road atlas available of England, Wales and Scotland. Hailed by Auto Express as 'the ultimate road atlas', the atlas shows every road and lane in Britain.

Street atlases currently available

England

Bedfordshire and Luton	Surrey
Berkshire	East Sussex
Birmingham and West Midlands	West Sussex
	Tyne and Wear
Bristol and Bath	Warwickshire and Coventry
Buckinghamshire and Milton Keynes	Wiltshire and Swindon
	Worcestershire
Cambridgeshire and Peterborough	East Yorkshire Northern Lincolnshire
Cheshire	North Yorkshire
Cornwall	South Yorkshire
Cumbria	West Yorkshire
Derbyshire	
Devon	**Wales**
Dorset	Anglesey, Conwy and Gwynedd
County Durham and Teesside	Cardiff, Swansea and The Valleys
Essex	Carmarthenshire, Pembrokeshire and Swansea
North Essex	
South Essex	Ceredigion and South Gwynedd
Gloucestershire and Bristol	
Hampshire	Denbighshire, Flintshire, Wrexham
North Hampshire	
South Hampshire	Herefordshire Monmouthshire
Herefordshire Monmouthshire	
	Powys
Hertfordshire	
Isle of Wight	**Scotland**
Kent	Aberdeenshire
East Kent	Ayrshire
West Kent	Dumfries and Galloway
Lancashire	Edinburgh and East Central Scotland
Leicestershire and Rutland	
	Fife and Tayside
Lincolnshire	Glasgow and West Central Scotland
Liverpool and Merseyside	
London	Inverness and Moray
Greater Manchester	Lanarkshire
Norfolk	Scottish Borders
Northamptonshire	
Northumberland	**Northern Ireland**
Nottinghamshire	County Antrim and County Londonderry
Oxfordshire	
Shropshire	County Armagh and County Down
Somerset	
Staffordshire	Belfast
Suffolk	County Tyrone and County Fermanagh

How to order

Philip's maps and atlases are available from bookshops, motorway services and petrol stations. You can order direct from the publisher by phoning **0207 531 8473** or online at **www.philips-maps.co.uk**
For bulk orders only, e-mail philips@philips-maps.co.uk